CRIMINAL PROCEDURE (SCOTLAND) ACT 1995 (UK)

Updated as of March 26, 2018

THE LAW LIBRARY

TABLE OF CONTENTS

Introductory Text

Criminal Procedure (Scotland) Act 1995

1995 CHAPTER 46

An Act to consolidate certain enactments relating to criminal procedure in Scotland.
[8th November 1995]
Be it enacted by the Queen's most Excellent Majesty, by and with the advice and consent of the Lords Spiritual and Temporal, and Commons, in this present Parliament assembled, and by the authority of the same, as follows:—

Extent Information

E1. Act extends to Scotland; for sections extending to England and Wales, Northern Ireland and the Isle of Man, see s. 309. (3)-(6).

Modifications etc. (not altering text)

C1. Act modified (1.4.1997) by S.I. 1996/3255, reg. 5

C2. Act amended (temp. from 1.4.1996) by 1995 c. 40, ss. 4, 7. (2), Sch. 3 Pt. II para. 5

C3. Act extended (S.) (1.4.1996) by 1995 c. 40, ss. 1, 2. (2), 7. (2)

C4. Act excluded (S.) (1.4.1996) by 1995 c. 39, ss. 46. (3), 53. (2)

C5. Act construed (S.) (1.4.1996) with 1995 c. 39, ss. 43. (2), 53. (2)

C6. Act applied (3.7.2001) by S.I. 2001/1701, reg. 17, Sch. 13 para. 14. (3);

Act applied (20.11.2002) by Copyright, Designs and Patents Act 1988 (c. 48), ss. 114. B(6), 204. B(6), 297. D(6) (as inserted by Copyright, etc. and Trade Marks (Offences and Enforcement) Act 2002 (c. 25), ss. 3, 4, 5; S.I. 2002/2749, art. 2)

Act applied (7.3.2005) by The Electromagnetic Compatibility Regulations 2005 (S.I. 2005/281), reg. 98. (3)

Act applied (S.) (5.10.2005) by The Mental Health (Cross border transfer: patients subject to detention requirement or otherwise in hospital)(Scotland) Regulations 2005 (S.S.I. 2005/467), {reg. 46. (1)}

Act modified (S.) (6.10.2006) by Animal Health and Welfare (Scotland) Act 2006 (asp 11), ss. 43. (1), 55. (1); S.S.I. 2006/482, art. 2 (subject to art. 4)

C7. Act modified (12.12.2007) by Animal Welfare Act 2006 (c. 45), ss. 49. (1), 68 (with ss. 1. (2), 58. (1), 59, 60); S.S.I. 2007/519, art. 2

C8. Act modified (S.) (10.3.2008, 2.6.2008, 8.12.2008, 23.2.2009, 14.12.2009 and 22.2.2010 for certain purposes, otherwise prosp.) by Criminal Proceedings etc. (Reform) (Scotland) Act 2007 (asp 6), ss. 62. (8), 84; S.S.I. 2008/42, art. 3, Sch.; S.S.I. 2008/192, art. 3, Sch.; S.S.I. 2008/362, art. 3, Sch.; S.S.I. 2009/432, art. 3, Schs. 1, 2

Act: power to apply conferred (S.) (10.12.2007) by Criminal Proceedings etc. (Reform) (Scotland) Act 2007 (asp 6), ss. 64. (5), 84; S.S.I. 2007/479, art. 3. (1), Sch. (as amended by S.S.I. 2007/527)

Act: power to modify conferred (S.) (10.12.2007) by Criminal Proceedings etc. (Reform) (Scotland) Act 2007 (asp 6), ss. 64. (6)(7), 84; S.S.I. 2007/479, art. 3. (1), Sch. (as amended by S.S.I. 2007/527)

C9various regulations applied by 1997 c. 43, Sch. 1 para. 19. B (as inserted (1.2.2015) by Offender Rehabilitation Act 2014 (c. 11), s. 22. (1), Sch. 3 para. 7 (with Sch. 7 para. 2); S.I. 2015/40, art. 2. (u))

C10. Act power to apply (with or without modifications) conferred by 2002 c. 29, s. 118. (2. B)(c) (as inserted (1.3.2016) by Serious Crime Act 2015 (c. 9), ss. 19. (1)(b), 88. (2)(a); S.S.I. 2016/11, reg. 2. (d) (with reg. 3))
Commencement Information
I1. Act wholly in force on 1.4.1996, see s. 309. (2)

Part I Criminal Courts

Part IS Criminal Courts

Jurisdiction and PowersS

1 Judges in the High Court.S
(1) The Lord President of the Court of Session shall be the Lord Justice General and shall perform his duties as the presiding judge of the High Court.
(2) Every person who is appointed to the office of one of the Senators of the College of Justice in Scotland shall, by virtue of such appointment, be a Lord Commissioner of Justiciary in Scotland.
(3) If any difference arises as to the rotation of judges in the High Court, it shall be determined by the Lord Justice General, whom failing by the Lord Justice Clerk.
(4) Any Lord Commissioner of Justiciary may preside alone at the trial of an accused before the High Court.
(5) Without prejudice to subsection (4) above, in any trial of difficulty or importance it shall be competent for two or more judges in the High Court to preside for the whole or any part of the trial.
2 Fixing of High Court sittings.S
(1) The High Court shall sit at such times and places as the Lord Justice General, whom failing the Lord Justice Clerk, may, after consultation with the Lord Advocate, determine.
(2) Without prejudice to subsection (1) above, the High Court shall hold such additional sittings as the Lord Advocate may require.
(3) Where an accused has been cited to [F1, or otherwise required to attend, a diet to be held at any] sitting of the High Court, the prosecutor may, at any time before the commencement of [F2the diet or, in the case of a trial diet, the trial] , apply to the Court to transfer the case to [F3a diet to be held at a sitting of the Court in another place] ; and a single judge of the High Court may—
    (a) after giving the accused or his counsel an opportunity to be heard; or
    (b) on the joint application of all parties,
make an order for the transfer of the case.
[F4. (3. C)The judge may proceed under subsection (3) above on a joint application of the parties without hearing the parties and, accordingly, he may dispense with any hearing previously appointed for the purpose of considering the application.]
(4) Where no [F5diets have been appointed to be held at] a sitting of the High Court or if it is no longer expedient that a sitting should take place, it shall not be necessary for the sitting to take place.
(5) If [F6in any case a diet remains appointed to be held at] a sitting which does not take place in pursuance of subsection (4) above, subsection (3) above shall apply in relation to the transfer of any other such case to another sitting.
[F7. (6)For the purposes of subsection (3) above—
    (a) a diet shall be taken to commence when it is called; and
    (b) a trial shall be taken to commence when the oath is administered to the jury.]

Amendments (Textual)

F1. Words in s. 2. (3) substituted (1.2.2005) by Criminal Procedure (Amendment) (Scotland) Act 2004 (asp 5), ss. 25, 27. (1), Sch. para. 2. (a)(i); S.S.I. 2004/405, art. 2, Sch. 1 (subject to arts. 3-5)

F2. Words in s. 2. (3) substituted (1.2.2005) by Criminal Procedure (Amendment) (Scotland) Act 2004 (asp 5), ss. 25, 27. (1), Sch. para. 2. (a)(ii); S.S.I. 2004/405, art. 2, Sch. 1 (subject to arts. 3-5)

F3. Words in s. 2. (3) substituted (1.2.2005) by Criminal Procedure (Amendment) (Scotland) Act 2004 (asp 5), ss. 25, 27. (1), Sch. para. 2. (a)(iii); S.S.I. 2004/405, art. 2, Sch. 1 (subject to arts. 3-5)

F4. S. 2. (3. C) inserted (1.2.2005) by Criminal Procedure (Amendment) (Scotland) Act 2004 (asp 5), ss. 25, 27. (1), Sch. para. 2. (b); S.S.I. 2004/405, art. 2, Sch. 1 (subject to arts. 3-5)

F5. Words in s. 2. (4) substituted (1.2.2005) by Criminal Procedure (Amendment) (Scotland) Act 2004 (asp 5), ss. 25, 27. (1), Sch. para. 2. (c); S.S.I. 2004/405, art. 2, Sch. 1 (subject to arts. 3-5)

F6. Words in s. 2. (5) substituted (1.2.2005) by Criminal Procedure (Amendment) (Scotland) Act 2004 (asp 5), ss. 25, 27. (1), Sch. para. 2. (d); S.S.I. 2004/405, art. 2, Sch. 1 (subject to arts. 3-5)

F7. S. 2. (6) inserted (1.2.2005) by Criminal Procedure (Amendment) (Scotland) Act 2004 (asp 5), ss. 25, 27. (1), Sch. para. 2. (e); S.S.I. 2004/405, art. 2, Sch. 1 (subject to arts. 3-5)

Solemn courts: generalS

3 Jurisdiction and powers of solemn courts.S

(1) The jurisdiction and powers of all courts of solemn jurisdiction, except so far as altered or modified by any enactment passed after the commencement of this Act, shall remain as at the commencement of this Act.

(2) Any crime or offence which is triable on indictment may be tried by the High Court sitting at any place in Scotland.

(3) The sheriff shall, without prejudice to any other or wider power conferred by statute, not be entitled, on the conviction on indictment of an accused, to pass a sentence of imprisonment for a term exceeding [F8five years].

(4) Subject to subsection (5) below, where under any enactment passed or made before 1st January 1988 (the date of commencement of section 58 of the M1. Criminal Justice (Scotland) Act 1987) an offence is punishable on conviction on indictment by imprisonment for a term exceeding two years but the enactment either expressly or impliedly restricts the power of the sheriff to impose a sentence of imprisonment for a term exceeding two years, it shall be competent for the sheriff to impose a sentence of imprisonment for a term exceeding two but not exceeding [F9five years].

[F10. (4. A)Subject to subsection (5) below, where under any enactment passed or made after 1st January 1988 but before the commencement of section 13 of the Crime and Punishment (Scotland) Act 1997 (increase in sentencing powers of sheriff courts) an offence is punishable on conviction on indictment for a term exceeding three years but the enactment either expressly or impliedly restricts the power of the sheriff to impose a sentence of imprisonment for a term exceeding three years, it shall be competent for the sheriff to impose a sentence of imprisonment for a term exceeding three but not exceeding five years.]

(5) Nothing in subsection (4) above shall authorise the imposition by the sheriff of a sentence in excess of the sentence specified by the enactment as the maximum sentence which may be imposed on conviction of the offence.

(6) Subject to any express exclusion contained in any enactment, it shall be lawful to indict in the sheriff court all crimes except murder, treason, rape [F11. (whether at common law or under section 1. (1) of the Sexual Offences (Scotland) Act 2009 (asp 9)), rape of a young child (under section 18 of that Act)] and breach of duty by magistrates.

Amendments (Textual)

F8. Words in s. 3. (3) substituted (1.5.2004) by 1997 c. 48, ss. 13. (1)(a), 65. (2); S.S.I. 2004/176, art. 2, (with art. 3)

F9. Words in s. 3. (4) substituted (1.5.2004) by 1997 c. 48, ss. 13. (1)(b), 65. (2); S.S.I. 2004/176, art. 2, (with art. 3)

F10. S. 3. (4. A) inserted (1.5.2004) by 1997 c. 48, ss. 13. (1)(c), 65. (2); S.S.I. 2004/176, art. 2, (with art. 3)

F11. Words in s. 3. (6) inserted (1.12.2010) by Sexual Offences (Scotland) Act 2009 (asp 9), ss. 61, 62. (2), Sch. 5 para. 2. (2); S.S.I. 2010/413, art. 2, Sch.

Marginal Citations

M11987 c.41.

The sheriffS

4 Territorial jurisdiction of sheriff.S

(1) Subject to the provisions of this section, the jurisdiction of the sheriffs, within their respective sheriffdoms shall extend to and include all navigable rivers, ports, harbours, creeks, shores and anchoring grounds in or adjoining such sheriffdoms and includes all criminal maritime causes and proceedings (including those applying to persons furth of Scotland) provided that the accused is, by virtue of any enactment or rule of law, subject to the jurisdiction of the sheriff before whom the case or proceeding is raised.

(2) Where an offence is alleged to have been committed in one district in a sheriffdom, it shall be competent to try that offence in a sheriff court in any other district in that sheriffdom.

(3) It shall not be competent for the sheriff to try any crime committed on the seas which it would not be competent for him to try if the crime had been committed on land.

(4) The sheriff shall have a concurrent jurisdiction with every other court of summary jurisdiction in relation to all offences competent for trial in such courts.

5 The sheriff: summary jurisdiction and powers.S

(1) The sheriff, sitting as a court of summary jurisdiction, shall continue to have all the jurisdiction and powers exercisable by him at the commencement of this Act.

(2) The sheriff shall, without prejudice to any other or wider powers conferred by statute, have power on convicting any person of a common law offence—

　(a) to impose a fine not exceeding the prescribed sum;

　(b) to ordain the accused to find caution for good behaviour for any period not exceeding 12 months to an amount not exceeding the prescribed sum either in lieu of or in addition to a fine or in addition to imprisonment;

　(c) failing payment of such fine, or on failure to find such caution, to award imprisonment in accordance with section 219 of this Act;

　(d) to impose imprisonment, for any period not exceeding [F1212] months.

(3) F13. . . . .

(4) It shall be competent to prosecute summarily in the sheriff court the following offences—

　(a) uttering a forged document;

　(b) wilful fire-raising;

　(c) robbery; and

　(d) assault with intent to rob.

Amendments (Textual)

F12. Word in s. 5. (2)(d) substituted (10.12.2007) by Criminal Proceedings etc. (Reform) (Scotland) Act 2007 (asp 6), ss. 43. (a), 84; S.S.I. 2007/479, art. 3. (1), Sch. (subject to art. 12)

F13. S. 5. (3) repealed (10.12.2007) by Criminal Proceedings etc. (Reform) (Scotland) Act 2007 (asp 6), ss. 43. (b), 84; S.S.I. 2007/479, art. 3. (1), Sch. (subject to art. 12)

[F14. JP courts] S

Amendments (Textual)

F14. S. 6 cross-heading substituted (10.3.2008, 2.6.2008, 8.12.2008, 23.2.2009 and 14.12.2009 for certain purposes, otherwise 22.2.2010) by Criminal Proceedings etc. (Reform) (Scotland) Act 2007 (asp 6), ss. 80, 84. (1), Sch. para. 9. (5)(a); S.S.I. 2008/42, art. 3, Sch.; S.S.I. 2008/192, art. 3, Sch.; S.S.I. 2008/329, art. 3, Sch.; S.S.I. 2008/362, art. 3, Sch.; S.S.I. 2009/432, art. 3, Schs. 1, 2

6[F15. JP courts: constitution and prosecutor].S

(1) F16. . . . .

(2) The jurisdiction and powers of the [F17. JP court] shall be exercisable by a [F18summary sheriff] or by one or more justices, and no decision of the court shall be questioned on the ground that it was not constituted as required by this subsection unless objection was taken on that ground by or on behalf of a party to the proceedings not later than the time when the proceedings or the alleged irregularity began.

(3) All prosecutions in a [F19. JP court] shall proceed at the instance of the procurator fiscal.

(4) F20. . . . .

[F21. (5)The authority of the procurator fiscal to prosecute in JP courts is without prejudice to the authority of any other person to take proceedings there in pursuance of section 43 (prosecutions and penalties) of the Education (Scotland) Act 1980 (c. 44).]

[F22. (6)In this section, "justice" means a justice of the peace.]

Amendments (Textual)

F15. S. 6 title substituted (10.3.2008, 2.6.2008, 8.12.2008, 23.2.2009 and 14.12.2009 for certain purposes, otherwise 22.2.2010) by Criminal Proceedings etc. (Reform) (Scotland) Act 2007 (asp 6), ss. 80, 84, Sch. para. 9. (5)(b); S.S.I. 2008/42, art. 3, Sch.; S.S.I. 2008/192, art. 3, Sch.; S.S.I. 2008/329, art. 3, Sch.; S.S.I. 2008/362, art. 3, Sch.; S.S.I. 2009/432, art. 3, Schs. 1, 2

F16. S. 6. (1) repealed (10.3.2008, 2.6.2008, 8.12.2008, 23.2.2009 and 14.12.2009 for certain purposes, otherwise 22.2.2010) by Criminal Proceedings etc. (Reform) (Scotland) Act 2007 (asp 6), ss. 80, 84, Sch. para. 9. (1)(a); S.S.I. 2008/42, art. 3, Sch.; S.S.I. 2008/192, art. 3, Sch.; S.S.I. 2008/329, art. 3, Sch.; S.S.I. 2008/362, art. 3, Sch.; S.S.I. 2009/432, art. 3, Schs. 1, 2

F17. Words in s. 6. (2) substituted (10.3.2008, 2.6.2008, 8.12.2008, 23.2.2009 and 14.12.2009 for certain purposes, otherwise 22.2.2010) by Criminal Proceedings etc. (Reform) (Scotland) Act 2007 (asp 6), ss. 80, 84, Sch. para. 9. (4); S.S.I. 2008/42, art. 3, Sch.; S.S.I. 2008/192, art. 3, Sch.; S.S.I. 2008/329, art. 3, Sch.; S.S.I. 2008/362, art. 3, Sch.; S.S.I. 2009/432, art. 3, Schs. 1, 2

F18. Words in s. 6. (2) substituted (1.4.2016) by Courts Reform (Scotland) Act 2014 (asp 18), s. 138. (2), sch. 5 para. 39. (2); S.S.I. 2016/13, art. 2 sch. (with art. 3)

F19. Words in s. 6. (3) substituted (10.3.2008, 2.6.2008, 8.12.2008, 23.2.2009 and 14.12.2009 for certain purposes, otherwise 22.2.2010) by Criminal Proceedings etc. (Reform) (Scotland) Act 2007 (asp 6), ss. 80, 84, Sch. para. 9. (1)(b); S.S.I. 2008/42, art. 3, Sch.; S.S.I. 2008/192, art. 3, Sch.; S.S.I. 2008/329, art. 3, Sch.; S.S.I. 2008/362, art. 3, Sch.; S.S.I. 2009/432, art. 3, Schs. 1, 2

F20. S. 6. (4) repealed (10.3.2008, 2.6.2008, 8.12.2008, 23.2.2009 and 14.12.2009 for certain purposes, otherwise 22.2.2010) by Criminal Proceedings etc. (Reform) (Scotland) Act 2007 (asp 6), ss. 80, 84, Sch. para. 9. (1)(c); S.S.I. 2008/42, art. 3, Sch.; S.S.I. 2008/192, art. 3, Sch.; S.S.I. 2008/329, art. 3, Sch.; S.S.I. 2008/362, art. 3, Sch.; S.S.I. 2009/432, art. 3, Schs. 1, 2

F21. S. 6. (5) substituted (10.3.2008, 2.6.2008, 8.12.2008, 23.2.2009 and 14.12.2009 for certain purposes, otherwise 22.2.2010) by Criminal Proceedings etc. (Reform) (Scotland) Act 2007 (asp 6), ss. 80, 84, Sch. para. 9. (1)(d); S.S.I. 2008/42, art. 3, Sch.; S.S.I. 2008/192, art. 3, Sch.; S.S.I. 2008/329, art. 3, Sch.; S.S.I. 2008/362, art. 3, Sch.; S.S.I. 2009/432, art. 3, Schs. 1, 2

F22. S. 6. (6) substituted (10.3.2008, 2.6.2008, 8.12.2008, 23.2.2009 and 14.12.2009 for certain purposes, otherwise 22.2.2010) by Criminal Proceedings etc. (Reform) (Scotland) Act 2007 (asp 6), ss. 80, 84, Sch. para. 9. (1)(e); S.S.I. 2008/42, art. 3, Sch.; S.S.I. 2008/192, art. 3, Sch.; S.S.I. 2008/329, art. 3, Sch.; S.S.I. 2008/362, art. 3, Sch.; S.S.I. 2009/432, art. 3, Schs. 1, 2

Modifications etc. (not altering text)

C1. S. 6. (2): power to amend conferred (prosp.) by Criminal Proceedings etc. (Reform) (Scotland) Act 2007 (asp 6), ss. 63. (2), 84

7[F23. JP courts: jurisdiction and powers].S

F24. (1). . . . .

F24. (2). . . . .

(3) Except in so far as any enactment (including this Act or an enactment passed after this Act) otherwise provides, it shall be competent for a [F25. JP court][F26 to—

(a) try any common law or statutory offence which is triable summarily;

(b) make such orders and grant such warrants as are appropriate to a court of summary jurisdiction;

(c) do anything else (by way of procedure or otherwise) as is appropriate to such a court]

(4) It shall be competent, whether or not the accused has been previously convicted of an offence inferring dishonest appropriation of property, for any of the following offences to be tried in the [F27. JP court]—

(a) theft or reset of theft;

(b) falsehood, fraud or wilful imposition;

(c) breach of trust or embezzlement,

where (in any such case) the amount concerned does not exceed level 4 on the standard scale.

F28. (5). . . . .

(6) The [F29. JP court] shall, without prejudice to any other or wider powers conferred by statute, be entitled on convicting of a common law offence—

(a) to impose imprisonment for any period not exceeding 60 days;

(b) to impose a fine not exceeding level 4 on the standard scale;

(c) to ordain the accused (in lieu of or in addition to such imprisonment or fine) to find caution for good behaviour for any period not exceeding six months and to an amount not exceeding level 4 on the standard scale;

(d) failing payment of such fine or on failure to find such caution, to award imprisonment in accordance with section 219 of this Act,

but in no case shall the total period of imprisonment imposed in pursuance of this subsection exceed 60 days.

(7) Without prejudice to any other or wider power conferred by any enactment, it shall not be competent for a [F30. JP court], as respects any statutory offence—

(a) to impose a sentence of imprisonment for a period exceeding 60 days;

(b) to impose a fine of an amount exceeding level 4 on the standard scale; or

(c) to ordain an accused person to find caution for any period exceeding six months or to an amount exceeding level 4 on the standard scale.

(8) The [F31. JP court] shall not have jurisdiction to try or to pronounce sentence in the case of any person—

(a) F32. . . . .

(b) brought before it accused or suspected of having committed within its jurisdiction any of the following offences—

(i) murder, culpable homicide, robbery, rape [F33. (whether at common law or under section 1. (1) of the Sexual Offences (Scotland) Act 2009 (asp 9)), rape of a young child (under section 18 of that Act)], wilful fire-raising, or attempted wilful fire-raising;

(ii) theft by housebreaking, or housebreaking with intent to steal;

(iii) theft or reset, falsehood fraud or wilful imposition, breach of trust or embezzlement, where the value of the property is an amount exceeding level 4 on the standard scale;

(iv) assault causing the fracture of a limb, assault with intent to ravish, assault to the danger of life, or assault by stabbing;

(v) uttering forged documents or uttering forged bank or banker's notes, or offences under the Acts relating to coinage.

(9) Without prejudice to subsection (8) above, where either in the preliminary investigation or in the course of the trial of any offence it appears that the offence is one which—

(a) cannot competently be tried in the court before which an accused is brought; or

(b) in the opinion of the court in view of the circumstances of the case, should be dealt with by a higher court,

the court may take cognizance of the offence and commit the accused to prison for examination for any period not exceeding four days.

(10) Where an accused is committed as mentioned in subsection (9) above, the prosecutor in the court which commits the accused shall forthwith give notice of the committal to the procurator fiscal of the [F34area] within which the offence was committed or to such other official as is entitled to take cognizance of the offence in order that the accused may be dealt with according to law.

Amendments (Textual)

F23. S. 7 title substituted (10.3.2008, 2.6.2008, 8.12.2008, 23.2.2009 and 14.12.2009 for certain purposes, otherwise 22.2.2010) by Criminal Proceedings etc. (Reform) (Scotland) Act 2007 (asp 6), ss. 80, 84, Sch. para. 9. (5)(c); S.S.I. 2008/42, art. 3, Sch.; S.S.I. 2008/192, art. 3, Sch.; S.S.I. 2008/329, art. 3, Sch.; S.S.I. 2008/362, art. 3, Sch.; S.S.I. 2009/432, art. 3, Schs. 1, 2

F24. S. 7. (1)(2) repealed (10.3.2008, 2.6.2008, 8.12.2008, 23.2.2009 and 14.12.2009 for certain purposes, otherwise 22.2.2010) by Criminal Proceedings etc. (Reform) (Scotland) Act 2007 (asp 6), ss. 80, 84, Sch. para. 9. (2)(a); S.S.I. 2008/42, art. 3, Sch.; S.S.I. 2008/192, art. 3, Sch.; S.S.I. 2008/329, art. 3, Sch.; S.S.I. 2008/362, art. 3, Sch.; S.S.I. 2009/432, art. 3, Schs. 1, 2

F25. Words in s. 7. (3)-(8) substituted (10.3.2008, 2.6.2008, 8.12.2008, 23.2.2009 and 14.12.2009 for certain purposes, otherwise 22.2.2010) by Criminal Proceedings etc. (Reform) (Scotland) Act 2007 (asp 6), ss. 80, 84, Sch. para. 9. (4); S.S.I. 2008/42, art. 3, Sch.; S.S.I. 2008/192, art. 3, Sch.; S.S.I. 2008/329, art. 3, Sch.; S.S.I. 2008/362, art. 3, Sch.; S.S.I. 2009/432, art. 3, Schs. 1, 2

F26. Words in s. 7. (3) substituted (10.3.2008, 2.6.2008, 8.12.2008, 23.2.2009 and 14.12.2009 for certain purposes, otherwise 22.2.2010) by Criminal Proceedings etc. (Reform) (Scotland) Act 2007 (asp 6), ss. 80, 84, Sch. para. 9. (2)(b); S.S.I. 2008/42, art. 3, Sch.; S.S.I. 2008/192, art. 3, Sch.; S.S.I. 2008/329, art. 3, Sch.; S.S.I. 2008/362, art. 3, Sch.; S.S.I. 2009/432, art. 3, Schs. 1, 2

F27. Words in s. 7. (3)-(8) substituted (10.3.2008, 2.6.2008, 8.12.2008, 23.2.2009 and 14.12.2009 for certain purposes, otherwise 22.2.2010) by Criminal Proceedings etc. (Reform) (Scotland) Act 2007 (asp 6), ss. 80, 84, Sch. para. 9. (4); S.S.I. 2008/42, art. 3, Sch.; S.S.I. 2008/192, art. 3, Sch.; S.S.I. 2008/329, art. 3, Sch.; S.S.I. 2008/362, art. 3, Sch.; S.S.I. 2009/432, art. 3, Schs. 1, 2

F28. S. 7. (5) repealed (1.4.2016) by Courts Reform (Scotland) Act 2014 (asp 18), s. 138. (2), sch. 5 para. 39. (3); S.S.I. 2016/13, art. 2 sch. (with art. 3)

F29. Words in s. 7. (3)-(8) substituted (10.3.2008, 2.6.2008, 8.12.2008, 23.2.2009 and 14.12.2009 for certain purposes, otherwise 22.2.2010) by Criminal Proceedings etc. (Reform) (Scotland) Act 2007 (asp 6), ss. 80, 84, Sch. para. 9. (4); S.S.I. 2008/42, art. 3, Sch.; S.S.I. 2008/192, art. 3, Sch.; S.S.I. 2008/329, art. 3, Sch.; S.S.I. 2008/362, art. 3, Sch.; S.S.I. 2009/432, art. 3, Schs. 1, 2

F30. Words in s. 7. (3)-(8) substituted (10.3.2008, 2.6.2008, 8.12.2008, 23.2.2009 and 14.12.2009 for certain purposes, otherwise 22.2.2010) by Criminal Proceedings etc. (Reform) (Scotland) Act 2007 (asp 6), ss. 80, 84, Sch. para. 9. (4); S.S.I. 2008/42, art. 3, Sch.; S.S.I. 2008/192, art. 3, Sch.; S.S.I. 2008/329, art. 3, Sch.; S.S.I. 2008/362, art. 3, Sch.; S.S.I. 2009/432, art. 3, Schs. 1, 2

F31. Words in s. 7. (3)-(8) substituted (10.3.2008, 2.6.2008, 8.12.2008, 23.2.2009 and 14.12.2009 for certain purposes, otherwise 22.2.2010) by Criminal Proceedings etc. (Reform) (Scotland) Act 2007 (asp 6), ss. 80, 84, Sch. para. 9. (4); S.S.I. 2008/42, art. 3, Sch.; S.S.I. 2008/192, art. 3, Sch.; S.S.I. 2008/329, art. 3, Sch.; S.S.I. 2008/362, art. 3, Sch.; S.S.I. 2009/432, art. 3, Schs. 1, 2

F32. S. 7. (8)(a) and word repealed (10.3.2008, 2.6.2008, 8.12.2008, 23.2.2009 and 14.12.2009 for certain purposes, otherwise 22.2.2010) by Criminal Proceedings etc. (Reform) (Scotland) Act 2007 (asp 6), ss. 80, 84, Sch. para. 9. (2)(d); S.S.I. 2008/42, art. 3, Sch.; S.S.I. 2008/192, art. 3, Sch.; S.S.I. 2008/329, art. 3, Sch.; S.S.I. 2008/362, art. 3, Sch.; S.S.I. 2009/432, art. 3, Schs. 1, 2

F33. Words in s. 7. (8)(b)(i) inserted (1.12.2010) by Sexual Offences (Scotland) Act 2009 (asp 9), ss. 61, 62. (2), Sch. 5 para. 2. (3); S.S.I. 2010/413, art. 2, Sch.

F34. Word in s. 7. (10) substituted (10.3.2008, 2.6.2008, 8.12.2008, 23.2.2009 and 14.12.2009 for certain purposes, otherwise 22.2.2010) by Criminal Proceedings etc. (Reform) (Scotland) Act 2007 (asp 6), ss. 80, 84, Sch. para. 9. (2)(e); S.S.I. 2008/42, art. 3, Sch.; S.S.I. 2008/192, art. 3, Sch.; S.S.I. 2008/329, art. 3, Sch.; S.S.I. 2008/362, art. 3, Sch.; S.S.I. 2009/432, art. 3, Schs. 1, 2

[F35. Sittings of sheriff and JP courts]S

Amendments (Textual)

F35. S. 8 cross-heading substituted (10.3.2008, 2.6.2008, 8.12.2008, 23.2.2009 and 14.12.2009 for certain purposes, otherwise 22.2.2010) by Criminal Proceedings etc. (Reform) (Scotland) Act 2007 (asp 6), ss. 80, 84, Sch. para. 9. (5)(d); S.S.I. 2008/42, art. 3, Sch.; S.S.I. 2008/192, art. 3, Sch.; S.S.I. 2008/329, art. 3, Sch.; S.S.I. 2008/362, art. 3, Sch.; S.S.I. 2009/432, art. 3, Schs. 1, 2

8[F36. Sittings of sheriff and JP courts].S

(1) Notwithstanding any enactment or rule of law, a sheriff court or a [F37. JP court]—

(a) shall not be required to sit on any Saturday or Sunday or on a day which by virtue of subsection (2) or (3) below is a court holiday; but

(b) may sit on any day for the disposal of criminal business.

(2) A sheriff principal may in an order made under [F38section 28. (1) of the Courts Reform (Scotland) Act 2014] prescribe in respect of criminal business not more than [F3911] days, other than Saturdays and Sundays, in a calendar year as court holidays in the sheriff courts within his jurisdiction; and may in the like manner prescribe as an additional court holiday any day which has been proclaimed, under section 1. (3) of the M2. Banking and Financial Dealings Act 1971, to be a bank holiday either throughout the United Kingdom or in a place or locality in the United Kingdom within his jurisdiction.

(3) [F40. A sheriff principal may] prescribe not more than [F3911] days, other than Saturdays and Sundays, in a calendar year as court holidays in the [F41. JP courts] within his jurisdiction; and he may F42. . . . prescribe as an additional holiday any day which has been proclaimed, under section 1. (3) of the said Banking and Financial Dealings Act 1971, to be a bank holiday either throughout the United Kingdom or in a place or locality in the United Kingdom within his jurisdiction.

(4) A sheriff principal may in pursuance of subsection (2) or (3) above prescribe different days as court holidays in relation to different sheriff or [F43. JP courts] .

Amendments (Textual)

F36. S. 8 title substituted (10.3.2008, 2.6.2008, 8.12.2008, 23.2.2009 and 14.12.2009 for certain purposes, otherwise 22.2.2010) by Criminal Proceedings etc. (Reform) (Scotland) Act 2007 (asp 6), ss. 80, 84, Sch. para. 9. (5)(e); S.S.I. 2008/42, art. 3, Sch.; S.S.I. 2008/192, art. 3, Sch.; S.S.I. 2008/329, art. 3, Sch.; S.S.I. 2008/362, art. 3, Sch.; S.S.I. 2009/432, art. 3, Schs. 1, 2

F37. Words in s. 8. (1) substituted (10.3.2008, 2.6.2008, 8.12.2008, 23.2.2009 and 14.12.2009 for certain purposes, otherwise 22.2.2010) by Criminal Proceedings etc. (Reform) (Scotland) Act 2007 (asp 6), ss. 80, 84, Sch. para. 9. (4); S.S.I. 2008/42, art. 3, Sch.; S.S.I. 2008/192, art. 3, Sch.; S.S.I. 2008/329, art. 3, Sch.; S.S.I. 2008/362, art. 3, Sch.; S.S.I. 2009/432, art. 3, Schs. 1, 2

F38. Words in s. 8. (2) substituted (1.4.2015) by The Courts Reform (Scotland) Act 2014 (Consequential Provisions) Order 2015 (S.S.I. 2015/150), art. 1, sch. para. 5

F39. Word in s. 8. (2)(3) substituted (16.3.2009) by Judiciary and Courts (Scotland) Act 2008 (asp 6), ss. 59. (2), 76; S.S.I. 2009/83, art. 2

F40. Words in s. 8. (3) substituted (10.3.2008, 2.6.2008, 8.12.2008, 23.2.2009 and 14.12.2009 for certain purposes, otherwise 22.2.2010) by Criminal Proceedings etc. (Reform) (Scotland) Act 2007 (asp 6), ss. 80, 84, Sch. para. 9. (3)(a); S.S.I. 2008/42, art. 3, Sch.; S.S.I. 2008/192, art. 3, Sch.; S.S.I. 2008/329, art. 3, Sch.; S.S.I. 2008/362, art. 3, Sch.; S.S.I. 2009/432, art. 3, Schs. 1, 2

F41. Words in s. 8. (3)(4) substituted (10.3.2008, 2.6.2008, 8.12.2008, 23.2.2009 and 14.12.2009 for certain purposes, otherwise 22.2.2010) by Criminal Proceedings etc. (Reform) (Scotland) Act 2007 (asp 6), ss. 80, 84, Sch. para. 9. (4); S.S.I. 2008/42, art. 3, Sch.; S.S.I. 2008/192, art. 3, Sch.; S.S.I. 2008/329, art. 3, Sch.; S.S.I. 2008/362, art. 3, Sch.; S.S.I. 2009/432, art. 3, Schs. 1, 2

F42. Words in s. 8. (3) repealed (10.3.2008, 2.6.2008, 8.12.2008, 23.2.2009 and 14.12.2009 for certain purposes, otherwise 22.2.2010) by Criminal Proceedings etc. (Reform) (Scotland) Act 2007 (asp 6), ss. 80, 84, Sch. para. 9. (3)(b); S.S.I. 2008/42, art. 3, Sch.; S.S.I. 2008/192, art. 3, Sch.; S.S.I. 2008/329, art. 3, Sch.; S.S.I. 2008/362, art. 3, Sch.; S.S.I. 2009/432, art. 3, Schs. 1, 2

F43. Words in s. 8. (3)(4) substituted (10.3.2008, 2.6.2008, 8.12.2008, 23.2.2009 and 14.12.2009 for certain purposes, otherwise 22.2.2010) by Criminal Proceedings etc. (Reform) (Scotland) Act 2007 (asp 6), ss. 80, 84, Sch. para. 9. (4); S.S.I. 2008/42, art. 3, Sch.; S.S.I. 2008/192, art. 3, Sch.;

S.S.I. 2008/329, art. 3, Sch.; S.S.I. 2008/362, art. 3, Sch.; S.S.I. 2009/432, art. 3, Schs. 1, 2
Marginal Citations
M21971 c.80.

Territorial jurisdiction: generalS

9 Boundaries of jurisdiction.S
(1) Where an offence is committed in any harbour, river, arm of the sea or other water (tidal or otherwise) which runs between or forms the boundary of the jurisdiction of two or more courts, the offence may be tried by any one of such courts.
(2) Where an offence is committed on the boundary of the jurisdiction of two or more courts, or within the distance of 500 metres of any such boundary, or partly within the jurisdiction of one court and partly within the jurisdiction of another court or courts, the offence may be tried by any one of such courts.
(3) Where an offence is committed against any person or in respect of any property in or on any carriage, cart or vehicle employed in a journey by road or railway, or on board any vessel employed in a river, loch, canal or inland navigation, the offence may be tried by any court through whose jurisdiction the carriage, cart, vehicle or vessel passed in the course of the journey or voyage during which the offence was committed.
(4) Where several offences, which if committed in one sheriff court district could be tried [F44together] , are alleged to have been committed by any person in different sheriff court districts, the accused may be tried for all or any of those [F45 offences—
  (a) under one indictment or complaint before the sheriff of any one of the districts; or
  (b) under one complaint in the JP court for any one of the districts.]
(5) Where an offence is authorised by this section to be tried by any court, it may be dealt with, heard, tried, determined, adjudged and punished as if the offence had been committed wholly within the jurisdiction of such court.
Amendments (Textual)
F44. Word in s. 9. (4) substituted (10.3.2008, 2.6.2008, 8.12.2008, 23.2.2009 and 14.12.2009 for certain purposes, otherwise 22.2.2010) by Criminal Proceedings etc. (Reform) (Scotland) Act 2007 (asp 6), ss. 80, 84, Sch. para. 9. (6)(a); S.S.I. 2008/42, art. 3, Sch.; S.S.I. 2008/192, art. 3, Sch.; S.S.I. 2008/329, art. 3, Sch.; S.S.I. 2008/362, art. 3, Sch.; S.S.I. 2009/432, art. 3, Schs. 1, 2
F45. Words in s. 9. (4) substituted (10.3.2008, 2.6.2008, 8.12.2008, 23.2.2009 and 14.12.2009 for certain purposes, otherwise 22.2.2010) by Criminal Proceedings etc. (Reform) (Scotland) Act 2007 (asp 6), ss. 80, 84, Sch. para. 9. (6)(b); S.S.I. 2008/42, art. 3, Sch.; S.S.I. 2008/192, art. 3, Sch.; S.S.I. 2008/329, art. 3, Sch.; S.S.I. 2008/362, art. 3, Sch.; S.S.I. 2009/432, art. 3, Schs. 1, 2
[F469. ACompetence of justice's actings outwith jurisdictionS
[F47. It is competent for a justice, even if not present within his jurisdiction, to sign any warrant, judgment, interlocutor or other document relating to proceedings within that jurisdiction provided that when he does so he is present within Scotland.]]
Amendments (Textual)
F46. S. 9. A inserted (27.6.2003) by Criminal Justice (Scotland) Act 2003 (asp 7), ss. 59, 89; S.S.I. 2003/288, art. 2, Sch.
F47. S. 9. A repealed (10.12.2007, 8.12.2008, 23.2.2009, 14.12.2009 and 22.2.2010 for certain purposes, otherwise prosp.) by Criminal Proceedings etc. (Reform) (Scotland) Act 2007 (asp 6), ss. 80, 84, Sch. para. 9. (7); S.S.I. 2007/479, art. 3. (1), Sch. (as amended by S.S.I. 2007/527); S.S.I. 2008/329, art. 3, Sch.; S.S.I. 2008/362, art. 3, Sch.; S.S.I. 2009/432, art. 3, Schs. 1, 2
10 Crimes committed in different districts.S
(1) Where a person is alleged to have committed in more than one sheriff court district a crime or crimes to which subsection (2) below applies, he may be [F48prosecuted in] the sheriff court [F49or JP court] of such one of those districts as the Lord Advocate determines.
(2) This subsection applies to—

(a) a crime committed partly in one sheriff court district and partly in another;

(b) crimes connected with each other but committed in different sheriff court districts;

(c) crimes committed in different sheriff court districts in succession which, if they had been committed in one such district, could have been tried [F50together] .

(3) Where, in pursuance of subsection (1) above, a case is tried in the sheriff court [F51or JP court] of any sheriff court district, the procurator fiscal of that district shall have power to prosecute in that case even if the crime was in whole or in part committed in a different district, and the procurator fiscal shall have the like powers in relation to such case, whether before, during or after the trial, as he has in relation to a case arising out of a crime or crimes committed wholly within his own district.

Amendments (Textual)

F48. Words in s. 10. (1) substituted (10.3.2008) by Criminal Proceedings etc. (Reform) (Scotland) Act 2007 (asp 6), ss. 80, 84, Sch. para. 10. (a)(i); S.S.I. 2008/42, art. 3, Sch.

F49. Words in s. 10. (1) inserted (10.3.2008) by Criminal Proceedings etc. (Reform) (Scotland) Act 2007 (asp 6), ss. 80, 84, Sch. para. 10. (a)(ii); S.S.I. 2008/42, art. 3, Sch.

F50. Word in s. 10. (2)(c) substituted (10.3.2008) by Criminal Proceedings etc. (Reform) (Scotland) Act 2007 (asp 6), ss. 80, 84, Sch. para. 10. (b); S.S.I. 2008/42, art. 3, Sch.

F51. Words in s. 10. (3) inserted (10.3.2008) by Criminal Proceedings etc. (Reform) (Scotland) Act 2007 (asp 6), ss. 80, 84, Sch. para. 10. (c); S.S.I. 2008/42, art. 3, Sch.

[F5210. AJurisdiction for transferred casesS

(1) A sheriff has jurisdiction for any cases which come before the sheriff by virtue of—

(a) section 34. A or 83 of this Act; or

(b) section 137. A, 137. B, 137. C or 137. D of this Act.

[F53. (1. A)The jurisdiction of a JP court includes jurisdiction for any cases which come before it by virtue of section 137. CA, 137. CB or 137. CC of this Act.]

(2) A procurator fiscal for a sheriff court district shall have—

(a) power to prosecute in any cases which come before a sheriff of that district by virtue of a provision mentioned in subsection (1) above; F54 ...

[F55. (aa)power to prosecute in any cases which come before a JP court of that district by virtue of a provision mentioned in subsection (1. A) above;]

(b) the like powers in relation to such cases as he has for the purposes of [F56the other cases which come before that sheriff when exercising criminal jurisdiction or (as the case may be) before that JP court].

[F57. (3)This section is without prejudice to sections 4 to 10 of this Act.]]

Amendments (Textual)

F52 S. 10. A inserted (10.3.2008) by Criminal Proceedings etc. (Reform) (Scotland) Act 2007 (asp 6) , ss. 80 , 84 , Sch. para. 11 ; S.S.I. 2008/42 , art. 3 , Sch.

F53 S. 10. A(1. A) inserted (28.3.2011) by Criminal Justice and Licensing (Scotland) Act 2010 (asp 13) , s. 206. (1) , sch. 7 para. 27. (a) ; S.S.I. 2011/178 , art. 2 , sch.

F54 Word in s. 10. A(2) repealed (28.3.2011) by Criminal Justice and Licensing (Scotland) Act 2010 (asp 13) , s. 206. (1) , sch. 7 para. 27. (b)(i) ; S.S.I. 2011/178 , art. 2 , sch.

F55 S. 10. A(2)(aa) inserted (28.3.2011) by Criminal Justice and Licensing (Scotland) Act 2010 (asp 13) , s. 206. (1) , sch. 7 para. 27. (b)(ii) ; S.S.I. 2011/178 , art. 2 , sch.

F56 Words in s. 10. A(2)(b) substituted (28.3.2011) by Criminal Justice and Licensing (Scotland) Act 2010 (asp 13) , s. 206. (1) , sch. 7 para. 27. (b)(iii) ; S.S.I. 2011/178 , art. 2 , sch.

F57 S. 10. A(3) substituted (28.3.2011) by Criminal Justice and Licensing (Scotland) Act 2010 (asp 13) , s. 206. (1) , sch. 7 para. 27. (c) ; S.S.I. 2011/178 , art. 2 , sch.

11 Certain offences committed outside Scotland.S

(1) Any British citizen or British subject who in a country outside the United Kingdom does any act or makes any omission which if done or made in Scotland would constitute the crime of murder or of culpable homicide shall be guilty of the same crime and subject to the same punishment as if the act or omission had been done or made in Scotland.

(2) Any British citizen or British subject employed in the service of the Crown who, in a foreign

country, when acting or purporting to act in the course of his employment, does any act or makes any omission which if done or made in Scotland would constitute an offence punishable on indictment shall be guilty of the same offence and subject to the same punishment, as if the act or omission had been done or made in Scotland.

(3) A person may be [F58prosecuted], tried and punished for an offence to which this section applies—

(a) in any sheriff court district in Scotland in which he is apprehended or is in custody; or

(b) in such sheriff court district as the Lord Advocate may determine,

as if the offence had been committed in that district, and the offence shall, for all purposes incidental to or consequential on the trial or punishment thereof, be deemed to have been committed in that district.

(4) Any person who—

(a) has in his possession in Scotland property which he has stolen in any other part of the United Kingdom; or

(b) in Scotland receives property stolen in any other part of the United Kingdom,

may be [F59prosecuted], tried and punished in Scotland in like manner as if he had stolen it in Scotland.

[F60. (5)Where a person in any part of the United Kingdom outside Scotland—

(a) steals or attempts to steal any mail-bag or postal packet in the course of its transmission by post, or any of the contents of such a mail-bag or postal packet; or

(b) in stealing or with intent to steal any such mail-bag or postal packet or any of its contents commits any robbery, attempted robbery or assault with intent to rob,

he is guilty of the offence mentioned in paragraph (a) or (b) as if he had committed it in Scotland and shall be liable to be prosecuted, tried and punished there without proof that the offence was committed there.

(6) Any expression used in subsection (5) and in the Postal Services Act 2000 has the same meaning in that subsection as it has in that Act.]

Amendments (Textual)

F58. Word in s. 11. (3) substituted (28.3.2011) by Criminal Justice and Licensing (Scotland) Act 2010 (asp 13), s. 206. (1), sch. 7 para. 28. (a); S.S.I. 2011/178, art. 2, sch.

F59. Word in s. 11. (4) substituted (28.3.2011) by Criminal Justice and Licensing (Scotland) Act 2010 (asp 13), s. 206. (1), sch. 7 para. 28. (b); S.S.I. 2011/178, art. 2, sch.

F60. S. 11. (5)(6) inserted (26.3.2001) by 2000 c. 26, s. 127. (4), Sch. 8 para. 24; S.I. 2001/1148, art. 2, Sch. (subject to arts. 3-42)

Modifications etc. (not altering text)

C2. S. 11. (3) applied (27.6.2003) by Criminal Justice (Scotland) Act 2003 (asp 7), ss. {69. (2)(c)}, 89; S.S.I. 2003/288, art. 2, Sch.

[F6111. A [F62. Conspiracy to commit offences outwith Scotland]S

(1) This section applies to any act done by a person in Scotland which would amount to conspiracy to commit an offence but for the fact that the criminal purpose is intended to occur [F63outwith Scotland].

(2) Where a person does an act to which this section applies, the criminal purpose shall be treated as the offence mentioned in subsection (1) above and he shall, accordingly, be guilty of conspiracy to commit the offence.

(3) A person is guilty of an offence by virtue of this section only if the criminal purpose would involve at some stage—

(a) an act by him or another party to the conspiracy; or

(b) the happening of some other event,

constituting an offence under [F64the relevant law]; and conduct punishable under [F65that law] is an offence under that law for the purposes of this section however it is described in that law.

[F66. (3. A)In subsection (3) above, "the relevant law" is—

(a) if the act or event was intended to take place in another part of the United Kingdom, the law in force in that part,

(b) if the act or event was intended to take place in a country or territory outwith the United Kingdom, the law in force in that country or territory.]

(4) Subject to subsection (6) below, a condition specified in subsection (3) above shall be taken to be satisfied unless, not later than such time as High Court may, by Act of Adjournal, prescribe, the accused serves on the prosecutor a notice—

(a) stating that, on the facts as alleged with respect to the relevant conduct, the condition is not in his opinion satisfied;

(b) setting out the grounds for his opinion; and

(c) requiring the prosecutor to prove that the condition is satisfied.

(5) In subsection (4) above " the relevant conduct " means the agreement to effect the criminal purpose.

(6) The court may permit the accused to require the prosecutor to prove that the condition mentioned in subsection (4) above is satisfied without the prior service of a notice under that subsection.

(7) In proceedings on indictment, the question whether a condition is satisfied shall be determined by the judge alone.

(8) Nothing in this section—

(a) applies to an act done before the day on which the Criminal Justice (Terrorism and Conspiracy) Act 1998 was passed, or

(b) imposes criminal liability on any person acting on behalf of, or holding office under, the Crown.]

Amendments (Textual)

F61. S. 11. A inserted (4.9.1998) by Criminal Justice (Terrorism and Conspiracy) Act 1998 (c. 40), s. 7

F62. S. 11. A title substituted (28.3.2011) by Criminal Justice and Licensing (Scotland) Act 2010 (asp 13), ss. 50. (1), 206. (1); S.S.I. 2011/178, art. 2, sch.

F63. Words in s. 11. A(1) substituted (28.3.2011) by Criminal Justice and Licensing (Scotland) Act 2010 (asp 13), ss. 50. (2)(a), 206. (1); S.S.I. 2011/178, art. 2, sch.

F64. Words in s. 11. A(3) substituted (28.3.2011) by Criminal Justice and Licensing (Scotland) Act 2010 (asp 13), ss. 50. (2)(b)(i), 206. (1); S.S.I. 2011/178, art. 2, sch.

F65. Words in s. 11. A(3) substituted (28.3.2011) by Criminal Justice and Licensing (Scotland) Act 2010 (asp 13), ss. 50. (2)(b)(ii), 206. (1); S.S.I. 2011/178, art. 2, sch.

F66. S. 11. A(3. A) inserted (28.3.2011) by Criminal Justice and Licensing (Scotland) Act 2010 (asp 13), ss. 50. (2)(c), 206. (1); S.S.I. 2011/178, art. 2, sch.

PART II Police Functions

PART IIS Police Functions

12 Instructions by Lord Advocate as to reporting of offences.S

The Lord Advocate may, from time to time, issue instructions to [F1the] chief constable with regard to the reporting, for consideration of the question of prosecution, of offences alleged to have been committed F2....

Amendments (Textual)

F1. Word in s. 12 substituted (1.4.2013) by Police and Fire Reform (Scotland) Act 2012 (asp 8), s. 129. (2), sch. 7 para. 12. (2)(a); S.S.I. 2013/51, art. 2 (with transitional provisions and savings in S.S.I. 2013/121)

F2. Words in s. 12 repealed (1.4.2013) by Police and Fire Reform (Scotland) Act 2012 (asp 8), s.

129. (2), sch. 7 para. 12. (2)(b); S.S.I. 2013/51, art. 2 (with transitional provisions and savings in S.S.I. 2013/121)

Detention and questioningS

13 Powers relating to suspects and potential witnesses.S

(1) Where a constable has reasonable grounds for suspecting that a person has committed or is committing an offence at any place, he may require—

(a) that person, if the constable finds him at that place or at any place where the constable is entitled to be, to give [F3the information mentioned in subsection (1. A) below] and may ask him for an explanation of the circumstances which have given rise to the constable's suspicion;

(b) any other person whom the constable finds at that place or at any place where the constable is entitled to be and who the constable believes has information relating to the offence, to give [F4the information mentioned in subsection (1. A) below].

[F5. (1. A)That information is—

(a) the person's name;

(b) the person's address;

(c) the person's date of birth;

(d) the person's place of birth (in such detail as the constable considers necessary or expedient for the purpose of establishing the person's identity); and

(e) the person's nationality.]

(2) The constable may require the person mentioned in paragraph (a) of subsection (1) above to remain with him while he (either or both)—

(a) subject to subsection (3) below, verifies any [F6information mentioned in subsection (1. A) above] given by the person;

(b) notes any explanation proffered by the person.

(3) The constable shall exercise his power under paragraph (a) of subsection (2) above only where it appears to him that such verification can be obtained quickly.

(4) A constable may use reasonable force to ensure that the person mentioned in paragraph (a) of subsection (1) above remains with him.

(5) A constable shall inform a person, when making a requirement of that person under—

(a) paragraph (a) of subsection (1) above, of his suspicion and of the general nature of the offence which he suspects that the person has committed or is committing;

(b) paragraph (b) of subsection (1) above, of his suspicion, of the general nature of the offence which he suspects has been or is being committed and that the reason for the requirement is that he believes the person has information relating to the offence;

(c) subsection (2) above, why the person is being required to remain with him;

(d) either of the said subsections, that failure to comply with the requirement may constitute an offence.

(6) A person mentioned in—

(a) paragraph (a) of subsection (1) above who having been required—

(i) under that subsection to give [F7the information mentioned in subsection (1. A) above]; or

(ii) under subsection (2) above to remain with a constable,

fails, without reasonable excuse, to do so, shall be guilty of an offence and liable on summary conviction to a fine not exceeding level 3 on the standard scale;

(b) paragraph (b) of the said subsection (1) who having been required under that subsection to give [F8the information mentioned in subsection (1. A) above] fails, without reasonable excuse, to do so shall be guilty of an offence and liable on summary conviction to a fine not exceeding level 2 on the standard scale.

F9. (7). . . . .

Amendments (Textual)
F3. Words in s. 13. (1)(a)(b) substituted (1.9.2006) by Police, Public Order and Criminal Justice (Scotland) Act 2006 (asp 10), ss. 81. (2), 104; S.S.I. 2006/432, art. 2. (e)
F4. Words in s. 13. (1)(a)(b) substituted (1.9.2006) by Police, Public Order and Criminal Justice (Scotland) Act 2006 (asp 10), ss. 81. (2), 104; S.S.I. 2006/432, art. 2. (e)
F5. S. 13. (1. A) inserted (1.9.2006) by Police, Public Order and Criminal Justice (Scotland) Act 2006 (asp 10), ss. 81. (3), 104; S.S.I. 2006/432, art. 2. (e)
F6. Words in s. 13. (2)(a) substituted (1.9.2006) by Police, Public Order and Criminal Justice (Scotland) Act 2006 (asp 10), ss. 81. (4), 104; S.S.I. 2006/432, art. 2. (e)
F7. Words in s. 13. (6)(a)(i)(b) substituted (1.9.2006) by Police, Public Order and Criminal Justice (Scotland) Act 2006 (asp 10), ss. 81. (5), 104; S.S.I. 2006/432, art. 2. (e)
F8. Words in s. 13. (6)(a)(i)(b) substituted (1.9.2006) by Police, Public Order and Criminal Justice (Scotland) Act 2006 (asp 10), ss. 81. (5), 104; S.S.I. 2006/432, art. 2. (e)
F9. S. 13. (7) repealed (25.1.2018) by Criminal Justice (Scotland) Act 2016 (asp 1), s. 117. (2), sch. 2 para. 2. (a); S.S.I. 2017/345, art. 3, sch.

F1014 Detention and questioning at police station.S

. . . .
Amendments (Textual)
F10. Ss. 14-17. A repealed (25.1.2018) by Criminal Justice (Scotland) Act 2016 (asp 1), s. 117. (2), sch. 2 para. 27. (a); S.S.I. 2017/345, art. 3, sch. (with arts. 4, 7)

F1014. AExtension of period of detention under section 14. S

. . . .
Amendments (Textual)
F10. Ss. 14-17. A repealed (25.1.2018) by Criminal Justice (Scotland) Act 2016 (asp 1), s. 117. (2), sch. 2 para. 27. (a); S.S.I. 2017/345, art. 3, sch. (with arts. 4, 7)

F1014. BExtension under section 14. A: procedureS

. . . .
Amendments (Textual)
F10. Ss. 14-17. A repealed (25.1.2018) by Criminal Justice (Scotland) Act 2016 (asp 1), s. 117. (2), sch. 2 para. 27. (a); S.S.I. 2017/345, art. 3, sch. (with arts. 4, 7)

F1015. Right of persons arrested or detained to have intimation sent to another personS

. . . .
Amendments (Textual)
F10. Ss. 14-17. A repealed (25.1.2018) by Criminal Justice (Scotland) Act 2016 (asp 1), s. 117. (2), sch. 2 para. 27. (a); S.S.I. 2017/345, art. 3, sch. (with arts. 4, 7)

F1015. ARight of suspects to have access to a solicitorS

. . . .
Amendments (Textual)
F10. Ss. 14-17. A repealed (25.1.2018) by Criminal Justice (Scotland) Act 2016 (asp 1), s. 117.

F1016 Drunken persons: power to take to designated place.S

. . . .

Amendments (Textual)

F10. Ss. 14-17. A repealed (25.1.2018) by Criminal Justice (Scotland) Act 2016 (asp 1), s. 117. (2), sch. 2 para. 27. (a); S.S.I. 2017/345, art. 3, sch. (with arts. 4, 7)

Arrest: access to solicitorS

F1017 Right of accused to have access to solicitor.S

. . . .

Amendments (Textual)

F10. Ss. 14-17. A repealed (25.1.2018) by Criminal Justice (Scotland) Act 2016 (asp 1), s. 117. (2), sch. 2 para. 27. (a); S.S.I. 2017/345, art. 3, sch. (with arts. 4, 7)

F1017. A Right of person accused of sexual offence to be told about restriction on conduct of defence: arrestS

. . . .

Amendments (Textual)

F10. Ss. 14-17. A repealed (25.1.2018) by Criminal Justice (Scotland) Act 2016 (asp 1), s. 117. (2), sch. 2 para. 27. (a); S.S.I. 2017/345, art. 3, sch. (with arts. 4, 7)

Prints and samplesS

18 Prints, samples etc. in criminal investigations.S

(1) This section applies where a person has been arrested and is in custody F11....

(2) A constable may take from the person [F12, or require the person to provide him with, such relevant physical data] as the constable may, having regard to the circumstances of the suspected offence [F13or the relevant offence (within the meaning of section 164. (3) of the Extradition Act 2003)] in respect of which the person has been arrested F14..., reasonably consider it appropriate to take [F15from him or require him to provide, and the person so required shall comply with that requirement].

[F16. (3)Subject to [F17subsections (3. A) and (4)] below [F18and [F19sections 18. A to [F2018. G]] of this Act], all record of any relevant physical data taken from or provided by a person under subsection (2) above, all samples taken under subsection (6) [F21or (6. A)] below and all information derived from such samples shall be destroyed as soon as possible following a decision not to institute criminal proceedings against the person or on the conclusion of such proceedings otherwise than with a conviction or an order under section 246. (3) of this Act.]

[F22. (3. A)(3. A) Subsection (3) does not apply to—

 (a) relevant physical data taken under subsection (2) from, or provided under that subsection by, a person arrested under an extradition arrest power (within the meaning of section 174. (2) of the Extradition Act 2003), and

 (b) any sample, or any information derived from a sample, taken under subsection (6) or (6. A) from a person arrested under such a power (but see section 18. H).]

(4) The duty under subsection (3) above to destroy samples taken under subsection (6) [F23or (6. A)] below and information derived from such samples shall not apply—

(a) where the destruction of the sample or the information could have the effect of destroying any sample, or any information derived therefrom, lawfully held in relation to a person other than the person from whom the sample was taken; or

(b) where the record, sample or information in question is of the same kind as a record, a sample or, as the case may be, information lawfully held by or on behalf of [F24the Police Service of Scotland] in relation to the person.

(5) No sample, or information derived from a sample, retained by virtue of subsection (4) above shall be used—

(a) in evidence against the person from whom the sample was taken; or

(b) for the purposes of the investigation of any offence.

(6) A constable may, with the authority of an officer of a rank no lower than inspector, take from the person—

(a) from the hair of an external part of the body other than pubic hair, by means of cutting, combing or plucking, a sample of hair or other material;

(b) from a fingernail or toenail or from under any such nail, a sample of nail or other material;

(c) from an external part of the body, by means of swabbing or rubbing, a sample of blood or other body fluid, of body tissue or of other material;

(d) F25. . . . .

[F26. (6. A)A constable, or at a constable's direction a police custody and security officer, may take from the inside of the person's mouth, by means of swabbing, a sample of saliva or other material.]

F27. (7). . . . .

[F28. (7. A) For the purposes of this section and [F29, subject to the modification in subsection (7. AA), sections 18. A to 19. C] of this Act "relevant physical data" means any—

(a) fingerprint;

(b) palm print;

(c) print or impression other than those mentioned in paragraph (a) and (b) above, of an external part of the body;

(d) record of a person's skin on an external part of the body created by a device approved by the Secretary of State.

[F30. (7. AA)The modification is that for the purposes of section 19. C as it applies in relation to relevant physical data taken from or provided by a person outwith Scotland, subsection (7. A) is to be read as if in paragraph (d) the words from "created" to the end were omitted.]

(7. B)The Secretary of State by order made by statutory instrument may approve a device for the purpose of creating such records as are mentioned in paragraph (d) of subsection (7. A) above.]

(8) Nothing in this section shall prejudice—

(a) any power of search;

(b) any power to take possession of evidence where there is imminent danger of its being lost or destroyed; or

(c) any power to take [F31relevant physical data] or samples under the authority of a warrant.

Amendments (Textual)

F11. Words in s. 18. (1) repealed (25.1.2018) by Criminal Justice (Scotland) Act 2016 (asp 1), s. 117. (2), sch. 2 para. 28. (1)(a); S.S.I. 2017/345, art. 3, sch. (with art. 4)

F12. Words in s. 18. (2) substituted (1.8.1997) by 1997 c. 48, s. 47. (1)(a)(i); S.I. 1997/1712, art. 3, Sch. (subject to arts. 4, 5)

F13. Words in s. 18. (2) inserted (25.1.2018) by The Criminal Justice (Scotland) Act 2016 (Consequential Provisions) Order 2018 (S.I. 2018/46), art. 2. (2)(a)(f), Sch. 5 para. 1. (2)

F14. Words in s. 18. (2) repealed (25.1.2018) by Criminal Justice (Scotland) Act 2016 (asp 1), s. 117. (2), sch. 2 para. 28. (1)(b); S.S.I. 2017/345, art. 3, sch. (with art. 4)

F15. Words in s. 18. (2) inserted (1.8.1997) by 1997 c. 48, s. 47. (1)(a)(ii); S.I. 1997/1712, art. 3,

Sch. (subject to arts. 4, 5)

F16. S. 18. (3) substituted (retrospective to 1.8.1997) by 1998 c. 37, ss. 119, 121. (2), Sch. 8 para. 117. (2)

F17. Words in s. 18. (3) substituted (25.1.2018) by The Criminal Justice (Scotland) Act 2016 (Consequential Provisions) Order 2018 (S.I. 2018/46), art. 2. (2)(a)(f), Sch. 5 para. 1. (3)

F18. Words in s. 18. (3) inserted (1.1.2007) by Police, Public Order and Criminal Justice (Scotland) Act 2006 (asp 10), ss. 83. (1), 104; S.S.I. 2006/607, art. 3, Sch.

F19. Words in s. 18. (3) substituted (28.3.2011) by Criminal Justice and Licensing (Scotland) Act 2010 (asp 13), ss. 77. (2)(a), 206. (1); S.S.I. 2011/178, art. 2, sch. (with art. 4)

F20. Word in s. 18. (3) substituted (31.10.2013) by Protection of Freedoms Act 2012 (c. 9), s. 120, Sch. 1 para. 6. (2) (with s. 97); S.I. 2013/1814, art. 2. (k)

F21. Words in s. 18. (3) inserted (1.9.2006) by Police, Public Order and Criminal Justice (Scotland) Act 2006 (asp 10), ss. 101, 104, Sch. 6 para. 4. (2); S.S.I. 2006/432, art. 2. (g)(h)

F22. S. 18. (3. A) inserted (25.1.2018) by The Criminal Justice (Scotland) Act 2016 (Consequential Provisions) Order 2018 (S.I. 2018/46), art. 2. (2)(a)(f), Sch. 5 para. 1. (4)

F23. Words in s. 18. (4) inserted (1.9.2006) by Police, Public Order and Criminal Justice (Scotland) Act 2006 (asp 10), ss. 101, 104, Sch. 6 para. 4. (2); S.S.I. 2006/432, art. 2. (g)(h)

F24. Words in s. 18. (4)(b) substituted (1.4.2013) by Police and Fire Reform (Scotland) Act 2012 (asp 8), s. 129. (2), sch. 7 para. 12. (3); S.S.I. 2013/51, art. 2 (with transitional provisions and savings in S.S.I. 2013/121)

F25. S. 18. (6)(d) repealed (27.6.2003) by Criminal Justice (Scotland) Act 2003 (asp 7), ss. {55. (2)(a)}, 89; S.S.I. 2003/288, art. 2, Sch.

F26. S. 18. (6. A) inserted (27.6.2003) by Criminal Justice (Scotland) Act 2003 (asp 7), ss. {55. (2)(b)}, 89; S.S.I. 2003/288, art. 2, Sch.

F27. S. 18. (7) repealed (17.11.1997) by 1997 c. 48, ss. 47. (1)(c), 62. (2), Sch. 3; S.I. 1997/2694, art. 2. (2)(a)(d)

F28. S. 18. (7. A)(7. B) inserted (1.8.1997) by 1997 c. 48, s. 47. (1)(d); S.I. 1997/1712, art. 3, Sch. (subject to arts. 4, 5)

F29. Words in s. 18. (7. A) substituted (1.8.2011) by Criminal Justice and Licensing (Scotland) Act 2010 (asp 13), ss. 77. (2)(b), 206. (1); S.S.I. 2011/178, art. 2, sch. (with art. 4)

F30. S. 18. (7. AA) inserted (1.8.2011) by Criminal Justice and Licensing (Scotland) Act 2010 (asp 13), ss. 77. (2)(c), 206. (1); S.S.I. 2011/178, art. 2, sch. (with art. 4)

F31. Words in s. 18. (8)(c) substituted (28.3.2011) by Criminal Justice and Licensing (Scotland) Act 2010 (asp 13), s. 206. (1), sch. 7 para. 30; S.S.I. 2011/178, art. 2, sch.

Modifications etc. (not altering text)

C1. S. 18 applied (with modifications) (19.2.2001) by 2000 c. 11, ss. 41, 53, Sch. 7 para. 6, Sch. 8 para. 20. (1); S.I. 2001/421, art. 2

C2. S. 18 applied (with modifications) by 1994 c. 33, s. 138. (2)(2. A)(6)-(9) (as substituted (15.7.2011) by The Criminal Procedure (Legal Assistance, Detention and Appeals) (Scotland) Act 2010 (Consequential Provisions) Order 2011 (S.I. 2011/1739), art. 1. (2), Sch. 2 para. 2. (3)(4) (with art. 6. (2)))

C3. S. 18. (3)-(5) applied (17.12.2001) by 2001 asp 13, s. 17, Sch. 4 para. 7 (with s. 29); S.S.I. 2001/456, art. 2

[F3218. A Retention of samples etc. : prosecutions for sexual and violent offences S

[F33. (1)This section applies to—

   (a) relevant physical data taken or provided under section 18. (2), and

   (b) any sample, or any information derived from a sample, taken under section 18. (6) or (6. A), where the condition in subsection (2) is satisfied.]

(2) That condition is that criminal proceedings in respect of a relevant sexual offence or a relevant

violent offence were instituted against the person from whom [F34the relevant physical data was taken or by whom it was provided or, as the case may be, from whom] the sample was taken but those proceedings concluded otherwise than with a conviction or an order under section 246. (3) of this Act.

(3) Subject to subsections (9) and (10) below, the [F35relevant physical data, sample or information derived from a sample] shall be destroyed no later than the destruction date.

(4) The destruction date is—

    (a) the date of expiry of the period of 3 years following the conclusion of the proceedings; or

    (b) such later date as an order under subsection (5) below may specify.

(5) On a summary application made by the [F36chief constable of the Police Service of Scotland] within the period of 3 months before the destruction date the sheriff may, if satisfied that there are reasonable grounds for doing so, make an order amending, or further amending, the destruction date.

(6) An application under subsection (5) above may be made to any sheriff—

    (a) in whose sheriffdom the person referred to in subsection (2) above resides;

    (b) in whose sheriffdom that person is believed by the applicant to be; or

    (c) to whose sheriffdom the person is believed by the applicant to be intending to come.

(7) An order under subsection (5) above shall not specify a destruction date more than 2 years later than the previous destruction date.

(8) The decision of the sheriff on an application under subsection (5) above may be appealed to the sheriff principal within 21 days of the decision; and the sheriff principal's decision on any such appeal is final.

[F37. (8. A)If the sheriff principal allows an appeal against the refusal of an application under subsection (5), the sheriff principal may make an order amending, or further amending, the destruction date.

(8. B)An order under subsection (8. A) must not specify a destruction date more than 2 years later than the previous destruction date.]

(9) Subsection (3) above does not apply where—

    (a) an application under subsection (5) above has been made but has not been determined;

    (b) the period within which an appeal may be brought under subsection (8) above against a decision to refuse an application has not elapsed; or

    (c) such an appeal has been brought but has not been withdrawn or finally determined.

(10) Where—

    (a) the period within which an appeal referred to in subsection (9)(b) above may be brought has elapsed without such an appeal being brought;

    (b) such an appeal is brought and is withdrawn or finally determined against the appellant; or

    (c) an appeal brought under subsection (8) above against a decision to grant an application is determined in favour of the appellant,

the [F38relevant physical data, sample or information derived from a sample] shall be destroyed as soon as possible thereafter.

(11) In this section—

F39...

"relevant sexual offence" and "relevant violent offence" have [F40, subject to the modification in subsection (12),] the same meanings as in section 19. A(6) of this Act and include any attempt, conspiracy or incitement to commit such an offence.]

[F41. (12)The modification is that the definition of "relevant sexual offence" in section 19. A(6) is to be read as if for paragraph (g) there were substituted—

    "(g)public indecency if it is apparent from the offence as charged in the indictment or complaint that there was a sexual aspect to the behaviour of the person charged;"]

Amendments (Textual)

F32. S. 18. A inserted (1.1.2007) by Police, Public Order and Criminal Justice (Scotland) Act 2006 (asp 10), ss. 83. (2), 104; S.S.I. 2006/607, art. 3, Sch.

F33. S. 18. A(1) substituted (28.3.2011) by Criminal Justice and Licensing (Scotland) Act 2010 (asp 13), ss. 77. (3)(a), 206. (1); S.S.I. 2011/178, art. 2, sch. (with art. 4)

F34. Words in s. 18. A(2) inserted (28.3.2011) by Criminal Justice and Licensing (Scotland) Act 2010 (asp 13), ss. 77. (3)(b), 206. (1); S.S.I. 2011/178, art. 2, sch. (with art. 4)

F35. Words in s. 18. A(3) substituted (28.3.2011) by Criminal Justice and Licensing (Scotland) Act 2010 (asp 13), ss. 77. (3)(c), 206. (1); S.S.I. 2011/178, art. 2, sch. (with art. 4)

F36. Words in s. 18. A(5) substituted (1.4.2013) by Police and Fire Reform (Scotland) Act 2012 (asp 8), s. 129. (2), sch. 7 para. 12. (4)(a); S.S.I. 2013/51, art. 2 (with transitional provisions and savings in S.S.I. 2013/121)

F37. S. 18. A(8. A)(8. B) inserted (28.3.2011) by Criminal Justice and Licensing (Scotland) Act 2010 (asp 13), ss. 77. (3)(d), 206. (1); S.S.I. 2011/178, art. 2, sch. (with art. 4)

F38. Words in s. 18. A(10) substituted (28.3.2011) by Criminal Justice and Licensing (Scotland) Act 2010 (asp 13), ss. 77. (3)(e), 206. (1); S.S.I. 2011/178, art. 2, sch. (with art. 4)

F39. Definition in s. 18. A(11) repealed (1.4.2013) by Police and Fire Reform (Scotland) Act 2012 (asp 8), s. 129. (2), sch. 7 para. 12. (4)(b); S.S.I. 2013/51, art. 2 (with transitional provisions and savings in S.S.I. 2013/121)

F40. Words in s. 18. A(11) inserted (28.3.2011) by Criminal Justice and Licensing (Scotland) Act 2010 (asp 13), ss. 77. (3)(f)(ii), 206. (1); S.S.I. 2011/178, art. 2, sch. (with art. 4)

F41. S. 18. A(12) inserted (28.3.2011) by Criminal Justice and Licensing (Scotland) Act 2010 (asp 13), ss. 77. (3)(g), 206. (1); S.S.I. 2011/178, art. 2, sch. (with art. 4)

[F4218. BRetention of samples etc. where offer under sections 302 to 303. ZA acceptedS

(1) This section applies to—

(a) relevant physical data taken from or provided by a person under section 18. (2), and

(b) any sample, or any information derived from a sample, taken from a person under section 18. (6) or (6. A),

where the conditions in subsection (2) are satisfied.

(2) The conditions are—

(a) the relevant physical data or sample was taken from or provided by the person while the person was [F43in custody] in connection with the offence or offences in relation to which a relevant offer is issued to the person, and

(b) the person—

(i) accepts a relevant offer, or

(ii) in the case of a relevant offer other than one of the type mentioned in paragraph (d) of subsection (3), is deemed to accept a relevant offer.

(3) In this section "relevant offer" means—

(a) a conditional offer under section 302,

(b) a compensation offer under section 302. A,

(c) a combined offer under section 302. B, or

(d) a work offer under section 303. ZA.

(4) Subject to subsections (6) and (7) and section 18. C(9) and (10), the relevant physical data, sample or information derived from a sample must be destroyed no later than the destruction date.

(5) In subsection (4), "destruction date" means—

(a) in relation to a relevant offer that relates only to—

(i) a relevant sexual offence,

(ii) a relevant violent offence, or

(iii) both a relevant sexual offence and a relevant violent offence, the date of expiry of the period of 3 years beginning with the date on which the relevant offer is issued or such later date as an order under section 18. C(2) or (6) may specify,

(b) in relation to a relevant offer that relates to—

(i) an offence or offences falling within paragraph (a), and

23

(ii) any other offence,

the date of expiry of the period of 3 years beginning with the date on which the relevant offer is issued or such later date as an order under section 18. C(2) or (6) may specify,

(c) in relation to a relevant offer that does not relate to an offence falling within paragraph (a), the date of expiry of the period of 2 years beginning with the date on which the relevant offer is issued.

(6) If a relevant offer is recalled by virtue of section 302. C(5) or a decision to uphold it is quashed under section 302. C(7)(a), all record of the relevant physical data, sample and information derived from a sample must be destroyed as soon as possible after—

(a) the prosecutor decides not to issue a further relevant offer to the person,

(b) the prosecutor decides not to institute criminal proceedings against the person, or

(c) the prosecutor institutes criminal proceedings against the person and those proceedings conclude otherwise than with a conviction or an order under section 246. (3).

(7) If a relevant offer is set aside by virtue of section 303. ZB, all record of the relevant physical data, sample and information derived from a sample must be destroyed as soon as possible after the setting aside.

(8) In this section, "relevant sexual offence" and "relevant violent offence" have, subject to the modification in subsection (9), the same meanings as in section 19. A(6) and include any attempt, conspiracy or incitement to commit such an offence.

(9) The modification is that the definition of "relevant sexual offence" in section 19. A(6) is to be read as if for paragraph (g) there were substituted—

"(g)public indecency if it is apparent from the relevant offer (as defined in section 18. B(3)) relating to the offence that there was a sexual aspect to the behaviour of the person to whom the relevant offer is issued;".]

Amendments (Textual)

F42. Ss. 18. B-18. C inserted (28.3.2011) by Criminal Justice and Licensing (Scotland) Act 2010 (asp 13), ss. 78, 206. (1); S.S.I. 2011/178, art. 2, sch. (with art. 5)

F43. Words in s. 18. B(2)(a) substituted (25.1.2018) by Criminal Justice (Scotland) Act 2016 (asp 1), s. 117. (2), sch. 2 para. 28. (2); S.S.I. 2017/345, art. 3, sch. (with art. 4)

[F4218. CSection 18. B: extension of retention period where relevant offer relates to certain sexual or violent offencesS

(1) This section applies where the destruction date for relevant physical data, a sample or information derived from a sample falls within section 18. B(5)(a) or (b).

(2) On a summary application made by the [F44chief constable of the Police Service of Scotland] within the period of 3 months before the destruction date, the sheriff may, if satisfied that there are reasonable grounds for doing so, make an order amending, or further amending, the destruction date.

(3) An application under subsection (2) may be made to any sheriff—

(a) in whose sheriffdom the appropriate person resides,

(b) in whose sheriffdom that person is believed by the applicant to be, or

(c) to whose sheriffdom the person is believed by the applicant to be intending to come.

(4) An order under subsection (2) must not specify a destruction date more than 2 years later than the previous destruction date.

(5) The decision of the sheriff on an application under subsection (2) may be appealed to the sheriff principal within 21 days of the decision.

(6) If the sheriff principal allows an appeal against the refusal of an application under subsection (2), the sheriff principal may make an order amending, or further amending, the destruction date.

(7) An order under subsection (6) must not specify a destruction date more than 2 years later than the previous destruction date.

(8) The sheriff principal's decision on an appeal under subsection (5) is final.

(9) Section 18. B(4) does not apply where—

(a) an application under subsection (2) has been made but has not been determined,

(b) the period within which an appeal may be brought under subsection (5) against a decision to refuse an application has not elapsed, or

(c) such an appeal has been brought but has not been withdrawn or finally determined.

(10) Where—

(a) the period within which an appeal referred to in subsection (9)(b) may be brought has elapsed without such an appeal being brought,

(b) such an appeal is brought and is withdrawn or finally determined against the appellant, or

(c) an appeal brought under subsection (5) against a decision to grant an application is determined in favour of the appellant,

the relevant physical data, sample or information derived from a sample must be destroyed as soon as possible after the period has elapsed, or, as the case may be, the appeal is withdrawn or determined.

(11) In this section—

"appropriate person" means the person from whom the relevant physical data was taken or by whom it was provided or from whom the sample was taken,

"destruction date" has the meaning given by section 18. B(5),

F45...]

Amendments (Textual)

F42. Ss. 18. B-18. C inserted (28.3.2011) by Criminal Justice and Licensing (Scotland) Act 2010 (asp 13), ss. 78, 206. (1); S.S.I. 2011/178, art. 2, sch. (with art. 5)

F44. Words in s. 18. C(2) substituted (1.4.2013) by Police and Fire Reform (Scotland) Act 2012 (asp 8), s. 129. (2), sch. 7 para. 12. (5)(a); S.S.I. 2013/51, art. 2 (with transitional provisions and savings in S.S.I. 2013/121)

F45. Definition in s. 18. C(11) repealed (1.4.2013) by Police and Fire Reform (Scotland) Act 2012 (asp 8), s. 129. (2), sch. 7 para. 12. (5)(b); S.S.I. 2013/51, art. 2 (with transitional provisions and savings in S.S.I. 2013/121)

[F4618. DRetention of samples etc. taken or provided in connection with certain fixed penalty offencesS

(1) This section applies to—

(a) relevant physical data taken from or provided by a person under section 18. (2), and

(b) any sample, or any information derived from a sample, taken from a person under section 18. (6) or (6. A),

where the conditions in subsection (2) are satisfied.

(2) The conditions are—

(a) the person was arrested F47... in connection with a fixed penalty offence,

(b) the relevant physical data or sample was taken from or provided by the person while the person was [F48in custody] in connection with that offence,

(c) after the relevant physical data or sample was taken from or provided by the person, a constable gave the person under section 129. (1) of the 2004 Act—

(i) a fixed penalty notice in respect of that offence (the "main FPN"), or

(ii) the main FPN and one or more other fixed penalty notices in respect of fixed penalty offences arising out of the same circumstances as the offence to which the main FPN relates, and

(d) the person, in relation to the main FPN and any other fixed penalty notice of the type mentioned in paragraph (c)(ii)—

(i) pays the fixed penalty, or

(ii) pays any sum that the person is liable to pay by virtue of section 131. (5) of the 2004 Act.

(3) Subject to subsections (4) and (5), the relevant physical data, sample or information derived from a sample must be destroyed before the end of the period of 2 years beginning with—

(a) where subsection (2)(c)(i) applies, the day on which the main FPN is given to the person,

(b) where subsection (2)(c)(ii) applies and—

(i) the main FPN and any other fixed penalty notice are given to the person on the same day, that day,

(ii) the main FPN and any other fixed penalty notice are given to the person on different days, the later day.

(4) Where—

(a) subsection (2)(c)(i) applies, and

(b) the main FPN is revoked under section 133. (1) of the 2004 Act,

the relevant physical data, sample or information derived from a sample must be destroyed as soon as possible after the revocation.

(5) Where—

(a) subsection (2)(c)(ii) applies, and

(b) the main FPN and any other fixed penalty notices are revoked under section 133. (1) of the 2004 Act,

the relevant physical data, sample or information derived from a sample must be destroyed as soon as possible after the revocations.

(6) In this section—

"the 2004 Act" means the Antisocial Behaviour etc. (Scotland) Act 2004 (asp 8),

"fixed penalty notice" has the meaning given by section 129. (2) of the 2004 Act,

"fixed penalty offence" has the meaning given by section 128. (1) of the 2004 Act.]

Amendments (Textual)

F46. S. 18. D inserted (28.3.2011) by Criminal Justice and Licensing (Scotland) Act 2010 (asp 13), ss. 79, 206. (1); S.S.I. 2011/178, art. 2, sch. (with art. 6)

F47. Words in s. 18. D(2)(a) repealed (25.1.2018) by Criminal Justice (Scotland) Act 2016 (asp 1), s. 117. (2), sch. 2 para. 28. (3)(a); S.S.I. 2017/345, art. 3, sch. (with art. 4)

F48. Words in s. 18. D(2)(b) substituted (25.1.2018) by Criminal Justice (Scotland) Act 2016 (asp 1), s. 117. (2), sch. 2 para. 28. (3)(b); S.S.I. 2017/345, art. 3, sch. (with art. 4)

[F4918. ERetention of samples etc.: children referred to children's hearingsS

(1) This section applies to—

(a) relevant physical data taken from or provided by a child under section 18. (2); and

(b) any sample, or any information derived from a sample, taken from a child under section 18. (6) or (6. A),

where [F50subsection (3), (4) or (5) applies.]

F51. (2). . . . .

[F52. (3)This subsection applies where—

(a) in relation to a children's hearing arranged in relation to the child under section 69. (2) of the 2011 Act, a section 67 ground is that the child has committed an offence mentioned in subsection (6) (a "relevant offence"),

(b) the ground is accepted by the child and each relevant person in relation to the child under section 91. (1) or 105. (1) of that Act, and

(c) no application to the sheriff under section 93. (2)(a) or 94. (2)(a) of that Act is made in relation to that ground.

(4) This subsection applies where—

(a) in relation to a children's hearing arranged in relation to the child under section 69. (2) of the 2011 Act, a section 67 ground is that the child has committed a relevant offence,

(b) the sheriff, on an application under section 93. (2)(a) or 94. (2)(a) of that Act, determines under section 108 of that Act that the ground is established, and

(c) no application to the sheriff under section 110. (2) of that Act is made in relation to the ground.

(5) This subsection applies where, on an application under section 110. (2) of the 2011 Act in relation to the child—

(a) the sheriff is satisfied under section 114. (2) or 115. (1)(b) of that Act that a section 67 ground which constitutes a relevant offence is established or accepted by the child and each relevant person in relation to the child, or

(b) the sheriff determines under section 117. (2)(a) of that Act that—

(i) a section 67 ground which was not stated in the statement of grounds which gave rise to the grounds determination is established, and

(ii) the ground constitutes a relevant offence.]

(6) A relevant offence is such relevant sexual offence or relevant violent offence as the Scottish Ministers may by order made by statutory instrument prescribe.

(7) An order under subsection (6) may prescribe a relevant violent offence by reference to a particular degree of seriousness.

(8) Subject to section 18. F(8) and (9), the relevant physical data, sample or information derived from a sample must be destroyed no later than the destruction date.

(9) The destruction date is—

(a) the date of expiry of the period of 3 years following—

[F53. (i)where subsection (3) applies, the date on which the section 67 ground was accepted as mentioned in that subsection,

(ii) where subsection (4) applies, the date on which the section 67 ground was established as mentioned in that subsection,

(iii) where the section 67 ground is established as mentioned in paragraph (a) of subsection (5), the date on which that ground was established under section 108 of the 2011 Act or, as the case may be, accepted under section 91. (1) or 105. (1) of that Act, or

(iv) where the section 67 ground is established as mentioned in paragraph (b) of subsection (5), the date on which that ground was established as mentioned in that paragraph,]

(b) such later date as an order under section 18. F(1) may specify.

(10) No statutory instrument containing an order under subsection (6) may be made unless a draft of the instrument has been laid before, and approved by resolution of, the Scottish Parliament.

(11) In this section—

[F54"the 2011 Act" means the Children's Hearings (Scotland) Act 2011 (asp 1),

"grounds determination" has the meaning given by section 110. (1) of the 2011 Act;]

"relevant person" has the same meaning as in section [F55200. (1) of the 2011 Act except that it includes a person deemed to be a relevant person by virtue of section 81. (3), 160. (4)(b) or 164. (6) of that Act];

"relevant sexual offence" and "relevant violent offence" have, subject to the modification in subsection (12), the same meanings as in section 19. A(6) and include any attempt, conspiracy or incitement to commit such an offence.

[F56"section 67 ground" has the meaning given by section 67. (1) of the 2011 Act;

"statement of grounds" has the meaning given by section 89. (3) of the 2011 Act.]

(12) The modification is that the definition of "relevant sexual offence" in section 19. A(6) is to be read as if for paragraph (g) there were substituted—

""(g)public indecency if it is apparent from the [F57section 67 ground] relating to the offence that there was a sexual aspect to the behaviour of the child;"".

Amendments (Textual)

F49. Ss. 18. E, 18. F inserted (13.12.2010 for the insertion of s. 18. E(6)(7)(10), 15.4.2011 in so far as not already in force) by Criminal Justice and Licensing (Scotland) Act 2010 (asp 13), ss. 80, 206. (1); S.S.I. 2010/413, art. 2, sch.; S.S.I. 2011/178, art. 2, sch. (with art. 7)

F50. Words in s. 18. E(1) substituted (24.6.2013) by The Childrens Hearings (Scotland) Act 2011 (Modification of Primary Legislation) Order 2013 (S.S.I. 2013/211), art. 1, sch. 1 para. 10. (2)(a)

F51. S. 18. E(2) repealed (24.6.2013) by The Childrens Hearings (Scotland) Act 2011 (Modification of Primary Legislation) Order 2013 (S.S.I. 2013/211), art. 1, sch. 1 para. 10. (2)(b)

F52. S. 18. E(3)-(5) substituted (24.6.2013) by The Childrens Hearings (Scotland) Act 2011 (Modification of Primary Legislation) Order 2013 (S.S.I. 2013/211), art. 1, sch. 1 para. 10. (2)(c)

F53. S. 18. E(9)(a)(i)-(iv) substituted (24.6.2013) by The Childrens Hearings (Scotland) Act 2011 (Modification of Primary Legislation) Order 2013 (S.S.I. 2013/211), art. 1, sch. 1 para. 10. (2)(d)

F54. Definitions in s. 18. E(11) inserted (24.6.2013) by The Childrens Hearings (Scotland) Act 2011 (Modification of Primary Legislation) Order 2013 (S.S.I. 2013/211), art. 1, sch. 1 para. 10. (2)(e)(i)

F55. Words in s. 18. E(11) substituted (24.6.2013) by The Childrens Hearings (Scotland) Act 2011 (Modification of Primary Legislation) Order 2013 (S.S.I. 2013/211), art. 1, sch. 1 para. 10. (2)(e)(ii)

F56. Definitions in s. 18. E(11) inserted (24.6.2013) by The Childrens Hearings (Scotland) Act 2011 (Modification of Primary Legislation) Order 2013 (S.S.I. 2013/211), art. 1, sch. 1 para. 10. (2)(e)(iii)

F57. Words in s. 18. E(12) substituted (24.6.2013) by The Childrens Hearings (Scotland) Act 2011 (Modification of Primary Legislation) Order 2013 (S.S.I. 2013/211), art. 1, sch. 1 para. 10. (2)(f)

18. FRetention of samples etc. relating to children: appealsS

(1) On a summary application made by the [F58chief constable of the Police Service of Scotland] within the period of 3 months before the destruction date the sheriff may, if satisfied that there are reasonable grounds for doing so, make an order amending, or further amending, the destruction date.

(2) An application under subsection (1) may be made to any sheriff—

    (a) in whose sheriffdom the child mentioned in section 18. E(1) resides;

    (b) in whose sheriffdom that child is believed by the applicant to be; or

    (c) to whose sheriffdom that child is believed by the applicant to be intending to come.

(3) An order under subsection (1) must not specify a destruction date more than 2 years later than the previous destruction date.

(4) The decision of the sheriff on an application under subsection (1) may be appealed to the sheriff principal within 21 days of the decision.

(5) If the sheriff principal allows an appeal against the refusal of an application under subsection (1), the sheriff principal may make an order amending, or further amending, the destruction date.

(6) An order under subsection (5) must not specify a destruction date more than 2 years later than the previous destruction date.

(7) The sheriff principal's decision on an appeal under subsection (4) is final.

(8) Section 18. E(8) does not apply where—

    (a) an application under subsection (1) has been made but has not been determined;

    (b) the period within which an appeal may be brought under subsection (4) against a decision to refuse an application has not elapsed; or

    (c) such an appeal has been brought but has not been withdrawn or finally determined.

(9) Where—

    (a) the period within which an appeal referred to in subsection (8)(b) may be brought has elapsed without such an appeal being brought;

    (b) such an appeal is brought and is withdrawn or finally determined against the appellant; or

    (c) an appeal brought under subsection (4) against a decision to grant an application is determined in favour of the appellant,

the relevant physical data, sample or information derived from a sample must be destroyed as soon as possible after the period has elapsed or, as the case may be, the appeal is withdrawn or determined.

(10) In this section—

"destruction date" has the meaning given by section 18. E(9); and

F59...]

Amendments (Textual)

F49. Ss. 18. E, 18. F inserted (13.12.2010 for the insertion of s. 18. E(6)(7)(10), 15.4.2011 in so far as not already in force) by Criminal Justice and Licensing (Scotland) Act 2010 (asp 13), ss. 80, 206. (1); S.S.I. 2010/413, art. 2, sch.; S.S.I. 2011/178, art. 2, sch. (with art. 7)

F58. Words in s. 18. F(1) substituted (1.4.2013) by Police and Fire Reform (Scotland) Act 2012 (asp 8), s. 129. (2), sch. 7 para. 12. (6)(a); S.S.I. 2013/51, art. 2 (with transitional provisions and savings in S.S.I. 2013/121)

F59. Definition in s. 18. F(10) repealed (1.4.2013) by Police and Fire Reform (Scotland) Act 2012 (asp 8), s. 129. (2), sch. 7 para. 12. (6)(b); S.S.I. 2013/51, art. 2 (with transitional provisions and savings in S.S.I. 2013/121)

[F6018. GRetention of samples etc: national securityS

(1) This section applies to—

(a) relevant physical data taken from or provided by a person under section 18. (2) (including any taken or provided by virtue of paragraph 20 of Schedule 8 to the Terrorism Act 2000),

(b) any sample, or any information derived from a sample, taken from a person under section 18. (6) or (6. A) (including any taken by virtue of paragraph 20 of Schedule 8 to the Terrorism Act 2000),

(c) any relevant physical data, sample or information derived from a sample taken from, or provided by, a person under section 19. AA(3),

(d) any relevant physical data, sample or information derived from a sample which is held by virtue of section 56 of the Criminal Justice (Scotland) Act 2003, and

(e) any relevant physical data, sample or information derived from a sample taken from a person—

(i) by virtue of any power of search,

(ii) by virtue of any power to take possession of evidence where there is immediate danger of its being lost or destroyed, or

(iii) under the authority of a warrant.

(2) The relevant physical data, sample or information derived from a sample may be retained for so long as a national security determination made by the relevant chief constable has effect in relation to it.

(3) A national security determination is made if the relevant chief constable determines that is necessary for the relevant physical data, sample or information derived from a sample to be retained for the purposes of national security.

(4) A national security determination—

(a) must be made in writing,

(b) has effect for a maximum of 2 years beginning with the date on which the determination is made, and

(c) may be renewed.

(5) Any relevant physical data, sample or information derived from a sample which is retained in pursuance of a national security determination must be destroyed as soon as possible after the determination ceases to have effect (except where its retention is permitted by any other enactment).

(6) In this section, "the relevant chief constable" means the chief constable of the police force of which the constable who took the relevant physical data, or to whom it was provided, or who took or directed the taking of the sample, was a member.]

Amendments (Textual)

F60. S. 18. G inserted (31.10.2013) by Protection of Freedoms Act 2012 (c. 9), s. 120, Sch. 1 para. 6. (3) (with s. 97); S.I. 2013/1814, art. 2. (k)

[F6118. HRetention of samples etc.: extraditionS

(1) This section applies to—

(a) relevant physical data taken under section 18. (2) from, or provided under that subsection by, a person arrested under an extradition arrest power (within the meaning of section 174. (2) of the Extradition Act 2003), and

(b) any sample, or any information derived from a sample, taken under section 18. (6) or (6. A) from a person arrested under an extradition arrest power (within the meaning of section 174. (2) of the Extradition Act 2003).

(2) All record of any relevant physical data, all samples and all information derived from such samples must be destroyed as soon as possible following the final determination of the extradition proceedings.

(3) The duty under subsection (2) to destroy samples taken under section 18. (6) or (6. A) and information derived from such samples does not apply where the circumstances in paragraph (a) or (b) of section 18. (4) apply to the sample or information (and where such circumstances apply, the restrictions in section 18. (5) apply to the sample or information retained).

(4) For the purposes of this section, extradition proceedings are finally determined—

(a) if the person is extradited, on the day of the extradition,

(b) if the person is discharged and there is no right of appeal under the Extradition Act 2003 against the decision which resulted in the order for the person's discharge, when the person is discharged, on the day of the discharge,

(c) where the person is discharged at an extradition hearing or by the Scottish Ministers under section 93 of the Extradition Act 2003—

(i) if no application is made to the High Court for leave to appeal against the decision within the period during which such an application may be made, at the end of that period,

(ii) if such an application is made and is refused, on the day of the refusal,

(d) where the High Court orders the person's discharge or dismisses an appeal against a decision to discharge the person—

(i) if no application is made to the High Court for permission to appeal to the Supreme Court within the 28 day period starting with the day of the High Court's decision, at the end of that period,

(ii) if such an application is made to the High Court and is refused, and no application is made to the Supreme Court for permission to appeal to the Supreme Court within the period of 28 days starting with the day of the refusal, at the end of that period,

(iii) if such an application is made to the Supreme Court and is refused, on the day of the refusal,

(iv) if permission to appeal to the Supreme Court is granted, but no appeal is made within the period of 28 days starting with the day on which permission is granted, at the end of that period,

(v) if there is an appeal to the Supreme Court against the High Court's decision, on the day on which the appeal is refused, is abandoned or is upheld with the effect that the person is discharged,

(e) if an appeal to the Supreme Court is upheld with the effect that the person is discharged, on the day of the decision to uphold the appeal.

(5) In subsection (4)—

"extradition hearing" has the meaning given by section 68 or as the case may be section 140 of the Extradition Act 2003,

"extradition proceedings" means proceedings under the Extradition Act 2003.]

Amendments (Textual)

F61. S. 18. H inserted (25.1.2018) by The Criminal Justice (Scotland) Act 2016 (Consequential Provisions) Order 2018 (S.I. 2018/46), art. 2. (2)(a)(f), Sch. 5 para. 1. (5) (with art. 9. (3)(4))

19 Prints, samples etc. in criminal investigations: supplementary provisions.S

(1) [F62. Without prejudice to any power exercisable under section 19. A of this Act, this] section

applies where a person convicted of an offence—

(a) has not, since the conviction, had [F63taken from him, or been required to provide, any relevant physical data or had any impression or sample] taken from him; or

(b) has [F64at any time had—

(i) taken from him or been required (whether under paragraph (a) above or under section 18 [F65, 19. A or 19. AA] of this Act or otherwise) to provide any relevant physical data; or

(ii) any F66... sample taken from him,

which was not suitable for the means of analysis for which the data were taken or required or the F66... sample was taken] or, though suitable, was insufficient (either in quantity or in quality) to enable information to be obtained by that means of analysis.

(2) Where this section applies, a constable may, within the permitted period—

[F67. (a)take from or require the convicted person to provide him with such relevant physical data as he reasonably considers it appropriate to take or, as the case may be, require the provision of]; F68. . .

(b) with the authority of an officer of a rank no lower than inspector, take from the person any sample mentioned in any of paragraphs (a) to [F69. (c)] of subsection (6) of section 18 of this Act by the means specified in that paragraph in relation to that sample [F70 and]

[F71. (c)take, or direct a police custody and security officer to take, from the person any sample mentioned in subsection (6. A) of that section by the means specified in that subsection.]

(3) A constable—

(a) may require the convicted person to attend a police station for the purposes of subsection (2) above;

(b) may, where the convicted person is in legal custody by virtue of section 295 of this Act, exercise the powers conferred by subsection (2) above in relation to the person in the place where he is for the time being.

(4) In subsection (2) above, "the permitted period" means—

(a) in a case to which paragraph (a) of subsection (1) above applies, the period of one month beginning with the date of the conviction;

(b) in a case to which paragraph (b) of that subsection applies, the period of one month beginning with the date on which a constable of the [F72. Police Service of Scotland] receives written intimation that [F73the relevant physical data were or] the sample, F74. . .was unsuitable or, as the case may be, insufficient as mentioned in that paragraph.

(5) A requirement under subsection (3)(a) above—

(a) shall give the person at least seven days' notice of the date on which he is required to attend;

(b) may direct him to attend at a specified time of day or between specified times of day.

(6) Any constable may arrest without warrant a person who fails to comply with a requirement under subsection (3)(a) above.

Amendments (Textual)

F62. Words in s. 19. (1) substituted (17.11.1997) by 1997 c. 48, s. 48. (1); S.I. 1997/2694, art. 2. (2)(b)

F63. Words in s. 19. (1)(a) substituted (1.8.1997) by 1997 c. 48, s. 47. (2)(a)(i); S.I. 1997/1712, art. 3, Sch. (subject to arts. 4, 5)

F64. Words and s. 19. (1)(b)(i)(ii) substituted (1.8.1997) for words in s. 19. (1)(b) by 1997 c. 48, s. 47. (2)(a)(ii); S.I. 1997/1712, art. 3, Sch. (subject to arts. 4, 5)

F65. Words in s. 19. (1)(b)(i) substituted (1.9.2006) by Police, Public Order and Criminal Justice (Scotland) Act 2006 (asp 10), ss. 77. (3), 104; S.S.I. 2006/432, art. 2. (d)

F66. Words in s. 19. (1)(b) repealed (28.3.2011) by Criminal Justice and Licensing (Scotland) Act 2010 (asp 13), s. 206. (1), sch. 7 para. 31; S.S.I. 2011/178, art. 2, sch.

F67. S. 19. (2)(a) substituted (1.8.1997) by 1997 c. 48, s. 47. (2)(b); S.I. 1997/1712, art. 3, Sch. (subject to arts. 4, 5)

F68. Word in s. 19. (2) repealed (27.6.2003) by Criminal Justice (Scotland) Act 2003 (asp 7), ss. {55. (3)(a)}, 89; S.S.I. 2003/288, art. 2, Sch.

F69. Word in s. 19. (2)(b) substituted (27.6.2003) by Criminal Justice (Scotland) Act 2003 (asp 7), ss. {55. (3)(b)}, 89; S.S.I. 2003/288, art. 2, Sch.

F70. S. 19. (2)(c) and word added (27.6.2003) by Criminal Justice (Scotland) Act 2003 (asp 7), ss. {55. (3)(c)}, 89; S.S.I. 2003/288, art. 2, Sch.

F71. S. 19. (2)(c) and word added (27.6.2003) by Criminal Justice (Scotland) Act 2003 (asp 7), ss. {55. (3)(c)}, 89; S.S.I. 2003/288, art. 2, Sch.

F72. Words in s. 19. (4)(b) substituted (1.4.2013) by Police and Fire Reform (Scotland) Act 2012 (asp 8), s. 129. (2), sch. 7 para. 12. (7); S.S.I. 2013/51, art. 2 (with transitional provisions and savings in S.S.I. 2013/121)

F73. Words in s. 19. (4)(b) inserted (1.8.1997) by 1997 c. 48, s. 47. (2)(c)(i); S.I. 1997/1712, art. 3, Sch. (subject to arts. 4, 5)

F74. Words in s. 19. (4)(b) repealed (1.8.1997) by 1997 c. 48, ss. 47. (2)(c)(ii), 62. (2), Sch. 3; S.I. 1997/1712, art. 3, Sch. (subject to arts. 4, 5)

[F7519. A Samples etc. from persons convicted of sexual and violent offences. S

(1) This section applies where a person—

(a) is convicted on or after the relevant date of a relevant offence and is sentenced to imprisonment;

(b) was convicted before the relevant date of a relevant offence, was sentenced to imprisonment and is serving that sentence on or after the relevant date;

(c) was convicted before the relevant date of a specified relevant offence, was sentenced to imprisonment, is not serving that sentence on that date or at any time after that date but was serving it at any time during the period of five years ending with the day before that date.

(2) Subject to subsections (3) and (4) below, where this section applies a constable may—

(a) take from the person or require the person to provide him with such relevant physical data as the constable reasonably considers appropriate; F76 . . .

(b) with the authority of an officer of a rank no lower than inspector, take from the person any sample mentioned in any of paragraphs (a) to [F77. (c)] of subsection (6) of section 18 of this Act by the means specified in that paragraph in relation to that sample [F78 and]

[F79. (c)take, or direct a police custody and security officer to take, from the person any sample mentioned in subsection (6. A) of that section by the means specified in that subsection.]

(3) The power conferred by subsection (2) above shall not be exercised where the person has previously had taken from him or been required to provide relevant physical data or any sample under [F80subsection (2) of section 19 of this Act in a case where the power conferred by that subsection was exercised by virtue of subsection (1)(a) of that section][F81, under this section or under section 19. AA(3) of this Act] unless the data so taken or required have been or, as the case may be, the sample so taken or required has been lost or destroyed.

(4) Where this section applies by virtue of—

(a) paragraph (a) or (b) of subsection (1) above, the powers conferred by subsection (2) above may be exercised at any time when the person is serving his sentence; and

(b) paragraph (c) of the said subsection (1), those powers may only be exercised within a period of three months beginning on the relevant date.

(5) Where a person in respect of whom the power conferred by subsection (2) above may be exercised—

(a) is no longer serving his sentence of imprisonment, subsections (3)(a), (5) and (6);

(b) is serving his sentence of imprisonment, subsection (3)(b),

of section 19 of this Act shall apply for the purposes of subsection (2) above as they apply for the purposes of subsection (2) of that section.

(6) In this section—

"conviction" includes—

- an acquittal [F82by reason of the special defence set out in section 51. A of this Act;]

- a finding under section 55. (2) of this Act,

and "convicted" shall be construed accordingly;

"relevant date" means the date on which section 48 of the M1 Crime and Punishment (Scotland) Act 1997 is commenced;

"relevant offence" means any relevant sexual offence or any relevant violent offence;

"relevant sexual offence" means any of the following offences—

- rape [F83at common law];
- clandestine injury to women;
- abduction of a woman with intent to rape;
- [F84abduction with intent to commit the statutory offence of rape;]
- assault with intent to rape or ravish;
- [F85assault with intent to commit the statutory offence of rape;]
- indecent assault;
- lewd, indecent or libidinous behaviour or practices;
- [F86public indecency if the court, in imposing sentence or otherwise disposing of the case, determined for the purposes of paragraph 60 of Schedule 3 to the Sexual Offences Act 2003 (c.42) that there was a significant sexual aspect to the offender's behaviour in committing the offence;]
- sodomy; F87 . . .
- any offence which consists of a contravention of any of the following statutory provisions—

section 52 of the M2 Civic Government (Scotland) Act 1982 (taking and distribution of indecent images of children);

section 52. A of that Act (possession of indecent images of children);

[F88section 311 of the Mental Health (Care and Treatment)(Scotland) Act 2003 (non consensual sexual acts);]

[F89section 313 of that Act (persons providing care services: sexual offences);]

section 1 of the M3 Criminal Law (Consolidation)(Scotland) Act 1995 (incest);

section 2 of that Act (intercourse with step-child);

section 3 of that Act (intercourse with child under 16 years by person in position of trust);

section 5. (1) or (2) of that Act (unlawful intercourse with girl under 13 years);

section 5. (3) of that Act (unlawful intercourse with girl aged between 13 and 16 years);

section 6 of that Act (indecent behaviour towards girl between 12 and 16 years);

section 7 of that Act (procuring);

section 8 of that Act (abduction and unlawful detention of women and girls);

section 9 of that Act (permitting use of premises for unlawful sexual intercourse);

section 10 of that Act (liability of parents etc in respect of offences against girls under 16 years);

section 11. (1)(b) of that Act (soliciting for immoral purpose);

section 13. (5)(b) and (c) of that Act (homosexual offences); [F90 and

- any offence which consists of a contravention of any of the following provisions of the Sexual Offences (Scotland) Act 2009 (asp 9)—

section 1 (rape),

section 2 (sexual assault by penetration),

section 3 (sexual assault),

section 4 (sexual coercion),

section 5 (coercing a person into being present during a sexual activity),

section 6 (coercing a person into looking at a sexual image),

section 7. (1) (communicating indecently),

section 7. (2) (causing a person to see or hear an indecent communication),

section 8 (sexual exposure),

section 9 (voyeurism),

section 18 (rape of a young child),

section 19 (sexual assault on a young child by penetration),

section 20 (sexual assault on a young child),

section 21 (causing a young child to participate in a sexual activity), section 22 (causing a young child to be present during a sexual activity),

section 23 (causing a young child to look at a sexual image),

section 24. (1) (communicating indecently with a young child),

section 24. (2) (causing a young child to see or hear an indecent communication),

section 25 (sexual exposure to a young child),

section 26 (voyeurism towards a young child),

section 28 (having intercourse with an older child),

section 29 (engaging in penetrative sexual activity with or towards an older child),

section 30 (engaging in sexual activity with or towards an older child),

section 31 (causing an older child to participate in a sexual activity),

section 32 (causing an older child to be present during a sexual activity),

section 33 (causing an older child to look at a sexual image),

section 34. (1) (communicating indecently with an older child),

section 34. (2) (causing an older child to see or hear an indecent communication),

section 35 (sexual exposure to an older child),

section 36 (voyeurism towards an older child),

section 37. (1) (engaging while an older child in sexual conduct with or towards another older child),

section 37. (4) (engaging while an older child in consensual sexual conduct with another older child),

section 42 (sexual abuse of trust) but only if the condition set out in section 43. (6) of that Act is fulfilled,

section 46 (sexual abuse of trust of a mentally disordered person);]

"relevant violent offence" means any of the following offences—

- murder or culpable homicide;

- uttering a threat to the life of another person;

- perverting the course of justice in connection with an offence of murder;

- fire raising;

- assault;

- reckless conduct causing actual injury;

- abduction; and

- any offence which consists of a contravention of any of the following statutory provisions—

sections 2 (causing explosion likely to endanger life) or 3 (attempting to cause such an explosion) of the M4 Explosive Substances Act 1883;

section 12 of the M5 Children and Young Persons (Scotland) Act 1937 (cruelty to children);

sections 16 (possession of firearm with intent to endanger life or cause serious injury), 17 (use of firearm to resist arrest) or 18 (having a firearm for purpose of committing an offence listed in Schedule 2) of the M6 Firearms Act 1968;

section 6 of the M7 Child Abduction Act 1984 (taking or sending child out of the United Kingdom); and

[F91section 47. (1) (possession of offensive weapon in public place), 49. (1) (possession of article with blade or point in public place), 49. A(1) or (2) (possession of article with blade or point or offensive weapon on school premises) or 49. C(1) (possession of offensive weapon or article with blade or point in prison) of the Criminal Law (Consolidation) (Scotland) Act 1995 (c.39);]

"sentence of imprisonment" means the sentence imposed in respect of the relevant offence and includes—

- a [F92compulsion] order, a restriction order, a hospital direction and any order under section 57. (2)(a) or (b) of this Act; and

- a sentence of detention imposed under section 207 or 208 of this Act,

and "sentenced to imprisonment" shall be construed accordingly; and any reference to a person serving his sentence shall be construed as a reference to the person being detained in a prison, hospital or other place in pursuance of a sentence of imprisonment; and

"specified relevant offence" means—

- any relevant sexual offence mentioned in paragraphs (a), (b), (f) and (i)(viii) of the definition of that expression and any such offence as is mentioned in paragraph (h) of that definition where the person against whom the offence was committed did not consent; and
- any relevant violent offence mentioned in paragraph (a) or (g) of the definition of that expression and any such offence as is mentioned in paragraph (e) of that definition where the assault is to the victim's severe injury,
but, notwithstanding subsection (7) below, does not include—
- conspiracy or incitement to commit; and
- aiding and abetting, counselling or procuring the commission of,
any of those offences.
[F93. (6. A)In subsection (6)—
(a) the references to "rape" in paragraphs (c) and (d) of the definition of "relevant sexual offence" are to the offence of rape at common law; and
(b) the references in paragraphs (ca) and (da) of that subsection to "the statutory offence of rape" are (as the case may be) to?
(i) the offence of rape under section 1 of the Sexual Offences (Scotland) Act 2009, or
(ii) the offence of rape of a young child under section 18 of that Act.]
(7) In this section—
(a) any reference to a relevant offence includes a reference to any attempt, conspiracy or incitement to commit such an offence; and
(b) any reference to—
(i) a relevant sexual offence mentioned in paragraph (i) [F94or (j)]; or
(ii) a relevant violent offence mentioned in paragraph (h),
of the definition of those expressions in subsection (6) above includes a reference to aiding and abetting, counselling or procuring the commission of such an offence.]
Amendments (Textual)
F75. S. 19. A inserted (17.11.1997) by 1997 c. 48, s. 48. (2); S.I. 1997/2694, art. 2. (2)(b)
F76. Word in s. 19. A(2) repealed (27.6.2003) by Criminal Justice (Scotland) Act 2003 (asp 7), ss. {55. (3)(a)}, 89; S.S.I. 2003/288, art. 2, Sch.
F77. Word in s. 19. A(2) substituted (27.6.2003) by Criminal Justice (Scotland) Act 2003 (asp 7), ss.{55. (3)(b)}, 89; S.S.I. 2003/288, art. 2, Sch.
F78. S. 19. A(2)(c) and word added (27.6.2003) by Criminal Justice (Scotland) Act 2003 (asp 7), ss.{55. (3)(c)}, 89; S.S.I. 2003/288, art. 2, Sch.
F79. S. 19. A(2)(c) and word added (27.6.2003) by Criminal Justice (Scotland) Act 2003 (asp 7), ss. {55. (3)(c)}, 89; S.S.I. 2003/288, art. 2, Sch.
F80. Words in s. 19. A(3) substituted (1.9.2006) by Police, Public Order and Criminal Justice (Scotland) Act 2006 (asp 10), ss. 101, 104, Sch. 6 para. 4. (3); S.S.I. 2006/432, art. 2. (g)(h)
F81. Words in s. 19. A(3) substituted (1.9.2006) by Police, Public Order and Criminal Justice (Scotland) Act 2006 (asp 10), ss. 77. (4), 104; S.S.I. 2006/432, art. 2. (d)
F82. Words in s. 19. A(6) substituted (with application in accordance with art. 3 of the commencing S.S.I.) by Criminal Justice and Licensing (Scotland) Act 2010 (asp 13), s. 206. (1), sch. 7 para. 32; S.S.I. 2012/160, art. 3, sch.
F83. Words in s. 19. A(6)(a) inserted (1.12.2010) by Sexual Offences (Scotland) Act 2009 (asp 9), ss. 61, 62. (2), Sch. 5 para. 2. (4)(a)(i); S.S.I. 2010/413, art. 2, Sch.
F84. S. 19. A(6): words in definition of "relevant sexual offence" inserted (1.12.2010) by The Sexual Offences (Scotland) Act 2009 (Supplemental and Consequential Provision) Order 2010 (S.S.I. 2010/421), art. 2, Sch. para. 1. (2)(a)(i)
F85. S. 19. A(6): words in definition of "relevant sexual offence" inserted (1.12.2010) by The Sexual Offences (Scotland) Act 2009 (Supplemental and Consequential Provision) Order 2010 (S.S.I. 2010/421), art. 2, Sch. para. 1. (2)(a)(ii)
F86. Words in s. 19. A(6) substituted (28.3.2011) by Criminal Justice and Licensing (Scotland) Act 2010 (asp 13), ss. 81. (a), 206. (1); S.S.I. 2011/178, art. 2, sch. (with art. 8)
F87. Word in s. 19. A(6) repealed (1.12.2010) by Sexual Offences (Scotland) Act 2009 (asp 9), ss.

61, 62. (2), Sch. 5 para. 2. (4)(a)(ii); S.S.I. 2010/413, art. 2, Sch.

F88. S. 19. A(6)(i): words in the definition of "relevant sexual offence" substituted (27.9.2005) by The Mental Health (Care and Treatment) (Scotland) Act 2003 (Modification of Enactments) Order 2005 (S.S.I. 2005/465), art. 2, Sch. 1 para. 27. (2)(a)(i)

F89. S. 19. A(6)(i): words in the definition of "relevant sexual offence" substituted (27.9.2005) by The Mental Health (Care and Treatment) (Scotland) Act 2003 (Modification of Enactments) Order 2005 (S.S.I. 2005/465), art. 2, Sch. 1 para. 27. (2)(a)(ii)

F90. S. 19. A(6)(j) and word inserted (1.12.2010) by Sexual Offences (Scotland) Act 2009 (asp 9), ss. 61, 62. (2), {Sch. 5 para. 2 (4)(a)(iii)}; S.S.I. 2010/413, art. 2, Sch.

F91. Words in s. 19. A(6) inserted (28.3.2011) by Criminal Justice and Licensing (Scotland) Act 2010 (asp 13), ss. 81. (b), 206. (1); S.S.I. 2011/178, art. 2, sch. (with art. 8)

F92. S. 19. A(6)(i): word in the definition of "sentence of imprisonment" substituted and the word "hospital" omitted (27.9.2005) by virtue of The Mental Health (Care and Treatment) (Scotland) Act 2003 (Modification of Enactments) Order 2005 (S.S.I. 2005/465), art. 2, Sch. 1 para. 27. (2)(b)

F93. S. 19. A(6. A) inserted (1.12.2010) by The Sexual Offences (Scotland) Act 2009 (Supplemental and Consequential Provision) Order 2010 (S.S.I. 2010/421), art. 2, Sch. para. 1. (2)(b)

F94. Words in s. 19. A(7)(b)(i) inserted (1.12.2010) by Sexual Offences (Scotland) Act 2009 (asp 9), ss. 61, 62. (2), Sch. 5 para. 4. (b); S.S.I. 2010/413, art. 2, Sch.

Marginal Citations

M11997 c.48.
M21982 c.45.
M31995 c.39.
M41883 c.3.
M51937 c.37.
M61968 c.27.
M71984 c.37.

[F9519. AASamples etc. from sex offendersS

(1) This section applies where a person is subject to—

(a) the notification requirements of Part 2 of the 2003 Act;

(b) an order under section 2 of the Protection of Children and Prevention of Sexual Offences (Scotland) Act 2005 (asp 9)(a risk of sexual harm order); or

(c) an order under section [F96122. A or] 123 of the 2003 Act (which makes provision for England and Wales and Northern Ireland corresponding to section 2 of that Act of 2005).

(2) This section applies regardless of whether the person became subject to those requirements or that order before or after the commencement of this section.

(3) Subject to subsections (4) to (8) below, where this section applies a constable may—

(a) take from the person or require the person to provide him with such relevant physical data as the constable considers reasonably appropriate;

(b) with the authority of an officer of a rank no lower than inspector, take from the person any sample mentioned in any of paragraphs (a) to (c) of subsection (6) of section 18 of this Act by the means specified in that paragraph in relation to that sample;

(c) take, or direct a police custody and security officer to take, from the person any sample mentioned in subsection (6. A) of that section by the means specified in that subsection.

(4) Where this section applies by virtue of subsection (1)(c) above, the power conferred by subsection (3) shall not be exercised unless the constable reasonably believes that the person's sole or main residence is in Scotland.

(5) The power conferred by subsection (3) above shall not be exercised where the person has previously had taken from him or been required to provide relevant physical data or any sample

under section 19. (2) or 19. A(2) of this Act unless the data so taken or required have been or, as the case may be, the sample so taken has been, lost or destroyed.

(6) The power conferred by subsection (3) above shall not be exercised where the person has previously had taken from him or been required to provide relevant physical data or any sample under that subsection unless the data so taken or required or, as the case may be, the sample so taken—

(a) have or has been lost or destroyed; or

(b) were or was not suitable for the particular means of analysis or, though suitable, were or was insufficient (either in quantity or quality) to enable information to be obtained by that means of analysis.

(7) The power conferred by subsection (3) above may be exercised only—

(a) in a police station; or

(b) where the person is in legal custody by virtue of section 295 of this Act, in the place where the person is for the time being.

(8) The power conferred by subsection (3) above may be exercised in a police station only—

(a) where the person is present in the police station in pursuance of a requirement made by a constable to attend for the purpose of the exercise of the power; or

(b) while the person is in custody in the police station following his arrest F97... in connection with any offence.

(9) A requirement under subsection (8)(a) above—

(a) shall give the person at least seven days' notice of the date on which he is required to attend;

(b) may direct him to attend at a specified time of day or between specified times of day; and

(c) where this section applies by virtue of subsection (1)(b) or (c) above, shall warn the person that failure, without reasonable excuse, to comply with the requirement or, as the case may be, to allow the taking of or to provide any relevant physical data, or to provide any sample, under the power, constitutes an offence.

(10) A requirement under subsection (8)(a) above in a case where the person has previously had taken from him or been required to provide relevant physical data or any sample under subsection (3) above shall contain intimation that the relevant physical data were or the sample was unsuitable or, as the case may be, insufficient, as mentioned in subsection (6)(b) above.

(11) Before exercising the power conferred by subsection (3) above in a case to which subsection (8)(b) above applies, a constable shall inform the person of that fact.

(12) Any constable may arrest without warrant a person who fails to comply with a requirement under subsection (8)(a) above.

(13) This section does not prejudice the generality of section 18 of this Act.

(14) In this section, "the 2003 Act" means the Sexual Offences Act 2003 (c. 42).

Amendments (Textual)

F95. Ss. 19. AA, 19. AB inserted (1.9.2006) by Police, Public Order and Criminal Justice (Scotland) Act 2006 (asp 10), ss. 77. (2), 104; S.S.I. 2006/432, art. 2. (d)

F96. Words in s. 19. AA(1)(c) inserted (8.3.2015) by Anti-social Behaviour, Crime and Policing Act 2014 (c. 12), s. 185. (1), Sch. 11 para. 51 (with ss. 21, 33, 42, 58, 75, 93); S.I. 2015/373, art. 2. (g)(i)

F97. Words in s. 19. AA(8)(b) repealed (25.1.2018) by Criminal Justice (Scotland) Act 2016 (asp 1), s. 117. (2), sch. 2 para. 28. (4); S.S.I. 2017/345, art. 3, sch. (with art. 4)

19. ABSection 19. AA: supplementary provision in risk of sexual harm order casesS

(1) This section applies where section 19. AA of this Act applies by virtue of subsection (1)(b) or (c) of that section.

(2) A person who fails without reasonable excuse—

(a) to comply with a requirement made of him under section 19. AA(8)(a) of this Act; or

(b) to allow relevant physical data to be taken from him, to provide relevant physical data, or to allow a sample to be taken from him, under section 19. AA(3) of this Act,
shall be guilty of an offence.

(3) A person guilty of an offence under subsection (2) above shall be liable on summary conviction to the following penalties—

(a) a fine not exceeding level 4 on the standard scale;

(b) imprisonment for a period—

(i) where the conviction is in the district court, not exceeding 60 days; or

(ii) where the conviction is in the sheriff court, not exceeding 3 months; or

(c) both such fine and such imprisonment.

(4) Subject to subsection (6) below, all record of any relevant physical data taken from or provided by a person under section 19. AA(3) of this Act, all samples taken from a person under that subsection and all information derived from such samples shall be destroyed as soon as possible following the person ceasing to be a person subject to any risk of sexual harm orders.

(5) For the purpose of subsection (4) above, a person does not cease to be subject to a risk of sexual harm order where the person would be subject to such an order but for an order under section 6. (2) of the 2005 Act or any corresponding power of a court in England and Wales or in Northern Ireland.

(6) Subsection (4) above does not apply if before the duty to destroy imposed by that subsection would apply, the person—

(a) is convicted of an offence; or

(b) becomes subject to the notification requirements of Part 2 of the 2003 Act.

(7) In this section—

"risk of sexual harm order" means an order under—

- section 2 of the 2005 Act; or

- section 123 of the 2003 Act; [F98and also includes an order under section 122. A of the 2003 Act (sexual risk orders);]

"the 2005 Act" means the Protection of Children and Prevention of Sexual Offences (Scotland) Act 2005 (asp 9);

"the 2003 Act" has the meaning given by section 19. AA(14) of this Act; and

"convicted" shall be construed in accordance with section 19. A(6) of this Act.]

Amendments (Textual)

F95. Ss. 19. AA, 19. AB inserted (1.9.2006) by Police, Public Order and Criminal Justice (Scotland) Act 2006 (asp 10), ss. 77. (2), 104; S.S.I. 2006/432, art. 2. (d)

F98. Words in s. 19. AB(7) inserted (8.3.2015) by Anti-social Behaviour, Crime and Policing Act 2014 (c. 12), s. 185. (1), Sch. 11 para. 52 (with ss. 21, 33, 42, 58, 75, 93); S.I. 2015/373, art. 2. (g)(i)

[F9919. B Power of constable in obtaining relevant physical data etc.S

[F100. (1)]A constable may use reasonable force in—

(a) taking any relevant physical data from a person or securing a person's compliance with a requirement made under section 18. (2), 19. (2)(a) or 19. A(2)(a) of this Act [F101, or under subsection (3)(a) of section 19. AA of this Act where that section applies by virtue of subsection (1)(a) of that section];

(b) exercising any power conferred by section 18. (6), 19. (2)(b) or 19. A(2)(b) of this Act [F102, or under subsection (3)(b) of section 19. AA of this Act where that section applies by virtue of subsection (1)(a) of that section].

[F103. (2)A constable may, with the authority of an officer of a rank no lower than inspector, use reasonable force in (himself) exercising any power conferred by section 18. (6. A), 19. (2)(c) or 19. A(2)(c) of this Act [F104, or under subsection (3)(c) of section 19. AA of this Act where that section applies by virtue of subsection (1)(a) of that section].]]

Amendments (Textual)

F99. S. 19. (B) inserted (17.11.1997) by 1997 c. 48, s. 48. (2); S.I. 1997/2694, art. 2. (2)(b)

F100. S. 19. B renumbered as s. 19. B(1) (27.6.2003) by virtue of Criminal Justice (Scotland) Act 2003 (asp 7), ss. 55. (4), 89; S.S.I. 2003/288, art. 2, Sch.

F101. Words in s. 19. B(1)(a) inserted (1.9.2006) by Police, Public Order and Criminal Justice (Scotland) Act 2006 (asp 10), ss. 77. (5)(a)(i), 104; S.S.I. 2006/432, art. 2. (d)

F102. Words in s. 19. B(1)(b) inserted (1.9.2006) by Police, Public Order and Criminal Justice (Scotland) Act 2006 (asp 10), ss. 77. (5)(a)(ii), 104; S.S.I. 2006/432, art. 2. (d)

F103. S. 19. B(2) added (27.6.2003) by Criminal Justice (Scotland) Act 2003 (asp 7), ss. 55. (4), 89; S.S.I. 2003/288, art. 2, Sch.

F104. Words in s. 19. B(2) inserted (1.9.2006) by Police, Public Order and Criminal Justice (Scotland) Act 2006 (asp 10), ss. 77. (5)(b), 104; S.S.I. 2006/432, art. 2. (d)

[F10519. CSections 18 and 19 to 19. AA: use of samples etc.S

(1) Subsection (2) applies to—

(a) relevant physical data taken or provided under section 18. (2), 19. (2)(a), 19. A(2)(a) or 19. AA(3)(a), [F106. (including any taken or provided by virtue of paragraph 20 of Schedule 8 to the Terrorism Act 2000)]

(b) a sample, or any information derived from a sample, taken under section 18. (6) or (6. A), 19. (2)(b) or (c), 19. A(2)(b) or (c) or 19. AA(3)(b) or (c),

(c) relevant physical data or a sample taken from a person—

(i) by virtue of any power of search,

(ii) by virtue of any power to take possession of evidence where there is immediate danger of its being lost or destroyed, or

(iii) under the authority of a warrant,

(d) information derived from a sample falling within paragraph (c), and

(e) relevant physical data, a sample or information derived from a sample taken from, or provided by, a person outwith Scotland which is given by any person to—

[F107. (i)the Police Service of Scotland ("the Police Service"),]

(ii) the Scottish Police [F108. Authority ("the Authority"),] or

(iii) a person acting on behalf of [F109the Police Service or the Authority].

(2) The relevant physical data, sample or information derived from a sample may be used—

(a) for the prevention or detection of crime, the investigation of an offence or the conduct of a prosecution, F110...

(b) for the identification of a deceased person or a person from whom the relevant physical data or sample came.

[F111. (c)in the interests of national security, or

(d) for the purposes of a terrorist investigation]

(3) Subsections (4) and (5) apply to relevant physical data, a sample or information derived from a sample falling within any of paragraphs (a) to (d) of subsection (1) ("relevant material").

(4) If the relevant material is held by [F112the Police Service, the Authority or a person acting on behalf of the Police Service or the Authority, the Police Service] or, as the case may be, the Authority or person may give the relevant material to another person for use by that person in accordance with subsection (2).

(5) [F113. The Police Service, the Authority or a person acting on behalf of the Police Service or the Authority] may, in using the relevant material in accordance with subsection (2), check it against other relevant physical data, samples and information derived from samples received from another person.

(6) In subsection (2)—

(a) the reference to crime includes a reference to—

(i) conduct which constitutes a criminal offence or two or more criminal offences (whether under the law of a part of the United Kingdom or a country or territory outside the United Kingdom), or (ii) conduct which is, or corresponds to, conduct which, if it all took place in any one part of the United Kingdom would constitute a criminal offence or two or more criminal offences,

(b) the reference to an investigation includes a reference to an investigation outside Scotland of a crime or suspected crime, F114...

(c) the reference to a prosecution includes a reference to a prosecution brought in respect of a crime in a country or territory outside Scotland [F115, and

(d) "terrorist investigation" has the meaning given by section 32 of the Terrorism Act 2000.]
(7) This section is without prejudice to any other power relating to the use of relevant physical data, samples or information derived from a sample.]

Amendments (Textual)

F105. S. 19. C inserted (1.8.2011) by Criminal Justice and Licensing (Scotland) Act 2010 (asp 13), ss. 82. (1), 206. (1); S.S.I. 2011/178, art. 2, sch. (with art. 9)

F106. Words in s. 19. C(1)(a) inserted (16.9.2011) by The Criminal Justice and Licensing (Scotland) Act 2010 (Consequential Provisions and Modifications) Order 2011 (S.I. 2011/2298), art. 1. (3), Sch. para. 1. (a) (with art. 4. (1)(4))

F107. S. 19. C(1)(e)(i) substituted (1.4.2013) by Police and Fire Reform (Scotland) Act 2012 (asp 8), s. 129. (2), sch. 7 para. 12. (8)(a)(i); S.S.I. 2013/51, art. 2 (with transitional provisions and savings in S.S.I. 2013/121)

F108. Words in s. 19. C(1)(e)(ii) substituted (1.4.2013) by Police and Fire Reform (Scotland) Act 2012 (asp 8), s. 129. (2), sch. 7 para. 12. (8)(a)(ii); S.S.I. 2013/51, art. 2 (with transitional provisions and savings in S.S.I. 2013/121)

F109. Words in s. 19. C(1)(e)(iii) substituted (1.4.2013) by Police and Fire Reform (Scotland) Act 2012 (asp 8), s. 129. (2), sch. 7 para. 12. (8)(a)(iii); S.S.I. 2013/51, art. 2 (with transitional provisions and savings in S.S.I. 2013/121)

F110. Word in s. 19. C(2)(a) omitted (16.9.2011) by virtue of The Criminal Justice and Licensing (Scotland) Act 2010 (Consequential Provisions and Modifications) Order 2011 (S.I. 2011/2298), art. 1. (3), Sch. para. 1. (b)(i) (with art. 4. (1)(4))

F111. S. 19. C(2)(c)(d) inserted (16.9.2011) by The Criminal Justice and Licensing (Scotland) Act 2010 (Consequential Provisions and Modifications) Order 2011 (S.I. 2011/2298), art. 1. (3), Sch. para. 1. (b)(ii) (with art. 4. (1)(4))

F112. Words in s. 19. C(4) substituted (1.4.2013) by Police and Fire Reform (Scotland) Act 2012 (asp 8), s. 129. (2), sch. 7 para. 12. (8)(b); S.S.I. 2013/51, art. 2 (with transitional provisions and savings in S.S.I. 2013/121)

F113. Words in s. 19. C(5) substituted (1.4.2013) by Police and Fire Reform (Scotland) Act 2012 (asp 8), s. 129. (2), sch. 7 para. 12. (8)(c); S.S.I. 2013/51, art. 2 (with transitional provisions and savings in S.S.I. 2013/121)

F114. Word in s. 19. C(6)(b) omitted (16.9.2011) by virtue of The Criminal Justice and Licensing (Scotland) Act 2010 (Consequential Provisions and Modifications) Order 2011 (S.I. 2011/2298), art. 1. (3), Sch. para. 1. (c)(i) (with art. 4. (1)(4))

F115. S. 19. C(6)(d) and word inserted (16.9.2011) by The Criminal Justice and Licensing (Scotland) Act 2010 (Consequential Provisions and Modifications) Order 2011 (S.I. 2011/2298), art. 1. (3), Sch. para. 1. (c)(ii) (with art. 4. (1)(4))

F11620 Use of prints, samples etc.S

. . . .

Amendments (Textual)

F116. S. 20 repealed (1.8.2011) by Criminal Justice and Licensing (Scotland) Act 2010 (asp 13), s. 206. (1), sch. 7 para. 33; S.S.I. 2011/178, art. 2, sch.

Modifications etc. (not altering text)

C4. S. 20 applied (with modifications) (prosp.) by the Terrorism Act 2002 (c. 11), Sch. 8 para. 21 (as inserted by Counter-Terrorism Act 2008 (c. 28), ss. 17. (3), 91, 100) (with s. 101. (2))

[F117. Testing for Class A drugsS

Amendments (Textual)
F117. Ss. 20. A, 20. B and preceding cross-heading inserted (1.1.2007 for certain purposes, 25.2.2007 in regard to the inserted s. 20. B(3), and otherwise in force at 12.6.2007) by Police, Public Order and Criminal Justice (Scotland) Act 2006 (asp 10), ss. 84, 104; S.S.I. 2006/607, art. 3, Sch.; S.S.I. 2007/84, {art. 3. (1)(a)(4))(a)}

20. AArrested persons: testing for certain Class A drugsS

(1) Subject to subsection (2) below, where subsection (3) below applies an appropriate officer may—
(a) require a person who has been arrested and is in custody in a police station to provide him with a sample of urine; or
(b) take from the inside of the mouth of such a person, by means of swabbing, a sample of saliva or other material,
which the officer may subject to analysis intended to reveal whether there is any relevant Class A drug in the person's body.
(2) The power conferred by subsection (1) above shall not be exercised where the person has previously been required to provide or had taken from him a sample under that subsection in the same period in custody.
(3) This subsection applies where—
(a) the person is of 16 years of age or more;
(b) the period in custody in the police station has not exceeded 6 hours;
(c) the police station is situated in an area prescribed by order made by statutory instrument by the Scottish Ministers; and
(d) either—
(i) the person's arrest was on suspicion of committing or having committed a relevant offence; or
(ii) a senior police officer who has appropriate grounds has authorised the making of the requirement to provide or the taking of the sample.
(4) Before exercising the power conferred by subsection (1) above, an appropriate officer shall—
(a) warn the person in respect of whom it is to be exercised that failure, without reasonable excuse, to comply with the requirement or, as the case may be, allow the sample to be taken constitutes an offence; and
(b) in a case within subsection (3)(d)(ii) above, inform the person of the giving of the authorisation and the grounds for the suspicion.
(5) Where—
(a) a person has been required to provide or has had taken a sample under subsection (1) above;
(b) any of the following is the case—
(i) the sample was not suitable for the means of analysis to be used to reveal whether there was any relevant Class A drug in the person's body;
(ii) though suitable, the sample was insufficient (either in quantity or quality) to enable information to be obtained by that means of analysis; or
(iii) the sample was destroyed during analysis and the means of analysis failed to produce reliable information; and
(c) the person remains in custody in the police station (whether or not the period of custody has exceeded 6 hours),
an appropriate officer may require the person to provide or as the case may be take another sample of the same kind by the same method.

41

(6) Before exercising the power conferred by subsection (5) above, an appropriate officer shall warn the person in respect of whom it is to be exercised that failure, without reasonable excuse, to comply with the requirement or, as the case may be, allow the sample to be taken constitutes an offence.

(7) A person who fails without reasonable excuse—

    (a) to comply with a requirement made of him under subsection (1)(a) or (5) above; or

    (b) to allow a sample to be taken from him under subsection (1)(b) or (5) above,

shall be guilty of an offence.

(8) In this section—

"appropriate grounds" means reasonable grounds for suspecting that the misuse by the person of any relevant Class A drug caused or contributed to the offence on suspicion of which the person was arrested;

"appropriate officer" means—

    - a constable; or

    - a police custody and security officer acting on the direction of a constable;

"misuse" has the same meaning as in the Misuse of Drugs Act 1971 (c. 38);

"relevant Class A drug" means any of the following substances, preparations and products—

    - cocaine or its salts;

    - any preparation or other product containing cocaine or its salts;

    - diamorphine or its salts;

    - any preparation or other product containing diamorphine or its salts;

"relevant offence" means any of the following offences—

    - theft;

    - assault;

    - robbery;

    - fraud;

    - reset;

    - uttering a forged document;

    - embezzlement;

    - an attempt, conspiracy or incitement to commit an offence mentioned in paragraphs (a) to (g);

    - an offence under section 4 of the Misuse of Drugs Act 1971 (c. 38) (restriction on production and supply of controlled drugs) committed in respect of a relevant Class A drug;

    - an offence under section 5. (2) of that Act of 1971 (possession of controlled drug) committed in respect of a relevant Class A drug;

    - an offence under section 5. (3) of that Act of 1971 (possession of controlled drug with intent to supply) committed in respect of a relevant Class A drug;

"senior police officer" means a police officer of a rank no lower than inspector.

20. BSection 20. A: supplementaryS

(1) Section 20. A of this Act does not prejudice the generality of section 18 of this Act.

(2) Each person carrying out a function under section 20. A of this Act must have regard to any guidance issued by the Scottish Ministers—

    (a) about the carrying out of the function; or

    (b) about matters connected to the carrying out of the function.

(3) An order under section 20. A(3)(c) shall be subject to annulment in pursuance of a resolution of the Scottish Parliament.

(4) An authorisation for the purposes of section 20. A of this Act may be given orally or in writing but, if given orally, the person giving it shall confirm it in writing as soon as is reasonably practicable.

(5) If a sample is provided or taken under section 20. A of this Act by virtue of an authorisation, the authorisation and the grounds for the suspicion are to be recorded in writing as soon as is

reasonably practicable after the sample is provided or taken.

(6) A person guilty of an offence under section 20. A of this Act shall be liable on summary conviction to the following penalties—

(a) a fine not exceeding level 4 on the standard scale;

(b) imprisonment for a period—

(i) where conviction is in the district court, not exceeding 60 days; or

(ii) where conviction is in the sheriff court, not exceeding 3 months; or

(c) both such fine and imprisonment.

(7) Subject to subsection (8) below, a sample provided or taken under section 20. A of this Act shall be destroyed as soon as possible following its analysis for the purpose for which it was taken.

(8) Where an analysis of the sample reveals that a relevant Class A drug is present in the person's body, the sample may be retained so that it can be used, and supplied to others, for the purpose of any proceedings against the person for an offence under section 88 of the Police, Public Order and Criminal Justice (Scotland) Act 2006 (asp 10); but—

(a) the sample may not be used, or supplied, for any other purpose; and

(b) the sample shall be destroyed as soon as possible once it is no longer capable of being used for that purpose.

(9) Information derived from a sample provided by or taken from a person under section 20. A of this Act may be used and disclosed only for the following purposes—

(a) for the purpose of proceedings against the person for an offence under section 88 of the Police, Public Order and Criminal Justice (Scotland) Act 2006 (asp 10);

(b) for the purpose of informing any decision about granting bail in any criminal proceedings to the person;

(c) for the purpose of informing any decision of a children's hearing arranged to consider the person's case;

(d) where the person is convicted of an offence, for the purpose of informing any decision about the appropriate sentence to be passed by a court and any decision about the person's supervision or release;

(e) for the purpose of ensuring that appropriate advice and treatment is made available to the person.

(10) Subject to subsection (11) below, the Scottish Ministers may by order made by statutory instrument modify section 20. A(8) of this Act for either of the following purposes—

(a) for the purpose of adding an offence to or removing an offence from those for the time being listed in the definition of "relevant offence";

(b) for the purpose of adding a substance, preparation or product to or removing a substance, preparation or product from those for the time being listed in the definition of "relevant Class A drug".

(11) An order under subsection (10)(b) may add a substance, preparation or product only if it is a Class A drug (that expression having the same meaning as in the Misuse of Drugs Act 1971 (c. 38)).

(12) An order under subsection (10) above shall not be made unless a draft of the statutory instrument containing it has been laid before and approved by resolution of the Scottish Parliament.]

Schedule 1 offencesS

F11821 Schedule 1 offences: power of constable to take offender into custody.S

. . . .

F119...S

F12022 Liberation by police.S

. . . .

F12022. ZAOffences where undertaking breachedS

. . . .

F12022. ZBEvidential and procedural provisionS

. . . .

PART III Bail

PART IIIS Bail

[F122. A Consideration of bail on first appearanceS

(1) On the first occasion on which—

(a) a person accused on petition is brought before the sheriff prior to committal until liberated in due course of law; or

(b) a person charged on complaint with an offence is brought before a judge having jurisdiction to try the offence,

the sheriff or, as the case may be, the judge shall, after giving that person and the prosecutor an opportunity to be heard F2. . . , either admit or refuse to admit that person to bail.

[F3. (2)Admittance to or refusal of bail shall be determined before the end of the day (not being a Saturday or Sunday, or a court holiday prescribed for the court which is to determine the question of bail, unless that court is sitting on that day for the disposal of criminal business) after the day on which the person accused or charged is brought before the sheriff or judge.]

(3) If, by [F4that time], the sheriff or judge has not admitted or refused to admit the person accused or charged to bail, then that person shall be forthwith liberated.

(4) This section applies whether or not the person accused or charged is in custody when that person is brought before the sheriff or judge.]

Amendments (Textual)

F1. S. 22. A inserted before s. 23 (9.8.2000) by 2000 asp 9, s. 1

F2. Words in s. 22. A(1) repealed (10.12.2007) by Criminal Proceedings etc. (Reform) (Scotland) Act 2007 (asp 6), ss. 6. (1)(a), 84; S.S.I. 2007/479, art. 3. (1), Sch. (as amended by S.S.I. 2007/527)

F3. S. 22. A(2) substituted (10.12.2007) by Criminal Proceedings etc. (Reform) (Scotland) Act 2007 (asp 6), ss. 6. (1)(b), 84; S.S.I. 2007/479, art. 3. (1), Sch. (as amended by S.S.I. 2007/527)

F4. Words in s. 22. A(3) substituted (10.12.2007) by Criminal Proceedings etc. (Reform) (Scotland) Act 2007 (asp 6), ss. 6. (1)(c), 84; S.S.I. 2007/479, art. 3. (1), Sch. (as amended by S.S.I. 2007/527)

23 Bail applications.S

(1) Any person accused on petition of a crime F5. . . shall be entitled immediately, on any [F6. (other than the first)] occasion on which he is brought before the sheriff prior to his committal until liberated in due course of law, to apply to the sheriff for bail, and the prosecutor shall be entitled to be heard against any such application.

(2) The sheriff shall be entitled in his discretion to refuse such application before the person accused is committed until liberated in due course of law.

(3) Where an accused is admitted to bail without being committed until liberated in due course of law, it shall not be necessary so to commit him, and it shall be lawful to serve him with an indictment or complaint without his having been previously so committed.

(4) Where bail is refused before committal until liberation in due course of law on an application under subsection (1) above, the application for bail may be renewed after such committal.

(5) Any sheriff having jurisdiction to try the offence or to commit the accused until liberated in due course of law may, at his discretion, on the application of any person who has been committed until liberation in due course of law for any crime or offence, F7. . ., and having given the prosecutor an opportunity to be heard, admit or refuse to admit the person to bail.

[F8. (6)Any person charged on complaint with an offence shall, on any (other than the first) occasion on which he is brought before a judge having jurisdiction to try the offence, be entitled to apply to the judge for bail and the prosecutor shall be entitled to be heard against any such application.]

(7) An application under subsection (5) or (6) above shall be disposed of [F9before the end of the day (not being a Saturday or Sunday, or a court holiday prescribed for the court which is to determine the question of bail, unless that court is sitting on that day for the disposal of criminal business) after the day of] its presentation to the judge, failing which the accused shall be forthwith liberated.

(8) This section applies whether or not the accused is in custody at the time he appears for disposal of his application.

Amendments (Textual)

F5. Words in s. 23. (1) repealed (9.8.2000) by 2000 asp 9, s. 12, Sch. para. 7. (1)(a)(i)

F6. Words in s. 23. (1) inserted (9.8.2000) by 2000 asp 9, s. 12, Sch. para. 7. (1)(a)(ii)

F7. Words in s. 23. (5) repealed (9.8.2000) by 2000 asp 9, s. 12, Sch. para. 7. (1)(b)

F8. S. 23. (6) substituted (9.8.2000) by 2000 asp 9, s. 12, Sch. para. 7. (1)(c)

F9. Words in s. 23. (7) substituted (10.12.2007) by Criminal Proceedings etc. (Reform) (Scotland) Act 2007 (asp 6), ss. 6. (2), 84; S.S.I. 2007/479, art. 3. (1), Sch. (as amended by S.S.I. 2007/527)

[F1023. A Bail and liberation where person already in custodyS

(1) A person may be admitted to bail under section 22. A , [F1123, 65. (8. C) or 107. A(7)(b)] of this Act although in custody—

(a) having been refused bail in respect of another crime or offence; or

(b) serving a sentence of imprisonment.

(2) A decision to admit a person to bail by virtue of subsection (1) above does not liberate the person from the custody mentioned in that subsection.

(3) The liberation under section [F1222. A(3), 23. (7) or 107. A(7)(b)] of this Act of a person who may be admitted to bail by virtue of subsection (1) above does not liberate that person from the custody mentioned in that subsection.

(4) In subsection (1) above, "another crime or offence" means a crime or offence other than that giving rise to the consideration of bail under section 22. A , [F1323, 65. (8. C) or 107. A(7)(b)] of this Act.]

Amendments (Textual)

F10. S. 23. A inserted (9.8.2000) by 2000 asp 9, s. 2

F11. Words in s. 23. A(1) substituted (28.3.2011) by Criminal Justice and Licensing (Scotland) Act 2010 (asp 13), s. 206. (1), sch. 7 para. 35. (a); S.S.I. 2011/178, art. 2, sch.

F12. Words in s. 23. A(3) substituted (28.3.2011) by Criminal Justice and Licensing (Scotland) Act 2010 (asp 13), s. 206. (1), sch. 7 para. 35. (b); S.S.I. 2011/178, art. 2, sch.

F13. Words in s. 23. A(4) substituted (28.3.2011) by Criminal Justice and Licensing (Scotland) Act 2010 (asp 13), s. 206. (1), sch. 7 para. 35. (a); S.S.I. 2011/178, art. 2, sch.

[F1423. BEntitlement to bail and the court's functionS

(1) Bail is to be granted to an accused person—

(a) except where—

(i) by reference to section 23. C of this Act; and

(ii) having regard to the public interest,

there is good reason for refusing bail;

(b) subject to section 23. D of this Act.

(2) In determining a question of bail in accordance with subsection (1) above, the court is to consider the extent to which the public interest could, if bail were granted, be safeguarded by the imposition of bail conditions.

(3) Reference in subsections (1)(a)(ii) and (2) above to the public interest includes (without prejudice to the generality of the public interest) reference to the interests of public safety.

(4) The court must (without prejudice to any other right of the parties to be heard) give the prosecutor and the accused person an opportunity to make submissions in relation to a question of bail.

(5) The attitude of the prosecutor towards a question of bail (including as to bail conditions) does not restrict the court's exercise of its discretion in determining the question in accordance with subsection (1) above.

(6) For the purpose of so determining a question of bail (including as to bail conditions), the court may request the prosecutor or the accused person's solicitor or counsel to provide it with information relevant to the question.

(7) However, whether that party gives the court opinion as to any risk of something occurring (or any likelihood of something not occurring) is a matter for that party to decide.

Amendments (Textual)

F14. Ss. 23. B-23. D inserted (10.12.2007) by Criminal Proceedings etc. (Reform) (Scotland) Act 2007 (asp 6), ss. 1, 84; S.S.I. 2007/479, art. 3. (1), Sch. (as amended by S.S.I. 2007/527)

23. CGrounds relevant as to question of bailS

(1) In any proceedings in which a person is accused of an offence, the following are grounds on which it may be determined that there is good reason for refusing bail—

    (a) any substantial risk that the person might if granted bail—

(i) abscond; or

(ii) fail to appear at a diet of the court as required;

    (b) any substantial risk of the person committing further offences if granted bail;

    (c) any substantial risk that the person might if granted bail—

(i) interfere with witnesses; or

(ii) otherwise obstruct the course of justice,

in relation to himself or any other person;

    (d) any other substantial factor which appears to the court to justify keeping the person in custody.

(2) In assessing the grounds specified in subsection (1) above, the court must have regard to all material considerations including (in so far as relevant in the circumstances of the case) the following examples—

    (a) the—

(i) nature (including level of seriousness) of the offences before the court;

(ii) probable disposal of the case if the person were convicted of the offences;

    (b) whether the person was subject to a bail order when the offences are alleged to have been committed;

    (c) whether the offences before the court are alleged to have been committed—

(i) while the person was subject to another court order;

(ii) while the person was on release on licence or parole;

(iii) during a period for which sentence of the person was deferred;

    (d) the character and antecedents of the person, in particular—

(i) the nature of any previous convictions of the person (including convictions [F15by courts outside the European Union]);

(ii) whether the person has previously contravened a bail order or other court order (by committing an offence or otherwise);

(iii) whether the person has previously breached the terms of any release on licence or parole (by committing an offence or otherwise);

(iv) whether the person is serving or recently has served a sentence of imprisonment in connection with a matter referred to in sub-paragraphs (i) to (iii) above;

    (e) the associations and community ties of the person.

Amendments (Textual)

F14. Ss. 23. B-23. D inserted (10.12.2007) by Criminal Proceedings etc. (Reform) (Scotland) Act 2007 (asp 6), ss. 1, 84; S.S.I. 2007/479, art. 3. (1), Sch. (as amended by S.S.I. 2007/527)

F15. Words in s. 23. C(2)(d)(i) substituted (13.12.2010 for all purposes in respect of offences committed on or after this date) by Criminal Justice and Licensing (Scotland) Act 2010 (asp 13), ss. 71. (1), 206. (1), Sch. 4 para. 2; S.S.I. 2010/413, art. 2, Sch.

23. DRestriction on bail in certain solemn casesS

(1) Where subsection (2) or (3) below applies, a person is to be granted bail in solemn proceedings only if there are exceptional circumstances justifying bail.

(2) This subsection applies where the person—

    (a) is accused in the proceedings of a violent or sexual offence; and

    (b) has a previous conviction on indictment for a violent or sexual offence.

(3) This subsection applies where the person—

    (a) is accused in the proceedings of a drug trafficking offence; and

(b) has a previous conviction on indictment for a drug trafficking offence.

(4) For the purposes of this section—

"drug trafficking offence" has the meaning given by section 49. (5) of the Proceeds of Crime (Scotland) Act 1995 (c. 43);

"sexual offence" has the meaning given by section 210. A(10) and (11) of this Act;

"violent offence" means any offence (other than a sexual offence) inferring personal violence.

(5) Any reference in this section to a conviction on indictment for a violent or sexual offence or a drug trafficking offence includes—

(a) a conviction on indictment in England and Wales or Northern Ireland for an equivalent offence;

(b) a conviction in a member State of the European Union (other than the United Kingdom) which is equivalent to conviction on indictment for an equivalent offence.

(6) Any issue of equivalence arising in pursuance of subsection (5) above is for the court to determine.

(7) This section is without prejudice to section 23. C of this Act.]

Amendments (Textual)

F14. Ss. 23. B-23. D inserted (10.12.2007) by Criminal Proceedings etc. (Reform) (Scotland) Act 2007 (asp 6), ss. 1, 84; S.S.I. 2007/479, art. 3. (1), Sch. (as amended by S.S.I. 2007/527)

24 Bail and bail conditions.S

(1) All crimes and offences F16. . . are bailable.

(2) Nothing in this Act shall affect the right of the Lord Advocate or the High Court to admit to bail any person charged with any crime or offence.

[F17. (2. A)Whenever the court grants or refuses bail, it shall state its reasons.

(2. B)Where the court—

(a) grants bail to a person accused of a sexual offence (having the meaning given by section 210. A(10) and (11) of this Act); and

(b) does so without imposing on the accused further conditions under subsection (4)(b)(i) below,

the court shall also state why it considers in the circumstances of the case that such conditions are unnecessary.]

(3) It shall not be lawful to grant bail or release for a pledge or deposit of money, and—

(a) release on bail may be granted only on conditions which subject to subsection (6) below, shall not include a pledge or deposit of money;

(b) liberation may be granted by the police under [F18section 25 of the Criminal Justice (Scotland) Act 2016].

(4) In granting bail the court or, as the case may be, the Lord Advocate shall impose on the accused—

(a) the standard conditions; and

(b) such further conditions as the court or, as the case may be, the Lord Advocate considers necessary to secure—

(i) that the standard conditions are observed; F19...

F19. (ii). . . . .

(5) The standard conditions referred to in subsection (4) above are conditions that the accused—

(a) appears at the appointed time at every diet relating to the offence with which he is charged of which he is given due notice; [F20 or at which he is required by this Act to appear]

(b) does not commit an offence while on bail;

(c) does not interfere with witnesses or otherwise obstruct the course of justice whether in relation to himself or any other person; F21. . .

[F22. (ca)does not behave in a manner which causes, or is likely to cause, alarm or distress to witnesses;]

[F23. (cb)whenever reasonably instructed by a constable to do so—
(i) participates in an identification parade or other identification procedure; and
(ii) allows any print, impression or sample to be taken from the accused;]

(d) makes himself available for the purpose of enabling enquiries or a report to be made to assist the court in dealing with him for the offence with which he is charged [F24; and

(e) where the (or an) offence in respect of which he is admitted to bail is one to which section 288. C of this Act applies, does not seek to obtain, otherwise than by way of a solicitor, any precognition of or statement by the complainer in relation to the subject matter of the offence.]

(6) The court or, as the case may be, the Lord Advocate may impose as one of the conditions of release on bail a requirement that the accused or a cautioner on his behalf deposits a sum of money in court, but only where the court or, as the case may be, the Lord Advocate is satisfied that the imposition of such condition is appropriate to the special circumstances of the case.

[F25. (6. A)Subsection (6) above does not apply in relation to an accused admitted to bail under section 65. (8. C) of this Act.]

(7) In any enactment, including this Act and any enactment passed after this Act—

(a) any reference to bail shall be construed as a reference to release on conditions in accordance with this Act or to conditions imposed on bail, as the context requires;

(b) any reference to an amount of bail fixed shall be construed as a reference to conditions, including a sum required to be deposited under subsection (6) above;

(c) any reference to finding bail or finding sufficient bail shall be construed as a reference to acceptance of conditions imposed or the finding of a sum required to be deposited under subsection (6) above.

[F26. (7. A)In subsection (5)(e) above, "complainer" has the same meaning as in section 274 of this Act.]

(8) In this section and sections 25 and 27 to 29 of this Act, references to an accused and to appearance at a diet shall include references respectively to an appellant and to appearance at the court on the day fixed for the hearing of an appeal.

Amendments (Textual)

F16. Words in s. 24. (1) repealed (9.8.2000) by 2000 asp 9, s. 3. (1)

F17. S. 24. (2. A)(2. B) inserted (10.12.2007) by Criminal Proceedings etc. (Reform) (Scotland) Act 2007 (asp 6), ss. 2. (1)(a), 84; S.S.I. 2007/479, art. 3. (1), Sch. (as amended by S.S.I. 2007/527)

F18. Words in s. 24. (3)(b) substituted (25.1.2018) by The Criminal Justice (Scotland) Act 2016 (Consequential and Supplementary Modifications) Regulations 2017 (S.S.I. 2017/452), reg. 1, sch. para. 12. (2) (with reg. 2. (2))

F19. S. 24. (4)(b)(ii) and preceding word repealed (28.3.2011) by Criminal Justice and Licensing (Scotland) Act 2010 (asp 13), ss. 58. (a), 206. (1); S.S.I. 2011/178, art. 2, sch.

F20. Words in s. 24. (5)(a) inserted (1.2.2005) by Criminal Procedure (Amendment) (Scotland) Act 2004 (asp 5), ss. 25, 27. (1), Sch. para. 5. (a); S.S.I. 2004/405, art. 2 Sch. 1 (subject to arts. 3-5)

F21. Word in s. 24. (5) repealed (1.11.2002) by Sexual Offences (Procedure and Evidence) (Scotland) Act 2002 (asp 9), s. 5. (1)(a); S.S.I. 2002/443, art. 3

F22. S. 24. (5)(ca) inserted (10.12.2007) by Criminal Proceedings etc. (Reform) (Scotland) Act 2007 (asp 6), ss. 2. (1)(c), 84; S.S.I. 2007/479, art. 3. (1), Sch. (as amended by S.S.I. 2007/527)

F23. S. 24. (5)(cb) inserted (28.3.2011) by Criminal Justice and Licensing (Scotland) Act 2010 (asp 13), ss. 58. (b), 206. (1); S.S.I. 2011/178, art. 2, sch.

F24. S. 24. (5)(e) and preceding word inserted (1.11.2002) by Sexual Offences (Procedure and Evidence) (Scotland) Act 2002 (asp 9), s. 5. (1)(b); S.S.I. 2002/443, art. 3

F25. S. 24. (6. A) inserted (1.2.2005) by Criminal Procedure (Amendment) (Scotland) Act 2004 (asp 5), ss. 25, 27. (1), Sch. para. 5. (b); S.S.I. 2004/405, art. 2 Sch. 1 (subject to arts. 3-5)

F26. S. 24. (7. A) inserted (1.11.2002) by Sexual Offences (Procedure and Evidence) (Scotland) Act 2002 (asp 9), s. 5. (2); S.S.I. 2002/443, art. 3

24. ABail conditions: remote monitoring of restrictions on movementsS

F27. . . . .

Amendments (Textual)

F27. Ss. 24. A-24. E repealed (13.12.2010) by Criminal Justice and Licensing (Scotland) Act 2010 (asp 13), ss. 59, 206. (1); S.S.I. 2010/413, art. 2, Sch.

24. BRegulations as to power to impose remote monitoring requirements under section 24. AS

F28. . . . .

Amendments (Textual)

F28. Ss. 24. A-24. E repealed (13.12.2010) by Criminal Justice and Licensing (Scotland) Act 2010 (asp 13), ss. 59, 206. (1); S.S.I. 2010/413, art. 2, Sch.

24. CMonitoring of compliance in pursuance of requirements imposed under section 24. AS

F29. . . . .

Amendments (Textual)

F29. Ss. 24. A-24. E repealed (13.12.2010) by Criminal Justice and Licensing (Scotland) Act 2010 (asp 13), ss. 59, 206. (1); S.S.I. 2010/413, art. 2, Sch.

24. DRemote monitoringS

F30. . . . .

Amendments (Textual)

F30. Ss. 24. A-24. E repealed (13.12.2010) by Criminal Justice and Licensing (Scotland) Act 2010 (asp 13), ss. 59, 206. (1); S.S.I. 2010/413, art. 2, Sch.

24. EDocumentary evidence in proceedings for breach of bail conditions being remotely monitoredS

F31. . . . .

Amendments (Textual)

F31. Ss. 24. A-24. E repealed (13.12.2010) by Criminal Justice and Licensing (Scotland) Act 2010 (asp 13), ss. 59, 206. (1); S.S.I. 2010/413, art. 2, Sch.

[F32[F3324. F]Bail: extradition proceedingsS

(1) In the application of the provisions of this Part by virtue of section 9. (2) or 77. (2) of the Extradition Act 2003 (judge's powers at extradition hearing), those provisions apply with the modifications that—

(a) references to the prosecutor are to be read as references to a person acting on behalf of the territory to which extradition is sought;

(b) the right of the Lord Advocate mentioned in section 24. (2) of this Act applies to a person subject to extradition proceedings as it applies to a person charged with any crime or offence;

(c) the following do not apply—

(i) paragraph (b) of section 24. (3); and

(ii) subsection (3) of section 30; and

(d) sections 28. (1) and 33 apply to a person subject to extradition proceedings as they apply to an accused.

(2) Section 32 of this Act applies in relation to a refusal of bail, the amount of bail or a decision to allow bail or ordain appearance in proceedings under this Part as the Part applies by virtue of the sections of that Act of 2003 mentioned in subsection (1) above.

(3) The Scottish Ministers may, by order, for the purposes of section 9. (2) or 77. (2) of the Extradition Act 2003 make such amendments to this Part as they consider necessary or expedient.

(4) The order making power in subsection (3) above shall be exercisable by statutory instrument subject to annulment in pursuance of a resolution of the Scottish Parliament.]

Amendments (Textual)

F32. S. 24. A inserted (1.1.2004) by Extradition Act 2003 (c. 41), ss. 199, 221; S.I. 2003/3103, art. 2 (subject to arts. 3-5)

F33. S. 24. F: s. 24. A renumbered as 24. F (31.1.2005) by The Criminal Procedure (Amendment) (Scotland) Act 2004 (Incidental, Supplemental and Consequential Provisions) Order 2005 (S.S.I. 2005/40), art. 4. (2)

25 Bail conditions: supplementary.S

[F34. (A1)When granting bail, the court shall (if the accused is present) explain to the accused in ordinary language—

(a) the effect of the conditions imposed;

(b) the effect of the requirement under subsection (2. B) below; and

(c) the consequences which may follow a breach of any of those conditions or that requirement.

(B1) The accused shall (whether or not the accused is present when bail is granted) be given a written explanation in ordinary language of the matters mentioned in paragraphs (a) to (c) of subsection (A1) above.

(C1) Such a written explanation may be contained in the copy of the bail order given to the accused or in another document.]

(1) The court shall specify in the order granting bail, a copy of which shall be given to the accused—

(a) the conditions imposed; and

[F35. (aa)that breach of a condition imposed is an offence and renders the accused liable to arrest, prosecution and punishment under this Act;]

(b) an address, within the United Kingdom (being the accused's normal place of residence or such other place as the court may, on cause shown, direct) which, subject to subsection (2) below, shall be his proper domicile of citation.

(2) The court may on application in writing by the accused while he is on bail alter the address specified in the order granting bail, and this new address shall, as from such date as the court may direct, become his proper domicile of citation; and the court shall notify the accused of its decision on any application under this subsection.

[F36. (2. A)Where an application is made under subsection (2) above—

(a) the application shall be intimated by the accused immediately and in writing to the Crown Agent and for that purpose the application shall be taken to be intimated to the Crown Agent if intimation of it is sent to the procurator fiscal for the sheriff court district in which bail was granted ; and

(b) the court shall, before determining the application, give the prosecutor an opportunity to be heard.]

[F37. (2. B)Where the domicile of citation specified in an order granting bail ceases to be the accused's normal place of residence, the accused must make an application under subsection (2) above within 7 days of that happening.

(2. C)A person who without reasonable excuse contravenes subsection (2. B) above is guilty of an offence and is liable—

(a) on conviction in the JP court, to a fine not exceeding level 3 on the standard scale or to imprisonment for a period not exceeding 60 days or to both;

(b) in any other case, to a fine not exceeding level 3 on the standard scale or to imprisonment for a period not exceeding 12 months or to both.]

(3) In this section "proper domicile of citation" means the address at which the accused may be cited to appear at any diet relating to the offence with which he is charged or an offence charged in the same proceedings as that offence or to which any other intimation or document may be sent; and any citation at or the sending of an intimation or document to the proper domicile of citation shall be presumed to have been duly carried out.

[F38. (4)In this section, references to the court (other than in subsection (2. A)) shall, in relation to a person who has been admitted to bail by the Lord Advocate, be read as if they were references to the Lord Advocate.]

Amendments (Textual)

F34. S. 25. (A1)-(C1) inserted (10.12.2007) by Criminal Proceedings etc. (Reform) (Scotland) Act 2007 (asp 6), ss. 2. (2)(a), 84; S.S.I. 2007/479, art. 3. (1), Sch. (as amended by S.S.I. 2007/527)

F35. S. 25. (1)(aa) inserted (10.12.2007) by Criminal Proceedings etc. (Reform) (Scotland) Act 2007 (asp 6), ss. 2. (2)(b), 84; S.S.I. 2007/479, art. 3. (1), Sch. (as amended by S.S.I. 2007/527)

F36. S. 25. (2. A) inserted (1.2.2005) by Criminal Procedure (Amendment) (Scotland) Act 2004 (asp 5), ss. 18. (2), 27. (1); S.S.I. 2004/405, art. 2, Sch. 1 (subject to arts. 3-5) (as amended by S.S.I. 2005/40, art. 3. (4))

F37. S. 25. (2. B)(2. C) inserted (10.12.2007) by Criminal Proceedings etc. (Reform) (Scotland) Act 2007 (asp 6), ss. 2. (2)(c), 84; S.S.I. 2007/479, art. 3. (1), Sch. (as amended by S.S. I. 2007/527)

F38. S. 25. (4) inserted (4.10.2004) by Criminal Procedure (Amendment) (Scotland) Act 2004 (asp 5), ss. 25, 27. (1), Sch. para. 6; S.S.I. 2004/405, art. 2, Sch. 1 (subject to arts. 3-5)

Modifications etc. (not altering text)

C1. S. 25. (2. C)(a) applied (10.12.2007) by The District Courts and Justices of the Peace (Scotland) Order 2007 (S.S.I. 2007/480), art. 4. (1)(a)

[F3925. AFailure to accept conditions of bail under section 65(8. C): continued detention of accusedS

An accused who—

(a) is, by virtue of subsection (4) of section 65 of this Act, entitled to be admitted to bail; but

(b) fails to accept any of the conditions imposed by the court on bail under subsection (8. C) of that section,

shall continue to be detained under the committal warrant for so long as he fails to accept any of those conditions.]

Amendments (Textual)

F39. S. 25. A inserted (1.2.2005) by Criminal Procedure (Amendment) (Scotland) Act 2004 (asp 5), ss. 25, 27. (1), Sch. para. 7; S.S.I. 2004/405, art. 2 Sch. 1 (subject to arts. 3-5)

F4026. . . . . .S

Amendments (Textual)

F40. S. 26 repealed (9.8.2000) by 2000 asp 9, s. 3. (2)

27 Breach of bail conditions: offences.S

(1) Subject to subsection (7) below, an accused who having been granted bail fails without reasonable excuse—

(a) to appear at the time and place appointed for any diet of which he has been given due notice [F41or at which he is required by this Act to appear]; or

(b) to comply with any other condition imposed on bail,

shall, subject to subsection (3) below, be guilty of an offence and liable on conviction to the penalties specified in subsection (2) below.

(2) The penalties mentioned in subsection (1) above are—

(a) a fine not exceeding level 3 on the standard scale; and

(b) imprisonment for a period—

(i) where conviction is in the [F42. JP court], not exceeding 60 days; or

(ii) in any other case, not exceeding [F4312] months.

(3) Where, and to the extent that, the failure referred to in subsection (1)(b) above consists in the accused having committed an offence while on bail (in this section referred to as "the subsequent offence"), he shall not be guilty of an offence under that subsection but, subject to subsection (4) below, the court which sentences him for the subsequent offence shall, in determining the appropriate sentence or disposal for that offence, have regard to—

(a) the fact that the offence was committed by him while on bail and the number of bail orders to which he was subject when the offence was committed;

(b) any previous conviction of the accused of an offence under subsection (1)(b) above; and

(c) the extent to which the sentence or disposal in respect of any previous conviction of the accused differed, by virtue of this subsection, from that which the court would have imposed but for this subsection.

[F44. (3. A)The reference in subsection (3)(b) to any previous conviction of an offence under subsection (1)(b) includes any previous conviction by a court in England and Wales, Northern Ireland or a member State of the European Union other than the United Kingdom of an offence that is equivalent to an offence under subsection (1)(b).

(3. B)The references in subsection (3)(c) to subsection (3) are to be read, in relation to a previous conviction by a court referred to in subsection (3. A), as references to any provision that is equivalent to subsection (3).

(3. C)Any issue of equivalence arising in pursuance of subsection (3. A) or (3. B) is for the court to determine.]

(4) The court shall not, under subsection (3) above, have regard to the fact that the subsequent offence was committed while the accused was on bail unless that fact is libelled in the indictment or, as the case may be, specified in the complaint.

[F45. (4. A)The fact that the subsequent offence was committed while the accused was on bail shall, unless challenged—

(a) in the case of proceedings on indictment, by giving notice of a preliminary objection [F46in accordance with section 71. (2) or 72. (6)(b)(i)] of this Act; or

(b) in summary proceedings, by preliminary objection before his plea is recorded,

be held as admitted.]

[F47. (4. B)In any proceedings in relation to an offence under subsection (1) above or subsection 7 below, the fact that (as the case may be) an accused—

(a) was on bail;

(b) was subject to any particular condition of bail;

(c) failed to appear at a diet; or

(d) was given due notice of a diet,

shall, unless challenged in the manner described in paragraph (a) or (b) of subsection (4. A) above, be held as admitted.]

(5) Where the maximum penalty in respect of the subsequent offence is specified by or by virtue of any enactment, that maximum penalty shall, for the purposes of the court's determination, by virtue of subsection (3) above, of the appropriate sentence or disposal in respect of that offence, be increased—

(a) where it is a fine, by the amount for the time being equivalent to level 3 on the standard scale; and

(b) where it is a period of imprisonment—

(i) as respects a conviction in the High Court or the sheriff court, by 6 months; and

(ii) as respects a conviction in the [F42. JP court], by 60 days,

notwithstanding that the maximum penalty as so increased exceeds the penalty which it would otherwise be competent for the court to impose.

(6) Where the sentence or disposal in respect of the subsequent offence is, by virtue of subsection (3) above, different from that which the court would have imposed but for that subsection, the court shall state the extent of and the reasons for that difference.

[F48. (6. A)Where, despite the requirement to have regard to the matters specified in paragraphs (a) to (c) of subsection (3) above, the sentence or disposal in respect of the subsequent offence is not different from that which the court would have imposed but for that subsection, the court shall state (as appropriate, by reference to those matters) the reasons for there being no difference.]

(7) An accused who having been granted bail in relation to solemn proceedings fails without reasonable excuse to appear at the time and place appointed for any diet of which he has been given due notice (where such diet is in respect of solemn proceedings) shall be guilty of an offence and liable on conviction on indictment to the following penalties—

(a) a fine; and

(b) imprisonment for a period not exceeding [F495] years.

(8) At any time before the trial of an accused under solemn procedure for the original offence, it shall be competent—

(a) to amend the indictment to include an additional charge of an offence under this section;

(b) to include in the list of witnesses or productions relating to the original offence, witnesses or productions relating to the offence under this section.

[F50. (8. A)At any time before the trial of an accused in summary proceedings for the original offence, it is competent to amend the complaint to include an additional charge of an offence under this section.]

(9) [F51. A penalty under subsection (2) or (7) above shall] be imposed in addition to any other penalty which it is competent for the court to impose, notwithstanding that the total of penalties imposed may exceed the maximum penalty which it is competent to impose in respect of the original offence.

[F52. (9. A)The reference in subsection (9) above to a penalty being imposed in addition to another penalty means, in the case of sentences of imprisonment or detention—

(a) where the sentences are imposed at the same time (whether or not in relation to the same complaint or indictment), framing the sentences so that they have effect consecutively;

(b) where the sentences are imposed at different times, framing the sentence imposed later so that (if the earlier sentence has not been served) the later sentence has effect consecutive to the earlier sentence.

(9. B)Subsection (9. A)(b) above is subject to section 204. A of this Act.]

(10) A court which finds an accused guilty of an offence under this section may remit the accused for sentence in respect of that offence to any court which is considering the original offence.

(11) In this section "the original offence" means the offence with which the accused was charged when he was granted bail or an offence charged in the same proceedings as that offence.

Amendments (Textual)

F41. Words in s. 27. (1)(a) inserted (1.2.2005) by Criminal Procedure (Amendment) (Scotland) Act 2004 (asp 5), ss. 25, 27. (1), Sch. para. 8. (a); S.S.I. 2004/405, art. 2, Sch. 1 (subject to arts. 3-5)

F42. Words in s. 27. (2)(b)(i)(5)(b)(ii) substituted (10.3.2008, 2.6.2008, 8.12.2008, 23.2.2009 and 14.12.2009 for certain purposes, otherwise 22.2.2010) by Criminal Proceedings etc. (Reform) (Scotland) Act 2007 (asp 6), ss. 80, 84, Sch. para. 26. (c); S.S.I. 2008/42, art. 3, Sch.; S.S.I. 2008/192, art. 3, Sch.; S.S.I. 2008/329, art. 3, Sch.; S.S.I. 2008/362, art. 3, Sch.; S.S.I. 2009/432, art. 3, Schs. 1, 2

F43. Word in s. 27. (2)(b)(ii) substituted (10.12.2007) by Criminal Proceedings etc. (Reform) (Scotland) Act 2007 (asp 6), ss. 3. (1)(a), 84; S.S.I. 2007/479, art. 3. (1), Sch. (as amended by S.S. I. 2007/527)

F44. S. 27. (3. A)-(3. C) inserted (13.12.2010 for all purposes in respect of offences committed on or after this date) by Criminal Justice and Licensing (Scotland) Act 2010 (asp 13), ss. 71. (1), 206. (1), Sch. 4 para. 3; S.S.I. 2010/413, art. 2, Sch.

F45. S. 27. (4. A) inserted (4.7.1996) by 1996 c. 25, s. 73. (2)

F46. Words in s. 27. (4. A)(a) substituted (1.2.2005) by Criminal Procedure (Amendment) (Scotland) Act 2004 (asp 5), ss. 25, 27. (1), Sch. para. 8. (b); S.S.I. 2004/405, art. 2, Sch. 1 (subject to arts. 3-5)

F47. S. 27. (4. B) inserted (10.12.2007) by Criminal Proceedings etc. (Reform) (Scotland) Act 2007 (asp 6), ss. 3. (1)(b), 84 (as amended by S.S.I. 2007/540, art. 3); S.S.I. 2007/479, art. 3. (1), Sch. (as amended by S.S.I. 2007/527)

F48. S. 27. (6. A) inserted (10.12.2007) by Criminal Proceedings etc. (Reform) (Scotland) Act 2007 (asp 6), ss. 3. (1)(c), 84; S.S.I. 2007/479, art. 3. (1), Sch. (as amended by S.S. I. 2007/527)

F49. Word in s. 27. (7)(b) substituted (10.12.2007) by Criminal Proceedings etc. (Reform) (Scotland) Act 2007 (asp 6), ss. 3. (1)(d), 84; S.S.I. 2007/479, art. 3. (1), Sch. (as amended by S.S. I. 2007/527)

F50. S. 27. (8. A) inserted (28.3.2011) by Criminal Justice and Licensing (Scotland) Act 2010 (asp 13), ss. 62. (1), 206. (1); S.S.I. 2011/178, art. 2, sch.

F51. Words in s. 27. (9) substituted (10.12.2007) by Criminal Proceedings etc. (Reform) (Scotland) Act 2007 (asp 6), ss. 3. (1)(e), 84; S.S.I. 2007/479, art. 3. (1), Sch. (as amended by S.S. I. 2007/527)

F52. S. 27. (9. A)(9. B) inserted (10.12.2007) by Criminal Proceedings etc. (Reform) (Scotland) Act 2007 (asp 6), ss. 3. (1)(f), 84; S.S.I. 2007/479, art. 3. (1), Sch. (as amended by S.S. I. 2007/527)

28 Breach of bail conditions: arrest of offender, etc.S

(1) A constable may arrest without warrant an accused who has been released on bail where the constable has reasonable grounds for suspecting that the accused has broken, is breaking, or is likely to break any condition imposed on his bail.

[F53. (1. ZA)Where—

(a) a constable who is not in uniform arrests a person under subsection (1), and

(b) the person asks to see the constable's identification,

the constable must show identification to the person as soon as reasonably practicable.]

[F54. (1. A)Where an accused who has been released on bail is arrested by a constable (otherwise than under subsection (1) above), the accused may be detained in custody under this subsection if the constable has reasonable grounds for suspecting that the accused has breached, or is likely to breach, any condition imposed on his bail.

(1. B)Subsection (1. A) above—

(a) is without prejudice to any other power to detain the accused;

(b) applies even if release of the accused would be required but for that subsection.]

(2) An accused who is arrested under [F55subsection (1) above, or is detained under subsection (1. A) above,] shall wherever practicable be brought before the court to which his application for bail was first made not later than in the course of the first day after his arrest, such day not being, subject to subsection (3) below, a Saturday, a Sunday or a court holiday prescribed for that court under section 8 of this Act.

(3) Nothing in subsection (2) above shall prevent an accused being brought before a court on a Saturday, a Sunday or such a court holiday where the court is, in pursuance of the said section 8, sitting on such day for the disposal of criminal business.

[F56. (3. A)If—

(a) a person is in custody only by virtue of subsection (1) or (1. A), and

(b) in the opinion of a constable there are no reasonable grounds for suspecting that the person has broken, or is likely to break, a condition imposed on the person's bail,

the person must be released from custody immediately.

(3. B)An accused is deemed to be brought before a court under subsection (2) or (3) if the accused appears before it by means of a live television link (by virtue of a determination by the court that the person is to do so by such means).]

(4) Where an accused is brought before a court under subsection (2) or (3) above, the court, after hearing the parties, may—

(a) recall the order granting bail;

(b) release the accused under the original order granting bail; or

(c) vary the order granting bail so as to contain such conditions as the court thinks it necessary to impose to secure that the accused complies with the requirements of paragraphs (a) to (d) of section 24. (5) of this Act.

[F57. (4. A)In the case of an accused released on bail by virtue of section 65. (8. C) of this Act—

(a) subsection (2) above shall have effect as if the reference to the court to which his application for bail was first made were a reference to the court or judge which admitted him to bail under that section; and

(b) subsection (4) above shall not apply and subsection (4. B) below shall apply instead.

(4. B)Where an accused referred to in subsection (4. A) above is, under subsection (2) or (3) above, brought before the court or judge which admitted him to bail under section 65. (8. C)—

(a) the court or judge shall give the prosecutor an opportunity to make an application under section 65. (5) of this Act; and

(b) if the prosecutor does not make such an application, or if such an application is made but is refused, the court or judge may—

(i) release the accused under the original order granting bail; or

(ii) vary the order granting bail so as to contain such conditions as the court or judge thinks necessary to impose to secure that the accused complies with the requirements of paragraphs (a) to (d) of section 24. (5) of this Act.]

(5) The same rights of appeal shall be available against any decision of the court under subsection (4) above as were available against the original order of the court relating to bail.

(6) For the purposes of this section and section 27 of this Act, an extract from the minute of proceedings, containing the order granting bail and bearing to be signed by the clerk of court, shall be sufficient evidence of the making of that order and of its terms and of the acceptance by the accused of the conditions imposed under section 24 of this Act.

Amendments (Textual)

F53. S. 28. (1. ZA) inserted (25.1.2018) by Criminal Justice (Scotland) Act 2016 (asp 1), s. 117. (2), sch. 2 para. 29. (a); S.S.I. 2017/345, art. 3, sch.

F54. S. 28. (1. A)(1. B) inserted (10.12.2007) by Criminal Proceedings etc. (Reform) (Scotland) Act 2007 (asp 6), ss. 3. (2)(a), 84; S.S.I. 2007/479, art. 3. (1), Sch. (as amended by S.S.I. 2007/527)

F55. Words in s. 28. (2) substituted (10.12.2007) by Criminal Proceedings etc. (Reform) (Scotland) Act 2007 (asp 6), ss. 3. (2)(b), 84; S.S.I. 2007/479, art. 3. (1), Sch. (as amended by S.S.I. 2007/527)

F56. S. 28. (3. A)(3. B) inserted (25.1.2018) by Criminal Justice (Scotland) Act 2016 (asp 1), s. 117. (2), sch. 2 para. 29. (b); S.S.I. 2017/345, art. 3, sch.

F57. S. 28. (4. A)(4. B) inserted (1.2.2005) by Criminal Procedure (Amendment) (Scotland) Act 2004 (asp 5), ss. 25, 27. (1), Sch. para. 9; S.S.I. 2004/405, art. 2, Sch. 1 (subject to arts. 3-5)

[F5828. AApplication of the Criminal Justice (Scotland) Act 2016 to persons arrested and detained under section 28. S

(1) Section 7. (2) of the Criminal Justice (Scotland) Act 2016 ("the 2016 Act") does not apply to an accused who has been arrested under section 28. (1) of this Act.

(2) The following provisions of the 2016 Act apply in relation to a person who is to be brought before a court under section 28. (2) or (3) of this Act as they apply in relation to a person who is to be brought before a court in accordance with section 21. (2) of the 2016 Act—

(a) section 22,

(b) section 23,

(c) section 24.

(3) In relation to a person who is to be brought before a court under section 28. (2) or (3) of this Act, the 2016 Act applies as though—

(a) in section 23. (2)—

(i) for paragraph (c) there were substituted—

"(c)that the person is to be brought before the court under section 28 of the 1995 Act in order for the person's bail to be considered.", and

(ii) paragraph (d) were omitted,

(b) in section 24—

(i) in subsection (3)(c), for the words "after being officially accused" there were substituted " after being informed that the person is to be brought before a court under section 28. (2) or (3) of the 1995 Act ", and

(ii) in subsection (4), for paragraph (c) there were substituted—

"(c)that the person is to be brought before the court under section 28 of the 1995 Act in order for the person's bail to be considered.",

(c) in section 43. (1), for paragraph (d) there were substituted—

"(d)the court before which the person is to be brought under section 28. (2) or (3) of the 1995 Act and the date on which the person is to be brought before that court.".]

Amendments (Textual)

F58. S. 28. A inserted (25.1.2018) by Criminal Justice (Scotland) Act 2016 (asp 1), s. 117. (2), sch. 2 para. 30; S.S.I. 2017/345, art. 3, sch.

29 Bail: monetary conditions.S

(1) Without prejudice to section 27 of this Act, where the accused or a cautioner on his behalf has deposited a sum of money in court under section 24. (6) of this Act, then—

(a) if the accused fails to appear at the time and place appointed for any diet of which he has been given due notice, the court may, on the motion of the prosecutor, immediately order forfeiture of the sum deposited;

(b) if the accused fails to comply with any other condition imposed on bail, the court may, on conviction of an offence under section 27. (1)(b) of this Act and on the motion of the prosecutor, order forfeiture of the sum deposited.

(2) If the court is satisfied that it is reasonable in all the circumstances to do so, it may recall an order made under subsection (1)(a) above and direct that the money forfeited shall be refunded, and any decision of the court under this subsection shall be final and not subject to review.

(3) A cautioner, who has deposited a sum of money in court under section 24. (6) of this Act, shall be entitled, subject to subsection (4) below, to recover the sum deposited at any diet of the court at which the accused appears personally.

(4) Where the accused has been charged with an offence under section 27. (1)(b) of this Act, nothing in subsection (3) above shall entitle a cautioner to recover the sum deposited unless and until—

(a) the charge is not proceeded with; or

(b) the accused is acquitted of the charge; or

(c) on the accused's conviction of the offence, the court has determined not to order forfeiture of the sum deposited.

(5) The references in subsections (1)(b) and (4)(c) above to conviction of an offence shall include references to the making of an order in respect of the offence under section 246. (3) of this Act.

30 Bail review.S

(1) This section applies where a court has refused to admit a person to bail or, where a court has so admitted a person, the person has failed to accept the conditions imposed or that a sum required to be deposited under section 24. (6) of this Act has not been so deposited.

[F59. (1. A)This section also applies where a person who has accepted the conditions imposed on his bail wants to have any of them removed or varied.]

(2) A court shall, on the application of any person mentioned in subsection (1) [F60 or (1. A) above, have power to review (in favour of the person) its decision as to bail, or its decision as to the conditions imposed, if—

    (a) the circumstances of the person have changed materially; or

    (b) the person puts before the court material information which was not available to it when its decision was made.]

[F61[F62. (2. A)On receipt of an application under subsection (2), the court must—

    (a) intimate the application to the prosecutor, and

    (b) before determining the application, give the prosecutor an opportunity to be heard.

(2. AA)Despite subsection (2. A)(b), the court may grant the application without having heard the prosecutor if the prosecutor consents.]

(2. B)Subsection (2. C) below applies where an application is made under subsection (2) above by a person convicted on indictment pending the 5determination of—

    (a) his appeal;

    (b) any relevant appeal by the Lord Advocate under section 108 or 108. A of this Act; or

    (c) the sentence to be imposed on, or other method of dealing with, him.

(2. C)Where this subsection applies the application shall be—

    (a) intimated by the person making it immediately and in writing to the Crown Agent; and

    (b) [F63determined] not less than 7 days after the date of that intimation.]

(3) An application under this section, where it relates to the original decision of the court, shall not be made before the fifth day after that decision and, where it relates to a subsequent decision, before the fifteenth day thereafter.

(4) Nothing in this section shall affect any right of a person to appeal against the decision of a court in relation to admitting to bail or to the conditions imposed.

Amendments (Textual)

F59. S. 30. (1. A) inserted (10.12.2007) by Criminal Proceedings etc. (Reform) (Scotland) Act 2007 (asp 6), ss. 4. (1)(a), 84; S.S.I. 2007/479, art. 3. (1), Sch. (as amended by S.S.I. 2007/527)

F60. Words in s. 30. (02) substituted (10.12.2007) by Criminal Proceedings etc. (Reform) (Scotland) Act 2007 (asp 6), ss. 4. (1)(b), 84; S.S.I. 2007/479, art. 3. (1), Sch. (as amended by S.S.I. 2007/527)

F61. S. 30. (2. A)-(2. C) inserted (1.2.2005) by Criminal Procedure (Amendment) (Scotland) Act 2004 (asp 5), ss. 18. (3), 27. (1); S.S.I. 2004/405, art. 2 Sch. 1 (subject to arts. 3-5)

F62. S. 30. (2. A)(2. AA) substituted for s. 30. (2. A) (28.3.2011) by Criminal Justice and Licensing (Scotland) Act 2010 (asp 13), ss. 57. (2)(a), 206. (1); S.S.I. 2011/178, art. 2, sch.

F63. Word in s. 30. (2. C)(b) substituted (28.3.2011) by Criminal Justice and Licensing (Scotland) Act 2010 (asp 13), ss. 57. (2)(b), 206. (1); S.S.I. 2011/178, art. 2, sch.

31 Bail review on prosecutor's application.S

(1) On an application by the prosecutor at any time after a court has granted bail to a person the court may, where the prosecutor puts before the court material information which was not available to it when it granted bail to that person, review its decision.

(2) On receipt of an application under subsection (1) above the court shall—

    (a) intimate the application to the person granted bail;

    (b) fix a diet for hearing the application and cite that person to attend the diet; and

    (c) where it considers that the interests of justice so require, grant warrant to arrest that person.

[F64. (2. ZA)Despite subsection (2)(b), the court may grant the application without fixing a hearing if the person granted bail consents.]

[F65. (2. A)Subsection (2. B) below applies to an application under subsection (1) above where the person granted bail—

    (a) was convicted on indictment; and

    (b) was granted bail pending the determination of—

(i) his appeal;

(ii) any relevant appeal by the Lord Advocate under section 108 or 108. A of this Act; or

(iii) the sentence to be imposed on, or other method of dealing with, him.

(2. B)Where this subsection applies, the application shall be heard not more than 7 days after the day on which it is made.]

(3) On F66... an application under subsection (1) above the court may—

    (a) withdraw the grant of bail and remand the person in question in custody; or

    (b) grant bail, or continue the grant of bail, either on the same or on different conditions.

[F67. (3. A)In relation to an accused admitted to bail under section 65. (8. C) of this Act—

    (a) an application may be made under subsection (1) above only in relation to the conditions imposed on bail; and

    (b) paragraph (a) of subsection (3) above shall not apply in relation to any such application.]

(4) Nothing in the foregoing provisions of this section shall affect any right of appeal against the decision of a court in relation to bail.

Amendments (Textual)

F64. S. 31. (2. ZA) inserted (28.3.2011) by Criminal Justice and Licensing (Scotland) Act 2010 (asp 13), ss. 57. (3)(a), 206. (1); S.S.I. 2011/178, art. 2, sch.

F65. S. 31. (2. A)(2. B) inserted (1.2.2005) by Criminal Procedure (Amendment) (Scotland) Act 2004 (asp 5), ss. 18. (4), 27. (1); S.S.I. 2004/405, art. 2, Sch. 1 (subject to arts. 3-5)

F66. Word in s. 31. (3) repealed (28.3.2011) by Criminal Justice and Licensing (Scotland) Act 2010 (asp 13), ss. 57. (3)(b), 206. (1); S.S.I. 2011/178, art. 2, sch.

F67. S. 31. (3. A) inserted (1.2.2005) by Criminal Procedure (Amendment) (Scotland) Act 2004 (asp 5), ss. 25, 27. (1), Sch. para. 10; S.S.I. 2004/405, art. 2, Sch. 1 (subject to arts. 3-5)

32 Bail appeal.S

(1) [F68. Where, in any case, bail] is refused or where the [F69accused] is dissatisfied with the amount of bail fixed, he may appeal to the [F70appropriate Appeal Court] which may, in its discretion order intimation to the Lord Advocate or, as the case may be, the prosecutor.

(2) Where, in any case, F71. . . bail is granted, or, in summary proceedings an accused is ordained to appear, the public prosecutor, if dissatisfied—

    (a) with the decision allowing bail;

    (b) with the amount of bail fixed; or

    (c) in summary proceedings, that the accused has been ordained to appear,

may appeal to the [F72appropriate Appeal Court], and the [F69accused] shall not be liberated, subject to subsection (7) below, until the appeal by the prosecutor is disposed of.

[F73. (2. A)The public prosecutor may, in relation to an accused admitted to bail under section 65. (8. C) of this Act, appeal under subsection (2) above only in relation to the conditions imposed on bail.]

(3) Written notice of appeal shall be immediately given to the opposite party by a party appealing under this section.

[F74. (3. A)A notice of appeal under this section is to be lodged with the clerk of the court from which the appeal is to be taken.

(3. B)When an appeal is made under this section, that clerk shall without delay—

(a) send a copy of the notice of appeal to the judge whose decision is the subject of the appeal; and

(b) request the judge to provide a report of the reasons for that decision.

(3. C)The judge shall, as soon as is reasonably practicable, provide that clerk with the judge's report of those reasons.

[F75. (3. CA)The clerk of the court from which the appeal is to be taken (unless that clerk is the Clerk of Justiciary) must—

(a) send the notice of appeal without delay to the clerk of the appropriate Appeal Court, and

(b) before the end of the day after the day of receipt of the notice of appeal, send the judge's report (if provided by then) to the clerk of the appropriate Appeal Court.]

(3. F)The [F76clerk of the appropriate Appeal Court] shall, upon receipt of the notice of appeal, without delay fix a diet for the hearing of the appeal.

(3. G)The [F77clerk of the appropriate Appeal Court] shall send a copy of the judge's report to—

(a) the accused or his solicitor; and

(b) the Crown Agent.

(3. H)[F78. In a case where the Sheriff Appeal Court is the appropriate Appeal Court, if] the judge's report is not sent as mentioned in subsection [F79. (3. CA)] above—

(a) the [F80appropriate Appeal Court] may call for the report to be submitted to it within such period as it may specify; or

(b) if it thinks fit, hear and determine the appeal without the report.

(3. I)Subject to subsection (3. G) above, the judge's report shall be available only to the [F81appropriate Appeal Court], the parties and, on such conditions as may be prescribed by Act of Adjournal, such other persons or classes of person as may be so prescribed.]

(4) An appeal under this section shall be disposed of by the [F82appropriate Appeal Court] or any [F83judge of the appropriate Appeal Court] in court or in chambers after such inquiry and hearing of parties as shall seem just.

(5) Where an [F69accused] in an appeal under this section is under 21 years of age, section 51 of this Act shall apply to the [F84appropriate Appeal Court] or, as the case may be, the [F85judge of the appropriate Appeal Court] when disposing of the appeal as it applies to a court when remanding or committing a person of the [F69accused's] age for trial or sentence.

(6) In the event of the appeal of the public prosecutor under this section being refused, the court may award expenses against him.

(7) When an appeal is taken by the public prosecutor either against the grant of bail or against the amount fixed, the [F69accused] to whom bail has been granted [F86. (other than an accused to whom subsection (7. B) below applies)] shall, if the bail fixed has been found by him, be liberated after 72 hours from the granting of [F87bail], whether the appeal has been disposed of or not, unless the [F88appropriate Appeal Court] grants an order for his further detention in custody.

[F89. (7. B)Where, in relation to an accused admitted to bail under section 65. (8. C) of this Act, the public prosecutor appeals against the conditions imposed on bail, the accused—

(a) may continue to be detained under the committal warrant for no more than 72 hours from the granting of bail or for such longer period as [F90the appropriate Appeal Court] may allow; and

(b) on expiry of that period, shall, whether the appeal has been disposed of or not, be released on bail subject to the conditions imposed.]

(8) In computing the period mentioned in subsection (7) above, Sundays and public holidays, whether general or court holidays, shall be excluded.

(9) When an appeal is taken under this section by the prosecutor in summary proceedings against the fact that the accused has been ordained to appear, subsections (7) and (8) above shall apply as they apply in the case of an appeal against the granting of bail or the amount fixed.

(10) Notice to the governor of the prison of the issue of an order such as is mentioned in subsection (7) above within the time mentioned in that subsection bearing to be sent by the [F91clerk of the appropriate Appeal Court] or the Crown Agent shall be sufficient warrant for the

detention of the [F69accused] pending arrival of the order in due course of post.

[F92. (11)In this section—

"appropriate Appeal Court" means—

- in the case of an appeal under this section against a bail decision of the High Court or a judge of the High Court, that Court,

- in the case of an appeal under this section against a bail decision of the Sheriff Appeal Court, the High Court,

- in the case of an appeal under this section against a bail decision of a sheriff (whether in solemn or summary proceedings) or a JP court, the Sheriff Appeal Court,

"judge of the appropriate Appeal Court" means—

- in a case where the High Court is the appropriate Appeal Court, judge of that Court,

- in a case where the Sheriff Appeal Court is the appropriate Appeal Court, Appeal Sheriff,

"the clerk of the appropriate Appeal Court" means—

- in a case where the High Court is the appropriate Appeal Court, the Clerk of Justiciary,

- in a case where the Sheriff Appeal Court is the appropriate Appeal Court, the Clerk of that Court.

(12) In a case where the Sheriff Appeal Court is the appropriate Appeal Court, the references in subsections (3. G)(b) and (10) to the Crown Agent are to be read as references to the prosecutor.]

Amendments (Textual)

F68. Words in s. 32. (1) substituted (9.8.2000) by 2000 asp 9, s. 4

F69. Words in s. 32. (1)(2)(5)(7)(10) substituted (9.8.2000) by 2000 asp 9, s. 12, Sch. para. 7. (2)(a)

F70. Words in s. 32. (1) substituted (22.9.2015) by Courts Reform (Scotland) Act 2014 (asp 18), ss. 122. (2), 138. (2); S.S.I. 2015/247, art. 2, sch. (with art. 7)

F71. Words in s. 32. (2) repealed (9.8.2000) by 2000 asp 9, s. 12, Sch. para. 7. (2)(b)

F72. Words in s. 32. (2) substituted (22.9.2015) by Courts Reform (Scotland) Act 2014 (asp 18), ss. 122. (2), 138. (2); S.S.I. 2015/247, art. 2, sch. (with art. 7)

F73. S. 32. (2. A) inserted (1.2.2005) by Criminal Procedure (Amendment) (Scotland) Act 2004 (asp 5), ss. 25, 27. (1), Sch. para. 11. (a); S.S.I. 2004/405, art. 2, Sch. 1 (subject to arts. 3-5)

F74. S. 32. (3. A)-(3. I) inserted (10.12.2007) by Criminal Proceedings etc. (Reform) (Scotland) Act 2007 (asp 6), ss. 4. (2), 84; S.S.I. 2007/479, art. 3. (1), Sch. (as amended by S.S.I. 2007/527)

F75. S. 32. (3. CA) substituted for s. 32. (3. D)(3. E) (22.9.2015) by Courts Reform (Scotland) Act 2014 (asp 18), ss. 122. (3), 138. (2); S.S.I. 2015/247, art. 2, sch. (with art. 7)

F76. Words in s. 32. (3. F) substituted (22.9.2015) by Courts Reform (Scotland) Act 2014 (asp 18), ss. 122. (4), 138. (2); S.S.I. 2015/247, art. 2, sch. (with art. 7)

F77. Words in s. 32. (3. G) substituted (22.9.2015) by Courts Reform (Scotland) Act 2014 (asp 18), ss. 122. (4), 138. (2); S.S.I. 2015/247, art. 2, sch. (with art. 7)

F78. Words in s. 32. (3. H) substituted (22.9.2015) by Courts Reform (Scotland) Act 2014 (asp 18), ss. 122. (5)(a), 138. (2); S.S.I. 2015/247, art. 2, sch. (with art. 7)

F79. Word in s. 32. (3. H) substituted (22.9.2015) by Courts Reform (Scotland) Act 2014 (asp 18), ss. 122. (5)(b), 138. (2); S.S.I. 2015/247, art. 2, sch. (with art. 7)

F80. Words in s. 32. (3. H)(a) substituted (22.9.2015) by Courts Reform (Scotland) Act 2014 (asp 18), ss. 122. (2), 138. (2); S.S.I. 2015/247, art. 2, sch. (with art. 7)

F81. Words in s. 32. (3. I) substituted (22.9.2015) by Courts Reform (Scotland) Act 2014 (asp 18), ss. 122. (2), 138. (2); S.S.I. 2015/247, art. 2, sch. (with art. 7)

F82. Words in s. 32. (4) substituted (22.9.2015) by Courts Reform (Scotland) Act 2014 (asp 18), ss. 122. (2), 138. (2); S.S.I. 2015/247, art. 2, sch. (with art. 7)

F83. Words in s. 32. (4) substituted (22.9.2015) by Courts Reform (Scotland) Act 2014 (asp 18), ss. 122. (6), 138. (2); S.S.I. 2015/247, art. 2, sch. (with art. 7)

F84. Words in s. 32. (5) substituted (22.9.2015) by Courts Reform (Scotland) Act 2014 (asp 18), ss. 122. (2), 138. (2); S.S.I. 2015/247, art. 2, sch. (with art. 7)

F85. Words in s. 32. (5) substituted (22.9.2015) by Courts Reform (Scotland) Act 2014 (asp 18), ss. 122. (6), 138. (2); S.S.I. 2015/247, art. 2, sch. (with art. 7)

F86. Words s. 32. (7) inserted (1.2.2005) by Criminal Procedure (Amendment) (Scotland) Act 2004 (asp 5), ss. 25, 27. (1), Sch. para. 11. (b); S.S.I. 2004/405, art. 2, Sch. 1 (subject to arts. 3-5)

F87. Words in s. 32. (7) substituted (9.8.2000) by 2000 asp 9, s. 12, Sch. para. 7. (2)(c)

F88. Words in s. 32. (7) substituted (22.9.2015) by Courts Reform (Scotland) Act 2014 (asp 18), ss. 122. (2), 138. (2); S.S.I. 2015/247, art. 2, sch. (with art. 7)

F89. S. 32. (7. B) inserted (1.2.2005) by Criminal Procedure (Amendment) (Scotland) Act 2004 (asp 5), ss. 25, 27. (1), Sch. para. 11. (c); S.S.I. 2004/405, art. 2, Sch. 1 (subject to arts. 3-5)

F90. Words in s. 32. (7. B)(a) substituted (22.9.2015) by Courts Reform (Scotland) Act 2014 (asp 18), ss. 122. (7), 138. (2); S.S.I. 2015/247, art. 2, sch. (with art. 7)

F91. Words in s. 32. (10) substituted (22.9.2015) by Courts Reform (Scotland) Act 2014 (asp 18), ss. 122. (4), 138. (2); S.S.I. 2015/247, art. 2, sch. (with art. 7)

F92. S. 32. (11)(12) inserted (22.9.2015) by Courts Reform (Scotland) Act 2014 (asp 18), ss. 122. (8), 138. (2); S.S.I. 2015/247, art. 2, sch. (with art. 7)

[F9332. ABail after conviction: prosecutor's attitudeS

(1) Where—
    (a) a person has been convicted in any proceedings of an offence; and
    (b) a question of bail (including as to bail conditions) subsequently arises in the proceedings
(whether before sentencing or pending appeal or otherwise),
the prosecutor and the convicted person must be given an opportunity to make submissions in relation to the question.
(2) But the attitude of the prosecutor towards the question does not restrict the court's exercise of its discretion in determining the question in accordance with the rules applying in the case.
(3) Despite subsection (1) above, the prosecutor need not be given an opportunity to make submissions in relation to a question of bail arising under section 245. J of this Act.
(4) This section is without prejudice to any other right of the parties to be heard.]

Amendments (Textual)

F93. S. 32. A inserted (10.12.2007) by Criminal Proceedings etc. (Reform) (Scotland) Act 2007 (asp 6), ss. 5, 84; S.S.I. 2007/479, art. 3. (1), Sch. (as amended by S.S.I. 2007/527)

33 Bail: no fees exigible.S

No clerks fees, court fees or other fees or expenses shall be exigible from or awarded against an accused in respect of [F94a decision on bail under section 22. A above, an] application for bail or of the appeal of such [F95a decision or] application to the High Court.

Amendments (Textual)

F94. Words in s. 33 substituted (9.8.2000) by 2000 asp 9, s. 12, Sch. para. 7. (3)(a)

F95. Words in s. 33 inserted (9.8.2000) by 2000 asp 9, s. 12, Sch. para. 7. (3)(b)

PART IV Petition Procedure

PART IVS Petition Procedure

34 Petition for warrant.S

(1) A petition for warrant to arrest and commit a person suspected of or charged with crime may be in the forms—

(a) set out in Schedule 2 to this Act; or

(b) prescribed by Act of Adjournal,

or as nearly as may be in such form; and Schedule 3 to this Act shall apply to any such petition as it applies to the indictment.

(2) If on the application of the procurator fiscal, a sheriff is satisfied that there is reasonable ground for suspecting that an offence has been or is being committed by a body corporate, the sheriff shall have the like power to grant warrant for the citation of witnesses and the production of documents and articles as he would have if a petition charging an individual with the commission of the offence were presented to him.

[F1. Petition proceedings outwith sheriffdomS

Amendments (Textual)

F1. S. 34. A and preceding cross-heading inserted (10.3.2008) by Criminal Proceedings etc. (Reform) (Scotland) Act 2007 (asp 6), ss. 31, 84; S.S.I. 2008/42, art. 3, Sch.

34. APetition proceedings outwith sheriffdomS

(1) Where the prosecutor believes—

(a) that, because of exceptional circumstances (and without an order under subsection (3) below), it is likely that there would be an unusually high number of accused persons appearing from custody for the first calling of cases on petition in the sheriff courts in the sheriffdom; and

(b) that it would not be practicable for those courts to deal with all the cases involved,

the prosecutor may apply to the sheriff principal for the order referred to in subsection (2) below.

(2) For the purposes of subsection (1) above, the order is for authority for petition proceedings against some or all of the accused persons to be—

(a) taken at a sheriff court in another sheriffdom; and

(b) maintained—

(i) there; or

(ii) at any of the sheriff courts referred to in subsection (1) above as may at the first calling of the case be appointed for further proceedings.

(3) On an application under subsection (1) above, the sheriff principal may make the order sought with the consent of the sheriff principal of the other sheriffdom.

(4) An order under subsection (3) above may be made by reference to a particular period or particular circumstances.

(5) This section does not confer jurisdiction for any subsequent proceedings on indictment.]

Judicial examinationS

35 Judicial examination.S

(1) The accused's solicitor shall be entitled to be present at the examination.

(2) The sheriff may delay the examination for a period not exceeding 48 hours from and after the time of the accused's arrest, in order to allow time for the attendance of the solicitor.

F2. (3). . . . .

F3. (4). . . . .

[F4. (4. A)An accused charged with a sexual offence to which section 288. C of this Act applies shall, as soon as he is brought before the sheriff for examination on the charge, be told—

[F5. (a)that his case at, or for the purposes of, any relevant hearing (within the meaning of section 288. C(1. A)) in the course of the proceedings may be conducted only by a lawyer,]

(b) that it is, therefore, in his interests, if he has not already done so, to get the professional assistance of a solicitor; and

(c) that, if he does not engage a solicitor for the purposes of [F6the conduct of his case at or for the purposes of the] [F7hearing], the court will do so.

(4. B)A failure to comply with subsection (4. A) above does not affect the validity or lawfulness of the examination or of any other element of the proceedings against the accused.]

F8. (5). . . . .

(6) Where the accused is brought before the sheriff for further examination the sheriff may delay that examination for a period not exceeding 24 hours in order to allow time for the attendance of the accused's solicitor.

[F9. (6. A)In proceedings before the sheriff in examination or further examination, the accused is not to be given an opportunity to make a declaration in respect of any charge.]

(7) Any proceedings before the sheriff in examination or further examination shall be conducted in chambers and outwith the presence of any co-accused.

(8) This section applies to procedure on petition, without prejudice to the accused being tried summarily by the sheriff for any offence in respect of which he has been committed until liberated in due course of law.

Amendments (Textual)

F2. S. 35. (3) repealed (17.1.2017) by Criminal Justice (Scotland) Act 2016 (asp 1), ss. 78. (2)(a), 117. (2); S.S.I. 2016/426, art. 2, sch.

F3. S. 35. (4) repealed (17.1.2017) by Criminal Justice (Scotland) Act 2016 (asp 1), ss. 78. (2)(a), 117. (2); S.S.I. 2016/426, art. 2, sch.

F4 S. 35. (4. A)(4. B) inserted (1.11.2002) by Sexual Offences (Procedure and Evidence) (Scotland) Act 2002 (asp 9), s. 3, Sch. para. 3; S.S.I. 2002/443, art. 3 (with art. 4. (3))

F5 S. 35. (4. A)(a) substituted for s. 35. (4. A)(za)(a) (28.3.2011) by Criminal Justice and Licensing (Scotland) Act 2010 (asp 13), s. 206. (1), sch. 7 para. 36. (a); S.S.I. 2011/178, art. 2, sch.

F6 Words in s. 35. (4. A)(c) inserted (4.12.2004) by Criminal Procedure (Amendment) (Scotland) Act 2004 (asp 5), ss. 25, 27. (1), Sch. para. 12. (b); S.S.I. 2004/405, art. 2, Sch. 1 (subject to arts. 3-5)

F7 Word in s. 35. (4. A)(c) substituted (28.3.2011) by Criminal Justice and Licensing (Scotland) Act 2010 (asp 13), s. 206. (1), sch. 7 para. 36. (b); S.S.I. 2011/178, art. 2, sch.

F8. S. 35. (5) repealed (17.1.2017) by Criminal Justice (Scotland) Act 2016 (asp 1), ss. 78. (2)(a), 117. (2); S.S.I. 2016/426, art. 2, sch.

F9. S. 35. (6. A) inserted (17.1.2017) by Criminal Justice (Scotland) Act 2016 (asp 1), ss. 78. (1), 117. (2); S.S.I. 2016/426, art. 2, sch.

F1036 Judicial examination: questioning by prosecutor.S

. . . .

Amendments (Textual)

F10. S. 36 repealed (17.1.2017) by Criminal Justice (Scotland) Act 2016 (asp 1), ss. 78. (2)(b), 117. (2); S.S.I. 2016/426, art. 2, sch. (with art. 3)

F1137 Judicial examination: record of proceedings.S

. . . .

Amendments (Textual)

F11. S. 37 repealed (17.1.2017) by Criminal Justice (Scotland) Act 2016 (asp 1), ss. 78. (2)(b), 117. (2); S.S.I. 2016/426, art. 2, sch. (with art. 3)

F1238 Judicial examination: rectification of record of proceedings.S

. . . .

Amendments (Textual)
F12. S. 38 repealed (17.1.2017) by Criminal Justice (Scotland) Act 2016 (asp 1), ss. 78. (2)(b), 117. (2); S.S.I. 2016/426, art. 2, sch. (with art. 3)

39 Judicial examination: charges arising in different districts.S

(1) An accused against whom there are charges in more than one sheriff court district may be brought before the sheriff of any one such district at the instance of the procurator fiscal of such district for examination on all or any of the charges.

(2) Where an accused is brought for examination as mentioned in subsection (1) above, he may be dealt with in every respect as if all of the charges had arisen in the district where he is examined.

(3) This section is without prejudice to the power of the Lord Advocate under section 10 of this Act to determine the court before which the accused shall be tried on such charges.

CommittalS

40 Committal until liberated in due course of law.S

(1) Every petition shall be signed and no accused shall be committed until liberated in due course of law for any crime or offence without a warrant in writing expressing the particular charge in respect of which he is committed.

(2) Any such warrant for imprisonment which either proceeds on an unsigned petition or does not express the particular charge shall be null and void.

(3) The accused shall immediately be given a true copy of the warrant for imprisonment signed by the constable or person executing the warrant before imprisonment or by the prison officer receiving the warrant.

PART V Children and Young Persons

PART V Children and Young Persons

41 Age of criminal responsibility.S

It shall be conclusively presumed that no child under the age of eight years can be guilty of any offence.

[F141. AProsecution of children under 12.

(1) A child under the age of 12 years may not be prosecuted for an offence.

(2) A person aged 12 years or more may not be prosecuted for an offence which was committed at a time when the person was under the age of 12 years.]

Amendments (Textual)

42 Prosecution of children.S

(1) [F2. A child aged 12 years or more but under 16 years may not] be prosecuted for any offence except on the instructions of the Lord Advocate, or at [F3the instance of the Lord Advocate]; and no court other than the High Court and the sheriff court shall have jurisdiction over [F4such a child] for an offence.

(2) Where a child is charged with any offence, his parent or guardian may in any case, and shall, if he can be found and resides within a reasonable distance, be required to attend at the court before which the case is heard or determined during all the stages of the proceedings, unless the court is satisfied that it would be unreasonable to require his attendance.

F5. (3). . . . .

(4) For the purpose of enforcing the attendance of a parent or guardian and enabling him to take part in the proceedings and enabling orders to be made against him, rules may be made under section 305 of this Act, for applying, with the necessary adaptations and modifications, such of the provisions of this Act relating to summary proceedings as appear appropriate for the purpose.

(5) The parent or guardian whose attendance is required under this section is—

   (a) the parent who has parental responsibilities or parental rights (within the meaning of sections 1. (3) and 2. (4) respectively of the M1. Children (Scotland) Act 1995) in relation to the child; or

   (b) the guardian having actual possession and control of him.

(6) The attendance of the parent of a child shall not be required under this section in any case where the child was before the institution of the proceedings removed from the care or charge of his parent by an order of a court.

F6. (7). . . . .

(8) Where a local authority receive notification under [F7section 24 of the Criminal Justice (Scotland) Act 2016] they shall make such investigations and submit to the court a report which shall contain such information as to the home surroundings of the child as appear to them will assist the court in the disposal of his case, and the report shall contain information, which the appropriate education authority shall have a duty to supply, as to the school record, health and character of the child.

(9) Any child F8... being conveyed to or from any criminal court, or waiting before or after attendance in such court, shall be prevented from associating with an adult (not being a relative) who is charged with any offence other than an offence with which the child is jointly charged.

F9. (10). . . . .

F9. S. 42. (10) repealed (25.1.2018) by Criminal Justice (Scotland) Act 2016 (asp 1), s. 117. (2), sch. 2 para. 31. (e); S.S.I. 2017/345, art. 3, sch. (with art. 4)
Marginal Citations
M11995 c.36.

F1043 Arrangements where children arrested.S

. . . .
Amendments (Textual)
F10. S. 43 repealed (25.1.2018) by Criminal Justice (Scotland) Act 2016 (asp 1), s. 117. (2), sch. 2 para. 27. (c); S.S.I. 2017/345, art. 3, sch. (with arts. 4, 5)

44 Detention of children.

(1) Where a child appears before the sheriff in summary proceedings and pleads guilty to, or is found guilty of, an offence to which this section applies, the sheriff may order that he be detained in residential accommodation provided under Part II of the M2. Children (Scotland) Act 1995 by the appropriate local authority for such period not exceeding one year as may be specified in the order in such place (in any part of the United Kingdom) as the local authority may, from time to time, consider appropriate.

(2) This section applies to any offence [F11. (other than, if the child is under the age of 16 years, an offence under section 9. (1) of the Antisocial Behaviour etc. (Scotland) Act 2004 (asp 8) or that section as applied by section 234. AA(11) of this Act)] in respect of which it is competent to impose imprisonment on a person of the age of 21 years or more.

(3) Where a child in respect of whom an order is made under this section is detained by the appropriate local authority, that authority shall have the same powers and duties in respect of the child as they would have if he were subject to a [F12compulsory supervision order].

(4) Where a child in respect of whom an order is made under this section is also subject to a [F13compulsory supervision order or interim compulsory supervision order], subject to subsection (6) below, the [F13compulsory supervision order or interim compulsory supervision order] shall be of no effect during any period for which he is required to be detained under the order.

(5) The Secretary of State may, by regulations made by statutory instrument subject to annulment in pursuance of a resolution of either House of Parliament, make such provision as he considers necessary as regards the detention in secure accommodation of children in respect of whom orders have been made under this section.

(6) Where a child is detained in residential accommodation in pursuance of an order under—

(a) subsection (1) above, he shall be released from such detention not later than the date by which half the period specified in the order has (following commencement of the detention) elapsed but, without prejudice to subsection (7) below, until the entire such period has so elapsed may be required by the local authority to submit to supervision in accordance with such conditions as they consider appropriate;

(b) subsection (1) above or (8) below, the local authority may at any time review his case and may, in consequence of such review and after having regard to the best interests of the child and the need to protect members of the public, release the child—

(i) for such period and on such conditions as the local authority consider appropriate; or

(ii) unconditionally.

(7) Where a child released under paragraph (a) or (b)(ii) of subsection (6) above is subject to a [F13compulsory supervision order or interim compulsory supervision order], the effect of that [F14order] shall commence or, as the case may be, resume upon such release.

(8) If, while released under paragraph (a) or (b) of subsection (6) above (and before the date on which the entire period mentioned in the said paragraph (a) has, following the commencement of the detention, elapsed), a child commits an offence to which this section applies and (whether

before or after that date) pleads guilty to or is found guilty of it a court may, instead of or in addition to making any other order in respect of that plea or finding, order that he be returned to the residential accommodation provided by the authority which released him and that his detention in that accommodation or any other such accommodation provided by that authority shall continue for the whole or any part of the period which—

(a) begins with the date of the order for his return; and

(b) is equal in length to the period between the date on which the new offence was committed and the date on which that entire period elapses.

(9) An order under subsection (8) above for return to residential accommodation provided by the appropriate local authority—

(a) shall be taken to be an order for detention in residential accommodation for the purpose of this Act and any appeal; and

(b) shall, as the court making that order may direct, either be for a period of detention in residential accommodation before and to be followed by, or to be concurrent with, any period of such detention to be imposed in respect of the new offence (being in either case disregarded in determining the appropriate length of the period so imposed).

(10) Where a local authority consider it appropriate that a child in respect of whom an order has been made under subsection (1) or (8) above should be detained in a place in any part of the United Kingdom outside Scotland, the order shall be a like authority as in Scotland to the person in charge of the place to restrict the child's liberty to such an extent as that person may consider appropriate having regard to the terms of the order.

(11) In this section—

"the appropriate local authority" means—

- where the child usually resides in Scotland, the local authority for the area in which he usually resides;

- in any other case, the local authority for the area in which the offence was committed; and

[F15"secure accommodation" means accommodation provided for the purpose of restricting the liberty of children which—

- in Scotland, is provided in a residential establishment approved in accordance with regulations made under section 78. (2) of the Public Service Reform (Scotland) Act 2010;

- in England, is provided in a children's home within the meaning of the [F16. Care Standards Act 2000] in respect of which a person is registered under Part 2 of that Act, that before the coming into force of section 107. (2) of the Health and Social Care (Community Health Standards) Act 2003, "secure accommodation" means accommodation in relation to England which—

is provided in a children's home, within the meaning of the [F16. Care Standards Act 2000], in respect of which a person is registered under Part 2 of that Act; and

is approved by the Secretary of State for the purpose of restricting the liberty of children; and

- in Wales, is provided in a children's home within the meaning of the [F16. Care Standards Act 2000] in respect of which a person is registered under Part 2 of that Act;]

Amendments (Textual)

F11. Words in s. 44. (2) inserted (S.) (28.10.2004) by Antisocial Behaviour etc. (Scotland) Act 2004 (asp 8), ss. 10. (2), 145. (2); S.S.I. 2004/420, art. 3, Sch. 1

F12. Words in s. 44. (3) substituted (24.6.2013) by The Children's Hearings (Scotland) Act 2011 (Consequential and Transitional Provisions and Savings) Order 2013 (S.I. 2013/1465), art. 1. (2), Sch. 3 para. 2. (a)

F13. Words in s. 44. (4)(7) substituted (24.6.2013) by The Children's Hearings (Scotland) Act 2011 (Consequential and Transitional Provisions and Savings) Order 2013 (S.I. 2013/1465), art. 1. (2), Sch. 3 para. 2. (b)

F14. Word in s. 44. (7) substituted (24.6.2013) by The Children's Hearings (Scotland) Act 2011 (Consequential and Transitional Provisions and Savings) Order 2013 (S.I. 2013/1465), art. 1. (2), Sch. 3 para. 2. (c)

F15. Definition in s. 44. (11) substituted (24.6.2013) by The Children's Hearings (Scotland) Act 2011 (Consequential and Transitional Provisions and Savings) Order 2013 (S.I. 2013/1465), art. 1.

(2), Sch. 3 para. 2. (d)

F16. Words in s. 44. (11) substituted (S.) (30.9.2015) by Children and Young People (Scotland) Act 2014 (asp 8), s. 102. (3), sch. 5 para. 5. (2); S.S.I. 2015/317, art. 2, sch. and (E.W.N.I) (30.9.2015) by The Children and Young People (Scotland) Act 2014 (Consequential and Saving Provisions) Order 2015 (S.I. 2015/907), arts. 1. (4), 3

Modifications etc. (not altering text)

C1. S. 44 modified (1.4.1997) by S.I. 1996/3255, art. 13. (1)

Marginal Citations

M21995 c.36.

[F1744. AAppeal against detention in secure accommodation

(1) A child, or a relevant person in relation to the child, may appeal to the sheriff against a decision by a local authority to detain the child in secure accommodation in pursuance of an order made under section 44 of this Act.

(2) An appeal under subsection (1) may be made jointly by—

(a) the child and one or more relevant persons in relation to the child; or

(b) two or more relevant persons in relation to the child.

(3) An appeal must not be held in open court.

(4) The sheriff may determine an appeal by—

(a) confirming the decision to detain the child in secure accommodation; or

(b) quashing that decision and directing the local authority to move the child to be detained in residential accommodation which is not secure accommodation.

(5) The Scottish Ministers may by regulations make further provision about appeals under subsection (1).

(6) Regulations under subsection (5) may in particular—

(a) specify the period within which an appeal may be made;

(b) make provision about the hearing of evidence during an appeal;

(c) provide for appeals to the [F18. Sheriff Appeal Court] and Court of Session against the determination of an appeal.

(7) Regulations under subsection (5) are subject to the affirmative procedure.

(8) In this section—

"relevant person", in relation to a child, means any person who is a relevant person in relation to the child for the purposes of the Children's Hearings (Scotland) Act 2011 (including anyone deemed to be a relevant person in relation to the child by virtue of section 81. (3), 160. (4)(b) or 164. (6) of that Act);

"secure accommodation" has the same meaning as in section 44 of this Act.]

Amendments (Textual)

F17. S. 44. A inserted (1.8.2014 for specified purposes, 1.2.2016 in so far as not already in force) by Children and Young People (Scotland) Act 2014 (asp 8), ss. 91, 102. (3); S.S.I. 2014/131, art. 2. (2)(3), sch.; S.S.I. 2015/406, art. 3. (1) (with art. 4)

F18. Words in s. 44. A(6)(c) substituted (1.1.2016) by The Courts Reform (Scotland) Act 2014 (Consequential and Supplemental Provisions) Order 2015 (S.S.I. 2015/402), art. 1, sch. para. 3 (with art. 5)

45 Security for child's good behaviour.S

(1) Where a child has been charged with an offence the court may order his parent or guardian to give security for his co-operation in securing the child's good behaviour.

(2) Subject to subsection (3) below, an order under this section shall not be made unless the parent or guardian has been given the opportunity of being heard.

(3) Where a parent or guardian has been required to attend and fails to do so, the court may make

an order under this section.

(4) Any sum ordered to be paid by a parent or guardian on the forfeiture of any security given under this section may be recovered from him by civil diligence or imprisonment in like manner as if the order had been made on the conviction of the parent or guardian of the offence with which the child was charged.

(5) In this section "parent" means either of the child's parents, if that parent has parental responsibilities or parental rights (within the meaning of sections 1. (3) and 2. (4) respectively of the Children (Scotland) Act 1995) in relation to him.

46 Presumption and determination of age of child.S

(1) Where a person charged with an offence [F19, whose age is not specified in the indictment or complaint in relation to that offence,]is brought before a court other than for the purpose of giving evidence, and it appears to the court that he is a child, the court shall make due enquiry as to the age of that person, and for that purpose shall take such evidence as may be forthcoming at the hearing of the case, and the age presumed or declared by the court to be the age of that person shall, for the purposes of this Act or the M3. Children and Young Persons (Scotland) Act 1937, be deemed to be the true age of that person.

(2) The court in making any inquiry in pursuance of subsection (1) above shall have regard to the definition of child for the purposes of this Act.

(3) [F20. Without prejudice to section 255. A of this Act,]Where in an indictment or complaint for—

    (a) an offence under the Children and Young Persons (Scotland) 1937;

    (b) any of the offences mentioned in paragraphs 3 and 4 of Schedule 1 to this Act; or

    (c) an offence under section 1, 10. (1) to (3) or 12 of the M4. Criminal Law (Consolidation) (Scotland) Act 1995,

it is alleged that the person by or in respect of whom the offence was committed was a child or was under or had attained any specified age, and he appears to the court to have been at the date of the commission of the alleged offence a child, or to have been under or to have attained the specified age, as the case may be, he shall for the purposes of this Act or the M5. Children and Young Persons (Scotland) Act 1937 or Part I of the Criminal Law (Consolidation) (Scotland) Act 1995 be presumed at that date to have been a child or to have been under or to have attained that age, as the case may be, unless the contrary is proved.

(4) Where, in an indictment or complaint for an offence under the Children and Young Persons (Scotland) Act 1937 or any of the offences mentioned in Schedule 1 to this Act, it is alleged that the person in respect of whom the offence was committed was a child or was a young person, it shall not be a defence to prove that the person alleged to have been a child was a young person or the person alleged to have been a young person was a child in any case where the acts constituting the alleged offence would equally have been an offence if committed in respect of a young person or child respectively.

(5) An order or judgement of the court shall not be invalidated by any subsequent proof that—

    (a) the age of a person mentioned in subsection (1) above has not been correctly stated to the court; or

    (b) the court was not informed that at the material time the person was subject to a [F21compulsory supervision order or interim compulsory supervision order] or that his case had been referred to a children's hearing by virtue of regulations made under [F22section 190 of the Children's Hearings (Scotland) Act 2011 (asp 1).]

(6) Where it appears to the court that a person mentioned in subsection (1) above has attained the age of 17 years, he shall for the purposes of this Act or the Children and Young Persons (Scotland) Act 1937 be deemed not to be a child.

(7) In subsection (3) above, references to a child (other than a child charged with an offence) shall be construed as references to a child under the age of 17 years; but except as aforesaid references

in this section to a child shall be construed as references to a child within the meaning of section 307 of this Act.

Amendments (Textual)

F19. Words in s. 46. (1) inserted (1.8.1997) by 1997 c. 48, s. 62. (1), Sch. 1 para. 21. (4)(a); S.I. 1997/1712, art. 3, Sch. (subject to arts. 4, 5)

F20. Words in s. 46. (3) inserted (1.8.1997) by 1997 c. 48, s. 62. (1), Sch. 1 para. 21. (4)(a); S.I. 1997/1712, art. 3, Sch. (subject to arts. 4, 5)

F21. Words in s. 46. (5)(b) substituted (24.6.2013) by The Childrens Hearings (Scotland) Act 2011 (Modification of Primary Legislation) Order 2013 (S.S.I. 2013/211), art. 1, sch. 1 para. 10. (3)(a)

F22. Words in s. 46. (5)(b) substituted (24.6.2013) by The Childrens Hearings (Scotland) Act 2011 (Modification of Primary Legislation) Order 2013 (S.S.I. 2013/211), art. 1, sch. 1 para. 10. (3)(b)

Marginal Citations

M31937 c.37.

M41995 c.39.

M51937 c.37.

47 Restriction on report of proceedings involving children.

(1) Subject to subsection (3) below, no newspaper report of any proceedings in a court shall reveal the name, address or school, or include any particulars calculated to lead to the identification, of any person under the age of [F2318] years concerned in the proceedings, either—

(a) as being a person against or in respect of whom the proceedings are taken; or

(b) as being a witness in the proceedings.

(2) Subject to subsection (3) below, no picture which is, or includes, a picture of a person under the age of [F2418] years concerned in proceedings as mentioned in subsection (1) above shall be published in any newspaper in a context relevant to the proceedings.

(3) The requirements of subsections (1) and (2) above shall be applied in any case mentioned in any of the following paragraphs to the extent specified in that paragraph—

(a) where a person under the age of [F2518] years is concerned in the proceedings as a witness only and no one against whom the proceedings are taken is under the age of [F2518] years, the requirements shall not apply unless the court so directs;

(b) where, at any stage of the proceedings, the court, if it is satisfied that it is in the public interest so to do, directs that the requirements (including the requirements as applied by a direction under paragraph (a) above) shall be dispensed with to such extent as the court may specify; and

(c) where the Secretary of State, after completion of the proceedings, if satisfied as mentioned in paragraph (b) above, by order dispenses with the requirements to such extent as may be specified in the order.

(4) This section shall, with the necessary modifications, apply in relation to sound and television programmes included in a programme service (within the meaning of the M6. Broadcasting Act 1990) as it applies in relation to newspapers.

(5) A person who publishes matter in contravention of this section shall be guilty of an offence and liable on summary conviction to a fine not exceeding level 4 of the standard scale.

(6) In this section, references to a court shall not include a court in England, Wales or Northern Ireland.

Amendments (Textual)

F23. Word in s. 47. (1) substituted (1.9.2015) by Victims and Witnesses (Scotland) Act 2014 (asp 1), ss. 15, 34; S.S.I. 2015/200, art. 2. (2), sch.

F24. Word in s. 47. (2) substituted (1.9.2015) by Victims and Witnesses (Scotland) Act 2014 (asp 1), ss. 15, 34; S.S.I. 2015/200, art. 2. (2), sch.

F25. Word in s. 47. (3)(a) substituted (1.9.2015) by Victims and Witnesses (Scotland) Act 2014

(asp 1), ss. 15, 34; S.S.I. 2015/200, art. 2. (2), sch.
Modifications etc. (not altering text)
C2. S. 47 modified (S.) (31.3.2006) by Antisocial Behaviour etc. (Scotland) Act 2004 (asp 8), ss.
111. (6), 145. (2); S.S.I. 2004/420, art. 2 (as amended by S.S.I. 2005/553, art. 2)
Marginal Citations
M61990 c.42.

48 Power to refer certain children to reporter.S

(1) A court by or before which a person is convicted of having committed an offence to which this section applies may refer—

(a) a child in respect of whom an offence mentioned in paragraph (a) or (b) of subsection (2) below has been committed; or

(b) any child who is, or who is likely to become, a member of the same household as the person who has committed an offence mentioned in paragraph (b) or (c) of that subsection or the person in respect of whom the offence so mentioned was committed,

to the Principal Reporter, and certify that the offence shall be a ground established for the purposes of [F26the Children's Hearings (Scotland) Act 2011 (asp 1).]

(2) This section applies to an offence—

(a) under section 21 of the M7. Children and Young Persons (Scotland) Act 1937;

(b) mentioned in Schedule 1 to this Act; or

(c) in respect of a person aged 17 years or over which constitutes the crime of incest.

Amendments (Textual)
F26. Words in s. 48. (1) substituted (24.6.2013) by The Childrens Hearings (Scotland) Act 2011
(Modification of Primary Legislation) Order 2013 (S.S.I. 2013/211), art. 1, sch. 1 para. 10. (4)
Marginal Citations
M71937 c.37.

49 Reference or remit to children's hearing.S

(1) Where a child who is not subject to a [F27compulsory supervision order or interim compulsory supervision order] pleads guilty to, or is found guilty of, an offence the court—

(a) instead of making an order on that plea or finding, may remit the case to the Principal Reporter to arrange for the disposal of the case by a children's hearing; or

(b) on that plea or finding may request the Principal Reporter to arrange a children's hearing for the purposes of obtaining their advice as to the treatment of the child.

(2) Where a court has acted in pursuance of paragraph (b) of subsection (1) above, the court, after consideration of the advice received from the children's hearing may, as it thinks proper, itself dispose of the case or remit the case as mentioned in paragraph (a) of that subsection.

(3) Where a child who is subject to a [F28compulsory supervision order or interim compulsory supervision order] pleads guilty to, or is found guilty of, an offence the court dealing with the case if it is—

(a) the High Court, may; and

(b) the sheriff [F29. JP court] , shall,

request the Principal Reporter to arrange a children's hearing for the purpose of obtaining their advice as to the treatment of the child, and on consideration of that advice may, as it thinks proper, itself dispose of the case or remit the case as mentioned in subsection (1)(a) above [F30except that where [F31section 51. A of the Firearms Act 1968 or section 29 of the Violent Crime Reduction Act 2006 applies] it shall itself dispose of the case] .

(4) [F32. Subject to any appeal against any decision to remit made under subsection (1)(a) above or (7)(b) below,] where a court has remitted a case to the Principal Reporter under this section, the jurisdiction of the court in respect of the child shall cease, and his case shall stand referred to a

children's hearing.

(5) Nothing in this section shall apply to a case in respect of an offence the sentence for which is fixed by law.

(6) Where a person who is—

(a) not subject to a [F33compulsory supervision order or interim compulsory supervision order] ;

(b) over the age of 16; and

(c) not within six months of attaining the age of 18,

is charged summarily with an offence and pleads guilty to, or has been found guilty of, the offence the court may request the Principal Reporter to arrange a children's hearing for the purpose of obtaining their advice as to the treatment of the person.

(7) On consideration of any advice obtained under subsection (6) above, the court may, as it thinks proper—

(a) itself dispose of the case; or

(b) where the hearing have so advised, remit the case to the Principal Reporter for the disposal of the case by a children's hearing.

Amendments (Textual)

F27. Words in s. 49. (1) substituted (24.6.2013) by The Childrens Hearings (Scotland) Act 2011 (Modification of Primary Legislation) Order 2013 (S.S.I. 2013/211), art. 1, sch. 1 para. 10. (5)

F28. Words in s. 49. (3) substituted (24.6.2013) by The Childrens Hearings (Scotland) Act 2011 (Modification of Primary Legislation) Order 2013 (S.S.I. 2013/211), art. 1, sch. 1 para. 10. (5)

F29. Words in s. 49. (3)(b) substituted (10.3.2008, 2.6.2008, 8.12.2008, 23.2.2009 and 14.12.2009 for certain purposes, otherwise 22.2.2010) by Criminal Proceedings etc. (Reform) (Scotland) Act 2007 (asp 6), ss. 80, 84, Sch. para. 26. (d); S.S.I. 2008/42, art. 3, Sch.; S.S.I. 2008/192, art. 3, Sch.; S.S.I. 2008/329, art. 3, Sch.; S.S.I. 2008/362, art. 3, Sch.; S.S.I. 2009/432, art. 3, Schs. 1, 2

F30. Words in s. 49. (3) inserted (22.1.2004) by Criminal Justice Act 2003 (c. 44), ss. 290. (2), 336; S.I. 2004/81, art. 3. (2)(b)

F31. Words in s. 49. (3) substituted (6.4.2007) by Violent Crime Reduction Act 2006 (c. 38), ss. 49, 66. (2), Sch. 1 para. 4. (2); S.I. 2007/858, art. 2. (g)

F32. Words in s. 49. (4) inserted (1.8.1997) by 1997 c. 48, s. 23. (a); S.I. 1997/1712, art. 3, Sch. (subject to arts. 4, 5)

F33. Words in s. 49. (6)(a) substituted (24.6.2013) by The Childrens Hearings (Scotland) Act 2011 (Modification of Primary Legislation) Order 2013 (S.S.I. 2013/211), art. 1, sch. 1 para. 10. (5)

Modifications etc. (not altering text)

C3. S. 49. (3): power to amend conferred (22.1.2004) by Criminal Justice Act 2003 (c. 44), ss. 291. (1)(c), 336; S.I. 2004/81, art. 3. (2)(b)

50 Children and certain proceedings.S

(1) No child under 14 years of age (other than an infant in arms) shall be permitted to be present in court during any proceedings against any other person charged with an offence unless his presence is required as a witness or otherwise for the purposes of justice [F34or the court consents to his presence].

(2) Any child present in court when, under subsection (1) above, he is not to be permitted to be so shall be ordered to be removed.

(3) Where, in any proceedings in relation to an offence against, or any conduct contrary to, decency or morality, a person who, in the opinion of the court, is a child is called as a witness, the court may direct that all or any persons, not being—

(a) members or officers of the court;

(b) parties to the case before the court, their counsel or solicitors or persons otherwise directly concerned in the case;

(c) bona fide representatives of news gathering or reporting organisations present for the purpose of the preparation of contemporaneous reports of the proceedings; or

(d) such other persons as the court may specially authorise to be present,

shall be excluded from the court during the taking of the evidence of that witness.

(4) The powers conferred on a court by subsection (3) above shall be in addition and without prejudice to any other powers of the court to hear proceedingsin camera.

(5) Where in any proceedings relating to any of the offences mentioned in Schedule 1 to this Act, the court is satisfied that the attendance before the court of any person under the age of 17 years in respect of whom the offence is alleged to have been committed is not essential to the just hearing of the case, the case may be proceeded with and determined in the absence of that person.

(6) Every court in dealing with a child who is brought before it as an offender shall have regard to the welfare of the child and shall in a proper case take steps for removing him from undesirable surroundings.

Amendments (Textual)

F34. Words in s. 50. (1) inserted (27.9.1999) by 1999 c. 22, ss. 73. (2), 108. (3)(b) (with s. 107, Sch. 14 para. 7. (2))

51 Remand and committal of children and young persons.S

(1) Where a court remands or commits for trial or for sentence a person under 21 years of age who is charged with or convicted of an offence and is not released on bail or ordained to appear, then, except as otherwise expressly provided by this section, the following provisions shall have effect—

(a) F35. . . if he is under 16 years of age F36[F37. . . , the court shall] commit him to the local authority [F38which it considers appropriate] to be detained—

(i) where the court so requires, in secure accommodation [F39. (as defined in section 202. (1) of the Children's Hearings (Scotland) Act 2011 (asp 1))] ; and

(ii) in any other case, in a suitable place of safety chosen by the authority;

[F40. (aa)if the person [F41has attained the age of 16 years and is] subject to a [F42compulsory supervision order or interim compulsory supervision order] , the court may F43. . . commit him to the local authority which it considers appropriate to be detained as mentioned in sub-paragraphs (i) or (ii) of paragraph (a) above [F44or may commit him either to prison or to a young offenders institution] ;]

[F45. (b)if he is a person who has attained the age of 16 years and to whom paragraph (aa) above does not apply, then where—

(i) the court has been notified by the Scottish Ministers that a remand centre is available for the reception from that court of persons of his class or description, it shall commit him to a remand centre; or

(ii) the court has not been so notified, it may commit him either to prison or to a young offenders institution;

(bb) F46. . . . .]

(2) Where any person is committed to a local authority F47. . . under any provision of this Act, that authority F48. . . shall be specified in the warrant, and he shall be detained by the authority F49. . . for the period for which he is committed or until he is liberated in due course of law.

[F50. (2. A)F51. . . Where any person is committed to a remand centre under any provision of this Act, he shall be detained in a remand centre for the period for which he is committed or until he is liberated in due course of law.]

(3) F52. . . . .

(4) F52. . . . .

[F53. (4. A)The local authority which may be appropriate in relation to a power to commit a person under paragraphs (a) or (aa) of subsection (1) F54. . . may, without prejudice to the generality of those powers, be—

(a) the local authority for the area in which the court is situated;

(b) if the person is usually resident in Scotland, the local authority for the area in which he is usually resident;

(c) if the person is subject to a [F55compulsory supervision order or interim compulsory supervision order, the implementation authority (as defined in section 202. (1) of the Children's Hearings (Scotland) Act 2011 (asp 1).]

[F56. (5)Where by virtue of subsection [F57. (1)(aa) or (b)(ii)] of this section a person is committed either to prison or to a young offenders institution, the warrant issued by the court is warrant also, without further application to the court in that regard, for committal to whichever of the two the court does not specify.]]

Amendments (Textual)

F35. Words in s. 51. (1)(a) repealed (27.6.2003) by Criminal Justice (Scotland) Act 2003 (asp 7), ss. 23. (3)(a)(i), 89; S.S.I. 2003/288, art. 2, Sch.

F36. Words in s. 51. (1)(a) repealed (13.12.2010) by Criminal Justice and Licensing (Scotland) Act 2010 (asp 13), ss. 64. (2)(a)(i), 206. (1); S.S.I. 2010/413, art. 2, Sch.

F37. Words in s. 51. (1)(a) substituted (27.6.2003) by Criminal Justice (Scotland) Act 2003 (asp 7), ss.{23. (3)(a)(ii)}, 89; S.S.I. 2003/288, art. 2, Sch.

F38. Words in s. 51. (1)(a) substituted (1.8.1997) by 1997 c. 48, s. 56. (2)(a); S.I. 1997/1712, art. 3, Sch. (subject to arts. 4, 5)

F39. Words in s. 51. (1)(a)(i) substituted (24.6.2013) by The Childrens Hearings (Scotland) Act 2011 (Modification of Primary Legislation) Order 2013 (S.S.I. 2013/211), art. 1, sch. 1 para. 10. (6)(a)

F40. S. 51. (1)(aa) inserted (1.8.1997) by 1997 c. 48, s. 56. (2)(b); S.I. 1997/1712, art. 3, Sch. (subject to arts. 4, 5)

F41. Words in s. 51. (1)(aa) substituted (27.6.2003) by Criminal Justice (Scotland) Act 2003 (asp 7), ss.{23. (3)(b)(i)}, 89; S.S.I. 2003/288, art. 2, Sch.

F42. Words in s. 51. (1)(aa) substituted (24.6.2013) by The Childrens Hearings (Scotland) Act 2011 (Modification of Primary Legislation) Order 2013 (S.S.I. 2013/211), art. 1, sch. 1 para. 10. (6)(b)

F43. Words in s. 51. (1)(aa) repealed (27.6.2003) by Criminal Justice (Scotland) Act 2003 (asp 7), ss.{23. (3)(b)(ii)}, 89; S.S.I. 2003/288, art. 2, Sch.

F44. Words in s. 51. (1)(aa) added (27.6.2003) by Criminal Justice (Scotland) Act 2003 (asp 7), ss.{23. (3)(b)(iii)}, 89; S.S.I. 2003/288, art. 2, Sch.

F45. S. 51. (1)(b)(bb) substituted for (b) (27.6.2003) by Criminal Justice (Scotland) Act 2003 (asp 7), ss.{23. (3)(c)}, 89; S.S.I. 2003/288, art. 2, Sch.

F46. S. 51. (1)(bb) repealed (13.12.2010) by Criminal Justice and Licensing (Scotland) Act 2010 (asp 13), ss. 64. (2)(a)(ii), 206. (1); S.S.I. 2010/413, art. 2, Sch.

F47. Words in s. 51. (2) repealed (27.6.2003) by Criminal Justice (Scotland) Act 2003 (asp 7), ss.{23. (4)}, 89; S.S.I. 2003/288, art. 2, Sch.

F48. Words in s. 51. (2) repealed (27.6.2003) by Criminal Justice (Scotland) Act 2003 (asp 7), ss.{23. (4)}, 89; S.S.I. 2003/288, art. 2, Sch.

F49. Words in s. 51. (2) repealed (27.6.2003) by Criminal Justice (Scotland) Act 2003 (asp 7), ss.{23. (4)}, 89; S.S.I. 2003/288, art. 2, Sch.

F50. S. 51. (2. A) inserted (27.6.2003) by Criminal Justice (Scotland) Act 2003 (asp 7), ss.{23. (5)}, 89; S.S.I. 2003/288, art. 2, Sch.

F51. Words in s. 51. (2. A) repealed (13.12.2010) by Criminal Justice and Licensing (Scotland) Act 2010 (asp 13), ss. 64. (2)(b), 206. (1); S.S.I. 2010/413, art. 2, Sch.

F52. S. 51. (3)(4) repealed (13.12.2010) by Criminal Justice and Licensing (Scotland) Act 2010 (asp 13), ss. 64. (2)(c), 206. (1); S.S.I. 2010/413, art. 2, Sch.

F53. S. 51. (4. A) inserted (1.8.1997) by 1997 c. 48, s. 56. (4); S.I. 1997/1712, art. 3, Sch. (subject to arts. 4, 5)

F54. Words in s. 51. (4. A) repealed (13.12.2010) by Criminal Justice and Licensing (Scotland) Act 2010 (asp 13), ss. 64. (2)(d), 206. (1); S.S.I. 2010/413, art. 2, Sch.

F55. Words in s. 51. (4. A)(c) substituted (24.6.2013) by The Childrens Hearings (Scotland) Act

2011 (Modification of Primary Legislation) Order 2013 (S.S.I. 2013/211), art. 1, sch. 1 para. 10. (6)(c)

F56. S. 51. (5) added (27.6.2003) by Criminal Justice (Scotland) Act 2003 (asp 7), ss.{23. (8)}, 89; S.S.I. 2003/288, art. 2, Sch.

F57. Words in s. 51. (5) substituted (13.12.2010) by Criminal Justice and Licensing (Scotland) Act 2010 (asp 13), ss. 64. (3), 206. (1); S.S.I. 2010/413, art. 2, Sch.

Modifications etc. (not altering text)

C4. S. 51 applied (1.12.2014) by The Mutual Recognition of Supervision Measures in the European Union (Scotland) Regulations 2014 (S.S.I. 2014/337), reg. 1, sch. 2 para. 18. (1)

C5. S. 51. (1)(a)(ii) modified (1.4.1997) by S.I. 1996/3255, reg. 14. (1)(a)

S. 51. (4)(b) modified (1.4.1997) by S.I. 1996/3255, reg. 14. (1)(a)

PART VI Mental Disorder

PART VIS Mental Disorder

Amendments (Textual)

F1. Ss. 51. A, 51. B and cross-headings inserted (with application in accordance with art. 3 of the commencing S.S.I.) by Criminal Justice and Licensing (Scotland) Act 2010 (asp 13), ss. 168, 206. (1); S.S.I. 2012/160, art. 3, sch. (with art. 4)

51. ACriminal responsibility of persons with mental disorderS

(1) A person is not criminally responsible for conduct constituting an offence, and is to be acquitted of the offence, if the person was at the time of the conduct unable by reason of mental disorder to appreciate the nature or wrongfulness of the conduct.

(2) But a person does not lack criminal responsibility for such conduct if the mental disorder in question consists only of a personality disorder which is characterised solely or principally by abnormally aggressive or seriously irresponsible conduct.

(3) The defence set out in subsection (1) is a special defence.

(4) The special defence may be stated only by the person charged with the offence and it is for that person to establish it on the balance of probabilities.

(5) In this section, "conduct" includes acts and omissions.

Modifications etc. (not altering text)

C1. S. 51. A modified (27.11.2015 for specified purposes, 1.4.2016 in so far as not already in force) by Human Trafficking and Exploitation (Criminal Justice and Support for Victims) Act (Northern Ireland) 2015 (c. 2), s. 28. (3), Sch. 3 para. 23. (6); S.R. 2015/376, art. 2; S.R. 2016/61, art. 2

Diminished responsibilityS

51. BDiminished responsibilityS

(1) A person who would otherwise be convicted of murder is instead to be convicted of culpable homicide on grounds of diminished responsibility if the person's ability to determine or control conduct for which the person would otherwise be convicted of murder was, at the time of the conduct, substantially impaired by reason of abnormality of mind.

(2) For the avoidance of doubt, the reference in subsection (1) to abnormality of mind includes

mental disorder.

(3) The fact that a person was under the influence of alcohol, drugs or any other substance at the time of the conduct in question does not of itself—

(a) constitute abnormality of mind for the purposes of subsection (1), or

(b) prevent such abnormality from being established for those purposes.

(4) It is for the person charged with murder to establish, on the balance of probabilities, that the condition set out in subsection (1) is satisfied.

(5) In this section, "conduct" includes acts and omissions.]

Committal of mentally disordered personsS

52 Power of court to commit to hospital an accused suffering from mental disorder.S

(1) Where it appears to the prosecutor in any court before which a person is charged with an offence that the person may be suffering from mental disorder, it shall be the duty of the prosecutor to bring before the court such evidence as may be available of the mental condition of that person.

(2) F2. . . . .

(3) F3. . . . .

(4) F4. . . . .

(5) F5. . . . .

(6) F6. . . . .

(7) F7. . . . .

Amendments (Textual)

F2. S. 52. (2)-(7) repealed (5.10.2005) by Mental Health (Care and Treatment) (Scotland) Act 2003 (asp 13), ss. 331. (2)(3), 333. (1)-(4), Sch. 5 Pt. 1; S.S.I. 2005/161, art. 3 (with savings for s. 52. (2)-(7) by virtue of S.S.I. 2005/452, art. 33. (12))

F3. S. 52. (2)-(7) repealed (5.10.2005) by Mental Health (Care and Treatment) (Scotland) Act 2003 (asp 13), ss. 331. (2)(3), 333. (1)-(4), Sch. 5 Pt. 1; S.S.I. 2005/161, art. 3 (with savings for s. 52. (2)-(7) by virtue of S.S.I. 2005/452, art. 33. (12))

F4. S. 52. (2)-(7) repealed (5.10.2005) by Mental Health (Care and Treatment) (Scotland) Act 2003 (asp 13), ss. 331. (2)(3), 333. (1)-(4), Sch. 5 Pt. 1; S.S.I. 2005/161, art. 3 (with savings for s. 52. (2)-(7) by virtue of S.S.I. 2005/452, art. 33. (12))

F5. S. 52. (2)-(7) repealed (5.10.2005) by Mental Health (Care and Treatment) (Scotland) Act 2003 (asp 13), ss. 331. (2)(3), 333. (1)-(4), Sch. 5 Pt. 1; S.S.I. 2005/161, art. 3 (with savings for s. 52. (2)-(7) by virtue of S.S.I. 2005/452, art. 33. (12))

F6. S. 52. (2)-(7) repealed (5.10.2005) by Mental Health (Care and Treatment) (Scotland) Act 2003 (asp 13), ss. 331. (2)(3), 333. (1)-(4), Sch. 5 Pt. 1; S.S.I. 2005/161, art. 3 (with savings for s. 52. (2)-(7) by virtue of S.S.I. 2005/452, art. 33. (12))

F7. S. 52. (2)-(7) repealed (5.10.2005) by Mental Health (Care and Treatment) (Scotland) Act 2003 (asp 13), ss. 331. (2)(3), 333. (1)-(4), Sch. 5 Pt. 1; S.S.I. 2005/161, art. 3 (with savings for s. 52. (2)-(7) by virtue of S.S.I. 2005/452, art. 33. (12))

[F8. Remit of mentally disordered persons from district courtS

Amendments (Textual)

F8. Ss. 52. A-52. U inserted (5.10.2005) by Mental Health (Care and Treatment) (Scotland) Act 2003 (asp 13), ss. {130}, 333. (1)-(4); S.S.I. 2005/161, art. 3 (as amended (27.9.2005) by S.S.I. 2005/465, art. 2, Sch. 1 para. 32. (13)(a)(i)(ii) and {Sch. 2})

52. ARemit of certain mentally disordered persons from district court to sheriff courtS

Where—

(a) a person has been charged in a [F9. JP court] with an offence punishable by imprisonment; and

(b) it appears to the court that the person has a mental disorder,

the [F9. JP court] shall remit the person to the sheriff in the manner provided by section 7. (9) and (10) of this Act.

Amendments (Textual)

F9. Words in s. 52. A substituted (10.3.2008, 2.6.2008, 8.12.2008, 23.2.2009 and 14.12.2009 for certain purposes, otherwise 22.2.2010) by Criminal Proceedings etc. (Reform) (Scotland) Act 2007 (asp 6), ss. 80, 84, Sch. para. 26. (e); S.S.I. 2008/42, art. 3, Sch.; S.S.I. 2008/192, art. 3, Sch.; S.S.I. 2008/329, art. 3, Sch.; S.S.I. 2008/362, art. 3, Sch.; S.S.I. 2009/432, art. 3, Schs. 1, 2

Assessment ordersS

52. BProsecutor's power to apply for assessment orderS

(1) Where—

(a) a person has been charged with an offence;

(b) a relevant disposal has not been made in the proceedings in respect of the offence; and

(c) it appears to the prosecutor that the person has a mental disorder,

the prosecutor may apply to the court for an order under section 52. D(2) of this Act (in this Act referred to as an "assessment order") in respect of that person.

(2) Where the prosecutor applies for an assessment order under subsection (1) above, the prosecutor shall, as soon as reasonably practicable after making the application, inform the persons mentioned in subsection (3) below of the making of the application.

(3) Those persons are—

(a) the person in respect of whom the application is made;

(b) any solicitor acting for the person; and

(c) in a case where the person is [F10remanded] in custody, the Scottish Ministers.

(4) In this section—

"court" means any court, other than a [F11. JP court], competent to deal with the case; and "relevant disposal" means—

- the liberation in due course of law of the person charged;
- the desertion of summary proceedings pro loco et tempore or simpliciter;
- the desertion of solemn proceedings simpliciter;
- the acquittal of the person charged; or
- the conviction of the person charged.

Amendments (Textual)

F10. Word in s. 52. B(3)(c) inserted (30.6.2017) by Mental Health (Scotland) Act 2015 (asp 9), ss. 38. (2)(a), 61. (2); S.S.I. 2017/197, art. 2, sch.

F11. Words in s. 52. B(4) substituted (10.3.2008, 2.6.2008, 8.12.2008, 23.2.2009 and 14.12.2009 for certain purposes, otherwise 22.2.2010) by Criminal Proceedings etc. (Reform) (Scotland) Act 2007 (asp 6), ss. 80, 84, Sch. para. 26. (f); S.S.I. 2008/42, art. 3, Sch.; S.S.I. 2008/192, art. 3, Sch.; S.S.I. 2008/329, art. 3, Sch.; S.S.I. 2008/362, art. 3, Sch.; S.S.I. 2009/432, art. 3, Schs. 1, 2

52. CScottish Ministers' power to apply for assessment orderS

(1) Where—

    (a) a person has been charged with an offence;

    (b) the person has not been sentenced;

    (c) the person is [F12remanded] in custody; and

    (d) it appears to the Scottish Ministers that the person has a mental disorder,

the Scottish Ministers may apply to the court for an assessment order in respect of that person.

(2) Where the Scottish Ministers apply for an order under subsection (1) above, they shall, as soon as reasonably practicable after making the application, inform the persons mentioned in subsection (3) below of the making of the application.

(3) Those persons are—

    (a) the person in respect of whom the application is made;

    (b) any solicitor acting for the person; and

    (c) in a case where a relevant disposal has not been made in the proceedings in respect of the offence with which the person is charged, the prosecutor.

(4) In this section, "court" and "relevant disposal" have the same meanings as in section 52. B of this Act.

Amendments (Textual)

F12. Word in s. 52. C(1)(c) inserted (30.6.2017) by Mental Health (Scotland) Act 2015 (asp 9), ss. 38. (2)(b), 61. (2); S.S.I. 2017/197, art. 2, sch.

52. DAssessment orderS

(1) This section applies where an application for an assessment order is made under section 52. B(1) or 52. C(1) of this Act.

(2) If the court is satisfied—

    (a) on the written or oral evidence of a medical practitioner, as to the matters mentioned in subsection (3) below; and

    (b) that, having regard to the matters mentioned in subsection (4) below, it is appropriate,

it may, subject to subsection (5) below, make an assessment order authorising the measures mentioned in subsection (6) below and specifying any matters to be included in the report under section 52. G(1) of this Act.

(3) The matters referred to in subsection (2)(a) above are—

    (a) that there are reasonable grounds for believing—

(i) that the person in respect of whom the application is made has a mental disorder;

(ii) that it is necessary to detain the person in hospital to assess whether the conditions mentioned in subsection (7) below are met in respect of the person; and

(iii) that if the assessment order were not made there would be a significant risk to the health, safety or welfare of the person or a significant risk to the safety of any other person;

    (b) that the hospital proposed by the medical practitioner is suitable for the purpose of assessing whether the conditions mentioned in subsection (7) below are met in respect of the person;

    (c) that, if an assessment order were made, the person could be admitted to such hospital before the expiry of the period of 7 days beginning with the day on which the order is made; and

    (d) that it would not be reasonably practicable to carry out the assessment mentioned in paragraph (b) above unless an order were made.

(4) The matters referred to in subsection (2)(b) above are—

    (a) all the circumstances (including the nature of the offence with which the person in respect of whom the application is made is charged or, as the case may be, of which the person was convicted); and

    (b) any alternative means of dealing with the person.

(5) The court may make an assessment order only if the person in respect of whom the application is made has not been sentenced.

(6) The measures are—

(a) in the case of a person who, when the assessment order is made, has not been admitted to the specified hospital, the removal, before the [F13end of the day following the] 7 days beginning with the day on which the order is made, of the person to the specified hospital by—

(i) a constable;

(ii) a person employed in, or contracted to provide services in or to, the specified hospital who is authorised by the managers of that hospital to remove persons to hospital for the purposes of this section; or

(iii) a specified person;

(b) the detention, for the [F14relevant period given by subsection (6. A) below], of the person in the specified hospital; and

(c) during the [F14relevant period given by subsection (6. A) below], the giving to the person, in accordance with Part 16 of the Mental Health (Care and Treatment) (Scotland) Act 2003 (asp 13), of medical treatment.

[F15. (6. A)For the purpose of subsection (6)(b) and (c) above, the relevant period is the period—

(a) beginning with the day on which the order is made,

(b) expiring at the end of the 28 days following that day.]

(7) The conditions referred to in paragraphs (a)(ii) and (b) of subsection (3) above are—

(a) that the person in respect of whom the application is made has a mental disorder;

(b) that medical treatment which would be likely to—

(i) prevent the mental disorder worsening; or

(ii) alleviate any of the symptoms, or effects, of the disorder,

is available for the person; and

(c) that if the person were not provided with such medical treatment there would be a significant risk—

(i) to the health, safety or welfare of the person; or

(ii) to the safety of any other person.

(8) The court may make an assessment order in the absence of the person in respect of whom the application is made only if—

(a) the person is represented by counsel or a solicitor;

(b) that counsel or solicitor is given an opportunity of being heard; and

(c) the court is satisfied that it is—

(i) impracticable; or

(ii) inappropriate,

for the person to be brought before it.

(9) An assessment order may include such directions as the court thinks fit for the removal of the person subject to the order to, and detention of the person in, a place of safety pending the person's admission to the specified hospital.

(10) The court shall, as soon as reasonably practicable after making an assessment order, give notice of the making of the order to—

(a) the person subject to the order;

(b) any solicitor acting for the person;

(c) in a case where—

(i) the person has been charged with an offence; and

(ii) a relevant disposal has not been made in the proceedings in respect of the offence,

the prosecutor;

(d) in a case where the person, immediately before the order was made, was [F16remanded] in custody, the Scottish Ministers; and

(e) the Mental Welfare Commission.

(11) In this section—

"court" has the same meaning as in section 52. B of this Act;

"medical treatment" has the meaning given by section 329. (1) of the Mental Health (Care and Treatment) (Scotland) Act 2003 (asp 13);

"relevant disposal" has the same meaning as in section 52. B of this Act; and

"specified" means specified in the assessment order.

Amendments (Textual)

F13. Words in s. 52. D(6)(a) substituted (30.9.2017) by Mental Health (Scotland) Act 2015 (asp 9), ss. 40. (2)(a)(i), 61. (2); S.S.I. 2017/197, art. 2, sch.

F14. Words in s. 52. D(6)(b)(c) substituted (30.9.2017) by Mental Health (Scotland) Act 2015 (asp 9), ss. 40. (2)(a)(ii), 61. (2); S.S.I. 2017/197, art. 2, sch.

F15. S. 52. D(6. A) inserted (30.9.2017) by Mental Health (Scotland) Act 2015 (asp 9), ss. 40. (2)(b), 61. (2); S.S.I. 2017/197, art. 2, sch.

F16. Word in s. 52. D(10)(d) inserted (30.6.2017) by Mental Health (Scotland) Act 2015 (asp 9), ss. 38. (2)(c), 61. (2); S.S.I. 2017/197, art. 2, sch.

52. EAssessment order made ex proprio motu: application of section 52. DS

(1) Where—

    (a) a person has been charged with an offence;

    (b) the person has not been sentenced; and

    (c) it appears to the court that the person has a mental disorder,

the court may, subject to subsections (2) and (3) below, make an assessment order in respect of that person.

(2) The court may make an assessment order under subsection (1) above only if it would make one under subsections (2) to (11) of section 52. D of this Act; and those subsections shall apply for the purposes of subsection (1) above as they apply for the purposes of subsection (1) of that section, references in those subsections to the person in respect of whom the application is made being construed as references to the person in respect of whom it is proposed to make an assessment order.

(3) An assessment order made under subsection (1) above shall, for the purposes of this Act and the Mental Health (Care and Treatment) (Scotland) Act 2003 (asp 13), be treated as if made under section 52. D(2) of this Act.

(4) In this section, "court" has the same meaning as in section 52. B of this Act.

52. FAssessment order: supplementaryS

(1) If, before the [F17end of the day following the] 7 days beginning with the day on which an assessment order is made—

    (a) in the case of a person who, immediately before the order was made, was [F18remanded] in custody, it appears to the Scottish Ministers; or

    (b) in any other case, it appears to the court,

that, by reason of emergency or other special circumstances, it is not reasonably practicable for the person to be admitted to the hospital specified in the order, the Scottish Ministers, or, as the case may be, the court, may direct that the person be admitted to the hospital specified in the direction.

(2) Where the court makes a direction under subsection (1) above, it shall, as soon as reasonably practicable after making the direction, inform the person having custody of the person subject to the assessment order of the making of the direction.

(3) Where the Scottish Ministers make a direction under subsection (1) above, they shall, as soon as reasonably practicable after making the direction, inform—

    (a) the court;

    (b) the person having custody of the person subject to the assessment order; and

    (c) in a case where—

(i) the person has been charged with an offence; and

(ii) a relevant disposal has not been made in the proceedings in respect of the offence,
the prosecutor,
of the making of the direction.

(4) Where a direction is made under subsection (1) above, the assessment order shall have effect as if the hospital specified in the direction were the hospital specified in the order.

(5) In this section—

"court" means the court which made the assessment order; and

"relevant disposal" has the same meaning as in section 52. B of this Act.

Amendments (Textual)

F17. Words in s. 52. F(1) substituted (30.9.2017) by Mental Health (Scotland) Act 2015 (asp 9), ss. 40. (3), 61. (2); S.S.I. 2017/197, art. 2, sch. (with art. 19. (a))

F18. Word in s. 52. F(1)(a) inserted (30.6.2017) by Mental Health (Scotland) Act 2015 (asp 9), ss. 38. (2)(d), 61. (2); S.S.I. 2017/197, art. 2, sch.

52. GReview of assessment orderS

(1) The responsible medical officer shall, before the [F19end of the day following the] 28 days beginning with the day on which the assessment order is made, submit a report in writing to the court—

(a) as to whether the conditions mentioned in section 52. D(7) of this Act are met in respect of the person subject to the order; and

(b) as to any matters specified by the court under section 52. D(2) of this Act.

(2) The responsible medical officer shall, at the same time as such officer submits the report to the court, send a copy of such report—

(a) to the person in respect of whom the report is made;

(b) to any solicitor acting for the person;

(c) in a case where—

(i) the person has been charged with an offence; and

(ii) a relevant disposal has not been made in the proceedings in respect of the offence,
to the prosecutor; and

(d) to the Scottish Ministers.

(3) Subject to subsection (4) below, the court shall, on receiving a report submitted under subsection (1) above, revoke the assessment order and—

(a) subject to subsections (7) and (8) below, make a treatment order; or

(b) commit the person to prison or such other institution to which the person might have been committed had the assessment order not been made or otherwise deal with the person as the court considers appropriate.

(4) If, on receiving a report submitted under subsection (1) above, the court is satisfied that further time is necessary to assess whether the conditions mentioned in section 52. D(7) of this Act are met in respect of the person subject to the assessment order, it may, on one occasion only, make an order extending the assessment order for a period not exceeding [F20the relevant period given by subsection (4. A) below].

[F21. (4. A)For the purpose of subsection (4) above, the relevant period is the period—

(a) beginning with the day on which the order would otherwise cease to authorise the detention of the person in hospital,

(b) expiring at the end of the 14 days following that day.]

(5) The court may, under subsection (4) above, extend an assessment order in the absence of the person subject to the order only if—

(a) the person is represented by counsel or a solicitor;

(b) that counsel or solicitor is given an opportunity of being heard; and

(c) the court is satisfied that it is—

(i) impracticable; or

(ii) inappropriate,

for the person to be brought before it.

(6) Where the court makes an order under subsection (4) above, it shall, as soon as reasonably practicable after making the order, give notice of the making of the order to—

(a) the persons mentioned in paragraphs (a) and (b) of subsection (2) above;

(b) in a case where—

(i) the person has been charged with an offence; and

(ii) a relevant disposal has not been made in the proceedings in respect of the offence,

the prosecutor;

(c) the Scottish Ministers; and

(d) the person's responsible medical officer.

(7) The court shall make a treatment order under subsection (3)(a) above only if it would make one under subsections (2) to (10) of section 52. M of this Act; and those subsections shall apply for the purposes of subsection (3)(a) above as they apply for the purposes of that section, references in those subsections to the person in respect of whom the application is made being construed as references to the person in respect of whom it is proposed to make a treatment order.

(8) A treatment order made under subsection (3)(a) above shall, for the purposes of this Act and the Mental Health (Care and Treatment) (Scotland) Act 2003 (asp 13), be treated as if made under section 52. M(2) of this Act.

(9) The responsible medical officer shall, where that officer is satisfied that there has been a change of circumstances since the assessment order was made which justifies the variation of the order, submit a report to the court in writing.

(10) Where a report is submitted under subsection (9) above, the court shall—

(a) if satisfied that the person need not be subject to an assessment order, revoke the order and take any action mentioned in subsection (3)(b) above; or

(b) if not so satisfied—

(i) confirm the order;

(ii) vary the order; or

(iii) revoke the order and take any action mentioned in subsection (3)(b) above.

(11) Sections 52. D, 52. F, 52. H and 52. J of this Act and subsections (1) to (3) above apply to the variation of an order under subsection (10)(b)(ii) above as they apply to an assessment order.

(12) In this section—

"court" means the court which made the assessment order;

"relevant disposal" has the same meaning as in section 52. B of this Act; and

"responsible medical officer" means the person's responsible medical officer appointed under section 230 of the Mental Health (Care and Treatment) (Scotland) Act 2003 (asp 13).

Amendments (Textual)

F19. Words in s. 52. G(1) substituted (30.9.2017) by Mental Health (Scotland) Act 2015 (asp 9), ss. 40. (4)(a), 61. (2); S.S.I. 2017/197, art. 2, sch. (with art. 19. (b))

F20. Words in s. 52. G(4) substituted (30.9.2017) by Mental Health (Scotland) Act 2015 (asp 9), ss. 40. (4)(b), 61. (2); S.S.I. 2017/197, art. 2, sch.

F21. S. 52. G(4. A) inserted (30.9.2017) by Mental Health (Scotland) Act 2015 (asp 9), ss. 40. (4)(c), 61. (2); S.S.I. 2017/197, art. 2, sch.

52. HEarly termination of assessment orderS

(1) This section applies where—

(a) in the case of a person who, when the assessment order is made, has not been removed to the hospital specified in the order, the [F22relevant period given by subsection (1. A) below] has not expired;

(b) in the case of a person—

(i) who, when the assessment order is made, has been admitted to the hospital specified in the order; or

(ii) who has been removed under paragraph (a) of subsection (6) of section 52. D of this Act to the hospital so specified,

the [F23relevant period given by subsection (1. A) below] has not expired; or

(c) in the case of a person in respect of whom the court has made an order under section 52. G(4) of this Act extending the assessment order for a period, the period for which the order was extended has not expired.

[F24. (1. A)For the purpose of subsection (1)(a) and (b) above, the relevant period is the period—

(a) beginning with the day on which the order is made,

(b) expiring—

(i) as regards subsection (1)(a) above, at the end of the 7 days following the day mentioned in paragraph (a) of this subsection,

(ii) as regards subsection (1)(b) above, at the end of the 28 days following the day mentioned in paragraph (a) of this subsection.]

(2) An assessment order shall cease to have effect on the occurrence of any of the following events—

(a) the making of a treatment order in respect of the person subject to the assessment order;

(b) in a case where—

(i) the person subject to the assessment order has been charged with an offence; and

(ii) a relevant disposal had not been made in the proceedings in respect of that offence when the order was made,

the making of a relevant disposal in such proceedings;

(c) in a case where the person subject to the assessment order has been convicted of an offence but has not been sentenced—

(i) the deferral of sentence by the court under section 202. (1) of this Act;

(ii) the making of one of the orders mentioned in subsection (3) below or

(iii) the imposition of any sentence.

(3) The orders are—

(a) an interim compulsion order;

(b) a compulsion order;

(c) a guardianship order;

(d) a hospital direction;

(e) any order under section 57 of this Act; F25. . .

(f) F26. . . . .

(4) In this section, "relevant disposal" has the same meaning as in section 52. B of this Act.

Amendments (Textual)

F22. Words in s. 52. H(1)(a) substituted (30.9.2017) by Mental Health (Scotland) Act 2015 (asp 9), ss. 40. (5)(a)(i), 61. (2); S.S.I. 2017/197, art. 2, sch. (with art. 19. (c))

F23. Words in s. 52. H(1)(b) substituted (30.9.2017) by Mental Health (Scotland) Act 2015 (asp 9), ss. 40. (5)(a)(ii), 61. (2); S.S.I. 2017/197, art. 2, sch. (with art. 19. (c))

F24. S. 52. H(1. A) inserted (30.9.2017) by Mental Health (Scotland) Act 2015 (asp 9), ss. 40. (5)(b), 61. (2); S.S.I. 2017/197, art. 2, sch. (with art. 19. (c))

F25. Word in s. 52. H(3) repealed (1.2.2011) by Criminal Justice and Licensing (Scotland) Act 2010 (asp 13), ss. 14. (2), 206. (1), Sch. 2 para. 2. (a); S.S.I. 2010/413, art. 2, Sch. (with art. 3)

F26. S. 52. H(3)(f) repealed (1.2.2011) by Criminal Justice and Licensing (Scotland) Act 2010 (asp 13), ss. 14. (2), 206. (1), Sch. 2 para. 2. (b); S.S.I. 2010/413, art. 2, Sch. (with art. 3)

52. JPower of court on assessment order ceasing to have effectS

(1) Where, otherwise than by virtue of section 52. G(3) or (10) or 52. H(2) of this Act, an assessment order ceases to have effect the court shall commit the person who was subject to the order to prison or such other institution to which the person might have been committed had the

order not been made or otherwise deal with the person as the court considers appropriate.

(2) In this section, "court" has the same meaning as in section 52. B of this Act.

Treatment ordersS

52. KProsecutor's power to apply for treatment orderS

(1) Where—

    (a) a person has been charged with an offence;

    (b) a relevant disposal has not been made in the proceedings in respect of the offence; and

    (c) it appears to the prosecutor that the person has a mental disorder,

the prosecutor may apply to the court for an order under section 52. M of this Act (in this Act referred to as a "treatment order") in respect of that person.

(2) Where the prosecutor applies for a treatment order under subsection (1) above, the prosecutor shall, as soon as reasonably practicable after making the application, inform the persons mentioned in subsection (3) below of the making of the application.

(3) Those persons are—

    (a) the person in respect of whom the application is made;

    (b) any solicitor acting for the person; and

    (c) in a case where the person is [F27remanded] in custody, the Scottish Ministers.

(4) In this section, "court" and "relevant disposal" have the same meanings as in section 52. B of this Act.

Amendments (Textual)

F27. Word in s. 52. K(3)(c) inserted (30.6.2017) by Mental Health (Scotland) Act 2015 (asp 9), ss. 38. (2)(e), 61. (2); S.S.I. 2017/197, art. 2, sch.

52. LScottish Ministers' power to apply for treatment orderS

(1) Where—

    (a) a person has been charged with an offence;

    (b) the person has not been sentenced;

    (c) the person is [F28remanded] in custody; and

    (d) it appears to the Scottish Ministers that the person has a mental disorder,

the Scottish Ministers may apply to the court for a treatment order in respect of that person.

(2) Where the Scottish Ministers apply for an order under subsection (1) above, they shall, as soon as reasonably practicable after making the application, inform the persons mentioned in subsection (3) below of the making of the application.

(3) Those persons are—

    (a) the person in respect of whom the application is made;

    (b) any solicitor acting for the person; and

    (c) in a case where a relevant disposal has not been made in the proceedings in respect of the offence with which the person is charged, the prosecutor.

(4) In this section, "court" and "relevant disposal" have the same meanings as in section 52. B of this Act.

Amendments (Textual)

F28. Word in s. 52. L(1)(c) inserted (30.6.2017) by Mental Health (Scotland) Act 2015 (asp 9), ss. 38. (2)(f), 61. (2); S.S.I. 2017/197, art. 2, sch.

52. MTreatment orderS

(1) This section applies where an application for a treatment order is made under section 52. K(1) or 52. L(1) of this Act.

(2) If the court is satisfied—

(a) on the written or oral evidence of two medical practitioners, as to the matters mentioned in subsection (3) below; and

(b) that, having regard to the matters mentioned in subsection (4) below, it is appropriate, it may, subject to subsection (5) below, make a treatment order authorising the measures mentioned in subsection (6) below.

(3) The matters referred to in subsection (2)(a) above are—

(a) that the conditions mentioned in subsection (7) of section 52. D of this Act are met in relation to the person in respect of whom the application is made;

(b) that the hospital proposed by the approved medical practitioner and the medical practitioner is suitable for the purpose of giving medical treatment to the person; and

(c) that, if a treatment order were made, such person could be admitted to such hospital before the [F29end of the day following the] 7 days beginning with the day on which the order is made.

(4) The matters referred to in subsection (2)(b) above are—

(a) all the circumstances (including the nature of the offence with which the person in respect of whom the application is made is charged or, as the case may be, of which the person was convicted); and

(b) any alternative means of dealing with the person.

(5) The court may make a treatment order only if the person in respect of whom the application is made has not been sentenced.

(6) The measures are—

(a) in the case of a person who, when the treatment order is made, has not been admitted to the specified hospital, the removal, before the [F30end of the day following the] 7 days beginning with the day on which the order is made, of the person to the specified hospital by—

(i) a constable;

(ii) a person employed in, or contracted to provide services in or to, the specified hospital who is authorised by the managers of that hospital to remove persons to hospital for the purposes of this section; or

(iii) a specified person;

(b) the detention of the person in the specified hospital; and

(c) the giving to the person, in accordance with Part 16 of the Mental Health (Care and Treatment) (Scotland) Act 2003 (asp 13), of medical treatment.

(7) The court may make a treatment order in the absence of the person in respect of whom the application is made only if—

(a) the person is represented by counsel or solicitor;

(b) that counsel or solicitor is given an opportunity of being heard; and

(c) the court is satisfied that it is—

(i) impracticable; or

(ii) inappropriate,

for the person to be brought before it.

(8) A treatment order may include such directions as the court thinks fit for the removal of the person subject to the order to, and detention of the person in, a place of safety pending the person's admission to the specified hospital.

(9) The court shall, as soon as reasonably practicable after making a treatment order, give notice of the making of the order to—

(a) the person subject to the order;

(b) any solicitor acting for the person;

(c) in a case where—

(i) the person has been charged with an offence; and

(ii) a relevant disposal has not been made in the proceedings in respect of the offence, the prosecutor;

(d) in a case where the person, immediately before the order was made—

(i) was [F31remanded] in custody ; or

(ii) was subject to an assessment order and, immediately before that order was made, was [F31remanded] in custody,

the Scottish Ministers; and

(e) the Mental Welfare Commission.

(10) In this section—

"court" has the same meaning as in section 52. B of this Act;

"medical treatment" has the same meaning as in section 52. D of this Act; and

"specified" means specified in the treatment order.

Amendments (Textual)

F29. Words in s. 52. M(3)(c) substituted (30.9.2017) by Mental Health (Scotland) Act 2015 (asp 9), ss. 41. (2)(a), 61. (2); S.S.I. 2017/197, art. 2, sch.

F30. Words in s. 52. M(6)(a) substituted (30.9.2017) by Mental Health (Scotland) Act 2015 (asp 9), ss. 41. (2)(b), 61. (2); S.S.I. 2017/197, art. 2, sch.

F31. Word in s. 52. M(9)(d)(i)(ii) inserted (30.6.2017) by Mental Health (Scotland) Act 2015 (asp 9), ss. 38. (2)(g), 61. (2); S.S.I. 2017/197, art. 2, sch.

52. NTreatment order made ex proprio motu: application of section 52. MS

(1) Where—

(a) a person has been charged with an offence;

(b) the person has not been sentenced; and

(c) it appears to the court that the person has a mental disorder,

the court may, subject to subsections (2) and (3) below, make a treatment order in respect of that person.

(2) The court may make a treatment order under subsection (1) above only if it would make one under subsections (2) to (10) of section 52. M of this Act; and those subsections shall apply for the purposes of subsection (1) above as they apply for the purposes of subsection (1) of that section, references in those subsections to the person in respect of whom the application is made being construed as references to the person in respect of whom it is proposed to make a treatment order.

(3) A treatment order made under subsection (1) above shall, for the purposes of this Act and the Mental Health (Care and Treatment) (Scotland) Act 2003 (asp 13), be treated as if made under section 52. M(2) of this Act.

(4) In this section, "court" has the same meaning as in section 52. B of this Act.

52. PTreatment order: supplementaryS

(1) If, before the [F32end of the day following the] 7 days beginning with the day on which the treatment order is made—

(a) in the case of a person to whom subsection (2) below applies, it appears to the Scottish Ministers; or

(b) in any other case, it appears to the court,

that, by reason of emergency or other special circumstances, it is not reasonably practicable for the person to be admitted to the hospital specified in the order, the Scottish Ministers, or, as the case may be, the court, may direct that the person be admitted to the hospital specified in the direction.

(2) This subsection applies to—

(a) a person who is [F33remanded] in custody immediately before the treatment order is made; or

(b) a person—

(i) who was subject to an assessment order immediately before the treatment order is made; and

(ii) who was [F34remanded] in custody immediately before that assessment order was made.

(3) Where the court makes a direction under subsection (1) above, it shall, as soon as reasonably practicable after making the direction, inform the person having custody of the person subject to the treatment order of the making of the direction.

(4) Where the Scottish Ministers make a direction under subsection (1) above, they shall, as soon as reasonably practicable after making the direction, inform—

    (a) the court;

    (b) the person having custody of the person subject to the treatment order; and

    (c) in a case where—

(i) the person has been charged with an offence; and

(ii) a relevant disposal has not been made in the proceedings in respect of the offence,

the prosecutor,

of the making of the direction.

(5) Where a direction is made under subsection (1) above, the treatment order shall have effect as if the hospital specified in the direction were the hospital specified in the order.

(6) In this section—

"court" means the court which made the treatment order; and

"relevant disposal" has the same meaning as in section 52. B of this Act.

Amendments (Textual)

F32. Words in s. 52. P(1) substituted (30.9.2017) by Mental Health (Scotland) Act 2015 (asp 9), ss. 41. (3), 61. (2); S.S.I. 2017/197, art. 2, sch. (with art. 20. (a))

F33. Word in s. 52. P(2)(a) inserted (30.6.2017) by Mental Health (Scotland) Act 2015 (asp 9), ss. 38. (2)(h), 61. (2); S.S.I. 2017/197, art. 2, sch.

F34. Word in s. 52. P(2)(b)(ii) inserted (30.6.2017) by Mental Health (Scotland) Act 2015 (asp 9), ss. 38. (2)(h), 61. (2); S.S.I. 2017/197, art. 2, sch.

52. QReview of treatment orderS

(1) The responsible medical officer shall, where that officer is satisfied—

    (a) that any of the conditions mentioned in section 52. D(7) of this Act are no longer met in respect of the person subject to the treatment order; or

    (b) that there has otherwise been a change of circumstances since the order was made which makes the continued detention of the person in hospital by virtue of the order no longer appropriate,

submit a report in writing to the court.

(2) Where a report is submitted under subsection (1) above, the court shall—

    (a) if satisfied that the person need not be subject to the treatment order—

(i) revoke the order; and

(ii) commit the person to prison or such other institution to which the person might have been committed had the order not been made or otherwise deal with the person as the court considers appropriate; or

    (b) if not so satisfied—

(i) confirm the order;

(ii) vary the order; or

(iii) revoke the order and take any action mentioned in paragraph (a)(ii) above.

(3) Sections 52. M, 52. P, this section and sections 52. R and 52. S of this Act apply to the variation of a treatment order under subsection (2)(b)(ii) above as they apply to a treatment order.

(4) In this section—

"court" means the court which made the treatment order; and

"responsible medical officer" means the person's responsible medical officer appointed under section 230 of the Mental Health (Care and Treatment) (Scotland) Act 2003 (asp 13).

52. RTermination of treatment orderS

(1) This section applies—

(a) where, in the case of a person who, when the treatment order is made, has not been removed to the hospital specified in the order, the [F35relevant period given by subsection (1. A) below] has not expired; or

(b) in the case of a person—

(i) who, when the treatment order is made, has been admitted to the hospital specified in the order; or

(ii) who has been removed under paragraph (a) of subsection (6) of section 52. M of this Act to the hospital so specified.

[F36. (1. A)For the purpose of subsection (1)(a) above, the relevant period is the period—

(a) beginning with the day on which the order is made,

(b) expiring at the end of the 7 days following that day.]

(2) A treatment order shall cease to have effect on the occurrence of any of the following events—

(a) in a case where—

(i) the person subject to the treatment order has been charged with an offence; and

(ii) a relevant disposal had not been made in the proceedings in respect of such offence when the order was made,

the making of a relevant disposal in such proceedings;

(b) in a case where the person subject to the treatment order has been convicted of an offence but has not been sentenced—

(i) the deferral of sentence by the court under section 202. (1) of this Act;

(ii) the making of one of the orders mentioned in subsection (3) below; or

(iii) the imposition of any sentence.

(3) The orders are—

(a) an interim compulsion order;

(b) a compulsion order;

(c) a guardianship order;

(d) a hospital direction;

(e) any order under section 57 of this Act; F37. . .

(f) F38. . . . .

(4) In this section, "relevant disposal" has the same meaning as in section 52. B of this Act.

Amendments (Textual)

F35. Words in s. 52. R(1)(a) substituted (30.9.2017) by Mental Health (Scotland) Act 2015 (asp 9), ss. 41. (4)(a), 61. (2); S.S.I. 2017/197, art. 2, sch. (with art. 20. (b))

F36. S. 52. R(1. A) inserted (30.9.2017) by Mental Health (Scotland) Act 2015 (asp 9), ss. 41. (4)(b), 61. (2); S.S.I. 2017/197, art. 2, sch. (with art. 20. (b))

F37. Word in s. 52. R(3) repealed (1.2.2011) by Criminal Justice and Licensing (Scotland) Act 2010 (asp 13), ss. 14. (2), 206. (1), Sch. 2 para. 3. (a); S.S.I. 2010/413, art. 2, Sch. (with art. 3)

F38. S. 52. R(3)(f) repealed (1.2.2011) by Criminal Justice and Licensing (Scotland) Act 2010 (asp 13), ss. 14. (2), 206. (1), Sch. 2 para. 3. (b); S.S.I. 2010/413, art. 2, Sch. (with art. 3)

52. SPower of court on treatment order ceasing to have effectS

(1) Where, otherwise than by virtue of section 52. Q(2) or 52. R(2) of this Act, a treatment order ceases to have effect the court shall commit the person who was subject to the order to prison or such other institution to which the person might have been committed had the order not been made or otherwise deal with the person as the court considers appropriate.

(2) In this section, "court" has the same meaning as in section 52. B of this Act.

Prevention of delay in trialsS

52. TPrevention of delay in trials: assessment orders and treatment ordersS

(1) Subsections (4) to (9) of section 65 of this Act shall apply in the case of a person committed for an offence until liberated in due course of law who is detained in hospital by virtue of an assessment order or a treatment order as those subsections apply in the case of an accused who is—

   (a) committed for an offence until liberated in due course of law; and

   (b) detained by virtue of that committal.

(2) Section 147 of this Act shall apply in the case of a person charged with an offence in summary proceedings who is detained in hospital by virtue of an assessment order or a treatment order as it applies in the case of an accused who is detained in respect of that offence.

(3) Any period during which, under—

   (a) section 221 (as read with sections 222 and 223) of the Mental Health (Care and Treatment) (Scotland) Act 2003 (asp 13); or

   (b) section 224 (as read with sections 225 and 226) of that Act,

a patient's detention is not authorised shall be taken into account for the purposes of the calculation of any of the periods mentioned in subsection (4) below.

(4) Those periods are—

   (a) the total periods of 80 days, 110 days and 140 days referred to in subsection (4) of section 65 of this Act as applied by subsection (1) above;

   (b) those total periods as extended under subsection (5) or, on appeal, under subsection (8) of that section as so applied;

   (c) the total of 40 days referred to in section 147 of this Act (prevention of delay in trials in summary proceedings) as applied by subsection (2) above; and

   (d) that period as extended under subsection (2) of that section or, on appeal, under subsection (3) of that section as so applied.

Effect of assessment and treatment orders on pre-existing mental health ordersS

52. UEffect of assessment order and treatment order on pre-existing mental health orderS

(1) This section applies where—

   (a) a patient is subject to a relevant order; and

   (b) an assessment order or a treatment order is made in respect of the patient.

(2) The relevant order shall cease to authorise the measures specified in it for the period during which the patient is subject to the assessment order or, as the case may be, treatment order.

(4) In this section, a "relevant order" means—

   (a) an interim compulsory treatment order made under section 65. (2) of the 2003 Act; and

   (b) a compulsory treatment order made under section 64. (4)(a) of that Act.]

[F39. Interim compulsion orders]S

Amendments (Textual)
F39. Ss. 53-53. D and cross-heading substituted (5.10.2005) for s. 53 and cross-heading by Mental Health (Care and Treatment) (Scotland) Act 2003 (asp 13), ss. 131, 333. (1)-(4); S.S.I. 2005/161, art. 3 (with savings for s. 53 by virtue of S.S.I. 2005/452, art. 33. (14))

[F4053 Interim compulsion order.S

(1) This section applies where a person (referred to in this section and in sections 53. A to 53. D of this Act as an "offender")—

(a) is convicted in the High Court or the sheriff court of an offence punishable by imprisonment (other than an offence the sentence for which is fixed by law); or

(b) is remitted to the High Court by the sheriff under any enactment for sentence for such an offence.

(2) If the court is satisfied—

(a) on the written or oral evidence of two medical practitioners—

(i) that the offender has a mental disorder; and

(ii) as to the matters mentioned in subsection (3) below; and

(b) that, having regard to the matters mentioned in subsection (4) below, it is appropriate, it may, subject to subsection (7) below, make an order (in this Act referred to as an "interim compulsion order") authorising the measures mentioned in subsection (8) below and specifying any matters to be included in the report under section 53. B(1) of this Act.

(3) The matters referred to in subsection (2)(a)(ii) above are—

(a) that there are reasonable grounds for believing—

(i) that the conditions mentioned in subsection (5) below are likely to be met in respect of the offender; and

(ii) that the offender's mental disorder is such that it would be appropriate to make one of the disposals mentioned in subsection (6) below in relation to the offender;

(b) that the hospital to be specified in the order is suitable for the purpose of assessing whether the conditions mentioned in subsection (5) below are met in respect of the offender;

(c) that, were an interim compulsion order made, the offender could be admitted to such hospital before the [F41end of the day following the] 7 days beginning with the day on which the order is made; and

(d) that it would not be reasonably practicable for the assessment mentioned in paragraph (b) above to be made unless an order were made.

(4) The matters referred to in subsection (2)(b) above are—

(a) all the circumstances (including the nature of the offence of which the offender is convicted); and

(b) any alternative means of dealing with the offender.

(5) The conditions referred to in paragraphs (a)(i) and (b) of subsection (3) above are—

(a) that medical treatment which would be likely to—

(i) prevent the mental disorder worsening; or

(ii) alleviate any of the symptoms, or effects, of the disorder, is available for the offender;

(b) that if the offender were not provided with such medical treatment there would be a significant risk—

(i) to the health, safety or welfare of the offender; or

(ii) to the safety of any other person; and

(c) that the making of an interim compulsion order in respect of the offender is necessary.

(6) The disposals are—

(a) both a compulsion order that authorises detention in hospital by virtue of section 57. A(8)(a) of this Act and a restriction order; or

(b) a hospital direction.

(7) An interim compulsion order may authorise detention in a state hospital only if, on the written or oral evidence of the two medical practitioners mentioned in subsection (2)(a) above, it appears to the court—

(a) that the offender requires to be detained in hospital under conditions of special security; and

(b) that such conditions of special security can be provided only in a state hospital.

(8) The measures are—

(a) in the case of an offender who, when the interim compulsion order is made, has not been admitted to the specified hospital, the removal, before the [F42end of the day following the] 7 days beginning with the day on which the order is made, of the offender to the specified hospital by—

(i) a constable;

(ii) a person employed in, or contracted to provide services in or to, the specified hospital who is authorised by the managers of that hospital to remove persons to hospital for the purposes of this section; or

(iii) a specified person;

(b) the detention, for a period not exceeding [F43the relevant period given by subsection (8. A) below], of the offender in the specified hospital; and

(c) during the [F44relevant period given by subsection (8. A) below], the giving to the offender, in accordance with Part 16 of the Mental Health (Care and Treatment)(Scotland) Act 2003 (asp 13), of medical treatment.

[F45. (8. A)For the purpose of subsection (8)(b) and (c) above, the relevant period is the period—

(a) beginning with the day on which the order is made,

(b) expiring at the end of the 12 weeks following that day.]

(9) An interim compulsion order may include such directions as the court thinks fit for the removal of the offender to, and the detention of the offender in, a place of safety pending the offender's admission to the specified hospital.

(10) The court may make an interim compulsion order in the absence of the offender only if—

(a) the offender is represented by counsel or solicitor;

(b) that counsel or solicitor is given an opportunity of being heard; and

(c) the court is satisfied that it is—

(i) impracticable; or

(ii) inappropriate,

for the offender to be brought before it.

(11) The court shall, as soon as reasonably practicable after making an interim compulsion order, give notice of the making of the order to—

(a) the person subject to the order;

(b) any solicitor acting for that person;

(c) the Scottish Ministers; and

(d) the Mental Welfare Commission.

(12) Where a court makes an interim compulsion order in relation to an offender, the court—

(a) shall not, at the same time—

(i) make an order under section 200 of this Act;

(ii) impose a fine;

(iii) pass sentence of imprisonment;

(iv) make a compulsion order;

(v) make a guardianship order;

[F46. (vi)impose a community payback order;

(vii) make a drug treatment and testing order; or

(viii)make a restriction of liberty order,]

in relation of the offender;

(b) may make any other order which it has power to make apart from this section.

(13) In this section—

"medical treatment" has the same meaning as in section 52. D of this Act;

"sentence of imprisonment" includes any sentence or order for detention; and

"specified" means specified in the interim compulsion order.]

Amendments (Textual)

F40. Ss. 53-53. D and cross-heading substituted (5.10.2005) for s. 53 and cross-heading by Mental Health (Care and Treatment) (Scotland) Act 2003 (asp 13), ss. 131, 333. (1)-(4); S.S.I. 2005/161, art. 3 (with savings for s. 53 by virtue of S.S.I. 2005/452, art. 33. (14))

F41. Words in s. 53. (3)(c) substituted (30.9.2017) by Mental Health (Scotland) Act 2015 (asp 9), ss. 42. (2)(a), 61. (2); S.S.I. 2017/197, art. 2, sch.

F42. Words in s. 53. (8)(a) substituted (30.9.2017) by Mental Health (Scotland) Act 2015 (asp 9), ss. 42. (2)(b)(i), 61. (2); S.S.I. 2017/197, art. 2, sch.

F43. Words in s. 53. (8)(b) substituted (30.9.2017) by Mental Health (Scotland) Act 2015 (asp 9), ss. 42. (2)(b)(ii), 61. (2); S.S.I. 2017/197, art. 2, sch.

F44. Words in s. 53. (8)(c) substituted (30.9.2017) by Mental Health (Scotland) Act 2015 (asp 9), ss. 42. (2)(b)(iii), 61. (2); S.S.I. 2017/197, art. 2, sch.

F45. S. 53. (8. A) inserted (30.9.2017) by Mental Health (Scotland) Act 2015 (asp 9), ss. 42. (2)(c), 61. (2); S.S.I. 2017/197, art. 2, sch.

F46. S. 53. (12)(a)(vi)-(viii) substituted for s. 53. (12)(a)(vi)(vii) (1.2.2011) by Criminal Justice and Licensing (Scotland) Act 2010 (asp 13), ss. 14. (2), 206. (1), Sch. 2 para. 4; S.S.I. 2010/413, art. 2, Sch. (with art. 3)

[F4753. AInterim compulsion order: supplementaryS

(1) If, before the [F48end of the day following the] 7 days beginning with the day on which the interim compulsion order is made, it appears to the court, or, as the case may be, the Scottish Ministers, that, by reason of emergency or other special circumstances, it is not reasonably practicable for the offender to be admitted to the hospital specified in the order, the court, or, as the case may be, the Scottish Ministers, may direct that the offender be admitted to the hospital specified in the direction.

(2) Where—

(a) the court makes a direction under subsection (1) above, it shall, as soon as reasonably practicable after making the direction, inform the person having custody of the offender; and

(b) the Scottish Ministers make such a direction, they shall, as soon as reasonably practicable after making the direction, inform—

(i) the court; and

(ii) the person having custody of the offender.

(3) Where a direction is made under subsection (1) above, the interim compulsion order shall have effect as if the hospital specified in the direction were the hospital specified in the order.

(4) In this section, "court" means the court which made the interim compulsion order.]

Amendments (Textual)

F47. Ss. 53-53. D and cross-heading substituted (5.10.2005) for s. 53 and cross-heading by Mental Health (Care and Treatment) (Scotland) Act 2003 (asp 13), ss. 131, 333. (1)-(4); S.S.I. 2005/161, art. 3 (with savings for s. 53 by virtue of S.S.I. 2005/452, art. 33. (14))

F48. Words in s. 53. A(1) substituted (30.9.2017) by Mental Health (Scotland) Act 2015 (asp 9), ss. 42. (3), 61. (2); S.S.I. 2017/197, art. 2, sch. (with art. 21. (a))

[F4953. BReview and extension of interim compulsion orderS

(1) The responsible medical officer shall, before the expiry of the period specified by the court under section 53. (8)(b) of this Act, submit a report in writing to the court—

(a) as to the matters mentioned in subsection (2) below; and

(b) as to any matters specified by the court under section 53. (2) of this Act.

(2) The matters are—

(a) whether the conditions mentioned in section 53. (5) of this Act are met in respect of the offender;

(b) the type (or types) of mental disorder that the offender has; and

(c) whether it is necessary to extend the interim compulsion order to allow further time for the assessment mentioned in section 53. (3)(b) of this Act.

(3) The responsible medical officer shall, at the same time as such officer submits the report to the court, send a copy of such report to—

(a) the offender; and

(b) any solicitor acting for the offender.

(4) The court may, on receiving the report submitted under subsection (1) above,

[F50. (a) if satisfied that the extension of the order is necessary, extend the order for such period [F51not exceeding the relevant period given by subsection (4. A) below] as the court may specify][F52, and

(b) if it seems appropriate to do so, direct that the offender be admitted to the hospital specified in the direction.]

[F53. (4. A)For the purpose of subsection (4) above, the relevant period is the period—

(a) beginning with the day on which the order would cease to have effect if it were not extended,

(b) expiring at the end of the 12 weeks following that day.]

(5) The court may extend an interim compulsion order under subsection (4) above for a period only if, by doing so, the total period for which the offender will be subject to the order does not exceed [F54the period—

(a) beginning with the day on which the order was first made,

(b) expiring at the end of the 12 months following that day.]

(6) The court may, under subsection (4) above, extend an interim compulsion order [F55or make a direction specifying a hospital] in the absence of the offender only if—

(a) the offender is represented by counsel or a solicitor;

(b) that counsel or solicitor is given an opportunity of being heard; and

(c) the court is satisfied that it is—

(i) impracticable; or

(ii) inappropriate,

for the offender to be brought before it.

(7) Subsections (1) to (9) of this section shall apply for the purposes of an interim compulsion order extended under subsection (4) above as they apply for the purposes of an interim compulsion order, references in those subsections to the period specified by the court under section 53. (8)(b) of this Act being construed as references to the period specified by the court under subsection (4) above.

[F56. (7. A)Where a direction is made under subsection (4) above, the interim compulsion order has effect as if the hospital specified in the direction were the hospital specified in the order.]

(8) Where a report is submitted under subsection (1) above, the court may, before the expiry of the period specified by the court under section 53. (8)(b) of this Act—

(a) revoke the interim compulsion order and make one of the disposals mentioned in section 53. (6) of this Act; or

(b) revoke the interim compulsion order and deal with the offender in any way (other than by making an interim compulsion order) in which the court could have dealt with the offender if no such order had been made.

(9) In this section—

"court" means the court which made the interim compulsion order; and

"responsible medical officer" means the responsible medical officer appointed in respect of the offender under section 230 of the Mental Health (Care and Treatment)(Scotland) Act 2003 (asp 13).]

Amendments (Textual)

F49. Ss. 53-53. D and cross-heading substituted (5.10.2005) for s. 53 and cross-heading by Mental

Health (Care and Treatment) (Scotland) Act 2003 (asp 13), ss. 131, 333. (1)-(4); S.S.I. 2005/161, art. 3 (with savings for s. 53 by virtue of S.S.I. 2005/452, art. 33. (14))

F50. Words in s. 53. B(4) renumbered as s. 53. B(4)(a) (30.9.2017) by Mental Health (Scotland) Act 2015 (asp 9), ss. 45. (2)(a)(i), 61. (2); S.S.I. 2017/197, art. 2, sch.

F51. Words in s. 53. B(4) substituted (30.9.2017) by Mental Health (Scotland) Act 2015 (asp 9), ss. 42. (4)(a), 61. (2); S.S.I. 2017/197, art. 2, sch.

F52. S. 53. B(4)(b) and word inserted (30.9.2017) by Mental Health (Scotland) Act 2015 (asp 9), ss. 45. (2)(a)(ii), 61. (2); S.S.I. 2017/197, art. 2, sch.

F53. S. 53. B(4. A) inserted (30.9.2017) by Mental Health (Scotland) Act 2015 (asp 9), ss. 42. (4)(b), 61. (2); S.S.I. 2017/197, art. 2, sch.

F54. Words in s. 53. B(5) substituted (30.9.2017) by Mental Health (Scotland) Act 2015 (asp 9), ss. 42. (4)(c), 61. (2); S.S.I. 2017/197, art. 2, sch.

F55. Words in s. 53. B(6) inserted (30.9.2017) by Mental Health (Scotland) Act 2015 (asp 9), ss. 45. (2)(b), 61. (2); S.S.I. 2017/197, art. 2, sch.

F56. S. 53. B(7. A) inserted (30.9.2017) by Mental Health (Scotland) Act 2015 (asp 9), ss. 45. (2)(c), 61. (2); S.S.I. 2017/197, art. 2, sch.

[F5753. CEarly termination of interim compulsion orderS

(1) An interim compulsion order shall cease to have effect if the court—
    (a) makes a compulsion order in relation to the offender;
    (b) makes a hospital direction in relation to the offender; or
    (c) deals with the offender in some other way, including the imposing of a sentence of imprisonment on the offender.
(2) In this section, "court" means the court which made the interim compulsion order.]
Amendments (Textual)
F57. Ss. 53-53. D and cross-heading substituted (5.10.2005) for s. 53 and cross-heading by Mental Health (Care and Treatment) (Scotland) Act 2003 (asp 13), ss. 131, 333. (1)-(4); S.S.I. 2005/161, art. 3 (with savings for s. 53 by virtue of S.S.I. 2005/452, art. 33. (14))

[F5853. DPower of court on interim compulsion order ceasing to have effectS

(1) Where, otherwise than by virtue of section 53. B(8) or 53. C of this Act, an interim compulsion order ceases to have effect the court may deal with the offender who was subject to the order in any way (other than the making of a new interim compulsion order) in which it could have dealt with the offender if no such order had been made.
(2) In this section, "court" means the court which made the interim compulsion order.]
Amendments (Textual)
F58. Ss. 53-53. D and cross-heading substituted (5.10.2005) for s. 53 and cross-heading by Mental Health (Care and Treatment) (Scotland) Act 2003 (asp 13), ss. 131, 333. (1)-(4); S.S.I. 2005/161, art. 3 (with savings for s. 53 by virtue of S.S.I. 2005/452, art. 33. (14))

[F59. Acquittal involving mental disorderS

Amendments (Textual)
F59. S. 53. E and cross-heading inserted (with application in accordance with art. 3 of the commencing S.S.I.) by Criminal Justice and Licensing (Scotland) Act 2010 (asp 13), ss. 169, 206. (1); S.S.I. 2012/160, art. 3, sch.

53. EAcquittal involving mental disorderS

(1) Where the prosecutor accepts a plea (by the person charged with the commission of an offence) of the special defence set out in section 51. A of this Act, the court must declare that the person is acquitted by reason of the special defence.

(2) Subsection (3) below applies where—

(a) the prosecutor does not accept such a plea, and

(b) evidence tending to establish the special defence set out in section 51. A of this Act is brought before the court.

(3) Where this subsection applies the court is to—

(a) in proceedings on indictment, direct the jury to find whether the special defence has been established and, if they find that it has, to declare whether the person is acquitted on that ground,

(b) in summary proceedings, state whether the special defence has been established and, if it states that it has, declare whether the person is acquitted on that ground.]

[F60. Unfitness for trialS

Amendments (Textual)

F60. S. 53. F and cross-heading inserted (with application in accordance with art. 3 of the commencing S.S.I.) by Criminal Justice and Licensing (Scotland) Act 2010 (asp 13), ss. 170. (1), 206. (1); S.S.I. 2012/160, art. 3, sch.

53. FUnfitness for trialS

(1) A person is unfit for trial if it is established on the balance of probabilities that the person is incapable, by reason of a mental or physical condition, of participating effectively in a trial.

(2) In determining whether a person is unfit for trial the court is to have regard to—

(a) the ability of the person to—

(i) understand the nature of the charge,

(ii) understand the requirement to tender a plea to the charge and the effect of such a plea,

(iii) understand the purpose of, and follow the course of, the trial,

(iv) understand the evidence that may be given against the person,

(v) instruct and otherwise communicate with the person's legal representative, and

(b) any other factor which the court considers relevant.

(3) The court is not to find that a person is unfit for trial by reason only of the person being unable to recall whether the event which forms the basis of the charge occurred in the manner described in the charge.

(4) In this section "the court" means—

(a) as regards a person charged on indictment, the High Court or the sheriff court,

(b) as regards a person charged summarily, the sheriff court.]

F61...S

Amendments (Textual)

F61. S. 54 cross-heading omitted (with application in accordance with art. 3 of the commencing S.S.I.) by virtue of Criminal Justice and Licensing (Scotland) Act 2010 (asp 13), ss. 170. (2), 206. (1); S.S.I. 2012/160, art. 3, sch.

54 [F62. Unfitness for trial: further provision] .S

(1) Where the court is satisfiedF63... that a person charged with the commission of an offence is [F64unfit for trial] so that his trial cannot proceed or, if it has commenced, cannot continue, the

court shall, subject to subsection (2) below—

(a) make a finding to that effect and state the reasons for that finding;

(b) discharge the trial diet [F65or, in proceedings on indictment where the finding is made at or before the first diet (in the case of proceedings in the sheriff court) or the preliminary hearing (in the case of proceedings in the High Court), that diet or, as the case may be, hearing] and order that a diet (in this Act referred to as an "an examination of facts") be held under section 55 of this Act; and

(c) remand the person in custody or on bail or, where the court is satisfied—

(i) on the written or oral evidence of two medical practitioners, that [F66the conditions mentioned in subsection (2. A) below are met in respect of the person] ; and

(ii) that a hospital is available for his admission and suitable for his detention,

make an order (in this section referred to as a [F67temporary compulsion order]) [F68authorising the measures mentioned in subsection (2. B) below in respect of the person] until the conclusion of the examination of facts.

(2) Subsection (1) above is without prejudice to the power of the court, on an application by the prosecutor, to desert the dietpro loco et tempore.

[F69. (2. A)The conditions referred to in subsection (1)(c)(i) above are—

(a) that the person has a mental disorder;

(b) that medical treatment which would be likely to—

(i) prevent the mental disorder worsening; or

(ii) alleviate any of the symptoms, or effects, of the disorder,

is available for the person; and

(c) that if the person were not provided with such medical treatment there would be a significant risk—

(a) to the health, safety or welfare of the person; or

(b) to the safety of any other person.

(2. B)The measures referred to in subsection (1)(c) above are—

(a) in the case of a person who, when the temporary compulsion order is made, has not been admitted to the specified hospital, the removal, before the [F70end of the day following the] 7 days beginning with the day on which the order is made of the person to the specified hospital by—

(i) a constable;

(ii) a person employed in, or contracted to provide services in or to, the specified hospital who is authorised by the managers of that hospital to remove persons to hospital for the purposes of this section; or

(iii) a specified person;

(b) the detention of the person in the specified hospital; and

(c) the giving to the person, in accordance with Part 16 of the Mental Health (Care and Treatment)(Scotland) Act 2003 (asp 13), of medical treatment.]

(3) The court may, before making a finding under subsection (1) above as to [F71whether a person is unfit for trial] , adjourn the case in order that investigation of his mental [F72or physical] condition may be carried out.

(4) The court which made a temporary [F73compulsion] order may, at any time while the order is in force, review the order on the ground that there has been a change of circumstances since the order was made and, on such review—

(a) where the court considers that such an order is no longer required in relation to a person, it shall revoke the order and may remand him in custody or on bail;

(b) in any other case, the court may—

(i) confirm or vary the order; or

(ii) revoke the order and make such other order, under subsection (1)(c) above or any other provision of this Act, as the court considers appropriate.

(5) Where it appears to a court that it is not practicable or appropriate for the accused to be brought before it for the purpose of determining whether he is [F74unfit for trial] so that his trial

cannot proceed, then, if no objection to such a course is taken by or on behalf of the accused, the court may order that the case be proceeded with in his absence.

F75. (6)............................

F75. (7)............................

(8) In this section

[F76"medical treatment" has the same meaning as in section 52. D of this Act;

"specified" means specified in the temporary compulsion order; and],

"the court" means—

- as regards a person charged on indictment, the High Court or the sheriff court;

- as regards a person charged summarily, the sheriff court.

Amendments (Textual)

F62. S. 54 heading substituted (with application in accordance with art. 3 of the commencing S.S.I.) by Criminal Justice and Licensing (Scotland) Act 2010 (asp 13), ss. 170. (2), 206. (1); S.S.I. 2012/160, art. 3, sch.

F63. Words in s. 54. (1) repealed (with application in accordance with art. 3 of the commencing S.S.I.) by Criminal Justice and Licensing (Scotland) Act 2010 (asp 13), ss. 170. (2)(a)(i), 206. (1); S.S.I. 2012/160, art. 3, sch.

F64. Words in s. 54. (1) substituted (with application in accordance with art. 3 of the commencing S.S.I.) by Criminal Justice and Licensing (Scotland) Act 2010 (asp 13), ss. 170. (2)(a)(ii), 206. (1); S.S.I. 2012/160, art. 3, sch.

F65. Words in s. 54. (1)(b) inserted (1.2.2005) by Criminal Procedure (Amendment) (Scotland) Act 2004 (asp 5), ss. 25, 27. (1), Sch. para. 13; S.S.I. 2004/405, art. 2, Sch. 1 (subject to arts. 3-5)

F66. Words in s. 54. (1)(c)(i) substituted (5.10.2005) by Mental Health (Care and Treatment) (Scotland) Act 2003 (asp 13), ss. 331. (1), 333. (1)-(4), Sch. 4 para. 8. (2)(a)(i); S.S.I. 2005/161, art. 3 (with savings for s. 54. (1)(c) by virtue of S.S.I. 2005/452, art. 33. (18))

F67. Words in s. 54. (1)(c) substituted (5.10.2005) by Mental Health (Care and Treatment) (Scotland) Act 2003 (asp 13), ss. 331. (1), 333. (1)-(4), Sch. 4 para. 8. (2)(a)(ii); S.S.I. 2005/161, art. 3 (with savings for s. 54. (1)(c) by virtue of S.S.I. 2005/452, art. 33. (18))

F68. Words in s. 54. (1)(c) substituted (5.10.2005) by Mental Health (Care and Treatment) (Scotland) Act 2003 (asp 13), ss. 331. (1), 333. (1)-(4), Sch. 4 para. 8. (2)(a)(iii); S.S.I. 2005/161, art. 3 (with savings for s. 54. (1)(c) by virtue of S.S.I. 2005/452, art. 33. (18))

F69. S. 54. (2. A)(2. B) inserted (5.10.2005) by Mental Health (Care and Treatment) (Scotland) Act 2003 (asp 13), ss. 331. (1), 333. (1)-(4), Sch. 4 para. 8. (2)(b); S.S.I. 2005/161, art. 3 (as amended (27.9.2005) by the repeal of "(i)" in the inserted subsection (2. B) by virtue of S.S.I. 2005/465, art. 3, Sch. 2) (with savings for s. 54. (2. A)(2. B) by virtue of S.S.I. 2005/452, art. 33. (18))

F70. Words in s. 54. (2. B)(a) substituted (30.9.2017) by Mental Health (Scotland) Act 2015 (asp 9), ss. 42. (5), 61. (2); S.S.I. 2017/197, art. 2, sch. (with art. 21. (b))

F71. Words in s. 54. (3) substituted (with application in accordance with art. 3 of the commencing S.S.I.) by Criminal Justice and Licensing (Scotland) Act 2010 (asp 13), ss. 170. (2)(b)(i), 206. (1); S.S.I. 2012/160, art. 3, sch.

F72. Words in s. 54. (3) inserted (with application in accordance with art. 3 of the commencing S.S.I.) by Criminal Justice and Licensing (Scotland) Act 2010 (asp 13), ss. 170. (2)(b)(ii), 206. (1); S.S.I. 2012/160, art. 3, sch.

F73. Word in s. 54. (4) substituted (5.10.2005) by Mental Health (Care and Treatment) (Scotland) Act 2003 (asp 13), ss. 331. (1), 333. (1)-(4), Sch. 4 para. 8. (2)(c); S.S.I. 2005/161, art. 3 (with savings for s. 54. (4) by virtue of S.S.I. 2005/452, art. 33. (18))

F74. Words in s. 54. (5) substituted (with application in accordance with art. 3 of the commencing S.S.I.) by Criminal Justice and Licensing (Scotland) Act 2010 (asp 13), ss. 170. (2)(c), 206. (1); S.S.I. 2012/160, art. 3, sch.

F75. S. 54. (6)(7) repealed (with application in accordance with art. 3 of the commencing S.S.I.) by Criminal Justice and Licensing (Scotland) Act 2010 (asp 13), ss. 170. (3), 206. (1); S.S.I. 2012/160, art. 3, sch.

F76. Words in s. 54. (8) inserted (5.10.2005) by Mental Health (Care and Treatment) (Scotland) Act 2003 (asp 13), ss. 331. (1), 333. (1)-(4), Sch. 4 para. 8. (2)(d); S.S.I. 2005/161, art. 3 (with savings for s. 54. (8) by virtue of S.S.I. 2005/452, art. 33. (18))

Examination of factsS

55 Examination of facts.S

(1) At an examination of facts ordered under section 54. (1)(b) of this Act the court shall, on the basis of the evidence (if any) already given in the trial and such evidence, or further evidence, as may be led by either party, determine whether it is satisfied—

(a) beyond reasonable doubt, as respects any charge on the indictment or, as the case may be, the complaint in respect of which the accused was being or was to be tried, that he did the act or made the omission constituting the offence; and

(b) on the balance of probabilities, that there are no grounds for acquitting him.

(2) Where the court is satisfied as mentioned in subsection (1) above, it shall make a finding to that effect.

(3) Where the court is not so satisfied it shall, subject to subsection (4) below, acquit the person of the charge.

(4) Where, as respects a person acquitted under subsection (3) above, the court is satisfied as to the matter mentioned in subsection (1)(a) above but it appears to the court that the person was [F77not, because of section 51. A of this Act, criminally responsible for the conduct] constituting the offence, the court shall state whether the acquittal is [F78by reason of the special defence set out in that section] .

(5) Where it appears to the court that it is not practical or appropriate for the accused to attend an examination of facts the court may, if no objection is taken by or on behalf of the accused, order that the examination of facts shall proceed in his absence.

(6) Subject to the provisions of this section, section 56 of this Act and any Act of Adjournal the rules of evidence and procedure and the powers of the court shall, in respect of an examination of facts, be as nearly as possible those applicable in respect of a trial.

(7) For the purposes of the application to an examination of facts of the rules and powers mentioned in subsection (6) above, an examination of facts—

(a) commences when the indictment or, as the case may be, complaint is called; and

(b) concludes when the court—

(i) acquits the person under subsection (3) above;

(ii) makes an order under subsection (2) of section 57 of this Act; or

(iii) decides, under paragraph (e) of that subsection, not to make an order.

Amendments (Textual)

F77. Words in s. 55. (4) substituted (with application in accordance with art. 3 of the commencing S.S.I.) by Criminal Justice and Licensing (Scotland) Act 2010 (asp 13), s. 206. (1), sch. 7 para. 37. (a); S.S.I. 2012/160, art. 3, sch.

F78. Words in s. 55. (4) substituted (with application in accordance with art. 3 of the commencing S.S.I.) by Criminal Justice and Licensing (Scotland) Act 2010 (asp 13), s. 206. (1), sch. 7 para. 37. (b); S.S.I. 2012/160, art. 3, sch.

56 Examination of facts: supplementary provisions.S

(1) An examination of facts ordered under section 54. (1)(b) of this Act may, where the order is made at the trial diet [F79or, in proceedings on indictment, at the first diet (in the case of proceedings in the sheriff court) or the preliminary hearing (in the case of proceedings in the High

Court)] , be held immediately following the making of the order and, where it is so held, the citation of the accused and any witness to the trial diet [F80, first diet or, as the case may be, preliminary hearing] shall be a valid citation to the examination of facts.

(2) F81. . . . .

(3) Where an accused person is not legally represented at an examination of facts the court shall appoint counsel or a solicitor to represent his interests.

(4) The court may, on the motion of the prosecutor and after hearing the accused, order that the examination of facts shall proceed in relation to a particular charge, or particular charges, in the indictment or, as the case may be, complaint in priority to other such charges.

(5) The court may, on the motion of the prosecutor and after hearing the accused, at any time desert the examination of facts pro loco et tempore as respects either the whole indictment or, as the case may be, complaint or any charge therein.

(6) Where, and to the extent that, an examination of facts has, under subsection (5) above, been deserted pro loco et tempore—

(a) in the case of proceedings on indictment, the Lord Advocate may, at any time, raise and insist in a new indictment; or

(b) in the case of summary proceedings, the prosecutor may at any time raise a fresh libel, notwithstanding any time limit which would otherwise apply in respect of prosecution of the alleged offence.

(7) If, in a case where a court has made a finding under subsection (2) of section 55 of this Act, a person is subsequently charged, whether on indictment or on a complaint, with an offence arising out of the same act or omission as is referred to in subsection (1) of that section, any order made under section 57. (2) of this Act shall, with effect from the commencement of the later proceedings, cease to have effect.

(8) For the purposes of subsection (7) above, the later proceedings are commenced when the indictment or, as the case may be, the complaint is served.

Amendments (Textual)

F79. Words in s. 56. (1) inserted (1.2.2005) by Criminal Procedure (Amendment) (Scotland) Act 2004 (asp 5), ss. 25, 27. (1), Sch. para. 14. (a)(i); S.S.I. 2004/405, art. 2, Sch. 1 (subject to arts. 3-5)

F80. Words in s. 56. (1) inserted (1.2.2005) by Criminal Procedure (Amendment) (Scotland) Act 2004 (asp 5), ss. 25, 27. (1), Sch. para. 14. (a)(ii); S.S.I. 2004/405, art. 2, Sch. 1 (subject to arts. 3-5)

F81. S. 56. (2) repealed (1.2.2005) by Criminal Procedure (Amendment) (Scotland) Act 2004 (asp 5), ss. 25, 27. (1), Sch. para. 14. (b); S.S.I. 2004/405, art. 2, Sch. 1 (subject to arts. 3-5)

Disposal [F82where accused found not criminally responsible] S

Amendments (Textual)

F82. Words in s. 57 cross-heading substituted (with application in accordance with art. 3 of the commencing S.S.I.) by Criminal Justice and Licensing (Scotland) Act 2010 (asp 13), s. 206. (1), sch. 7 para. 38; S.S.I. 2012/160, art. 3, sch.

57 Disposal of case where accused found [F83not criminally responsible or unfit for trial].S

(1) This section applies where—

(a) a person is [F84acquitted by reason of the special defence set out in section 51. A of this Act]; or

(b) following an examination of facts under section 55, a court makes a finding under subsection (2) of that section.

(2) Subject to subsection (3) below, where this section applies the court may, as it thinks fit—

(a) [F85subject to subsection (4) below, make a compulsion order [F86. (whether or not authorising the detention of the person in a hospital)]]];

[F87. (b)subject to subsection (4. A) below, make a restriction order in respect of the person (that is, in addition to a compulsion order authorising the detention of the person in a hospital);]

[F88[F89. (bb)subject to subsections (3. A) and (4. B) below, make an interim compulsion order in respect of the person;]]]

(c) [F90subject to subsections (4. C) and (6) below, make a guardianship order in respect of the person];

(d) [F91subject to subsection (5) below,] make a supervision and treatment order (within the meaning of paragraph 1. (1) of Schedule 4 to this Act [F92in respect of the person]); or

(e) make no order.

[F93. (3)Where the court is satisfied, having regard to a report submitted in respect of the person following an interim [F94compulsion] order, that, on a balance of probabilities, the risk his being at liberty presents to the safety of the public at large is high, it shall make orders under both paragraphs (a) and (b) of subsection (2) above in respect of that person.]

[F95. (3. A)The court may make an interim compulsion order under paragraph (bb) of subsection (2) above in respect of a person only where it has not previously made such an order in respect of the person under that paragraph.]

[F96. (4)For the purposes of subsection (2)(a) above—

(a) subsections (2) to (16) of section 57. A of this Act shall apply as they apply for the purposes of subsection (1) of that section, subject to the following modifications—
(i) references to the offender shall be construed as references to the person to whom this section applies; and
(ii) in subsection (4)(b)(i), the reference to the offence of which the offender was convicted shall be construed as a reference to the offence with which the person to whom this section applies was charged;

(b) section 57. B of this Act shall have effect subject to the modification that references to the offender shall be construed as references to the person to whom this section applies;

(c) section 57. C of this Act shall have effect subject to the following modifications—
(i) references to the offender shall be construed as references to the person to whom this section applies; and
(ii) references to section 57. A of this Act shall be construed as references to subsection (2)(a) above; and

(d) section 57. D of this Act shall have effect subject to the modification that references to the offender shall be construed as references to the person to whom this section applies.

(4. A)For the purposes of subsection (2)(b) above, section 59 of this Act shall have effect.

(4. B)For the purposes of subsection (2)(bb) above—

(a) subsections (2) to (13) of section 53 of this Act shall apply as they apply for the purposes of subsection (1) of that section, subject to the following modifications—
(i) references to the offender shall be construed as references to the person to whom this section applies;
(ii) in subsection (3)(a)(ii), the reference to one of the disposals mentioned in subsection (6) of that section shall be construed as a reference to the disposal mentioned in subsection (6)(a) of that section;
(iii) in subsection (4)(a), the reference to the offence of which the offender is convicted shall be construed as a reference to the offence with which the person to whom this section applies is charged; and
(iv) subsection (6)(b) shall not apply;

(b) section 53. A of this Act shall have effect subject to the modification that references to the offender shall be construed as references to the person to whom this section applies;

(c) section 53. B of this Act shall have effect subject to the following modifications—
(i) references to the offender shall be construed as references to the person to whom this section

applies; and

(ii) for paragraphs (a) and (b) of subsection (8) there shall be substituted ", revoke the interim compulsion order and—

(a) make an order in respect of the person under paragraph (a), (b), (c) or (d) of subsection (2) of section 57 of this Act; or

(b) decide, under paragraph (e) of that subsection, to make no order in respect of the person.";

(d) section 53. C of this Act shall have effect subject to the following modifications—

(i) references to the offender shall be construed as references to the person to whom this section applies; and

(ii) for paragraphs (a) to (c) of subsection (1) there shall be substituted—

"(a)makes an order in respect of the person under paragraph (a), (b), (c) or (d) of subsection (2) of section 57 of this Act; or

(b) decides, under paragraph (e) of that subsection, to make no order in respect of the person."; and

(e) section 53. D of this Act shall have effect subject to the modification that the reference to the offender shall be construed as a reference to the person to whom this section applies.

(4. C)For the purposes of subsection (2)(c) above, subsections (1. A), (6) to (8) and (11) of section 58 of this Act shall apply, subject to the modifications that the reference to a person convicted and any references to the offender shall be construed as references to the person to whom this section applies.]

(5) Schedule 4 to this Act shall have effect as regards supervision and treatment orders.

[F97. (6)Section 58. A of this Act shall have effect as regards guardianship orders made under subsection (2)(c) of this section.]

Amendments (Textual)

F83. Words in s. 57 heading substituted (with application in accordance with art. 3 of the commencing S.S.I.) by Criminal Justice and Licensing (Scotland) Act 2010 (asp 13), s. 206. (1), sch. 7 para. 38; S.S.I. 2012/160, art. 3, sch.

F84. Words in s. 57. (1)(a) substituted (with application in accordance with art. 3 of the commencing S.S.I.) by Criminal Justice and Licensing (Scotland) Act 2010 (asp 13), s. 206. (1), sch. 7 para. 39; S.S.I. 2012/160, art. 3, sch.

F85. Words in s. 57. (2)(a) substituted (5.10.2005) by Mental Health (Care and Treatment) (Scotland) Act 2003 (asp 13), ss. 331. (1), 333. (1)-(4), Sch. 4 para. 8. (3)(a)(i); S.S.I. 2005/161, art. 3

F86. Words in s. 57. (2)(a) substituted (30.6.2017) by Mental Health (Scotland) Act 2015 (asp 9), ss. 39. (2)(a), 61. (2); S.S.I. 2017/197, art. 2, sch.

F87. S. 57. (2)(b) substituted (30.6.2017) by Mental Health (Scotland) Act 2015 (asp 9), ss. 39. (2)(b), 61. (2); S.S.I. 2017/197, art. 2, sch.

F88. S. 57. (2)(bb) inserted (4.10.2005) by Criminal Justice (Scotland) Act 2003 (asp 7), ss. 2. (a), 89; S.S.I. 2005/433, art. 2

F89. S. 57. (2)(bb) substituted (5.10.2005) by Mental Health (Care and Treatment) (Scotland) Act 2003 (asp 13), ss. 331. (1), 333. (1)-(4), Sch. 4 para. 8. (3)(a)(iii); S.S.I. 2005/161, art. 3

F90. Words in s. 57. (2)(c) substituted (5.10.2005) by Mental Health (Care and Treatment) (Scotland) Act 2003 (asp 13), ss. 331. (1), 333. (1)-(4), Sch. 4 para. 8. (3)(a)(iv); S.S.I. 2005/161, art. 3

F91. Words in s. 57. (2)(d) inserted (5.10.2005) by Mental Health (Care and Treatment) (Scotland) Act 2003 (asp 13), ss. 331. (1), 333. (1)-(4), Sch. 4 para. 8. (3)(a)(v)(A); S.S.I. 2005/161, art. 3

F92. Words in s. 57. (2)(d) inserted (5.10.2005) by Mental Health (Care and Treatment) (Scotland) Act 2003 (asp 13), ss. 331. (1), 333. (1)-(4), Sch. 4 para. 8. (3)(a)(v)(B); S.S.I. 2005/161, art. 3

F93. S. 57. (3) substituted (27.6.2003) by Criminal Justice (Scotland) Act 2003 (asp 7), ss. {2. (b)}, 89; S.S.I. 2003/288, art. 2, Sch.

F94. Word in s. 57. (3) substituted (5.10.2005) by Mental Health (Care and Treatment) (Scotland) Act 2003 (asp 13), ss. 331. (1), 333. (1)-(4), Sch. 4 para. 8. (3)(b); S.S.I. 2005/161, art. 3

F95. S. 57. (3. A) substituted (5.10.2005) by Mental Health (Care and Treatment) (Scotland) Act

2003 (asp 13), ss. 331. (1), 333. (1)-(4), Sch. 4 para. 8. (3)(c); S.S.I. 2005/161, art. 3

F96. S. 57. (4)-(4. C) substituted (5.10.2005) for s. 57. (4) by Mental Health (Care and Treatment) (Scotland) Act 2003 (asp 13), ss. 331. (1), 333. (1)-(4), Sch. 4 para. 8. (3)(d); S.S.I. 2005/161, art. 3

F97. S. 57. (6) inserted (1.4.2002) by 2000 asp 4, s. 88. (2), Sch. 5 para. 26. (1)(c); S.S.I. 2001/81, art. 3, Sch. 2

Modifications etc. (not altering text)

C2. S. 57. (2)(a) extended (1.1.1998) by 1997 c. 48, s. 9. (1)(a) (subject to s. 9. (2)); S.I. 1997/2323, art. 4, Sch. 2 (subject to art. 7)

[F98. Compulsion ordersS

Amendments (Textual)

F98. Ss. 57. A-57. D and cross-heading inserted (21.3.2005 for certain purposes and otherwise 5.10.2005) by Mental Health (Care and Treatment) (Scotland) Act 2003 (asp 13), ss. 133, 333. (1)-(4); S.S.I. 2005/161, arts. 2, 3, Sch. 1 (as amended (27.9.2005) by S.S.I. 2005/465, art. 2, Sch. 1 para. 32. (14))

57. ACompulsion orderS

(1) This section applies where a person (in this section and in sections 57. B to 57. D of this Act, referred to as the "offender")—

(a) is convicted in the High Court or the sheriff court of an offence punishable by imprisonment (other than an offence the sentence for which is fixed by law); or

(b) is remitted to the High Court by the sheriff under any enactment for sentence for such an offence.

(2) If the court is satisfied—

(a) on the written or oral evidence of two medical practitioners, that the conditions mentioned in subsection (3) below are met in respect of the offender; and

(b) that, having regard to the matters mentioned in subsection (4) below, it is appropriate,

it may, subject to subsection (5) below, make an order (in this Act referred to as a "compulsion order") authorising, subject to subsection (7) below, for the [F99relevant period given by subsection (2. A) below] such of the measures mentioned in subsection (8) below as may be specified in the order.

[F100. (2. A)For the purpose of subsection (2) above, the relevant period is the period—

(a) beginning with the day on which the order is made,

(b) expiring at the end of the 6 months following that day.]

(3) The conditions referred to in subsection (2)(a) above are—

(a) that the offender has a mental disorder;

(b) that medical treatment which would be likely to—

(i) prevent the mental disorder worsening; or

(ii) alleviate any of the symptoms, or effects, of the disorder,

is available for the offender;

(c) that if the offender were not provided with such medical treatment there would be a significant risk—

(i) to the health, safety or welfare of the offender; or

(ii) to the safety of any other person; and

(d) that the making of a compulsion order in respect of the offender is necessary.

(4) The matters referred to in subsection (2)(b) above are—

(a) the mental health officer's report, prepared in accordance with section 57. C of this Act, in respect of the offender;

(b) all the circumstances, including—

(i) the nature of the offence of which the offender was convicted; and
(ii) the antecedents of the offender; and
(c) any alternative means of dealing with the offender.
(5) The court may, subject to subsection (6) below, make a compulsion order authorising the detention of the offender in a hospital by virtue of subsection (8)(a) below only if satisfied, on the written or oral evidence of the two medical practitioners mentioned in subsection (2)(a) above, that—
(a) the medical treatment mentioned in subsection (3)(b) above can be provided only if the offender is detained in hospital;
(b) the offender could be admitted to the hospital to be specified in the order before the [F101end of the day following the] 7 days beginning with the day on which the order is made; and
(c) the hospital to be so specified is suitable for the purpose of giving the medical treatment to the offender.
(6) A compulsion order may authorise detention in a state hospital only if, on the written or oral evidence of the two medical practitioners mentioned in subsection (2)(a) above, it appears to the court—
(a) that the offender requires to be detained in hospital under conditions of special security; and
(b) that such conditions of special security can be provided only in a state hospital.
(7) Where the court—
(a) makes a compulsion order in respect of an offender; and
(b) also makes a restriction order in respect of the offender,
the compulsion order shall authorise the measures specified in it without limitation of time.
(8) The measures mentioned in subsection (2) above are—
(a) the detention of the offender in the specified hospital;
(b) the giving to the offender, in accordance with Part 16 of the Mental Health (Care and Treatment)(Scotland) Act 2003 (asp 13), of medical treatment;
(c) the imposition of a requirement on the offender to attend—
(i) on specified or directed dates; or
(ii) at specified or directed intervals,
specified or directed places with a view to receiving medical treatment;
(d) the imposition of a requirement on the offender to attend—
(i) on specified or directed dates; or
(ii) at specified or directed intervals,
specified or directed places with a view to receiving community care services, relevant services or any treatment, care or service;
(e) subject to subsection (9) below, the imposition of a requirement on the offender to reside at a specified place;
(f) the imposition of a requirement on the offender to allow—
(i) the mental health officer;
(ii) the offender's responsible medical officer; or
(iii) any person responsible for providing medical treatment, community care services, relevant services or any treatment, care or service to the offender who is authorised for the purposes of this paragraph by the offender's responsible medical officer,
to visit the offender in the place where the offender resides;
(g) the imposition of a requirement on the offender to obtain the approval of the mental health officer to any change of address; and
(h) the imposition of a requirement on the offender to inform the mental health officer of any change of address before the change takes effect.
(9) The court may make a compulsion order imposing, by virtue of subsection (8)(e) above, a requirement on an offender to reside at a specified place which is a place used for the purpose of providing a care home service only if the court is satisfied that the person providing the care home service is willing to receive the offender.
(10) The Scottish Ministers may, by regulations made by statutory instrument, make provision for

measures prescribed by the regulations to be treated as included among the measures mentioned in subsection (8) above.

(11) The power conferred by subsection (10) above may be exercised so as to make different provision for different cases or descriptions of case or for different purposes.

(12) No regulations shall be made under subsection (10) above unless a draft of the statutory instrument containing them has been laid before, and approved by a resolution of, the Scottish Parliament.

(13) The court shall be satisfied as to the condition mentioned in subsection (3)(a) above only if the description of the offender's mental disorder by each of the medical practitioners mentioned in subsection (2)(a) above specifies, by reference to the appropriate paragraph (or paragraphs) of the definition of "mental disorder" in section 328. (1) of the Mental Health (Care and Treatment)(Scotland) Act 2003 (asp 13), at least one type of mental disorder that the offender has that is also specified by the other.

(14) A compulsion order—

(a) shall specify—

(i) by reference to the appropriate paragraph (or paragraphs) of the definition of "mental disorder" in section 328. (1) of the Mental Health (Care and Treatment)(Scotland) Act 2003 (asp 13), the type (or types) of mental disorder that each of the medical practitioners mentioned in subsection (2)(a) above specifies that the offender has that is also specified by the other; and

(ii) if the order does not, by virtue of subsection (8)(a) above, authorise the detention of the offender in hospital, the name of the hospital the managers of which are to have responsibility for appointing the offender's responsible medical officer; and

(b) may include—

(i) in a case where a compulsion order authorises the detention of the offender in a specified hospital by virtue of subsection (8)(a) above; or

(ii) in a case where a compulsion order imposes a requirement on the offender to reside at a specified place by virtue of subsection (8)(e) above,

such directions as the court thinks fit for the removal of the offender to, and the detention of the offender in, a place of safety pending the offender's admission to the specified hospital or, as the case may be, place.

(15) Where the court makes a compulsion order in relation to an offender, the court—

(a) shall not—

(i) make an order under section 200 of this Act;

(ii) make an interim compulsion order;

(iii) make a guardianship order;

(iv) pass a sentence of imprisonment;

(v) impose a fine;

[F102. (vi)impose a community payback order;

(vii) make a drug treatment and testing order; or

(viii)make a restriction of liberty order,]

in relation to the offender;

(b) may make any other order that the court has power to make apart from this section.

(16) In this section—

"care home service" has the meaning given by [F103paragraph 2 of schedule 12 to the Public Services Reform (Scotland) Act 2010] ;

"community care services" has the meaning given by section [F10412. A(8)] of the Social Work (Scotland) Act 1968 (c. 49);

"medical treatment" has the same meaning as in section 52. D of this Act;

"relevant services" has the meaning given by section [F10520. (2)] of the Children (Scotland) Act 1995 (c. 36);

"responsible medical officer", in relation to an offender, means the responsible medical officer appointed in respect of the offender under section 230 of the Mental Health (Care and Treatment)(Scotland) Act 2003 (asp 13);

"restriction order" means an order under section 59 of this Act;

"sentence of imprisonment" includes any sentence or order for detention; and

"specified" means specified in the compulsion order.

Amendments (Textual)

F99. Words in s. 57. A(2) substituted (30.9.2017) by Mental Health (Scotland) Act 2015 (asp 9), ss. 43. (2)(a), 61. (2); S.S.I. 2017/197, art. 2, sch.

F100. S. 57. A(2. A) inserted (30.9.2017) by Mental Health (Scotland) Act 2015 (asp 9), ss. 43. (2)(b), 61. (2); S.S.I. 2017/197, art. 2, sch.

F101. Words in s. 57. A(5)(b) substituted (30.9.2017) by Mental Health (Scotland) Act 2015 (asp 9), ss. 43. (2)(c), 61. (2); S.S.I. 2017/197, art. 2, sch.

F102. S. 57. A(15)(a)(vi)-(viii) substituted for s. 57. A(15)(a)(vi)(vii) (1.2.2011) by Criminal Justice and Licensing (Scotland) Act 2010 (asp 13), ss. 14. (2), 206. (1), Sch. 2 para. 5; S.S.I. 2010/413, art. 2, Sch. (with art. 3)

F103. Words in s. 57. A(16) substituted (1.4.2011) by The Public Services Reform (Scotland) Act 2010 (Consequential Modifications) Order 2011 (S.S.I. 2011/211), art. 1, sch. 1 para. 7

F104. Word in s. 57. A(16) substituted (1.4.2015) by The Public Bodies (Joint Working) (Scotland) Act 2014 (Consequential Modifications and Saving) Order 2015 (S.S.I. 2015/157), art. 1. (1), sch. para. 3

F105. Word in s. 57. A(16) substituted (1.4.2017) by Children and Young People (Scotland) Act 2014 (asp 8), s. 102. (3), sch. 5 para. 5. (3); S.S.I. 2016/254, art. 3. (3)(c)

57. BCompulsion order authorising detention in hospital or requiring residence at place: ancillary provisionS

(1) Where a compulsion order—

    (a) authorises the detention of an offender in a specified hospital; or

    (b) imposes a requirement on an offender to reside at a specified place,

this section authorises the removal, before the [F106end of the day following the] 7 days beginning with the day on which the order is made, of the offender to the specified hospital or place, by any of the persons mentioned in subsection (2) below.

(2) Those persons are—

    (a) a constable;

    (b) a person employed in, or contracted to provide services in or to, the specified hospital who is authorised by the managers of that hospital to remove persons to hospital for the purposes of this section; and

    (c) a specified person.

(3) In this section, "specified" means specified in the compulsion order.

Amendments (Textual)

F106. Words in s. 57. B(1) substituted (30.9.2017) by Mental Health (Scotland) Act 2015 (asp 9), ss. 43. (3), 61. (2); S.S.I. 2017/197, art. 2, sch. (with art. 22. (a))

57. CMental health officer's reportS

(1) This section applies where the court is considering making a compulsion order in relation to an offender under section 57. A of this Act.

(2) If directed to do so by the court, the mental health officer shall—

    (a) subject to subsection (3) below, interview the offender; and

    (b) prepare a report in relation to the offender in accordance with subsection (4) below.

(3) If it is impracticable for the mental health officer to comply with the requirement in subsection (2)(a) above, the mental health officer need not do so.

(4) The report shall state—

(a) the name and address of the offender;

(b) if known by the mental health officer, the name and address of the offender's primary carer;

(c) in so far as relevant for the purposes of section 57. A of this Act, details of the personal circumstances of the offender; and

(d) any other information that the mental health officer considers relevant for the purposes of that section.

(5) In this section—

"carer", and "primary", in relation to a carer, have the meanings given by section 329. (1) of the Mental Health (Care and Treatment)(Scotland) Act 2003 (asp 13);

"mental health officer" means a person appointed (or deemed to be appointed) under section 32. (1) of that Act; and

"named person" has the meaning given by section 329. (1) of that Act.

57. DCompulsion order: supplementaryS

(1) If, before the [F107end of the day following the] 7 days beginning with the day on which a compulsion order authorising detention of the offender in a hospital is made, it appears to the court, or, as the case may be, the Scottish Ministers, that, by reason of emergency or other special circumstances, it is not reasonably practicable for the offender to be admitted to the hospital specified in the order, the court, or, as the case may be, the Scottish Ministers, may direct that the offender be admitted to the hospital specified in the direction.

(2) Where—

(a) the court makes a direction under subsection (1) above, it shall inform the person having custody of the offender; and

(b) the Scottish Ministers make such a direction, they shall inform—

(i) the court; and

(ii) the person having custody of the offender.

(3) Where a direction is made under subsection (1) above, the compulsion order shall have effect as if the hospital specified in the direction were the hospital specified in the order.

(4) In this section, "court" means the court which made the compulsion order.]

Amendments (Textual)

F107. Words in s. 57. D(1) substituted (30.9.2017) by Mental Health (Scotland) Act 2015 (asp 9), ss. 43. (4), 61. (2); S.S.I. 2017/197, art. 2, sch. (with art. 22. (b))

Modifications etc. (not altering text)

C3. S. 57. D(1) modified (5.10.2005) by The Mental Health (Care and Treatment) (Scotland) Act 2003 (Transitional and Savings Provisions) Order 2005 (S.S.I. 2005/452), art. 9. (5)

Hospital orders and guardianshipS

58 Order for hospital admission or guardianship.S

[F108. (1)F109. . . . .

(1. A)Where a person is convicted [F110in the High Court or the sheriff court of an offence, other than an offence the sentence for which is fixed by law, punishable by that court with imprisonment,] and the court is satisfied—

(a) on the evidence of two medical practitioners (complying with section 61 of this Act and with any requirements imposed under section 57. (3) of the Adults with Incapacity (Scotland) Act 2000 (asp 4)) that the grounds set out in section 58. (1)(a) of that Act apply in relation to the offender;

(b) that no other means provided by or under this Act would be sufficient to enable the offender's interests in his personal welfare to be safeguarded or promoted, the court may, subject to subsection (2) below, by order place the offender's personal welfare under the guardianship of such local authority or of such other person approved by a local authority as may be specified in the order.]

(2) Where the case is remitted by the sheriff to the High Court for sentence under any enactment, the power to make an order under [F111subsection F112. . . (1. A)] above shall be exercisable by that court.

(3) Where in the case of a person charged summarily in the sheriff court with an act or omission constituting an offence the court would have power, on convicting him, to make an order under [F111subsection F112. . . (1. A)] above, then, if it is satisfied that the person did the act or made the omission charged, the court may, if it thinks fit, make such an order without convicting him.

(4) F113. . . . .

(5) F113. . . . .

[F114. (6)An order placing a person under the guardianship of a local authority or of any other person (in this Act referred to as "a guardianship order") shall not be made under this section unless the court is satisfied—

(a) on the report of a mental health officer (complying with any requirements imposed by section 57. (3) of the Adults with Incapacity (Scotland) Act 2000 (asp 4)) giving his opinion as to the general appropriateness of the order sought, based on an interview and assessment of the person carried out not more than 30 days before it makes the order, that it is necessary in the interests of the personal welfare of the person that he should be placed under guardianship;

(b) that any person nominated to be appointed a guardian is suitable to be so appointed;

(c) that the authority or person is willing to receive that person into guardianship; and

(d) that there is no other guardianship order, under this Act or the Adults with Incapacity (Scotland) Act 2000 (asp 4), in force relating to the [F115person's personal welfare which makes the same provision as the guardianship order which the court proposes to make under this section] .]

(7) A F116. . . guardianship order [F117made under this section] shall specify [F118 (by reference to the appropriate paragraph (or paragraphs) of the definition of "mental disorder" in section 328. (1) of the Mental Health (Care and Treatment)(Scotland) Act 2003 (asp 13)) the type (or types) of mental disorder that the [F119person] has] ; and no such order shall be made unless [F120the descriptions of the [F119person's] mental disorder by each of the medical practitioners, whose evidence is taken into account under subsection (1. A)(a) above, specifies at least one type of mental disorder that is also specified by the other].

(8) Where an order is made under this section, the court shall not pass sentence of imprisonment or impose a fine or [F121impose a community payback order or make a drug treatment and testing order] in respect of the offence, but may make any other order which the court has power to make apart from this section; and for the purposes of this subsection "sentence of imprisonment" includes any sentence or order for detention.

(9) F122. . . . .

(10) F122. . . . .

[F123. (11)Section 58. A of this Act shall have effect as regards guardianship orders made under F124. . . this section.]

Amendments (Textual)

F108. S. 58. (1)(1. A) substituted for s. 58. (1) (1.4.2002) by 2000 asp 4, s. 88. (2), Sch. 5 para. 26. (2)(a); S.S.I. 2001/81, art. 3, Sch. 2

F109. S. 58. (1) repealed (5.10.2005) by Mental Health (Care and Treatment) (Scotland) Act 2003 (asp 13), ss. 331. (2)(3), 333. (1)-(4), Sch. 5 Pt. 1; S.S.I. 2005/161, art. 3

F110. Words in s. 58. (1. A) substituted (5.10.2005) by Mental Health (Care and Treatment) (Scotland) Act 2003 (asp 13), ss. 331. (1), 333. (1)-(4), Sch. 4 para. 8. (4)(a); S.S.I. 2005/161, art. 3

F111. Words in s. 58. (2)(3)(10) substituted (1.4.2002) by 2000 asp 4, s. 88. (2), Sch. 5 para. 26. (2)(b); S.S.I. 2001/81, art. 3, Sch. 2

F112. Words in s. 58. (2)(3) repealed (5.10.2005) by Mental Health (Care and Treatment)

(Scotland) Act 2003 (asp 13), ss. 331. (2)(3), 333. (1)-(4), Sch. 5 Pt. 1; S.S.I. 2005/161, art. 3

F113. S. 58. (4)(5) repealed (5.10.2005) by Mental Health (Care and Treatment) (Scotland) Act 2003 (asp 13), ss. 331. (2)(3), 333. (1)-(4), Sch. 5 Pt. 1; S.S.I. 2005/161, art. 3

F114. S. 58. (6) substituted (1.4.2002) by 2000 asp 4, s. 88. (2), Sch. 5 para. 26. (2)(d); S.S.I. 2001/81, art. 3, Sch. 2

F115. Words in s. 58. (6)(d) substituted (5.10.2007) by Adult Support and Protection (Scotland) Act 2007 (asp 10), ss. 77. (1), 79, Sch. 1 para. 4. (a); S.S.I. 2007/334, art. 2. (b), Sch. 2

F116. Words in s. 58. (7) repealed (5.10.2005) by Mental Health (Care and Treatment) (Scotland) Act 2003 (asp 13), ss. 331. (2)(3), 333. (1)-(4), Sch. 5 Pt. 1; S.S.I. 2005/161, art. 3

F117. Words in s. 58. (7) inserted (5.10.2007) by Adult Support and Protection (Scotland) Act 2007 (asp 10), ss. 77. (1), 79, Sch. 1 para. 4. (b)(i); S.S.I. 2007/334, art. 2. (b), Sch. 2

F118. Words in s. 58. (7) substituted (5.10.2005) by Mental Health (Care and Treatment) (Scotland) Act 2003 (asp 13), ss. 331. (1), 333. (1)-(4), Sch. 4 para. 8. (4)(b)(i); S.S.I. 2005/161, art. 3

F119. Word in s. 58. (7) substituted (5.10.2007) by Adult Support and Protection (Scotland) Act 2007 (asp 10), ss. 77. (1), 79, Sch. 1 para. 4. (b)(ii); S.S.I. 2007/334, art. 2. (b), Sch. 2

F120. Words in s. 58. (7) substituted (5.10.2005) by Mental Health (Care and Treatment) (Scotland) Act 2003 (asp 13), ss. 331. (1), 333. (1)-(4), Sch. 4 para. 8. (4)(b)(ii); S.S.I. 2005/161, art. 3

F121. Words in s. 58. (8) substituted (1.2.2011) by Criminal Justice and Licensing (Scotland) Act 2010 (asp 13), ss. 14. (2), 206. (1), Sch. 2 para. 6; S.S.I. 2010/413, art. 2, Sch. (with art. 3)

F122. S. 58. (9)(10) repealed (5.10.2005) by Mental Health (Care and Treatment) (Scotland) Act 2003 (asp 13), ss. 331. (2)(3), 333. (1)-(4), Sch. 5 Pt. 1; S.S.I. 2005/161, art. 3

F123. S. 58. (11) inserted (1.4.2002) by 2000 asp 4, s. 88. (2), Sch. 5 para. 26. (2)(e); S.S.I. 2001/81, art. 3, Sch. 2

F124. Words in s. 58. (11) repealed (5.10.2005) by Mental Health (Care and Treatment) (Scotland) Act 2003 (asp 13), ss. 331. (2)(3), 333. (1)-(4), Sch. 5 Pt. 1; S.S.I. 2005/161, art. 3

Modifications etc. (not altering text)

C4. S. 58 extended (1.1.1998) by 1997 c. 48, s. 9. (1)(b) (subject to s. 9. (2)); S.I. 1997/2323, art. 4, Sch. 2 (subject to art. 7)

[F12558. A Application of Adults with Incapacity (Scotland) Act 2000. S

(1) Subject to the provisions of this section, the provisions of Parts 1, 5, 6 and 7 of the Adults with Incapacity (Scotland) Act 2000 (asp 4) ("the 2000 Act") apply—

(a) to a guardian appointed by an order of the court under section 57. (2)(c), 58. (1) or 58. (1. A) of this Act (in this section referred to as a "guardianship order") whether appointed before or after the coming into force of these provisions, as they apply to a guardian with powers relating to the personal welfare of an adult appointed under section 58 of that Act;

(b) to a person authorised under an intervention order under section [F12660. B] of this Act as they apply to a person so authorised under section 53 of that Act.

(2) In making a guardianship order the court shall have regard to any regulations made by the Scottish Ministers under section 64. (11) of the 2000 Act and—

(a) shall confer powers, which it shall specify in the order, relating only to the personal welfare of the person;

(b) may appoint a joint guardian;

(c) may appoint a substitute guardian;

(d) may make such consequential or ancillary order, provision or direction as it considers appropriate.

(3) Without prejudice to the generality of subsection (2), or to any other powers conferred by this Act, the court may—

(a) make any order granted by it subject to such conditions and restrictions as appear to it to be appropriate;

(b) order that any reports relating to the person who will be the subject of the order be lodged with the court or that the person be assessed or interviewed and that a report of such assessment or interview be lodged;

(c) make such further inquiry or call for such further information as appears to it to be appropriate;

(d) make such interim order as appears to it to be appropriate pending the disposal of the proceedings.

(4) Where the court makes a guardianship order it shall forthwith send a copy of the interlocutor containing the order to the Public Guardian who shall—

(a) enter prescribed particulars of the appointment in the register maintained by him under section 6. (2)(b)(iv) of the 2000 Act;

(b) unless he considers that the notification would be likely to pose a serious risk to the person's health notify the person of the appointment of the guardian; and

(c) notify the local authority and the Mental Welfare Commission of the terms of the interlocutor.

(5) A guardianship order shall continue in force for a period of 3 years or such other period (including an indefinite period) as, on cause shown, the court may determine.

(6) Where any proceedings for the appointment of a guardian under section 57. (2)(c) or 58. (1) of this Act have been commenced and not determined before the date of coming into force of section 84 of, and paragraph 26 of schedule 5 to, the Adults with Incapacity (Scotland) Act 2000 (asp 4) they shall be determined in accordance with this Act as it was immediately in force before that date.]

Amendments (Textual)

F125. S. 58. A inserted (1.4.2002) by 2000 asp 4, s. 84. (2); S.S.I. 2001/81, art. 3, Sch. 2

F126. S. 58. A: "In section 84 (applications to guardians appointed under Criminal Procedure (Scotland) Act 1995 (c. 46), in subsection (1)(b) of the section prospectively inserted by subsection (2), for the words "60. A" there is substituted "60. B"" (1.4.2002) by virtue of 2001 asp 8, s. 79, Sch. 3 para. 23. (5); S.S.I. 2002/162, art. 2. (h) (subject to arts. 3-13)

59 Hospital orders: restrictions on discharge.S

(1) Where a [F127compulsion order authorising the detention of a person in a hospital by virtue of paragraph (a) of section 57. A(8) of this Act] is made in respect of a person, and it appears to the court—

(a) having regard to the nature of the offence with which he is charged;

(b) the antecedents of the person; and

(c) the risk that as a result of his mental disorder he would commit offences if set at large, that it is necessary for the protection of the public from serious harm so to do, the court may, subject to the provisions of this section, further order that the person shall be subject to the special restrictions set out in [F128. Part 10 of the Mental Health (Care and Treatment)(Scotland) Act 2003 (asp 13)] , without limit of time.

(2) An order under this section (in this Act referred to as "a restriction order") shall not be made in the case of any person unless the [F129approved medical practitioner] , whose evidence is taken into account by the court under [F130section 57. A(2)(a)] of this Act, has given evidence orally before the court.

[F131. (2. A)The court may, in the case of a person in respect of whom it did not, before making the compulsion order, make an interim compulsion order, make a restriction order in respect of the person only if satisfied that, in all the circumstances, it was not appropriate to make an interim compulsion order in respect of the person.]

(3) F132. . . . .

Amendments (Textual)

F127. Words in s. 59. (1) substituted (5.10.2005) by Mental Health (Care and Treatment) (Scotland) Act 2003 (asp 13), ss. 331. (1), 333. (1)-(4), Sch. 4 para. 8. (5)(a)(i); S.S.I. 2005/161, art. 3

F128. Words in s. 59. (1) substituted (5.10.2005) by Mental Health (Care and Treatment) (Scotland) Act 2003 (asp 13), ss. 331. (1), 333. (1)-(4), Sch. 4 para. 8. (5)(a)(ii); S.S.I. 2005/161, art. 3

F129. Words in s. 59. (2) substituted (5.10.2005) by Mental Health (Care and Treatment) (Scotland) Act 2003 (asp 13), ss. 331. (1), 333. (1)-(4), Sch. 4 para. 8. (5)(b)(i); S.S.I. 2005/161, art. 3

F130. Words in s. 59. (2) substituted (5.10.2005) by Mental Health (Care and Treatment) (Scotland) Act 2003 (asp 13), ss. 331. (1), 333. (1)-(4), Sch. 4 para. 8. (5)(b)(ii); S.S.I. 2005/161, art. 3

F131. S. 59. (2. A) inserted (5.10.2005) by Mental Health (Care and Treatment) (Scotland) Act 2003 (asp 13), ss. 331. (1), 333. (1)-(4), Sch. 4 para. 8. (5)(c); S.S.I. 2005/161, art. 3

F132. S. 59. (3) repealed (5.10.2005) by Mental Health (Care and Treatment) (Scotland) Act 2003 (asp 13), ss. 331. (2)(3), 333. (1)(-(4), {Sch. 5 Pt. 1}; S.S.I. 2005/161 {art. 3}

[F133. Hospital directions]S

Amendments (Textual)

F133. Ss. 59. A-59. C and preceding cross-heading substituted for s. 59. A (5.10.2005) by Mental Health (Care and Treatment) (Scotland) Act 2003 (asp 13), ss. 331. (1), 333. (1)-(4), Sch. 4 para. 8. (6); S.S.I. 2005/161, art. 3

[F13459. AHospital directionS

(1) This section applies where a person, not being a child, (in this section and in sections 59. B and 59. C of this Act referred to as the "offender") is convicted on indictment in—

    (a) the High Court; or

    (b) the sheriff court,

of an offence punishable by imprisonment.

(2) If the court is satisfied—

    (a) on the written or oral evidence of two medical practitioners—

(i) that the conditions mentioned in subsection (3) below are met in respect of the offender; and

(ii) as to the matters mentioned in subsection (4) below; and

    (b) that, having regard to the matters mentioned in subsection (5) below, it is appropriate,

the court may, in addition to any sentence of imprisonment which it has the power or the duty to impose, make, subject to subsection (6) below, a direction (in this Act referred to as a "hospital direction") authorising the measures mentioned in subsection (7) below.

(3) The conditions referred to in subsection (2)(a)(i) above are—

    (a) that the offender has a mental disorder;

    (b) that medical treatment which would be likely to—

(i) prevent the mental disorder worsening; or

(ii) alleviate any of the symptoms, or effects, of the disorder,

is available for the offender;

    (c) that if the offender were not provided with such medical treatment there would be a significant risk—

(i) to the health, safety or welfare of the offender; or

(ii) to the safety of any other person; and

    (d) that the making of a hospital direction in respect of the offender is necessary.

(4) The matters referred to in subsection (2)(a)(ii) above are—

(a) that the hospital proposed by the two medical practitioners mentioned in subsection (2)(a) above is suitable for the purpose of giving the medical treatment mentioned in paragraph (b) of subsection (3) above to the offender; and

(b) that, were a hospital direction made, the offender could be admitted to such hospital before the [F135end of the day following the] 7 days beginning with the day on which the direction is made.

(5) The matters referred to in subsection (2)(b) above are—

(a) the mental health officer's report, prepared in accordance with section 59. B of this Act, in respect of the offender;

(b) all the circumstances, including—

(i) the nature of the offence of which the offender was convicted; and

(ii) the antecedents of the offender; and

(c) any alternative means of dealing with the offender.

(6) A hospital direction may authorise detention in a state hospital only if, on the written or oral evidence of the two medical practitioners mentioned in subsection (2)(a) above, it appears to the court—

(a) that the offender requires to be detained in a state hospital under conditions of special security; and

(b) that such conditions of special security can be provided only in a state hospital.

(7) The measures mentioned in subsection (2) above are—

(a) in the case of an offender who, when the hospital direction is made, has not been admitted to the specified hospital, the removal, before the [F136end of the day following the] 7 days beginning with the day on which the direction is made, of the offender to the specified hospital by—

(i) a constable;

(ii) a person employed in, or contracted to provide services in or to, the specified hospital who is authorised by the managers of that hospital to remove persons to hospital for the purposes of this section; or

(iii) a specified person;

(b) the detention of the offender in the specified hospital; and

(c) the giving to the offender, in accordance with Part 16 of the Mental Health (Care and Treatment) (Scotland) Act 2003 (asp 13), of medical treatment.

(8) The court shall be satisfied as to the condition mentioned in subsection (3)(a) above only if the description of the offender's mental disorder by each of the medical practitioners mentioned in subsection (2)(a) above specifies, by reference to the appropriate paragraph (or paragraphs) of the definition of "mental disorder" in section 328. (1) of the Mental Health (Care and Treatment) (Scotland) Act 2003 (asp 13), at least one type of mental disorder that the offender has that is also specified by the other.

(9) A hospital direction—

(a) shall specify, by reference to the appropriate paragraph (or paragraphs) of the definition of "mental disorder" in section 328. (1) of the Mental Health (Care and Treatment) (Scotland) Act 2003 (asp 13), the type (or types) of mental disorder that each of the medical practitioners mentioned in subsection (2)(a) above specifies that is also specified by the other; and

(b) may include such directions as the court thinks fit for the removal of the offender to, and the detention of the offender in, a place of safety pending the offender's admission to the specified hospital.

(10) In this section—

"medical treatment" has the same meaning as in section 52. D of this Act; and

"specified" means specified in the hospital direction.]

Amendments (Textual)

F134. Ss. 59. A-59. C and preceding cross-heading substituted for s. 59. A (5.10.2005) by Mental Health (Care and Treatment) (Scotland) Act 2003 (asp 13), ss. 331. (1), 333. (1)-(4), Sch. 4 para. 8. (6); S.S.I. 2005/161, art. 3

[F13759. BHospital direction: mental health officer's reportS

(1) This section applies where the court is considering making a hospital direction in relation to an offender under section 59. A of this Act.

(2) If directed to do so by the court, the mental health officer shall—

    (a) subject to subsection (3) below, interview the offender; and

    (b) prepare a report in relation to the offender in accordance with subsection (4) below.

(3) If it is impracticable for the mental health officer to comply with the requirement in subsection (2)(a) above, the mental health officer need not do so.

(4) The report shall state—

    (a) the name and address of the offender;

    (b) if known by the mental health officer, the name and address of the offender's primary carer;

    (c) in so far as relevant for the purposes of section 59. A of this Act, details of the personal circumstances of the offender; and

    (d) any other information that the mental health officer considers relevant for the purposes of that section.

(5) In this section, "carer", "primary", in relation to a carer, and "mental health officer" have the same meanings as in section 57. C of this Act.]

Amendments (Textual)

[F13859. CHospital direction: supplementaryS

(1) If, before the [F139end of the day following the] 7 days beginning with the day on which a hospital direction is made, it appears to the court, or, as the case may be, the Scottish Ministers, that, by reason of emergency or other special circumstances, it is not reasonably practicable for the offender to be admitted to the hospital specified in the hospital direction, the court, or, as the case may be, the Scottish Ministers, may direct that the offender be admitted to such other hospital as is specified.

(2) Where—

    (a) the court makes a direction under subsection (1) above, it shall inform the person having custody of the offender; and

    (b) the Scottish Ministers make such a direction, they shall inform—

(i) the court; and

(ii) the person having custody of the offender.

(3) Where a direction is made under subsection (1) above, the hospital direction shall have effect as if the hospital specified in the hospital direction were the hospital specified by the court, or, as the case may be, the Scottish Ministers, under subsection (1) above.

(4) In this section, "court" means the court which made the hospital direction.]

Amendments (Textual)

60 Appeals against hospital orders.S

Where a [F140compulsion] order, interim [F140compulsion] order (but not a [F141extension] thereof), guardianship order [F142, a restriction order or a hospital direction] has been made by a court in respect of a person charged or brought before it, he may without prejudice to any other form of appeal under any rule of law (or, where an interim [F140compulsion] order has been made, to any right of appeal against any other order or sentence which may be imposed), appeal against that [F143order or, as the case may be, direction in] the same manner as against sentence.
Amendments (Textual)
F140. Word in s. 60 substituted (5.10.2005) by Mental Health (Care and Treatment) (Scotland) Act 2003 (asp 13), ss. 331. (1), 333. (1)-(4), Sch. 4 para. 8. (7)(a); S.S.I. 2005/161 {art. 3} (with savings for s. 60 by virtue of S.S.I. 2005/452, art. 33. (19))
F141. Word in s. 60 substituted (5.10.2005) by Mental Health (Care and Treatment) (Scotland) Act 2003 (asp 13), ss. 331. (1), 333. (1)-(4), Sch. 4 para. 8. (7)(b); S.S.I. 2005/161 {art. 3} (with savings for s. 60 by virtue of S.S.I. 2005/452, art. 33. (19))
F142. Words in s. 60 substituted (1.1.1998) by 1997 c. 48, s. 6. (2)(a)(b); S.I. 1997/2323, art. 4, Sch. 2 (subject to art. 7)
F143. Words in s. 60 substituted (1.1.1998) by 1997 c. 48, s. 6. (2)(a)(b); S.I. 1997/2323, art. 4, Sch. 2 (subject to art. 7)

[F14460. A Appeal by prosecutor against hospital orders etc.S

(1) This section applies where the court, in respect of a person charged or brought before it, has made—
   [F145. (a)a compulsion order;
   (b) a restriction order;
   (c) a guardianship order;
   (d) a decision under section 57. (2)(e) of this Act to make no order; or
   (e) a hospital direction.]
(2) Where this section applies, the prosecutor may appeal against any such order, decision or direction as is mentioned in subsection (1) above—
   (a) if it appears to him that the order, decision or direction was inappropriate; or
   (b) on a point of law,
and an appeal under this section shall be treated in the same manner as an appeal against sentence under section 108 of this Act.]
Amendments (Textual)
F144. S. 60. A inserted (1.1.1998) by 1997 c. 48, s. 22; S.I. 1997/2323, art. 4, Sch. 2 (subject to art. 7)
F145. S. 60. A(1)(a)-(e) substituted (5.10.2005) for s. 60. A(1)(a)(b) by Mental Health (Care and Treatment) (Scotland) Act 2003 (asp 13), ss. 331. (1), 333. (1)-(4), Sch. 4 para. 8. (8); S.S.I. 2005/161 {art. 3}

[F14660. B Intervention ordersS

The court may instead of making a [F147compulsion] order F148. . . or a guardianship order under section 57. (2)(c) or 58. (1. A) of this Act, make an intervention order(as defined in section 53. (1) of the Adults with Incapacity (Scotland) Act 2000 (asp 4) where it considers that it would be appropriate to do so.]
Amendments (Textual)
F146. S. 60. B inserted (1.4.2002) by 2000 asp 4, s. 88. (2), Sch. 5 para. 26. (3) (as amended

(1.4.2002) by 2001 asp 8, s. 79, Sch. 3 para. 23. (7); S.S.I. 2001/304, art. 2); S.S.I. 2001/81, art. 3, Sch. 2

F147. Word in s. 60. B substituted (5.10.2005) by Mental Health (Care and Treatment) (Scotland) Act 2003 (asp 13), ss. 331. (1), 333. (1)-(4), Sch. 4 para. 8. (9); S.S.I. 2005/161 {art. 3}

F148. Words in s. 60. B repealed (5.10.2007) by Adult Support and Protection (Scotland) Act 2007 (asp 10), ss. 77. (1), 79, Sch. 1 para. 4. (c); S.S.I. 2007/334, art. 2. (b), Sch. 2

X1[F14960. CAcquitted persons: detention for medical examinationS

(1) Subject to subsection (7) below, this section applies where a person charged with an offence is acquitted.

(2) If the court by or before which the person is acquitted is satisfied—

(a) on the written or oral evidence of two medical practitioners that the conditions mentioned in subsection (3) below are met in respect of the person; and

(b) that it is not practicable to secure the immediate examination of the person by a medical practitioner,

the court may, immediately after the person is acquitted, make an order authorising the measures mentioned in subsection (4) below for the purpose of enabling arrangements to be made for a medical practitioner to carry out a medical examination of the person.

(3) The conditions referred to in subsection (2)(a) above are—

(a) that the person has a mental disorder;

(b) that medical treatment which would be likely to—

(i) prevent the mental disorder worsening; or

(ii) alleviate any of the symptoms, or effects, of the disorder,

is available for the person; and

(c) that if the person were not provided with such medical treatment there would be a significant risk—

(i) to the health, safety or welfare of the person; or

(ii) to the safety of any other person.

(4) The measures referred to in subsection (2) above are—

(a) the removal of the person to a place of safety by—

(i) a constable; or

(ii) a person specified by the court; and

(b) the detention, subject to subsection (6) below, of the person in that place of safety for a period of 6 hours beginning with the time at which the order under subsection (2) above is made.

(5) If the person absconds—

(a) while being removed to a place of safety under subsection (4) above; or

(b) from the place of safety,

a constable or the person specified by the court under paragraph (a) of that subsection may, at any time during the period mentioned in paragraph (b) of that subsection, take the person into custody and remove the person to a place of safety.

(6) An order under this section ceases to authorise detention of a person if, following the medical examination of the person, a medical practitioner grants—

(a) an emergency detention certificate under section 36 of the Mental Health (Care and Treatment) (Scotland) Act 2003 (asp 13); or

(b) a short-term detention certificate under section 44 of that Act.

(7) This section does not apply [F150in a case where the person is acquitted by reason of the special defence set out in section 51. A of this Act.]

F151. (a). . . . .

F151. (b). . . . .

(8) In this section, "medical treatment" has the same meaning as in section 52. D of this Act.

Editorial Information

X1. S. 60. C: With effect from 5.10.2005 s. 60. C became subsumed by new cross-heading" Hospital directions ". Versions of this provision as it stood at any time before that date cannot be accessed directly by navigation from this version. To view those versions, it is recommended that users either conduct an 'advanced search' specifying an 'as at' date earlier than 5.10.2005 or navigate via the Part VI heading.

Amendments (Textual)

F149. Ss. 60. C, 60. D inserted (21.3.2005 for specified purpose and otherwise 5.10.2005) by Mental Health (Care and Treatment) (Scotland) Act 2003 (asp 13), ss. 134, 333. (1)-(4); S.S.I. 2005/161, arts. {2}, {3}

F150. Words in s. 60. C(7) inserted (with application in accordance with art. 3 of the commencing S.S.I.) by Criminal Justice and Licensing (Scotland) Act 2010 (asp 13), s. 206. (1), sch. 7 para. 40. (a); S.S.I. 2012/160, art. 3, sch.

F151. S. 60. C(7)(a)(b) repealed (with application in accordance with art. 3 of the commencing S.S.I.) by Criminal Justice and Licensing (Scotland) Act 2010 (asp 13), s. 206. (1), sch. 7 para. 40. (b); S.S.I. 2012/160, art. 3, sch.

60. DNotification of detention under section 60. CS

(1) This section applies where a person has been removed to a place of safety under section 60. C of this Act.

(2) The court shall, before the expiry of the period of 14 days beginning with the day on which the order under section 60. C(2) of this Act is made, ensure that the Mental Welfare Commission is given notice of the matters mentioned in subsection (3) below.

(3) Those matters are—

    (a) the name and address of the person removed to the place of safety;

    (b) the date on and time at which the person was so removed;

    (c) the address of the place of safety;

    (d) if the person is removed to a police station, the reason why the person was removed there; and

    (e) any other matter that the Scottish Ministers may, by regulations made by statutory instrument, prescribe.

(4) The power conferred by subsection (3)(e) above may be exercised so as to make different provision for different cases or descriptions of case or for different purposes.

(5) A statutory instrument containing regulations under subsection (3)(e) above shall be subject to annulment in pursuance of a resolution of the Scottish Parliament.]

Amendments (Textual)

F149. Ss. 60. C, 60. D inserted (21.3.2005 for specified purpose and otherwise 5.10.2005) by Mental Health (Care and Treatment) (Scotland) Act 2003 (asp 13), ss. 134, 333. (1)-(4); S.S.I. 2005/161, arts. {2}, {3}

[F152. Miscellaneous provision]S

Amendments (Textual)

F152. S. 61 crossheading substituted (30.6.2017) by Mental Health (Scotland) Act 2015 (asp 9), ss. 46. (2), 61. (2); S.S.I. 2017/197, art. 2, sch.

61 Requirements as to medical evidence.S

F153. (1)Of the medical practitioners whose evidence is taken into account [F154in making a finding F155... under any of the relevant provisions], at least one shall be [F156an approved medical practitioner] .

[F157. (1. A)Of the medical practitioners whose evidence is taken into account under section [F15852. M(2)(a), 53. (2)(a)] , 54. (1)(c), [F15957. A(2)(a)] or 59. A(3)(a) and (b) of this Act, at least one shall be employed at the hospital which is to be specified in the order or, as the case may be, direction.]

F160. (2)Written or oral evidence given for the purposes of [F161section 52. D(2)(a) or][F162any of the relevant provisions] shall include a statement as to whether the person giving the evidence is related to the accused and of any pecuniary interest which that person may have in the admission of the accused to hospital or his reception into guardianship.

F153. (3)For the purposes of [F163making a finding under section [F16452. D(2)(a)] F165... of this Act or of any of the relevant provisions] a report in writing purporting to be signed by a medical practitioner may, subject to the provisions of this section, be received in evidence without proof of the signature or qualifications of the practitioner; but the court may, in any case, require that the practitioner by whom such a report was signed be called to give oral evidence.

(4) Where any such report as aforesaid is tendered in evidence, otherwise than by or on behalf of the accused, then—

(a) if the accused is represented by counsel or solicitor, a copy of the report shall be given to his counsel or solicitor;

(b) if the accused is not so represented, the substance of the report shall be disclosed to the accused or, where he is a child under 16 years of age, to his parent or guardian if present in court;

(c) in any case, the accused may require that the practitioner by whom the report was signed be called to give oral evidence, and evidence to rebut the evidence contained in the report may be called by or on behalf of the accused,

and where the court is of the opinion that further time is necessary in the interests of the accused for consideration of that report, or the substance of any such report, it shall adjourn the case.

(5) For the purpose of calling evidence to rebut the evidence contained in any such report as aforesaid, arrangements may be made by or on behalf of an accused person detained in a hospital or, as respects a report for the purposes of [F166section 54. (1)(c) of this Act] , remanded in custody for his examination by any medical practitioner, and any such examination may be made in private.

[F167. (6)In this section the "relevant provisions" means sections [F16852. M(2)(a), 53. (2)(a), 54. (1)(c), 57. A(2)(a), 58. (1. A)(a), 59. A(2)(a) and 60. C(2)(a)] of this Act.

[F169. (7)In this section, "approved medical practitioner" has the meaning given by section 22 of the Mental Health (Care and Treatment)(Scotland) Act 2003 (asp 13).]]

Amendments (Textual)

F153. S. 61. (1)(3): It is provided that for "and 58. (1)(a)" there shall be substituted ", 58. (1)(a) and 58. (1. A)(a)" (1.4.2002) by 2000 asp 4, s. 88. (2), Sch. 5 para. 26. (4)(a)(c); S.S.I. 2001/81, art. 3, Sch. 2

F154. Words in s. 61. (1) substituted (1.1.1998) by 1997 c. 48, s. 10. (2)(a); S.I. 1997/2323, art. 4, Sch. 2 (subject to art. 7)

F155. Words in s. 61. (1) repealed (with application in accordance with art. 3 of the commencing S.S.I.) by Criminal Justice and Licensing (Scotland) Act 2010 (asp 13), s. 206. (1), sch. 7 para. 41. (a); S.S.I. 2012/160, art. 3, sch.

F156. Words in s. 61. (1) substituted (5.10.2005) by Mental Health (Care and Treatment) (Scotland) Act 2003 (asp 13), ss. 331. (1), 333. (1)-(4), Sch. 4 para. 8. (10)(a); S.S.I. 2005/161, art. 3

F157. S. 61. (1. A) inserted (1.1.1998) by 1997 c. 48, s. 10. (2)(b); S.I. 1997/2323, art. 4, Sch. 2 (subject to art. 7)

F158. Words in s. 61. (1. A) substituted (5.10.2005) by Mental Health (Care and Treatment) (Scotland) Act 2003 (asp 13), ss. 331. (1), 333. (1)-(4), Sch. 4 para. 8. (10)(b)(i); S.S.I. 2005/161, art. 3

F159. Words in s. 61. (1. A) substituted (5.10.2005) by Mental Health (Care and Treatment) (Scotland) Act 2003 (asp 13), ss. 331. (1), 333. (1)-(4), Sch. 4 para. 8. (10)(b)(ii); S.S.I. 2005/161, art. 3

F160. S. 61. (2): It is provided that after "section 58. (1)(a)" there shall be inserted "or 58. (1. A)(a)" (1.4.2002) by 2000 asp 4, s. 88. (2), Sch, 5 para. 26. (4)(b); S.S.I. 2001/81, art. 3, Sch. 2

F161. Words in s. 61. (2) inserted (5.10.2005) by Mental Health (Care and Treatment) (Scotland) Act 2003 (asp 13), ss. 331. (1), 333. (1)-(4), Sch. 4 para. 8. (10)(c); S.S.I. 2005/161, art. 3

F162. Words in s. 61. (2) substituted (1.1.1998) by 1997 c. 48, s. 10. (2)(c); S.I. 1997/2323, art. 4, Sch. 2 (subject to art. 7)

F163. Words in s. 61. (3) substituted (1.1.1998) by 1997 c. 48, s. 10. (2)(d); S.I. 1997/2323, art. 4, Sch. 2 (subject to art. 7)

F164. Words in s. 61. (3) inserted (5.10.2005) by Mental Health (Care and Treatment) (Scotland) Act 2003 (asp 13), ss. 331. (1), 333. (1)-(4), Sch. 4 para. 8. (10)(d); S.S.I. 2005/161, art. 3

F165. Words in s. 61. (3) repealed (with application in accordance with art. 3 of the commencing S.S.I.) by Criminal Justice and Licensing (Scotland) Act 2010 (asp 13), s. 206. (1), sch. 7 para. 41. (b); S.S.I. 2012/160, art. 3, sch.

F166. Words in s. 61. (5) substituted (with application in accordance with art. 3 of the commencing S.S.I.) by Criminal Justice and Licensing (Scotland) Act 2010 (asp 13), s. 206. (1), sch. 7 para. 41. (c); S.S.I. 2012/160, art. 3, sch.

F167. S. 61. (6) added (1.1.1998) by 1997 c. 48, s. 10. (2)(e); S.I. 1997/2323, art. 4, Sch. 2 (subject to art. 7)

F168. Words in s. 61. (6) substituted (5.10.2005) by Mental Health (Care and Treatment) (Scotland) Act 2003 (asp 13), ss. 331. (1), 333. (1)-(4), Sch. 4 para. 8. (10)(e); S.S.I. 2005/161, art. 3

F169. S. 61. (7) inserted (5.10.2005) by Mental Health (Care and Treatment) (Scotland) Act 2003 (asp 13), ss. 331. (1), 333. (1)-(4), Sch. 4 para. 8. (10)(f); S.S.I. 2005/161, art. 3

[F17061. ATransfer of person to suitable hospitalS

(1) Subsection (2) below applies in relation to a person who is subject to—
    (a) an assessment order,
    (b) a treatment order,
    (c) an interim compulsion order, or
    (d) a temporary compulsion order (see section 54. (1)(c) of this Act).
(2) The person's responsible medical officer may transfer the person from the specified hospital to another hospital.
(3) The responsible medical officer may transfer the person only if satisfied that, for the purpose for which the order in question is made—
    (a) the specified hospital is not suitable, and
    (b) the other hospital is suitable.
(4) In considering the suitability of each hospital, the responsible medical officer is to have particular regard to the specific requirements and needs in the person's case.
(5) As far before the transfer as practicable, the responsible medical officer must—
    (a) inform the person of the reason for the transfer,
    (b) notify the managers of the specified hospital, and
    (c) obtain the consent of—
(i) the managers of the other hospital, and
(ii) the Scottish Ministers.
(6) As soon after the transfer as practicable, the responsible medical officer must notify—
    (a) any solicitor known by the officer to be acting for the person, and
    (b) the court which made the order in question.
(7) A person may be transferred under subsection (2) above only once with respect to the order in question.
(8) Where a person is transferred under subsection (2) above, the order in question has effect as if

the other hospital were the specified hospital.

(9) In this section—

"managers" has the meaning given by section 329. (1) of the Mental Health (Treatment and Care) Scotland) Act 2003,

"responsible medical officer" has the meaning given by section 329. (4) of that Act,

"specified hospital" means hospital to which the person is admitted by virtue of the order in question.]

Amendments (Textual)

F170. S. 61. A inserted (30.6.2017) by Mental Health (Scotland) Act 2015 (asp 9), ss. 46. (3), 61. (2); S.S.I. 2017/197, art. 2, sch.

[F17161. BSpecification of hospital unitS

(1) A reference in this Part to a hospital may be read as a reference to a hospital unit.

(2) In the operation of section 61. A of this Act in relation to a transfer from one hospital unit to another within the same hospital—

   (a) subsection (2) of that section applies by virtue of subsection (1) of that section where the order in question specifies the hospital unit in which the person is to be detained,

   (b) in subsection (5) of that section—

(i) paragraph (b) is to be ignored,

(ii) in paragraph (c)(i), the reference to the managers of the other hospital is to be read as a reference to the managers of the hospital in which the person is detained.

(3) For the purposes of this section, "hospital unit" means any part of a hospital which is treated as a separate unit.]

Amendments (Textual)

F171. S. 61. B inserted (30.6.2017) by virtue of Mental Health (Scotland) Act 2015 (asp 9), ss. 47. (2), 61. (2); S.S.I. 2017/197, art. 2, sch.

Appeals under Part VIS

62 Appeal by accused [F172not criminally responsible or unfit for trial] .S

(1) A person may appeal to the [F173appropriate Appeal Court] against—

   (a) a finding made under section 54. (1) of this Act that he is [F174unfit for trial] so that his trial cannot proceed or continue, or the refusal of the court to make such a finding;

   (b) a finding under section 55. (2) of this Act; or

   (c) an order made under section 57. (2) of this Act.

(2) An appeal under subsection (1) above shall be—

   (a) in writing; and

   (b) lodged—

(i) in the case of an appeal under paragraph (a) of that subsection, not later than seven days after the date of the finding or refusal which is the subject of the appeal;

(ii) in the case of an appeal under paragraph (b), or both paragraphs (b) and (c) of that subsection, not later than 28 days after the conclusion of the examination of facts;

(iii) in the case of an appeal under paragraph (c) of that subsection against an order made on an acquittal, by [F175reason of the special defence set out in section 51. A of this Act] , not later than 14 days after the date of the acquittal;

(iv) in the case of an appeal under that paragraph against an order made on a finding under section 55. (2), not later than 14 days after the conclusion of the examination of facts, or within such longer period as the [F176appropriate Appeal Court] may, on cause shown, allow.

(3) Where the examination of facts was held in connection with proceedings on indictment, subsections (1)(a) and (2)(b)(i) above are without prejudice to section 74. (1) of this Act.

(4) Where an appeal is taken under subsection (1) above, the period from the date on which the appeal was lodged until it is withdrawn or disposed of shall not count towards any time limit applying in respect of the case.

(5) An appellant in an appeal under this section shall be entitled to be present at the hearing of the appeal unless the [F177appropriate Appeal Court] determines that his presence is not practicable or appropriate.

(6) In disposing of an appeal under subsection (1) above the [F178appropriate Appeal Court] may—

(a) affirm the decision of the court of first instance;

(b) make any other finding or order which that court could have made at the time when it made the finding [F179, order or other disposal] which is the subject of the appeal; or

(c) remit the case to that court with such directions in the matter as the [F178appropriate Appeal Court] thinks fit.

(7) Section 60 of this Act shall not apply in relation to any order as respects which a person has a right of appeal under subsection (1)(c) above.

[F180. (8)In this section, "appropriate Appeal Court" means—

(a) in the case of an appeal under subsection (1) against a finding or refusal, or an order made, in proceedings on indictment, the High Court;

(b) in the case of an appeal under subsection (1) against a finding or refusal, or an order made, in summary proceedings, the Sheriff Appeal Court.]

Amendments (Textual)

F172. Words in s. 62 heading substituted (with application in accordance with art. 3 of the commencing S.S.I.) by Criminal Justice and Licensing (Scotland) Act 2010 (asp 13), s. 206. (1), sch. 7 para. 42; S.S.I. 2012/160, art. 3, sch.

F173. Words in s. 62. (1) substituted (22.9.2015) by The Courts Reform (Scotland) Act 2014 (Consequential Provisions No. 2) Order 2015 (S.S.I. 2015/338), art. 1, sch. 2 para. 5. (2)(a) (with art. 4)

F174. Words in s. 62. (1)(a) substituted (with application in accordance with art. 3 of the commencing S.S.I.) by Criminal Justice and Licensing (Scotland) Act 2010 (asp 13), s. 206. (1), sch. 7 para. 42. (a); S.S.I. 2012/160, art. 3, sch.

F175. Words in s. 62. (2)(b)(iii) substituted (with application in accordance with art. 3 of the commencing S.S.I.) by Criminal Justice and Licensing (Scotland) Act 2010 (asp 13), s. 206. (1), sch. 7 para. 42. (b); S.S.I. 2012/160, art. 3, sch.

F176. Words in s. 62. (2) substituted (22.9.2015) by The Courts Reform (Scotland) Act 2014 (Consequential Provisions No. 2) Order 2015 (S.S.I. 2015/338), art. 1, sch. 2 para. 5. (2)(a) (with art. 4)

F177. Words in s. 62. (5) substituted (22.9.2015) by The Courts Reform (Scotland) Act 2014 (Consequential Provisions No. 2) Order 2015 (S.S.I. 2015/338), art. 1, sch. 2 para. 5. (2)(a) (with art. 4)

F178. Words in s. 62. (6) substituted (22.9.2015) by The Courts Reform (Scotland) Act 2014 (Consequential Provisions No. 2) Order 2015 (S.S.I. 2015/338), art. 1, sch. 2 para. 5. (2)(a) (with art. 4)

F179. Words in s. 62. (6)(b) substituted (1.1.1998) by 1997 c. 48, s. 62. (1), Sch. 1 para. 21. (7); S.I. 1997/2323, art. 4, Sch. 2 (subject to art. 7)

F180. S. 62. (8) inserted (22.9.2015) by The Courts Reform (Scotland) Act 2014 (Consequential Provisions No. 2) Order 2015 (S.S.I. 2015/338), art. 1, sch. 2 para. 5. (2)(b) (with art. 4)

63 Appeal by prosecutor [F181where accused found not criminally responsible or unfit for trial].S

(1) The prosecutor may appeal to the [F182appropriate Appeal Court] on a point of law against—

(a) a finding under subsection (1) of section 54 of this Act that an accused is [F183unfit for trial] so that his trial cannot proceed or continue;

[F184. (b)an acquittal by reason of the special defence set out in section 51. A of this Act;]

(c) an acquittal under section 55. (3) of this Act (whether or not [F185by reason of the special defence set out in section 51. A of this Act]); or

F186. (d). . . . .

(2) An appeal under subsection (1) above shall be—

(a) in writing; and

(b) lodged—

(i) in the case of an appeal under paragraph (a) or (b) of that subsection, not later than seven days after the finding or, as the case may be, the acquittal which is the subject of the appeal;

(ii) in the case of an appeal under paragraph (c) F187. . .of that subsection, not later than seven days after the conclusion of the examination of facts,

or within such longer period as the [F188appropriate Appeal Court] may, on cause shown, allow.

(3) Where the examination of facts was held in connection with proceedings on indictment, subsections (1)(a) and (2)(b)(i) above are without prejudice to section 74. (1) of this Act.

(4) A respondent in an appeal under this subsection shall be entitled to be present at the hearing of the appeal unless the [F189appropriate Appeal Court] determines that his presence is not practicable or appropriate.

(5) In disposing of an appeal under subsection (1) above the [F190appropriate Appeal Court] may—

(a) affirm the decision of the court of first instance;

(b) make any other finding [F191order or disposal] which that court could have made at the time when it made the finding [F191or acquittal] which is the subject of the appeal; or

(c) remit the case to that court with such directions in the matter as the [F190appropriate Appeal Court] thinks fit.

(6) In this section, "the prosecutor" means, in relation to proceedings on indictment, the Lord Advocate.

[F192. (7)In this section, "appropriate Appeal Court" means—

(a) in the case of an appeal under subsection (1) against a finding or an acquittal made in proceedings on indictment, the High Court;

(b) in the case of an appeal under subsection (1) against a finding or an acquittal made in summary proceedings, the Sheriff Appeal Court.]

Amendments (Textual)

F181. Words in s. 63 heading substituted (with application in accordance with art. 3 of the commencing S.S.I.) by Criminal Justice and Licensing (Scotland) Act 2010 (asp 13), s. 206. (1), sch. 7 para. 43; S.S.I. 2012/160, art. 3, sch.

F182. Words in s. 63. (1) substituted (22.9.2015) by The Courts Reform (Scotland) Act 2014 (Consequential Provisions No. 2) Order 2015 (S.S.I. 2015/338), art. 1, sch. 2 para. 5. (3)(a) (with art. 4)

F183. Words in s. 63. (1)(a) substituted (with application in accordance with art. 3 of the commencing S.S.I.) by Criminal Justice and Licensing (Scotland) Act 2010 (asp 13), s. 206. (1), sch. 7 para. 43. (a); S.S.I. 2012/160, art. 3, sch.

F184. S. 63. (1)(b) substituted (with application in accordance with art. 3 of the commencing S.S.I.) by Criminal Justice and Licensing (Scotland) Act 2010 (asp 13), s. 206. (1), sch. 7 para. 43. (b); S.S.I. 2012/160, art. 3, sch.

F185. Words in s. 63. (1)(c) substituted (with application in accordance with art. 3 of the commencing S.S.I.) by Criminal Justice and Licensing (Scotland) Act 2010 (asp 13), s. 206. (1), sch. 7 para. 43. (c); S.S.I. 2012/160, art. 3, sch.

F186. S. 63. (1)(d) repealed (1.1.1998) by 1997 c. 48, s. 62. (1)(2), Sch. 1 para. 21. (8)(a), Sch. 3; S.I. 1997/2323, art. 4, Sch. 2 (subject to art. 7)

F187. Words in s. 63. (2)(b)(ii) repealed (1.1.1998) by 1997 c. 48, s. 62. (1)(2), Sch. 1 para. 21. (8)(b), Sch. 3; S.I. 1997/2323, art. 4, Sch. 2 (subject to art. 7)

F188. Words in s. 63. (2) substituted (22.9.2015) by The Courts Reform (Scotland) Act 2014 (Consequential Provisions No. 2) Order 2015 (S.S.I. 2015/338), art. 1, sch. 2 para. 5. (3)(a) (with art. 4)

F189. Words in s. 63. (4) substituted (22.9.2015) by The Courts Reform (Scotland) Act 2014 (Consequential Provisions No. 2) Order 2015 (S.S.I. 2015/338), art. 1, sch. 2 para. 5. (3)(a) (with art. 4)

F190. Words in s. 63. (5) substituted (22.9.2015) by The Courts Reform (Scotland) Act 2014 (Consequential Provisions No. 2) Order 2015 (S.S.I. 2015/338), art. 1, sch. 2 para. 5. (3)(a) (with art. 4)

F191. Words in s. 63. (5)(b) substituted (1.1.1998) by 1997 c. 48, s. 62. (1), Sch. 1 para. 21. (8)(c)(i)(ii); S.I. 1997/2323, art. 4, Sch. 2 (subject to art. 7)

F192. S. 63. (7) inserted (22.9.2015) by The Courts Reform (Scotland) Act 2014 (Consequential Provisions No. 2) Order 2015 (S.S.I. 2015/338), art. 1, sch. 2 para. 5. (3)(b) (with art. 4)

Appeals under Part VI

62 Appeal by accused [F1not criminally responsible or unfit for trial] .S

(1) A person may appeal to the [F2appropriate Appeal Court] against—

(a) a finding made under section 54. (1) of this Act that he is [F3unfit for trial] so that his trial cannot proceed or continue, or the refusal of the court to make such a finding;

(b) a finding under section 55. (2) of this Act; or

(c) an order made under section 57. (2) of this Act.

(2) An appeal under subsection (1) above shall be—

(a) in writing; and

(b) lodged—

(i) in the case of an appeal under paragraph (a) of that subsection, not later than seven days after the date of the finding or refusal which is the subject of the appeal;

(ii) in the case of an appeal under paragraph (b), or both paragraphs (b) and (c) of that subsection, not later than 28 days after the conclusion of the examination of facts;

(iii) in the case of an appeal under paragraph (c) of that subsection against an order made on an acquittal, by [F4reason of the special defence set out in section 51. A of this Act] , not later than 14 days after the date of the acquittal;

(iv) in the case of an appeal under that paragraph against an order made on a finding under section 55. (2), not later than 14 days after the conclusion of the examination of facts,

or within such longer period as the [F5appropriate Appeal Court] may, on cause shown, allow.

(3) Where the examination of facts was held in connection with proceedings on indictment, subsections (1)(a) and (2)(b)(i) above are without prejudice to section 74. (1) of this Act.

(4) Where an appeal is taken under subsection (1) above, the period from the date on which the appeal was lodged until it is withdrawn or disposed of shall not count towards any time limit applying in respect of the case.

(5) An appellant in an appeal under this section shall be entitled to be present at the hearing of the appeal unless the [F6appropriate Appeal Court] determines that his presence is not practicable or appropriate.

(6) In disposing of an appeal under subsection (1) above the [F7appropriate Appeal Court] may—

(a) affirm the decision of the court of first instance;

(b) make any other finding or order which that court could have made at the time when it made the finding [F8, order or other disposal] which is the subject of the appeal; or

(c) remit the case to that court with such directions in the matter as the [F7appropriate Appeal Court] thinks fit.

(7) Section 60 of this Act shall not apply in relation to any order as respects which a person has a right of appeal under subsection (1)(c) above.

[F9. (8)In this section, "appropriate Appeal Court" means—

(a) in the case of an appeal under subsection (1) against a finding or refusal, or an order made, in proceedings on indictment, the High Court;

(b) in the case of an appeal under subsection (1) against a finding or refusal, or an order made, in summary proceedings, the Sheriff Appeal Court.]

Amendments (Textual)

F1. Words in s. 62 heading substituted (with application in accordance with art. 3 of the commencing S.S.I.) by Criminal Justice and Licensing (Scotland) Act 2010 (asp 13), s. 206. (1), sch. 7 para. 42; S.S.I. 2012/160, art. 3, sch.

F2. Words in s. 62. (1) substituted (22.9.2015) by The Courts Reform (Scotland) Act 2014 (Consequential Provisions No. 2) Order 2015 (S.S.I. 2015/338), art. 1, sch. 2 para. 5. (2)(a) (with art. 4)

F3. Words in s. 62. (1)(a) substituted (with application in accordance with art. 3 of the commencing S.S.I.) by Criminal Justice and Licensing (Scotland) Act 2010 (asp 13), s. 206. (1), sch. 7 para. 42. (a); S.S.I. 2012/160, art. 3, sch.

F4. Words in s. 62. (2)(b)(iii) substituted (with application in accordance with art. 3 of the commencing S.S.I.) by Criminal Justice and Licensing (Scotland) Act 2010 (asp 13), s. 206. (1), sch. 7 para. 42. (b); S.S.I. 2012/160, art. 3, sch.

F5. Words in s. 62. (2) substituted (22.9.2015) by The Courts Reform (Scotland) Act 2014 (Consequential Provisions No. 2) Order 2015 (S.S.I. 2015/338), art. 1, sch. 2 para. 5. (2)(a) (with art. 4)

F6. Words in s. 62. (5) substituted (22.9.2015) by The Courts Reform (Scotland) Act 2014 (Consequential Provisions No. 2) Order 2015 (S.S.I. 2015/338), art. 1, sch. 2 para. 5. (2)(a) (with art. 4)

F7. Words in s. 62. (6) substituted (22.9.2015) by The Courts Reform (Scotland) Act 2014 (Consequential Provisions No. 2) Order 2015 (S.S.I. 2015/338), art. 1, sch. 2 para. 5. (2)(a) (with art. 4)

F8. Words in s. 62. (6)(b) substituted (1.1.1998) by 1997 c. 48, s. 62. (1), Sch. 1 para. 21. (7); S.I. 1997/2323, art. 4, Sch. 2 (subject to art. 7)

F9. S. 62. (8) inserted (22.9.2015) by The Courts Reform (Scotland) Act 2014 (Consequential Provisions No. 2) Order 2015 (S.S.I. 2015/338), art. 1, sch. 2 para. 5. (2)(b) (with art. 4)

63 Appeal by prosecutor [F10where accused found not criminally responsible or unfit for trial].S

(1) The prosecutor may appeal to the [F11appropriate Appeal Court] on a point of law against—

(a) a finding under subsection (1) of section 54 of this Act that an accused is [F12unfit for trial] so that his trial cannot proceed or continue;

[F13. (b)an acquittal by reason of the special defence set out in section 51. A of this Act;]

(c) an acquittal under section 55. (3) of this Act (whether or not [F14by reason of the special defence set out in section 51. A of this Act]); or

F15. (d). . . . .

(2) An appeal under subsection (1) above shall be—

(a) in writing; and

(b) lodged—

(i) in the case of an appeal under paragraph (a) or (b) of that subsection, not later than seven days after the finding or, as the case may be, the acquittal which is the subject of the appeal;

(ii) in the case of an appeal under paragraph (c) F16. . .of that subsection, not later than seven days after the conclusion of the examination of facts,
or within such longer period as the [F17appropriate Appeal Court] may, on cause shown, allow.
(3) Where the examination of facts was held in connection with proceedings on indictment, subsections (1)(a) and (2)(b)(i) above are without prejudice to section 74. (1) of this Act.
(4) A respondent in an appeal under this subsection shall be entitled to be present at the hearing of the appeal unless the [F18appropriate Appeal Court] determines that his presence is not practicable or appropriate.
(5) In disposing of an appeal under subsection (1) above the [F19appropriate Appeal Court] may—

(a) affirm the decision of the court of first instance;

(b) make any other finding [F20order or disposal] which that court could have made at the time when it made the finding [F20or acquittal] which is the subject of the appeal; or

(c) remit the case to that court with such directions in the matter as the [F19appropriate Appeal Court] thinks fit.

(6) In this section, "the prosecutor" means, in relation to proceedings on indictment, the Lord Advocate.

[F21. (7)In this section, "appropriate Appeal Court" means—

(a) in the case of an appeal under subsection (1) against a finding or an acquittal made in proceedings on indictment, the High Court;

(b) in the case of an appeal under subsection (1) against a finding or an acquittal made in summary proceedings, the Sheriff Appeal Court.]

Amendments (Textual)

F10. Words in s. 63 heading substituted (with application in accordance with art. 3 of the commencing S.S.I.) by Criminal Justice and Licensing (Scotland) Act 2010 (asp 13), s. 206. (1), sch. 7 para. 43; S.S.I. 2012/160, art. 3, sch.

F11. Words in s. 63. (1) substituted (22.9.2015) by The Courts Reform (Scotland) Act 2014 (Consequential Provisions No. 2) Order 2015 (S.S.I. 2015/338), art. 1, sch. 2 para. 5. (3)(a) (with art. 4)

F12. Words in s. 63. (1)(a) substituted (with application in accordance with art. 3 of the commencing S.S.I.) by Criminal Justice and Licensing (Scotland) Act 2010 (asp 13), s. 206. (1), sch. 7 para. 43. (a); S.S.I. 2012/160, art. 3, sch.

F13. S. 63. (1)(b) substituted (with application in accordance with art. 3 of the commencing S.S.I.) by Criminal Justice and Licensing (Scotland) Act 2010 (asp 13), s. 206. (1), sch. 7 para. 43. (b); S.S.I. 2012/160, art. 3, sch.

F14. Words in s. 63. (1)(c) substituted (with application in accordance with art. 3 of the commencing S.S.I.) by Criminal Justice and Licensing (Scotland) Act 2010 (asp 13), s. 206. (1), sch. 7 para. 43. (c); S.S.I. 2012/160, art. 3, sch.

F15. S. 63. (1)(d) repealed (1.1.1998) by 1997 c. 48, s. 62. (1)(2), Sch. 1 para. 21. (8)(a), Sch. 3; S.I. 1997/2323, art. 4, Sch. 2 (subject to art. 7)

F16. Words in s. 63. (2)(b)(ii) repealed (1.1.1998) by 1997 c. 48, s. 62. (1)(2), Sch. 1 para. 21. (8)(b), Sch. 3; S.I. 1997/2323, art. 4, Sch. 2 (subject to art. 7)

F17. Words in s. 63. (2) substituted (22.9.2015) by The Courts Reform (Scotland) Act 2014 (Consequential Provisions No. 2) Order 2015 (S.S.I. 2015/338), art. 1, sch. 2 para. 5. (3)(a) (with art. 4)

F18. Words in s. 63. (4) substituted (22.9.2015) by The Courts Reform (Scotland) Act 2014 (Consequential Provisions No. 2) Order 2015 (S.S.I. 2015/338), art. 1, sch. 2 para. 5. (3)(a) (with art. 4)

F19. Words in s. 63. (5) substituted (22.9.2015) by The Courts Reform (Scotland) Act 2014 (Consequential Provisions No. 2) Order 2015 (S.S.I. 2015/338), art. 1, sch. 2 para. 5. (3)(a) (with art. 4)

F20. Words in s. 63. (5)(b) substituted (1.1.1998) by 1997 c. 48, s. 62. (1), Sch. 1 para. 21. (8)(c)(i)(ii); S.I. 1997/2323, art. 4, Sch. 2 (subject to art. 7)

F21. S. 63. (7) inserted (22.9.2015) by The Courts Reform (Scotland) Act 2014 (Consequential Provisions No. 2) Order 2015 (S.S.I. 2015/338), art. 1, sch. 2 para. 5. (3)(b) (with art. 4)

PART VII Solemn Proceedings

PART VIIS Solemn Proceedings

64 Prosecution on indictment.S

(1) All prosecutions for the public interest before the High Court or before the sheriff sitting with a jury shall proceed on indictment [F1at the instance] of Her Majesty's Advocate.

(2) The indictment may be in the forms—

(a) set out in Schedule 2 to this Act; or

(b) prescribed by Act of Adjournal,

or as nearly as may be in such form.

(3) Indictments in proceedings before the High Court shall be signed by the Lord Advocate or one of his deputes.

(4) Indictments in proceedings before the sheriff sitting with a jury shall be signed by the procurator fiscal, and the words "By Authority of Her Majesty's Advocate" shall be prefixed to the signature of the procurator fiscal.

(5) The principal record and service copies of indictments and all notices of citation, lists of witnesses, productions and jurors, and all other official documents required in a prosecution on indictment may be either written or printed or partly written and partly printed.

(6) Schedule 3 to this Act shall have effect as regards indictments under this Act.

Amendments (Textual)

F1. Words in s. 64. (1) substituted (13.12.2010) by Criminal Justice and Licensing (Scotland) Act 2010 (asp 13), ss. 60. (2), 206. (1); S.S.I. 2010/413, art. 2, Sch. (with art. 5)

65 Prevention of delay in trials.S

(1) Subject to subsections (2) and (3) below, an accused shall not be tried on indictment for any offence unless

[F2. (a)where an indictment has been served on the accused in respect of the High Court, a preliminary hearing is commenced within the period of 11 months; and

[F3. (aa)where an indictment has been served on the accused in respect of the sheriff court, a first diet is commenced within the period of 11 months;]

(b) in any case, the trial is commenced within the period of 12 months,

of the first appearance of the accused on petition in respect of the offence.]

[F4. (1. A)If the preliminary hearing (where subsection (1)(a) above applies) [F5, the first diet (where subsection (1)(aa) above applies)] or the trial is not so commenced,] the accused

[F6. (a)shall be discharged forthwith from any indictment as respects the offence; and

(b) shall not at any time be proceeded against on indictment as respects the offence]

(2) Nothing in subsection (1) [F7or (1. A)] above shall bar the trial of an accused for whose [F8apprehension] a warrant has been granted for failure to appear at a diet in the case.

(3) On an application made for the purpose,

[F9. (a)where an indictment has been served on the accused in respect of the High Court, a single judge of that court may, on cause shown, extend either or both of the periods of 11 and 12 months specified in subsection (1) above; or

(b) in any other case, the sheriff may, on cause shown, extend [F10either or both of the periods

125

of 11 and] 12 months specified in that subsection.]

[F11. (3. A)An application under subsection (3) shall not be made at any time when an appeal made with leave under section 74. (1) of this Act has not been disposed of by the High Court.]

(4) Subject to subsections (5) to (9) below, an accused who is committed for any offence until liberated in due course of law shall not be detained by virtue of that committal for a total period of more than—

(a) 80 days, unless within that period the indictment is served on him, which failing he shall be [F12entitled to be admitted to bail]; or

[F13. (aa)where an indictment has been served on the accused in respect of the High Court—

(i) 110 days, unless a preliminary hearing in respect of the case is commenced within that period, which failing he shall be entitled to be admitted to bail; or

(ii) 140 days, unless the trial of the case is commenced within that period, which failing he shall be entitled to be admitted to bail;]

(b) [F14where an indictment has been served on the accused in respect of the sheriff court,] [F15110 days]

[F15. (i)110 days, unless a first diet in respect of the case is commenced within that period, which failing he shall be entitled to be admitted to bail; or

(ii) 140 days], unless the trial of the case is commenced within that period, which failing he shall be [F16entitled to be admitted to bail].

[F17. (4. A)Where an indictment has been served on the accused in respect of the High Court, subsections (1)(a) and (4)(aa)(i) above shall not apply if the preliminary hearing has been dispensed with under section 72. B(1) of this Act.]

[F18. (5)On an application made for the purpose—

(a) in a case where, at the time the application is made, an indictment has not been served on the accused, a single judge of the High Court; or

(b) in any other case, the court specified in the notice served under section 66. (6) of this Act, may, on cause shown, extend any period mentioned in subsection (4) above.

(5. A)Before determining an application under subsection (3) or (5) above, the judge or, as the case may be, the court shall give the parties an opportunity to be heard.

(5. B)However, where all the parties join in the application, the judge or, as the case may be, the court may determine the application without hearing the parties and, accordingly, may dispense with any hearing previously appointed for the purpose of considering the application.]

F19. (6). . . . .

F19. (7). . . . .

(8) The grant or refusal of any application to extend the periods mentioned in this section may be appealed against by note of appeal presented to the High Court; and that Court may affirm, reverse or amend the determination made on such application.

[F20. (8. A)Where an accused is, by virtue of subsection (4) above, entitled to be admitted to bail, the accused shall, unless he has been admitted to bail by the Lord Advocate, be brought forthwith before—

(a) in a case where an indictment has not yet been served on the accused, a single judge of the High Court; or

(b) in any other case, the court specified in the notice served under section 66. (6) of this Act.

(8. B)Where an accused is brought before a judge or court under subsection (8. A) above, the judge or, as the case may be, the court shall give the prosecutor an opportunity to make an application under subsection (5) above.

(8. C)If the prosecutor does not make such an application or, if such an application is made but is refused, the judge or, as the case may be, the court shall, after giving the prosecutor an opportunity to be heard, admit the accused to bail.

(8. D)Where such an application is made but is refused and the prosecutor appeals against the refusal, the accused—

(a) may continue to be detained under the committal warrant for no more than 72 hours from the granting of bail under subsection (8. C) above or for such longer period as the High Court may allow; and

(b) on expiry of that period, shall, whether the appeal has been disposed of or not, be released on bail subject to the conditions imposed.]

(9) For the purposes of this section,

[F21. (a)where the accused is cited in accordance with subsection (4)(b) of section 66 of this Act, the indictment shall be deemed to have been served on the accused;

(b) a preliminary hearing shall be taken to commence when it is called; [F22and]

[F23. (ba)a first diet shall be taken to commence when it is called;]

(c)] a trial shall be taken to commence when the oath is administered to the jury.

(10) In calculating the [F24periods of 11 and] months specified in subsections (1) and (3) above there shall be left out of account any period during which the accused is detained, other than while serving a sentence of imprisonment or detention, in any other part of the United Kingdom or in any of the Channel Islands or the Isle of Man in any prison or other institution or place mentioned in subsection (1) or (1. A) of section 29 of the M1. Criminal Justice Act 1961 (transfer of prisoners for certain judicial purposes).

Amendments (Textual)

F2. S. 65. (1)(a)(b)(1. A) substituted (1.2.2005) for words by Criminal Procedure (Amendment) (Scotland) Act 2004 (asp 5), ss. 6. (2), 27. (1); S.S.I. 2004/405, art. 2, Sch. 1 (subject to arts. 3-5)

F3. S. 65. (1)(aa) inserted (29.5.2017 for specified purposes) by Criminal Justice (Scotland) Act 2016 (asp 1), ss. 79. (2)(a), 117. (2); S.S.I. 2017/99, art. 3. (1)(2) (with art. 6)

F4. S. 65. (1)(a)(b)(1. A) substituted (1.2.2005) for words by Criminal Procedure (Amendment) (Scotland) Act 2004 (asp 5), ss. 6. (2), 27. (1); S.S.I. 2004/405, art. 2, Sch. 1 (subject to arts. 3-5)

F5. Words in s. 65. (1. A) inserted (29.5.2017 for specified purposes) by Criminal Justice (Scotland) Act 2016 (asp 1), ss. 79. (2)(b), 117. (2); S.S.I. 2017/99, art. 3. (1)(2) (with art. 6)

F6. S. 65. (1)(a)(b) substituted (4.7.1996) for words by 1996 c. 25, s. 73. (3) (with s. 78. (1))

F7. Words in s. 65. (2) inserted (1.2.2005) by Criminal Procedure (Amendment) (Scotland) Act 2004 (asp 5), ss. 6. (3), 27. (1); S.S.I. 2004/405, art. 2, Sch. 1 (subject to arts. 3-5)

F8. Word in s. 65. (2) substituted (10.12.2007) by Criminal Proceedings etc. (Reform) (Scotland) Act 2007 (asp 6), ss. 80, 84, Sch. para. 12. (1); S.S.I. 2007/479, art. 3. (1), Sch. (as amended by S.S.I. 2007/527)

F9. S. 65. (3)(a)(b) substituted (1.2.2005) for words by Criminal Procedure (Amendment) (Scotland) Act 2004 (asp 5), ss. 6. (4), 27. (1); S.S.I. 2004/405, art. 2, Sch. 1 (subject to arts. 3-5)

F10. Words in s. 65. (3)(b) substituted (10.12.2007) by Criminal Proceedings etc. (Reform) (Scotland) Act 2007 (asp 6), ss. 26, 84; S.S.I. 2007/479, art. 3. (1), Sch. (as amended by S.S.I. 2007/527)

F11. S. 65. (3. A) inserted (1.8.1997) by 1997 c. 48, s. 62. (1), Sch. 1 para. 21. (9); S.I. 1997/1712, art. 3, Sch. (subject to arts. 4, 5)

F12. Words in s. 65. (4)(a) substituted (1.2.2005) by Criminal Procedure (Amendment) (Scotland) Act 2004 (asp 5), ss. 6. (5)(a), 27. (1); S.S.I. 2004/405, art. 2, Sch. 1 (subject to arts. 3-5)

F13. S. 65. (4)(aa) inserted (1.2.2005) by Criminal Procedure (Amendment) (Scotland) Act 2004 (asp 5), ss. 6. (5)(b), 27. (1); S.S.I. 2004/405, art. 2, Sch. 1 (subject to arts. 3-5)

F14. Words in s. 65. (4)(b) inserted (1.2.2005) by Criminal Procedure (Amendment) (Scotland) Act 2004 (asp 5), ss. 6. (5)(c)(i), 27. (1); S.S.I. 2004/405, art. 2, Sch. 1 (subject to arts. 3-5)

F15. S. 65. (4)(b)(i)(ii) substituted for words (29.5.2017 for specified purposes) by Criminal Justice (Scotland) Act 2016 (asp 1), ss. 79. (2)(c), 117. (2); S.S.I. 2017/99, art. 3. (1)(2) (with art. 6)

F16. Words in s. 65. (4)(b) substituted (1.2.2005) by Criminal Procedure (Amendment) (Scotland) Act 2004 (asp 5), ss. 6. (5)(c)(ii), 27. (1); S.S.I. 2004/405, art. 2, Sch. 1 (subject to arts. 3-5)

F17. S. 65. (4. A) inserted (1.2.2005) by Criminal Procedure (Amendment) (Scotland) Act 2004 (asp 5), ss. 6. (6), 27. (1); S.S.I. 2004/405, art. 2, Sch. 1 (subject to arts. 3-5)

F18. S. 65. (5)-(5. B) substituted (1.2.2005) for s. 65. (5) by Criminal Procedure (Amendment) (Scotland) Act 2004 (asp 5), ss. 6. (7), 27. (1); S.S.I. 2004/405, art. 2, Sch. 1 (subject to arts. 3-5)

F19. S. 65. (6)(7) repealed (1.2.2005) by Criminal Procedure (Amendment) (Scotland) Act 2004 (asp 5), ss. 6. (8), 27. (1); S.S.I. 2004/405, art. 2, Sch. 1 (subject to arts. 3-5)

F20. S. 65. (8. A)-(8. D) inserted (1.2.2005) by Criminal Procedure (Amendment) (Scotland) Act 2004 (asp 5), ss. 6. (9), 27. (1); S.S.I. 2004/405, art. 2, Sch. 1 (subject to arts. 3-5)

F21. Words in s. 65. (9) inserted (1.2.2005) by Criminal Procedure (Amendment) (Scotland) Act 2004 (asp 5), ss. 6. (10), 27. (1); S.S.I. 2004/405, art. 2, Sch. 1 (subject to arts. 3-5)

F22. Word in s. 65. (9) repealed (29.5.2017 for specified purposes) by Criminal Justice (Scotland) Act 2016 (asp 1), ss. 79. (2)(d)(i), 117. (2); S.S.I. 2017/99, art. 3. (1)(2) (with art. 6)

F23. S. 65. (9)(ba) inserted (29.5.2017 for specified purposes) by Criminal Justice (Scotland) Act 2016 (asp 1), ss. 79. (2)(d)(ii), 117. (2); S.S.I. 2017/99, art. 3. (1)(2) (with art. 6)

F24. Words in s. 65. (10) substituted (1.2.2005) by Criminal Procedure (Amendment) (Scotland) Act 2004 (asp 5), ss. 6. (11), 27. (1); S.S.I. 2004/405, art. 2, Sch. 1 (subject to arts. 3-5)

Modifications etc. (not altering text)

C1. S. 65 extended (1.10.1997) by 1997 c. 43, s. 41, Sch. 1 Pt. II para. 10. (1)(a); S.I. 1997/2200, art. 2. (1)(g)

C2. S. 65 modified (1.10.1997) by 1997 c. 43, s. 41, Sch. 1 Pt. II para. 11. (1)(a); S.I. 1997/2200, art. 2. (1)(g) (subject to transitional provisions in art. 5)

C3. S. 65 applied (with modifications) (1.10.1997) by S.I. 1997/1776, arts. 1, 2, Sch. 1 paras. 5-7; S.I. 1997/2200, art. 2. (1)(g) (subject to transitional provisions in art. 5)

C4. S. 65. (4)(aa)(b) applied (28.11.2011) by Double Jeopardy (Scotland) Act 2011 (asp 16), ss. 6. (7)(8)(a), 17. (3); S.S.I. 2011/365, art. 3

C5. S. 65. (4. A)-(9) applied (28.11.2011) by Double Jeopardy (Scotland) Act 2011 (asp 16), ss. 6. (7)(8)(a), 17. (3); S.S.I. 2011/365, art. 3

Marginal Citations

M11961 c.39.

66 Service and lodging of indictment, etc.S

[F25. (1)This Act shall be sufficient warrant for—

(a) the citation of the accused and witnesses to—

(i) any diet of the High Court to be held on any day, and at any place, the Court is sitting;

(ii) any diet of the sheriff court to be held on any day the court is sitting; or

(iii) any adjournment of a diet specified in sub-paragraph (i) or (ii) above; and

(b) the citation of jurors for any trial to be held—

(i) in the High Court; or

(ii) under solemn procedure in the sheriff court.]

(2) The execution of the citation against an accused, witness or juror shall be in such form as may be prescribed by Act of Adjournal, or as nearly as may be in such form.

(3) A witness may be cited by sending the citation to the witness by ordinary or registered post or by the recorded delivery service and a written execution in the form prescribed by Act of Adjournal or as nearly as may be in such form, purporting to be signed by the person who served such citation together with, where appropriate, the relevant post office receipt shall be sufficient evidence of such citation.

[F26. (4)The accused may be cited either—

(a) by being served with a copy of the indictment and of the list of the names and addresses of the witnesses to be adduced by the prosecution [F27 and of the list of productions (if any) to be put in evidence by the prosecution]; or

(b) [F28if the accused, at the time of citation, is not in custody,] by a constable affixing to the door of the [F29relevant premises] a notice in such form as may be prescribed by Act of Adjournal, or as nearly as may be in such form—

(i) specifying the date on which it was so affixed;

(ii) informing the accused that he may collect a copy of the indictment and of such [F30lists as are] mentioned in paragraph (a) above from a police station specified in the notice; and

(iii) calling upon him to appear and answer to the indictment at such diet as shall be so specified.

[F31. (4. ZA) In subsection (4)(b) above, "the relevant premises" means—

(a) where the accused, at the time of citation, has been admitted to bail, his proper domicile of citation as specified for the purposes of section 25 of this Act; or

(b) in any other case, any premises which the constable reasonably believes to be the accused's dwelling-house or place of business.]

(4. A)Where a date is specified by virtue of sub-paragraph (i) of subsection (4)(b) above, that date shall be deemed the date on which the indictment is served; and the copy of the indictment referred to in sub-paragraph (ii) of that subsection shall, for the purposes of subsections (12) and (13) below be deemed the service copy.

(4. B)Paragraphs (a) and (b) of subsection (6) below shall apply for the purpose of specifying a diet by virtue of subsection (4)(b)(iii) above as they apply for the purpose of specifying a diet in any notice under subsection (6).]

[F32. (4. C)Where—

(a) the accused is cited in accordance with subsection (4)(b) above; and

(b) the charge in the indictment is of committing a sexual offence to which section 288. C of this Act applies,

the accused shall, on collecting the indictment, be given a notice containing intimation of the matters specified in subsection (6. A)(a) below.]

(5) Except in a case to which section 76 of this Act applies, the prosecutor shall on or before the date of service of the indictment lodge the record copy of the indictment with the clerk of court before which the trial is to take place, together with a copy of the list of witnesses and a copy of the list of productions.

(6) [F33. If the accused is cited by being served with a copy of the indictment, then except where such service is] under section 76. (1) of this Act, a notice shall be served on the accused with the indictment calling upon him to appear and answer to the indictment—

(a) where the case is to be tried in the sheriff court

F34 [[F35. (i)]at a first diet not less than 15 clear days after the service of the indictment and not less than 10 clear days before the trial diet [F36; and

(ii) at a trial diet not less than 29 clear days after service of the indictment,]] [F35at a first diet not less than 29 clear days after the service of the indictment,]

[F37. (b)where the indictment is in respect of the High Court, at a diet not less than 29 clear days after the service of the indictment (such a diet being referred to in this Act as a "preliminary hearing").]

[F38. (6. A)Where the charge in the indictment is of committing a sexual offence to which section 288. C of this Act applies, the notice served under subsection (6) above shall—

(a) contain intimation to the accused—

[F39. (i)that his case at, or for the purposes of, any relevant hearing (within the meaning of section 288. C(1. A)) in the course of the proceedings (including at any commissioner proceedings) may be conducted only by a lawyer,]

(ii) that it is, therefore, in his interests, if he has not already done so, to get the professional assistance of a solicitor; and

(iii) that if he does not engage a solicitor for the purposes of [F40the conduct of his case at or for the purposes of the] [F41hearing] [F42. (or at any related commissioner proceedings)], the court will do so; F43. . .

    F43. (b) . . . .

[F44. (6. AA)A notice affixed under subsection (4)(b) above or served under subsection (6) above shall, where the accused is a body corporate, also contain intimation to the accused—

(a) where the indictment is in respect of the High Court, that, if it does not appear as mentioned in section 70. (4) of this Act or by counsel or a solicitor at the preliminary hearing—

(i) the hearing may proceed; and

(ii) a trial diet may be appointed,

in its absence; and

(b) in any case (whether the indictment is in respect of the High Court or the sheriff court), that if it does not appear as mentioned in paragraph (a) above at the trial diet, the trial may proceed in its absence.]

[F45. (6. AB)A notice affixed under subsection (4)(b) or served under subsection (6), where the indictment is in respect of the sheriff court, must contain intimation to the accused that the first diet may proceed and a trial diet may be appointed in the accused's absence.]

(6. B)A failure to comply with subsection [F46. (4. C), (6. A) [F47or (6. AA)] [F47, (6. AA) or (6. AB)]] above does not affect the validity or lawfulness of any [F48notice affixed under subsection (4)(b) above or served under subsection (6) above] or any other element of the proceedings against the accused.]

[F49. (6. C)An accused shall be taken to be served with—

(a) the indictment and lists of witnesses and productions; and

(b) the notice referred to in subsection (6) above,

if they are served on the solicitor specified in subsection (6. D) below at that solicitor's place of business.

(6. D)The solicitor referred to in subsection (6. C) above is any solicitor who—

(a) has notified in writing the procurator fiscal for the district in which the charge against the accused was being investigated that he is engaged by the accused for the purposes of his defence; and

(b) has not informed that procurator fiscal that he has been dismissed by, or has withdrawn from acting for, the accused.

(6. E)It is the duty of a solicitor who has, before service of an indictment, notified a procurator fiscal that he is engaged by the accused for the purposes of his defence to inform that procurator fiscal in writing forthwith if he is dismissed by, or withdraws from acting for, the accused.]

(7) [F50. Subject to subsection (4)(b) above,] service of the indictment, lists of witnesses and productions, and any notice or intimation to the accused, and the citation of witnesses, whether for precognition or trial, may be effected by any officer of law.

F51. (8) . . . .

(9) The citation of witnesses may be effected by any officer of law duly authorised; and in any proceedings, the evidence on oath of the officer shall, subject to subsection (10) below, be sufficient evidence of the execution of the citation.

F52. (10) . . . .

(11) No objection to the competency of the officer who served the indictment [F53, or who executed a citation under subsection (4)(b) above,] to give evidence in respect of such service [F54or execution] shall be upheld on the ground that his name is not included in the list of witnesses served on the accused.

(12) Any deletion or correction made before service on the record or service copy of an indictment shall be sufficiently authenticated by the initials of the person who has signed, or could by law have signed, the indictment.

(13) Any deletion or correction made on a service copy of an indictment, or on any notice of citation, postponement, adjournment or other notice F55 . . . served on an accused shall be sufficiently authenticated by the initials of any procurator fiscal or of the person serving the same.

(14) Any deletion or correction made on any execution of citation or notice [F56or] other document [F57so] served shall be sufficiently authenticated by the initials of the person serving the same.

[F58. (15) In subsection (6. A) above, "commissioner proceedings" means proceedings before a commissioner appointed under section 271. I(1) or by virtue of section 272. (1)(b) of this Act.]

Amendments (Textual)

F25 S. 66. (1) substituted (1.2.2005) by Criminal Procedure (Amendment) (Scotland) Act 2004 (asp 5), ss. 7. (2), 27. (1); S.S.I. 2004/405, art. 2, Sch. 1 (subject to arts. 3-5)

F26 S. 66. (4)-(4. B) substituted (27.6.2003) for s. 66. (4) by Criminal Justice (Scotland) Act 2003 (asp 7), ss. 61. (1)(a), 89; S.S.I. 2003/288, art. 2, Sch.

F27 Words in s. 66. (4)(a) inserted (1.2.2005) by Criminal Procedure (Amendment) (Scotland) Act

2004 (asp 5), ss. 25, 27. (1), Sch. para. 15. (a)(i); S.S.I. 2004/405, art. 2, Sch. 1 (subject to arts. 3-5)

F28 Words in s. 66. (4)(b) inserted (1.2.2005) by Criminal Procedure (Amendment) (Scotland) Act 2004 (asp 5), ss. 7. (3)(a), 27. (1); S.S.I. 2004/405, art. 2, Sch. 1 (subject to arts. 3-5)

F29 Words in s. 66. (4)(b) substituted (1.2.2005) by Criminal Procedure (Amendment) (Scotland) Act 2004 (asp 5), ss. 7. (3)(b), 27. (1); S.S.I. 2004/405, art. 2, Sch. 1 (subject to arts. 3-5)

F30 Words in s. 66. (4)(b) substituted (1.2.2005) by Criminal Procedure (Amendment) (Scotland) Act 2004 (asp 5), ss. 25, 27. (1), Sch. para. 15. (a)(ii); S.S.I. 2004/405, art. 2, Sch. 1 (subject to arts. 3-5)

F31 S. 66. (4. ZA) inserted (1.2.2005) by Criminal Procedure (Amendment) (Scotland) Act 2004 (asp 5), ss. 7. (4), 27. (1); S.S.I. 2004/405, art. 2, Sch. 1 (subject to arts. 3-5)

F32 S. 66. (4. C) inserted (1.2.2005) by Criminal Procedure (Amendment) (Scotland) Act 2004 (asp 5), ss. 25, 27. (1), Sch. para. 15. (b); S.S.I. 2004/405, art. 2, Sch. 1 (subject to arts. 3-5)

F33 Words in s. 66 (6) substituted (27.6.2003) by Criminal Justice (Scotland) Act 2003 (asp 7), ss. 61. (1)(b)(i), 89; S.S.I. 2003/288, art. 2, Sch.

F34 Words in s. 66. (6)(a) renumbered as s. 66. (6)(a)(i) (1.2.2005) by virtue of Criminal Procedure (Amendment) (Scotland) Act 2004 (asp 5), ss. 1. (1)(a)(i), 27. (1); S.S.I. 2004/405, art. 2, Sch. 1 (subject to arts. 3-5)

F35. Words in s. 66. (6)(a) substituted for s. 66. (6)(a)(i)(ii) (29.5.2017 for specified purposes) by Criminal Justice (Scotland) Act 2016 (asp 1), ss. 79. (3), 117. (2); S.S.I. 2017/99, art. 3. (1)(2) (with arts. 3. (3)(4), 6)

F36 S. 66. (6)(a)(ii) and word inserted (1.2.2005) by Criminal Procedure (Amendment) (Scotland) Act 2004 (asp 5), ss. 1. (1)(a)(ii), 27. (1); S.S.I. 2004/405, art. 2, Sch. 1 (subject to arts. 3-5)

F37 S. 66. (6)(b) substituted (1.2.2005) by Criminal Procedure (Amendment) (Scotland) Act 2004 (asp 5), ss. 1. (1)(b), 27. (1); S.S.I. 2004/405, art. 2, Sch. 1 (subject to arts. 3-5)

F38 S. 66. (6. A)(6. B) inserted (1.11.2002) by Sexual Offences (Procedure and Evidence) (Scotland) Act 2002 (asp 9), s. 3, Sch. para. 4; S.S.I. 2002/443, art. 3

F39 S. 66. (6. A)(a)(i) substituted for s. 66. (6. A)(a)(zi)(i) (28.3.2011) by Criminal Justice and Licensing (Scotland) Act 2010 (asp 13), s. 206. (1), sch. 7 para. 44. (a); S.S.I. 2011/178, art. 2, sch.

F40 Words in s. 66. (6. A)(a)(iii) inserted (1.2.2005) by Criminal Procedure (Amendment) (Scotland) Act 2004 (asp 5), ss. 25, 27. (1), Sch. para. 15. (c)(ii); S.S.I. 2004/405, art. 2, Sch. 1 (subject to arts. 3-5)

F41 Word in s. 66. (6. A)(a)(iii) substituted (28.3.2011) by Criminal Justice and Licensing (Scotland) Act 2010 (asp 13), s. 206. (1), sch. 7 para. 44. (b); S.S.I. 2011/178, art. 2, sch.

F42 Words in s. 66. (6. A)(a)(iii) inserted (23.4.2007) by Criminal Proceedings etc. (Reform) (Scotland) Act 2007 (asp 6), ss. 35. (1)(a)(ii), 84; S.S.I. 2007/250, art. 3. (a)

F43 S. 66. (6. A)(b) and preceding word repealed (1.2.2005) by Criminal Procedure (Amendment) (Scotland) Act 2004 (asp 5), ss. 1. (2), 27. (1); S.S.I. 2004/405, art. 2, Sch. 1 (subject to arts. 3-5)

F44 S. 66. (6. AA) inserted (1.2.2005) by Criminal Procedure (Amendment) (Scotland) Act 2004 (asp 5), ss. 10. (5), 27. (1); S.S.I. 2004/405, art. 2, Sch. 1 (subject to arts. 3-5)

F45. S. 66. (6. AB) inserted (29.5.2017 for specified purposes) by Criminal Justice (Scotland) Act 2016 (asp 1), ss. 81. (2)(a), 117. (2); S.S.I. 2017/99, art. 3. (1)(2) (with arts. 3. (5), 6)

F46 Words in s. 66. (6. B) substituted (1.2.2005) by Criminal Procedure (Amendment) (Scotland) Act 2004 (asp 5), ss. 25, 27. (1), Sch. para. 15. (d)(i); S.S.I. 2004/405, art. 2, Sch. 1 (subject to arts. 3-5)

F47. Words in s. 66. (6. B) substituted (29.5.2017 for specified purposes) by Criminal Justice (Scotland) Act 2016 (asp 1), ss. 81. (2)(b), 117. (2); S.S.I. 2017/99, art. 3. (1)(2) (with art. 6)

F48 Words in s. 66. (6. B) substituted (1.2.2005) by Criminal Procedure (Amendment) (Scotland) Act 2004 (asp 5), ss. 25, 27. (1), Sch. para. 15. (d)(ii); S.S.I. 2004/405, art. 2, Sch. 1 (subject to arts. 3-5)

F49 S. 66. (6. C)-(6. E) inserted (1.2.2005) by Criminal Procedure (Amendment) (Scotland) Act 2004 (asp 5), ss. 7. (5), 27. (1); S.S.I. 2004/405, art. 2, Sch. 1 (subject to arts. 3-5)

F50 Words in s. 66 (7) inserted (27.6.2003) by Criminal Justice (Scotland) Act 2003 (asp 7), ss. 61. (1)(c), 89; S.S.I. 2003/288, art. 2, Sch.

F51 S. 66. (8) repealed (1.2.2005) by Criminal Procedure (Amendment) (Scotland) Act 2004 (asp 5), ss. 7. (6), 27. (1); S.S.I. 2004/405, art. 2, Sch. 1 (subject to arts. 3-5)

F52 S. 66. (10) repealed (1.2.2005) by Criminal Procedure (Amendment) (Scotland) Act 2004 (asp 5), ss. 25, 27. (1), Sch. para. 15. (e); S.S.I. 2004/405, art. 2, Sch. 1 (subject to arts. 3-5)

F53 Words in s. 66. (11) inserted (27.6.2003) by Criminal Justice (Scotland) Act 2003 (asp 7), ss. 61. (1)(e)(i), 89; S.S.I. 2003/288, art. 2, Sch.

F54 Words in s. 66. (11) inserted (27.6.2003) by Criminal Justice (Scotland) Act 2003 (asp 7), ss. 61. (1)(e)(ii), 89; S.S.I. 2003/288, art. 2, Sch.

F55 Words in s. 66. (13) repealed (27.6.2003) by Criminal Justice (Scotland) Act 2003 (asp 7), ss. 61. (1)(f), 89; S.S.I. 2003/288, art. 2, Sch.

F56 Words in s. 66. (14) substituted (27.6.2003) by Criminal Justice (Scotland) Act 2003 (asp 7), ss. 61. (1)(g)(i), 89; S.S.I. 2003/288, art. 2, Sch.

F57 Words in s. 66. (14) substituted (27.6.2003) by Criminal Justice (Scotland) Act 2003 (asp 7), ss. 61. (1)(g)(ii), 89; S.S.I. 2003/288, art. 2, Sch.

F58 S. 66. (15) added (23.4.2007) by Criminal Proceedings etc. (Reform) (Scotland) Act 2007 (asp 6), ss. 35. (1)(b), 84; S.S.I. 2007/250, art. 3. (a)

67 Witnesses.S

(1) The list of witnesses shall consist of the names of the witnesses together with an address at which they can be contacted for the purposes of precognition.

(2) It shall not be necessary to include in the list of witnesses the names of any witnesses to the declaration of the accused or the names of any witnesses to prove that an extract conviction applies to the accused, but witnesses may be examined in regard to these matters without previous notice.

(3) Any objection in respect of misnomer or misdescription of—

(a) any person named in the indictment; or

(b) any witness in the list of witnesses,

shall be intimated in writing to the court before which the trial is to take place, to the prosecutor and to any other accused, where the case is to be tried in the sheriff court, at or before the first diet and, where the case is to be tried in the High Court, not less than [F59seven] clear days before the [F60preliminary hearing]; and, except on cause shown, no such objection shall be admitted F61. . . unless so intimated.

(4) Where such intimation has been given or cause is shown and the court is satisfied that the accused making the objection has not been supplied with sufficient information to enable him to identify the person named in the indictment or to find such witness in sufficient time to precognosce him before the trial, the court may grant such remedy by postponement, adjournment or otherwise as appears to it to be appropriate.

[F62. (4. A)The prosecutor shall have a duty to cite a witness included in the list only if—

(a) it has been ascertained under—

(i) in the case of proceedings in the High Court, section 72. (6)(d); or

(ii) in the case of proceedings in the sheriff court, section 71. (1. C)(a),

of this Act that the witness is required by the prosecutor or the accused to attend the trial; or

(b) where, in the case of proceedings in the High Court, the preliminary hearing has been dispensed with under subsection (1) of section 72. B of this Act, the witness was identified in the application under that subsection as being required by the prosecutor or the accused to attend the trial.]

(5) Without prejudice to—

(a) any enactment or rule of law permitting the prosecutor to examine any witness not included in the list of witnesses; or

(b) subsection (6) below,

in any trial it shall be competent with the leave of the court for the prosecutor to examine any witness or to put in evidence any production not included in the lists lodged by him, provided that written notice, containing in the case of a witness his name and address as mentioned in subsection (1) above, has been given to the accused [F63by the relevant time.]

[F64. (5. A)In subsection (5) above, "the relevant time" means—

(a) where the case is to be tried in the High Court—

(i) not less then seven clear days before the preliminary hearing; or

(ii) such later time, before the jury is sworn to try the case, as the court may, on cause shown, allow;

(b) where the case is to be tried in the sheriff court,]

not less than two clear days before the day on which the jury is sworn to try the case.

(6) It shall be competent for the prosecutor to examine any witness or put in evidence any production included in any list or notice lodged by the accused, and it shall be competent for an accused to examine any witness or put in evidence any production included in any list or notice lodged by the prosecutor or by a co-accused.

Amendments (Textual)

F59. Word in s. 67. (3) substituted (1.2.2005) by Criminal Procedure (Amendment) (Scotland) Act 2004 (asp 5), ss. 25, 27. (1), Sch. para. 16. (a)(i); S.S.I. 2004/405, art. 2, Sch. 1 (subject to arts. 3-5)

F60. Words in s. 67. (3) substituted (1.2.2005) by Criminal Procedure (Amendment) (Scotland) Act 2004 (asp 5), ss. 25, 27. (1), Sch. para. 16. (a)(ii); S.S.I. 2004/405, art. 2, Sch. 1 (subject to arts. 3-5)

F61. Words in s. 67. (3) repealed (1.2.2005) by Criminal Procedure (Amendment) (Scotland) Act 2004 (asp 5), ss. 25, 27. (1), Sch. para. 16. (a)(iii); S.S.I. 2004/405, art. 2, Sch. 1 (subject to arts. 3-5)

F62. S. 67. (4. A) inserted (1.2.2005) by Criminal Procedure (Amendment) (Scotland) Act 2004 (asp 5), ss. 25, 27. (1), Sch. para. 16. (b); S.S.I. 2004/405, art. 2, Sch. 1 (subject to arts. 3-5)

F63. S. 67: words, including words forming part of a new subsection (5. A), expressed to be inserted in subsection (5) (1.2.2005) by Criminal Procedure (Amendment) (Scotland) Act 2004 (asp 5), ss. 25, 27. (1), Sch. para. 16. (c); S.S.I. 2004/405, art. 2, Sch. 1 (subject to arts. 3-5)

F64. S. 67: words, including words forming part of a new subsection (5. A), expressed to be inserted in subsection (5) (1.2.2005) by Criminal Procedure (Amendment) (Scotland) Act 2004 (asp 5), ss. 25, 27. (1), Sch. para. 16. (c); S.S.I. 2004/405, art. 2, Sch. 1 (subject to arts. 3-5)

67. A Failure of witness to attend for, or give evidence on, precognition.S

F65. . . . .

Amendments (Textual)

F65. S. 67. A repealed (4.10.2004) by Criminal Procedure (Amendment) (Scotland) Act 2004 (asp 5), ss. 25, 27. (1), Sch. para. 17; S.S.I. 2004/405, art. 2, Sch. 1 (subject to arts. 3-5)

68 Productions.S

F66. (1). . . . .

(2) The accused shall be entitled to see the productions according to the existing law and practice in the office of the sheriff clerk of the district in which the court of the trial diet is situated or, where the trial diet is to be in the High Court in Edinburgh, in the Justiciary Office.

(3) Where a person who has examined a production is adduced to give evidence with regard to it and the production has been lodged [F67, where the case is to be tried in the sheriff court,] at least

eight days before the trial diet [F68or, where the case is to be tried in the High Court, at least 14 days before the preliminary hearing,] , it shall not be necessary to prove—

(a) that the production was received by him in the condition in which it was taken possession of by the procurator fiscal or the police and returned by him after his examination of it to the procurator fiscal or the police; or

(b) that the production examined by him is that taken possession of by the procurator fiscal or the police,

unless the accused, [F69where the case is to be tried in the sheriff court,] at least four days before the trial diet [F70or, where the case is to be tried in the High Court, at least seven days before the preliminary hearing,] , gives in accordance with subsection (4) below written notice that he does not admit that the production was received or returned as aforesaid or, as the case may be, that it is that taken possession of as aforesaid.

(4) The notice mentioned in subsection (3) above shall be given—

(a) where [F71the case is to be tried in the High Court] , to the Crown Agent; and

(b) where [F72the case is to be tried in the sheriff court] , to the procurator fiscal.

Amendments (Textual)

F66. S. 68. (1) repealed (17.1.2017) by Criminal Justice (Scotland) Act 2016 (asp 1), ss. 78. (2)(c), 117. (2); S.S.I. 2016/426, art. 2, sch. (with art. 3)

F67. Words in s. 68. (3) inserted (1.2.2005) by Criminal Procedure (Amendment) (Scotland) Act 2004 (asp 5), ss. 25, 27. (1), Sch. para. 18. (a)(i); S.S.I. 2004/405, art. 2, Sch. 1 (subject to arts. 3-5)

F68. Words in s. 68. (3) inserted (1.2.2005) by Criminal Procedure (Amendment) (Scotland) Act 2004 (asp 5), ss. 25, 27. (1), Sch. para. 18. (a)(ii); S.S.I. 2004/405, art. 2, Sch. 1 (subject to arts. 3-5)

F69. Words in s. 68. (3) inserted (1.2.2005) by Criminal Procedure (Amendment) (Scotland) Act 2004 (asp 5), ss. 25, 27. (1), Sch. para. 18. (a)(iii); S.S.I. 2004/405, art. 2, Sch. 1 (subject to arts. 3-5)

F70. Words in s. 68. (3) inserted (1.2.2005) by Criminal Procedure (Amendment) (Scotland) Act 2004 (asp 5), ss. 25, 27. (1), Sch. para. 18. (a)(iv); S.S.I. 2004/405, art. 2, Sch. 1 (subject to arts. 3-5)

F71. Words in s. 68. (4)(a) substituted (1.2.2005) by Criminal Procedure (Amendment) (Scotland) Act 2004 (asp 5), ss. 25, 27. (1), Sch. para. 18. (b)(i); S.S.I. 2004/405, art. 2, Sch. 1 (subject to arts. 3-5)

F72. Words in s. 68. (4)(b) substituted (1.2.2005) by Criminal Procedure (Amendment) (Scotland) Act 2004 (asp 5), ss. 25, 27. (1), Sch. para. 18. (b)(ii); S.S.I. 2004/405, art. 2, Sch. 1 (subject to arts. 3-5)

69 Notice of previous convictions.S

(1) No mention shall be made in the indictment of previous convictions, nor shall extracts of previous convictions be included in the list of productions annexed to the indictment.

(2) If the prosecutor intends to place before the court any previous conviction, he shall cause to be served on the accused along with the indictment a notice in the form set out in an Act of Adjournal or as nearly as may be in such form, and any conviction specified in the notice shall be held to apply to the accused unless he gives, in accordance with subsection (3) below, written intimation objecting to such conviction on the ground that it does not apply to him or is otherwise inadmissible.

(3) Intimation objecting to a conviction under subsection (2) above shall be given—

(a) where the accused is [F73indicted to the High Court, to the Crown Agent not less than seven clear days before the preliminary hearing;]

[F73. (b)where the accused is indicted to the sheriff court, to the procurator fiscal at least five clear days before the first day of the sitting in which the trial diet is to be held.]

(4) Where notice is given by the accused under section 76 of this Act of his intention to plead guilty and the prosecutor intends to place before the court any previous conviction, he shall cause to be served on the accused along with the indictment a notice in the form set out in an Act of Adjournal or as nearly as may be in such form.

[F74. (4. A)A notice served under subsection (2) or (4) above shall include any details which the prosecutor proposes to provide under section 101. (3. A) of this Act; and subsection (3) above shall apply in relation to intimation objecting to the provision of such details, on the grounds that they do not apply to the accused or are otherwise inadmissible, as it applies in relation to intimation objecting to a conviction.]

(5) Where the accused pleads guilty at any diet, no objection to any conviction of which notice has been served on him under this section [F75, or to the provision of such details as are, by virtue of subsection (4. A) above, included in a notice so served,] shall be entertained unless he has, at least two clear days before the diet, given intimation to the procurator fiscal of the district to the court of which the accused is cited for the diet.

[F76. (6)This section applies in relation to the alternative disposals mentioned in subsection (7) below as it applies in relation to previous convictions.

(7) Those alternative disposals are—

   (a) a—

(i) fixed penalty under section 302. (1) of this Act;

(ii) compensation offer under section 302. A(1) of this Act,

that has been accepted (or deemed to have been accepted) by the accused in the two years preceding the date of an offence charged;

   (b) a work order under section 303. ZA(6) of this Act that has been completed in the two years preceding the date of an offence charged.][F77;

   (c) a restoration notice given under subsection (4) of section 20. A of the Nature Conservation (Scotland) Act 2004 (asp 6) in respect of which the accused has given notice of intention to comply under subsection (5) of that section in the two years preceding the date of an offence charged.]

Amendments (Textual)

F73. S. 69. (3)(b) and words substituted (1.2.2005) by Criminal Procedure (Amendment) (Scotland) Act 2004 (asp 5), ss. 25, 27. (1), Sch. para. 19; S.S.I. 2004/405, art. 2. (1), Sch. 1 (subject to arts. 3-5)

F74. S. 69. (4. A) inserted (19.6.2006 for certain purposes and otherwise prosp.) by Criminal Justice (Scotland) Act 2003 (asp 7), ss. 1. (2), 89, Sch. 1 para. 2. (2)(a); S.S.I. 2006/332, art. 2. (1)(2)

F75. Words in s. 69. (5) inserted (19.6.2006 for certain purposes and otherwise prosp.) by Criminal Justice (Scotland) Act 2003 (asp 7), ss. 1. (2), 89, Sch. 1 para. 2. (2)(b); S.S.I. 2006/332, art. 2. (1)(2)

F76. S. 69. (6)(7) added (10.3.2008) by Criminal Proceedings etc. (Reform) (Scotland) Act 2007 (asp 6), ss. 53. (1), 84; S.S.I. 2008/42, art. 3, Sch.

F77. S. 69. (7)(c) and semi colon inserted (29.6.2011) by Wildlife and Natural Environment (Scotland) Act 2011 (asp 6), ss. 40. (3)(a), 43. (1) (with s. 41. (1)); S.S.I. 2011/279, art. 2. (1)(q)

70 Proceedings against [F78organisations].S

(1) This section applies to proceedings on indictment against [F79an organisation].

[F80. (2)The indictment may be served by delivery of a copy of the indictment together with notice to appear at—

   (a) in the case of a body of trustees—

(i) the dwelling-house or place of business of any of the trustees, or

(ii) if the solicitor of the body of trustees is known, the place of business of the solicitor,

[F81. (aa)in the case of a partnership prosecuted by virtue of section 1 of the Partnerships (Prosecution) (Scotland) Act 2013, the dwelling-house or place of business of any of the partners,]

(b) in the case of any other organisation, the registered office or, if there is no registered office or the registered office is not in the United Kingdom, at the principal place of business in the United Kingdom of the organisation.]

(3) Where a letter containing a copy of the indictment has been sent by registered post or by the recorded delivery service to [F82any place], an acknowledgement or certificate of the delivery of the letter issued by the [F83postal operator] shall be sufficient evidence of the delivery of the letter at [F84that place] on the day specified in such acknowledgement or certificate.

(4) [F85. An organisation] may, for the purpose of—

(a) stating objections to the competency or relevancy of the indictment or proceedings; or

(b) tendering a plea of guilty or not guilty; or

(c) making a statement in mitigation of sentence,

appear by a representative F86....

(5) Where at the trial diet the [F87organisation] does not appear as mentioned in subsection (4) above, or by counsel or a solicitor, the court [F88 may—

(a) on the motion of the prosecutor; and

(b) if satisfied as to the matters specified in subsection (5. A) below,

proceed with the trial] and dispose of the case in the absence of the [F87organisation].

[F89. (5. A)The matters referred to in subsection (5)(b) above are—

(a) that the [F90organisation] was cited in accordance with section 66 of this Act as read with subsection (2) above; and

(b) that it is in the interests of justice to proceed as mentioned in subsection (5) above.]

(6) Where [F91an organisation] is sentenced to a fine, the fine may be recovered in like manner in all respects as if a copy of the sentence certified by the clerk of the court were an extract decree of the Court of Session for the payment of the amount of the fine by [F92the organisation] to the Queen's and Lord Treasurer's Remembrancer.

F93. (7). . . . .

[F94. (8) In subsection (4) above, "representative" means—

(a) in the case of a body corporate (other than a limited liability partnership), the managing director, secretary or other person in charge, or locally in charge, of its affairs;

(b) in the case of a limited liability partnership, a member of the partnership;

(ba) [F95in the case of a partnership (other than a limited liability partnership), a partner or other person in charge, or locally in charge, of the partnership's affairs;

(bb) in the case of an unincorporated association, the secretary or other person in charge, or locally in charge, of the association's affairs;

(c) in the case of any other organisation, an employee, officer or official of the organisation duly appointed by it for the purposes of the proceedings.]

(9) For the purposes of subsection (8)(c) above, a statement—

(a) in the case of a body corporate (other than a limited liability partnership), purporting to be signed by an officer of the body;

(b) in the case of a limited liability partnership, purporting to be signed by a member of the partnership,

[F96. (c)in the case of a partnership (other than a limited liability partnership), purporting to be signed by a partner;

(d) in the case of an unincorporated association, purporting to be signed by an officer of the association;

(e) in the case of a government department or a part of the Scottish Administration, purporting to be signed by a senior officer in the department or part,]

to the effect that the person named in the statement has been appointed as the representative for the purposes of any proceedings to which this section applies is sufficient evidence of such appointment.]

Amendments (Textual)

F78. Word in s. 70 title substituted (28.3.2011) by Criminal Justice and Licensing (Scotland) Act 2010 (asp 13), ss. 66. (1), 206. (1); S.S.I. 2011/178, art. 2, sch.

F79. Words in s. 70. (1) substituted (28.3.2011) by Criminal Justice and Licensing (Scotland) Act 2010 (asp 13), ss. 66. (3), 206. (1); S.S.I. 2011/178, art. 2, sch.

F80. S. 70. (2) substituted (28.3.2011) by Criminal Justice and Licensing (Scotland) Act 2010 (asp 13), ss. 66. (4), 206. (1); S.S.I. 2011/178, art. 2, sch.

F81. S. 70. (2)(aa) inserted (26.4.2013) by Partnerships (Prosecution) (Scotland) Act 2013 (c. 21), ss. 6. (4), 8. (2) (with s. 8. (3)(4))

F82. Words in s. 70. (3) substituted (28.3.2011) by Criminal Justice and Licensing (Scotland) Act 2010 (asp 13), ss. 66. (5)(a), 206. (1); S.S.I. 2011/178, art. 2, sch.

F83. Words in s. 70. (3) substituted (26.3.2001) by S.I. 2001/1149, art. 3. (1), Sch. 1 para. 104. (2) (subject to art. 1. (3))

F84. Words in s. 70. (3) substituted (28.3.2011) by Criminal Justice and Licensing (Scotland) Act 2010 (asp 13), ss. 66. (5)(b), 206. (1); S.S.I. 2011/178, art. 2, sch.

F85. Words in s. 70. (4) substituted (28.3.2011) by Criminal Justice and Licensing (Scotland) Act 2010 (asp 13), ss. 66. (6)(a), 206. (1); S.S.I. 2011/178, art. 2, sch.

F86. Words in s. 70. (4) repealed (28.3.2011) by Criminal Justice and Licensing (Scotland) Act 2010 (asp 13), ss. 66. (6)(b), 206. (1); S.S.I. 2011/178, art. 2, sch.

F87. Word in s. 70. (5) substituted (28.3.2011) by Criminal Justice and Licensing (Scotland) Act 2010 (asp 13), ss. 66. (7), 206. (1); S.S.I. 2011/178, art. 2, sch.

F88. Words in s. 70. (5) substituted (1.2.2005) by Criminal Procedure (Amendment) (Scotland) Act 2004 (asp 5), ss. 10. (6)(a), 27. (1); S.S.I. 2004/405, art. 2, Sch. 1 (subject to arts. 3-5)

F89. S. 70. (5. A) inserted (1.2.2005) by Criminal Procedure (Amendment) (Scotland) Act 2004 (asp 5), ss. 10. (6)(b), 27. (1); S.S.I. 2004/405, art. 2, Sch. 1 (subject to arts. 3-5)

F90. Word in s. 70. (5. A)(a) substituted (28.3.2011) by Criminal Justice and Licensing (Scotland) Act 2010 (asp 13), ss. 66. (8), 206. (1); S.S.I. 2011/178, art. 2, sch.

F91. Words in s. 70. (6) substituted (28.3.2011) by Criminal Justice and Licensing (Scotland) Act 2010 (asp 13), ss. 66. (9)(a), 206. (1); S.S.I. 2011/178, art. 2, sch.

F92. Words in s. 70. (6) substituted (28.3.2011) by Criminal Justice and Licensing (Scotland) Act 2010 (asp 13), ss. 66. (9)(b), 206. (1); S.S.I. 2011/178, art. 2, sch.

F93. S. 70. (7) repealed (17.1.2017) by Criminal Justice (Scotland) Act 2016 (asp 1), ss. 83. (a), 117. (2); S.S.I. 2016/426, art. 2, sch.

F94. S. 70. (8)(9) substituted (10.3.2008) for s. 70. (8) by Criminal Proceedings etc. (Reform) (Scotland) Act 2007 (asp 6), ss. 28, 84; S.S.I. 2008/42, art. 3, Sch.

F95. S. 70. (8)(ba)-(c) substituted for s. 70. (8)(c) (28.3.2011) by Criminal Justice and Licensing (Scotland) Act 2010 (asp 13), ss. 66. (11), 206. (1); S.S.I. 2011/178, art. 2, sch.

F96. S. 70. (9)(c)-(e) inserted (28.3.2011) by Criminal Justice and Licensing (Scotland) Act 2010 (asp 13), ss. 66. (12), 206. (1); S.S.I. 2011/178, art. 2, sch.

Modifications etc. (not altering text)

C6. S. 70 extended (6.1.1997) by S.I. 1996/2827, reg. 70. (4)

C7. S. 70 applied (18.6.2001) by 2000 c. 8, s. 403. (4)(b); S.I. 2001/1820, art. 2, Sch.

S. 70 applied (with modifications) (16.2.2001) by 2000 c. 41, s. 153. (4); S.I. 2001/222, art. 2, Sch. 1 Pt. 1

S. 70 applied (31.5.2002) by Anti-terrorism, Crime and Security Act 2001 (c. 24), s. 69. (4)(b); S.I. 2002/1279, art. 2

S. 70 applied (1.4.2005) by Gangmasters (Licensing) Act 2004 (c. 11), ss. {21. (4)(b)}, {22. (6)(b)}, 29; S.I. 2005/447, art. 1

C8. S. 70 applied (26.7.2007 for certain purposes and 26.7.2008 otherwise) by The Civil Aviation (Access to Air Travel for Disabled Persons and Persons with Reduced Mobility) Regulations 2007 (S.I. 2007/1895), regs. 1, 6. (4)

S. 70 applied (15.12.2007) by The Money Laundering Regulations 2007 (S.I. 2007/2157), reg. 47. (8)(b)

S. 70 applied (15.12.2007) by The Transfer of Funds (Information on the Payer) Regulations 2007

(S.I. 2007/3298), reg. 16. (8)(b)

S. 70 applied (6.4.2008) by Serious Crime Act 2007 (c. 27), ss. 31. (6)(b)(ii), 94; S.I. 2008/755, art. 15. (1) (subject to paras. (2)(3))

S. 70 applied (6.4.2008) by Serious Crime Act 2007 (c. 27), ss. 32. (5)(b)(ii), 94; S.I. 2008/755, art. 15. (1) (subject to paras. (2)(3))

C9. S. 70 applied (20.1.2007, 6.4.2007, 1.10.2007, 6.4.2008, 1.10.2008 for certain purposes and 1.10.2009 otherwise) by Companies Act 2006 (c. 46), ss. 1130. (2)(b)(ii), 1300 (with savings in s. 1133); S.I. 2006/3428, art. 3. (2) (subject to Sch. 1 (which was revoked (1.10.2009) by S.I. 2008/2860, art. 6 subject to savings in Sch. 2)); S.I. 2007/1093, art. 2. (2)(c) (subject to Sch. 1. (which was revoked (1.10.2009) by S.I. 2008/2860, art. 6 subject to savings in Sch. 2)); S.I. 2007/2194, art. 2. (1)(l)(3)(h)(subject to art. 12, Sch. 1. (which Sch. 1 was revoked (1.10.2009) by S.I. 2008/2860, art. 6 subject to savings in Sch. 2)); S.I. 2007/3495, arts. {3. (3)(g)},{5. (3)(a)}(subject to arts. 7, 12, Sch. 1 (which Sch. 1 was revoked (1.10.2009) by S.I. 2008/2860, art. 6 subject to savings in Sch. 2)); S.I. 2008/2860, art. 3. (s) (with arts. 5, 7, 8, Sch. 2 (as amended by S.I. 2009/1802, art. 18 and S.I. 2009/2476, reg. 2)).

C10. S. 70 applied (20.1.2007 for certain purposes and 6.4.2008 otherwise) by Companies Act 2006 (c. 46), ss. 1257. (5), 1300; S.I. 2006/3428, art. 3. (3) (subject to arts. 5, 6, Sch. 1 (which Sch. 1 was revoked (1.10.2009) by S.I. 2008/2860, art. 6 subject to savings in Sch. 2)); S.I. 2007/3495, art. 3. (1)(u) (with arts. 7, 12, Sch. 4 paras. 37-42)

C11. S. 70 applied (5.2.2008) by The Transport Act 1968 (c. 73), s. 102. B(4)(b) (as inserted by The Passenger and Goods Vehicles (Recording Equipment) (Downloading and Retention of Data) Regulations 2008 (S.I. 2008/198), reg. 3)

C12. S. 70 applied (27.11.2008) by Counter-Terrorism Act 2008 (c. 28), ss. 62, 91, 100, Sch. 7 para. 37. (2)(b) (with s. 101. (2) and Sch. 7 para. 43)

C13. S. 70 applied (9.3.2009) by The Ozone-Depleting Substances (Qualifications) Regulations 2009 (S.I. 2009/ 216), {reg. 10. (4)}

S. 70 applied (9.3.2009) by The Ozone-Depleting Substances (Qualifications) Regulations 2009 (S.I. 2009/ 216), {reg. 10. (6)(ii)}

C14. S. 70 applied (9.3.2009) by The Fluorinated Greenhouse Gases Regulations 2009 (S.I. 2009/261), regs. 1. (1)(b)(4), 52. (4)

S. 70 applied (9.3.2009) by The Fluorinated Greenhouse Gases Regulations 2009 (S.I. 2009/261), regs. 1. (1)(b)(4), 52. (6)(b)(ii)

C15. S. 70 applied (27.4.2009) by The Organic Products Regulations 2009 (S.I. 2009/842), reg. 28. (4)(b)

C16. S. 70 applied (1.1.2010) by The Common Agricultural Policy Single Payment and Support Schemes (Integrated Administration and Control System) Regulations 2009 (S.I. 2009/3263), reg. 12. (2)(b)(ii)

C17. S. 70 applied (prosp.) by Pensions Act 2008 (c. 30), ss. 47. (2)(b)(ii), 149

C18. S. 70 applied (1.5.2009 for certain purposes, otherwise 1.11.2009) by The Payment Services Regulations 2009 (S.I. 2009/209), {regs. 1. (2)(b)(xiii)(c), 118. (4)(b)}

C19. S. 70 applied (8.3.2010) by The Mercury Export and Data (Enforcement) Regulations 2010 (S.I. 2010/265), reg. 7. (7)(b)(ii)

C20. S. 70 applied (6.4.2010) by The Detergents Regulations 2010 (S.I. 2010/740), reg. 24. (2)(b)(ii)

C21. S. 70 applied (17.12.2010) by Terrorist Asset-Freezing etc. Act 2010 (c. 38), ss. 38. (5)(b)(6), 55. (1) (with s. 44)

C22. S. 70 applied (1.7.2011) by Bribery Act 2010 (c. 23), ss. 15. (2)(b)(iii), 19. (1) (with ss. 16, 19. (5)); S.I. 2011/1418, art. 2

C23. S. 70 applied (with modifications) (30.12.2011) by The Wine Regulations 2011 (S.I. 2011/2936), regs. 1. (2), 16. (2)(c) (with reg. 3. (9))

C24. S. 70 applied (30.6.2012) by Pensions Act 2008 (c. 30), ss. 47. (2)(b)(ii), 149. (1); S.I. 2012/1682, art. 2, Sch. 2

C25. S. 70 applied (1.2.2007 for W. for specified purposes, 2.4.2007 for W. for specified

138

purposes, 1.7.2007 for E. for specified purposes, 22.4.2008 for E.W.S. for specified purposes, 13.12.2008 for W. for specified purposes, 1.8.2012 for N.I. for specified purposes) by Health Act 2006 (c. 28), ss. 77. (4)(b), 83. (4)(a)(6)(b)(7); S.I. 2007/204, arts. 2. (c), 3. (c); S.I. 2007/1375, art. 2. (b); S.I. 2008/1147, art. 3. (b)(c); S.I. 2008/3171, art. 2. (b); S.R. 2012/307, art. 2. (b)

C26. S. 70 applied (with modifications) (1.3.2014) by The Olive Oil (Marketing Standards) Regulations 2014 (S.I. 2014/195), regs. 1, 15. (2)(c)

C27. S. 70 applied (12.12.2014) by The Immigration Act 2014 (Bank Accounts) Regulations 2014 (S.I. 2014/3085), regs. 1, 23. (4)(b)

C28. S. 70 applied (7.3.2015 for specified purposes) by The Ozone-Depleting Substances Regulations 2015 (S.I. 2015/168), regs. 1. (2), 11. (5)(8)(b)(ii) (with regs. 1. (3), 2. (7), 12. (7))

C29. S. 70 applied (19.3.2015 for specified purposes) by The Fluorinated Greenhouse Gases Regulations 2015 (S.I. 2015/310), regs. 1. (1)(b)(2), 30. (6)(b)(ii)

C30. S. 70 applied (13.4.2015) by The Electricity and Gas (Market Integrity and Transparency) (Criminal Sanctions) Regulations 2015 (S.I. 2015/979), regs. 1, 8. (2)(b)

C31. S. 70 applied (with modifications) (16.11.2015) by The Single Common Market Organisation (Emergency Aid for Milk Producers) Regulations 2015 (S.I. 2015/1896), regs. 1. (2), 13. (2)(c)

C32. S. 70 applied (1.1.2016) by The Small and Medium Sized Business (Finance Platforms) Regulations 2015 (S.I. 2015/1946), regs. 1. (2), 35. (4)(b)

C33. S. 70 applied (1.1.2016) by The Small and Medium Sized Business (Credit Information) Regulations 2015 (S.I. 2015/1945), regs. 1. (2), 38. (4)(b)

C34. S. 70 applied (13.7.2016) by The Financial Services and Markets Act 2000 (Transparency of Securities Financing Transactions and of Reuse) Regulations 2016 (S.I. 2016/715), regs. 1. (2), 27. (4)(b)

C35. S. 70 applied (25.11.2016) by Immigration Act 2016 (c. 19), ss. 30. (3)(b)(ii), 94. (1); S.I. 2016/1037, reg. 4. (c)

C36. S. 70 applied (25.11.2016) by Immigration Act 2016 (c. 19), ss. 29. (4)(b)(ii), 94. (1); S.I. 2016/1037, reg. 4. (c)

C37. S. 70 applied (13.10.2017) by The Payment Services Regulations 2017 (S.I. 2017/752), regs. 1. (3)(d), 146. (4)(b) (with reg. 3)

[F9770. ADefence statementsS

(1) This section applies where an indictment is served on an accused.

(2) The accused must lodge a defence statement at least 14 days before the first diet.

(3) The accused must lodge a defence statement at least 14 days before the preliminary hearing.

(4) At least 7 days before the trial diet the accused must—

   (a) where there has been no material change in circumstances in relation to the accused's defence since the last defence statement was lodged, lodge a statement stating that fact,

   (b) where there has been a material change in circumstances in relation to the accused's defence since the last defence statement was lodged, lodge a defence statement.

(5) If after lodging a statement under subsection (2), (3) or (4) there is a material change in circumstances in relation to the accused's defence, the accused must lodge a defence statement.

(6) Where subsection (5) requires a defence statement to be lodged, it must be lodged before the trial diet begins unless on cause shown the court allows it to be lodged during the trial diet.

(7) The accused may lodge a defence statement—

   (a) at any time before the trial diet, or

   (b) during the trial diet if the court on cause shown allows it.

(8) As soon as practicable after lodging a defence statement or a statement under subsection (4)(a), the accused must send a copy of the statement to the prosecutor and any co-accused.

(9) In this section, "defence statement" means a statement setting out—

   (a) the nature of the accused's defence, including any particular defences on which the accused intends to rely,

(b) any matters of fact on which the accused takes issue with the prosecution and the reason for doing so,

(c) particulars of the matters of fact on which the accused intends to rely for the purposes of the accused's defence,

(d) any point of law which the accused wishes to take and any authority on which the accused intends to rely for that purpose,

(e) by reference to the accused's defence, the nature of any information that the accused requires the prosecutor to disclose, and

(f) the reasons why the accused considers that disclosure by the prosecutor of any such information is necessary.]

Amendments (Textual)

F97. S. 70. A inserted (6.6.2011) by Criminal Justice and Licensing (Scotland) Act 2010 (asp 13), ss. 124. (3), 206. (1) (with s. 124. (1)); S.S.I. 2011/178, art. 2, sch.

Pre-trial proceedingsS

71 First diet.S

[F98. (A1)At a first diet [F99in proceedings to which subsection (B1) below applies], the court shall, F100. . . ascertain whether [F101the accused] has engaged a solicitor for the purposes of [F102the conduct of his case at any relevant hearing in the course of the proceedings].]

[F103. (B1)This subsection applies to proceedings—

(a) in which the accused is charged with a sexual offence to which section 288. C of this Act applies,

(b) to which section 288. E of this Act applies, or

(c) in which an order under section 288. F(2) of this Act has been made [F104in relation to any hearing in the course of the proceedings].]

(1) At a first diet the court shall, so far as is reasonably practicable, ascertain F105...—

(a) the state of preparation of the prosecutor and of the accused with respect to their cases; and

(b) the extent to which the prosecutor and the accused have complied with the duty under section 257. (1) of this Act.

[F106. (1. ZA)If a written record has been lodged in accordance with section 71. C, the court must have regard to the written record when ascertaining the state of preparation of the parties.]

[F107. (1. A)At a first diet, the court shall also—

(a) ascertain whether subsection (1. B) below applies to any person who is to give evidence at or for the purposes of [F108any hearing in the course of the proceedings] or to the accused, and

(b) if so, consider whether it should make an order under section 271. A(7) or 271. D(2) of this Act in relation to the person or, as the case may be, the accused.

(1. B)This subsection applies—

(a) to a person who is to give evidence at or for the purposes of [F109any hearing in the course of the proceedings] if that person is, or is likely to be, a vulnerable witness,

(b) to the accused if, were he to give evidence at or for the purposes of the trial, he would be, or would be likely to be, a vulnerable witness.]

[F110. (1. C)At a first diet, the court—

(a) shall ascertain which of the witnesses included in the list of witnesses are required by the prosecutor or the accused to attend the trial; and

(b) shall, where the accused has been admitted to bail, review the conditions imposed on his bail and may—

(i) after giving the parties an opportunity to be heard; and

(ii) if it considers it appropriate to do so,

fix bail on different conditions.]

(2) In addition to the matters mentioned in subsection (1) [F111, (1. A) and (1. C)] above the court shall, at a first diet, consider any [F112preliminary plea or preliminary issue (within the meanings given to those terms in section 79. (2) of this Act)] of which a party has, not less than two clear days before the first diet, given notice to the court and to the other parties.

[F113. (2. XA)At a first diet the court shall also dispose of any [F114vulnerable] witness notice under section 271. A(2) or vulnerable witness application under section 271. C(2) appointed to be disposed of at that diet.]

[F115. (2. YA)At a first diet, the court shall also ascertain whether there is any objection to the admissibility of any evidence which any party wishes to raise despite not having given the notice referred to in subsection (2) above, and—

(a) if so, decide whether to grant leave under section 79. (1) of this Act for the objection to be raised; and

(b) if leave is granted, dispose of the objection unless it considers it inappropriate to do so at the first diet.

(2. ZA)Where the court, having granted leave for the objection to be raised, decides not to dispose of it at the first diet, the court may—

(a) appoint a further diet to be held before the trial diet for the purpose of disposing of the objection; or

(b) appoint the objection to be disposed of at the trial diet.]

[F116. (2. A)At a first diet the court may consider an application for the purposes of subsection (1) of section 275 of this Act.]

(3) At a first diet the court may ask the prosecutor and the accused any question in connection with any matter which it is required to ascertain or consider under subsection (1) [F117, (1. A)][F118, (1. C)][F119, (2) or (2. YA)] above [F120or which is relevant to an application for the purposes of subsection (1) of the said section 275].

(4) The accused shall attend a first diet of which he has been given notice F121. . .

(5) A first diet may proceed [F122, and a trial diet may be appointed,] notwithstanding the absence of the accused.

[F123. (5. A)Where, however—

[F124. (a)the proceedings in which the first diet is being held are proceedings to which subsection (B1) above applies;]

(b) the court has not ascertained (whether at that diet or earlier) that he has engaged a solicitor for the purposes of [F125the conduct of his case at any relevant hearing in the course of the proceeding],

a first diet may not proceed in his absence; and, in such a case, the court shall adjourn the diet and ordain the accused then to attend.]

(6) [F126. Where the accused appears at the first diet, the accused is to be required at that diet] to state how he pleads to the indictment, and section 77 of this Act shall apply where he tenders a plea of guilty.

F127. (7). . . . .

[F128. (7. A)In subsections (A1) and (5. A)(b), "relevant hearing" means—

(a) in relation to proceedings mentioned in paragraph (a) of subsection (B1), any hearing at, or for the purposes of, which a witness is to give evidence,

(b) in relation to proceedings mentioned in paragraph (b) of that subsection, a hearing referred to in section 288. E(2. A),

(c) in relation to proceedings mentioned in paragraph (c) of that subsection, a hearing in respect of which an order is made under section 288. F.]

F129. (8). . . . .

F129. (8. A). . . . .

(9) In this section [F130and section 71. B] "the court" means the sheriff court.

Amendments (Textual)

F98. S. 71. (A1) inserted (1.11.2002) by Sexual Offences (Procedure and Evidence) (Scotland)

Act 2002 (asp 9), s. 3, Sch. para. 5. (a); S.S.I. 2002/443, art. 3

F99. Words in s. 71. (A1) inserted (1.4.2005 for certain purposes and 1.4.2006 for further certain purposes and otherwise prosp.) by Vulnerable Witnesses (Scotland) Act 2004 (asp 3), ss. 7. (1)(a)(i), 25; S.S.I. 2005/168, art. 2, Sch. (with art. 4); S.S.I. 2006/59, art. 2, Sch. (with art. 4. (1))

F100. Words in s. 71. (A1) repealed (1.4.2005 for certain purposes and 1.4.2006 for further certain purposes and otherwise prosp.) by Vulnerable Witnesses (Scotland) Act 2004 (asp 3), ss. 7. (1)(a)(ii), 25; S.S.I. 2005/168, art. 2, Sch. (with art. 4); S.S.I. 2006/59, art. 2, Sch. (with art. 4. (1))

F101. Word in s. 71. (A1) substituted (1.4.2005 for certain purposes and 1.4.2006 for further certain purposes and otherwise prosp.) by Vulnerable Witnesses (Scotland) Act 2004 (asp 3), ss. 7. (1)(a)(iii), 25; S.S.I. 2005/168, art. 2, Sch. (with art. 4); S.S.I. 2006/59, art. 2, Sch. (with art. 4. (1))

F102. Words in s. 71. (A1) substituted (28.3.2011) by Criminal Justice and Licensing (Scotland) Act 2010 (asp 13), s. 206. (1), sch. 7 para. 45. (a); S.S.I. 2011/178, art. 2, sch.

F103. S. 71. (B1) inserted (1.4.2005 for certain purposes and 1.4.2006 for further certain purposes and otherwise prosp.) by Vulnerable Witnesses (Scotland) Act 2004 (asp 3), ss. 7. (1)(b), 25; S.S.I. 2005/168, art. 2, Sch. (with art. 4); S.S.I. 2006/59, art. 2, Sch. (with art. 4. (1))

F104. Words in s. 71. (B1)(c) substituted (28.3.2011) by Criminal Justice and Licensing (Scotland) Act 2010 (asp 13), s. 206. (1), sch. 7 para. 45. (b); S.S.I. 2011/178, art. 2, sch.

F105. Words in s. 71. (1) repealed (31.7.2017) by Criminal Justice (Scotland) Act 2016 (asp 1), ss. 81. (3)(a), 117. (2); S.S.I. 2017/99, art. 4. (1) (with arts. 4. (2), 6)

F106. S. 71. (1. ZA) inserted (29.5.2017 for specified purposes) by Criminal Justice (Scotland) Act 2016 (asp 1), ss. 80. (2), 117. (2); S.S.I. 2017/99, art. 3. (1)(2) (with art. 6)

F107. S. 71. (1. A)(1. B) inserted (1.4.2005 and 1.4.2006 for certain purposes, otherwise 1.4.2008) by Vulnerable Witnesses (Scotland) Act 2004 (asp 3), ss. 2. (1)(a), 25; S.S.I. 2005/168, art. 2, Sch. (with art. 4); S.S.I. 2006/59, art. 2, Sch. (with art 4. (1)); S.S.I. 2008/57, art. 2 (with art. 3)

F108. Words in s. 71. (1. A)(a) substituted (28.3.2011) by Criminal Justice and Licensing (Scotland) Act 2010 (asp 13), s. 206. (1), sch. 7 para. 45. (c); S.S.I. 2011/178, art. 2, sch.

F109. Words in s. 71. (1. B)(a) substituted (28.3.2011) by Criminal Justice and Licensing (Scotland) Act 2010 (asp 13), s. 206. (1), sch. 7 para. 45. (d); S.S.I. 2011/178, art. 2, sch.

F110. S. 71. (1. C) inserted after (1. B) (1.2.2005) by Criminal Procedure (Amendment) (Scotland) Act 2004 (asp 5), ss. 19. (2), 27. (1); S.S.I. 2004/405, art. 2, Sch. 1 (subject to arts. 3-5)

F111. Words in s. 71. (2) substituted (1.2.2005) by Criminal Procedure (Amendment) (Scotland) Act 2004 (asp 5), ss. 19. (3), 27. (1); S.S.I. 2004/405, art. 2, Sch. 1 (subject to arts. 3-5)

F112. Words in s. 71. (2) substituted (1.2.2005) by Criminal Procedure (Amendment) (Scotland) Act 2004 (asp 5), ss. 25, 27. (1), Sch. para. 20. (a); S.S.I. 2004/405, art. 2, Sch. 1 (subject to arts. 3-5)

F113. S. 71. (2. XA) inserted (1.2.2005 for certain purposes in accordance with art. 1. (3) of the amending S.S.I.) by The Criminal Procedure (Amendment) (Scotland) Act 2004 (Incidental, Supplemental and Consequential Provisions) Order 2005 (S.S.I. 2005/40), art. 4. (3); S.S.I. 2004/405, art. 2, Schs. 1, 2

F114. Word in s. 71. (2. XA) substituted (1.9.2015) by Victims and Witnesses (Scotland) Act 2014 (asp 1), ss. 11. (1), 34; S.S.I. 2015/200, art. 2. (2), sch. (with arts. 1. (3), 4)

F115. S. 71. (2. YA)(2. ZA) inserted (1.2.2005) by Criminal Procedure (Amendment) (Scotland) Act 2004 (asp 5), ss. 14. (1)(a), 27. (1); S.S.I. 2004/405, art. 2, Sch. 1 (subject to arts. 3-5)

F116. S. 71. (2. A) inserted (1.11.2002) by Sexual Offences (Procedure and Evidence) (Scotland) Act 2002 (asp 9), s. 8. (2)(a); S.S.I. 2002/443, art. 3 (with art. 4. (5))

F117. Words in s. 71. (3) inserted (1.4.2005 and 1.4.2006 for certain purposes and otherwise 1.4.2008) by Vulnerable Witnesses (Scotland) Act 2004 (asp 3), ss. 2. (1)(c), 25; S.S.I. 2005/168, art. 2, Sch. (with art. 4); S.S.I. 2006/59, art. 2, Sch. (with art. 4. (1)); S.S.I. 2008/57, art. 2 (with art. 3)

F118. Words in s. 71. (3) inserted (1.2.2005) by Criminal Procedure (Amendment) (Scotland) Act 2004 (asp 5), ss. 19. (4), 27. (1); S.S.I. 2004/405, art. 2, Sch. 1 (subject to arts. 3-5)

F119. Words in s. 71. (3) substituted (1.2.2005) by Criminal Procedure (Amendment) (Scotland) Act 2004 (asp 5), ss. 14. (1)(b), 27. (1); S.S.I. 2004/405, art. 2, Sch. 1 (subject to arts. 3-5)

F120. Words in s. 71. (3) inserted (1.11.2002) by Sexual Offences (Procedure and Evidence) (Scotland) Act 2002 (asp 9), s. 8. (2)(b); S.S.I. 2002/443, art. 3 (with art. 4. (5))

F121. Words in s. 71. (4) repealed (10.12.2007) by Criminal Proceedings etc. (Reform) (Scotland) Act 2007 (asp 6), ss. 80, 84, Sch. para. 12. (2); S.S.I. 2007/479, art. 3. (1), Sch. (as amended by S.S.I. 2007/527)

F122. Words in s. 71. (5) inserted (31.7.2017) by Criminal Justice (Scotland) Act 2016 (asp 1), ss. 81. (3)(b), 117. (2); S.S.I. 2017/99, art. 4. (1) (with arts. 4. (2), 6)

F123. S. 71. (5. A) inserted (1.11.2002) by Sexual Offences (Procedure and Evidence) (Scotland) Act 2002 (asp 9), s. 3, Sch. para. 5. (b); S.S.I. 2002/443, art. 3

F124. S. 71. (5. A)(a) substituted (1.4.2005 for certain purposes and 1.4.2006 for further certain purposes and otherwise prosp.) by Vulnerable Witnesses (Scotland) Act 2004 (asp 3), ss. 7. (1)(c), 25; S.S.I. 2005/168, art. 2, Sch. (with art. 4); S.S.I. 2006/59, art. 2, Sch. (with art. 4. (1))

F125. Words in s. 71. (5. A)(b) substituted (28.3.2011) by Criminal Justice and Licensing (Scotland) Act 2010 (asp 13), s. 206. (1), sch. 7 para. 45. (e); S.S.I. 2011/178, art. 2, sch.

F126. Words in s. 71. (6) substituted (31.7.2017) by Criminal Justice (Scotland) Act 2016 (asp 1), ss. 81. (3)(c), 117. (2); S.S.I. 2017/99, art. 4. (1) (with arts. 4. (2), 6)

F127. S. 71. (7) repealed (31.7.2017) by Criminal Justice (Scotland) Act 2016 (asp 1), ss. 81. (3)(d), 117. (2); S.S.I. 2017/99, art. 4. (1) (with arts. 4. (2), 6)

F128. S. 71. (7. A) inserted (28.3.2011) by Criminal Justice and Licensing (Scotland) Act 2010 (asp 13), s. 206. (1), sch. 7 para. 45. (f); S.S.I. 2011/178, art. 2, sch.

F129. S. 71. (8)(8. A) repealed (1.2.2005) by Criminal Procedure (Amendment) (Scotland) Act 2004 (asp 5), ss. 25, 27. (1), Sch. para. 20. (b); S.S.I. 2004/405, art. 2, Sch. 1 (subject to arts. 3-5)

F130. Words in s. 71. (9) inserted (31.7.2017) by Criminal Justice (Scotland) Act 2016 (asp 1), ss. 81. (3)(e), 117. (2); S.S.I. 2017/99, art. 4. (1) (with arts. 4. (2), 6)

[F13171. A Further pre-trial diet: dismissal or withdrawal of solicitor representing accused in case of sexual offenceS

F132. . . . .]

Amendments (Textual)

F131. S. 71. A inserted (1.11.2002) by Sexual Offences (Procedure and Evidence) (Scotland) Act 2002 (asp 9), s. 3, Sch. para. 6; S.S.I. 2002/443, art. 3

F132. S. 71. A repealed (4.12.2004) by Criminal Procedure (Amendment) (Scotland) Act 2004 (asp 5), ss. 25, 27. (1), Sch. para. 21; S.S.I. 2004/405, art. 2, Sch. 1 (subject to arts. 3-5)

[F13371. BFirst diet: appointment of trial dietS

(1) At a first diet, unless a plea of guilty is tendered and accepted, the court must—

    (a) after complying with section 71, and

    (b) subject to subsections (3) to (7),

appoint a trial diet.

(2) Where a trial diet is appointed at a first diet, the accused must appear at the trial diet and answer the indictment.

(3) In appointing a trial diet under subsection (1), in any case in which the 12 month period applies (whether or not the 140 day period also applies in the case)—

    (a) if the court considers that the case would be likely to be ready to proceed to trial within that period, it must, subject to subsections (5) to (7), appoint a trial diet for a date within that period, or

    (b) if the court considers that the case would not be likely to be so ready, it must give the prosecutor an opportunity to make an application to the court under section 65. (3) for an extension of the 12 month period.

(4) Where paragraph (b) of subsection (3) applies—

(a) if such an application as is mentioned in that paragraph is made and granted, the court must, subject to subsections (5) to (7), appoint a trial diet for a date within the 12 month period as extended, or

(b) if no such application is made or if one is made but is refused by the court—

(i) the court may desert the first diet simpliciter or pro loco et tempore, and

(ii) where the accused is committed until liberated in due course of law, the accused must be liberated forthwith.

(5) Subsection (6) applies in any case in which—

(a) the 140 day period as well as the 12 month period applies, and

(b) the court is required, by virtue of subsection (3)(a) or (4)(a) to appoint a trial diet within the 12 month period.

(6) In such a case—

(a) if the court considers that the case would be likely to be ready to proceed to trial within the 140 day period, it must appoint a trial diet for a date within that period as well as within the 12 month period, or

(b) if the court considers that the case would not be likely to be so ready, it must give the prosecutor an opportunity to make an application under section 65. (5) for an extension of the 140 day period.

(7) Where paragraph (b) of subsection (6) applies—

(a) if such an application as is mentioned in that paragraph is made and granted, the court must appoint a trial diet for a date within the 140 day period as extended as well as within the 12 month period,

(b) if no such application is made or if one is made but is refused by the court—

(i) the court must proceed under subsection (3)(a) or (as the case may be) (4)(a) to appoint a trial diet for a date within the 12 month period, and

(ii) the accused is then entitled to be admitted to bail.

(8) Where an accused is, by virtue of subsection (7)(b)(ii), entitled to be admitted to bail, the court must, before admitting the accused to bail, give the prosecutor an opportunity to be heard.

(9) On appointing a trial diet under this section in a case where the accused has been admitted to bail (otherwise than by virtue of subsection (7)(b)(ii)), the court, after giving the parties an opportunity to be heard—

(a) must review the conditions imposed on the accused's bail, and

(b) having done so, may, if it considers it appropriate to do so, fix bail on different conditions.

(10) In this section—

"the 12 month period" means the period specified in subsection (1)(b) of section 65 and, in any case in which that period has been extended under subsection (3) of that section, includes that period as so extended,

"the 140 day period" means the period specified in subsection (4)(b)(ii) of section 65 and, in any case in which that period has been extended under subsection (5) of that section, includes that period as so extended.]

Amendments (Textual)

F133. S. 71. B inserted (31.7.2017) after s. 71 by virtue of Criminal Justice (Scotland) Act 2016 (asp 1), ss. 81. (4), 117. (2); S.S.I. 2017/99, art. 4. (1) (with arts. 4. (2), 6)

[F13471. CWritten record of state of preparation: sheriff courtS

(1) Subsection (2) applies where—

(a) the accused is indicted to the sheriff court, and

(b) a solicitor—

(i) has notified the court under section 72. F(1) that the solicitor has been engaged by the accused for the purposes of conducting the accused's defence, and

(ii) has not subsequently been dismissed by the accused or withdrawn.

(2) The prosecutor and the accused's legal representative must, within the period described in subsection (3), communicate with each other and jointly prepare a written record of their state of preparation with respect to their cases (referred to in this section as "the written record").

(3) The period referred to in subsection (2) begins on the day the accused is served with an indictment and expires at the end of the day falling 14 days later.

(4) The written record must—

    (a) be in such form, or as nearly as may be in such form,

    (b) contain such information, and

    (c) be lodged in such manner,

as may be prescribed by act of adjournal.

(5) The written record must state the manner in which the communication required by subsection (2) was conducted (for example, by telephone, email or a meeting in person).

(6) In subsection (2), "the accused's legal representative" means—

    (a) the solicitor referred to in subsection (1), or

    (b) where the solicitor has instructed counsel for the purposes of the conduct of the accused's case, either the solicitor or that counsel, or both of them.

(7) In subsection (6)(b), "counsel" includes a solicitor who has a right of audience in the High Court of Justiciary under section 25. A of the Solicitors (Scotland) Act 1980.]

Amendments (Textual)

F134. S. 71. C inserted (29.5.2017 for specified purposes) by Criminal Justice (Scotland) Act 2016 (asp 1), ss. 80. (3), 117. (2); S.S.I. 2017/99, art. 3. (1)(2) (with art. 6)

[F13572 Preliminary hearing: procedure up to appointment of trial dietS

(1) A preliminary hearing shall be conducted in accordance with this section and section 72. A.

(2) The court shall—

    (a) where the accused is charged with an offence to which section 288. C of this Act applies; or

    (b) in any case—

(i) in respect of which section 288. E of this Act applies; or

(ii) in which an order has been made under section 288. F(2) of this Act,

before taking any further step under this section, ascertain whether the accused has engaged a solicitor for the purposes of the conduct of his case at or for the purposes of the preliminary hearing.

(3) After complying with subsection (2) above, the court shall dispose of any preliminary pleas (within the meaning of section 79. (2)(a) of this Act) of which a party has given notice not less than 7 clear days before the preliminary hearing to the court and to the other parties.

(4) After disposing of any preliminary pleas under subsection (3) above, the court shall require the accused to state how he pleads to the indictment.

(5) If the accused tenders a plea of guilty, section 77 of this Act shall apply.

(6) After the accused has stated how he pleads to the indictment, the court shall, unless a plea of guilty is tendered and accepted—

    (a) in any case—

(i) where the accused is charged with an offence to which section 288. C of this Act applies;

(ii) in respect of which section 288. E of this Act applies; or

(iii) in which an order has been made under section 288. F(2) of this Act,

ascertain whether the accused has engaged a solicitor for the purposes of his defence at the trial;

    (b) unless it considers it inappropriate to do so at the preliminary hearing, dispose of—

(i) any preliminary issues (within the meaning of section 79. (2)(b) of this Act) of which a party has given notice not less than 7 clear days before the preliminary hearing to the court and to the other parties;

(ii) any [F136vulnerable] witness notice under section 271. A(2) or vulnerable witness application under section 271. C(2) appointed to be disposed of at the preliminary hearing;

(iii) subject to subsection (8) below, any application under section 275. (1) or 288. F(2) of this Act made before the preliminary hearing; and

(iv) any other matter which, in the opinion of the court, could be disposed of with advantage before the trial;

(c) ascertain whether there is any objection to the admissibility of any evidence which any party wishes to raise despite not having given the notice referred to in paragraph (b)(i) above, and—

(i) if so, decide whether to grant leave under section 79. (1) of this Act for the objection to be raised; and

(ii) if leave is granted, dispose of the objection unless it considers it inappropriate to do so at the preliminary hearing;

(d) ascertain which of the witnesses included in the list of witnesses are required by the prosecutor or the accused to attend the trial;

(e) ascertain whether subsection (7) below applies to any person who is to give evidence at or for the purposes of the trial or to the accused and, if so, consider whether it should make an order under section 271. A(7) or 271. D(2) of this Act in relation to the person or, as the case may be, the accused; and

(f) ascertain, so far as is reasonably practicable—

(i) the state of preparation of the prosecutor and the accused with respect to their cases; and

(ii) the extent to which the prosecutor and the accused have complied with the duty under section 257. (1) of this Act.

(7) This subsection applies—

(a) to a person who is to give evidence at or for the purposes of the trial if that person is, or is likely to be, a vulnerable witness;

(b) to the accused if, were he to give evidence at or for the purposes of the trial, he would be, or would be likely to be, a vulnerable witness.

(8) Where any application or notice such as is mentioned in subsection (6)(b)(iii) above is required by the provision under which it is made or lodged, or by any other provision of this Act, to be made or lodged by a certain time, the court—

(a) shall not be required under that subsection to dispose of it unless it has been made or lodged by that time; but

(b) shall have power to dispose of it to the extent that the provision under which it was made, or any other provision of this Act, allows it to be disposed of notwithstanding that it was not made or lodged in time.

(9) Where the court decides not to dispose of any preliminary issue, application, notice, objection or other matter referred to in subsection (6)(b) or (c) above at the preliminary hearing, it may—

(a) appoint a further diet, to be held before the trial diet appointed under section 72. A of this Act, for the purpose of disposing of the issue, application, notice, objection or matter; or

(b) appoint the issue, application, notice, objection or other matter to be disposed of at the trial diet.]

Amendments (Textual)

F135. Ss. 72-72. D substituted for ss. 72-73. A (1.2.2005, 1.4.2005, 1.4.2006, 1.4.2007 and 2.7.2007 for certain purposes, otherwise 1.4.2008) by Criminal Procedure (Amendment) (Scotland) Act 2004 (asp 5), ss. 1. (3), 27. (1); S.S.I. 2004/405, art. 2, Sch. 1 (subject to arts. 3-5); S.S.I. 2005/168, art. 2, Sch. (with art. 4); S.S.I. 2006/59, art. 2, Sch. (with art. 4. (1)); S.S.I. 2007/101, art. 2, Sch. (with art. 4); S.S.I. 2007/329, art. 2, Sch. (with art. 4)); S.S.I. 2008/57, art. 2 (with art. 3)

F136. Word in s. 72. (6)(b)(ii) substituted (1.9.2015) by Victims and Witnesses (Scotland) Act 2014 (asp 1), ss. 11. (2), 34; S.S.I. 2015/200, art. 2. (2), sch. (with arts. 1. (3), 4)

[F137[F13872. A Preliminary hearing: appointment of trial dietS

(1) [F139. In any case in which subsection (6) of section 72] applies, the court shall, at the preliminary hearing—

(a) after complying with that subsection;

(b) having regard to earlier proceedings at the preliminary hearing; and

(c) subject to subsections (3) to (7) below,

appoint a trial diet.

F140. (1. A). . . . .

(2) In appointing a trial diet under subsection (1) above, the court may, if satisfied that it is appropriate to do so, indicate that the diet is to be a floating diet for the purposes of section 83. A of this Act.

(3) In any case in which the 12 month period applies (whether or not the 140 day period also applies in the case)—

(a) if the court considers that the case would be likely to be ready to proceed to trial within that period, it shall, subject to subsections (5) to (7) below, appoint a trial diet for a date within that period; or

(b) if the court considers that the case would not be likely to be so ready, it shall give the prosecutor an opportunity to make an application to the court under section 65. (3) of this Act for an extension of the 12 month period.

(4) Where paragraph (b) of subsection (3) above applies—

(a) if such an application as is mentioned in that paragraph is made and granted, the court shall, subject to subsections (5) to (7) below, appoint a trial diet for a date within the 12 month period as extended; or

(b) if no such application is made or if one is made but is refused by the court—

(i) the court may desert the preliminary hearing simpliciter or pro loco et tempore; and

(ii) where the accused is committed until liberated in due course of law, he shall be liberated forthwith.

(5) Subsection (6) below applies in any case in which—

(a) the 140 day period as well as the 12 month period applies; and

(b) the court is required, by virtue of subsection (3)(a) or (4)(a) above, to appoint a trial diet within the 12 month period.

(6) In such a case—

(a) if the court considers that the case would be likely to be ready to proceed to trial within the 140 day period, it shall appoint a trial diet for a date within that period as well as within the 12 month period; or

(b) if the court considers that the case would not be likely to be so ready, it shall give the prosecutor an opportunity to make an application under section 65. (5) of this Act for an extension of the 140 day period.

(7) Where paragraph (b) of subsection (6) above applies—

(a) if such an application as is mentioned in that paragraph is made and granted, the court shall appoint a trial diet for a date within the 140 day period as extended as well as within the 12 month period;

(b) if no such application is made or if one is made but is refused by the court—

(i) the court shall proceed under subsection (3)(a) or, as the case may be, (4)(a) above to appoint a trial diet for a date within the 12 month period; and

(ii) the accused shall then be entitled to be admitted to bail.

(8) Where an accused is, by virtue of subsection (7)(b)(ii) above, entitled to be admitted to bail, the court shall, before admitting him to bail, give the prosecutor an opportunity to be heard.

(9) On appointing a trial diet under this section in a case where the accused has been admitted to bail (otherwise than by virtue of subsection (7)(b)(ii) above), the court, after giving the parties an opportunity to be heard—

(a) shall review the conditions imposed on his bail; and

(b) having done so, may, if it considers it appropriate to do so, fix bail on different conditions.

(10) In this section—

"the 12 month period" means the period specified in subsection (1)(b) of section 65 of this Act and, in any case in which that period has been extended under subsection (3) of that section, includes that period as so extended; and

"the 140 day period" means the period specified in subsection (4)(aa)(ii) of that section and, in any case in which that period has been extended under subsection (5) of that section, includes that period as so extended.]]

Amendments (Textual)

F137. S. 72. A inserted (1.11.2002) by Sexual Offences (Procedure and Evidence) (Scotland) Act 2002 (asp 9), s. 3, Sch. para. 7; S.S.I. 2002/443, art. 3

F138. Ss. 72-72. D substituted for ss. 72-73. A (1.2.2005, 1.4.2005, 1.4.2006, 1.4.2007 and 2.7.2007 for certain purposes, otherwise 1.4.2008) by Criminal Procedure (Amendment) (Scotland) Act 2004 (asp 5), ss. 1. (3), 27. (1); S.S.I. 2004/405, art. 2, Sch. 1 (subject to arts. 3-5); S.S.I. 2005/168, art. 2, Sch. (with art. 4); S.S.I. 2006/59, art. 2, Sch. (with art. 4. (1)); S.S.I. 2007/101, art. 2, Sch. (with art. 4); S.S.I. 2007/329, art. 2, Sch. (with art. 4)); S.S.I. 2008/57, art. 2 (with art. 3)

F139. Words in s. 72. A(1) substituted (17.1.2017) by Criminal Justice (Scotland) Act 2016 (asp 1), ss. 82. (a), 117. (2); S.S.I. 2016/426, art. 2, sch.

F140. S. 72. A(1. A) repealed (17.1.2017) by Criminal Justice (Scotland) Act 2016 (asp 1), ss. 82. (b), 117. (2); S.S.I. 2016/426, art. 2, sch.

[F14172. BPower to dispense with preliminary hearingS

(1) The court may, on an application made to it jointly by the parties, dispense with a preliminary hearing and appoint a trial diet if the court is satisfied on the basis of the application that—

(a) the state of preparation of the prosecutor and the accused with respect to their cases is such that the case is likely to be ready to proceed to trial on the date to be appointed for the trial diet;

(b) there are no preliminary pleas, preliminary issues or other matters which require to be, or could with advantage be, disposed of before the trial; and

(c) there are no persons to whom section 72. (7) of this Act applies.

(2) An application under subsection (1) above shall identify which (if any) of the witnesses included in the list of witnesses are required by the prosecutor or the accused to attend the trial.

(3) Where a trial diet is to be appointed under subsection (1) above, it shall be appointed in accordance with such procedure as may be prescribed by Act of Adjournal.

(4) Where a trial diet is appointed under subsection (1) above, the accused shall appear at the diet and answer the indictment.

(5) The fact that a preliminary hearing in any case has been dispensed with under subsection (1) above shall not affect the calculation in that case of any time limit for the giving of any notice or the doing of any other thing under this Act, being a time limit fixed by reference to the preliminary hearing.

(6) Accordingly, any such time limit shall have effect in any such case as if it were fixed by reference to the date on which the preliminary hearing would have been held if it had not been dispensed with.

Amendments (Textual)

F141. Ss. 72-72. D substituted for ss. 72-73. A (1.2.2005, 1.4.2005, 1.4.2006, 1.4.2007 and 2.7.2007 for certain purposes, otherwise 1.4.2008) by Criminal Procedure (Amendment) (Scotland) Act 2004 (asp 5), ss. 1. (3), 27. (1); S.S.I. 2004/405, art. 2, Sch. 1 (subject to arts. 3-5); S.S.I. 2005/168, art. 2, Sch. (with art. 4); S.S.I. 2006/59, art. 2, Sch. (with art. 4. (1)); S.S.I. 2007/101, art. 2, Sch. (with art. 4); S.S.I. 2007/329, art. 2, Sch. (with art. 4)); S.S.I. 2008/57, art. 2 (with art. 3)

72. CProcedure where preliminary hearing does not proceedS

(1) The prosecutor shall not raise a fresh libel in any case in which the court has deserted a preliminary hearing simpliciter unless the court's decision has been reversed on appeal.

(2) Where a preliminary hearing is deserted pro loco et tempore, the court may appoint a further preliminary hearing for a later date and the accused shall appear and answer the indictment at that hearing.

(3) Subsection (4) below applies where, at a preliminary hearing—

(a) the hearing has been deserted pro loco et tempore for any reason and no further preliminary hearing has been appointed under subsection (2) above; or

(b) the indictment is for any reason not proceeded with and the hearing has not been adjourned or postponed.

(4) Where this subsection applies, the prosecutor may, at any time within the period of two months after the relevant date, give notice to the accused on another copy of the indictment to appear and answer the indictment—

(a) at a further preliminary hearing in the High Court not less than seven clear days after the date of service of the notice; or

[F142. (b)at—

(i) a first diet not less than 15 clear days after the service of the notice and not less than 10 clear days before the trial diet; and

(ii) a trial diet not less than 29 clear days after the service of the notice,

in the sheriff court where the charge is one that can lawfully be tried in that court.]

[F142. (b)where the charge is one that can lawfully be tried in the sheriff court, at a first diet in that court not less than 29 clear days after the service of the notice.]

(5) Where notice is given to the accused under subsection (4)(b) above, then for the purposes of section 65. (4) of this Act—

(a) the giving of the notice shall be taken to be service of an indictment in respect of the sheriff court; and

(b) the previous service of the indictment in respect of the High Court shall be disregarded.

(6) In subsection (4) above, "the relevant date" means—

(a) where paragraph (a) of subsection (3) above applies, the date on which the diet was deserted as mentioned in that paragraph; or

(b) where paragraph (b) of that subsection applies, the date of the preliminary hearing referred to in that paragraph.

(7) A notice referred to in subsection (4) above shall be in such form as may be prescribed by Act of Adjournal, or as nearly as may be in such form.

Amendments (Textual)

F141. Ss. 72-72. D substituted for ss. 72-73. A (1.2.2005, 1.4.2005, 1.4.2006, 1.4.2007 and 2.7.2007 for certain purposes, otherwise 1.4.2008) by Criminal Procedure (Amendment) (Scotland) Act 2004 (asp 5), ss. 1. (3), 27. (1); S.S.I. 2004/405, art. 2, Sch. 1 (subject to arts. 3-5); S.S.I. 2005/168, art. 2, Sch. (with art. 4); S.S.I. 2006/59, art. 2, Sch. (with art. 4. (1)); S.S.I. 2007/101, art. 2, Sch. (with art. 4); S.S.I. 2007/329, art. 2, Sch. (with art. 4)); S.S.I. 2008/57, art. 2 (with art. 3)

F142. S. 72. C(4)(b) substituted (29.5.2017 for specified purposes) by Criminal Justice (Scotland) Act 2016 (asp 1), ss. 79. (4), 117. (2); S.S.I. 2017/99, art. 3. (1)(2) (with art. 3. (3)(4), 6)

72. DPreliminary hearing: further provisionS

(1) The court may, on cause shown, allow a preliminary hearing to proceed notwithstanding the absence of the accused.

(2) Where—

(a) the accused is a body corporate;

(b) it fails to appear at a preliminary hearing;

(c) the court allows the hearing to proceed in its absence under subsection (1) above; and

(d) no plea is entered on its behalf at the hearing,

it shall be treated for the purposes of proceedings at the preliminary hearing as having pled not guilty.

(3) Where, at a preliminary hearing, a trial diet is appointed, the accused shall appear at the trial diet and answer the indictment.

(4) At a preliminary hearing, the court—

(a) shall take into account any written record lodged under section 72. E of this Act; and

(b) may ask the prosecutor and the accused any question in connection with any matter which it is required to dispose of or ascertain under section 72 of this Act.

(5) The proceedings at a preliminary hearing shall be recorded by means of shorthand notes or by mechanical means.

(6) Subsections (2) to (4) of section 93 of this Act shall apply for the purposes of the recording of proceedings at a preliminary hearing in accordance with subsection (5) above as they apply for the purposes of the recording of proceedings at the trial in accordance with subsection (1) of that section.

(7) The Clerk of Justiciary shall prepare, in such form and manner as may be prescribed by Act of Adjournal, a minute of proceedings at a preliminary hearing, which shall record, in particular, whether any preliminary pleas or issues were disposed of and, if so, how they were disposed of.

(8) In this section, references to a preliminary hearing include an adjourned preliminary hearing.

(9) In this section and sections 72 to 72. C, "the court" means the High Court.]

Amendments (Textual)

F141. Ss. 72-72. D substituted for ss. 72-73. A (1.2.2005, 1.4.2005, 1.4.2006, 1.4.2007 and 2.7.2007 for certain purposes, otherwise 1.4.2008) by Criminal Procedure (Amendment) (Scotland) Act 2004 (asp 5), ss. 1. (3), 27. (1); S.S.I. 2004/405, art. 2, Sch. 1 (subject to arts. 3-5); S.S.I. 2005/168, art. 2, Sch. (with art. 4); S.S.I. 2006/59, art. 2, Sch. (with art. 4. (1)); S.S.I. 2007/101, art. 2, Sch. (with art. 4); S.S.I. 2007/329, art. 2, Sch. (with art. 4)); S.S.I. 2008/57, art. 2 (with art. 3)

[F14372. EWritten record of state of preparation in certain casesS

(1) This section applies where, in any proceedings in the High Court, a solicitor has notified the Court under section 72. F(1) of this Act that he has been engaged by the accused for the purposes of the conduct of his case at the preliminary hearing.

(2) The prosecutor and the accused's legal representative shall, not less than two days before the preliminary hearing—

(a) communicate with each other with a view to jointly preparing a written record of their state of preparation with respect to their cases (referred to in this section as "the written record"); and

(b) lodge the written record with the Clerk of Justiciary.

(3) The High Court may, on cause shown, allow the written record to be lodged after the time referred to in subsection (2) above.

(4) The written record shall—

(a) be in such form, or as nearly as may be in such form;

(b) contain such information; and

(c) be lodged in such manner,

as may be prescribed by Act of Adjournal.

(5) The written record may contain, in addition to the information required by virtue of subsection (4)(b) above, such other information as the prosecutor and the accused's legal representative consider appropriate.

(6) In this section—

"the accused's legal representative" means—

- the solicitor referred to in subsection (1) above; or

- where the solicitor has instructed counsel for the purposes of the conduct of the accused's case at the preliminary hearing, either the solicitor or that counsel, or both of them; and "counsel" includes a solicitor who has a right of audience in the High Court of Justiciary under section 25. A (rights of audience in various courts including the High Court of Justiciary) of the Solicitors (Scotland) Act 1980 (c. 46).]

Amendments (Textual)

F143. S. 72. E inserted (1.2.2005) by Criminal Procedure (Amendment) (Scotland) Act 2004 (asp 5), ss. 2, 27. (1); S.S.I. 2004/405, art. 2, Sch. 1 (subject to arts. 3-5)

[F14472. FEngagement, dismissal and withdrawal of solicitor representing accusedS

(1) In any [F145solemn proceedings] , it is the duty of a solicitor who is engaged by the accused for the purposes of his defence at any part of the proceedings to notify the court and the prosecutor of that fact forthwith in writing.

(2) A solicitor is to be taken to have complied with the duty under subsection (1) to notify the prosecutor of his engagement if, before service of the indictment, he—

(a) notified in writing the procurator fiscal for the district in which the charge against the accused was then being investigated that he was then engaged by the accused for the purposes of his defence; and

(b) had not notified that procurator fiscal in writing that he had been dismissed by the accused or had withdrawn from acting.

(3) Where any such solicitor as is referred to in subsection (1) above—

(a) is dismissed by the accused; or

(b) withdraws,

it is the duty of the solicitor to inform the court and the prosecutor of those facts forthwith in writing.

(4) The prosecutor shall, for the purposes of subsections (1) and (3), be taken to be notified or informed of any fact in accordance with those subsections if—

(a) in proceedings in the High Court, the Crown Agent; or

(b) in [F146solemn proceedings] in the sheriff court, the procurator fiscal for the district in which the trial diet is to be held,

is so notified or, as the case may be, informed of the fact.

(5) On being informed in accordance with subsection (3) above of the dismissal or withdrawal of the accused's solicitor in any case to which subsections (6) and (7) below apply, the court shall order that, before the trial diet, there shall be a further pre-trial diet under this section.

(6) This subsection applies to any case—

(a) where the accused is charged with an offence to which section 288. C of this Act applies;

(b) in respect of which section 288. E of this Act applies; or

(c) in which an order has been made under section 288. F(2) of this Act.

(7) This subsection applies to any case in which—

(a) the solicitor was engaged for the purposes of the defence of the accused—

(i) in the case of proceedings in the High Court, at the time of a preliminary hearing or, if a preliminary hearing was dispensed with under section 72. B(1) of this Act, at the time it was so dispensed with;

(ii) in the case of solemn proceedings in the sheriff court, at the time of a first diet;

(iii) at the time of a diet under this section; or

(iv) in the case of a diet which, under subsection (11) below, is dispensed with, at the time when it was so dispensed with; and

(b) the court is informed as mentioned in subsection (3) above after that time but before the trial diet.

(8) At a diet under this section, the court shall ascertain whether or not the accused has engaged another solicitor for the purposes of his defence at the trial.

(9) A diet under this section shall be not less than 10 clear days before the trial diet.

(10) A court may, at a diet under this section, postpone the trial diet for such period as appears to it to be appropriate and may, if it thinks fit, direct that such period (or some part of it) shall not count towards any time limit applying in respect of the case.

(11) The court may dispense with a diet under this section previously ordered, but only if a solicitor engaged by the accused for the purposes of the defence of the accused at the trial has, in writing—

(a) confirmed his engagement for that purpose; and

(b) requested that the diet be dispensed with.]

Amendments (Textual)

F144. S. 72. F inserted (4.12.2004) "after s. 72. E" by virtue of Criminal Procedure (Amendment) (Scotland) Act 2004 (asp 5), ss. 8, 27. (1); S.S.I. 2004/405, art. 2, Sch. 1 (subject to arts. 3-5)

F145. Words in s. 72. F(1) substituted (10.12.2007) by Criminal Proceedings etc. (Reform) (Scotland) Act 2007 (asp 6), ss. 80, 84, Sch. para. 13. (1); S.S.I. 2007/479, art. 3. (1), Sch. (as amended by S.S.I. 2007/527)

F146. Words in s. 72. F(4)(b) substituted (10.12.2007) by Criminal Proceedings etc. (Reform) (Scotland) Act 2007 (asp 6), ss. 80, 84, Sch. para. 13. (1); S.S.I. 2007/479, art. 3. (1), Sch. (as amended by S.S.I. 2007/527)

[F14772. GService etc. on accused through a solicitorS

(1) In any [F148solemn proceedings] , anything which is to be served on or given, notified or otherwise intimated to, the accused shall be taken to be so served, given, notified or intimated if it is, in such form and manner as may be prescribed by Act of Adjournal, served on or given, notified or intimated to (as the case may be) the solicitor described in subsection (2) below at that solicitor's place of business.

(2) That solicitor is any solicitor—

(a) who—

(i) has notified the prosecutor under subsection (1) of section 72. F of this Act that he is engaged by the accused for the purposes of his defence; and

(ii) has not informed the prosecutor under subsection (3) of that section that he has been dismissed by, or has withdrawn from acting for, the accused; or

(b) who—

(i) has been appointed to act for the purposes of the accused's defence at the trial under section 92 or 288. D of this Act; and

(ii) has not been relieved of the appointment by the court.]

Amendments (Textual)

F147. S. 72. G inserted (4.12.2004) by Criminal Procedure (Amendment) (Scotland) Act 2004 (asp 5), ss. 12, 27. (1); S.S.I. 2004/405, art. 2, Sch. 1 (subject to arts. 3-5)

F148. Words in s. 72. G(1) substituted (10.12.2007) by Criminal Proceedings etc. (Reform) (Scotland) Act 2007 (asp 6), ss. 80, 84, Sch. para. 13. (2); S.S.I. 2007/479, art. 3. (1), Sch. (as amended by S.S.I. 2007/527)

73. . . . .

74 Appeals in connection with preliminary diets.S

(1) Without prejudice [F152to any right of appeal under section 106 or 108 a party may,] in accordance with such procedure as may be prescribed by Act of Adjournal, appeal to the High Court against a decision at a first diet or a preliminary [F153hearing].

(2) An appeal under subsection (1) above—

(a) may not be taken against a decision to adjourn the first [F154diet] or, as the case may be, preliminary [F155hearing] or to [F156accelerate or] postpone the trial diet;

[F157. (aza)may not be taken against a decision taken by virtue of section 35 of the Criminal Justice (Scotland) Act 2016;]

[F158. (aa)may not be taken against a decision taken by virtue of—
(i) in the case of a first diet, section 71. (1. A),
(ii) in the case of a preliminary [F159hearing, section 72. (6)(e)],
of this Act;]

[F160. (ab)may not be taken against a decision at a preliminary hearing, in appointing a trial diet, to appoint or not to appoint it as a floating diet for the purposes of section 83. A(2) of this Act;]

(b) must be taken not later than [F161seven] days after the decision.

[F162. (2. A)An appeal under subsection (1) may be taken—

(a) in the case of a decision to dismiss the indictment or any part of it, by the prosecutor without the leave of the court,

(b) in any other case, only with the leave of the court of first instance (granted on the motion of a party or ex proprio motu).]

(3) Where an appeal is taken under subsection (1) above, the High Court may postpone [F163any trial diet that has been appointed] for such period as appears to it to be appropriate and may, if it thinks fit, direct that such period (or some part of it) shall not count towards any time limit applying in respect of the case.

[F164. (3. A)Where an appeal is taken under subsection (1) above against a decision at a preliminary hearing, the High Court may adjourn, or further adjourn, the preliminary hearing for such period as appears to it to be appropriate and may, if it thinks fit, direct that such period (or some part of it) shall not count towards any time limit applying in respect of the case.]

(4) In disposing of an appeal under subsection (1) above the High Court—

(a) may affirm the decision of the court of first instance or may remit the case to it with such directions in the matter as it thinks fit; F165. . .

(b) where the court of first instance has dismissed the indictment or any part of it, may reverse that decision and direct that the court of first instance fix

[F166. (i)where the indictment is in respect of the High Court, a further preliminary hearing; or
(ii) where the indictment is in respect of the sheriff court,]

a trial diet, if it has not already fixed one as regards so much of the indictment as it has not dismissed.

[F167. (c)may on cause shown extend the period mentioned in section 65. (1) of this Act.]

Amendments (Textual)

F152. Words in s. 74. (1) substituted (17.1.2017) by Criminal Justice (Scotland) Act 2016 (asp 1), ss. 88. (a), 117. (2); S.S.I. 2016/426, art. 2, sch.

F153. Word in s. 74. (1) substituted (1.2.2005) by Criminal Procedure (Amendment) (Scotland) Act 2004 (asp 5), ss. 3. (2), 27. (1); S.S.I. 2004/405, art. 2, Sch. 1

F154. Word in s. 74. (2)(a) inserted (1.2.2005) by Criminal Procedure (Amendment) (Scotland) Act 2004 (asp 5), ss. 3. (3)(a)(i), 27. (1); S.S.I. 2004/405, art. 2, Sch. 1

F155. Word in s. 74. (2)(a) substituted (1.2.2005) by Criminal Procedure (Amendment) (Scotland) Act 2004 (asp 5), ss. 3. (3)(a)(ii), 27. (1); S.S.I. 2004/405, art. 2, Sch. 1

F156. Words in s. 74. (2)(a) inserted (1.2.2005) by Criminal Procedure (Amendment) (Scotland) Act 2004 (asp 5), ss. 25, 27. (1), Sch. para. 22; S.S.I. 2004/405, art. 2, Sch. 1 (subject to arts. 3-5)

F157. S. 74. (2)(aza) inserted (25.1.2018) by Criminal Justice (Scotland) Act 2016 (asp 1), s. 117. (2), sch. 2 para. 32; S.S.I. 2017/345, art. 3, sch.

F158. S. 74. (2)(aa) inserted (1.4.2005 and 1.4.2006 for certain purposes and otherwise 1.4.2008) by Vulnerable Witnesses (Scotland) Act 2004 (asp 3), ss. 2. (4), 25; S.S.I. 2005/168, art. 2, Sch. (with art. 4); S.S.I. 2006/59, art. 2, Sch. (with art 4. (1)); S.S.I. 2008/57, art. 2 (with art. 3)

F159. Words s. 74. (2)(aa)(ii) substituted (1.2.2005) by Criminal Procedure (Amendment)

(Scotland) Act 2004 (asp 5), ss. 3. (3)(a), 27. (1); S.S.I. 2004/405, art. 2, Sch. 1

F160. S. 74. (2)(ab) inserted (1.2.2005) after (aa) by Criminal Procedure (Amendment) (Scotland) Act 2004 (asp 5), ss. 3. (3)(c), 27. (1); S.S.I. 2004/405, art. 2, Sch. 1

F161. Word in s. 74. (2)(b) substituted (28.3.2011) by Criminal Justice and Licensing (Scotland) Act 2010 (asp 13), ss. 72. (2), 206. (1); S.S.I. 2011/178, art. 2, sch.

F162. S. 74. (2. A) inserted (17.1.2017) by Criminal Justice (Scotland) Act 2016 (asp 1), ss. 88. (b), 117. (2); S.S.I. 2016/426, art. 2, sch.

F163. Words in s. 74. (3) substituted (1.2.2005) by Criminal Procedure (Amendment) (Scotland) Act 2004 (asp 5), ss. 3. (4), 27. (1); S.S.I. 2004/405, art. 2, Sch. 1

F164. S. 74. (3. A) inserted (1.2.2005) by Criminal Procedure (Amendment) (Scotland) Act 2004 (asp 5), ss. 3. (5), 27. (1); S.S.I. 2004/405, art. 2, Sch. 1

F165. Word in s. 74. (4) repealed (1.8.1997) by 1997 c. 48, s. 62. (1)(2), Sch. 1 para. 21. (10)(a), Sch. 3; S.I. 1997/1712, art. 3, Sch. (subject to arts. 4, 5)

F166. Words in s. 74. (4)(b) inserted (1.2.2005) by Criminal Procedure (Amendment) (Scotland) Act 2004 (asp 5), ss. 3. (6), 27. (1); S.S.I. 2004/405, art. 2, Sch. 1

F167. S. 74. (4)(c) inserted (1.8.1997) by 1997 c. 48, s. 62. (1)(2), Sch. 1 para. 21. (10)(b); S.I. 1997/1712, art. 3, Sch. (subject to arts. 4, 5)

75 Computation of certain periods.S

Where the last day of any period mentioned in section 66. (6), 67. (3), [F16871. C(3)] F169. . . or 74 of this Act falls on a Saturday, Sunday or court holiday, such period shall extend to and include the next day which is not a Saturday, Sunday or court holiday.

Amendments (Textual)

F168. Word in s. 75 inserted (29.5.2017 for specified purposes) by Criminal Justice (Scotland) Act 2016 (asp 1), ss. 80. (4), 117. (2); S.S.I. 2017/99, art. 3. (1)(2) (with art. 6)

F169. Word in s. 75. (1) repealed (1.2.2005) by Criminal Procedure (Amendment) (Scotland) Act 2004 (asp 5), ss. 25, 27. (1), Sch. para. 23; S.S.I. 2004/405, art. 2, Sch. 1 (subject to arts. 3-5)

[F170. Adjournment and alteration of dietsS

Amendments (Textual)

F170. S. 75. A and crossheading inserted (1.2.2005) by Criminal Procedure (Amendment) (Scotland) Act 2004 (asp 5), ss. 15, 27. (1); S.S.I. 2004/405, art. 2, Sch. 1 (subject to arts. 3-5)

[F17175. AAdjournment and alteration of dietsS

(1) This section applies where any diet has been fixed in any proceedings on indictment.

(2) The court may, if it considers it appropriate to do so, adjourn the diet.

(3) However—

(a) in the case of a trial diet, the court may adjourn the diet under subsection (2) above only if the indictment is not brought to trial at the diet;

(b) if the court adjourns any diet under that subsection by reason only that, following enquiries for the purpose of ascertaining whether the accused has engaged a solicitor for the purposes of the conduct of his defence at or for the purposes of a preliminary hearing or at a trial, it appears to the court that he has not done so, the adjournment shall be for a period of not more than 48 hours.

(4) A trial diet in the High Court may be adjourned under subsection (2) above to a diet to be held at a sitting of the Court in another place.

(5) The court may, on the application of any party to the proceedings made at any time before commencement of any diet—

(a) discharge the diet; and

(b) fix a new diet for a date earlier or later than that for which the discharged diet was fixed.

(6) Before determining an application under subsection (5) above, the court shall give the parties an opportunity to be heard.

(7) However, where all the parties join in an application under that subsection, the court may determine the application without hearing the parties and, accordingly, may dispense with any hearing previously appointed for the purpose of subsection (6) above.

(8) Where there is a hearing for the purpose of subsection (6) above, the accused shall attend it unless the court permits the hearing to proceed notwithstanding the absence of the accused.

(9) In appointing a new trial diet under subsection (5)(b) above, the court—

(a) shall have regard to the state of preparation of the prosecutor and the accused with respect to their cases and, in particular, to the likelihood of the case being ready to proceed to trial on the date to be appointed for the trial diet; and

(b) may, if it appears to the court that there are any preliminary pleas, preliminary issues or other matters which require to be, or could with advantage be, disposed of or ascertained before the trial, appoint a diet to be held before the trial diet for the purpose of disposing of or, as the case may be, ascertaining them.

(10) A date for a new diet may be fixed under subsection (5)(b) above notwithstanding that the holding of the diet on that date would result in any provision of this Act as to the minimum or maximum period within which the diet is to be held or to commence not being complied with.

(11) In subsections (5) to (9) above, "the court" means—

(a) in the case of proceedings in the High Court, a single judge of that Court; and

(b) in the case of proceedings in the sheriff court, that court.

(12) For the purposes of subsection (5) above—

(a) a diet other than a trial diet shall be taken to commence when it is called; and

(b) a trial diet shall be taken to commence when the jury is sworn.]]

Amendments (Textual)

F171. S. 75. A and crossheading inserted (1.2.2005) by Criminal Procedure (Amendment) (Scotland) Act 2004 (asp 5), ss. 15, 27. (1); S.S.I. 2004/405, art. 2, Sch. 1 (subject to arts. 3-5)

[F17275. B[F173. Refixing diets: non-sitting days]S

(1) This section applies where in any proceedings on indictment any diet has been fixed for a non-sitting day.

(2) The court may at any time before the non-sitting day—

(a) discharge the diet; and

(b) fix a new diet for a date earlier or later than that for which the discharged diet was fixed.

(3) That is, by acting—

(a) of the court's own accord; and

(b) without the need for a hearing for the purpose.

(4) In the case of a trial diet—

(a) the prosecutor;

(b) the accused,

shall be entitled to an adjournment of the new diet fixed if the court is satisfied that it is not practicable for that party to proceed with the case on that date.

(5) The power of the court under subsection (1) above is not exercisable for the sole purpose of ensuring compliance with a time limit applying in the proceedings.

(6) In subsections (1) and (2) above, a "non-sitting day" is a day on which the court is under this Act not required to sit.

(7) In subsections (2) to (5) above, "the court" means—

(a) in the case of proceedings in the High Court, a single judge of that Court;

(b) in the case of proceedings in the sheriff court, that court.]

Amendments (Textual)

F172. S. 75. B inserted (10.12.2007) by Criminal Proceedings etc. (Reform) (Scotland) Act 2007 (asp 6), ss. 39. (1), 84; S.S.I. 2007/479, art. 3. (1), Sch. (as amended by S.S.I. 2007/527)
F173. S. 75. B heading substituted (30.1.2012) by Act of Adjournal (Amendment of the Criminal Procedure (Scotland) Act 1995) (Refixing diets) 2011 (S.S.I. 2011/430), ss. 1. (2), 2. (3)

[F17475. CRefixing diets: non-suitable daysS

(1) Where in any proceedings on indictment any diet has been fixed for a day which is no longer suitable to the court, it may, of its own accord, at any time before that diet—
    (a) discharge the diet; and
    (b) fix a new diet for a date earlier or later than that for which the discharged diet was fixed.
(2) Before proceeding as mentioned in subsection (1) the court shall give the parties an opportunity to be heard.
(3) In subsections (1) and (2), "the court" means—
    (a) in the case of proceedings in the High Court, a single judge of that Court;
    (b) in the case of proceedings in the sheriff court, that court.]

Amendments (Textual)
F174. S. 75. C inserted (30.1.2012) by Act of Adjournal (Amendment of the Criminal Procedure (Scotland) Act 1995) (Refixing diets) 2011 (S.S.I. 2011/430), ss. 1. (2), 2. (2)

Plea of guiltyS

76 Procedure where accused desires to plead guilty.S

(1) Where an accused intimates in writing to the Crown Agent that he intends to plead guilty and desires to have his case disposed of at once, the accused may be served with an indictment (unless one has already been served) and a notice to appear at a diet of the appropriate court not less than four clear days after the date of the notice; and it shall not be necessary to lodge or give notice of any list of witnesses or productions.
(2) In subsection (1) above, "appropriate court" means—
    (a) in a case where at the time of the intimation mentioned in that subsection an indictment had not been served, either the High Court or the sheriff court; and
    (b) in any other case, the court specified in the notice served under section 66. (6) of this Act on the accused.
(3) If at any such diet the accused pleads not guilty to the charge or pleads guilty only to a part of the charge, and the prosecutor declines to accept such restricted plea, the diet shall be desertedpro loco et tempore and thereafter the cause may proceed in accordance with the other provisions of this Part of this Act; except that in a case mentioned in paragraph (b) of subsection (2) above the court may postpone the trial diet [F175[F176or, where the accused has been indicted to the High Court,] [F176, the first diet or (as the case may be)] the preliminary hearing] and the period of such postponement shall not count towards any time limit applying in respect of the case.

Amendments (Textual)
F175. Words in s. 76. (3) inserted (1.2.2005) by Criminal Procedure (Amendment) (Scotland) Act 2004 (asp 5), ss. 25, 27. (1), Sch. para. 24; S.S.I. 2004/405, art. 2, Sch. 1 (subject to arts. 3-5)
F176. Words in s. 76. (3) substituted (29.5.2017 for specified purposes) by Criminal Justice (Scotland) Act 2016 (asp 1), ss. 81. (5), 117. (2); S.S.I. 2017/99, art. 3. (1)(2) (with art. 6)

77 Plea of guilty.S

(1) Where at any diet the accused tenders a plea of guilty to the indictment or any part thereof he

shall do so in open court F177....

(2) Where the plea is to part only of the charge and the prosecutor does not accept the plea, such non-acceptance shall be recorded.

(3) Where an accused charged on indictment with any offence tenders a plea of guilty to any other offence of which he could competently be found guilty on the trial of the indictment, and that plea is accepted by the prosecutor, it shall be competent to convict the accused of the offence to which he has so pled guilty and to sentence him accordingly.

Amendments (Textual)

F177. Words in s. 77. (1) repealed (17.1.2017) by Criminal Justice (Scotland) Act 2016 (asp 1), ss. 83. (b), 117. (2); S.S.I. 2016/426, art. 2, sch.

Notice by accusedS

78 Special defences, incrimination and notice of witnesses, etc.S

(1) It shall not be competent for an accused to state a special defence or to lead evidence calculated to exculpate the accused by incriminating a co-accused unless—

(a) a plea of special defence or, as the case may be, notice of intention to lead such evidence has been lodged and intimated in writing in accordance with subsection (3) belowF178. . .

(b) the court, on cause shown, otherwise directs.

[F179. (1. A)Subsection (1) does not apply where—

(a) the accused lodges a defence statement under section 70. A, and

(b) the accused's defence consists of or includes a special defence.]

(2) Subsection (1) above shall apply [F180to a plea of diminished responsibility or] to a defence of automatism [F181, coercion or, in a prosecution for an offence to which section 288. C of this Act applies, consent] as if it were a special defence.

[F182. (2. A)In subsection (2) above, the reference to a defence of consent is a reference to the defence which is stated by reference to the complainer's consent to the act which is the subject matter of the charge or the accused's belief as to that consent.

(2. B)In subsection (2. A) above, "complainer" has the same meaning as in section 274 of this Act.]

(3) A plea or notice is lodged and intimated in accordance with this subsection—

(a) where [F183the case is to be tried in the High Court] , by lodging the plea or notice with the Clerk of Justiciary and by intimating the plea or notice to the Crown Agent and to any co-accused not less than [F184seven clear days before the preliminary hearing] ;

(b) where the [F185case is to be tried in the sheriff court] , by lodging the plea or notice with the sheriff clerk and by intimating it to the procurator fiscal and to any co-accused at or before the first diet.

(4) It shall not be competent for the accused to examine any witnesses or to put in evidence any productions not included in the lists lodged by the prosecutor unless—

(a) written notice of the names and addresses of such witnesses and of such productions has been given—

(i) where the case is to be tried in the sheriff court, to the procurator fiscal of the district of the trial diet at or before the first diet; and

(ii) where the case is to be tried in the High Court, to the Crown Agent at least [F186seven clear days before the preliminary hearing]

(b) the court, on cause shown, otherwise directs.

(5) A copy of every written notice required by subsection (4) above shall be lodged by the accused with the sheriff clerk of the district in which the trial diet is to be held, or in any case the trial diet of which is to be held in the High Court in Edinburgh with the Clerk of Justiciary, at or before

[F187. (a)where the case is to be tried in the High Court, the preliminary hearing;

(b) where the case is to be tried in the sheriff court, the trial diet,

for the use of the court.] .

Amendments (Textual)

F178. Words in s. 78. (1)(a) repealed (1.2.2005) by Criminal Procedure (Amendment) (Scotland) Act 2004 (asp 5), ss. 25, 27. (1), Sch. para. 25. (a); S.S.I. 2004/405, art. 2, Sch. 1 (subject to arts. 3-5)

F179. S. 78. (1. A) inserted (6.6.2011) by Criminal Justice and Licensing (Scotland) Act 2010 (asp 13), ss. 124. (4), 206. (1) (with s. 124. (1)); S.S.I. 2011/178, art. 2, sch.

F180. Words in s. 78. (2) inserted (with application in accordance with art. 3 of the commencing S.S.I.) by Criminal Justice and Licensing (Scotland) Act 2010 (asp 13), s. 206. (1), sch. 7 para. 46; S.S.I. 2012/160, art. 3, sch.

F181. Words in s. 78. (2) substituted (1.11.2002) by Sexual Offences (Procedure and Evidence) (Scotland) Act 2002 (asp 9), s. 6. (1)(a); S.S.I. 2002/443, art. 3 (with art. 4. (4))

F182. S. 78. (2. A)(2. B) inserted (1.11.2002) by Sexual Offences (Procedure and Evidence) (Scotland) Act 2002 (asp 9), s. 6. (1)(b); S.S.I. 2002/443, art. 3 (with art. 4. (4))

F183. Words in s. 78. (3)(a) substituted (1.2.2005) by Criminal Procedure (Amendment) (Scotland) Act 2004 (asp 5), ss. 25, 27. (1), Sch. para. 25. (b)(i)(A); S.S.I. 2004/405, art. 2, Sch. 1 (subject to arts. 3-5)

F184. Words in s. 78. (3)(a) substituted (1.2.2005) by Criminal Procedure (Amendment) (Scotland) Act 2004 (asp 5), ss. 25, 27. (1), Sch. para. 25. (b)(i)(B); S.S.I. 2004/405, art. 2, Sch. 1 (subject to arts. 3-5)

F185. Words in s. 78. (3)(b) substituted (1.2.2005) by Criminal Procedure (Amendment) (Scotland) Act 2004 (asp 5), ss. 25, 27. (1), Sch. para. 25. (b)(ii); S.S.I. 2004/405, art. 2, Sch. 1 (subject to arts. 3-5)

F186. Words in s. 78. (4)(a)(ii) substituted (1.2.2005) by Criminal Procedure (Amendment) (Scotland) Act 2004 (asp 5), ss. 25, 27. (1), Sch. para. 25. (c); S.S.I. 2004/405, art. 2, Sch. 1 (subject to arts. 3-5)

F187. Words in s. 78. (5) substituted (1.2.2005) by Criminal Procedure (Amendment) (Scotland) Act 2004 (asp 5), ss. 25, 27. (1), Sch. para. 25. (d); S.S.I. 2004/405, art. 2, Sch. 1 (subject to arts. 3-5)

[F18879 Preliminary pleas and preliminary issues.S

(1) Except by leave of the court on cause shown, no preliminary plea or preliminary issue shall be made, raised or submitted in any proceedings on indictment by any party unless his intention to do so has been stated in a notice under section 71. (2) or, as the case may be, 72. (3) or (6)(b)(i) of this Act.

[F189. (1. A)Subsection (1) is subject to section 271. Q(8).]

(2) For the purposes of this section and those sections—

(a) the following are preliminary pleas, namely—

(i) a matter relating to the competency or relevancy of the indictment;

(ii) an objection to the validity of the citation against a party, on the ground of any discrepancy between the record copy of the indictment and the copy served on him, or on account of any error or deficiency in such service copy or in the notice of citation; and

(iii) a plea in bar of trial; and

(b) the following are preliminary issues, namely—

(i) an application for separation or conjunction of charges or trials;

[F190. (ii)a preliminary objection under any of the provisions listed in subsection (3. A);]

[F191. (iia)an application for a witness anonymity order under section 271. P of this Act;]

F192. (iii). . . . .

(iv) an objection by a party to the admissibility of any evidence;

(v) an assertion by a party that there are documents the truth of the contents of which ought to be admitted, or that there is any other matter which in his view ought to be agreed; and

(vi) any other point raised by a party, as regards any matter not mentioned in sub-paragraphs (i) to (v) above, which could in his opinion be resolved with advantage before the trial.

(3) No discrepancy, error or deficiency such as is mentioned in subsection (2)(a)(ii) above shall entitle an accused to object to plead to the indictment unless the court is satisfied that the discrepancy, error or deficiency tended substantially to mislead and prejudice the accused.

[F193. (3. A)For the purpose of subsection (2)(b)(ii), the provisions are—

(a) section 27. (4. A)(a) or (4. B), 90. C(2. A), 255 or 255. A of this Act,

(b) section 9. (6) of the Antisocial Behaviour etc. (Scotland) Act 2004 or that section as applied by section 234. AA(11) of this Act,

(c) paragraph 6. (5)(b) of schedule 1 to the Criminal Justice (Scotland) Act 2016.]

(4) Where the court, under subsection (1) above, grants leave for a party to make, raise or submit a preliminary plea or preliminary issue (other than an objection to the admissibility of any evidence) without his intention to do so having been stated in a notice as required by that subsection, the court may—

(a) if it considers it appropriate to do so, appoint a diet to be held before the trial diet for the purpose of disposing of the plea or issue; or

(b) appoint the plea or issue to be disposed of at the trial diet.]

Amendments (Textual)

F188. S. 79 substituted (1.2.2005) by Criminal Procedure (Amendment) (Scotland) Act 2004 (asp 5), ss. 13. (1), 27. (1); S.S.I. 2004/405, art. 2, Sch. 1 (subject to arts. 3-5)

F189. S. 79. (1. A) inserted (28.3.2011) by Criminal Justice and Licensing (Scotland) Act 2010 (asp 13), ss. 90. (2)(a)(i), 206. (1); S.S.I. 2011/178, art. 2, sch.

F190. S. 79. (2)(b)(ii) substituted (25.1.2018) by Criminal Justice (Scotland) Act 2016 (asp 1), s. 117. (2), sch. 2 para. 33. (a); S.S.I. 2017/345, art. 3, sch.

F191. S. 79. (2)(b)(iia) inserted (28.3.2011) by Criminal Justice and Licensing (Scotland) Act 2010 (asp 13), ss. 90. (2)(a)(ii), 206. (1); S.S.I. 2011/178, art. 2, sch.

F192. S. 79. (2)(b)(iii) repealed (17.1.2017) by Criminal Justice (Scotland) Act 2016 (asp 1), ss. 78. (2)(d), 117. (2); S.S.I. 2016/426, art. 2, sch. (with art. 3)

F193. S. 79. (3. A) inserted (25.1.2018) by Criminal Justice (Scotland) Act 2016 (asp 1), s. 117. (2), sch. 2 para. 33. (b); S.S.I. 2017/345, art. 3, sch.

[F19479. AObjections to admissibility of evidence raised after first diet or preliminary hearingS

(1) This section applies where a party seeks to raise an objection to the admissibility of any evidence after—

(a) in proceedings in the High Court, the preliminary hearing; or

(b) in proceedings on indictment in the sheriff court, the first diet.

(2) The court shall not, under section 79. (1) of this Act, grant leave for the objection to be raised if the party seeking to raise it has not given written notice of his intention to do so to the other parties.

(3) However, the court may, where the party seeks to raise the objection after the commencement of the trial, dispense with the requirement under subsection (2) above for written notice to be given.

(4) Where the party seeks to raise the objection after the commencement of the trial, the court shall not, under section 79. (1) of this Act, grant leave for the objection to be raised unless it considers that it could not reasonably have been raised before that time.

(5) Where the party seeks to raise the objection before the commencement of the trial and the court, under section 79. (1), grants leave for it to be raised, the court shall—

(a) if it considers it appropriate to do so, appoint a diet to be held before the commencement of the trial for the purpose of disposing of the objection; or

(b) dispose of the objection at the trial diet.

(6) In appointing a diet under subsection (5)(a) above, the court may postpone the trial diet for such period as appears to it to be appropriate and may, if it thinks fit, direct that such period (or some part of it) shall not count towards any time limit applying in respect of the case.

(7) The accused shall appear at any diet appointed under subsection (5)(a) above.

(8) For the purposes of this section, the trial shall be taken to commence when the jury is sworn.]

Amendments (Textual)

F194. S. 79. A inserted (1.2.2005) by Criminal Procedure (Amendment) (Scotland) Act 2004 (asp 5), ss. 14. (2), 27. (1); S.S.I. 2004/405, art. 2, Sch. 1

Alteration, etc, of dietS

80 Alteration and postponement of trial diet.S

F195. . . . .

Amendments (Textual)

F195. S. 80 repealed (1.2.2005) by Criminal Procedure (Amendment) (Scotland) Act 2004 (asp 5), ss. 25, 27. (1), Sch. para. 26; S.S.I. 2004/405, art. 2, Sch. 1 (subject to arts. 3-5)

[F19681 Procedure where trial diet does not proceed.S

(1) The prosecutor shall not raise a fresh libel in a case in which the court has deserted the trial simpliciter unless the court's decision has been reversed on appeal.

(2) Where a trial diet in any proceedings on indictment is deserted pro loco et tempore the court may appoint a further trial diet for a later date and the accused shall appear and answer the indictment at that diet.

(3) In appointing a further trial diet under subsection (2) above, the court—

(a) shall have regard to the state of preparation of the prosecutor and the accused with respect to their cases and, in particular, to the likelihood of the case being ready to proceed to trial on the date to be appointed for the trial diet; and

(b) may, if it appears to the court that there are any preliminary pleas, preliminary issues or other matters which require to be, or could with advantage be, disposed of or ascertained before the trial diet, appoint a diet to be held before the trial diet for the purpose of disposing of or, as the case may be, ascertaining them.

(4) Subsection (5) below applies where, in any proceedings on indictment in which a trial diet has been appointed F197...—

(a) the diet has been deserted pro loco et tempore for any reason and no further trial diet has been appointed under subsection (2) above; or

(b) the indictment falls or is for any other reason not brought to trial and the diet has not been continued, adjourned or postponed.

(5) Where this subsection applies, the prosecutor may, at any time within the period of two months after the relevant date, give notice to the accused on another copy of the indictment to appear and answer the indictment—

(a) where the trial diet referred to in subsection (4) above was in the High Court—

(i) at a further preliminary hearing in that Court not less than seven clear days after service of the notice; or

[F198. (ii)where the charge is one that can lawfully be tried in the sheriff court, at a first diet in that court not less than 21 clear days after service of the notice; or]

(b) where the trial diet referred to in subsection (4) was in the sheriff court—

(i) at a [F199first diet] in that court not less than seven clear days after service of the notice; or

(ii) at a preliminary hearing in the High Court not less than 21 clear days after service of the notice.

(6) Where notice is given to the accused under paragraph (a)(ii) or (b)(ii) of subsection (5) above, then for the purposes of section 65. (4) of this Act—

(a) the giving of the notice shall be taken to be service of an indictment in respect of—

(i) in the case of a notice under paragraph (a)(ii) of subsection (5) above, the sheriff court; or

(ii) in the case of a notice under paragraph (b)(ii) of that subsection, the High Court; and

(b) the previous service of the indictment in respect of—

(i) in the case of a notice under paragraph (a)(ii) of subsection (5), the High Court; or

(ii) in the case of a notice under paragraph (b)(ii) of that subsection, the sheriff court,

shall be disregarded.

(7) A notice under subsection (5) above shall be in such form as may be prescribed by Act of Adjournal, or as nearly as may be in such form.

(8) In subsection (5) above, "the relevant date" means—

(a) where paragraph (a) of subsection (4) applies, the date on which the trial diet was deserted as mentioned in that paragraph; or

(b) where paragraph (b) of that subsection applies, the date of the trial diet referred to in that subsection.]

Amendments (Textual)

F196. S. 81 substituted (1.2.2005) by Criminal Procedure (Amendment) (Scotland) Act 2004 (asp 5), ss. 9, 27. (1); S.S.I. 2004/405, art. 2, Sch. 1 (subject to arts. 3-5) (as amended (31.1.2005) by S.S.I. 2005/40, art. 3. (2) (subject to art. 1. (3)))

F197. Words in s. 81. (4) omitted (31.7.2017) by virtue of The Criminal Justice (Scotland) Act 2016 (Consequential and Transitional Provisions) Regulations 2017 (S.S.I. 2017/221), regs. 1. (1), 2. (2)(a) (with reg. 3)

F198. S. 81. (5)(a)(ii) substituted (31.7.2017) by The Criminal Justice (Scotland) Act 2016 (Consequential and Transitional Provisions) Regulations 2017 (S.S.I. 2017/221), regs. 1. (1), 2. (2)(b) (with reg. 4)

F199. Words in s. 81. (5)(b)(i) substituted (31.7.2017) by The Criminal Justice (Scotland) Act 2016 (Consequential and Transitional Provisions) Regulations 2017 (S.S.I. 2017/221), regs. 1. (1), 2. (2)(c)

82 Desertion or postponement where accused in custody.S

Where—

(a) a diet is deserted pro loco et tempore;

(b) a diet is [F200continued, accelerated,] postponed or adjourned; or

[F201. (c)an order is issued changing the place at which the trial is to take place,]

the warrant of committal on which the accused is at the time in custody till liberated in due course of law shall continue in force.

Amendments (Textual)

F200. Words in s. 82. (b) inserted (1.2.2005) by Criminal Procedure (Amendment) (Scotland) Act 2004 (asp 5), ss. 25, 27. (1), Sch. para. 27. (a); S.S.I. 2004/405, art. 2, Sch. 1 (subject to arts. 3-5)

F201. S. 82. (c) substituted (31.7.2017) by The Criminal Justice (Scotland) Act 2016 (Consequential and Transitional Provisions) Regulations 2017 (S.S.I. 2017/221), regs. 1. (1), 2. (3)

83 Transfer of sheriff court solemn proceedings.S

(1) Where an accused person has been cited to attend a [F202diet] of the sheriff court the prosecutor may [F203apply to the sheriff for an order for the transfer of the proceedings to a sheriff court in another district in that sheriffdom F204. . . and for adjournment to a [F202diet] of that court] .

[F205. (1. A)Where—

(a) an accused person has been cited to attend a [F206diet] of the sheriff court; or

(b) paragraph (a) above does not apply but it is competent so to cite an accused person,

and the prosecutor is informed by the sheriff clerk that, because of exceptional circumstances which could not reasonably have been foreseen, it is not practicable for that court (in subsection (2. A)(b)(i) below referred to as the "relevant court") or any other sheriff court in that sheriffdom to proceed with the case, the prosecutor—

(i) may, where paragraph (b) above applies, so cite the accused; and

(ii) shall, where paragraph (a) above applies or the accused is so cited by virtue of paragraph (i) above, as soon as practicable apply to the sheriff principal for an order for the transfer of the proceedings to a sheriff court in another sheriffdom F207. . . and for adjournment to a [F206diet] of that court.]

(2) On an application under subsection (1) above the sheriff may—

(a) after giving the accused or his counsel or solicitor an opportunity to be heard; or

(b) on the joint application of the parties,

[F208make such order as is mentioned in that subsection].

[F209. (2. A)On an application under subsection (1. A) above the sheriff principal may make the order sought—

(a) provided that the sheriff principal of the other sheriffdom consents; but

(b) in a case where the trial (or part of the trial) would be transferred, shall do so only—

(i) if the sheriff of the relevant court, after giving the accused or his counsel an opportunity to be heard, consents to the transfer; or

(ii) on the joint application of the parties.

(2. B)On the application of the prosecutor, a sheriff principal who has made an order under subsection (2. A) above may, if the sheriff principal of the other sheriffdom mentioned in that subsection consents—

(a) revoke; or

(ii) vary so as to restrict the effect of,

that order.]

[F210. (2. C)The sheriff may proceed under subsection (2) above on a joint application of the parties without hearing the parties and, accordingly, he may dispense with any hearing previously appointed for the purposes of considering the application.]

(3) F211. . . . .

Amendments (Textual)

F202. Words in s. 83. (1) substituted (1.2.2005) by Criminal Procedure (Amendment) (Scotland) Act 2004 (asp 3), ss. 25, 27. (1), Sch. para. 28. (a)(i); S.S.I. 2004/405, art. 2, Sch. 1 (subject to arts. 3-5)

F203. Words in s. 83. (1) substituted (27.6.2003) by Criminal Justice (Scotland) Act 2003 (asp 7), ss. 58. (1)(a), 89; S.S.I. 2003/288, art. 2, Sch.

F204. Words in s. 83. (1) repealed (1.2.2005) by Criminal Procedure (Amendment) (Scotland) Act 2004 (asp 3), ss. 25, 27. (1), Sch. para. 28. (a)(ii); S.S.I. 2004/405, art. 2, Sch. 1 (subject to arts. 3-5)

F205. S. 83. (1. A) inserted (27.6.2003) by Criminal Justice (Scotland) Act 2003 (asp 7), ss. 58. (1)(b), 89; S.S.I. 2003/288, art. 2, Sch.

F206. Words in s. 83. (1. A) substituted (1.2.2005) by Criminal Procedure (Amendment) (Scotland) Act 2004 (asp 3), ss. 25, 27. (1), Sch. para. 28. (b)(i); S.S.I. 2004/405, art. 2, Sch. 1 (subject to arts. 3-5)

F207. Words in s. 83. (1. A)(ii) repealed (1.2.2005) by Criminal Procedure (Amendment) (Scotland) Act 2004 (asp 3), ss. 25, 27. (1), Sch. para. 28. (b)(ii); S.S.I. 2004/405, art. 2, Sch. 1 (subject to arts. 3-5)

F208. Words in s. 83. (2) substituted (27.6.2003) by Criminal Justice (Scotland) Act 2003 (asp 7), ss. 58. (1)(c), 89; S.S.I. 2003/288, art. 2, Sch.

F209. S. 83. (2. A)-(2. B) inserted (27.6.2003) by Criminal Justice (Scotland) Act 2003 (asp 7), ss.

58. (1)(d), 89; S.S.I. 2003/288, art. 2, Sch.

F210. S. 83. (2. C) inserted (1.2.2005) by Criminal Procedure (Amendment) (Scotland) Act 2004 (asp 3), ss. 25, 27. (1), Sch. para. 28. (c); S.S.I. 2004/405, art. 2, Sch. 1 (subject to arts. 3-5)

F211. S. 83. (3) repealed (1.2.2005) by Criminal Procedure (Amendment) (Scotland) Act 2004 (asp 3), ss. 25, 27. (1), Sch. para. 28. (d); S.S.I. 2004/405, art. 2, Sch. 1 (subject to arts. 3-5)

[F212[F213. Continuation of trial diet]S

Amendments (Textual)

F212. S. 83. A and crossheading inserted (1.2.2005) by Criminal Procedure (Amendment) (Scotland) Act 2004 (asp 5), ss. 5, 27. (1); S.S.I. 2004/405, art. 2, Sch. 1 (subject to arts. 3-5)

F213. S. 83. A crossheading substituted (28.8.2017) by Criminal Justice (Scotland) Act 2016 (asp 1), ss. 81. (7), 117. (2); S.S.I. 2017/99, art. 5

[F21483. AContinuation of trial diet in the High CourtS

(1) Where, in any case which is to be tried in the High Court, the trial diet does not commence on the day appointed for the holding of the diet, the indictment shall fall.

(2) However, where, in appointing a day for the holding of the trial diet, the Court has indicated that the diet is to be a floating diet, the diet and, if it is adjourned, the adjourned diet may, without having been commenced, be continued from sitting day to sitting day—

(a) by minute, in such form as may be prescribed by Act of Adjournal, signed by the Clerk of Justiciary; and

(b) up to such maximum number of sitting days after the day originally appointed for the trial diet as may be so prescribed.

(3) If such a trial diet or adjourned diet is not commenced by the end of the last sitting day to which it may be continued by virtue of subsection (2)(b) above, the indictment shall fall.

(4) For the purposes of this section, a trial diet or adjourned trial diet shall be taken to commence when it is called.

(5) In this section, "sitting day" means any day on which the court is sitting, but does not include any Saturday or Sunday or any day which is a court holiday.]]

Amendments (Textual)

F214. S. 83. A and crossheading inserted (1.2.2005) by Criminal Procedure (Amendment) (Scotland) Act 2004 (asp 5), ss. 5, 27. (1); S.S.I. 2004/405, art. 2, Sch. 1 (subject to arts. 3-5)

[F21583. BContinuation of trial diet in the sheriff courtS

(1) In the sheriff court a trial diet and, if it is adjourned, the adjourned diet, may, without having been commenced, be continued from sitting day to sitting day—

(a) by minute, in such form as may be prescribed by act of adjournal, signed by the sheriff clerk,

(b) up to such maximum number of sitting days after the day originally appointed for the trial diet as may be so prescribed.

(2) The indictment falls if a trial diet, or adjourned diet, is not commenced by the end of the last sitting day to which it may be continued by virtue of subsection (1).

(3) For the purposes of this section, a trial diet or adjourned trial diet is to be taken to commence when it is called.

(4) In this section, "sitting day" means any day on which the court is sitting but does not include any Saturday or Sunday or any day which is a court holiday.]

Amendments (Textual)

F215. S. 83. B inserted (28.8.2017) by Criminal Justice (Scotland) Act 2016 (asp 1), ss. 81. (6), 117. (2); S.S.I. 2017/99, art. 5

Jurors for sittingsS

84 Juries: returns of jurors and preparation of lists.S

(1) For the purposes of a trial, the sheriff principal shall return such number of jurors as he thinks fit or, in relation to a trial in the High Court, such other number as the Lord Justice Clerk or any Lord Commissioner of Justiciary may direct.

(2) The Lord Justice General, whom failing the Lord Justice Clerk, may give directions as to the areas from which and the proportions in which jurors are to be summoned for trials to be held in the High Court, and for any such trial the sheriff principal of the sheriffdom in which the trial is to take place shall requisition the required number of jurors from the areas and in the proportions so specified.

(3) Where a sitting of the High Court is to be held at a town in which the High Court does not usually sit, the jury summoned to try any case in such a sitting shall be summoned from the [F216lists] of potential jurors of the sheriff court district in which the town is situated.

[F217. (4)For the purpose of a trial in the sheriff court, the sheriff principal must furnish the clerk of court with a list of names, containing the number of persons required, from lists of potential jurors of—

(a) the sheriff court district in which the trial is to be held (the "local district"), and

(b) if the sheriff principal considers it appropriate, any other sheriff court district or districts in the sheriffdom in which the trial is to be held ("other districts").

(4. A)Where the sheriff principal furnishes a list containing names of potential jurors of other districts, the sheriff principal may determine the proportion as between the local district and the other districts in which jurors are to be summoned.]

(5) The sheriff principal, in any return of jurors made by him to a court, shall take the names in regular order, beginning at the top of the [F218lists] of potential jurors in each of the sheriff court districts, as required; and as often as a juror is returned to him, he shall mark or cause to be marked, in the [F218lists] of potential jurors of the respective sheriff court districts the date when any such juror was returned to serve; and in any such return he shall commence with the name immediately after the last in the preceding return, without regard to the court to which the return was last made, and taking the subsequent names in the order in which they are entered, as directed by this subsection, and so to the end of the lists respectively.

(6) Where a person whose name has been entered in the lists of potential jurors dies, or ceases to be qualified to serve as a juror, the sheriff principal, in making returns of jurors in accordance with the M3. Jurors (Scotland) Act 1825, shall pass over the name of that person, but the date at which his name has been so passed over, and the reason therefor, shall be entered at the time in the lists of potential jurors.

(7) F219. . . . .

(8) The persons to serve as jurors at [F220trials in the High Court sitting at a particular place on a particular day] shall be listed and their names and addresses shall be inserted in one roll F221. . . , and the list made up under this section shall be known as the "list of assize".

(9) When more than one case is set down for trial [F222in the High Court sitting at a particular place on a particular day] , it shall not be necessary to prepare more than one list of assize, and such list F223. . . shall be the list of assize for [F224all trials to be held in the High Court sitting in that particular place on that particular day] ; and the persons included in such list shall be summoned to serve generally for [F225all such trials] , and only one general execution of citation shall be returned against them; and a copy of the list of assize, certified by one of the clerks of court, shall have the like effect, for all purposes for which the list may be required, as the principal list of assize authenticated as aforesaid.

(10) No irregularity in—

(a) making up the lists in accordance with the provisions of this Act;

(b) transmitting the lists;

(c) F226. . . . .

(d) summoning jurors; or

(e) in returning any execution of citation,

shall constitute an objection to jurors whose names are included in the jury list, subject to the ruling of the court in relation to the effect of an objection as to any criminal act by which jurors may be returned to serve in any case contrary to this Act or the M4. Jurors (Scotland) Act 1825.

Amendments (Textual)

F216. Word in s. 84. (3) substituted (13.12.2010) by Criminal Justice and Licensing (Scotland) Act 2010 (asp 13), ss. 93. (2)(a), 206. (1); S.S.I. 2010/413, art. 2, Sch.

F217. S. 84. (4)(4. A) substituted for s. 84. (4) (13.12.2010) by Criminal Justice and Licensing (Scotland) Act 2010 (asp 13), ss. 93. (2)(b), 206. (1); S.S.I. 2010/413, art. 2, Sch.

F218. Word in s. 84. (5) substituted (13.12.2010) by Criminal Justice and Licensing (Scotland) Act 2010 (asp 13), ss. 93. (2)(c), 206. (1); S.S.I. 2010/413, art. 2, Sch.

F219. S. 84. (7) repealed (13.12.2010) by Criminal Justice and Licensing (Scotland) Act 2010 (asp 13), ss. 93. (2)(d), 206. (1); S.S.I. 2010/413, art. 2, Sch.

F220. Words in s. 84. (8) substituted (1.2.2005) by Criminal Procedure (Amendment) (Scotland) Act 2004 (asp 3), ss. 25, 27. (1), Sch. para. 29. (a)(i); S.S.I. 2004/405, art. 2, Sch. 1 (subject to arts. 3-5)

F221. Words in s. 84. (8) repealed (1.2.2005) by Criminal Procedure (Amendment) (Scotland) Act 2004 (asp 3), ss. 25, 27. (1), Sch. para. 29. (a)(ii); S.S.I. 2004/405, art. 2, Sch. 1 (subject to arts. 3-5)

F222. Words in s. 84. (9) substituted (1.2.2005) by Criminal Procedure (Amendment) (Scotland) Act 2004 (asp 3), ss. 25, 27. (1), Sch. para. 29. (b)(i); S.S.I. 2004/405, art. 2, Sch. 1 (subject to arts. 3-5)

F223. Words in s. 84. (9) repealed (1.2.2005) by Criminal Procedure (Amendment) (Scotland) Act 2004 (asp 3), ss. 25, 27. (1), Sch. para. 29. (b)(ii); S.S.I. 2004/405, art. 2, Sch. 1 (subject to arts. 3-5)

F224. Words in s. 84. (9) substituted (1.2.2005) by Criminal Procedure (Amendment) (Scotland) Act 2004 (asp 3), ss. 25, 27. (1), Sch. para. 29. (b)(iii); S.S.I. 2004/405, art. 2, Sch. 1 (subject to arts. 3-5)

F225. Words in s. 84. (9) substituted (1.2.2005) by Criminal Procedure (Amendment) (Scotland) Act 2004 (asp 3), ss. 25, 27. (1), Sch. para. 29. (b)(iv); S.S.I. 2004/405, art. 2, Sch. 1 (subject to arts. 3-5)

F226. S. 84. (10)(c) repealed (1.2.2005) by Criminal Procedure (Amendment) (Scotland) Act 2004 (asp 3), ss. 25, 27. (1), Sch. para. 29. (c); S.S.I. 2004/405, art. 2, Sch. 1 (subject to arts. 3-5)

Marginal Citations

M36 Geo. 4. 1825 c.22.

M46 Geo 4. 1825 c.22.

85 Juries: citation and attendance of jurors.S

(1) It shall not be necessary to serve any list of jurors upon the accused, F227. . ..

[F228[F229. (2)A list of jurors shall—

(a) be prepared and kept in such form and manner; and

(b) contain such minimum number of names,

as may be prescribed by Act of Adjournal.]

(2. A)The clerk of the court before which the trial is take place shall, on an application made to him by or on behalf of an accused, supply the accused, free of charge, on the day on which the trial diet is called, and before the oath has been administered to the jurors for the trial of the accused, with a copy of a list of jurors prepared under subsection (2) above.

(2. B)Where an accused has been supplied under subsection (2. A) above with a list of jurors—

(a) neither he nor any person acting on his behalf shall make a copy of that list, or any part thereof; and

(b) he or his representative shall return the list to the clerk of the court after the oath has been administered to the jurors for his trial.

(2. C)A person who fails to comply with subsection (2. B) above shall be guilty of an offence and shall be liable on summary conviction to a fine not exceeding level 1 on the standard scale.]

(3) It shall not be necessary to summon all the jurors contained in any list of jurors under this Act, but it shall be competent to summon such jurors only, commencing from the top of the list, as may be necessary to ensure a sufficient number for the trial of the cases which remain for trial at the date of the citation of the jurors, and such number shall be fixed by the clerk of the court in which the trial diet is to be called, or in any case in the High Court by the Clerk of Justiciary, and the jurors who are not so summoned shall be placed upon the next list issued, until they have attended to serve.

(4) [F230 The sheriff clerk of—

(a) the sheriffdom in which the High Court is to sit, or

(b) the sheriff court district in which a trial in the sheriff court is to be held,

shall] fill up and sign a proper citation addressed to each F231. . . juror, and shall cause the same to be transmitted to him by letter, sent to him at his place of residence as stated in the lists of potential jurors F232... or to be served on him by an officer of law; and a certificate under the hand of such sheriff clerk of the citation of any jurors or juror in the manner provided in this subsection shall be a legal citation.

[F233. (4. A)Citation of a juror may also be effected by an electronic citation which is sent—

(a) by or on behalf of the sheriff clerk; and

(b) by means of electronic communication,

to the home or business email address of the juror.

(4. B)Citation under subsection (4. A) above is a legal citation if the sheriff clerk possesses a legible version of an electronic communication which—

(a) is signed by electronic signature by the person who signed the citation;

(b) includes the citation; and

(c) bears to have been sent to the home or business email address of the juror being cited.

(4. C)In subsection (4. A) above, an "electronic citation" is a citation in electronic form which—

(a) is capable of being kept in legible form; and

(b) is signed by electronic signature by or on behalf of the sheriff clerk.]

(5) The sheriff clerk of the sheriffdom in which [F234the High Court is to sit on any particular day] shall issue citations to the whole jurors required for [F235trials to be held in the High Court sitting in the sheriffdom on that day] , whether the jurors reside in that or in any other sheriffdom.

(6) Persons cited to attend as jurors may, unless they have been excused in respect thereof under section 1 [F236or 1. A] of the M5. Law Reform (Miscellaneous Provisions) (Scotland) Act 1980, be fined up to level 3 on the standard scale if they fail to attend in compliance with the citation.

(7) A fine imposed under subsection (6) above may, on application, be remitted—

(a) by a Lord Commissioner of Justiciary where imposed in the High Court;

(b) by the sheriff court where imposed in the sheriff court,

and no court fees or expenses shall be exigible in respect of any such application.

(8) A person shall not be exempted by sex or marriage from the liability to serve as a juror.

Amendments (Textual)

F227. Words in s. 85. (1) repealed (1.8.1997) by 1997 c. 48, ss. 58. (2), 62. (2), Sch. 3; S.I. 1997/1712, art. 3, Sch. (subject to arts. 4, 5)

F228. S. 85. (2)(2. A)(2. B)(2. C) substituted (1.8.1997) for s. 85. (2) by 1997 c. 48, s. 58. (3); S.I. 1997/1714, art. 3, Sch. (subject to arts. 4, 5)

F229. S. 85. (2) substituted (1.2.2005) by Criminal Procedure (Amendment) (Scotland) Act 2004 (asp 3), ss. 25, 27. (1), Sch. para. 30. (a); S.S.I. 2004/405, art. 2, Sch. 1 (subject to arts. 3-5)

F230. Words in s. 85. (4) substituted (13.12.2010) by Criminal Justice and Licensing (Scotland)

Act 2010 (asp 13), ss. 93. (3)(a), 206. (1); S.S.I. 2010/413, art. 2, Sch.
F231. Word in s. 85. (4) repealed (13.12.2010) by Criminal Justice and Licensing (Scotland) Act 2010 (asp 13), ss. 93. (3)(b), 206. (1); S.S.I. 2010/413, art. 2, Sch.
F232. Words in s. 85. (4) repealed (1.4.2015) by Courts Reform (Scotland) Act 2014 (asp 18), s. 138. (2), sch. 5 para. 44; S.S.I. 2015/77, art. 2. (2)(3), sch.
F233. S. 85. (4. A)-(4. C) inserted (1.11.2012) by Criminal Proceedings etc. (Reform) (Scotland) Act 2007 (asp 6), ss. 29, 84. (1); S.S.I. 2012/274, art. 2, sch.
F234. Words in s. 85. (5) substituted (1.2.2005) by Criminal Procedure (Amendment) (Scotland) Act 2004 (asp 3), ss. 25, 27. (1), Sch. para. 30. (c)(i); S.S.I. 2004/405, art. 2, Sch. 1 (subject to arts. 3-5)
F235. Words in s. 85. (5) substituted (1.2.2005) by Criminal Procedure (Amendment) (Scotland) Act 2004 (asp 3), ss. 25, 27. (1), Sch. para. 30. (c)(ii); S.S.I. 2004/405, art. 2, Sch. 1 (subject to arts. 3-5)
F236. Words in s. 85. (6) inserted (10.1.2011) by Criminal Justice and Licensing (Scotland) Act 2010 (asp 13), ss. 203, 206. (1), Sch. 7 para. 48; S.S.I. 2010/413, art. 2, Sch.
Marginal Citations
M51980 c.55.

86 Jurors: excusal and objections.S

(1) Where, before a juror is sworn to serve, the parties jointly apply for him to be excused the court shall, notwithstanding that no reason is given in the application, excuse that juror from service.

(2) Nothing in subsection (1) above shall affect the right of the accused or the prosecutor to object to any juror on cause shown.

(3) If any objection is taken to a juror on cause shown and such objection is founded on the want of sufficient qualification as provided by section 1. (1) of the M6. Law Reform (Miscellaneous Provisions) (Scotland) Act 1980, such objection shall be proved only by the oath of the juror objected to.

(4) No objection to a juror shall be competent after he has been sworn to serve.
Marginal Citations
M61980 c.55.

Non-availability of judgeS

87 Non-availability of judge.S

(1) Where the court is unable to proceed owing to the death, illness or absence of the presiding judge, the clerk of court may convene the court (if necessary) and—
    (a) in a case where no evidence has been led, adjourn the diet and any other diet appointed for [F237the same day] to—
(i) a time later the same day, or a date not more than seven days later, when he believes a judge will be available; or
(ii) a later [F238date] not more than two months after the date of the adjournment; or
    (b) in a case where evidence has been led—
(i) adjourn the diet and any other diet appointed for [F239the same day] to a time later the same day, or a date not more than seven days later, when he believes a judge will be available; or
(ii) with the consent of the parties, desert the diet pro loco et tempore.

(2) Where a diet has been adjourned under sub-paragraph (i) of either paragraph (a) or paragraph (b) of subsection (1) above the clerk of court may, where the conditions of that subsection

continue to be satisfied, further adjourn the diet under that sub-paragraph; but the total period of such adjournments shall not exceed seven days.

(3) Where a diet has been adjourned under subsection (1)(b)(i) above the court may, at the adjourned diet—

(a) further adjourn the diet; or

(b) desert the diet pro loco et tempore.

(4) Where a diet is deserted in pursuance of subsection (1)(b)(ii) or (3)(b) above, the Lord Advocate may raise and insist in a new indictment, and—

(a) where the accused is in custody it shall not be necessary to grant a new warrant for his incarceration, and the warrant or commitment on which he is at the time in custody till liberation in due course of law shall continue in force; and

(b) where the accused is at liberty on bail, his bail shall continue in force.

Amendments (Textual)

F237. Words in s. 87. (1)(a) substituted (1.2.2005) by Criminal Procedure (Amendment) (Scotland) Act 2004 (asp 3), ss. 25, 27. (1), Sch. para. 31. (a)(i); S.S.I. 2004/405, art. 2, Sch. 1 (subject to arts. 3-5)

F238. Words in s. 87. (1)(a)(ii) substituted (1.2.2005) by Criminal Procedure (Amendment) (Scotland) Act 2004 (asp 3), ss. 25, 27. (1), Sch. para. 31. (a)(ii); S.S.I. 2004/405, art. 2, Sch. 1 (subject to arts. 3-5)

F239. Words in s. 87. (1)(b)(i) substituted (1.2.2005) by Criminal Procedure (Amendment) (Scotland) Act 2004 (asp 3), ss. 25, 27. (1), Sch. para. 31. (b); S.S.I. 2004/405, art. 2, Sch. 1 (subject to arts. 3-5)

[F24087. ADisposal of preliminary matters at trial dietS

Where—

(a) any preliminary plea or issue; or

(b) in a case to be tried in the High Court, any application, notice or other matter referred to in section 72. (6)(b)(iii) or (iv) of this Act,

is to be disposed of at the trial diet, it shall be so disposed of before the jury is sworn, unless, where it is a preliminary issue consisting of an objection to the admissibility of any evidence, the court at the trial diet considers it is not capable of being disposed of before then.]

Amendments (Textual)

F240. S. 87. A inserted (1.2.2005) by Criminal Procedure (Amendment) (Scotland) Act 2004 (asp 3), ss. 13. (2), 27. (1); S.S.I. 2004/405, art. 2, Sch. 1

Jury for trialS

88 Plea of not guilty, balloting and swearing of jury, etc.S

(1) Where the accused pleads not guilty, the clerk of court shall record that fact and proceed to ballot the jury.

(2) The jurors for the trial shall be chosen in open court by ballot from the list of persons summoned in such manner as shall be prescribed by Act of Adjournal, and the persons so chosen shall be the jury to try the accused, and their names shall be recorded in the minutes of the proceedings.

(3) It shall not be competent for the accused or the prosecutor to object to a juror on the ground that the juror has not been duly cited to attend.

(4) Notwithstanding subsection (1) above, the jurors chosen for any particular trial may, when that trial is disposed of, without a new ballot serve on the trials of other accused, provided that—

(a) the accused and the prosecutor consent;

(b) the names of the jurors are contained in the list of jurors; and

(c) the jurors are duly sworn to serve on each successive trial.

(5) When the jury has been balloted, the clerk of court shall inform the jury of the charge against the accused—

(a) by reading the words of the indictment (with the substitution of the third person for the second); or

(b) if the presiding judge, because of the length or complexity of the indictment, so directs, by reading to the jury a summary of the charge approved by the judge,

and copies of the indictment shall be provided for each member of the jury without lists of witnesses or productions.

(6) After reading the charge as mentioned in subsection (5) above and any special defence as mentioned in section 89. (1) of this Act, the clerk of court shall administer the oath in common form.

(7) The court may excuse a juror from serving on a trial where the juror has stated the ground for being excused in open court.

(8) Where a trial which is proceeding is adjourned from one day to another, the jury shall not be secluded during the adjournment, unless, on the motion of the prosecutor or the accused or ex proprio motu the court sees fit to order that the jury be kept secluded.

Modifications etc. (not altering text)

C38. S. 88. (1) excluded by S.I. 1996/513, Sch. 2 rule 14.1. A(1) (as inserted (1.6.2010) by Act of Adjournal (Criminal Procedure Rules Amendment) (Miscellaneous) 2010 (S.S.I. 2010/184), para. 3)

89 Jury to be informed of special defence.S

(1) Subject to subsection (2) below, where the accused has lodged a plea of special defence, the clerk of court shall, after informing the jury, in accordance with section 88. (5) of this Act, of the charge against the accused, and before administering the oath, read to the jury the plea of special defence.

(2) Where the presiding judge on cause shown so directs, the plea of special defence shall not be read over to the jury in accordance with subsection (1) above; and in any such case the judge shall inform the jury of the lodging of the plea and of the general nature of the special defence.

(3) Copies of a plea of special defence shall be provided for each member of the jury.

90 Death or illness of jurors.S

(1) Where in the course of a trial—

(a) a juror dies; or

(b) the court is satisfied that it is for any reason inappropriate for any juror to continue to serve as a juror,

the court may in its discretion, on an application made by the prosecutor or an accused, direct that the trial shall proceed before the remaining jurors (if they are not less than twelve in number), and where such direction is given the remaining jurors shall be deemed in all respects to be a properly constituted jury for the purpose of the trial and shall have power to return a verdict accordingly whether unanimous or, subject to subsection (2) below, by majority.

(2) The remaining jurors shall not be entitled to return a verdict of guilty by majority unless at least eight of their number are in favour of such verdict and if, in any such case, the remaining jurors inform the court that—

(a) fewer than eight of their number are in favour of a verdict of guilty; and

(b) there is not a majority in favour of any other verdict,

they shall be deemed to have returned a verdict of not guilty.

[F241. Obstructive witnessesS

Amendments (Textual)

F241. Ss. 90. A-90. E inserted (1.2.2005 for specified purposes and otherwise prosp.) by Criminal Procedure (Amendment) (Scotland) Act 2004 (asp 5), ss. 11, 27. (1); S.S.I. 2004/405, art. 2, Sch. 1 (with transitional provision in arts. 3-5)

90. AApprehension of witnesses in proceedings on indictmentS

(1) In any proceedings on indictment, the court may, on the application of any of the parties, issue a warrant for the apprehension of a witness if subsection (2) or (3) below applies in relation to the witness.

(2) This subsection applies if the witness, having been duly cited to any diet in the proceedings, deliberately and obstructively fails to appear at the diet.

(3) This subsection applies if the court is satisfied by evidence on oath that the witness is being deliberately obstructive and is not likely to attend to give evidence at any diet in the proceedings without being compelled to do so.

(4) For the purposes of subsection (2) above, a witness who, having been duly cited to any diet, fails to appear at the diet is to be presumed, in the absence of any evidence to the contrary, to have so failed deliberately and obstructively.

(5) An application under subsection (1) above—

  (a) may be made orally or in writing;

  (b) if made in writing—

(i) shall be in such form as may be prescribed by Act of Adjournal, or as nearly as may be in such form; and

(ii) may be disposed of in court or in chambers after such inquiry or hearing (if any) as the court considers appropriate.

(6) A warrant issued under this section shall be in such form as may be prescribed by Act of Adjournal or as nearly as may be in such form.

(7) A warrant issued under this section in the form mentioned in subsection (6) above shall imply warrant to officers of law—

  (a) to search for and apprehend the witness in respect of whom it is issued;

  (b) to bring the witness before the court;

  (c) in the meantime, to detain the witness in a police station, police cell or other convenient place; and

  (d) so far as is necessary for the execution of the warrant, to break open shut and lockfast places.

(8) It shall not be competent, in any proceedings on indictment, for a court to issue a warrant for the apprehension of a witness otherwise than in accordance with this section.

(9) A person apprehended under a warrant issued under this section shall wherever practicable be brought before the court not later than in the course of the first day on which—

  (a) in the case of a warrant issued by a single judge of the High Court, that Court;

  (b) in any other case, the court,

is sitting after he is taken into custody.

(10) In this section and section 90. B, "the court" means F242. . .

  (a) where the witness is to give evidence in proceedings in the High Court, a single judge of that Court; or

  (b) where the witness is to give evidence in proceedings on indictment in the sheriff court, any sheriff court with jurisdiction in relation to the proceedings.

Amendments (Textual)

F242. Words in s. 90. A(10) repealed (10.12.2007) by Criminal Proceedings etc. (Reform)

(Scotland) Act 2007 (asp 6), ss. 80, 84, Sch. para. 15. (1); S.S.I. 2007/479, art. 3. (1), Sch. (as amended by S.S. I. 2007/527)

90. BOrders in respect of witnesses apprehended under section 90. AS

(1) Where a witness is brought before the court in pursuance of a warrant issued under section 90. A of this Act, the court shall, after giving the parties and the witness an opportunity to be heard, make an order—

(a) detaining the witness until the conclusion of the diet at which the witness is to give evidence;

(b) releasing the witness on bail; or

(c) liberating the witness.

(2) The court may make an order under subsection (1)(a) or (b) above only if it is satisfied that—

(a) the order is necessary with a view to securing that the witness appears at the diet at which the witness is to give evidence; and

(b) it is appropriate in all the circumstances to make the order.

[F243. (2. A)Whenever the court makes an order under subsection (1) above, it shall state the reasons for the terms of the order.]

(3) Subsection (1) above is without prejudice to any power of the court to—

(a) make a finding of contempt of court in respect of any failure of a witness to appear at a diet to which he has been duly cited; and

(b) dispose of the case accordingly.

(4) Where—

(a) an order under subsection (1)(a) above has been made in respect of a witness; and

(b) at, but before the conclusion of, the diet at which the witness is to give evidence, the court in which the diet is being held excuses the witness,

that court, on excusing the witness, may recall the order under subsection (1)(a) above and liberate the witness.

(5) On making an order under subsection (1)(b) above in respect of a witness, the court shall impose such conditions as it considers necessary with a view to securing that the witness appears at the diet at which he is to give evidence.

(6) However, the court may not impose as such a condition a requirement that the witness or a cautioner on his behalf deposit a sum of money in court.

(7) Where the court makes an order under subsection (1)(a) above in respect of a witness, the court shall, on the application of the witness—

(a) consider whether the imposition of a remote monitoring requirement would enable it to make an order under subsection (1)(b) above releasing the witness on bail subject to a movement restriction condition; and

(b) if so—

(i) make an order under subsection (1)(b) above releasing the witness on bail subject to such a condition (as well as such other conditions required to be imposed under subsection (5) above); and

(ii) in the order, impose, as a further condition under subsection (5) above, a remote monitoring requirement.

(8) Subsections (7) to (19) of section 24. A of this Act apply in relation to remote monitoring requirements imposed under subsection (7)(b)(ii) above and to the imposing of such requirements as they apply to remote monitoring requirements imposed under section 24. A(1) or (2) of this Act and the imposing of such requirements, but with the following modifications—

(a) references to a remote monitoring requirement imposed under section 24. A(1) or (2) of this Act shall be read as if they included references to a remote monitoring requirement imposed under subsection (7)(b)(ii) above;

(b) references to the accused shall be read as if they were references to the witness in respect of whom the order under subsection (1)(b) above is made.

(9) The powers conferred and duties imposed by sections 24. B to 24. D of this Act are exercisable in relation to remote monitoring requirements imposed under subsection (7)(b)(ii) above as they are exercisable in relation to remote monitoring requirements imposed under subsection (1) or (2) of section 24. A of this Act; and—

(a) references in those sections to remote monitoring requirements shall be read accordingly; and

(b) references to the imposition of any requirement as a further condition of bail shall be read as if they were references to the imposition of the requirement as a further condition under subsection (5) above.

(10) Section 25 of this Act (which makes provision for an order granting bail to specify the conditions imposed on bail and the accused's proper domicile of citation) shall apply in relation to an order under subsection (1)(b) above as it applies to an order granting bail, but with the following modifications—

(a) references to the accused shall be read as if they were references to the witness in respect of whom the order under subsection (1)(b) above is made;

(b) references to the order granting bail shall be read as if they were references to the order under subsection (1)(b) above;

(c) subsection (3) shall be read as if for the words from "relating" to "offence" in the third place where it occurs there were substituted at which the witness is to give evidence.

(11) In this section—

(a) "a movement restriction condition" means, in relation to a witness released on bail under subsection (1)(b) above, a condition imposed under subsection (5) above restricting the witness's movements, including such a condition requiring the witness to be, or not to be, in any place or description of place for, or during, any period or periods or at any time; and

(b) "a remote monitoring requirement" means, in relation to a movement restriction condition, a requirement that compliance with the condition be remotely monitored.

Amendments (Textual)

F243. S. 90. B(2. A) inserted (10.12.2007) by Criminal Proceedings etc. (Reform) (Scotland) Act 2007 (asp 6), ss. 27. (1), 84; S.S.I. 2007/479, art. 3. (1), Sch. (as amended by S.S. I. 2007/527)

90. CBreach of bail under section 90. B(1)(b)S

(1) A witness who, having been released on bail by virtue of an order under subsection (1)(b) of section 90. B of this Act, fails without reasonable excuse—

(a) to appear at any diet to which he has been cited; or

(b) to comply with any condition imposed under subsection (5) of that section,

shall be guilty of an offence and liable on conviction on indictment to the penalties specified in subsection (2) below.

(2) Those penalties are—

(a) a fine; and

(b) imprisonment for a period not exceeding two years.

[F244. (2. A)In any proceedings in relation to an offence under subsection (1) above, the fact that (as the case may be) a person—

(a) was on bail;

(b) was subject to any particular condition of bail;

(c) failed to appear at a diet;

(d) was cited to a diet,

shall, unless challenged by giving notice of a preliminary objection in accordance with section 71. (2) or 72. (6)(b)(i) of this Act, be held as admitted.]

(3) Subsection (4) below applies in proceedings against a witness for an offence under paragraph

(b) of subsection (1) above where the condition referred to in that paragraph is—

(a) a movement restriction condition (within the meaning of section 90. B(11) of this Act) in respect of which a remote monitoring requirement has been imposed under section 90. B(7)(b)(ii) of this Act; or

(b) a requirement imposed under section 24. D(3)(b)(as extended by section 90. B(9)) of this Act.

(4) In proceedings in which this subsection applies, evidence of—

(a) in the case referred to in subsection (3)(a) above, the presence or absence of the witness at a particular place at a particular time; or

(b) in the case referred to in subsection (3)(b) above, any tampering with or damage to a device worn or carried by the witness for the purpose of remotely monitoring his whereabouts,

may, subject to subsections (7) and (8) below, be given by the production of the document or documents referred to in subsection (5) below.

(5) That document or those documents is or are a document or documents bearing to be—

(a) a statement automatically produced by a device specified in regulations made under section 24. D(4)(as extended by section 90. B(9)) of this Act by which the witness's whereabouts were remotely monitored; and

(b) a certificate signed by a person nominated for the purpose of this paragraph by the Scottish Ministers that the statement relates to—

(i) in the case referred to in subsection (3)(a) above, the whereabouts of the witness at the dates and times shown in the statement; or

(ii) in the case referred to in subsection (3)(b) above, any tampering with or damage to the device.

(6) The statement and certificate mentioned in subsection (5) above shall, when produced in the proceedings, be sufficient evidence of the facts set out in them.

(7) Neither the statement nor the certificate mentioned in subsection (5) above shall be admissible in evidence unless a copy of both has been served on the witness prior to the trial.

(8) Without prejudice to subsection (7) above, where it appears to the court that the witness has had insufficient notice of the statement or certificate, it may adjourn the trial or make an order which it thinks appropriate in the circumstances.

(9) In subsections (7) and (8), "the trial" means the trial in the proceedings against the witness referred to in subsection (3) above.

(10) Section 28 of this Act shall apply in respect of a witness who has been released on bail by virtue of an order under section 90. B(1)(b) of this Act as it applies to an accused released on bail, but with the following modifications—

(a) references to an accused shall be read as if they were references to the witness;

(b) in subsection (2), the reference to the court to which the accused's application for bail was first made shall be read as if it were a reference to the court which made the order under section 90. B(1)(b) of this Act in respect of the witness; and

(c) in subsection (4)—

(i) references to the order granting bail and original order granting bail shall be read as if they were references to the order under section 90. B(1)(b) and the original such order respectively;

(ii) paragraph (a) shall be read as if at the end there were inserted "and make an order under section 90. B(1)(a) or (c) of this Act in respect of the witness"; and

(iii) paragraph (c) shall be read as if for the words from "complies" to the end there were substituted "appears at the diet at which the witness is to give evidence".

Amendments (Textual)

F244. S. 90. C(2. A) inserted (10.12.2007) by Criminal Proceedings etc. (Reform) (Scotland) Act 2007 (asp 6), ss. 27. (2), 84; S.S.I. 2007/479, art. 3. (1), Sch. (subject to art. 9) (as amended by S.S. I. 2007/527)

90. DReview of orders under section 90. B(1)(a) or (b)S

(1) Where a court has made an order under subsection (1)(a) of section 90. B of this Act, the court may, on the application of the witness in respect of whom the order was made, F245. . . and after giving the parties and the witness an opportunity to be heard—

(a) recall the order; and

(b) make an order under subsection (1)(b) or (c) of that section in respect of the witness.

(2) Where a court has made an order under subsection (1)(b) of section 90. B of this Act, the court may, after giving the parties and the witness an opportunity to be heard—

(a) on the application of the witness in respect of whom the order was made F246. . . —

(i) review the conditions imposed under subsection (5) of that section at the time the order was made; and

(ii) make a new order under subsection (1)(b) of that section and impose different conditions under subsection (5) of that section;

(b) on the application of the party who made the application under section 90. A(1) of this Act in respect of the witness, review the order and the conditions imposed under subsection (5) of [F247section 90. B] at the time the order was made, and

(i) recall the order and make an order under subsection (1)(a) of that section in respect of the witness; or

(ii) make a new order under subsection (1)(b) of that section and impose different conditions under subsection (5) of that section.

(3) The court may not review an order by virtue of subsection [F248 (1) or (2) above unless—

(a) in the case of an application by the witness, the circumstances of the witness have changed materially; or

(b) in that or [F249any other] case, the witness or] party making the application puts before the court material information which was not available to it when it made the order which is the subject of the application.

(4) An application under this section by a witness—

(a) where it relates to the first order made under section 90. B(1)(a) or (b) of this Act in respect of the witness, shall not be made before the fifth day after that order is made;

(b) where it relates to any subsequent such order, shall not be made before the fifteenth day after the order is made.

(5) On receipt of an application under subsection (2)(b) above the court shall—

(a) intimate the application to the witness in respect of whom the order which is the subject of the application was made;

(b) fix a diet for hearing the application and cite the witness to attend the diet; and

(c) where it considers that the interests of justice so require, grant warrant to arrest the witness.

(6) Nothing in this section shall affect any right of a person to appeal against an order under section 90. B(1).

Amendments (Textual)

F245. Words in s. 90. D(1) repealed (10.12.2007) by Criminal Proceedings etc. (Reform) (Scotland) Act 2007 (asp 6), ss. 27. (3)(a), 84; S.S.I. 2007/479, art. 3. (1), Sch. (as amended by S.S. I. 2007/527)

F246. Words in s. 90. D(2)(a) repealed (10.12.2007) by Criminal Proceedings etc. (Reform) (Scotland) Act 2007 (asp 6), ss. 27. (3)(b), 84; S.S.I. 2007/479, art. 3. (1), Sch. (as amended by S.S. I. 2007/527)

F247. Words in s. 90. D(2)(b) substituted (10.12.2007) by Criminal Proceedings etc. (Reform) (Scotland) Act 2007 (asp 6), ss. 80, 84, Sch. para. 15. (2); S.S.I. 2007/479, art. 3. (1), Sch. (as amended by S.S. I. 2007/527)

F248. Words in s. 90. D(3) substituted (10.12.2007) by virtue of Criminal Proceedings etc. (Reform) (Scotland) Act 2007 (asp 6), ss. 27. (3)(c), 84; S.S.I. 2007/479, art. 3. (1), Sch. (as amended by S.S. I. 2007/527)

F249. Words in s. 90. D(3)(b) substituted (13.12.2010) by Criminal Justice and Licensing (Scotland) Act 2010 (asp 13) ss. 203, 206. (1), {Sch. 7 para. 49}; S.S.I. 2010/413, art. 2, Sch.

90. EAppeals in respect of orders under section 90. B(1)S

(1) Any of the parties specified in subsection (2) below may appeal to the High Court against—

    (a) any order made under subsection (1)(a) or (c) of section 90. B of this Act; or

    (b) where an order is made under subsection (1)(b) of that section—

(i) the order;

(ii) any of the conditions imposed under subsection (5) of that section on the making of the order; or

(iii) both the order and any such conditions.

(2) The parties referred to in subsection (1) above are—

    (a) the witness in respect of whom the order which is the subject of the appeal was made;

    (b) the prosecutor; and

    (c) the accused.

(3) A party making an appeal under subsection (1) above shall intimate it to the other parties specified in subsection (2) above and, for that purpose, intimation to the [F250. Crown Agent] shall be sufficient intimation to the prosecutor.

(4) An appeal under this section shall be disposed of by the High Court or any Lord Commissioner of Justiciary in court or in chambers after such inquiry and hearing of the parties as shall seem just.

(5) Where the witness in respect of whom the order which is the subject of an appeal under this section was made is under 21 years of age, section 51 of this Act shall apply to the High Court or, as the case may be, the Lord Commissioner of Justiciary when disposing of the appeal as it applies to a court when remanding or committing a person of the witness's age for trial or sentence.]

Amendments (Textual)

F250. Words in s. 90. E(3) substituted (10.12.2007) by Criminal Proceedings etc. (Reform) (Scotland) Act 2007 (asp 6), ss. 80, 84, Sch. para. 15. (3); S.S.I. 2007/479, art. 3. (1), Sch. (as amended by S.S. I. 2007/527)

TrialS

91 Trial to be continuous.S

Every trial shall proceed from day to day until it is concluded unless the court sees cause to adjourn over a day or days.

92 Trial in presence of accused.S

(1) Without prejudice to section 54 of this Act, and subject to [F251subsections (2) and (2. A)] below, no part of a trial shall take place outwith the presence of the accused.

(2) If during the course of his trial an accused so misconducts himself that in the view of the court a proper trial cannot take place unless he is removed, the court may order—

    (a) that he is removed from the court for so long as his conduct makes it necessary; and

    (b) that the trial proceeds in his absence,

but if he is not legally represented the court shall appoint F252. . . a solicitor to represent his interests during such absence.

[F253. (2. A)If—

    (a) after evidence has been led which substantially implicates the accused in respect of the offence charged in the indictment or, where two or more offences are charged in the indictment, any of them, the accused fails to appear at the trial diet; and

    (b) the failure to appear occurred at a point in proceedings where the court is satisfied that it is in the interests of justice to do so,

then the court may, on the motion of the prosecutor and after hearing the parties on the motion, proceed with the trial and dispose of the case in the absence of the accused.

(2. B)Where a motion is made under subsection (2. A) above, the court shall—

    (a) if satisfied that there is a solicitor with authority to act for the purposes of—

(i) representing the accused's interests at the hearing on the motion; and

(ii) if the motion is granted, the accused's defence at the trial,

allow that solicitor to act for those purposes; or

    (b) if there is no such solicitor, at its own hand appoint a solicitor to act for those purposes.

(2. C)It is the duty of a solicitor appointed under subsection (2) or (2. B)(b) above to act in the best interests of the accused.

(2. D)In all other respects, a solicitor so appointed has, and may be made subject to, the same obligations and has, and may be given, the same authority as if engaged by the accused; and any employment of and instructions given to counsel by the solicitor shall proceed and be treated accordingly.

(2. E)Where the court is satisfied that—

    (a) a solicitor allowed to act under subsection (2. B)(a) above no longer has authority to act; or

    (b) a solicitor appointed under subsection (2) or (2. B)(b) above is no longer able to act in the best interests of the accused,

the court may relieve that solicitor and appoint another solicitor for the purposes referred to in subsection (2) or, as the case may be, (2. B) above.

(2. F)Subsections (2. B)(b) and (2. E) above shall not apply in the case of proceedings—

    (a) in respect of a sexual offence to which section 288. C of this Act applies; or

    (b) in respect of which section 288. E of this Act applies; or

    (c) in which an order has been made under section 288. F(2) of this Act.]

(3) From the commencement of the leading of evidence in a trial for rape or the like the judge may, if he thinks fit, cause all persons other than the accused and counsel and solicitors to be removed from the court-room.

[F254. (4)In this section—

    (a) references to a solicitor appointed under subsection (2) or (2. B)(b) above include references to a solicitor appointed under subsection (2. E) above;

    (b) " counsel " includes, in relation to the High Court of Justiciary, a solicitor who has a right of audience in that Court under section 25. A of the Solicitors (Scotland) Act 1980 (c. 46).]

Amendments (Textual)

F251. Words in s. 92. (1) substituted (1.2.2005) by Criminal Procedure (Amendment) (Scotland) Act 2004 (asp 5), ss. 10. (1), 27. (1); S.S.I. 2004/405, art. 2, Sch. 1 (with savings in arts. 3-5)

F252. Words in s. 92. (2) repealed (1.2.2005) by Criminal Procedure (Amendment) (Scotland) Act 2004 (asp 5), ss. 10. (2), 27. (1); S.S.I. 2004/405, art. 2, Sch. 1 (with savings in arts. 3-5)

F253. S. 92. (2. A)-(2. F) inserted (1.2.2005) by Criminal Procedure (Amendment) (Scotland) Act 2004 (asp 5), ss. 10. (3), 27. (1); S.S.I. 2004/405, art. 2, Sch. 1 (with savings in arts. 3-5) (as amended (31.1.2005) by S.S.I. 2005/40, art. 3. (3) (subject to art. 1. (3)))

F254. S. 92. (4) inserted (1.2.2005) by Criminal Procedure (Amendment) (Scotland) Act 2004 (asp 5), ss. 10. (4), 27. (1); S.S.I. 2004/405, art. 2, Sch. 1 (with savings in arts. 3-5)

93 Record of trial.S

(1) The proceedings at the trial of any person who, if convicted, is entitled to appeal under Part VIII of this Act, shall be recorded by means of shorthand notes or by mechanical means.

(2) A shorthand writer shall—

    (a) sign the shorthand notes taken by him of such proceedings and certify them as being complete and correct; and

    (b) retain the notes.

(3) A person recording such proceedings by mechanical means shall—

(a) certify that the record is true and complete;

(b) specify in the certificate the proceedings or, as the case may be, the part of the proceedings to which the record relates; and

(c) retain the record.

(4) The cost of making a record under subsection (1) above shall be defrayed, in accordance with scales of payment fixed for the time being by Treasury, out of money provided by Parliament.

(5) In subsection (1) above "proceedings at the trial" means the whole proceedings including, without prejudice to that generality—

(a) discussions—

(i) on any objection to the relevancy of the indictment;

(ii) with respect to any challenge of jurors; and

(iii) on all questions arising in the course of the trial;

(b) the decision of the court on any matter referred to in paragraph (a) above;

(c) the evidence led at the trial;

(d) any statement made by or on behalf of the accused whether before or after the verdict;

(e) the judge's charge to the jury;

(f) the speeches of counsel or agent;

(g) the verdict of the jury;

(h) the sentence by the judge.

Modifications etc. (not altering text)

C39. S. 93. (2)-(4) applied (3.11.2003 but only in respect of summary proceedings) by Criminal Justice (Scotland) Act 2003 (asp 7), ss. 21. (6), 89; S.S.I. 2003/475, art. 2, Sch.

94 Transcripts of record and documentary productions.S

(1) The Clerk of Justiciary may direct that a transcript of a record made under section 93. (1) of this Act, or any part thereof, be made and delivered to him for the use of any judge.

(2) Subject to subsection (3) below, the Clerk of Justiciary shall, if requested to do so by—

(a) the Secretary of State [F255or, subject to subsection (2. B) below, the prosecutor] ; or

(b) any other person [F256, not being a person convicted at the trial,] on payment of such charges as may be fixed for the time being by Treasury,

direct that such a transcript be made and sent to the person who requested it.

[F257. (2. A)If—

(a) on the written application of a person convicted at the trial and granted leave to appeal; and

[F258. (b)either of the conditions in subsection (2. AZA) is met or it is otherwise in the interests of justice to do so,]

a judge of the High Court [F259may order, and in that event] the Clerk of Justiciary shall direct, on payment of such charges as are mentioned in paragraph (b) of subsection (2) above, that such a transcript be made and sent to that person.

[F260. (2. AZA)The conditions mentioned in subsection (2. A)(b) are that—

(a) a ground of appeal, for which leave to appeal has been granted, reveals a significant dispute between that ground and the report of the trial judge on the nature and extent of the evidence, speech or other part of the record to which the application relates; or

(b) the trial judge's report does not, in relation to a ground of appeal for which leave to appeal has been granted, provide a sufficient narrative of the nature and extent of the evidence, speech or other part of the record to which the application relates.]

[F261. (2. AA)Subsection (2. A) applies to a person mentioned in subsection (2. AB) as it applies to a person convicted at the trial, with the modification that the reference to the transcript in subsection (2. A) is to be construed as a reference to the transcript of the record made of proceedings at the trial resulting in the acquittal mentioned in subsection (2. AB)(b).

(2. AB)The person mentioned in subsection (2. AA) is a person who—

(a) is convicted of the offence mentioned in subsection (1) of section 11 of the Double Jeopardy (Scotland) Act 2011 (asp 16));

(b) is subsequently acquitted of an offence mentioned in subsection (2) of that section; and

(c) desires to appeal, under subsection (7) of that section, against the conviction of the offence mentioned in paragraph (a).]

(2. B)Where, as respects any person convicted at the trial, the Crown Agent has received intimation under section 107. (10) of this Act, the prosecutor shall not be entitled to make a request under subsection (2)(a) above; but if, on the written application of the prosecutor and on cause shown, a judge of the High Court so orders, the Clerk of Justiciary shall direct that such a transcript be made and sent to the prosecutor.

(2. C)Any application under subsection (2. A) above shall—

(a) be made within 14 days after the date on which leave to appeal was granted or within such longer period after that date as a judge of the High Court may, on written application and on cause shown, allow; and

[F262. (aa)set out, for each ground of appeal to which the application relates, the particular evidence, speech or other part of the record required; and]

(b) be intimated forthwith by the applicant to the prosecutor.

(2. D)The prosecutor may, within 7 days after receiving intimation under subsection (2. C)(b) above, make written representations to the court as respects the application under subsection (2. A) above (the application being determined without a hearing).

(2. E)Any application under subsection (2. B) above shall—

(a) be made within 14 days after the receipt of intimation mentioned in that subsection or within such longer period after that receipt as a judge of the High Court may, on written application and on cause shown, allow; and

(b) be intimated forthwith by the prosecutor to the person granted leave to appeal.

(2. F)The person granted leave to appeal may, within 7 days after receiving intimation under subsection (2. E)(b) above, make written representations to the court as respects the application under subsection (2. B) above (the application being determined without a hearing).]

(3) The Secretary of State may, after consultation with the Lord Justice General, by order made by statutory instrument provide that in any class of proceedings specified in the order the Clerk of Justiciary shall only make a direction under subsection (2)(b) above if satisfied that the person requesting the transcript is of a class of person so specified and, if purposes for which the transcript may be used are so specified, intends to use it only for such a purpose; and different purposes may be so specified for different classes of proceedings or classes of person.

(4) Where subsection (3) above applies as respects a direction, the person to whom the transcript is sent shall, if purposes for which that transcript may be used are specified by virtue of that subsection, use it only for such a purpose.

(5) A statutory instrument containing an order under subsection (3) above shall be subject to annulment in pursuance of a resolution of either House of Parliament.

(6) A direction under subsection (1) or (2) above may require that the transcript be made by the person who made the record or by such competent person as may be specified in the direction; and that person shall comply with the direction.

(7) A transcript made in compliance with a direction under subsection (1) or (2) above—

(a) shall be in legible form; and

(b) shall be certified by the person making it as being a correct and complete transcript of the whole or, as the case may be, the part of the record purporting to have been made and certified, and in the case of shorthand notes signed, by the person who made the record.

(8) The cost of making a transcript in compliance with a direction under subsection (1) or (2)(a) above shall be defrayed, in accordance with scales of payment fixed for the time being by the Treasury, out of money provided by Parliament.

(9) The Clerk of Justiciary shall, on payment of such charges as may be fixed for the time being by the Treasury, provide a copy of any documentary production lodged in connection with an appeal under this Part of this Act to such of the following persons as may request it—

(a) the prosecutor;

(b) any person convicted in the proceedings;

(c) any other person named in, or immediately affected by, any order made in the proceedings; and

(d) any person authorised to act on behalf of any of the persons mentioned in paragraphs (a) to (c) above.

Amendments (Textual)

F255. Word in s. 94. (2)(a) added (27.6.2003) by Criminal Justice (Scotland) Act 2003 (asp 7), ss. 65. (a)(i), 89; S.S.I. 2003/288, art. 2, Sch.

F256. Words s. 94. (2)(b) inserted (27.6.2003) by Criminal Justice (Scotland) Act 2003 (asp 7), ss. 65. (a)(ii), 89; S.S.I. 2003/288, art. 2, Sch.

F257. S. 94. (2. A)-(2. F) inserted (27.6.2003) by Criminal Justice (Scotland) Act 2003 (asp 7), ss. 65. (b), 89; S.S.I. 2003/288, art. 2, Sch.

F258. S. 94. (2. A)(b) substituted (12.11.2012) by Act of Adjournal (Amendment of the Criminal Procedure (Scotland) Act 1995) (Transcripts) 2012 (S.S.I. 2012/272), paras. 1. (2), 2. (2)(a) (with para. 3)

F259. Words in s. 94. (2. A) substituted (12.11.2012) by Act of Adjournal (Amendment of the Criminal Procedure (Scotland) Act 1995) (Transcripts) 2012 (S.S.I. 2012/272), paras. 1. (2), 2. (2)(b) (with para. 3)

F260. S. 94. (2. AZA) inserted (12.11.2012) by Act of Adjournal (Amendment of the Criminal Procedure (Scotland) Act 1995) (Transcripts) 2012 (S.S.I. 2012/272), paras. 1. (2), 2. (3) (with para. 3)

F261. S. 94. (2. AA)(2. AB) inserted (28.11.2011) by Double Jeopardy (Scotland) Act 2011 (asp 16), s. 17. (3), sch. para. 7; S.S.I. 2011/365, art. 3

F262. S. 94. (2. C)(aa) inserted (12.11.2012) by Act of Adjournal (Amendment of the Criminal Procedure (Scotland) Act 1995) (Transcripts) 2012 (S.S.I. 2012/272), paras. 1. (2), 2. (4) (with para. 3)

95 Verdict by judge alone.S

(1) Where, at any time after the jury has been sworn to serve in a trial, the prosecutor intimates to the court that he does not intend to proceed in respect of an offence charged in the indictment, the judge shall acquit the accused of that offence and the trial shall proceed only in respect of any other offence charged in the indictment.

(2) Where, at any time after the jury has been sworn to serve in a trial, the accused intimates to the court that he is prepared to tender a plea of guilty as libelled, or such other plea as the Crown is prepared to accept, in respect of any offence charged in the indictment, the judge shall accept the plea tendered and shall convict the accused accordingly.

(3) Where an accused is convicted under subsection (2) above of an offence—

(a) the trial shall proceed only in respect of any other offence charged in the indictment; and

(b) without prejudice to any other power of the court to adjourn the case or to defer sentence, the judge shall not sentence him or make any other order competent following conviction until a verdict has been returned in respect of every other offence mentioned in paragraph (a) above.

96 Amendment of indictment.S

(1) No trial shall fail or the ends of justice be allowed to be defeated by reason of any discrepancy or variance between the indictment and the evidence.

(2) It shall be competent at any time prior to the determination of the case, unless the court see just cause to the contrary, to amend the indictment by deletion, alteration or addition, so as to—

(a) cure any error or defect in it;

(b) meet any objection to it; or

(c) cure any discrepancy or variance between the indictment and the evidence.

(3) Nothing in this section shall authorise an amendment which changes the character of the offence charged, and, if it appears to the court that the accused may in any way be prejudiced in his defence on the merits of the case by any amendment made under this section, the court shall grant such remedy to the accused by adjournment or otherwise as appears to the court to be just.

(4) An amendment made under this section shall be sufficiently authenticated by the initials of the clerk of the court.

97 No case to answer.S

(1) Immediately after the close of the evidence for the prosecution, the accused may intimate to the court his desire to make a submission that he has no case to answer both—

    (a) on an offence charged in the indictment; and

    (b) on any other offence of which he could be convicted under the indictment.

(2) If, after hearing both parties, the judge is satisfied that the evidence led by the prosecution is insufficient in law to justify the accused being convicted of the offence charged in respect of which the submission has been made or of such other offence as is mentioned, in relation to that offence, in paragraph (b) of subsection (1) above, he shall acquit him of the offence charged in respect of which the submission has been made and the trial shall proceed only in respect of any other offence charged in the indictment.

(3) If, after hearing both parties, the judge is not satisfied as is mentioned in subsection (2) above, he shall reject the submission and the trial shall proceed, with the accused entitled to give evidence and call witnesses, as if such submission had not been made.

(4) A submission under subsection (1) above shall be heard by the judge in the absence of the jury.

[F26397. ASubmissions as to sufficiency of evidenceS

(1) Immediately after one or other (but not both) of the appropriate events, the accused may make either or both of the submissions mentioned in subsection (2) in relation to an offence libelled in an indictment (the "indicted offence").

(2) The submissions are—

    (a) that the evidence is insufficient in law to justify the accused's being convicted of the indicted offence or any other offence of which the accused could be convicted under the indictment (a "related offence"),

    (b) that there is no evidence to support some part of the circumstances set out in the indictment.

(3) For the purposes of subsection (1), "the appropriate events" are—

    (a) the close of the whole of the evidence,

    (b) the conclusion of the prosecutor's address to the jury on the evidence.

(4) A submission made under this section must be heard by the judge in the absence of the jury.

Amendments (Textual)

F263. Ss. 97. A-97. D inserted (28.3.2011) by Criminal Justice and Licensing (Scotland) Act 2010 (asp 13), ss. 73, 206. (1); S.S.I. 2011/178, art. 2, sch.

97. BAcquittals etc. on section 97. A(2)(a) submissionsS

(1) This section applies where the accused makes a submission of the kind mentioned in section 97. A(2)(a).

(2) If the judge is satisfied that the evidence is insufficient in law to justify the accused's being convicted of the indicted offence, then—

    (a) where the judge is satisfied that the evidence is also insufficient in law to justify the accused's being convicted of a related offence—

(i) the judge must acquit the accused of the indicted offence, and

(ii) the trial is to proceed only in respect of any other offence libelled in the indictment,

    (b) where the judge is satisfied that the evidence is sufficient in law to justify the accused's being convicted of a related offence, the judge must direct that the indictment be amended accordingly.

(3) If the judge is not satisfied as is mentioned in subsection (2)—

    (a) the judge must reject the submission, and

    (b) the trial is to proceed as if the submission had not been made.

(4) The judge may make a decision under this section only after hearing both (or all) parties.

(5) An amendment made by virtue of this section must be sufficiently authenticated by the initials of the judge or the clerk of court.

(6) In this section, "indicted offence" and "related offence" have the same meanings as in section 97. A.

Amendments (Textual)

F263. Ss. 97. A-97. D inserted (28.3.2011) by Criminal Justice and Licensing (Scotland) Act 2010 (asp 13), ss. 73, 206. (1); S.S.I. 2011/178, art. 2, sch.

97. CDirections etc. on section 97. A(2)(b) submissionsS

(1) This section applies where the accused makes a submission of the kind mentioned in section 97. A(2)(b).

(2) If the judge is satisfied that there is no evidence to support some part of the circumstances set out in the indictment, the judge must direct that the indictment be amended accordingly.

(3) If the judge is not satisfied as is mentioned in subsection (2)—

    (a) the judge must reject the submission, and

    (b) the trial is to proceed as if the submission had not been made.

(4) The judge may make a decision under this section only after hearing both (or all) parties.

(5) An amendment made by virtue of this section must be sufficiently authenticated by the initials of the judge or the clerk of court.

Amendments (Textual)

F263. Ss. 97. A-97. D inserted (28.3.2011) by Criminal Justice and Licensing (Scotland) Act 2010 (asp 13), ss. 73, 206. (1); S.S.I. 2011/178, art. 2, sch.

97. DNo acquittal on "no reasonable jury" groundsS

(1) A judge has no power to direct the jury to return a not guilty verdict on any charge on the ground that no reasonable jury, properly directed on the evidence, could convict on the charge.

(2) Accordingly, no submission based on that ground or any ground of like effect is to be allowed.]

Amendments (Textual)

F263. Ss. 97. A-97. D inserted (28.3.2011) by Criminal Justice and Licensing (Scotland) Act 2010 (asp 13), ss. 73, 206. (1); S.S.I. 2011/178, art. 2, sch.

98 Defence to speak last.S

In any trial the accused or, where he is legally represented, his counsel or solicitor shall have the right to speak last.

99 Seclusion of jury to consider verdict.S

(1) When the jury retire to consider their verdict, the clerk of court shall enclose the jury in a room

by themselves and, except in so far as provided for, or is made necessary, by an instruction under subsection (4) below, neither he nor any other person shall be present with the jury [F264while] they are enclosed.

(2) Except in so far as is provided for, or is made necessary, by an instruction under subsection (4) below, [F265while the jury are enclosed and until they] intimate that they are ready to return their verdict—

(a) subject to subsection (3) below, no person shall visit the jury or communicate with them; and

(b) no juror shall come out of the jury room other than to receive or seek a direction from the judge or to make a request—

(i) for an instruction under subsection (4)(a), (c) or (d) below; or

(ii) regarding any matter in the cause.

(3) Nothing in paragraph (a) of subsection (2) above shall prohibit the judge, or any person authorised by him for the purpose, communicating with the jury for the purposes—

(a) of giving a direction, whether or not sought under paragraph (b) of that subsection; or

(b) responding to a request made under that paragraph.

(4) The judge may give such instructions as he considers appropriate as regards—

(a) the provision of meals and refreshments for the jury;

(b) the making of arrangements for overnight accommodation for the jury and [F266, unless under subsection (7) below the court permits them to separate,] for their continued seclusion if such accommodation is provided;

(c) the communication of a personal or business message, unconnected with any matter in the cause, from a juror to another person (or vice versa); or

(d) the provision of medical treatment, or other assistance, immediately required by a juror.

(5) If the prosecutor or any other person contravenes the provisions of this section, the accused shall be acquitted of the crime with which he is charged.

(6) During the period in which the jury are retired to consider their verdict, the judge may sit in any other proceedings; and the trial shall not fail by reason only of his so doing.

[F267. (7)The court may, if it thinks fit, permit the jury to separate even after they have retired to consider their verdict.]

Amendments (Textual)

F264. Word in s. 99. (1) substituted (27.6.2003) by Criminal Justice (Scotland) Act 2003 (asp 7), ss. 79. (a), 89; S.S.I. 2003/288, art. 2, Sch.

F265. Words in s. 99. (2) substituted (27.6.2003) by Criminal Justice (Scotland) Act 2003 (asp 7), ss. 79. (b), 89; S.S.I. 2003/288, art. 2, Sch.

F266. Words in s. 99. (4)(b) inserted (27.6.2003) by Criminal Justice (Scotland) Act 2003 (asp 7), ss. 79. (c), 89; S.S.I. 2003/288, art. 2, Sch.

F267. S. 99. (7) added (27.6.2003) by Criminal Justice (Scotland) Act 2003 (asp 7), ss. 79. (d), 89; S.S.I. 2003/288, art. 2, Sch.

Verdict and convictionS

100 Verdict of jury.S

(1) The verdict of the jury, whether the jury are unanimous or not, shall be returned orally by the foreman of the jury unless the court directs a written verdict to be returned.

(2) Where the jury are not unanimous in their verdict, the foreman shall announce that fact so that the relative entry may be made in the record.

(3) The verdict of the jury may be given orally through the foreman of the jury after consultation in the jury box without the necessity for the jury to retire.

101 Previous convictions: solemn proceedings.S

(1) Previous convictions against the accused shall not [F268, subject to subsection (2) below and section 275. A(2) of this Act,] be laid before the jury, nor shall reference be made to them in presence of the jury before the verdict is returned.

(2) Nothing in subsection (1) above shall prevent the prosecutor—

(a) asking the accused questions tending to show that he has been convicted of an offence other than that with which he is charged, where he is entitled to do so under section 266 of this Act; or

(b) leading evidence of previous convictions where it is competent to do so under section 270 of this Act,

and nothing in this section or in section 69 of this Act shall prevent evidence of previous convictions being led in any case where such evidence is competent in support of a substantive charge.

(3) Previous convictions shall not [F269, subject to section 275. A(1) of this Act,] be laid before the presiding judge until the prosecutor moves

[F270. (a)]for sentence [F271; or]

[F272. (b)for a risk assessment order (or the court at its own instance proposes to make such an order)],

and in that event the prosecutor shall lay before the judge a copy of the notice referred to in subsection (2) or (4) of section 69 of this Act.

[F273. (3. A)Where, under paragraph (b) of subsection (3) above, the prosecutor lays previous convictions before the judge, he shall also provide the judge with such details regarding the offences in question as are available to him.]

(4) On the conviction of the accused it shall be competent for the court, subject to subsection (5) below, to amend a notice of previous convictions so laid by deletion or alteration for the purpose of curing any error or defect.

F274. (5). . . . .

(6) Any conviction which is admitted in evidence by the court shall be entered in the record of the trial.

(7) Where a person is convicted of an offence, the court may have regard to any previous conviction in respect of that person in deciding on the disposal of the case.

(8) Where any such intimation as is mentioned in section 69 of this Act is given by the accused, it shall be competent to prove any previous conviction included in a notice under that section in the manner specified in section 285 [F275, or as the case may be 286. A,] of this Act, and the provisions of the [F276section in question] shall apply accordingly.

[F277. (9)This section, except subsection (2) above, applies in relation to the alternative disposals mentioned in subsection (10) below as it applies in relation to previous convictions.

(10) Those alternative disposals are—

(a) a—

(i) fixed penalty under section 302. (1) of this Act;

(ii) compensation offer under section 302. A(1) of this Act,

that has been accepted (or deemed to have been accepted) by the accused in the two years preceding the date of an offence charged;

(b) a work order under section 303. ZA(6) of this Act that has been completed in the two years preceding the date of an offence charged[F278;

(c) a restoration notice given under subsection (4) of section 20. A of the Nature Conservation (Scotland) Act 2004 (asp 6) in respect of which the accused has given notice of intention to comply under subsection (5) of that section in the two years preceding the date of an offence charged.]

(11) Nothing in this section or in section 69 of this Act shall prevent the prosecutor, following conviction of an accused of an offence—

(a) to which a fixed penalty offer made under section 302. (1) of this Act related;

(b) to which a compensation offer made under section 302. A(1) of this Act related; F279...

(c) to which a work offer made under section 303. ZA(1) of this Act related[F280; or

(d) to which a restoration notice given under section 20. A(4) of the Nature Conservation (Scotland) Act 2004 (asp 6) related,]

providing the judge with information about the making of the offer (including the terms of the offer) [F281or, as the case may be, about the giving of the notice (including the terms of the notice).]]

Amendments (Textual)

F268. Words in s. 101. (1) inserted (1.11.2002) by Sexual Offences (Procedure and Evidence) (Scotland) Act 2002 (asp 9), s. 10. (1)(a); S.S.I. 2002/443, art. 3 (with art. 4. (5))

F269. Words in s. 101. (3) inserted (1.11.2002) by Sexual Offences (Procedure and Evidence) (Scotland) Act 2002 (asp 9), s. 10. (1)(b); S.S.I. 2002/443, art. 3 (with art. 4. (5))

F270. Words in s. 101. (3) renumbered as s. 101. (3)(a) (19.6.2006) by virtue of Criminal Justice (Scotland) Act 2003 (asp 7), ss. 1. (2), 89, Sch. 1 para. 2. (3)(a); S.S.I. 2006/332, art. 2. (1)(2)

F271. Word in s. 101. (3) inserted (19.6.2006) by Criminal Justice (Scotland) Act 2003 (asp 7), ss. 1. (2), 89, Sch. 1 para. 2. (3)(a); S.S.I. 2006/332, art. 2. (1)(2)

F272. S. 101. (3)(b) inserted (19.6.2006) by Criminal Justice (Scotland) Act 2003 (asp 7), ss. 1. (2), 89, Sch. 1 para. 2. (3)(a); S.S.I. 2006/332, art. 2. (1)(2)

F273. S. 101. (3. A) inserted (19.6.2006) by Criminal Justice (Scotland) Act 2003 (asp 7), ss. 1. (2), 89, Sch. 1 para. 2. (3)(b); S.S.I. 2006/332, art. 2. (1)(2)

F274. S. 101. (5) repealed (1.8.1997) by 1997 c. 48, ss. 31, 62. (2), Sch. 3; S.I. 1997/1712, art. 3, Sch. (subject to arts. 4, 5)

F275. Words in s. 101. (8) inserted (27.6.2003) by Criminal Justice (Scotland) Act 2003 (asp 7), ss. 57. (2)(a), 89; S.S.I. 2003/288, art. 2, Sch.

F276. Words in s. 101. (8) substituted (27.6.2003) by Criminal Justice (Scotland) Act 2003 (asp 7), ss. 57. (2)(b), 89; S.S.I. 2003/288, art. 2, Sch.

F277. S. 101. (9)-(11) added (10.3.2008) by Criminal Proceedings etc. (Reform) (Scotland) Act 2007 (asp 6), ss. 53. (2), 84; S.S.I. 2008/42, art. 3, Sch.

F278. S. 101. (10)(c) and semi colon inserted (29.6.2011) by Wildlife and Natural Environment (Scotland) Act 2011 (asp 6), ss. 40. (3)(b)(i), 43. (1) (with s. 41. (1)); S.S.I. 2011/279, art. 2. (1)(q)

F279. Word in s. 101. (11) repealed (29.6.2011) by Wildlife and Natural Environment (Scotland) Act 2011 (asp 6), ss. 40. (3)(b)(ii)(A), 43. (1) (with s. 41. (1)); S.S.I. 2011/279, art. 2. (1)(q)

F280. S. 101. (11)(d) and word inserted (29.6.2011) by Wildlife and Natural Environment (Scotland) Act 2011 (asp 6), ss. 40. (3)(b)(ii)(B), 43. (1) (with s. 41. (1)); S.S.I. 2011/279, art. 2. (1)(q)

F281. Words in s. 101. (11) inserted (29.6.2011) by Wildlife and Natural Environment (Scotland) Act 2011 (asp 6), ss. 40. (3)(b)(ii)(C), 43. (1) (with s. 41. (1)); S.S.I. 2011/279, art. 2. (1)(q)

[F282101. APost-offence convictions etc.S

(1) This section applies where an accused person is convicted of an offence ("offence O") on indictment.

(2) The court may, in deciding on the disposal of the case, have regard to—

(a) any conviction in respect of the accused which occurred on or after the date of offence O but before the date of conviction in respect of that offence,

(b) any of the alternative disposals in respect of the accused that are mentioned in subsection (3).

(3) Those alternative disposals are—

(a) a—

(i) fixed penalty under section 302. (1) of this Act, or

(ii) compensation offer under section 302. A(1) of this Act,

that has been accepted (or deemed to have been accepted) on or after the date of offence O but before the date of conviction in respect of that offence,

(b) a work order under section 303. ZA(6) of this Act that has been completed on or after the date of offence O but before the date of conviction in respect of that offence.

(4) The court may have regard to any such conviction or alternative disposal only if it is—

(a) specified in a notice laid before the court by the prosecutor, and

(b) admitted by the accused or proved by the prosecutor (on evidence adduced then or at another diet).

(5) A reference in this section to a conviction which occurred on or after the date of offence O is a reference to such a conviction by a court in any part of the United Kingdom or in any other member State of the European Union.]

Amendments (Textual)

F282. S. 101. A inserted (28.3.2011) by Criminal Justice and Licensing (Scotland) Act 2010 (asp 13), ss. 70. (1), 206. (1); S.S.I. 2011/178, art. 2, sch.

102 Interruption of trial for other proceedings.S

(1) When the jury have retired to consider their verdict, and the diet in another criminal cause has been called, then, subject to subsection (3) below, if it appears to the judge presiding at the trial to be appropriate, he may interrupt the proceedings in such other cause—

(a) in order to receive the verdict of the jury in the preceding trial, and thereafter to dispose of the case;

(b) to give a direction to the jury in the preceding trial upon any matter upon which the jury may wish a direction from the judge or to hear any request from the jury regarding any matter in the cause.

(2) Where in any case the diet of which has not been called, the accused intimates to the clerk of court that he is prepared to tender a plea of guilty as libelled or such qualified plea as the Crown is prepared to accept, or where a case is remitted to the High Court for sentence, then, subject to subsection (3) below, any trial then proceeding may be interrupted for the purpose of receiving such plea or dealing with the remitted case and pronouncing sentence or otherwise disposing of any such case.

(3) In no case shall any proceedings in the preceding trial take place in the presence of the jury in the interrupted trial, but in every case that jury shall be directed to retire by the presiding judge.

(4) On the interrupted trial being resumed the diet shall be called de novo.

(5) In any case an interruption under this section shall not be deemed an irregularity, nor entitle the accused to take any objection to the proceedings.

[F283. Failure of accused to appearS

Amendments (Textual)

F283. S. 102. A inserted (10.12.2007) by Criminal Proceedings etc. (Reform) (Scotland) Act 2007 (asp 6), ss. 32, 84; S.S.I. 2007/479, art. 3. (1), Sch. (as amended by S.S. I. 2007/527)

102. AFailure of accused to appearS

(1) In proceedings on indictment, an accused person who without reasonable excuse fails to appear at a diet of which the accused has been given due notice (apart from a diet which the accused is not required to attend) is—

(a) guilty of an offence; and

(b) liable on conviction on indictment to a fine or to imprisonment for a period not exceeding 5 years or to both.

(2) In proceedings on indictment, where an accused person fails to appear at a diet of which the

accused has been given due notice (apart from a diet which the accused is not required to attend), the court may grant a warrant to apprehend the accused.

(3) It is not, otherwise than under subsection (2) above, competent in any proceedings on indictment for a court to grant a warrant for the apprehension of an accused person for failure to appear at a diet.

(4) However, it remains competent for a court to grant a warrant on petition (as referred to in section 34 of this Act) in respect of an offence under—

 (a) subsection (1) above;

 [F284. (b)section 27. (7) of this Act,]

whether or not a warrant has been granted under subsection (2) above in respect of the same failure to appear to which that offence relates.

(5) Where a warrant to apprehend an accused person is granted under subsection (2) above [F285at any stage prior to conviction], the indictment falls as respects that accused.

(6) Subsection (5) above is subject to any order to different effect made by the court when granting the warrant.

(7) An order under subsection (6) above—

 (a) for the purpose of proceeding with the trial in the absence of the accused under section 92. (2. A) (where the warrant is granted at a trial diet), may be made on the motion of the prosecutor;

 (b) for any other purpose, may be made on the motion of the prosecutor or of the court's own accord.

(8) A warrant granted under subsection (2) above shall be in such form as may be prescribed by Act of Adjournal or as nearly as may be in such form.

(9) A warrant granted under subsection (2) above (in the form mentioned in subsection (8) above) shall imply warrant to officers of law—

 (a) to search for and apprehend the accused;

 (b) to bring the accused before the court;

 (c) in the meantime, to detain the accused in a police station, police cell or other convenient place; and

 (d) so far as is necessary for the execution of the warrant, to break open shut and lockfast places.

(10) An accused apprehended under a warrant granted under subsection (2) above shall wherever practicable be brought before the court not later than in the course of the first day on which the court is sitting after the accused is taken into custody.

(11) Where the accused is brought before the court in pursuance of a warrant granted under subsection (2) above, the court shall make an order—

 (a) detaining the accused until liberated in due course of law; or

 (b) releasing the accused on bail.

(12) For the purposes of subsection (11) above, the court is to have regard to the terms of the indictment in relation to which the warrant was granted even if that indictment has fallen.

(13) In a case where a warrant is granted under subsection (2) above, any period of time during which the accused was detained in custody—

 (a) as regards that case; and

 (b) prior to the making of an order under subsection (11) above,

does not count towards any time limit applying in that case by virtue of section 65. (4) of this Act.

(14) For the purposes of subsection (13) above—

 (a) detention as regards a case includes, in addition to detention as regards the indictment in relation to which the warrant was granted (whether or not that indictment has fallen), detention as regards any preceding petition;

 (b) it is immaterial whether or not further proceedings are on a fresh indictment.

(15) At any time before the trial of an accused person on indictment, it is competent—

 (a) to amend the indictment so as to include an additional charge of an offence under subsection (1) above;

 (b) to include, in the list of witnesses or productions associated with the indictment, witnesses or productions relating to that offence.

(16) In this section, " the court " means—

(a) where the accused failed to appear at the High Court—

(i) for the purposes of subsections (10) to (12) above, that Court (whether or not constituted by a single judge);

(ii) otherwise, a single judge of that Court;

(b) where the accused failed to appear at a sheriff court, any sheriff court with jurisdiction in relation to the proceedings.]

Amendments (Textual)

F284. S. 102. A(4)(b) substituted (28.3.2011) by Criminal Justice and Licensing (Scotland) Act 2010 (asp 13), s. 206. (1), sch. 7 para. 50; S.S.I. 2011/178, art. 2, sch.

F285. Words in s. 102. A(5) inserted (10.3.2008) by The Criminal Proceedings etc. (Reform) (Scotland) Act 2007 (Supplemental Provisions) Order 2008 (S.S.I. 2008/109), art. 2. (b)

PART VIII Appeals from Solemn Proceedings

PART VIIIS Appeals from Solemn Proceedings

Modifications etc. (not altering text)

C1 Pt. 8 (ss. 103-132): power to modify or apply (with modifications) conferred (1.3.2007) by Police, Public Order and Criminal Justice (Scotland) Act 2006 (asp 10) , ss. 94. (2) , 104 ; S.S.I. 2007/84 , art. 3. (2)

103 Appeal sittings.S

(1) The High Court shall hold both during session and during vacation such sittings as are necessary for the disposal of appeals and other proceedings under this Part of this Act.

(2) Subject to subsection (3) below, for the purpose of hearing and determining any appeal or other proceeding under this Part of this Act three of the Lords Commissioners of Justiciary shall be a quorum of the High Court, and the determination of any question under this Part of this Act by the court shall be according to the votes of the majority of the members of the court sitting, including the presiding judge, and each judge so sitting shall be entitled to pronounce a separate opinion.

(3) For the purpose of hearing and determining any appeal under section 106. (1)(b) to (e) of this Act, or any proceeding connected therewith, two of the Lords Commissioners of Justiciary shall be a quorum of the High Court, and each judge shall be entitled to pronounce a separate opinion; but where the two Lords Commissioners of Justiciary are unable to reach agreement on the disposal of the appeal, or where they consider it appropriate, the appeal shall be heard and determined in accordance with [F1subsection (2)] above.

(4) Subsections (1) [F2to (3)] above shall apply to cases certified to the High Court by a single judge of the said court and to appeals by way of advocation in like manner as they apply to appeals under this Part of this Act.

(5) The powers of the High Court under this Part of this Act—

(a) to extend the time within which intimation of intention to appeal and note of appeal may be given;

(b) to allow the appellant to be present at any proceedings in cases where he is not entitled to be present without leave; and

(c) to admit an appellant to bail,

may be exercised by any judge of the High Court, sitting and acting wherever convenient, in the same manner as they may be exercised by the High Court, and subject to the same provisions.

(6) Where a judge acting under subsection (5) above refuses an application by an appellant to exercise under that subsection any power in his favour, the appellant shall be entitled to have the application determined by the High Court.

[F3. (6. A)Where a judge acting under subsection (5)(c) above grants an application by an appellant to exercise that power in his favour, the prosecutor shall be entitled to have the application determined by the High Court.]

(7) Subject to subsection (5) [F4, (6) and (6. A)] above and without prejudice to it, preliminary and interlocutory proceedings incidental to any appeal or application may be disposed of by a single judge.

(8) In all proceedings before a judge under section (5) above, and in all preliminary and interlocutory proceedings and applications except such as are heard before the full court, the parties may be represented and appear by a solicitor alone.

Amendments (Textual)

F1 Words in s. 103. (3) substituted (1.8.1997) by 1997 c. 48 , s. 62. (1) , Sch. 1 para. 21. (13)(a) ; S.I. 1997/1712 , art. 3 , Sch. (subject to arts. 4 , 5)

F2 Words in s. 103. (4) substituted (1.8.1997) by 1997 c. 48 , s. 62. (1) , Sch. 1 para. 21. (13)(b) ; S.I. 1997/1712 , art. 3 , Sch. (subject to arts. 4 , 5)

F3 S. 103. (6. A) inserted (27.6.2003) by Criminal Justice (Scotland) Act 2003 (asp 7) , ss. 66. (2)(a) , 89 ; S.S.I. 2003/288 , art. 2 , Sch.

F4 Words in s. 103. (7) substituted (27.6.2003) by Criminal Justice (Scotland) Act 2003 (asp 7) , ss. 66. (2)(b) , 89 ; S.S.I. 2003/288 , art. 2 , Sch.

104 Power of High Court in appeals.S

(1) Without prejudice to any existing power of the High Court, it may for the purposes of an appeal under section 106. (1)[F5, 107. A, 107. B] or 108 of this Act—

    (a) order the production of any document or other thing connected with the proceedings;

    (b) hear any F6. . .evidence relevant to any alleged miscarriage of justice or order such evidence to be heard by a judge of the High Court or by such other person as it may appoint for that purpose;

    (c) take account of any circumstances relevant to the case which were not before the trial judge;

    (d) remit to any fit person to enquire and report in regard to any matter or circumstance affecting the appeal;

    (e) appoint a person with expert knowledge to act as assessor to the High Court in any case where it appears to the court that such expert knowledge is required for the proper determination of the case.

(2) The evidence of any witnesses ordered to be examined before the High Court or before any judge of the High Court or other person appointed by the High Court shall be taken in accordance with the existing law and practice as to the taking of evidence in criminal trials in Scotland.

(3) The appellant or applicant and the respondent or counsel on their behalf shall be entitled to be present at and take part in any examination of any witness to which this section relates.

Amendments (Textual)

F5. Words in s. 104. (1) inserted (28.3.2011) by Criminal Justice and Licensing (Scotland) Act 2010 (asp 13), ss. 75, 206. (1); S.S.I. 2011/178, art. 2, sch.

F6 Word in s. 104. (1)(b) repealed (1.8.1997) by 1997 c. 48 , s. 62. (1)(2) , Sch. 1 para. 21. (14) , Sch. 3 ; S.I. 1997/1712 , art. 3 , Sch. (subject to arts. 4 , 5)

105 Appeal against refusal of application.S

(1) When an application or applications have been dealt with by a judge of the High Court, under section 103. (5) of this Act, the Clerk of Justiciary shall—

    (a) notify to the applicant the decision in the form prescribed by Act of Adjournal or as nearly as may be in such form; and

(b) where all or any of such applications have been refused, forward to the applicant the prescribed form for completion and return forthwith if he desires to have the application or applications determined by the High Court as fully constituted for the hearing of appeals under this Part of this Act.

(2) Where the applicant does not desire a determination as mentioned in subsection (1)(b) above, or does not return within five days to the Clerk the form duly completed by him, the refusal of his application or applications by the judge shall be final.

(3) Where an applicant who desires a determination by the High Court as mentioned in subsection (1)(b) above—

(a) is not legally represented, he may be present at the hearing and determination by the High Court of the application;

(b) is legally represented, he shall not be entitled to be present without leave of the court.

[F7. (3. A)Subsection (3) does not entitle an applicant to be present at the hearing and determination of an application under section 111. (2) unless the High Court has made a direction under section 111. (4)(b).]

(4) When an applicant duly completes and returns to the Clerk of Justiciary within the prescribed time the form expressing a desire to be present at the hearing and determination by the court of the applications mentioned in this section, the form shall be deemed to be an application by the applicant for leave to be so present, and the Clerk of Justiciary, on receiving the form, shall take the necessary steps for placing the application before the court.

[F8. (4. A)An application by a convicted person for a determination by the High Court of a decision of a judge acting under section 103. (5)(c) of this Act to refuse to admit him to bail shall be intimated by him immediately and in writing to the Crown Agent.]

(5) If the application to be present is refused by the court, the Clerk of Justiciary shall notify the applicant; and if the application is granted, he shall notify the applicant and the Governor of the prison where the applicant is in custody and the Secretary of State.

(6) For the purpose of constituting a Court of Appeal, the judge who has refused any application may sit as a member of the court, and take part in determining the application.

Amendments (Textual)

F7. S. 105. (3. A) inserted (17.1.2017) by Criminal Justice (Scotland) Act 2016 (asp 1), ss. 90. (1), 117. (2); S.S.I. 2016/426, art. 2, sch.

F8 S. 105. (4. A) inserted (27.6.2003) by Criminal Justice (Scotland) Act 2003 (asp 7) , ss. 66. (3) , 89 ; S.S.I. 2003/288 , art. 2 , Sch.

[F9105. AAppeal against granting of applicationS

(1) Where the prosecutor desires a determination by the High Court as mentioned in subsection (6. A) of section 103 of this Act, he shall apply to the judge immediately after the power in subsection (5)(c) of that section is exercised in favour of the appellant.

(2) Where a judge acting under section 103. (5)(c) of this Act has exercised that power in favour of the appellant but the prosecutor has made an application under subsection (1) above—

(a) the appellant shall not be liberated until the determination by the High Court; and

(b) that application by the prosecutor shall be heard not more than seven days after the making of the application,

and the Clerk of the Justiciary shall forward to the appellant the prescribed form for completion and return forthwith if he desires to be present at the hearing.

(3) At a hearing and determination as mentioned in subsection (2) above, if the appellant—

(a) is not legally represented, he may be present;

(b) is legally represented, he shall not be entitled to be present without leave of the court.

(4) If the appellant completes and returns the form mentioned in subsection (2) above indicating a desire to be present at the hearing, the form shall be deemed to be an application by the appellant

for leave to be so present, and the Clerk of Justiciary, on receiving the form, shall take the necessary steps for placing the application before the court.

(5) If the application to be present is refused by the court, the Clerk of Justiciary shall notify the appellant; and if the application is granted, he shall notify the appellant and the Governor of the prison where the applicant is in custody and the Scottish Ministers.

(6) For the purposes of constituting a Court of Appeal, the judge who exercised the power in section 103. (5)(c) of this Act in favour of the appellant may sit as a member of the court, and take part in determining the application of the prosecutor.]

Amendments (Textual)

F9 S. 105. A inserted (27.6.2003) by Criminal Justice (Scotland) Act 2003 (asp 7) , ss. 66. (4) , 89 ; S.S.I. 2003/288 , art. 2 , Sch.

106 Right of appeal.S

(1) Any person convicted on indictment may, with leave granted in accordance with section 107 of this Act, appeal in accordance with this Part of this Act, to the High Court—

  (a) against such conviction;

  (b) subject to subsection (2) below, against the sentence passed on such conviction;

  [F10. (ba)against the making of an order for lifelong restriction;]

  [F11. (bb)against any decision not to exercise the power conferred by section 205. A(3), [F12or 205. B(3)] of this Act;]

  (c) against his absolute discharge or admonition;

  [F13. (d)against any drug treatment and testing order;

  (dza) against any disposal under section 227. ZC(7)(a) to (c) or (e) or (8)(a) of this Act;]

  [F14. (da)against any decision to remit made under section 49. (1)(a) of this Act;]

  F15. (db). . . . .

  F15. (dc). . . . .

  (e) against any order deferring sentence; or

  (f) against

[F16. (i)]both such conviction and, subject to subsection (2) below, such sentence or disposal or order.

F17. (ii). . . . .

F17. (iii). . . . .

(2) There shall be no appeal against any sentence fixed by law.

[F18. (3)By an appeal under subsection (1) above a person may bring under review of the High Court any alleged miscarriage of justice, which may include such a miscarriage based on—

  (a) subject to subsections (3. A) to (3. D) below, the existence and significance of evidence which was not heard at the original proceedings; and

  (b) the jury's having returned a verdict which no reasonable jury, properly directed, could have returned.

(3. A)Evidence such as is mentioned in subsection (3)(a) above may found an appeal only where there is a reasonable explanation of why it was not so heard.

(3. B)Where the explanation referred to in subsection (3. A) above or, as the case may be, (3. C) below is that the evidence was not admissible at the time of the original proceedings, but is admissible at the time of the appeal, the court may admit that evidence if it appears to the court that it would be in the interests of justice to do so.

(3. C)Without prejudice to subsection (3. A) above, where evidence such as is mentioned in paragraph (a) of subsection (3) above is evidence—

  (a) which is—

(i) from a person; or

(ii) of a statement (within the meaning of section 259. (1) of this Act) by a person,

who gave evidence at the original proceedings; and

(b) which is different from, or additional to, the evidence so given,

it may not found an appeal unless there is a reasonable explanation as to why the evidence now sought to be adduced was not given by that person at those proceedings, which explanation is itself supported by independent evidence.

(3. D) For the purposes of subsection (3. C) above, " independent evidence " means evidence which—

(a) was not heard at the original proceedings;

(b) is from a source independent of the person referred to in subsection (3. C) above; and

(c) is accepted by the court as being credible and reliable.]

(4) Any document, production or other thing lodged in connection with the proceedings on the trial of any person who, if convicted, is entitled or may be authorised to appeal under this Part of this Act, shall, in accordance with subsections (5) to (9) below, be kept in the custody of the court in which the conviction took place.

(5) All documents and other productions produced at the trial of a convicted person shall be kept in the custody of the court of trial in such manner as it may direct until any period allowed under or by virtue of this Part of this Act for lodging intimation of intention to appeal has elapsed.

(6) Where no direction is given as mentioned in subsection (5) above, such custody shall be in the hands of the sheriff clerk of the district of the court of the second diet to whom the clerk of court shall hand them over at the close of the trial, unless otherwise ordered by the High Court on an intimation of intention to appeal being lodged, and if within such period there has been such lodgement under this Part of this Act, they shall be so kept until the appeal, if it is proceeded with, is determined.

(7) Notwithstanding subsections (5) and (6) above, the judge of the court in which the conviction took place may, on cause shown, grant an order authorising any of such documents or productions to be released on such conditions as to custody and return as he may deem it proper to prescribe.

(8) All such documents or other productions so retained in custody or released and returned shall, under supervision of the custodian thereof, be made available for inspection and for the purpose of making copies of documents or productions to a person who has lodged an intimation of intention to appeal or as the case may be, to the convicted person's counsel or agent, and to the Crown Agent and the procurator fiscal or his deputes.

(9) Where no intimation of intention to appeal is lodged within the period mentioned in subsection (6) above, all such documents and productions shall be dealt with as they are dealt with according to the existing law and practice at the conclusion of a trial; and they shall be so dealt with if, there having been such intimation, the appeal is not proceeded with.

Amendments (Textual)

F10 S. 106. (1)(ba) inserted (19.6.2006 for certain purpose and otherwise prosp.) by Criminal Justice (Scotland) Act 2003 (asp 7), ss. 1. (2), 89, Sch. 1 para. 2. (4); S.S.I. 2006/332, art. 2

F11 S. 106. (1)(bb) inserted (20.10.1997) by 1997 c. 48, s. 18. (1); S.I. 1997/2323, art. 3, Sch. 1

F12 Words in s. 106. (1)(bb) substituted (30.9.1998) by 1998 c. 37, s. 119, Sch. 8 para. 119; S.I. 1998/2327, art. 2. (1)(y)(2)(kk)

F13 S. 106. (1)(d)(dza) substituted for s. 106. (1)(d) (1.2.2011) by Criminal Justice and Licensing (Scotland) Act 2010 (asp 13), ss. 14. (2), 206. (1), Sch. 2 para. 7; S.S.I. 2010/413, art. 2, Sch. (with art. 3)

F14 S. 106. (1)(da) inserted (1.8.1997) by 1997 c. 48, s. 23. (b); S.I. 1997/1712, art. 3, Sch. (subject to arts. 4 , 5)

F15 S. 106. (1)(db) (dc) repealed (28.2.2011) by Protection of Vulnerable Groups (Scotland) Act 2007 (asp 14), s. 101. (2), sch. 4 para. 14. (a) (with ss. 90, 99); S.S.I. 2011/157, art. 2. (a) (with art. 5. (1))

F16 Words in s. 106. (1)(f) become s. 106. (1)(f)(i) (10.1.2005) by virtue of Protection of Children (Scotland) Act 2003 (asp 5), ss. 16. (2)(b), 22. (2); S.S.I. 2004/522, art. 2

F17 S. 106. (1)(f)(ii) (iii) repealed (28.2.2011) by Protection of Vulnerable Groups (Scotland) Act 2007 (asp 14), s. 101. (2), sch. 4 para. 14. (b) (with ss. 90, 99); S.S.I. 2011/157, art. 2. (a) (with art. 5. (1))

F18 S. 106. (3)-(3. D) substituted (1.8.1997) for s. 106. (3) by 1997 c. 48, s. 17. (1); S.I. 1997/1712, art. 3, Sch. (subject to arts. 4 , 5)
Modifications etc. (not altering text)
C2 S. 106 amended (1.4.1996) by 1995 c. 43, ss. 10. (5), 50. (2)
 S. 106 amended (24.3.2003) by Proceeds of Crime Act 2002 (c. 29), ss. 100. (7), 458; S.S.I. 2003/210, art. 2 (with arts. 3-7)
C3 S. 106 extended (19.2.2001) by 2000 c. 11, ss. 7. (4)(b), 8. (1)(c)(ii); S.I. 2001/421, art. 2
 S. 106 extended (11.3.2005) by Prevention of Terrorism Act 2005 (c. 2), s. 12. (5)(c)
C4. S. 106 extended (15.12.2011) by Terrorism Prevention and Investigation Measures Act 2011 (c. 23), s. 31. (2), Sch. 3 para. 4. (3)(c) (with Sch. 8)
C5. S. 106 applied (12.2.2015) by Counter-Terrorism and Security Act 2015 (c. 6), s. 52. (5), Sch. 4 para. 4. (3)(c)

[F19106. A Appeal against automatic sentences where earlier conviction quashed.S

(1) This subsection applies where—
    (a) a person has been sentenced under section 205. A(2) of this Act;
    (b) he had, at the time at which the offence for which he was so sentenced was committed, only one previous conviction for a qualifying offence or a relevant offence within the meaning of that section; and
    (c) after he has been so sentenced, the conviction mentioned in paragraph (b) above has been quashed.
(2) This subsection applies where—
    (a) a person has been sentenced under section 205. B(2) of this Act;
    (b) he had, at the time at which the offence for which he was so sentenced was committed, only two previous convictions for class A drug trafficking offences within the meaning of that section; and
    (c) after he has been so sentenced, one of the convictions mentioned in paragraph (b) above has been quashed.
(3) Where subsection (1) or (2) above applies, the person may appeal under section 106. (1)(b) of this Act against the sentence imposed on him under section 205. A(2) or, as the case may be, 205. B(2) of this Act.
(4) An appeal under section 106. (1)(b) of this Act by virtue of subsection (3) above—
    (a) may be made notwithstanding that the person has previously appealed under that section; and
    (b) shall be lodged within two weeks of the quashing of the conviction as mentioned in subsection (1)(c) or, as the case may be, (2)(c) above.
(5) Where an appeal is made under section 106. (1)(b) by virtue of this section, the following provisions of this Act shall not apply in relation to such an appeal, namely—
    (a) section 121; and
    (b) section 126.]
Amendments (Textual)
F19 S. 106. A inserted (20.10.1997 for specified purposes and otherwise prosp.) by 1997 c. 48 , ss. 19. (1) , 65. (2) ; S.I. 1997/2323 , art. 3 , Sch. 1

107 Leave to appeal.S

(1) The decision whether to grant leave to appeal for the purposes of section 106. (1) of this Act shall be made by a judge of the High Court who shall—
    (a) if he considers that the documents mentioned in subsection (2) below disclose arguable

grounds of appeal, grant leave to appeal and make such comments in writing as he considers appropriate; and

(b) in any other case—

(i) refuse leave to appeal and give reasons in writing for the refusal; and

(ii) where the appellant is on bail and the sentence imposed on his conviction is one of imprisonment, grant a warrant to apprehend and imprison him.

(2) The documents referred to in subsection (1) above are—

(a) the note of appeal lodged under section 110. (1)(a) of this Act;

(b) in the case of an appeal against conviction or sentence in a sheriff court, the certified copy or, as the case may be, the record of the proceedings at the trial;

(c) where the judge who presided at the trial furnishes a report under section 113 of this Act, that report; and

(d) where, by virtue of section 94. (1) of this Act, a transcript of the charge to the jury of the judge who presided at the trial is delivered to the Clerk of Justiciary, that transcript.

[F20. (2. A)In respect of an appeal by virtue of section 11. (7) of the Double Jeopardy (Scotland) Act 2011 (asp 16), the "report under section 113" in subsection (2)(c) means—

(a) the report of the judge who presided at the trial resulting in the appellant's acquittal for an offence mentioned in section 11. (2) of that Act;

(b) where an appeal against conviction was taken before that acquittal, the report of the judge who presided at the trial resulting in the conviction in respect of which leave to appeal is sought prepared at that time; and

(c) any other report of that judge furnished under section 113.]

(3) A warrant granted under subsection (1)(b)(ii) above shall not take effect until the expiry of the period of 14 days mentioned in subsection (4) below [F21. (and if that period is extended under subsection (4. A) below before the period being extended expires, until the expiry of the period as so extended)] without an application to the High Court for leave to appeal having been lodged by the appellant under [F22subsection (4)] .

(4) Where leave to appeal is refused under subsection (1) above the appellant may, within 14 days of intimation under [F23subsection (10)] below, apply to the High Court for leave to appeal.

[F24. (4. A)The High Court may, on cause shown, extend the period of 14 days mentioned in subsection (4) above, or that period as extended under this subsection, whether or not the period to be extended has expired (and if that period of 14 days has expired, whether or not it expired before section 62 of the Criminal Justice (Scotland) Act 2003 (asp 7) came into force).]

(5) In deciding an application under subsection (4) above the High Court shall—

(a) if, after considering the documents mentioned in subsection (2) above and the reasons for the refusal, the court is of the opinion that there are arguable grounds of appeal, grant leave to appeal and make such comments in writing as the court considers appropriate; and

(b) in any other case—

(i) refuse leave to appeal and give reasons in writing for the refusal; and

(ii) where the appellant is on bail and the sentence imposed on his conviction is one of imprisonment, grant a warrant to apprehend and imprison him.

(6) Consideration whether to grant leave to appeal under subsection (1) or (5) above shall take place in chambers without the parties being present.

(7) Comments in writing made under subsection (1)(a) or (5)(a) above may, without prejudice to the generality of that provision, specify the arguable grounds of appeal (whether or not they are contained in the note of appeal) on the basis of which leave to appeal is granted.

(8) Where the arguable grounds of appeal are specified by virtue of subsection (7) above it shall not, except by leave of the High Court on cause shown, be competent for the appellant to found any aspect of his appeal on any ground of appeal contained in the note of appeal but not so specified.

(9) Any application by the appellant for the leave of the High Court under subsection (8) above—

(a) shall be made [F25within 14 days of the date of intimation under subsection (10) below] ; and

(b) shall, [F26within 14 days of] that date, be intimated by the appellant to the Crown Agent. [F27. (9. A)The High Court may, on cause shown, extend the periods of 14 days mentioned in subsection (9) above.]

(10) The Clerk of Justiciary shall forthwith intimate—

(a) a decision under subsection (1) or (5) above; and

(b) in the case of a refusal of leave to appeal, the reasons for the decision,

to the appellant or his solicitor and to the Crown Agent.

Amendments (Textual)

F20. S. 107. (2. A) inserted (28.11.2011) by Double Jeopardy (Scotland) Act 2011 (asp 16), s. 17. (3), sch. para. 8; S.S.I. 2011/365, art. 3

F21. Words in s. 107. (3) inserted (27.6.2003) by Criminal Justice (Scotland) Act 2003. (asp 7), {ss. 62. (a)(i)}, 89; S.S.I. 2003.288, {art. 2}

F22 Words in s. 107. (3) substituted (27.6.2003) by Criminal Justice (Scotland) Act 2003 (asp 7), ss. 62. (a)(ii), 89; S.S.I. 2003/288, art. 2

F23 Words in s. 107. (4) substituted (1.8.1997) by 1997 c. 48, s. 62. (1), Sch. 1 para. 21. (15); S.I. 1997/1712, art. 3, Sch. (subject to arts. 4, 5)

F24 S. 107. (4. A) inserted (27.6.2003) by Criminal Justice (Scotland) Act 2003 (asp 7), ss. 62. (b), 89; S.S.I. 2003/288, art. 2

F25 Words in s. 107. (9)(a) substituted (23.4.2007) by Criminal Proceedings etc. (Reform) (Scotland) Act 2007 (asp 6), ss. 80, 84, Sch. para. 16. (1)(a)(i); S.S.I. 2007/250, art. 3. (i) (subject to art. 4. (2))

F26 Words in s. 107. (9)(b) substituted (23.4.2007) by Criminal Proceedings etc. (Reform) (Scotland) Act 2007 (asp 6), ss. 80, 84, Sch. para. 16. (1)(a)(ii); S.S.I. 2007/250, art. 3. (i) (subject to art. 4. (2))

F27 S. 107. (9. A) inserted (23.4.2007) by Criminal Proceedings etc. (Reform) (Scotland) Act 2007 (asp 6), ss. 80, 84, Sch. para. 16. (1)(b); S.S.I. 2007/250, art. 3. (i) (subject to art. 4. (2))

Modifications etc. (not altering text)

C6 S. 107 applied (with modifications) (26.8.2002) by Act of Adjournal (Criminal Procedure Rules) 1996 (S.I. 1996/513), rule 15 .15. (4) (as inserted (26.8.2002) by Act of Adjournal (Criminal Appeals) 2002 (S.S.I. 2002/387), para. 3. (4))

C7 S. 107. (1)(a) modified (27.10.2003) by S.I. 1996/513, rule 19. B .1. (3) (as inserted by Act of Adjournal (Criminal Procedure Rules Amendment No. 2) (Miscellaneous) 2003 (S.S.I. 2003/468), rule 2. (10))

[F28107. AProsecutor's right of appeal: decisions on section 97 and 97. A submissionsS

(1) The prosecutor may appeal to the High Court against—

(a) an acquittal under section 97 or 97. B(2)(a), or

(b) a direction under section 97. B(2)(b) or 97. C(2).

(2) If, immediately after an acquittal under section 97 or 97. B(2)(a), the prosecutor moves for the trial diet to be adjourned for no more than 2 days in order to consider whether to appeal against the acquittal under subsection (1), the court of first instance must grant the motion unless the court considers that there are no arguable grounds of appeal.

(3) If, immediately after the giving of a direction under section 97. B(2)(b) or 97. C(2), the prosecutor moves for the trial diet to be adjourned for no more than 2 days in order to consider whether to appeal against the direction under subsection (1), the court of first instance must grant the motion unless the court considers that it would not be in the interests of justice to do so.

(4) In considering whether it would be in the interests of justice to grant a motion for adjournment under subsection (3), the court must have regard, amongst other things, to—

(a) whether, if an appeal were to be made and to be successful, continuing with the diet would have any impact on any subsequent or continued prosecution,

(b) whether there are any arguable grounds of appeal.

(5) An appeal may not be brought under subsection (1) unless the prosecutor intimates intention to appeal—

(a) immediately after the acquittal or, as the case may be, the giving of the direction,

(b) if a motion to adjourn the trial diet under subsection (2) or (3) is granted, immediately upon resumption of the diet, or

(c) if such a motion is refused, immediately after the refusal.

(6) Subsection (7) applies if—

(a) the prosecutor intimates an intention to appeal under subsection (1)(a), or

(b) the trial diet is adjourned under subsection (2).

(7) Where this subsection applies, the court of first instance must suspend the effect of the acquittal and may—

(a) make an order under section 4. (2) of the Contempt of Court Act 1981 (c.49) (which gives a court power, in some circumstances, to order that publication of certain reports be postponed) as if proceedings for the offence of which the person was acquitted were pending or imminent,

(b) after giving the parties an opportunity of being heard, order the detention of the person in custody or admit him to bail.

(8) The court may, under subsection (7)(b), order the detention of the person in custody only if the court considers that there are arguable grounds of appeal.

Amendments (Textual)

F28. Ss. 107. A-107. F inserted (28.3.2011) by Criminal Justice and Licensing (Scotland) Act 2010 (asp 13), ss. 74, 206. (1); S.S.I. 2011/178, art. 2, sch.

107. BProsecutor's right of appeal: decisions on admissibility of evidenceS

(1) The prosecutor may appeal to the High Court against a finding, made after the jury is empanelled and before the close of the evidence for the prosecution, that evidence that the prosecution seeks to lead is inadmissible.

(2) The appeal may be made only with the leave of the court of first instance, granted—

(a) on the motion of the prosecutor, or

(b) on that court's initiative.

(3) Any motion for leave to appeal must be made before the close of the case for the prosecution.

(4) In determining whether to grant leave to appeal the court must consider—

(a) whether there are arguable grounds of appeal, and

(b) what effect the finding has on the strength of the prosecutor's case.

Amendments (Textual)

F28. Ss. 107. A-107. F inserted (28.3.2011) by Criminal Justice and Licensing (Scotland) Act 2010 (asp 13), ss. 74, 206. (1); S.S.I. 2011/178, art. 2, sch.

107. CAppeals under section 107. A and 107. B: general provisionsS

(1) In an appeal brought under section 107. A or 107. B the High Court may review not only the acquittal, direction or finding appealed against but also any direction, finding, decision, determination or ruling in the proceedings at first instance if it has a bearing on the acquittal, direction or finding appealed against.

(2) The test to be applied by the High Court in reviewing the acquittal, direction or finding appealed against is whether it was wrong in law.

Amendments (Textual)

F28. Ss. 107. A-107. F inserted (28.3.2011) by Criminal Justice and Licensing (Scotland) Act

107. DExpedited appealsS

(1) Subsection (2) applies where—

(a) the prosecutor intimates intention to appeal under section 107. A or leave to appeal is granted by the court under section 107. B, and

(b) the court is able to obtain confirmation from the Keeper of the Rolls that it would be practicable for the appeal to be heard and determined during an adjournment of the trial diet.

(2) The court must inform both parties of that fact and, after hearing them, must decide whether or not the appeal is to be heard and determined during such an adjournment.

(3) An appeal brought under section 107. A or 107. B which is heard and determined during such an adjournment is referred to in this Act as an "expedited appeal".

(4) If the court decides that the appeal is to be an expedited appeal the court must, pending the outcome of the appeal—

(a) adjourn the trial diet, and

(b) where the appeal is against an acquittal, suspend the effect of the acquittal.

(5) Where the court cannot obtain from the Keeper of the Rolls confirmation of the kind mentioned in subsection (1)(b), the court must inform the parties of that fact.

(6) Where the High Court in an expedited appeal determines that an acquittal of an offence libelled in the indictment was wrong in law it must quash the acquittal and direct that the trial is to proceed in respect of the offence.

Amendments (Textual)

F28. Ss. 107. A-107. F inserted (28.3.2011) by Criminal Justice and Licensing (Scotland) Act 2010 (asp 13), ss. 74, 206. (1); S.S.I. 2011/178, art. 2, sch.

107. EOther appeals under section 107. A: appeal against acquittalS

(1) This section applies where—

(a) an appeal brought under section 107. A is not an expedited appeal,

(b) the appeal is against an acquittal, and

(c) the High Court determines that the acquittal was wrong in law.

(2) The court must quash the acquittal.

(3) If the prosecutor seeks leave to bring a new prosecution charging the accused with the same offence as that libelled in the indictment, or a similar offence arising out of the same facts as the offence libelled in the indictment, the High Court must grant the prosecutor authority to do so in accordance with section 119, unless the court considers that it would be contrary to the interests of justice to do so.

(4) If—

(a) no motion is made under subsection (3), or

(b) the High Court does not grant a motion made under that subsection,

the High Court must in disposing of the appeal acquit the accused of the offence libelled in the indictment.

Amendments (Textual)

F28. Ss. 107. A-107. F inserted (28.3.2011) by Criminal Justice and Licensing (Scotland) Act 2010 (asp 13), ss. 74, 206. (1); S.S.I. 2011/178, art. 2, sch.

107. F Other appeals under section 107. A or 107. B: appeal against directions etc. S

(1) This section applies where—

(a) an appeal brought under section 107. A or 107. B is not an expedited appeal, and

(b) the appeal is not against an acquittal.

(2) The court of first instance must desert the diet pro loco et tempore in relation to any offence to which the appeal relates.

(3) The trial is to proceed only if another offence of which the accused has not been acquitted and to which the appeal does not relate is libelled in the indictment.

(4) However, if the prosecutor moves for the diet to be deserted pro loco et tempore in relation to such other offence, the court must grant the motion.

(5) If the prosecutor seeks leave to bring a new prosecution charging the accused with the same offence as that libelled in the indictment, or a similar offence arising out of the same facts as the offence libelled in the indictment, the High Court must grant the prosecutor authority to do so in accordance with section 119, unless the court considers that it would be contrary to the interests of justice to do so.]

Amendments (Textual)

F28. Ss. 107. A-107. F inserted (28.3.2011) by Criminal Justice and Licensing (Scotland) Act 2010 (asp 13), ss. 74, 206. (1); S.S.I. 2011/178, art. 2, sch.

[F29108 Lord Advocate's right of appeal against disposal.S

(1) Where a person has been convicted on indictment, the Lord Advocate may, in accordance with subsection (2) below, appeal against any of the following disposals, namely—

(a) a sentence passed on conviction;

(b) a decision under section 209. (1)(b) of this Act not to make a supervised release order;

(c) a decision under section 234. A(2) of this Act not to make a non-harassment order;

[F30. (ca)a decision under section 92 of the Proceeds of Crime Act 2002 not to make a confiscation order;.]

[F31. (cb)a decision under section 22. A of the Serious Crime Act 2007 not to make a serious crime prevention order;]

[F32. (cb)a decision under section 36. (2) of the Regulatory Reform (Scotland) Act 2014 not to make a publicity order;

(cc) a decision under section 41. (2) of that Act not to make a remediation order;]

[F33. (cd)a decision under section 97. B(2) of the Proceeds of Crime Act 2002 to make or not to make a compliance order;]

[F34. (cd)a decision under section 30. (2) of the Health (Tobacco, Nicotine etc. and Care) (Scotland) Act 2016 not to make a remedial order,

(ce) a decision under section 30. (2) of that Act not to make a publicity order,]

F35. (d) . . . .

[F36. (dd)a drug treatment and testing order;]

F35. (e) . . . .

(f) a decision to remit to the Principal Reporter made under section 49. (1)(a) of this Act;

(g) an order deferring sentence;

(h) an admonition; or

(i) an absolute discharge.

(2) An appeal under subsection (1) above may be made—

(a) on a point of law;

(b) where it appears to the Lord Advocate, in relation to an appeal under—

(i) paragraph (a), (h) or (i) of that subsection, that the disposal was unduly lenient;

(ii) paragraph (b) [F37, (c) [F38, (ca), (cb) [F39, (cc) or (cd)] [F40, (cc), (cd) or (ce)]]] of that subsection, that the decision not to make the order in question was inappropriate;

(iii) paragraph [F41. (cd) or] [F42. (dd)] of that subsection, that the making of the order concerned was unduly lenient or was on unduly lenient terms;

(iv) under paragraph (f) of that subsection, that the decision to remit was inappropriate;

(v) under paragraph (g) of that subsection, that the deferment of sentence was inappropriate or was on unduly lenient conditions.

[F43. (2. A)In deciding whether to appeal under subsection (1) in any case, the Lord Advocate must have regard to any sentencing guidelines which are applicable in relation to the case.]

[F44. (3)For the purposes of subsection (2)(b)(i) above in its application to a confiscation order by virtue of section 92. (11) of the Proceeds of Crime Act 2002, the reference to the disposal being unduly lenient is a reference to the amount required to be paid by the order being unduly low.]]

Amendments (Textual)

F29 S. 108 substituted (1.8.1997) by 1997 c. 48, s. 21. (1); S.I. 1997/1712, art. 3, Sch. (subject to arts. 4, 5)

F30 S. 108. (1)(ca) inserted (24.3.2003) by Proceeds of Crime Act 2002 (c. 29), ss. 115. (2), 458; S.S.I. 2003/210, art. 2 (subject to arts. 3-7)

F31. S. 108. (1)(cb) inserted (1.3.2016) by Serious Crime Act 2015 (c. 9), s. 88. (1), Sch. 4 para. 14; S.I. 2016/148, reg. 3. (g)

F32. S. 108. (1)(cb)(cc) inserted (30.6.2014) by Regulatory Reform (Scotland) Act 2014 (asp 3), ss. 44. (2)(a), 61. (2); S.S.I. 2014/160, art. 2. (1)(2), sch.

F33. S. 108. (1)(cd) inserted (1.3.2016) by Serious Crime Act 2015 (c. 9), ss. 17. (2)(a), 88. (2)(a); S.S.I. 2016/11, reg. 2. (b)

F34. S. 108. (1)(cd)(ce) inserted (1.10.2017) by Health (Tobacco, Nicotine etc. and Care) (Scotland) Act 2016 (asp 14), ss. 31. (2)(a), 36. (2); S.S.I. 2017/294, reg. 2, sch.

F35 S. 108. (1)(d)(e) repealed (1.2.2011) by Criminal Justice and Licensing (Scotland) Act 2010 (asp 13), ss. 14. (2), 206. (1), Sch. 2 para. 8. (a); S.S.I. 2010/413, art. 2, Sch. (with art. 3)

F36 S. 108. (1)(dd) inserted (30.9.1998) by 1998 c. 37, s. 94. (2), Sch. 6 Pt. II para. 6. (2); S.I. 1998/2327, art. 2. (1)(s)

F37 Words in s. 108. (2)(b)(ii) substituted (24.3.2003) by Proceeds of Crime Act 2002 (c. 29), ss. 115. (3), 458; S.S.I. 2003/210, art. 2 (subject to arts. 3-7)

F38. Words in s. 108. (2)(b)(ii) substituted (30.6.2014) by Regulatory Reform (Scotland) Act 2014 (asp 3), ss. 44. (2)(b), 61. (2); S.S.I. 2014/160, art. 2. (1)(2), sch.

F39. Words in s. 108. (2)(b)(ii) substituted (1.3.2016) by Serious Crime Act 2015 (c. 9), ss. 17. (2)(b)(i), 88. (2)(a); S.S.I. 2016/11, reg. 2. (b)

F40. Words in s. 108. (2)(b)(ii) substituted (1.10.2017) for "or (cc)" by Health (Tobacco, Nicotine etc. and Care) (Scotland) Act 2016 (asp 14), ss. 31. (2)(b), 36. (2); S.S.I. 2017/294, reg. 2, sch.

F41. Words in s. 108. (2)(b)(iii) inserted (1.3.2016) by Serious Crime Act 2015 (c. 9), ss. 17. (2)(b)(ii), 88. (2)(a); S.S.I. 2016/11, reg. 2. (b)

F42. Words in s. 108. (2)(b)(iii) substituted (1.2.2011) by Criminal Justice and Licensing (Scotland) Act 2010 (asp 13), ss. 14. (2), 206. (1), Sch. 2 para. 8. (b); S.S.I. 2010/413, art. 2, Sch. (with art. 3)

F43. S. 108. (2. A) inserted (19.10.2015) by Criminal Justice and Licensing (Scotland) Act 2010 (asp 13), ss. 6. (7), 206. (1); S.S.I. 2015/336, art. 2. (a)

F44 S. 108. (3) inserted (24.3.2003) by Proceeds of Crime Act 2002 (c. 29), ss. 115. (4), 458; S.S.I. 2003/210, art. 2 (subject to arts. 3-7)

[F45108. A Lord Advocate's appeal against decision not to impose automatic sentence in certain cases.S

Where the court has exercised the power conferred by section or [F46or 205. B(3)] of this Act, the Lord Advocate may appeal against that decision.]

Amendments (Textual)

F45 S. 108. A inserted (20.10.1997 for specified purposes and otherwise prosp.) by 1997 c. 48 , s. 18. (2) ; S.I. 1997/2323 , art. 3 , Sch. 1

F46 Words in s. 108. A substituted (30.9.1998) by 1998 c. 37 , s. 119 , Sch. 8 para. 120 ; S.I.

109 Intimation of intention to appeal.S

(1) Subject to section 111. (2) of this Act and to [F47section 99 of the Proceeds of Crime Act 2002 (postponement)] , where a person desires to appeal under section 106. (1)(a) or (f) of this Act, he shall within two weeks of the final determination of the proceedings, lodge with the Clerk of Justiciary written intimation of intention to appeal which shall identify the proceedings and be in as nearly as may be the form prescribed by Act of Adjournal.

[F48. (1. A)Where a person desires to appeal under section 106. (1)(a) of this Act by virtue of section 11. (7) of the Double Jeopardy (Scotland) Act 2011 (asp 16), subsection (1) applies with the following modifications—

    (a) for the words "two weeks of the final determination of the proceedings" substitute " two weeks of the date on which the person is acquitted of an offence mentioned in section 11. (2) of the Double Jeopardy (Scotland) Act 2011 (asp 16) "; and

    (b) the reference to identifying the proceedings is to be construed as a reference to identifying—
(i) the proceedings which resulted in the conviction desired to be appealed; and
(ii) the proceedings which resulted in the person's acquittal as mentioned in section 11. (7) of the Double Jeopardy (Scotland) Act 2011 (asp 16).

(1. B)Subsections (5) to (9) of section 106 of this Act do not apply where the modifications specified in subsection (1. A) apply.]

(2) A copy of intimation given under subsection (1) above shall be sent to the Crown Agent.

(3) On intimation under subsection (1) above being lodged by a person in custody, the Clerk of Justiciary shall give notice of the intimation to the Secretary of State.

(4) Subject to subsection (5) below, for the purposes of subsection (1) above and section 106. (5) to (7) of this Act, proceedings shall be deemed finally determined on the day on which sentence is passed in open court.

(5) Where in relation to an appeal under section 106. (1)(a) of this Act sentence is deferred under section 202 of this Act, the proceedings shall be deemed finally determined on the day on which sentence is first so deferred in open court.

(6) Without prejudice to section 10 of the said Act of 1995, the reference in subsection (4) above to "the day on which sentence is passed in open court" shall, in relation to any case in which, under subsection (1) of that section, a decision has been postponed for a period, be construed as a reference to the day on which that decision is made, whether or not a confiscation order is then made or any other sentence is then passed.

Amendments (Textual)

F47 Words in s. 109. (1) substituted (24.3.2003) by Proceeds of Crime Act 2002 (c. 29) , ss. 456 , 458 , Sch. 11 para. 29. (2) ; S.S.I. 2003/210 , art. 2 , Sch. (subject to arts. 3-7)

F48. S. 109. (1. A)(1. B) inserted (28.11.2011) by Double Jeopardy (Scotland) Act 2011 (asp 16), s. 17. (3), sch. para. 9; S.S.I. 2011/365, art. 3

Modifications etc. (not altering text)

C8 S. 109. (1) restricted (1.4.1996) by 1995 c. 43 , ss. 10. (4) , 50. (2)

C9 S. 109. (1) modified (24.3.2003) by Proceeds of Crime Act 2002 (c. 29) , ss. 100. (6) , 458 ; S.S.I. 2003/210 , art. 2 (subject to arts. 3-7)

110 Note of appeal.S

(1) Subject to section 111. (2) of this Act—

    (a) within [F49eight] weeks of lodging intimation of intention to appeal or, in the case of an appeal under section 106. (1)(b) to (e) of this Act F50. . . , within two weeks of the [F51appropriate date (being, as the case may be, the date on which sentence was passed, the order disposing of the case was made, sentence was deferred F52... or the previous conviction was quashed as mentioned in section 106. A(1)(c) or (2)(c) of this Act)] in open court, the convicted person may lodge a written note of appeal with the Clerk of Justiciary who shall send a copy to the judge who presided at the trial and to the Crown Agent; or, as the case may be,

(b) within four weeks of the passing of the sentence in open court, the Lord Advocate may lodge such a note with the Clerk of Justiciary, who shall send a copy to the said judge and to the convicted person or that person's solicitor.

[F53. (c)where the prosecutor intimates intention to appeal under section 107. A(1), within 7 days after the acquittal or direction appealed against, the prosecutor may, except in the case of an expedited appeal, lodge such a note with the Clerk of Justiciary, who must send a copy to the judge and to the accused or to the accused's solicitor,

(d) within 7 days after leave to appeal under section 107. B(1) is granted, the prosecutor may, except in the case of an expedited appeal, lodge such a note with the Clerk of Justiciary, who must send a copy to the judge and to the accused or to the accused's solicitor,

(e) in the case of an expedited appeal, as soon as practicable after the decision as to hearing and determining the case is made under section 107. D(2), the prosecutor may—
(i) lodge such a note with the Clerk of Justiciary, and
(ii) provide a copy to the judge and to the accused or to the accused's solicitor.]
(2) The period of [F54eight] weeks mentioned in paragraph (a) of subsection (1) above may be extended, before it expires, by the Clerk of Justiciary.
(3) A note of appeal shall—
(a) identify the proceedings;
(b) contain a full statement of all the grounds of appeal; and
(c) be in as nearly as may be the form prescribed by Act of Adjournal.
[F55. (3. A)In respect of a written note of appeal relating to an appeal by virtue of section 11. (7) of the Double Jeopardy (Scotland) Act 2011 (asp 16)—
(a) subsection (1) applies as if the reference to the judge who presided at the trial were a reference to—
(i) the judge who presided at the trial resulting in the conviction to which the written note of appeal relates; and
(ii) the judge who presided at the trial for an offence mentioned in section 11. (2) of that Act resulting in the convicted person's acquittal; and
(b) subsection (3)(a) applies as if the reference to the proceedings were a reference to—
(i) the proceedings which resulted in the conviction to which the written note of appeal relates; and
(ii) the proceedings which resulted in the convicted person's acquittal.]
(4) Except by leave of the High Court on cause shown, it shall not be competent for an appellant to found any aspect of his appeal on a ground not contained in the note of appeal.
(5) Subsection (4) above shall not apply as respects any ground of appeal specified as an arguable ground of appeal by virtue of subsection (7) of section 107 of this Act.
(6) On a note of appeal under section 106. (1)(b) to (e) of this Act being lodged by an appellant in custody the Clerk of Justiciary shall give notice of that fact to the Secretary of State.

Amendments (Textual)

F49 Word in s. 110. (1)(a) substituted (26.8.2002) by Act of Adjournal (Criminal Appeals) 2002 (S.S.I. 2002/387) , para. 2

F50 Words in s. 110. (1)(a) repealed (10.12.2007) by Criminal Proceedings etc. (Reform) (Scotland) Act 2007 (asp 6) , ss. 80 , 84 , Sch. para. 16. (2)(a) ; S.S.I. 2007/479 , art. 3. (1) , Sch. (as amended by S.S.I. 2007/527)

F51 Words in s. 110. (1) substituted (20.10.1997) by 1997 c. 48 , s. 19. (2) ; S.I. 1997/2323 , art. 3 , Sch. 1

F52 Words in s. 110. (1)(a) repealed (28.2.2011) by Protection of Vulnerable Groups (Scotland) Act 2007 (asp 14) , s. 101. (2) , sch. 4 para. 15 (with ss. 90 , 99); S.S.I. 2011/157 , art. 2. (a) (with art. 5. (1))

F53. S. 110. (1)(c)-(e) added (28.3.2011) by Criminal Justice and Licensing (Scotland) Act 2010 (asp 13), ss. 76. (1), 206. (1); S.S.I. 2011/178, art. 2, sch.

F54 Word in s. 110. (2) substituted (26.8.2002) by Act of Adjournal (Criminal Appeals) 2002 (S.S.I. 2002/387) , para. 2

F55. S. 110. (3. A) inserted (28.11.2011) by Double Jeopardy (Scotland) Act 2011 (asp 16), s. 17. (3), sch. para. 10; S.S.I. 2011/365, art. 3

Modifications etc. (not altering text)

C10 S. 110. (2)-(4)(6) applied (27.10.2003) by S.I. 1996/513 , rule 19. B .1. (2) (as inserted by Act of Adjournal (Criminal Procedure Rules Amendment No. 2) (Miscellaneous) 2003 (S.S.I. 2003/468) , rule 2. (10))

111 Provisions supplementary to sections 109 and 110.S

(1) Where the last day of any period mentioned in sections 109. (1) and 110. (1) of this Act falls on a day on which the office of the Clerk of Justiciary is closed, such period shall extend to and include the next day on which such office is open.

(2) Any period mentioned in section 109. (1) or 110. (1)(a) of this Act may be extended at any time by the High Court in respect of any convicted person; and an application for such extension may be made under this subsection and shall be in as nearly as may be the form prescribed by Act of Adjournal.

[F56. (2. ZA)Where an application under subsection (2) is received after the period to which it relates has expired, the High Court may extend the period only if it is satisfied that doing so is justified by exceptional circumstances.

(2. ZB)In considering whether there are exceptional circumstances for the purpose of subsection (2. ZA), the High Court must have regard to—

    (a) the length of time that has elapsed between the expiry of the period and the making of the application,

    (b) the reasons stated in accordance with subsection (2. A)(a)(i),

    (c) the proposed grounds of appeal.]

[F57. (2. A)An application under subsection (2) F58... must—

    (a) state—

(i) the reasons why the applicant failed [F59, or expects to fail,] to comply with the time limit F60..., and

(ii) the proposed grounds of appeal, and

    (b) be intimated in writing by the applicant to the Crown Agent.

(2. B)If the prosecutor so requests within 7 days of receipt of intimation of the application under subsection (2. A)(b), the prosecutor must be given an opportunity to make representations before the application is determined.

F61. (2. C). . . . .]

F62. (3). . . . .

[F63. (4)An application under subsection (2) is to be dealt with by the High Court—

    (a) in chambers, and

    (b) unless the Court directs otherwise, without the parties being present.

(5) If the High Court extends a period under subsection (2), it must—

    (a) give reasons for the decision in writing, and

    (b) give the reasons in ordinary language.]

Amendments (Textual)

F56. S. 111. (2. ZA)(2. ZB) inserted (17.1.2017) by Criminal Justice (Scotland) Act 2016 (asp 1), ss. 90. (3), 117. (2); S.S.I. 2016/426, art. 2, sch.

F57 S. 111. (2. A)-(2. C) inserted (30.10.2010) by Criminal Procedure (Legal Assistance, Detention and Appeals) (Scotland) Act 2010 (asp 15), ss. 5. (2), 9 (with s. 5. (4))

F58. Words in s. 111. (2. A) repealed (17.1.2017) by Criminal Justice (Scotland) Act 2016 (asp 1), ss. 90. (4)(a), 117. (2); S.S.I. 2016/426, art. 2, sch.

F59. Words in s. 111. (2. A)(a)(i) inserted (17.1.2017) by Criminal Justice (Scotland) Act 2016 (asp 1), ss. 90. (4)(b)(i), 117. (2); S.S.I. 2016/426, art. 2, sch.

F60. Words in s. 111. (2. A)(a)(i) repealed (17.1.2017) by Criminal Justice (Scotland) Act 2016 (asp 1), ss. 90. (4)(b)(ii), 117. (2); S.S.I. 2016/426, art. 2, sch.

F61. S. 111. (2. C) repealed (17.1.2017) by Criminal Justice (Scotland) Act 2016 (asp 1), ss. 90. (5), 117. (2); S.S.I. 2016/426, art. 2, sch.

F62 S. 111. (3) repealed (28.2.2011) by Protection of Vulnerable Groups (Scotland) Act 2007 (asp 14), s. 101. (2), sch. 4 para. 16 (with ss. 90, 99); S.S.I. 2011/157, art. 2. (a) (with art. 5. (1))

F63. S. 111. (4)(5) inserted (17.1.2017) by Criminal Justice (Scotland) Act 2016 (asp 1), ss. 90. (6), 117. (2); S.S.I. 2016/426, art. 2, sch.

112 Admission of appellant to bail.S

(1) Subject to [F64subsections (2), (2. A) and (9)] below, the High Court may, if it thinks fit, on the application of a convicted person, admit him to bail pending the determination of—

(a) his appeal; or

(b) any relevant appeal by the Lord Advocate under section 108 [F65or 108. A] of this Act.

[F66. (2)The High Court shall not admit a convicted person to bail under subsection (1) above unless—

(a) the application for bail—

(i) states reasons why it should be granted; and

(ii) where he is the appellant and has not lodged a note of appeal in accordance with section 110. (1)(a) of this Act, sets out the proposed grounds of appeal; F67 . . .

(b) F68 . . . .

(2. A)Where—

(a) the convicted person is the appellant and has not lodged a note of appeal in accordance with section 110. (1)(a) of this Act; or

(b) the Lord Advocate is the appellant,

the High Court shall not admit the convicted person to bail under subsection (1) above unless it considers there to be exceptional circumstances justifying admitting him to bail.]

(3) A person who is admitted to bail under subsection (1) above shall, unless the High Court otherwise directs, appear personally in court on the day or days fixed for the hearing of the appeal.

(4) Where an appellant fails to appear personally in court as mentioned in subsection (3) above, the court may—

(a) if he is the appellant—

(i) decline to consider the appeal; and

(ii) dismiss it summarily; or

(b) whether or not he is the appellant—

(i) consider and determine the appeal; or

(ii) without prejudice to section 27 of this Act, make such other order as the court thinks fit.

(5) For the purposes of subsections (1), (3) and (4) above, "appellant" includes not only a person who has lodged a note of appeal but also one who has lodged an intimation of intention to appeal.

[F69. (6)Subject to [F70subsections (7) and (9)] below, the High Court may, if it thinks fit, on the application of a convicted person, admit him to bail pending the determination of any appeal under [F71section 288. AA of this Act or] paragraph 13. (a) of Schedule 6 to the Scotland Act 1998 and the disposal of the proceedings by the High Court thereafter.

(7) The High Court shall not admit a convicted person to bail under subsection (6) above unless

F72 [(a)] the application for bail states reasons why it should be granted and the High Court considers there to be exceptional circumstances justifying admitting the convicted person to bail[F73 and

(b) where the appeal relates to conviction on indictment, the prosecutor has had an opportunity to be heard on the application.]

(8) A person who is admitted to bail under subsection (6) above shall, unless the High Court

otherwise directs, appear personally in the High Court at any subsequent hearing in the High Court in relation to the proceedings; and if he fails to do so the court may, without prejudice to section 27 of this Act, make such order as it thinks fit.]

[F74. (9)An application for the purposes of subsection (1) or (6) above by a person convicted on indictment shall be—

    (a) intimated by him immediately and in writing to the Crown Agent; and

    (b) heard not less than seven days after the date of that intimation.]

Amendments (Textual)

F64 Words in s. 112. (1) substituted (27.6.2003) by virtue of Criminal Justice (Scotland) Act 2003 (asp 7) , ss. 66. (5)(a) , 89 ; S.S.I. 2003/288 , art. 2

F65 Words in s. 112. (1) inserted (20.10.1997) by 1997 c. 48 , s. 18. (3) ; S.I. 1997/2323 , art. 3 , Sch. 1

F66 S. 112. (2)(2. A) substituted (27.6.2003) for s. 112. (2) by Criminal Justice (Scotland) Act 2003 (asp 7) , ss. 66. (5)(b) , 89 ; S.S.I. 2003/288 , art. 2

F67 S. 112. (2)(b) and preceding word repealed (10.12.2007) by Criminal Proceedings etc. (Reform) (Scotland) Act 2007 (asp 6) , ss. 80 , 84 , Sch. para. 16. (3) ; S.S.I. 2007/479 , art. 3. (1) , Sch. (as amended by S.S. I. 2007/527)

F68 S. 112. (2)(b) and preceding word repealed (10.12.2007) by Criminal Proceedings etc. (Reform) (Scotland) Act 2007 (asp 6) , ss. 80 , 84 , Sch. para. 16. (3) ; S.S.I. 2007/479 , art. 3. (1) , Sch. (as amended by S.S. I. 2007/527)

F69 S. 112. (6)-(8) inserted (6.5.1999) by S.I. 1999/1042 , arts. 1. (2)(a) , 3 , Sch. 1 Pt. I para. 13. (2)

F70 Words in s. 112. (6) substituted (27.6.2003) by virtue of Criminal Justice (Scotland) Act 2003 (asp 7) , ss. 66. (5)(c) , 89 ; S.S.I. 2003/288 , art. 2

F71. Words in s. 112. (6) inserted (22.4.2013) by Scotland Act 2012 (c. 11), ss. 36. (10), 44. (5); S.I. 2013/6, art. 2. (c)

F72 Words in s. 112. (7) renumbered as s. 112. (7)(a) (27.6.2003) by virtue of Criminal Justice (Scotland) Act 2003 (asp 7) , ss. 66. (5)(d)(i) , 89 ; S.S.I. 2003/288 , art. 2

F73 S. 112. (7)(b) and word inserted (27.6.2003) by Criminal Justice (Scotland) Act 2003 (asp 7) , ss. 66. (5)(d)(ii) , 89 ; S.S.I. 2003/288 , art. 2

F74 S. 112. (9) added (27.6.2003) by Criminal Justice (Scotland) Act 2003 (asp 7) , ss. 66. (5)(e) , 89 ; S.S.I. 2003/288 , art. 2

113 Judge's report.S

(1) [F75. Subject to subsections (1. A) to (1. D),] As soon as is reasonably practicable after receiving the copy note of appeal sent to him under [F76any of paragraphs (a) to (d) of] section 110. (1) of this Act, the judge who presided at the trial shall furnish the Clerk of Justiciary with a written report giving the judge's opinion on the case generally and on the grounds contained in the note of appeal.

[F77. (1. A)Subsections (1. B) to (1. D) apply where the copy note of appeal mentioned in subsection (1) relates to an appeal by virtue of section 11. (7) of the Double Jeopardy (Scotland) Act 2011 (asp 16).

(1. B)The reference in subsection (1) to the judge who presided at the trial is to be construed as a reference to—

    (a) the judge who presided at the trial for an offence mentioned in section 11. (2) of that Act resulting in the appellant's acquittal; and

    (b) where subsection (1. C) applies, the judge who presided at the trial resulting in the conviction to which the copy note of appeal relates.

(1. C)This subsection applies—

    (a) where, in connection with the appeal, the High Court calls for the report to be furnished by the judge mentioned in subsection (1. B)(b); and

(b) it is reasonably practicable for the judge to furnish the report.

(1. D)For the purposes of subsections (1) to (1. C), it is irrelevant whether or not the judge mentioned in subsection (1. B)(b) had previously furnished a report under subsection (1).]

(2) The Clerk of Justiciary shall send a copy of the judge's report—

    (a) to the convicted person or his solicitor;

    (b) to the Crown Agent; and

    (c) in a case referred under [F78. Part XA of this Act, to the Commission].

(3) Where the judge's report is not furnished as mentioned in [F79subsections (1) to (1. D)] above, the High Court may call for the report to be furnished within such period as it may specify or, if it thinks fit, hear and determine the appeal without the report.

(4) Subject to subsection (2) above, the report of the judge shall be available only to the High Court, the parties and, on such conditions as may be prescribed by Act of Adjournal, such other persons or classes of persons as may be so prescribed.

Amendments (Textual)

F75. Words in s. 113. (1) inserted (28.11.2011) by Double Jeopardy (Scotland) Act 2011 (asp 16), s. 17. (3), sch. para. 11. (a); S.S.I. 2011/365, art. 3

F76. Words in s. 113. (1) inserted (28.3.2011) by Criminal Justice and Licensing (Scotland) Act 2010 (asp 13), ss. 76. (2), 206. (1); S.S.I. 2011/178, art. 2, sch.

F77. S. 113. (1. A)-(1. D) inserted (28.11.2011) by Double Jeopardy (Scotland) Act 2011 (asp 16), s. 17. (3), sch. para. 11. (b); S.S.I. 2011/365, art. 3

F78 Words in s. 113. (2)(c) substituted (1.4.1999) by 1997 c. 48 , s. 62. (1) , Sch. 1 para. 21. (16) ; S.I. 1999/652 , art. 2 , Sch. (subject to savings and transitional provisions in art. 3)

F79. Words in s. 113. (3) substituted (28.11.2011) by Double Jeopardy (Scotland) Act 2011 (asp 16), s. 17. (3), sch. para. 11. (c); S.S.I. 2011/365, art. 3

Modifications etc. (not altering text)

C11 S. 113. (2)-(4) applied (26.8.2002) by Act of Adjournal (Criminal Procedure Rules) 1996 (S.I. 1996/513) , rule 15 .15. (3) (as inserted (26.8.2002) by Act of Adjournal (Criminal Appeals) 2002 (S.S.I. 2002/387) , para. 3. (4))

[F80113. AJudge's observations in expedited appealS

(1) On receiving a note of appeal given under section 110. (1)(e), the judge who presided at the trial may give the Clerk of Justiciary any written observations that the judge thinks fit on—

    (a) the case generally,

    (b) the grounds contained in the note of appeal.

(2) The High Court may hear and determine the appeal without any such written observations.

(3) If written observations are given under subsection (1), the Clerk of Justiciary must give a copy of them to—

    (a) the accused or the accused's solicitor, and

    (b) the prosecutor.

(4) The written observations of the judge are available only to—

    (a) the High Court,

    (b) the parties, and

    (c) any other person or classes of person prescribed by Act of Adjournal, in accordance with any conditions prescribed by Act of Adjournal.]

Amendments (Textual)

F80. S. 113. A inserted (28.3.2011) by Criminal Justice and Licensing (Scotland) Act 2010 (asp 13), ss. 76. (3), 206. (1); S.S.I. 2011/178, art. 2, sch.

114 Applications made orally or in writing.S

Subject to any provision of this Part of this Act [F81or to rules made under section 305 of this

Act] to the contrary, any application to the High Court may be made by the appellant or respondent as the case may be or by counsel on his behalf, orally or in writing.
Amendments (Textual)
F81 Words in s. 114 inserted (1.9.2003) by Act of Adjournal (Criminal Appeals) 2003 (S.S.I. 2003/387) , para. 2. (2)

115 Presentation of appeal in writing.S

(1) [F82. Subject to rules made under section 305 of this Act,] if an appellant, F83. . . desires to present his case and his argument in writing instead of orally he shall, at least four days before the diet fixed for the hearing of the appeal—
    (a) intimate this desire to the Clerk of Justiciary;
    (b) lodge with the Clerk of Justiciary three copies of his case and argument; and
    (c) send a copy of the intimation, case and argument to the Crown Agent.
(2) Any case or argument presented as mentioned in subsection (1) above shall be considered by the High Court.
(3) Unless the High Court otherwise directs, the respondent shall not make a written reply to a case and argument presented as mentioned in subsection (1) above, but shall reply orally at the diet fixed for the hearing of the appeal.
(4) Unless the High Court otherwise allows, an appellant who has presented his case and argument in writing shall not be entitled to submit in addition an oral argument to the court in support of the appeal.
Amendments (Textual)
F82 Words in s. 115. (1) inserted (1.9.2003) by Act of Adjournal (Criminal Appeals) 2003 (S.S.I. 2003/387) , para. 2. (3)(a)
F83 Words in s. 115. (1) omitted (1.9.2003) by virtue of Act of Adjournal (Criminal Appeals) 2003 (S.S.I. 2003/387) , para. 2. (3)(b)

116 Abandonment of appeal.S

(1) An appellant may abandon his appeal by lodging with the Clerk of Justiciary a notice of abandonment in as nearly as may be the form prescribed by Act of Adjournal; and on such notice being lodged the appeal shall be deemed to have been dismissed by the court.
[F84. (2)A person who has appealed against both conviction and sentence (or, as the case may be, against both conviction and a decision mentioned in section 106. (1)(bb) or both conviction and disposal and order) may abandon the appeal in so far as it is against conviction and may proceed with it against sentence (or, as the case may be, decision, disposal or order) alone.]
Amendments (Textual)
F84 S. 116. (2) substituted (28.2.2011) by Protection of Vulnerable Groups (Scotland) Act 2007 (asp 14) , s. 101. (2) , sch. 4 para. 17 (with ss. 90 , 99); S.S.I. 2011/157 , art. 2. (a) (with art. 5. (1))

117 Presence of appellant or applicant at hearing.S

(1) Where an appellant or applicant is in custody the Clerk of Justiciary shall notify—
    (a) the appellant or applicant;
    (b) the Governor of the prison in which the appellant or applicant then is; and
    (c) the Secretary of State,
of the probable day on which the appeal or application will be heard.
(2) The Secretary of State shall take steps to transfer the appellant or applicant to a prison convenient for his appearance before the High Court at such reasonable time before the hearing as

shall enable him to consult his legal adviser, if any.

(3) A convicted appellant, notwithstanding that he is in custody, shall be entitled to be present if he desires it, at the hearing of his appeal.

(4) When an appellant or applicant is to be present at any diet—

    (a) before the High Court or any judge of that court; or

    (b) for the taking of additional evidence before a person appointed for that purpose under section 104. (1)(b) of this Act, or

    (c) for an examination or investigation by a special commissioner in terms of section 104. (1)(d) of this Act,

the Clerk of Justiciary shall give timeous notice to the Secretary of State, in the form prescribed by Act of Adjournal or as nearly as may be in such form.

(5) A notice under subsection (4) above shall be sufficient warrant to the Secretary of State for transmitting the appellant or applicant in custody from prison to the place where the diet mentioned in that subsection or any subsequent diet is to be held and for reconveying him to prison at the conclusion of such diet.

F85. (6). . . . .

(7) Where the Lord Advocate is the appellant, subsections (1) to [F86. (5)] above shall apply in respect of the convicted person, if in custody, as they apply to an appellant or applicant in custody.

(8) The Secretary of State shall, on notice under subsection (4) above from the Clerk of Justiciary, ensure that sufficient male and female prison officers attend each sitting of the court, having regard to the list of appeals for the sitting.

(9) When the High Court fixes the date for the hearing of an appeal, or of an application under section 111. (2) of this Act, the Clerk of Justiciary shall give notice to the Crown Agent and to the solicitor of the convicted person, or to the convicted person himself if he has no known solicitor.

Amendments (Textual)

F85. S. 117. (6) repealed (17.1.2017) by Criminal Justice (Scotland) Act 2016 (asp 1), ss. 110. (2)(a)(i), 117. (2); S.S.I. 2016/426, art. 2, sch.

F86. Word in s. 117. (7) substituted (17.1.2017) by Criminal Justice (Scotland) Act 2016 (asp 1), ss. 110. (2)(a)(ii), 117. (2); S.S.I. 2016/426, art. 2, sch.

118 Disposal of appeals.S

(1) The High Court may, subject to subsection (4) below, dispose of an appeal against conviction by—

    (a) affirming the verdict of the trial court;

    (b) setting aside the verdict of the trial court and either quashing the conviction or, subject to subsection (2) below, substituting therefor an amended verdict of guilty; or

    (c) setting aside the verdict of the trial court and quashing the conviction and granting authority to bring a new prosecution in accordance with section 119 of this Act.

[F87. (1. A)Where an appeal against conviction is by virtue of section 11. (7) of the Double Jeopardy (Scotland) Act 2011 (asp 16), paragraph (c) of subsection (1) does not apply.]

(2) An amended verdict of guilty substituted under subsection (1) above must be one which could have been returned on the indictment before the trial court.

(3) In setting aside, under subsection (1) above, a verdict the High Court may quash any sentence imposed on the appellant (or, as the case may be, any disposal or order made) as respects the indictment, and—

    (a) in a case where it substitutes an amended verdict of guilty, whether or not the sentence (or disposal or order) related to the verdict set aside; or

    (b) in any other case, where the sentence (or disposal or order) did not so relate,

may pass another (but not more severe) sentence or make another (but not more severe) disposal or order in substitution for the sentence, disposal or order so quashed.

(4) The High Court may, subject to subsection (5) below, dispose of an appeal against sentence

by—

(a) affirming such sentence; or

(b) if the Court thinks that, having regard to all the circumstances, including any F88 . . . evidence such as is mentioned in section 106. (3) of this Act, a different sentence should have been passed, quashing the sentence and passing another sentence whether more or less severe in substitution therefor,

and, in this subsection, "appeal against sentence" shall, without prejudice to the generality of the expression, be construed as including an appeal under [F89section [F90106. (1)(ba), (bb), (c), (d), (da), (e) or (f)]], and any appeal under section 108, of this Act; and other references to sentence shall be construed accordingly.

F91. (4. AA). . . . .

[F92. (4. A)On an appeal under section 108. A of this Act, the High Court may dispose of the appeal—

(a) by affirming the decision and any sentence or order passed;

(b) where it is of the opinion mentioned in section 205. A(3) or, as the case may be, 205. B(3) of this Act but it considers that a different sentence or order should have been passed, by affirming the decision but quashing any sentence or order passed and passing another sentence or order whether more or less severe in substitution therefor; or

(c) in any other case, by setting aside the decision appealed against and any sentence or order passed by the trial court and where the decision appealed against was taken under—

(i) subsection (3) of section 205. A of this Act, by passing the sentence mentioned in subsection (2) of that section;

(ii) subsection (3) of section 205. B of this Act, by passing a sentence of imprisonment of at least the length mentioned in subsection (2) of that section; or

F93. (iii). . . . .]

(5) In relation to any appeal under section 106. (1) of this Act, the High Court shall, where it appears to it that the appellant committed the act charged against him but that he was [F94not, because of section 51. A of this Act, criminally responsible for it], dispose of the appeal by—

(a) setting aside the verdict of the trial court and substituting therefor a verdict of acquittal [F95by reason of the special defence set out in section 51. A of this Act]; and

(b) quashing any sentence imposed on the appellant (or disposal or order made) as respects the indictment and—

(i) making, in respect of the appellant, any order mentioned in section 57. (2)(a) to (d) of this Act; or

(ii) making no order.

(6) Subsections [F96. (3) to (6)] of section 57 of this Act shall apply to an order made under subsection (5)(b)(i) above as they apply to an order made under subsection (2) of that section.

(7) In disposing of an appeal under section 106. (1)(b) to (f) or 108 of this Act the High Court may, without prejudice to any other power in that regard, pronounce an opinion on

F97[(a)] the sentence or other disposal or order which is appropriate in any similar case [F98 ; F99 ...,

F100. (b). . . . .]

(8) No conviction, sentence, judgment, order of court or other proceeding whatsoever in or for the purposes of solemn proceedings under this Act—

(a) shall be quashed for want of form; or

(b) where the accused had legal assistance in his defence, shall be suspended or set aside in respect of any objections to—

(i) the relevancy of the indictment, or the want of specification therein; or

(ii) the competency or admission or rejection of evidence at the trial in the inferior court, unless such objections were timeously stated.

[F101. (9)The High Court may give its reasons for the disposal of any appeal in writing without giving those reasons orally.]

Amendments (Textual)

F87. S. 118. (1. A) inserted (28.11.2011) by Double Jeopardy (Scotland) Act 2011 (asp 16), s. 17. (3), sch. para. 12; S.S.I. 2011/365, art. 3

F88 S. 118. (4)(b) repealed (1.8.1997) by 1997 c. 48, s. 62. (1), Sch. 1 para. 21. (17)(a); S.I. 1997/1712, art. 3, Sch. (subject to arts. 4, 5)

F89 Words in s. 118. (4) substituted (20.10.1997) by 1997 c. 48, s. 18. (5)(a); S.I. 1997/2323, art. 3, Sch. 1

F90. Words in s. 118. (4) substituted (28.2.2011) by Protection of Vulnerable Groups (Scotland) Act 2007 (asp 14), s. 101. (2), sch. 4 para. 18. (a) (with ss. 90, 99); S.S.I. 2011/157, art. 2. (a) (with art. 5. (1))

F91. S. 118. (4. AA) repealed (28.2.2011) by Protection of Vulnerable Groups (Scotland) Act 2007 (asp 14), s. 101. (2), sch. 4 para. 18. (b) (with ss. 90, 99); S.S.I. 2011/157, art. 2. (a) (with art. 5. (1))

F92 S. 118. (4. A) inserted (20.10.1997 for specified purposes and otherwise prosp.) by 1997 c. 48, s. 18. (5)(b); S.I. 1997/2323, art. 3, Sch. 1

F93 S. 118. (4. A)(c)(iii) repealed (30.9.1998) by 1998 c. 37, ss. 119, 120. (2), Sch. 8 para. 121, Sch. 10; S.I. 1998/2327, art. 2. (1)(y)(2)(kk)(3)(w)

F94. Words in s. 118. (5) substituted (with application in accordance with art. 3 of the commencing S.S.I.) by Criminal Justice and Licensing (Scotland) Act 2010 (asp 13), s. 206. (1), sch. 7 para. 51. (a); S.S.I. 2012/160, art. 3, sch.

F95. Words in s. 118. (5) substituted (with application in accordance with art. 3 of the commencing S.S.I.) by Criminal Justice and Licensing (Scotland) Act 2010 (asp 13), s. 206. (1), sch. 7 para. 51. (b); S.S.I. 2012/160, art. 3, sch.

F96 Words in s. 118. (6) substituted (5.10.2005) by Mental Health (Care and Treatment) (Scotland) Act 2003 (asp 13), ss. 331. (1), 333. (1)-(4), (Sch. 4 para. 8. (11)); S.S.I. 2005/161, art. 3

F97 Words in s. 118. (7) becomes s. 118. (7)(a) (10.1.2005) by virtue of Protection of Children (Scotland) Act 2003 (asp 5), ss. 16. (4)(b), 22. (2); S.S.I. 2004/522, art. 2

F98 S. 118. (7)(b) and words inserted (10.1.2005) by Protection of Children (Scotland) Act 2003 (asp 5), ss. 16. (4)(c), 22. (2); S.S.I. 2004/522, art. 2

F99. Words in s. 118. (7)(a) repealed (28.2.2011) by Protection of Vulnerable Groups (Scotland) Act 2007 (asp 14), s. 101. (2), sch. 4 para. 18. (c)(i) (with ss. 90, 99); S.S.I. 2011/157, art. 2. (a) (with art. 5. (1))

F100. S. 118. (7)(b) repealed (28.2.2011) by Protection of Vulnerable Groups (Scotland) Act 2007 (asp 14), s. 101. (2), sch. 4 para. 18. (c)(ii) (with ss. 90, 99); S.S.I. 2011/157, art. 2. (a) (with art. 5. (1))

F101 S. 118. (9) inserted (1.8.1997) by 1997 c. 48, s. 62. (1), Sch. 1 para. 21. (17)(b); S.I. 1997/1712, art. 3, Sch. (subject to arts. 4, 5)

119 Provision where High Court authorises new prosecution.S

(1) Subject to subsection (2) below, where authority is granted under section 118. (1)(c) [F102 or 107. E(3) or 107. F(5)] of this Act, a new prosecution may be brought charging the accused with the same or any similar offence arising out of the same facts; and the proceedings out of which the appeal arose shall not be a bar to such new prosecution.

[F103. (2)In a new prosecution under this section—

(a) where authority for the prosecution is granted under section 118. (1)(c), the accused must not be charged with an offence more serious than that of which the accused was convicted in the earlier proceedings,

(b) where authority for the prosecution is granted under section 107. E(3), the accused must not be charged with an offence more serious than that of which the accused was acquitted in the earlier proceedings,

(c) where authority for the prosecution is granted under section 107. F(5), the accused must not be charged with an offence more serious than that originally libelled in the indictment in the earlier proceedings.]

[F104. (2. A)In a new prosecution under this section brought by virtue of section 107. F(5), the circumstances set out in the indictment are not to be inconsistent with any direction given under section 97. B(2)(b) or 97. C(2) in the proceedings which gave rise to the appeal in question unless the High Court, in disposing of that appeal, determined that the direction was wrong in law.]

(3) No sentence may be passed on conviction under the new prosecution which could not have been passed on conviction under the earlier proceedings.

(4) A new prosecution may be brought under this section, notwithstanding that any time limit, other than the time limit mentioned in subsection (5) below, for the commencement of such proceedings has elapsed.

(5) Proceedings in a prosecution under this section shall be commenced within two months of the date on which authority to bring the prosecution was granted.

(6) In proceedings in a new prosecution under this section it shall, subject to subsection (7) below, be competent for either party to lead any evidence which it was competent for him to lead in the earlier proceedings.

(7) The indictment in a new prosecution under this section shall identify any matters as respects which the prosecutor intends to lead evidence by virtue of subsection (6) above which would not have been competent but for that subsection.

(8) For the purposes of subsection (5) above, proceedings shall be deemed to be commenced—
    [F105. (a)in a case where a warrant to apprehend the accused is granted—
(i) on the date on which the warrant is executed; or
(ii) if it is executed without unreasonable delay, on the date on which it is granted;
    (b) in any other case, on the date on which the accused is cited.]

(9) Where the two months mentioned in subsection (5) above elapse and no new prosecution has been brought under this section, the order under section 118. (1)(c) of this Act setting aside the verdict [F106or under section 107. E(3) or 107. F(5) granting authority to bring a new prosecution] shall have the effect, for all purposes, of an acquittal.

(10) On granting authority under section 118. (1)(c) [F107or 107. E(3) or 107. F(5)] of this Act to bring a new prosecution, the High Court shall, after giving the parties an opportunity of being heard, order the detention of the accused person in custody or admit him to bail.

(11) [F108. Section 65. (4)(aa) and (b) and (4. A) to (9)] of this Act (prevention of delay in trials) shall apply to an accused person who is detained under subsection (10) above as they apply to an accused person detained by virtue of being committed until liberated in due course of law.

Amendments (Textual)

F102. Words in s. 119. (1) inserted (28.3.2011) by Criminal Justice and Licensing (Scotland) Act 2010 (asp 13), ss. 76. (4)(a), 206. (1); S.S.I. 2011/178, art. 2, sch.

F103. S. 119. (2) substituted (28.3.2011) by Criminal Justice and Licensing (Scotland) Act 2010 (asp 13), ss. 76. (4)(b), 206. (1); S.S.I. 2011/178, art. 2, sch.

F104. S. 119. (2. A) inserted (28.3.2011) by Criminal Justice and Licensing (Scotland) Act 2010 (asp 13), ss. 76. (4)(c), 206. (1); S.S.I. 2011/178, art. 2, sch.

F105 S. 119. (8)(a)(b) substituted (1.2.2005) by Criminal Procedure (Amendment) (Scotland) Act 2004 (asp 5) , ss. 25 , 27. (1) , Sch. para. 32 ; S.S.I. 2004/405 , art. 2 , Sch. 1 (with savings in arts. 3-5)

F106. Words in s. 119. (9) inserted (28.3.2011) by Criminal Justice and Licensing (Scotland) Act 2010 (asp 13), ss. 76. (4)(d), 206. (1); S.S.I. 2011/178, art. 2, sch.

F107. Words in s. 119. (10) inserted (28.3.2011) by Criminal Justice and Licensing (Scotland) Act 2010 (asp 13), ss. 76. (4)(a), 206. (1); S.S.I. 2011/178, art. 2, sch.

F108 Words in s. 119. (11) substituted (10.12.2007) by Criminal Proceedings etc. (Reform) (Scotland) Act 2007 (asp 6) , ss. 80 , 84 , Sch. para. 16. (6) (subject to art. 14); S.S.I. 2007/479 , art. 3. (1) , Sch. (as amended by S.S. I. 2007/527)

120 Appeals: supplementary provisions.S

(1) Where—

  (a) intimation of the diet appointed for the hearing of the appeal has been made to the appellant;

  (b) no appearance is made by or on behalf of an appellant at the diet; and

  (c) no case or argument in writing has been timeously lodged,

the High Court shall dispose of the appeal as if it had been abandoned.

(2) The power of the High Court to pass any sentence under this Part of this Act may be exercised notwithstanding that the appellant (or, where the Lord Advocate is the appellant, the convicted person) is for any reason not present.

(3) When the High Court has heard and dealt with any application under this Part of this Act, the Clerk of Justiciary shall (unless it appears to him unnecessary so to do) give to the applicant if he is in custody and has not been present at the hearing of such application notice of the decision of the court in relation to the said application.

(4) On the final determination of any appeal under this Part of this Act or of any matter under section 103. (5) of this Act, the Clerk of Justiciary shall give notice of such determination—

  (a) to the appellant or applicant if he is in custody and has not been present at such final determination;

  (b) to the clerk of the court in which the conviction took place; and

  (c) to the Secretary of State.

121 Suspension of disqualification, forfeiture, etc. S

(1) Any disqualification, forfeiture or disability which attaches to a person by reason of a conviction shall not attach—

  (a) for the period of four weeks from the date of the verdict against him; or

  (b) where an intimation of intention to appeal or, in the case of an appeal under section 106. (1)(b) to (e) [F109, 108 or 108. A] of this Act, a note of appeal is lodged, until the appeal, if it is proceeded with, is determined.

(2) The destruction or forfeiture or any order for the destruction or forfeiture of any property, matter or thing which is the subject of or connected with any prosecution following upon a conviction shall be suspended—

  (a) for the period of four weeks after the date of the verdict in the trial; or

  (b) where an intimation of intention to appeal or, in the case of an appeal under section 106. (1)(b) to (e) [F110, 108 or 108. A] of this Act, a note of appeal is lodged, until the appeal, if it is proceeded with, is determined.

(3) This section does not apply in the case of any disqualification, destruction or forfeiture or order for destruction or forfeiture under or by virtue of any enactment which makes express provision for the suspension of the disqualification, destruction or forfeiture or order for destruction or forfeiture pending the determination of an appeal against conviction or sentence.

(4) Where, upon conviction, a fine has been imposed on a person or a compensation order has been made against him under section 249 of this Act, then, for a period of four weeks from the date of the verdict against such person or, in the event of an intimation of intention to appeal (or in the case of an appeal under section 106. (1)(b) to (e) [F111, 108 or 108. A] of this Act a note of appeal) being lodged under this Part of this Act, until such appeal, if it is proceeded with, is determined—

  (a) the fine or compensation order shall not be enforced against that person and he shall not be liable to make any payment in respect of the fine or compensation order; and

  (b) any money paid by that person under the compensation order shall not be paid by the clerk of court to the person entitled to it under subsection (9) of the said section 249.

[F112. (5)In this section–

  (a) "appeal" includes an appeal under [F113section 288. AA of this Act or] paragraph 13. (a) of

Schedule 6 to the Scotland Act 1998; and

(b) in relation to such an appeal, references to an appeal being determined are to be read as references to the disposal of the proceedings by the High Court following determination of the appeal.]

Amendments (Textual)

F109 Words in s. 121. (1)(b) substituted (20.10.1997) by 1997 c. 48 , s. 18. (6)(a) ; S.I. 1997/2323 , art. 3 , Sch. 1

F110 Words in s. 121. (2)(b) substituted (20.10.1997) by 1997 c. 48 , s. 18. (6)(b) ; S.I. 1997/2323 , art. 3 , Sch. 1

F111 Words in s. 121. (4) substituted (20.10.1997) by 1997 c. 48 , s. 18. (6)(c) ; S.I. 1997/2323 , art. 3 , Sch. 1

F112 S. 121. (5) inserted (6.5.1999) by S.I. 1999/1042 , arts. 1. (2)(a) , 3 , Sch. 1 Pt. I para. 13. (3)

F113. Words in s. 121. (5)(a) inserted (22.4.2013) by Scotland Act 2012 (c. 11), ss. 36. (10), 44. (5); S.I. 2013/6, art. 2. (c)

Modifications etc. (not altering text)

C12. S. 121 excluded (28.11.2011) by Double Jeopardy (Scotland) Act 2011 (asp 16), ss. 11. (9), 17. (3) (with s. 14); S.S.I. 2011/365, art. 3

[F114121. A Suspension of certain sentences pending determination of appeal.S

(1) Where an intimation of intention to appeal or, in the case of an appeal under section 106. (1)(b) to (e) F115 [F116 ...] , 108 or 108. A of this Act, a note of appeal is lodged, the court may on the application of the appellant direct that the whole, or any remaining part, of a relevant sentence shall be suspended until the appeal, if it is proceeded with, is determined.

(2) Where the court has directed the suspension of the whole or any remaining part of a person's relevant sentence, the person shall, unless the High Court otherwise directs, appear personally in court on the day or days fixed for the hearing of the appeal.

(3) Where a person fails to appear personally in court as mentioned in subsection (2) above, the court may—

(a) if he is the appellant—

(i) decline to consider the appeal; and

(ii) dismiss it summarily; or

(b) whether or not he is the appellant—

(i) consider and determine the appeal; or

(ii) make such other order as the court thinks fit.

(4) In this section " relevant sentence " means any one or more of the following—

[F117. (aa)a community payback order;]

(d) a restriction of liberty order.]

[F118. (5)Subsections (1), (2) and (4) above apply to an appeal under [F119section 288. AA of this Act or] paragraph 13. (a) of Schedule 6 to the Scotland Act 1998 and, in relation to such an appeal–

(a) references to an appeal being determined are to be read as references to the disposal of the proceedings by the High Court following determination of the appeal; and

(b) the reference in subsection (2) to the hearing of the appeal is to be read as a reference to any subsequent hearing in the High Court in relation to the proceedings.

(6) Where a person fails to appear personally in court as mentioned in subsection (2) as read with subsection (5) above, the court may make such order as it thinks fit.]

Amendments (Textual)

F114 S. 121. A inserted (1.8.1997 for specified purposes otherwise and 1.7.1998) by 1997 c. 48 , s. 24. (1) ; S.I. 1997/1712 , art. 3 , Sch. (subject to arts. 4 , 5); S.I. 1997/2323 , art. 5. (1)

F115. Words in s. 121. A(1) repealed (28.2.2011) by Protection of Vulnerable Groups (Scotland)

Act 2007 (asp 14), s. 101. (2), sch. 4 para. 19 (with ss. 90, 99); S.S.I. 2011/157, art. 2. (a) (with art. 5. (1))

F116 Words in s. 121. A(1) inserted (10.1.2005) by Protection of Children (Scotland) Act 2003 (asp 5) , ss. 16. (5) , 22. (2) ; S.S.I. 2004/522 , art. 2

F117 S. 121. A(4)(aa) substituted for s. 121. A(4)(a)-(c) (1.2.2011) by Criminal Justice and Licensing (Scotland) Act 2010 (asp 13) , ss. 14. (2) , 206. (1) , Sch. 2 para. 10 ; S.S.I. 2010/413 , art. 2 , Sch. (with art. 3)

F118 S. 121. A(5)(6) inserted (6.5.1999) by S.I. 1999/1042 , arts. 1. (2)(a) , 3 , Sch. 1 Pt. I para. 13. (4)

F119. Words in s. 121. A(5) inserted (22.4.2013) by Scotland Act 2012 (c. 11), ss. 36. (10), 44. (5); S.I. 2013/6, art. 2. (c)

122 Fines and caution.S

(1) Where a person has on conviction been sentenced to payment of a fine and in default of payment to imprisonment, the person lawfully authorised to receive the fine shall, on receiving it, retain it until the determination of any appeal in relation to the conviction or sentence.

(2) If a person sentenced to payment of a fine remains in custody in default of payment of the fine he shall be deemed, for the purposes of this Part of this Act, to be a person sentenced to imprisonment.

(3) An appellant who has been sentenced to the payment of a fine, and has paid it in accordance with the sentence, shall, in the event of his appeal being successful, be entitled, subject to any order of the High Court, to the return of the sum paid or any part of it.

(4) A convicted person who has been sentenced to the payment of a fine and has duly paid it shall, if an appeal against sentence by the Lord Advocate [F120or any appeal by the Lord Advocate or the Advocate General for Scotland under [F121section 288. AA of this Act or] paragraph 13. (a) of Schedule 6 to the Scotland Act 1998]results in the sentence being quashed and no fine, or a lesser fine than that paid, being imposed, be entitled, subject to any order of the High Court, to the return of the sum paid or as the case may be to the return of the amount by which that sum exceeds the amount of the lesser fine.

[F122. (5)In subsections (1) and (3) above, "appeal" includes an appeal under [F123section 288. AA of this Act or] paragraph 13. (a) of Schedule 6 to the Scotland Act 1998.]

Amendments (Textual)

F120 Words in s. 122. (4) inserted (6.5.1999) by S.I. 1999/1042 , arts. 1. (2)(a) , 3 , Sch. 1 Pt. I para. 13. (5)(a)

F121. Words in s. 122. (4) inserted (22.4.2013) by Scotland Act 2012 (c. 11), ss. 36. (10), 44. (5); S.I. 2013/6, art. 2. (c)

F122 S. 122. (5) inserted (6.5.1999) by S.I. 1999/1042 , arts. 1. (2)(a) , 3 , Sch. 1 Pt. I para. 13. (5)(b)

F123. Words in s. 122. (5) inserted (22.4.2013) by Scotland Act 2012 (c. 11), ss. 36. (10), 44. (5); S.I. 2013/6, art. 2. (c)

123 Lord Advocate's reference.S

(1) Where a person tried on indictment is acquitted or convicted of a charge, the Lord Advocate may refer a point of law which has arisen in relation to that charge to the High Court for their opinion; and the Clerk of Justiciary shall send to the person and to any solicitor who acted for the person at the trial, a copy of the reference and intimation of the date fixed by the Court for a hearing.

(2) The person may, not later than seven days before the date so fixed, intimate in writing to the Clerk of Justiciary and to the Lord Advocate either—

    (a) that he elects to appear personally at the hearing; or

(b) that he elects to be represented thereat by counsel,

but, except by leave of the Court on cause shown, and without prejudice to his right to attend, he shall not appear or be represented at the hearing other than by and in conformity with an election under this subsection.

(3) Where there is no intimation under subsection (2)(b) above, the High Court shall appoint counsel to act at the hearing as amicus curiae .

(4) The costs of representation elected under subsection (2)(b) above or of an appointment under subsection (3) above shall, after being taxed by the Auditor of the Court of Session, be paid by the Lord Advocate.

(5) The opinion on the point referred under subsection (1) above shall not affect the acquittal or, as the case may be, conviction in the trial.

124 Finality of proceedings and Secretary of State's reference.S

(1) Nothing in this Part [F124or Part XA] of this Act shall affect the prerogative of mercy.

(2) Subject to [F125. Part XA and [F126section 288. AA] of this Act] [F127and paragraph 13. (a) of Schedule 6 to the Scotland Act 1998], every interlocutor and sentence pronounced by the High Court under this Part of this Act shall be final and conclusive and not subject to review by any court whatsoever and [F128, except for the purposes of F129... an appeal under [F130section 288. AA of this Act or] paragraph 13. (a) of that Schedule,] it shall be incompetent to stay or suspend any execution or diligence issuing from the High Court under this Part of this Act.

F131. (3). . . . .

F131. (4). . . . .

F131. (5). . . . .

Amendments (Textual)

F124 Words in s. 124. (1) inserted (1.4.1999) by 1997 c. 48, s. 62. (1), Sch. 1 para. 21. (18)(a); S.I. 1999/652, art. 2, Sch. (subject to savings and transitional provisions in art. 3)

F125 Words in s. 124. (2) substituted (1.4.1999) by 1997 c. 48, s. 62. (1), Sch. 1 para. 21. (18)(b); S.I. 1999/652, art. 2, Sch. (subject to savings and transitional provisions in art. 3)

F126. Words in s. 124. (2) substituted (17.1.2017) by Criminal Justice (Scotland) Act 2016 (asp 1), ss. 94. (a), 117. (2); S.S.I. 2016/426, art. 2, sch.

F127 S. 124. (2): By S.I. 1999/1042, arts. 1. (2)(a), 3, Sch. 1 Pt. I para. 13. (6)(a) it is provided (6.5.1999) that after "subsection (3) below" there is inserted "and paragraph 13. (a) of Schedule 6 to the Scotland Act 1998"

F128 Words in s. 124. (2) inserted (6.5.1999) by S.I. 1999/1042, arts. 1. (2)(a), 3, Sch. 1 Pt. I para. 13. (6)(b)

F129. Words in s. 124. (2) repealed (17.1.2017) by Criminal Justice (Scotland) Act 2016 (asp 1), ss. 94. (b), 117. (2); S.S.I. 2016/426, art. 2, sch.

F130. Words in s. 124. (2) inserted (22.4.2013) by Scotland Act 2012 (c. 11), ss. 36. (11)(c), 44. (5); S.I. 2013/6, art. 2. (c)

F131 S. 124. (3)-(5) repealed (1.4.1999) by 1997 c. 48, s. 62. (1)(2), Sch. 1 para. 21. (18)(c), Sch. 3; S.I. 1999/652, art. 2, Sch. Table (subject to savings and transitional provisions in art. 3)

125 Reckoning of time spent pending appeal.S

(1) Subject to subsection (2) below, where a convicted person is admitted to bail under section 112 of this Act, the period beginning with the date of his admission to bail and ending on the date of his readmission to prison in consequence of the determination or abandonment of—

(a) his appeal; or, as the case may be,

(b) any relevant appeal by the Lord Advocate under section 108 [F132or 108. A] of this Act,

shall not be reckoned as part of any term of imprisonment under his sentence.

(2) The time, including any period consequent on the recall of bail, during which an appellant is in

custody pending the determination of his appeal or, as the case may be, of any relevant appeal by the Lord Advocate under section 108 [F133or 108. A] of this Act shall, subject to any direction which the High Court may give to the contrary, be reckoned as part of any term of imprisonment under his sentence.

(3) Subject to any direction which the High Court may give to the contrary, imprisonment of an appellant or, where the appellant is the Lord Advocate, of a convicted person—

(a) who is in custody in consequence of the conviction or sentence appealed against, shall be deemed to run as from the date on which the sentence was passed;

(b) who is in custody other than in consequence of such conviction or sentence, shall be deemed to run or to be resumed as from the date on which his appeal was determined or abandoned;

(c) who is not in custody, shall be deemed to run or to be resumed as from the date on which he is received into prison under the sentence.

(4) In this section references to a prison and imprisonment shall include respectively references to a young offenders institution or place of safety or, as respects a child sentenced to be detained under section 208 of this Act, the place directed by the Secretary of State and to detention in such institution, centre or place of safety, or, as respects such a child, place directed by the Secretary of State and any reference to a sentence shall be construed as a reference to a sentence passed by the court imposing sentence or by the High Court on appeal as the case may require.

Amendments (Textual)

F132 Words in s. 125. (1)(b) inserted (20.10.1997) by 1997 c. 48 , s. 18. (7)(a) ; S.I. 1997/2323 , art. 3 , Sch. 1

F133 Words in s. 125. (2) inserted (20.10.1997) by 1997 c. 48 , s. 18. (7)(b) ; S.I. 1997/2323 , art. 3 , Sch. 1

126 Extract convictions.S

No extract conviction shall be issued—

(a) during the period of four weeks after the day on which the conviction took place, except in so far as it is required as a warrant for the detention of the person convicted under any sentence which has been pronounced against him; nor

(b) where an intimation of intention to appeal or, in the case of an appeal under section 106. (1)(b) to (e) [F134, 108 or 108. A]of this Act, a note of appeal is lodged, until the appeal, if it is proceeded with, is determined.

Amendments (Textual)

F134 Words in s. 126. (b) substituted (20.10.1997) by 1997 c. 48 , s. 18. (8) ; S.I. 1997/2323 , art. 3 , Sch. 1

127 Forms in relation to appeals.S

(1) The Clerk of Justiciary shall furnish the necessary forms and instructions in relation to intimations of intention to appeal, notes of appeal or notices of application under this Part of this Act to—

(a) any person who demands them; and

(b) to officers of courts, governors of prisons, and such other officers or persons as he thinks fit.

(2) The governor of a prison shall cause the forms and instructions mentioned in subsection (1) above to be placed at the disposal of prisoners desiring to appeal or to make any application under this Part of this Act.

(3) The governor of a prison shall, if requested to do so by a prisoner, forwarded on the prisoner's behalf to the Clerk of Justiciary any intimation, note or notice mentioned in subsection (1) above given by the prisoner.

128 Fees and expenses.S

Except as otherwise provided in this Part of this Act, no court fees, or other fees or expenses shall be exigible from or awarded against an appellant or applicant in respect of an appeal or application under this Part of this Act.

129 Non-compliance with certain provisions may be waived.S

(1) Non-compliance with—
    (a) the provisions of this Act set out in subsection (3) below; or
    (b) any rule of practice for the time being in force under this Part of this Act relating to appeals,
shall not prevent the further prosecution of an appeal if the High Court or a judge thereof considers it just and proper that the non-compliance is waived or, in the manner directed by the High Court or judge, remedied by amendment or otherwise.
(2) Where the High Court or a judge thereof directs that the non-compliance is to be remedied, and the remedy is carried out, the appeal shall proceed.
(3) The provisions of this Act referred to in subsection (1) above are:—
section 94
section 103. (1), (4), (6) and (7)
section 104. (2) and (3)
section 105
section 106. (4)
section 111
section 114
section 115
section 116
section 117
section 120. (1), (3) and (4)
section 121
section 122
section 126
section 128.
(4) This section does not apply to any rule of practice relating to appeals under section 60 of this Act.

130 Bill of suspension not competent.S

It shall not be competent to appeal to the High Court by bill of suspension against any conviction, sentence, judgement or order pronounced in any proceedings on indictment in the sheriff court.

[F135130. ABill of advocation not competent in respect of certain decisionsS

It is not competent to bring under review of the High Court by way of bill of advocation a decision taken at a first diet or a preliminary hearing.]
Amendments (Textual)
F135. S. 130. A inserted (17.1.2017) by Criminal Justice (Scotland) Act 2016 (asp 1), ss. 92, 117. (2); S.S.I. 2016/426, art. 2, sch.

131 Prosecution appeal by bill of advocation.S

(1) Without prejudice to section 74 of this Act, the prosecutor's right to bring a decision under review of the High Court by way of bill of advocation in accordance with existing law and practice shall extend to the review of a decision of any court of solemn jurisdiction.

(2) Where a decision to which a bill of advocation relates is reversed on the review of the decision the prosecutor may, whether or not there has already been a trial diet at which evidence has been led, proceed against the accused by serving him with an indictment containing, subject to subsection (3) below, the charge or charges which were affected by the decision.

(3) The wording of the charge or charges referred to in subsection (2) above shall be as it was immediately before the decision appealed against.

132 Interpretation of Part VIII.S

In this Part of this Act, unless the context otherwise requires—

" appellant " includes a person who has been convicted and desires to appeal under this Part of the Act;

" sentence " includes any order of the High Court made on conviction with reference to the person convicted or his wife or children, and any recommendation of the High Court as to the making of a deportation order in the case of a person convicted and the power of the High Court to pass a sentence includes a power to make any such order of the court or recommendation, and a recommendation so made by the High Court shall have the same effect for the purposes of Articles 20 and 21 of the Aliens Order 1953 as the certificate and recommendation of the convicting court.

Interpretation of Part VIII.

132 Interpretation of Part VIII.S

In this Part of this Act, unless the context otherwise requires—

" appellant " includes a person who has been convicted and desires to appeal under this Part of the Act;

" sentence " includes any order of the High Court made on conviction with reference to the person convicted or his wife or children, and any recommendation of the High Court as to the making of a deportation order in the case of a person convicted and the power of the High Court to pass a sentence includes a power to make any such order of the court or recommendation, and a recommendation so made by the High Court shall have the same effect for the purposes of Articles 20 and 21 of the Aliens Order 1953 as the certificate and recommendation of the convicting court.

PART IX Summary Proceedings

PART IXS Summary Proceedings

133 Application of Part IX of Act.S

(1) This Part of this Act applies to summary proceedings in respect of any offence which might prior to the passing of this Act, or which may under the provisions of this or any Act, whether passed before or after the passing of this Act, be tried summarily.

(2) Without prejudice to subsection (1) above, this Part of this Act also applies to procedure in all courts of summary jurisdiction in so far as they have jurisdiction in respect of—

(a) any offence or the recovery of a penalty under any enactment or rule of law which does not exclude summary procedure as well as, in accordance with section 211. (3) and (4) of this Act, to the enforcement of a fine imposed in solemn proceedings; and

(b) any order ad factum praestandum, or other order of court or warrant competent to a court of summary jurisdiction.

(3) Where any statute provides for summary proceedings to be taken under any public general or local enactment, such proceedings shall be taken under this Part of this Act.

(4) Nothing in this Part of this Act shall—

(a) extend to any complaint or other proceeding under or by virtue of any statutory provision for the recovery of any rate, tax, or impost whatsoever; or

(b) affect any right to raise any civil proceedings.

(5) Except where any enactment otherwise expressly provides, all prosecutions under this Part of this Act shall be brought at the instance of the procurator fiscal.

134 Incidental applications.S

(1) This section applies to any application to a court for any warrant or order of court—

(a) as incidental to proceedings by complaint; or

(b) where a court has power to grant any warrant or order of court, although no subsequent proceedings by complaint may follow thereon.

(2) An application to which this section applies may be made by petition at the instance of the prosecutor in the form prescribed by Act of Adjournal.

(3) Where it is necessary for the execution of a warrant or order granted under this section, warrant to break open shut and lockfast places shall be implied.

Modifications etc. (not altering text)

C1 S. 134 applied (20.11.2002) by Copyright, Designs and Patents Act 1988 (c. 48) , ss. 114. B(2)(a) , 204. B(2)(a) , 297. D(2)(a) (as inserted by Copyright, etc. and Trade Marks (Offences and Enforcement) Act 2002 (c. 25) , ss. 3 , 4 , 5 ; S.I. 2002/2749 , art. 2)

S. 134 applied (7.3.2005) by The Electromagnetic Compatibility Regulations 2005 (S.I. 2005/281) , reg. 98. (1)

135 Warrants of apprehension and search.S

(1) A warrant of apprehension or search may be in the form prescribed by Act of Adjournal or as nearly as may be in such form, and any warrant of apprehension or search shall, where it is necessary for its execution, imply warrant to officers of law to break open shut and lockfast places.

(2) A warrant of apprehension of an accused in the form mentioned in subsection (1) above shall imply warrant to officers of law to search for and to apprehend the accused, and to bring him before the court issuing the warrant, or before any other court competent to deal with the case, to answer to the charge on which such warrant is granted, and, in the meantime, until he can be so brought, to detain him in a police station, police cell, or other convenient place.

F1. (3). . . . .

F2. (4). . . . .

(5) A warrant of apprehension or other warrant shall not be required for the purpose of bringing before the court an accused who has been apprehended without a written warrant or who attends without apprehension in answer to any charge made against him.

Amendments (Textual)

F1 S. 135. (3) repealed (25.1.2018) by Criminal Justice (Scotland) Act 2016 (asp 1), s. 117. (2), sch. 2 para. 27. (d); S.S.I. 2017/345, art. 3, sch. (with arts. 4, 5)

F2 S. 135. (4) repealed (10.12.2007) by Criminal Proceedings etc. (Reform) (Scotland) Act 2007 (asp 6), ss. 80, 84, Sch. para. 17. (b); S.S.I. 2007/479, art. 3. (1), Sch. (as amended by S.S. I. 2007/527)

136 Time limit for certain offences.S

(1) Proceedings under this Part of this Act in respect of any offence to which this section applies shall be commenced—

(a) within six months after the contravention occurred;

(b) in the case of a continuous contravention, within six months after the last date of such contravention,

and it shall be competent in a prosecution of a contravention mentioned in paragraph (b) above to include the entire period during which the contravention occurred.

(2) This section applies to any offence triable only summarily and consisting of the contravention of any enactment, unless the enactment fixes a different time limit.

(3) For the purposes of this section proceedings shall be deemed to be commenced on the date on which a warrant to apprehend or to cite the accused is granted, if the warrant is executed without undue delay.

Modifications etc. (not altering text)

C2 S. 136. (3) savings for effects of S.I. 2011/548 art. 15. (3)(b) by S.I. 2011/548 art. 19 (as inserted (3.3.2011) by The Libya (Asset-Freezing) Regulations 2011 (S.I. 2011/605), regs. 1. (1), 20 (with reg. 18))

C3 S. 136 excluded (1.4.1999) by 1998 c. 39 , s. 33. (4) ; S.I. 1998/2574, art. 2. (2), Sch. 2
 S. 136 excluded (3.6.1999) by S.I. 1999/1516, reg. 9. (5)
 S. 136 excluded (25.10.1999) by 1973 c. 35, s. 11. A(3) (as inserted (25.10.1999) by 1999 c. 26, s. 31, Sch. 7 para. 5); S.I. 1999/2830, art. 2. (1), Sch. 1, Pt. I
 S. 136 excluded (16.2.2001) by 2000 c. 41, s. 151. (3); S.I. 2001/222, art. 2, Sch. 1 Pt. I (subject to transitional provisions in Sch. 1 Pt. II)
 S. 136 excluded (16.3.2001 in accordance with art. 1. (2)(3) of the amending S.I.) by S.I. 2001/947, art. 16. (8)
 S. 136 excluded (10.10.2001 in accordance with art. 1. (2) of the amending S.I.) by S.I. 2001/3365, art. 10. (6)
 S. 136 excluded (25.1.2002) by S.I. 2002/111, art. 20. (9)
 S. 136 excluded (24.10.2002) by S.I. 2002/2628, art. 16. (8)
 S. 136 excluded (14.6.2003) by S.I. 2003/1519, art. 20. (8)
 S. 136 excluded (13.2.2004) by S.I. 2004/348, art. 15. (8)
 S. 136 excluded (11.2.2005) by S.I. 2005/253, art. 9. (8)
 S. 136 excluded (7.3.2005) by S.I. 2005/281, reg. 93
 S. 136 excluded (1.10.2005) by S.I. 2005/1803, reg. 41. (2)
 S. 136 excluded (20.7.2007) by S.I. 2006/3418, reg. 54 (with savings in regs. 7-14, 63, 64)

C4 S. 136 excluded (26.5.2008) by The Business Protection from Misleading Marketing Regulations 2008 (S.I. 2008/1276), reg. 10. (4)(5)

C5 S. 136 excluded (26.5.2008) by The Consumer Protection from Unfair Trading Regulations 2008 (S.I. 2008/1277), reg. 14. (4)(5) (with reg. 28. (2)(3))

C6 S. 136 restricted (26.11.2008) by Planning Act 2008 (c. 29), ss. 58. (6)(7), 236, 241, Sch. 12 para. 9 (with s. 226)

C7 S. 136 excluded (10.4.2009) by The Iran (United Nations Sanctions) Order 2009 (S.I. 2009/886), art. 12. (7)

C8 S. 136 excluded (10.7.2009) by The North Korea (United Nations Sanctions) Order 2009 (S.I. 2009/1749), art. 14. (7) (as amended by S.I. 2009/3213)

C9. S. 136 excluded (30.4.2012) by The Civil Aviation (Air Travel Organisers' Licensing) Regulations 2012 (S.I. 2012/1017), regs. 1. (2), 71. (2) (with regs. 73, 74)

C10. S. 136 excluded (8.5.2012) by The Textile Products (Labelling and Fibre Composition)

Regulations 2012 (S.I. 2012/1102), regs. 1, 7. (4)

C11. S. 136 excluded (18.12.2013) by Scottish Independence Referendum Act 2013 (asp 14), ss. 15. (2), 36

C12. S. 136 applied (1.7.2016) by Air Weapons and Licensing (Scotland) Act 2015 (asp 10), ss. 32, 88. (2) (with s. 37); S.S.I. 2016/130, art. 2, sch. (with arts. 5, 6)

C13. S. 136 excluded by 2006 c. 36, s. 107. (3. C)(c) (as inserted (27.6.2017) by Digital Economy Act 2017 (c. 30), ss. 13. (2), 118. (2) (with s. 13. (4)))

C14 S. 136. (1) modified (21.7.1997) by 1997 c. 22, s. 21. (4)(c); S.I. 1997/1672, art. 2

C15 S. 136. (3) applied (1.4.1999) by 1998 c. 39, s. 33. (5)(b); S.I. 1998/2574, art. 2. (2), Sch. 2

S. 136. (3) applied (30.4.1998) by S.I. 1998/955, reg. 8. (4)

S. 136. (3) applied (1.7.1996) by S.I. 1996/1500, reg. 16. (5)

S. 136. (3) applied (1.8.1996) by S.I. 1996/2005, reg. 11. (4)

S. 136. (3) applied (3.12.1996) by S.I. 1996/2999, reg. 11. (4)

S. 136. (3) applied (2.8.1999) by S.I. 1999/1872, reg. 109. (5)

S. 136. (3) applied (16.12.1999) by S.I. 1999/3315, reg. 8. (5)

S. 136. (3) applied (17.12.1999) by S.S.I. 1999/186, reg. 8. (6)

S. 136. (3) applied (29.1.2001) by S.S.I. 2000/448, reg. 14. (4)

S. 136. (3) applied (10.10.2001 in accordance with art. 1. (2) of the amending S.I.) by S.I. 2001/3365, art. 10. (6)

S. 136. (3) applied (19.3.2001) by S.S.I. 2001/40, reg. 11. (4) (which S.S.I. was revoked 2.7.2001 by S.S.I. 2001/220, art. 13)

S. 136. (3) applied (12.5.2001) by S.S.I. 2001/140, reg. 16. (5)

S. 136. (3) applied (2.7.2001) by S.S.I. 2001/220, reg. 11. (4)

S. 136. (3) applied (28.9.2001) by S.S.I. 2001/300, reg. 17. (4)

S. 136. (3) applied (1.1.2002) by S.S.I. 2001/445, reg. 24. (2)

S. 136. (3) applied (22.3.2002) by S.S.I. 2002/139, reg. 20. (2)

S. 136. (3) applied (28.6.2002) by S.S.I. 2002/278, reg.15. (4)

S. 136. (3) applied (1.4.2002) by 1980 c. 45, s. 72. (3. C) (as inserted (1.4.2002) by 2002 asp 3, s. 65. (3) (with s. 67)); S.S.I. 2002/118, art. 2. (3)

S. 136. (3) applied (1.10.2004) by 1999 c. 33, s. 92. B(7) (as inserted (1.10.2004) by 2004 c. 19, ss. 39. (7), 48. (1)-(3)); S.I. 2004/2523, art. 2, Sch.)

S. 136. (3) applied (5.12.2005) by Civil Partnership Act 2004 (c. 33), ss. 100. (5), 263; S.S.I. 2005/604, art. 2

S. 136. (3) applied (18.3.2004) by S.I. 2004/70, reg. 21. (2)

S. 136. (3) applied (31.12.2005) by S.S.I. 2005/613, art. 45. (9)

C16 S. 136. (3) extended (1.4.1996) by 1995 c. 39, ss. 4. (3), 53. (2)

S. 136. (3) extended (4.5.1999) by S.I. 1999/1110, reg. 7. (6)

S. 136. (3) applied (at 0600 hours) by Smoking, Health and Social Care (Scotland) Act 2005 (asp 13), ss.26.3.2006 5. (2), 43 (with s. 10); S.S.I. 2005/492, art. 3. (d)

S. 136. (3) applied (1.3.2005) by S.I. 2005/218, reg. 12. (10)

S. 136. (3) applied (18.4.2005) by S.S.I. 2005/143, reg. 25, Sch. 4 para. 9. (2)

S. 136. (3) applied (12.5.2005) by S.I. 2005/1259, art. 10. (3)

S. 136. (3) applied (15.5.2005) by S.S.I. 2005/225, reg. 21. (4)

S. 136. (3) applied (9.6.2005) by S.I. 2005/1517, art. 10. (3)

S. 136. (3) applied (1.10.2005) by S.I. 2005/1803, reg. 41. (3)

S. 136. (3) applied (16.12.2005) by S.I. 2005/3432, art. 12. (3)(b)

S. 136. (3) applied (2.12.2005) by S.S.I. 2005/569, reg. 21. (2)

S. 136. (3) applied (1.9.2006) by Human Tissue (Scotland) Act 2006 (asp 4), ss. 21. (2), 62; S.S.I. 2006/251, art. 3

S. 136. (3) applied (1.7.2006) by S.S.I. 2006/319, art. 10. (7)

S. 136. (3) applied (9.6.2006) by S.I. 2006/1454, art. 13. (3)(b)

S. 136. (3) applied (9.10.2006) by S.I. 2002/3026, reg. 30. (2. C) (as inserted by S.I. 2006/2530, reg. 11. (2))

S. 136. (3) applied (12.10.2006) by S.I. 2006/2657, art. 14. (3)(b) (with arts. 18, 19)

S. 136. (3) applied (16.11.2006) by S.I. 2006/2952, art. 14. (3)(b) (with art. 18)

S. 136. (3) applied (16.11.2006) by S.I. 2006/2958, art. 13. (3)(b) (with art. 17)

C17 S. 136. (3) applied (9.2.2007) by The Iran (Financial Sanctions) Order 2007 (S.I. 2007/281), art. 13. (3)(b) (with art. 17)

S. 136. (3) applied (3.5.2007) by The Iran (European Community Financial Sanctions) Regulations 2007 (S.I. 2007/1374), reg. 13. (3)(b) (with reg. 16)

S. 136. (3) applied (28.9.2007) by The Less Favoured Area Support Scheme (Scotland) Regulations 2007 (S.S.I. 2007/439), reg. 21. (2)

C18 S. 136. (3) applied (20.1.2007, 6.4.2007, 1.10.2007, 6.4.2008, 1.10.2008 for certain purposes and 1.10.2009 otherwise) by Companies Act 2006 (c. 46), ss. 1128. (2), 1300 (with savings in s. 1133); S.I. 2006/3428, art. 3. (2) (with art. 6); S.I. 2007/1093, art. 2. (2)(c) (with arts. 4, 11); S.I. 2007/2194, art. 2. (1)(l)(3)(h) (with art. 12); S.I. 2007/3495, arts. {3. (3)(g)}, {5. (3)(a)} (with arts. 7, 12); S.I. 2008/2860, art. 3. (s) (with arts. 5, 7, 8, Sch. 2 (as amended by S.I. 2009/1802, art. 18, S.I. 2009/1941, art. 13, S.I. 2009/2476, reg. 2))

C19 S. 136. (3) applied (22.3.2008) by The Leader Grants (Scotland) Regulations 2008 (S.S.I. 2008/66), reg. 23. (4)

C20 S. 136. (3) applied (24.3.2008) by The Agricultural Processing, Marketing and Co-operation Grants (Scotland) Regulations 2008 (S.I. 2008/64), reg. 12. (4)

C21 S. 136. (3) applied (29.3.2008) by The Rural Development Contracts (Rural Priorities) (Scotland) Regulations 2008 (S.S.I. 2008/100), reg. 22. (4)

C22 S. 136. (3) applied (15.5.2008) by The Rural Development Contracts (Land Managers Options) (Scotland) Regulations 2008 (S.S.I. 2008/159), regs. 1. (1), 21. (4)

C23 S. 136. (3) applied (18.5.2008) by The Land Managers Skills Development Grants (Scotland) Regulations 2008 (S.S.I. 2008/162), reg. 13. (4)

C24 S. 136. (3) applied (27.11.2008) Counter- Terrorism Act 2008 (c. 28), ss. 62, 100, Sch. 7 para. 35. (2) (with s. 101. (2), Sch. 7 para. 43)

C25 S. 136. (3) applied (26.1.2009) by The Operation of Air Services in the Community Regulations 2009 (S.I. 2009/41), reg. 30. (5)

C26 S. 136. (3) applied (10.4.2009) by The Iran (United Nations Sanctions) Order 2009 (S.I. 2009/886), art. 12. (7)

C27. S. 136. (3) applied (24.4.2009) by The Zimbabwe (Financial Sanctions) Regulations 2009 (S.I. 2009/ 847), {reg. 14. (3)(b)}

C28 S. 136. (3) applied (10.8.2009) by The Terrorism (United Nations Measures) Order 2009 (S.I. 2009/1747), art. 22. (3)(b) (with art. 25)

C29 S. 136. (3) applied (1.10.2009) by Criminal Justice Act 1993 (c. 36), s. 61. A(3) (as inserted by The Companies Act 2006 (Consequential Amendments, Transitional Provisions and Savings) Order 2009 (S.I. 2009/1941), art. 2. (1), Sch. 1 para. 141 (with art. 10))

C30 S. 136. (3) applied (1.1.2010) by The Common Agricultural Policy Single Payment and Support Schemes (Integrated Administration and Control System) Regulations 2009 (S.I. 2009/3263), reg. 10. (7)

C31 S. 136. (3) applied by Child Support Act 1991 (c. 48), s. 14. A(8) (as inserted (14.1.2010) by Welfare Reform Act 2009 (c. 24), ss. 55. (3), 61; S.I. 2010/45, art. 2. (3))

C32 S. 136. (3) applied (8.4.2010) by The Al- Qaida and Taliban (Asset-Freezing) Regulations 2010 (S.I. 2010/1197), regs. 1. (1), 11. (3)(b) (with reg. 13)

C33 S. 136. (3) applied (2.7.2010) by The Less Favoured Area Support Scheme (Scotland) Regulations 2010 (S.S.I. 2010/273), regs. 1. (1), 21. (2) (with reg. 1. (3))

C34 S. 136. (3) applied (17.12.2010) by Terrorist Asset- Freezing etc. Act 2010 (c. 38), ss. 36. (2)(b), 55 (with s. 44)

C35 S. 136. (3) applied (4.1.2011) by The Somalia (Asset-Freezing) Regulations 2010 (S.I. 2010/2956), reg. 16. (3)(b) (with reg. 19)

C36 S. 136. (3) applied (27.2.2011) by Libya (Financial Sanctions) Order 2011 (S.I. 2011/548), arts. 1. (1), 15. (3)(b) (with art. 18)

C37 S. 136. (3) applied (3.3.2011) by The Libya (Asset-Freezing) Regulations 2011 (S.I. 2011/605), regs. 1. (1), 15. (3)(b) (with reg. 18)

C38. S. 136. (3) applied (7.4.2011) by Ivory Coast (Asset-Freezing) Regulations 2011 (S.I. 2011/1086), regs. 1. (1), 15. (3)(b) (with reg. 18)

C39. S. 136. (3) applied (15.4.2011 at 1.00 pm) by Iran (Asset-Freezing) Regulations 2011 (S.I. 2011/1129), regs. 1. (1), 15. (3)(b) (with reg. 18)

C40. S. 136. (3) applied (27.4.2011) by Democratic People's Republic of Korea (Asset-Freezing) Regulations 2011 (S.I. 2011/1094), regs. 1. (1), 15. (3)(b) (with art. 18)

C41. S. 136. (3) applied (10.5.2011 at 6.00 pm) by Syria (Asset-Freezing) Regulations 2011 (S.I. 2011/1244), regs. 1. (1), 15. (3)(b) (with reg. 18)

C42. S. 136. (3) applied (5.8.2011) by The Afghanistan (Asset-Freezing) Regulations 2011 (S.I. 2011/1893), regs. 1. (1), 15. (3)(b) (with reg. 18)

C43. S. 136. (3) applied (16.11.2011) by The Al-Qaida (Asset-Freezing) Regulations 2011 (S.I. 2011/2742), regs. 1. (1), 15. (3)(b)

C44. S. 136. (3) applied (1.1.2012) by The Common Agricultural Policy Single Farm Payment and Support Schemes (Scotland) Regulations 2011 (S.S.I. 2011/416), reg. 1. (1), sch. 2 para. 9. (2) (with reg. 14. (2))

C45. S. 136. (3) applied (26.3.2012) by The Iran (European Union Financial Sanctions) Regulations 2012 (S.I. 2012/925), regs. 1. (1), 22. (3)(b) (with reg. 26. (1)(2)(4))

C46. S. 136. (3) applied (30.4.2012) by The Civil Aviation (Air Travel Organisers' Licensing) Regulations 2012 (S.I. 2012/1017), regs. 1. (2), 71. (3) (with regs. 73, 74)

C47. S. 136. (3) applied (8.5.2012) by The Textile Products (Labelling and Fibre Composition) Regulations 2012 (S.I. 2012/1102), regs. 1, 7. (5)

C48. S. 136. (3) applied (6.6.2012) by The Guinea-Bissau (Asset-Freezing) Regulations 2012 (S.I. 2012/1301), regs. 1. (1), 14. (3)(b)

C49. S. 136. (3) applied (2.7.2012) by The Iraq (Asset-Freezing) Regulations 2012 (S.I. 2012/1489), regs. 1. (1), 14. (3)(b) (with reg. 17)

C50. S. 136. (3) applied (4.7.2012) by The Republic of Guinea (Asset-Freezing) Regulations 2012 (S.I. 2012/1508), regs. 1. (1), 14. (3)(b) (with reg. 17)

C51. S. 136. (3) applied (4.7.2012) by The Belarus (Asset-Freezing) Regulations 2012 (S.I. 2012/1509), regs. 1. (1), 14. (3)(b) (with reg. 17)

C52. S. 136. (3) applied (4.7.2012) by The Sudan (Asset-Freezing) Regulations 2012 (S.I. 2012/1507), regs. 1. (1), 14. (3)(b) (with reg. 17)

C53. S. 136. (3) applied (5.7.2012) by The Eritrea (Asset-Freezing) Regulations 2012 (S.I. 2012/1515), regs. 1. (1), 14. (3)(b) (with reg. 17. (1)-(4))

C54. S. 136. (3) applied (5.7.2012) by The Democratic Republic of the Congo (Asset-Freezing) Regulations 2012 (S.I. 2012/1511), regs. 1. (1), 14. (3)(b) (with reg. 17)

C55. S. 136. (3) applied (5.7.2012) by The Liberia (Asset-Freezing) Regulations 2012 (S.I. 2012/1516), regs. 1. (1), 14. (3)(b) (with reg. 17. (1)-(4))

C56. S. 136. (3) applied (5.7.2012) by The Lebanon and Syria (Asset-Freezing) Regulations 2012 (S.I. 2012/1517), regs. 1. (1), 14. (3)(b) (with reg. 17. (1)-(4))

C57. S. 136. (3) applied (14.8.2012) by The Human Medicines Regulations 2012 (S.I. 2012/1916), regs. 1. (2), 339. (2) (with Sch. 32)

C58. S. 136. (3) applied (2.1.2013) by The Restriction of the Use of Certain Hazardous Substances in Electrical and Electronic Equipment Regulations 2012 (S.I. 2012/3032), regs. 1, 42. (2)(b) (with regs. 5, 8)

C59. S. 136. (3) applied (21.2.2013) by The Belarus (Asset-Freezing) Regulations 2013 (S.I. 2013/164), regs. 1. (1), 14. (3)(b) (with reg. 17)

C60. S. 136. (3) applied by S.S.I. 2004/520, reg. 19. A(5) (as inserted (31.5.2013) by The Environmental Information (Scotland) Amendment Regulations 2013 (S.S.I. 2013/127), regs. 1. (1), 2. (2))

C61. S. 136. (3) applied (11.7.2013) by The Cosmetic Products Enforcement Regulations 2013 (S.I. 2013/1478), regs. 1. (2), 22. (2)(b) (with reg. 6. (5))

C62. S. 136. (3) applied (16.8.2013) by The Democratic People's Republic of Korea (European Union Financial Sanctions) Regulations 2013 (S.I. 2013/1877), regs. 1. (1), 17. (3)(b)

C63. S. 136. (3) applied (1.3.2014) by The Olive Oil (Marketing Standards) Regulations 2014 (S.I. 2014/195), regs. 1, 13. (4)

C64. S. 136. (3) applied (14.3.2014) by The Central African Republic (European Union Financial Sanctions) Regulations 2014 (S.I. 2014/587), regs. 1. (1), 13. (3)(b) (with reg. 17)

C65. S. 136. (3) applied (18.3.2014 at 3.30 p.m.) by The Ukraine (European Union Financial Sanctions) (No.2) Regulations 2014 (S.I. 2014/693), regs. 1. (1), 13. (3)(b) (with reg. 17)

C66. S. 136. (3) applied (1.4.2014) by Energy Act 2013 (c. 32), s. 156. (1), Sch. 10 para. 4. (3)(c); S.I. 2014/251, art. 4

C67. S. 136. (3) applied (6.4.2014 at 3.30 p.m.) by The Ukraine (European Union Financial Sanctions) Regulations 2014 (S.I. 2014/507), regs. 1. (1), 13. (3)(b) (with reg. 17)

C68. S. 136. (3) applied (11.7.2014 at 3.30 p.m.) by The Sudan (European Union Financial Sanctions) Regulations 2014 (S.I. 2014/1826), regs. 1. (1), 13. (3)(b) (with reg. 17)

C69. S. 136. (3) applied (11.7.2014 at 3.30 p.m.) by The South Sudan (European Union Financial Sanctions) Regulations 2014 (S.I. 2014/1827), regs. 1. (1), 13. (3)(b) (with reg. 17. (1)-(4))

C70. S. 136. (3) applied (1.8.2014 at 3.00 p.m.) by The Ukraine (European Union Financial Sanctions) (No.3) Regulations 2014 (S.I. 2014/2054), regs. 1. (1), 7. (3)(b) (with reg. 10)

C71. S. 136. (3) applied (19.12.2014 at 2.00 p.m.) by The Yemen (European Union Financial Sanctions) Regulations 2014 (S.I. 2014/3349), regs. 1. (1), 13. (5)(b) (with reg. 17)

C72. S. 136. (3) applied by 2003 c. 21, s. 127. (6) (as inserted (13.4.2015) by Criminal Justice and Courts Act 2015 (c. 2), ss. 51. (1), 95. (1) (with s. 51. (2)); S.I. 2015/778, art. 3, Sch. 1 para. 42)

C73. S. 136. (3) applied (with effect in accordance with reg. 1 of the amending S.I.) by The South Sudan (European Union Financial Sanctions) (No. 2) Regulations 2015 (S.I. 2015/1361), regs. 1. (1), 13. (5)(b) (with reg. 17)

C74. S. 136. (3) applied (17.8.2015) by The Pyrotechnic Articles (Safety) Regulations 2015 (S.I. 2015/1553), regs. 1, 66. (2)(b)

C75. S. 136. (3) applied (2.10.2015 at 3.00 p.m.) by The Burundi (European Union Financial Sanctions) Regulations 2015 (S.I. 2015/1740), regs. 1. (1), 13. (5)(b) (with reg. 17. (1)-(4))

C76. S. 136. (3) applied (12.10.2015) by The Nagoya Protocol (Compliance) Regulations 2015 (S.I. 2015/821), regs. 1. (3), 16. (8) (with regs. 1. (5), 12)

C77. S. 136. (3) applied (16.11.2015) by The Single Common Market Organisation (Emergency Aid for Milk Producers) Regulations 2015 (S.I. 2015/1896), regs. 1. (2), 11. (7)

C78. S. 136. (3) applied (30.11.2015) by The European Maritime and Fisheries Fund (Grants) (Scotland) Regulations 2015 (S.S.I. 2015/359), regs. 1. (1), 16. (6)

C79. S. 136. (3) applied (18.1.2016 at 4.00 p.m.) by The Iran (European Union Financial Sanctions) Regulations 2016 (S.I. 2016/36), regs. 1. (1), 14. (5)(b) (with regs. 18, 21)

C80. S. 136. (3) applied (20.1.2016) by The Libya (European Union Financial Sanctions) Regulations 2016 (S.I. 2016/45), regs. 1. (1), 13. (5)(b) (with reg. 17)

C81. S. 136. (3) applied (30.11.2016) by Bankruptcy (Scotland) Act 2016 (asp 21), ss. 220. (3), 237. (2) (with ss. 232, 234. (3), 235, 236); S.S.I. 2016/294, reg. 2

C82. S. 136. (3) applied (8.12.2016) by The Electromagnetic Compatibility Regulations 2016 (S.I. 2016/1091), regs. 1, 70. (2)(b) (with regs. 74, 75. (5))

C83. S. 136. (3) applied (8.12.2016) by The Electrical Equipment (Safety) Regulations 2016 (S.I. 2016/1101), regs. 1, 54. (2)(b) (with reg. 3)

C84. S. 136. (3) applied (8.12.2016) by The Pressure Equipment (Safety) Regulations 2016 (S.I. 2016/1105), regs. 1, 80. (2)(b) (with reg. 88)

C85. S. 136. (3) applied (8.12.2016) by The Lifts Regulations 2016 (S.I. 2016/1093), regs. 1, 74. (2)(b) (with regs. 3-5)

C86. S. 136. (3) applied (8.12.2016) by The Simple Pressure Vessels (Safety) Regulations 2016 (S.I. 2016/1092), regs. 1, 68. (2)(b) (with regs. 3, 68. (6))

C87. S. 136. (3) applied (8.12.2016) by The Equipment and Protective Systems Intended for Use in Potentially Explosive Atmospheres Regulations 2016 (S.I. 2016/1107), regs. 1. (1), 65. (2)(b)

C88. S. 136. (3) applied (1.3.2017) by The Democratic Peoples Republic of Korea (European Union Financial Sanctions) Regulations 2017 (S.I. 2017/218), regs. 1. (1), 27. (5)(b) (with regs. 31, 33)

C89. S. 136. (3) applied (temp.) (6.4.2017) by The Reporting on Payment Practices and Performance Regulations 2017 (S.I. 2017/395), regs. 1. (2), 10. (3)

C90. S. 136. (3) applied by 2006 c. 36, s. 107. (3. D) (as inserted (27.6.2017) by Digital Economy Act 2017 (c. 30), ss. 13. (2), 118. (2) (with s. 13. (4)))

C91. S. 136. (3) applied (3.8.2017) by The Recreational Craft Regulations 2017 (S.I. 2017/737), regs. 1, 82. (2)(b) (with reg. 89)

C92. S. 136. (3) applied (31.10.2017) by The Republic of Mali (European Union Financial Sanctions) Regulations 2017 (S.I. 2017/972), regs. 1. (1), 13. (5)(b) (with reg. 17)

C93. S. 136. (3) applied (6.12.2017) by The Venezuela (European Union Financial Sanctions) Regulations 2017 (S.I. 2017/1094), regs. 1. (1), 13. (5)(b) (with reg. 17)

C94. S. 136. (3) applied (26.12.2017) by The Radio Equipment Regulations 2017 (S.I. 2017/1206), regs. 1, 69. (2)(b) (with regs. 3-5, 77)

[F3136. ATime limits for transferred and related casesS

(1) This section applies where the prosecutor recommences proceedings by complaint containing both—

(a) a charge to which proceedings—

(i) transferred to a court by authority of an order made [F4under section 137. A or 137. CA] of this Act; or

(ii) transferred to, or taken at, a court by authority of an order made [F5under 137. B or 137. CB] of this Act,

relate; and

(b) a charge to which previous proceedings at that court relate.

(2) Where this section applies, proceedings for an offence charged in that complaint are, for the purposes of—

(a) section 136 of this Act (so far as applying to the offence);

(b) any provision of any other enactment for a time limit within which proceedings are to be commenced (so far as applying to the offence); and

(c) any rule of law relating to delay in bringing proceedings (so far as applying to the offence), to be regarded as having been commenced when any previous proceedings for the offence were first commenced.]

Amendments (Textual)

F3 S. 136. A inserted (10.3.2008) by Criminal Proceedings etc. (Reform) (Scotland) Act 2007 (asp 6), ss. 23, 84 ; S.S.I. 2008/42, art. 3, Sch. (subject to arts. 4 - 6)

F4 Words in s. 136. A(1)(a)(i) substituted (28.3.2011) by Criminal Justice and Licensing (Scotland) Act 2010 (asp 13), s. 206. (1), sch. 7 para. 52. (a) ; S.S.I. 2011/178, art. 2, sch.

F5 Words in s. 136. A(1)(a)(ii) substituted (28.3.2011) by Criminal Justice and Licensing (Scotland) Act 2010 (asp 13), s. 206. (1), sch. 7 para. 52. (b) ; S.S.I. 2011/178, art. 2, sch.

[F6136. B Time limits where fixed penalty offer etc. made S

(1) For the purposes of section 136 of this Act, and any provision of any other enactment for a time limit within which proceedings are to be commenced, in calculating the period since a contravention occurred—

(a) where a fixed penalty offer is made under section 302. (1) of this Act, the period between the date of the offer and—

(i) the receipt by the procurator fiscal of a notice under section 302. (4) of this Act;

(ii) a recall of the fixed penalty by virtue of section 302. C of this Act, shall be disregarded;

(b) where a compensation offer is made under section 302. A(1) of this Act, the period between the date of the offer and—

(i) the receipt by the procurator fiscal of a notice under section 302. A(4) of this Act;

(ii) a recall of the offer by virtue of section 302. C of this Act,

shall be disregarded;

(c) where a work offer is made under section 303. ZA(1) of this Act, the period between the date of the offer and—

(i) if the alleged offender does not accept the offer in the manner described in section 303. ZA(5) of this Act, the last date for notice of acceptance of the offer;

(ii) if the alleged offender accepts the offer as so described, but fails to complete the subsequent work order, the date specified for completion of the order,

shall be disregarded.

(2) A certificate purporting to be signed by or on behalf of the prosecutor which states a period to be disregarded by virtue of subsection (1) above is sufficient authority for the period to be disregarded.]

Amendments (Textual)

F6 S. 136. B inserted (10.3.2008) by Criminal Proceedings etc. (Reform) (Scotland) Act 2007 (asp 6) , ss. 54 , 84 ; S.S.I. 2008/42 , art. 3 , Sch. (subject to art. 6)

137 Alteration of diets.S

(1) Where a diet has been fixed in a summary prosecution, it shall be competent for the court, on a joint application in writing by the parties or their solicitors, to discharge the diet and fix an earlier diet in lieu.

(2) Where the prosecutor and the accused make joint application to the court (orally or in writing) for postponement of a diet which has been fixed, the court shall discharge the diet and fix a later diet in lieu unless the court considers that it should not do so because there has been unnecessary delay on the part of one of more of the parties.

(3) Where all the parties join in an application under subsection (2) above, the court may proceed under that subsection without hearing the parties.

(4) Where the prosecutor has intimated to the accused that he desires to postpone or accelerate a diet which has been fixed, and the accused refuses, or any of the accused refuse, to make a joint application to the court for that purpose, the prosecutor may make an incidental application for that purpose under section 134 of this Act; and after giving the parties an opportunity to be heard, the court may discharge the diet and fix a later diet or, as the case may be, an earlier diet in lieu.

(5) Where an accused had intimated to the prosecutor and to all the other accused that he desires such postponement or acceleration and the prosecutor refuses, or any of the other accused refuse, to make a joint application to the court for that purpose, the accused who has so intimated may apply to the court for that purpose; and, after giving the parties an opportunity to be heard, the court may discharge the diet and fix a later diet or, as the case may be, an earlier diet in lieu.

[F7137. ZA[F8. Refixing diets: non-sitting days]S

(1) This section applies where in a summary prosecution any diet has been fixed for a non-sitting day.

(2) The court may at any time before the non-sitting day—

(a) discharge the diet; and

(b) fix a new diet for a date earlier or later than that for which the discharged diet was fixed.

(3) That is, by acting—

(a) of the court's own accord; and

(b) without the need for a hearing for the purpose.

(4) In the case of a trial diet—

    (a) the prosecutor;

    (b) the accused,

shall be entitled to an adjournment of the new diet fixed if the court is satisfied that it is not practicable for that party to proceed with the case on that date.

(5) The power of the court under subsection (1) above is not exercisable for the sole purpose of ensuring compliance with a time limit applying in the proceedings.

(6) In subsections (1) and (2) above, a "non-sitting day" is a day on which the court is under this Act not required to sit.]

Amendments (Textual)

F7 S. 137. ZA inserted (10.12.2007) by Criminal Proceedings etc. (Reform) (Scotland) Act 2007 (asp 6), ss. 39. (2), 84; S.S.I. 2007/479, art. 3. (1), Sch. (as amended by S.S. I. 2007/527)

F8. S. 137. ZA heading substituted (30.1.2012) by Act of Adjournal (Amendment of the Criminal Procedure (Scotland) Act 1995) (Refixing diets) 2011 (S.S.I. 2011/430), ss. 1. (2), 2. (5)

[F9137. ZBRefixing diets: non-suitable daysS

(1) Where in a summary prosecution any diet has been fixed for a day which is no longer suitable to the court it may, of its own accord, at any time before that diet—

    (a) discharge the diet; and

    (b) fix a new diet for a date earlier or later than that for which the discharged diet was fixed.

(2) Before proceeding as mentioned in subsection (1) the court shall give the parties an opportunity to be heard.]

Amendments (Textual)

F9. S. 137. ZB inserted (30.1.2012) by Act of Adjournal (Amendment of the Criminal Procedure (Scotland) Act 1995) (Refixing diets) 2011 (S.S.I. 2011/430), ss. 1. (2), 2. (4)

[F10137. ATransfer of sheriff court summary proceedings within sheriffdomS

(1) Where [F11this subsection applies,] the prosecutor may apply to the sheriff for an order for the transfer of the proceedings to a sheriff court in any other district in that sheriffdom and for adjournment to a diet of that court.

[F12. (1. A)Subsection (1) above applies—

    (a) where the accused person has been cited in summary proceedings to attend a diet of the court; or

    (b) if the accused person has not been cited to such a diet, where summary proceedings against the accused have been commenced in the court.]

(2) On an application under subsection (1) above the sheriff may make such order as is mentioned in that subsection.

Amendments (Textual)

F10 Ss. 137. A, 137. B inserted (27.6.2003) by Criminal Justice (Scotland) Act 2003 (asp 7) , ss. 58. (2) , 89 ; S.S.I. 2003/288 , art. 2 , Sch.

F11 Words in s. 137. A(1) substituted (10.3.2008) by Criminal Proceedings etc. (Reform) (Scotland) Act 2007 (asp 6) , ss. 22. (1)(a) , 84 ; S.S.I. 2008/42 , art. 3 , Sch. (subject to arts. 4 - 6)

F12 S. 137. A(1. A) inserted (10.3.2008) by Criminal Proceedings etc. (Reform) (Scotland) Act 2007 (asp 6) , ss. 22. (1)(b) , 84 ; S.S.I. 2008/42 , art. 3 , Sch. (subject to arts. 4 - 6)

137. BTransfer of sheriff court summary proceedings outwith sheriffdomS

[F13. (1)Where the sheriff clerk informs the prosecutor that, because of exceptional circumstances which could not reasonably have been foreseen, it is not practicable for the sheriff court or any other sheriff court in the sheriffdom to proceed with some or all of the summary cases due to call at a diet, the prosecutor shall as soon as practicable apply to the sheriff principal for an order for—

(a) the transfer of the proceedings to a sheriff court in another sheriffdom; and

(b) adjournment to a diet of that court.]

[F14. (1. A)Where this subsection applies, the prosecutor may apply to the sheriff for an order for—

(a) the transfer of the proceedings to a sheriff court in another sheriffdom; and

(b) adjournment to a diet of that court,

if there are also summary proceedings against the accused person in that court in the other sheriffdom.

(1. B)Subsection (1. A) above applies—

(a) where the accused person has been cited in summary proceedings to attend a diet of the court; or

(b) if the accused person has not been cited to such a diet, where summary proceedings against the accused have been commenced in the court.

(1. C)Where the prosecutor intends to take summary proceedings against an accused person in the sheriff court, the prosecutor may apply to the sheriff for an order for authority for the proceedings to be taken at a sheriff court in another sheriffdom if there are also summary proceedings against the accused person in that court in the other sheriffdom.]

(2) On an application under subsection (1) above the sheriff principal may make the order sought, provided that the sheriff principal of the other sheriffdom consents.

[F15. (2. A)On an application under subsection (1. A) or (1. C) above, the sheriff is to make the order sought if—

(a) the sheriff considers that it would be expedient for the different cases involved to be dealt with by the same court; and

(b) a sheriff of the other sheriffdom consents.]

(3) On the application of the prosecutor, a sheriff principal who has made an order under subsection (2) above may, if the sheriff principal of the other sheriffdom mentioned in that subsection consents—

(a) revoke; or

(b) vary so as to restrict the effect of,

that order.

[F16. (4)On the application of the prosecutor, [F17the sheriff who has made an order under subsection (2. A) above (or another sheriff of the same sheriffdom)] may, if a sheriff of the other sheriffdom mentioned in paragraph (b) of that subsection consents—

(a) revoke; or

(b) vary so as to restrict the effect of,

that order.]]

Amendments (Textual)

F10 Ss. 137. A, 137. B inserted (27.6.2003) by Criminal Justice (Scotland) Act 2003 (asp 7) , ss. 58. (2) , 89 ; S.S.I. 2003/288 , art. 2 , Sch.

F13 S. 137. B(1) substituted (10.3.2008) by Criminal Proceedings etc. (Reform) (Scotland) Act 2007 (asp 6) , ss. 22. (2)(a) , 84 ; S.S.I. 2008/42 , art. 3 , Sch.

F14 S. 137. B(1. A)-(1. C) inserted (10.3.2008) by Criminal Proceedings etc. (Reform) (Scotland) Act 2007 (asp 6) , ss. 22. (2)(b) , 84 ; S.S.I. 2008/42 , art. 3 , Sch.

F15 S. 137. B(2. A) inserted (10.3.2008) by Criminal Proceedings etc. (Reform) (Scotland) Act 2007 (asp 6) , ss. 22. (2)(c) , 84 ; S.S.I. 2008/42 , art. 3 , Sch.

F16 S. 137. B(4) added (10.3.2008) by Criminal Proceedings etc. (Reform) (Scotland) Act 2007 (asp 6) , ss. 22. (2)(d) , 84 ; S.S.I. 2008/42 , art. 3 , Sch.

F17 Words in s. 137. B(4) substituted (28.3.2011) by Criminal Justice and Licensing (Scotland) Act 2010 (asp 13) , s. 206. (1) , sch. 7 para. 53 ; S.S.I. 2011/178 , art. 2 , sch.

[F18137. CCustody cases: initiating proceedings outwith sheriffdomS

(1) Where the prosecutor believes—

(a) that, because of exceptional circumstances (and without an order under subsection (3) below), it is likely that there would be an unusually high number of accused persons appearing from custody for the first calling of cases in summary prosecutions in the sheriff courts in the sheriffdom; and

(b) that it would not be practicable for those courts to deal with all the cases involved,

the prosecutor may apply to the sheriff principal for the order referred to in subsection (2) below.

(2) For the purposes of subsection (1) above, the order is for authority for summary proceedings against some or all of the accused persons to be—

(a) taken at a sheriff court in another sheriffdom; and

(b) maintained—

(i) there; or

(ii) at any of the sheriff courts referred to in subsection (1) above as may at the first calling of the case be appointed for further proceedings.

(3) On an application under subsection (1) above, the sheriff principal may make the order sought with the consent of the sheriff principal of the other sheriffdom.

(4) An order under subsection (3) above may be made by reference to a particular period or particular circumstances.]

Amendments (Textual)

F18 Ss. 137. C, 137. D inserted (10.3.2008) by Criminal Proceedings etc. (Reform) (Scotland) Act 2007 (asp 6) , ss. 22. (3) , 84 ; S.S.I. 2008/42 , art. 3 , Sch. (subject to arts. 4 - 6)

[F19137. CATransfer of JP court proceedings within sheriffdomS

(1) Subsection (2) applies—

(a) where the accused person has been cited in summary proceedings to attend a diet of a JP court, or

(b) if the accused person has not been cited to such a diet, where summary proceedings against the accused have been commenced in a JP court.

(2) The prosecutor may apply to a justice for an order for the transfer of the proceedings to another JP court in the sheriffdom (and for adjournment to a diet of that court).

(3) On an application under subsection (2), the justice may make the order sought.

(4) In this section and sections 137. CB and 137. CC, " justice " does not include the sheriff.

Amendments (Textual)

F19 Ss. 137. CA-137. CC inserted (28.3.2011) by Criminal Justice and Licensing (Scotland) Act 2010 (asp 13) , ss. 61 , 206. (1) ; S.S.I. 2011/178 , art. 2 , sch.

137. CBTransfer of JP court proceedings outwith sheriffdomS

(1) Subsection (2) applies where the clerk of a JP court informs the prosecutor that, because of exceptional circumstances which could not reasonably have been foreseen, it is not practicable for the JP court or any other JP court in the sheriffdom to proceed with some or all of the summary cases due to call at a diet.

(2) The prosecutor shall as soon as practicable apply to the sheriff principal for an order for the transfer of the proceedings to a JP court in another sheriffdom (and for adjournment to a diet of that court).

(3) Subsection (4) applies where—

(a) either—

(i) the accused person has been cited in summary proceedings to attend a diet of a JP court, or

(ii) if the accused person has not been cited to such a diet, summary proceedings against the accused have been commenced in a JP court, and

(b) there are also summary proceedings against the accused person in a JP court in another sheriffdom.

(4) The prosecutor may apply to a justice for an order for the transfer of the proceedings to a JP court in the other sheriffdom (and for adjournment to a diet of that court).

(5) Subsection (6) applies where—

(a) the prosecutor intends to take summary proceedings against an accused person in a JP court, and

(b) there are also summary proceedings against the accused person in a JP court in another sheriffdom.

(6) The prosecutor may apply to a justice for an order for authority for the proceedings to be taken at a JP court in the other sheriffdom.

(7) On an application under subsection (2), the sheriff principal may make the order sought with the consent of the sheriff principal of the other sheriffdom.

(8) On an application under subsection (4) or (6), the justice is to make the order sought if—

(a) the justice considers that it would be expedient for the different cases involved to be dealt with by the same court, and

(b) a justice of the other sheriffdom consents.

(9) On the application of the prosecutor, the sheriff principal who has made an order under subsection (7) may, with the consent of the sheriff principal of the other sheriffdom—

(a) revoke the order, or

(b) vary it so as to restrict its effect.

(10) On the application of the prosecutor, the justice who has made an order under subsection (8) (or another justice of the same sheriffdom) may, with the consent of a justice of the other sheriffdom—

(a) revoke the order, or

(b) vary it so as to restrict its effect.

Amendments (Textual)

F19 Ss. 137. CA-137. CC inserted (28.3.2011) by Criminal Justice and Licensing (Scotland) Act 2010 (asp 13) , ss. 61 , 206. (1) ; S.S.I. 2011/178 , art. 2 , sch.

137. CCCustody cases: initiating JP court proceedings outwith sheriffdomS

(1) Subsection (2) applies where the prosecutor believes—

(a) that, because of exceptional circumstances (and without an order under subsection (3)), it is likely that there would be an unusually high number of accused persons appearing from custody for the first calling of cases in summary prosecutions in the JP courts in the sheriffdom, and

(b) that it would not be practicable for those courts to deal with all the cases involved.

(2) The prosecutor may apply to the sheriff principal for an order authorising summary proceedings against some or all of the accused persons to be—

(a) taken at a JP court in another sheriffdom, and

(b) maintained—

(i) at that JP court, or

(ii) at any of the JP courts referred to in subsection (1) as may at the first calling of the case be appointed for further proceedings.

(3) On an application under subsection (2), the sheriff principal may make the order sought with the consent of the sheriff principal of the other sheriffdom.

(4) An order under subsection (3) may be made by reference to a particular period or particular

circumstances.]
Amendments (Textual)
F19 Ss. 137. CA-137. CC inserted (28.3.2011) by Criminal Justice and Licensing (Scotland) Act 2010 (asp 13) , ss. 61 , 206. (1) ; S.S.I. 2011/178 , art. 2 , sch.

[F18137. DTransfer of JP court proceedings to the sheriff courtS

(1) Where an accused person is due to be sentenced at a sheriff court for an offence, the prosecutor may apply to the sheriff for an order for—

(a)the transfer to the sheriff court of any case against the accused in respect of which sentencing is pending at any JP court in the sheriffdom; and

(b) the case to call at a diet of the sheriff court.

(2) On an application under subsection (1) above, the sheriff is to make the order sought if the sheriff considers that it would be expedient for the different cases to be disposed of at the same court at the same time.

(3) If, in a case transferred under subsection (1) above, the finding of guilt was before a justice of the peace, the sentencing powers of the sheriff in the case are restricted to those of the justice.]
Modifications etc. (not altering text)
C95 S. 137. D(1)(a) applied (10.12.2007) by The District Courts and Justices of the Peace (Scotland) Order 2007 (S.S.I. 2007/480) , art. 4. (1)(b)

ComplaintsS

138 Complaints.S

(1) All proceedings under this Part of this Act for the trial of offences or recovery of penalties shall be instituted by complaint signed by the prosecutor or by a solicitor on behalf of a prosecutor other than the procurator fiscal.

(2) The complaint shall be in the form—

(a) set out in Schedule 5 to this Act; or

(b) prescribed by Act of Adjournal,

or as nearly as may be in such form.

(3) A solicitor may appear for and conduct any prosecution on behalf of a prosecutor other than the procurator fiscal.

(4) Schedule 3 to this Act shall have effect as regards complaints under this Act.

139 Complaints: orders and warrants.S

(1) On any complaint under this Part of this Act being laid before a judge of the court in which the complaint is brought, he shall have power on the motion of the prosecutor—

(a) to pronounce an order assigning a diet for the disposal of the case to which the accused may be cited as mentioned in section 141 of this Act;

(b) to grant warrant to apprehend the accused where this appears to the judge expedient;

(c) to grant warrant to search the person, dwelling-house and repositories of the accused and any place where he may be found for any documents, articles, or property likely to afford evidence of his guilt of, or guilty participation in, any offence charged in the complaint, and to take possession of such documents, articles or property;

(d) to grant any other order or warrant of court or warrant which may be competent in the circumstances.

(2) The power of a judge under subsection (1) above—

(a) to pronounce an order assigning a diet for the disposal of the case may be exercised on his behalf by the clerk of court;

(b) to grant a warrant to apprehend the accused shall be exercisable notwithstanding that there is power whether at common law or under any Act to apprehend him without a warrant.

CitationS

140 Citation.S

(1) This Act shall be a sufficient warrant for [F20—

(a) F21. . . . .

(b)]the citation of the accused and witnesses in a summary prosecution to any ordinary sitting of the court or to any special diet fixed by the court or any adjournment thereof.

(2) [F22. Without prejudice to section 141. (2. A) of this Act,]such citation shall be in the form prescribed by Act of Adjournal or as nearly as may be in such form and shall, in the case of the accused, proceed on an induciae of at least 48 hours unless in the special circumstances of the case the court fixes a shorter induciae.

[F23. (2. A)Where the charge in the complaint in respect of which an accused is cited is of committing a sexual offence to which section 288. C of this Act applies, the citation shall include or be accompanied by notice to the accused—

[F24. (a)that his case at, or for the purposes of, any relevant hearing (within the meaning of section 288. C(1. A)) in the course of the proceedings (including at any commissioner proceedings) may be conducted only by a lawyer,]

(b) that it is, therefore, in his interests, if he has not already done so, to get the professional assistance of a solicitor; and

(c) that, if he does not engage a solicitor for the purposes of [F25the conduct of his case at, or for the purposes of, the hearing] [F26. (or at any related commissioner proceedings)] , the court will do so.

(2. B)A failure to comply with subsection (2. A) above does not affect the validity or lawfulness of any such citation or any other element of the proceedings against the accused.]

[F27. (2. C) In subsection (2. A) above, " commissioner proceedings " means proceedings before a commissioner appointed under section 271. I(1) or by virtue of section 272. (1)(b) of this Act.]

F28. (3). . . . .

Amendments (Textual)

F20. S. 140. (1)(a) and "(b)" inserted (1.8.1997) by 1997 c. 48, s. 57. (2)(a); S.I. 1997/1712, art. 3, Sch. (subject to arts. 4, 5)

F21. S. 140. (1)(a) repealed (4.10.2004) by Criminal Procedure (Amendment) (Scotland) Act 2004 (asp 5), ss. 25, 27. (1), Sch. para. 33; S.S.I. 2004/405, art. 2, Sch. 1 (with savings in arts. 3-5)

F22. Words in s. 140. (2) inserted (27.6.2003) by Criminal Justice (Scotland) Act 2003 (asp 7), ss. 61. (2), 89; S.S.I. 2003/288, art. 2, Sch.

F23. S. 140. (2. A)(2. B) inserted (1.11.2002) by Sexual Offences (Procedure and Evidence) (Scotland) Act 2002 (asp 9), s. 3, Sch. para. 8; S.S.I. 2002/443, art. 3

F24. S. 140. (2. A)(a) substituted (28.3.2011) by Criminal Justice and Licensing (Scotland) Act 2010 (asp 13), s. 206. (1), sch. 7 para. 54. (a); S.S.I. 2011/178, art. 2, sch.

F25. Words in s. 140. (2. A)(c) substituted (28.3.2011) by Criminal Justice and Licensing (Scotland) Act 2010 (asp 13), s. 206. (1), sch. 7 para. 54. (b); S.S.I. 2011/178, art. 2, sch.

F26. Words in s. 140. (2. A)(c) inserted (23.4.2007) by Criminal Proceedings etc. (Reform) (Scotland) Act 2007 (asp 6), ss. 35. (2)(a)(ii), 84; S.S.I. 2007/250, art. 3. (a)

F27. S. 140. (2. C) added (23.4.2007) by Criminal Proceedings etc. (Reform) (Scotland) Act 2007 (asp 6), ss. 35. (2)(b), 84; S.S.I. 2007/250, art. 3. (a)

F28. S. 140. (3) repealed (1.8.1997) by 1997 c. 48, ss. 57. (2)(b), 62. (2), Sch. 3; S.I. 1997/1712,

141 Manner of citation.S

[F29. (1)The citation of the accused or a witness in a summary prosecution to any ordinary sitting of the court or to any special diet fixed by the court or to any adjourned sitting or diet shall be effected by an officer of law or other person—

(a) delivering the citation to him personally; or

(b) leaving it for him—

(i) at his dwelling-house or place of business with a resident or (as the case may be) employee there; or

(ii) where he has no known dwelling-house or place of business, at any other place in which he may be resident at the time.]

(2) Notwithstanding subsection (1) above, citation may also be effected—

(a) where the accused or witness is the master of, or a seaman or person employed in a vessel, if the citation is left with a person on board the vessel and connected with it;

(b) where the accused is [F30an organisation other than a body of trustees] [F31or a partnership prosecuted by virtue of section 1 of the Partnerships (Prosecution) (Scotland) Act 2013]—

(i) if the citation is left at its ordinary place of business with a partner, director, secretary or other official; or

(ii) if it is cited in the same manner as if the proceedings were in a civil court; F32...

(c) where the accused is a body of trustees, if the citation is left with any one of them who is resident in Scotland or with their known solicitor in Scotland [F33or

(d) where the accused is a partnership prosecuted by virtue of section 1 of the Partnerships (Prosecution) (Scotland) Act 2013, if the citation is left with any one of the partners who is resident in Scotland;]

[F34; and in sub-paragraph (b)(i) of this subsection references to the director or secretary or other official, in relation to a limited liability partnership, are to any member of the limited liability partnership]

[F35. (2. A)Notwithstanding subsection (1) above and section 140. (2) of this Act, citation of the accused may also be effected by an officer of law affixing to the door of the accused's dwelling-house or place of business a notice in such form as may be prescribed by Act of Adjournal, or as nearly as may be in such form—

(a) specifying the date on which it was so affixed;

(b) informing the accused that he may collect a copy of the complaint from a police station specified in the notice; and

(c) calling upon him to appear and answer the complaint at such diet as shall be so specified.

(2. B)Where the citation of the accused is effected by notice under subsection (2. A) above, the induciae shall be reckoned from the date specified by virtue of paragraph (a) of that subsection.]

(3) Subject to subsection (4) below [F36and without prejudice to the effect of any other manner of citation], the citation of the accused or a witness to a sitting or diet or adjourned sitting or diet as mentioned in subsection (1) above shall be effective if it is F37. . .—

(a) in the case of the accused, [F38signed by the prosecutor and] sent by post in a registered envelope or through the recorded delivery service [F39or by ordinary post]; and

(b) in the case of a witness, sent [F38by or on behalf of the prosecutor] by ordinary post, to the dwelling-house or place of business of the accused or witness or, if he has no known dwelling-house or place of business, to any other place in which he may be resident at the time.

[F40. (3. A)Subject to subsection (4) below and without prejudice to the effect of any other manner of citation, the citation of the accused or a witness to a sitting or diet or adjourned sitting or diet as mentioned in subsection (1) above shall also be effective if an electronic citation is sent—

(a) by or on behalf of the prosecutor; and

(b) by means of electronic communication,

to the home or business email address of the person.]

(4) Where the accused fails to appear at a diet or sitting or adjourned diet or sitting to which he has been cited in the manner provided by this section, [F41sections 143. (7), 150. (3) and 150. A(1)] of this Act shall not apply unless it is proved to the court that he received the citation or that its contents came to his knowledge.

(5) The production in court of any letter or other communication [F42. (including a legible version of an electronic communication)] purporting to be written by or on behalf of an accused who has been cited as mentioned in subsection [F43. (2. A) or] (3) above in such terms as to infer that the contents of such citation came to his knowledge, shall be admissible as evidence of that fact for the purposes of subsection (4) above.

[F44. (5. ZA)The production in court of a legible version of an electronic communication which—

(a) bears to have come from an accused's email address; and

(b) is in such terms as to infer that the contents of an electronic citation sent as mentioned in subsection (3. A) above came to the accused's knowledge,

shall (even if not purporting to be written by or on behalf of the accused) be admissible as evidence of those facts for the purposes of subsection (4) above.]

[F45. (5. A)The citation of a witness to a sitting or diet or adjourned sitting or diet as mentioned in subsection (1) above shall be effective [F46 if—

(a) it is sent by or on behalf of the accused's solicitor by ordinary post—

(i) to the dwelling-house or place of business of the witness; or

(ii) if he has no known dwelling-house or place of business, to any other place in which he may be resident at the time; or

(b) an electronic citation is sent by or on behalf of the accused's solicitor by means of electronic communication to the home or business email address of the witness.]]

[F47. (5. B)Where a witness fails to appear at a diet or sitting or adjourned diet or sitting to which he has been cited in the manner provided by this section, subsection (2) of section 156 of this Act shall not apply unless it is proved to the court that he received the citation or that its contents came to his knowledge.]

(6) When the citation of any person is effected by post in terms of this section or any other provision of this Act to which this section is applied, the induciae shall be reckoned from 24 hours after the time of posting.

[F48. (6. A)When the citation of any person is effected by electronic citation under subsection (3. A) above, the induciae shall be reckoned from the end of the day on which the citation was sent.]

(7) It shall be sufficient evidence that

[F49. (a)]a citation has been sent by post in terms of this section or any other provision of this Act mentioned in subsection (6) above, if there is produced in court a written execution, signed by the person who signed the citation in the form prescribed by Act of Adjournal, or as nearly as may be in such form, together with the post office receipt for the relative registered or recorded delivery letter[F50; or]

[F51. (b)citation has been effected by notice under subsection (2. A) above, if there is produced in court a written execution, in such form as may be prescribed by Act of Adjournal, or as nearly as may be in such form, signed by the officer of law who affixed the notice.]

[F52. (7. A)It shall be sufficient evidence that citation has been effected electronically under subsection (3. A) or (5. A)(b) above if there is produced in court a legible version of an electronic communication which—

(a) is signed by electronic signature by the person who signed the citation;

(b) includes the citation; and

(c) bears to have been sent to the home or business email address of the person being cited.

(7. B)In this section, an "electronic citation" is a citation in electronic form which—

(a) is capable of being kept in legible form; and

(b) is signed by electronic signature—

(i) in the case of citation of the accused, by the prosecutor;

(ii) in the case of citation of a witness, by or on behalf of the prosecutor or the accused's solicitor.]

Amendments (Textual)

F29. S. 141. (1) substituted (10.12.2007) by Criminal Proceedings etc. (Reform) (Scotland) Act 2007 (asp 6), ss. 8. (a), 84; S.S.I. 2007/479, art. 3. (1), Sch. (as amended by S.S. I. 2007/527)

F30. Words in s. 141. (2)(b) substituted (28.3.2011) by Criminal Justice and Licensing (Scotland) Act 2010 (asp 13), ss. 68, 206. (1); S.S.I. 2011/178, art. 2, sch.

F31. Words in s. 141. (2)(b) inserted (26.4.2013) by Partnerships (Prosecution) (Scotland) Act 2013 (c. 21), ss. 6. (5)(a), 8. (2) (with s. 8. (3)(4))

F32. Word in s. 141. (2) omitted (26.4.2013) by virtue of Partnerships (Prosecution) (Scotland) Act 2013 (c. 21), ss. 6. (5)(b), 8. (2) (with s. 8. (3)(4))

F33. S. 141. (2)(d) and word inserted (26.4.2013) by Partnerships (Prosecution) (Scotland) Act 2013 (c. 21), ss. 6. (5)(c), 8. (2) (with s. 8. (3)(4))

F34. Words in s. 141. (2) inserted (6.4.2001) by S.S.I. 2001/128, reg. 5, Sch. 4 para. 2

F35. S. 141. (2. A)(2. B) inserted (27.6.2003) by Criminal Justice (Scotland) Act 2003 (asp 7), ss. 61. (3)(a), 89; S.S.I. 2003/288, art. 2, Sch.

F36. Words in s. 141. (3) inserted (27.6.2003) by Criminal Justice (Scotland) Act 2003 (asp 7), ss. 61. (3)(b), 89; S.S.I. 2003/288, art. 2, Sch.

F37. Words in s. 141. (3) repealed (1.8.1997) by 1997 c. 48, s. 62. (1)(2), Sch. 1 para. 21. (19)(a)(i), Sch. 3; S.I. 1997/1712, art. 3, Sch. (subject to arts. 4, 5)

F38. Words in s. 141. (3)(a)(b) inserted (1.8.1997) by 1997 c. 48, s. 62. (1), Sch. 1 para. 21. (19)(a)(ii)(iii); S.I. 1997/1712, art. 3, Sch. (subject to arts. 4, 5)

F39. Words in s. 141. (3)(a) inserted (10.12.2007) by Criminal Proceedings etc. (Reform) (Scotland) Act 2007 (asp 6), ss. 8. (b), 84; S.S.I. 2007/479, art. 3. (1), Sch. (as amended by S.S. I. 2007/527)

F40. S. 141. (3. A) inserted (10.12.2007) by Criminal Proceedings etc. (Reform) (Scotland) Act 2007 (asp 6), ss. 8. (c), 84; S.S.I. 2007/479, art. 3. (1), Sch. (as amended by S.S. I. 2007/527)

F41. Words in s. 141. (4) substituted (10.12.2007) by Criminal Proceedings etc. (Reform) (Scotland) Act 2007 (asp 6), ss. 14. (1), 84; S.S.I. 2007/479, art. 3. (1), Sch. (as amended by S.S. I. 2007/527)

F42. Words in s. 141. (5) substituted (10.12.2007) by Criminal Proceedings etc. (Reform) (Scotland) Act 2007 (asp 6), ss. 8. (d), 84; S.S.I. 2007/479, art. 3. (1), Sch. (as amended by S.S. I. 2007/527)

F43. Words in s. 141. (5) inserted (27.6.2003) by Criminal Justice (Scotland) Act 2003 (asp 7), ss. 61. (3)(c), 89; S.S.I. 2003/288, art. 2, Sch.

F44. S. 141. (5. ZA) inserted (10.12.2007) by Criminal Proceedings etc. (Reform) (Scotland) Act 2007 (asp 6), ss. 8. (e), 84; S.S.I. 2007/479, art. 3. (1), Sch. (as amended by S.S. I. 2007/527)

F45. S. 141. (5. A) inserted (1.8.1997) by 1997 c. 48, s. 62. (1), Sch. 1 para. 21. (19)(b); S.I. 1997/1712, art. 3, Sch. (subject to arts. 4, 5)

F46. Words in s. 141. (5. A) substituted (10.12.2007) by Criminal Proceedings etc. (Reform) (Scotland) Act 2007 (asp 6), ss. 8. (f), 84; S.S.I. 2007/479, art. 3. (1), Sch.

F47. S. 141. (5. B) inserted (10.12.2007) by Criminal Proceedings etc. (Reform) (Scotland) Act 2007 (asp 6), ss. 8. (g), 84; S.S.I. 2007/479, art. 3. (1), Sch. (as amended by S.S. I. 2007/527)

F48. S. 141. (6. A) inserted (10.12.2007) by Criminal Proceedings etc. (Reform) (Scotland) Act 2007 (asp 6), ss. 8. (h), 84; S.S.I. 2007/479, art. 3. (1), Sch. (as amended by S.S. I. 2007/527)

F49. Words in s. 141. (7) renumbered as s. 141. (7)(a) (27.6.2003) by virtue of Criminal Justice (Scotland) Act 2003 (asp 7), ss. 61. (3)(d)(i), 89; S.S.I. 2003/288, art. 2, Sch.

F50. Word in s. 141. (7) added (27.6.2003) by Criminal Justice (Scotland) Act 2003 (asp 7), ss. 61. (3)(d)(ii), 89; S.S.I. 2003/288, art. 2, Sch.

F51. S. 141. (7)(b) added (27.6.2003) by Criminal Justice (Scotland) Act 2003 (asp 7), ss. 61. (3)(d)(ii), 89; S.S.I. 2003/288, art. 2, Sch.

F52. S. 141. (7. A)(7. B) added (10.12.2007) by Criminal Proceedings etc. (Reform) (Scotland) Act 2007 (asp 6), ss. 8. (i), 84; S.S.I. 2007/479, art. 3. (1), Sch. (as amended by S.S. I. 2007/527)

Modifications etc. (not altering text)

ChildrenS

142 Summary proceedings against children.S

(1) Where summary proceedings are brought in respect of an offence alleged to have been committed by a child, the sheriff shall sit either in a different building or room from that in which he usually sits or on different days from those on which other courts in the building are engaged in criminal proceedings: and no person shall be present at any sitting for the purposes of such proceedings except—
    (a) members and officers of the court;
    (b) parties to the case before the court, their solicitors and counsel, and witnesses and other persons directly concerned in that case;
    (c) bona fide representatives of news gathering or reporting organisations present for the purpose of the preparation of contemporaneous reports of the proceedings;
    (d) such other persons as the court may specially authorise to be present.
(2) A sheriff sitting summarily for the purpose of hearing a charge against, or an application relating to, a person who is believed to be a child may, if he thinks fit to do so, proceed with the hearing and determination of the charge or application, notwithstanding that it is discovered that the person in question is not a child.
(3) When a sheriff sitting summarily has remanded a child for information to be obtained with respect to him, any sheriff sitting summarily in the same place—
    (a) may in his absence extend the period for which he is remanded provided that he appears before a sheriff or a justice at least once every 21 days;
    (b) when the required information has been obtained, may deal with him finally,
and where the sheriff by whom he was originally remanded has recorded a finding that he is guilty of an offence charged against him it shall not be necessary for any court which subsequently deals with him under this subsection to hear evidence as to the commission of that offence, except in so far as it may consider that such evidence will assist the court in determining the manner in which he should be dealt with.
(4) Any direction in any enactment that a charge shall be brought before a juvenile court shall be construed as a direction that he shall be brought before the sheriff sitting as a court of summary jurisdiction, and no such direction shall be construed as restricting the powers of any justice or justices to entertain an application for bail or for a remand, and to hear such evidence as may be necessary for that purpose.
(5) This section does not apply to summary proceedings before the sheriff in respect of an offence where a child has been charged jointly with a person who is not a child.

CompaniesS

143 Prosecution of companies, etc.S

(1) Without prejudice to any other or wider powers conferred by statute, this section shall apply in relation to the prosecution by summary procedure of [F53an organisation].
(2) Proceedings may be taken against the [F54organisation in its] corporate capacity, and in that event any penalty imposed shall be recovered by civil diligence in accordance with section 221 of this Act.

(3) Proceedings may be taken against an individual representative of a partnership, association or body corporate as follows:—

(a) in the case of a partnership or firm, any one of the partners, or the manager or the person in charge or locally in charge of its affairs;

(b) in the case of an association or body corporate, the managing director or the secretary or other person in charge, or locally in charge, of its affairs,

may be dealt with as if he was the person offending, and the offence shall be deemed to be the offence of the partnership, association or body corporate [F55; and in paragraph 3. (b) of this subsection references to the managing director or the secretary, in relation to a limited liability partnership, are to any member of the limited liability partnership].

[F56. (4)[F57. An organisation] may, for the purpose of—

(a) stating objections to the competency or relevancy of the complaint or proceedings;

(b) tendering a plea of guilty or not guilty;

(c) making a statement in mitigation of sentence,

appear by a representative.

(5) In subsection (4) above, " representative " means—

(a) an individual representative as mentioned in subsection (3) above; or

(b) an employee [F58, officer or official of the organisation] duly appointed by it for the purpose of the proceedings.

(6) For the purposes of subsection (5)(b) above, a statement—

(a) in the case of a body corporate (other than a limited liability partnership), purporting to be signed by an officer of the body;

(b) in the case of a limited liability partnership, purporting to be signed by a member of the partnership;

(c) in the case of a partnership (other than a limited liability partnership), purporting to be signed by a partner of the partnership;

(d) in the case of an association, purporting to be signed by an officer of the association,

[F59. (e)in the case of a government department or part of the Scottish Administration, purporting to be signed by a senior officer in the department or part,]

to the effect that the person named in the statement has been appointed as the representative for the purposes of any proceedings to which this section applies is sufficient evidence of such appointment.

(7) Where at a diet (apart from a diet fixed for the first calling of the case) [F60an organisation] does not appear as mentioned in subsection (4) above, or by counsel or a solicitor, the court may—

(a) on the motion of the prosecutor or, in relation to sentencing, of its own accord; and

(b) if satisfied as to the matters specified in subsection (8) below,

proceed to hear and dispose of the case in the absence of the [F61organisation].

(8) The matters referred to in subsection (7)(b) above are—

(a) that citation has been effected or other intimation of the diet has been received; and

(b) that it is in the interests of justice to proceed as mentioned in subsection (7) above.

(9) The reference in subsection (7) above to proceeding to hear and dispose of the case includes, in relation to a trial diet, proceeding with the trial.]

Amendments (Textual)

F53. Words in s. 143. (1) substituted (28.3.2011) by Criminal Justice and Licensing (Scotland) Act 2010 (asp 13), ss. 67. (2), 206. (1); S.S.I. 2011/178, art. 2, sch.

F54. Words in s. 143. (2) substituted (28.3.2011) by Criminal Justice and Licensing (Scotland) Act 2010 (asp 13), ss. 67. (3), 206. (1); S.S.I. 2011/178, art. 2, sch.

F55. Words in s. 143. (3) inserted (6.4.2001) by S.S.I. 2001/128, reg. 5, Sch. 4 para. 3

F56. S. 143. (4)-(9) added (10.3.2008) by Criminal Proceedings etc. (Reform) (Scotland) Act 2007 (asp 6), ss. 17, 84; S.S.I. 2008/42, art. 3, Sch.

F57. Words in s. 143. (4) substituted (28.3.2011) by Criminal Justice and Licensing (Scotland) Act 2010 (asp 13), ss. 67. (4), 206. (1); S.S.I. 2011/178, art. 2, sch.

F58. Words in s. 143. (5)(b) substituted (28.3.2011) by Criminal Justice and Licensing (Scotland)

Act 2010 (asp 13), ss. 67. (5), 206. (1); S.S.I. 2011/178, art. 2, sch.

F59. S. 143. (6)(e) inserted (28.3.2011) by Criminal Justice and Licensing (Scotland) Act 2010 (asp 13), ss. 67. (6), 206. (1); S.S.I. 2011/178, art. 2, sch.

F60. Words in s. 143. (7) substituted (28.3.2011) by Criminal Justice and Licensing (Scotland) Act 2010 (asp 13), ss. 67. (7)(a), 206. (1); S.S.I. 2011/178, art. 2, sch.

F61. Word in s. 143. (7) substituted (28.3.2011) by Criminal Justice and Licensing (Scotland) Act 2010 (asp 13), ss. 67. (7)(b), 206. (1); S.S.I. 2011/178, art. 2, sch.

Modifications etc. (not altering text)

C97. S. 143 applied (31.5.2002) by Anti-terrorism, Crime and Security Act 2001 (c. 24), s. 69. (4)(b); S.I. 2002/1279, art. 2

S. 143 applied (1.4.2005) by Gangmasters (Licensing) Act 2004 (c. 11), ss. 21, 29; S.I. 2005/447, arts. 1, 2

S. 143 applied (1.4.2005) by Gangmasters (Licensing) Act 2004 (c. 11), ss. 22, 29; S.I. 2005/447, arts. 1, 2

S. 143 applied (20.1.2007, 6.4.2007, 1.10.2007, 6.4.2008, 1.10.2008 for certain purposes and 1.10.2009 otherwise) by Companies Act 2006 (c. 46), ss. 1130. (2)(b)(ii), 1300 (with savings in s. 1133); S.I. 2006/3428, art. 3. (2) (with art. 6); S.I. 2007/1093, art. 2. (2)(c) (with arts. 4, 11); S.I. 2007/2194, art. 2. (1)(l)(3)(h) (with art. 12); S.I. 2007/3495, arts. {3. (3)(g)},{5. (3)(a)} (with arts. 7, 12); S.I. 2008/2860, art. 3. (s) (with arts. 5,7,8, Sch. 2) (as amended by S.I. 2009/1802, art. 18, S.I. 2009/2476, reg. 2)

C98. S. 143 applied (6.4.2008) by Serious Crime Act 2007 (c. 27), ss. 31. (6)(b)(ii), 94; S.I. 2008/755, art. 15. (1) (subject to paras. (2)(3))

S. 143 applied (6.4.2008) by Serious Crime Act 2007 (c. 27), ss. 32. (5)(b)(ii), 94; S.I. 2008/755, art. 15. (1) (subject to paras. (2)(3))

C99. S. 143 applied (1.1.2010) by The Common Agricultural Policy Single Payment and Support Schemes (Integrated Administration and Control System) Regulations 2009 (S.I. 2009/3263), reg. 12. (2)(b)(ii)

C100. S. 143 applied (6.4.2010) by The Detergents Regulations 2010 (S.I. 2010/740), reg. 24. (2)(b)(ii)

C101. S. 143 applied (with modifications) (30.12.2011) by The Wine Regulations 2011 (S.I. 2011/2936), regs. 1. (2), 16. (2)(c) (with reg. 3. (9))

C102. S. 143 applied (1.2.2007 for W. for specified purposes, 2.4.2007 for W. for specified purposes, 1.7.2007 for E. for specified purposes, 22.4.2008 for E.W.S. for specified purposes, 13.12.2008 for W. for specified purposes, 1.8.2012 for N.I. for specified purposes) by Health Act 2006 (c. 28), ss. 77. (4)(b), 83. (4)(a)(6)(b)(7); S.I. 2007/204, arts. 2. (c), 3. (c); S.I. 2007/1375, art. 2. (b); S.I. 2008/1147, art. 3. (b)(c); S.I. 2008/3171, art. 2. (b); S.R. 2012/307, art. 2. (b)

C103. S. 143 applied (with modifications) (1.3.2014) by The Olive Oil (Marketing Standards) Regulations 2014 (S.I. 2014/195), regs. 1, 15. (2)(c)

C104. S. 143 applied (12.12.2014) by The Immigration Act 2014 (Bank Accounts) Regulations 2014 (S.I. 2014/3085), regs. 1, 23. (4)(b)

C105. S. 143 applied (with modifications) (16.11.2015) by The Single Common Market Organisation (Emergency Aid for Milk Producers) Regulations 2015 (S.I. 2015/1896), regs. 1. (2), 13. (2)(c)

C106. S. 143 applied (1.1.2016) by The Small and Medium Sized Business (Finance Platforms) Regulations 2015 (S.I. 2015/1946), regs. 1. (2), 35. (4)(b)

C107. S. 143 applied (1.1.2016) by The Small and Medium Sized Business (Credit Information) Regulations 2015 (S.I. 2015/1945), regs. 1. (2), 38. (4)(b)

C108. S. 143 applied (13.7.2016) by The Financial Services and Markets Act 2000 (Transparency of Securities Financing Transactions and of Reuse) Regulations 2016 (S.I. 2016/715), regs. 1. (2), 27. (4)(b)

C109. S. 143 applied (25.11.2016) by Immigration Act 2016 (c. 19), ss. 29. (4)(b)(ii), 94. (1); S.I. 2016/1037, reg. 4. (c)

C110. S. 143 applied (25.11.2016) by Immigration Act 2016 (c. 19), ss. 30. (3)(b)(ii), 94. (1); S.I.

First dietS

144 Procedure at first diet.S

(1) Where the accused is present at the first calling of the case in a summary prosecution and—

(a) the complaint has been served on him, or

(b) the complaint or the substance thereof has been read to him, or

(c) he has legal assistance in his defence,

he shall, unless the court adjourns the case under the section 145 [F62or 145. ZA] of this Act and subject to subsection (4) below, be asked to plead to the charge.

(2) Where the accused is not present at a calling of the case in a summary prosecution and either—

(a) the prosecutor produces to the court written intimation that the accused pleads not guilty or pleads guilty F63. . .

(b) counsel or a solicitor, or a person not being counsel or a solicitor who satisfies the court that he is authorised by the accused, appears on behalf of the accused and tenders a plea of not guilty or a plea of guilty,

subsection (3) below shall apply.

(3) Where this subsection applies—

(a) in the case of a plea of not guilty, this Part of this Act except section 146. (2) shall apply in like manner as if the accused had appeared and tendered the plea; and

(b) in the case of a plea of guilty, the court may, if the prosecutor accepts the plea, proceed to hear and dispose of the case in the absence of the accused in like manner as if he had appeared and pled guilty, or may, if it thinks fit, continue the case to another diet and require the attendance of the accused with a view to pronouncing sentence in his presence.

[F64. (3. ZA)Where the prosecutor is not satisfied, in relation to a written intimation of a plea—

(a) that the intimation of the plea has been made or authorised by the accused; or

(b) that the terms of the plea are clear,

the court may continue the case to another diet.

(3. ZB)The clerk of court may perform the functions of the court under—

(a) subsections (2) and (3) above in relation to a plea of not guilty;

(b) subsection (3. ZA) above,

without the court being properly constituted.]

[F65. (3. A)Where an accused charged with a sexual offence to which section 288. C of this Act applies is present, whether or not with a solicitor, at a calling of the case in a summary prosecution, he shall be told—

[F66. (a)that his case at, or for the purposes of, any relevant hearing (within the meaning of section 288. C(1. A)) in the course of the proceedings may be conducted only by a lawyer,]

(b) that it is, therefore, in his interests, if he has not already done so, to get the professional assistance of a solicitor; and

(c) that if he does not engage a solicitor for the purposes of [F67the conduct of his case at, or for the purposes of, the hearing], the court will do so.

(3. B)A failure to comply with subsection (3. A) above does not affect the validity or lawfulness of anything done at the calling of the case or any other element of the proceedings against the accused.]

(4) Any objection to the competency or relevancy of a summary complaint or the proceedings thereon, or any denial that the accused is the person charged by the police with the offence shall be stated before the accused pleads to the charge or any plea is tendered on his behalf.

(5) No objection or denial such as is mentioned in subsection (4) above shall be allowed to be stated or issued at any future diet in the case except with the leave of the court, which may be

granted only on cause shown.

(6) Where in pursuance of subsection (3)(b) above the court proceeds to hear and dispose of a case in the absence of the accused, it shall not pronounce a sentence of imprisonment or of detention in a young offenders institution, remand centre or other establishment.

(7) In this section a reference to a plea of guilty shall include a reference to a plea of guilty to only part of the charge, but where a plea of guilty to only part of a charge is not accepted by the prosecutor it shall be deemed to be a plea of not guilty.

(8) It shall not be competent for any person appearing to answer a complaint, or for counsel or a solicitor appearing for the accused in his absence, to plead want of due citation or informality therein or in the execution thereof.

(9) In this section, a reference to the first calling of a case includes a reference to any adjourned diet fixed by virtue of section 145 [F68, 145. ZA][F69or 145. A] of this Act.

Amendments (Textual)

F62. Words in s. 144. (1) inserted (30.6.2007) by Adult Support and Protection (Scotland) Act 2007 (asp 10), ss. 75. (a)(i), 79; S.S.I. 2007/334, art. 2. (a), Sch. 1

F63. Words in s. 144. (2)(a) repealed (10.12.2007) by Criminal Proceedings etc. (Reform) (Scotland) Act 2007 (asp 6), ss. 9. (1)(a), 84; S.S.I. 2007/479, art. 3. (1), Sch. (as amended by S.S. I. 2007/527)

F64. S. 144. (3. ZA)(3. ZB) inserted (10.12.2007) by Criminal Proceedings etc. (Reform) (Scotland) Act 2007 (asp 6), ss. 9. (1)(b), 84; S.S.I. 2007/479, art. 3. (1), Sch. (as amended by S.S. I. 2007/527)

F65. S. 144. (3. A)(3. B) inserted (1.11.2002) by Sexual Offences (Procedure and Evidence) (Scotland) Act 2002 (asp 9), s. 3, Sch. para. 9; S.S.I. 2002/443, art. 3

F66. S. 144. (3. A)(a) substituted (28.3.2011) by Criminal Justice and Licensing (Scotland) Act 2010 (asp 13), s. 206. (1), sch. 7 para. 55. (a); S.S.I. 2011/178, art. 2, sch.

F67. Words in s. 144. (3. A)(c) substituted (28.3.2011) by Criminal Justice and Licensing (Scotland) Act 2010 (asp 13), s. 206. (1), sch. 7 para. 55. (b); S.S.I. 2011/178, art. 2, sch.

F68. Words in s. 144. (9) inserted (30.6.2007) by Adult Support and Protection (Scotland) Act 2007 (asp 10), ss. 75. (a)(ii), 79; S.S.I. 2007/334, art. 2. (a), Sch. 1

F69. Words in s. 144. (9) inserted (27.6.2003) by Criminal Justice (Scotland) Act 2003 (asp 7), ss. 63. (2), 89; S.S.I. 2003/288, art. 2, Sch.

145 Adjournment for inquiry at first calling.S

(1) [F70. Where the accused is present] at the first calling of a case in a summary prosecution the court may, in order to allow time for inquiry into the case or for any other cause which it considers reasonable, adjourn the case under this section, for such period as it considers appropriate, without calling on the accused to plead to any charge against him but remanding him in custody or on bail or ordaining him to appear at the diet thus fixed; and, subject to subsections (2) and (3) below, the court may from time to time so adjourn the case.

(2) Where the accused is remanded in custody, the total period for which he is so remanded under this section shall not exceed 21 days and no one period of adjournment shall, except on special cause shown, exceed 7 days.

(3) Where the accused is remanded on bail or ordained to appear, no one period of adjournment shall exceed 28 days.

Amendments (Textual)

F70. Words in s. 145. (1) substituted (27.6.2003) by Criminal Justice (Scotland) Act 2003 (asp 7), ss. 63. (3), 89; S.S.I. 2003/288, art. 2, Sch.

[F71145. ZAAdjournment where assessment order made at first callingS

Where the accused is present at the first calling of a case in a summary prosecution the court may, where it makes an assessment order in respect of the accused, adjourn the case under this section for a period not exceeding 28 days without calling on the accused to plead to any charge against him; and the court may so adjourn the case for a further period not exceeding 7 days.]

Amendments (Textual)

F71. S. 145. ZA inserted (30.6.2007) by Adult Support and Protection (Scotland) Act 2007 (asp 10), ss. 75. (b), 79; S.S.I. 2007/334, art. 2. (a), Sch. 1

[F72145. AAdjournment at first calling to allow accused to appear etc.S

(1) Without prejudice to section [F73150] of this Act, where the accused is not present at the first calling of the case in a summary prosecution, the court may (whether or not the prosecutor is able to provide evidence that the accused has been duly cited) adjourn the case under this section for such period as it considers appropriate; and subject to subsections (2) and (3) below, the court may from time to time so adjourn the case.

(2) An adjournment under this section shall be—

(a) for the purposes of allowing—

(i) the accused to appear in answer to the complaint; or

(ii) time for inquiry into the case; or

(b) for any other cause the court considers reasonable.

(3) No one period of adjournment under this section shall exceed 28 days.

[F74. (4)The clerk of court may perform the functions of the court under subsection (1) above without the court being properly constituted.]]

Amendments (Textual)

F72. S. 145. A inserted (27.6.2003) by Criminal Justice (Scotland) Act 2003 (asp 7), ss. 63. (4), 89; S.S.I. 2003/288, art. 2, Sch.

F73. Words in s. 145. A(1) substituted (10.12.2007) by Criminal Proceedings etc. (Reform) (Scotland) Act 2007 (asp 6), ss. 14. (2), 84; S.S.I. 2007/479, art. 3. (1), Sch. (as amended by S.S. I. 2007/527)

F74. S. 145. A(4) added (10.12.2007) by Criminal Proceedings etc. (Reform) (Scotland) Act 2007 (asp 6), ss. 9. (2), 84; S.S.I. 2007/479, art. 3. (1), Sch. (as amended by S.S. I. 2007/527)

146 Plea of not guilty.S

(1) This section applies where the accused in a summary prosecution—

(a) pleads not guilty to the charge; or

(b) pleads guilty to only part of the charge and the prosecutor does not accept the partial plea.

(2) The court may proceed to trial at once unless either party moves for an adjournment and the court considers it expedient to grant it.

(3) The court may adjourn the case for trial to as early a diet as is consistent with the just interest of both parties, and the prosecutor shall, if requested by the accused, furnish him with a copy of the complaint if he does not already have one.

[F75. (3. ZA)Where a case is adjourned under subsection (3) above, the court shall intimate to the accused the trial diet assigned and any intermediate diet fixed.

(3. ZB)When intimating a diet under subsection (3. ZA) above, the court shall inform the accused that, if he fails to appear at any diet in the proceedings in respect of the case, the court might hear and dispose of the case in his absence.]

[F76. (3. A)Where, under subsection (3) above, the prosecutor furnishes an accused charged with a sexual offence to which section 288. C of this Act applies with a copy of the complaint, it shall be accompanied by a notice to the accused—

[F77. (a)that his case at, or for the purposes of, any relevant hearing (within the meaning of section 288. C(1. A)) in the course of the proceedings may be conducted only by a lawyer,]

(b) that it is, therefore, in his interests, if he has not already done so, to get the professional assistance of a solicitor; and

(c) that, if he does not engage a solicitor for the purposes of [F78the conduct of his case at, or for the purposes of, the hearing], the court will do so.

(3. B)A failure to comply with subsection (3. A) above does not affect the validity or lawfulness of any such copy complaint or any other element of the proceedings against the accused.]

(4) Where the accused is brought before the court from custody the court shall inform the accused of his right to an adjournment of the case for not less than 48 hours and if he requests such adjournment before the prosecutor has commenced his proof, subject to subsection (5) below, the adjournment shall be granted.

(5) Where the court considers that it is necessary to secure the examination of witnesses who otherwise would not be available, the case may proceed to trial at once or on a shorter adjournment than 48 hours.

(6) Where the accused is in custody, he may be committed to prison or to legalised police cells or to any other place to which he may lawfully be committed pending trial—

(a) if he is neither granted bail nor ordained to appear; or

(b) if he is granted bail on a condition imposed under section 24. (6) of this Act that a sum of money is deposited in court, until the accused or a cautioner on his behalf has so deposited that sum.

(7) The court may from time to time at any stage of the case on the motion of either party or ex proprio motu grant such adjournment as may be necessary for the proper conduct of the case, and where from any cause a diet has to be continued from day to day it shall not be necessary to intimate the continuation to the accused.

(8) It shall not be necessary for the prosecutor to establish a charge or part of a charge to which the accused pleads guilty.

(9) The court may, in any case where it considers it expedient, permit any witness for the defence to be examined prior to evidence for the prosecution having been led or concluded, but in any such case the accused shall be entitled to lead additional evidence after the case for the prosecution is closed.

Amendments (Textual)

F75. S. 146. (3. ZA)(3. ZB) added (10.12.2007) by Criminal Proceedings etc. (Reform) (Scotland) Act 2007 (asp 6), ss. 10, 84; S.S.I. 2007/479, art. 3. (1), Sch. (as amended by S.S. I. 2007/527)

F76. S. 146. (3. A)(3. B) inserted (1.11.2002) by Sexual Offences (Procedure and Evidence) (Scotland) Act 2002 (asp 9), s. 3, Sch. para. 10; S.S.I. 2002/443, art. 3

F77. S. 146. (3. A)(a) substituted (28.3.2011) by Criminal Justice and Licensing (Scotland) Act 2010 (asp 13), s. 206. (1), sch. 7 para. 56. (a); S.S.I. 2011/178, art. 2, sch.

F78. Words in s. 146. (3. A)(c) substituted (28.3.2011) by Criminal Justice and Licensing (Scotland) Act 2010 (asp 13), s. 206. (1), sch. 7 para. 56. (b); S.S.I. 2011/178, art. 2, sch.

Pre-trial procedureS

147 Prevention of delay in trials.S

(1) Subject to subsections (2) and (3) below, a person charged with an offence in summary proceedings shall not be detained in that respect for a total of more than 40 days after the bringing of the complaint in court unless his trial is commenced within that period, failing which he shall be liberated forthwith and thereafter he shall be for ever free from all question or process for that offence.

[F79. (2)On an application made for the purpose, the sheriff may, on cause shown—

    (a) extend the period mentioned in subsection (1) above; and

    (b) order the accused to be detained awaiting trial,

for such period as the sheriff thinks fit.

(2. A)Before determining an application under subsection (2) above, the sheriff shall give the parties an opportunity to be heard.

(2. B)However, where all the parties join in the application, the sheriff may determine the application without hearing the parties and, accordingly, may dispense with any hearing previously appointed for the purpose of considering the application.]

(3) The grant or refusal of any application to extend the period mentioned in subsection (1) above may be appealed against by note of appeal presented to the [F80. Sheriff Appeal Court]; and that Court may affirm, reverse or amend the determination made on such application.

(4) For the purposes of this section, a trial shall be taken to commence when the first witness is sworn.

Amendments (Textual)

F79. S. 147. (2)-(2. B) substituted (10.3.2008) for s. 147. (2) by Criminal Proceedings etc. (Reform) (Scotland) Act 2007 (asp 6), ss. 11, 84; S.S.I. 2008/42, art. 3, (subject to art. 4)

F80. Words in s. 147. (3) substituted (22.9.2015) by The Courts Reform (Scotland) Act 2014 (Consequential Provisions No. 2) Order 2015 (S.S.I. 2015/338), art. 1, sch. 2 para. 5. (4) (with art. 4)

Modifications etc. (not altering text)

C111. S. 147 applied (with modifications) (1.10.1997) by S.I. 1997/1776, art. 2, Sch. 1 paras. 5-7; S.I. 1997/2200, arts. 1, 2 (subject to transitional provisions in art. 5)

S. 147 extended (1.10.1997) by 1997 c. 43, s. 41, Sch. 1 Pt. II para. 10. (1)(a); S.I. 1997/2200, art. 2 (subject to transitional provisions in art. 5)

S. 147 modified (1.10.1997) by 1997 c. 43, s. 41, Sch. 1 Pt. II para. 11. (1)(a); S.I. 1997/2200, art. 2 (subject to transitional provisions in art. 5)

C112. S. 147 applied (28.11.2011) by Double Jeopardy (Scotland) Act 2011 (asp 16), ss. 6. (7)(8)(b), 17. (3); S.S.I. 2011/365, art. 3

148 Intermediate diet.S

(1) [F81. The court may, when adjourning a case for trial in terms of section 146. (3) of this Act, and may also, at any time thereafter, whether before, on or after any date assigned as a trial diet], fix a diet (to be known as an intermediate diet) for the purpose of ascertaining, so far as is reasonably practicable, whether the case is likely to proceed to trial on [F81any date assigned as a trial diet] and, in particular—

    (a) the state of preparation of the prosecutor and of the accused with respect to their cases;

    (b) whether the accused intends to adhere to the plea of not guilty; and

    [F82. (ba)how many witnesses are required by—

(i) the prosecutor;

(ii) the accused,

to attend the trial;]

    (c) the extent to which the prosecutor and the accused have complied with the duty under section 257. (1) of this Act.

[F83. (1. A)At an intermediate diet in summary proceedings in the sheriff court, the court shall also—

    (a) ascertain whether subsection (1. B) below applies to any person who is to give evidence at or for the purposes of the trial or to the accused, and

    (b) if so, consider whether it should make an order under section 271. A(7) or 271. D(2) of this Act in relation to person or, as the case may be, the accused.

(1. B)This subsection applies—

(a) to a person who is to give evidence at or for the purposes of the trial if that person is, or is likely to be, a vulnerable witness,

(b) to the accused if, were he to give evidence at or for the purposes of the trial, he would be, or would be likely to be, a vulnerable witness.]

(2) Where at an intermediate diet the court concludes that the case is unlikely to proceed to trial on the date assigned for the trial diet, the court—

(a) [F84may] postpone the trial diet; and

(b) may fix a further intermediate diet.

(3) [F85. The] court may, if it considers it appropriate to do so, adjourn an intermediate diet.

[F86. (3. AA)At an intermediate diet, the court shall also dispose of any application for a witness anonymity order under section 271. P of this Act of which notice has been given in accordance with section 271. Q(2)(a) of this Act.]

[F87. (3. A)At an intermediate diet, the court may consider an application for the purposes of subsection (1) of section 275 of this Act; and, notwithstanding subsection (1) above, the court may fix a diet under that subsection for the purpose only of considering such an application.

(3. B)Subsection (3. A) above shall not operate so as to relieve any court prescribed by order under subsection (7) below of its duty, which arises by virtue of the operation of that subsection, to fix an intermediate diet for the purpose mentioned in subsection (1) above.]

[F88. (4)At an intermediate diet, the court shall make such enquiry of the parties as is reasonably required for the purposes of subsections (1) and (3. A) above.]

(5) The accused shall attend an intermediate diet of which he has received intimation or to which he has been cited unless—

(a) he is legally represented; and

[F89. (b)the court considers that, on cause shown, he need not attend.]

(6) A plea of guilty may be tendered at the intermediate diet.

(7) The foregoing provisions of this section shall have effect as respects any court prescribed by the Secretary of State by order, in relation to proceedings commenced after such date as may be so prescribed, with the following modifications—

(a) in subsection (1), for the word "may" [F90where it first appears,] there shall be substituted "shall, subject to subsection (1. A) below,"; and

(b) after subsection (1) there shall be inserted the following subsections—

"(1. A)If, on a joint application by the prosecutor and the accused made at any time before the commencement of the intermediate diet, the court considers it inappropriate to have such a diet, the duty under subsection (1) above shall not apply and the court shall discharge any such diet already fixed.

(1. B)The court may consider an application under subsection (1. A) above without hearing the parties.".

(8) An order under subsection (7) above shall be made by statutory instrument, which shall be subject to annulment in pursuance of a resolution of either House of Parliament.

Amendments (Textual)

F81. Words in s. 148. (1) substituted (retrospective to 1.4.1996) by 1998 c. 10, s. 1. (1)(a)(i)(ii)(2)

F82. S. 148. (1)(ba) inserted (10.12.2007) by Criminal Proceedings etc. (Reform) (Scotland) Act 2007 (asp 6), ss. 18. (a), 84; S.S.I. 2007/479, art. 3. (1), Sch. (as amended by S.S. I. 2007/527)

F83. S. 148. (1. A)(1. B) inserted (1.4.2007 for certain purposes and otherwise 1.4.2008) by Vulnerable Witnesses (Scotland) Act 2004 (asp 3), ss. 2. (5)(a), 25; S.S.I. 2007/101, art. 2, Sch. (with art. 4); S.S.I. 2008/57, art. 2 (with art. 3)

F84. Words in s. 148. (2)(a) substituted (10.12.2007) by Criminal Proceedings etc. (Reform) (Scotland) Act 2007 (asp 6), ss. 18. (b), 84; S.S.I. 2007/479, art. 3. (1), Sch. (as amended by S.S. I. 2007/527)

F85. Word in s. 148. (3) substituted (10.12.2007) by Criminal Proceedings etc. (Reform) (Scotland) Act 2007 (asp 6), ss. 18. (c), 84; S.S.I. 2007/479, art. 3. (1), Sch. (as amended by S.S. I. 2007/527)

F86. S. 148. (3. AA) inserted (28.3.2011) by Criminal Justice and Licensing (Scotland) Act 2010 (asp 13), ss. 90. (2)(b), 206. (1); S.S.I. 2011/178, art. 2, sch.

F87. S. 148. (3. A)(3. B) inserted (1.11.2002) by Sexual Offences (Procedure and Evidence) (Scotland) Act 2002 (asp 9), s. 8. (5)(a); S.S.I. 2002/443, art. 3 (with art. 4. (5))

F88. S. 148. (4) substituted (10.12.2007) by Criminal Proceedings etc. (Reform) (Scotland) Act 2007 (asp 6), ss. 18. (d), 84; S.S.I. 2007/479, art. 3. (1), Sch. (as amended by S.S. I. 2007/527)

F89. S. 148. (5)(b) substituted (10.10.2014) by Act of Adjournal (Amendment of the Criminal Procedure (Scotland) Act 1995 and Criminal Procedure Rules 1996) (Miscellaneous) 2014 (S.S.I. 2014/242), para. 2. (2)

F90. Words in s. 148. (7)(a) inserted (retrospective to 1.4.1996) by 1998 c. 10, s. 1. (1)(b)(2)

[F91148. A Interim diet: sexual offence to which section 288. C of this Act appliesS

(1) Where, in a case which is adjourned for trial, the charge is of committing a sexual offence to which section 288. C of this Act applies, the court shall order that, before the trial diet, there shall be a diet under this section and ordain the accused then to attend.

(2) At a diet under this section, the court shall ascertain whether or not the accused has engaged a solicitor for the purposes of his defence at the trial.

(3) Where, following inquiries for the purposes of subsection (2) above, it appears to the court that the accused has not engaged a solicitor for the purposes of his defence at his trial, it may adjourn the diet under this section for a period of not more than 48 hours and ordain the accused then to attend.

(4) A diet under this section may be conjoined with an intermediate diet.

(5) A court may, at a diet under this section, postpone the trial diet.

(6) The court may dispense with a diet under this section previously ordered, but only if a solicitor engaged by the accused for the purposes of the defence of the accused at the trial has, in writing—

    (a) confirmed his engagement for that purpose; and

    (b) requested that the diet be dispensed with.

(7) Where—

    (a) a solicitor has requested, under subsection (6) above, that a diet under this section be dispensed with; and

    (b) before that diet has been held or dispensed with, the solicitor—

(i) is dismissed by the accused; or

(ii) withdraws,

the solicitor shall forthwith inform the court in writing of those facts.

(8) It is the duty of a solicitor who—

    (a) was engaged for the purposes of the defence of the accused at the trial—

(i) at the time of a diet under this section; or

(ii) in the case of a diet which, under subsection (6) above, is dispensed with, at the time when it was so dispensed with; and

    (b) after that time but before the trial diet—

(i) is dismissed by the accused; or

(ii) withdraws,

forthwith to inform the court in writing of those facts.

(9) On being so informed, the court shall order a further diet under this section.]

Amendments (Textual)

F91. S. 148. A inserted (1.11.2002) by Sexual Offences (Procedure and Evidence) (Scotland) Act 2002 (asp 9), s. 3, Sch. para. 11; S.S.I. 2002/443, art. 3

[F92148. BPre-trial procedure in sheriff court where no intermediate diet is fixedS

(1) Where, in any summary proceedings in the sheriff court, no intermediate diet is fixed, the court shall, at the trial diet before the first witness is sworn—

(a) ascertain whether subsection (2) below applies to any person who is to give evidence at or for the purposes of the trial or to the accused and, if so, consider whether it should make an order under section 271. A(7) or 271. D(2) of this Act in relation to the person or, as the case may be, the accused, and

(b) if—

(i) section 288. E of this Act applies to the proceedings, or

(ii) an order under section 288. F(2) has been made in the proceedings,

ascertain whether or not the accused has engaged a solicitor for the purposes of his defence at the trial.

(2) This subsection applies—

(a) to a person who is to give evidence at or for the purposes of the trial if that person is, or is likely to be, a vulnerable witness,

(b) to the accused if, were he to give evidence at or for the purposes of the trial, he would be, or be likely to be, a vulnerable witness.

(3) Where, following inquiries for the purposes of subsection (1)(b) above, it appears to the court that the accused has not engaged a solicitor for the purposes of his defence at the trial, the court may adjourn the trial diet for a period of not more than 48 hours and ordain the accused then to attend.

(4) At the trial diet, the court may ask the prosecutor and the accused any question in connection with any matter which it is required to ascertain or consider under subsection (1) above.]

Amendments (Textual)

F92. S. 148. B inserted (1.4.2007 for certain purposes and otherwise 1.4.2008) by Vulnerable Witnesses (Scotland) Act 2004 (asp 3), ss. 9, 25; S.S.I. 2007/101, art. 2 (with art. 4); S.S.I. 2008/57, art. 2 (with art. 3)

[F93148. CEngagement, dismissal and withdrawal of solicitor representing accusedS

(1) In summary proceedings, it is the duty of a solicitor who is engaged by the accused for the purposes of his defence at trial to notify the court and the prosecutor of that fact forthwith in writing.

(2) The duty under subsection (1) above shall be regarded as having been complied with if the solicitor has represented the accused at the first calling of the case—

(a) by submitting a written intimation of the accused's plea as described in subsection (2)(a) of section 144 of this Act; or

(b) by appearing on behalf of the accused—

(i) as described in subsection (2)(b) of that section; or

(ii) with the accused present,

and has, when acting as described in paragraph (a) or (b) above, notified the court and the prosecutor orally or in writing that the solicitor is also engaged by the accused for the purposes of his defence at trial.

(3) Where a solicitor referred to in subsection (1) above—

(a) is dismissed by the accused; or

(b) withdraws,

it is the duty of the solicitor to notify the court and the prosecutor of that fact forthwith in writing.

Amendments (Textual)

F93. Ss. 148. C, 148. D inserted (10.12.2007) by Criminal Proceedings etc. (Reform) (Scotland) Act 2007 (asp 6), ss. 21, 84; S.S.I. 2007/479, art. 3. (1), Sch. (as amended by S.S.I. 2007/527)

148. DService etc. on accused through a solicitorS

(1) In summary proceedings, anything which is to be served on or given, notified or otherwise intimated to, the accused (except service of a complaint) shall be taken to be so served, given, notified or intimated if it is, in such form and manner as may be prescribed by Act of Adjournal, served on or given, notified or intimated to (as the case may be) the solicitor described in subsection (2) below at that solicitor's place of business.

(2) That solicitor is any solicitor—

(a) who—

(i) has given notice under subsection (1) of section 148. C of this Act that that solicitor is engaged by the accused for the purposes of the accused's defence at the trial; and

(ii) has not given notice under subsection (3) of that section;

(b) who has represented the accused as mentioned in subsection (2) of that section; and—

(i) has given notice as mentioned in that subsection; and

(ii) has not given notice under subsection (3) of that section; or

(c) who—

(i) has been appointed to act for the purposes of the accused's defence at the trial under section 150. A(4)(b) or (7) or 288. D of this Act; and

(ii) has not been relieved of the appointment by the court.]

Amendments (Textual)

F93. Ss. 148. C, 148. D inserted (10.12.2007) by Criminal Proceedings etc. (Reform) (Scotland) Act 2007 (asp 6), ss. 21, 84; S.S.I. 2007/479, art. 3. (1), Sch. (as amended by S.S.I. 2007/527)

149. . . . .

F96149. A. . . . .

[F97149. BNotice of defencesS

(1) It is not competent for an accused in a summary prosecution to found on a defence to which this subsection applies unless—

(a) notice of the defence has been given to the prosecutor in accordance with subsection (5) below; or

(b) the court, on cause shown, allows the accused to found on the defence despite the failure so to give notice of it.

(2) Subsection (1) above applies—

(a) to a special defence;

(b) to a defence which may be made out by leading evidence calculated to exculpate the accused by incriminating a co-accused;

(c) to a defence of automatism or coercion;

(d) in a prosecution for an offence to which section 288. C of this Act applies, to a defence of consent.

[F98. (2. A)Subsection (1) does not apply where—

(a) the accused lodges a defence statement under section 125 of the Criminal Justice and Licensing (Scotland) Act 2010 (asp 13),

(b) the statement is lodged—

(i) where an intermediate diet is to be held, at or before the diet, or

(ii) where such a diet is not to be held, no later than 10 clear days before the trial diet, and

(c) the accused's defence consists of or includes a defence to which that subsection applies.]

(3) In subsection (2)(d) above, the reference to a defence of consent is a reference to the defence which is stated by reference to the complainer's consent to the act which is the subject matter of the charge or the accused's belief as to that consent.

(4) In subsection (3) above, "complainer" has the same meaning as in section 274 of this Act.

(5) Notice of a defence is given in accordance with this subsection if it is given—

  (a) where an intermediate diet is to be held, at or before that diet; or

  (b) where such a diet is not to be held, no later than 10 clear days before the trial diet,

together with the particulars mentioned in subsection (6) below.

(6) The particulars are—

  (a) in relation to a defence of alibi, particulars as to time and place; and

  (b) in relation to that or any other defence, particulars of the witnesses who may be called to give evidence in support of the defence.

(7) Where notice of a defence to which subsection (1) above applies is given to the prosecutor, the prosecutor is entitled to an adjournment of the case.

(8) The entitlement to an adjournment under subsection (7) above may be exercised whether or not—

  (a) the notice was given in accordance with subsection (5) above;

  (b) the entitlement could have been exercised at an earlier diet.]

Amendments (Textual)

F97. S. 149. B substituted (10.12.2007) for ss. 149, 149. A by Criminal Proceedings etc. (Reform) (Scotland) Act 2007 (asp 6), ss. 19, 84; S.S.I. 2007/479, art. 3. (1) , Sch. (subject to art. 7) (as amended by S.S.I. 2007/527)

F98. S. 149. B(2. A) inserted (6.6.2011) by Criminal Justice and Licensing (Scotland) Act 2010 (asp 13), ss. 125. (7), 206. (1) (with s. 125. (1)); S.S.I. 2011/178, art. 2, sch.

Failure of accused to appearS

150 Failure of accused to appear.S

(1) This section applies where the accused in a summary prosecution fails to appear at any diet of which he has received intimation, or to which he has been cited other than a diet which, by virtue of section 148. (5) of this Act, he is not required to attend.

(2) The court may adjourn the proceedings to another diet, and order the accused to attend at such diet, and appoint intimation of the diet to be made to him.

(3) The court may grant warrant to apprehend the accused.

[F99. (3. A)The grant, under subsection (3) above, at an intermediate diet [F100or a diet under section 148. A of this Act] of a warrant to apprehend the accused has the effect of discharging the trial diet as respects that accused.

(3. B)Subsection (3. A) above is subject to any order to different effect made by the court when granting the warrant.]

[F101. (3. C)An order under subsection (3. B) above—

  (a) for the purpose of having a trial in absence of the accused under section 150. A of this Act, may be made on the motion of the prosecutor;

  (b) for any other purpose, may be made on the motion of the prosecutor or of the court's own accord.]

(4) Intimation under subsection (2) above shall be sufficiently given by an officer of law, or by letter signed by the clerk of court or prosecutor and sent to the accused at his last known address by registered post or by the recorded delivery service, and the production in court of the written execution of such officer or of an acknowledgement or certificate of the delivery of the letter issued by the [F102postal operator] shall be sufficient evidence of such intimation having been duly given.

(5) F103. . . . .

(6) F103. . . . .

(7) F103. . . . .

(8) An accused who without reasonable excuse fails to attend any diet of which he has been given due notice, shall be guilty of an offence and liable on summary conviction—

    (a) to a fine not exceeding level 3 on the standard scale; and

    (b) to a period of imprisonment not exceeding—

(i) in the [F104. JP court] , 60 days; or

(ii) in the sheriff court, [F10512] months.

(9) [F106. A penalty under subsection (8) above shall] be imposed in addition to any other penalty which it is competent for the court to impose, notwithstanding that the total of penalties imposed may exceed the maximum penalty which it is competent to impose in respect of the original offence.

[F107. (9. A)The reference in subsection (9) above to a penalty being imposed in addition to another penalty means, in the case of sentences of imprisonment or detention—

    (a) where the sentences are imposed at the same time (whether or not in relation to the same complaint), framing the sentences so that they have effect consecutively;

    (b) where the sentences are imposed at different times, framing the sentence imposed later so that (if the earlier sentence has not been served) the later sentence has effect consecutive to the earlier sentence.

(9. B)Subsection (9. A)(b) above is subject to section 204. A of this Act.

(9. C)In any proceedings in relation to an offence under subsection (8) above, the fact that (as the case may be) an accused—

    (a) failed to appear at a diet; or

    (b) was given due notice of a diet,

shall, unless challenged by preliminary objection before his plea is recorded, be held as admitted.]

[F108. (10)At any time before the trial in the prosecution in which the failure to appear occurred, it is competent to amend the complaint to include an additional charge of an offence under subsection (8).]

Amendments (Textual)

F99. S. 150. (3. A)(3. B) inserted (retrospectively) by Criminal Procedure (Amendment) (Scotland) Act 2002 (asp 4), s. 1. (1)(2) (with s. 1. (4))

F100. Words in s. 150. (3. A) inserted (1.11.2002) by Sexual Offences (Procedure and Evidence) (Scotland) Act 2002 (asp 9), s. 3, Sch. para. 12; S.S.I. 2002/443, art. 3

F101. S. 150. (3. C) inserted (10.12.2007) by Criminal Proceedings etc. (Reform) (Scotland) Act 2007 (asp 6), ss. 14. (3)(a), 84; S.S.I. 2007/479, art. 3. (1), Sch. (as amended by S.S. I. 2007/527)

F102. Words in s. 150. (4) substituted (26.3.2001) by S.I. 2001/1149, art. 3. (1), Sch. 1 para. 104. (3) (subject to art. 1. (3))

F103. S. 150. (5)-(7) repealed (10.12.2007) by Criminal Proceedings etc. (Reform) (Scotland) Act 2007 (asp 6), ss. 14. (3)(b), 84; S.S.I. 2007/479, art. 3. (1), Sch. (as amended by S.S. I. 2007/527)

F104. Words in s. 150. (8)(b)(i) substituted (10.3.2008, 2.6.2008, 8.12.2008, 23.2.2009 and 14.12.2009 for certain purposes, otherwise 22.2.2010) by Criminal Proceedings etc. (Reform) (Scotland) Act 2007 (asp 6), ss. 80, 84, Sch. para. 26. (g); S.S.I. 2008/42, art. 3, Sch.; S.S.I. 2008/192, art. 3, Sch.; S.S.I. 2008/329, art. 3, Sch.; S.S.I. 2008/362, art. 3, Sch.; S.S.I. 2009/432, art. 3, Schs. 1, 2

F105. Word in s. 150. (8)(b)(ii) substituted (10.12.2007) by Criminal Proceedings etc. (Reform) (Scotland) Act 2007 (asp 6), ss. 15. (a), 84; S.S.I. 2007/479, art. 3. (1), Sch. (subject to art. 6) (as amended by S.S. I. 2007/527)

F106. Words in s. 150. (9) substituted (10.12.2007) by Criminal Proceedings etc. (Reform) (Scotland) Act 2007 (asp 6), ss. 15. (b), 84; S.S.I. 2007/479, art. 3. (1), Sch. (subject to art. 6) (as amended by S.S. I. 2007/527)

F107. S. 150. (9. A)-(9. C) inserted (10.12.2007) by Criminal Proceedings etc. (Reform) (Scotland) Act 2007 (asp 6), ss. 15. (c), 84; S.S.I. 2007/479, art. 3. (1), Sch. (subject to art. 6) (as amended by S.S. I. 2007/527)

F108. S. 150. (10) substituted (28.3.2011) by Criminal Justice and Licensing (Scotland) Act 2010 (asp 13), ss. 62. (2), 206. (1); S.S.I. 2011/178, art. 2, sch.

[F109150. AProceedings in absence of accusedS

(1) Where the accused does not appear at a diet (apart from a diet fixed for the first calling of the case), the court—

(a) on the motion of the prosecutor or, in relation to sentencing, of its own accord; and

(b) if satisfied as to the matters specified in subsection (2) below,

may proceed to hear and dispose of the case in the absence of the accused in like manner as if the accused were present.

(2) The matters referred in subsection (1)(b) above are—

(a) that citation of the accused has been effected or the accused has received other intimation of the diet; and

(b) that it is in the interests of justice to proceed as mentioned in subsection (1) above.

(3) In subsection (1) above, the reference to proceeding to hear and dispose of the case includes, in relation to a trial diet, proceeding with the trial.

(4) Where the court is considering whether to proceed in pursuance of subsection (1) above, it shall—

(a) if satisfied that there is a solicitor with authority to act—

(i) for the purposes of representing the accused's interests at the hearing on whether to proceed that way; and

(ii) if it proceeds that way, for the purposes of representing the accused's further interests at the diet (including, in relation to a trial diet, presenting a defence at the trial),

allow that solicitor to act for those purposes; or

(b) if there is no such solicitor, at its own hand appoint a solicitor to act for those purposes if it considers that it is in the interests of justice to do so.

(5) It is the duty of a solicitor appointed under subsection (4)(b) above to act in the best interests of the accused.

(6) In all other respects, a solicitor so appointed has, and may be made subject to, the same obligations and has, and may be given, the same authority as if engaged by the accused; and any employment of and instructions given to counsel by the solicitor shall proceed and be treated accordingly.

(7) Where the court is satisfied that—

(a) a solicitor allowed to act under subsection (4)(a) above no longer has authority to act; or

(b) a solicitor appointed under subsection (4)(b) above is no longer able to act in the best interests of the accused,

the court may relieve that solicitor and appoint another solicitor for the purposes referred to in subsection (4) above.

(8) Subsections (4)(b) and (7) above do not apply in the case of proceedings—

(a) in respect of a sexual offence to which section 288. C of this Act applies;

(b) in respect of which section 288. E of this Act applies; or

(c) in which an order has been made under section 288. F(2) of this Act.

(9) Reference in this section to a solicitor appointed under subsection (4)(b) above includes reference to a solicitor appointed under subsection (7) above.

(10) Where the court proceeds in pursuance of subsection (1) above, it shall not in the absence of the accused pronounce a sentence of imprisonment or detention.

(11) Nothing in this section prevents—

(a) a warrant being granted at any stage of proceedings for the apprehension of the accused;

(b) a case subsequently being adjourned (in particular, with a view to having the accused present at any proceedings).]

248

Amendments (Textual)
F109. S. 150. A inserted (10.12.2007) by Criminal Proceedings etc. (Reform) (Scotland) Act 2007 (asp 6), ss. 14. (4), 84; S.S.I. 2007/479, art. 3. (1), Sch. (as amended by S.S. I. 2007/527)

Non-availability of judgeS

151 Death, illness or absence of judge.S

(1) Where the court is unable to proceed owing to the death, illness or absence of the presiding judge, it shall be lawful for the clerk of court—
    (a) where the diet has not been called, to convene the court and adjourn the diet;
    (b) where the diet has been called but no evidence has been led, to adjourn the diet; and
    (c) where the diet has been called and evidence has been led—
(i) with the agreement of the parties, to desert the diet pro loco et tempore; or
(ii) to adjourn the diet.
(2) Where, under subsection (1)(c)(i) above, a diet has been deserted pro loco et tempore, any new prosecution charging the accused with the same or any similar offence arising out of the same facts shall be brought within two months of the date on which the diet was deserted notwithstanding that any other time limit for the commencement of such prosecution has elapsed.
(3) For the purposes of subsection (2) above, a new prosecution shall be deemed to commence on the date on which a warrant to apprehend or to cite the accused is granted, if such warrant is executed without undue delay.

Trial dietS

152 Desertion of diet.S

(1) It shall be competent at the diet of trial, at any time before the first witness is sworn, for the court, on the application of the prosecutor, to desert the diet pro loco et tempore.
(2) If, at a diet of trial, the court refuses an application by the prosecutor to adjourn the trial or to desert the dietpro loco et tempore, and the prosecutor is unable or unwilling to proceed with the trial, the court shall desert the diet simpliciter.
(3) Where the court has deserted a diet simpliciter under subsection (2) above (and the court's decision in that regard has not been reversed on appeal), it shall not be competent for the prosecutor to raise a fresh libel.

[F110152. AComplaints triable togetherS

(1) Where—
    (a) two or more complaints against an accused call for trial in the same court on the same day; and
    (b) they each contain one or more charges to which the accused pleads not guilty,
the prosecutor may apply to the court for those charges to be tried together at that diet despite the fact that they are not all contained in the one complaint.
(2) On an application under subsection (1) above, the court is to try those charges together if it appears to the court that it is expedient to do so.
(3) For the purposes of subsections (1) and (2) above, any other charges contained in the complaints are (without prejudice to further proceedings as respects those other charges) to be disregarded.

(4) Where charges are tried together under this section, they are to be treated (including, in particular, for the purposes of and in connection with the leading of evidence, proof and verdict) as if they were contained in one complaint.

(5) But the complaints mentioned in subsection (1)(a) above are, for the purposes of further proceedings (including as to sentence), to be treated as separate complaints.]

Amendments (Textual)

F110. S. 152. A inserted (10.12.2007) by Criminal Proceedings etc. (Reform) (Scotland) Act 2007 (asp 6), ss. 13, 84; S.S.I. 2007/479, art. 3. (1), Sch. (as amended by S.S. I. 2007/527)

153 Trial in presence of accused.S

(1) [F111. Subject to section 150. A of this Act and] subsection (2) below, no part of a trial shall take place outwith the presence of the accused.

(2) If during the course of his trial an accused so misconducts himself that in the view of the court a proper trial cannot take place unless he is removed, the court may order—

(a) that he is removed from the court for so long as his conduct makes it necessary; and

(b) that the trial proceeds in his absence,

but if he is not legally represented the court shall appoint counsel or a solicitor to represent his interests during such absence.

Amendments (Textual)

F111. Words in s. 153. (1) substituted (10.12.2007) by Criminal Proceedings etc. (Reform) (Scotland) Act 2007 (asp 6), ss. 14. (5), 84; S.S.I. 2007/479, art. 3. (1), Sch. (as amended by S.S. I. 2007/527)

F112154. . . . . .S

Amendments (Textual)

F112. S. 154 repealed (1.8.1997) by 1997 c. 48, ss. 28. (1), 62. (2), Sch. 3; S.I. 1997/1712, art. 3, Sch. (subject to arts. 4, 5)

155 Punishment of witness for contempt.S

(1) If a witness in a summary prosecution—

(a) wilfully fails to attend after being duly cited; or

(b) unlawfully refuses to be sworn; or

(c) after the oath has been administered to him refuses to answer any question which the court may allow; or

(d) prevaricates in his evidence,

he shall be deemed guilty of contempt of court and be liable to be summarily punished forthwith for such contempt by a fine not exceeding level 3 on the standard scale or by imprisonment for any period not exceeding 21 days.

(2) Where punishment is summarily imposed as mentioned in subsection (1) above, the clerk of court shall enter in the record of the proceedings the acts constituting the contempt or the statements forming the prevarication.

(3) Subsections (1) and (2) above are without prejudice to the right of the prosecutor to proceed by way of formal complaint for any such contempt where a summary punishment, as mentioned in the said subsection (1), is not imposed.

(4) Any witness who, having been duly cited in accordance with section 140 of this Act—

(a) fails without reasonable excuse, after receiving at least 48 hours' notice, to attend for precognition by a prosecutor at the time and place mentioned in the citation served on him; or

(b) refuses when so cited to give information within his knowledge regarding any matter relative to the commission of the offence in relation to which such precognition is taken, shall be liable to the like punishment as is provided in subsection (1) above.

[F113156 Apprehension of witness.S

(1) In any summary proceedings, the court may, on the application of any of the parties, issue a warrant for the apprehension of a witness if subsection (2) or (3) below applies in relation to the witness.

(2) This subsection applies if the witness, having been duly cited to any diet in the proceedings, deliberately and obstructively fails to appear at the diet.

(3) This subsection applies if the court is satisfied by evidence on oath that the witness is being deliberately obstructive and is not likely to attend to give evidence at any diet in the proceedings without being compelled to do so.

(4) For the purposes of subsection (2) above, a witness who, having been duly cited to any diet, fails to appear at the diet is to be presumed, in the absence of any evidence to the contrary, to have so failed deliberately and obstructively.

(5) An application under subsection (1) above—

(a) may be made orally or in writing;

(b) if made in writing—

(i) shall be in such form as may be prescribed by Act of Adjournal, or as nearly as may be in such form; and

(ii) may be disposed of in court or in chambers after such enquiry or hearing (if any) as the court considers appropriate.

(6) A warrant issued under this section shall be in such form as may be prescribed by Act of Adjournal or as nearly as may be in such form.

(7) A warrant issued under this section in the form mentioned in subsection (6) above shall imply warrant to officers of law—

(a) to search for and apprehend the witness in respect of whom it is issued;

(b) to bring the witness before the court;

(c) in the meantime, to detain the witness in a police station, police cell or other convenient place; and

(d) so far as necessary for the execution of the warrant, to break open shut and lockfast places.

(8) It shall not be competent in summary proceedings for a court to issue a warrant for the apprehension of a witness otherwise than in accordance with this section.

(9) Section 135. (3) of this Act makes provision as to bringing before the court a person apprehended under a warrant issued under this section.

(10) In this section and section 156. A, "the court" means the court in which the witness is to give evidence.]

Amendments (Textual)

F113. Ss. 156-156. D substituted (10.3.2008) for s. 156 by Criminal Proceedings etc. (Reform) (Scotland) Act 2007 (asp 6), ss. 16, 84; S.S.I. 2008/42, art. 3, Sch.

Modifications etc. (not altering text)

C113. S. 156 applied (26.4.2004) by Crime (International Co-operation) Act 2003 (c. 32), ss. 15, 30, 31, 94, Sch. 1 para. 2, Sch. 2 para. 2; S.I. 2004/786, art. 3

C114. S. 156 modified (31.7.2017) by The Criminal Justice (European Investigation Order) Regulations 2017 (S.I. 2017/730), reg. 1. (1), Sch. 6 para. 3 (with reg. 3)

C115. S. 156 applied (31.7.2017) by The Criminal Justice (European Investigation Order) Regulations 2017 (S.I. 2017/730), reg. 1. (1), Sch. 5 para. 3 (with reg. 3)

[F114156. AOrders in respect of witnesses apprehended under section 156. S

(1) Where a witness is brought before the court in pursuance of a warrant issued under section 156 of this Act, the court shall, after giving the parties and the witness an opportunity to be heard, make an order—

(a) detaining the witness until the conclusion of the diet at which the witness is to give evidence;

(b) releasing the witness on bail; or

(c) liberating the witness.

(2) The court may make an order under subsection (1)(a) or (b) above only if it is satisfied that—

(a) the order is necessary with a view to securing that the witness appears at the diet at which the witness is to give evidence; and

(b) it is appropriate in all the circumstances to make the order.

(3) Whenever the court makes an order under subsection (1) above, it shall state the reasons for the terms of the order.

(4) Subsection (1) above is without prejudice to any power of the court to—

(a) make a finding of contempt of court in respect of any failure of a witness to appear at a diet to which he has been duly cited; and

(b) dispose of the case accordingly.

(5) Where—

(a) an order under subsection (1)(a) above has been made in respect of a witness; and

(b) at, but before the conclusion of, the diet at which the witness is to give evidence, the court in which the diet is being held excuses the witness,

that court, on excusing the witness, may recall the order under subsection (1)(a) above and liberate the witness.

(6) On making an order under subsection (1)(b) above in respect of a witness, the court shall impose such conditions as it considers necessary with a view to securing that the witness appears at the diet at which he is to give evidence.

(7) However, the court may not impose as such a condition a requirement that the witness or a cautioner on his behalf deposit a sum of money in court.

(8) Section 25 of this Act shall apply in relation to an order under subsection (1)(b) above as it applies to an order granting bail, but with the following modifications—

(a) references to the accused shall be read as if they were references to the witness in respect of whom the order under subsection (1)(b) above is made;

(b) references to the order granting bail shall be read as if they were references to the order under subsection (1)(b) above;

(c) subsection (3) shall be read as if for the words from "relating" to "offence" in the third place where it occurs there were substituted " at which the witness is to give evidence ".]

Amendments (Textual)

F114. Ss. 156-156. D substituted (10.3.2008) for s. 156 by Criminal Proceedings etc. (Reform) (Scotland) Act 2007 (asp 6), ss. 16, 84; S.S.I. 2008/42, art. 3, Sch.

[F115156. BBreach of bail under section 156. A(1)(b)S

(1) A witness who, having been released on bail by virtue of an order under subsection (1)(b) of section 156. A of this Act, fails without reasonable excuse—

(a) to appear at any diet to which he has been cited; or

(b) to comply with any condition imposed under subsection (6) of that section,

shall be guilty of an offence and liable on summary conviction to the penalties specified in subsection (2) below.

(2) Those penalties are—

(a) a fine not exceeding level 3 on the standard scale; and

(b) imprisonment for a period—

(i) where conviction is in the JP court, not exceeding 60 days;

(ii) where conviction is in the sheriff court, not exceeding 12 months.

(3) In any proceedings in relation to an offence under subsection (1) above, the fact that (as the case may be) a person—

(a) was on bail;

(b) was subject to any particular condition of bail;

(c) failed to appear at a diet;

(d) was cited to a diet,

shall, unless challenged by preliminary objection before his plea is recorded, be held as admitted.

(4) Section 28 of this Act shall apply in respect of a witness who has been released on bail by virtue of an order under section 156. A(1)(b) of this Act as it applies to an accused released on bail, but with the following modifications—

(a) references to an accused shall be read as if they were references to the witness;

(b) in subsection (2), the reference to the court to which the accused's application for bail was first made shall be read as if it were a reference to the court which made the order under section 156. A(1)(b) of this Act in respect of the witness;

(c) in subsection (4)—

(i) references to the order granting bail and original order granting bail shall be read as if they were references to the order under section 156. A(1)(b) of this Act and the original such order respectively;

(ii) paragraph (a) shall be read as if at the end there were inserted " and make an order under section 156. A(1)(a) or (c) of this Act in respect of the witness ";

(iii) paragraph (c) shall be read as if for the words from "complies" to the end there were substituted " appears at the diet at which the witness is to give evidence ".]

Amendments (Textual)

F115. Ss. 156-156. D substituted (10.3.2008) for s. 156 by Criminal Proceedings etc. (Reform) (Scotland) Act 2007 (asp 6), ss. 16, 84; S.S.I. 2008/42, art. 3, Sch.

Modifications etc. (not altering text)

C116. S. 156. B(2)(b)(i) applied (10.12.2007) by The District Courts and Justices of the Peace (Scotland) Order 2007 (S.S.I. 2007/480), art. 4. (1)(c)

[F116156. CReview of orders under section 156. A(1)(a) or (b)S

(1) Where a court has made an order under subsection (1)(a) of section 156. A of this Act, the court may, on the application of the witness in respect of whom the order was made and after giving the parties and the witness an opportunity to be heard—

(a) recall the order; and

(b) make an order under subsection (1)(b) or (c) of that section in respect of the witness.

(2) Where a court has made an order under subsection (1)(b) of section 156. A of this Act, the court may, after giving the parties and the witness an opportunity to be heard—

(a) on the application of the witness in respect of whom the order was made—

(i) review the conditions imposed under subsection (6) of that section at the time the order was made; and

(ii) make a new order under subsection (1)(b) of that section and impose different conditions under subsection (6) of that section;

(b) on the application of the party who made the application under section 156. (1) of this Act in respect of the witness, review the order and the conditions imposed under subsection (6) of section 156. A of this Act at the time the order was made, and—

(i) recall the order and make an order under subsection (1)(a) of that section in respect of the witness; or

(ii) make a new order under subsection (1)(b) of that section and impose different conditions under subsection (6) of that section.

(3) The court may not review an order by virtue of subsection (1) or (2) above unless—

(a) in the case of an application by the witness, the circumstances of the witness have changed materially; or

(b) in that or any other case, the witness or party making the application puts before the court material information which was not available to it when it made the order which is the subject of the application.

(4) An application under this section by a witness—

(a) where it relates to the first order made under section 156. A(1)(a) or (b) of this Act in respect of the witness, shall not be made before the fifth day after that order is made;

(b) where it relates to any subsequent such order, shall not be made before the fifteenth day after the order is made.

(5) On receipt of an application under subsection (2)(b) above the court shall—

(a) intimate the application to the witness in respect of whom the order which is the subject of the application was made;

(b) fix a diet for hearing the application and cite the witness to attend the diet; and

(c) where it considers that the interests of justice so require, grant warrant to arrest the witness.

(6) Nothing in this section shall affect any right of a person to appeal against an order under section 156. A(1).]

Amendments (Textual)

F116. Ss. 156-156. D substituted (10.3.2008) for s. 156 by Criminal Proceedings etc. (Reform) (Scotland) Act 2007 (asp 6), ss. 16, 84; S.S.I. 2008/42, art. 3, Sch.

[F117156. DAppeals in respect of orders under section 156. A(1)S

(1) Any of the parties specified in subsection (2) below may appeal to the [F118. Sheriff Appeal Court] against—

(a) any order made under subsection (1)(a) or (c) of section 156. A of this Act;

(b) where an order is made under subsection (1)(b) of that section—

(i) the order;

(ii) any of the conditions imposed under subsection (6) of that section on the making of the order; or

(iii) both the order and any such conditions.

(2) The parties referred to in subsection (1) above are—

(a) the witness in respect of whom the order which is the subject of the appeal was made;

(b) the prosecutor; and

(c) the accused.

(3) A party making an appeal under subsection (1) above shall intimate it to the other parties specified in subsection (2) above; and, for that purpose, intimation to the Crown Agent shall be sufficient intimation to the prosecutor.

(4) An appeal under this section shall be disposed of by [F119. Sheriff Appeal Court or any Appeal Sheriff] in court or in chambers after such enquiry and hearing of the parties as shall seem just.

(5) Where the witness in respect of whom the order which is the subject of an appeal under this section was made is under 21 years of age, section 51 of this Act shall apply to the [F120. Sheriff Appeal Court or, as the case may be, Appeal Sheriff] when disposing of the appeal as it applies to a court when remanding or committing a person of the witness's age for trial and sentence.]

Amendments (Textual)

F117. Ss. 156-156. D substituted (10.3.2008) for s. 156 by Criminal Proceedings etc. (Reform) (Scotland) Act 2007 (asp 6), ss. 16, 84; S.S.I. 2008/42, art. 3, Sch.

F118. Words in s. 156. D(1) substituted (22.9.2015) by The Courts Reform (Scotland) Act 2014 (Consequential Provisions No. 2) Order 2015 (S.S.I. 2015/338), art. 1, sch. 2 para. 5. (5)(a) (with art. 4)

F119. Words in s. 156. D(4) substituted (22.9.2015) by The Courts Reform (Scotland) Act 2014 (Consequential Provisions No. 2) Order 2015 (S.S.I. 2015/338), art. 1, sch. 2 para. 5. (5)(b) (with art. 4)
F120. Words in s. 156. D(5) substituted (22.9.2015) by The Courts Reform (Scotland) Act 2014 (Consequential Provisions No. 2) Order 2015 (S.S.I. 2015/338), art. 1, sch. 2 para. 5. (5)(c) (with art. 4)

157 Record of proceedings.S

(1) Proceedings in a summary prosecution shall be conducted summarily viva voce and, except where otherwise provided and subject to subsection (2) below, no record need be kept of the proceedings other than the complaint, or a copy of the complaint certified as a true copy by the procurator fiscal, the plea, a note of any documentary evidence produced, and the conviction and sentence or other finding of the court.

(2) Any objection taken to the competency or relevancy of the complaint or proceedings, or to the competency or [F121. (subject to subsection (3) below)] admissibility of evidence, shall, if either party desires it, be entered in the record of the proceedings.

[F122. (3)An application for the purposes of subsection (1) of section 275 of this Act, together with the court's decision on it, the reasons stated therefor and any conditions imposed and directions issued under subsection (7) of that section shall be entered in the record of the proceedings.]

Amendments (Textual)
F121. Words in s. 157. (2) inserted (1.11.2002) by Sexual Offences (Procedure and Evidence) (Scotland) Act 2002 (asp 9), s. 8. (6)(a); S.S.I. 2002/443, art. 3 (with art. 4. (5))
F122. S. 157. (3) inserted (1.11.2002) by Sexual Offences (Procedure and Evidence) (Scotland) Act 2002 (asp 9), s. 8. (6)(b); S.S.I. 2002/443, art. 3 (with art. 4. (5))

158 Interruption of summary proceedings for verdict in earlier trial.S

Where the sheriff is sitting in summary proceedings during the period in which the jury in a criminal trial in which he has presided are retired to consider their verdict, it shall be lawful, if he considers it appropriate to do so, to interrupt those proceedings—

    (a) in order to receive the verdict of the jury and dispose of the cause to which it relates;

    (b) to give a direction to the jury on any matter on which they may wish one from him, or to hear a request from them regarding any matter,

and the interruption shall not affect the validity of the proceedings nor cause the instance to fall in respect of any person accused in the proceedings.

159 Amendment of complaint.S

(1) It shall be competent at any time prior to the determination of the case, unless the court see just cause to the contrary, to amend the complaint or any notice of previous conviction relative thereto by deletion, alteration or addition, so as to—

    (a) cure any error or defect in it;

    (b) meet any objection to it; or

    (c) cure any discrepancy or variance between the complaint or notice and the evidence.

(2) Nothing in this section shall authorise an amendment which changes the character of the offence charged, and, if it appears to the court that the accused may in any way be prejudiced in his defence on the merits of the case by any amendment made under this section, the court shall grant such remedy to the accused by adjournment or otherwise as appears to the court to be just.

(3) An amendment made under this section shall be sufficiently authenticated by the initials of the clerk of the court.

160 No case to answer.S

(1) Immediately after the close of the evidence for the prosecution, the accused may intimate to the court his desire to make a submission that he has no case to answer both—
    (a) on an offence charged in the complaint; and
    (b) on any other offence of which he could be convicted under the complaint were the offence charged the only offence so charged.
(2) If, after hearing both parties, the judge is satisfied that the evidence led by the prosecution is insufficient in law to justify the accused being convicted of the offence charged in respect of which the submission has been made or of such other offence as is mentioned, in relation to that offence, in paragraph (b) of subsection (1) above, he shall acquit him of the offence charged in respect of which the submission has been made and the trial shall proceed only in respect of any other offence charged in the complaint.
(3) If, after hearing both parties, the judge is not satisfied as is mentioned in subsection (2) above, he shall reject the submission and the trial shall proceed, with the accused entitled to give evidence and call witnesses, as if such submission had not been made.

161 Defence to speak last.S

In any trial the accused or, where he is legally represented, his counsel or solicitor shall have the right to speak last.

Verdict and convictionS

162 Judges equally divided.S

In a summary prosecution in a court consisting of more than one judge, if the judges are equally divided in opinion as to the guilt of the accused, the accused shall be found not guilty of the charge or part thereof on which such division of opinion exists.

163 Conviction: miscellaneous provisions.S

(1) Where imprisonment is authorised by the sentence of a court of summary jurisdiction, an extract of the finding and sentence in the form prescribed by Act of Adjournal shall be a sufficient warrant for the apprehension and commitment of the accused, and no such extract shall be void or liable to be set aside on account of any error or defect in point of form.
(2) In any proceedings in a court of summary jurisdiction consisting of more than one judge, the signature of one judge shall be sufficient in all warrants or other proceedings prior or subsequent to conviction, and it shall not be necessary that the judge so signing shall be one of the judges trying or dealing with the case otherwise.

164 Conviction of part of charge.S

A conviction of a part or parts only of the charge or charges libelled in a complaint shall imply dismissal of the rest of the complaint.

165"Conviction" and "sentence" not to be used for children.S

The words "conviction" and "sentence" shall not be used in relation to children dealt with summarily and any reference in any enactment, whether passed before or after the commencement of this Act, to a person convicted, a conviction or a sentence shall in the case of a child be construed as including a reference to a person found guilty of an offence, a finding of guilt or an order made upon such a finding as the case may be.

166 Previous convictions: summary proceedingsS

(1) This section shall apply where the accused in a summary prosecution has been previously convicted of any offence and the prosecutor has decided to lay a previous conviction before the court.

(2) A notice in the form prescribed by Act of Adjournal or as nearly as may be in such form specifying the previous conviction shall be served on the accused with the complaint where he is cited to a diet, and where he is in custody the complaint and such a notice shall be served on him before he is asked to plead.

(3) The previous conviction shall not [F123, subject to section 275. A(1) of this Act,] be laid before the judge until he is satisfied that the charge is proved.

(4) If a plea of guilty is tendered or if, after a plea of not guilty, the accused is convicted the prosecutor shall lay the notice referred to in subsection (2) above before the judge, and—

   (a) in a case where the plea of guilty is tendered in writing the accused shall be deemed to admit any previous conviction set forth in the notice, unless he expressly denies it in the writing by which the plea is tendered;

   (b) in any other case the judge or the clerk of court shall ask the accused whether he admits the previous conviction,

and if such admission is made or deemed to be made it shall be entered in the record of the proceedings; and it shall not be necessary for the prosecutor to produce extracts of any previous convictions so admitted.

(5) Where the accused does not admit any previous conviction, the prosecutor unless he withdraws the conviction shall adduce evidence in proof thereof either then or at any other diet.

(6) A copy of any notice served on the accused under this section shall be entered in the record of the proceedings.

(7) Where a person is convicted of an offence, the court may have regard to any previous conviction in respect of that person in deciding on the disposal of the case.

(8) Nothing in this section shall prevent the prosecutor—

   (a) asking the accused questions tending to show that the accused has been convicted of an offence other than that with which he is charged, where he is entitled to do so under section 266 of this Act; or

   (b) leading evidence of previous convictions where it is competent to do so—
(i) F124. . . . .
(ii) under section 270 of this Act.

[F125. (9)This section, except subsection (8) above, applies in relation to the alternative disposals mentioned in subsection (10) below as it applies in relation to previous convictions.

(10) Those alternative disposals are—

   (a) a—
(i) fixed penalty under section 302. (1) of this Act;
(ii) compensation offer under section 302. A(1) of this Act,
that has been accepted (or deemed to have been accepted) by the accused in the two years preceding the date of an offence charged;

   (b) a work order under section 303. ZA(6) of this Act that has been completed in the two years preceding the date of an offence charged [F126;

(c) a restoration notice given under subsection (4) of section 20. A of the Nature Conservation (Scotland) Act 2004 (asp 6) in respect of which the accused has given notice of intention to comply under subsection (5) of that section in the two years preceding the date of an offence charged.]

(11) Nothing in this section shall prevent the prosecutor, following conviction of an accused of an offence—

(a) to which a fixed penalty offer made under section 302. (1) of this Act related;

(b) to which a compensation offer made under section 302. A(1) of this Act related; F127...

(c) to which a work offer made under section 303. ZA(1) of this Act related [F128; or

(d) to which a restoration notice given under section 20. A(4) of the Nature Conservation (Scotland) Act 2004 (asp 6) related,]

providing the judge with information about the making of the offer (including the terms of the offer) [F129or, as the case may be, about the giving of the notice (including the terms of the notice).]]

Amendments (Textual)

F123 Words in s. 166. (3) inserted (1.11.2002) by Sexual Offences (Procedure and Evidence) (Scotland) Act 2002 (asp 9), s. 10. (2); S.S.I. 2002/443, art. 3 (with art. 4. (5))

F124 S. 166. (8)(b)(i) and following word repealed (10.12.2007) by Criminal Proceedings etc. (Reform) (Scotland) Act 2007 (asp 6), ss. 12. (1), 84; S.S.I. 2007/479, art. 3. (1), Sch. (as amended by S.S.I. 2007/527)

F125 S. 166. (9)-(11) added (10.3.2008) by Criminal Proceedings etc. (Reform) (Scotland) Act 2007 (asp 6), ss. 53. (3), 84; S.S.I. 2008/42, art. 3, Sch. (subject to art. 6)

F126. S. 166. (10)(c) and semi colon inserted (29.6.2011) by Wildlife and Natural Environment (Scotland) Act 2011 (asp 6), ss. 40. (3)(c)(i), 43. (1) (with s. 41. (1)); S.S.I. 2011/279, art. 2. (1)(q)

F127. Word in s. 166. (11) repealed (29.6.2011) by Wildlife and Natural Environment (Scotland) Act 2011 (asp 6), ss. 40. (3)(c)(ii)(A), 43. (1) (with s. 41. (1)); S.S.I. 2011/279, art. 2. (1)(q)

F128. S. 166. (11)(d) and word inserted (29.6.2011) by Wildlife and Natural Environment (Scotland) Act 2011 (asp 6), ss. 40. (3)(c)(ii)(B), 43. (1) (with s. 41. (1)); S.S.I. 2011/279, art. 2. (1)(q)

F129. Words in s. 166. (11) inserted (29.6.2011) by Wildlife and Natural Environment (Scotland) Act 2011 (asp 6), ss. 40. (3)(c)(ii)(C), 43. (1) (with s. 41. (1)); S.S.I. 2011/279, art. 2. (1)(q)

[F130[F131166. A Post-offence convictions etc. S

(1) This section applies where an accused person is convicted of an offence ("offence O") on summary complaint.

(2) The court may, in deciding on the disposal of the case, have regard to—

(a) any conviction in respect of the accused which occurred on or after the date of offence O but before the date of conviction in respect of that offence,

(b) any of the alternative disposals in respect of the accused that are mentioned in subsection (3).

(3) Those alternative disposals are—

(a) a—

(i) fixed penalty under section 302. (1) of this Act, or

(ii) compensation offer under section 302. A(1) of this Act,

that has been accepted (or deemed to have been accepted) on or after the date of offence O but before the date of conviction in respect of that offence,

(b) a work order under section 303. ZA(6) of this Act that has been completed on or after the date of offence O but before the date of conviction in respect of that offence.

(4) The court may have regard to any such conviction or alternative disposal only if it is—

(a) specified in a notice laid before the court by the prosecutor, and

(b) admitted by the accused or proved by the prosecutor (on evidence adduced then or at another diet).

(5) A reference in this section to a conviction which occurred on or after the date of offence O is a reference to such a conviction by a court in any part of the United Kingdom or in any other member State of the European Union.]]

Amendments (Textual)

F130 S. 166. A inserted (10.3.2008) by Criminal Proceedings etc. (Reform) (Scotland) Act 2007 (asp 6) , ss. 12. (2) , 84 ; S.S.I. 2008/42 , art. 3 , Sch. (subject to art. 5)

F131 S. 166. A substituted (28.3.2011) by Criminal Justice and Licensing (Scotland) Act 2010 (asp 13) , ss. 70. (2) , 206. (1) ; S.S.I. 2011/178 , art. 2 , sch.

[F132166. BCharges which disclose convictionsS

(1) Nothing in section 166 of this Act prevents—

(a) the prosecutor leading evidence of previous convictions where it is competent to do so as evidence in support of a substantive charge;

(b) the prosecutor proceeding with a charge—

(i) which discloses a previous conviction; or

(ii) in support of which evidence of a previous conviction may competently be led,

on a complaint which includes a charge in relation to which the conviction is irrelevant; or

(c) the court trying a charge—

(i) which discloses a previous conviction; or

(ii) in support of which evidence of a previous conviction may competently be led,

together with a charge on another complaint in relation to which the conviction is irrelevant.

(2) But subsections (1)(b) and (c) above apply only if the charges are of offences which—

(a) relate to the same occasion; or

(b) are of a similar character and amount to (or form part of) a course of conduct.

(3) The reference in subsection (1)(c) above to trying a charge together with a charge on another complaint means doing so under section 152. A of this Act.]

Amendments (Textual)

F132 S. 166. B inserted (10.12.2007) by Criminal Proceedings etc. (Reform) (Scotland) Act 2007 (asp 6) , ss. 12. (2) , 84 ; S.S.I. 2007/479 , art. 3. (1) , Sch. (as amended by S.S.I. 2007/527)

167 Forms of finding and sentence.S

(1) Every sentence imposed by a court of summary jurisdiction shall unless otherwise provided be pronounced in open court in the presence of the accused, but need not be written out or signed in his presence.

(2) The finding and sentence and any order of a court of summary jurisdiction, as regards both offences at common law and offences under any enactment, shall be entered in the record of the proceedings in the form, as nearly as may be, prescribed by Act of Adjournal.

(3) The record of the proceedings shall be sufficient warrant for all execution on a finding, sentence or order and for the clerk of court to issue extracts containing such executive clauses as may be necessary for implement thereof.

(4) When imprisonment forms part of any sentence or other judgement, warrant for the apprehension and interim detention of the accused pending his being committed to prison shall, where necessary, be implied.

(5) Where a fine imposed by a court of summary jurisdiction is paid at the bar it shall not be necessary for the court to refer to the period of imprisonment applicable to the non-payment thereof.

(6) Where several charges at common law or under any enactment are embraced in one complaint, a cumulo penalty may be imposed in respect of all or any of such charges of which the accused is convicted.

(7) [F133. Subject to section 204. A of this Act,] a court of summary jurisdiction may frame—

(a) a sentence following on conviction; or

(b) an order for committal in default of payment of any sum of money or for contempt of court, so as to take effect on the expiry of any previous sentence [F134for a term] or order which, at the date of the later conviction or order, the accused is undergoing.

[F135. (7. A)Where the court imposes a sentence as mentioned in paragraph (a) of subsection (7) above for an offence committed after the coming into force of this subsection, the court may—

(a) if the person is serving or is liable to serve the punishment part of a previous sentence, frame the sentence to take effect on the day after that part of that sentence is or would be due to expire; or

(b) if the person is serving or is liable to serve the punishment parts of two or more previous sentences, frame the sentence to take effect on the day after the later or (as the case may be) latest expiring of those parts is or would be due to expire.

(7. B)Where it falls to the court to sentence a person who is subject to a previous sentence in respect of which a punishment part requires to be (but has not been) specified, the court shall not sentence the person until such time as the part is either specified or no longer requires to be specified.

(7. C)In subsections (7. A) and (7. B) above, any reference to a punishment part of a sentence shall be construed by reference to—

(a) the punishment part of the sentence as is specified in an order mentioned in section 2. (2) of the 1993 Act; or

(b) any part of the sentence which has effect, by virtue of section 10 of the 1993 Act or the schedule to the Convention Rights (Compliance)(Scotland) Act 2001 (asp 7), as if it were the punishment part so specified,

and " the 1993 Act " means the Prisoners and Criminal Proceedings (Scotland) Act 1993 (c. 9).]

(8) It shall be competent at any time before imprisonment has followed on a sentence for the court to alter or modify it; but no higher sentence than that originally pronounced shall be competent, and—

(a) the signature of the judge or clerk of court to any sentence shall be sufficient also to authenticate the findings on which such sentence proceeds; and

(b) the power conferred by this subsection to alter or modify a sentence may be exercised without requiring the attendance of the accused.

Amendments (Textual)

F133 Words in s. 167. (7) inserted (30.9.1998) by 1998 c. 37 , s. 119 , Sch. 8 para. 122 ; S.I. 1998/2327 , art. 2. (1)(y)(2)(kk) (subject to arts. 5-8)

F134 Words in s. 167. (7)(b) inserted (1.12.2003) by Criminal Justice (Scotland) Act 2003 (asp 7) , ss. 26. (2)(a) , 89 ; S.S.I. 2003/475 , art. 2 , Sch.

F135 S. 167. (7. A)-(7. C) inserted (1.12.2003) by Criminal Justice (Scotland) Act 2003 (asp 7) , ss. 26. (2)(b) , 89 ; S.S.I. 2003/475 , art. 2 , Sch.

168 Caution.S

(1) This section applies with regard to the finding, forfeiture, and recovery of caution in any proceedings under this Part of this Act.

(2) Caution may be found by consignation of the amount with the clerk of court, or by bond of caution signed by the cautioner.

(3) Where caution becomes liable to forfeiture, forfeiture may be granted by the court on the motion of the prosecutor, and, where necessary, warrant granted for the recovery of the caution.

(4) Where a cautioner fails to pay the amount due under his bond within six days after he has received a charge to that effect, the court may—

(a) order him to be imprisoned for the maximum period applicable in pursuance of section 219 of this Act to that amount or until payment is made; or

(b) if it considers it expedient, on the application of the cautioner grant time for payment; or

(c) instead of ordering imprisonment, order recovery by civil diligence in accordance with section 221 of this Act.

169 Detention in precincts of court.S

F136 . . . .

Amendments (Textual)

F136 S. 169 repealed (13.12.2010 in respect of offences committed on or after this date) by Criminal Justice and Licensing (Scotland) Act 2010 (asp 13) , ss. 16. (2) , 206. (1) ; S.S.I. 2010/413 , art. 2 , Sch.

MiscellaneousS

170 Damages in respect of summary proceedings.S

(1) No judge, clerk of court or prosecutor in the public interest shall be found liable by any court in damages for or in respect of any proceedings taken, act done, or judgment, decree or sentence pronounced in any summary proceedings under this Act, unless—

(a) the person suing has suffered imprisonment in consequence thereof; and

(b) such proceedings, act, judgment, decree or sentence has been quashed; and

(c) the person suing specifically avers and proves that such proceeding, act, judgment, decree or sentence was taken, done or pronounced maliciously and without probable cause.

(2) No such liability as aforesaid shall be incurred or found where such judge, clerk of court or prosecutor establishes that the person suing was guilty of the offence in respect whereof he had been convicted, or on account of which he had been apprehended or had otherwise suffered, and that he had undergone no greater punishment than was assigned by law to such offence.

(3) No action to enforce such liability as aforesaid shall lie unless it is commenced within two months after the proceeding, act, judgment, decree or sentence founded on, or in the case where the Act under which the action is brought fixes a shorter period, within that shorter period.

(4) In this section "judge" shall not include "sheriff", and the provisions of this section shall be without prejudice to the privileges and immunities possessed by sheriffs.

171 Recovery of penalties.S

(1) All penalties, for the recovery of which no special provision has been made by any enactment may be recovered by the public prosecutor in any court having jurisdiction.

(2) Where a court has power to take cognisance of an offence the penalty attached to which is not defined, the punishment therefore shall be regulated by that applicable to common law offences in that court.

172 Forms of procedure.S

(1) The forms of procedure for the purposes of summary proceedings under this Act and appeals therefrom shall be in such forms as are prescribed by Act of Adjournal or as nearly as may be in such forms.

(2) All warrants (other than warrants of apprehension or search), orders of court, and sentences may be signed either by the judge or by the clerk of court, and execution upon any warrant, order of court, or sentence may proceed either upon such warrant, order of court, or sentence itself or upon an extract thereof issued and signed by the clerk of court.

(3) Where, preliminary to any procedure, a statement on oath is required, the statement may be given before any judge, whether the subsequent procedure is in his court or another court.

Application of Part IX of Act.

133 Application of Part IX of Act.S

(1) This Part of this Act applies to summary proceedings in respect of any offence which might prior to the passing of this Act, or which may under the provisions of this or any Act, whether passed before or after the passing of this Act, be tried summarily.

(2) Without prejudice to subsection (1) above, this Part of this Act also applies to procedure in all courts of summary jurisdiction in so far as they have jurisdiction in respect of—

(a) any offence or the recovery of a penalty under any enactment or rule of law which does not exclude summary procedure as well as, in accordance with section 211. (3) and (4) of this Act, to the enforcement of a fine imposed in solemn proceedings; and

(b) any order ad factum praestandum, or other order of court or warrant competent to a court of summary jurisdiction.

(3) Where any statute provides for summary proceedings to be taken under any public general or local enactment, such proceedings shall be taken under this Part of this Act.

(4) Nothing in this Part of this Act shall—

(a) extend to any complaint or other proceeding under or by virtue of any statutory provision for the recovery of any rate, tax, or impost whatsoever; or

(b) affect any right to raise any civil proceedings.

(5) Except where any enactment otherwise expressly provides, all prosecutions under this Part of this Act shall be brought at the instance of the procurator fiscal.

PART X Appeals from Summary Proceedings

PART XS Appeals from Summary Proceedings

Modifications etc. (not altering text)

C1. Pt. X (ss. 173-194) excluded (19.2.2001) by 2000 c. 11, ss. 7. (7), 8. (1)(f)(ii); S.I. 2001/421, art. 2

C2. Pt. 10 referred (11.3.2005) by Prevention of Terrorism Act 2005 (c. 2), s. 12. (6)(e)

C3. Pt. X extended (15.12.2011) by Terrorism Prevention and Investigation Measures Act 2011 (c. 23), s. 31. (2), Sch. 3 para. 4. (4)(e) (with Sch. 8)

C4. Pt. X applied (12.2.2015) by Counter-Terrorism and Security Act 2015 (c. 6), s. 52. (5), Sch. 4 para. 4. (4)(e)

173 [F1. Quorum of Sheriff Appeal Court in relation to appeals.]S

(1) For the purpose of hearing and determining any appeal under this Part of this Act, or any proceeding connected therewith, three of the [F2. Appeal Sheriffs] shall be a quorum of the [F3. Sheriff Appeal Court], and the determination of any question under this Part of this Act by the court shall be according to the votes of the majority of the members of the court sitting, including the presiding [F4. Appeal Sheriff], and each [F4. Appeal Sheriff] so sitting shall be entitled to pronounce a separate opinion.

(2) For the purpose of hearing and determining appeals under section [F5175. (2)(b), (c) or (cza)]

F6... of this Act, or any proceeding connected therewith, two of the [F7. Appeal Sheriffs] shall be a quorum of the [F8. Sheriff Appeal Court], and each [F9. Appeal Sheriff] shall be entitled to pronounce a separate opinion; but where the two [F7. Appeal Sheriffs] are unable to reach agreement on the disposal of the appeal, or where they consider it appropriate, the appeal shall be heard and determined in accordance with subsection (1) above.

Amendments (Textual)

F1. S. 173 title substituted (22.9.2015) by Courts Reform (Scotland) Act 2014 (asp 18), s. 138. (2), sch. 3 para. 2. (2); S.S.I. 2015/247, art. 2, sch. (with art. 6)

F2. Words in s. 173. (1) substituted (22.9.2015) by Courts Reform (Scotland) Act 2014 (asp 18), s. 138. (2), sch. 3 para. 2. (3)(c); S.S.I. 2015/247, art. 2, sch. (with art. 6)

F3. Words in s. 173. (1) substituted (22.9.2015) by Courts Reform (Scotland) Act 2014 (asp 18), s. 138. (2), sch. 3 para. 2. (3)(a); S.S.I. 2015/247, art. 2, sch. (with art. 6)

F4. Words in s. 173. (1) substituted (22.9.2015) by Courts Reform (Scotland) Act 2014 (asp 18), s. 138. (2), sch. 3 para. 2. (3)(b); S.S.I. 2015/247, art. 2, sch. (with art. 6)

F5. Words in s. 173. (2) substituted (1.2.2011) by Criminal Justice and Licensing (Scotland) Act 2010 (asp 13), ss. 14. (2), 206. (1), Sch. 2 para. 11; S.S.I. 2010/413, art. 2, Sch. (with art. 3)

F6. Words in s. 173. (2) repealed (28.2.2011) by Protection of Vulnerable Groups (Scotland) Act 2007 (asp 14), s. 101. (2), sch. 4 para. 20 (with ss. 90, 99); S.S.I. 2011/157, art. 2. (a) (with art. 5. (1))

F7. Words in s. 173. (2) substituted (22.9.2015) by Courts Reform (Scotland) Act 2014 (asp 18), s. 138. (2), sch. 3 para. 2. (3)(c); S.S.I. 2015/247, art. 2, sch. (with art. 6)

F8. Words in s. 173. (2) substituted (22.9.2015) by Courts Reform (Scotland) Act 2014 (asp 18), s. 138. (2), sch. 3 para. 2. (3)(a); S.S.I. 2015/247, art. 2, sch. (with art. 6)

F9. Words in s. 173. (2) substituted (22.9.2015) by Courts Reform (Scotland) Act 2014 (asp 18), s. 138. (2), sch. 3 para. 2. (3)(b); S.S.I. 2015/247, art. 2, sch. (with art. 6)

174 Appeals relating to preliminary pleas.S

(1) Without prejudice to any right of appeal under section 175. (1) to (6) or 191 of this Act, a party may, F10... in accordance with such procedure as may be prescribed by Act of Adjournal, appeal to the [F11. Sheriff Appeal Court] against a decision of the court of first instance (other than a decision not to grant leave under [F12subsection (1. A)(b)]) which relates to such objection or denial as is mentioned in section 144. (4) of this Act; but such appeal must be taken not later than [F13seven] days after such decision.

[F14. (1. A)An appeal under subsection (1) may be taken—

(a) in the case of a decision to dismiss the complaint or any part of it, by the prosecutor without the leave of the court,

(b) in any other case, only with the leave of the court of first instance (granted on the motion of a party or ex proprio motu).]

(2) Where an appeal is taken under subsection (1) above, the [F15. Sheriff Appeal Court] may postpone the trial diet (if one has been fixed) for such period as appears to it to be appropriate and may, if it thinks fit, direct that such period (or some part of it) shall not count towards any time limit applying in respect of the case.

[F16. (2. A)Subsection (3) applies where—

(a) the court grants leave to appeal under subsection (1), or

(b) the prosecutor—

(i) indicates an intention to appeal under subsection (1), and

(ii) by virtue of subsection (1. A)(a), does not require the leave of the court.]

(3) [F17. Where this subsection applies, the court of first instance] shall not proceed to trial at once under subsection (2) of section 146 of this Act; and subsection (3) of that section shall be construed as requiring sufficient time to be allowed for the appeal to be taken.

(4) In disposing of an appeal under subsection (1) above the [F18. Sheriff Appeal Court] may

affirm the decision of the court of first instance or may remit the case to it with such directions in the matter as it thinks fit; and where the court of first instance had dismissed the complaint, or any part of it, may reverse that decision and direct that the court of first instance fix a trial diet (if it has not already fixed one as regards so much of the complaint as it has not dismissed.)

Amendments (Textual)

F10. Words in s. 174. (1) repealed (17.1.2017) by Criminal Justice (Scotland) Act 2016 (asp 1), ss. 87. (2)(a), 117. (2); S.S.I. 2016/426, art. 2, sch.

F11. Words in s. 174. (1) substituted (22.9.2015) by Courts Reform (Scotland) Act 2014 (asp 18), s. 138. (2), sch. 3 para. 3; S.S.I. 2015/247, art. 2, sch. (with art. 6)

F12. Words in s. 174. (1) substituted (17.1.2017) by Criminal Justice (Scotland) Act 2016 (asp 1), ss. 87. (2)(b), 117. (2); S.S.I. 2016/426, art. 2, sch.

F13. Word in s. 174. (1) substituted (28.3.2011) by Criminal Justice and Licensing (Scotland) Act 2010 (asp 13), ss. 72. (3), 206. (1); S.S.I. 2011/178, art. 2, sch.

F14. S. 174. (1. A) inserted (17.1.2017) by Criminal Justice (Scotland) Act 2016 (asp 1), ss. 87. (3), 117. (2); S.S.I. 2016/426, art. 2, sch.

F15. Words in s. 174. (2) substituted (22.9.2015) by Courts Reform (Scotland) Act 2014 (asp 18), s. 138. (2), sch. 3 para. 3; S.S.I. 2015/247, art. 2, sch. (with art. 6)

F16. S. 174. (2. A) inserted (17.1.2017) by Criminal Justice (Scotland) Act 2016 (asp 1), ss. 87. (4), 117. (2); S.S.I. 2016/426, art. 2, sch.

F17. Words in s. 174. (3) substituted (17.1.2017) by Criminal Justice (Scotland) Act 2016 (asp 1), ss. 87. (5), 117. (2); S.S.I. 2016/426, art. 2, sch.

F18. Words in s. 174. (4) substituted (22.9.2015) by Courts Reform (Scotland) Act 2014 (asp 18), s. 138. (2), sch. 3 para. 3; S.S.I. 2015/247, art. 2, sch. (with art. 6)

175 Right of appeal.S

(1) This section is without prejudice to any right of appeal under section 191 of this Act.

(2) Any person convicted, or found to have committed an offence, in summary proceedings may, with leave granted in accordance with section 180 or, as the case may be, 187 of this Act, appeal under this section to the [F19. Sheriff Appeal Court]—

    (a) against such conviction, or finding;

    (b) against the sentence passed on such conviction;

    (c) against his absolute discharge or admonition or any [F20drug treatment and testing order] or any order deferring sentence; F21...

    [F22. (cza)against any disposal under section 227. ZC(7)(a) to (c) or (e) or (8)(a) of this Act;]

    [F23. (ca)against any decision to remit made under section 49. (1)(a) or (7)(b) of this Act;]

    [F24. (cb)F25... or]

    (d) against

[F26. (i)]both such conviction and such sentence or disposal or order.

F27. (ii)................................

F27. (iii)................................

(3) The prosecutor in summary proceedings may appeal under this section to the [F28. Sheriff Appeal Court] on a point of law—

    (a) against an acquittal in such proceedings; or

    (b) against a sentence passed on conviction in such proceedings.

[F29. (4)The prosecutor in summary proceedings, in any class of case specified by order made by the Secretary of State, may, in accordance with subsection (4. A) below, appeal to the [F30. Sheriff Appeal Court] against any of the following disposals, namely—

    (a) a sentence passed on conviction;

    (b) a decision under section 209. (1)(b) of this Act not to make a supervised release order;

    (c) a decision under section 234. A(2) of this Act not to make a non-harassment order;

    [F31. (ca)a decision under section 92 of the Proceeds of Crime Act 2002 not to make a confiscation order;.]

[F32. (cb)a decision under section 22. A of the Serious Crime Act 2007 not to make a serious crime prevention order;]

[F33. (cb)a decision under section 36. (2) of the Regulatory Reform (Scotland) Act 2014 not to make a publicity order;

(cc) a decision under section 41. (2) of that Act not to make a remediation order;]

[F34. (cd)a decision under section 97. B(2) of the Proceeds of Crime Act 2002 to make or not to make a compliance order;]

[F35. (cd)a decision under section 30. (2) of the Health (Tobacco, Nicotine etc. and Care) (Scotland) Act 2016 not to make a remedial order,

(ce) a decision under section 30. (2) of that Act not to make a publicity order,]

F36. (d). . . . .

[F37. (dd)a drug treatment and testing order;]

F36. (e). . . . .

(f) a decision to remit to the Principal Reporter made under section 49. (1)(a) or (7)(b) of this Act;

(g) an order deferring sentence;

(h) an admonition; or

(i) an absolute discharge.

(4. A)An appeal under subsection (4) above may be made—

(a) on a point of law;

(b) where it appears to the Lord Advocate, in relation to an appeal under—

(i) paragraph (a), (h) or (i) of that subsection, that the disposal was unduly lenient;

(ii) paragraph (b) [F38, (c) [F39[F40 , (ca) or (cb)], (cb) [F41, (cc) or (cd)] [F42, (cc), (cd) or (ce)]]] of that subsection, that the decision not to make the order in question was inappropriate;

(iii) paragraph [F43. (cd) or] [F44. (dd)] of that subsection, that the making of the order concerned was unduly lenient or was on unduly lenient terms;

(iv) under paragraph (f) of that subsection, that the decision to remit was inappropriate;

(v) under paragraph (g) of that subsection, that the deferment of sentence was inappropriate or was on unduly lenient conditions.]

[F45. (4. B)For the purposes of subsection (4. A)(b)(i) above in its application to a confiscation order by virtue of section 92. (11) of the Proceeds of Crime Act 2002, the reference to the disposal being unduly lenient is a reference to the amount required to be paid by the order being unduly low.]

[F46. (4. C)In deciding whether to appeal under subsection (4) in any case, the prosecutor must have regard to any sentencing guidelines which are applicable in relation to the case.]

[F47. (5)By an appeal under subsection (2) above, an appellant may bring under review of the [F48. Sheriff Appeal Court] any alleged miscarriage of justice which may include such a miscarriage based, subject to subsections (5. A) to (5. D) below, on the existence and significance of evidence which was not heard at the original proceedings.

(5. A)Evidence which was not heard at the original proceedings may found an appeal only where there is a reasonable explanation of why it was not so heard.

(5. B)Where the explanation referred to in subsection (5. A) above or, as the case may be, (5. C) below is that the evidence was not admissible at the time of the original proceedings, but is admissible at the time of the appeal, the court may admit that evidence if it appears to the court that it would be in the interests of justice to do so.

(5. C)Without prejudice to subsection (5. A) above, where evidence such as is mentioned in F49. . . subsection (5) above is evidence—

(a) which is—

(i) from a person; or

(ii) of a statement (within the meaning of section 259. (1) of this Act) by a person, who gave evidence at the original proceedings; and

(b) which is different from, or additional to, the evidence so given, it may not found an appeal unless there is a reasonable explanation as to why the evidence now sought to be adduced was not given by that person at those proceedings, which explanation is itself supported by independent evidence.

(5. D) For the purposes of subsection (5. C) above, "independent evidence" means evidence which—

(a) was not heard at the original proceedings;

(b) is from a source independent of the person referred to in subsection (5. C) above; and

(c) is accepted by the court as being credible and reliable.

(5. E)By an appeal against acquittal under subsection (3) above a prosecutor may bring under review of the [F50. Sheriff Appeal Court] any alleged miscarriage of justice.]

(6) The power of the Secretary of State to make an order under subsection (4) above shall be exercisable by statutory instrument; and any order so made shall be subject to annulment in pursuance of a resolution of either House of Parliament.

(7) Where a person desires to appeal under subsection (2)(a) or (d) or (3) above, he shall pursue such appeal in accordance with sections 176 to 179, 181 to 185, 188, 190 and 192. (1) and (2) of this Act.

(8) A person who has appealed [F51against both conviction and sentence may abandon the appeal in so far as it is against conviction and may proceed with it against sentence alone,] subject to such procedure as may be prescribed by Act of Adjournal.

(9) Where a convicted person or as the case may be a person found to have committed an offence desires to appeal under subsection (2)(b) or (c) F52... above, or the prosecutor desires so to appeal by virtue of subsection (4) above, he shall pursue such appeal in accordance with sections 186, 189. (1) to (6), 190 and 192. (1) and (2) of this Act; but nothing in this section shall prejudice any right to proceed by bill of suspension, or as the case may be advocation, against an alleged fundamental irregularity relating to the imposition of sentence.

(10) Where any statute provides for an appeal from summary proceedings to be taken under any public general or local enactment, such appeal shall be taken under this Part of this Act.

Amendments (Textual)

F19. Words in s. 175. (2) substituted (22.9.2015) by Courts Reform (Scotland) Act 2014 (asp 18), s. 138. (2), sch. 3 para. 4; S.S.I. 2015/247, art. 2, sch. (with art. 6)

F20. Words in s. 175. (2)(c) substituted (1.2.2011) by Criminal Justice and Licensing (Scotland) Act 2010 (asp 13), ss. 14. (2), 206. (1), Sch. 2 para. 12. (a)(i); S.S.I. 2010/413, art. 2, Sch. (with art. 3)

F21. Word in s. 175. (2)(c) repealed (10.1.2005) by Protection of Children (Scotland) Act 2003 (asp 5), ss. 16. (7)(a), 22. (2); S.S.I. 2004/522, art. 2 (as amended by S.S.I. 2004/556, art. 2)

F22. S. 175. (2)(cza) inserted (1.2.2011) by Criminal Justice and Licensing (Scotland) Act 2010 (asp 13), ss. 14. (2), 206. (1), Sch. 2 para. 12. (a)(ii); S.S.I. 2010/413, art. 2, Sch. (with art. 3)

F23. S. 175. (2)(ca) inserted (1.8.1997) by 1997 c. 48, s. 23. (c); S.I. 1997/1712, art. 3, Sch. (subject to arts. 4, 5)

F24. S. 175. (2)(cb) inserted (10.1.2005) by Protection of Children (Scotland) Act 2003 (asp 5), ss. 16. (7)(b), 22. (2); S.S.I. 2004/522, art. 2 (as amended by S.S.I. 2004/556, art. 2)

F25. S. 175. (2)(cb) repealed (28.2.2011) by Protection of Vulnerable Groups (Scotland) Act 2007 (asp 14), s. 101. (2), sch. 4 para. 21. (a)(i) (with ss. 90, 99); S.S.I. 2011/157, art. 2. (a) (with art. 5. (1))

F26. S. 175. (2): words in para. (d) become s. 175. (2)(d)(i) (10.1.2005) by virtue of Protection of Children (Scotland) Act 2003 (asp 5) {ss. 16. (7)(c)}, 22. (2); S.S.I. 2004/522, art. 2 (as amended by S.S.I. 2004/556, art. 2)

F27. S. 175. (2)(d)(ii)(iii) repealed (28.2.2011) by Protection of Vulnerable Groups (Scotland) Act 2007 (asp 14), s. 101. (2), sch. 4 para. 21. (a)(ii) (with ss. 90, 99); S.S.I. 2011/157, art. 2. (a) (with art. 5. (1))

F28. Words in s. 175. (3) substituted (22.9.2015) by Courts Reform (Scotland) Act 2014 (asp 18), s. 138. (2), sch. 3 para. 4; S.S.I. 2015/247, art. 2, sch. (with art. 6)

F29. S. 175. (4)(4. A) substituted (1.8.1997) for s. 175. (4) by 1997 c. 48, s. 21. (2); S.I.

1997/1712, art. 3, Sch. (subject to arts. 4, 5)

F30. Words in s. 175. (4) substituted (22.9.2015) by Courts Reform (Scotland) Act 2014 (asp 18), s. 138. (2), sch. 3 para. 4; S.S.I. 2015/247, art. 2, sch. (with art. 6)

F31. S. 175. (4)(ca) inserted (24.3.2003) by Proceeds of Crime Act 2002 (c. 29), ss. 115. (6), 458; S.S.I. 2003/210, art. 2. (1)(a) (subject to arts. 3-7)

F32. S. 175. (4)(cb) inserted (1.3.2016) by Serious Crime Act 2015 (c. 9), s. 88. (1), Sch. 4 para. 15. (2); S.I. 2016/148, reg. 3. (g)

F33. S. 175. (4)(cb)(cc) inserted (30.6.2014) by Regulatory Reform (Scotland) Act 2014 (asp 3), ss. 44. (3)(a), 61. (2); S.S.I. 2014/160, art. 2. (1)(2), sch.

F34. S. 175. (4)(cd) inserted (1.3.2016) by Serious Crime Act 2015 (c. 9), ss. 17. (3)(a), 88. (2)(a); S.S.I. 2016/11, reg. 2. (b)

F35. S. 175. (4)(cd)(ce) inserted (1.10.2017) by Health (Tobacco, Nicotine etc. and Care) (Scotland) Act 2016 (asp 14), ss. 31. (3)(a), 36. (2); S.S.I. 2017/294, reg. 2, sch.

F36. S. 175. (4)(d)(e) repealed (1.2.2011) by Criminal Justice and Licensing (Scotland) Act 2010 (asp 13), ss. 14. (2), 206. (1), Sch. 2 para. 12. (b); S.S.I. 2010/413, art. 2, Sch. (with art. 3)

F37. S. 175. (4)(dd) inserted (30.9.1998) by 1998 c. 37, s. 94. (2), Sch. 6 Pt. II para. 7. (3); S.I. 1998/2327, art. 2. (1)(s) (subject to arts. 5-8)

F38. Words in s. 175. (4. A)(b)(ii) substituted (24.3.2003) by Proceeds of Crime Act 2002 (c. 29), ss. 115. (7), 458; S.S.I. 2003/210, art. 2. (1)(a) (subject to arts. 3-7)

F39. Words in s. 175. (4. A)(b)(ii) substituted (30.6.2014) by Regulatory Reform (Scotland) Act 2014 (asp 3), ss. 44. (3)(b), 61. (2); S.S.I. 2014/160, art. 2. (1)(2), sch.

F40. Words in s. 175. (4. A)(b)(ii) substituted (1.3.2016) by Serious Crime Act 2015 (c. 9), s. 88. (1), Sch. 4 para. 15. (3); S.I. 2016/148, reg. 3. (g)

F41. Words in s. 175. (4. A)(b)(ii) substituted (1.3.2016) by Serious Crime Act 2015 (c. 9), ss. 17. (3)(b)(i), 88. (2)(a); S.S.I. 2016/11, reg. 2. (b)

F42. Words in s. 175. (4. A)(b)(ii) substituted (1.10.2017) for "or (cc)" by Health (Tobacco, Nicotine etc. and Care) (Scotland) Act 2016 (asp 14), ss. 31. (3)(b), 36. (2); S.S.I. 2017/294, reg. 2, sch.

F43. Words in s. 175. (4. A)(b)(iii) inserted (1.3.2016) by Serious Crime Act 2015 (c. 9), ss. 17. (3)(b)(ii), 88. (2)(a); S.S.I. 2016/11, reg. 2. (b)

F44. Words in s. 175. (4. A)(b)(iii) substituted (1.2.2011) by Criminal Justice and Licensing (Scotland) Act 2010 (asp 13), ss. 14. (2), 206. (1), Sch. 2 para. 12. (c); S.S.I. 2010/413, art. 2, Sch. (with art. 3)

F45. S. 175. (4. B) inserted (24.3.2003) by Proceeds of Crime Act 2002 (c. 29), ss. 115. (8), 458; S.S.I. 2003/210, art. 2. (1)(a) (subject to arts. 3-7)

F46. S. 175. (4. C) inserted (19.10.2015) by Criminal Justice and Licensing (Scotland) Act 2010 (asp 13), ss. 6. (8), 206. (1); S.S.I. 2015/336, art. 2. (a)

F47. S. 175. (5)-(5. E) substituted (1.8.1997) for s. 175. (5) by 1997 c. 48, s. 17. (2); S.I. 1997/1712, art. 3, Sch. (subject to arts. 4, 5)

F48. Words in s. 175. (5) substituted (22.9.2015) by Courts Reform (Scotland) Act 2014 (asp 18), s. 138. (2), sch. 3 para. 4; S.S.I. 2015/247, art. 2, sch. (with art. 6)

F49. Words in s. 175. (5. C) repealed (30.9.1998) by 1998 c. 37, ss. 119, 120. (2), Sch. 8 para. 123, Sch. 10; S.I. 1998/2327, art. 2. (1)(y)(aa)(2)(kk)(3)(w) (subject to arts. 5-8)

F50. Words in s. 175. (5. E) substituted (22.9.2015) by Courts Reform (Scotland) Act 2014 (asp 18), s. 138. (2), sch. 3 para. 4; S.S.I. 2015/247, art. 2, sch. (with art. 6)

F51. Words in s. 175. (8) substituted (28.2.2011) by Protection of Vulnerable Groups (Scotland) Act 2007 (asp 14), s. 101. (2), sch. 4 para. 21. (b) (with ss. 90, 99); S.S.I. 2011/157, art. 2. (a) (with art. 5. (1))

F52. Words in s. 175. (9) repealed (28.2.2011) by Protection of Vulnerable Groups (Scotland) Act 2007 (asp 14), s. 101. (2), sch. 4 para. 21. (c) (with ss. 90, 99); S.S.I. 2011/157, art. 2. (a) (with art. 5. (1))

Modifications etc. (not altering text)

C5. S. 175. (2)(b) amended (24.3.2003) by Proceeds of Crime Act 2002 (c. 29), ss. 100. (9), 458;

S.S.I. 2003/210, art. 2. (1)(a) (subject to arts. 3-7)

C6. S. 175. (3)(b) amended (24.3.2003) by Proceeds of Crime Act 2002 (c. 29), ss. 100. (9), 458;
S.S.I. 2003/210, art. 2. (1)(a) (subject to arts. 3-7)

[F53175. APower to refer points of law for the opinion of the High CourtS

(1) In an appeal under this Part, the Sheriff Appeal Court may refer a point of law to the High Court for its opinion if it considers that the point is a complex or novel one.

(2) The Sheriff Appeal Court may make a reference under subsection (1)—

(a) on the application of a party to the appeal proceedings, or

(b) on its own initiative.

(3) On giving its opinion on a reference under subsection (1), the High Court may also give a direction as to further procedure in, or disposal of, the appeal.]

Amendments (Textual)

F53. S. 175. A inserted (22.9.2015) by Courts Reform (Scotland) Act 2014 (asp 18), ss. 120, 138. (2); S.S.I. 2015/247, art. 2, sch.

Stated caseS

176 Stated case: manner and time of appeal.S

(1) An appeal under section 175. (2)(a) or (d) or (3) of this Act shall be by application for a stated case, which application shall—

(a) be made within one week of the final determination of the proceedings;

(b) contain a full statement of all the matters which the appellant desires to bring under review and, where the appeal is also against sentence or disposal or order, the ground of appeal against that sentence or disposal or order; and

(c) be signed by the appellant or his solicitor and lodged with the clerk of court,

and a copy of the application shall, within the period mentioned in paragraph (a) above, be sent by the appellant to the respondent or the respondent's solicitor.

(2) The clerk of court shall enter in the record of the proceedings the date when an application under subsection (1) above was lodged.

(3) The appellant may, at any time within the period of three weeks mentioned in subsection (1) of section 179 of this Act, or within any further period afforded him by virtue of section 181. (1) of this Act, amend any matter stated in his application or add a new matter; and he shall intimate any such amendment, or addition, to the respondent or the respondent's solicitor.

(4) Where such an application has been made by the person convicted, and the judge by whom he was convicted dies before signing the case or is precluded by illness or other cause from doing so, it shall be competent for the convicted person to present a bill of suspension to the [F54. Sheriff Appeal Court] and to bring under the review of that court any matter which might have been brought under review by stated case.

(5) The record of the procedure in the inferior court in an appeal mentioned in subsection (1) above shall be as nearly as may be in the form prescribed by Act of Adjournal.

Amendments (Textual)

F54. Words in s. 176. (4) substituted (22.9.2015) by Courts Reform (Scotland) Act 2014 (asp 18), s. 138. (2), sch. 3 para. 5; S.S.I. 2015/247, art. 2, sch. (with art. 6)

Modifications etc. (not altering text)

C7. S. 176. (1) modified (24.3.2003) by Proceeds of Crime Act 2002 (c. 29), ss. 100. (8), 458;
S.S.I. 2003/210, art. 2. (1)(a) (subject to transitional provisions and savings in arts. 3-7)

[F55176. AApplication of section 176 in relation to certain appealsS

(1) Section 176 applies in relation to an appeal under section 175. (2)(a) by virtue of section 11. (7) of the Double Jeopardy (Scotland) Act 2011 (asp 16) with the following modifications.

(2) In subsection (1)(a), for the words "one week of the final determination of the proceedings" substitute " one week of the date on which the appellant is acquitted of an offence mentioned in section 11. (2) of the Double Jeopardy (Scotland) Act 2011 (asp 16) ".

(3) In subsection (2), the reference to the proceedings is to be construed as a reference to the proceedings resulting in the appellant's acquittal as mentioned in section 11. (7) of the Double Jeopardy (Scotland) Act 2011 (asp 16).

(4) In subsection (5), the reference to the inferior court is to be construed as a reference to the court which acquitted the appellant of an offence under section 11. (2) of the Double Jeopardy (Scotland) Act 2011 (asp 16).]

Amendments (Textual)

F55. S. 176. A inserted (28.11.2011) by Double Jeopardy (Scotland) Act 2011 (asp 16), s. 17. (3), sch. para. 13; S.S.I. 2011/365, art. 3

177 Procedure where appellant in custody.S

(1) If an appellant making an application under section 176 of this Act is in custody, the court of first instance may—

    (a) grant bail;

    (b) grant a sist of execution;

    (c) make any other interim order.

(2) An application for bail shall be disposed of by the court [F56before the end of the day (not being a Saturday or Sunday, or a court holiday prescribed for the court which is to determine the question of bail, unless that court is sitting on that day for the disposal of criminal business) after the day on which the application is] made.

(3) If bail is refused or the appellant is dissatisfied with the conditions imposed, he may, within 24 hours after the judgment of the court, appeal against it by a note of appeal written on the complaint and signed by himself or his solicitor, and the complaint and proceedings shall thereupon be transmitted to the [F57. Clerk of the Sheriff Appeal Court], and the [F58. Sheriff Appeal Court] or any [F59. Appeal Sheriff] thereof, either in court or in chambers, shall F60. . . have power to review the decision of the inferior court and to grant bail on such conditions as the Court or [F59. Appeal Sheriff] may think fit, or to refuse bail.

(4) No clerks' fees, court fees or other fees or expenses shall be exigible from or awarded against an appellant in custody in respect of an appeal to the [F61. Sheriff Appeal Court] against the conditions imposed or on account of refusal of bail by a court of summary jurisdiction.

(5) If an appellant who has been granted bail does not thereafter proceed with his appeal, the inferior court shall have power to grant warrant to apprehend and imprison him for such period of his sentence as at the date of his bail remained unexpired and, subject to subsection (6) below, such period shall run from the date of his imprisonment under the warrant or, on the application of the appellant, such earlier date as the court thinks fit, not being a date later than the date of expiry of any term or terms of imprisonment imposed subsequently to the conviction appealed against.

(6) Where an appellant who has been granted bail does not thereafter proceed with his appeal, the court from which the appeal was taken shall have power, where at the time of the abandonment of the appeal the person is in custody or serving a term or terms of imprisonment imposed subsequently to the conviction appealed against, to order that the sentence or, as the case may be, the unexpired portion of that sentence relating to that conviction should run from such date as the

court may think fit, not being a date later than the date on which any term or terms of imprisonment subsequently imposed expired.

(7) The court shall not make an order under subsection (6) above to the effect that the sentence or, as the case may be, unexpired portion of the sentence shall run other than concurrently with the subsequently imposed term of imprisonment without first notifying the appellant of its intention to do so and considering any representations made by him or on his behalf.

[F62. (8)Subsections (6) and (7) of section 112 of this Act (bail pending determination of appeals under [F63section 288. AA of this Act or] paragraph 13. (a) of Schedule 6 to the Scotland Act 1998) shall apply to appeals arising in summary proceedings as they do to appeals arising in solemn proceedings.]

Amendments (Textual)

F56. Words in s. 177. (2) substituted (10.12.2007) by Criminal Proceedings etc. (Reform) (Scotland) Act 2007 (asp 6), ss. 6. (3), 84; S.S.I. 2007/479, art. 3. (1), Sch. (as amended by S.S. I. 2007/527)

F57. Words in s. 177. (3) substituted (22.9.2015) by Courts Reform (Scotland) Act 2014 (asp 18), s. 138. (2), sch. 3 para. 6. (2)(a); S.S.I. 2015/247, art. 2, sch. (with art. 6)

F58. Words in s. 177. (3) substituted (22.9.2015) by Courts Reform (Scotland) Act 2014 (asp 18), s. 138. (2), sch. 3 para. 6. (3); S.S.I. 2015/247, art. 2, sch. (with art. 6)

F59. Words in s. 177. (3) substituted (22.9.2015) by Courts Reform (Scotland) Act 2014 (asp 18), s. 138. (2), sch. 3 para. 6. (2)(b); S.S.I. 2015/247, art. 2, sch. (with art. 6)

F60. Words in s. 177. (3) repealed (10.12.2007) by Criminal Proceedings etc. (Reform) (Scotland) Act 2007 (asp 6), ss. 80, 84, Sch. para. 18. (1); S.S.I. 2007/479, art. 3. (1), Sch. (as amended by S.S. I. 2007/527)

F61. Words in s. 177. (4) substituted (22.9.2015) by Courts Reform (Scotland) Act 2014 (asp 18), s. 138. (2), sch. 3 para. 6. (3); S.S.I. 2015/247, art. 2, sch. (with art. 6)

F62. S. 177. (8) inserted (6.5.1999) by S.I. 1999/1042, arts. 1. (2)(a), 3, Sch. 1 Pt. I para. 13. (7)

F63. Words in s. 177. (8) inserted (22.4.2013) by Scotland Act 2012 (c. 11), ss. 36. (10), 44. (5); S.I. 2013/6, art. 2. (c)

Modifications etc. (not altering text)

C8. S. 177. (2) applied (1.9.2001) by 2001 c. 17, s. 10. (6); S.I. 2001/2161, art. 2 (subject to art. 3) (as amended by S.I. 2001/2304, art. 2)

178 Stated case: preparation of draft.S

(1) Within three weeks of the final determination of proceedings in respect of which an application for a stated case is made under section 176 of this Act—

(a) where the appeal is taken from the [F64. JP court] and the trial was presided over by a justice of the peace or justices of the peace, the Clerk of Court; or

(b) in any other case the judge who presided at the trial,

shall prepare a draft stated case, and the clerk of the court concerned shall forthwith issue the draft to the appellant or his solicitor and a duplicate thereof to the respondent or his solicitor.

[F65. (1. A)Where an application for a stated case under section 176 of this Act relates to an appeal by virtue of section 11. (7) of the Double Jeopardy (Scotland) Act 2011 (asp 16)—

(a) the reference in subsection (1) to the final determination of proceedings is to be construed as a reference to the date on which the appellant is acquitted of an offence mentioned in section 11. (2) of that Act; and

(b) the reference in subsection (1)(b) to the judge who presided at the trial is to be construed as a reference to the judge who presided at the trial resulting in the conviction in respect of which the application for a stated case is made.]

(2) A stated case shall be, as nearly as may be, in the form prescribed by Act of Adjournal, and shall set forth the particulars of any matters competent for review which the appellant desires to bring under the review of the [F66. Sheriff Appeal Court], and of the facts, if any, proved in the

case, and any point of law decided, and the grounds of the decision.

Amendments (Textual)

F64. Words in s. 178. (1)(a) substituted (10.3.2008, 2.6.2008, 8.12.2008, 23.2.2009 and 14.12.2009 for certain purposes, otherwise 22.2.2010) by Criminal Proceedings etc. (Reform) (Scotland) Act 2007 (asp 6), ss. 80, 84, Sch. para. 26. (h); S.S.I. 2008/42, art. 3, Sch.; S.S.I. 2008/192, art. 3, Sch.; S.S.I. 2008/329, art. 3, Sch.; S.S.I. 2008/362, art. 3, Sch.; S.S.I. 2009/432, art. 3, Schs. 1, 2

F65. S. 178. (1. A) inserted (28.11.2011) by Double Jeopardy (Scotland) Act 2011 (asp 16), s. 17. (3), sch. para. 14; S.S.I. 2011/365, art. 3

F66. Words in s. 178. (2) substituted (22.9.2015) by Courts Reform (Scotland) Act 2014 (asp 18), s. 138. (2), sch. 3 para. 7; S.S.I. 2015/247, art. 2, sch. (with art. 6)

179 Stated case: adjustment and signature.S

(1) Subject to section 181. (1) of this Act, within three weeks of the issue of the draft stated case under section 178 of this Act, each party shall cause to be transmitted to the court and to the other parties or their solicitors a note of any adjustments he proposes be made to the draft case or shall intimate that he has no such proposal.

(2) The adjustments mentioned in subsection (1) above shall relate to evidence heard or purported to have been heard at the trial and not to such F67. . . evidence as is mentioned in section 175. (5) of this Act.

(3) Subject to section 181. (1) of this Act, if the period mentioned in subsection (1) above has expired and the appellant has not lodged adjustments and has failed to intimate that he has no adjustments to propose, he shall be deemed to have abandoned his appeal; and subsection (5) of section 177 of this Act shall apply accordingly.

(4) If adjustments are proposed under subsection (1) above or if the judge desires to make any alterations to the draft case there shall, within one week of the expiry of the period mentioned in that subsection or as the case may be of any further period afforded under section 181. (1) of this Act, be a hearing (unless the appellant has, or has been deemed to have, abandoned his appeal) for the purpose of considering such adjustments or alterations.

(5) Where a party neither attends nor secures that he is represented at a hearing under subsection (4) above, the hearing shall nevertheless proceed.

(6) Where at a hearing under subsection (4) above—

(a) any adjustment proposed under subsection (1) above by a party (and not withdrawn) is rejected by the judge; or

(b) any alteration proposed by the judge is not accepted by all the parties,

that fact shall be recorded in the minute of the proceedings of the hearing.

(7) Within two weeks of the date of the hearing under subsection (4) above or, where there is no hearing, within two weeks of the expiry of the period mentioned in subsection (1) above, the judge shall (unless the appellant has been deemed to have abandoned the appeal) state and sign the case and shall append to the case—

(a) any adjustment, proposed under subsection (1) above, which is rejected by him, a note of any evidence rejected by him which is alleged to support that adjustment and the reasons for his rejection of that adjustment and evidence; and

(b) a note of the evidence upon which he bases any finding of fact challenged, on the basis that it is unsupported by the evidence, by a party at the hearing under subsection (4) above.

(8) As soon as the case is signed under subsection (7) above the clerk of court—

(a) shall send the case to the appellant or his solicitor and a duplicate thereof to the respondent or his solicitor; and

[F68. (b)shall transmit a certified copy of the complaint, the minute of proceedings and any other relevant documents to the [F69. Clerk of the Sheriff Appeal Court].]

(9) Subject to section 181. (1) of this Act, within one week of receiving the case the appellant or

his solicitor, as the case may be, shall cause it to be lodged with the [F70. Clerk of the Sheriff Appeal Court].

(10) Subject to section 181. (1) of this Act, if the appellant or his solicitor fails to comply with subsection (9) above the appellant shall be deemed to have abandoned the appeal; and subsection (5) of section 177 of this Act shall apply accordingly.

[F71. (11)In relation to a draft stated case under section 178 of this Act relating to an appeal by virtue of section 11. (7) of the Double Jeopardy (Scotland) Act 2011 (asp 16)—

(a) the reference in subsection (1) to the court is to be construed as a reference to the court by which the appellant was convicted; and

(b) the references in this section to the judge are to be construed as references to the judge who presided at the trial resulting in that conviction.]

Amendments (Textual)

F67. Word in s. 179. (2) repealed (1.8.1997) by 1997 c. 48, s. 62. (1)(2), Sch. 1 para. 21. (20), Sch. 3; S.I. 1997/1712, art. 3, Sch. (subject to arts. 4, 5)

F68. S. 179. (8)(b) substituted (8.4.2009) by Act of Adjournal (Amendment of the Criminal Procedure (Scotland) Act 1995) (Appeals by Stated Case) 2009 (S.S.I. 2009/108), {rule 2}

F69. Words in s. 179. (8)(b) substituted (22.9.2015) by Courts Reform (Scotland) Act 2014 (asp 18), s. 138. (2), sch. 3 para. 8; S.S.I. 2015/247, art. 2, sch. (with art. 6)

F70. Words in s. 179. (9) substituted (22.9.2015) by Courts Reform (Scotland) Act 2014 (asp 18), s. 138. (2), sch. 3 para. 8; S.S.I. 2015/247, art. 2, sch. (with art. 6)

F71. S. 179. (11) inserted (28.11.2011) by Double Jeopardy (Scotland) Act 2011 (asp 16), s. 17. (3), sch. para. 15; S.S.I. 2011/365, art. 3

Modifications etc. (not altering text)

C9. S. 179. (8) excluded by 2006 asp 10, s. 96. A(5) (as inserted (22.9.2015) by The Courts Reform (Scotland) Act 2014 (Consequential Provisions No. 2) Order 2015 (S.S.I. 2015/338), art. 1, sch. 2 para. 9. (6) (with art. 4))

180 Leave to appeal against conviction etc.S

(1) The decision whether to grant leave to appeal for the purposes of section 175. (2)(a) or (d) of this Act shall be made by [F72an Appeal Sheriff] of the [F73. Sheriff Appeal Court] who shall—

(a) if he considers that the documents mentioned in subsection (2) below disclose arguable grounds of appeal, grant leave to appeal and make such comments in writing as he considers appropriate; and

(b) in any other case—

(i) refuse leave to appeal and give reasons in writing for the refusal; and

(ii) where the appellant is on bail and the sentence imposed on his conviction is one of imprisonment, grant a warrant to apprehend and imprison him.

(2) The documents referred to in subsection (1) above are—

(a) the stated case lodged under subsection (9) of section 179 of this Act; and

(b) the documents transmitted to the [F74. Clerk of the Sheriff Appeal Court] under subsection (8)(b) of that section.

(3) A warrant granted under subsection (1)(b)(ii) above shall not take effect until the expiry of the period of 14 days mentioned in subsection (4) below [F75. (and if that period is extended under subsection (4. A) below before the period being extended expires, until the expiry of the period as so extended)] without an application to the [F76. Sheriff Appeal Court] for leave to appeal having been lodged by the appellant under [F77subsection (4) below].

(4) Where leave to appeal is refused under subsection (1) above the appellant may, within 14 days of intimation under subsection (10) below, apply to the [F78. Sheriff Appeal Court] for leave to appeal.

[F79. (4. A)The [F78. Sheriff Appeal Court] may, on cause shown, extend the period of 14 days mentioned in subsection (4) above, or that period as extended under this subsection, whether or not the period to be extended has expired (and if that period of 14 days has expired, whether or not it expired before section 25. (1) of the Criminal Proceedings etc. (Reform) (Scotland) Act 2007 (asp 6) came into force).]

(5) In deciding an application under subsection (4) above the [F80. Sheriff Appeal Court] shall—

(a) if, after considering the documents mentioned in subsection (2) above and the reasons for the refusal, the court is of the opinion that there are arguable grounds of appeal, grant leave to appeal and make such comments in writing as the court considers appropriate; and

(b) in any other case—

(i) refuse leave to appeal and give reasons in writing for the refusal; and

(ii) where the appellant is on bail and the sentence imposed on his conviction is one of imprisonment, grant a warrant to apprehend and imprison him.

(6) The question whether to grant leave to appeal under subsection (1) or (5) above shall be considered and determined in chambers without the parties being present.

(7) Comments in writing made under subsection (1)(a) or (5)(a) above may, without prejudice to the generality of that provision, specify the arguable grounds of appeal (whether or not they are contained in the stated case) on the basis of which leave to appeal is granted.

(8) Where the arguable grounds of appeal are specified by virtue of subsection (7) above it shall not, except by leave of the [F81. Sheriff Appeal Court] on cause shown, be competent for the appellant to found any aspect of his appeal on any ground of appeal contained in the stated case but not so specified.

(9) Any application by the appellant for the leave of the [F82. Sheriff Appeal Court] under subsection (8) above—

(a) shall be made [F83within 14 days of the date of intimation under subsection (10) below]; and

(b) shall, [F84within 14 days of] that date, be intimated by the appellant to the [F85prosecutor].

[F86. (9. A)The [F87. Sheriff Appeal Court] may, on cause shown, extend the periods of 14 days mentioned in subsection (9) above.]

(10) The [F88. Clerk of the Sheriff Appeal Court] shall forthwith intimate—

(a) a decision under subsection (1) or (5) above; and

(b) in the case of a refusal of leave to appeal, the reasons for the decision,

to the appellant or his solicitor and to the [F89prosecutor].

Amendments (Textual)

F72. Words in s. 180. (1) substituted (22.9.2015) by Courts Reform (Scotland) Act 2014 (asp 18), s. 138. (2), sch. 3 para. 9. (2); S.S.I. 2015/247, art. 2, sch. (with art. 6)

F73. Words in s. 180. (1) substituted (22.9.2015) by Courts Reform (Scotland) Act 2014 (asp 18), s. 138. (2), sch. 3 para. 9. (3); S.S.I. 2015/247, art. 2, sch. (with art. 6)

F74. Words in s. 180. (2)(b) substituted (22.9.2015) by Courts Reform (Scotland) Act 2014 (asp 18), s. 138. (2), sch. 3 para. 9. (4); S.S.I. 2015/247, art. 2, sch. (with art. 6)

F75. Words in s. 180. (3) inserted (10.12.2007) by Criminal Proceedings etc. (Reform) (Scotland) Act 2007 (asp 6), ss. 25. (1)(a)(i), 84; S.S.I. 2007/479, art. 3. (1), Sch. (as amended by S.S.I. 2007/527)

F76. Words in s. 180. (3) substituted (22.9.2015) by Courts Reform (Scotland) Act 2014 (asp 18), s. 138. (2), sch. 3 para. 9. (3); S.S.I. 2015/247, art. 2, sch. (with art. 6)

F77. Words in s. 180. (3) substituted (10.12.2007) by Criminal Proceedings etc. (Reform) (Scotland) Act 2007 (asp 6), ss. 25. (1)(a)(ii), 84; S.S.I. 2007/479, art. 3. (1), Sch. (as amended by S.S.I. 2007/527)

F78. Words in s. 180. (4)(4. A) substituted (22.9.2015) by Courts Reform (Scotland) Act 2014 (asp 18), s. 138. (2), sch. 3 para. 9. (3); S.S.I. 2015/247, art. 2, sch. (with art. 6); S.S.I. 2015/247, art. 2, sch. (with art. 6)

F79. S. 180. (4. A) inserted (10.12.2007) by Criminal Proceedings etc. (Reform) (Scotland) Act 2007 (asp 6), ss. 25. (1)(b), 84; S.S.I. 2007/479, art. 3. (1), Sch. (as amended by S.S.I. 2007/527)

F80. Words in s. 180. (5) substituted (22.9.2015) by Courts Reform (Scotland) Act 2014 (asp 18), s. 138. (2), sch. 3 para. 9. (3); S.S.I. 2015/247, art. 2, sch. (with art. 6)

F81. Words in s. 180. (8) substituted (22.9.2015) by Courts Reform (Scotland) Act 2014 (asp 18), s. 138. (2), sch. 3 para. 9. (3); S.S.I. 2015/247, art. 2, sch. (with art. 6)

F82. Words in s. 180. (9) substituted (22.9.2015) by Courts Reform (Scotland) Act 2014 (asp 18), s. 138. (2), sch. 3 para. 9. (3); S.S.I. 2015/247, art. 2, sch. (with art. 6)

F83. Words in s. 180. (9)(a) substituted (23.4.2007) by Criminal Proceedings etc. (Reform) (Scotland) Act 2007 (asp 6), ss. 80, 84, Sch. para. 18. (2)(a)(i); S.S.I. 2007/250, art. 3. (h)(i) (subject to art. 4. (2))

F84. Words in s. 180. (9)(b) substituted (23.4.2007) by Criminal Proceedings etc. (Reform) (Scotland) Act 2007 (asp 6), ss. 80, 84, Sch. para. 18. (2)(a)(ii); S.S.I. 2007/250, art. 3. (h)(i) (subject to art. 4. (2))

F85. Word in s. 180. (9)(b) substituted (22.9.2015) by Courts Reform (Scotland) Act 2014 (asp 18), s. 138. (2), sch. 3 para. 9. (5); S.S.I. 2015/247, art. 2, sch. (with art. 6)

F86. S. 180. (9. A) inserted (23.4.2007) by Criminal Proceedings etc. (Reform) (Scotland) Act 2007 (asp 6), ss. 80, 84, Sch. para. 18. (2)(b); S.S.I. 2007/250, art. 3. (h)(i) (subject to art. 4. (2))

F87. Words in s. 180. (9. A) substituted (22.9.2015) by Courts Reform (Scotland) Act 2014 (asp 18), s. 138. (2), sch. 3 para. 9. (3); S.S.I. 2015/247, art. 2, sch. (with art. 6)

F88. Words in s. 180. (10) substituted (22.9.2015) by Courts Reform (Scotland) Act 2014 (asp 18), s. 138. (2), sch. 3 para. 9. (4); S.S.I. 2015/247, art. 2, sch. (with art. 6)

F89. Word in s. 180. (10) substituted (22.9.2015) by Courts Reform (Scotland) Act 2014 (asp 18), s. 138. (2), sch. 3 para. 9. (5); S.S.I. 2015/247, art. 2, sch. (with art. 6)

Modifications etc. (not altering text)

C10. S. 180. (10) excluded by 2006 asp 10, s. 96. A(5) (as inserted (22.9.2015) by The Courts Reform (Scotland) Act 2014 (Consequential Provisions No. 2) Order 2015 (S.S.I. 2015/338), art. 1, sch. 2 para. 9. (6) (with art. 4))

181 [F90. Stated case: directions by Sheriff Appeal Court.]S

(1) Without prejudice to any other power of relief which the [F91. Sheriff Appeal Court] may have, where it appears to that court on application made in accordance with subsection (2) below, that the applicant has failed to comply with any of the requirements of—

(a) subsection (1) of section 176 of this Act; or

(b) subsection (1) or (9) of section 179 of this Act,

the [F91. Sheriff Appeal Court] may direct that such further period of time as it may think proper be afforded to the applicant to comply with any requirement of the aforesaid provisions.

[F92. (1. A)Where an application for a direction under subsection (1)—

(a) is made by the person convicted, and

(b) relates to the requirements of section 176. (1),

the Sheriff Appeal Court may make a direction only if it is satisfied that doing so is justified by exceptional circumstances.

(1. B)In considering whether there are exceptional circumstances for the purpose of subsection (1. A), the Sheriff Appeal Court must have regard to—

(a) the length of time that has elapsed between the expiry of the period mentioned in section 176. (1)(a) and the making of the application,

(b) the reasons stated in accordance with subsection (2. A)(a)(i),

(c) the proposed grounds of appeal.]

(2) Any application for a direction under subsection (1) above shall be made in writing to the [F93. Clerk of the Sheriff Appeal Court] and shall state the ground for the application, and, in the case of an application for the purposes of paragraph (a) of subsection (1) above, notification of the application shall be made by the appellant or his solicitor to the clerk of the court from which the appeal is to be taken, and the clerk shall thereupon transmit the complaint, documentary productions and any other proceedings in the cause to the [F93. Clerk of the Sheriff Appeal Court].

[F94. (2. A)An application for a direction under subsection (1) in relation to the requirements of section 176. (1) of this Act must—

(a) state—

(i) the reasons why the applicant failed to comply with the requirements of section 176. (1), and

(ii) the proposed grounds of appeal, and

(b) be intimated in writing by the applicant to the respondent or the respondent's solicitor.

(2. B)If the respondent so requests within 7 days of receipt of intimation of the application under subsection (2. A)(b), the respondent must be given an opportunity to make representations before the application is determined.

F95. (2. C). . . . .]

(3) The [F96. Sheriff Appeal Court] shall dispose of any application under subsection (1) above in like manner as an application to review the decision of an inferior court on a grant of bail, but shall have power—

(a) to dispense with a hearing F97...; and

(b) to make such enquiry in relation to the application as the court may think fit,

and when the [F96. Sheriff Appeal Court] has disposed of the application the [F98. Clerk of the Sheriff Appeal Court] shall inform the clerk of the inferior court of the result.

F99. (4). . . . .

[F100. (5)If the Sheriff Appeal Court makes a direction under subsection (1), it must—

(a) give reasons for the decision in writing, and

(b) give the reasons in ordinary language.]

Amendments (Textual)

F90. S. 181 title substituted (22.9.2015) by Courts Reform (Scotland) Act 2014 (asp 18), s. 138. (2), sch. 3 para. 10. (2); S.S.I. 2015/247, art. 2, sch. (with art. 6)

F91. Words in s. 181. (1) substituted (22.9.2015) by Courts Reform (Scotland) Act 2014 (asp 18), s. 138. (2), sch. 3 para. 10. (3); S.S.I. 2015/247, art. 2, sch. (with art. 6)

F92. S. 181. (1. A)(1. B) inserted (17.1.2017) by Criminal Justice (Scotland) Act 2016 (asp 1), ss. 89. (2), 117. (2); S.S.I. 2016/426, art. 2, sch.

F93. Words in s. 181. (2) substituted (22.9.2015) by Courts Reform (Scotland) Act 2014 (asp 18), s. 138. (2), sch. 3 para. 10. (6); S.S.I. 2015/247, art. 2, sch. (with art. 6)

F94. S. 181. (2. A)-(2. C) inserted (30.10.2010) by Criminal Procedure (Legal Assistance, Detention and Appeals) (Scotland) Act 2010 (asp 15), ss. 5. (3)(a), 9 (with s. 5. (4))

F95. S. 181. (2. C) repealed (17.1.2017) by Criminal Justice (Scotland) Act 2016 (asp 1), ss. 89. (3), 117. (2); S.S.I. 2016/426, art. 2, sch.

F96. Words in s. 181. (3) substituted (22.9.2015) by Courts Reform (Scotland) Act 2014 (asp 18), s. 138. (2), sch. 3 para. 10. (7)(a); S.S.I. 2015/247, art. 2, sch. (with art. 6)

F97. Words in s. 181. (3)(a) repealed (17.1.2017) by Criminal Justice (Scotland) Act 2016 (asp 1), ss. 89. (4), 117. (2); S.S.I. 2016/426, art. 2, sch.

F98. Words in s. 181. (3) substituted (22.9.2015) by Courts Reform (Scotland) Act 2014 (asp 18), s. 138. (2), sch. 3 para. 10. (7)(b); S.S.I. 2015/247, art. 2, sch. (with art. 6)

F99. S. 181. (4) repealed (28.2.2011) by Protection of Vulnerable Groups (Scotland) Act 2007 (asp 14), s. 101. (2), sch. 4 para. 22 (with ss. 90, 99); S.S.I. 2011/157, art. 2. (a) (with art. 5. (1))

F100. S. 181. (5) inserted (17.1.2017) by Criminal Justice (Scotland) Act 2016 (asp 1), ss. 89. (5), 117. (2); S.S.I. 2016/426, art. 2, sch.

182 Stated case: hearing of appeal.S

(1) A stated case under this Part of this Act shall be heard by the [F101. Sheriff Appeal Court] on such date as it may fix.

(2) For the avoidance of doubt, where an appellant, in his application under section 176. (1) of this Act (or in a duly made amendment or addition to that application), refers to an alleged miscarriage of justice, but in stating a case under section 179. (7) of this Act the inferior court is unable to take

the allegation into account, the [F102. Sheriff Appeal Court] may nevertheless have regard to the allegation at a hearing under subsection (1) above.

(3) Except by leave of the [F103. Sheriff Appeal Court] on cause shown, it shall not be competent for an appellant to found any aspect of his appeal on a matter not contained in his application under section 176. (1) of this Act (or in a duly made amendment or addition to that application).

(4) Subsection (3) above shall not apply as respects any ground of appeal specified as an arguable ground of appeal by virtue of subsection (7) of section 180 of this Act.

(5) Without prejudice to any existing power of the [F104. Sheriff Appeal Court], that court may in hearing a stated case—

(a) order the production of any document or other thing connected with the proceedings;

(b) hear any F105. . .evidence relevant to any alleged miscarriage of justice or order such evidence to be heard by [F106an Appeal Sheriff] at the [F104. Sheriff Appeal Court] or by such other person as it may appoint for that purpose;

(c) take account of any circumstances relevant to the case which were not before the trial judge;

(d) remit to any fit person to enquire and report in regard to any matter or circumstance affecting the appeal;

(e) appoint a person with expert knowledge to act as assessor to the [F104. Sheriff Appeal Court] in any case where it appears to the court that such expert knowledge is required for the proper determination of the case;

(f) take account of any matter proposed in any adjustment rejected by the trial judge and of the reasons for such rejection;

(g) take account of any evidence contained in a note of evidence such as is mentioned in section 179. (7) of this Act.

(6) The [F107. Sheriff Appeal Court] may at the hearing remit the stated case back to the inferior court to be amended and returned.

Amendments (Textual)

F101. Words in s. 182. (1) substituted (22.9.2015) by Courts Reform (Scotland) Act 2014 (asp 18), s. 138. (2), sch. 3 para. 11. (2); S.S.I. 2015/247, art. 2, sch. (with art. 6)

F102. Words in s. 182. (2) substituted (22.9.2015) by Courts Reform (Scotland) Act 2014 (asp 18), s. 138. (2), sch. 3 para. 11. (2); S.S.I. 2015/247, art. 2, sch. (with art. 6)

F103. Words in s. 182. (3) substituted (22.9.2015) by Courts Reform (Scotland) Act 2014 (asp 18), s. 138. (2), sch. 3 para. 11. (2); S.S.I. 2015/247, art. 2, sch. (with art. 6)

F104. Words in s. 182. (5) substituted (22.9.2015) by Courts Reform (Scotland) Act 2014 (asp 18), s. 138. (2), sch. 3 para. 11. (2); S.S.I. 2015/247, art. 2, sch. (with art. 6)

F105. Word in s. 182. (5)(b) repealed (1.8.1997) by 1997 c. 48, s. 62. (1)(2), Sch. 1 para. 21. (21), Sch. 3; S.I. 1997/1712, art. 3, Sch. (subject to arts. 4 and 5)

F106. Words in s. 182. (5)(b) substituted (22.9.2015) by Courts Reform (Scotland) Act 2014 (asp 18), s. 138. (2), sch. 3 para. 11. (3); S.S.I. 2015/247, art. 2, sch. (with art. 6)

F107. Words in s. 182. (6) substituted (22.9.2015) by Courts Reform (Scotland) Act 2014 (asp 18), s. 138. (2), sch. 3 para. 11. (2); S.S.I. 2015/247, art. 2, sch. (with art. 6)

Modifications etc. (not altering text)

C11. S. 182 applied (1.7.2013) by The Construction Products Regulations 2013 (S.I. 2013/1387), regs. 1, 9. (9)

C12. S. 182. (5)(a)-(e) applied (1.4.1996) by 1984 c. 12, s. 81. (8) (as substituted (1.4.1996) by 1995 c. 40, ss. 5, 7. (2), Sch. 4 para. 48. (3))

S. 182. (5)(a)-(e) applied (1.7.1997) by S.I. 1997/831, reg. 19. (1)-(4), Sch. 15 para. 5. (8)

S. 182. (5)(a)-(e) applied (3.7.2001) by S.I. 2001/1701, reg. 17, Sch. 13 para. 14. (8)

S. 182. (5)(a)-(e) applied (20.11.2002) by Copyright, Designs and Patents Act 1988 (c. 48), ss. 114. B(10), 204. B(10), 297. D(10) (as inserted by Copyright, etc. and Trade Marks (Offences and Enforcement) Act 2002 (c. 25), ss. 3, 4, 5; S.I. 2002/2749, art. 2)

S. 182. (5)(a)-(e) applied (7.3.2005) by The Electromagnetic Compatibility Regulations 2005 (S.I. 2005/281), reg. 98. (8)

C13. S. 182. (5)(a)-(e) applied (8.4.2000) by S.I. 2000/730, reg. 18, Sch. 9 para. 4. (8) (which amendment was superseded by S.I. 2003/3144, reg. 2. (10))

S. 182. (5)(a)-(e) applied (29.12.2003) by S.I. 2000/730, Sch. 9 para. 22. (8) (as substituted (29.12.2003) by S.I. 2003/3144, reg. 2. (10))

S. 182. (5)(a)-(e) applied (20.7.2007) by The Electromagnetic Compatibility Regulations 2006 (S.I. 2006/3418), reg. 59. (8) (with savings in regs. 7-14, 63, 64)

C14. S. 182. (5)(a)-(e) applied (1.12.2008) by The REACH Enforcement Regulations 2008 (S.I. 2008/2852), reg. 9. (1), Sch. 6 Pt. 3 para. 36 (with reg. 19)

C15. S. 182. (5)(a)-(e) applied by 1949 c. 88, s. 35. ZD(10) (as inserted (1.10.2014) by Intellectual Property Act 2014 (c. 18), ss. 13, 24. (1); S.I. 2014/2330, art. 3, Sch.)

C16. S. 182. (5)(a)-(e) applied (1.12.2008) by The REACH Enforcement Regulations 2008 (S.I. 2008/2852), reg. 9. (1), Sch. 6 Pt. 3 para. 36 (with reg. 19)

C17. S. 182. (5)(a)-(e) applied (1.12.2008) by The REACH Enforcement Regulations 2008 (S.I. 2008/2852), reg. 9. (1), Sch. 6 Pt. 3 para. 36 (with reg. 19)

C18. S. 182. (5)(a)-(e) applied (1.12.2008) by The REACH Enforcement Regulations 2008 (S.I. 2008/2852), reg. 9. (1), Sch. 6 Pt. 3 para. 36 (with reg. 19)

C19. S. 182. (5)(a)-(e) applied (1.12.2008) by The REACH Enforcement Regulations 2008 (S.I. 2008/2852), reg. 9. (1), Sch. 6 Pt. 3 para. 36 (with reg. 19)

183 Stated case: disposal of appeal.S

(1) The [F108. Sheriff Appeal Court] may, subject to subsection (3) below and to section 190. (1) of this Act, dispose of a stated case by—

(a) remitting the cause to the inferior court with its opinion and any direction thereon;

(b) affirming the verdict of the inferior court;

(c) setting aside the verdict of the inferior court and either quashing the conviction or, subject to subsection (2) below, substituting therefor an amended verdict of guilty; or

(d) setting aside the verdict of the inferior court and granting authority to bring a new prosecution in accordance with section 185 of this Act.

[F109. (1. A)Where an appeal against conviction is by virtue of section 11. (7) of the Double Jeopardy (Scotland) Act 2011 (asp 16), paragraphs (a) and (d) of subsection (1) do not apply.]

(2) An amended verdict of guilty substituted under subsection (1)(c) above must be one which could have been returned on the complaint before the inferior court.

(3) The [F110. Sheriff Appeal Court] shall, in an appeal—

(a) against both conviction and sentence, subject to section 190. (1) of this Act, dispose of the appeal against sentence; or

(b) by the prosecutor, against sentence, dispose of the appeal,

by exercise of the power mentioned in section 189. (1) of this Act.

(4) In setting aside, under subsection (1) above, a verdict the [F111. Sheriff Appeal Court] may quash any sentence imposed on the appellant as respects the complaint, and—

(a) in a case where it substitutes an amended verdict of guilty, whether or not the sentence related to the verdict set aside; or

(b) in any other case, where the sentence did not so relate,

may pass another (but not more severe) sentence in substitution for the sentence so quashed.

(5) For the purposes of subsections (3) and (4) above, "sentence" shall be construed as including disposal or order.

(6) Where an appeal against acquittal is sustained, the [F112. Sheriff Appeal Court] may—

(a) convict and, subject to subsection (7) below, sentence the respondent;

(b) remit the case to the inferior court with instructions to convict and sentence the respondent, who shall be bound to attend any diet fixed by the court for such purpose; or

(c) remit the case to the inferior court with their opinion thereon.

(7) Where the [F113. Sheriff Appeal Court] sentences the respondent under subsection (6)(a) above it shall not in any case impose a sentence beyond the maximum sentence which could have

been passed by the inferior court.

(8) Any reference in subsection (6) above to convicting and sentencing shall be construed as including a reference to—

(a) convicting and making some other disposal; or

(b) convicting and deferring sentence.

(9) The [F114. Sheriff Appeal Court] shall have power in an appeal under this Part of this Act to award such expenses both in the [F114. Sheriff Appeal Court] and in the inferior court as it may think fit.

(10) Where, following an appeal, other than an appeal under section 175. (2)(b) or (3) of this Act, the appellant remains liable to imprisonment or detention under the sentence of the inferior court, or is so liable under a sentence passed in the appeal proceedings the [F115. Sheriff Appeal Court] shall have the power where at the time of disposal of the appeal the appellant—

(a) was at liberty on bail, to grant warrant to apprehend and imprison or detain the appellant for a term, to run from the date of such apprehension, not longer than that part of the term or terms of imprisonment or detention specified in the sentence brought under review which remained unexpired at the date of liberation;

(b) is serving a term or terms of imprisonment or detention imposed in relation to a conviction subsequent to the conviction appealed against, to exercise the like powers in regard to him as may be exercised, in relation to an appeal which has been abandoned, by a court of summary jurisdiction in pursuance of section 177. (6) of this Act.

Amendments (Textual)

F108. Words in s. 183. (1) substituted (22.9.2015) by Courts Reform (Scotland) Act 2014 (asp 18), s. 138. (2), sch. 3 para. 12; S.S.I. 2015/247, art. 2, sch. (with art. 6)

F109. S. 183. (1. A) inserted (28.11.2011) by Double Jeopardy (Scotland) Act 2011 (asp 16), s. 17. (3), sch. para. 16; S.S.I. 2011/365, art. 3

F110. Words in s. 183. (3) substituted (22.9.2015) by Courts Reform (Scotland) Act 2014 (asp 18), s. 138. (2), sch. 3 para. 12; S.S.I. 2015/247, art. 2, sch. (with art. 6)

F111. Words in s. 183. (4) substituted (22.9.2015) by Courts Reform (Scotland) Act 2014 (asp 18), s. 138. (2), sch. 3 para. 12; S.S.I. 2015/247, art. 2, sch. (with art. 6)

F112. Words in s. 183. (6) substituted (22.9.2015) by Courts Reform (Scotland) Act 2014 (asp 18), s. 138. (2), sch. 3 para. 12; S.S.I. 2015/247, art. 2, sch. (with art. 6)

F113. Words in s. 183. (7) substituted (22.9.2015) by Courts Reform (Scotland) Act 2014 (asp 18), s. 138. (2), sch. 3 para. 12; S.S.I. 2015/247, art. 2, sch. (with art. 6)

F114. Words in s. 183. (9) substituted (22.9.2015) by Courts Reform (Scotland) Act 2014 (asp 18), s. 138. (2), sch. 3 para. 12; S.S.I. 2015/247, art. 2, sch. (with art. 6)

F115. Words in s. 183. (10) substituted (22.9.2015) by Courts Reform (Scotland) Act 2014 (asp 18), s. 138. (2), sch. 3 para. 12; S.S.I. 2015/247, art. 2, sch. (with art. 6)

184 Abandonment of appeal.S

(1) An appellant in an appeal such as is mentioned in section 176. (1) of this Act may at any time prior to lodging the case with the [F116. Clerk of the Sheriff Appeal Court] abandon his appeal by minute signed by himself or his solicitor, written on the complaint or lodged with the clerk of the inferior court, and intimated to the respondent or the respondent's solicitor, but such abandonment shall be without prejudice to any other competent mode of appeal, review, advocation or suspension.

(2) Subject to section 191 of this Act, on the case being lodged with the [F117. Clerk of the Sheriff Appeal Court], the appellant shall be held to have abandoned any other mode of appeal which might otherwise have been open to him.

Amendments (Textual)

F116. Words in s. 184. (1) substituted (22.9.2015) by Courts Reform (Scotland) Act 2014 (asp 18), s. 138. (2), sch. 3 para. 13; S.S.I. 2015/247, art. 2, sch. (with art. 6)

F117. Words in s. 184. (2) substituted (22.9.2015) by Courts Reform (Scotland) Act 2014 (asp 18), s. 138. (2), sch. 3 para. 13; S.S.I. 2015/247, art. 2, sch. (with art. 6)

New prosecutionS

185 Authorisation of new prosecution.S

(1) Subject to subsection (2) below, where authority is granted under section 183. (1)(d) of this Act, a new prosecution may be brought charging the accused with the same or any similar offence arising out of the same facts; and the proceedings out of which the stated case arose shall not be a bar to such prosecution.

(2) In a new prosecution under this section the accused shall not be charged with an offence more serious than that of which he was convicted in the earlier proceedings.

(3) No sentence may be passed on conviction under the new prosecution which could not have been passed on conviction under the earlier proceedings.

(4) A new prosecution may be brought under this section, notwithstanding that any time limit (other than the time limit mentioned in subsection (5) below) for the commencement of such proceedings has elapsed.

(5) Proceedings in a prosecution under this section shall be commenced within two months of the date on which authority to bring the prosecution was granted.

(6) In proceedings in a new prosecution under this section it shall, subject to subsection (7) below, be competent for either party to lead any evidence which it was competent for him to lead in the earlier proceedings.

(7) The complaint in a new prosecution under this section shall identify any matters as respects which the prosecutor intends to lead evidence by virtue of subsection (6) above which would not have been competent but for that subsection.

(8) For the purposes of subsection (5) above, proceedings shall be deemed to be commenced—

　(a) in a case where such warrant is executed without unreasonable delay, on the date on which a warrant to apprehend or to cite the accused is granted; and

　(b) in any other case, on the date on which the warrant is executed.

(9) Where the two months mentioned in subsection (5) above elapse and no new prosecution has been brought under this section, the order under section 183. (1)(d) of this Act setting aside the verdict shall have the effect, for all purposes, of an acquittal.

(10) On granting authority under section 183. (1)(d) of this Act to bring a new prosecution, the [F118. Sheriff Appeal Court] may, after giving the parties an opportunity of being heard, order the detention of the accused person in custody; but an accused person may not be detained by virtue of this subsection for a period of more than 40 days.

Amendments (Textual)

F118. Words in s. 185. (10) substituted (22.9.2015) by Courts Reform (Scotland) Act 2014 (asp 18), s. 138. (2), sch. 3 para. 14; S.S.I. 2015/247, art. 2, sch. (with art. 6)

Appeals against sentenceS

186 Appeals against sentence only.S

(1) An appeal under section [F119175. (2)(b), (c) or (cza)] F120..., or by virtue of section 175. (4), of this Act shall be by note of appeal, which shall state the ground of appeal.

(2) The note of appeal shall, where the appeal is—

　(a) under section [F119175. (2)(b), (c) or (cza)] F120... be lodged, within one week of—

(i) the passing of the sentence; F121. . . [F122 or]

(ii) the making of the order disposing of the case or deferring sentence; F123...

F123. (iii). . . . .

with the clerk of the court from which the appeal is to be taken; or

(b) by virtue of section 175. (4) be so lodged within four weeks of such passing or making.

(3) The clerk of court on receipt of the note of appeal shall—

(a) send a copy of the note to the respondent or his solicitor; and

(b) obtain a report from the judge who sentenced the convicted person or, as the case may be, who disposed of the case or deferred sentence.

(4) Subject to subsection (5) below, the clerk of court shall within two weeks of the passing of the sentence or within two weeks of the disposal or order against which the appeal is taken—

(a) send to the [F124. Clerk of the Sheriff Appeal Court] the note of appeal, together with the report mentioned in subsection (3)(b) above, a certified copy of the complaint, the minute of proceedings and any other relevant documents; and

(b) send copies of that report to the appellant and respondent or their solicitors.

(5) [F125. The sheriff principal of the sheriffdom in which the judgment was pronounced may, on cause shown,] extend the period of two weeks specified in subsection (4) above for such period as he considers reasonable.

(6) Subject to subsection (4) above, the report mentioned in subsection (3)(b) above shall be available only to the [F126. Sheriff Appeal Court], the parties and, on such conditions as may be prescribed by Act of Adjournal, such other persons or classes of persons as may be so prescribed.

(7) Where the judge's report is not furnished within the period mentioned in subsection (4) above or such period as extended under subsection (5) above, the [F127. Sheriff Appeal Court] may extend such period, or, if it thinks fit, hear and determine the appeal without the report.

(8) Section 181 of this Act shall apply where an appellant fails to comply with the requirement of subsection (2)(a) above as they apply where an applicant fails to comply with any of the requirements of section 176. (1) of this Act.

(9) An appellant under section [F119175. (2)(b), (c) or (cza)] F128..., or by virtue of section 175. (4), of this Act may at any time prior to the hearing of the appeal abandon his appeal by minute, signed by himself or his solicitor, lodged—

(a) in a case where the note of appeal has not yet been sent under subsection (4)(a) above to the [F129. Clerk of the Sheriff Appeal Court], with the clerk of court;

(b) in any other case, with the [F130. Clerk of the Sheriff Appeal Court],

and intimated to the respondent.

(10) Sections 176. (5), 177 and 182. (5)(a) to (e) of this Act shall apply to appeals under section [F119175. (2)(b), (c) or (cza)] F128..., or by virtue of section 175. (4), of this Act as they apply to appeals under section 175. (2)(a) or (d) of this Act, except that, for the purposes of such application to any appeal by virtue of section 175. (4), references in subsections (1) to (4) of section 177 to the appellant shall be construed as references to the convicted person and subsections (6) and (7) of that section shall be disregarded.

Amendments (Textual)

F119. Words in s. 186. (1)(2)(a)(9)(10) substituted (1.2.2011) by Criminal Justice and Licensing (Scotland) Act 2010 (asp 13), ss. 14. (2), 206. (1), Sch. 2 para. 13; S.S.I. 2010/413, art. 2, Sch. (with art. 3)

F120. Words in s. 186. (1)(2) repealed (28.2.2011) by Protection of Vulnerable Groups (Scotland) Act 2007 (asp 14), s. 101. (2), sch. 4 para. 23. (a) (with ss. 90, 99); S.S.I. 2011/157, art. 2. (a) (with art. 5. (1))

F121. Word in s. 186. (2)(a) repealed (4.10.2004) by Criminal Procedure (Amendment) (Scotland) Act 2004 (asp 5), ss. 24. (5)(a), 27. (1); S.S.I. 2004/405, art. 2, Sch. 1 (subject to arts. 3-5)

F122. Word in s. 186. (2)(a)(i) inserted (28.2.2011) by Protection of Vulnerable Groups (Scotland) Act 2007 (asp 14), s. 101. (2), sch. 4 para. 23. (b)(i) (with ss. 90, 99); S.S.I. 2011/157, art. 2. (a) (with art. 5. (1))

F123. S. 186. (2)(a)(iii) repealed (28.2.2011) by Protection of Vulnerable Groups (Scotland) Act

2007 (asp 14), s. 101. (2), sch. 4 para. 23. (b)(ii) (with ss. 90, 99); S.S.I. 2011/157, art. 2. (a) (with art. 5. (1))

F124. Words in s. 186. (4)(a) substituted (22.9.2015) by Courts Reform (Scotland) Act 2014 (asp 18), s. 138. (2), sch. 3 para. 15. (2); S.S.I. 2015/247, art. 2, sch. (with art. 6)

F125. Words in s. 186. (5) substituted (10.12.2007) by Criminal Proceedings etc. (Reform) (Scotland) Act 2007 (asp 6), ss. 25. (2), 84; S.S.I. 2007/479, art. 3. (1), Sch. (as amended by S.S.I. 2007/527)

F126. Words in s. 186. (6) substituted (22.9.2015) by Courts Reform (Scotland) Act 2014 (asp 18), s. 138. (2), sch. 3 para. 15. (3); S.S.I. 2015/247, art. 2, sch. (with art. 6)

F127. Words in s. 186. (7) substituted (22.9.2015) by Courts Reform (Scotland) Act 2014 (asp 18), s. 138. (2), sch. 3 para. 15. (3); S.S.I. 2015/247, art. 2, sch. (with art. 6)

F128. Words in s. 186. (9)(10) repealed (28.2.2011) by Protection of Vulnerable Groups (Scotland) Act 2007 (asp 14), s. 101. (2), sch. 4 para. 23. (a) (with ss. 90, 99); S.S.I. 2011/157, art. 2. (a) (with art. 5. (1))

F129. Words in s. 186. (9)(a) substituted (22.9.2015) by Courts Reform (Scotland) Act 2014 (asp 18), s. 138. (2), sch. 3 para. 15. (2); S.S.I. 2015/247, art. 2, sch. (with art. 6)

F130. Words in s. 186. (9)(b) substituted (22.9.2015) by Courts Reform (Scotland) Act 2014 (asp 18), s. 138. (2), sch. 3 para. 15. (2); S.S.I. 2015/247, art. 2, sch. (with art. 6)

Modifications etc. (not altering text)

C20. S. 186. (4)(b) excluded by 2006 asp 10, s 96. A(5) (as inserted (22.9.2015) by The Courts Reform (Scotland) Act 2014 (Consequential Provisions No. 2) Order 2015 (S.S.I. 2015/338), art. 1, sch. 2 para. 9. (6) (with art. 4))

187 Leave to appeal against sentence.S

(1) The decision whether to grant leave to appeal for the purposes of section [F131175. (2)(b), (c) or (cza)] F132... of this Act shall be made by [F133an Appeal Sheriff] of the [F134. Sheriff Appeal Court] who shall—

(a) if he considers that the note of appeal and other documents sent to the [F135. Clerk of the Sheriff Appeal Court] under section 186. (4)(a) of this Act disclose arguable grounds of appeal, grant leave to appeal and make such comments in writing as he considers appropriate; and

(b) in any other case—

(i) refuse leave to appeal and give reasons in writing for the refusal; and

(ii) where the appellant is on bail and the sentence imposed on his conviction is one of imprisonment, grant a warrant to apprehend and imprison him.

(2) A warrant granted under subsection (1)(b)(ii) above shall not take effect until the expiry of the period of 14 days mentioned in subsection (3) below [F136. (and if that period is extended under subsection (3. A) below before the period being extended expires, until the expiry of the period as so extended)] without an application to the [F137. Sheriff Appeal Court] for leave to appeal having been lodged by the appellant under [F138subsection (3) below].

(3) Where leave to appeal is refused under subsection (1) above the appellant may, within 14 days of intimation under subsection (9) below, apply to the [F139. Sheriff Appeal Court] for leave to appeal.

[F140. (3. A)The [F141. Sheriff Appeal Court] may, on cause shown, extend the period of 14 days mentioned in subsection (3) above, or that period as extended under this subsection, whether or not the period to be extended has expired (and if that period of 14 days has expired, whether or not it expired before section 25. (3) of the Criminal Proceedings etc. (Reform) (Scotland) Act 2007 (asp 6) came into force).]

(4) In deciding an application under subsection (3) above the [F142. Sheriff Appeal Court] shall—

(a) if, after considering the note of appeal and other documents mentioned in subsection (1) above and the reasons for the refusal, it is of the opinion that there are arguable grounds of appeal, grant leave to appeal and make such comments in writing as he considers appropriate; and

(b) in any other case—

(i) refuse leave to appeal and give reasons in writing for the refusal; and

(ii) where the appellant is on bail and the sentence imposed on his conviction is one of imprisonment, grant a warrant to apprehend and imprison him.

(5) The question whether to grant leave to appeal under subsection (1) or (4) above shall be considered and determined in chambers without the parties being present.

(6) Comments in writing made under subsection (1)(a) or (4)(a) above may, without prejudice to the generality of that provision, specify the arguable grounds of appeal (whether or not they are contained in the note of appeal) on the basis of which leave to appeal is granted.

(7) Where the arguable grounds of appeal are specified by virtue of subsection (6) above it shall not, except by leave of the [F143. Sheriff Appeal Court] on cause shown, be competent for the appellant to found any aspect of his appeal on any ground of appeal contained in the note of appeal but not so specified.

(8) Any application by the appellant for the leave of the [F144. Sheriff Appeal Court] under subsection (7) above—

(a) shall be made [F145within 14 days of the date of intimation under subsection (9) below]; and

(b) shall, [F146within 14 days of] that date, be intimated by the appellant to the [F147prosecutor].

[F148. (8. A)The [F149. Sheriff Appeal Court] may, on cause shown, extend the periods of 14 days mentioned in subsection (8) above.]

(9) The [F150. Clerk of the Sheriff Appeal Court] shall forthwith intimate—

(a) a decision under subsection (1) or (4) above; and

(b) in the case of a refusal of leave to appeal, the reasons for the decision,

to the appellant or his solicitor and to the [F151prosecutor].

Amendments (Textual)

F131. Words in s. 187. (1) substituted (1.2.2011) by Criminal Justice and Licensing (Scotland) Act 2010 (asp 13), ss. 14. (2), 206. (1), Sch. 2 para. 14; S.S.I. 2010/413, art. 2, Sch. (with art. 3)

F132. Words in s. 187. (1) repealed (28.2.2011) by Protection of Vulnerable Groups (Scotland) Act 2007 (asp 14), s. 101. (2), sch. 4 para. 24 (with ss. 90, 99); S.S.I. 2011/157, art. 2. (a) (with art. 5. (1))

F133. Words in s. 187. (1) substituted (22.9.2015) by Courts Reform (Scotland) Act 2014 (asp 18), s. 138. (2), sch. 3 para. 16. (2); S.S.I. 2015/247, art. 2, sch. (with art. 6)

F134. Words in s. 187. (1) substituted (22.9.2015) by Courts Reform (Scotland) Act 2014 (asp 18), s. 138. (2), sch. 3 para. 16. (3); S.S.I. 2015/247, art. 2, sch. (with art. 6)

F135. Words in s. 187. (1)(a) substituted (22.9.2015) by Courts Reform (Scotland) Act 2014 (asp 18), s. 138. (2), sch. 3 para. 16. (4); S.S.I. 2015/247, art. 2, sch. (with art. 6)

F136. Words in s. 187. (2) inserted (10.12.2007) by Criminal Proceedings etc. (Reform) (Scotland) Act 2007 (asp 6), ss. 25. (3)(a)(i), 84; S.S.I. 2007/479, art. 3. (1), Sch. (as amended by S.S.I. 2007/527)

F137. Words in s. 187. (2) substituted (22.9.2015) by Courts Reform (Scotland) Act 2014 (asp 18), s. 138. (2), sch. 3 para. 16. (3); S.S.I. 2015/247, art. 2, sch. (with art. 6)

F138. Words in s. 187. (2) substituted (10.12.2007) by Criminal Proceedings etc. (Reform) (Scotland) Act 2007 (asp 6), ss. 25. (3)(a)(ii), 84; S.S.I. 2007/479, art. 3. (1), Sch. (as amended by S.S.I. 2007/527)

F139. Words in s. 187. (3) substituted (22.9.2015) by Courts Reform (Scotland) Act 2014 (asp 18), s. 138. (2), sch. 3 para. 16. (3); S.S.I. 2015/247, art. 2, sch. (with art. 6)

F140. S. 187. (3. A) inserted (10.12.2007) by Criminal Proceedings etc. (Reform) (Scotland) Act 2007 (asp 6), ss. 25. (3)(b), 84; S.S.I. 2007/479, art. 3. (1), Sch. (as amended by S.S.I. 2007/527)

F141. Words in s. 187. (3. A) substituted (22.9.2015) by Courts Reform (Scotland) Act 2014 (asp 18), s. 138. (2), sch. 3 para. 16. (3); S.S.I. 2015/247, art. 2, sch. (with art. 6)

F142. Words in s. 187. (4) substituted (22.9.2015) by Courts Reform (Scotland) Act 2014 (asp 18), s. 138. (2), sch. 3 para. 16. (3); S.S.I. 2015/247, art. 2, sch. (with art. 6)

F143. Words in s. 187. (7) substituted (22.9.2015) by Courts Reform (Scotland) Act 2014 (asp 18), s. 138. (2), sch. 3 para. 16. (3); S.S.I. 2015/247, art. 2, sch. (with art. 6)

F144. Words in s. 187. (8) substituted (22.9.2015) by Courts Reform (Scotland) Act 2014 (asp 18), s. 138. (2), sch. 3 para. 16. (3); S.S.I. 2015/247, art. 2, sch. (with art. 6)

F145. Words in s. 187. (8)(a) substituted (23.4.2007) by Criminal Proceedings etc. (Reform) (Scotland) Act 2007 (asp 6), ss. 80, 84, Sch. para. 18. (3)(a)(i); S.S.I. 2007/250, art. 3. (h)(i) (subject to art. 4. (2))

F146. Words in s. 187. (8)(b) substituted (23.4.2007) by Criminal Proceedings etc. (Reform) (Scotland) Act 2007 (asp 6), ss. 80, 84, Sch. para. 18. (3)(a)(ii); S.S.I. 2007/250, art. 3. (h)(i) (subject to art. 4. (2))

F147. Word in s. 187. (8)(b) substituted (22.9.2015) by Courts Reform (Scotland) Act 2014 (asp 18), s. 138. (2), sch. 3 para. 16. (5); S.S.I. 2015/247, art. 2, sch. (with art. 6)

F148. S. 187. (8. A) inserted (23.4.2007) by Criminal Proceedings etc. (Reform) (Scotland) Act 2007 (asp 6), ss. 80, 84, Sch. para. 18. (3)(b); S.S.I. 2007/250, art. 3. (h)(i) (subject to art. 4. (2))

F149. Words in s. 187. (8. A) substituted (22.9.2015) by Courts Reform (Scotland) Act 2014 (asp 18), s. 138. (2), sch. 3 para. 16. (3); S.S.I. 2015/247, art. 2, sch. (with art. 6)

F150. Words in s. 187. (9) substituted (22.9.2015) by Courts Reform (Scotland) Act 2014 (asp 18), s. 138. (2), sch. 3 para. 16. (4); S.S.I. 2015/247, art. 2, sch. (with art. 6)

F151. Word in s. 187. (9) substituted (22.9.2015) by Courts Reform (Scotland) Act 2014 (asp 18), s. 138. (2), sch. 3 para. 16. (5); S.S.I. 2015/247, art. 2, sch. (with art. 6)

Modifications etc. (not altering text)

C21. S. 187. (9) excluded by 2006 asp 10, s 96. A(5) (as inserted (22.9.2015) by The Courts Reform (Scotland) Act 2014 (Consequential Provisions No. 2) Order 2015 (S.S.I. 2015/338), art. 1, sch. 2 para. 9. (6) (with art. 4))

Disposal of appealsS

188 Setting aside conviction or sentence: prosecutor's consent or application.S

(1) Without prejudice to section 175. (3) or (4) of this Act, where—

(a) an appeal has been taken under section 175. (2) of this Act or by suspension or otherwise and the prosecutor is not prepared to maintain the judgment appealed against he may, by a relevant minute, consent to the conviction or sentence or, as the case may be, conviction and sentence ("sentence" being construed in this section as including disposal or order) being set aside either in whole or in part; or

(b) no such appeal has been taken but the prosecutor is, at any time, not prepared to maintain the judgment on which a conviction is founded or the sentence imposed following such conviction he may, by a relevant minute, apply for the conviction or sentence or, as the case may be, conviction and sentence to be set aside.

(2) For the purposes of subsection (1) above, a "relevant minute" is a minute, signed by the prosecutor—

(a) setting forth the grounds on which he is of the opinion that the judgment cannot be maintained; and

(b) written on the complaint or lodged with the clerk of court.

(3) A copy of any minute under subsection (1) above shall be sent by the prosecutor to the convicted person or his solicitor and the clerk of court shall—

(a) thereupon ascertain and note on the record, whether that person or solicitor desires to be heard by the [F152. Sheriff Appeal Court] before the appeal, or as the case may be application, is disposed of; and

(b) thereafter transmit the complaint and relative proceedings to the [F153. Clerk of the Sheriff Appeal Court].

(4) The [F154. Clerk of the Sheriff Appeal Court], on receipt of a complaint and relative proceedings transmitted under subsection (3) above, shall lay them before any [F155. Appeal Sheriff] of the [F156. Sheriff Appeal Court] either in court or in chambers who, after hearing parties if they desire to be heard, may—

(a) set aside the conviction or the sentence, or both, either in whole or in part and—

(i) award such expenses to the convicted person, both in the [F156. Sheriff Appeal Court] and in the inferior court, as the [F155. Appeal Sheriff] may think fit;

(ii) where the conviction is set aside in part, pass another (but not more severe) sentence in substitution for the sentence imposed in respect of that conviction; and

(iii) where the sentence is set aside, pass another (but not more severe) sentence; or

(b) refuse to set aside the conviction or sentence or, as the case may be, conviction and sentence, in which case the complaint and proceedings shall be returned to the clerk of the inferior court.

(5) Where an appeal has been taken and the complaint and proceedings in respect of that appeal returned under subsection (4)(b) above, the appellant shall be entitled to proceed with the appeal as if it had been marked on the date of their being received by the clerk of the inferior court on such return.

(6) Where an appeal has been taken and a copy minute in respect of that appeal sent under subsection (3) above, the preparation of the draft stated case shall be delayed pending the decision of the [F157. Sheriff Appeal Court].

(7) The period from an application being made under subsection (1)(b) above until its disposal under subsection (4) above (including the day of application and the day of disposal) shall, in relation to the conviction to which the application relates, be disregarded in any computation of time specified in any provision of this Part of this Act.

Amendments (Textual)

F152. Words in s. 188. (3)(a) substituted (22.9.2015) by Courts Reform (Scotland) Act 2014 (asp 18), s. 138. (2), sch. 3 para. 17. (2); S.S.I. 2015/247, art. 2, sch. (with art. 6)

F153. Words in s. 188. (3)(b) substituted (22.9.2015) by Courts Reform (Scotland) Act 2014 (asp 18), s. 138. (2), sch. 3 para. 17. (3); S.S.I. 2015/247, art. 2, sch. (with art. 6)

F154. Words in s. 188. (4) substituted (22.9.2015) by Courts Reform (Scotland) Act 2014 (asp 18), s. 138. (2), sch. 3 para. 17. (3); S.S.I. 2015/247, art. 2, sch. (with art. 6)

F155. Words in s. 188. (4) substituted (22.9.2015) by Courts Reform (Scotland) Act 2014 (asp 18), s. 138. (2), sch. 3 para. 17. (4); S.S.I. 2015/247, art. 2, sch. (with art. 6)

F156. Words in s. 188. (4) substituted (22.9.2015) by Courts Reform (Scotland) Act 2014 (asp 18), s. 138. (2), sch. 3 para. 17. (2); S.S.I. 2015/247, art. 2, sch. (with art. 6)

F157. Words in s. 188. (6) substituted (22.9.2015) by Courts Reform (Scotland) Act 2014 (asp 18), s. 138. (2), sch. 3 para. 17. (2); S.S.I. 2015/247, art. 2, sch. (with art. 6)

189 Disposal of appeal against sentence.S

(1) An appeal against sentence by note of appeal shall be heard by the [F158. Sheriff Appeal Court] on such date as it may fix, and the [F158. Sheriff Appeal Court] may, subject to section 190. (1) of this Act, dispose of such appeal by—

(a) affirming the sentence; or

(b) if the Court thinks that, having regard to all the circumstances, including any F159. . . . evidence such as is mentioned in section 175. (5) of this Act, a different sentence should have been passed, quashing the sentence and, subject to subsection (2) below, passing another sentence, whether more or less severe, in substitution therefor.

(2) In passing another sentence under subsection (1)(b) above, the Court shall not in any case increase the sentence beyond the maximum sentence which could have been passed by the inferior

court.

F160. (2. A)...............................

(3) The [F161. Sheriff Appeal Court] shall have power in an appeal by note of appeal to award such expenses both in the [F161. Sheriff Appeal Court] and in the inferior court as it may think fit.

(4) Where, following an appeal under section 175. (2)(b) or (c), or by virtue of section 175. (4), of this Act, the convicted person remains liable to imprisonment or detention under the sentence of the inferior court or is so liable under a sentence passed in the appeal proceedings, the [F162. Sheriff Appeal Court] shall have power where at the time of disposal of the appeal the convicted person—

(a) was at liberty on bail, to grant warrant to apprehend and imprison or detain the appellant for a term, to run from the date of such apprehension, not longer than that part of the term or terms of imprisonment or detention specified in the sentence brought under review which remained unexpired at the date of liberation; or

(b) is serving a term or terms of imprisonment or detention imposed in relation to a conviction subsequent to the conviction in respect of which the sentence appealed against was imposed, to exercise the like powers in regard to him as may be exercised, in relation to an appeal which has been abandoned, by a court of summary jurisdiction in pursuance of section 177. (6) of this Act.

(5) In subsection (1) above, "appeal against sentence" shall, without prejudice to the generality of the expression, be construed as including an appeal under section 175. (2)(c) [F163or (cza)], and any appeal by virtue of section 175. (4), of this Act; and without prejudice to subsection (6) below, other references to sentence in that subsection and in subsection (4) above shall be construed accordingly.

(6) In disposing of any appeal in a case where the accused has not been convicted, the [F164. Sheriff Appeal Court] may proceed to convict him; and where it does, the reference in subsection (4) above to the conviction in respect of which the sentence appealed against was imposed shall be construed as a reference to the disposal or order appealed against.

(7) In disposing of an appeal under section 175. (2)(b) to (d), (3)(b) or (4) of this Act the [F165. Sheriff Appeal Court] may, without prejudice to any other power in that regard, pronounce an opinion on

[F166. (a)]the sentence or other disposal or order which is appropriate in any similar case; F167...

  F168. (b)...............................

Amendments (Textual)

F158. Words in s. 189. (1) substituted (22.9.2015) by Courts Reform (Scotland) Act 2014 (asp 18), s. 138. (2), sch. 3 para. 18; S.S.I. 2015/247, art. 2, sch. (with art. 6)

F159. Word in s. 189. (1)(b) repealed (1.8.1997) by 1997 c. 48, s. 62. (1)(2), Sch. 1 para. 21. (22), Sch. 3; S.I. 1997/1712, art. 3, Sch. (subject to arts. 4, 5)

F160. S. 189. (2. A) repealed (28.2.2011) by Protection of Vulnerable Groups (Scotland) Act 2007 (asp 14), s. 101. (2), sch. 4 para. 25. (a) (with ss. 90, 99); S.S.I. 2011/157, art. 2. (a) (with art. 5. (1))

F161. Words in s. 189. (3) substituted (22.9.2015) by Courts Reform (Scotland) Act 2014 (asp 18), s. 138. (2), sch. 3 para. 18; S.S.I. 2015/247, art. 2, sch. (with art. 6)

F162. Words in s. 189. (4) substituted (22.9.2015) by Courts Reform (Scotland) Act 2014 (asp 18), s. 138. (2), sch. 3 para. 18; S.S.I. 2015/247, art. 2, sch. (with art. 6)

F163. Words in s. 189. (5) inserted (1.2.2011) by Criminal Justice and Licensing (Scotland) Act 2010 (asp 13), ss. 14. (2), 206. (1), Sch. 2 para. 15; S.S.I. 2010/413, art. 2, Sch. (with art. 3)

F164. Words in s. 189. (6) substituted (22.9.2015) by Courts Reform (Scotland) Act 2014 (asp 18), s. 138. (2), sch. 3 para. 18; S.S.I. 2015/247, art. 2, sch. (with art. 6)

F165. Words in s. 189. (7) substituted (22.9.2015) by Courts Reform (Scotland) Act 2014 (asp 18), s. 138. (2), sch. 3 para. 18; S.S.I. 2015/247, art. 2, sch. (with art. 6)

F166. S. 189. (7): words "become" para. (a) (10.1.2005) by virtue of Protection of Children (Scotland) Act 2003 (asp 5), ss. 16. (10)(b), 22. (2); S.S.I. 2004/522, art. 2 (as amended by S.S.I. 2004/556, art. 2)

F167. Words in s. 189. (7)(a) repealed (28.2.2011) by Protection of Vulnerable Groups (Scotland) Act 2007 (asp 14), s. 101. (2), sch. 4 para. 25. (b)(i) (with ss. 90, 99); S.S.I. 2011/157, art. 2. (a) (with art. 5. (1))

F168. S. 189. (7)(b) repealed (28.2.2011) by Protection of Vulnerable Groups (Scotland) Act 2007 (asp 14), s. 101. (2), sch. 4 para. 25. (b)(ii) (with ss. 90, 99); S.S.I. 2011/157, art. 2. (a) (with art. 5. (1))

190 Disposal of appeal where appellant [F169not criminally responsible].S

(1) In relation to any appeal under section 175. (2) of this Act, the [F170. Sheriff Appeal Court] shall, where it appears to it that the appellant committed the act charged against him but that he was [F171not, because of section 51. A of this Act, criminally responsible for it], dispose of the appeal by—

(a) setting aside the verdict of the inferior court and substituting therefor a verdict of acquittal [F172by reason of the special defence set out in section 51. A of this Act]; and

(b) quashing any sentence imposed on the appellant as respects the complaint and—

(i) making, in respect of the appellant, any order mentioned in section 57. (2)(a) to (d) of this Act; or

(ii) making no order.

(2) [F173. Subsections (3) to (6)] of section 57 of this Act shall apply to an order made under subsection (1)(b)(i) above as it applies to an order made under subsection (2) of that section.

Amendments (Textual)

F169. Words in s. 190 heading substituted (with application in accordance with art. 3 of the commencing S.S.I.) by Criminal Justice and Licensing (Scotland) Act 2010 (asp 13), s. 206. (1), sch. 7 para. 57; S.S.I. 2012/160, art. 3, sch.

F170. Words in s. 190. (1) substituted (22.9.2015) by Courts Reform (Scotland) Act 2014 (asp 18), s. 138. (2), sch. 3 para. 19; S.S.I. 2015/247, art. 2, sch. (with art. 6)

F171. Words in s. 190. (1) substituted (with application in accordance with art. 3 of the commencing S.S.I.) by Criminal Justice and Licensing (Scotland) Act 2010 (asp 13), s. 206. (1), sch. 7 para. 58. (a); S.S.I. 2012/160, art. 3, sch.

F172. Words in s. 190. (1) substituted (with application in accordance with art. 3 of the commencing S.S.I.) by Criminal Justice and Licensing (Scotland) Act 2010 (asp 13), s. 206. (1), sch. 7 para. 58. (b); S.S.I. 2012/160, art. 3, sch.

F173. Words in s. 190. (2) substituted (5.10.2005) by Mental Health (Care and Treatment) (Scotland) Act 2003 (asp 13), ss. 331. (1), 333. (2)-(4), Sch. 4 para. 8. (12); S.S.I. 2005/161, art. 3

MiscellaneousS

191 Appeal by suspension or advocation on ground of miscarriage of justice.S

(1) Notwithstanding section 184. (2) of this Act, a party to a summary prosecution may, where an appeal under section 175 of this Act would be incompetent or would in the circumstances be inappropriate, appeal to the [F174. Sheriff Appeal Court], by bill of suspension against a conviction or, as the case may be, by advocation against an acquittal on the ground of an alleged miscarriage of justice in the proceedings.

(2) Where the alleged miscarriage of justice is referred to in an application under section 176. (1) of this Act, for a stated case as regards the proceedings (or in a duly made amendment or addition to that application), an appeal under subsection (1) above shall not proceed without the leave of

the [F175. Sheriff Appeal Court] until the appeal to which the application relates has been finally disposed of or abandoned.

(3) Sections 182. (5)(a) to (e), 183. (1)(d) and (4) and 185 of this Act shall apply to appeals under this section as they apply to appeals such as are mentioned in section 176. (1) of this Act.

(4) This section is without prejudice to any rule of law relating to bills of suspension or advocation in so far as such rule of law is not inconsistent with this section.

Amendments (Textual)

F174. Words in s. 191. (1) substituted (22.9.2015) by Courts Reform (Scotland) Act 2014 (asp 18), s. 138. (2), sch. 3 para. 20; S.S.I. 2015/247, art. 2, sch. (with art. 6)

F175. Words in s. 191. (2) substituted (22.9.2015) by Courts Reform (Scotland) Act 2014 (asp 18), s. 138. (2), sch. 3 para. 20; S.S.I. 2015/247, art. 2, sch. (with art. 6)

[F176191. ATime limit for lodging bills of advocation and bills of suspensionS

(1) This section applies where a party wishes—

(a) to appeal to the [F177. Sheriff Appeal Court] under section 191. (1) of this Act by bill of suspension against a conviction or by advocation against an acquittal, or

(b) to appeal to the [F178. Sheriff Appeal Court] against, or to bring under review of the [F178. Sheriff Appeal Court], any other decision in a summary prosecution by bill of suspension or by advocation.

(2) The party must lodge the bill of suspension or bill of advocation within 3 weeks of the date of the conviction, acquittal or, as the case may be, other decision to which the bill relates.

(3) The [F179. Sheriff Appeal Court] may, on the application of the party, extend the time limit in subsection (2).

(4) An application under subsection (3) must—

(a) state—

(i) the reasons why the applicant failed to comply with the time limit in subsection (2), and

(ii) the proposed grounds of appeal or review, and

(b) be intimated in writing by the applicant to the other party to the prosecution.

(5) If the other party so requests within 7 days of receipt of intimation of the application under subsection (4)(b), the other party must be given an opportunity to make representations before the application is determined.

(6) Any representations may be made in writing or, if the other party so requests, orally at a hearing; and if a hearing is fixed, the applicant must also be given an opportunity to be heard.]

Amendments (Textual)

F176. S. 191. A inserted (30.10.2010) by Criminal Procedure (Legal Assistance, Detention and Appeals) (Scotland) Act 2010 (asp 15), ss. 6. (1), 9 (with s. 6. (2))

F177. Words in s. 191. A(1)(a) substituted (22.9.2015) by Courts Reform (Scotland) Act 2014 (asp 18), s. 138. (2), sch. 3 para. 21; S.S.I. 2015/247, art. 2, sch. (with art. 6)

F178. Words in s. 191. A(1)(b) substituted (22.9.2015) by Courts Reform (Scotland) Act 2014 (asp 18), s. 138. (2), sch. 3 para. 21; S.S.I. 2015/247, art. 2, sch. (with art. 6)

F179. Words in s. 191. A(3) substituted (22.9.2015) by Courts Reform (Scotland) Act 2014 (asp 18), s. 138. (2), sch. 3 para. 21; S.S.I. 2015/247, art. 2, sch. (with art. 6)

[F180191. BBill of advocation not competent in respect of certain decisionsS

It is not competent to bring under review of the Sheriff Appeal Court by way of bill of advocation a decision of the court of first instance that relates to such objection or denial as is mentioned in section 144. (4).]

Amendments (Textual)

F180. S. 191. B inserted (17.1.2017) by Criminal Justice (Scotland) Act 2016 (asp 1), ss. 93, 117. (2); S.S.I. 2016/426, art. 2, sch.

192 Appeals: miscellaneous provisions.S

(1) Where an appellant has been granted bail, whether his appeal is under this Part of this Act or otherwise, he shall appear personally in court at the diet appointed for the hearing of the appeal.

(2) Where an appellant who has been granted bail does not appear at such a diet, the [F181. Sheriff Appeal Court] shall either—

(a) dispose of the appeal as if it had been abandoned (in which case subsection (5) of section 177 of this Act shall apply accordingly); or

(b) on cause shown permit the appeal to be heard in his absence.

(3) No conviction, sentence, judgement, order of court or other proceeding whatsoever in or for the purposes of summary proceedings under this Act—

(a) shall be quashed for want of form; or

(b) where the accused had legal assistance in his defence, shall be suspended or set aside in respect of any objections to—

(i) the relevancy of the complaint, or to the want of specification therein; or

(ii) the competency or admission or rejection of evidence at the trial in the inferior court, unless such objections were timeously stated.

(4) The provisions regulating appeals shall, subject to the provisions of this Part of this Act, be without prejudice to any other mode of appeal competent.

(5) Any officer of law may serve any bill of suspension or other writ relating to an appeal.

Amendments (Textual)

F181. Words in s. 192. (2) substituted (22.9.2015) by Courts Reform (Scotland) Act 2014 (asp 18), s. 138. (2), sch. 3 para. 23; S.S.I. 2015/247, art. 2, sch. (with art. 6)

193 Suspension of disqualification, forfeiture etc.S

(1) Where upon conviction of any person—

(a) any disqualification, forfeiture or disability attaches to him by reason of such conviction; or

(b) any property, matters or things which are the subject of the prosecution or connected therewith are to be or may be ordered to be destroyed or forfeited,

if the court before which he was convicted thinks fit, the disqualification, forfeiture or disability or, as the case may be, destruction or forfeiture or order for destruction or forfeiture shall be suspended pending the determination of any appeal against conviction or sentence (or disposal or order).

(2) Subsection (1) above does not apply in respect of any disqualification, forfeiture or, as the case may be, destruction or forfeiture or order for destruction or forfeiture under or by virtue of any enactment which contains express provision for the suspension of such disqualification, forfeiture or, as the case may be, destruction or forfeiture or order for destruction or forfeiture pending the determination of any appeal against conviction or sentence (or disposal or order).

(3) Where, upon conviction, a fine has been imposed upon a person or a compensation order has been made against him under section 249 of this Act—

(a) the fine or compensation order shall not be enforced against him and he shall not be liable to make any payment in respect of the fine or compensation order; and

(b) any money paid under the compensation order shall not be paid by the clerk of court to the entitled person under subsection (9) of that section,

pending the determination of any appeal against conviction or sentence (or disposal or order).

Modifications etc. (not altering text)

C22. S. 193 excluded (28.11.2011) by Double Jeopardy (Scotland) Act 2011 (asp 16), ss. 11. (9),

17. (3) (with s. 14); S.S.I. 2011/365, art. 3

[F182 193. A Suspension of certain sentences pending determination of appeal.S

(1) Where a convicted person or the prosecutor appeals to the [F183. Sheriff Appeal Court] under section 175 of this Act F184..., the court may on the application of the appellant direct that the whole, or any remaining part, of a relevant sentence shall be suspended until the appeal, if it is proceeded with, is determined.

(2) Where the court has directed the suspension of the whole or any remaining part of a person's relevant sentence, the person shall, unless the [F185. Sheriff Appeal Court] otherwise directs, appear personally in court on the day or days fixed for the hearing of the appeal.

(3) Where a person fails to appear personally in court as mentioned in subsection (2) above, the court may—

(a) if he is the appellant—

(i) decline to consider the appeal; and

(ii) dismiss it summarily; or

(b) whether or not he is the appellant—

(i) consider and determine the appeal; or

(ii) make such other order as the court thinks fit.

(4) In this section "relevant sentence" means any one or more of the following—

[F186. (aa)a community payback order;]

(d) a restriction of liberty order.

F187. (e)..............................]

Amendments (Textual)

F182. S. 193. A inserted (1.8.1997 except s. 193. A(4)(d) which is in force on 1.7.1998) by 1997 c. 48, s. 24. (2); S.I. 1997/1712, art. 3, Sch. (subject to arts. 4, 5); S.I. 1997/2323, art. 5. (1)

F183. Words in s. 193. A(1) substituted (22.9.2015) by Courts Reform (Scotland) Act 2014 (asp 18), s. 138. (2), sch. 3 para. 24; S.S.I. 2015/247, art. 2, sch. (with art. 6)

F184. Words in s. 193. A(1) repealed (28.2.2011) by Protection of Vulnerable Groups (Scotland) Act 2007 (asp 14), s. 101. (2), sch. 4 para. 26 (with ss. 90, 99); S.S.I. 2011/157, art. 2. (a) (with art. 5. (1))

F185. Words in s. 193. A(2) substituted (22.9.2015) by Courts Reform (Scotland) Act 2014 (asp 18), s. 138. (2), sch. 3 para. 24; S.S.I. 2015/247, art. 2, sch. (with art. 6)

F186. S. 193. A(4)(aa) substituted (1.2.2011) for s. 193. A(4)(a)-(c) by Criminal Justice and Licensing (Scotland) Act 2010 (asp 13), ss. 14. (2), 206. (1), Sch. 2 para. 16. (a); S.S.I. 2010/413, art. 2, Sch. (with art. 3)

F187. S. 193. A(4)(e) repealed (1.2.2011) by Criminal Justice and Licensing (Scotland) Act 2010 (asp 13), ss. 14. (2), 206. (1), Sch. 2 para. 16. (b); S.S.I. 2010/413, art. 2, Sch. (with art. 3)

194 Computation of time.S

(1) If any period of time specified in any provision of this Part of this Act relating to appeals expires on a Saturday, Sunday or court holiday prescribed for the relevant court, the period shall be extended to expire on the next day which is not a Saturday, Sunday or such court holiday.

(2) [F188. The sheriff principal of the sheriffdom in which the judgment was pronounced may, on cause shown,] extend any period specified in sections 178. (1) and 179. (4) and (7) of this Act for such period as he considers reasonable.

(3) For the purposes of sections 176. (1)(a) and 178. (1) of this Act, summary proceedings shall be deemed to be finally determined on the day on which sentence is passed in open court; except that, where in relation to an appeal—

(a) under section 175. (2)(a) or (3)(a); or

(b) in so far as it is against conviction, under section 175. (2)(d),

of this Act sentence is deferred under section 202 of this Act, they shall be deemed finally determined on the day on which sentence is first so deferred in open court.

Amendments (Textual)

F188. Words in s. 194. (2) substituted (10.12.2007) by Criminal Proceedings etc. (Reform) (Scotland) Act 2007 (asp 6), ss. 25. (4), 84; S.S.I. 2007/479, art. 3. (1), Sch. (as amended by S.S.I. 2007/527)

PART 10ZA APPEALS FROM SHERIFF APPEAL COURT

[F1. PART 10. ZAAPPEALS FROM SHERIFF APPEAL COURT

Amendments (Textual)

F1. Pt. 10. ZA inserted (1.4.2015 for specified purposes, 22.9.2015 in so far as not already in force) by Courts Reform (Scotland) Act 2014 (asp 18), ss. 119, 138. (2); S.S.I. 2015/77, art. 2. (2)(3), sch.; S.S.I. 2015/247, art. 2, sch.

194. ZBAppeal from the Sheriff Appeal Court

(1) An appeal on a point of law may be taken to the High Court against any decision of the Sheriff Appeal Court in criminal proceedings, but only with the permission of the High Court.

(2) An appeal under subsection (1) may be taken by any party to the appeal in the Sheriff Appeal Court.

(3) The High Court may give permission for an appeal under subsection (1) only if the Court considers that—

(a) the appeal would raise an important point of principle or practice, or

(b) there is some other compelling reason for the Court to hear the appeal.

(4) An application for permission for an appeal under subsection (1) must be made before the end of the period of 14 days beginning with the day on which the decision of the Sheriff Appeal Court that would be the subject of the appeal was made.

(5) The High Court may extend the period of 14 days mentioned in subsection (4) if satisfied that doing so is justified by exceptional circumstances.

194. ZCAppeals: applications and procedure

(1) An appeal under section 194. ZB(1) is to be made by way of note of appeal.

(2) A note of appeal must specify the point of law on which the appeal is being made.

(3) For the purposes of considering and deciding an appeal under section 194. ZB(1)—

(a) three of the judges of the High Court are to constitute a quorum of the Court,

(b) decisions are to be taken by a majority vote of the members of the Court sitting (including the presiding judge),

(c) each judge sitting may pronounce a separate opinion.

194. ZDApplication for permission for appeal: determination by single judge

(1) An application to the High Court for permission for an appeal under section 194. ZB(1) is to be determined by a single judge of the High Court.

(2) If the judge gives permission for the appeal, the judge may make comments in writing in relation to the appeal.

(3) If the judge refuses permission for the appeal—

(a) the judge must give reasons in writing for the refusal, and

(b) where the appellant is on bail and the sentence imposed on the appellant on conviction is one of imprisonment, the judge must grant a warrant to apprehend and imprison the appellant.

(4) A warrant under subsection (3)(b) does not take effect until the expiry of the period of 14 days mentioned in section 194. ZE(1) (or, where that period is extended under section 194. ZE(2) before the period being extended expires, until the expiry of the period as so extended) without an application for permission having been lodged by the appellant under section 194. ZE(1).

194. ZEFurther application for permission where single judge refuses permission

(1) Where the judge refuses permission for the appeal under section 194. ZD, the appellant may, within the period of 14 days beginning with the day on which intimation of the decision is given under section 194. ZF(2), apply again to the High Court for permission for the appeal.

(2) The High Court may extend the period of 14 days mentioned in subsection (1), or that period as extended under this subsection, whether or not the period to be extended has expired.

(3) The High Court may extend a period under subsection (2) only if satisfied that doing so is justified by exceptional circumstances.

(4) Three of the judges of the High Court are to constitute a quorum for the purposes of considering an application under subsection (1).

(5) If the High Court gives permission for the appeal, the Court may make comments in writing in relation to the appeal.

(6) If the High Court refuses permission for the appeal—

(a) the Court must give reasons in writing for the refusal, and

(b) where the appellant is on bail and the sentence imposed on the appellant on conviction is one of imprisonment, the Court must grant a warrant to apprehend and imprison the appellant.

194. ZFApplications for permission: further provision

(1) An application for permission for an appeal under section 194. ZB(1) is to be considered and determined (whether under section 194. ZD or 194. ZE)—

(a) in chambers without the parties being present,

(b) by reference to section 194. ZB(3), and

(c) on the basis of consideration of—

(i) the note of appeal under section 194. ZC(1), and

(ii) such other document or information (if any) as may be specified by act of adjournal.

(2) The Clerk of Justiciary must, as soon as possible, intimate to the appellant or the appellant's solicitor and to the Crown Agent—

(a) a decision under section 194. ZD or 194. ZE determining the application for permission for an appeal, and

(b) in the case of a refusal of permission for the appeal, the reasons for the decision.

194. ZGRestriction of grounds of appeal

(1) Comments in writing made under section 194. ZD(2) or 194. ZE(5) may specify the arguable

grounds of appeal (whether or not they were stated in the note of appeal) on the basis of which permission for the appeal was given.

(2) Where the arguable grounds of appeal are specified under subsection (1), the appellant may not, except with the permission of the High Court on cause shown, found any aspect of the appeal on a ground of appeal stated in the application for permission but not specified under subsection (1).

(3) An application by the appellant for permission under subsection (2) must—

(a) be made before the end of the period of 14 days beginning with the date of intimation under section 194. ZF(2), and

(b) be intimated by the appellant to the Crown Agent before the end of that period.

(4) The High Court may extend the period of 14 days mentioned in subsection (3) if satisfied that doing so is justified by exceptional circumstances.

(5) The appellant may not, except with the permission of the High Court on cause shown, found any aspect of the appeal on a matter not stated in the note of appeal (or in a duly made amendment or addition to the note of appeal).

(6) Subsection (5) does not apply in relation to a matter specified as an arguable ground of appeal under subsection (1).

194. ZHDisposal of appeals

(1) In disposing of an appeal under section 194. ZB(1), the High Court may—

(a) remit the case back to the Sheriff Appeal Court with its opinion and any direction as to further procedure in, or disposal of, the case, or

(b) exercise any power that the Sheriff Appeal Court could have exercised in relation to disposal of the appeal proceedings before that Court.

(2) So far as necessary for the purposes or in consequence of the exercise of a power by the High Court by virtue of subsection (1)(b)—

(a) references in Part X to the Sheriff Appeal Court are to be read as including references to the High Court, and

(b) references in Part X to a verdict of or sentence passed by the inferior court are to be read as incuding references to a verdict of or sentence passed by the Sheriff Appeal Court in disposing of the appeal before it.

(3) Subsections (1)(b) and (2) do not affect any power in relation to the consideration or disposal of appeals that the High Court has apart from those subsections.

194. ZIProcedure where appellant in custody

(1) Section 177 (procedure where appellant in custody) applies in the case where a party making an appeal (other than an excepted appeal) under section 194. ZB(1) is in custody as it applies in the case where an appellant making an application under section 176 is in custody.

(2) In subsection (1), "excepted appeal" means an appeal against a decision of the Sheriff Appeal Court in—

(a) an appeal under section 32, or

(b) an appeal under section 177. (3).

194. ZJAbandonment of appeal

An appellant in an appeal under section 194. ZB(1) may at any time abandon the appeal by minute to that effect—

(a) signed by the appellant or the appellant's solicitor,

(b) lodged with the Clerk of Justiciary, and

(c) intimated to the respondent or the respondent's solicitor.

194. ZKFinality of proceedings

(1) Every interlocutor and sentence (including disposal or order) pronounced by the High Court in disposing of an appeal relating to summary proceedings is final and conclusive and not subject to review by any court whatsoever.
(2) Subsection (1) is subject to—
    (a) Part XA and section 288. AA, and
    (b) paragraph 13. (a) of Schedule 6 to the Scotland Act 1998.
(3) It is incompetent to stay or suspend any execution or diligence issuing from the High Court under this Part, except for the purposes of an appeal under—
    (a) section 288. AA, or
    (b) paragraph 13. (a) of Schedule 6 to the Scotland Act 1998.

194. ZLComputation of time

If any period of time specified in this Part expires on a Saturday, Sunday or court holiday prescribed for the relevant court, the period is extended to expire on the next day which is not a Saturday, Sunday or such a court holiday.]

Part XA Scottish Criminal Cases Review Commission

[F1. Part XAS Scottish Criminal Cases Review Commission

Amendments (Textual)
F1. Pt. XA (ss. 194. A-194. L) inserted (1.1.1998 for the purpose of inserting ss. 194. A, 194. E and 194. G, otherwise 1.4.1999) by 1997 c. 48, s. 25. (1); S.I. 1997/3004, art. 2, Sch.; S.I. 1999/652, art. 2, Sch. (subject to art. 3)
Modifications etc. (not altering text)
C1. Pt. XA (ss. 194. A-194. L) extended (1.4.1999) by S.I. 1999/1181, art. 2

F2194. A Scottish Criminal Cases Review Commission.S

(1) There shall be established a body corporate to be known as the Scottish Criminal Cases Review Commission (in this Act referred to as "the Commission").
(2) The Commission shall not be regarded as the servant or agent of the Crown or as enjoying any status, immunity or privilege of the Crown; and the Commission's property shall not be regarded as property of, or held on behalf of, the Crown.
(3) The Commission shall consist of not fewer than three members.
(4) The members of the Commission shall be appointed by Her Majesty on the recommendation of the Secretary of State.
(5) At least one third of the members of the Commission shall be persons who are legally qualified; and for this purpose a person is legally qualified if he is an advocate or solicitor of at least ten years' standing.
(6) At least two thirds of the members of the Commission shall be persons who appear to the Secretary of State to have knowledge or experience of any aspect of the criminal justice system;

and for the purposes of this subsection the criminal justice system includes, in particular, the investigation of offences and the treatment of offenders.

(7) Schedule 9. A to this Act, which makes further provision as to the Commission, shall have effect.

Amendments (Textual)

F2. S. 194. A inserted (1.1.1998) by 1997 c. 48, s. 25. (1); S.I. 1997/3004, art. 2, Sch.

References to High CourtS

194. B [F3. References by the Commission]S

(1) The Commission on the consideration of any conviction of a person or of the sentence (other than sentence of death) passed on a person who has been convicted on indictment [F4or complaint] may, if they think fit, at any time, and whether or not an appeal against such conviction or sentence has previously been heard and determined by the High Court [F5or the Sheriff Appeal Court], refer the whole case to the High Court and F6... the case shall be heard and determined, subject to any directions the High Court may make, as if it were an appeal under Part VIII [F7or, as the case may be, Part X] of this Act.

(2) The power of the Commission under this section to refer to the High Court the case of a person convicted shall be exercisable whether or not that person has petitioned for the exercise of Her Majesty's prerogative of mercy.

(3) This section shall apply in relation to a finding under section 55. (2) and an order under section 57. (2) of this Act as it applies, respectively, in relation to a conviction and a sentence.

[F8. (3. A)For the purposes of an appeal under Part X of this Act in a case referred to the High Court under subsection (1)—

(a) the High Court may exercise in the case all the powers and jurisdiction that the Sheriff Appeal Court would, had the case been an appeal to that Court, have had in relation to the case by virtue of section 118 of the Courts Reform (Scotland) Act 2014, and

(b) accordingly, Part X of this Act has effect in relation to the case subject to the following modifications—

(i) references to the Sheriff Appeal Court are to be read as references to the High Court,

(ii) references to an Appeal Sheriff are to be read as references to a judge of the High Court,

(iii) references to the Clerk of the Sheriff Appeal Court are to be read as reference to the Clerk of Justiciary.]

(4) For the purposes of this section "person" includes a person who is deceased.

Amendments (Textual)

F3. S. 194. B title substituted (17.1.2017) by Criminal Justice (Scotland) Act 2016 (asp 1), ss. 96. (3), 117. (2); S.S.I. 2016/426, art. 2, sch.

F4. Words in s. 194. B(1) inserted (1.4.1999) by S.I. 1999/1181, art. 3. (a)

F5. Words in s. 194. B(1) inserted (22.9.2015) by Courts Reform (Scotland) Act 2014 (asp 18), ss. 121. (2), 138. (2); S.S.I. 2015/247, art. 2, sch.

F6. Words in s. 194. B(1) repealed (17.1.2017) by Criminal Justice (Scotland) Act 2016 (asp 1), ss. 96. (2), 117. (2); S.S.I. 2016/426, art. 2, sch.

F7. Words in s. 194. B(1) inserted (1.4.1999) by S.I. 1999/1181, art. 3. (b)

F8. S. 194. B(3. A) inserted (22.9.2015) by Courts Reform (Scotland) Act 2014 (asp 18), ss. 121. (3), 138. (2); S.S.I. 2015/247, art. 2, sch.

194. C Grounds for reference.S

[F9. (1)]The grounds upon which the Commission may refer a case to the High Court are that they believe—

(a) that a miscarriage of justice may have occurred; and

(b) that it is in the interests of justice that a reference should be made.

F10. (2). . . . .

Amendments (Textual)

F9. S. 194. C renumbered as s. 194. C(1) (30.10.2010) by Criminal Procedure (Legal Assistance, Detention and Appeals) (Scotland) Act 2010 (asp 15), ss. 7. (3)(a), 9

F10. S. 194. C(2) repealed (17.1.2017) by Criminal Justice (Scotland) Act 2016 (asp 1), ss. 96. (4), 117. (2); S.S.I. 2016/426, art. 2, sch.

F11194. D Further provision as to references.S

(1) A reference of a conviction, sentence or finding may be made under section 194. B of this Act whether or not an application has been made by or on behalf of the person to whom it relates.

(2) In considering whether to make a reference the Commission shall have regard to—

(a) any application or representations made to the Commission by or on behalf of the person to whom it relates;

(b) any other representations made to the Commission in relation to it: and

(c) any other matters which appear to the Commission to be relevant.

(3) In considering whether to make a reference the Commission may at any time refer to the High Court for the Court's opinion any point on which they desire the Court's assistance; and on a reference under this subsection the High Court shall consider the point referred and furnish the Commission with their opinion on the point.

(4) Where the Commission make a reference to the High Court under section 194. B of this Act they shall—

(a) give to the Court a statement of their reasons for making the reference; and

(b) send a copy of the statement to every person who appears to them to be likely to be a party to any proceedings on the appeal arising from the reference.

[F12. (4. A)The grounds for an appeal arising from a reference to the High Court under section 194. B of this Act must relate to one or more of the reasons for making the reference contained in the Commission's statement of reasons.

(4. B)Despite subsection (4. A), the High Court may, if it considers it is in the interests of justice to do so, grant leave for the appellant to found the appeal on additional grounds.

(4. C)An application by the appellant for leave under subsection (4. B) must be made and intimated to the Crown Agent within 21 days after the date on which a copy of the Commission's statement of reasons is sent under subsection (4)(b).

(4. D)The High Court may, on cause shown, extend the period of 21 days mentioned in subsection (4. C).

(4. E)The Clerk of Justiciary must intimate to the persons mentioned in subsection (4. F)—

(a) a decision under subsection (4. B), and

(b) in the case of a refusal to grant leave for the appeal to be founded on additional grounds, the reasons for the decision.

(4. F)Those persons are—

(a) the appellant or the appellant's solicitor, and

(b) the Crown Agent.]

(5) In every case in which—

(a) an application has been made to the Commission by or on behalf of any person for the reference by them of any conviction, sentence or finding; but

(b) the Commission decide not to make a reference of the conviction, sentence or finding, they shall give a statement of the reasons for their decision to the person who made the application.

Amendments (Textual)

F11. S. 194. D inserted (1.4.1999) by 1997 c. 48, s. 25. (1); S.I. 1999/652, art. 2, Sch. (subject to art. 3)

F12. S. 194. D(4. A)-(4. F) inserted (5.11.2010) by Criminal Justice and Licensing (Scotland) Act 2010 (asp 13), ss. 83, 206. (1); S.S.I. 2010/385, art. 2 (with arts. 3, 4)

F13194. DAHigh Court's power to reject a reference made by the CommissionS

. . . .

Amendments (Textual)

F13. S. 194. DA repealed (17.1.2017) by Criminal Justice (Scotland) Act 2016 (asp 1), ss. 96. (5), 117. (2); S.S.I. 2016/426, art. 2, sch.

F14194. E Extension of Commission's remit to summary cases.S

(1) The Secretary of State may by order provide for this Part of this Act to apply in relation to convictions, sentences and findings made in summary proceedings as they apply in relation to convictions, sentences and findings made in solemn proceedings, and may for that purpose make in such an order such amendments to the provisions of this Part as appear to him to be necessary or expedient.

(2) An order under this section shall be made by statutory instrument, and shall not have effect unless a draft of it has been laid before and approved by a resolution of each House of Parliament.

Amendments (Textual)

F14. S. 194. E inserted (1.1.1998) by 1997 c. 48, s. 25. (1); S.I. 1997/3004, art. 2, Sch.

F15194. F Further powers.S

The Commission may take any steps which they consider appropriate for assisting them in the exercise of any of their functions and may, in particular—

(a) themselves undertake inquiries and obtain statements, opinions or reports; or

(b) request the Lord Advocate or any other person to undertake such inquiries or obtain such statements, opinions and reports.

Amendments (Textual)

F15. S. 194. F inserted (1.4.1999) by 1997 c. 48, s. 25. (1); S.I. 1999/652, art. 2, Sch. (subject to art. 3)

F16194. G Supplementary provision.S

(1) The Secretary of State may by order make such incidental, consequential, transitional or supplementary provisions as may appear to him to be necessary or expedient for the purpose of bringing this Part of this Act into operation, and, without prejudice to the generality of the foregoing, of dealing with any cases being considered by him under section 124 of this Act at the time when this Part comes into force, and an order under this section may make different provision in relation to different cases or classes of case.

(2) An order under this section shall be made by statutory instrument subject to annulment in pursuance of a resolution of either House of Parliament.

Amendments (Textual)

F16. S. 194. G inserted (1.1.1998) by 1997 c. 48, s. 25. (1); S.I. 1997/3004, art. 2, Sch.

Powers of investigation of CommissionS

F17194. H Power to request precognition on oath.S

(1) Where it appears to the Commission that a person may have information which they require for the purposes of carrying out their functions, and the person refuses to make any statement to them, they may apply to the sheriff under this section.

(2) On an application made by the Commission under this section, the sheriff may, if he is satisfied that it is reasonable in the circumstances, grant warrant to cite the person concerned to appear before the sheriff in chambers at such time or place as shall be specified in the citation, for precognition on oath by a member of the Commission or a person appointed by them to act in that regard.

(3) Any person who, having been duly cited to attend for precognition under subsection (2) above and having been given at least 48 hours notice, fails without reasonable excuse to attend shall be guilty of an offence and liable on summary conviction to a fine not exceeding level 3 on the standard scale or to imprisonment for a period not exceeding 21 days; and the court may issue a warrant for the apprehension of the person concerned ordering him to be brought before a sheriff for precognition on oath.

(4) Any person who, having been duly cited to attend for precognition under subsection (2) above, attends but—

(a) refuses to give information within his knowledge or to produce evidence in his possession; or

(b) prevaricates in his evidence,

shall be guilty of an offence and shall be liable to be summarily subjected to a fine not exceeding level 3 on the standard scale or to imprisonment for a period not exceeding 21 days.

Amendments (Textual)

F17. S. 194. H inserted (1.4.1999) by 1997 c. 48, s. 25. (1); S.I. 1999/652, art. 2, Sch. (subject to art. 3)

F18194. I Power to obtain documents etc.S

(1) Where the Commission believe that a person or a public body has possession or control of a document or other material which may assist them in the exercise of any of their functions, they may apply to the High Court for an order requiring that person or body—

(a) to produce the document or other material to the Commission or to give the Commission access to it; and

(b) to allow the Commission to take away the document or other material or to make and take away a copy of it in such form as they think appropriate,

and such an order may direct that the document or other material must not be destroyed, damaged or altered before the direction is withdrawn by the Court.

(2) The duty to comply with an order under this section is not affected by any obligation of secrecy or other limitation on disclosure (including any such obligation or limitation imposed by or by virtue of any enactment) which would otherwise prevent the production of the document or other material to the Commission or the giving of access to it to the Commission.

(3) The documents and other material covered by this section include, in particular, any document or other material obtained or created during any investigation or proceedings relating to—

(a) the case in relation to which the Commission's function is being or may be exercised; or

(b) any other case which may be in any way connected with that case (whether or not any function of the Commission could be exercised in relation to that other case).

(4) In this section—

"Minister" means a Minister of the Crown as defined by section 8 of the Ministers of the Crown Act 1975;

F19...

"public body" means

   - [F20the Police Service of Scotland;]

   - any government department, local authority or other body constituted for the purposes of the public service, local government or the administration of justice; or

   - any other body whose members are appointed by Her Majesty, any Minister [F21, the Scottish Ministers] or any government department or whose revenues consist wholly or mainly of money provided by Parliament.

Amendments (Textual)

F18. S. 194. I inserted (1.4.1999) by 1997 c. 48, s. 25. (1); S.I. 1999/652, art. 2, Sch. (subject to art. 3)

F19. Definition in s. 194. I(4) repealed (1.4.2013) by Police and Fire Reform (Scotland) Act 2012 (asp 8), s. 129. (2), sch. 8 Pt. 1; S.S.I. 2013/51, art. 2 (with transitional provisions and savings in S.S.I. 2013/121)

F20. Words in s. 194. I(4) substituted (1.4.2013) by Police and Fire Reform (Scotland) Act 2012 (asp 8), s. 129. (2), sch. 7 para. 12. (9); S.S.I. 2013/51, art. 2 (with transitional provisions and savings in S.S.I. 2013/121)

F21. Words in s. 194. I(4) inserted (1.7.1999) by S.I. 1999/1820, arts. 1. (2), 4, Sch. 2 Pt. 1 para. 122. (2); S.I. 1998/3178, art. 3

[F22194. IAPower to request assistance in obtaining information abroadS

(1) Where it appears to the Commission that there may be information which they require for the purposes of carrying out their functions, and the information is outside the United Kingdom, they may apply to the High Court to request assistance.

(2) On an application made by the Commission under subsection (1), the High Court may request assistance if satisfied that it is reasonable in the circumstances.

(3) In this section, "request assistance" means request assistance in obtaining outside the United Kingdom any information specified in the request for use by the Commission for the purposes of carrying out their functions.

(4) Section 8 of the Crime (International Co-operation) Act 2003 (c.32) (sending requests for assistance) applies to requests for assistance under this section as it applies to requests for assistance under section 7 of that Act.

(5) Subsections (2), (3) and (6) of section 9 of that Act (use of evidence obtained) apply to information obtained pursuant to a request for assistance under this section as they apply under subsection (1) of that section to evidence obtained pursuant to a request for assistance under section 7 of that Act.]

Amendments (Textual)

F22. S. 194. IA inserted (13.12.2010) by Criminal Justice and Licensing (Scotland) Act 2010 (asp 13), ss. 105, 206. (1); S.S.I. 2010/413, art. 2, Sch.

Disclosure of informationS

F23194. J Offence of disclosure.S

(1) A person who is or has been a member or employee of the Commission shall not disclose any information obtained by the Commission in the exercise of any of their functions unless the disclosure of the information is excepted from this section by section 194. K [F24or 194. M] of this Act.

(2) A member of the Commission shall not authorise the disclosure by an employee of the Commission of any information obtained by the Commission in the exercise of any of their functions unless the authorisation of the disclosure of the information is excepted from this section by section 194. K [F25or 194. M] of this Act.

(3) A person who contravenes this section is guilty of an offence and liable on summary conviction to a fine of an amount not exceeding level 5 on the standard scale.

Amendments (Textual)

F23. S. 194. J inserted (1.4.1999) by 1997 c. 48, s. 25. (1); S.I. 1999/652, art. 2, Sch. (subject to art. 3)

F24. Words in s. 194. J(1) inserted (24.9.2012) by Criminal Cases (Punishment and Review) (Scotland) Act 2012 (asp 7), ss. 3. (2), 5. (2); S.S.I. 2012/249, art. 2

F25. Words in s. 194. J(2) inserted (24.9.2012) by Criminal Cases (Punishment and Review) (Scotland) Act 2012 (asp 7), ss. 3. (2), 5. (2); S.S.I. 2012/249, art. 2

F26194. K Exceptions from obligations of non-disclosure.S

(1) The disclosure of information, or the authorisation of the disclosure of information, is excepted from section 194. J of this Act by this section if the information is disclosed, or is authorised to be disclosed—

(a) for the purposes of any criminal, disciplinary or civil proceedings;

(b) in order to assist in dealing with an application made to the Secretary of State for compensation for a miscarriage of justice;

(c) by a person who is a member or an employee of the Commission to another person who is a member or an employee of the Commission;

(d) in any statement or report required by this Act;

(e) in or in connection with the exercise of any function under this Act; or

(f) in any circumstances in which the disclosure of information is permitted by an order made by the Secretary of State.

(2) The disclosure of information is also excepted from section 194. J of this Act by this section if the information is disclosed by an employee of the Commission who is authorised to disclose the information by a member of the Commission.

(3) The disclosure of information, or the authorisation of the disclosure of information, is also excepted from section 194. J of this Act by this section if the information is disclosed, or is authorised to be disclosed, for the purposes of—

(a) the investigation of an offence; or

(b) deciding whether to prosecute a person for an offence,

unless the disclosure is or would be prevented by an obligation or other limitation on disclosure (including any such obligation or limitation imposed by, under or by virtue of any enactment) arising otherwise than under that section.

(4) Where the disclosure of information is excepted from section 194. J of this Act by subsection (1) or (2) above, the disclosure of the information is not prevented by any obligation of secrecy or other limitation on disclosure (including any such obligation or limitation imposed by, under or by virtue of any enactment) arising otherwise than under that section.

(5) The power to make an order under subsection (1)(f) above is exercisable by statutory instrument which shall be subject to annulment in pursuance of a resolution of either House of Parliament.

Amendments (Textual)

F26. S. 194. K inserted (1.4.1999) by 1997 c. 48, s. 25. (1); S.I. 1999/652, art. 2, Sch. (subject to art. 3)

[F27194. L Consent to disclosure.S

(1) Where a person or body is required by an order under section 194. I of this Act to produce or allow access to a document or other material to the Commission and notifies them that any information contained in the document or other material to which the order relates is not to be disclosed by the Commission without his or its prior consent, the Commission shall not disclose the information without such consent.

(2) Such consent may not be withheld unless—

(a) (apart from section 194. I of this Act) the person would have been prevented by any obligation of secrecy or other limitation on disclosure from disclosing the information without such consent; and

(b) it is reasonable for the person to withhold his consent to disclosure of the information by the Commission.

(3) An obligation of secrecy or other limitation on disclosure which applies to a person only where disclosure is not authorised by another person shall not be taken for the purposes of subsection (2)(a) above to prevent the disclosure by the person of information to the Commission unless—

(a) reasonable steps have been taken to obtain the authorisation of the other person; or

(b) such authorisation could not reasonably be expected to be obtained.]]

Amendments (Textual)

F27. S. 194. L inserted (1.4.1999) by 1997 c. 48, s. 25. (1); S.I. 1999/652, art. 2, Sch. (subject to art. 3)

[F28. Special circumstances for disclosureS

Amendments (Textual)

F28. Ss. 194. M-194. T and cross-heading inserted (24.9.2012) by Criminal Cases (Punishment and Review) (Scotland) Act 2012 (asp 7), ss. 3. (3), 5. (2); S.S.I. 2012/249, art. 2

194. MFurther exception to section 194. JS

(1) The disclosure of information, or the authorisation of disclosure of information, is excepted from section 194. J by this section if—

(a) the conditions specified in subsection (2) are met, and

(b) the Commission have determined that it is appropriate in the whole circumstances for the information to be disclosed.

(2) The conditions are that—

(a) the information relates to a case that has been referred to the High Court under section 194. B(1),

(b) the reference concerns—

(i) a conviction, or

(ii) a finding under section 55. (2), and

(c) the case has fallen, or has been abandoned, under the provisions or other rules applying by virtue of section 194. B(1).

194. NEffect of the exceptionS

(1) Where the disclosure of information is excepted from section 194. J by section 194. M, the disclosure of the information is not prevented by any obligation of confidentiality or other limitation on disclosure arising otherwise than under section 194. J.

(2) For the purpose of subsection (1), such an obligation or limitation does not include one imposed—

(a) by, under or by virtue of any enactment, or

(b) by any interdict or other court order applying in connection with this section.

194. ONotification and representations etc.S

(1) When considering for the purpose of section 194. M(1) the question of whether it is appropriate for the information to be disclosed, the Commission have the following duties.

(2) The Commission must—

(a) so far as practicable, take reasonable measures to—

(i) notify each of the affected persons of the possibility that the information may be disclosed, and

(ii) seek the views of each of them on the question, and

(b) to such extent (and in such manner) as they think fit, consult the other interested persons.

(3) The Commission must—

(a) allow the prescribed period for each of the affected and other interested persons involved to take steps (including legal action) in their own favour in relation to the question, and

(b) have regard to any material representations made to them on the question by any of those affected and other interested persons within the prescribed period.

(4) The Commission must have regard to any other factors that they believe to be significant in relation to the question.

(5) In subsections (2) and (3)—

(a) the references to the affected persons are to the persons—

(i) to whom the information directly relates, or

(ii) from whom the information was obtained, whether directly or indirectly,

(b) the references to the other interested persons are to (so far as not among the affected persons)—

(i) the Lord Advocate, and

(ii) such additional persons (if any) as appear to the Commission to have a substantial interest in the question.

(6) In subsection (3), the references to the prescribed period in relation to a particular person are to—

(a) the period of 6 weeks, or

(b) such longer period as the Commission may set,

starting with the date on which the notification was sent to, or (as the case may be) consultation was initiated with respect to, the person.

(7) Subsections (3) and (6) are inapplicable in relation to a particular person if the Commission cannot reasonably ascertain the person's whereabouts.

194. PConsent if UK interestS

(1) Unless subsection (3) is complied with, section 194. M(1) is of no effect in relation to any information falling within subsection (2).

(2) Information falls within this subsection if it—

(a) is held by the Commission, and

(b) at any time, has been supplied by the UK Government under arrangements of any kind.

(3) This subsection is complied with if, at any time, the UK Government has in connection with section 194. M(1) given its consent to disclosure of the information.

(4) In this section, "the UK Government" means a Minister of the Crown or a department of the Government of the United Kingdom.

194. QConsent if foreign interestS

(1) Unless subsection (3) is complied with, section 194. M(1) is of no effect in relation to any information falling within subsection (2).

(2) Information falls within this subsection if it—

(a) is held by the Commission, and

(b) at any time, has been supplied by a designated foreign authority under arrangements of any kind.

(3) This subsection is complied with if the designated foreign authority has in connection with section 194. M(1) given its consent to disclosure of the information, by virtue of—

(a) the arrangements concerned, or

(b) subsection (4).

(4) Where not previously given by virtue of those arrangements, it is for the Commission to seek the designated foreign authority's consent to disclosure of the information.

(5) Subsection (1) does not apply if the information also falls within section 194. P(2).

194. RDesignated foreign authorityS

(1) The references in section 194. Q to a designated foreign authority are to a current or previous authority of a prosecutorial, judicial or other character which is or was located within a country or territory outwith the United Kingdom.

(2) But, if in connection with subsection (4) of that section—

(a) the Commission cannot reasonably identify or find the particular authority in question, or

(b) they are unsuccessful in their reasonable attempts to communicate with it,

the references in subsections (3) and (4) of that section to the designated foreign authority are to be read as if they were to the relevant foreign government.

(3) In the application of subsection (2), paragraph (a) of subsection (3) of that section is to be ignored.

(4) In subsection (2)—

(a) the references to the Commission include their acting with the Lord Advocate's help,

(b) the reference to the relevant foreign government—

(i) is to the government of the other country or territory,

(ii) in the event of doubt as to the status or operation of a governmental system in the other country or territory, is to be regarded as being to the body described in subsection (5).

(5) That is, the principal body in it (for the time being (if any)) that is recognised by the Government of the United Kingdom as having responsibility for exercising governmental control centrally.

194. SDisapplication of sections 194. O to 194. RS

(1) Sections 194. O to 194. R cease to have effect if subsection (2) prevails.

(2) This subsection prevails where, on their preliminary examination of the question to which section 194. O(1) relates, the Commission determine for the purpose of section 194. M(1) that it is manifestly inappropriate for the information to be disclosed.

(3) But—

(a) if there is a material change in any significant factor on which the determination depended, it is open to the Commission to re-examine the question (and this is to be regarded as another preliminary examination of the question),

(b) where they choose to re-examine the question, the effect of sections 194. O to 194. R is restored unless subsection (2) again prevails.

194. TFinal disclosure-related mattersS

(1) If the Commission decide in pursuance of section 194. M(1) to disclose the information—

(a) subsection (2) applies initially, and

(b) subsection (3) applies subsequently.

(2) Before disclosing the information, the Commission must—

(a) so far as practicable, take reasonable measures to notify of the decision—

(i) each of the affected persons, and

(ii) to the same extent as they were consulted under section 194. O(2)(b), the other interested persons, and

(b) allow the prescribed period for each of the affected and other interested persons involved to take steps (including legal action) in their own favour in relation to the decision.

(3) In disclosing the information, the Commission must—

(a) explain the context in which the information is being disclosed by them (including by describing the background to the case), and

(b) where (for any reason) other information relating to the case remains undisclosed by them, explicitly state that fact,

and do so along with the material by which the disclosure is made.

(4) In subsection (2), the references to the affected and other interested persons are to be construed in accordance with section 194. O(5).

(5) In subsection (2)(b), the reference to the prescribed period in relation to a particular person is to—

(a) the period of 6 weeks, or

(b) such longer period as the Commission may set,

starting with the date on which the notification was sent to the person.

(6) Subsections (2)(b) and (5) are inapplicable in relation to a particular person if the Commission cannot reasonably ascertain the person's whereabouts.

(7) In subsection (3)(b), the reference to other information is to any other information obtained by the Commission in the exercise of their functions.]

PART XI Sentencing

PART XI Sentencing

195 Remit to High Court for sentence.S

(1) Where at any diet in proceedings on indictment in the sheriff court, sentence falls to be imposed but the sheriff holds that any competent sentence which he can impose is inadequate [F1or it appears to him that the criteria mentioned in section 210. E of this Act (that is to say, the risk criteria) may be met] so that [F2, in either case,] the question of sentence is appropriate for the High Court, he shall—

(a) endorse upon the record copy of the indictment a certificate of the plea or the verdict, as the case may be;

(b) by interlocutor written on the record copy remit the convicted person to the High Court for sentence; and

(c) append to the interlocutor a note of his reasons for the remit,

and a remit under this section shall be sufficient warrant to bring the accused before the High Court for sentence and shall remain in force until the person is sentenced.

(2) Where under any enactment an offence is punishable on conviction on indictment by imprisonment for a term exceeding [F3five years] but the enactment either expressly or impliedly restricts the power of the sheriff to impose a sentence of imprisonment for a term exceeding [F3five years], it shall be competent for the sheriff to remit the accused to the High Court for sentence under subsection (1) above; and it shall be competent for the High Court to pass any

sentence which it could have passed if the person had been convicted before it.

(3) When the Clerk of Justiciary receives the record copy of the indictment he shall send a copy of the note of reasons to the convicted person or his solicitor and to the Crown Agent.

(4) Subject to subsection (3) above, the note of reasons shall be available only to the High Court and the parties.

Amendments (Textual)

F1. Words in s. 195. (1) inserted (19.6.2006 for certain purposes and otherwise prosp.) by Criminal Justice (Scotland) Act 2003 (asp 7), ss. 1. (2), 89, Sch. 1 para. 2. (5)(a): S.S.I. 2006/332, art. 2

F2. Words in s. 195. (1) inserted (19.6.2006 for certain purposes and otherwise prosp.) by Criminal Justice (Scotland) Act 2003 (asp 7), ss. 1. (2), 89, Sch. 1 para. 2. (5)(b); S.S.I. 2006/332, art. 2

F3. Words in s. 195. (2) substituted (1.5.2004) by 1997 c. 48, ss. 13. (3), 65. (2); S.S.I. 2004/176, art. 2

196 Sentence following guilty plea.S

[F4. (1)] In determining what sentence to pass on, or what other disposal or order to make in relation to, an offender who has pled guilty to an offence, a court [F5shall] take into account—

(a) the stage in the proceedings for the offence at which the offender indicated his intention to plead guilty, and

(b) the circumstances in which that indication was given.

[F6. (1. A)In passing sentence on an offender referred to in subsection (1) above, the court shall—

(a) state whether, having taken account of the matters mentioned in paragraphs (a) and (b) of that subsection, the sentence imposed in respect of the offence is different from that which the court would otherwise have imposed; and

(b) if it is not, state reasons why it is not.]

[F7. (2)Where the court is passing sentence on an offender under section 205. B(2) of this Act and that offender has pled guilty to the offence for which he is being so sentenced, the court may, after taking into account the matters mentioned in paragraphs (a) and (b) of subsection (1) above, pass a sentence of less than seven years imprisonment or, as the case may be, detention but any such sentence shall not be of a term of imprisonment or period of detention of less than five years, two hundred and nineteen days.]

Amendments (Textual)

F4. S. 196 renumbered as s. 196. (1) (20.10.1997) by 1997 c. 48, s. 2. (2)(a); S.I. 1997/2323, art. 3, Sch. 1

F5. Word in s. 196. (1) substituted (4.10.2004) by Criminal Procedure (Amendment) (Scotland) Act 2004 (asp 5), ss. 20. (2), 27. (1); S.S.I. 2004/405, art. 2, Sch. 1 (subject to savings in arts. 3-5)

F6. S. 196. (1. A) inserted (4.10.2004) by Criminal Procedure (Amendment) (Scotland) Act 2004 (asp 5), ss. 20. (3), 27. (1); S.S.I. 2004/405, art. 2, Sch. 1 (subject to savings in arts. 3-5)

F7. S. 196. (2) inserted (20.10.1997) by 1997 c. 48, s. 2. (2)(b); S.I. 1997/2323, art. 3, Sch. 1

197 Sentencing guidelines.S

Without prejudice to any rule of law, a court in passing sentence shall have regard to any relevant opinion pronounced under section 118. (7) or section 189. (7) of this Act.

198 Form of sentence.S

(1) In any case the sentence to be pronounced shall be announced by the judge in open court and shall be entered in the record in the form prescribed by Act of Adjournal.

(2) In recording a sentence of imprisonment, it shall be sufficient to minute the term of imprisonment to which the court sentenced the accused, without specifying the prison in which the sentence is to be carried out; and an entry of sentence, signed by the clerk of court, shall be full warrant and authority for any subsequent execution of the sentence and for the clerk to issue extracts for the purposes of execution or otherwise.

(3) In extracting a sentence of imprisonment, the extract may be in the form set out in an Act of Adjournal or as nearly as may be in such form.

199 Power to mitigate penalties.S

(1) Subject to subsection (3) below, where a person is convicted of the contravention of an enactment and the penalty which may be imposed involves—

    (a) imprisonment;

    (b) the imposition of a fine;

    (c) the finding of caution for good behaviour or otherwise whether or not imposed in addition to imprisonment or a fine,

subsection (2) below shall apply.

(2) Where this subsection applies, the court, in addition to any other power conferred by statute, shall have power—

    (a) to reduce the period of imprisonment;

    (b) to substitute for imprisonment a fine (either with or without the finding of caution for good behaviour);

    (c) to substitute for imprisonment or a fine the finding of caution;

    (d) to reduce the amount of the fine;

    (e) to dispense with the finding of caution.

(3) Subsection (2) above shall not apply—

    (a) in relation to an enactment which carries into effect a treaty, convention, or agreement with a foreign state which stipulates for a fine of a minimum amount; or

    (b) to proceedings taken under any Act relating to any of Her Majesty's regular or auxiliary forces. [F8; or

    (c) to any proceedings in which the court on conviction is under a duty to impose a sentence under section 205. A(2) or 205. B(2) of this Act.]

(4) Where, in summary proceedings, a fine is imposed in substitution for imprisonment, the fine—

    (a) in the case of an offence which is triable either summarily or on indictment, shall not exceed the prescribed sum; and

    (b) in the case of an offence triable only summarily, shall not exceed level 4 on the standard scale.

(5) Where the finding of caution is imposed under this section—

    (a) in respect of an offence which is triable only summarily, the amount shall not exceed level 4 on the standard scale and the period shall not exceed that which the court may impose under this Act; and

    (b) in any other case, the amount shall not exceed the prescribed sum and the period shall not exceed 12 months.

Amendments (Textual)

F8. S. 199. (3)(c) and the preceding word "; or" inserted (20.10.1997 for specified purposes and otherwise prosp.) by 1997 c. 48, ss. 62. (1), 65. (2), Sch. 1 para. 21. (23); S.I. 1997/2323, art. 3, Sch. 1

Modifications etc. (not altering text)

C1. S. 199. (2)(b) excluded (1.12.2010) by Sexual Offences (Scotland) Act 2009 (asp 9), ss. 48. (2), 62. (2); S.S.I. 2010/357, art. 2

Pre-sentencing procedureS

200 Remand for inquiry into physical or mental condition.S

(1) Without prejudice to any powers exercisable by a court under section 201 of this Act, where—

(a) the court finds that an accused has committed an offence punishable with imprisonment; and

(b) it appears to the court that before the method of dealing with him is determined an inquiry ought to be made into his physical or mental condition,

subsection (2) below shall apply.

(2) Where this subsection applies the court shall—

(a) for the purpose of inquiry solely into his physical condition, remand him in custody or on bail;

(b) for the purpose of inquiry into his mental condition (whether or not in addition to his physical condition), remand him in custody or on bail or, where the court is satisfied—

(i) on the written or oral evidence of a medical practitioner, that the person appears to be suffering from a mental disorder; and

[F9. (ii)that the accused could be admitted to a hospital that is suitable for his detention,] make an order committing him to that hospital,

for such period or periods, no single period exceeding three weeks, as the court thinks necessary to enable a medical examination and report to be made.

(3) Where the court is of the opinion that a person ought to continue to be committed to hospital for the purpose of inquiry into his mental condition following the expiry of the period specified in an order for committal to hospital under paragraph (b) of subsection (2) above, the court may—

(a) if the condition in sub-paragraph (i) of that paragraph continues to be satisfied and [F10he could be admitted to a hospital that is suitable] for his continued detention, renew the order for such further period not exceeding three weeks as the court thinks necessary to enable a medical examination and report to be made; and

(b) in any other case, remand the person in custody or on bail in accordance with subsection (2) above.

(4) An order under subsection (3)(a) above may, unless objection is made by or on behalf of the person to whom it relates, be made in his absence.

(5) Where, before the expiry of the period specified in an order for committal to hospital under subsection (2)(b) above, the court considers, on an application made to it, that committal to hospital is no longer required in relation to the person, the court shall revoke the order and may make such other order, under subsection (2)(a) above or any other provision of this Part of this Act, as the court considers appropriate.

(6) Where an accused is remanded on bail under this section, it shall be a condition of the order granting bail that he shall—

(a) undergo a medical examination by a duly qualified registered medical practitioner or, where the inquiry is into his mental condition, and the order granting bail so specifies, two such practitioners; and

(b) for the purpose of such examination, attend at an institution or place, or on any such practitioner specified in the order granting bail and, where the inquiry is into his mental condition, comply with any directions which may be given to him for the said purpose by any person so specified or by a person of any class so specified,

and, if arrangements have been made for his reception, it may be a condition of the order granting bail that the person shall, for the purpose of the examination, reside in an institution or place specified as aforesaid, not being an institution or place to which he could have been remanded in custody, until the expiry of such period as may be so specified or until he is discharged therefrom, whichever first occurs.

(7) On exercising the powers conferred by this section to remand in custody or on bail the court shall—

(a) where the person is remanded in custody, send to the institution or place in which he is detained; and

(b) where the person is released on bail, send to the institution or place at which or the person by whom he is to be examined,

a statement of the reasons for which it appears to the court that an inquiry ought to be made into his physical or mental condition, and of any information before the court about his physical or mental condition.

(8) On making an order of committal to hospital under subsection (2)(b) above the court shall send to the hospital specified in the order a statement of the reasons for which the court is of the opinion that an inquiry ought to be made into the mental condition of the person to whom it relates, and of any information before the court about his mental condition.

(9) A person remanded under this section may [F11, before the expiry of the period of 24 hours beginning with his remand,] appeal [F12to the [F13appropriate Appeal Court] by note of appeal] against the refusal of bail or against the conditions imposed and a person committed to hospital under this section may [F14, at any time during the period when the order for his committal, or, as the case may be, renewal of such order, is in force,] appeal [F12to the [F13appropriate Appeal Court] by note of appeal] against the order of committal F15. . . F16. . ., and the [F13appropriate Appeal Court], either in court or in chambers, may after hearing parties—

(a) review the order and grant bail on such conditions as it thinks fit; or

(b) confirm the order; or

(c) in the case of an appeal against an order of committal to hospital, revoke the order and remand the person in custody.

[F17. (9. A)A note of appeal under subsection (9) above is to be—

(a) lodged with the clerk of the court from which the appeal is to be taken; and

(b) sent without delay by that clerk (where not the [F18clerk of the appropriate Appeal Court]) to the [F18clerk of the appropriate Appeal Court].]

(10) The court may, on cause shown, vary an order for committal to hospital under subsection (2)(b) above by substituting another hospital for the hospital specified in the order.

(11) Subsection (2)(b) above shall apply to the variation of an order under subsection (10) above as it applies to the making of an order for committal to hospital.

[F19. (12)In this section—

"appropriate Appeal Court" means—

- in the case of an appeal under subsection (9) against a decision of the High Court, that Court;

- in the case of an appeal under subsection (9) against a decision of a sheriff (whether in solemn or summary proceedings) or a JP court, the Sheriff Appeal Court; and

"the clerk of the appropriate Appeal Court" means—

- in a case where the High Court is the appropriate Appeal Court, the Clerk of Justiciary;

- in a case where the Sheriff Appeal Court is the appropriate Appeal Court, the Clerk of that Court.]

Amendments (Textual)

F9. S. 200. (2)(b)(ii) substituted (5.10.2005) by Mental Health (Care and Treatment) (Scotland) Act 2003 (asp 13), ss. 331. (1), 333. (2)-(4), Sch. 4 para. 8. (13)(a); S.S.I. 2005/161, art. 3

F10. Words in s. 200. (3)(a) substituted (5.10.2005) by Mental Health (Care and Treatment) (Scotland) Act 2003 (asp 13), ss. 331. (1), 333. (2)-(4), Sch. 4 para. 8. (13)(b); S.S.I. 2005/161, art. 3

F11. Words in s. 200. (9) inserted (5.10.2005) by Mental Health (Care and Treatment) (Scotland) Act 2003 (asp 13), ss. 132. (a), 333. (2)-(4); S.S.I. 2005/161, art. 3

F12. Words in s. 200. (9) inserted (10.12.2007) by Criminal Proceedings etc. (Reform) (Scotland) Act 2007 (asp 6), ss. 6. (4)(a)(i), 84; S.S.I. 2007/479, art. 3. (1), Sch. (as amended by S.S.I. 2007/527)

F13. Words in s. 200. (9) substituted (22.9.2015) by The Courts Reform (Scotland) Act 2014 (Consequential Provisions No. 2) Order 2015 (S.S.I. 2015/338), art. 1, sch. 2 para. 5. (6)(a) (with art. 4)

F14. Words in s. 200. (9) inserted (5.10.2005) by Mental Health (Care and Treatment) (Scotland) Act 2003 (asp 13), ss. 132. (b), 333. (2)-(4); S.S.I. 2005/161, art. 3

F15. Words in s. 200. (9) repealed (5.10.2005) by Mental Health (Care and Treatment) (Scotland) Act 2003 (asp 13), ss. 132. (c), 331. (2), 333. (2)-(4), Sch. 5; S.S.I. 2005/161, art. 3

F16. Words in s. 200. (9) repealed (10.12.2007) by Criminal Proceedings etc. (Reform) (Scotland) Act 2007 (asp 6), ss. 6. (4)(a)(ii), 84; S.S.I. 2007/479, art. 3. (1), Sch. (as amended by S.S.I. 2007/527)

F17. S. 200. (9. A) added (10.12.2007) by Criminal Proceedings etc. (Reform) (Scotland) Act 2007 (asp 6), ss. 6. (4)(b), 84; S.S.I. 2007/479, art. 3. (1), Sch. (as amended by S.S.I. 2007/527)

F18. Words in s. 200. (9. A)(b) substituted (22.9.2015) by The Courts Reform (Scotland) Act 2014 (Consequential Provisions No. 2) Order 2015 (S.S.I. 2015/338), art. 1, sch. 2 para. 5. (6)(b) (with art. 4)

F19. S. 200. (12) inserted (22.9.2015) by The Courts Reform (Scotland) Act 2014 (Consequential Provisions No. 2) Order 2015 (S.S.I. 2015/338), art. 1, sch. 2 para. 5. (6)(c) (with art. 4)

201 Power of court to adjourn case before sentence.S

(1) Where an accused has been convicted or the court has found that he committed the offence and before he has been sentenced or otherwise dealt with, subject to subsection (3) below, the court may adjourn the case for the purpose of enabling inquiries to be made or of determining the most suitable method of dealing with his case.

(2) Where the court adjourns a case solely for the purpose mentioned in subsection (1) above, it shall remand the accused in custody or on bail or ordain him to appear at the adjourned diet.

(3) [F20. Subject to section 21. (9) of the Criminal Justice (Scotland) Act 2003 (asp 7),] a court shall not adjourn the hearing of a case as mentioned in subsection (1) above for any single period [F21exceeding four weeks or, on cause shown, eight weeks.]

(4) An accused who is remanded under this section may appeal [F22to the [F23appropriate Appeal Court]] against the refusal of bail or against the conditions imposed within 24 hours of his remand, by note of appeal F24. . . , and the [F23appropriate Appeal Court], either in court or in chambers, may F25. . . —

(a) review the order appealed against and either grant bail on such conditions as it thinks fit or ordain the accused to appear at the adjourned diet; or

(b) confirm the order.

[F26. (5)A note of appeal under subsection (4) above is to be—

(a) lodged with the clerk of the court from which the appeal is to be taken; and

(b) sent without delay by that clerk (where not the [F27clerk of the appropriate Appeal Court]) to the [F27clerk of the appropriate Appeal Court].]

[F28. (6)In this section—

"appropriate Appeal Court" means—

- in the case of an appeal under subsection (4) against a decision of the High Court, that Court;

- in the case of an appeal under subsection (4) against a decision of a sheriff (whether in solemn or summary proceedings) or a JP court, the Sheriff Appeal Court; and

"the clerk of the appropriate Appeal Court" means—

- in a case where the High Court is the appropriate Appeal Court, the Clerk of Justiciary;

- in a case where the Sheriff Appeal Court is the appropriate Appeal Court, the Clerk of that Court.]

Amendments (Textual)

F20. Words in s. 201. (3) inserted (10.6.2004) by Criminal Justice (Scotland) Act 2003 (asp 7), ss. 21. (10), 89; S.S.I. 2004/240, art. 2

F21. Words in s. 201. (3) substituted (27.6.2003) by Criminal Justice (Scotland) Act 2003 (asp 7), ss. 67, 89; S.S.I. 2003/288, art. 2, Sch.

F22. Words in s. 201. (4) inserted (10.12.2007) by Criminal Proceedings etc. (Reform) (Scotland)

Act 2007 (asp 6), ss. 6. (5)(a)(i), 84; S.S.I. 2007/479, art. 3. (1), Sch. (as amended by S.S.I. 2007/527)

F23. Words in s. 201. (4) substituted (22.9.2015) by The Courts Reform (Scotland) Act 2014 (Consequential Provisions No. 2) Order 2015 (S.S.I. 2015/338), art. 1, sch. 2 para. 5. (7)(a) (with art. 4)

F24. Words in s. 201. (4) repealed (10.12.2007) by Criminal Proceedings etc. (Reform) (Scotland) Act 2007 (asp 6), ss. 6. (5)(a)(ii), 84; S.S.I. 2007/479, art. 3. (1), Sch. (as amended by S.S.I. 2007/527)

F25. Words in s. 201. (4) repealed (10.12.2007) by Criminal Proceedings etc. (Reform) (Scotland) Act 2007 (asp 6), ss. 80, 84, Sch. para. 18. (4); S.S.I. 2007/479, art. 3. (1), Sch. (as amended by S.S.I. 2007/527)

F26. S. 201. (5) added (10.12.2007) by Criminal Proceedings etc. (Reform) (Scotland) Act 2007 (asp 6), ss. 6. (5)(b), 84; S.S.I. 2007/479, art. 3. (1), Sch. (as amended by S.S.I. 2007/527)

F27. Words in s. 201. (5)(b) substituted (22.9.2015) by The Courts Reform (Scotland) Act 2014 (Consequential Provisions No. 2) Order 2015 (S.S.I. 2015/338), art. 1, sch. 2 para. 5. (7)(b) (with art. 4)

F28. S. 201. (6) inserted (22.9.2015) by The Courts Reform (Scotland) Act 2014 (Consequential Provisions No. 2) Order 2015 (S.S.I. 2015/338), art. 1, sch. 2 para. 5. (7)(c) (with art. 4)

Modifications etc. (not altering text)

C2. S. 201. (3) modified (10.6.2004) by Criminal Justice (Scotland) Act 2003 (asp 7), ss. 21. (9), 89; S.S.I. 2004/240, art. 2

202 Deferred sentence.S

(1) It shall be competent for a court to defer sentence after conviction for a period and on such conditions as the court may determine.

(2) If it appears to the court which deferred sentence on an accused under subsection (1) above that he has been convicted during the period of deferment, by a court in any part of [F29the United Kingdom or in another member State of the European Union] of an offence committed during that period and has been dealt with for that offence, the court which deferred sentence may—

(a) issue a warrant for the arrest of the accused; or

(b) instead of issuing such a warrant in the first instance, issue a citation requiring him to appear before it at such time as may be specified in the citation,

and on his appearance or on his being brought before the court it may deal with him in any manner in which it would be competent for it to deal with him on the expiry of the period of deferment.

(3) Where a court which has deferred sentence on an accused under subsection (1) above convicts him of another offence during the period of deferment, it may deal with him for the original offence in any manner in which it would be competent for it to deal with him on the expiry of the period of deferment, as well as for the offence committed during the said period.

Amendments (Textual)

F29. Words in s. 202. (2) substituted (13.12.2010 for all purposes in respect of offences committed on or after this date) by Criminal Justice and Licensing (Scotland) Act 2010 (asp 13), ss. 71. (1), 206. (1), Sch. 4 para. 4; S.S.I. 2010/413, art. 2, Sch.

203 Reports.S

(1) Where a person specified in section 27. (1)(b)(i) to (vi) of the M1. Social Work (Scotland) Act 1968 commits an offence, the court shall not dispose of the case without obtaining from the local authority in whose area the person resides a report as to—

(a) the circumstances of the offence; and

(b) the character of the offender, including his behaviour while under the supervision, or as the case may be subject to the order, so specified in relation to him.

[F30. (1. A)However, if there is available to the court a report from a local authority—

(a) of the kind described in subsection (1)(b) above; and

(b) which was prepared in relation to the person not more than 3 months before the person was convicted of the offence,

the court need not obtain another report of that kind before disposing of the case unless it considers, following representations made by or on behalf of the person as to the person's circumstances, that it is appropriate to obtain another report.

(1. B)Nothing in subsection (1) or (1. A) above requires the court to obtain a report if the court is satisfied, having regard to its likely method of dealing with the case before it for disposal, that the report would not be of any material assistance.]

(2) In subsection (1) above, "the court" does not include a [F31. JP court] .

(3) Where, in any case, a report by an officer of a local authority is made to the court with a view to assisting the court in determining the most suitable method of dealing with any person in respect of an offence, a copy of the report shall be given by the clerk of the court to

[F32. (a)the offender,

(b) the offender's solicitor (if any), and

(c) the prosecutor.]

Amendments (Textual)

F30. S. 203. (1. A)(1. B) inserted (10.12.2007) by Criminal Proceedings etc. (Reform) (Scotland) Act 2007 (asp 6), ss. 24, 84; S.S.I. 2007/479, art. 3. (1), Sch. (as amended by S.S.I. 2007/527)

F31. Words in s. 203. (2) substituted (10.3.2008, 2.6.2008, 8.12.2008, 23.2.2009 and 14.12.2009 for certain purposes, otherwise 22.2.2010) by Criminal Proceedings etc. (Reform) (Scotland) Act 2007 (asp 6), ss. 80, 84, Sch. para. 26. (i); S.S.I. 2008/42, art. 3, Sch.; S.S.I. 2008/192, art. 3, Sch.; S.S.I. 2008/329, art. 3, Sch.; S.S.I. 2008/362, art. 3, Sch.; S.S.I. 2009/432, art. 3, Schs. 1, 2

F32. Words in s. 203. (3) substituted (1.2.2011) by Criminal Justice and Licensing (Scotland) Act 2010 (asp 13), ss. 20. (2), 206. (1); S.S.I. 2010/413, art. 2, Sch. (with art. 3)

Marginal Citations

M11968 c.49.

[F33203. AReports about organisationsS

(1) This section applies where an organisation is convicted of an offence.

(2) Before dealing with the organisation in respect of the offence, the court may obtain a report into the organisation's financial affairs and structural arrangements.

(3) The report is to be prepared by a person appointed by the court.

(4) The person appointed to prepare the report is referred to in this section as the "reporter".

(5) The court may issue directions to the reporter about—

(a) the information to be contained in the report,

(b) the particular matters to be covered by the report,

(c) the time by which the report is to be submitted to the court.

(6) The court may order the organisation to give the reporter and any person acting on the reporter's behalf—

(a) access at all reasonable times to the organisation's books, documents and other records,

(b) such information or explanation as the reporter thinks necessary.

(7) The reporter's costs in preparing the report are to be paid by the clerk of court, but the court may order the organisation to reimburse to the clerk all or a part of those costs.

(8) An order under subsection (7) may be enforced by civil diligence as if it were a fine.

(9) On submission of the report to the court, the clerk of court must provide a copy of the report to—

(a) the organisation,

(b) the organisation's solicitor (if any), and

(c) the prosecutor.

(10) The court must have regard to the report in deciding how to deal with the organisation in respect of the offence.

(11) If the court decides to impose a fine, the court must, in determining the amount of the fine, have regard to—

(a) the report, and

(b) if the court makes an order under subsection (7), the amount of costs that the organisation is required to reimburse under the order.

(12) Where the court—

(a) makes an order under subsection (7), and

(b) imposes a fine on the organisation,

any payment by the organisation is first to be applied in satisfaction of the order under subsection (7).

(13) Where the court also makes a compensation order in respect of the offence, any payment by the organisation is first to be applied in satisfaction of the compensation order before being applied in accordance with subsection (12).]

Amendments (Textual)

F33. S. 203. A inserted (28.3.2011) by Criminal Justice and Licensing (Scotland) Act 2010 (asp 13), ss. 22, 206. (1); S.S.I. 2011/178, art. 2, sch.

Imprisonment, etc.

204 Restrictions on passing sentence of imprisonment or detention.S

(1) A court shall not pass a sentence of imprisonment or of detention in respect of any offence, nor impose imprisonment, or detention, under section 214. (2) of this Act in respect of failure to pay a fine, on an accused who is not legally represented in that court and has not been previously sentenced to imprisonment or detention by a court in any part of the United Kingdom [F34or in another member State of the European Union], unless the accused either—

(a) applied for legal aid and the application was refused on the ground that he was not financially eligible; or

(b) having been informed of his right to apply for legal aid, and having had the opportunity, failed to do so.

(2) A court shall not pass a sentence of imprisonment on a person of or over twenty-one years of age who has not been previously sentenced to imprisonment or detention by a court in any part of the United Kingdom [F34or in another member State of the European Union] unless the court considers that no other method of dealing with him is appropriate; F35. . ..

[F36. (2. A)For the purpose of determining under subsection (2) above whether any other method of dealing with such a person is appropriate, the court [F37, unless it has made a risk assessment order in respect of the person,] shall take into account—

(a) such information as it has been able to obtain from an officer of a local authority or otherwise about his circumstances;

(b) any information before it concerning his character and mental and physical condition;

(c) its power to make a hospital direction in addition to imposing a sentence of imprisonment.]

(3) Where a court of summary jurisdiction passes a sentence of imprisonment on any such person as is mentioned in subsection (2) above, the court shall state the reason for its opinion that no other method of dealing with him is appropriate, and shall have that reason entered in the record of the proceedings.

[F38. (3. A)A court must not pass a sentence of imprisonment for a term of 3 months or less on a person unless the court considers that no other method of dealing with the person is appropriate.

(3. B)Where a court passes such a sentence, the court must—

(a) state its reasons for the opinion that no other method of dealing with the person is appropriate, and

(b) have those reasons entered in the record of the proceedings.

(3. C)The Scottish Ministers may by order made by statutory instrument substitute for the number of months for the time being specified in subsection (3. A) another number of months.

(3. D)An order under subsection (3. C) is not to be made unless a draft of the statutory instrument containing the order has been laid before and approved by resolution of the Scottish Parliament.]

(4) The court shall, for the purpose of determining whether a person has been previously sentenced to imprisonment or detention by a court in any part of the United Kingdom—

(a) disregard a previous sentence of imprisonment which, having been suspended, has not taken effect under section 23 of the M2. Powers of Criminal Courts Act 1973 or under section 19 of the M3. Treatment of Offenders Act (Northern Ireland) 1968;

(b) construe detention as meaning —

(i) in relation to Scotland, detention in a young offenders institution or detention centre;

(ii) in relation to England and Wales a sentence of youth custody, borstal training or detention in a young offender institution or detention centre; and

(iii) in relation to Northern Ireland, detention in a young offenders centre.

[F39. (4. A)The court shall, for the purpose of determining whether a person has been previously sentenced to imprisonment or detention by a court in a member State of the European Union other than the United Kingdom—

(a) disregard any previous sentence of imprisonment which, being the equivalent of a suspended sentence, has not taken effect;

(b) construe detention as meaning an equivalent sentence to any of those mentioned in subsection (4)(b).

(4. B)Any issue of equivalence arising in pursuance of subsection (4. A) is for the court to determine.]

(5) This section does not affect the power of a court to pass sentence on any person for an offence the sentence for which is fixed by law.

(6) In this section—

"legal aid" means legal aid for the purposes of any part of the proceedings before the court;

"legally represented" means represented by counsel or a solicitor at some stage after the accused is found guilty and before he is dealt with as referred to in subsection (1) above.

Amendments (Textual)

F34. Words in s. 204. (1)(2) inserted (13.12.2010 for all purposes in respect of offences committed on or after this date) by Criminal Justice and Licensing (Scotland) Act 2010 (asp 13), ss. 71. (1), 206. (1), Sch. 4 para. 5. (a); S.S.I. 2010/413, art. 2, Sch.

F35. Words in s. 204. (2) repealed (1.8.1997) by 1997 c. 48, s. 62. (2), Sch. 3; S.I. 1997/1712, art. 3, Sch. (subject to arts. 4, 5) and expressed to be repealed (1.1.1998) by 1997 c. 48, s. 6. (3)(a); S.I. 1997/2323, art. 4, Sch. 2 (subject to art. 7)

F36. S. 204. (2. A) inserted (1.1.1998) by 1997 c. 48, s. 6. (3)(b); S.I. 1997/2323, art. 4, Sch. 2 (subject to art. 7)

F37. Words in s. 204. (2. A) inserted (19.6.2006 for certain purposes and otherwise prosp.) by Criminal Justice (Scotland) Act 2003 (asp 7), ss. 1. (2), 89, Sch. 1 para. 2. (6); S.S.I. 2006/332, art. 2

F38. S. 204. (3. A)-(3. D) inserted (1.2.2011for all purposes in respect of offences committed on or after this date) by Criminal Justice and Licensing (Scotland) Act 2010 (asp 13), ss. 17, 206. (1); S.S.I. 2010/413, art. 2, Sch.

F39. S. 204. (4. A)(4. B) inserted (13.12.2010 for all purposes in respect of offences committed on or after this date) by Criminal Justice and Licensing (Scotland) Act 2010 (asp 13), ss. 71. (1), 206. (1), Sch. 4 para. 5. (b); S.S.I. 2010/413, art. 2, Sch.

Marginal Citations

M21973 c.62.

[F40204. A Restriction on consecutive sentences for released prisoners.S

A court sentencing a person to imprisonment or other detention shall not order or direct that the term of imprisonment or detention shall commence on the expiration of any other such sentence from which he has been released at any time under the existing or new provisions within the meaning of Schedule 6 to the M4. Prisoners and Criminal Proceedings (Scotland) Act 1993.]
Amendments (Textual)
F40. S. 204. A inserted (30.9.1998) by 1998 c. 37, s. 112; S.I. 1998/2327, art. 2. (1)(x)
Marginal Citations
M41993 c.9.

[F41204. BConsecutive sentences: life prisoners etc.S

(1) This section applies in respect of sentencing for offences committed after the coming into force of this section.
(2) Where, in solemn proceedings, the court sentences a person to imprisonment or other detention, the court may—

(a) if the person is serving or is liable to serve the punishment part of a previous sentence, frame the sentence to take effect on the day after that part of that sentence is or would be due to expire; or

(b) if the person is serving or is liable to serve the punishment parts of two or more previous sentences, frame the sentence to take effect on the day after the later or (as the case may be) latest expiring of those parts is or would be due to expire.

(3) Where, in such proceedings, it falls to the court to sentence a person who is subject to a previous sentence in respect of which a punishment part requires to be (but has not been) specified, the court shall not sentence the person until such time as the part is either specified or no longer requires to be specified.

(4) Where the court sentences a person to a sentence of imprisonment or other detention for life, for an indeterminate period or without limit of time, the court may, if the person is serving or is liable to serve for any offence—

(a) a previous sentence of imprisonment or other detention the term of which is not treated as part of a single term under section 27. (5) of the 1993 Act; or

(b) two or more previous sentences of imprisonment or other detention the terms of which are treated as a single term under that section of that Act,

frame the sentence to take effect on the day after the person would (but for the sentence so framed and disregarding any subsequent sentence) be entitled to be released under the provisions referred to in section 204. A of this Act as respects the sentence or sentences.

(5) Subsection (4)(a) above shall not apply where the sentence is a sentence from which he has been released at any time under the provisions referred to in section 204. A of this Act.

(6) In this section, any reference to a punishment part of a sentence shall be construed by reference to—

(a) the punishment part of the sentence as is specified in an order mentioned in section 2. (2) of the 1993 Act; or

(b) any part of the sentence which has effect, by virtue of section 10 of the 1993 Act or the schedule to the Convention Rights (Compliance)(Scotland) Act 2001 (asp 7), as if it were the punishment part so specified,

and " the 1993 Act " means the Prisoners and Criminal Proceedings (Scotland) Act 1993 (c. 9).

(7) This section is without prejudice to any other power under any enactment or rule of law as

respects sentencing.]

Amendments (Textual)

F41. S. 204. B inserted (1.12.2003) by Criminal Justice (Scotland) Act 2003 (asp 7), ss. 26. (1), 89; S.S.I. 2003/475, art. 2, Sch.

205 Punishment for murder.S

(1) Subject to subsections (2) and (3) [F42and section 205. D]below, a person convicted of murder shall be sentenced to imprisonment for life.

(2) Where a person convicted of murder is under the age of 18 years he shall not be sentenced to imprisonment for life but to be detained without limit of time and shall be liable to be detained in such place, and under such conditions, as the Secretary of State may direct.

(3) Where a person convicted of murder has attained the age of 18 years but is under the age of 21 years he shall not be sentenced to imprisonment for life but to be detained in a young offenders institution and shall be liable to be detained for life.

F43. (4). . . . .

F43. (5). . . . .

F43. (6). . . . .

Amendments (Textual)

F42. Words in s. 205. (1) inserted (17.12.2001) by 2001 asp 7, s. 2. (1)(a); S.S.I. 2001/456, art. 2

F43. S. 205. (4)-(6) repealed (17.12.2001) by 2001 asp 7, s. 2. (1)(b); S.S.I. 2001/456 art. 2

[F44205. B Minimum sentence for third conviction of certain offences relating to drug trafficking.S

(1) This section applies where—

(a) a person is convicted on indictment in the High Court of a class A drug trafficking offence committed after the commencement of section 2 of the Crime and Punishment (Scotland) Act 1997;

(b) at the time when that offence was committed, he had attained the age of at least 18 years and had [F45two previous convictions for relevant offences], irrespective of—

(i) whether either of those offences was committed before or after the commencement of section 2 of the Crime and Punishment (Scotland) Act 1997;

(ii) the court in which any such conviction was obtained; and

(iii) his age at the time of the commission of either of those offences; and

(c) one of the offences mentioned in paragraph (b) above was committed after he had been convicted of the other.

[F46. (1. A) In subsection (1), " relevant offence " means—

(a) in relation to a conviction by a court in any part of the United Kingdom, a class A drug trafficking offence;

(b) in relation to a conviction by a court in a member State of the European Union other than the United Kingdom, an offence that is equivalent to a class A drug trafficking offence.

(1. B)Any issue of equivalence arising in pursuance of subsection (1. A)(b) is for the court to determine.]

(2) Subject to subsection (3) below, where this section applies the court shall sentence the person—

(a) where he has attained the age of 21 years, to a term of imprisonment of at least seven years; and

(b) where he has attained the age of 18 years but is under the age of 21 years, to detention in a young offenders institution for a period of at least seven years.

(3) The court shall not impose the sentence otherwise required by subsection (2) above where it is

of the opinion that there are specific circumstances which—

    (a) relate to any of the offences or to the offender; and

    (b) would make that sentence unjust.

(4) For the purposes of section 106. (2) of this Act a sentence passed under subsection (2) above in respect of a conviction for a class A drug trafficking offence shall not be regarded as a sentence fixed by law for that offence.

(5) In this section " class A drug trafficking offence " means a drug trafficking offence committed in respect of a class A drug; and for this purpose—

" class A drug " has the same meaning as in the M5 Misuse of Drugs Act 1971;

[F47 " drug trafficking offence " means an offence specified in paragraph 2 or (so far as it relates to that paragraph) paragraph 10 of Schedule 4 to the Proceeds of Crime Act 2002;]]

Amendments (Textual)

F44. S. 205. B inserted (20.10.1997) by 1997 c. 48, s. 2. (1); S.I. 1997/2323, art. 3, Sch. 1

F45. Words in s. 205. B(1)(b) substituted (13.12.2010 for all purposes in respect of offences committed on or after this date) by Criminal Justice and Licensing (Scotland) Act 2010 (asp 13), ss. 71. (1), 206. (1), Sch. 4 para. 6. (a); S.S.I. 2010/413, art. 2, Sch.

F46. S. 205. B(1. A)(1. B) inserted (13.12.2010 for all purposes in respect of offences committed on or after this date) by Criminal Justice and Licensing (Scotland) Act 2010 (asp 13), ss. 71. (1), 206. (1), Sch. 4 para. 6. (b); S.S.I. 2010/413, art. 2, Sch.

F47. In s. 205. B(5) definition of "drug trafficking offence" substituted (24.3.2003) by Proceeds of Crime Act 2002 (c. 29), ss. 456, 458, Sch. 11 para. 29. (3); S.S.I. 2003/210, art. 2, Sch. (subject to arts. 3-7)

Marginal Citations

M51971 c.38.

[F48205. C Meaning of "conviction" for purposes of sections 205. A and 205. B.S

(1) For the purposes of paragraph (b) of subsection (1) of each of sections 205. A and 205. B of this Act " conviction " includes—

    (a) a finding of guilt in respect of which the offender was admonished under section 181 of the M6. Criminal Procedure (Scotland) Act 1975 (admonition); and

    (b) a conviction for which an order is made placing the offender on probation,

and related expressions shall be construed accordingly.

(2) This subsection applies where a person has at any time been convicted of an offence under—

    (a) section 70 of the M7. Army Act 1955;

    (b) section 70 of the M8. Air Force Act 1955; or

    (c) section 42 of the M9. Naval Discipline Act 1957.

(3) Where subsection (2) above applies and the corresponding civil offence (within the meaning of the Act under which the offence was committed) was—

    (a) a relevant offence within the meaning of section 205. A of this Act; or

    (b) a Class A drug trafficking offence within the meaning of section 205. B of this Act,

that section shall have effect as if he had been convicted in England and Wales of the corresponding civil offence.]

Amendments (Textual)

F48. S. 205. C inserted (20.10.1997 for specified purposes and otherwise prosp.) by 1997 c. 48, ss. 3, 65. (2); S.I. 1997/2323, art. 3, Sch. 1

Marginal Citations

M61975 c. 21.

M71955 c.18.

M81955 c.19.

M91957 c. 53.

[F49205. D Only one sentence of imprisonment for life to be imposed in any proceedingsS

Where a person is convicted on the same indictment of more than one offence for which the court must impose or would, apart from this section, have imposed a sentence of imprisonment for life, only one such sentence shall be imposed in respect of those offences.]
Amendments (Textual)
F49. S. 205. D inserted (8.10.2001) by 2001 asp 7, s. 2. (2); S.S.I. 2001/274, art. 3. (3)

206 Minimum periods of imprisonment.S

(1) No person shall be sentenced to imprisonment by a court of summary jurisdiction for a period of less than [F5015] days.
(2) F51. . . . .
(3) F51. . . . .
(4) F51. . . . .
(5) F51. . . . .
(6) F51. . . . .
Amendments (Textual)
F50. Word in s. 206. (1) substituted (13.12.2010 for all purposes in respect of offences committed on or after this date) by Criminal Justice and Licensing (Scotland) Act 2010 (asp 13), ss. 16. (3)(a), 206. (1); S.S.I. 2010/413, art. 2, Sch.
F51. S. 206. (2)-(6) repealed (13.12.2010 for all purposes in respect of offences committed on or after this date) by Criminal Justice and Licensing (Scotland) Act 2010 (asp 13), ss. 16. (3)(b), 206. (1); S.S.I. 2010/413, art. 2, Sch.

207 Detention of young offenders.S

(1) It shall not be competent to impose imprisonment on a person under 21 years of age.
(2) Subject to [F52sections 205. (2) and (3), 205. A(2)(b) and 205. B(2)(b)] of this Act and to subsections (3) and (4) below, a court may impose detention (whether by way of sentence or otherwise) on a person, who is not less than 16 but under 21 years of age, where but for subsection (1) above the court would have power to impose a period of imprisonment; and a period of detention imposed under this section on any person shall not [F53be less than the minimum nor more than]the maximum period of imprisonment which might otherwise have been imposed.
(3) The court shall not under subsection (2) above impose detention on an offender unless it is of the opinion that no other method of dealing with him is appropriate; and the court shall state its reasons for that opinion, and, except in the case of the High Court, those reasons shall be entered in the record of proceedings.
[F54. (3. A)Subsections (2) and (3) above are subject to—
    (a) section 51. A(2) of the Firearms Act 1968 (minimum sentences for certain firearms offences); and
    (b) section 29. (8) of the Violent Crime Reduction Act 2006 (minimum sentence of detention for certain offences relating to dangerous weapons).]
(4) To enable the court to form an opinion under subsection (3) above, it shall obtain from an officer of a local authority or otherwise such information as it can about the offender's circumstances; and it shall also take into account any information before it concerning the offender's character and physical and mental condition.
[F55. (4. A)In forming an opinion under subsection (3) above the court shall take into account its power to make a hospital direction in addition to imposing a period of detention.]

[F56. (4. B)Subsections (4) and (4. A) above apply to the forming of an opinion under the enactments mentioned in subsection (3. A) above as they apply to the forming of an opinion under subsection (3) above.]

(5) A sentence of detention imposed under this section shall be a sentence of detention in a young offenders institution.

Amendments (Textual)

F52. Words in s. 207. (2) substituted (20.10.1997 for specified purposes and otherwise prosp.) by 1997 c. 48, ss. 62. (1), 65. (2), Sch. 1 para. 21. (25)(a); S.I. 1997/2323, art. 3, Sch. 1

F53. Words in s. 207. (2) substituted (20.10.1997 for specified purposes and otherwise prosp.) by 1997 c. 48, ss. 62. (1), 65. (2), Sch. 1 para. 21. (25)(b); S.I. 1997/2323, art. 3, Sch. 1

F54. S. 207. (3. A) inserted (6.4.2007) by Violent Crime Reduction Act 2006 (c. 38), ss. 49, 66. (2), Sch. 1 para. 4. (3)(a); S.I. 2007/858, art. 2. (g)

F55. S. 207. (4. A) inserted (1.1.1998) by 1997 c. 48, s. 6. (4); S.I. 1997/2323, art. 4, Sch. 2 (subject to art. 7)

F56. S. 207. (4. B) inserted (6.4.2007) by Violent Crime Reduction Act 2006 (c. 38), ss. 49, 66. (2), Sch. 1 para. 4. (3)(b); S.I. 2007/858, art. 2. (g)

208 Detention of children convicted on indictment.S

[F57. (1)]Subject to section 205 of this Act [F58and subsection (3) below] , where a child is convicted on indictment and the court is of the opinion that no other method of dealing with him is appropriate, it may sentence him to be detained for a period which it shall specify in the sentence; and the child shall during that period be liable to be detained in such place and on such conditions as the Secretary of State may direct.

[F59. (1. A)Where the court imposes a sentence of detention on a child, the court must—

(a) state its reasons for the opinion that no other method of dealing with the child is appropriate, and

(b) have those reasons entered in the record of the proceedings.]

[F60. (2)[F61. Subsections (1) and (1. A) above are] subject to—

(a) section 51. A(2) of the Firearms Act 1968 (minimum sentences for certain firearms offences); and

(b) section 29. (9) of the Violent Crime Reduction Act 2006 (minimum sentence of detention for certain offences relating to dangerous weapons).]

[F62. (3)If the child is under the age of 16 years, the power conferred by subsection (1) above shall not be exercisable in respect of a conviction for an offence under section 9. (1) of the Antisocial Behaviour etc. (Scotland) Act 2004 (asp 8) or that section as applied by section 234. AA(11) of this Act.]

Amendments (Textual)

F57. S. 208 renumbered (22.1.2004) as s. 208. (1) by Criminal Justice Act 2003 (c. 44), ss. 290. (3), 336; S.I. 2004/81, art. 3

F58. Words in s. 208 inserted (28.10.2004) by Antisocial Behaviour etc. (Scotland) Act 2004 (asp 8), ss. 10. (3), 145. (2); S.S.I. 2004/420, art. 3, Sch. 1

F59. S. 208. (1. A) inserted (1.2.2011 for all purposes in respect of offences committed on or after this date) by Criminal Justice and Licensing (Scotland) Act 2010 (asp 13), ss. 21. (2), 206. (1); S.S.I. 2010/413, art. 2, Sch.

F60. S. 208. (2) substituted (6.4.2007) by Violent Crime Reduction Act 2006 (c. 38), ss. 49, 66. (2), Sch. 1 para. 4. (4); S.I. 2007/858, art. 2. (g)

F61. Words in s. 208. (2) substituted (1.2.2011 for all purposes in respect of offences committed on or after this date) by Criminal Justice and Licensing (Scotland) Act 2010 (asp 13), ss. 21. (3), 206. (1); S.S.I. 2010/413, art. 2, Sch.

F62. S. 208. (3) added (28.10.2004) by Antisocial Behaviour etc. (Scotland) Act 2004 (asp 8), ss. 10. (4), 145. (2); S.S.I. 2004/420, art. 3, Sch. 1

209 Supervised release orders.

(1) Where a person is convicted [F63on indictment]of an offence [F63, other than a sexual offence within the meaning of section 210. A of this Act,]and is sentenced to imprisonment for a term of F64... less than four years, the court on passing sentence may, if it considers that it is necessary to do so to protect the public from serious harm from the offender on his release, make such order as is mentioned in subsection (3) below.

(2) A court shall, before making an order under subsection (1) above, consider a report by a relevant officer of a local authority about the offender and his circumstances and, if the court thinks it necessary, hear that officer.

(3) The order referred to in subsection (1) above (to be known as a "supervised release order") is that the person, during a relevant period—

(a) be under the supervision F65... of a relevant officer of a local authority or of [F66an officer of a local probation board] appointed for or assigned to a petty sessions area [F67or (as the case may be) an officer of a provider of probation services acting in a local justice area](such local authority or the justices for such area to be designated under section 14. (4) or 15. (1) of the M10. Prisoners and Criminal Proceedings (Scotland) Act 1993);

(b) comply with;

(i) such requirements as may be imposed by the court in the order; and

(ii) such requirements as that officer may reasonably specify,

for the purpose of securing the good conduct of the person or preventing, or lessening the possibility of, his committing a further offence (whether or not an offence of the kind for which he was sentenced); and

(c) comply with the standard requirements imposed by virtue of subsection (4)(a)(i) below.

(4) A supervised release order—

(a) shall—

(i) without prejudice to subsection (3)(b) above, contain such requirements (in this section referred to as the "standard requirements"); and

(ii) be as nearly as possible in such form,

as may be prescribed by Act of Adjournal;

(b) for the purposes of any appeal or review constitutes part of the sentence of the person in respect of whom the order is made; and

(c) shall have no effect during any period in which the person is subject to a licence under Part I of the said Act of 1993.

(5) Before making a supervised release order as respects a person the court shall explain to him, in as straightforward a way as is practicable, the effect of the order and the possible consequences for him of any breach of it.

(6) The clerk of the court by which a supervised release order is made in respect of a person shall—

(a) forthwith send a copy of the order to the person and to the Secretary of State; and

(b) within seven days after the date on which the order is made, send to the Secretary of State such documents and information relating to the case and to the person as are likely to be of assistance to a supervising officer.

(7) In this section—

"relevant officer" has the same meaning as in Part I of the M11. Prisoners and Criminal Proceedings (Scotland) Act 1993;

"relevant period" means such period as may be specified in the supervised release order, being a period—

- not exceeding twelve months after the date of the person's release; and

- no part of which is later than the date by which the entire term of imprisonment specified in his sentence has elapsed; and

"supervising officer" means, where an authority has or justices have been designated as is mentioned in subsection (3)(a) above for the purposes of the order, any relevant officer or, as the case may be, [F68officer of a local probation board][F69or officer of a provider of probation services] who is for the time being supervising for those purposes the person released.
[F70. (7. A)Where a person—

(a) is serving a sentence of imprisonment and on his release from that sentence will be subject to a supervised release order; and

(b) is sentenced to a further term of imprisonment, whether that term is to run consecutively or concurrently with the sentence mentioned in paragraph (a) above,

the relevant period for any supervised release order made in relation to him shall begin on the date when he is released from those terms of imprisonment; and where there is more than one such order he shall on his release be subject to whichever of them is for the longer or, as the case may be, the longest period.]

(8) This section applies to a person sentenced under section 207 of this Act as it applies to a person sentenced to a period of imprisonment.

Extent Information

E1. S. 209. (3)and(7) extend to G.B., see s. 309. (4)

Amendments (Textual)

F63. Words in s. 209. (1) inserted (30.9.1998) by 1998 c. 37, s. 86. (2)(a)(b); S.I. 1998/2327, art. 2. (1)(s) (subject to arts. 5-8)

F64. Words in s. 209. (1) repealed (30.9.1998) by 1998 c. 37, ss. 86. (2)(c), 120. (2), Sch. 10; S.I. 1998/2327, art. 2. (1)(s)(aa)(3)(w) (subject to arts. 5-8)

F65. Word in s. 209. (3)(a) omitted (1.4.2008) by virtue of The Offender Management Act 2007 (Consequential Amendments) Order 2008 (S.I. 2008/912), art. 3, Sch. 1 para. 11. (2)(a)

F66. Words in s. 209. (3)(a) substituted (1.4.2001) by 2000 c. 43, s. 74, Sch. 7 para. 4. (1)(a)(2); S.I. 2001/919, art. 2. (f)(ii)

F67. Words in s. 209. (3)(a) inserted (1.4.2008) by The Offender Management Act 2007 (Consequential Amendments) Order 2008 (S.I. 2008/912), art. 3, Sch. 1 para. 11. (2)(a)

F68. Words in s. 209. (7) substituted (1.4.2001) by 2000 c. 43, s. 74, Sch. 7 para. 121; S.I. 2001/919, art. 2. (f)(ii)

F69. Words in s. 209. (7) inserted (1.4.2008) by The Offender Management Act 2007 (Consequential Amendments) Order 2008 (S.I. 2008/912), art. 3, Sch. 1 para. 11. (2)(b)

F70. S. 209. (7. A) inserted (1.4.1999) by 1997 c. 48, s. 62. (1), Sch. 1 para. 21. (26)S.I. 1999/652, art. 2, Sch. (subject to savings and transitional provisions in art. 3)

Marginal Citations

M101993 c.9.

M111993 c.9.

210 Consideration of time spent in custody.S

(1) A court, in passing a sentence of imprisonment or detention on a person for an offence, shall—

(a) in determining the period of imprisonment or detention, have regard to any period of time spent in custody by the person on remand awaiting trial or sentence, or spent in custody awaiting extradition to the United Kingdom [F71otherwise than from a category 1 territory] [F72, or spent in hospital awaiting trial or sentence by virtue [F73of an assessment order, a treatment order or an interim compulsion order or by virtue] of an order made under section F74. . . 200 of this Act];

(b) specify the date of commencement of the sentence; and

(c) if the person—

(i) has spent a period of time in custody on remand awaiting trial or sentence; or

(ii) is an extradited prisoner [F75who was extradited to the United Kingdom otherwise than from a category 1 territory], [F76; or

(iii) has spent a period of time in hospital awaiting trial or sentence by virtue [F77of an assessment order, a treatment order or an interim compulsion order or by virtue] of an order made under section F74. . . 200 of this Act,]

and the date specified under paragraph (b) above is not earlier than the date on which sentence was passed, state its reasons for not specifying an earlier date [F78so however that a period of time spent both in custody on remand and, by virtue of section 47. (1) of the Crime (International Co-operation) Act 2003 [F79or regulation 20 or 54 of the Criminal Justice (European Investigation Order) Regulations 2017], abroad is not for any reason to be discounted in a determination under paragraph (a) above or specification under paragraph (b) above].

[F80. (1. A)Subsection (1. B) applies where—

(a) a court is passing a sentence of imprisonment or detention on a person for an offence, and

(b) the person is an extradited prisoner who was extradited to the United Kingdom from a category 1 territory.

(1. B)The court shall specify—

(a) the period of time spent in custody awaiting extradition, and

(b) the date of commencement of the sentence in accordance with subsection (1. C).

(1. C)The date of commencement of the sentence is to be a date the relevant number of days earlier than the date the sentence would have commenced had the person not spent time in custody awaiting extradition.

(1. D)In subsection (1. C), "the relevant number of days" means the number of days in the period specified under subsection (1. B)(a).]

(2) A prisoner is an extradited prisoner for the purposes of this section if—

(a) he was tried for the offence in respect of which his sentence of imprisonment was imposed—

(i) after having been extradited to the United Kingdom; and

(ii) without having first been restored to the state from which he was extradited or having had an opportunity of leaving the United Kingdom; and

(b) he was for any period in custody while awaiting such extradition.

[F81. (2. A)In this section, "category 1 territory" means a territory designated under the Extradition Act 2003 for the purposes of Part 1 of that Act.]

F82. (3). . . . .

Amendments (Textual)

F71. Words in s. 210. (1)(a) inserted (21.7.2014) by Anti-social Behaviour, Crime and Policing Act 2014 (c. 12), ss. 172. (2)(a), 185. (1) (with ss. 21, 33, 42, 58, 75, 93); S.I. 2014/1916, art. 2. (q)

F72. Words in s. 210. (1) inserted (1.8.1997) by 1997 c. 48, s. 12. (a); S.I. 1997/1712, art. 3, Sch. (subject to arts. 4, 5)

F73. Words in s. 210. (1)(a) inserted (5.10.2005) by Mental Health (Care and Treatment) (Scotland) Act 2003 (asp 13), ss. 331. (1),333. (2)-(4), {Sch. 4 para. 8. (14)(a)}; S.S.I. 2005/161, art. 3

F74. Words in s. 210. (1)(a)(c)(iii) repealed (5.10.2005)by Mental Health (Care and Treatment) (Scotland) Act 2003 (asp 13), ss. 331. (2)(3), 333. (2)-(4), Sch. 5 Pt. 1; S.S.I. 2005/161, art. 3

F75. Words in s. 210. (1)(c)(ii) substituted (21.7.2014) by Anti-social Behaviour, Crime and Policing Act 2014 (c. 12), ss. 172. (2)(b), 185. (1) (with ss. 21, 33, 42, 58, 75, 93); S.I. 2014/1916, art. 2. (q)

F76. S. 210. (1)(c)(iii) and the preceding word ";or" inserted (1.8.1997) by 1997 c. 48, s. 12. (b); S.I. 1997/1712, art. 3, Sch. (subject to arts. 4, 5)

F77. Words in s. 210. (1)(c)(iii) inserted (5.10.2005) by Mental Health (Care and Treatment) (Scotland) Act 2003 (asp 13), ss. 331. (1), 333. (2)-(4), Sch. 4 para. 8. (14)(b); S.S.I. 2005/161, art. 3

F78. Words in s. 210. (1)(c) inserted (26.4.2004) by Crime (International Co-operation) Act 2003 (c. 32), ss. 91, 94, Sch. 5 para. 65; S.I. 2004/786, art. 3

F79. Words in s. 210. (1)(c) inserted (31.7.2017) by The Criminal Justice (European Investigation Order) Regulations 2017 (S.I. 2017/730), reg. 1. (1), Sch. 3 para. 3. (2) (with reg. 3)

F80. S. 210. (1. A)-(1. D) inserted (21.7.2014) by Anti-social Behaviour, Crime and Policing Act 2014 (c. 12), ss. 172. (3), 185. (1) (with ss. 21, 33, 42, 58, 75, 93); S.I. 2014/1916, art. 2. (q)
F81. S. 210. (2. A) inserted (21.7.2014) by Anti-social Behaviour, Crime and Policing Act 2014 (c. 12), ss. 172. (4), 185. (1) (with ss. 21, 33, 42, 58, 75, 93); S.I. 2014/1916, art. 2. (q)
F82. S. 210. (3) repealed (21.7.2014) by Anti-social Behaviour, Crime and Policing Act 2014 (c. 12), ss. 172. (5), 185. (1) (with ss. 21, 33, 42, 58, 75, 93); S.I. 2014/1916, art. 2. (q)

[F83210. A Extended sentences for sex and violent offenders.S

(1) Where a person is convicted on indictment of a sexual or violent offence, the court may, if it—
    (a) intends, in relation to—
(i) a sexual offence, to pass a determinate sentence of imprisonment; or
(ii) a violent offence, to pass such a sentence for a term of four years or more; and
    (b) considers that the period (if any) for which the offender would, apart from this section, be subject to a licence would not be adequate for the purpose of protecting the public from serious harm from the offender,
pass an extended sentence on the offender.
(2) An extended sentence is a sentence of imprisonment which is the aggregate of—
    (a) the term of imprisonment (" the custodial term ") which the court would have passed on the offender otherwise than by virtue of this section; and
    (b) a further period (" the extension period ") for which the offender is to be subject to a licence and which is, subject to the provisions of this section, of such length as the court considers necessary for the purpose mentioned in subsection (1)(b) above.
(3) The extension period shall not exceed, in the case of—
    (a) a sexual offence, ten years; and
    (b) a violent offence, [F84ten] years.
(4) A court shall, before passing an extended sentence, consider a report by a relevant officer of a local authority about the offender and his circumstances and, if the court thinks it necessary, hear that officer.
(5) The term of an extended sentence passed for a statutory offence shall not exceed the maximum term of imprisonment provided for in the statute in respect of that offence.
(6) Subject to subsection (5) above, a sheriff may pass an extended sentence which is the aggregate of a custodial term not exceeding the maximum term of imprisonment which he may impose and an extension period not exceeding [F85five years].
(7) The Secretary of State may by order—
    (a) amend paragraph (b) of subsection (3) above by substituting a different period, not exceeding ten years, for the period for the time being specified in that paragraph; and
    (b) make such transitional provision as appears to him to be necessary or expedient in connection with the amendment.
(8) The power to make an order under subsection (7) above shall be exercisable by statutory instrument; but no such order shall be made unless a draft of the order has been laid before, and approved by a resolution of, each House of Parliament.
(9) An extended sentence shall not be imposed where the sexual or violent offence was committed before the commencement of section 86 of the Crime and Disorder Act 1998.
(10) For the purposes of this section—
" licence " and " relevant officer " have the same meaning as in Part I of the M12 Prisoners and Criminal Proceedings (Scotland) Act 1993;
" sexual offence " means—
  - rape [F86at common law];
  - clandestine injury to women;
  - abduction of a woman or girl with intent to rape or ravish;
  - [F87abduction with intent to commit the statutory offence of rape;]

- assault with intent to rape or ravish;
- [F88assault with intent to commit the statutory offence of rape;]
- indecent assault;
- lewd, indecent or libidinous behaviour or practices;
- F89. . . . .
- sodomy;
- an offence under section 170 of the M13. Customs and Excise Management Act 1979 in relation to goods prohibited to be imported under section 42 of the M14. Customs Consolidation Act 1876, but only where the prohibited goods include indecent photographs of persons;
- an offence under section 52 of the M15. Civic Government (Scotland) Act 1982 (taking and distribution of indecent images of children);
- an offence under section 52. A of that Act (possession of indecent images of children);
- an offence under section 1 of the M16. Criminal Law (Consolidation) (Scotland) Act 1995 (incest);
- an offence under section 2 of that Act (intercourse with a stepchild);
- an offence under section 3 of that Act (intercourse with child under 16 by person in position of trust);
- an offence under section 5 of that Act (unlawful intercourse with girl under 16);
- an offence under section 6 of that Act (indecent behaviour towards girl between 12 and 16);
- an offence under section 8 of that Act (abduction of girl under 18 for purposes of unlawful intercourse);
- an offence under section 10 of that Act (person having parental responsibilities causing or encouraging sexual activity in relation to a girl under 16); F90. . .
- an offence under subsection (5) of section 13 of that Act (homosexual offences); F91[F92. . .
- an offence under section 3 of the Sexual Offences (Amendment) Act 2000 (abuse of position of trust)]F93[F94. . .
- an offence under section 311. (1) of the Mental Health (Care and Treatment)(Scotland) Act 2003 (asp 13)(non-consensual sexual acts).]
- [F95an offence under section 1 of the Protection of Children and Prevention of Sexual Offences (Scotland) Act 2005 (asp 9) (meeting a child following certain preliminary conduct);
- an offence under section 9 of that Act (paying for sexual services of a child);
- an offence under section 10 of that Act (causing or inciting provision by child of sexual services or child pornography);
- an offence under section 11 of that Act (controlling a child providing sexual services or involved in pornography);
- an offence under section 12 of that Act (arranging or facilitating provision by child of sexual services or child pornography).][F96 and
- an offence which consists of a contravention of any of the following provisions of the Sexual Offences (Scotland) Act 2009 (asp 9)—
section 1 (rape),
section 2 (sexual assault by penetration),
section 3 (sexual assault),
section 4 (sexual coercion),
section 5 (coercing a person into being present during a sexual activity),
section 6 (coercing a person into looking at a sexual image),
section 7. (1) (communicating indecently),
section 7. (2) (causing a person to see or hear an indecent communication),
section 8 (sexual exposure),
section 9 (voyeurism),
section 11 (administering a substance for sexual purposes),
section 18 (rape of a young child),
section 19 (sexual assault on a young child by penetration),
section 20 (sexual assault on a young child),

section 21 (causing a young child to participate in a sexual activity),

section 22 (causing a young child to be present during a sexual activity)

section 23 (causing a young child to look at a sexual image),

section 24. (1) (communicating indecently with a young child),

section 24. (2) (causing a young child to see or hear an indecent communication),

section 25 (sexual exposure to a young child),

section 26 (voyeurism towards a young child),

section 28 (having intercourse with an older child),

section 29 (engaging in penetrative sexual activity with or towards an older child),

section 30 (engaging in sexual activity with or towards an older child),

section 31 (causing an older child to participate in a sexual activity),

section 32 (causing an older child to be present during a sexual activity),

section 33 (causing an older child to look at a sexual image),

section 34. (1) (communicating indecently with an older child),

section 34. (2) (causing an older child to see or hear an indecent communication),

section 35 (sexual exposure to an older child),

section 36 (voyeurism towards an older child),

section 37. (1) (engaging while an older child in sexual conduct with or towards another older child),

section 37. (4) (engaging while an older child in consensual sexual conduct with another older child),

section 42 (sexual abuse of trust),

section 46 (sexual abuse of trust of a mentally disordered person);

- [F97an offence (other than one mentioned in the preceding paragraphs) where the court determines for the purposes of this paragraph that there was a significant sexual aspect to the offender's behaviour in committing the offence;]]

" imprisonment " includes—

- detention under section 207 of this Act; and

- detention under section 208 of this Act; and

" violent offence " means any offence (other than an offence which is a sexual offence within the meaning of this section) inferring personal violence.

[F98. (11)In subsection (10)

(a) any reference to a " sexual offence " includes?

(i) a reference to any attempt, conspiracy or incitement to commit that offence; and

(ii) except in the case of an offence under paragraphs (i) to (viii) of the definition of "sexual offence" in that subsection, a reference to aiding and abetting, counselling or procuring the commission of that offence;

(b) the references to "rape" in paragraphs (iii) and (iv) of the definition of "sexual offence" are to the offence of rape at common law; and

(c) the references to "the statutory offence of rape" in paragraphs (iiia) and (iva) of that definition are (as the case may be) to?

(i) the offence of rape under section 1 of the Sexual Offences (Scotland) Act 2009, or

(ii) the offence of rape of a young child under section 18 of that Act.]

[F99. (12)An extended sentence may be passed by reference to paragraph (xxviii) only if the offender is or is to become, by virtue of Schedule 3 to the Sexual Offences Act 2003 (c.42), subject to the notification requirements of Part 2 of that Act.]]

Amendments (Textual)

F83. S. 210. A inserted (30.9.1998) by 1998 c. 37, s. 86. (1); S.I. 1998/2327, art. 2. (1)(s) (subject to arts. 5-8)

F84. Word in s. 210. A(3)(b) substituted (28.1.2003) by The Extended Sentences for Violent Offenders (Scotland) Order 2003 (S.S.I. 2003/48), art. 2 (with art. 1. (2))

F85. Words in s. 210. A(6) substituted (4.10.2004) by Criminal Procedure (Amendment) (Scotland) Act 2004 (asp 5), ss. 21, 27. (1); S.S.I. 2004/405, art. 2, Sch. 1 (subject to savings in arts. 3-5)

F86. Words in s. 210. A(10) inserted (1.12.2010) by Sexual Offences (Scotland) Act 2009 (asp 9), ss. 61, 62. (2), Sch. 5 para. 2. (6)(a); S.S.I. 2010/357, art. 2. (a)

F87. S. 210. A(10): words in the definition of "sexual offence" inserted (1.12.2010) by The Sexual Offences (Scotland) Act 2009 (Supplemental and Consequential Provisions) Order 2010 (S.S.I. 2010/421), art. 2, Sch. para. 1. (3)(a)(i)

F88. S. 210. A(10): words in the definition of "sexual offence" inserted (1.12.2010) by The Sexual Offences (Scotland) Act 2009 (Supplemental and Consequential Provisions) Order 2010 (S.S.I. 2010/421), art. 2, Sch. para. 1. (3)(a)(ii)

F89. Words in s. 210. A(10) repealed (1.12.2010) by Sexual Offences (Scotland) Act 2009 (asp 9), ss. 61, 62. (2), Sch. 6; S.S.I. 2010/357, art. 2. (a)

F90. S. 210. A: word "and"immediately preceding s. 210. A(10) para. (xix) omitted (8.1.2001) by virtue of 2000 c. 44, s. 6. (2); S.S.I. 2000/452, art. 2. (f)

F91. Word in s. 210. A(10) in definition of "sexual offence" omitted (5.10.2005) by virtue of Mental Health (Care and Treatment) (Scotland) Act 2003 (asp 13), ss. 312. (a), 333. (2)-(4); S.S.I. 2005/161, art. 3

F92. S. 210. A(xx) and the preceding "and"inserted (8.1.2001) by 2000 c. 44, s. 6. (2); S.S.I. 2000/452, art. 2. (f)

F93. S. 210. A(10): word repealed (23.4.2007) by Criminal Proceedings etc. (Reform) (Scotland) Act 2007 (asp 6), ss. 80, 84, Sch. para. 19. (a); S.S.I. 2007/250, art. 3. (i) (subject to art. 4)

F94. Words in s. 210. A(10) in definition of "sexual offence" added (5.10.2005) by Mental Health (Care and Treatment) (Scotland) Act 2003 (asp 13), ss. 312. (b), 333. (2)-(4); S.S.I. 2005/161, art. 3

F95. S. 210. A(10): words added (23.4.2007) by Criminal Proceedings etc. (Reform) (Scotland) Act 2007 (asp 6), ss. 80, 84, Sch. para. 19. (b); S.S.I. 2007/250, art. 3. (i) (subject to art. 4)

F96. S. 210. A(10)(xxvii) and word inserted (1.12.2010) by Sexual Offences (Scotland) Act 2009 (asp 9), ss. 61, 62. (2), Sch. 5 para. 2. (6)(b); S.S.I. 2010/357, art. 2. (a)

F97. S. 210. A(10): words in the definition of "sexual offence" added (13.12.2010 for all purposes in respect of offences committed on or after this date) by Criminal Justice and Licensing (Scotland) Act 2010 (asp 13), ss. 23. (a), 206. (1); S.S.I. 2010/413, art. 2, Sch.

F98. S. 210. A(11) substituted (1.12.2010) by The Sexual Offences (Scotland) Act 2009 (Supplemental and Consequential Provisions) Order 2010 (S.S.I. 2010/421), art. 2, Sch. para. 1. (3)(b)

F99. S. 210. A(12) added (13.12.2010 for all purposes in respect of offences committed on or after this date) by Criminal Justice and Licensing (Scotland) Act 2010 (asp 13), ss. 23. (b), 206. (1); S.S.I. 2010/413, art. 2, Sch.

Modifications etc. (not altering text)

C3. S. 210. A restricted (15.3.2007) by The Criminal Proceedings etc. (Reform) (Scotland) Act 2007 (Commencement and Savings) Order 2007 (S.S.I. 2007/250), art. 4

Marginal Citations

M121993 c.9.

M131979 c.2.

M141876 c.36.

M151982 c.45.

M161995 c.39.

[F100210. AAExtended sentences for certain other offendersS

Where a person is convicted on indictment of abduction but the offence is other than is mentioned in paragraph (iii) of the definition of "sexual offence" in subsection (10) of section 210. A of this Act, that section shall apply in relation to the person as it applies in relation to a person so convicted of a violent offence.]

Amendments (Textual)
F100. S. 210. AA inserted (27.6.2003) by Criminal Justice (Scotland) Act 2003 (asp 7), ss. 20, 89; S.S.I. 2003/288, art. 2, Sch.

[F101. Risk assessmentS

Amendments (Textual)
F101. Ss. 210. B-210. H and cross-headings inserted (19.6.2006 for specified purposes) by Criminal Justice (Scotland) Act 2003 (asp 7), ss. 1, 89 (as amended with regards to ss. 210. B, 210. D and 210. G (27.9.2005) by S.S.I. 2005/465, art. 2, Sch. 1 para. 34. (2)); S.S.I. 2006/332, art. 2

210. BRisk assessment orderS

(1) This subsection applies where it falls to the High Court to impose sentence on a person convicted of an offence other than murder and that offence—

(a) is (any or all)—

(i) a sexual offence (as defined in section 210. A(10) of this Act);

(ii) a violent offence (as so defined);

(iii) an offence which endangers life; or

(b) is an offence the nature of which, or circumstances of the commission of which, are such that it appears to the court that the person has a propensity to commit any such offence as is mentioned in sub-paragraphs (i) to (iii) of paragraph (a) above.

(2) Where subsection (1) above applies, the court, at its own instance or (provided that the prosecutor has given the person notice of his intention in that regard) on the motion of the prosecutor, if it considers that the risk criteria may be met, shall make an order under this subsection (a " risk assessment order ") unless—

(a) the court makes an interim compulsion order by virtue of section 210. D(1) of this Act in respect of the person; or

(b) the person is subject to an order for lifelong restriction previously imposed.

(3) A risk assessment order is an order—

(a) for the convicted person to be taken to a place specified in the order, so that there may be prepared there—

(i) by a person accredited for the purposes of this section by the Risk Management Authority; and

(ii) in such manner as may be so accredited,

a risk assessment report (that is to say, a report as to what risk his being at liberty presents to the safety of the public at large); and

(b) providing for him to be remanded in custody there for so long as is necessary for those purposes and thereafter there or elsewhere until such diet as is fixed for sentence.

(4) On making a risk assessment order, the court shall adjourn the case for a period not exceeding ninety days.

(5) The court may on one occasion, on cause shown, extend the period mentioned in subsection (4) above by not more than ninety days; and it may exceptionally, where by reason of circumstances outwith the control of the person to whom it falls to prepare the risk assessment report (the " assessor "), or as the case may be of any person instructed under section 210. C(5) of this Act to prepare such a report, the report in question has not been completed, grant such further extension as appears to it to be appropriate.

(6) There shall be no appeal against a risk assessment order or against any refusal to make such an order.

210. CRisk assessment reportS

(1) The assessor may, in preparing the risk assessment report, take into account not only any previous conviction of the convicted person but also any allegation that the person has engaged in criminal behaviour (whether or not that behaviour resulted in prosecution and acquittal).

(2) Where the assessor, in preparing the risk assessment report, takes into account any allegation that the person has engaged in criminal behaviour, the report is to—

    (a) list each such allegation;

    (b) set out any additional evidence which supports the allegation; and

    (c) explain the extent to which the allegation and evidence has influenced the opinion included in the report under subsection (3) below.

(3) The assessor shall include in the risk assessment report his opinion as to whether the risk mentioned in section 210. B(3)(a) of this Act is, having regard to such standards and guidelines as are issued by the Risk Management Authority in that regard, high, medium or low.

(4) The assessor shall submit the risk assessment report to the High Court by sending it, together with such documents as are available to the assessor and are referred to in the report, to the Principal Clerk of Justiciary, who shall then send a copy of the report and of those documents to the prosecutor and to the convicted person.

(5) The convicted person may, during the period of his detention at the place specified in the risk assessment order, himself instruct the preparation (by a person other than the assessor) of a risk assessment report; and if such a report is so prepared then the person who prepares it shall submit it to the court by sending it, together with such documents as are available to him (after any requirement under subsection (4) above is met) and are referred to in the report, to the Principal Clerk of Justiciary, who shall then send a copy of it and of those documents to the prosecutor.

(6) When the court receives the risk assessment report submitted by the assessor a diet shall be fixed for the convicted person to be brought before it for sentence.

(7) If, within such period after receiving a copy of that report as may be prescribed by Act of Adjournal, the convicted person intimates, in such form, or as nearly as may be in such form, as may be so prescribed—

    (a) that he objects to the content or findings of that report; and

    (b) what the grounds of his objection are,

the prosecutor and he shall be entitled to produce and examine witnesses with regard to—

(i) that content or those findings; and

(ii) the content or findings of any risk assessment report instructed by the person and duly submitted under subsection (5) above.

210. DInterim hospital order and assessment of riskS

(1) Where subsection (1) of section 210. B of this Act applies, the High Court, if—

    (a) it may make an interim compulsion order in respect of the person under section 53 of this Act; and

    (b) it considers that the risk criteria may be met,

shall make such an order unless the person is subject to an order for lifelong restriction previously imposed.

(2) Where an interim compulsion order is made by virtue of subsection (1) above, a report as to the risk the convicted person's being at liberty presents to the safety of the public at large shall be prepared by a person accredited for the purposes of this section by the Risk Management Authority and in such manner as may be so accredited.

(3) Section 210. C(1) to (4) and (7)(except paragraph (ii)) of this Act shall apply in respect of any such report as it does in respect of a risk assessment report.

210. EThe risk criteriaS

For the purposes of sections 195. (1), 210. B(2), 210. D(1) and 210. F(1) and (3) of this Act, the risk criteria are that the nature of, or the circumstances of the commission of, the offence of which the convicted person has been found guilty either in themselves or as part of a pattern of behaviour are such as to demonstrate that there is a likelihood that he, if at liberty, will seriously endanger the lives, or physical or psychological well-being, of members of the public at large.

[F102210. EAApplication of certain sections of this Act to proceedings under section 210. C(7)S

(1) Sections 271 to 271. M, 274 to 275. C and 288. C to 288. F of this Act (in this section referred to as the " applied sections ") apply in relation to proceedings under section 210. C(7) of this Act as they apply in relation to proceedings in or for the purposes of a trial, references in the applied sections to the "trial" and to the "trial diet" being construed accordingly.

(2) But for the purposes of this section the references—

(a) in sections 271. (1)(a) and 271. B(1)(b) to the date of commencement of the proceedings in which the trial is being held or is to be held; and

(b) in section 288. E(2)(b) to the date of commencement of the proceedings,

are to be construed as references to the date of commencement of the proceedings in which the person was convicted of the offence in respect of which sentence falls to be imposed (such proceedings being in this section referred to as the " original proceedings ").

(3) And for the purposes of this section any reference in the applied sections to—

(a) an "accused" (or to a person charged with an offence) is to be construed as a reference to the convicted person except that the reference in section 271. (2)(e)(iii) to an accused is to be disregarded;

(b) an "alleged" offence is to be construed as a reference to any or all of the following—

(i) the offence in respect of which sentence falls to be imposed;

(ii) any other offence of which the convicted person has been convicted;

(iii) any alleged criminal behaviour of the convicted person; and

(c) a " complainer " is to be construed as a reference to any or all of the following—

(i) the person who was the complainer in the original proceedings;

(ii) in the case of any such offence as is mentioned in paragraph (b)(ii) above, the person who was the complainer in the proceedings relating to that offence;

(iii) in the case of alleged criminal behaviour if it was alleged behaviour directed against a person, the person in question.

(4) Where—

(a) any person who is giving or is to give evidence at an examination under section 210. C(7) of this Act gave evidence at the trial in the original proceedings; and

(b) a special measure or combination of special measures was used by virtue of section 271. A, 271. C or 271. D of this Act for the purpose of taking the person's evidence at that trial,

that special measure or, as the case may be, combination of special measures is to be treated as having been authorised, by virtue of the same section, to be used for the purpose of taking the person's evidence at or for the purposes of the examination.

(5) Subsection (4) above does not affect the operation, by virtue of subsection (1) above, of section 271. D of this Act.]

Amendments (Textual)

F102. S. 210. EA inserted (20.6.2006 for specified purposes) by Management of Offenders etc. (Scotland) Act 2005 (asp 14), ss. 19, 24; S.S.I. 2006/331, art. 3. (1) (subject to art. 3. (2))

Order for lifelong restriction etc.S

210. F[F103. Order for lifelong restriction or compulsion order]S

(1) The High Court, at its own instance or on the motion of the prosecutor, if it is satisfied, having regard to—

(a) [F104any] risk assessment report submitted under section 210. C(4) or (5) of this Act;

(b) any report submitted by virtue of section 210. D of this Act;

(c) any evidence given under section 210. C(7) of this Act; and

(d) any other information before it,

that, on a balance of probabilities, the risk criteria are met, shall [F105, in a case where it may make a compulsion order in respect of the convicted person under section 57. A of this Act, either make such an order or make an order for lifelong restriction in respect of that person and in any other case make an order for lifelong restriction in respect of that person.]

(2) An order for lifelong restriction constitutes a sentence of imprisonment, or as the case may be detention, for an indeterminate period.

(3) The prosecutor may, on the grounds that on a balance of probabilities the risk criteria are met, appeal against any refusal of the court to make an order for lifelong restriction.

Amendments (Textual)

F103. S. 210. F title substituted (20.6.2006 for specified purposes) by virtue of Management of Offenders etc. (Scotland) Act 2005 (asp 14) {ss. 14. (3)}, 24; S.S.I. 2006/331, art. 3. (1) (subject to art. 3. (2))

F104. Word in s. 210. F(1)(a) substituted (20.6.2006 for specified purposes) by Management of Offenders etc. (Scotland) Act 2005 (asp 14), ss. 14. (2)(a), 24; S.S.I. 2006/331, art. 3. (1) (subject to art. 3. (2))

F105. Words in s. 210. F(1) substituted (20.6.2006 for specified purposes) by Management of Offenders etc. (Scotland) Act 2005 (asp 14), ss. 14. (2)(b), 24; S.S.I. 2006/331, art. 3. (1) (subject to art. 3. (2)) [Editorial Note: the word "shall" immediately preceding the substituted text is treated as not having been removed despite the wording of the amending section, by virtue of the decision of the Appeal Court, High Court of Justiciary, in the case of Brian Johnstone v HM Advocate 5 July 2011 [2011] HCJAC 66]

210. GDisposal of case where certain orders not madeS

(1) Where, in respect of a convicted person—

(a) a risk assessment order is not made under section 210. B(2) of this Act, or (as the case may be) an interim compulsion order is not made by virtue of section 210. D(1) of this Act, because the court does not consider that the risk criteria may be met; or

(b) the court considers that the risk criteria may be met but a risk assessment order, or (as the case may be) an interim compulsion order, is not so made because the person is subject to an order for lifelong restriction previously imposed,

the court shall dispose of the case as it considers appropriate.

(2) Where, in respect of a convicted person, an order for lifelong restriction is not made under section 210. F of this Act because the court is not satisfied (in accordance with subsection (1) of that section) that the risk criteria are met, the court, in disposing of the case, shall not impose on the person a sentence of imprisonment for life, detention for life or detention without limit of time.

Report of judgeS

210. HReport of judgeS

(1) This subsection applies where a person falls to be sentenced—

(a) in the High Court for an offence (other than murder) mentioned in section 210. B(1) of this Act; or

(b) in the sheriff court for such an offence prosecuted on indictment.

(2) Where subsection (1) above applies, the court shall, as soon as reasonably practicable, prepare a report in writing, in such form as may be prescribed by Act of Adjournal—

(a) as to the circumstances of the case; and

(b) containing such other information as it considers appropriate,

but no such report shall be prepared if a report is required to be prepared under section 21. (4) of the Criminal Justice (Scotland) Act 2003 (asp 7).]

FinesS

211 Fines.S

(1) Where an accused who is convicted on indictment of any offence (whether triable only on indictment or triable either on indictment or summarily other than by virtue of section 292. (6) of this Act) would apart from this subsection be liable to a fine of or not exceeding a specified amount, he shall by virtue of this subsection be liable to a fine of any amount.

(2) Where any Act confers a power by subordinate instrument to make a person liable on conviction on indictment of any offence mentioned in subsection (1) above to a fine or a maximum fine of a specified amount, or which shall not exceed a specified amount, the fine which may be imposed in the exercise of that power shall by virtue of this subsection be a fine of an unlimited amount.

(3) Any sentence or decree for any fine or expenses pronounced by a sheriff court or [F106. JP court] may be enforced against the person or effects of any party against whom the sentence or decree was awarded—

(a) in the district where the sentence or decree was pronounced; or

(b) in any other such district.

(4) A fine imposed by the High Court shall be remitted for enforcement to, and shall be enforceable as if it had been imposed by—

(a) where the person upon whom the fine was imposed resides in Scotland, the sheriff for the district where that person resides; and

(b) where that person resides outwith Scotland, the sheriff before whom he was brought for examination in relation to the offence for which the fine was imposed.

(5) F107. . . . .

(6) [F108. Except where the provisions of section 223. R(2) apply,] all fines and expenses imposed in F109. . . proceedings under this Act shall be paid to the [F110clerk of any court, or to any other person (or class of person) authorised by the Scottish Ministers for the purpose,] to be accounted for F111. . . to the person entitled to such fines and expenses, and it shall not be necessary to specify in any sentence the person entitled to payment of such fines or expenses unless it is necessary to provide for the division of the penalty.

(7) A court in determining the amount of any fine to be imposed on an offender shall take into consideration, amongst other things, the means of the offender so far as known to the court.

Amendments (Textual)

F106. Words in s. 211. (3) substituted (10.3.2008, 2.6.2008, 8.12.2008, 23.2.2009 and 14.12.2009 for certain purposes, otherwise 22.2.2010) by Criminal Proceedings etc. (Reform) (Scotland) Act 2007 (asp 6), ss. 80, 84, Sch. para. 26. (j); S.S.I. 2008/42, art. 3, Sch.; S.S.I. 2008/192, art. 3, Sch.; S.S.I. 2008/329, art. 3, Sch.; S.S.I. 2008/362, art. 3, Sch.; S.S.I. 2009/432, art. 3, Schs. 1, 2

F107. S. 211. (5) repealed (10.3.2008) by Criminal Proceedings etc. (Reform) (Scotland) Act 2007 (asp 6), ss. 80, 84, Sch. para. 20. (1)(a); S.S.I. 2008/42, art. 3, Sch.

F108. Words in s. 211. (6) inserted (12.10.2009) by The Mutual Recognition of Criminal Financial

Penalties in the European Union (Scotland) Order 2009 (S.S.I. 2009/342), art. 7 (with art. 2)
F109. Word in s. 211. (6) repealed (10.3.2008) by Criminal Proceedings etc. (Reform) (Scotland) Act 2007 (asp 6), ss. 80, 84, Sch. para. 20. (1)(b)(i); S.S.I. 2008/42, art. 3, Sch.
F110. Words in s. 211. (6) substituted (10.3.2008 for certain purposes and otherwise prosp.) by Criminal Proceedings etc. (Reform) (Scotland) Act 2007 (asp 6), ss. 80, 84, Sch. para. 20. (1)(b)(ii); S.S.I. 2008/42, art. 3, Sch.
F111. Words in s. 211. (6) repealed (10.3.2008) by Criminal Proceedings etc. (Reform) (Scotland) Act 2007 (asp 6), ss. 80, 84, Sch. para. 20. (1)(b)(iii); S.S.I. 2008/42, art. 3, Sch.
Modifications etc. (not altering text)
C4. S. 211. (3)-(6) applied (1.4.1996) by 1995 c. 43, ss. 14. (1), 34, 50. (2), Sch. 1 para. 4. (4)
S. 211. (3)-(6) applied (24.3.2003) by Proceeds of Crime Act 2002 (c. 29), ss. 118. (1)(2)(a), 458; S.S.I. 2003/210, art. 2 (subject to transitional provisions in arts. 3-7)

212 Fines in summary proceedings.S

(1) Where a court of summary jurisdiction imposes a fine on an offender, the court may order him to be searched, and any money found on him on apprehension or when so searched or when taken to prison or to a young offenders institution in default of payment of the fine, may, unless the court otherwise directs and subject to subsection (2) below, be applied towards payment of the fine, and the surplus if any shall be returned to him.
(2) Money shall not be applied as mentioned in subsection (1) above if the court is satisfied that it does not belong to the person on whom it was found or that the loss of the money will be more injurious to his family than his imprisonment or detention.
(3) When a court of summary jurisdiction, which has adjudged that a sum of money shall be paid by an offender, considers that any money found on the offender on apprehension, or after he has been searched by order of the court, should not be applied towards payment of such sum, the court, shall make a direction in writing to that effect which shall be written on the extract of the sentence which imposes the fine before it is issued by the clerk of the court.
(4) An accused may make an application to such a court either orally or in writing, through the governor of the prison in whose custody he may be at that time, that any sum of money which has been found on his person should not be applied in payment of the fine adjudged to be paid by him.
(5) A person who alleges that any money found on the person of an offender is not the property of the offender, but belongs to that person, may apply to such court either orally or in writing for a direction that the money should not be applied in payment of the fine adjudged to be paid, and the court after enquiry may so direct.
(6) A court of summary jurisdiction, which has adjudged that a sum of money shall be paid by an offender, may order the attendance in court of the offender, if he is in prison, for the purpose of ascertaining the ownership of money which has been found on his person.
(7) A notice in the form prescribed by Act of Adjournal, or as nearly as may be in such form, addressed to the governor of the prison in whose custody an offender may be at the time, signed by the judge of a court of summary jurisdiction shall be a sufficient warrant to the governor of such prison for conveying the offender to the court.

213 Remission of fines.S

(1) A fine may at any time be remitted in whole or in part by—
    (a) in a case where a transfer of fine order under section 222 of this Act is effective and the court by which payment is enforceable is, in terms of the order, a court of summary jurisdiction in Scotland, that court; or
    (b) in any other case, the court which imposed the fine or, where that court was the High Court, by which payment was first enforceable.
(2) Where the court remits the whole or part of a fine after imprisonment has been imposed under

section 214. (2) or (4) of this Act, it shall also remit the whole period of imprisonment or, as the case may be, reduce the period by an amount which bears the same proportion to the whole period as the amount remitted bears to the whole fine.

(3) The power conferred by subsection (1) above shall be exercisable without requiring the attendance of the accused.

214 Fines: time for payment and payment by instalments.S

(1) Where a court has imposed a fine on an offender or ordered him to find caution the court shall, subject to subsection (2) below, allow him at least seven days to pay the fine or the first instalment thereof or, as the case may be, to find caution; and any reference in this section and section 216 of this Act to a failure to pay a fine or other like expression shall include a reference to a failure to find caution.

(2) If on the occasion of the imposition of a fine—

(a) the offender appears to the court to possess sufficient means to enable him to pay the fine forthwith; or

(b) on being asked by the court whether he wishes to have time for payment, he does not ask for time; or

(c) he fails to satisfy the court that he has a fixed abode; or

(d) the court is satisfied for any other special reason that no time should be allowed for payment,

the court may refuse him time to pay the fine and, if the offender fails to pay, may exercise its power to impose imprisonment and, if it does so, shall state the special reason for its decision.

(3) In all cases where time is not allowed by a court for payment of a fine, the reasons of the court for not so allowing time shall be stated in the extract of the finding and sentence as well as in the finding and sentence itself.

(4) Where time is allowed for payment of a fine or payment by instalments is ordered, the court shall not, on the occasion of the imposition of a fine, impose imprisonment in the event of a future default in paying the fine or an instalment thereof unless the offender is before it and the court determines that, having regard to the gravity of the offence or to the character of the offender, or to other special reason, it is expedient that he should be imprisoned without further inquiry in default of payment; and where a court so determines, it shall state the special reason for its decision.

(5) Where a court has imposed imprisonment in accordance with subsection (4) above, then, if at any time the offender asks the court to commit him to prison, the court may do so notwithstanding subsection (1) of this section.

(6) Nothing in the foregoing provisions of this section shall affect any power of the court to order a fine to be recovered by civil diligence.

(7) Where time has been allowed for payment of a fine imposed by the court, it may, on an application by or on behalf of the offender, and after giving the prosecutor an opportunity of being heard, allow further time for payment.

(8) Without prejudice to subsection (2) above, where a court has imposed a fine on an offender, the court may, of its own accord or on the application of the offender, order payment of that fine by instalments of such amounts and at such time as it may think fit.

(9) Where the court has ordered payment of a fine by instalments it may—

(a) allow further time for payment of any instalment thereof;

(b) order payment thereof by instalments of lesser amounts, or at longer intervals, than those originally fixed,

and the powers conferred by this subsection shall be exercisable without requiring the attendance of the accused.

Modifications etc. (not altering text)

C5. S. 214 applied (with modifications) (1.4.1996) by 1995 c. 43, ss. 14. (2)(a), 50. (2)

C6. S. 214. (2) modified (1.4.1996) by 1995 c. 43, ss. 15. (2), 50. (2)

C7. S. 214. (4)-(6) applied (with modifications) (24.3.2003) by Proceeds of Crime Act 2002 (c. 29), ss. 118. (1)(2)(b), 458; S.S.I. 2003/210, art. 2 (with transitional provisions in arts. 3-7)

215 Application for further time to pay fine.S

(1) An application by an offender for further time in which to pay a fine imposed on him by a court, or of instalments thereof, shall be made, subject to subsection (2) below, to that court.
(2) Where a transfer of fine order has been made under section 222 of this Act, section 90 of the M17. Magistrates' Courts Act 1980 or Article 95 of the M18. Magistrates' Courts (Northern Ireland) Order 1981, an application under subsection (1) above shall be made to the court specified in the transfer order, or to the court specified in the last transfer order where there is more than one transfer.
(3) A court to which an application is made under this section shall allow further time for payment of the fine or of instalments thereof, unless it is satisfied that the failure of the offender to make payment has been wilful or that the offender has no reasonable prospect of being able to pay if further time is allowed.
(4) An application made under this section may be made orally or in writing.
Modifications etc. (not altering text)
C8. S. 215 applied (with modifications) (1.4.1996) by 1995 c. 43, ss. 14. (2)(b), 50. (2)
Marginal Citations
M171980 c.43.
M18. S.I. 1981/1675 (N.I. 26)

216 Fines: restriction on imprisonment for default.S

(1) Where a court has imposed a fine or ordered the finding of caution without imposing imprisonment in default of payment, subject to subsection (2) below, it shall not impose imprisonment on an offender for failing to make payment of the fine or, as the case may be, to find caution, unless on an occasion subsequent to that sentence the court has enquired into in his presence the reason why the fine has not been paid or, as the case may be, caution has not been found.
(2) Subsection (1) above shall not apply where the offender is in prison.
(3) A court may, for the purpose of enabling enquiry to be made under this section—
    (a) issue a citation requiring the offender to appear before the court at a time and place appointed in the citation; or
    (b) issue a warrant of apprehension.
(4) On the failure of the offender to appear before the court in response to a citation under this section, the court may issue a warrant of apprehension.
(5) The citation of an offender to appear before a court in terms of subsection (3)(a) above shall be effected in like manner, mutatis mutandis, as the citation of an accused to a sitting or diet of the court under section 141 of this Act, and—
    (a) the citation shall be signed by the clerk of the court before which the offender is required to appear, instead of by the prosecutor; and
    (b) the forms relating to the citation of an accused shall not apply to such citation.
(6) The following matters shall be, or as nearly as may be, in such form as is prescribed by Act of Adjournal—
    (a) the citation of an offender under this section;
    (b) if the citation of the offender is effected by an officer of law, the written execution, if any, of that officer of law;
    (c) a warrant of apprehension issued by a court under subsection (4) above; and
    (d) the minute of procedure in relation to an enquiry into the means of an offender under this section.

(7) Where a child would, if he were an adult, be liable to be imprisoned in default of payment of any fine the court may, if it considers that none of the other methods by which the case may legally be dealt with is suitable, order that the child be detained for such period, not exceeding one month, as may be specified in the order in a place chosen by the local authority in whose area the court is situated.

Modifications etc. (not altering text)

C9. S. 216 applied (with modifications) (1.4.1996) by 1995 c. 43, ss. 14. (2)(c), 50. (2)

S. 216 applied (with modifications) (24.3.2003) by Proceeds of Crime Act 2002 (c. 29), ss. 118. (1)(2)(c), 458; S.S.I. 2003/210, art. 2 (with transitional provisions in arts. 3-7)

C10. S. 216. (7) modified (1.4.1997) by S.I. 1996/3255, reg. 14. (1)

217 Fines: supervision pending payment.S

(1) Where an offender has been allowed time for payment of a fine, the court may, either on the occasion of the imposition of the fine or on a subsequent occasion, order that he be placed under the supervision of such person, in this section referred to as the "supervising officer", as the court may from time to time appoint for the purpose of assisting and advising the offender in regard to payment of the fine.

(2) An order made in pursuance of subsection (1) above shall remain in force so long as the offender to whom it relates remains liable to pay the fine or any part of it unless the order ceases to have effect or is discharged under subsection (3) below.

(3) An order under this section shall cease to have effect on the making of a transfer of fine order under section 222 of this Act in respect of the fine or may be discharged by the court that made it without prejudice, in either case, to the making of a new order.

(4) Where an offender under 21 years of age has been allowed time for payment of a fine, the court shall not order the form of detention appropriate to him in default of payment of the fine unless—

(a) he has been placed under supervision in respect of the fine; or

(b) the court is satisfied that it is impracticable to place him under supervision.

(5) Where a court, on being satisfied as mentioned in subsection (4)(b) above, orders the detention of a person under 21 years of age without an order under this section having been made, the court shall state the grounds on which it is so satisfied.

(6) Where an order under this section is in force in respect of an offender, the court shall not impose imprisonment in default of the payment of the fine unless before doing so it has—

(a) taken such steps as may be reasonably practicable to obtain from the supervising officer a report, which may be oral, on the offender's conduct and means, and has considered any such report; and

(b) in a case where an enquiry is required by section 216 of this Act, considered such enquiry.

(7) When a court appoints a different supervising officer under subsection (1) above, a notice shall be sent by the clerk of the court to the offender in such form, as nearly as may be, as is prescribed by Act of Adjournal.

(8) The supervising officer shall communicate with the offender with a view to assisting and advising him in regard to payment of the fine, and unless the fine or any instalment thereof is paid to the clerk of the court within the time allowed by the court for payment, the supervising officer shall report to the court without delay after the expiry of such time, as to the conduct and means of the offender.

[F112. (9)Where an enforcement order has been made under section 226. B of this Act in relation to payment of the fine, the supervising officer shall, instead of reporting under subsection (8) above to the court, report under that subsection to the fines enforcement officer dealing with the order.]

Amendments (Textual)

F112. S. 217. (9) inserted (10.3.2008) by Criminal Proceedings etc. (Reform) (Scotland) Act 2007

(asp 6), ss. 80, 84, Sch. para. 20. (2); S.S.I. 2008/42, art. 3, Sch.
Modifications etc. (not altering text)
C11. S. 217 applied (with modifications) (1.4.1996) by 1995 c. 43, ss. 14. (2)(d), 50. (2)
S. 217 applied (24.3.2003) by Proceeds of Crime Act 2002 (c. 29), ss. 118. (1)(2)(d), 458; S.S.I.
2003/210, art.2 (with transitional provisions in arts 3-7)

218 Fines: supplementary provisions as to payment.S

(1) Where under the provisions of section 214 or 217 of this Act a court is required to state a special reason for its decision or the grounds on which it is satisfied that it is undesirable or impracticable to place an offender under supervision, the reason or, as the case may be, the grounds shall be entered in the record of the proceedings along with the finding and sentence.
(2) Any reference in the said sections 214 and 217 to imprisonment shall be construed, in the case of an offender on whom by reason of his age imprisonment may not lawfully be imposed, as a reference to the lawful form of detention in default of payment of a fine appropriate to that person, and any reference to prison shall be construed accordingly.
(3) Where a warrant has been issued for the apprehension of an offender for non-payment of a fine, the offender may, notwithstanding section 211. (6) of this Act, pay such fine in full to a constable; and the warrant shall not then be enforced and the constable shall remit the fine to the clerk of court.
Modifications etc. (not altering text)
C12. S. 218. (2)(3) applied (with modifications) (1.4.1996) by 1995 c. 43, ss. 14. (2)(e), 50. (2)
S. 218. (2)(3) applied (24.3.2006) by Proceeds of Crime Act 2002 (c. 29), ss. 118. (1)(2)(e), 458;
S.S.I. 2003/210, art. 2 (with transitional provisions in arts. 3-7)

219 Fines: periods of imprisonment for non-payment.S

(1) Subject to sections 214 to 218 of this Act [F113and subsection (1. A) below]—
    (a) a court may, when imposing a fine, impose a period of imprisonment in default of payment;
or
    (b) where no order has been made under paragraph (a) above and a person fails to pay a fine, or any part or instalment of a fine, by the time ordered by the court (or, where section 214. (2) of this Act applies, immediately) the court may, subject to section 235. (1) of this Act, impose a period of imprisonment for such failure either with immediate effect or to take effect in the event of the person failing to pay the fine or any part or instalment of it by such further time as the court may order,
whether or not the fine is imposed under an enactment which makes provision for its enforcement or recovery.
[F114. (1. A)Subsection (1) shall not apply to a fine imposed for an offence under section 107 of the Antisocial Behaviour etc. (Scotland) Act 2004 (asp 8).]
(2) Subject to the following subsections of this section, the maximum period of imprisonment which may be imposed under subsection (1) above or for failure to find caution, shall be as follows—

Amount of Fine or Caution	Maximum Period of Imprisonment
Not exceeding £200	7 days
Exceeding £200 but not exceeding £500	14 days
Exceeding £500 but not exceeding £1,000	28 days
Exceeding £1,000 but not exceeding £2,500	45 days
Exceeding £2,500 but not exceeding £5,000	3 months
Exceeding £5,000 but not exceeding £10,000	6 months
Exceeding £10,000 but not exceeding £20,000	12 months
Exceeding £20,000 but not exceeding £50,000	18 months

Exceeding £50,000 but not exceeding £100,000................... | 2 years |

Exceeding £100,000 but not exceeding £250,000................... | 3 years |

Exceeding £250,000 but not exceeding £1 Million................... | 5 years |

Exceeding £1 Million................... | 10 years |

(3) Where an offender is fined on the same day before the same court for offences charged in the same indictment or complaint or in separate indictments or complaints, the amount of the fine shall, for the purposes of this section, be taken to be the total of the fines imposed.

(4) Where a court has imposed a period of imprisonment in default of payment of a fine, and—

    (a) an instalment of the fine is not paid at the time ordered; or

    (b) part only of the fine has been paid within the time allowed for payment,

the offender shall be liable to imprisonment for a period which bears to the period so imposed the same proportion, as nearly as may be, as the amount outstanding at the time when warrant is issued for imprisonment of the offender in default bears to the original fine.

(5) Where no period of imprisonment in default of payment of a fine has been imposed and—

    (a) an instalment of the fine is not paid at the time ordered; or

    (b) part only of the fine has been paid within the time allowed for payment,

the offender shall be liable to imprisonment for a maximum period which bears, as nearly as may be, the same proportion to the maximum period of imprisonment which could have been imposed by virtue of the Table in subsection (2) above in default of payment of the original fine as the amount outstanding at the time when he appears before the court bears to the original fine.

(6) If in any sentence or extract sentence the period of imprisonment inserted in default of payment of a fine or on failure to find caution is in excess of that competent under this Part of this Act, such period of imprisonment shall be reduced to the maximum period under this Part of this Act applicable to such default or failure, and the judge who pronounced the sentence shall have power to order the sentence or extract to be corrected accordingly.

(7) The provisions of this section shall be without prejudice to the operation of section 220 of this Act.

(8) Where in any case—

    (a) the sheriff considers that the imposition of imprisonment for the number of years for the time being specified in section 3. (3) of this Act would be inadequate; and

    (b) the maximum period of imprisonment which may be imposed under subsection (1) above (or under that subsection as read with either or both of sections 252. (2) of this Act and section [F115118. (2) [F116, (2. A) and (2. B)] of the Proceeds of Crime Act 2002] exceeds that number of years,

he shall remit the case to the High Court for sentence.

Amendments (Textual)

F113. Words in s. 219. (1) inserted (4.4.2005) by Antisocial Behaviour etc. (Scotland) Act 2004 (asp 8), ss. 144. (1), 145. (2), Sch. 4 para. 5. (4)(a); S.S.I. 2004/420, art. 3, Sch. 5

F114. S. 219. (1. A) inserted (4.4.2005) by Antisocial Behaviour etc. (Scotland) Act 2004 (asp 8), ss. 144. (1), 145. (2), Sch. 4 para. 5. (4)(b); S.S.I. 2004/420, art. 3, Sch. 5

F115. Words in s. 219. (8)(b) substituted (24.3.2003) by Proceeds of Crime Act 2002 (c. 29), ss. 456, 458, Sch. 11 para. 29. (4); S.S.I. 2003/210, art. 2, Sch. (subject to arts. 3-7)

F116. Words in s. 219. (8)(b) inserted (1.3.2016) by Serious Crime Act 2015 (c. 9), ss. 19. (3), 88. (2)(a); S.S.I. 2016/11, reg. 2. (d) (with reg. 3)

Modifications etc. (not altering text)

C13. S. 219 applied (with modifications) (1.4.1996) by 1995 c. 43, ss. 14. (2)(f), 50. (2)

S. 219 applied (with modifications) (24.3.2003) by Proceeds of Crime Act 2002 (c. 29), ss. 118. (1)(2)(f)(5), 458; S.S.I. 2003/210, art. 2 (subject to arts. 3-7)

C14. S. 219. (2)(2. A): power to amend conferred by 2002 c. 29, s. 118. (2. B)(a)(b) (as inserted (1.3.2016) by Serious Crime Act 2015 (c. 9), ss. 19. (1)(b), 88. (2)(a); S.S.I. 2016/11, reg. 2. (d) (with reg. 3))

C15. S. 219. (2) modified by 2002 c. 29, s. 118. (2. A) (as inserted (1.3.2016) by Serious Crime Act 2015 (c. 9), ss. 19. (1)(b), 88. (2)(a); S.S.I. 2016/11, reg. 2. (d) (with reg. 3))

220 Fines: part payment by prisoners.S

(1) Where a person committed to prison or otherwise detained for failure to pay a fine imposed by a court pays to the governor of the prison, under conditions prescribed by rules made under the M19. Prisons (Scotland) Act 1989, any sum in part satisfaction of the fine, the term of imprisonment [F117imposed under section 219 of this Act in respect of the fine] shall be reduced (or as the case may be further reduced) by a number of days bearing as nearly as possible the same proportion to such term as the sum so paid bears to the amount of the fine outstanding at the commencement of the imprisonment.

(2) The day on which any sum is paid as mentioned in subsection (1) above shall not be regarded as a day served by the prisoner as part of the said term of imprisonment.

(3) All sums paid under this section shall be handed over on receipt by the governor of the prison to the clerk of the court in which the conviction was obtained, and thereafter paid and applied pro tanto in the same manner and for the same purposes as sums adjudged to be paid by the conviction and sentence of the court, and paid and recovered in terms thereof, are lawfully paid and applied.

(4) In this section references to a prison and to the governor thereof shall include respectively references to any other place in which a person may be lawfully detained in default of payment of a fine, and to an officer in charge thereof.

Amendments (Textual)

F117. Words in s. 220. (1) inserted (27.6.2003) by Criminal Justice (Scotland) Act 2003 (asp 7), ss. 85, 89, Sch. 4 para. 3. (3); S.S.I. 2003/288, art. 2, Sch.

Modifications etc. (not altering text)

C16. S. 220 applied (with modifications) (1.4.1996) by 1995 c. 43, ss. 14. (2)(g), 50. (2)

S. 220 applied (with modifications) (24.3.2003) by Proceeds of Crime Act 2002 (c. 29), ss. 118. (1)(2)(g), 458; S.S.I. 2003/210, art. 2 (with transitional provisions in arts. 3-7)

Marginal Citations

M191989 c.45.

221 Fines: recovery by civil diligence.S

(1) Where any fine falls to be recovered by civil diligence in pursuance of this Act or in any case in which a court may think it expedient to order a fine to be recovered by civil diligence, there shall be added to the finding of the court imposing the fine a warrant for civil diligence in a form prescribed by Act of Adjournal which shall have the effect of authorising—

(a) the charging of the person who has been fined to pay the fine within the period specified in the charge and, in the event of failure to make such payment within that period,

[F118. (i)the execution of an arrestment;

(ii) the attachment of articles belonging to him; and

(iii) the execution of a money attachment ,]

and, if necessary for the purpose of executing the [F119attachment][F120 or the money attachment], the opening of shut and lockfast places;

(b) an arrestment other than an arrestment of earnings in the hands of his employer, and such diligence, whatever the amount of the fine imposed, may be executed in the same manner as if the proceedings were on an extract decree of the sheriff in a summary cause.

(2) Subject to subsection (3) below, proceedings by civil diligence under this section may be taken at any time after the imposition of the fine to which they relate.

(3) No such proceedings shall be authorised after the offender has been imprisoned in consequence of his having defaulted in payment of the fine.

(4) Where proceedings by civil diligence for the recovery of a fine or caution are taken, imprisonment for non-payment of the fine or for failure to find such caution shall remain competent and such proceedings may be authorised after the court has imposed imprisonment for,

or in the event of, the non-payment or the failure but before imprisonment has followed such imposition.

Amendments (Textual)

F118. S. 221. (1)(a)(i)-(iii) substituted for words (23.11.2009) by Bankruptcy and Diligence etc. (Scotland) Act 2007 (asp 3), ss. 226, 227, Sch. 5 para. 23. (a) (with s. 223); S.S.I. 2009/369, art. 3. (2)(3), Sch. 1

F119. Words in s. 221. (1)(a) substituted (30.12.2002) by Debt Arrangement and Attachment (Scotland) Act 2002 (asp 17), s. 61, Sch. 3 Pt. 1 para. 25 (with s. 63)

F120. Words in s. 221. (1)(a) inserted (23.11.2009) by Bankruptcy and Diligence etc. (Scotland) Act 2007 (asp 3), ss. 226, 227, Sch. 5 para. 23. (b) (with s. 223); S.S.I. 2009/369, art. 3. (2)(3), Sch. 1

Modifications etc. (not altering text)

C17. S. 221 applied (with modifications) (1.4.1996) by 1995 c. 43, ss. 14. (2)(h), 50. (2)
S. 221 applied (1.1.2003) by Fur Farming (Prohibition) (Scotland) Act 2002 (asp 10), s. 3. (2); S.S.I. 2002/519, art. 2

C18. S. 221 applied (24.3.2003) by Proceeds of Crime Act 2002 (c. 29), ss. 118. (1)(2)(h), 458; S.S.I. 2003/210, art. 2 (with transitional provisions in arts. 3-7) (as amended (1.3.2016) by Serious Crime Act 2015 (c. 9), ss. 19. (1)(a), 88. (2)(a); S.S.I. 2016/11, reg. 2. (d) (with reg. 3))

C19. S. 221 applied (1.3.2007) by The Sea Fishing (Prohibition on the Removal of Shark Fins) (Scotland) Order 2007 (S.S.I. 2007/39), art. 4. (3)

C20. S. 221 applied (29.11.2012) by Glasgow Commonwealth Games Act 2008 (asp 4), ss. 36. (3), 49; S.S.I. 2012/261, art. 2, sch.

222 Transfer of fine orders.S

(1) Where a court has imposed a fine on a person convicted of an offence and it appears to [F121the clerk of court] that he is residing—

    (a) within the jurisdiction of another court in Scotland; or

    (b) in any petty sessions area in England and Wales; or

    (c) in any petty sessions district in Northern Ireland,

[F122that clerk] may order that payment of the fine shall be enforceable by that other court or in that petty sessions area or petty sessions district as the case may be.

[F123. (1. A)Where a court has imposed a fine on a person convicted of an offence, and it appears to the clerk of court that there is a fine imposed by another court (of whatever kind) in the same sheriffdom, that clerk may order that payment of the fine is to be enforceable by that other court.]

(2) An order under this section (in this section referred to as a "transfer of fine order") shall specify the court by which or the petty sessions area or petty sessions district in which payment is to be enforceable and, where the court to be specified in a transfer of fine order is a court of summary jurisdiction, it shall, in any case where the order is made by [F124the sheriff clerk], be a sheriff court.

(3) Subject to subsections (4) and (5) below, where a transfer of fine order is made with respect to any fine under this section, any functions under any enactment relating to that sum which, if no such order had been made, would have been exercisable by the court which made the order or by the clerk of that court shall cease to be so exercisable.

(4) Where [F125, in relation to a transfer of fine order made under subsection (1)(a) above]—

    (a) the [F126clerk of the court specified in the order] is satisfied, after inquiry, that the offender is not residing within the jurisdiction of that court; and

    (b) the clerk of that court, within 14 days of receiving the notice required by section 223. (1) of this Act, sends to the clerk of the court which made the order notice to that effect,

the order shall cease to have effect.

(5) Where a transfer of fine order ceases to have effect by virtue of subsection (4) above, the functions referred to in subsection (3) above shall again be exercisable by the court which made

the order or, as the case may be, by the clerk of that court.

(6) Where a transfer of fine order under this section, section 90 of the M20. Magistrates' Courts Act 1980 or Article 95 of the M21. Magistrates' Courts (Northern Ireland) Order 1981 specifies a court of summary jurisdiction in Scotland, that court and the clerk of that court shall have all the like functions under this Part of this Act in respect of the fine or the sum in respect of which that order was made (including the power to make any further order under this section) as if the fine or the sum were a fine imposed by that court and as if any order made under this section, the said Act of 1980 or the said Order of 1981 in respect of the fine or the sum before the making of the transfer of fine order had been made by that court.

(7) The functions of the court to which subsection (6) above relates shall be deemed to include the court's power to apply to the Secretary of State under any regulations made by him under section 24. (1)(a) of the M22. Criminal Justice Act 1991 (power to deduct fines etc from income support).

(8) Where a transfer of fine order under section 90 of the Magistrates' Courts Act 1980, Article 95 of the Magistrates' Courts (Northern Ireland) Order 1981, or this section provides for the enforcement by a sheriff court in Scotland of a fine imposed by the Crown Court, the term of imprisonment which may be imposed under this Part of this Act shall be the term fixed in pursuance of [F127section 139 of the Powers of Criminal Courts (Sentencing) Act 2000] by the Crown Court or a term which bears the same proportion to the term so fixed as the amount of the fine remaining due bears to the amount of the fine imposed by that court, notwithstanding that the term exceeds the period applicable to the case under section 219 of this Act.

Amendments (Textual)

F121. Words in s. 222. (1) substituted (10.3.2008) by Criminal Proceedings etc. (Reform) (Scotland) Act 2007 (asp 6), ss. 80, 84, Sch. para. 20. (3)(a)(i); S.S.I. 2008/42, art. 3, Sch.

F122. Words in s. 222. (1) substituted (10.3.2008) by Criminal Proceedings etc. (Reform) (Scotland) Act 2007 (asp 6), ss. 80, 84, Sch. para. 20. (3)(a)(ii); S.S.I. 2008/42, art. 3, Sch.

F123. S. 222. (1. A) inserted (10.3.2008, 2.6.2008, 8.12.2008, 23.2.2009 and 14.12.2009 for certain purposes, otherwise 22.2.2010) by Criminal Proceedings etc. (Reform) (Scotland) Act 2007 (asp 6), ss. 80, 84, Sch. para. 20. (3)(b); S.S.I. 2008/42, art. 3, Sch.; S.S.I. 2008/192, art. 3, Sch.; S.S.I. 2008/329, art. 3, Sch.; S.S.I. 2008/362, art. 3, Sch.; S.S.I. 2009/432, art. 3, Schs. 1, 2

F124. Words in s. 222. (2) substituted (10.3.2008) by Criminal Proceedings etc. (Reform) (Scotland) Act 2007 (asp 6), ss. 80, 84, Sch. para. 20. (3)(c); S.S.I. 2008/42, art. 3, Sch.

F125. Words in s. 222. (2) substituted (10.3.2008) by Criminal Proceedings etc. (Reform) (Scotland) Act 2007 (asp 6), ss. 80, 84, Sch. para. 20. (3)(d)(i); S.S.I. 2008/42, art. 3, Sch.

F126. Words in s. 222. (2) substituted (10.3.2008) by Criminal Proceedings etc. (Reform) (Scotland) Act 2007 (asp 6), ss. 80, 84, Sch. para. 20. (3)(d)(ii); S.S.I. 2008/42, art. 3, Sch.

F127. Words in s. 222. (8) substituted (1.3.2016) by Serious Crime Act 2015 (c. 9), s. 88. (2)(c), Sch. 4 para. 16; S.S.I. 2016/11, reg. 2. (j)

Modifications etc. (not altering text)

C21. S. 222 applied (with modifications) (1.4.1996) by 1995 c. 43, ss. 14. (2)(i), 50. (2)

S. 222 applied (with modifications) (24.3.2003) by Proceeds of Crime Act 2002 (c. 29), ss. 118. (1)(2)(i), 458; S.S.I. 2003/210, art. 2 (with transitional provisions in arts. 3-7)

C22. S. 222 applied (E.) (12.8.2009) by The Sea Fishing (Landing and Weighing of Herring, Mackerel and Horse Mackerel) Order 2009 (S.I. 2009/1850), arts. 1, 10. (3)

C23. S. 222. (8) modified by 2002 c. 29, s. 118. (2. C)(2. D) (as inserted (1.3.2016) by Serious Crime Act 2015 (c. 9), ss. 19. (1)(b), 88. (2)(a); S.S.I. 2016/11, reg. 2. (d) (with reg. 3))

Marginal Citations

M201980 c.43.

M21. S.I. 1981/1675

M221991 c.53.

223 Transfer of fines: procedure for clerk of court.S

(1) Where [F128the clerk of] a court makes a transfer of fine order under section 222 of this Act, [F129that clerk] shall send to the clerk of the court specified in the order—

(a) a notice in the form prescribed by Act of Adjournal, or as nearly as may be in such form;

(b) a statement of the offence of which the offender was convicted; and

(c) a statement of the steps, if any, taken to recover the fine,

and shall give him such further information, if any, as, in his opinion, is likely to assist the court specified in the order in recovering the fine.

(2) In the case of a further transfer of fine order, the clerk [F130of court who] made the order shall send to the clerk of the court by which the fine was imposed a copy of the notice sent to the clerk of the court specified in the order.

(3) The clerk of court specified in a transfer of fine order shall, as soon as may be after he has received the notice mentioned in subsection (1)(a) above, send an intimation to the offender in the form prescribed by Act of Adjournal or as nearly as may be in such form.

(4) The clerk of court specified in a transfer of fine order shall remit or otherwise account for any payment received in respect of [F131a fine imposed by a court outwith Scotland] to the clerk of the court by which the fine was imposed, and if the sentence has been enforced otherwise than by payment of the fine, he shall inform the clerk of court how the sentence was enforced.

Amendments (Textual)

F128. Words in s. 223. (1) inserted (10.3.2008) by Criminal Proceedings etc. (Reform) (Scotland) Act 2007 (asp 6), ss. 80, 84, Sch. para. 20. (4)(a)(i); S.S.I. 2008/42, art. 3, Sch.

F129. Words in s. 223. (1) substituted (10.3.2008) by Criminal Proceedings etc. (Reform) (Scotland) Act 2007 (asp 6), ss. 80, 84, Sch. para. 20. (4)(a)(ii); S.S.I. 2008/42, art. 3, Sch.

F130. Words in s. 223. (2) substituted (10.3.2008) by Criminal Proceedings etc. (Reform) (Scotland) Act 2007 (asp 6), ss. 80, 84, Sch. para. 20. (4)(b); S.S.I. 2008/42, art. 3, Sch.

F131. Words in s. 223. (4) substituted (10.3.2008) by Criminal Proceedings etc. (Reform) (Scotland) Act 2007 (asp 6), ss. 80, 84, Sch. para. 20. (4)(c); S.S.I. 2008/42, art. 3, Sch.

Modifications etc. (not altering text)

C24. S. 223 applied (1.4.1996) by 1995 c. 43, ss. 14. (2)(j), 50. (2)

S. 223 applied (24.3.2003) by Proceeds of Crime Act 2002 (c. 29), ss. 118. (1)(2)(j), 458; S.S.I. 2003/210, art. 2 (with transitional provisions in arts. 3-7)

[F132. The mutual recognition of criminal financial penaltiesS

Amendments (Textual)

F132. Ss. 223. A-223. T and cross-heading inserted (12.10.2009) by The Mutual Recognition of Criminal Financial Penalties in the European Union (Scotland) Order 2009 (S.S.I. 2009/342), art. 3 (with art. 2)

223. ARecognition of financial penalties: requests to other member StatesS

(1) The designated officer of the competent authority for Scotland may issue a certificate, in a form prescribed by Act of Adjournal, requesting enforcement under the Framework Decision on financial penalties where—

(a) a person is required to pay a financial penalty;

(b) the financial penalty is not paid in full within the time allowed for payment;

(c) there is no appeal outstanding in relation to the financial penalty; and

(d) it appears to the designated officer of the competent authority for Scotland that the person is normally resident, or has property or income, in a member State other than the United Kingdom.

(2) For the purposes of subsection (1)(c), there is no appeal outstanding in relation to a financial penalty if—

(a) no appeal has been brought in relation to the imposition of the financial penalty within the time allowed for making such an appeal; or

(b) such an appeal has been brought but the proceedings on appeal have been concluded.

(3) In subsections (1)(c) and (2) "appeal" in respect of financial penalties mentioned in subsection (5)(b) and (c) includes a request made under section 302. C of this Act that such a penalty be recalled.

(4) Where the person required to pay the financial penalty is a body corporate or a partnership (including a Scottish partnership) subsection (1)(d) applies as if the reference to the member State in which the person appears to be normally resident were a reference to the member State in which the person appears to have its registered office or, as the case may be, its principal office of the partnership.

(5) In this section "financial penalty" means—

(a) any sum payable under a compensation order imposed under section 249 of this Act;

(b) any sum payable as a fixed penalty in a conditional offer made under section 302. (1) of this Act and accepted, or deemed to be accepted, in accordance with that section;

(c) any sum payable under a compensation offer made under section 302. A(1) of this Act and accepted, or deemed to be accepted, in accordance with that section;

(d) a fine, which is to be construed in accordance with section 307 of this Act, imposed by a court in Scotland on a person's conviction of an offence;

(e) a fine or other sum imposed by a court in England and Wales, or Northern Ireland, on a person's conviction of an offence which, following a transfer of fine order by virtue of section 90 of the Magistrates' Courts Act 1980 F133 or Article 95 of the Magistrates' Courts (Northern Ireland) Order 1981 F134, respectively, is enforceable in Scotland;

(f) a penalty in respect of which a fixed penalty notice is given under section 54 (giving notices for fixed penalty offences), or section 62 (fixing notices to vehicles) of the Road Traffic Offenders Act 1988 F135, which has been registered in Scotland for enforcement as a fine by virtue of section 71 of that Act;

(g) a fixed penalty notice given under section 129 (fixed penalty notices) of the Antisocial Behaviour etc. (Scotland) Act 2004 F136 in respect of which section 131. (5) of that Act applies; and

(h) expenses imposed in connection with proceedings relating to a conviction as mentioned in paragraphs (d) and (e).

Amendments (Textual)

F1331980 c.43; section 90 was amended by the Criminal Justice and Public Order Act 1994 (c.33), section 47. (2); the Access to Justice Act 1999 (c.22), section 90, Schedule 13, paragraphs 95, 108 (with section 107, Schedule 14, paragraph 7. (2)); S.I. 1995/127 and S.I. 2001/916.

F134. S.I. 1981/1675 (N.I. 26).

F1351988 c.53; section 54 was amended by the Road Traffic Act 1991 (c.40), sections 48 and 83, Schedule 4, paragraph 103. (2) and (3) and Schedule 8; the Police Reform Act 2002 (c.30), sections 38, 41, 76. (2), 108. (2) to (5), Schedule 4, paragraph 1. (2)(b) and Schedule 5, paragraph 1. (2)(a); S.I. 1990/144; S.I. 1992/1286; S.I. 2002/2750; S.I. 2002/2306 and section 62 was amended by the Road Safety Act 2006 (c.49), section 5, Schedule 1, paragraph 7.

F1362004 asp 8.

223. BRequests to other member States: procedure on issue of certificateS

(1) This section applies where the designated officer of the competent authority for Scotland issues a certificate under section 223. A(1) of this Act requesting enforcement under the Framework Decision on financial penalties.

(2) The designated officer of the competent authority for Scotland must give the central authority for Scotland the certificate, together with a certified copy, or extract, of the decision requiring

payment of the financial penalty.

(3) On receipt of the documents mentioned in subsection (2), the central authority for Scotland must give those documents to the central authority, or the competent authority, of the member State other than the United Kingdom in which the person appears to be normally resident or, as the case may be, has property or income.

(4) Where the documents mentioned in subsection (2) are given to the central authority, or the competent authority, of the member State other than the United Kingdom in accordance with subsection (3)—

    (a) no further steps to enforce the financial penalty may be taken in Scotland; and

    (b) no further such documents may be given under subsection (2);

unless subsection (5) applies.

(5) This subsection applies where any of the events mentioned in Article 15. (2) of the Framework Decision on financial penalties occurs; and accordingly the right to enforce the financial penalty reverts to the appropriate competent authority for Scotland.

(6) Where the person required to pay the financial penalty is a body corporate or a partnership (including a Scottish partnership) subsection (3) applies as if the reference to the member State in which the person appears to be normally resident were a reference to the member State in which the person appears to have its registered office or, as the case may be, its principal office of the partnership.

223. CRequests to other member States: application of provisions relating to finesS

Where the designated officer of the competent authority for Scotland has issued a certificate under section 223. A(1) of this Act in respect of a financial penalty mentioned in—

    (a) section 223. A(5)(d) or (h) of this Act;

    (b) section 223. A(5)(e) of this Act (in terms of the application of section 222. (6) of this Act);
or

    (c) section 223. A(5)(f) of this Act,

the provisions of section 217. (3) of this Act (supervision pending payment of fine) shall apply except that the reference to the making of a transfer of fine order under section 222 of this Act shall instead be a reference to the issuing of a certificate under sections 223. A(1) or 226. HA(4) of this Act.

223. DRequests to other member States: application of provisions relating to compensation ordersS

(1) This section applies where the designated officer of the competent authority for Scotland has issued a certificate under section 223. A(1) of this Act in respect of a financial penalty mentioned in section 223. A(5)(a).

(2) Section 252 of this Act shall apply, but the reference in subsection (2) of that section to section 217 is to be construed as a reference to that section modified as mentioned in section 223. C of this Act.

223. ERequests to other member States: application of provisions relating to fixed penaltiesS

(1) This section applies where the designated officer of the competent authority for Scotland has issued a certificate under section 223. A(1) of this Act in respect of a financial penalty mentioned in section 223. A(5)(b) or (c).

(2) Section 303 of this Act shall apply, but in the application of this Act to the outstanding amounts mentioned in subsection (1) of that section (which fall to be treated as fines by virtue of that subsection), the provisions mentioned in section [F137223. C] of this Act apply modified as mentioned in that section.

Amendments (Textual)

F137. Word in s. 223. E(2) substituted (1.12.2014) by The Mutual Recognition of Criminal Financial Penalties in the European Union (Scotland) (No. 1) Order 2014 (S.S.I. 2014/322), arts. 1, 3

223. FRecognition of financial penalties: requests from other member StatesS

(1) This section applies where—

(a) the competent authority, or central authority, of a member State ("the issuing State") other than the United Kingdom gives the central authority for Scotland—

(i) a certificate requesting enforcement under the Framework Decision on financial penalties; and

(ii) the decision, or a certified copy of the decision, requiring payment of the financial penalty to which the certificate relates; and

(b) the penalty is suitable for enforcement in Scotland.

(2) If the certificate states that the person against whom the decision has been made is normally resident in Scotland, the central authority for Scotland must give the documents mentioned in subsection (1)(a) to the designated officer of the competent authority for Scotland based upon the person's residence.

(3) If the certificate states otherwise than as mentioned in subsection (2), the central authority for Scotland must, subject to section 223. P(2) and (3) of this Act, give those documents to the designated officer of such competent authority for Scotland as appears appropriate based on the terms of the certificate.

(4) Where the central authority for Scotland acts under subsection (2) or (3), the central authority for Scotland must also give the designated officer of the competent authority for Scotland mentioned in those subsections a notice—

(a) stating whether the central authority thinks that any of the grounds for refusal specified in Schedule 12 apply; and

(b) giving reasons for that opinion.

(5) Where the person required to pay the financial penalty is a body corporate or a partnership (including a Scottish partnership), subsection (2) applies as if the reference to the competent authority for Scotland were a reference to the competent authority for Scotland within whose jurisdiction it appears that the person has its registered office or, as the case may be, its principal office of the partnership.

(6) Where—

(a) the competent authority, or central authority, of the issuing State gives the central authority for England and Wales, or the central authority for Northern Ireland, the documents mentioned in subsection (1)(a); and

(b) without taking any action to enforce the financial penalty in England and Wales, or Northern Ireland, the central authority for England and Wales or, as the case may be, the central authority for Northern Ireland gives those documents to the central authority for Scotland;

this section applies as if the competent authority, or central authority, of the issuing State gave the documents to the central authority for Scotland.

(7) Schedule 11 to this Act, which specifies when a financial penalty is suitable for enforcement in Scotland for the purposes of subsection (1)(b), has effect.

[F138223. FARequests from other member States: procedure

where no certificateS

(1) Subsection (2) applies where—

    (a) a requesting authority has—

(i) given the central authority for Scotland a decision, or a certified copy of a decision, requiring payment of a financial penalty; and

(ii) asked that the decision be enforced in any part of the United Kingdom under the Framework Decision on financial penalties; and

    (b) the central authority for Scotland has not been given anything purporting to be a certificate relating to the decision.

(2) The central authority for Scotland must immediately notify the requesting authority that the decision will not be enforced in Scotland unless a certificate relating to the decision is given to the central authority for Scotland.

(3) For the purpose of this section, a requesting authority is to be treated as having given a decision, or a certified copy of a decision, requiring payment of a financial penalty to the central authority for Scotland if—

    (a) the requesting authority gave the decision, or the certified copy, to—

(i) the central authority for England and Wales; or

(ii) the central authority for Northern Ireland; and

    (b) the central authority given the decision, or the certified copy, by the requesting authority—

(i) has not taken any action to enforce the financial penalty; and

(ii) has given the decision, or the certified copy, to the central authority for Scotland.

(4) In this section, "requesting authority" means the competent authority, or central authority, of a member State other than the United Kingdom.]

Amendments (Textual)

F138. S. 223. FA inserted (1.12.2014) by The Mutual Recognition of Criminal Financial Penalties in the European Union (Scotland) (No. 1) Order 2014 (S.S.I. 2014/322), arts. 1, 4

F139223. GRequests from other member States: return of certificateS

. . . .

Amendments (Textual)

F139. S. 223. G repealed (1.12.2014) by The Mutual Recognition of Criminal Financial Penalties in the European Union (Scotland) (No. 1) Order 2014 (S.S.I. 2014/322), arts. 1, 5

223. HRequests from other member States: procedure on receipt of certificateS

(1) This section applies where the central authority for Scotland gives the designated officer of the competent authority for Scotland—

    (a) a certificate, as mentioned in section 223. F, requesting enforcement under the Framework Decision on financial penalties;

    (b) the decision, or a certified copy of the decision, requiring payment of the financial penalty to which the certificate relates; and

    (c) a notice under section 223. F(4).

(2) The designated officer of the competent authority for Scotland must refer the matter to the competent authority for Scotland mentioned in section 223. Q(2).

(3) The competent authority for Scotland must decide whether it is satisfied that any of the grounds for refusal, as mentioned in Schedule 12, apply.

[F140. (3. A)The competent authority for Scotland may not decide that a ground for refusal specified in subsection (3. B) applies unless the authority which signed the certificate referred to in subsection (1)(a) has—

(a) been informed that the competent authority for Scotland may be minded to make that decision;

(b) been consulted; and

(c) where appropriate, been given an opportunity to supply any information that is necessary if the financial penalty is to be enforced in Scotland.

(3. B)The specified grounds for refusal referred to in subsection (3. A) are the grounds for refusal mentioned in [F141paragraphs 5. A, 6 and 6. A] of Schedule 12.]

F142. (4). . . . .

(5) Schedule 12 to this Act, which specifies the grounds for refusal to enforce financial penalties for the purposes of subsection (3) and section 223. F(4), has effect.

Amendments (Textual)

F140. S. 223. H(3. A)(3. B) inserted (1.12.2014) by The Mutual Recognition of Criminal Financial Penalties in the European Union (Scotland) (No. 1) Order 2014 (S.S.I. 2014/322), arts. 1, 6. (a)

F141. Words in s. 223. H(3. B) substituted (1.12.2014) by The Mutual Recognition of Criminal Financial Penalties in the European Union (Scotland) (No. 2) Order 2014 (S.S.I. 2014/336), arts. 1, 3

F142. S. 223. H(4) repealed (1.12.2014) by The Mutual Recognition of Criminal Financial Penalties in the European Union (Scotland) (No. 1) Order 2014 (S.S.I. 2014/322), arts. 1, 6. (b)

223. IRequests from other member States: action undertaken under certificateS

(1) Where the competent authority for Scotland to whom a matter has been referred under section 223. H(2) of this Act is satisfied that none of the grounds for refusal to enforce the financial penalty, as mentioned in Schedule 12, apply then the competent authority for Scotland shall forthwith, and without any further formality being required, seek the enforcement in Scotland of the financial penalty.

(2) Where the competent authority for Scotland to whom a matter has been referred under section 223. H(2) of this Act is satisfied that one or more of the grounds for refusal to enforce the financial penalty as mentioned in Schedule 12 applies—

(a) the designated officer of the competent authority for Scotland shall return the documents mentioned in section 223. H(1) to the central authority for Scotland; and

(b) subsection (3) shall apply.

(3) Where the documents have been given to the central authority for Scotland by virtue of subsection (2) the central authority for Scotland shall [F143immediately return any of them which are of a type mentioned in subsection (1)(a) of section 223. F to the authority which signed the certificate referred to in that subsection.]

Amendments (Textual)

F143. Words in s. 223. I(3) substituted (1.12.2014) by The Mutual Recognition of Criminal Financial Penalties in the European Union (Scotland) (No. 1) Order 2014 (S.S.I. 2014/322), arts. 1, 7

223. JRequests from other member States: application of provisions in relation to finesS

Where section 223. I(1) applies, the provisions of this Act specified in section 223. K shall, subject to any necessary modifications and to the qualifications mentioned in that section, apply in relation to—

the financial penalties as they apply in relation to—

- fines imposed by the High Court;
- sentences or decrees for fines or expenses pronounced by a sheriff court or JP court;
- fines adjudged to be paid by offenders; and

persons liable to pay financial penalties as they apply in relation to persons or offenders in relation to whom a fine has been imposed.

223. KRequests from other member States: supplementary provisions in relation to finesS

(1) The provisions mentioned in section 223. J are—

(a) section 199 (power to mitigate penalties), except that in subsection (2) the reference to the court shall be construed as a reference to the competent authority for Scotland;

(b) section 211. (3) and (4) (enforcement of fines), except that—

(i) in paragraph (a) of subsection (3) the reference to the district in which the sentence or decree was pronounced shall be construed as a reference to the district in which the person required to pay the fine or expenses appears to be normally resident or have property or income or, in the case where that person is a body corporate or partnership (including a Scottish partnership), the district in which that person has its registered office or, as the case may be, its principal office of the partnership; and

(ii) in subsection (4) the reference to the district in which the person resides shall be construed as a reference to the district in which the person required to pay the fine appears to be normally resident or have property or income or, in the case where that person is a body corporate or partnership (including a Scottish partnership), the district in which that person has its registered office or, as the case may be, its principal office of the partnership;

(c) section 213 (power to remit fines), except that in paragraph (b) of subsection (1) the references to the court which imposed the fine and the court by which payment was first enforceable shall be construed as a reference to the competent authority for Scotland and subsection (2) shall be construed accordingly;

(d) section 215 (further time for payment), except that, in its application to financial penalties, the references in subsection (2) to the court specified in the transfer order (or, where relevant, the last transfer order) shall be construed as references to the competent authority for Scotland;

(e) section 216 (reasons for default), except that the court may only impose imprisonment on a person in default of payment of a financial penalty where section 223. L applies;

(f) section 217 (supervision pending payment of fine), except that the court mentioned in that section may, in relation to the person who is liable to pay the financial penalty—

(i) place such a person under supervision by virtue of subsection (1) of that section; or

(ii) order the detention of such a person under 21 years of age as mentioned in subsection (5) of that section,

only where section 223. L applies;

(g) section 219 (maximum period of imprisonment for non-payment of fine), but subject to the modification that the references to the maximum periods of imprisonment specified in the table in subsection (2) shall be construed as references to the maximum period as stated in the certificate;

(h) section 220 (payment of fine in part by prisoner), except that in subsection (3) the reference to the court in which the conviction was obtained shall be construed as a reference to the competent authority for Scotland;

(i) section 221 (recovery by civil diligence);

(j) section 224 (discharge from imprisonment to be specified); and

(k) sections 235 to 237 (supervised attendance).

(2) The competent authority for Scotland, and the designated officer of the competent authority, shall have all the like functions under this Act in respect of the financial penalty as if it were a penalty imposed by that competent authority.

223. LRequests from other member States: action for enforcement where financial penalty not recoveredS

This section applies where—
a member State other than the United Kingdom has allowed for—
- supervision pending payment of the financial penalty;
- the imposition of a supervised attendance order, or detention or imprisonment in default of payment of the financial penalty,
within the certificate referred to in section 223. F; and
that measure does not exceed any maximum level for such disposal as specified in that certificate.

223. MRequests from other member States: application of provisions relating to orders for compensationS

Where section 223. I(1) applies, the provisions of this Act specified in section 223. N shall, subject to any necessary modifications and to the qualifications mentioned in that section, apply in relation to financial penalties as they apply in relation to any sum payable under compensation orders imposed under section 249 of this Act.

223. NRequests from other member States: supplementary provisions in relation to orders for compensationS

The provisions mentioned in section 223. M are—
section 249. (9) (payment of sum payable under compensation order), but that section is subject to section 223. S of this Act;
section 250. (2) to (4) (compensation orders: supplementary provisions);
section 251 (review of compensation order), except that in paragraph (b) of subsection (2) the reference to the court which made the compensation order, or by which the order was first enforceable, shall be construed as a reference to the competent authority for Scotland in respect of which the financial penalty was referred under section 223. H(2);
section 252 (enforcement of compensation orders), except that the provisions listed in subsection (2), as modified and qualified, shall be construed as if the modifications and qualifications made to the provisions which are listed in section 223. K have been so made; and
section 253. (3) (award of damages in civil proceedings subsequent to imposition of compensation order).

223. ORequests from other member States: application of provisions relating to fixed penaltiesS

(1) Where section 223. I(1) applies, the provision of this Act specified in subsection (2) shall, subject to any necessary modifications and to the qualifications mentioned in that subsection, apply in relation to the financial penalties as it applies in relation to any sums payable under fixed penalties issued under this Act.
(2) The provision mentioned in subsection (1) is section 303. (1) to (3) (fixed penalty: enforcement) of this Act, except that—
(a) the references to fixed penalty offers and compensation offers shall be construed as references to financial penalties; and
(b) the modifications and qualifications made by section 223. K to the provisions as specified there shall be applicable where those provisions of this Act apply by virtue of section 303 of this

Act.

223. PTransfer of certificates to central authority for England and Wales, or to central authority for Northern IrelandS

(1) This section applies where—

(a) the competent authority, or central authority, of a member State other than the United Kingdom gives the central authority for Scotland—

(i) a certificate requesting enforcement under the Framework Decision on financial penalties; and

(ii) the decision, or a certified copy of the decision, requiring payment of the financial penalty to which the certificate relates; but

(b) the central authority for Scotland is not required by section 223. F(2) or (3) to give the documents to the competent authority for Scotland.

(2) If the certificate states that the person to whom the certificate relates is normally resident or has property or income in England or Wales only or, in the case of a body corporate or partnership, has its registered office or its principal office of the partnership there, the central authority for Scotland may give the documents to the central authority for England and Wales.

(3) If the certificate states that the person is normally resident or has property or income in Northern Ireland only or, in the case of a body corporate or partnership, has its registered office or its principal office of the partnership there, the central authority for Scotland may give the documents to the central authority for Northern Ireland.

223. QThe competent authority for ScotlandS

(1) In sections 223. A to 223. E of this Act "the competent authority for Scotland" is—

(a) in respect of a financial penalty mentioned in—

(i) section 223. A(5)(a) or (d) of this Act;

(ii) paragraph (h) of subsection (5) of section 223. A of this Act, where that financial penalty is imposed in connection with proceedings relating to a conviction mentioned in paragraph (d) of that subsection,

the court in respect of which the financial penalty was imposed or pronounced;

(b) in respect of a financial penalty mentioned in section 223. A(5)(b) or (c) of this Act, the court the clerk of which is specified in the notice issued under section 302 or, as the case may be, 302. A of this Act;

(c) in respect of a financial penalty mentioned in—

(i) section 223. A(5)(e); or

(ii) paragraph (h) of subsection (5) of section 223. A, where that financial penalty is imposed in connection with proceedings relating to a conviction as mentioned in paragraph (e) of that subsection,

the court specified in the transfer of fine order made under section 90 of the Magistrates' Courts Act 1980 or Article 95 of the Magistrates' Courts (Northern Ireland) Order 1981 as being the court by which the financial penalty is enforceable;

(d) in respect of a financial penalty mentioned in section 223. A(5)(f) of this Act—

(i) the court in which the financial penalty has been registered for enforcement by virtue of section 71. (2)(a) of the Road Traffic Offenders Act 1988 F144; or

(ii) the court in respect of which the registration certificate, as mentioned in section 71. (2) of the Road Traffic Offenders Act 1988, has been sent by virtue of section 71. (2)(b) of that Act; and

(e) in respect of a financial penalty mentioned in section 223. A(5)(g) of this Act, the JP court specified in the fixed penalty notice which has been issued by virtue of section 129 of the Antisocial Behaviour (Scotland) Act 2004.

(2) In sections 223. F, 223. H, 223. I, 223. K, 223. P and 223. S "the competent authority for

Scotland" is—

(a) the sheriff; or

(b) the JP court;

having jurisdiction for the area in respect of which the person to whom the certificate is issued under section 223. F(1) relates appears to normally reside or have property or income, or in the case of a body corporate or a partnership (including a Scottish partnership) the area in respect of which the person has its registered office or, as the case may be, its principal office of the partnership.

Amendments (Textual)

F1441988 c.53; section 71 was amended by the Access to Justice Act 1999 (c.22), section 90, Schedule 13, paragraph 150. (2).

223. RAccrual of monies obtained from the enforcement of financial penaltiesS

(1) Subject to subsection (4), where a certificate requesting enforcement under the Framework Decision on financial penalties has been—

(a) issued under sections 223. A or 226. HA(4) of this Act, subsection (2) shall apply; or

(b) received under section 223. F of this Act, subsection (3) shall apply.

(2) Where this subsection applies the sum in respect of which the financial penalty relates shall be paid and treated as if that penalty were a penalty imposed in the member State other than the United Kingdom to which the certificate was issued.

(3) Where this subsection applies the sum in respect of which the financial penalty relates shall be paid and treated as if that penalty had been imposed or pronounced on the liable person or otherwise adjudged to be paid by that person under this Act.

(4) This section shall not apply where—

(a) an agreement has been made between the United Kingdom and the member State other than the United Kingdom in respect of the treatment of the financial penalty, and that agreement provides for payment otherwise than as provided for in subsection (2) or (3); or

(b) the financial penalty is one in respect of which section 223. S applies.

223. STreatment of compensation moniesS

(1) This section applies to those financial penalties mentioned in—

(a) section 223. A(5)(a) and (c) of this Act; and

(b) Article 1. (b)(ii) and (iv) of the Framework Decision on financial penalties.

(2) Payment of any sum under a financial penalty mentioned in subsection (1) shall be made by the central authority for Scotland or, as the case may be, by the competent authority for Scotland—

(a) to the victim; or

(b) in cases where the victim resides outwith Scotland, to the central authority of the member State, other than the United Kingdom, in which the victim of the offence to which the financial penalty relates resides.

(3) In this section "victim" has the same meaning as given in section 249. (1. A) of this Act.

223. TInterpretation of sections 223. A to 223. SS

(1) In sections 223. A to 223. S of this Act—

"central authority", in relation to a member State other than the United Kingdom, means an authority designated by that member State as a central authority for the purposes of the Framework Decision on financial penalties;

"central authority for England and Wales" means the authority designated for England and Wales as the central authority for the purposes of the Framework Decision on financial penalties;

"central authority for Northern Ireland" means the authority designated for Northern Ireland as the central authority for the purposes of the Framework Decision on financial penalties;

"central authority for Scotland" means the sheriff clerk of Lothian and Borders at Edinburgh;

"certificate" means the certificate as is provided for by Article 4 of the Framework Decision on financial penalties;

"decision" shall have the meaning given in Article 1 of the Framework Decision on financial penalties;

"Framework Decision on financial penalties" means Council Framework Decision 2005/214/JHAof 24 February 2005 on the application of the principle of mutual recognition to financial penalties [F145as amended by Council Framework Decision 2009/299/JHA]; and

"member State" means a member State of the European Union.

(2) Unless the context otherwise requires, in sections 223. F to 223. P, 223. R and 223. S of this Act "financial penalty" has the same meaning as given in Article 1. (b) of the Framework Decision on financial penalties.

(3) In sections 223. A to 223. C of this Act, "designated officer" of the competent authority for Scotland—

(a) in the case of financial penalties mentioned in—

(i) section 223. A(5)(a) or (d) of this Act; and

(ii) paragraph (h) of subsection (5) of section 223. A of this Act, where that financial penalty is imposed in connection with proceedings relating to a conviction mentioned in paragraph (d) of that subsection,

means the clerk of court in respect of which the financial penalty was imposed or pronounced;

(b) in the case of financial penalties mentioned in section 223. A(5)(b) or (c) of this Act means the clerk of court specified in the notice, issued under section 302 or 302. A, respectively, of this Act;

(c) in the case of financial penalties mentioned in—

(i) section 223. A(5)(e) of this Act; and

(ii) paragraph (h) of subsection (5) of section 223. A of this Act, where that financial penalty is imposed in connection with proceedings relating to a conviction as mentioned in paragraph (e) of that subsection,

means the clerk of the court specified in the transfer of fine order made under section 90 of the Magistrates' Courts Act 1980 or Article 95 of the Magistrates' Courts (Northern Ireland) Order 1981 to which the financial penalty has been transferred for enforcement;

(d) in the case of financial penalties mentioned in section 223. A(5)(f) of this Act means—

(i) the clerk of the court in which the financial penalty has been registered for enforcement by virtue of section 71. (2)(a) of the Road Traffic Offenders Act 1988; or

(ii) the clerk of the court in respect of which the registration certificate, as mentioned in section 71. (2) of the Road Traffic Offenders Act 1988, has been sent by virtue of section 71. (2)(b) of that Act;

(e) in the case of financial penalties mentioned in section 223. A(5)(g) of this Act, means the clerk of the JP court specified in the fixed penalty notice which has been issued by virtue of section 129 of the Antisocial Behaviour (Scotland) Act 2004; and

(f) in the case of a FEO acting in accordance with section 226. HA of this Act, is to be construed as if references to such an officer were references to a FEO.

(4) In sections 223. F, 223. H, 223. I and 223. K of this Act, "designated officer" of the competent authority for Scotland means the clerk of the court mentioned in section 223. Q(2) of this Act or, as the case may be, a FEO acting in accordance with section 226. A to 226. G of this Act in respect of a financial penalty.]

Amendments (Textual)

F145. Words in s. 223. T(1) inserted (1.12.2014) by The Mutual Recognition of Criminal Financial Penalties in the European Union (Scotland) (No. 2) Order 2014 (S.S.I. 2014/336), arts.

[F146. Fines: discharge from imprisonment and penaltiesS

Amendments (Textual)
F146. Ss. 223. A-223. T and cross-headings inserted (12.10.2009) by The Mutual Recognition of Criminal Financial Penalties in the European Union (Scotland) Order 2009 (S.S.I. 2009/342), art. 3 (with art. 2)

224 Discharge from imprisonment to be specified.S

All warrants of imprisonment in default of payment of a fine, or on failure to find caution, shall specify a period at the expiry of which the person sentenced shall be discharged, notwithstanding the fine has not been paid, or caution found.

Modifications etc. (not altering text)
C25. S. 224 applied (1.4.1996) by 1995 c. 43, ss. 14. (2)(k), 50. (2)
S. 224 applied (24.3.2003) by Proceeds of Crime Act 2002 (c. 29), ss. 118. (1)(2)(k), 458; S.S.I. 2003/210, art. 2 (with transitional provisions in arts. 3-7)

225 Penalties: standard scale, prescribed sum and uprating.S

(1) There shall be a standard scale of fines for offences triable only summarily, which shall be known as " the standard scale ".

(2) The standard scale is shown below—

Level on the scale	Amount of Fine
1	£ 200
2	£ 500
3	£1,000
4	£2,500
5	£5,000

(3) Any reference in any enactment, whenever passed or made, to a specified level on the standard scale shall be construed as referring to the amount which corresponds to that level on the standard scale referred to in subsection (2) above.

(4) If it appears to the Secretary of State that there has been a change in the value of money since the relevant date, he may by order substitute for the sum or sums for the time being specified in the provisions mentioned in subsection (5) below such other sum or sums as appear to him justified by the change.

(5) The provisions referred to in subsection (4) above are—

    (a) subsection (2) above;

    (b) subsection (8) below;

    (c) section 219. (2) of this Act;

    (d) column 5 or 6 of Schedule 4 to the M23. Misuse of Drugs Act 1971 so far as the column in question relates to the offences under provisions of that Act specified in column 1 of that Schedule in respect of which the maximum fines were increased by Part II of Schedule 8 to the M24. Criminal Justice and Public Order Act 1994.

(6) In subsection (4) above " the relevant date " means—

    (a) in relation to the first order made under that subsection, the date the last order was made under section 289. D(1) of the M25. Criminal Procedure (Scotland) Act 1975; and

    (b) in relation to each subsequent order, the date of the previous order.

(7) An order under subsection (4) above—

    (a) shall be made by statutory instrument subject to annulment in pursuance of a resolution of either House of Parliament and may be revoked by a subsequent order thereunder; and

(b) without prejudice to Schedule 14 to the M26. Criminal Law Act 1977, shall not affect the punishment for an offence committed before that order comes into force.

(8) In this Act " the prescribed sum " means [F147 £10,000] or such sum as is for the time being substituted in this definition by an order in force under subsection (4) above.

Amendments (Textual)

F147. Words in s. 225. (8) substituted (10.12.2007) by Criminal Proceedings etc. (Reform) (Scotland) Act 2007 (asp 6), ss. 48, 84; S.S.I. 2007/479, art. 3. (1), Sch. (subject to art. 12) (as amended by S.S.I. 2007/527)

Marginal Citations

M231971 c.38.

M241994 c.33.

M251975 c.21.

M261977 c.45.

226 Penalties: exceptionally high maximum fines.S

(1) The Secretary of State may by order amend an enactment specifying a sum to which this subsection applies so as to substitute for that sum such other sum as appears to him—

(a) to be justified by a change in the value of money appearing to him to have taken place since the last occasion on which the sum in question was fixed; or

(b) to be appropriate to take account of an order altering the standard scale which has been made or is proposed to be made.

(2) Subsection (1) above applies to any sum which—

(a) is higher than level 5 on the standard scale; and

(b) is specified as the fine or the maximum fine which may be imposed on conviction of an offence which is triable only summarily.

(3) The Secretary of State may by order amend an enactment specifying a sum to which this subsection applies so as to substitute for that sum such other sum as appears to him—

(a) to be justified by a change in the value of money appearing to him to have taken place since the last occasion on which the sum in question was fixed; or

(b) to be appropriate to take account of an order made or proposed to be made altering the statutory maximum.

(4) Subsection (3) above applies to any sum which—

(a) is higher than the statutory maximum; and

(b) is specified as the maximum fine which may be imposed on summary conviction of an offence triable either on indictment or summarily.

(5) An order under this section—

(a) shall be made by statutory instrument subject to annulment in pursuance of a resolution of either House of Parliament; and

(b) shall not affect the punishment for an offence committed before that order comes into force.

(6) In this section " enactment " includes an enactment contained in an Act or subordinate instrument passed or made after the commencement of this Act.]

[F148. Enforcement of fines etc.: fines enforcement officersS

Amendments (Textual)

F148. Ss. 226. A-226. I and preceding cross-heading inserted (10.3.2008 for certain purposes and otherwise prosp.) by Criminal Proceedings etc. (Reform) (Scotland) Act 2007 (asp 6), ss. 55, 84; S.I. 2008/42, art. 3, Sch.

226. AFines enforcement officersS

(1) The Scottish Ministers may authorise persons (including classes of person) to act as fines enforcement officers for any or all of the purposes of this section and sections 226. B to 226. H of this Act.

(2) A FEO has the general functions of—

(a) providing information and advice to offenders as regards payment of relevant penalties;

(b) securing compliance of offenders with enforcement orders (including as varied under section 226. C(1) of this Act).

(3) Where an offender is subject to two or more relevant penalties, a FEO—

(a) in exercising the function conferred by subsection (2)(b) above;

(b) in considering whether or not to vary an enforcement order under section 226. C(1) of this Act,

shall have regard to that fact and to the total amount which the offender is liable to pay in respect of them.

(4) Where an enforcement order as respects an offender has been made in a sheriff court district other than that in which the offender resides, a FEO for the district in which the offender resides may (whether or not those districts are in the same sheriffdom) take responsibility for exercising functions in relation to the order.

(5) A FEO taking responsibility for exercising functions by virtue of subsection (4) above is to notify that fact to—

(a) the offender; and

(b) any FEO for the district in which the enforcement order was made.

(6) Notification under subsection (5)(b) above has the effect of transferring functions in relation to the enforcement order—

(a) from any FEO for the district in which the order was made; and

(b) to a FEO for the district in which the offender resides.

(7) The Scottish Ministers may by regulations make further provision as to FEOs and their functions.

(8) Regulations under subsection (7) above are not made unless a draft of the statutory instrument containing the regulations has been laid before, and approved by a resolution of, the Scottish Parliament.

226. BEnforcement ordersS

(1) When a court grants time to pay (or further time to pay) a relevant penalty (or an instalment of it) under section 214 or 215 of this Act, the court shall make an enforcement order under this subsection in relation to payment of the penalty.

(2) Despite subsection (1) above, a court need not make an enforcement order where it considers that it would not be appropriate to do so in the circumstances of the case.

(3) Where, by virtue of subsection (2) above, a court does not make an enforcement order under subsection (1) above, it may subsequently make an enforcement order under that subsection in relation to payment of the penalty.

(4) Where—

(a) a person has accepted (or is deemed to have accepted)—

(i) a fixed penalty offer under section 302. (1) of this Act; or

(ii) a compensation offer under section 302. A(1) of this Act; and

(b) payment (or payment of an instalment) has not been made as required by the offer,

the relevant court may make an enforcement order under this subsection in relation to the payment due.

(5) Where—

(a) a person is liable to pay—

(i) a fixed penalty notice given under section 54 (giving notices for fixed penalty offences), or section 62 (fixing notices to vehicles) of the Road Traffic Offenders Act 1988 (c. 53), which has been registered under section 71 of that Act; or

(ii) by virtue of section 131. (5) of the Antisocial Behaviour etc. (Scotland) Act 2004 (asp 8), a fixed penalty notice given under section 129 (fixed penalty notices) of that Act; and

(b) payment (or payment of an instalment) has not been made as required by the penalty,

the relevant court may make an enforcement order under this subsection in relation to the payment due.

(6) Where there is transferred to a court in Scotland a fine—

(a) imposed by a court in England and Wales; and

(b) in relation to which a collection order (within the meaning of Part 4 of Schedule 5 to the Courts Act 2003 (c. 39)) has been made,

the relevant court may make an enforcement order under this subsection in relation to payment of the fine.

[F149. (6. A)Where—

(a) a certificate requesting enforcement under the Framework Decision on financial penalties and a decision, or a certified copy of the decision, requiring payment of the financial penalty to which the certificate relates has been referred to the competent authority for Scotland by virtue of section 223. H(2) of this Act; and

(b) by virtue of section 223. I(1) the competent authority for Scotland is satisfied that none of the grounds for refusal to enforce the financial penalty as specified in Schedule 12 to this Act apply,

the relevant court may make an enforcement order under this subsection in relation to payment of the financial penalty (which, for the purposes of this subsection, is deemed to be a relevant penalty).]

(7) An enforcement order under subsection (4), (5) [F150, (6) or (6. A)] above may be made—

(a) on the oral or written application of the clerk of court; and

(b) without the offender being present.

(8) An enforcement order shall—

(a) state the amount of the relevant penalty;

(b) require payment of the relevant penalty in accordance with—

(i) such arrangements as to the amount of the instalments by which the relevant penalty should be paid and as to the intervals at which such instalments should be paid;

(ii) such other arrangements,

as the order may specify;

(c) provide contact details for the FEO dealing with the enforcement order;

(d) explain the effect of the enforcement order.

(9) Where a court makes (or is to make) an enforcement order in relation to a fine—

(a) a court may not impose imprisonment—

(i) under section 214. (4) of this Act; or

(ii) under section 219. (1) of this Act,

in respect of the fine;

(b) a court may not—

(i) allow further time for payment under subsection (9)(a) of section 214 of this Act; or

(ii) make an order under subsection (9)(b) of that section,

in respect of the fine;

(c) the offender may not make an application under section 215. (1) of this Act in respect of the fine.

(10) Paragraphs (a) to (c) of subsection (9) above apply for so long as the enforcement order continues to have effect.

(11) An enforcement order ceases to have effect if—

(a) the relevant penalty is paid (including by application of any proceeds of enforcement action); or

(b) it is revoked under section 226. G(9)(a) of this Act.

Amendments (Textual)

F149. S. 226. B(6. A) inserted (12.10.2009) by The Mutual Recognition of Criminal Financial Penalties in the European Union (Scotland) Order 2009 (S.S.I. 2009/342), art. 5. (a) (with art. 2)

F150. Words in s. 226. B(7) substituted (12.10.2009) by The Mutual Recognition of Criminal Financial Penalties in the European Union (Scotland) Order 2009 (S.S.I. 2009/342), art. 5. (b) (with art. 2)

226. CVariation for further time to payS

(1) A FEO dealing with an enforcement order may—
    (a) on the application of the offender; and
    (b) having regard to the circumstances of the offender,
vary the arrangements specified in the order for payment of the relevant penalty.
(2) That is, by—
    (a) allowing the offender further time to pay the penalty (or any instalment of it);
    (b) allowing the offender to pay the penalty by instalments of such lesser amounts, or at such longer intervals, as those specified in the enforcement order.
(3) An application by an offender for the purpose of subsection (1) above may be made orally or in writing.
(4) A FEO shall notify the offender concerned of any—
    (a) variation under subsection (1) above;
    (b) refusal of an application for variation under that subsection.

226. DSeizure of vehiclesS

(1) A FEO may, for the purpose mentioned in subsection (2) below, direct that a motor vehicle belonging to the offender be—
    (a) immobilised;
    (b) impounded.
(2) The purpose is of obtaining the amount of a relevant penalty which has not been paid in accordance with an enforcement order.
(3) For the purposes of this section—
    (a) a vehicle belongs to an offender if it is registered under the Vehicle Excise and Registration Act 1994 (c. 22) in the offender's name;
    (b) a reference—
(i) to a vehicle being immobilised is to its being fitted with an immobilisation device in accordance with regulations made under subsection (12) below;
(ii) to a vehicle being impounded is to its being taken to a place of custody in accordance with regulations made under that subsection;
    (c) a direction under subsection (1) above is referred to as a " seizure order ".
(4) A FEO shall notify the offender concerned that a seizure order has been carried out.
(5) Where—
    (a) a seizure order has been carried out; and
    (b) at the end of such period as may be specified in regulations made under subsection (12) below, any part of the relevant penalty remains unpaid,
a FEO may apply to the relevant court for an order under subsection (6) below.
(6) The court may make an order under this subsection—
    (a) for the sale or other disposal of the vehicle in accordance with regulations made under subsection (12) below;
    (b) for any proceeds of the disposal to be applied in accordance with regulations made under that subsection in payment of or towards the unpaid amount of the relevant penalty;

(c) for any remainder of those proceeds to be applied in accordance with regulations made under that subsection in payment of or towards any reasonable expenses incurred by the FEO in relation to the seizure order;

(d) subject to paragraphs (b) and (c) above, for any balance to be given to the offender.

(7) Where, before a vehicle which is the subject of a seizure order is disposed of—

(a) a third party claims to own the vehicle; and

(b) either—

(i) a FEO is satisfied that the claim is valid (and that there are no reasonable grounds for believing that the claim is disputed by the offender or any other person from whose possession the vehicle was taken); or

(ii) the sheriff, on an application by the third party, makes an order that the sheriff is so satisfied, the seizure order ceases to have effect.

(8) An application for the purposes of subsection (7)(b)(ii) above does not preclude any other proceedings for recovery of the vehicle.

(9) A person commits an offence if, without lawful authority or reasonable excuse, the person removes or attempts to remove—

(a) an immobilisation device fitted;

(b) a notice fixed,

to a motor vehicle in pursuance of a seizure order.

(10) A person guilty of an offence under subsection (9) above is liable on summary conviction to a fine not exceeding level 3 on the standard scale.

(11) A seizure order must not be made in respect of a vehicle—

(a) which displays a valid disabled person's badge; or

(b) in relation to which there are reasonable grounds for believing that it is used primarily for the carriage of a disabled person.

(12) The Scottish Ministers may make regulations for the purposes of and in connection with this section.

(13) Regulations under subsection (12) above may, in particular, include provision—

(a) as to circumstances in which a seizure order may (or may not) be made;

(b) as regards the value of a vehicle seizable compared to the amount of a relevant penalty which is unpaid;

(c) by reference to subsection (3)(a) and (7) above or otherwise, for protecting the interests of owners of vehicles apart from offenders;

(d) relating to subsections (3)(b), (5)(b) and (6) above;

(e) as to the fixing of notices to vehicles to which an immobilisation device has been fitted;

(f) as to the keeping and release of vehicles immobilised or impounded (including as to conditions of release);

(g) as to the payment of reasonable fees, charges or other costs in relation to—

(i) the immobilisation or impounding of vehicles;

(ii) the keeping, release or disposal of vehicles immobilised or impounded.

(14) Regulations under subsection (12) above shall be made by statutory instrument subject to annulment in pursuance of a resolution of the Scottish Parliament.

(15) In this section—

" disabled person's badge " means a badge issued, or having effect as if issued, under regulations made under section 21 of the Chronically Sick and Disabled Persons Act 1970 (c. 44);

" immobilisation device " has the same meaning as in section 104. (9) of the Road Traffic Regulation Act 1984 (c. 27);

" motor vehicle " means a mechanically propelled vehicle intended or adapted for use on roads (except that section 189 of the Road Traffic Act 1988 (c. 52) applies for the purposes of this section as it applies for the purposes of that Act).

226. EDeduction from benefitsS

(1) A FEO may, for the purpose mentioned in subsection (2) below, request the relevant court to make an application under regulations made under section 24. (1)(a) of the Criminal Justice Act 1991 (c. 53) for deductions as described in that section.

(2) The purpose is of obtaining the amount of a relevant penalty which has not been paid in accordance with an enforcement order.

226. FPowers of diligenceS

(1) When a court makes an enforcement order, it shall grant a warrant for civil diligence in the form prescribed by Act of Adjournal.

(2) A warrant granted under subsection (1) above authorises a FEO to execute the types of diligence mentioned in subsection (3) below for the purpose mentioned in subsection (4) below.

(3) The types of diligence are—

    (a) arrestment of earnings; and

    (b) arrestment of funds standing in accounts held at any bank or other financial institution.

(4) The purpose is of obtaining the amount of a relevant penalty which has not been paid in accordance with an enforcement order.

(5) The types of diligence mentioned in subsection (3) above may (whatever the amount of the relevant penalty concerned) be executed by an FEO in the same manner as if authorised by a warrant granted by the sheriff in a summary cause.

(6) However, the power of FEOs to execute the types of diligence mentioned in subsection (3) above is subject to such provision as the Scottish Ministers may by regulations make.

(7) Provision in regulations under subsection (6) above may, in particular—

    (a) specify circumstances in which the types of diligence mentioned in subsection (3) above are (or are not) to be executed by a FEO;

    (b) modify the application of any enactment (including subsection (5) above) or rule of law applying in relation to those types of diligence in so far as they may be executed by a FEO.

(8) Regulations under subsection (6) above shall be made by statutory instrument subject to annulment in pursuance of a resolution of the Scottish Parliament.

226. GReference of case to courtS

(1) A FEO may refer an enforcement order to the relevant court where—

    (a) the FEO believes that payment of a relevant penalty, or any remaining part of a relevant penalty, to which an enforcement order relates is unlikely to be obtained;

    (b) for any other reason (including failure of the offender to co-operate with the FEO) the FEO considers it expedient to do so.

(2) A FEO may make a reference under subsection (1) above at any time from the day after the enforcement order is made.

(3) When making a reference under subsection (1) above, the FEO shall provide the court with a report on the circumstances of the case.

(4) A report under subsection (3) above shall include, in particular—

    (a) a copy of any report from a supervising officer received by the FEO under section 217. (9) of this Act; and

    (b) information about—

(i) the steps taken by the enforcement officer to obtain payment of or towards the relevant penalty; and

(ii) any effort (or lack of effort) made by the offender to make payment of or towards the penalty.

(5) Where a reference is made under subsection (1) above, the relevant court shall enquire of the offender as to the reason why the relevant penalty (or an instalment of it) has not been paid.

(6) Subsection (5) above does not apply where the offender is in prison.

(7) Subsections (3) to (7) of section 216 of this Act apply in relation to subsection (5) above as they apply in relation to subsection (1) of that section.

(8) After the court has considered—

(a) the report provided by the FEO under subsection (3) above; and

(b) any information obtained by enquiry under subsection (5) above,

the court may dispose of the case as mentioned in subsection (9) below.

(9) That is, the court may—

(a) revoke the enforcement order and deal with the offender as if the enforcement order had never been made;

(b) vary the enforcement order;

(c) confirm the enforcement order as previously made;

(d) direct the FEO to take specified steps to secure payment of or towards the relevant penalty in accordance with the enforcement order (including as varied under paragraph (b) above);

(e) make such other order as it thinks fit.

226. HReview of actions of FEOS

(1) The offender may apply to the relevant court for review—

(a) in relation to an enforcement order—

(i) of any variation under section 226. C(1) of this Act;

(ii) of any refusal of an application for variation under that section;

(b) of the making of a seizure order under section 226. D(1) of this Act.

(2) An application under subsection (1) above requires to be made within 7 days of notification under section 226. C(4) of this Act or (as the case may be) section 226. D(4) of this Act.

(3) On an application under subsection (1) above, the relevant court may—

(a) confirm, vary or quash the decision of the FEO;

(b) make such other order as it thinks fit.

[F151226. HA Judicial co-operation in criminal matters: mutual recognition of financial penalties: requests to other member States

(1) Subsection (4) applies where—

(a) an offender is subject to a relevant penalty (including such a penalty in relation to the payment of which an enforcement order has been made);

(b) the relevant penalty is not paid (or, where relevant, has not been paid in accordance with the enforcement order);

(c) there is no appeal outstanding in relation to the relevant penalty;

(d) a FEO is exercising (or intends to exercise) the function conferred—

(i) by paragraph (a) of section 226. A(2) of this Act in respect of the relevant penalty; or

(ii) by paragraph (b) of that section in respect of any enforcement order relating to the relevant penalty; and

(e) it appears to the FEO that the offender is normally resident, or has property or income, in a member State of the European Union other than the United Kingdom.

(2) For the purposes of subsection (1)(c), there is no appeal outstanding in relation to a financial penalty if—

(a) no appeal has been brought in relation to the imposition of the financial penalty within the time allowed for making such an appeal; or

(b) such an appeal has been brought but the proceedings on appeal have been concluded.

(3) In subsections (1)(c) and (2) "appeal" in respect of financial penalties mentioned in section 223. A(5)(b) and (c) includes a request made under section 302. C of this Act that such a penalty be recalled.

(4) The FEO may issue a certificate as mentioned in section 223. A(1) of this Act.

(5) Subsection (4) does not apply where the designated officer of the competent authority for Scotland has issued such a certificate in respect of the financial penalty.

(6) The FEO must give the central authority for Scotland any certificate issued under subsection (4), together with a copy, or extract, of the decision requiring payment of the relevant penalty.

(7) Where the central authority for Scotland receives the documents mentioned in subsection (6) above, subsections (3) to (6) of section 223. B of this Act apply as if the documents had been given under subsection (2) of that section.]

Amendments (Textual)

F151. S. 226. HA inserted (12.10.2009) by The Mutual Recognition of Criminal Financial Penalties in the European Union (Scotland) Order 2009 (S.S.I. 2009/342), art. 4 (with art. 2)

226. IEnforcement of fines etc.: interpretationS

(1) [F152. Subject to subsection (1. A), in] this section and sections 226. A to [F153226. HA] of this Act—

[F154 " central authority for Scotland " means the sheriff clerk of Lothian and Borders at Edinburgh;

" certificate " has the meaning given in section 223. T(1) of this Act;

" competent authority for Scotland " is to be construed in accordance with section 223. Q of this Act;

" decision " has the meaning given in section 223. T(1) of this Act;]

" enforcement order " is to be construed in accordance with section 226. B(1) and (4) to [F155 (6. A)] of this Act;

" FEO " means a fines enforcement officer;

[F156 " financial penalty " has the meaning given in Article 1. (b) of the Framework Decision on financial penalties;

" Framework Decision on financial penalties " has the meaning given in section 223. T(1) of this Act;]

" offender " means the person who is liable to pay a relevant penalty;

"relevant court"—

- in the case of a fine or compensation order, means—

the court which imposed the penalty; or

where the penalty is transferred to another court, that other court;

- in the case of another relevant penalty (apart from a penalty specified by order for the purposes of this section), means—

the court whose clerk is specified in the notice to the offender; or

where the penalty is transferred to another court, that other court;

- in the case of a penalty specified by order for the purposes of this section, means—

the court whose clerk is specified in the notice to the offender;

where the penalty is transferred to another court, that other court; or

such other court as the order may specify for those purposes;

- [F157in the case of a penalty in respect of which subsection (6. A) applies, means the competent authority for Scotland to which the documents mentioned in that subsection have been referred in accordance with section 223. H(2) of this Act.]

" relevant penalty " means—

- a fine;

- a compensation order imposed under section 249 of this Act;

- a fixed penalty offer made under section 302. (1) of this Act;

- a compensation offer made under section 302. A(1) of this Act;

- a fixed penalty notice given under section 54 (giving notices for fixed penalty offences) or section 62 (fixing notices to vehicles) of the Road Traffic Offenders Act 1988 (c. 53);

- a fixed penalty notice given under section 129 (fixed penalty notices) of the Antisocial Behaviour etc. (Scotland) Act 2004 (asp 8);

- such other penalty as the Scottish Ministers may by order specify for the purposes of this section.

[F158. (1. A)Unless the context otherwise requires, in this section and in sections 226. A to 226. H of this Act "relevant penalty", where a FEO is acting in a case in respect of which section 226. B(6. A) applies, has the same meaning as "financial penalty.]

(2) An order specifying a penalty or a court for the purpose of this section shall be made by statutory instrument which shall be subject to annulment in pursuance of a resolution of the Scottish Parliament.]

Amendments (Textual)

F152. Words in s. 226. I(1) substituted (12.10.2009) by The Mutual Recognition of Criminal Financial Penalties in the European Union (Scotland) Order 2009 (S.S.I. 2009/342), art. 6. (a)(i) (with art. 2)

F153. Word in s. 226. I(1) substituted (12.10.2009) by The Mutual Recognition of Criminal Financial Penalties in the European Union (Scotland) Order 2009 (S.S.I. 2009/342), art. 6. (a)(ii) (with art. 2)

F154. S. 226. I(1): definitions inserted (12.10.2009) by The Mutual Recognition of Criminal Financial Penalties in the European Union (Scotland) Order 2009 (S.S.I. 2009/342), art. 6. (a)(iii) (with art. 2)

F155. Word in s. 226. I(1) substituted (12.10.2009) by The Mutual Recognition of Criminal Financial Penalties in the European Union (Scotland) Order 2009 (S.S.I. 2009/342), art. 6. (a)(iv) (with art. 2)

F156. S. 226. I(1): definitions inserted (12.10.2009) by The Mutual Recognition of Criminal Financial Penalties in the European Union (Scotland) Order 2009 (S.S.I. 2009/342), art. 6. (a)(v) (with art. 2)

F157. S. 226. I(1): Words in the definition of "relevant court" inserted (12.10.2009) by The Mutual Recognition of Criminal Financial Penalties in the European Union (Scotland) Order 2009 (S.S.I. 2009/342), art. 6. (a)(vi) (with art. 2)

F158. S. 226. I(1. A) inserted (12.10.2009) by The Mutual Recognition of Criminal Financial Penalties in the European Union (Scotland) Order 2009 (S.S.I. 2009/342), {art. 6. (b} (with art. 2)

CautionS

227 Caution.S

Where a person is convicted on indictment of an offence (other than an offence the sentence for which is fixed by law) the court may, instead of or in addition to imposing a fine or a period of imprisonment, ordain the accused to find caution for good behaviour for a period not exceeding 12 months and to such amount as the court considers appropriate.

[F159. Community payback ordersS

Amendments (Textual)

F159. Ss. 227. A-227. ZN and cross-headings inserted (1.2.2011 except for the insertion of s. 227. ZM, 1.4.2011 in so far as not already in force) by Criminal Justice and Licensing (Scotland) Act 2010 (asp 13), ss. 14. (1), 206. (1); S.S.I. 2010/413, art. 2, sch. (with art. 3. (1))

227. ACommunity payback ordersS

(1) Where a person (the "offender") is convicted of an offence punishable by imprisonment, the court may, instead of imposing a sentence of imprisonment, impose a community payback order

on the offender.

(2) A community payback order is an order imposing one or more of the following requirements—

    (a) an offender supervision requirement,

    (b) a compensation requirement,

    (c) an unpaid work or other activity requirement,

    (d) a programme requirement,

    (e) a residence requirement,

    (f) a mental health treatment requirement,

    (g) a drug treatment requirement,

    (h) an alcohol treatment requirement,

    (i) a conduct requirement.

(3) Subsection (4) applies where—

    (a) a person (the "offender") is convicted of an offence punishable by a fine (whether or not it is also punishable by imprisonment), and

    (b) where the offence is also punishable by imprisonment, the court decides not to impose—

(i) a sentence of imprisonment, or

(ii) a community payback order under subsection (1) instead of a sentence of imprisonment.

(4) The court may, instead of or as well as imposing a fine, impose a community payback order on the offender imposing one or more of the following requirements—

    (a) an offender supervision requirement,

    (b) a level 1 unpaid work or other activity requirement,

    (c) a conduct requirement.

(5) A justice of the peace court may only impose a community payback order imposing one or more of the following requirements—

    (a) an offender supervision requirement,

    (b) a compensation requirement,

    (c) an unpaid work or other activity requirement,

    (d) a residence requirement,

    (e) a conduct requirement.

(6) Subsection (5)(c) is subject to section 227. J(4).

(7) The Scottish Ministers may by order made by statutory instrument amend subsection (5) so as to add to or omit requirements that may be imposed by a community payback order imposed by a justice of the peace court.

(8) An order is not to be made under subsection (7) unless a draft of the statutory instrument containing the order has been laid before and approved by resolution of the Scottish Parliament.

(9) In this section and sections 227. B to 227. ZK, except where the context requires otherwise—

" court " means the High Court, the sheriff or a justice of the peace court,

" imprisonment " includes detention.

227. BCommunity payback order: procedure prior to impositionS

(1) This section applies where a court is considering imposing a community payback order on an offender.

(2) The court must not impose the order unless it is of the opinion that the offence, or the combination of the offence and one or more offences associated with it, was serious enough to warrant the imposition of such an order.

(3) Before imposing a community payback order imposing two or more requirements, the court must consider whether, in the circumstances of the case, the requirements are compatible with each other.

(4) The court must not impose the order unless it has obtained, and taken account of, a report from an officer of a local authority containing information about the offender and the offender's circumstances.

(5) An Act of Adjournal may prescribe—

    (a) the form of a report under subsection (4), and

    (b) the particular information to be contained in it.

(6) Subsection (4) does not apply where the court is considering imposing a community payback order—

    (a) imposing only a level 1 unpaid work or other activity requirement, or

    (b) under section 227. M(2).

(7) The clerk of the court must give a copy of any report obtained under subsection (4) to—

    (a) the offender,

    (b) the offender's solicitor (if any), and

    (c) the prosecutor.

(8) Before imposing the order, the court must explain to the offender in ordinary language—

    (a) the purpose and effect of each of the requirements to be imposed by the order,

    (b) the consequences which may follow if the offender fails to comply with any of the requirements imposed by the order, and

    (c) where the court proposes to include in the order provision under section 227. X for it to be reviewed, the arrangements for such a review.

(9) The court must not impose the order unless the offender has, after the court has explained those matters, confirmed that the offender—

    (a) understands those matters, and

    (b) is willing to comply with each of the requirements to be imposed by the order.

(10) Subsection (9)(b) does not apply where the court is considering imposing a community payback order under section 227. M(2).

227. CCommunity payback order: responsible officerS

(1) This section applies where a court imposes a community payback order on an offender.

(2) The court must, in imposing the order—

    (a) specify the locality in which the offender resides or will reside for the duration of the order,

    (b) require the local authority within whose area that locality is situated to nominate, within two days of its receiving a copy of the order, an officer of the authority as the responsible officer for the purposes of the order,

    (c) require the offender to comply with any instructions given by the responsible officer—

(i) about keeping in touch with the responsible officer, or

(ii) for the purposes of subsection (3),

    (d) require the offender to report to the responsible officer in accordance with instructions given by that officer,

    (e) require the offender to notify the responsible officer without delay of—

(i) any change of the offender's address, and

(ii) the times, if any, at which the offender usually works (or carries out voluntary work) or attends school or any other educational establishment, and

    (f) where the order imposes an unpaid work or other activity requirement, require the offender to undertake for the number of hours specified in the requirement such work or activity as the responsible officer may instruct, and at such times as may be so instructed.

(3) The responsible officer is responsible for—

    (a) making any arrangements necessary to enable the offender to comply with each of the requirements imposed by the order,

    (b) promoting compliance with those requirements by the offender,

    (c) taking such steps as may be necessary to enforce compliance with the requirements of the order or to vary, revoke or discharge the order.

(4) References in this Act to the responsible officer are, in relation to an offender on whom a community payback order has been imposed, the officer for the time being nominated in

pursuance of subsection (2)(b).

(5) In reckoning the period of two days for the purposes of subsection (2)(b), no account is to be taken of a Saturday or Sunday or any day which is a local or public holiday in the area of the local authority concerned.

227. DCommunity payback order: further provisionS

(1) Where a community payback order is imposed on an offender, the order is to be taken for all purposes to be a sentence imposed on the offender.

(2) On imposing a community payback order, the court must state in open court the reasons for imposing the order.

(3) The imposition by a court of a community payback order on an offender does not prevent the court imposing a fine or any other sentence (other than imprisonment), or making any other order, that it would be entitled to impose or make in respect of the offence.

(4) Where a court imposes a community payback order on an offender, the clerk of the court must ensure that—

    (a) a copy of the order is given to—

(i) the offender, and

(ii) the local authority within whose area the offender resides or will reside, and

    (b) a copy of the order and such other documents and information relating to the case as may be useful are given to the clerk of the appropriate court (unless the court imposing the order is that court).

(5) A copy of the order may be given to the offender—

    (a) by being delivered personally to the offender, or

    (b) by being sent—

(i) by a registered post service (as defined in section 125. (1) of the Postal Services Act 2000 (c.26)), or

(ii) by a postal service which provides for the delivery of the document to be recorded.

(6) A community payback order is to be in such form, or as nearly as may be in such form, as may be prescribed by Act of Adjournal.

227. ERequirement to avoid conflict with religious beliefs, work etc.S

(1) In imposing a community payback order on an offender, the court must ensure, so far as practicable, that any requirement imposed by the order avoids—

    (a) a conflict with the offender's religious beliefs,

    (b) interference with the times, if any, at which the offender normally works (or carries out voluntary work) or attends school or any other educational establishment.

(2) The responsible officer must ensure, so far as practicable, that any instruction given to the offender avoids such a conflict or interference.

227. FPayment of offenders' travelling and other expensesS

(1) The Scottish Ministers may by order made by statutory instrument provide for the payment to offenders of travelling or other expenses in connection with their compliance with requirements imposed on them by community payback orders.

(2) An order under subsection (1) may—

    (a) specify expenses or provide for them to be determined under the order,

    (b) provide for the payments to be made by or on behalf of local authorities,

    (c) make different provision for different purposes.

(3) An order under subsection (1) is subject to annulment in pursuance of a resolution of the Scottish Parliament.

Offender supervision requirementS

227. GOffender supervision requirementS

(1) In this Act, an "offender supervision requirement" is, in relation to an offender, a requirement that, during the specified period, the offender must attend appointments with the responsible officer or another person determined by the responsible officer, at such time and place as may be determined by the responsible officer, for the purpose of promoting the offender's rehabilitation.

(2) On imposing a community payback order, the court must impose an offender supervision requirement if—

(a) the offender is under 18 years of age at the time the order is imposed, or

(b) the court, in the order, imposes—

(i) a compensation requirement,

(ii) a programme requirement,

(iii) a residence requirement,

(iv) a mental health requirement,

(v) a drug treatment requirement,

(vi) an alcohol treatment requirement, or

(vii) a conduct requirement.

(3) The specified period must be at least 6 months and not more than 3 years.

(4) Subsection (3) is subject to subsection (5) and section 227. ZE(4).

(5) In the case of an offender supervision requirement imposed on a person aged 16 or 17 along with only a level 1 unpaid work or other activity requirement, the specified period must be no more than whichever is the greater of—

(a) the specified period under section 227. L in relation to the level 1 unpaid work or other activity requirement, and

(b) 3 months.

(6) In this section, " specified ", in relation to an offender supervision requirement, means specified in the requirement.

Compensation requirementS

227. HCompensation requirementS

(1) In this Act, a "compensation requirement" is, in relation to an offender, a requirement that the offender must pay compensation for any relevant matter in favour of a relevant person.

(2) In subsection (1)—

" relevant matter " means any personal injury, loss, damage or other matter in respect of which a compensation order could be made against the offender under section 249 of this Act, and

" relevant person " means a person in whose favour the compensation could be awarded by such a compensation order.

(3) A compensation requirement may require the compensation to be paid in a lump sum or in instalments.

(4) The offender must complete payment of the compensation before the earlier of the following—

(a) the end of the period of 18 months beginning with the day on which the compensation requirement is imposed,

(b) the beginning of the period of 2 months ending with the day on which the offender supervision requirement imposed under section 227. G(2) ends.

(5) The following provisions of this Act apply in relation to a compensation requirement as they apply in relation to a compensation order, and as if the references in them to a compensation order included a compensation requirement—

(a) section 249. (3), (4), (5) and (8) to (10),

(b) section 250. (2),

(c) section 251. (1), (1. A) and (2)(b), and

(d) section 253.

Unpaid work or other activity requirementS

227. IUnpaid work or other activity requirementS

(1) In this Act, an "unpaid work or other activity requirement" is, in relation to an offender, a requirement that the offender must, for the specified number of hours, undertake—

(a) unpaid work, or

(b) unpaid work and other activity.

(2) Whether the offender must undertake other activity as well as unpaid work is for the responsible officer to determine.

(3) The nature of the unpaid work and any other activity to be undertaken by the offender is to be determined by the responsible officer.

(4) The number of hours that may be specified in the requirement must be (in total)—

(a) at least 20 hours, and

(b) not more than 300 hours.

(5) An unpaid work or other activity requirement which requires the work or activity to be undertaken for a number of hours totalling no more than 100 is referred to in this Act as a "level 1 unpaid work or other activity requirement".

(6) An unpaid work or other activity requirement which requires the work or activity to be undertaken for a number of hours totalling more than 100 is referred to in this Act as a "level 2 unpaid work or other activity requirement".

(7) The Scottish Ministers may by order made by statutory instrument substitute another number of hours for any of the numbers of hours for the time being specified in subsections (4) to (6).

(8) An order under subsection (7) may only substitute for the number of hours for the time being specified in a provision mentioned in the first column of the following table a number of hours falling within the range set out in the corresponding entry in the second column.

Provision	Range	
	No fewer than	No more than
Subsection (4)(a)	10 hours	40 hours
Subsection (4)(b)	250 hours	350 hours
Subsections (5) and (6)	70 hours	150 hours

(9) An order under subsection (7) is subject to annulment in pursuance of a resolution of the Scottish Parliament.

(10) In this section, " specified ", in relation to an unpaid work or other activity requirement, means specified in the requirement.

227. JUnpaid work or other activity requirement: further provisionS

(1) A court may not impose an unpaid work or other activity requirement on an offender who is

under 16 years of age.

(2) A court may impose such a requirement on an offender only if the court is satisfied, after considering the report mentioned in section 227. B(4), that the offender is a suitable person to undertake unpaid work in pursuance of the requirement.

(3) Subsection (2) does not apply where the court is considering imposing a community payback order—

(a) imposing only a level 1 unpaid work or other activity requirement, or

(b) under section 227. M(2).

(4) A justice of the peace court may impose a level 2 unpaid work or other activity requirement only if—

(a) the Scottish Ministers by regulations made by statutory instrument so provide, and

(b) the requirement is imposed in such circumstances and subject to such conditions as may be specified in the regulations.

(5) Regulations are not to be made under subsection (4) unless a draft of the statutory instrument containing them has been laid before and approved by resolution of the Scottish Parliament.

227. KAllocation of hours between unpaid work and other activityS

(1) Subject to subsection (2), it is for the responsible officer to determine how many out of the number of hours specified in an unpaid work or other activity requirement are to be allocated to undertaking, respectively—

(a) unpaid work, and

(b) any other activity to be undertaken.

(2) The number of hours allocated to undertaking an activity other than unpaid work must not exceed whichever is the lower of—

(a) 30% of the number of hours specified in the requirement, and

(b) 30 hours.

(3) The Scottish Ministers may by order made by statutory instrument—

(a) substitute another percentage for the percentage for the time being specified in subsection (2)(a),

(b) substitute another number of hours for the number of hours for the time being specified in subsection (2)(b).

(4) An order is not to be made under subsection (3) unless a draft of the statutory instrument containing the order has been laid before and approved by resolution of the Scottish Parliament.

227. LTime limit for completion of unpaid work or other activityS

(1) The number of hours of unpaid work and any other activity that the offender is required to undertake in pursuance of an unpaid work or other activity requirement must be completed by the offender before the end of the specified period beginning with the imposition of the requirement.

(2) The "specified period" is—

(a) in relation to a level 1 unpaid work or other activity requirement, 3 months or such longer period as the court may specify in the requirement,

(b) in relation to a level 2 unpaid work or other activity requirement, 6 months or such longer period as the court may specify in the requirement.

227. MFine defaultersS

(1) This section applies where—

(a) a fine has been imposed on an offender in respect of an offence,

(b) the offender fails to pay the fine or an instalment of the fine,

(c) the offender is not serving a sentence of imprisonment, and

(d) apart from this section, the court would have imposed a period of imprisonment on the offender under section 219. (1) of this Act in respect of the failure to pay the fine or instalment.

(2) Instead of imposing a period of imprisonment under section 219. (1) of this Act, the court—

(a) where the amount of the fine or the instalment does not exceed level 2 on the standard scale, must impose a community payback order on the offender imposing a level 1 unpaid work or other activity requirement,

(b) where the amount of the fine or the instalment exceeds that level, may impose such a community payback order.

(3) The court, in imposing a community payback order under subsection (2) on a person aged 16 or 17, must also impose an offender supervision requirement.

(4) Where the amount of the fine or the instalment does not exceed level 1 on the standard scale, the number of hours specified in the requirement must not exceed 50.

(5) On completion of the hours of unpaid work and any other activity specified in an unpaid work or other activity requirement imposed under this section, the fine in respect of which the requirement was imposed is discharged (or, as the case may be, the outstanding instalments of the fine are discharged).

(6) If, after a community payback order is imposed on an offender under this section, the offender pays the fine or the full amount of any outstanding instalments, the appropriate court must discharge the order.

(7) Subsection (2) is subject to sections 227. J(1) and 227. N(2), (3) and (7).

(8) In this section, " court " does not include the High Court.

227. NOffenders subject to more than one unpaid work or other activity requirementS

(1) This section applies where—

(a) a court is considering imposing an unpaid work or other activity requirement on an offender (referred to as the " new requirement "), and

(b) at the time the court is considering imposing the requirement, there is already in effect one or more [F160of the following orders—

(i) a community payback order imposing such a requirement on the same offender;

(ii) a community service order under this Act in relation to the same offender;

(iii) a probation order under this Act imposing an unpaid work requirement on the same offender;

(iv) a supervised attendance order under this Act in relation to the same offender.]

[F161. (1. A)In this section references to an "existing requirement" are—

(a) in relation to a community payback order, to the unpaid work or other activity requirement imposed on the offender by the order;

(b) in relation to a community service order or a probation order, to the unpaid work requirement imposed on the offender by the order;

(c) in relation to a supervised attendance order, to the requirement imposed on the offender by the order by virtue of section 235. (2) of this Act.]

(2) The court may, in imposing the new requirement, direct that it is to be concurrent with any existing requirement.

(3) Where the court makes a direction under subsection (2), hours of unpaid work or other activity undertaken after the new requirement is imposed count for the purposes of compliance with that requirement and the existing requirement.

(4) Subsection (5) applies where the court does not make a direction under subsection (2).

(5) The maximum number of hours which may be specified in the new requirement is the number of hours specified in section 227. I(4)(b) less the aggregate of the number of hours F162... still to be completed under each existing requirement at the time the new requirement is imposed.

(6) In calculating that aggregate, if any existing requirement is concurrent with another (by virtue of a direction under subsection (2)), hours that count for the purposes of compliance with both (or, as the case may be, all) are to be counted only once.

(7) Where that maximum number is less than the minimum number of hours that can be specified by virtue of section 227. I(4)(a), the court must not impose the new requirement.

Amendments (Textual)

F160. Words in s. 227. N(1)(b) substituted (1.2.2011) by The Criminal Justice and Licensing (Scotland) Act 2010 (Consequential and Supplementary Provisions) Order 2011 (S.S.I. 2011/25), art. 1, sch. para. 1. (2)(a) (with art. 3)

F161. S. 227. N(1. A) inserted (1.2.2011) by The Criminal Justice and Licensing (Scotland) Act 2010 (Consequential and Supplementary Provisions) Order 2011 (S.S.I. 2011/25), art. 1, sch. para. 1. (2)(b) (with art. 3)

F162. Words in s. 227. N(5) repealed (1.2.2011) by The Criminal Justice and Licensing (Scotland) Act 2010 (Consequential and Supplementary Provisions) Order 2011 (S.S.I. 2011/25), art. 1, sch. para. 1. (2)(c) (with art. 3)

227. ORules about unpaid work and other activityS

(1) The Scottish Ministers may make rules by statutory instrument for or in connection with the undertaking of unpaid work and other activities in pursuance of unpaid work or other activity requirements.

(2) Rules under subsection (1) may in particular make provision for—

(a) limiting the number of hours of work or other activity that an offender may be required to undertake in any one day,

(b) reckoning the time spent undertaking unpaid work or other activity,

(c) the keeping of records of unpaid work and any other activity undertaken.

(3) Rules under subsection (1) may—

(a) confer functions on responsible officers,

(b) contain rules about the way responsible officers are to exercise functions under this Act.

(4) Rules under subsection (1) are subject to annulment in pursuance of a resolution of the Scottish Parliament.

Programme requirementS

227. PProgramme requirementS

(1) In this Act, a "programme requirement" is, in relation to an offender, a requirement that the offender must participate in a specified programme, at the specified place and on the specified number of days.

(2) In this section, " programme " means a course or other planned set of activities, taking place over a period of time, and provided to individuals or groups of individuals for the purpose of addressing offending behavioural needs.

(3) A court may impose a programme requirement on an offender only if the specified programme is one which has been recommended by an officer of a local authority as being suitable for the offender to participate in.

(4) If an offender's compliance with a proposed programme requirement would involve the co-operation of a person other than the offender, the court may impose the requirement only if the other person consents.

(5) A court may not impose a programme requirement that would require an offender to participate in a specified programme after the expiry of the period specified in the offender

supervision requirement to be imposed at the same time as the programme requirement (by virtue of section 227. G(2)(b)).

(6) Where the court imposes a programme requirement on an offender, the requirement is to be taken to include a requirement that the offender, while attending the specified programme, complies with any instructions given by or on behalf of the person in charge of the programme.

(7) In this section, " specified ", in relation to a programme requirement, means specified in the requirement.

Residence requirementS

227. QResidence requirementS

(1) In this Act, a "residence requirement" is, in relation to an offender, a requirement that, during the specified period, the offender must reside at a specified place.

(2) The court may, in a residence requirement, require an offender to reside at a hostel or other institution only if the hostel or institution has been recommended as a suitable place for the offender to reside in by an officer of a local authority.

(3) The specified period must not be longer than the period specified in the offender supervision requirement to be imposed at the same time as the residence requirement (by virtue of section 227. G(2)(b)).

(4) In this section, " specified ", in relation to a residence requirement, means specified in the requirement.

Mental health treatment requirementS

227. RMental health treatment requirementS

(1) In this Act, a "mental health treatment requirement" is, in relation to an offender, a requirement that the offender must submit, during the specified period, to treatment by or under the direction of a registered medical practitioner or a registered psychologist (or both) with a view to improving the offender's mental condition.

(2) The treatment to which an offender may be required to submit under a mental health treatment requirement is such of the kinds of treatment described in subsection (3) as is specified; but otherwise the nature of the treatment is not to be specified.

(3) Those kinds of treatment are—

(a) treatment as a resident patient in a hospital (other than a State hospital) within the meaning of the Mental Health (Care and Treatment) (Scotland) Act 2003 (asp 13) (" the 2003 Act "),

(b) treatment as a non-resident patient at such institution or other place as may be specified, or

(c) treatment by or under the direction of such registered medical practitioner or registered psychologist as may be specified.

(4) A court may impose a mental health treatment requirement on an offender only if the court is satisfied—

(a) on the written or oral evidence of an approved medical practitioner (within the meaning of the 2003 Act), that Condition A is met,

(b) on the written or oral evidence of the registered medical practitioner or registered psychologist by whom or under whose direction the treatment is to be provided, that Condition B is met, and

(c) that Condition C is met.

(5) Condition A is that—

(a) the offender suffers from a mental condition,

(b) the condition requires, and may be susceptible to, treatment, and

(c) the condition is not such as to warrant the offender's being subject to—

(i) a compulsory treatment order under section 64 of the 2003 Act, or

(ii) a compulsion order under section 57. A of this Act.

(6) Condition B is that the treatment proposed to be specified is appropriate for the offender.

(7) Condition C is that arrangements have been made for the proposed treatment including, where the treatment is to be of the kind mentioned in subsection (3)(a), arrangements for the offender's reception in the hospital proposed to be specified in the requirement.

(8) The specified period must not be longer than the period specified in the offender supervision requirement to be imposed at the same time as the mental health treatment requirement (by virtue of section 227. G(2)(b)).

(9) In this section, " specified ", in relation to a mental health treatment requirement, means specified in the requirement.

227. SMental health treatment requirements: medical evidenceS

(1) For the purposes of section 227. R(4)(a) or (b), a written report purporting to be signed by an approved medical practitioner (within the meaning of the Mental Health (Care and Treatment) (Scotland) Act 2003 (asp 13)) may be received in evidence without the need for proof of the signature or qualifications of the practitioner.

(2) Where such a report is lodged in evidence otherwise than by or on behalf of the offender, a copy of the report must be given to—

(a) the offender, and

(b) the offender's solicitor (if any).

(3) The court may adjourn the case if it considers it necessary to do so to give the offender further time to consider the report.

(4) Subsection (5) applies where the offender is—

(a) detained in a hospital under this Act, or

(b) remanded in custody.

(5) For the purpose of calling evidence to rebut any evidence contained in a report lodged as mentioned in subsection (2), arrangements may be made by or on behalf of the offender for an examination of the offender by a registered medical practitioner.

(6) Such an examination is to be carried out in private.

227. TPower to change treatmentS

(1) This section applies where—

(a) a mental health treatment requirement has been imposed on an offender, and

(b) the registered medical practitioner or registered psychologist by whom or under whose direction the offender is receiving the treatment to which the offender is required to submit in pursuance of the requirement is of the opinion mentioned in subsection (2).

(2) That opinion is—

(a) that the offender requires, or that it would be appropriate for the offender to receive, a different kind of treatment (whether in whole or in part) from that which the offender has been receiving, or

(b) that the treatment (whether in whole or in part) can be more appropriately given in or at a different hospital or other institution or place from that where the offender has been receiving treatment.

(3) The practitioner or, as the case may be, psychologist may make arrangements for the offender to be treated accordingly.

(4) Subject to subsection (5), the treatment provided under the arrangements must be of a kind

which could have been specified in the mental health treatment requirement.

(5) The arrangements may provide for the offender to receive treatment (in whole or in part) as a resident patient in an institution or place even though it is one that could not have been specified for that purpose in the mental health treatment requirement.

(6) Arrangements may be made under subsection (3) only if—

(a) the offender and the responsible officer agree to the arrangements,

(b) the treatment will be given by or under the direction of a registered medical practitioner or registered psychologist who has agreed to accept the offender as a patient, and

(c) where the treatment requires the offender to be a resident patient, the offender will be received as such.

(7) Where arrangements are made under subsection (3)—

(a) the responsible officer must notify the court of the arrangements, and

(b) the treatment provided under the arrangements is to be taken to be treatment to which the offender is required to submit under the mental health treatment requirement.

Drug treatment requirementS

227. UDrug treatment requirementS

(1) In this Act, a "drug treatment requirement" is, in relation to an offender, a requirement that the offender must submit, during the specified period, to treatment by or under the direction of a specified person with a view to reducing or eliminating the offender's dependency on, or propensity to misuse, drugs.

(2) The treatment to which an offender may be required to submit under a drug treatment requirement is such of the kinds of treatment described in subsection (3) as is specified (but otherwise the nature of the treatment is not to be specified).

(3) Those kinds of treatment are—

(a) treatment as a resident in such institution or other place as is specified,

(b) treatment as a non-resident at such institution or other place, and at such intervals, as is specified.

(4) The specified person must be a person who has the necessary qualifications or experience in relation to the treatment to be provided.

(5) The specified period must not be longer than the period specified in the offender supervision requirement to be imposed at the same time as the drug treatment requirement (by virtue of section 227. G(2)(b)).

(6) A court may impose a drug treatment requirement on an offender only if the court is satisfied that—

(a) the offender is dependent on, or has a propensity to misuse, any controlled drug (as defined in section 2. (1)(a) of the Misuse of Drugs Act 1971 (c.38)),

(b) the dependency or propensity requires, and may be susceptible to, treatment, and

(c) arrangements have been, or can be, made for the proposed treatment including, where the treatment is to be of the kind mentioned in subsection (3)(a), arrangements for the offender's reception in the institution or other place to be specified.

(7) In this section, " specified ", in relation to a drug treatment requirement, means specified in the requirement.

Alcohol treatment requirementS

227. VAlcohol treatment requirementS

(1) In this Act, an "alcohol treatment requirement" is, in relation to an offender, a requirement that the offender must submit, during the specified period, to treatment by or under the direction of a specified person with a view to the reduction or elimination of the offender's dependency on alcohol.

(2) The treatment to which an offender may be required to submit under an alcohol treatment requirement is such of the kinds of treatment described in subsection (3) as is specified (but otherwise the nature of the treatment is not to be specified).

(3) Those kinds of treatment are—

(a) treatment as a resident in such institution or other place as is specified,

(b) treatment as a non-resident at such institution or other place, and at such intervals, as is specified,

(c) treatment by or under the direction of such person as is specified.

(4) The person specified under subsection (1) or (3)(c) must be a person who has the necessary qualifications or experience in relation to the treatment to be provided.

(5) The specified period must not be longer than the period specified in the offender supervision requirement to be imposed at the same time as the alcohol treatment requirement (by virtue of section 227. G(2)(b)).

(6) A court may impose an alcohol treatment requirement on an offender only if the court is satisfied that—

(a) the offender is dependent on alcohol,

(b) the dependency requires, and may be susceptible to, treatment, and

(c) arrangements have been, or can be, made for the proposed treatment, including, where the treatment is to be of the kind mentioned in subsection (3)(a), arrangements for the offender's reception in the institution or other place to be specified.

(7) In this section, " specified ", in relation to an alcohol treatment requirement, means specified in the requirement.

Conduct requirementS

227. WConduct requirementS

(1) In this Act, a "conduct requirement" is, in relation to an offender, a requirement that the offender must, during the specified period, do or refrain from doing specified things.

(2) A court may impose a conduct requirement on an offender only if the court is satisfied that the requirement is necessary with a view to—

(a) securing or promoting good behaviour by the offender, or

(b) preventing further offending by the offender.

(3) The specified period must be not more than 3 years.

(4) The specified things must not include anything that—

(a) could be required by imposing one of the other requirements listed in section 227. A(2), or

(b) would be inconsistent with the provisions of this Act relating to such other requirements.

(5) In this section, " specified ", in relation to a conduct requirement, means specified in the requirement.

Community payback orders: review, variation etc.S

227. XPeriodic review of community payback ordersS

(1) On imposing a community payback order on an offender, the court may include in the order provision for the order to be reviewed at such time or times as may be specified in the order.

(2) A review carried out in pursuance of such provision is referred to in this section as a " progress review ".

(3) A progress review may be carried out by the court which imposed the community payback order or (if different) the appropriate court, and, where those courts are different, the court must specify in the order which of those courts is to carry out the reviews.

(4) A progress review is to be carried out in such manner as the court carrying out the review may determine.

(5) Before each progress review, the responsible officer must give the court a written report on the offender's compliance with the requirements imposed by the community payback order in the period to which the review relates.

(6) The offender must attend each progress review.

(7) If the offender fails to attend a progress review, the court may—

    (a) issue a citation requiring the offender's attendance, or

    (b) issue a warrant for the offender's arrest.

(8) The unified citation provisions apply in relation to a citation under subsection (7)(a) as they apply in relation to a citation under section 216. (3)(a) of this Act.

(9) Subsections (10) and (11) apply where, in the course of carrying out a progress review in respect of a community payback order, it appears to the court that the offender has failed to comply with a requirement imposed by the order.

(10) The court must—

    (a) provide the offender with written details of the alleged failure,

    (b) inform the offender that the offender is entitled to be legally represented, and

    (c) inform the offender that no answer need be given to the allegation before the offender—

(i) has been given an opportunity to take legal advice, or

(ii) has indicated that the offender does not wish to take legal advice.

(11) The court must then—

    (a) if it is the appropriate court, appoint another hearing for consideration of the alleged failure in accordance with section 227. ZC, or

    (b) if it is not the appropriate court, refer the alleged failure to that court for consideration in accordance with that section.

(12) On conclusion of a progress review in respect of a community payback order, the court may vary, revoke or discharge the order in accordance with section 227. Z.

227. YApplications to vary, revoke and discharge community payback ordersS

(1) The appropriate court may, on the application of either of the persons mentioned in subsection (2), vary, revoke or discharge a community payback order in accordance with section 227. Z.

(2) Those persons are—

    (a) the offender on whom the order was imposed,

    (b) the responsible officer in relation to the offender.

227. ZVariation, revocation and discharge: court's powersS

(1) This section applies where a court is considering varying, revoking or discharging a community payback order imposed on an offender.

(2) The court may vary, revoke or discharge the order only if satisfied that it is in the interests of justice to do so having regard to circumstances which have arisen since the order was imposed.

(3) Subsection (2) does not apply where the court is considering varying the order under section

227. ZC(7)(d).

(4) In varying an order, the court may, in particular—

    (a) add to the requirements imposed by the order,

    (b) revoke or discharge any requirement imposed by the order,

    (c) vary any requirement imposed by the order,

    (d) include provision for progress reviews under section 227. X,

    (e) where the order already includes such provision, vary that provision.

(5) In varying a requirement imposed by the order, the court may, in particular—

    (a) extend or shorten any period or other time limit specified in the requirement,

    (b) in the case of an unpaid work or other activity requirement, increase or decrease the number of hours specified in the requirement,

    (c) in the case of a compensation requirement, vary the amount of compensation or any instalment.

(6) The court may not, under subsection (5)(b), increase the number of hours beyond the appropriate maximum.

(7) The appropriate maximum is the number of hours specified in section 227. I(4)(b) at the time the unpaid work or other activity requirement being varied was imposed less the aggregate of the number of hours of unpaid work or other activity still to be completed under each other unpaid work or other activity requirement (if any) in effect in respect of the offender at the time of the variation (a "current requirement").

(8) In calculating that aggregate, if any current requirement is concurrent with another (by virtue of a direction under section 227. N(2)), hours that count for the purposes of compliance with both (or, as the case may be, all) are to be counted only once.

(9) The court may not, under subsection (5)(c), increase the amount of compensation beyond the maximum that could have been awarded at the time the requirement was imposed.

(10) Where the court varies a restricted movement requirement imposed by a community payback order, the court must give a copy of the order making the variation to the person responsible for monitoring the offender's compliance with the requirement.

(11) Where the court revokes a community payback order, the court may deal with the offender in respect of the offence in relation to which the order was imposed as it could have dealt with the offender had the order not been imposed.

(12) Subsection (11) applies in relation to a community payback order imposed under section 227. M(2) as if the reference to the offence in relation to which the order was imposed were a reference to the failure to pay in respect of which the order was imposed.

(13) Where the court is considering varying, revoking or discharging the order otherwise than on the application of the offender, the court must issue a citation to the offender requiring the offender to appear before the court (except where the offender is required to appear by section 227. X(6)) or 227. ZC(2)(b).

(14) If the offender fails to appear as required by the citation, the court may issue a warrant for the arrest of the offender.

(15) The unified citation provisions apply in relation to a citation under subsection (13) as they apply in relation to a citation under section 216. (3)(a) of this Act.

227. ZAVariation of community payback orders: further provisionS

(1) This section applies where a court is considering varying a community payback order imposed on an offender.

(2) The court must not make the variation unless it has obtained, and taken account of, a report from the responsible officer containing information about the offender and the offender's circumstances.

(3) An Act of Adjournal may prescribe—

(a) the form of a report under subsection (2), and

(b) the particular information to be contained in it.

(4) Subsection (2) does not apply where the court is considering varying a community payback order—

(a) so that it imposes only a level 1 unpaid work or other activity requirement, or

(b) imposed under section 227. M(2).

(5) The clerk of the court must give a copy of any report obtained under subsection (2) to—

(a) the offender,

(b) the offender's solicitor (if any).

(6) Before making the variation, the court must explain to the offender in ordinary language—

(a) the purpose and effect of each of the requirements to be imposed by the order as proposed to be varied,

(b) the consequences which may follow if the offender fails to comply with any of the requirements imposed by the order as proposed to be varied, and

(c) where the court proposes to include in the order as proposed to be varied provision for a progress review under section 227. X, or to vary any such provision already included in the order, the arrangements for such a review.

(7) The court must not make the variation unless the offender has, after the court has explained those matters, confirmed that the offender—

(a) understands those matters, and

(b) is willing to comply with each of the requirements to be imposed by the order as proposed to be amended.

(8) Where the variation would impose a new requirement—

(a) the court must not make the variation if the new requirement is not a requirement that could have been imposed by the order when it was imposed,

(b) if the new requirement is one which could have been so imposed, the court must, before making the variation take whatever steps the court would have been required to take before imposing the requirement had it been imposed by the order when it was imposed.

(9) Subsection (8)(a) does not prevent the imposition of a restricted movement requirement under section 227. ZC(7)(d).

(10) In determining for the purpose of subsection (8)(a) whether an unpaid work or other activity requirement is a requirement that could have been imposed by the order when the order was imposed, the effect of section 227. N(7) is to be ignored.

(11) Where the variation would vary any requirement imposed by the order, the court must not make the variation if the requirement as proposed to be varied could not have been imposed, or imposed in that way, by the order when it was imposed.

(12) Subsections (4) and (5) of section 227. D apply, with the necessary modifications, where a community payback order is varied as they apply where such an order is imposed.

227. ZBChange of offender's residence to new local authority areaS

(1) The section applies where—

(a) the offender on whom a community payback order has been imposed proposes to change, or has changed, residence to a locality ("the new locality") situated in the area of a different local authority from that in which the locality currently specified in the order is situated, and

(b) the court is considering varying the order so as to specify the new local authority area in which the offender resides or will reside.

(2) The court may vary the order only if satisfied that arrangements have been, or can be, made in the local authority area in which the new locality is situated for the offender to comply with the requirements imposed by the order.

(3) If the court considers that a requirement ("the requirement concerned") imposed by the order

cannot be complied with if the offender resides in the new locality, the court must not vary the order so as to specify the new local authority area unless it also varies the order so as to—

(a) revoke or discharge the requirement concerned, or

(b) substitute for the requirement concerned another requirement that can be so complied with.

(4) Where the court varies the order, the court must also vary the order so as to require the local authority for the area in which the new locality is situated to nominate an officer of the authority to be the responsible officer for the purposes of the order.

Breach of community payback orderS

227. ZCBreach of community payback orderS

(1) This section applies where it appears to the appropriate court that an offender on whom a community payback order has been imposed has failed to comply with a requirement imposed by the order.

(2) The court may—

(a) issue a warrant for the offender's arrest, or

(b) issue a citation to the offender requiring the offender to appear before the court.

(3) If the offender fails to appear as required by a citation issued under subsection (2)(b), the court may issue a warrant for the arrest of the offender.

(4) The unified citation provisions apply in relation to a citation under subsection (2)(b) as they apply in relation to a citation under section 216. (3)(a) of this Act.

(5) The court must, before considering the alleged failure—

(a) provide the offender with written details of the alleged failure,

(b) inform the offender that the offender is entitled to be legally represented, and

(c) inform the offender that no answer need be given to the allegation before the offender—

(i) has been given an opportunity to take legal advice, or

(ii) has indicated that the offender does not wish to take legal advice.

(6) Subsection (5) does not apply if the offender has previously been provided with those details and informed about those matters under section 227. X(10) of this Act.

(7) Where the order was imposed under section 227. A, if the court is satisfied that the offender has failed without reasonable excuse to comply with a requirement imposed by the order, the court may—

(a) impose on the offender a fine not exceeding level 3 on the standard scale,

(b) where the order was imposed under section 227. A(1), revoke the order and deal with the offender in respect of the offence in relation to which the order was imposed as it could have dealt with the offender had the order not been imposed,

(c) where the order was imposed under section 227. A(4), revoke the order and impose on the offender a sentence of imprisonment for a term not exceeding—

(i) where the court is a justice of the peace court, 60 days,

(ii) in any other case, 3 months,

(d) vary the order so as to impose a new requirement, vary any requirement imposed by the order or revoke or discharge any requirement imposed by the order, or

(e) both impose a fine under paragraph (a) and vary the order under paragraph (d).

(8) Where the order was imposed under section 227. M(2), if the court is satisfied that the offender has failed without reasonable excuse to comply with a requirement imposed by the order, the court may—

(a) revoke the order and impose on the offender a period of imprisonment for a term not exceeding—

(i) where the court is a justice of the peace court, 60 days,

(ii) in any other case, 3 months, or

(b) vary—

(i) the number of hours specified in the level 1 unpaid work or other activity requirement imposed by the order, and

(ii) where the order also imposes an offender supervision requirement, the specified period under section 227. G in relation to the requirement.

(9) Where the court revokes a community payback order under subsection (7)(b) or (c) and the offender is, in respect of the same offence, also subject to—

(a) a drug treatment and testing order, by virtue of section 234. J, or

(b) a restriction of liberty order, by virtue of section 245. D(3),

the court must, before dealing with the offender under subsection (7)(b) or (c), revoke the drug treatment and testing order or, as the case may be, restriction of liberty order.

[F163. (9. A)Where under subsection (8)(a) the court revokes the order and imposes on the offender a period of imprisonment, liability to pay the fine in respect of which the order was imposed (or, as the case may be, any instalments of the fine that are unpaid on the date that the period of imprisonment is imposed) is discharged.]

(10) If the court is satisfied that the offender has failed to comply with a requirement imposed by the order but had a reasonable excuse for the failure, the court may, subject to section 227. Z(2), vary the order so as to impose a new requirement, vary any requirement imposed by the order or revoke or discharge any requirement imposed by the order.

(11) Subsections (7)(b) and (c) and (9) are subject to section 42. (9) of the Criminal Justice (Scotland) Act 2003 (asp 7) (powers of drugs courts to deal with breach of community payback orders).

Amendments (Textual)

F163. S. 227. ZC(9. A) inserted (1.2.2011) by The Criminal Justice and Licensing (Scotland) Act 2010 (Consequential and Supplementary Provisions) Order 2011 (S.S.I. 2011/25), art. 1, sch. para. 1. (3) (with art. 3)

227. ZDBreach of community payback order: further provisionS

(1) Evidence of one witness is sufficient for the purpose of establishing that an offender has failed without reasonable excuse to comply with a requirement imposed by a community payback order.

(2) Subsection (3) applies in relation to a community payback order imposing a compensation requirement.

(3) A document bearing to be a certificate signed by the clerk of the appropriate court and stating that the compensation, or an instalment of the compensation, has not been paid as required by the requirement is sufficient evidence that the offender has failed to comply with the requirement.

(4) The appropriate court may, for the purpose of considering whether an offender has failed to comply with a requirement imposed by a community payback order, require the responsible officer to provide a report on the offender's compliance with the requirement.

Restricted movement requirementS

227. ZERestricted movement requirementS

(1) The requirements which the court may impose under section 227. ZC(7)(d) include a restricted movement requirement.

(2) If the court varies a community payback order under section 227. ZC(7)(d) so as to impose a restricted movement requirement, the court must also vary the order so as to impose an offender supervision requirement, unless an offender supervision requirement is already imposed by the order.

(3) The court must ensure that the specified period under section 227. G in relation to the offender supervision requirement is at least as long as the period for which the restricted movement requirement has effect and, where the community payback order already imposes an offender supervision requirement, must vary it accordingly, if necessary.

(4) The minimum period of 6 months in section 227. G(3) does not apply in relation to an offender supervision requirement imposed under subsection (2).

(5) Where the court varies the order so as to impose a restricted movement requirement, the court must give a copy of the order making the variation to the person responsible for monitoring the offender's compliance with the requirement.

(6) If during the period for which the restricted movement requirement is in effect it appears to the person responsible for monitoring the offender's compliance with the requirement that the offender has failed to comply with the requirement, the person must report the matter to the offender's responsible officer.

(7) On receiving a report under subsection (6), the responsible officer must report the matter to the court.

227. ZFRestricted movement requirement: effectS

(1) In this Act, a "restricted movement requirement" is, in relation to an offender, a requirement restricting the offender's movements to such extent as is specified.

(2) A restricted movement requirement may in particular require the offender—

    (a) to be in a specified place at a specified time or during specified periods, or

    (b) not to be in a specified place, or a specified class of place, at a specified time or during specified periods.

(3) In imposing a restricted movement requirement containing provision under subsection (2)(a), the court must ensure that the offender is not required, either by the requirement alone or the requirement taken together with any other relevant requirement or order, to be at any place for periods totalling more than 12 hours in any one day.

(4) In subsection (3), " other relevant requirement or order " means—

    (a) any other restricted movement requirement in effect in respect of the offender at the time the court is imposing the requirement referred to in subsection (3), and

    (b) any restriction of liberty order under section 245. A in effect in respect of the offender at that time.

(5) A restricted movement requirement—

    (a) takes effect from the specified day, and

    (b) has effect for such period as is specified.

(6) The period specified under subsection (5)(b) must be—

    (a) not less than 14 days, and

    (b) subject to subsections (7) and (8), not more than 12 months.

(7) Subsection (8) applies in the case of a restricted movement requirement imposed for failure to comply with a requirement of a community payback order—

    (a) where the offender was under 18 years of age at the time the order was imposed, or

    (b) where the only requirement imposed by the order is a level 1 unpaid work or other activity requirement.

(8) The period specified under subsection (5)(b) must be not more than—

    (a) where the order was imposed by a justice of the peace court, 60 days, or

    (b) in any other case, 3 months.

(9) A court imposing a restricted movement requirement must specify in it—

    (a) the method by which the offender's compliance with the requirement is to be monitored, and

    (b) the person who is to be responsible for monitoring that compliance.

(10) The Scottish Ministers may by regulations made by statutory instrument substitute—

    (a) for the number of hours for the time being specified in subsection (3) another number of hours,

(b) for the number of months for the time being specified in subsection (6)(b) another number of months.

(11) Regulations are not to be made under subsection (10) unless a draft of the statutory instrument containing the regulations has been laid before and approved by resolution of the Scottish Parliament.

(12) In this section, " specified ", in relation to a restricted movement requirement, means specified in the requirement.

227. ZGRestricted movement requirements: further provisionS

(1) A court may not impose a restricted movement requirement requiring the offender to be, or not to be, in a specified place unless it is satisfied that the offender's compliance with the requirement can be monitored by the method specified in the requirement.

(2) Before imposing a restricted movement requirement requiring the offender to be in a specified place, the appropriate court must obtain and consider a report by an officer of the local authority in whose area the place is situated on—

(a) the place, and

(b) the attitude of any person (other than the offender) likely to be affected by the enforced presence of the offender at the place.

(3) The court may, before imposing the requirement, hear the officer who prepared the report.

227. ZHVariation of restricted movement requirementS

(1) This section applies where—

(a) a community payback order which is in force in respect of an offender imposes a restricted movement requirement requiring the offender to be at a particular place specified in the requirement for any period, and

(b) the court is considering varying the requirement so as to require the offender to be at a different place ("the new place").

(2) Before making the variation, the appropriate court must obtain and consider a report by an officer of the local authority in whose area the new place is situated on—

(a) the new place, and

(b) the attitude of any person (other than the offender) likely to be affected by the enforced presence of the offender at the new place.

(3) The court may, before making the variation, hear the officer who prepared the report.

227. ZIRemote monitoringS

Section 245. C of this Act, and regulations made under that section, apply in relation to the imposition of, and compliance with, restricted movement requirements as they apply in relation to the imposition of, and compliance with, restriction of liberty orders.

227. ZJRestricted movement requirements: Scottish Ministers' functionsS

(1) The Scottish Ministers may by regulations made by statutory instrument prescribe—

(a) which courts, or class or classes of courts, may impose restricted movement requirements,

(b) the method or methods of monitoring compliance with a restricted movement requirement which may be specified in such a requirement,

(c) the class or classes of offender on whom such a requirement may be imposed.

(2) Regulations under subsection (1) may make different provision about the matters mentioned in paragraphs (b) and (c) of that subsection in relation to different courts or classes of court.

(3) Regulations under subsection (1) are subject to annulment in pursuance of a resolution of the Scottish Parliament.

(4) The Scottish Ministers must determine the person, or class or description of person, who may be specified in a restricted movement requirement as the person to be responsible for monitoring the offender's compliance with the requirement (referred to in this section as the "monitor").

(5) The Scottish Ministers may determine different persons, or different classes or descriptions of person, in relation to different methods of monitoring.

(6) The Scottish Ministers must notify each court having power to impose a restricted movement requirement of their determination.

(7) Subsection (8) applies where—

    (a) the Scottish Ministers make a determination under subsection (4) changing a previous determination made by them, and

    (b) a person specified in a restricted movement requirement in effect at the date the determination takes effect as the monitor is not a person, or is not of a class or description of person, mentioned in the determination as changed.

(8) The appropriate court must—

    (a) vary the restricted movement requirement so as to specify a different person as the monitor,

    (b) send a copy of the requirement as varied to that person and to the responsible officer, and

    (c) notify the offender of the variation.

227. ZKDocumentary evidence in proceedings for breach of restricted movement requirementS

(1) This section applies for the purposes of establishing in any proceedings whether an offender on whom a restricted movement requirement has been imposed has complied with the requirement.

(2) Evidence of the presence or absence of the offender at a particular place at a particular time may be given by the production of a document or documents bearing to be—

    (a) a statement automatically produced by a device specified in regulations made under section 245. C of this Act, by which the offender's whereabouts were remotely monitored, and

    (b) a certificate signed by a person nominated for the purposes of this paragraph by the Scottish Ministers that the statement relates to the whereabouts of the offender at the dates and times shown in the statement.

(3) The statement and certificate are, when produced in evidence, sufficient evidence of the facts stated in them.

(4) The statement and certificate are not admissible in evidence at any hearing unless a copy of them has been served on the offender before the hearing.

(5) Where it appears to any court before which the hearing is taking place that the offender has not had sufficient notice of the statement or certificate, the court may adjourn the hearing or make any order that it considers appropriate.

Local authorities: annual consultation about unpaid workS

227. ZLLocal authorities: annual consultations about unpaid workS

(1) Each local authority must, for each year, consult prescribed persons about the nature of unpaid work and other activities to be undertaken by offenders residing in the local authority's area on whom community payback orders are imposed.

(2) In subsection (1), " prescribed persons " means such persons, or class or classes of person, as may be prescribed by the Scottish Ministers by regulations made by statutory instrument.

(3) A statutory instrument containing regulations under subsection (2) is to be subject to annulment in pursuance of a resolution of the Scottish Parliament.

Annual reports on community payback ordersS

227. ZMAnnual reports on community payback ordersS

(1) Each local authority must, as soon as practicable after the end of each reporting year, prepare a report on the operation of community payback orders within their area during that reporting year, and send a copy of the report to [F164. Community Justice Scotland].

(2) The Scottish Ministers may issue directions to local authorities about the content of their reports under subsection (1); and local authorities must comply with any such directions.

(3) [F165. Community Justice Scotland] must, [F166in relation to] each reporting year, lay before the Scottish Parliament and publish a report that collates and summarises the data included in the various reports under subsection (1).

[F167. (3. A)A report under subsection (3) must be laid before the Parliament, and published, together with, or as part of, the corresponding report under section 27 of the Community Justice (Scotland) Act 2016.

(3. B)The reference in subsection (3. A) to the corresponding report under section 27 of the Community Justice (Scotland) Act 2016 is, in relation to a report under subsection (3) for a particular reporting year, a reference to the report under that section which requires to be published as soon as reasonably practicable after that 31 March.]

[F168. (4)In this section, "reporting year" means a year ending with 31 March.]

Amendments (Textual)

F164. Words in s. 227. ZM(1) substituted (1.4.2017) by Community Justice (Scotland) Act 2016 (asp 10), s. 41. (2), sch. 2 para. 2. (a); S.S.I. 2017/33, reg. 2. (3)

F165. Words in s. 227. ZM(3) substituted (1.4.2017) by Community Justice (Scotland) Act 2016 (asp 10), s. 41. (2), sch. 2 para. 2. (b)(i); S.S.I. 2017/33, reg. 2. (3)

F166. Words in s. 227. ZM(3) substituted (1.4.2017) by Community Justice (Scotland) Act 2016 (asp 10), s. 41. (2), sch. 2 para. 2. (b)(ii); S.S.I. 2017/33, reg. 2. (3)

F167. S. 227. ZM(3. A)(3. B) inserted (1.4.2017) by Community Justice (Scotland) Act 2016 (asp 10), s. 41. (2), sch. 2 para. 2. (c); S.S.I. 2017/33, reg. 2. (3)

F168. S. 227. ZM(4) substituted (1.4.2017) by Community Justice (Scotland) Act 2016 (asp 10), s. 41. (2), sch. 2 para. 2. (d); S.S.I. 2017/33, reg. 2. (3)

Community payback order: meaning of "the appropriate court"S

227. ZNMeaning of "the appropriate court"S

(1) In sections 227. A to 227. ZK, " the appropriate court " means, in relation to a community payback order—

(a) where the order was imposed by the High Court of Justiciary, that Court,

(b) where the order was imposed by a sheriff, a sheriff having jurisdiction in the locality mentioned in subsection (2),

(c) where the order was imposed by a justice of the peace court—

(i) the justice of the peace court having jurisdiction in that locality, or

(ii) if there is no justice of the peace court having jurisdiction in that locality, a sheriff having such jurisdiction.

(2) The locality referred to in subsection (1) is the locality for the time being specified in the community payback order under section 227. C(2)(a).]

[F169227. ZOCommunity payback orders: persons residing in England and Wales or Northern IrelandS

Schedule 13 to this Act, which makes provision for the transfer of community payback orders to England and Wales or Northern Ireland, has effect.]

Amendments (Textual)

F169. S. 227. ZO inserted (16.9.2011) by The Criminal Justice and Licensing (Scotland) Act 2010 (Consequential Provisions and Modifications) Order 2011 (S.I. 2011/2298), art. 1, Sch. para. 5 (with art. 4. (4))

ProbationS

228 Probation orders.S

F170. . . . .

Amendments (Textual)

F170. Ss. 228-234 repealed (1.2.2011) by Criminal Justice and Licensing (Scotland) Act 2010 (asp 13), ss. 14. (2), 206. (1), Sch. 2 para. 17; S.S.I. 2010/413, art. 2, Sch. (with art. 3)

229 Probation orders: additional requirements.S

F171. . . . .

Amendments (Textual)

F171. Ss. 228-234 repealed (1.2.2011) by Criminal Justice and Licensing (Scotland) Act 2010 (asp 13), ss. 14. (2), 206. (1), Sch. 2 para. 17; S.S.I. 2010/413, art. 2, Sch. (with art. 3)

229. AProbation progress reviewS

F172 . . . .

Amendments (Textual)

F172. Ss. 228-234 repealed (1.2.2011) by Criminal Justice and Licensing (Scotland) Act 2010 (asp 13), ss. 14. (2), 206. (1), Sch. 2 para. 17; S.S.I. 2010/413, art. 2, Sch. (with art. 3)

230 Probation orders: requirement of treatment for mental condition.S

F173. . . . .

Amendments (Textual)

F173. Ss. 228-234 repealed (1.2.2011) by Criminal Justice and Licensing (Scotland) Act 2010 (asp 13), ss. 14. (2), 206. (1), Sch. 2 para. 17; S.S.I. 2010/413, art. 2, Sch. (with art. 3)

230. ARequirement for remote monitoring in probation orderS

F174 . . . .

231 Probation orders: amendment and discharge.S

F175. . . . .

232 Probation orders: failure to comply with requirement.S

F176. . . . .

233 Probation orders: commission of further offence.S

F177. . . . .

F178. F179234 Probation orders: persons residing in England and Wales.

. . . .

[F180 Non-harassment orders]S

[F181234. A Non-harassment orders.S

[F182. (1)This section applies where a person is—
  (a) convicted of an offence involving misconduct towards another person ("the victim"),
  (b) acquitted of such an offence by reason of the special defence set out in section 51. A, or
  (c) found by a court to be unfit for trial under section 53. F in respect of such an offence and the court determines that the person has done the act or made the omission constituting the offence.
(1. A)The prosecutor may apply to the court to make (instead of or in addition to dealing with the person in any other way) a non-harassment order against the person.

(1. B)A non-harassment order is an order requiring the person to refrain, for such period (including an indeterminate period) as may be specified in the order, from such conduct in relation to the victim as may be specified in the order.]

(2) On an application under subsection [F183. (1. A)] above the court may, if it is satisfied on a balance of probabilities that it is appropriate to do so in order to protect the victim from [F184harassment (or further harassment)], make a non-harassment order.

[F185. (2. A)The court may, for the purpose of subsection (2) above, have regard to any information given to it for that purpose by the prosecutor—

(a) about any other offence involving misconduct towards the victim—

(i) of which the [F186person against whom the order is sought] has been convicted, or

(ii) as regards which the [F187person against whom the order is sought] has accepted (or has been deemed to have accepted) a fixed penalty or compensation offer under section 302. (1) or 302. A(1) or as regards which a work order has been made under section 303. ZA(6),

(b) in particular, by way of—

(i) an extract of the conviction along with a copy of the complaint or indictment containing the charge to which the conviction relates, or

(ii) a note of the terms of the charge to which the fixed penalty offer, compensation offer or work order relates.

(2. B)But the court may do so only if the court may, under section 101 or 101. A (in a solemn case) or section 166 or 166. A (in a summary case), have regard to the conviction or the offer or order.

[F188. (2. BA)The court may, for the purpose of subsection (2) above, have regard to any information given to it for that purpose by the prosecutor about any other offence involving misconduct towards the victim—

(a) in respect of which the person against whom the order is sought was acquitted by reason of the special defence set out in section 51. A, or

(b) in respect of which the person against whom the order is sought was found by a court to be unfit for trial under section 53. F and the court determined that the person had done the act or made the omission constituting the offence.]

(2. C)The court must give the [F189person against whom the order is sought] an opportunity to make representations in response to the application.]

[F190. (3)A non-harassment order made by a criminal court may be appealed against—

(a) if the order was made in a case falling within subsection (1)(a) above, as if the order were a sentence,

(b) if the order was made in a case falling within subsection (1)(b) or (c) above, as if the person had been convicted of the offence concerned and the order were a sentence passed on the person for the offence.

(3. A)A variation or revocation of a non-harassment order made under subsection (6) below may be appealed against—

(a) if the order was made in a case falling within subsection (1)(a) above, as if the variation or revocation were a sentence,

(b) if the order was made in a case falling within subsection (1)(b) or (c) above, as if the person had been convicted of the offence concerned and the variation or revocation were a sentence passed on the person for the offence.]

(4) Any person who is F191. . . in breach of a non-harassment order shall be guilty of an offence and liable—

(a) on conviction on indictment, to imprisonment for a term not exceeding 5 years or to a fine, or to both such imprisonment and such fine; and

(b) on summary conviction, to imprisonment for a period not exceeding 6 months or to a fine not exceeding the statutory maximum, or to both such imprisonment and such fine.

F192. (4. A). . . . .

F192. (4. B). . . . .

F193. (5). . . . .

(6) The person against whom a non-harassment order is made, or the prosecutor at whose instance the order is made, may apply to the court which made the order for its revocation or variation and, in relation to any such application the court concerned may, if it is satisfied on a balance of probabilities that it is appropriate to do so, revoke the order or vary it in such manner as it thinks fit, but not so as to increase the period for which the order is to run.

[F194. (7)For the purposes of this section—

"harassment" and "conduct" are to be construed in accordance with section 8 of the Protection from Harassment Act 1997 (c.40),

" misconduct " includes conduct that causes alarm or distress.]]

Amendments (Textual)

F181. S. 234. A inserted (16.6.1997) by 1997 c. 40, s. 11; S.I. 1997/1418, art. 2

F182. S. 234. A(1)-(1. B) substituted for s. 234. A(1) (24.4.2017) by Abusive Behaviour and Sexual Harm (Scotland) Act 2016 (asp 22), ss. 5. (2), 45. (2)(3) (with s. 44); S.S.I. 2017/93, reg. 2 (with reg. 4)

F183. Word in s. 234. A(2) substituted (24.4.2017) by Abusive Behaviour and Sexual Harm (Scotland) Act 2016 (asp 22), ss. 5. (3), 45. (2)(3) (with s. 44); S.S.I. 2017/93, reg. 2 (with reg. 4)

F184. Words in s. 234. A(2) substituted (28.3.2011) by Criminal Justice and Licensing (Scotland) Act 2010 (asp 13), ss. 15. (b), 206. (1); S.S.I. 2011/178, art. 2, sch.

F185. Ss. 234. A(2. A)-(2. C) inserted (28.3.2011) by Criminal Justice and Licensing (Scotland) Act 2010 (asp 13), ss. 15. (c), 206. (1); S.S.I. 2011/178, art. 2, sch.

F186. Words in s. 234. A(2. A)(a)(i) substituted (24.4.2017) by Abusive Behaviour and Sexual Harm (Scotland) Act 2016 (asp 22), ss. 5. (4)(a), 45. (2)(3) (with s. 44); S.S.I. 2017/93, reg. 2 (with reg. 4)

F187. Words in s. 234. A(2. A)(a)(ii) substituted (24.4.2017) by Abusive Behaviour and Sexual Harm (Scotland) Act 2016 (asp 22), ss. 5. (4)(b), 45. (2)(3) (with s. 44); S.S.I. 2017/93, reg. 2 (with reg. 4)

F188. S. 234. A(2. BA) inserted (24.4.2017) by Abusive Behaviour and Sexual Harm (Scotland) Act 2016 (asp 22), ss. 5. (5), 45. (2)(3) (with s. 44); S.S.I. 2017/93, reg. 2 (with reg. 4)

F189. Words in s. 234. A(2. C) substituted (24.4.2017) by Abusive Behaviour and Sexual Harm (Scotland) Act 2016 (asp 22), ss. 5. (6), 45. (2)(3) (with s. 44); S.S.I. 2017/93, reg. 2 (with reg. 4)

F190. S. 234. A(3)(3. A) substituted for s. 234. A(3) (24.4.2017) by Abusive Behaviour and Sexual Harm (Scotland) Act 2016 (asp 22), ss. 5. (7), 45. (2)(3) (with s. 44); S.S.I. 2017/93, reg. 2 (with reg. 4)

F191. Words in s. 234. A(4) repealed (27.6.2003) by Criminal Justice (Scotland) Act 2003 (asp 7), ss. 49. (1)(a), 89; S.S.I. 2003/288, art. 2, Sch.

F192. S. 234. A(4. A)(4. B) repealed (25.1.2018) by Criminal Justice (Scotland) Act 2016 (asp 1), s. 117. (2), sch. 2 para. 3. (1); S.S.I. 2017/345, art. 3, sch.

F193. S. 234. A(5) repealed (1.8.1997) by 1997 c. 48, s. 62. (1)(2), Sch. 1 para. 21. (30), Sch. 3; S.I. 1997/1712, art. 3 Sch. (subject to arts. 4, 5)

F194. S. 234. A(7) substituted (28.3.2011) by Criminal Justice and Licensing (Scotland) Act 2010 (asp 13), ss. 15. (d), 206. (1); S.S.I. 2011/178, art. 2, sch.

[F195. Antisocial behaviour ordersS

Amendments (Textual)

F195. Ss. 234. AA, 234. AB and cross-heading inserted (28.10.2004) by Antisocial Behaviour etc. (Scotland) Act 2004 (asp 8), ss. 118, 145. (2); S.S.I. 2004/420, art. 3, Sch. 1

234. AAAntisocial behaviour ordersS

(1) Where subsection (2) below applies, the court may, instead of or in addition to imposing any sentence which it could impose, make an antisocial behaviour order in respect of a person (the

"offender").

(2) This subsection applies where—

(a) the offender is convicted of an offence;

F196. (b). . . . .

(c) in committing the offence, he engaged in antisocial behaviour; and

(d) the court is satisfied, on a balance of probabilities, that the making of an antisocial behaviour order is necessary for the purpose of protecting other persons from further antisocial behaviour by the offender.

(3) For the purposes of subsection (2)(c) above, a person engages in antisocial behaviour if he—

(a) acts in a manner that causes or is likely to cause alarm or distress; or

(b) pursues a course of conduct that causes or is likely to cause alarm or distress,

to at least one person who is not of the same household as him.

(4) Subject to subsection (5) below, an antisocial behaviour order is an order which prohibits, indefinitely or for such period as may be specified in the order, the offender from doing anything described in the order.

(5) The prohibitions that may be imposed by an antisocial behaviour order are those necessary for the purpose of protecting other persons from further antisocial behaviour by the offender.

(6) Before making an antisocial behaviour order, the court shall explain to the offender in ordinary language—

(a) the effect of the order and the prohibitions proposed to be included in it;

(b) the consequences of failing to comply with the order;

(c) the powers the court has under subsection (8) below; and

(d) the entitlement of the offender to appeal against the making of the order.

(7) Failure to comply with subsection (6) shall not affect the validity of the order.

(8) On the application of the offender in respect of whom an antisocial behaviour order is made under this section, the court which made the order may, if satisfied on a balance of probabilities that it is appropriate to do so—

(a) revoke the order; or

(b) subject to subsection (9) below, vary it in such manner as it thinks fit.

(9) Where an antisocial behaviour order specifies a period, the court may not, under subsection (8)(b) above, vary the order by extending the period.

(10) An antisocial behaviour order made under this section, and any revocation or variation of such an order under subsection (8) above, shall be taken to be a sentence for the purposes of an appeal.

(11) [F197. Section 9 (breach of orders) of the Antisocial Behaviour etc. (Scotland) Act 2004 applies in relation to antisocial behaviour orders made under this section as that section applies] in relation to antisocial behaviour orders made under section 4 of that Act.

(12) In this section, "conduct" includes speech; and a course of conduct must involve conduct on at least two occasions.

Amendments (Textual)

F196. S. 234. AA(2)(b) repealed (28.3.2011) by Criminal Justice and Licensing (Scotland) Act 2010 (asp 13), ss. 52. (4), 206. (1); S.S.I. 2011/178, art. 2, sch.

F197. Words in s. 234. AA(11) substituted (25.1.2018) by Criminal Justice (Scotland) Act 2016 (asp 1), s. 117. (2), sch. 2 para. 3. (2); S.S.I. 2017/345, art. 3, sch.

234. ABAntisocial behaviour orders: notificationS

(1) Upon making an antisocial behaviour order under section 234. AA of this Act, the court shall—

(a) serve a copy of the order on the offender; and

(b) give a copy of the order to the local authority it considers most appropriate.

(2) Upon revoking an antisocial behaviour order under subsection (8)(a) of that section, the court

shall notify the local authority to whom a copy of the order was given under subsection (1)(b) above.

(3) Upon varying an antisocial behaviour order under subsection (8)(b) of that section, the court shall—

(a) serve a copy of the order as varied on the offender; and

(b) give a copy of the order as varied to the local authority to whom a copy of the order was given under subsection (1)(b) above.

(4) For the purposes of this section, a copy is served on an offender if—

(a) given to him; or

(b) sent to him by registered post or the recorded delivery service.

(5) A certificate of posting of a letter sent under subsection (4)(b) issued by the postal operator shall be sufficient evidence of the sending of the letter on the day specified in such certificate.

(6) In this section, " offender " means the person in respect of whom the antisocial behaviour order was made.

[F198234. B Drug treatment and testing order.S

(1) This section applies where a person of 16 years of age or more is convicted of an offence, other than one for which the sentence is fixed by law, committed on or after the date on which section 89 of the Crime and Disorder Act 1998 comes into force.

(2) Subject to the provisions of this section, the court by or before which the offender is convicted may, if it is of the opinion that it is expedient to do so instead of sentencing him, make an order (a " drug treatment and testing order ") which shall—

(a) have effect for a period specified in the order of not less than six months nor more than three years (" the treatment and testing period "); and

(b) include the requirements and provisions mentioned in section 234. C of this Act.

(3) A court shall not make a drug treatment and testing order unless it—

(a) has been notified by the Secretary of State that arrangements for implementing such orders are available in the area of the local authority proposed to be specified in the order under section 234. C(6) of this Act and the notice has not been withdrawn;

(b) has obtained a report by, and if necessary heard evidence from, an officer of the local authority in whose area the offender is resident about the offender and his circumstances; and

(c) is satisfied that—

(i) the offender is dependent on, or has a propensity to misuse, drugs;

(ii) his dependency or propensity is such as requires and is susceptible to treatment; and

(iii) he is a suitable person to be subject to such an order.

(4) For the purpose of determining for the purposes of subsection (3)(c) above whether the offender has any drug in his body, the court may by order require him to provide samples of such description as it may specify.

(5) A drug treatment and testing order or an order under subsection (4) above shall not be made unless the offender expresses his willingness to comply with its requirements.

(6) The Secretary of State may by order—

(a) amend paragraph (a) of subsection (2) above by substituting a different period for the minimum or the maximum period for the time being specified in that paragraph; and

(b) make such transitional provisions as appear to him necessary or expedient in connection with any such amendment.

(7) The power to make an order under subsection (6) above shall be exercisable by statutory instrument; but no such order shall be made unless a draft of the order has been laid before and approved by resolution of each House of Parliament.

(8) A drug treatment and testing order shall be as nearly as may be in the form prescribed by Act of Adjournal.]

Amendments (Textual)

F198. S. 234. B inserted (30.9.1998) by 1998 c. 37, s. 89; S.I. 1998/2327, art. 2. (1)(s) (subject to arts. 5-8)

[F199234. C Requirements and provisions of drug treatment and testing orders.S

(1) A drug treatment and testing order shall include a requirement (" the treatment requirement ") that the offender shall submit, during the whole of the treatment and testing period, to treatment by or under the direction of a specified person having the necessary qualifications or experience (" the treatment provider ") with a view to the reduction or elimination of the offender's dependency on or propensity to misuse drugs.

(2) The required treatment for any particular period shall be—

(a) treatment as a resident in such institution or place as may be specified in the order; or

(b) treatment as a non-resident in or at such institution or place, and at such intervals, as may be so specified;

but the nature of the treatment shall not be specified in the order except as mentioned in paragraph (a) or (b) above.

(3) A court shall not make a drug treatment and testing order unless it is satisfied that arrangements have been made for the treatment intended to be specified in the order (including arrangements for the reception of the offender where he is required to submit to treatment as a resident).

(4) A drug treatment and testing order shall include a requirement (" the testing requirement ") that, for the purpose of ascertaining whether he has any drug in his body during the treatment and testing period, the offender shall provide during that period, at such times and in such circumstances as may (subject to the provisions of the order) be determined by the treatment provider, samples of such description as may be so determined.

(5) The testing requirement shall specify for each month the minimum number of occasions on which samples are to be provided.

(6) A drug treatment and testing order shall specify the local authority in whose area the offender will reside when the order is in force and require that authority to appoint or assign an officer (a " supervising officer ") for the purposes of subsections (7) and (8) below.

(7) A drug treatment and testing order shall—

(a) provide that, for the treatment and testing period, the offender shall be under the supervision of a supervising officer;

(b) require the offender to keep in touch with the supervising officer in accordance with such instructions as he may from time to time be given by that officer, and to notify him of any change of address; and

(c) provide that the results of the tests carried out on the samples provided by the offender in pursuance of the testing requirement shall be communicated to the supervising officer.

(8) Supervision by the supervising officer shall be carried out to such extent only as may be necessary for the purpose of enabling him—

(a) to report on the offender's progress to the appropriate court;

(b) to report to that court any failure by the offender to comply with the requirements of the order; and

(c) to determine whether the circumstances are such that he should apply to that court for the variation or revocation of the order.]]

Amendments (Textual)

F199. S. 234. C inserted (30.9.1998) by 1998 c. 37, s. 90; S.I. 1998/2327, art. 2. (1)(s) (subject to arts. 5-8)

[F200234. CARequirement for remote monitoring in drug

treatment and testing orderS

(1) A drug treatment and testing order may include a requirement that during such period as may be specified in the requirement, being a period not exceeding twelve months, the offender comply with such restrictions as to his movements as the court thinks fit; and paragraphs (a) and (b) of subsection (2) of section 245. A of this Act (with the qualification of paragraph (a) which that subsection contains) shall apply in relation to any such requirement as they apply in relation to a restriction of liberty order.

(2) The clerk of the court shall cause a copy of a drug treatment and testing order which includes such a requirement to be sent to the person who is to be responsible for monitoring the offender's compliance with the requirement.

(3) If, within the period last specified by virtue of subsection (1) above or (6)(d) below, it appears to the person so responsible that the offender has failed to comply with the requirement the person shall so inform the supervising officer appointed by virtue of section 234. C(6) of this Act, who shall report the matter to the court.

(4) Section 245. H shall apply in relation to proceedings under section 234. G of this Act as respects a drug treatment and testing order which includes such a requirement as it applies in relation to proceedings under section 245. F of this Act.

(5) Sections 245. A(6) and (8) to (11), 245. B and 245. C of this Act shall apply in relation to the imposition of, or as the case may be compliance with, requirements included by virtue of subsection (1) above in a drug treatment and testing order as those sections apply in relation to the making of, or as the case may be compliance with, a restriction of liberty order.

(6) In relation to a drug testing order which includes such a requirement, section 234. E of this Act shall apply with the following modifications—

(a) the persons who may make an application under subsection (1) of that section shall include the person responsible for monitoring the offender's compliance with the requirement, but only in so far as the application relates to the requirement;

(b) the reference in subsection (2) of that section to the supervising officer shall be construed as a reference to either that officer or the person so responsible;

(c) where an application is made under subsection (1) of that section and relates to the requirement, the persons to be heard under subsection (3) of that section shall include the person so responsible;

(d) the ways of varying the order which are mentioned in subsection (3)(a) of that section shall include increasing or decreasing the period specified by virtue of subsection (1) above (or last specified by virtue of this paragraph) but not so as to increase that period above the maximum mentioned in subsection (1) above; and

(e) the reference in subsection (5) of that section—

(i) to the supervising officer shall be construed as a reference to either that officer or the person so responsible; and

(ii) to sections 234. B(5) and 234. D(1) shall be construed as including a reference to section 245. A(6) and (11).

(7) Where under section 234. E or 234. G(2)(b) of this Act the court varies such a requirement, the clerk of court shall cause a copy of the amended drug treatment and testing order to be sent—

(a) to the person responsible for monitoring the offender's compliance with the requirement; and

(b) where the variation comprises a change in who is designated for the purposes of such monitoring, to the person who, immediately before the order was varied, was so responsible.]

Amendments (Textual)

F200. S. 234. CA inserted (27.6.2003) by Criminal Justice (Scotland) Act 2003 (asp 7), ss. 47. (2), 89; S.S.I. 2003/288, art. 2, Sch.

[F201234. D Procedural matters relating to drug treatment and

testing orders.S

(1) Before making a drug treatment and testing order, a court shall explain to the offender in ordinary language—

(a) the effect of the order and of the requirements proposed to be included in it;

(b) the consequences which may follow under section 234. G of this Act or 42. (4) of the Criminal Justice (Scotland) Act 2003 (asp 7)(powers of drugs court)] if he fails to comply with any of those requirements;

(c) that the court has power under section 234. E of this Act to vary or revoke the order on the application of either the offender or the supervising officer; and

(d) that the order will be periodically reviewed at intervals provided for in the order.

(2) Upon making a drug treatment and testing order the court shall—

(a) give, or send by registered post or the recorded delivery service, a copy of the order to the offender;

(b) send a copy of the order to the treatment provider;

(c) send a copy of the order to the chief social work officer of the local authority specified in the order in accordance with section 234. C(6) of this Act; and

(d) where it is not the appropriate court, send a copy of the order (together with such documents and information relating to the case as are considered useful) to the clerk of the appropriate court.

(3) Where a copy of a drug treatment and testing order has under subsection (2)(a) been sent by registered post or by the recorded delivery service, an acknowledgment or certificate of delivery of a letter containing a copy order issued by the [F202postal operator] shall be sufficient evidence of the delivery of the letter on the day specified in such acknowledgement or certificate.

Amendments (Textual)

F201. S. 234. D inserted (30.9.1998) by 1998 c. 37, s. 91; S.I. 1998/2327, art. 2. (1)(s) (subject to arts. 5-8)

F202. Words in s. 234. D(3) substituted (26.3.2001) by S.I. 2001/1149, art. 3. (1), Sch. 1 para. 104. (5) (subject to art. 1. (3))

[F203234. E Amendment of drug treatment and testing order.S

(1) Where a drug treatment and testing order is in force either the offender or the supervising officer may apply to the appropriate court for variation or revocation of the order.

(2) Where an application is made under subsection (1) above by the supervising officer, the court shall issue a citation requiring the offender to appear before the court.

(2. A)The unified citation provisions apply in relation to a citation under this section as they apply in relation to a citation under section 216. (3)(a) of this Act.]

(3) On an application made under subsection (1) above and after hearing both the offender and the supervising officer, the court may by order, if it appears to it in the interests of justice to do so—

(a) vary the order by—

(i) amending or deleting any of its requirements or provisions;

(ii) inserting further requirements or provisions; or

(iii) subject to subsection (4) below, increasing or decreasing the treatment and testing period; or

(b) revoke the order.

(4) The power conferred by subsection (3)(a)(iii) above shall not be exercised so as to increase the treatment and testing period above the maximum for the time being specified in section 234. B(2)(a) of this Act, or to decrease it below the minimum so specified.

(5) Where the court, on the application of the supervising officer, proposes to vary (otherwise than by deleting a requirement or provision) a drug treatment and testing order, sections 234. B(5) and 234. D(1) of this Act shall apply to the variation of such an order as they apply to the making of such an order.

(6) If an offender fails to appear before the court after having been cited in accordance with

subsection (2) above, the court may issue a warrant for his arrest.

[F204. (7)This section is subject to section 234. CA(6) of this Act.]

Amendments (Textual)

F203. S. 234. E inserted (30.9.1998) by 1998 c. 37, s. 92; S.I. 1998/2327, art. 2. (1)(s) (subject to arts. 5-8)

F204. S. 234. E(7) added (27.6.2003) by Criminal Justice (Scotland) Act 2003 (asp 7), ss. 47. (3), 89; S.S.I. 2003/288, art. 2, Sch.

[F205234. F Periodic review of drug treatment and testing order.S

(1) A drug treatment and testing order shall—

(a) provide for the order to be reviewed periodically at intervals of not less than one month;

(b) provide for each review of the order to be made, subject to subsection (5) below, at a hearing held for the purpose by the appropriate court (a " review hearing ");

(c) require the offender to attend each review hearing;

(d) provide for the supervising officer to make to the court, before each review, a report in writing on the offender's progress under the order; and

(e) provide for each such report to include the test results communicated to the supervising officer under section 234. C(7)(c) of this Act and the views of the treatment provider as to the treatment and testing of the offender.

(1. A)A review hearing may be held whether or not the prosecutor elects to appear.]

(2) At a review hearing the court, after considering the supervising officer's report, may amend any requirement or provision of the order.

(3) The court—

(a) shall not amend the treatment or testing requirement unless the offender expresses his willingness to comply with the requirement as amended;

(b) shall not amend any provision of the order so as reduce the treatment and testing period below the minimum specified in section 234. B(2)(a) of this Act or to increase it above the maximum so specified; and

(c) except with the consent of the offender, shall not amend any requirement or provision of the order while an appeal against the order is pending.

(4) If the offender fails to express his willingness to comply with the treatment or testing requirement as proposed to be amended by the court, the court may revoke the order.

(5) If at a review hearing the court, after considering the supervising officer's report, is of the opinion that the offender's progress under the order is satisfactory, the court may so amend the order as to provide for each subsequent review to be made without a hearing.

(6) A review without a hearing shall take place in chambers without the parties being present.

(7) If at a review without a hearing the court, after considering the supervising officer's report, is of the opinion that the offender's progress is no longer satisfactory, the court may issue a warrant for the arrest of the offender or may, if it thinks fit, instead of issuing a warrant in the first instance, issue a citation requiring the offender to appear before that court as such time as may be specified in the citation.

(8) Where an offender fails to attend—

(a) a review hearing in accordance with a requirement contained in a drug treatment and testing order; or

(b) a court at the time specified in a citation under subsection (7) above,

the court may issue a warrant for his arrest.

(9) Where an offender attends the court at a time specified by a citation issued under subsection (7) above—

(a) the court may exercise the powers conferred by this section as if the court were conducting a review hearing; and

(b) so amend the order as to provide for each subsequent review to be made at a review hearing.

Amendments (Textual)

F205. S. 234. F inserted (30.9.1998) by 1998 c. 37, s. 92, S.I. 1998/2327, art. 2. (1)(s) (subject to arts. 5-8)

[F206234. G Breach of drug treatment testing order.S

(1) If at any time when a drug treatment and testing order is in force it appears to the appropriate court that the offender has failed to comply with any requirement of the order, the court may issue a citation requiring the offender to appear before the court at such time as may be specified in the citation or, if it appears to the court to be appropriate, it may issue a warrant for the arrest of the offender.

(1. A)The unified citation provisions apply in relation to a citation under this section as they apply in relation to a citation under section 216. (3)(a) of this Act.]

(2) If it is proved to the satisfaction of the appropriate court that the offender has failed without reasonable excuse to comply with any requirement of the order, the court may by order—

  (a) without prejudice to the continuation in force of the order, impose a fine not exceeding level 3 on the standard scale;

  (b) vary the order [F207so however that any extension of the period of a requirement imposed by virtue of section 234. CA of this Act shall not increase that period above the maximum mentioned in subsection (1) of that section] ; or

  (c) revoke the order.

[F208. (2. A)Subsections (6) and (11) of section 245. A of this Act apply to the variation, under paragraph (b) of subsection (2) above, of a requirement imposed as is mentioned in that paragraph as they apply to the making of a restriction of liberty order.]

(3) For the purposes of subsection (2) above, the evidence of one witness shall be sufficient evidence.

(4) A fine imposed under this section in respect of a failure to comply with the requirements of a drug treatment and testing order shall be deemed for the purposes of any enactment to be a sum adjudged to be paid by or in respect of a conviction or a penalty imposed on a person summarily convicted.

Amendments (Textual)

F206. S. 234. G inserted (30.9.1998) by 1998 c. 37, s. 93; S.I. 1998/2327, art. 2. (1)(s) (subject to arts. 5-8)

F207. Words in s. 234. G(2)(b) added (27.6.2003) by Criminal Justice (Scotland) Act 2003 (asp 7), ss. 47. (4)(a), 89; S.S.I. 2003/288, art. 2, Sch.

F208. S. 234. G(2. A) inserted (27.6.2003) by Criminal Justice (Scotland) Act 2003 (asp 7), ss. 47. (4)(b), 89; S.S.I. 2003/288, art. 2, Sch.

[F209234. H Disposal on revocation of drugs treatment and testing order.S

(1) Where the court revokes a [F210drug] treatment and testing order under section 234. E(3)(b), 234. F(4) or 234. G(2)(c) of this Act, it may dispose of the offender in any way which would have been competent at the time when the order was made.

(2) In disposing of an offender under subsection (1) above, the court shall have regard to the time for which the order has been in operation.

(3) Where the court revokes a drug treatment and testing order as mentioned in subsection (1) above and the offender is [F211, in respect of the same offence, also subject to a community payback order, by virtue of section 234. J, or a restriction of liberty order, by virtue of section 245. D, the court shall, before disposing of the offender under subsection (1) above, revoke the community payback order or restriction of liberty order (as the case may be).]

(4) This section is subject to section 42. (8) of the Criminal Justice (Scotland) Act 2003 (asp 7)(powers of drugs court).]

Amendments (Textual)

F209. S. 234. H inserted (30.9.1998) by 1998 c. 37, s. 93; S.I. 1998/2327, art. 2. (1)(s) (subject to arts. 5-8)

F210. Word in s. 234. H(1) substituted (1.2.2011) by Criminal Justice and Licensing (Scotland) Act 2010 (asp 13), ss. 14. (2), 206. (1), Sch. 2 para. 18. (a); S.S.I. 2010/413, art. 2, Sch. (with art. 3)

F211. Words in s. 234. H(3) substituted (1.2.2011) by Criminal Justice and Licensing (Scotland) Act 2010 (asp 13), ss. 14. (2), 206. (1), Sch. 2 para. 18. (b); S.S.I. 2010/413, art. 2, Sch. (with art. 3)

F212[234. J Concurrent drug treatment and testing and probation orders.S

(1) Notwithstanding [F213section] 234. B(2) of this Act, where the court considers it expedient that the offender should be subject to a drug treatment and testing order and to a [F214community payback order], it may make both such orders in respect of the offender.

(2) In deciding whether it is expedient for it to exercise the power conferred by subsection (1) above, the court shall have regard to the circumstances, including the nature of the offence and the character of the offender and to the report submitted to it under section 234. B(3)(b) of this Act.

(3) Where the court makes both a drug treatment and testing order and a [F215community payback order] by virtue of subsection (1) above, the clerk of the court shall send a copy of each of the orders to the following—

(a) the treatment provider within the meaning of section 234. C(1);

[F216. (ba)the local authority within whose area the offender will reside for the duration of each order.]

(4) Where the offender by an act or omission fails to comply with a requirement of an order made by virtue of subsection (1) above—

(a) if the failure relates to a requirement contained in a [F217community payback order and is dealt with under section 227. ZC(7)(d)] of this Act, the court may, in addition, exercise the power conferred by section 234. G(2)(b) of this Act in relation to the drug treatment and testing order; and

(b) if the failure relates to a requirement contained in a drug treatment and testing order and is dealt with under section 234. G(2)(b) of this Act, the court may, in addition, exercise the power conferred by section [F218227. ZC(7)(d) of this Act in relation to the community payback order].

(5) Where an offender by an act or omission fails to comply with both a requirement contained in a drug treatment and testing order and in a [F219community payback order] to which he is subject by virtue of subsection (1) above, he may, without prejudice to subsection (4) above, be dealt with as respects that act or omission either under section [F220227. ZC(7)] of this Act or under section 234. G(2) of this Act but he shall not be liable to be otherwise dealt with in respect of that act or omission.]

Amendments (Textual)

F212. S. 234. J inserted "after s. 234. H" (30.9.1998) by virtue of 1998 c. 37, s. 94. (1); S.I. 1998/2327, art. 2. (1)(s) (subject to arts. 5-8)

F213. Words in s. 234. J(1) substituted (1.2.2011) by Criminal Justice and Licensing (Scotland) Act 2010 (asp 13), ss. 14. (2), 206. (1), Sch. 2 para. 19. (2)(a); S.S.I. 2010/413, art. 2, Sch. (with art. 3)

F214. Words in s. 234. J(1) substituted (1.2.2011) by Criminal Justice and Licensing (Scotland) Act 2010 (asp 13), ss. 14. (2), 206. (1), Sch. 2 para. 19. (2)(b); S.S.I. 2010/413, art. 2, Sch. (with arts. 3-8)

F215. Words in s. 234. J(3) substituted (1.2.2011) by Criminal Justice and Licensing (Scotland)

Act 2010 (asp 13), ss. 14. (2), 206. (1), Sch. 2 para. 19. (3)(a); S.S.I. 2010/413, art. 2, Sch. (with art. 3)

F216. S. 234. J(3)(ba) substituted (1.2.2011) for s. 234. J(3)(b)(c) by Criminal Justice and Licensing (Scotland) Act 2010 (asp 13), ss. 14. (2), 206. (1), Sch. 2 para. 19. (3)(b); S.S.I. 2010/413, art. 2, Sch. (with art. 3)

F217. Words in s. 234. J(4)(a) substituted (1.2.2011) by Criminal Justice and Licensing (Scotland) Act 2010 (asp 13), ss. 14. (2), 206. (1), Sch. 2 para. 19. (4)(a); S.S.I. 2010/413, art. 2, Sch. (with art. 3)

F218. Words in s. 234. J(4)(b) substituted (1.2.2011) by Criminal Justice and Licensing (Scotland) Act 2010 (asp 13), ss. 14. (2), 206. (1), Sch. 2 para. 19. (4)(b); S.S.I. 2010/413, art. 2, Sch. (with art. 3)

F219. Words in s. 234. J(5) substituted (1.2.2011) by Criminal Justice and Licensing (Scotland) Act 2010 (asp 13), ss. 14. (2), 206. (1), Sch. 2 para. 19. (5)(a); S.S.I. 2010/413, art. 2, Sch. (with art. 3)

F220. Words in s. 234. J(5) substituted (1.2.2011) by Criminal Justice and Licensing (Scotland) Act 2010 (asp 13), ss. 14. (2), 206. (1), Sch. 2 para. 19. (5)(b); S.S.I. 2010/413, art. 2, Sch. (with art. 3)

F221[234. K Drug treatment and testing orders: interpretation.S

In sections 234. B to 234. J of this Act—

" the appropriate court " means—

- where the drug treatment and testing order has been made by the High Court, that court;

- in any other case, the court having jurisdiction in the area of the local authority for the time being specified in the order under section 234. C(6) of this Act, being a sheriff or [F222. JP court] according to whether the order has been made by a sheriff or [F222. JP court] , but in a case where an order has been made by a [F222. JP court] and there is no [F222. JP court] in that area, the sheriff court; and

" local authority " means a council constituted under section 2 of the M27 Local Government etc. (Scotland) Act 1994 and any reference to the area of such an authority is a reference to the local government area within the meaning of that Act for which it is so constituted.]

Amendments (Textual)

F221. S. 234. K inserted (30.9.1998) by 1998 c. 37, s. 95. (1); S.I. 1998/2327, art. 2. (1)(s) (subject to arts. 5-8)

F222. Words in s. 234. K(b) substituted (10.3.2008, 2.6.2008, 8.12.2008, 23.2.2009 and 14.12.2009 for certain purposes, otherwise 22.2.2010) by Criminal Proceedings etc. (Reform) (Scotland) Act 2007 (asp 6), ss. 80, 84, Sch. para. 26. (k); S.S.I. 2008/42, art. 3, Sch.; S.S.I. 2008/192, art. 3, Sch.; S.S.I. 2008/329, art. 3, Sch.; S.S.I. 2008/362, art. 3, Sch.; S.S.I. 2009/432, art. 3, Schs. 1, 2

Marginal Citations

M271994 c.39.

Supervised attendanceS

235 Supervised attendance orders.S

F223. . . . .

Amendments (Textual)

F223. Ss. 235-237 repealed (1.2.2011) by Criminal Justice and Licensing (Scotland) Act 2010 (asp 13), ss. 14. (2), 206. (1), Sch. 2 para. 20; S.S.I. 2010/413, art. 2, Sch. (with arts. 3-8)

236 Supervised attendance orders in place of fines for 16 and 17 year olds.S

F224. . . . .
Amendments (Textual)
F224. Ss. 235-237 repealed (1.2.2011) by Criminal Justice and Licensing (Scotland) Act 2010 (asp 13), ss. 14. (2), 206. (1), Sch. 2 para. 20; S.S.I. 2010/413, art. 2, Sch. (with arts. 3-8)

237 Supervised attendance orders where court allows further time to pay fine.S

F225. . . . .
Amendments (Textual)
F225. Ss. 235-237 repealed (1.2.2011) by Criminal Justice and Licensing (Scotland) Act 2010 (asp 13), ss. 14. (2), 206. (1), Sch. 2 para. 20; S.S.I. 2010/413, art. 2, Sch. (with arts. 3-8)

Community service by offenders

238 Community service orders.S

F226. . . . .
Amendments (Textual)
F226. Ss. 238-245 repealed (1.2.2011) by Criminal Justice and Licensing (Scotland) Act 2010 (asp 13), ss. 14. (2), 206. (1), Sch. 2 para. 20; S.S.I. 2010/413, art. 2, Sch. (with arts. 3-8)

239 Community service orders: requirements.S

F227. . . . .
Amendments (Textual)
F227. Ss. 238-245 repealed (1.2.2011) by Criminal Justice and Licensing (Scotland) Act 2010 (asp 13), ss. 14. (2), 206. (1), Sch. 2 para. 20; S.S.I. 2010/413, art. 2, Sch. (with arts. 3-8)

240 Community service orders: amendment and revocation etc.S

F228. . . . .
Amendments (Textual)
F228. Ss. 238-245 repealed (1.2.2011) by Criminal Justice and Licensing (Scotland) Act 2010 (asp 13), ss. 14. (2), 206. (1), Sch. 2 para. 20; S.S.I. 2010/413, art. 2, Sch. (with arts. 3-8)

241 Community service order: commission of offence while order in force.S

F229. . . . .
Amendments (Textual)
F229. Ss. 238-245 repealed (1.2.2011) by Criminal Justice and Licensing (Scotland) Act 2010 (asp 13), ss. 14. (2), 206. (1), Sch. 2 para. 20; S.S.I. 2010/413, art. 2, Sch. (with arts. 3-8)

242 Community service orders: persons residing in England and Wales.S

F230. . . . .

Amendments (Textual)

F230. Ss. 238-245 repealed (1.2.2011) by Criminal Justice and Licensing (Scotland) Act 2010 (asp 13), ss. 14. (2), 206. (1), Sch. 2 para. 20; S.S.I. 2010/413, art. 2, Sch. (with arts. 3-8)

243 Community service orders: persons residing in Northern Ireland.S

F231. . . . .

Amendments (Textual)

F231. Ss. 238-245 repealed (1.2.2011) by Criminal Justice and Licensing (Scotland) Act 2010 (asp 13), ss. 14. (2), 206. (1), Sch. 2 para. 20; S.S.I. 2010/413, art. 2, Sch. (with arts. 3-8)

F232. F233244 Community service orders: general provisions relating to persons living in England and Wales or Northern Ireland.

. . . .

Amendments (Textual)

F232. S. 244 repealed (S.) (1.2.2011) by Criminal Justice and Licensing (Scotland) Act 2010 (asp 13), ss. 14. (2), 206. (1), Sch. 2 para. 20; S.S.I. 2010/413, art. 2, Sch. (with arts. 3-8)

F233. S. 244 so far as still in force amended (E.W.N.I.) (16.9.2011) by The Criminal Justice and Licensing (Scotland) Act 2010 (Consequential Provisions and Modifications) Order 2011 (S.I. 2011/2298), art. 1, Sch. para. 7. (b) (with art. 4. (2)(4))

245 Community service orders: rules, annual report and interpretation.S

F234. . . . .

Amendments (Textual)

F234. Ss. 238-245 repealed (1.2.2011) by Criminal Justice and Licensing (Scotland) Act 2010 (asp 13), ss. 14. (2), 206. (1), Sch. 2 para. 20; S.S.I. 2010/413, art. 2, Sch. (with arts. 3-8)

[F235. Restriction of liberty orders]S

Amendments (Textual)

F235. Ss. 245. A-245. I and preceding cross-heading inserted (20.10.1997 for specified purposes and 1.7.1998 otherwise) by 1997 c. 48, s. 5; S.I. 1997/2323, arts. 3, 5. (1), Sch. 1

[F236245. A Restriction of liberty orders.S

(1) Without prejudice to section 245. D of this Act, where a person F237. . . is convicted of an offence [F238punishable by imprisonment] (other than an offence the sentence for which is fixed by law) the court, F239. . . may [F240, instead of imposing on him a sentence of, or including, imprisonment or any other form of detention,] make an order under this section (in this Act

referred to as a "restriction of liberty order") in respect of him. F241. . .

(2) A restriction of liberty order may restrict the offender's movements to such extent as the court thinks fit and, without prejudice to the generality of the foregoing, may include provision—

(a) requiring the offender to be in such place as may be specified for such period or periods in each day or week as may be specified;

(b) requiring the offender not to be in such place or places, or such class or classes of place or places, at such time or during such periods, as may be specified,
F242. . . .

[F243. (2. A)In making a restriction of liberty order containing provision under subsection (2)(a), the court must ensure that the offender is not required, either by the order alone or the order taken together with any other relevant order or requirement, to be in any place or places for a period or periods totalling more than 12 hours in any one day.

(2. B)In subsection (2. A), "other relevant order or requirement" means—

(a) any other restriction of liberty order in effect in respect of the offender at the time the court is making the order referred to in subsection (2. A), and

(b) any restricted movement requirement under section 227. ZF in effect in respect of the offender at that time.]

(3) A restriction of liberty order may be made for any period up to 12 months.

(4) Before making a restriction of liberty order, the court shall explain to the offender in ordinary language—

(a) the effect of the order, including any requirements which are to be included in the order under section 245. C of this Act;

(b) the consequences which may follow any failure by the offender to comply with the requirements of any order; and

(c) that the court has power under section 245. E of this Act to review the order on the application either of the offender or of any person responsible for monitoring the order,
and the court shall not make the order unless the offender agrees to comply with its requirements.

(5) The clerk of the court by which a restriction of liberty order is made shall—

(a) cause a copy of the order to be sent
[F244. (i)]to any person who is to be responsible for monitoring the offender's compliance with the order; [F245 and

(ii) if the offender resides (or is to reside) in a place outwith the jurisdiction of the court making the order, to the clerk of a court within whose jurisdiction that place is;] and

(b) cause a copy of the order to be given to the offender or sent to him by registered post or by the recorded delivery service; and an acknowledgment or certificate of delivery of a letter containing such copy order issued by the Post Office shall be sufficient evidence of the delivery of the letter on the day specified in such acknowledgment or certificate.

(6) Before making a restriction of liberty order which will require the offender to remain in a specified place or places the court shall [F246—

(a)] obtain and consider [F247 a report by an officer of a local authority about—

(i) the place or places proposed to be specified; and

(ii)] the attitude of persons likely to be affected by the enforced presence there of the offender [F248; and

(b) if it considers it necessary, hear the officer who prepared the report.]

(7) A restriction of liberty order shall be taken to be a sentence for the purposes of this Act and of any appeal.

(8) The Secretary of State may by regulations prescribe—

(a) which courts, or class or classes of courts, may make restriction of liberty orders;

(b) what method or methods of monitoring compliance with such orders may be specified in any such order by any such court; and

(c) the class or classes of offenders in respect of which restriction of liberty orders may be made,
and different provision may be made in relation to the matters mentioned in paragraphs (b) and (c)

above in relation to different courts or classes of court.

F249. (9). . . . .

(10) Regulations under subsection (8) above may make such transitional and consequential provisions, including provision in relation to the continuing effect of any restriction of liberty order in force when new regulations are made, as the Secretary of State considers appropriate.

(11) A court shall not make a restriction of liberty order which requires an offender to be in or, as the case may be, not to be in, a particular place or places unless it is satisfied that his compliance with that requirement can be monitored by the means of monitoring which it intends to specify in the order.

[F250. (11. A)A court shall not make a restriction of liberty order in respect of an offender who is under 16 years of age unless, having obtained a report on the offender from the local authority in whose area he resides, it is satisfied as to the services which the authority will provide for his support and rehabilitation during the period when he is subject to the order.]

(12) The Secretary of State may by regulations substitute for the period of—

    (a) hours for the time being mentioned in [F251subsection (2. A)] above; or

    (b) months for the time being mentioned in subsection (3) above,

such period of hours or, as the case may be, months as may be prescribed in the regulations.

(13) Regulations under this section shall be made by statutory instrument.

(14) A statutory instrument containing regulations made under subsection (8) above shall be subject to annulment in pursuance of a resolution of either House of Parliament.

(15) No regulations shall be made under subsection (12) above unless a draft of the regulations has been laid before, and approved by a resolution of, each House of Parliament.]

Amendments (Textual)

F236. Ss. 245. A-245. I and preceding cross-heading inserted (20.10.1997 for specified purposes and 1.7.1998 otherwise) by 1997 c. 48, s. 5; S.I. 1997/2323, arts. 3, 5. (1), Sch. 1

F237. Words in s. 245. A(1) repealed (4.4.2005) by Antisocial Behaviour etc. (Scotland) Act 2004 (asp 8), ss. 121. (2), 145. (2); S.S.I. 2004/420, art. 3, Sch. 5

F238. Words in s. 245. A(1) inserted (27.6.2003) by Criminal Justice (Scotland) Act 2003 (asp 7), ss. 50. (3)(a), 89; S.S.I. 2003/288, art. 2, Sch.

F239. Words in s. 245. A(1) repealed (27.6.2003) by Criminal Justice (Scotland) Act 2003 (asp 7), ss. 50. (3)(b), 89; S.S.I. 2003/288, art. 2, Sch.

F240. Words in s. 245. A(1) inserted (27.6.2003) by Criminal Justice (Scotland) Act 2003 (asp 7), ss. 50. (3)(c), 89; S.S.I. 2003/288, art. 2, Sch.

F241. Words in s. 245. A(1) repealed (4.4.2005) by Antisocial Behaviour etc. (Scotland) Act 2004 (asp 8), ss. 144. (2), 145. (2), Sch. 5; S.S.I. 2004/420, art. 3, Sch. 5

F242. Words in s. 245. A(2) repealed (1.2.2011) by Criminal Justice and Licensing (Scotland) Act 2010 (asp 13), ss. 14. (2), 206. (1), Sch. 2 para. 21. (2); S.S.I. 2010/413, art. 2, Sch. (with art. 3)

F243. S. 245. A(2. A)(2. B) inserted (1.2.2011) by Criminal Justice and Licensing (Scotland) Act 2010 (asp 13), ss. 14. (2), 206. (1), Sch. 2 para. 21. (3); S.S.I. 2010/413, art. 2, Sch. (with art. 3)

F244. Words in s. 245. A(5)(a) renumbered as s. 245. A(5)(a)(i) (27.6.2003) by Criminal Justice (Scotland) Act 2003 (asp 7), ss. 43. (2)(a), 89; S.S.I. 2003/288, art. 2, Sch.

F245. S. 245. A(5)(a)(ii) and preceding word inserted (27.6.2003) by Criminal Justice (Scotland) Act 2003 (asp 7), ss. 43. (2)(b), 89; S.S.I. 2003/288, art. 2, Sch.

F246. Words in s. 245. A(6) renumbered (4.10.2004) as s. 245. (6)(a) by virtue of Criminal Procedure (Amendment) (Scotland) Act 2004 (asp 5), ss. 25, 27. (1), Sch. para. 35. (a); S.S.I. 2004/405, art. 2, Sch. 1 (with savings in arts. 3-5)

F247. Words in s. 245. A(6)(a) substituted (4.10.2004) by Criminal Procedure (Amendment) (Scotland) Act 2004 (asp 5, ss. 25, 27. (1), {Sch. para. 35. (b)}; S.S.I. 2004/405, art. 2, Sch. 1 (with savings in arts. 3-5)

F248. S. 245. A(6)(b) and preceding word inserted (4.10.2004) by Criminal Procedure (Amendment) (Scotland) Act 2004 (asp 5), ss. 25, 27. (1), Sch. para. 35. (c); S.S.I. 2004/405, art. 2, Sch. 1 (with savings in arts. 3-5)

F249. S. 245. A(9) repealed (1.4.2016) by Courts Reform (Scotland) Act 2014 (asp 18), s. 138.

(2), sch. 5 para. 39. (4); S.S.I. 2016/13, art. 2, sch. (with art. 3)

F250. S. 245. A(11. A) inserted (4.4.2005) by Antisocial Behaviour etc. (Scotland) Act 2004 (asp 8), ss. 121. (3), 145. (2); S.S.I. 2004/420, art. 3, Sch. 5

F251. Words in s. 245. A(12)(a) substituted (1.2.2011) by Criminal Justice and Licensing (Scotland) Act 2010 (asp 13), ss. 14. (2), 206. (1), Sch. 2 para. 21. (4); S.S.I. 2010/413, art. 2, Sch. (with art. 3)

[F252245. B Monitoring of restriction of liberty orders.S

(1) Where the Secretary of State, in regulations made under section 245. A(8) of this Act, empowers a court or a class of court to make restriction of liberty orders he shall notify the court or each of the courts concerned of the person or class or description of persons who may be designated by that court for the purpose of monitoring an offender's compliance with any such order.

(2) A court which makes a restriction of liberty order in respect of an offender shall include provision in the order for making a person notified by the Secretary of State under subsection (1) above, or a class or description of persons so notified, responsible for the monitoring of the offender's compliance with it.

(3) Where the Secretary of State changes the person or class or description of persons notified by him under subsection (1) above, any court which has made a restriction of liberty order shall, if necessary, vary the order accordingly and shall notify the variation to the offender.]

Amendments (Textual)

F252. Ss. 245. A-245. I and preceding cross-heading inserted (20.10.1997 for specified purposes and 1.7.1998 otherwise) by 1997 c. 48, s. 5; S.I. 1997/2323, arts. 3, 5. (1), Sch. 1

[F253245. C Remote monitoring.S

(1) The Secretary of State may make such arrangements, including contractual arrangements, as he considers appropriate with such persons, whether legal or natural, as he thinks fit for the remote monitoring of the compliance of offenders with restriction of liberty orders, and different arrangements may be made in relation to different areas or different forms of remote monitoring.

(2) A court making a restriction of liberty order which is to be monitored remotely may include in the order a requirement that the offender [F254—

   (a)] shall, either continuously or for such periods as may be specified, wear or carry a device for the purpose of enabling the remote monitoring of his compliance with the order to be carried out [F255, and

   (b) shall not tamper with or intentionally damage the device or knowingly allow it to be tampered with or intentionally damaged.]

(3) The Secretary of State shall by regulations specify devices which may be used for the purpose of remotely monitoring the compliance of an offender with the requirements of a restriction of liberty order.

(4) Regulations under this section shall be made by statutory instrument subject to annulment in pursuance of a resolution of either House of Parliament.]

Amendments (Textual)

F253. Ss. 245. A-245. I and preceding cross-heading inserted (20.10.1997 for specified purposes and 1.7.1998 otherwise) by 1997 c. 48, s. 5; S.I. 1997/2323, arts. 3, 5. (1), Sch. 1

F254. Words in s. 245. C(2) renumbered as s. 245. C(2)(a) (4.10.2004) by virtue of Criminal Procedure (Amendment) (Scotland) Act 2004 (asp 8), ss. 25, 27. (1), Sch. para. 36. (a); S.S.I. 2004/405, art. 2, Sch. 1 (with savings in arts. 3-5)

F255. S. 245. C(2)(b) and preceding word inserted (4.10.2004) by Criminal Procedure (Amendment) (Scotland) Act 2004 (asp 5), ss. 25, 27. (1), Sch. para. 36. (b); S.S.I. 2004/405, art. 2, Sch. 1 (with savings in arts. 3-5)

Modifications etc. (not altering text)

C26. S. 245. C applied (12.1.2004) by Criminal Justice (Scotland) Act 2003 (asp 7), ss. 40. (7), 89; S.S.I. 2003/475, art. 2, Sch.

S. 245. C applied (8.2.2006 for certain purposes and 3.7.2006 for certain further purposes, otherwise 21.3.2008) by Prisoners and Criminal Proceedings (Scotland) Act 1993 (1993 c. 9), s. 12. AB (as inserted by Management of Offenders etc. (Scotland) Act 2005 (asp 14), ss. 15. (10), 24); S.S.I. 2006/48, art. 3. (1), Sch. Pt. 1 (subject to art. 3. (3)); S.S.I. 2006/331, art. 3. (4) (subject to art. 3. (5)); S.S.I. 2008/21, art. 2

C27. S. 245. C applied (prosp.) by Custodial Sentences and Weapons (Scotland) Act 2007 (asp 17), ss. 49. (2), 67

C28. S. 245. C applied by 1997 c. 43, Sch. 1 para. 19. B (as inserted (1.2.2015) by Offender Rehabilitation Act 2014 (c. 11), s. 22. (1), Sch. 3 para. 7 (with Sch. 7 para. 2); S.I. 2015/40, art. 2. (u))

C29. S. 245. C(1)(3) modified (prosp.) by Criminal Justice Act 2003 (c. 44), ss. 188, 336, Sch. 11 para. 23

S. 245. C(1)(3) modified (4.4.2005) by Criminal Justice Act 2003 (c. 44), ss. 188, 336, Sch. 13 para. 21; S.I. 2005/950, art. 2. (1), Sch. 1

C30. S. 245. C(1)(3) modified (prosp.) by Criminal Justice Act 2003 (c. 44), ss. 188, 336, Sch. 11 para. 23

S. 245. C(1)(3) modified (4.4.2005) by Criminal Justice Act 2003 (c. 44), ss. 188, 336, Sch. 13 para. 21; S.I. 2005/950, art. 2. (1), Sch. 1

[F256245. D Combination of restriction of liberty order with other orders.S

(1) Subsection (3) applies where the court—

(a) intends to make a restriction of liberty order under section 245. A(1) of this Act; and

(b) considers it expedient that the offender should also be subject to

[F257. (i)in the case of an offender who is under 16 years of age,] a [F258community payback order imposed under section 227. A(1)] of this Act

[F259. (ii)in the case of an offender who is 16 years of age or more, a [F260community payback order imposed under section 227. A(1) of this Act or]] a drug treatment and testing order made under section 234. B(2) of this Act F261. . . .

(2) In deciding whether it is expedient to make a [F262community payback order] or a drug treatment and testing order by virtue of paragraph (b) of subsection (1) above, the court shall—

(a) have regard to the circumstances, including the nature of the offence and the character of the offender; and

(b) obtain a report as to the circumstances and character of the offender.

(3) Where this subsection applies, the court, notwithstanding sections F263. . . 234. B(2) and 245. A(1) of this Act, may make a restriction of liberty order and

[F264. (a)in the case of an offender who is under 16 years of age, a [F265community payback order];

(b) in the case of an offender who is 16 years of age or more,] [F266either a community payback order or] a drug treatment and testing order.

(4) Where the court makes a restriction of liberty order and a [F267community payback order] by virtue of subsection (3) above, the clerk of the court shall send a copy of each order to—

(a) any person responsible for monitoring the offender's compliance with the restriction of liberty order; and

[F268. (b)the local authority within whose area the offender will reside for the duration of each order.]

(5) Where the court makes a restriction of liberty order and a drug treatment and testing order by virtue of subsection (3) above, the clerk of the court shall send a copy of each order to—

(a) any person responsible for monitoring the offender's compliance with the restriction of liberty order;

(b) the treatment provider, within the meaning of section 234. C(1) of this Act; and

(c) the officer of the local authority who is appointed or assigned to be the supervising officer under section 234. C(6) of this Act.

(6) F269. . . . .

(7) Where the offender by an act or omission fails to comply with a requirement of an order made by virtue of subsection (3) above—

(a) if the failure relates to a requirement [F270imposed by a community payback order and is dealt with under section 227. ZC(7)(d)] of this Act, the court may, in addition, exercise the powers conferred by section F271. . . 245. F(2) of this Act in relation to the restriction of liberty order;

(b) if the failure relates to a requirement contained in a drug treatment and testing order and is dealt with under section F272. . . 245. F(2)(b) of this Act in relation to the restriction of liberty order; and

(c) if the failure relates to a requirement contained in a restriction of liberty order and is dealt with under section 245. F(2)(b) of this Act, the court may, in addition, exercise the powers conferred by section [F273227. ZC(7)(d) of this Act in relation to a community payback order] and by section 234. G(2)(b) of this Act in relation to a drug treatment and testing order to which, in either case, the offender is subject by virtue of subsection (3) above.

(8) In any case to which this subsection applies, the offender may, without prejudice to subsection (7) above, be dealt with as respects that case under section [F274227. ZC] or, as the case may be, section 234. G or section 245. F(2) of this Act but he shall not be liable to be otherwise dealt with as respects that case.

(9) Subsection (8) applies in a case where—

(a) the offender by an act or omission fails to comply with both a requirement contained in a restriction of liberty order and in a [F275community payback order] to which he is subject by virtue of subsection (3) above;

(b) the offender by an act or omission fails to comply with both a requirement contained in a restriction of liberty order and in a drug treatment and testing order to which he is subject by virtue of subsection (3) above;

(c) F276. . . . .]

Amendments (Textual)

F256. S. 245. D substituted (30.9.1998) by 1998 c. 37, s. 94. (2), Sch. 6 Pt. I para. 3; S.I. 1998/2327, art. 2. (1)(s)

F257. Words in s. 245. D(1)(b) inserted (4.4.2005) by Antisocial Behaviour etc. (Scotland) Act 2004 (asp 8), ss. 144. (1), 145. (2), Sch. 4 para. 5. (7)(a)(i); S.S.I. 2004/420, art. 3, Sch. 5

F258. Words in s. 245. D(1)(b)(i) substituted (1.2.2011) by Criminal Justice and Licensing (Scotland) Act 2010 (asp 13), ss. 14. (2), 206. (1), Sch. 2 para. 22. (2)(a); S.S.I. 2010/413, art. 2, Sch. (with art. 3)

F259. Words in s. 245. D(1)(b) substituted (4.4.2005) for words by Antisocial Behaviour etc. (Scotland) Act 2004 (asp 8), ss. 144. (1), 145. (2), Sch. 4 para. 5. (7)(a)(ii); S.S.I. 2004/420, art. 3, Sch. 5

F260. Words in s. 245. D(1)(b)(ii) substituted (1.2.2011) by Criminal Justice and Licensing (Scotland) Act 2010 (asp 13), ss. 14. (2), 206. (1), Sch. 2 para. 22. (2)(b)(i); S.S.I. 2010/413, art. 2, Sch. (with art. 3)

F261. Words in s. 245. D(1)(b)(ii) repealed (1.2.2011) by Criminal Justice and Licensing (Scotland) Act 2010 (asp 13), ss. 14. (2), 206. (1), Sch. 2 para. 22. (2)(b)(ii); S.S.I. 2010/413, art. 2, Sch. (with arts. 3-8)

F262. Words in s. 245. D(2) substituted (1.2.2011) by Criminal Justice and Licensing (Scotland) Act 2010 (asp 13), ss. 14. (2), 206. (1), Sch. 2 para. 22. (3); S.S.I. 2010/413, art. 2, Sch. (with art. 3)

F263. Words in s. 245. D(3) repealed (1.2.2011) by Criminal Justice and Licensing (Scotland) Act 2010 (asp 13), ss. 14. (2), 206. (1), Sch. 2 para. 22. (4)(a); S.S.I. 2010/413, art. 2, Sch. (with art. 3)

F264. Words in s. 245. D(3) inserted (4.4.2005) by Antisocial Behaviour etc. (Scotland) Act 2004 (asp 8), ss. 144. (1), 145. (2), Sch. 4 para. 5. (7)(b); S.S.I. 2004/420, art. 3, Sch. 5

F265. Words in s. 245. D(3)(a) substituted (1.2.2011) by Criminal Justice and Licensing (Scotland) Act 2010 (asp 13), ss. 14. (2), 206. (1), Sch. 2 para. 22. (4)(b); S.S.I. 2010/413, art. 2, Sch. (with art. 3)

F266. Words in s. 245. D(3)(b) substituted (1.2.2011) by Criminal Justice and Licensing (Scotland) Act 2010 (asp 13), ss. 14. (2), 206. (1), Sch. 2 para. 22. (4)(c); S.S.I. 2010/413, art. 2, Sch. (with art. 3)

F267. Words in s. 245. D(4) substituted (1.2.2011) by Criminal Justice and Licensing (Scotland) Act 2010 (asp 13), ss. 14. (2), 206. (1), Sch. 2 para. 22. (5)(a); S.S.I. 2010/413, art. 2, Sch. (with art. 3)

F268. S. 245. D(4)(b) substituted (1.2.2011) by Criminal Justice and Licensing (Scotland) Act 2010 (asp 13), ss. 14. (2), 206. (1), Sch. 2 para. 22. (5)(b); S.S.I. 2010/413, art. 2, Sch. (with art. 3)

F269. S. 245. D(6) repealed (1.2.2011) by Criminal Justice and Licensing (Scotland) Act 2010 (asp 13), ss. 14. (2), 206. (1), Sch. 2 para. 22. (6); S.S.I. 2010/413, art. 2, Sch. (with art. 3)

F270. Words in s. 245. D(7)(a) substituted (1.2.2011) by Criminal Justice and Licensing (Scotland) Act 2010 (asp 13), ss. 14. (2), 206. (1), Sch. 2 para. 22. (7)(a)(i); S.S.I. 2010/413, art. 2, Sch. (with art. 3)

F271. Words in s. 245. D(7)(a) repealed (1.2.2011) by Criminal Justice and Licensing (Scotland) Act 2010 (asp 13), ss. 14. (2), 206. (1), Sch. 2 para. 22. (7)(a)(ii); S.S.I. 2010/413, art. 2, Sch. (with art. 3)

F272. Words in s. 245. D(7)(b) repealed (1.2.2011) by Criminal Justice and Licensing (Scotland) Act 2010 (asp 13), ss. 14. (2), 206. (1), Sch. 2 para. 22. (7)(b); S.S.I. 2010/413, art. 2, Sch. (with art. 3)

F273. Words in s. 245. D(7)(c) substituted (1.2.2011) by Criminal Justice and Licensing (Scotland) Act 2010 (asp 13), ss. 14. (2), 206. (1), Sch. 2 para. 22. (7)(c); S.S.I. 2010/413, art. 2, Sch. (with art. 3)

F274. Words in s. 245. D(8) substituted (1.2.2011) by Criminal Justice and Licensing (Scotland) Act 2010 (asp 13), ss. 14. (2), 206. (1), Sch. 2 para. 22. (8); S.S.I. 2010/413, art. 2, Sch. (with art. 3)

F275. Words in s. 245. D(9)(a) substituted (1.2.2011) by Criminal Justice and Licensing (Scotland) Act 2010 (asp 13), ss. 14. (2), 206. (1), Sch. 2 para. 22. (9)(a); S.S.I. 2010/413, art. 2, Sch. (with art. 3)

F276. S. 245. D(9)(c) repealed (1.2.2011) by Criminal Justice and Licensing (Scotland) Act 2010 (asp 13), ss. 14. (2), 206. (1), Sch. 2 para. 22. (9)(b); S.S.I. 2010/413, art. 2, Sch. (with art. 3)

[F277245. E Variation of restriction of liberty order.S

(1) Where a restriction of liberty order is in force either the offender or any person responsible for monitoring his compliance with the order may

[F278. (a)][F279except in a case to which paragraph (b) below applies,] apply to the court which made the order [F280 or]

[F281. (b)where a copy of the order was, under section 245. A(5)(a)(ii) of this Act or subsection (7)(a) below, sent to the clerk of a different court, [F282apply] to that different court (or, if there has been more than one such sending, the different court to which such a copy has most recently been so sent),]

for a review of it.

(2) On an application made under subsection (1) above, and after hearing both the offender and any person responsible for monitoring his compliance with the order, the court may by order, if it appears to it to be in the interests of justice to do so—

(a) vary the order by—

(i) amending or deleting any of its requirements;

(ii) inserting further requirements; or

(iii) subject to subsection (3) of section 245. A of this Act, increasing the period for which the order has to run; or

(b) revoke the order.

(3) Where the court, on the application of a person other than the offender, proposes to—

(a) exercise the power conferred by paragraph (a) of subsection (2) above to vary (otherwise than by deleting a requirement) a restriction of liberty order, it shall issue a citation requiring the offender to appear before the court and section 245. A(4) shall apply to the variation of such an order as it applies to the making of an order; and

(b) exercise the power conferred by subsection (2)(b) above to revoke such an order and deal with the offender under section 245. G of this Act, it shall issue a citation requiring him to appear before the court.

[F283. (3. A)The unified citation provisions apply in relation to a citation under this section as they apply in relation to a citation under section 216. (3)(a) of this Act.]

(4) If an offender fails to appear before the court after having been cited in accordance with subsection (3) above, the court may issue a warrant for his arrest.

[F284. (4. A)Before varying a restriction of liberty order so as to require the offender to remain in a specified place or places or so as to specify a different place or different places in which the offender is to remain, the court shall—

(a) obtain and consider a report by an officer of a local authority about—

(i) the place or places proposed to be specified, and

(ii) the attitude of persons likely to be affected by any enforced presence there of the offender; and

(b) if it considers it necessary, hear the officer who prepared the report.]

[F285. (5)Where a reason for an application by the offender under subsection (1) above is that he proposes to reside in a place outwith the jurisdiction of the court to which that application is made, and the court is satisfied that suitable arrangements can be made, in the district where that place is, for monitoring his compliance with the order it may—

(a) vary the order to permit or make practicable such arrangements; and

(b) where the change in residence necessitates or makes desirable a change in who is designated for the purpose of such monitoring, vary the order accordingly.

(6) Before varying a restriction of liberty order for the reason mentioned in subsection (5) above, the court shall—

(a) if the order will require the offender to remain in a specified place or in specified places—

[F286. (i)] obtain and consider [F287a report by an officer of a local authority about the place or places proposed to be specified and] the attitude of persons likely to be affected by any enforced presence there of the offender; [F288 and

(ii) if it considers it necessary, hear the officer who prepared the report;] and

(b) satisfy itself that his compliance with that requirement can be monitored by the means of monitoring specified, or which it intends to specify, in the order.

(7) Where a restriction of liberty order is varied as is mentioned in subsection (5) above, the clerk of the court shall send a copy of the order as so varied to—

(a) the clerk of a court within whose jurisdiction the place of proposed residence is;

(b) the person who, immediately before the order was varied, was responsible for monitoring the person's compliance with it; and

(c) the person who, in consequence of the variation, is to have that responsibility.

(8) If, in relation to an application made for such reason as is mentioned in subsection (5) above, the court is not satisfied as is mentioned in that subsection, it may—

(a) refuse the application; or

(b) revoke the order.]]

Amendments (Textual)

F277. Ss. 245. A-245. I and preceding cross-heading inserted (20.10.1997 for specified purposes and 1.7.1998 otherwise) by 1997 c. 48, s. 5; S.I. 1997/2323, arts. 3, 5. (1), Sch. 1

F278. Words in s. 245. E(1) renumbered as s. 245. E(1)(a) (27.6.2003) by virtue of Criminal

Justice (Scotland) Act 2003 (asp 7), ss. 43. (3)(a)(i), 89; S.S.I. 2003/288, art. 2, Sch.

F279. Words in s. 245. E(1) inserted (27.6.2003) by Criminal Justice (Scotland) Act 2003 (asp 7), ss. 43. (3)(a)(i), 89; S.S.I. 2003/288, art. 2, Sch.

F280. Word in s. 245. E(1) inserted (27.6.2003) by Criminal Justice (Scotland) Act 2003 (asp 7), ss. 43. (3)(a)(ii), 89; S.S.I. 2003/288, art. 2, Sch.

F281. S. 245. E(1)(b) inserted (27.6.2003) by Criminal Justice (Scotland) Act 2003 (asp 7), ss. 43. (3)(a)(ii), 89; S.S.I. 2003/288, art. 2, Sch.

F282. Word in s. 245. E(1)(b) inserted (4.4.2005) by Antisocial Behaviour etc. (Scotland) Act 2004 (asp 8), ss. 144. (1), 145. (2), Sch. 4 para. 5. (8); S.S.I. 2004/420, art. 3, Sch. 5

F283. S. 245. E(3. A) inserted (27.10.2003) by virtue of Criminal Justice (Scotland) Act 2003 (asp 7), ss. 60. (1)(g), 89; S.S.I. 2003/475, art. 2, Sch.

F284. S. 245. E(4. A) inserted (4.10.2004) by Criminal Procedure (Amendment) (Scotland) Act 2004 (asp 5), ss. 25, 27. (1), Sch. para. 37. (a); S.S.I. 2004/405, art. 2, Sch. 1 (with savings in arts. 3-5)

F285. S. 245. E(5)-(8) added (27.6.2003) by Criminal Justice (Scotland) Act 2003 (asp 7), ss. 43. (3)(b), 89; S.S.I. 2003/288, art. 2, Sch.

F286. Words in s. 245. E(6)(a) renumbered (4.10.2004) as s. 245. E(6)(a)(i) by virtue of Criminal Procedure (Amendment) (Scotland) Act 2004 (asp 5), ss. 25, 27. (1), Sch. para. 37. (b)(i); S.S.I. 2004/405, art. 2, Sch. 1 (with savings in arts. 3-5)

F287. Words in s. 245. E(6)(a)(i) substituted (4.10.2004) by Criminal Procedure (Amendment) (Scotland) Act 2004 (asp 5), ss. 25, 27. (1), Sch. para. 37. (b)(ii); S.S.I. 2004/405, art. 2, Sch. 1 (with savings in arts. 3-5)

F288. S. 245. E(6)(a)(ii) and preceding word inserted (4.10.2004) by Criminal Procedure (Amendment) (Scotland) Act 2004 (asp 5), ss. 25, 27. (1), Sch. para. 37. (b)(iii); S.S.I. 2004/405, art. 2, Sch. 1 (with savings in arts. 3-5)

[F289245. F Breach of restriction of liberty order.S

(1) If at any time when a restriction of liberty order is in force it appears

[F290. (a)][F291except in a case to which paragraph (b) below applies,] to the court which made the order[F292 or]

[F293. (b)where a copy of the order was, under section 245. A(5)(a)(ii) or 245. E(7)(a) of this Act, sent to the clerk of a different court, to that different court (or, if there has been more than one such sending, the different court to which such a copy has most recently been so sent),]

that the offender has failed to comply with any of the requirements of the order the court [F294in question] may issue a citation requiring the offender to appear before [F295it] at such time as may be specified in the citation or, if it appears to [F296that court] to be appropriate, it may issue a warrant for the arrest of the offender.

[F297. (1. A)The unified citation provisions apply in relation to a citation under this section as they apply in relation to a citation under section 216. (3)(a) of this Act.]

(2) If it is proved to the satisfaction of [F298that court] that the offender has failed without reasonable excuse to comply with any of the requirements of the order [F299it] may by order—

(a) without prejudice to the continuance in force of the order, impose a fine not exceeding level 3 on the standard scale;

(b) vary the restriction of liberty order; or

(c) revoke that order.

[F300. (2. A)For the purposes of subsection (2) above, evidence of one witness shall be sufficient evidence.]

(3) A fine imposed under this section in respect of a failure to comply with the requirements of a restriction of liberty order shall be deemed for the purposes of any enactment to be a sum adjudged to be paid by or in respect of a conviction or a penalty imposed on a person summarily convicted.

(4) Where [F301a court] varies a restriction of liberty order under subsection (2) above it may do so in any of the ways mentioned in paragraph (a) of section 245. E(2) of this Act.]

Amendments (Textual)

F289. Ss. 245. A-245. I and preceding cross-heading inserted (20.10.1997 for specified purposes and 1.7.1998 otherwise) by 1997 c. 48, s. 5; S.I. 1997/2323, arts. 3, 5. (1), Sch. 1

F290. Words in s. 245. F(1) renumbered (27.6.2003) as s. 245. F(1)(a) by Criminal Justice (Scotland) Act 2003 (asp 7), ss. 43. (1)(a)(i), 89; S.S.I. 2003/288, art. 2, Sch.

F291. Words in s. 245. F(1) inserted (27.6.2003) by Criminal Justice (Scotland) Act 2003 (asp 7), ss. 43. (4)(a)(i), 89; S.S.I. 2003/288, art. 2, Sch.

F292. Word in s. 245. F(1) inserted (27.6.2003) by Criminal Justice (Scotland) Act 2003 (asp 7), ss. 43. (4)(a)(ii), 89; S.S.I. 2003/288, art. 2, Sch.

F293. S. 245. F(1)(b) inserted (27.6.2003) by Criminal Justice (Scotland) Act 2003 (asp 7), ss. 43. (4)(a)(ii), 89; S.S.I. 2003/288, art. 2, Sch.

F294. Words in s. 245. F(1) inserted (27.6.2003) by Criminal Justice (Scotland) Act 2003 (asp 7), ss. 43. (4)(a)(iii), 89; S.S.I. 2003/288, art. 2, Sch.

F295. Words in s. 245. F(1) substituted (27.6.2003) by Criminal Justice (Scotland) Act 2003 (asp 7), ss. 43. (4)(a)(iv), 89; S.S.I. 2003/288, art. 2, Sch.

F296. Words in s. 245. F(1) substituted (27.6.2003) by Criminal Justice (Scotland) Act 2003 (asp 7), ss. 43. (4)(a)(v), 89; S.S.I. 2003/288, art. 2, Sch.

F297. S. 245. F(1. A) inserted (27.10.2003) by virtue of Criminal Justice (Scotland) Act 2003 (asp 7), ss. 60. (1)(h), 89; S.S.I. 2003/475, art. 2, Sch.

F298. Words in s. 245. F(2) substituted (27.6.2003) by Criminal Justice (Scotland) Act 2003 (asp 7), ss. 43. (4)(b)(i), 89; S.S.I. 2003/288, art. 2, Sch.

F299. Words in s. 245. F(2) substituted (27.6.2003) by Criminal Justice (Scotland) Act 2003 (asp 7), ss. 43. (4)(b)(ii), 89; S.S.I. 2003/288, art. 2, Sch.

F300. S. 245. F(2. A) inserted (10.12.2007) by Criminal Proceedings etc. (Reform) (Scotland) Act 2007 (asp 6), ss. 58, 84; S.S.I. 2007/479, art. 3. (1), Sch. (subject to art. 13) (as amended by S.S.I. 2007/527)

F301. Words in s. 245. F(4) substituted (27.6.2003) by Criminal Justice (Scotland) Act 2003 (asp 7), ss. 43. (4)(c), 89; S.S.I. 2003/288, art. 2, Sch.

[F302245. G Disposal on revocation of restriction of liberty order.S

(1) Where the court revokes a restriction of liberty order under section 245. E(2)(b) or 245. F(2) of this Act, it may dispose of the offender in any way which would have been competent at the time when the order was made, but in so doing the court shall have regard to the time for which the order has been in operation.

(2) Where the court revokes a restriction of liberty order as mentioned in subsection (1) above, and the offender is, [F303in respect of the same offence, also subject to a community payback order or a drug treatment and testing order, by virtue of section 245. D(3), it shall before disposing of the offender under subsection (1) above, revoke the community payback order or drug treatment and testing order.]

[F304. (3)Where the court orders a [F305community payback order] or a drug treatment and testing order revoked the clerk of the court shall forthwith give copies of that order to the persons mentioned in subsection (4) or, as the case may be, (5) of section 245. D of this Act.

(4) F306. . . . .]]

Amendments (Textual)

F302. Ss. 245. A-245. I inserted (20.10.1997 for specified purposes and 1.7.1998 otherwise) by 1997 c. 48, s. 5; S.I. 1997/2323, arts. 3, 5. (1), Sch. 1

F303. Words in s. 245. G(2) substituted (1.2.2011) by Criminal Justice and Licensing (Scotland) Act 2010 (asp 13), ss. 14. (2), 206. (1), Sch. 2 para. 23. (2); S.S.I. 2010/413, art. 2, Sch. (with art.

3)

F304. S. 245. G(3)(4) added (30.9.1998) by 1998 c. 37, s. 94. (2), Sch. 6 Pt. I para. 4. (3); S.I. 1998/2327, art. 2. (1)(s)

F305. Words in s. 245. G(3) substituted (1.2.2011) by Criminal Justice and Licensing (Scotland) Act 2010 (asp 13), ss. 14. (2), 206. (1), Sch. 2 para. 23. (3); S.S.I. 2010/413, art. 2, Sch. (with art. 3)

F306. S. 245. G(4) repealed (1.2.2011) by Criminal Justice and Licensing (Scotland) Act 2010 (asp 13), ss. 14. (2), 206. (1), Sch. 2 para. 23. (4); S.S.I. 2010/413, art. 2, Sch. (with art. 3)

[F307245. H Documentary evidence in proceedings under section 245. F.S

(1) Evidence of the presence or absence of the offender at a particular place at a particular time may, subject to the provisions of this section, be given by the production of a document or documents bearing to be—

(a) a statement automatically produced by a device specified in regulations made under section 245. C of this Act, by which the offender's whereabouts were remotely monitored; and

(b) a certificate signed by a person nominated for the purpose of this paragraph by the Secretary of State that the statement relates to the whereabouts of the [F308offender] at the dates and times shown in the statement.

(2) The statement and certificate mentioned in subsection (1) above shall, when produced at a hearing, be sufficient evidence of the facts set out in them.

(3) Neither the statement nor the certificate mentioned in subsection (1) above shall be admissible in evidence unless a copy of both has been served on the offender prior to the hearing and, without prejudice to the foregoing, where it appears to the court that the offender has had insufficient notice of the statement or certificate, it may adjourn a hearing or make any order which it thinks appropriate in the circumstances.]

Amendments (Textual)

F307. Ss. 245. A-245. I and preceding cross-heading inserted (20.10.1997 for specified purposes and 1.7.1998 otherwise) by 1997 c. 48, s. 5; S.I. 1997/2323, arts. 3, 5. (1), Sch. 1

F308. Word in s. 245. H substituted (4.4.2005) by Antisocial Behaviour etc. (Scotland) Act 2004 (asp 8), ss. 144. (1), 145. (2), Sch. 4 para. 5. (10); S.S.I. 2004/420, art. 3, Sch. 5

Modifications etc. (not altering text)

C31. S. 245. H applied (4.4.2005) by Criminal Justice Act 2003 (c. 44), ss. 194, 336, Sch. 13 para. 14. (5); S.I. 2005/950, art. 2. (1), Sch. 1

[F309245. I Procedure on variation or revocation of restriction of liberty order.S

Where a court exercises any power conferred by sections 232. (3. A), 245. E(2) or 245. F(2)(b) or (c) of this Act, the clerk of the court shall forthwith give copies of the order varying or revoking the restriction of liberty order to any person responsible for monitoring the offender's compliance with that order and that person shall give a copy of the order to the offender.]

Amendments (Textual)

F309. Ss. 245. A-245. I and preceding cross-heading inserted (20.10.1997 for specified purposes and 1.7.1998 otherwise) by 1997 c. 48, s. 5; S.I. 1997/2323, arts. 3, 5. (1), Sch. 1

[F310245. J[F310. Breach of certain orders: adjourning hearing and remanding in custody etc.]S

(1) Where [F311an] offender appears before the court in respect of his apparent failure to comply with a requirement of, as the case may be, a [F312community payback order], drug treatment and testing order, F313. . . or restriction of liberty order the court may, for the purpose of enabling inquiries to be made or of determining the most suitable method of dealing with him, adjourn the hearing.

(2) Where, under subsection (1) above, the court adjourns a hearing it shall remand the F314. . . offender in custody or on bail or ordain him to appear at the adjourned hearing.

(3) A court shall not so adjourn a hearing for any single period exceeding four weeks or, on cause shown, eight weeks.

(4) [F315. An] offender remanded under this section may appeal against the refusal of bail, or against the conditions imposed, within 24 hours of his remand.

(5) Any such appeal shall be [F316to the [F317appropriate Appeal Court] by note of appeal, and the [F317appropriate Appeal Court]], either in court or in chambers, may after hearing F318. . . the appellant—

    (a) review the order appealed against and either grant bail on such conditions as it thinks fit or ordain the appellant to appear at the adjourned hearing; or

    (b) confirm the order.

[F319. (6)A note of appeal under subsection (5) above is to be—

    (a) lodged with the clerk of the court from which the appeal is to be taken; and

    (b) sent without delay by that clerk (where not the [F320clerk of the appropriate Appeal Court]) to the [F320clerk of the appropriate Appeal Court].]

[F321. (7)In this section—

"appropriate Appeal Court" means—

    - in the case of an appeal under subsection (4) against a decision of the High Court, that Court;

    - in the case of an appeal under subsection (4) against a decision of a sheriff (whether in solemn or summary proceedings) or a JP court, the Sheriff Appeal Court; and

"the clerk of the appropriate Appeal Court" means—

    - in a case where the High Court is the appropriate Appeal Court, the Clerk of Justiciary;

    - in a case where the Sheriff Appeal Court is the appropriate Appeal Court, the Clerk of that Court.]]

Amendments (Textual)

F310. S. 245. J inserted (27.6.2003) by Criminal Justice (Scotland) Act 2003 (asp 7), ss. 48, 89; S.S.I. 2003/288, art. 2, Sch.

F311. Words in s. 245. J(1) substituted (1.2.2011) by Criminal Justice and Licensing (Scotland) Act 2010 (asp 13), ss. 14. (2), 206. (1), Sch. 2 para. 24. (a)(i); S.S.I. 2010/413, art. 2, Sch. (with art. 3)

F312. Words in s. 245. J(1) substituted (1.2.2011) by Criminal Justice and Licensing (Scotland) Act 2010 (asp 13), ss. 14. (2), 206. (1), Sch. 2 para. 24. (a)(ii); S.S.I. 2010/413, art. 2, Sch. (with arts. 3-8)

F313. Words in s. 245. J(1) repealed (1.2.2011) by Criminal Justice and Licensing (Scotland) Act 2010 (asp 13), ss. 14. (2), 206. (1), Sch. 2 para. 24. (a)(iii); S.S.I. 2010/413, art. 2, Sch. (with arts. 3-8)

F314. Words in s. 245. J(2) repealed (1.2.2011) by Criminal Justice and Licensing (Scotland) Act 2010 (asp 13), ss. 14. (2), 206. (1), Sch. 2 para. 24. (b); S.S.I. 2010/413, art. 2, Sch. (with art. 3)

F315. Words in s. 245. J(4) substituted (1.2.2011) by Criminal Justice and Licensing (Scotland) Act 2010 (asp 13), ss. 14. (2), 206. (1), Sch. 2 para. 24. (c); S.S.I. 2010/413, art. 2, Sch. (with art. 3)

F316. Words in s. 245. J(5) substituted (10.12.2007) by Criminal Proceedings etc. (Reform) (Scotland) Act 2007 (asp 6), ss. 6. (6)(a), 84; S.S.I. 2007/479, art. 3. (1), Sch. (as amended by S.S.I. 2007/527)

F317. Words in s. 245. J(5) substituted (22.9.2015) by The Courts Reform (Scotland) Act 2014 (Consequential Provisions No. 2) Order 2015 (S.S.I. 2015/338), art. 1, sch. 2 para. 5. (8)(a) (with art. 4)

F318. Words in s. 245. J(5) repealed (10.12.2007) by Criminal Proceedings etc. (Reform) (Scotland) Act 2007 (asp 6), ss. 80, 84, Sch. para. 21; S.S.I. 2007/479, art. 3. (1), Sch. (as amended by S.S.I. 2007/527)

F319. S. 245. J(6) added (10.12.2007) by Criminal Proceedings etc. (Reform) (Scotland) Act 2007 (asp 6), ss. 6. (6)(b), 84; S.S.I. 2007/479, art. 3. (1), Sch. (as amended by S.S.I. 2007/527)

F320. Words in s. 245. J(6)(b) substituted (22.9.2015) by The Courts Reform (Scotland) Act 2014 (Consequential Provisions No. 2) Order 2015 (S.S.I. 2015/338), art. 1, sch. 2 para. 5. (8)(b) (with art. 4)

F321. S. 245. J(7) inserted (22.9.2015) by The Courts Reform (Scotland) Act 2014 (Consequential Provisions No. 2) Order 2015 (S.S.I. 2015/338), art. 1, sch. 2 para. 5. (8)(c) (with art. 4)

[F322. Community reparation ordersS

Amendments (Textual)
F322. Ss. 245. K-245. Q and preceding cross-heading inserted (28.10.2004) by Antisocial Behaviour etc. (Scotland) Act 2004 (asp 8), ss. 120, 145. (2); S.S.I. 2004/420, art. 3, Sch. 1

245. KCommunity reparation ordersS

F323. . . . .
Amendments (Textual)
F323. Ss. 245. K-245. Q repealed (1.2.2011) by Criminal Justice and Licensing (Scotland) Act 2010 (asp 13), ss. 14. (2), 206. (1), Sch. 2 para. 25; S.S.I. 2010/413, art. 2, Sch. (with art. 3)

245. LCommunity reparation order: notificationS

F324. . . . .
Amendments (Textual)
F324. Ss. 245. K-245. Q repealed (1.2.2011) by Criminal Justice and Licensing (Scotland) Act 2010 (asp 13), ss. 14. (2), 206. (1), Sch. 2 para. 25; S.S.I. 2010/413, art. 2, Sch. (with art. 3)

245. MFailure to comply with community reparation order: extension of 12 month periodS

F325. . . . .
Amendments (Textual)
F325. Ss. 245. K-245. Q repealed (1.2.2011) by Criminal Justice and Licensing (Scotland) Act 2010 (asp 13), ss. 14. (2), 206. (1), Sch. 2 para. 25; S.S.I. 2010/413, art. 2, Sch. (with art. 3)

245. NFailure to comply with community reparation order: powers of courtS

F326. . . . .
Amendments (Textual)
F326. Ss. 245. K-245. Q repealed (1.2.2011) by Criminal Justice and Licensing (Scotland) Act 2010 (asp 13), ss. 14. (2), 206. (1), Sch. 2 para. 25; S.S.I. 2010/413, art. 2, Sch. (with art. 3)

245. PExtension, variation and revocation of orderS

F327. . . . .

F327. Ss. 245. K-245. Q repealed (1.2.2011) by Criminal Justice and Licensing (Scotland) Act 2010 (asp 13), ss. 14. (2), 206. (1), Sch. 2 para. 25; S.S.I. 2010/413, art. 2, Sch. (with art. 3)

245. QSections 245. L, 245. N and 245. P: meaning of "appropriate court"S

F328. . . . .]

F328. Ss. 245. K-245. Q repealed (1.2.2011) by Criminal Justice and Licensing (Scotland) Act 2010 (asp 13), ss. 14. (2), 206. (1), Sch. 2 para. 25; S.S.I. 2010/413, art. 2, Sch. (with art. 3)

Admonition and absolute dischargeS

246 Admonition and absolute discharge.S

(1) [F329. Subject to sections 205. A and 205. B of this Act,] a court may, if it appears to meet the justice of the case, dismiss with an admonition any person convicted by the court of any offence.
(2) Where a person is convicted on indictment of an offence (other than an offence the sentence for which is fixed by law), if it appears to the court, having regard to the circumstances including the nature of the offence and the character of the offender, that it is inexpedient to inflict punishment F330. . . it may instead of sentencing him make an order discharging him absolutely.
(3) Where a person is charged before a court of summary jurisdiction with an offence (other than an offence the sentence for which is fixed by law) and the court is satisfied that he committed the offence, the court, if it is of the opinion, having regard to the circumstances including the nature of the offence and the character of the offender, that it is inexpedient to inflict punishment F330. . . may without proceeding to conviction make an order discharging him absolutely.

F329. Words in s. 246. (1) inserted (20.10.1997 for specified purposes and otherwise prosp.) by 1997 c. 48, ss. 62. (1), 65. (2), Sch. 1 para. 21. (31); S.I. 1997/2323, art. 3, Sch. 1
F330. Words in s. 246. (2)(3) repealed (1.2.2011) by Criminal Justice and Licensing (Scotland) Act 2010 (asp 13), ss. 14. (2), 206. (1), Sch. 2 para. 26; S.S.I. 2010/413, art. 2, Sch. (with art. 3)
Modifications etc. (not altering text)
C32. Ss. 246, 247 excluded by 2007 c. 27, s. 36. A(5)(6) (as inserted (1.3.2016) by Serious Crime Act 2015 (c. 9), s. 88. (1), Sch. 1 para. 25; S.I. 2016/148, reg. 3. (f))
C33. S. 246 excluded (26.5.2016) by Psychoactive Substances Act 2016 (c. 2), ss. 32. (6)(b), 63. (2); S.I. 2016/553, reg. 2
C34. S. 246. (1)(2) restricted (1.4.1996) by 1995 c. 40, ss. 4, 7. (2), Sch. 3 Pt. II para. 9

247 Effect of probation and absolute discharge.S

(1) Subject to the following provisions of this section, a conviction of an offence for which an order is made [F331discharging the offender] absolutely shall be deemed not to be a conviction for any purpose other than the purposes of the proceedings in which the order is made and of laying it before a court as a previous conviction in subsequent proceedings for another offence.
(2) Without prejudice to subsection (1) above, the conviction of an offender who is F332... discharged absolutely as aforesaid shall in any event be disregarded for the purposes of any enactment which imposes any disqualification or disability upon convicted persons, or authorises or requires the imposition of any such disqualification or disability.

(3) Subsections (1) and (2) above shall not affect any right to appeal.

(4) Where a person charged with an offence has at any time previously been discharged absolutely in respect of the commission by him of an offence it shall be competent, in the proceedings for that offence, to lay before the court the order of absolute discharge in like manner as if the order were a conviction.

(5) Where an offender is discharged absolutely by a court of summary jurisdiction, he shall have the like right of appeal against the finding that he committed the offence as if that finding were a conviction.

F333. (6). . . . .

Amendments (Textual)

F331. Words in s. 247. (1) substituted (28.3.2011) by Criminal Justice and Licensing (Scotland) Act 2010 (asp 13), s. 206. (1), sch. 7 para. 59. (a); S.S.I. 2011/178, art. 2, sch.

F332. Words in s. 247. (2) repealed (28.3.2011) by Criminal Justice and Licensing (Scotland) Act 2010 (asp 13), s. 206. (1), sch. 7 para. 59. (b); S.S.I. 2011/178, art. 2, sch.

F333. S. 247. (6) repealed (28.3.2011) by Criminal Justice and Licensing (Scotland) Act 2010 (asp 13), s. 206. (1), sch. 7 para. 59. (c); S.S.I. 2011/178, art. 2, sch.

Modifications etc. (not altering text)

C32. Ss. 246, 247 excluded by 2007 c. 27, s. 36. A(5)(6) (as inserted (1.3.2016) by Serious Crime Act 2015 (c. 9), s. 88. (1), Sch. 1 para. 25; S.I. 2016/148, reg. 3. (f))

C35. S. 247 excluded (26.5.2016) by Psychoactive Substances Act 2016 (c. 2), ss. 32. (6)(b), 63. (2); S.I. 2016/553, reg. 2

C36. S. 247. (1) excluded (1.5.2004) by Sexual Offences Act 2003 (c. 42), ss. 134. (1)(c), 141 (with s. 134. (2)(3)); S.S.I. 2004/138, art. 2

C37. S. 247. (1)(2) excluded (6.4.2010) by Coroners and Justice Act 2009 (c. 25), ss. 158. (3)(c), 182 (with s. 180); S.I. 2010/816, art. 2, Sch. para. 11

C38. S. 247. (1)(2) excluded by 2005 asp 16 s. 129. (5) (as inserted (28.3.2011) by Criminal Justice and Licensing (Scotland) Act 2010 (asp 13), ss. 24. (5), 206. (1); S.S.I. 2011/178, art. 2, sch.)

C39. S. 247. (1) excluded by 2005 asp 16 s. 96. (2. A) (as inserted (28.3.2011) by Criminal Justice and Licensing (Scotland) Act 2010 (asp 13), ss. 24. (4), 206. (1); S.S.I. 2011/178, art. 2, sch.)

C40. S. 247. (1) excluded (28.11.2011) by Double Jeopardy (Scotland) Act 2011 (asp 16), ss. 1. (1)(4)(a), 17. (3) (with s. 14); S.S.I. 2011/365, art. 3

DisqualificationS

248 Disqualification where vehicle used to commit offence.S

(1) Where a person is convicted of an offence (other than one triable only summarily) and the court which passes sentence is satisfied that a motor vehicle was used for the purposes of committing or facilitating the commission of that offence, the court may order him to be disqualified for such a period as the court thinks fit from holding or obtaining a licence to drive a motor vehicle granted under Part III of the M28. Road Traffic Act 1988.

[F334. (2)A court which makes an order under subsection (1) above disqualifying a person from holding or obtaining a licence under Part III of the Road Traffic Act 1988 shall require him to produce—

(a) any such licence;

(b) any Community licence (within the meaning of that Part); and

(c) any counterpart of a licence mentioned in paragraph (a) or (b) above,

held by him.]

(3) Any reference in this section to facilitating the commission of an offence shall include a reference to the taking of any steps after it has been committed for the purpose of disposing of any

property to which it relates or of avoiding apprehension or detection.

(4) In relation to licences [F335, other than Community licences] which came into force before 1st June 1990, the reference in subsection (2) above to the counterpart of a licence shall be disregarded.

Amendments (Textual)

F334. S. 248. (2) substituted (1.1.1997) by S.I. 1996/1974, reg. 5, Sch. 4 para. 6. (2)

F335. Words in s. 248. (4) inserted (1.1.1997) by 1996/1974, reg. 5, Sch. 4 para. 6. (3)

Marginal Citations

M281988 c.52.

[F336248. A General power to disqualify offenders.S

(1) Subject to subsection (2) below, the court by or before which a person is convicted of an offence may, in addition to or instead of dealing with him in any other way, order him to be disqualified from holding or obtaining a licence to drive a motor vehicle granted under Part III of the M29. Road Traffic Act 1988 for such period as it thinks fit.

(2) Where the person is convicted of an offence for which the sentence is fixed by law, subsection (1) above shall have effect as if the words "or instead of" were omitted.

(3) Subsections (2) and (4) of section 248 of this Act shall apply for the purposes of this section as they apply for the purposes of that section.]

Amendments (Textual)

F336. Ss. 248. A-248. C inserted (20.10.1997 for specified purposes and otherwise 1.1.1998) by 1997 c. 48, s. 15. (1); S.I. 1997/2323, arts. 3, 4, Schs. 1, 2

Marginal Citations

M291988 c.52.

[F337248. B Power to disqualify fine defaulters.S

(1) This section applies where the court has power to impose a period of imprisonment in default of payment of a fine, or any part or instalment of a fine.

(2) Where this section applies, the court may, instead of imposing such a period of imprisonment as is mentioned in subsection (1) above, order that where the offender is in default he shall be disqualified from holding a licence to drive a motor vehicle granted under Part III of the Road Traffic Act 1988 for such period not exceeding twelve months as the court thinks fit.

(3) Where an order has been made under subsection (2) above in default of payment of any fine, or any part or instalment of a fine—

(a) on payment of the fine to any person authorised to receive it, the order shall cease to have effect; and

(b) on payment of any part of that fine to any such person, the period of disqualification to which the order relates shall be reduced (or, as the case may be, further reduced) by a number of days bearing as nearly as possible the same proportion to such period as the sum so paid bears to the amount of the fine outstanding at the commencement of that period.

(4) Subsections (2) and (4) of section 248 of this Act shall apply for the purposes of this section as they apply for the purposes of that section.

(5) Section 19 of the M30. Road Traffic Offenders Act 1988 (proof of disqualification in Scottish proceedings) shall apply to an order under subsection (2) above as it applies to a conviction or extract conviction.

(6) The Secretary of State may by order made by statutory instrument vary the period specified in subsection (2) above; but no such order shall be made unless a draft of the order has been laid before, and approved by a resolution of, each House of Parliament.]

Amendments (Textual)

F337. Ss. 248. A-248. C inserted (20.10.1997 for specified purposes and otherwise 1.1.1998) by

1997 c. 48, s. 15. (1); S.I. 1997/2323, arts. 3, 4, Schs. 1, 2
Marginal Citations
M301988 c.53.

[F338248. C Application of sections 248. A and 248. B.S

(1) The Secretary of State may by order prescribe which courts, or class or classes of courts, may make orders under section 248. A or 248. B of this Act F339....

(2) An order made under subsection (1) above shall be made by statutory instrument and any such instrument shall be subject to annulment in pursuance of a resolution of either House of Parliament.

(3) Where an order has been made under subsection (1) above, section 248. (1) of this Act shall not apply as respects any court, or class or classes of court prescribed by the order.]

Amendments (Textual)

F338. Ss. 248. A-248. C inserted (20.10.1997 for specified purposes and otherwise 1.1.1998) by 1997 c. 48, s. 15. (1); S.I. 1997/2323, arts. 3, 4, Schs. 1, 2

F339. Words in s. 248. C(1) repealed (1.4.2016) by Courts Reform (Scotland) Act 2014 (asp 18), s. 138. (2), sch. 5 para. 39. (5); S.S.I. 2016/13, art. 2, sch. (with art. 3)

Compensation

249 Compensation order against convicted person.S

(1) [F340. Where] a person is convicted of an offence the court, instead of or in addition to dealing with him in any other way, may make an order (in this Part of this Act referred to as "a compensation order") requiring him to pay compensation [F341in favour of the victim] for [F342 any—

(a) personal injury, loss or damage caused directly or indirectly; or

(b) alarm or distress caused directly,

to the victim.]

[F343. (1. A) For the purposes of subsection (1) above, "victim" means—

(a) a person against whom; or

(b) a person against whose property,

the acts which constituted the offence were directed.]

[F344. (1. B)Where a person is convicted of an offence, the court may (instead of or in addition to dealing with the person in any other way), in accordance with subsections (3. A) to (3. C), make a compensation order requiring the convicted person to pay compensation in favour of—

(a) the victim, or

(b) a person who is liable for funeral expenses in respect of which subsection (3. C)(b) allows a compensation order to be made.

(1. C) For the purposes of subsection (1. B)(a), "victim" means—

(a) a person who has suffered personal injury, loss or damage in respect of which a compensation order may be made by virtue of subsection (3. A), or

(b) a relative (as defined in Schedule 1 to the Damages (Scotland) Act 1976 (c.13)) who has suffered bereavement in respect of which subsection (3. C)(a) allows a compensation order to be made.]

(2) It shall not be competent for a court to make a compensation order—

(a) where, under section 246. (2) of this Act, it makes an order discharging him absolutely;

[F345. (ab)where, under section 227. A of this Act, it imposes a community payback order;]

(c) at the same time as, under section 202 of this Act, it defers sentence.

(3) Where, in the case of an offence involving dishonest appropriation, or the unlawful taking and using of property or a contravention of section 178. (1) of the M31. Road Traffic Act 1988 (taking motor vehicle without authority etc.) the property is recovered, but has been damaged while out of the owner's possession, that damage, however and by whomsoever it was in fact caused, shall be treated for the purposes of subsection (1) above as having been caused by the acts which constituted the offence.

[F346. (3. A)A compensation order may be made in respect of personal injury, loss or damage (apart from loss suffered by a person's dependents in consequence of a person's death) that was caused directly or indirectly by an accident arising out of the presence of a motor vehicle on a road if—

(a) it was being used in contravention of section 143. (1) of the Road Traffic Act 1988 (c.52), and

(b) no compensation is payable under arrangements to which the Secretary of State is a party.

(3. B)Where a compensation order is made by virtue of subsection (3) or (3. A), the order may include an amount representing the whole or part of any loss of (including reduction in) preferential rates of insurance if the loss is attributable to the accident.

(3. C)A compensation order may be made—

(a) for bereavement in connection with a person's death resulting from the acts which constituted the offence,

(b) for funeral expenses in connection with such a death,

except where the death was due to an accident arising out of the presence of a motor vehicle on a road.]

(4) [F347. Unless (and to the extent that) subsections (3) to (3. C) allow a compensation order to be made, no] compensation order shall be made in respect of—

(a) loss suffered in consequence of the death of any person; or

(b) injury, loss or damage due to an accident arising out of the presence of a motor vehicle on a road F348....

(5) In determining whether to make a compensation order against any person, and in determining the amount to be paid by any person under such order, the court shall take into consideration his means so far as known to the court.

F349. (6). . . . .

(7) In solemn proceedings there shall be no limit on the amount which may be awarded under a compensation order.

(8) In summary proceedings—

(a) a sheriff F350... F351. . . , shall have power to make a compensation order awarding in respect of each offence an amount not exceeding the prescribed sum;

(b) a judge of a [F352. JP court] F353... shall have power to make a compensation order awarding in respect of each offence an amount not exceeding level 4 on the standard scale.

[F354. (8. A)In summary proceedings before the sheriff, where the fine or maximum fine to which a person is liable on summary conviction of an offence exceeds the prescribed sum, the sheriff may make a compensation order awarding in respect of the offence an amount not exceeding the amount of the fine to which the person is so liable.]

(9) Payment of any amount under a compensation order shall be made to the clerk of the court who shall account for the amount to the person entitled thereto.

(10) Only the court shall have power to enforce a compensation order.

[F355. (11)This section is subject to section 34 of the Regulatory Reform (Scotland) Act 2014.]

Amendments (Textual)

F340. Word in s. 249. (1) substituted (28.3.2011) by Criminal Justice and Licensing (Scotland) Act 2010 (asp 13), ss. 115. (1)(a)(i), 206. (1); S.S.I. 2011/178, art. 2, sch.

F341. Word in s. 249. (1) inserted (28.3.2011) by Criminal Justice and Licensing (Scotland) Act 2010 (asp 13), ss. 115. (1)(a)(ii), 206. (1); S.S.I. 2011/178, art. 2, sch.

F342. Words in s. 249. (1) substituted (10.3.2008) by Criminal Proceedings etc. (Reform) (Scotland) Act 2007 (asp 6), ss. 49. (1)(a), 84; S.S.I. 2008/42, art. 3, Sch.

F343. S. 249. (1. A) inserted (10.3.2008) by Criminal Proceedings etc. (Reform) (Scotland) Act 2007 (asp 6), ss. 49. (1)(b), 84; S.S.I. 2008/42, art. 3, Sch.

F344. S. 249. (1. B)(1. C) inserted (28.3.2011) by Criminal Justice and Licensing (Scotland) Act 2010 (asp 13), ss. 115. (1)(b), 206. (1); S.S.I. 2011/178, art. 2, sch.

F345. S. 249. (2)(ab) substituted (1.2.2011) by Criminal Justice and Licensing (Scotland) Act 2010 (asp 13), ss. 14. (2), 206. (1), Sch. 2 para. 27; S.S.I. 2010/413, art. 2, Sch. (with art. 3)

F346. S. 249. (3. A)-(3. C) inserted (28.3.2011) by Criminal Justice and Licensing (Scotland) Act 2010 (asp 13), ss. 115. (1)(c), 206. (1); S.S.I. 2011/178, art. 2, sch.

F347. Words in s. 249. (4) substituted (28.3.2011) by Criminal Justice and Licensing (Scotland) Act 2010 (asp 13), ss. 115. (1)(d)(i), 206. (1); S.S.I. 2011/178, art. 2, sch.

F348. Words in s. 249. (4)(b) repealed (28.3.2011) by Criminal Justice and Licensing (Scotland) Act 2010 (asp 13), ss. 115. (1)(d)(ii), 206. (1); S.S.I. 2011/178, art. 2, sch.

F349. S. 249. (6) repealed (28.3.2011) by Criminal Justice and Licensing (Scotland) Act 2010 (asp 13), ss. 115. (1)(e), 206. (1); S.S.I. 2011/178, art. 2, sch.

F350. Words in s. 249. (8)(a) repealed (1.4.2016) by Courts Reform (Scotland) Act 2014 (asp 18), s. 138. (2), sch. 5 para. 39. (6)(a); S.S.I. 2016/13, art. 2, sch. (with art. 3)

F351. Words in s. 249. (8)(a) repealed(10.3.2008, 2.6.2008, 8.12.2008, 23.2.2009, 14.12.2009 for certain purposes, otherwise 22.2.2010) by Criminal Proceedings etc. (Reform) (Scotland) Act 2007 (asp 6), ss. 80, 84, Sch. para. 22. (a); S.S.I. 2008/42, art. 3, Sch.; S.S.I. 2008/192, art. 3, Sch.; S.S.I. 2008/329, art. 3, Sch.; S.S.I. 2008/362, art. 3, Sch.; S.S.I. 2009/432, art. 3, Schs. 1, 2

F352. Words in s. 249. (8)(b) substituted (10.3.2008, 2.6.2008, 8.12.2008, 23.2.2009 and 14.12.2009, otherwise 22.2.2010) by Criminal Proceedings etc. (Reform) (Scotland) Act 2007 (asp 6), ss. 80, 84, Sch. para. 26. (p); S.S.I. 2008/42, art. 3, Sch.; S.S.I. 2008/192, art. 3, Sch.; S.S.I. 2008/329, art. 3, Sch.; S.S.I. 2008/362, art. 3, Sch.; S.S.I. 2009/432, art. 3, Schs. 1, 2

F353. Words in s. 249. (8)(b) repealed (1.4.2016) by Courts Reform (Scotland) Act 2014 (asp 18), s. 138. (2), sch. 5 para. 39. (6)(b); S.S.I. 2016/13, art. 2, sch. (with art. 3)

F354. S. 249. (8. A) inserted (28.3.2011) by Criminal Justice and Licensing (Scotland) Act 2010 (asp 13), ss. 115. (1)(f), 206. (1); S.S.I. 2011/178, art. 2, sch.

F355. S. 249. (11) added (30.6.2014) by Regulatory Reform (Scotland) Act 2014 (asp 3), s. 61. (2), sch. 3 para. 12; S.S.I. 2014/160, art. 2. (1)(2), sch.

Modifications etc. (not altering text)

C41. S. 249 modified (30.6.2014) by Regulatory Reform (Scotland) Act 2014 (asp 3), ss. 34, 61. (2); S.S.I. 2014/160, art. 2. (1)(2), sch.

Marginal Citations

M311988 c.52.

250 Compensation orders: supplementary provisions.S

(1) Where a court considers that in respect of an offence it would be appropriate to impose a fine and to make a compensation order but the convicted person has insufficient means to pay both an appropriate fine and an appropriate amount in compensation the court should prefer a compensation order.

(2) Where a convicted person has both been fined and had a compensation order made against him in respect of the same offence or different offences in the same proceedings, a payment by the convicted person shall first be applied in satisfaction of the compensation order.

(3) For the purposes of any appeal or review, a compensation order is a sentence.

(4) Where a compensation order has been made against a person, a payment made to the court in respect of the order shall be retained until the determination of any appeal in relation to the order.

251 Review of compensation order.S

(1) Without prejudice to the power contained in section 213 of this Act, (as applied by section 252

of this Act), at any time before a compensation order has been complied with or fully complied with, the court, on the application of the person against whom the compensation order was made, may discharge the compensation order or reduce the amount that remains to be paid if it appears to the court that—

F356. (a). . . . .

(b) that property the loss of which is reflected in the compensation order has been recovered.
[F357. (1. A)On the application of the prosecutor at any time before a compensation order has been complied with (or fully complied with), the court may increase the amount payable under the compensation order if it is satisfied that the person against whom it was made—

(a) because of the availability of materially different information about financial circumstances, has more means than were made known to the court when the order was made, or

(b) because of a material change of financial circumstances, has more means than the person had then.]

(2) In subsection (1) above "the court" means—

(a) in a case where, as respects the compensation order, a transfer of fine order under section 222 of this Act (as applied by the said section 252) is effective and the court by which the compensation order is enforceable is in terms of the transfer of fine order a court of summary jurisdiction in Scotland, that court; or

(b) in any other case, the court which made the compensation order or, where that court was the High Court, by which the order was first enforceable.

Amendments (Textual)

F356. S. 251. (1)(a) repealed (28.3.2011) by Criminal Justice and Licensing (Scotland) Act 2010 (asp 13), ss. 115. (2)(a), 206. (1); S.S.I. 2011/178, art. 2, sch.

F357. S. 251. (1. A) inserted (28.3.2011) by Criminal Justice and Licensing (Scotland) Act 2010 (asp 13), ss. 115. (2)(b), 206. (1); S.S.I. 2011/178, art. 2, sch.

252 Enforcement of compensation orders: application of provisions relating to fines.

(1) The provisions of this Act specified in subsection (2) below shall, subject to any necessary modifications and to the qualifications mentioned in that subsection, apply in relation to compensation orders as they apply in relation to fines; and section 91 of the M32. Magistrates' Courts Act 1980 and article 96 of the M33. Magistrates' Courts (Northern Ireland) Order 1981 shall be construed accordingly.

(2) The provisions mentioned in subsection (1) above are—

section 211. (3), (4) and (7) to (9) (enforcement of fines);

section 212 (fines in summary proceedings);

section 213 (power to remit fines), with the omission of the words "or (4)" in subsection (2) of that section;

section 214 (time for payment) with the omission of—

(a) the words from "unless" to "its decision" in subsection (4); and

(b) subsection (5);

section 215 (further time for payment);

section 216 (reasons for default);

section 217 (supervision pending payment of fine);

section 218 (supplementary provisions), except that subsection (1) of that section shall not apply in relation to compensation orders made in solemn proceedings;

subject to subsection (3) below, section 219. (1)(b), (2), (3), (5), (6) and (8) (maximum period of imprisonment for non-payment of fine);

section 220 (payment of fine in part by prisoner);

section 221 (recovery by civil diligence);

section 222 (transfer of fine orders);

section 223 (action of clerk of court on transfer of fine order); [F358and]

section 224 (discharge from imprisonment to be specified) [F359; and.

section 248. B (driving disqualification for fine defaulters) so far as it relates to the power conferred by section 219. (1)(b).]

(3) In the application of the provisions of section 219 of this Act mentioned in subsection (2) above for the purposes of subsection (1) above—

(a) a court may impose imprisonment in respect of a fine and decline to impose imprisonment in respect of a compensation order but not vice versa; and

(b) where a court imposes imprisonment both in respect of a fine and of a compensation order the amounts in respect of which imprisonment is imposed shall, for the purposes of subsection (2) of the said section 219, be aggregated.

Extent Information

E2. S. 252 extends to UK for certain construction purposes, see. s. 252. (1).

Amendments (Textual)

F358. S. 252. (2): by 1997 c. 48, ss. 15. (2)(a), 62. (2), Sch. 3; S.I. 1997/2323, art. 4, Sch. 2 (subject to art. 7) it is provided (1.1.1998) that the word "and" in the third place where it occurs is repealed

F359. Entry in s. 252. (2) and preceding word "; and" inserted (1.1.1998) by 1997 c. 48, s. 15. (2)(b); S.I. 1997/2323, art. 4, Sch. 2 (subject to art. 7)

Marginal Citations

M321980 c.43.

M331981/1675 (N.I. 26.)

253 Effect of compensation order on subsequent award of damages in civil proceedings.S

(1) This section shall have effect where a compensation order or a service compensation order or award has been made in favour of any person in respect of any injury, loss [F360, damage, alarm or distress] and a claim by him in civil proceedings for damages in respect thereof subsequently falls to be determined.

(2) The damages in the civil proceedings shall be assessed without regard to the order or award; but where the whole or part of the amount awarded by the order or award has been paid, the damages awarded in the civil proceedings shall be restricted to the amount (if any) by which, as so assessed, they exceed the amount paid under the order or award.

(3) Where the whole or part of the amount awarded by the order or award remains unpaid and damages are awarded in a judgment in the civil proceedings, then, unless the person against whom the order or award was made has ceased to be liable to pay the amount unpaid (whether in consequence of an appeal, or of his imprisonment for default or otherwise), the court shall direct that the judgment—

(a) if it is for an amount not exceeding the amount unpaid under the order or award, shall not be enforced; or

(b) if it is for an amount exceeding the amount unpaid under the order or award, shall not be enforced except to the extent that it exceeds the amount unpaid,

without the leave of the court.

(4) In this section a "service compensation order or award" means—

(a) an order requiring the payment of compensation under paragraph 11 of—

(i) Schedule 5. A to the M34. Army Act 1955;

(ii) Schedule 5. A to the M35. Air Force Act 1955; or

(iii) Schedule 4. A to the M36. Naval Discipline Act 1957; or

(b) an award of stoppages payable by way of compensation under any of those Acts.

Amendments (Textual)

F360. Words in s. 253. (1) substituted (10.3.2008) by Criminal Proceedings etc. (Reform)

(Scotland) Act 2007 (asp 6), ss. 49. (3), 84; S.S.I. 2008/42, art. 3, Sch.
Marginal Citations
M341955 c.18.
M351955 c.19.
M361957 c.53.

[F361. Victim surcharge

Amendments (Textual)
F361. Ss. 253. F-253. J and cross-heading inserted (13.8.2014 for the insertion of ss. 253. F, 253.
G for specified purposes) by Victims and Witnesses (Scotland) Act 2014 (asp 1), ss. 26, 34; S.S.I.
2014/210, art. 2, sch.

253. FVictim surcharge

(1) This section applies where—
    (a) a person ("P") is convicted of an offence other than an offence, or offence of a class, that is prescribed by regulations by the Scottish Ministers,
    (b) the court does not make a restitution order, and
    (c) the court imposes a sentence, or sentence of a class, that is so prescribed.
(2) Except in such circumstances as may be prescribed by regulations by the Scottish Ministers, the court, in addition to dealing with P in any other way, must order P to pay a victim surcharge of such amount as may be so prescribed.
(3) Despite subsection (2), if P is convicted of two or more offences in the same proceedings, the court must order P to pay only one victim surcharge in respect of both or, as the case may be, all the offences.
(4) Any sum paid in respect of a victim surcharge is to be paid to the clerk of any court or any other person (or class of person) authorised by the Scottish Ministers for the purpose.
(5) Regulations under this section may make different provision for different cases and in particular may include provision—
    (a) prescribing different amounts for different descriptions of offender,
    (b) prescribing different amounts for different circumstances.
(6) Where provision is made by virtue of subsection (5), the Scottish Ministers may by regulations make provision for determining which victim surcharge is payable in the circumstances mentioned in subsection (3).
(7) Regulations under this section are subject to the affirmative procedure.

253. GThe Victim Surcharge Fund

(1) A person to whom any sum is paid under section 253. F(4) in respect of a victim surcharge must pay the sum to the Scottish Ministers.
(2) The Scottish Ministers must pay any sum received by virtue of subsection (1) into a fund to be known as the Victim Surcharge Fund.
(3) The Scottish Ministers must establish, maintain and administer the Victim Surcharge Fund for the purpose of securing the provision of support services for persons who are or appear to be the victims of crime and prescribed relatives of such persons.
(4) Any payment out of the fund may be made only to—
    (a) a person who is or appears to be the victim of crime,
    (b) a prescribed relative of a person who is or appears to be the victim of crime,
    (c) a person who provides or secures the provision of support services for persons who are or appear to be victims of crime, or

(d) the Scottish Ministers or, with the consent of the Scottish Ministers, a person specified by order by virtue of subsection (5) in respect of outlays incurred in administering the fund.

(5) The Scottish Ministers may delegate to such person as they may specify by order the duties imposed on them by subsection (3) of establishing, maintaining and administering the Victim Surcharge Fund.

(6) The Scottish Ministers may by regulations make further provision about the administration of the Victim Surcharge Fund including provision for or in connection with—

(a) the making of payments out of the fund,

(b) the keeping of financial and other records,

(c) the making of reports to the Scottish Government containing such information and in respect of such periods as may be specified.

(7) An order under subsection (5) and regulations under subsection (6) are subject to the affirmative procedure.

(8) In this section—

"prescribed" means prescribed by the Scottish Ministers by regulations,

"support services", in relation to a person who is or appears to be the victim of crime, means any type of service or treatment which is intended to benefit the physical or mental health or wellbeing of the person or a prescribed relative of the person.

(9) Regulations under subsections (3), (4) and (8) are subject to the negative procedure.

253. HApplication of receipts

(1) This section applies where the court orders the payment of a victim surcharge in relation to a person ("P") convicted of an offence and also in respect of the same offence or different offences in the same proceedings—

(a) imposes a fine and makes a compensation order, or

(b) imposes a fine or makes a compensation order.

(2) A payment by P must be applied in the following order—

(a) the payment must first be applied in satisfaction of the compensation order,

(b) the payment must next be applied in satisfaction of the victim surcharge,

(c) the payment must then be applied in satisfaction of the fine.

253. JEnforcement: application of certain provisions relating to fines

(1) The provisions of this Act specified in subsection (2) apply in relation to victim surcharges as they apply in relation to fines but subject to the modifications mentioned in subsection (2) and to any other necessary modifications.

(2) The provisions are—

(a) section 211. (3) and (4),

(b) section 212,

(c) section 213 (with the modification that subsection (2) is to be read as if the words "or (4)" were omitted),

(d) section 214. (1) to (4) and (6) to (9) (with the modification that subsection (4) is to be read as if the words from "unless" to "decision" were omitted),

(e) sections 215 to 218,

(f) subject to subsection (3) below, section 219. (1)(b), (2), (3), (5), (6) and (8),

(g) sections 220 to 224,

(h) section 248. B.

(3) In the application of the provisions of section 219 mentioned in subsection (2)(f) for the purposes of subsection (1)—

(a) a court may impose imprisonment in respect of a fine and decline to impose imprisonment in respect of a victim surcharge but not vice versa,

(b) where a court imposes imprisonment both in respect of a fine and a victim surcharge, the amounts in respect of which imprisonment is imposed are to be aggregated for the purposes of section 219. (2).]

ForfeitureS

254 Search warrant for forfeited articles.S

[F362. (1)Where a court has made an order for the forfeiture of an article, the court or any justice may, if satisfied on information on oath—

(a) that there is reasonable cause to believe that the article is to be found in any place or premises; and

(b) that admission to the place or premises has been refused or that a refusal of such admission is apprehended,

issue a warrant of search which may be executed according to law.]

[F363. (2)In subsection (1), "article" includes animal.]

Amendments (Textual)

F362. S. 254. (1): s. 254 renumbered as s. 254. (1) (28.3.2011) by Criminal Justice and Licensing (Scotland) Act 2010 (asp 13), s. 206. (1), sch. 7 para. 60. (a); S.S.I. 2011/178, art. 2, sch.

F363. S. 254. (2) inserted (28.3.2011) by Criminal Justice and Licensing (Scotland) Act 2010 (asp 13), s. 206. (1), sch. 7 para. 60. (b); S.S.I. 2011/178, art. 2, sch.

[F364. European Protection OrdersS

Amendments (Textual)

F364. Ss. 254. A-254. E and cross-heading inserted (11.3.2015) by The European Protection Order (Scotland) Regulations 2015 (S.S.I. 2015/107), regs. 1. (2), 2. (2)

254. A. European Protection Orders: interpretationS

In this section and in sections 254. B, 254. C, 254. D and 254. E, except where the context otherwise requires—

"competent authority" means the judicial or equivalent authority in a member state of the European Union which has power to issue and recognise a European Protection Order;

"European Protection Order" means a decision—

- taken in relation to a protection measure by a competent authority in a member state of the European Union; and

- on the basis of which the competent authority of another member state of the European Union may take any appropriate measure or measures under its own national law with a view to continuing the protection of the protected person,

"issuing state" in relation to a European Protection Order, means the member state of the European Union, other than the United Kingdom, whose competent authority has issued the Order;

"offender" in relation to a protection measure or, as the case may be, a non-harassment order made under section 254. D(1), means the individual whose conduct is the subject of the measure or order;

"protected person" in relation to a protection measure or, as the case may be, a non-harassment order made under section 254. D(1), means the individual who is the object of the protection given by the measure or order;

"protection measure" means a decision taken in criminal matters which is intended to protect a protected person from the criminal conduct of the offender by imposing one or more of the following prohibitions or restrictions—

- prohibiting the offender from entering certain localities, places or defined areas where the protected person resides or visits;

- prohibiting the offender from contacting, or regulating the offender's contact with, the protected person in any form (for example by telephone, electronic or ordinary mail or fax); or

- prohibiting the offender from coming closer than a prescribed distance to the protected person or regulating the approach of the offender to the protected person within such a distance.

254. B.Issuing of a European Protection OrderS

(1) A protected person, or an authorised representative of such a person, may apply to a court for a European Protection Order.

(2) A court may issue a European Protection Order in respect of a protected person if the court is satisfied that—

(a) a protection measure which has been taken in Scotland is in force; and

(b) the protected person—

(i) resides or stays in the executing state, or

(ii) has decided to reside or stay in the executing state.

(3) In deciding whether to issue a European Protection Order, the court must take into account—

(a) the period or periods of time during which the protected person intends to reside or stay in the executing state; and

(b) the seriousness of the need for protection of the protected person.

(4) Where the court decides not to issue a European Protection Order, the court must inform the protected person of that decision.

(5) Where a court issues a European Protection Order under subsection (2) the court must, as soon as reasonably practicable, transmit the European Protection Order to the competent authority of the executing state.

(6) Where a European Protection Order has been issued by a court under subsection (2) and the court subsequently modifies or revokes the protection measure on which it is based, the court must, as soon as reasonably practicable—

(a) modify or revoke the European Protection Order accordingly; and

(b) inform the competent authority of the executing state of that decision.

(7) For the purposes of this section—

"court" means the High Court [F365, the Sheriff Appeal Court], a sheriff or a justice of the peace court; and

"executing state" means a member state of the European Union, other than the United Kingdom in which the protected person resides, stays, or intends to reside or stay.

Amendments (Textual)

F365. Words in s. 254. B(7) inserted (22.9.2015) by The Courts Reform (Scotland) Act 2014 (Consequential Provisions No. 2) Order 2015 (S.S.I. 2015/338), art. 1, sch. 2 para. 5. (9) (with art. 4)

254. C.Recognition of a European Protection OrderS

(1) This section applies where a sheriff receives a European Protection Order from a competent authority of an issuing state.

(2) Except where one or more grounds specified in subsection (3) applies, the sheriff must recognise the European Protection Order.

(3) The grounds are—

(a) the sheriff, after complying with subsection (4), decides that the European Protection Order is incomplete;

(b) the European Protection Order does not relate to a protection measure;

(c) the prohibitions or restrictions contained in the European Protection Order have been adopted in relation to conduct that does not constitute a criminal offence in Scotland;

(d) the protection created by the prohibitions or restrictions contained in the European Protection Order derives from the execution of a penalty or measure that is covered by an amnesty under the law of Scotland;

(e) there is immunity conferred on the offender in Scotland, which would make it impossible to adopt a protection measure following recognition of the European Protection Order;

(f) criminal proceedings against the offender for the conduct in relation to which the prohibitions or restrictions contained in the European Protection Order have been adopted would be prohibited in Scotland under any enactment had the conduct occurred in Scotland;

(g) recognition of the European Protection Order would be inconsistent with the rule against double jeopardy provided for in section 1. (1) of the Double Jeopardy (Scotland) Act 2011;

(h) the offender, by reason of the offender's age, could not have been held criminally responsible for the conduct in relation to which the prohibitions or restrictions contained in the European Protection Order have been adopted had the conduct occurred in Scotland;

(i) the prohibitions or restrictions contained in the European Protection Order relate to a criminal offence which, under the law of Scotland, is regarded as having been committed, wholly or for a major or essential part, within Scotland.

(4) Where the sheriff considers that the European Protection Order is incomplete, the sheriff must—

(a) inform the competent authority of the issuing state in writing;

(b) request that the competent authority of the issuing state provide the missing information; and

(c) allow the competent authority of the issuing state such reasonable period of time as the sheriff may specify in order to comply with that request.

(5) Where the sheriff refuses to recognise a European Protection Order on any of the grounds specified in subsection (3), the sheriff must inform the competent authority of the issuing state and the protected person of the refusal and the grounds of refusal.

254. D.Implementation of a recognised European Protection OrderS

(1) Where a sheriff recognises a European Protection Order under section 254. C(2), the sheriff must make a non-harassment order in relation to the offender requiring the offender to refrain from such conduct in relation to the protected person as may be specified in the order for such period (which includes an indeterminate period) as may be so specified.

(2) Subsection (4) of section 234. A applies to a non-harassment order made under subsection (1) of this section as it applies to a non-harassment order made under section 234. A subject to the restrictions in paragraph 1. (1)(d) of Schedule 2 to the European Communities Act 1972.

(3) Subsections (4. A) and (4. B) of section 234. A apply to a non-harassment order made under subsection (1) of this section as they apply to a non-harassment order made under section 234. A.

(4) A non-harassment order made under subsection (1) may impose on the offender only such requirements as to the offender's conduct—

(a) as may constitute a protection measure; and

(b) which correspond, to the highest degree possible, to the prohibitions or restrictions contained in the European Protection Order.

(5) In considering which requirements to specify in a non-harassment order made under subsection (1), the sheriff must consider—

(a) the nature of the prohibitions or restrictions contained in the European Protection Order; and

(b) the duration of the prohibitions or restrictions contained in the European Protection Order.

(6) Where a sheriff makes a non-harassment order under subsection (1), the sheriff must provide the information in subsection (7) to—

(a) the offender;

(b) the competent authority of the issuing state; and

(c) the protected person.

(7) The information is—

(a) that the non-harassment order has been made;

(b) that a breach of the non-harassment order is an offence under section 234. A(4);

(c) information about the punishments to which the offender may be liable following conviction for an offence under section 234. A(4); and

(d) information about the powers of arrest available to a constable under section 234. A(4. A) and (4. B).

(8) Where the offender is convicted of an offence consisting of, or involving, a breach of a non-harassment order made under subsection (1), the convicting court must notify the competent authority of the issuing state.

254. E.Modification and revocation of non-harassment orders made under section 254. DS

(1) This section applies to non-harassment orders made under section 254. D(1).

(2) Where a sheriff is informed by a competent authority of an issuing state that the European Protection Order to which a non-harassment order relates has been modified, the sheriff must—

(a) modify the non-harassment order so that the requirements as to the offender's conduct contained in the modified non-harassment order correspond, to the highest degree possible, to the prohibitions or restrictions contained in the modified European Protection Order;

(b) where the information submitted by the competent authority of the issuing state in relation to the modification of the European Protection Order is incomplete, refuse to modify the non-harassment order until the missing information is provided by the competent authority of the issuing state; or

(c) where the prohibitions or restrictions contained in the modified European Protection Order no longer constitute a protection measure, revoke the non-harassment order.

(3) A sheriff may, on the application of an offender to whom a non-harassment order relates, modify the order on either or both of the following grounds—

(a) that the requirements as to the offender's conduct contained in the non-harassment order do not correspond, or do not correspond sufficiently, to the prohibitions or restrictions contained in the European Protection Order to which the non-harassment order relates;

(b) the European Protection Order to which the non-harassment order relates has been modified by the competent authority of the issuing state and the non-harassment order should be modified in a similar manner.

(4) Where a sheriff is informed by a competent authority of an issuing state that the European Protection Order to which a non-harassment order relates has been revoked or withdrawn, the sheriff must revoke the non-harassment order.

(5) A sheriff may, on the application of an offender to whom a non-harassment order relates, revoke the order on any of the following grounds—

(a) the recognition of the European Protection Order to which the non-harassment order relates should have been refused on one of the grounds specified in section 254. C(3);

(b) the protected person no longer resides or stays in Scotland;

(c) where the prohibitions or restrictions contained in the European Protection Order have been modified and no longer constitute a protection measure;

(d) the European Protection Order has been revoked or withdrawn by the competent authority of the issuing state; or

(e) a decision on supervision measures, within the meaning of Article 4 of Framework Decision

2009/829/JHA, which includes the prohibitions or restrictions contained in the European Protection Order, is transferred to Scotland after the recognition of the European Protection Order. (6) Where a sheriff modifies or revokes a non-harassment order under this section, the sheriff must inform—

(a) the competent authority of the issuing state; and

(b) where possible—

(i) the protected person, and

(ii) the offender.]

PART XII Evidence

PART XIIS Evidence

255 Special capacity.S

Where an offence is alleged to be committed in any special capacity, as by the holder of a licence, master of a vessel, occupier of a house, or the like, the fact that the accused possesses the qualification necessary to the commission of the offence shall, unless challenged—

(a) in the case of proceedings on indictment, by giving notice of a preliminary objection [F1in accordance with section 71. (2) or 72. (6)(b)(i)] of this Act; or

(b) in summary proceedings, by preliminary objection before his plea is recorded,

be held as admitted.

Amendments (Textual)

F1. Words in s. 255. (a) substituted (1.2.2005) by Criminal Procedure (Amendment) (Scotland) Act 2004 (asp 5), ss. 25, 27. (1), Sch. para. 38; S.S.I. 2004/405, art. 2, Sch. 1 (with savings in arts. 3-5)

[F2 Proof of ageS

Amendments (Textual)

F2. S. 255. A and preceding cross-heading inserted (1.8.1997) by 1997 c. 48, s. 27; S.I. 1997/1712, art. 3, Sch. 1 (subject to arts. 4, 5)

[F3255. A Proof of age.S

Where the age of any person is specified in an indictment or a complaint, it shall, unless challenged—

(a) in the case of proceedings on indictment by giving notice of a preliminary objection [F4in accordance with section 71. (2) or 72. (6)(b)(i)] of this Act; or

(b) in summary proceedings—

(i) by preliminary objection before the plea of the accused is recorded; or

(ii) by objection at such later time as the court may in special circumstances allow,

be held as admitted.]]

Amendments (Textual)

F3. S. 255. A and preceding cross-heading inserted (1.8.1997) by 1997 c. 48, s. 27; S.I. 1997/1712, art. 3, Sch. 1 (subject to arts. 4, 5)

F4. Words in s. 255. A(a) substituted (1.2.2005) by Criminal Procedure (Amendment) (Scotland) Act 2004 (asp 5), ss. 25, 27. (1), Sch. para. 39; S.S.I. 2004/405, art. 2, Sch. 1 (with savings in arts.

Agreed evidenceS

256 Agreements and admissions as to evidence.S

(1) In any trial it shall not be necessary for the accused or for the prosecutor—

(a) to prove any fact which is admitted by the other; or

(b) to prove any document, the terms and application of which are not in dispute between them,

and, without prejudice to paragraph 1 of Schedule 8 to this Act, copies of any documents may, by agreement of the parties, be accepted as equivalent to the originals.

(2) For the purposes of subsection (1) above, any admission or agreement shall be made by lodging with the clerk of court a minute in that behalf signed—

(a) in the case of an admission, by the party making the admission or, if that party is the accused and he is legally represented, by his counsel or solicitor; and

(b) in the case of an agreement, by the prosecutor and the accused or, if he is legally represented, his counsel or solicitor.

(3) Where a minute has been signed and lodged as aforesaid, any facts and documents admitted or agreed thereby shall be deemed to have been duly proved.

257 Duty to seek agreement of evidence.S

(1) Subject to subsection (2) below, the prosecutor and the accused (or each of the accused if more than one) shall each identify any facts which are facts—

(a) which he would, apart from this section, be seeking to prove;

(b) which he considers unlikely to be disputed by the other party (or by any of the other parties); and

(c) in proof of which he does not wish to lead oral evidence,

and shall, without prejudice to section 258 of this Act, take all reasonable steps to secure the agreement of the other party (or each of the other parties) to them; and the other party (or each of the other parties) shall take all reasonable steps to reach such agreement.

(2) Subsection (1) above shall not apply in relation to proceedings as respects which the accused (or any of the accused if more than one) is not legally represented.

(3) The duty under subsection (1) above applies—

(a) in relation to proceedings on indictment, from the date of service of the indictment until the swearing of the jury or, where intimation is given under section 76 of this Act, the date of that intimation; and

(b) in relation to summary proceedings, from the date on which the accused pleads not guilty until the swearing of the first witness or, where the accused tenders a plea of guilty at any time before the first witness is sworn, the date when he does so.

[F5. (4)Without prejudice to subsection (3) above, [F6in relation to proceedings on indictment], the parties to the proceedings shall, in complying with the duty under subsection (1) above, seek to ensure that the facts to be identified, and the steps to be taken in relation to those facts, [F7 are identified and taken—

(a) in the case of the High Court, before the preliminary hearing;

(b) in the case of the sheriff court, before the first diet]

[F8. (5)Without prejudice to subsection (3) above, in relation to summary proceedings, the parties to the proceedings shall, in complying with the duty under subsection (1) above, seek to ensure that the facts to be identified, and the steps to be taken in relation to those facts, are identified and taken before any intermediate diet that is to be held.]]

Amendments (Textual)

F5. S. 257. (4) inserted (1.2.2005) by Criminal Procedure (Amendment) (Scotland) Act 2004 (asp 5), ss. 25, 27. (1), Sch. para. 40; S.S.I. 2004/405, art. 2, Sch. 1

F6. Words in s. 257. (4) substituted (10.12.2007) by Criminal Proceedings etc. (Reform) (Scotland) Act 2007 (asp 6), ss. 30. (a), 84; S.S.I. 2007/479, art. 3. (1), Sch. (as amended by S.S.I. 2007/527)

F7. Words in s. 257. (4) substituted (10.12.2007) by Criminal Proceedings etc. (Reform) (Scotland) Act 2007 (asp 6), ss. 30. (b), 84; S.S.I. 2007/479, art. 3. (1), Sch. (as amended by S.S.I. 2007/527)

F8. S. 257. (5) added (10.12.2007) by Criminal Proceedings etc. (Reform) (Scotland) Act 2007 (asp 6), ss. 20. (1), 84; S.S.I. 2007/479, art. 3. (1), Sch. (subject to art. 7) (as amended by S.S.I. 2007/527)

258 Uncontroversial evidence.S

(1) This section applies where, in any criminal proceedings, a party (in this section referred to as "the first party") considers that facts which that party would otherwise be seeking to prove are unlikely to be disputed by the other parties to the proceedings.

(2) Where this section applies, the first party may prepare and sign a statement—

(a) specifying the facts concerned; or

(b) referring to such facts as set out in a document annexed to the statement,

and shall, not less than [F9the relevant period] before the [F10relevant] diet, serve a copy of the statement and any such document on every other party.

[F11. (2. ZA) In subsection (2) above, the "relevant period" means—

(a) where the relevant diet for the purpose of that subsection is an intermediate diet in summary proceedings, 7 days;

(b) in any other case, 14 days.]

[F12. (2. A) In subsection (2) above, "the relevant diet" means—

(a) in the case of proceedings in the High Court, the preliminary hearing;

[F13. (aa)in summary proceedings in which an intermediate diet is to be held, that diet;]

(b) in any other case, the trial diet.]

(3) Unless any other party serves on the first party, not more than seven days after the date of service of the copy on him under subsection (2) above or by such later time as the court may in special circumstances allow, a notice that he challenges any fact specified or referred to in the statement, the facts so specified or referred to shall be deemed to have been conclusively proved.

(4) Where a notice is served under subsection (3) above, the facts specified or referred to in the statement shall be deemed to have been conclusively proved only in so far as unchallenged in the notice.

[F14. (4. A)Where a notice is served under subsection (3) above F15. . . , the court may, on the application of any party to the proceedings made not less than 48 hours before the relevant diet, direct that any challenge in the notice to any fact is to be disregarded for the purposes of subsection (4) above if the court considers the challenge to be unjustified.

[F16. (4. AA)Where in summary proceedings the relevant diet for the purposes of subsection (4. A) above is an intermediate diet, an application under that subsection may be made at (or at any time before) that diet.]

(4. B) In subsection (4. A) above, "the relevant diet" means—

(a) in proceedings in the High Court, the preliminary hearing; F17. . .

(b) in [F18solemn] proceedings in the sheriff court, the first diet.

[F19. (c)in summary proceedings—

(i) in which an intermediate diet is to be held, that diet;

(ii) in which such a diet is not to be held, the trial diet.]

(4. C)In proceedings in the High Court, the Court may, on cause shown, allow an application

under subsection (4. A) above to be made after the time limit specified in that subsection.

[F20. (4. D)In summary proceedings, the court may allow an application under subsection (4. A) above to be made late if the court is satisfied that a timeous application would not have been practicable.]]

(5) Subsections (3) and (4) above shall not preclude a party from leading evidence of circumstances relevant to, or other evidence in explanation of, any fact specified or referred to in the statement.

(6) Notwithstanding subsections (3) and (4) above, the court—

(a) may, on the application of any party, where it is satisfied that there are special circumstances; and

(b) shall, on the joint application of all the parties,

direct that the presumptions in those subsections shall not apply in relation to such fact specified or referred to in the statement as is specified in the direction.

(7) An application under subsection (6) above may be made at any time after the commencement of the trial and before the commencement of the prosecutor's address to the court on the evidence.

(8) Where the court makes a direction under subsection (6) above it shall, unless all the parties otherwise agree, adjourn the trial and may, without prejudice to section 268 of this Act, permit any party to lead evidence as to any such fact as is specified in the direction, notwithstanding that a witness or production concerned is not included in any list lodged by the parties and that the notice required by sections 67. (5) and 78. (4) of this Act has not been given.

(9) A copy of a statement or a notice required, under this section, to be served on any party shall be served in such manner as may be prescribed by Act of Adjournal; and a written execution purporting to be signed by the person who served such copy or notice together with, where appropriate, the relevant post office receipt shall be sufficient evidence of such service.

Amendments (Textual)

F9. Words in s. 258. (2) substituted (10.12.2007) by Criminal Proceedings etc. (Reform) (Scotland) Act 2007 (asp 6), ss. 20. (2)(a), 84; S.S.I. 2007/479, art. 3. (1), Sch. (subject to art. 7) (as amended by S.S.I. 2007/527)

F10. Word in s. 258. (2) substituted (1.2.2005) by Criminal Procedure (Amendment) (Scotland) Act 2004 (asp 5), ss. 25, 27. (1), Sch. para. 41. (a); S.S.I. 2004/405, art. 2, Sch. 1 (with savings in arts. 3-5)

F11. S. 258. (2. ZA) inserted (10.12.2007) by Criminal Proceedings etc. (Reform) (Scotland) Act 2007 (asp 6), ss. 20. (2)(b), 84; S.S.I. 2007/479, art. 3. (1), Sch. (subject to art. 7) (as amended by S.S.I. 2007/527)

F12. S. 258. (2. A) inserted (1.2.2005) by Criminal Procedure (Amendment) (Scotland) Act 2004 (asp 5), ss. 25, 27. (1), Sch. para. 41. (b); S.S.I. 2004/405, art. 2, Sch. 1 (with savings in arts. 3-5)

F13. S. 258. (2. A)(aa) inserted (10.12.2007) by Criminal Proceedings etc. (Reform) (Scotland) Act 2007 (asp 6), ss. 20. (2)(c), 84; S.S.I. 2007/479, art. 3. (1), Sch. (subject to art. 7) (as amended by S.S.I. 2007/527)

F14. S. 258. (4. A)-(4. C) inserted (1.2.2005) by Criminal Procedure (Amendment) (Scotland) Act 2004 (asp 5), ss. 16, 27. (1); S.S.I. 2004/405, art. 2, Sch. 1 (with savings in arts. 3-5)

F15. Words in s. 258. (4. A) repealed (10.12.2007) by Criminal Proceedings etc. (Reform) (Scotland) Act 2007 (asp 6), ss. 20. (2)(d), 84; S.S.I. 2007/479, art. 3. (1), Sch. (subject to art. 7) (as amended by S.S.I. 2007/527)

F16. S. 258. (4. AA) inserted (28.3.2011) by Criminal Justice and Licensing (Scotland) Act 2010 (asp 13), s. 206. (1), sch. 7 para. 61; S.S.I. 2011/178, art. 2, sch.

F17. Word immediately following paragraph (a) in s. 258. (4. B) repealed (10.12.2007) by Criminal Proceedings etc. (Reform) (Scotland) Act 2007 (asp 6), ss. 20. (2)(e)(i), 84; S.S.I. 2007/479, art. 3. (1), Sch. (subject to art. 7) (as amended by S.S.I. 2007/527)

F18. Word in s. 258. (4. B)(b) inserted (10.12.2007) by Criminal Proceedings etc. (Reform) (Scotland) Act 2007 (asp 6), ss. 20. (2)(e)(ii), 84; S.S.I. 2007/479, art. 3. (1), Sch. (subject to art. 7) (as amended by S.S.I. 2007/527)

F19. S. 258. (4. B)(c) added (10.12.2007) by Criminal Proceedings etc. (Reform) (Scotland) Act

2007 (asp 6), ss. 20. (2)(e)(iii), 84; S.S.I. 2007/479, art. 3. (1), Sch. (subject to art. 7) (as amended by S.S.I. 2007/527)

F20. S. 258. (4. D) added (10.12.2007) by Criminal Proceedings etc. (Reform) (Scotland) Act 2007 (asp 6), ss. 20. (3), 84 (as added by S.S.I. 2007/540, art. 4); S.S.I. 2007/479, art. 3. (1), Sch. (subject to art. 7) (as amended by S.S.I. 2007/527)

HearsayS

259 Exceptions to the rule that hearsay evidence is inadmissible.S

(1) Subject to the following provisions of this section, evidence of a statement made by a person otherwise than while giving oral evidence in court in criminal proceedings shall be admissible in those proceedings as evidence of any matter contained in the statement where the judge is satisfied—

(a) that the person who made the statement will not give evidence in the proceedings of such matter for any of the reasons mentioned in subsection (2) below;

(b) that evidence of the matter would be admissible in the proceedings if that person gave direct oral evidence of it;

(c) that the person who made the statement would have been, at the time the statement was made, a competent witness in such proceedings; and

(d) that there is evidence which would entitle a jury properly directed, or in summary proceedings would entitle the judge, to find that the statement was made and that either—

(i) it is contained in a document; or

(ii) a person who gave oral evidence in the proceedings as to the statement has direct personal knowledge of the making of the statement.

(2) The reasons referred to in paragraph (a) of subsection (1) above are that the person who made the statement—

(a) is dead or is, by reason of his bodily or mental condition, unfit or unable to give evidence in any competent manner;

(b) is named and otherwise sufficiently identified, but is outwith the United Kingdom and it is not reasonably practicable to secure his attendance at the trial or to obtain his evidence in any other competent manner;

(c) is named and otherwise sufficiently identified, but cannot be found and all reasonable steps which, in the circumstances, could have been taken to find him have been so taken;

(d) having been authorised to do so by virtue of a ruling of the court in the proceedings that he is entitled to refuse to give evidence in connection with the subject matter of the statement on the grounds that such evidence might incriminate him, refuses to give such evidence; or

(e) is called as a witness and either—

(i) refuses to take the oath or affirmation; or

(ii) having been sworn as a witness and directed by the judge to give evidence in connection with the subject matter of the statement refuses to do so,

and in the application of this paragraph to a child, the reference to a witness refusing to take the oath or affirmation or, as the case may be, to having been sworn shall be construed as a reference to a child who has refused to accept an admonition to tell the truth or, having been so admonished, refuses to give evidence as mentioned above.

(3) Evidence of a statement shall not be admissible by virtue of subsection (1) above where the judge is satisfied that the occurrence of any of the circumstances mentioned in paragraphs (a) to (e) of subsection (2) above, by virtue of which the statement would otherwise be admissible, is caused by—

(a) the person in support of whose case the evidence would be given; or

(b) any other person acting on his behalf,

for the purpose of securing that the person who made the statement does not give evidence for the purposes of the proceedings either at all or in connection with the subject matter of the statement.

(4) Where in any proceedings evidence of a statement made by any person is admitted by reference to any of the reasons mentioned in paragraphs (a) to (c) and (e)(i) of subsection (2) above—

(a) any evidence which, if that person had given evidence in connection with the subject matter of the statement, would have been admissible as relevant to his credibility as a witness shall be admissible for that purpose in those proceedings;

(b) evidence may be given of any matter which, if that person had given evidence in connection with the subject matter of the statement, could have been put to him in cross-examination as relevant to his credibility as a witness but of which evidence could not have been adduced by the cross-examining party; and

(c) evidence tending to prove that that person, whether before or after making the statement, made in whatever manner some other statement which is inconsistent with it shall be admissible for the purpose of showing that he has contradicted himself.

(5) Subject to subsection (6) below, where a party intends to apply to have evidence of a statement admitted by virtue of subsection (1) above he shall, [F21by the relevant time], give notice in writing of—

(a) that fact;

(b) the witnesses and productions to be adduced in connection with such evidence; and

(c) such other matters as may be prescribed by Act of Adjournal,

to every other party to the proceedings and, for the purposes of this subsection, such evidence may be led notwithstanding that a witness or production concerned is not included in any list lodged by the parties and that the notice required by sections 67. (5) and 78. (4) of this Act has not been given.

[F22. (5. A)In subsection (5) above, "the relevant time" means—

(a) in the case of proceedings in the High Court—

(i) not less than 7 days before the preliminary hearing; or

(ii) such later time, before the trial diet, as the judge may on cause shown allow;

(b) in any other case, before the trial diet.]

(6) A party shall not be required to give notice as mentioned in subsection (5) above where—

(a) the grounds for seeking to have evidence of a statement admitted are as mentioned in paragraph (d) or (e) of subsection (2) above; or

(b) he satisfies the judge that there was good reason for not giving such notice.

(7) If no other party to the proceedings objects to the admission of evidence of a statement by virtue of subsection (1) above, the evidence shall be admitted without the judge requiring to be satisfied as mentioned in that subsection.

(8) For the purposes of the determination of any matter upon which the judge is required to be satisfied under subsection (1) above—

(a) except to the extent that any other party to the proceedings challenges them and insists in such challenge, it shall be presumed that the circumstances are as stated by the party seeking to introduce evidence of the statement; and

(b) where such a challenge is insisted in, the judge shall determine the matter on the balance of probabilities, and he may draw any reasonable inference—

(i) from the circumstances in which the statement was made or otherwise came into being; or

(ii) from any other circumstances, including, where the statement is contained in a document, the form and contents of the document.

(9) Where evidence of a statement has been admitted by virtue of subsection (1) above on the application of one party to the proceedings, without prejudice to anything in any enactment or rule of law, the judge may permit any party to lead additional evidence of such description as the judge may specify, notwithstanding that a witness or production concerned is not included in any list lodged by the parties and that the notice required by sections 67. (5) and 78. (4) of this Act has not been given.

(10) Any reference in subsections (5), (6) and (9) above to evidence shall include a reference to evidence led in connection with any determination required to be made for the purposes of subsection (1) above.

Amendments (Textual)

F21. Words in s. 259. (5) substituted (1.2.2005) by Criminal Procedure (Amendment) (Scotland) Act 2004 (asp 5), ss. 25, 27. (1), Sch. para. 42. (a); S.S.I. 2004/405, art. 2, Sch. 1 (with savings in arts. 3-5)

F22. S. 259. (5. A) inserted (1.2.2005) by Criminal Procedure (Amendment) (Scotland) Act 2004 (asp 5), ss. 25, 27. (1), Sch. para. 42. (b); S.S.I. 2004/405, art. 2, Sch. 1 (with savings in arts. 3-5)

Modifications etc. (not altering text)

C1. Ss. 259-261 excluded (1.4.1996) by 1995 c. 40, ss. 3, 7. (2), Sch. 3 Pt. II para. 14

260 Admissibility of prior statements of witnesses.S

(1) Subject to the following provisions of this section, where a witness gives evidence in criminal proceedings, any prior statement made by the witness shall be admissible as evidence of any matter stated in it of which direct oral evidence by him would be admissible if given in the course of those proceedings.

(2) A prior statement shall not be admissible under this section unless—

 (a) the statement is contained in a document;

 (b) the witness, in the course of giving evidence, indicates that the statement was made by him and that he adopts it as his evidence; and

 (c) at the time the statement was made, the person who made it would have been a competent witness in the proceedings.

(3) For the purposes of this section, any reference to a prior statement is a reference to a prior statement which, but for the provisions of this section, would not be admissible as evidence of any matter stated in it.

(4) Subsections (2) and (3) above do not apply to a prior statement—

 (a) contained in a precognition on oath; or

 (b) made in other proceedings, whether criminal or civil and whether taking place in the United Kingdom or elsewhere,

and, for the purposes of this section, any such statement shall not be admissible unless it is sufficiently authenticated.

[F23. (5)A prior statement made by a witness shall not, in any proceedings on indictment, be inadmissible by reason only that it is not included in any list of productions lodged by the parties.]

Amendments (Textual)

F23. S. 260. (5) inserted (4.10.2004) by Criminal Procedure (Amendment) (Scotland) Act 2004 (asp 5), ss. 23, 27. (1); S.S.I. 2004/405, art. 2, Sch. 1 (subject to savings in arts. 3-5)

Modifications etc. (not altering text)

C2. Ss. 259-261 excluded (1.4.1996) by 1995 c. 40, ss. 3, 7. (2), Sch. 3 Pt. II para. 14

C3. S. 260. (2)(c) modified (28.3.2011) by Criminal Justice and Licensing (Scotland) Act 2010 (asp 13), ss. 84, 206. (1); S.S.I. 2011/178, art. 2, sch.

261 [F24. Statements by co-accused]S

(1) Subject to the following provisions of this section, nothing in sections 259 and 260 of this Act shall apply to a statement made by the accused.

(2) Evidence of a statement made by an accused shall be admissible by virtue of the said section 259 at the instance of another accused in the same proceedings as evidence in relation to that other accused.

(3) For the purposes of subsection (2) above, the first mentioned accused shall be deemed—

 (a) where he does not give evidence in the proceedings, to be a witness refusing to give evidence in connection with the subject matter of the statement as mentioned in paragraph (e) of subsection (2) of the said section 259; and

(b) to have been, at the time the statement was made, a competent witness in the proceedings.

(4) Evidence of a statement shall not be admissible as mentioned in subsection (2) above unless the accused at whose instance it is sought to be admitted has given notice of his intention to do so as mentioned in subsection (5) of the said section 259; but subsection (6) of that section shall not apply in the case of notice required to be given by virtue of this subsection.

Amendments (Textual)

F24. S. 261 title substituted (25.1.2018) by Criminal Justice (Scotland) Act 2016 (asp 1), ss. 109. (2), 117. (2); S.S.I. 2017/345, art. 3, sch. (with art. 9)

Modifications etc. (not altering text)

C4. Ss. 259-261 excluded (1.4.1996) by 1995 c. 40, ss. 3, 7. (2), Sch. 3 Pt. II para. 14

[F25261. ZAStatements by accusedS

(1) Evidence of a statement to which this subsection applies is not inadmissible as evidence of any fact contained in the statement on account of the evidence's being hearsay.

(2) Subsection (1) applies to a statement made by the accused in the course of the accused's being questioned (whether as a suspect or not) by a constable, or another official, investigating an offence.

(3) Subsection (1) does not affect the issue of whether evidence of a statement made by one accused is admissible as evidence in relation to another accused.]

Amendments (Textual)

F25. S. 261. ZA inserted (25.1.2018) by Criminal Justice (Scotland) Act 2016 (asp 1), ss. 109. (1), 117. (2); S.S.I. 2017/345, art. 3, sch. (with art. 9)

[F26. Statements made after chargeS

Amendments (Textual)

F26. S. 261. ZB and cross-heading inserted (25.1.2018) by Criminal Justice (Scotland) Act 2016 (asp 1), s. 117. (2), sch. 2 para. 34; S.S.I. 2017/345, art. 3, sch.

261. ZBException to rule on inadmissiblityS

Evidence of a statement made by a person in response to questioning carried out in accordance with authorisation granted under section 35 of the Criminal Justice (Scotland) Act 2016 is not inadmissible on account of the statement's being made after the person has been charged with an offence.]

[F27. Witness statementsS

Amendments (Textual)

F27. S. 261. A and cross-heading inserted (6.6.2011) by Criminal Justice and Licensing (Scotland) Act 2010 (asp 13), ss. 85. (2), 206. (1); S.S.I. 2011/178, art. 2, sch.

261. AWitness statements: use during trialS

(1) Subsection (2) applies where—
    (a) a witness is giving evidence in criminal proceedings,
    (b) the witness has made a prior statement,
    (c) the prosecutor has seen or has been given an opportunity to see the statement, and

(d) the accused (or a solicitor or advocate acting on behalf of the accused in the proceedings) has seen or has been given an opportunity to see the statement.

(2) The court may allow the witness to refer to the statement while the witness is giving evidence.]

262 Construction of sections 259 to [F28261. A].S

(1) For the purposes of sections 259 to [F29261. A] of this Act, a "statement" includes—

(a) any representation, however made or expressed, of fact or opinion; and

(b) any part of a statement,

but does not include a statement in a precognition other than a precognition on oath.

(2) For the purposes of the said sections 259 to [F30261. A] a statement is contained in a document where the person who makes it—

(a) makes the statement in the document personally;

(b) makes a statement which is, with or without his knowledge, embodied in a document by whatever means or by any person who has direct personal knowledge of the making of the statement; or

(c) approves a document as embodying the statement.

(3) In the said sections 259 to [F30261. A]—

"criminal proceedings" include [F31. (other than in section 261. A)] any hearing by the sheriff of an application made [F32by virtue of section 93. (2)(a) or 94. (2)(a) of the Children's Hearings (Scotland) Act 2011 (asp 1) to determine whether a ground is established, in so far as the application relates to the commission of an offence by the child, or for a review of such a determination;]

"document" includes, in addition to a document in writing—

- any map, plan, graph or drawing;

- any photograph;

- any disc, tape, sound track or other device in which sounds or other data (not being visual images) are recorded so as to be capable (with or without the aid of some other equipment) of being reproduced therefrom; and

- any film, negative, tape, disc or other device in which one or more visual images are recorded so as to be capable (as aforesaid) of being reproduced therefrom;

"film" includes a microfilm;

"made" includes [F30. (other than in section 261. A)] allegedly made.

(4) Nothing in the said sections 259 to [F30261. A] shall prejudice the admissibility of a statement made by a person other than in the course of giving oral evidence in court which is admissible otherwise than by virtue of those sections.

Amendments (Textual)

F28. Word in s. 262 heading substituted (6.6.2011) by Criminal Justice and Licensing (Scotland) Act 2010 (asp 13), ss. 85. (3)(a), 206. (1); S.S.I. 2011/178, art. 2, sch.

F29. Word in s. 262. (1)-(4) substituted (6.6.2011) by Criminal Justice and Licensing (Scotland) Act 2010 (asp 13), ss. 85. (3)(b), 206. (1); S.S.I. 2011/178, art. 2, sch.

F30. Words in s. 262. (3) inserted (6.6.2011) by Criminal Justice and Licensing (Scotland) Act 2010 (asp 13), ss. 85. (3)(c)(ii), 206. (1); S.S.I. 2011/178, art. 2, sch.

F31. Words in s. 262. (3) inserted (6.6.2011) by Criminal Justice and Licensing (Scotland) Act 2010 (asp 13), ss. 85. (3)(c)(i), 206. (1); S.S.I. 2011/178, art. 2, sch.

F32. Words in s. 262. (3) substituted (24.6.2013) by The Childrens Hearings (Scotland) Act 2011 (Modification of Primary Legislation) Order 2013 (S.S.I. 2013/211), art. 1, sch. 1 para. 10. (7)

Modifications etc. (not altering text)

C5. S. 262 applied (with modifications) (6.6.2011) by Criminal Justice and Licensing (Scotland) Act 2010 (asp 13), ss. 54. (3), 206. (1); S.S.I. 2011/178, art. 2, sch.

WitnessesS

263 Examination of witnesses.S

(1) In any trial, it shall be competent for the party against whom a witness is produced and swornin causa to examine such witness both in cross andin causa.

(2) The judge may, on the motion of either party, on cause shown order that the examination of a witness for that party ("the first witness") shall be interrupted to permit the examination of another witness for that party.

(3) Where the judge makes an order under subsection (2) above he shall, after the examination of the other witness, permit the recall of the first witness.

(4) In a trial, a witness may be examined as to whether he has on any specified occasion made a statement on any matter pertinent to the issue at the trial different from the evidence given by him in the trial; and evidence may be led in the trial to prove that the witness made the different statement on the occasion specified.

(5) In any trial, on the motion of either party, the presiding judge may permit a witness who has been examined to be recalled.

[F33264. Spouse or civil partner of accused a compellable witnessS

(1) The spouse or civil partner of an accused is a competent and compellable witness for the prosecution, the accused or any co-accused in the proceedings against the accused.

(2) Subsection (1) is, if the spouse or civil partner is a co-accused in the proceedings, subject to any enactment or rule of law by virtue of which an accused need not (by reason of being an accused) give evidence in the proceedings.

(3) Subsection (1) displaces any other rule of law that would (but for that subsection) prevent or restrict, by reference to the relationship, the giving of evidence by the spouse or civil partner of an accused.]

Amendments (Textual)

F33. S. 264 substituted (28.3.2011) by Criminal Justice and Licensing (Scotland) Act 2010 (asp 13), ss. 86. (1), 206. (1); S.S.I. 2011/178, art. 2, sch.

265 Witnesses not excluded for conviction, interest, relationship, etc.S

(1) Every person adduced as a witness who is not otherwise by law disqualified from giving evidence, shall be admissible as a witness, and no objection to the admissibility of a witness shall be competent on the ground of—

    (a) conviction of or punishment for an offence;

    (b) interest;

    (c) agency or partial counsel;

    (d) the absence of due citation to attend; or

    (e) his having been precognosced subsequently to the date of citation.

(2) Where any person who is or has been an agent of the accused is adduced and examined as a witness for the accused, it shall not be competent for the accused to object, on the ground of confidentiality, to any question proposed to be put to such witness on matter pertinent to the issue of the guilt of the accused.

(3) No objection to the admissibility of a witness shall be competent on the ground that he or she is the father, mother, son, daughter, brother or sister, by consanguinity or affinity, or uncle, aunt, nephew or niece, by consanguinity of any party adducing the witness in any trial.

(4) It shall not be competent for any witness to decline to be examined and give evidence on the ground of any relationship mentioned in subsection (3) above.

266 Accused as witness.S

(1) Subject to subsections (2) to (8) below, the accused shall be a competent witness for the defence at every stage of the case, whether the accused is on trial alone or along with a co-accused.

(2) The accused shall not be called as a witness in pursuance of this section except upon his own application or in accordance with subsection (9) or (10) below.

(3) An accused who gives evidence on his own behalf in pursuance of this section may be asked any question in cross-examination notwithstanding that it would tend to incriminate him as to the offence charged.

(4) An accused who gives evidence on his own behalf in pursuance of this section shall not be asked, and if asked shall not be required to answer, any question tending to show that he has committed, or been convicted of, or been charged with, any offence other than that with which he is then charged, or is of bad character, unless—

(a) the proof that he has committed or been convicted of such other offence is admissible evidence to show that he is guilty of the offence with which he is then charged; or

(b) the accused or his counsel or solicitor has asked questions of the witnesses for the prosecution with a view to establishing the accused's good character or impugning the character of the complainer, or the accused has given evidence of his own good character, or the nature or conduct of the defence is such as to involve imputations on the character of the prosecutor or of the witnesses for the prosecution or of the complainer; or

(c) the accused has given evidence against any other person charged in the same proceedings.

(5) In a case to which paragraph (b) of subsection (4) above applies, the prosecutor shall be entitled to ask the accused a question of a kind specified in that subsection only if the court, on the application of the prosecutor, permits him to do so.

[F34. (5. A)Nothing in subsections (4) and (5) above shall prevent the accused from being asked, or from being required to answer, any question tending to show that he has been convicted of an offence other than that with which he is charged if his conviction for that other offence has been disclosed to the jury, or is to be taken into consideration by the judge, under section 275. A(2) of this Act.]

(6) An application under subsection (5) above in proceedings on indictment shall be made in the course of the trial but in the absence of the jury.

(7) In subsection (4) above, references to the complainer include references to a victim who is deceased.

(8) Every person called as a witness in pursuance of this section shall, unless otherwise ordered by the court, give his evidence from the witness box or other place from which the other witnesses give their evidence.

(9) The accused may—

(a) with the consent of a co-accused, call that other accused as a witness on the accused's behalf; or

(b) ask a co-accused any question in cross-examination if that co-accused gives evidence, but he may not do both in relation to the same co-accused.

(10) The prosecutor or the accused may call as a witness a co-accused who has pleaded guilty to or been acquitted of all charges against him which remain before the court (whether or not, in a case where the co-accused has pleaded guilty to any charge, he has been sentenced) or in respect of whom the diet has been deserted; and the party calling such co-accused as a witness shall not require to give notice thereof, but the court may grant any other party such adjournment or postponement of the trial as may seem just.

(11) Where, in any trial, the accused is to be called as a witness he shall be so called as the first

witness for the defence unless the court, on cause shown, otherwise directs.

Amendments (Textual)

F34. S. 266. (5. A) inserted (1.11.2002) by Sexual Offences (Procedure and Evidence) (Scotland) Act 2002 (asp 9), s. 10. (3); S.S.I. 2002/443, art. 3 (with art. 4. (5))

267 Witnesses in court during trial.S

(1) The court may, on an application by any party to the proceedings, permit a witness to be in court during the proceedings or any part of the proceedings before he has given evidence if it appears to the court that the presence of the witness would not be contrary to the interests of justice.

(2) Without prejudice to subsection (1) above, where a witness has, without the permission of the court and without the consent of the parties to the proceedings, been present in court during the proceedings, the court may, in its discretion, admit the witness, where it appears to the court that the presence of the witness was not the result of culpable negligence or criminal intent, and that the witness has not been unduly instructed or influenced by what took place during his presence, or that injustice will not be done by his examination.

[F35267. ACitation of witnesses for precognitionS

(1) This Act shall be sufficient warrant for the citation of witnesses for precognition by the prosecutor, whether or not any person has been charged with the offence in relation to which the precognition is taken.

[F36. (1. A)Subsection (1) extends to citation for precognition by the prosecutor where a European investigation order having effect by virtue of Part 3 of the Criminal Justice (European Investigation Order) Regulations 2017 contains a request for a person in Scotland to be heard under regulations 35 to 37 of those Regulations.]

(2) Such citation shall be in the form prescribed by Act of Adjournal or as nearly as may be in such form.

(3) A witness who, having been duly cited—

 (a) fails without reasonable excuse, after receiving at least 48 hours notice, to attend for precognition by a prosecutor at the time and place mentioned in the citation served on him; or

 (b) refuses when so cited to give information within his knowledge regarding any matter relative to the commission of the offence in relation to which the precognition is taken,

shall be guilty of an offence and shall be liable on summary conviction to a fine not exceeding level 3 on the standard scale or to a term of imprisonment not exceeding 21 days.]

Amendments (Textual)

F35. S. 267. A inserted (4.10.2004) by Criminal Procedure (Amendment) (Scotland) Act 2004 (asp 5), ss. 22, 27. (1); S.S.I. 2004/405, art. 2, Sch. 1 (subject to savings in arts. 3-5)

F36. S. 267. A(1. A) inserted (31.7.2017) by The Criminal Justice (European Investigation Order) Regulations 2017 (S.I. 2017/730), reg. 1. (1), Sch. 3 para. 3. (3) (with reg. 3)

[F37. Identification proceduresS

Amendments (Textual)

F37. S. 267. B and preceding cross-heading inserted (10.12.2007) by Criminal Proceedings etc. (Reform) (Scotland) Act 2007 (asp 6), ss. 34, 84; S.S.I. 2007/479, art. 3. (1), Sch. (as amended by S.S.I. 2007/527)

267. BOrder requiring accused to participate in identification procedureS

(1) The court may, on an application by the prosecutor in any proceedings, make an order requiring the accused person to participate in an identification parade or other identification procedure.

(2) The application may be made at any time after the proceedings have been commenced.

(3) The court—

(a) shall (if the accused is present) allow the accused to make representations in relation to the application;

(b) may, if it considers it appropriate to do so (where the accused is not present), fix a hearing for the purpose of allowing the accused to make such representations.

(4) Where an order is made under subsection (1) above, the clerk of court shall (if the accused is not present) have notice of the order effected as respects the accused without delay.

(5) Notice under subsection (4) above shall (in relation to any proceedings) be effected in the same manner as citation under section 141 of this Act.

(6) It is sufficient evidence that notice has been effected under subsection (5) above if there is produced a written execution—

(a) in the form prescribed by Act of Adjournal or as nearly as may be in such form; and

(b) signed by the person who effected notice.

(7) In relation to notice effected by means of registered post or the recorded delivery service, the relevant post office receipt requires to be produced along with the execution mentioned in subsection (6) above.

(8) A person who, having been given due notice of an order made under subsection (1) above, without reasonable excuse fails to comply with the order is—

(a) guilty of an offence; and

(b) liable on summary conviction to a fine not exceeding level 3 on the standard scale or to imprisonment for a period not exceeding 12 months or to both.

(9) For the purpose of subsection (5) above, section 141 of this Act is to be read with such modifications as are necessary for its application in the circumstances.

(10) In this section, "the court" means—

(a) in the case of proceedings in the High Court, a single judge of that Court;

(b) in any other case, any court with jurisdiction in relation to the proceedings.]

Additional evidence, etc.S

268 Additional evidence.S

(1) Subject to subsection (2) below, the judge may, on a motion of the prosecutor or the accused made—

(a) in proceedings on indictment, at any time before the commencement of the speeches to the jury;

(b) in summary proceedings, at any time before the prosecutor proceeds to address the judge on the evidence,

permit him to lead additional evidence.

(2) Permission shall only be granted under subsection (1) above where the judge—

(a) considers that the additional evidence is prima facie material; and

(b) accepts that at the commencement of the trial either—

(i) the additional evidence was not available and could not reasonably have been made available; or

(ii) the materiality of such additional evidence could not reasonably have been foreseen by the party.

(3) The judge may permit the additional evidence to be led notwithstanding that—

(a) in proceedings on indictment, a witness or production concerned is not included in any list lodged by the parties and that the notice required by sections 67. (5) and 78. (4) of this Act has not been given; or

(b) in any case, a witness must be recalled.

(4) The judge may, when granting a motion in terms of this section, adjourn or postpone the trial before permitting the additional evidence to be led.

(5) In this section "the commencement of the trial" means—

(a) in proceedings on indictment, the time when the jury is sworn; and

(b) in summary proceedings, the time when the first witness for the prosecution is sworn.

269 Evidence in replication.S

(1) The judge may, on a motion of the prosecutor made at the relevant time, permit the prosecutor to lead additional evidence for the purpose of—

(a) contradicting evidence given by any defence witness which could not reasonably have been anticipated by the prosecutor; or

(b) providing such proof as is mentioned in section 263. (4) of this Act.

(2) The judge may permit the additional evidence to be led notwithstanding that—

(a) in proceedings on indictment, a witness or production concerned is not included in any list lodged by the parties and that the notice required by sections 67. (5) and 78. (4) of this Act has not been given; or

(b) in any case, a witness must be recalled.

(3) The judge may when granting a motion in terms of this section, adjourn or postpone the trial before permitting the additional evidence to be led.

(4) In subsection (1) above, "the relevant time" means—

(a) in proceedings on indictment, after the close of the defence evidence and before the commencement of the speeches to the jury; and

(b) in summary proceedings, after the close of the defence evidence and before the prosecutor proceeds to address the judge on the evidence.

270 Evidence of criminal record and character of accused.S

(1) This section applies where—

(a) evidence is led by the defence, or the defence asks questions of a witness for the prosecution, with a view to establishing the accused's good character or impugning the character of the prosecutor, of any witness for the prosecution or of the complainer; or

(b) the nature or conduct of the defence is such as to tend to establish the accused's good character or to involve imputations on the character of the prosecutor, of any witness for the prosecution or of the complainer.

(2) Where this section applies the court may, without prejudice to section 268 of this Act, on the application of the prosecutor, permit the prosecutor to lead evidence that the accused has committed, or has been convicted of, or has been charged with, offences other than that for which he is being tried, or is of bad character, notwithstanding that, in proceedings on indictment, a witness or production concerned is not included in any list lodged by the prosecutor and that the notice required by sections 67. (5) and 78. (4) of this Act has not been given.

(3) In proceedings on indictment, an application under subsection (2) above shall be made in the course of the trial but in the absence of the jury.

(4) In subsection (1) above, references to the complainer include references to a victim who is deceased.

[F38. Special measures for child witnesses and other vulnerable

witnesses]S

Amendments (Textual)

F38. Ss. 271-271. M and preceding cross-heading substituted for s. 271 (1.4.2005, 30.11.2005, 1.4.2006. 1.4.2007 and 2.7.2007 for certain purposes and otherwise 1.4.2008) by Vulnerable Witnesses (Scotland) Act 2004 (asp 3), ss. 1, 25; S.S.I. 2005/168, art. 2, Sch. (with savings in art. 4); S.S.I. 2005/590, art. 2, Sch. (with art. 4); S.S.I. 2006/59, art. 2, Sch. (with art. 4. (1)); S.S.I. 2007/101, art. 2, Sch. (with art. 4); S.S.I. 2007/329, art. 2, Sch. (with art. 4); S.S.I. 2008/57, art. 2 (with art. 3)

[F39 271. Vulnerable witnesses: main definitionsS

[F40. (1)For the purposes of this Act, a person who is giving or is to give evidence at, or for the purposes of, a hearing in relevant criminal proceedings is a vulnerable witness if—

(a) the person is under the age of 18 on the date of commencement of the proceedings in which the hearing is being or is to be held,

(b) there is a significant risk that the quality of the evidence to be given by the person will be diminished by reason of—

(i) mental disorder (within the meaning of section 328 of the Mental Health (Care and Treatment) (Scotland) Act 2003), or

(ii) fear or distress in connection with giving evidence at the hearing,

(c) the offence is alleged to have been committed against the person in proceedings for—

(i) an offence listed in any of paragraphs 36 to 59. ZL of Schedule 3 to the Sexual Offences Act 2003,

(ii) an offence under section 22 of the Criminal Justice (Scotland) Act 2003 (traffic in prostitution etc.),

(iii) an offence under section 4 of the Asylum and Immigration (Treatment of Claimants, etc.) Act 2004 (trafficking people for exploitation),

[F41. (iiia)an offence of human trafficking (see section 1 of the Human Trafficking and Exploitation (Scotland) Act 2015),]

(iv) an offence the commission of which involves domestic abuse, or

(v) an offence of stalking, or

(d) there is considered to be a significant risk of harm to the person by reason only of the fact that the person is giving or is to give evidence in the proceedings.]

F42. (1. A). . . . .

[F43. (1. AA)The Scottish Ministers may by order subject to the affirmative procedure modify subsection (1)(c).]

(2) In determining whether a person is a vulnerable witness by virtue of subsection (1)(b) [F44or (d)] above, the court shall take into account—

(a) the nature and circumstances of the alleged offence to which the proceedings relate,

(b) the nature of the evidence which the person is likely to give,

(c) the relationship (if any) between the person and the accused,

(d) the person's age and maturity,

(e) any behaviour towards the person on the part of—

(i) the accused,

(ii) members of the family or associates of the accused,

(iii) any other person who is likely to be an accused or a witness in the proceedings, and

(f) such other matters, including—

(i) the social and cultural background and ethnic origins of the person,

(ii) the person's sexual orientation,

(iii) the domestic and employment circumstances of the person,

(iv) any religious beliefs or political opinions of the person, and

(v) any physical disability or other physical impairment which the person has, as appear to the court to be relevant.

(3) For the purposes of subsection (1)(a) above and section 271. B(1)(b) below, proceedings shall be taken to have commenced when the indictment or, as the case may be, complaint is served on the accused.

(4) In subsection (1)(b) above, the reference to the quality of evidence is to its quality in terms of completeness, coherence and accuracy.

[F45. (4. A)In determining whether a person is a vulnerable witness under subsection (1)(b) or (d), the court must—

(a) have regard to the best interests of the witness, and

(b) take account of any views expressed by the witness.]

(5) In this section and sections 271. A to 271. M of this Act—

[F46 "child witness" means a vulnerable witness referred to in subsection (1)(a),]

[F47 "deemed vulnerable witness" means a vulnerable witness referred to in subsection (1)(c),]

"court" means the High Court or the sheriff court,

[F48 "hearing in relevant criminal proceedings" means any hearing in the course of any criminal proceedings in the High Court or the sheriff court.]

F49 ...

(6) In sections 271. A to 271. M of this Act, "special measure" means any of the special measures set out in, or prescribed under, section 271. H below.]

Amendments (Textual)

F39. Ss. 271-271. M and preceding cross-heading substituted for s. 271 (1.4.2005, 30.11.2005, 1.4.2006. 1.4.2007 and 2.7.2007 for certain purposes, otherwise 1.4.2008) by Vulnerable Witnesses (Scotland) Act 2004 (asp 3), ss. 1, 25; S.S.I. 2005/168, art. 2, Sch. (with savings in art. 4); S.S.I. 2005/590, art. 2, Sch. (with art. 4); S.S.I. 2006/59, art. 2, Sch. (with art. 4. (1)); S.S.I. 2007/101, art. 2, Sch. (with art. 4); S.S.I. 2007/329, art. 2, Sch. (with art. 4); S.S.I. 2008/57, art. 2 (with art. 3)

F40. S. 271. (1) substituted (1.9.2015) by Victims and Witnesses (Scotland) Act 2014 (asp 1), ss. 10. (a), 34; S.S.I. 2015/200, art. 2. (2), sch. (with arts. 1. (3), 4)

F41. S. 271. (1)(c)(iiia) inserted (31.5.2016) by Human Trafficking and Exploitation (Scotland) Act 2015 (asp 12), s. 45. (2), sch. para. 1 (with s. 44); S.S.I. 2016/128, reg. 2, sch.

F42. S. 271. (1. A) repealed (1.9.2015) by Victims and Witnesses (Scotland) Act 2014 (asp 1), ss. 10. (c), 34; S.S.I. 2015/200, art. 2. (2), sch. (with arts. 1. (3), 4)

F43. S. 271. (1. AA) inserted (1.9.2015) by Victims and Witnesses (Scotland) Act 2014 (asp 1), ss. 10. (b), 34; S.S.I. 2015/200, art. 2. (2), sch. (with arts. 1. (3), 4)

F44. Words in s. 271. (2) inserted (1.9.2015) by Victims and Witnesses (Scotland) Act 2014 (asp 1), ss. 10. (d), 34; S.S.I. 2015/200, art. 2. (2), sch. (with arts. 1. (3), 4)

F45. S. 271. (4. A) inserted (1.9.2015) by Victims and Witnesses (Scotland) Act 2014 (asp 1), ss. 10. (e), 34; S.S.I. 2015/200, art. 2. (2), sch. (with arts. 1. (3), 4)

F46. Definition in s. 271. (5) inserted (1.9.2015) by Victims and Witnesses (Scotland) Act 2014 (asp 1), ss. 11. (3)(a), 34; S.S.I. 2015/200, art. 2. (2), sch. (with arts. 1. (3), 4)

F47. Definition in s. 271. (5) inserted (1.9.2015) by Victims and Witnesses (Scotland) Act 2014 (asp 1), ss. 11. (3)(b), 34; S.S.I. 2015/200, art. 2. (2), sch. (with arts. 1. (3), 4)

F48. Definition in s. 271. (5) inserted (28.3.2011) by Criminal Justice and Licensing (Scotland) Act 2010 (asp 13), ss. 87. (2)(b)(ii), 206. (1); S.S.I. 2011/178, art. 2, sch.

F49. Definition in s. 271. (5) repealed (28.3.2011) by Criminal Justice and Licensing (Scotland) Act 2010 (asp 13), ss. 87. (2)(b)(i), 206. (1); S.S.I. 2011/178, art. 2, sch.

Modifications etc. (not altering text)

C6. Ss. 271-271. M applied by Criminal Justice (Scotland) Act 2003 (asp 7), s. 15. A (as inserted (1.4.2005, 30.11.2005, 1.4.2006, 1.4.2007 and 2.7.2007 for certain purposes and 1.4.2008) by Vulnerable Witnesses (Scotland) Act 2004 (asp 3), ss. 3, 25; S.S.I. 2005/168, art. 2, Sch. (with savings in art. 4); S.S.I. 2005/590, art. 2, Sch. (with art. 4); S.S.I. 2006/59, art. 2, Sch. (with art. 4); S.S.I. 2007/101, art. 2, Sch. (with art. 4); S.S.I. 2007/329, art. 2, Sch. (with art. 4)); S.S.I. 2008/57, art. 2 (with art. 3)

C7. Ss. 271-271. M applied (with modifications) (23.12.2015) by The Justice of the Peace Courts (Special Measures) (Scotland) Order 2015 (S.S.I. 2015/447), arts. 1. (2), 3 (with art. 1. (3))

[F50271. A[F51. Child and deemed vulnerable witnesses]S

(1) Where a child witness [F52or a deemed vulnerable witness] is to give evidence at or for the purposes of [F53a hearing in relevant criminal proceedings], the F54... witness is entitled, subject to—

(a) subsections (2) to (13) below, and

(b) section 271. D of this Act,

to the benefit of one or more of the special measures for the purpose of giving evidence.

(2) A party citing or intending to cite a child witness [F55or a deemed vulnerable witness] shall, [F56by the required time], lodge with the court a notice (referred to in this Act as a "[F57vulnerable] witness notice")—

(a) specifying the special measure or measures which the party considers to be the most appropriate for the purpose of taking the F58... witness's evidence, or

(b) if the party considers that the F58... witness should give evidence without the benefit of any special measure, stating that fact.

(3) A [F59vulnerable] witness notice shall contain or be accompanied by—

(a) a summary of any views expressed for the purposes of section 271. E(2)(b) of this Act, and

(b) such other information as may be prescribed by Act of Adjournal.

[F60. (3. A)In the case where a vulnerable witness notice under subsection (2)(a) specifies only a standard special measure, subsection (3)(a) does not apply.]

(4) The court may, on cause shown, allow a [F61vulnerable] witness notice to be lodged after [F62the required time].

[F63. (4. A)Any party to the proceedings may, not later than 7 days after a vulnerable witness notice has been lodged, lodge with the court a notice (referred to in this section as an "objection notice") stating—

(a) an objection to any special measure (other than a standard special measure) specified in the vulnerable witness notice that the party considers to be inappropriate, and

(b) the reasons for that objection.

(4. B)The court may, on cause shown, allow an objection notice to be lodged after the period referred to in subsection (4. A).

(4. C)If an objection notice is lodged in accordance with subsection (4. A) or (4. B)—

(a) subsection (5)(a)(ii) does not apply to the vulnerable witness notice, and

(b) the court must make an order under subsection (5. A).]

(5) The court shall, not [F64earlier than 7 days and not later than 14] days after a [F65vulnerable] witness notice has been lodged, consider the notice in the absence of the parties and, subject to section [F66271. B] of this Act—

(a) in the case of a notice under subsection (2)(a) above—

(i) if a standard special measure is specified in the notice, make an order authorising the use of that measure for the purpose of taking the F67... witness's evidence, and

(ii) if any other special measure is specified in the notice and the court is satisfied on the basis of the notice that it is appropriate to do so, make an order authorising the use of the special measure (in addition to any authorised by virtue of an order under sub-paragraph (i) above) for the purpose of taking the F67... witness's evidence,

(b) in the case of a notice under subsection (2)(b) above, if—

(i) the summary of views accompanying the notice under subsection (3)(a) above indicates that the F68... witness has expressed a wish to give evidence without the benefit of any special measure, and

(ii) the court is satisfied on the basis of the notice that it is appropriate to do so, make an order authorising the giving of evidence by the F68... witness without the benefit of any special measure, or

(c) if—

(i) paragraph (a)(ii) or (b) above would apply but for the fact that the court is not satisfied as mentioned in that paragraph, or

(ii) in the case of a notice under subsection (2)(b), the summary of views accompanying the notice under subsection (3)(a) above indicates that the F69... witness has not expressed a wish to give evidence without the benefit of any special measure,

make an order [F70under subsection (5. A) below.]

[F71. (5. A)That order is an order—

(a) in the case of proceedings in the High Court where the preliminary hearing is yet to be held, appointing the [F72vulnerable] witness notice to be disposed of at that hearing;

(b) in the case of proceedings on indictment in the sheriff court where the first diet is yet to be held, appointing the [F73vulnerable] witness notice to be disposed of at that diet; or

(c) in any other case, appointing a diet to be held before [F74the hearing at which the evidence is to be given] and requiring the parties to attend the diet.]

(6) Subsection (7) below applies where—

(a) it appears to the court that a party intends to call a child witness [F75or a deemed vulnerable witness] to give evidence at or for the purposes of [F76a hearing in relevant criminal proceedings],

(b) the party has not lodged a [F77vulnerable] witness notice in respect of the F78... witness by the time specified in subsection (2) above, and

(c) the court has not allowed a [F79vulnerable] witness notice in respect of the F80... witness to be lodged after that time under subsection (4) above.

(7) Where this subsection applies, the court shall—

(a) order the party to lodge a [F81vulnerable] witness notice in respect of the F82... witness by such time as the court may specify, or

[F83. (b)where the court does not so order—

(i) in the case of proceedings on indictment where this subsection applies at or before the preliminary hearing or, as the case may be, the first diet, at that hearing or diet make an order under subsection (9) below; or

(ii) in any other case, make an order appointing a diet to be held before [F84the hearing at which the evidence is to be given] diet and requiring the parties to attend the diet.]

(8) On making an order under subsection [F85. (5. A)(c) or (7)(b)(ii)] above, the court may postpone [F86the hearing at which the evidence is to be given].

[F87. (8. A)Subsection (9) below applies to—

(a) a preliminary hearing or first diet, so far as the court is—

(i) by virtue of an order under subsection (5. A)(a) or (b) above, disposing of a [F88vulnerable] witness notice at the hearing or diet; or

(ii) by virtue of subsection (7)(b)(i) above, to make an order under subsection (9) F89... at the hearing or diet; and

(b) a diet appointed under subsection (5. A)(c) or (7)(b)(ii) above.]

(9) At a [F90hearing or diet to which this subsection applies], the court, after giving the parties an opportunity to be heard—

(a) in a case where any of the standard special measures has been authorised by an order under subsection (5)(a)(i) above, may make an order authorising the use of such further special measure or measures as it considers appropriate for the purpose of taking the F91... witness's evidence, and

(b) in any other case, shall make an order—

(i) authorising the use of such special measure or measures as the court considers to be the most appropriate for the purpose of taking the F91... witness's evidence, or

(ii) that the F91... witness is to give evidence without the benefit of any special measure.

(10) The court may make an order under subsection (9)(b)(ii) above only if satisfied—

(a) where the F92... witness has expressed a wish to give evidence without the benefit of any special measure, that it is appropriate for the F92... witness so to give evidence, or

(b) in any other case, that—

(i) the use of any special measure for the purpose of taking the evidence of the F92... witness would give rise to a significant risk of prejudice to the fairness of the trial or otherwise to the interests of justice, and

(ii) that risk significantly outweighs any risk of prejudice to the interests of the F92... witness if the order is made.

(11) A [F93hearing or diet to which subsection (9) above applies] may—

(a) on the application of the party citing or intending to cite the F94... witness in respect of whom the diet is to be held, or

(b) of the court's own motion,

be held in chambers.

(12) A diet [F95appointed under subsection (5. A)(c) or (7)(b)(ii) above in any case may be conjoined with any other diet to be held before [F96the hearing at which the evidence is to be given].]

(13) A party lodging a [F97vulnerable] witness notice [F98or an objection notice] shall, at the same time, intimate the notice to the other parties to the proceedings.

[F99. (13. A) In subsections (2) and (4) above, "the required time" means—

(a) in the case of proceedings in the High Court, no later than 14 clear days before the preliminary hearing;

(b) in the case of proceedings on indictment in the sheriff court, no later than 7 clear days before the first diet;

(c) in any other case, no later than 14 clear days before [F100the hearing at which the evidence is to be given].]

(14) In this section, references to a standard special measure are to any of the following special measures—

(a) the use of a live television link in accordance with section 271. J of this Act F101...

(b) the use of a screen in accordance with section 271. K of this Act, and

(c) the use of a supporter in accordance with section 271. L of this Act F102...

[F103. (15)The Scottish Ministers may, by order subject to the affirmative procedure—

(a) modify subsection (14),

(b) in consequence of any modification made under paragraph (a)—

(i) prescribe the procedure to be followed when standard special measures are used, and

(ii) so far as is necessary, modify sections 271. A to 271. M of this Act.]]

Amendments (Textual)

F50. Ss. 271-271. M and preceding cross-heading substituted for s. 271 (1.4.2005, 30.11.2005, 1.4.2006. 1.4.2007 and 2.7.2007 for certain purposes and otherwise 1.4.2008) by Vulnerable Witnesses (Scotland) Act 2004 (asp 3), ss. 1, 25; S.S.I. 2005/168, art. 2, Sch. (with savings in art. 4); S.S.I. 2005/590, art. 2, Sch. (with art. 4); S.S.I. 2006/59, art. 2, Sch. (with art. 4. (1)); S.S.I. 2007/101, art. 2, Sch. (with art. 4); S.S.I. 2007/329, art. 2, Sch. (with art. 4); S.S.I. 2008/57, art. 2 (with art. 3)

F51. S. 271. A title substituted (1.9.2015) by Victims and Witnesses (Scotland) Act 2014 (asp 1), ss. 11. (5), 34; S.S.I. 2015/200, art. 2. (2), sch. (with arts. 1. (3), 4)

F52. Words in s. 271. A(1) inserted (1.9.2015) by Victims and Witnesses (Scotland) Act 2014 (asp 1), ss. 11. (4)(a)(i), 34; S.S.I. 2015/200, art. 2. (2), sch. (with arts. 1. (3), 4)

F53. Words in s. 271. A(1) substituted (28.3.2011) by Criminal Justice and Licensing (Scotland) Act 2010 (asp 13), ss. 87. (3)(a), 206. (1); S.S.I. 2011/178, art. 2, sch.

F54. Word in s. 271. A(1) repealed (1.9.2015) by Victims and Witnesses (Scotland) Act 2014 (asp 1), ss. 11. (4)(a)(ii), 34; S.S.I. 2015/200, art. 2. (2), sch. (with arts. 1. (3), 4)

F55. Words in s. 271. A(2) inserted (1.9.2015) by Victims and Witnesses (Scotland) Act 2014 (asp 1), ss. 11. (4)(b)(i), 34; S.S.I. 2015/200, art. 2. (2), sch. (with arts. 1. (3), 4)

F56. Words in s. 271. A(2) substituted (1.4.2005, 1.4.2006, 1.4.2007 and 2.7.2007 for certain purposes and otherwise 1.4.2008) by Criminal Procedure (Amendment) (Scotland) Act 2004 (asp 5), ss. 25, 27. (1), Sch. para. 43. (a); S.S.I. 2004/405, art. 2. (2), Sch. 2 (with savings in arts. 3-5);

S.S.I. 2005/168, art. 2, Sch. (with savings in art. 4); S.S.I. 2006/59, art. 2, Sch. (with art. 4. (1));
S.S.I. 2007/101, art. 2, Sch. (with art. 4); S.S.I. 2007/329, art. 2, Sch. (with art. 4); S.S.I. 2008/57,
art. 2 (with art. 3)

F57. Word in s. 271. A(2) substituted (1.9.2015) by Victims and Witnesses (Scotland) Act 2014
(asp 1), ss. 11. (4)(b)(ii), 34; S.S.I. 2015/200, art. 2. (2), sch. (with arts. 1. (3), 4)

F58. Word in s. 271. A(2)(a)(b) repealed (1.9.2015) by Victims and Witnesses (Scotland) Act
2014 (asp 1), ss. 11. (4)(b)(iii), 34; S.S.I. 2015/200, art. 2. (2), sch. (with arts. 1. (3), 4)

F59. Word in s. 271. A(3) substituted (1.9.2015) by Victims and Witnesses (Scotland) Act 2014
(asp 1), ss. 11. (4)(c), 34; S.S.I. 2015/200, art. 2. (2), sch. (with arts. 1. (3), 4)

F60. S. 271. A(3. A) inserted (1.9.2015) by Victims and Witnesses (Scotland) Act 2014 (asp 1),
ss. 11. (4)(d), 34; S.S.I. 2015/200, art. 2. (2), sch. (with arts. 1. (3), 4)

F61. Word in s. 271. A(4) substituted (1.9.2015) by Victims and Witnesses (Scotland) Act 2014
(asp 1), ss. 11. (4)(c), 34; S.S.I. 2015/200, art. 2. (2), sch. (with arts. 1. (3), 4)

F62. Words in s. 271. A(4) substituted (1.4.2005, 1.4.2006, 1.4.2007 and 2.7.2007 for certain
purposes and otherwise 1.4.2008) by Criminal Procedure (Amendment) (Scotland) Act 2004 (asp
5), ss. 25, 27. (1), Sch. para. 43. (b); S.S.I. 2004/405, art. 2. (2), Sch. 2 (with savings in arts. 3-5);
S.S.I. 2005/168, art. 2, Sch. (with savings in art. 4); S.S.I. 2006/59, art. 2, Sch. (with art. 4. (1));
S.S.I. 2007/101, art. 2, Sch. (with art. 4); S.S.I. 2007/329, art. 2, Sch. (with art. 4); S.S.I. 2008/57,
art. 2 (with art. 3)

F63. S. 271. A(4. A)-(4. C) inserted (1.9.2015) by Victims and Witnesses (Scotland) Act 2014
(asp 1), ss. 13. (a), 34; S.S.I. 2015/200, art. 2. (2), sch. (with arts. 1. (3), 4)

F64. Words in s. 271. A(5) substituted (1.9.2015) by Victims and Witnesses (Scotland) Act 2014
(asp 1), ss. 13. (b), 34; S.S.I. 2015/200, art. 2. (2), sch. (with arts. 1. (3), 4)

F65. Word in s. 271. A(5) substituted (1.9.2015) by Victims and Witnesses (Scotland) Act 2014
(asp 1), ss. 11. (4)(e)(i), 34; S.S.I. 2015/200, art. 2. (2), sch. (with arts. 1. (3), 4)

F66. Word in s. 271. A(5) substituted (1.9.2015) by Victims and Witnesses (Scotland) Act 2014
(asp 1), ss. 14. (2), 34; S.S.I. 2015/200, art. 2. (2), sch. (with arts. 1. (3), 4)

F67. Word in s. 271. A(5)(a) repealed (1.9.2015) by Victims and Witnesses (Scotland) Act 2014
(asp 1), ss. 11. (4)(e)(ii), 34; S.S.I. 2015/200, art. 2. (2), sch. (with arts. 1. (3), 4)

F68. Word in s. 271. A(5)(b) repealed (1.9.2015) by Victims and Witnesses (Scotland) Act 2014
(asp 1), ss. 11. (4)(e)(ii), 34; S.S.I. 2015/200, art. 2. (2), sch. (with arts. 1. (3), 4)

F69. Word in s. 271. A(5)(c) repealed (1.9.2015) by Victims and Witnesses (Scotland) Act 2014
(asp 1), ss. 11. (4)(e)(ii), 34; S.S.I. 2015/200, art. 2. (2), sch. (with arts. 1. (3), 4)

F70. Words in s. 271. A(5) substituted (1.4.2005, 1.4.2006, 1.4.2007 and 2.7.2007 for certain
purposes and otherwise 1.4.2008) by Criminal Procedure (Amendment) (Scotland) Act 2004 (asp
5), ss. 25, 27. (1), Sch. para. 43. (c); S.S.I. 2004/405, art. 2. (2), Sch. 2 (with savings in arts. 3-5);
S.S.I. 2005/168, art. 2, Sch. (with savings in art. 4); S.S.I. 2006/59, art. 2, Sch. (with art. 4. (1));
S.S.I. 2007/101, art. 2, Sch. (with art. 4); S.S.I. 2007/329, art. 2, Sch. (with art. 4); S.S.I. 2008/57,
art. 2 (with art. 3)

F71. S. 271. A(5. A) inserted (1.4.2005, 1.4.2006, 1.4.2007 and 2.7.2007 for certain purposes and
otherwise 1.4.2008) by Criminal Procedure (Amendment) (Scotland) Act 2004 (asp 5), ss. 25, 27.
(1), Sch. para. 43. (d); S.S.I. 2004/405, art. 2. (2), Sch. 2 (with savings in arts. 3-5); S.S.I.
2005/168, art. 2, Sch. (with savings in art. 4); S.S.I. 2006/59, art. 2, Sch. (with art. 4. (1)) S.S.I.
2007/101, art. 2, Sch. (with art. 4); S.S.I. 2007/329, art. 2, Sch. (with art. 4); S.S.I. 2008/57, art. 2
(with art. 3)

F72. Word in s. 271. A(5. A)(a) substituted (1.9.2015) by Victims and Witnesses (Scotland) Act
2014 (asp 1), ss. 11. (4)(f)(i), 34; S.S.I. 2015/200, art. 2. (2), sch. (with arts. 1. (3), 4)

F73. Word in s. 271. A(5. A)(b) substituted (1.9.2015) by Victims and Witnesses (Scotland) Act
2014 (asp 1), ss. 11. (4)(f)(ii), 34; S.S.I. 2015/200, art. 2. (2), sch. (with arts. 1. (3), 4)

F74. Words in s. 271. A(5. A)(c) substituted (28.3.2011) by Criminal Justice and Licensing
(Scotland) Act 2010 (asp 13), ss. 87. (3)(b), 206. (1); S.S.I. 2011/178, art. 2, sch.

F75. Words in s. 271. A(6)(a) inserted (1.9.2015) by Victims and Witnesses (Scotland) Act 2014
(asp 1), ss. 11. (4)(g)(i), 34; S.S.I. 2015/200, art. 2. (2), sch. (with arts. 1. (3), 4)

F76. Words in s. 271. A(6)(a) substituted (28.3.2011) by Criminal Justice and Licensing (Scotland) Act 2010 (asp 13), ss. 87. (3)(c), 206. (1); S.S.I. 2011/178, art. 2, sch.

F77. Word in s. 271. A(6)(b) substituted (1.9.2015) by Victims and Witnesses (Scotland) Act 2014 (asp 1), ss. 11. (4)(g)(ii), 34; S.S.I. 2015/200, art. 2. (2), sch. (with arts. 1. (3), 4)

F78. Word in s. 271. A(6)(b) repealed (1.9.2015) by Victims and Witnesses (Scotland) Act 2014 (asp 1), ss. 11. (4)(g)(iii), 34; S.S.I. 2015/200, art. 2. (2), sch. (with arts. 1. (3), 4)

F79. Word in s. 271. A(6)(c) substituted (1.9.2015) by Victims and Witnesses (Scotland) Act 2014 (asp 1), ss. 11. (4)(g)(iv), 34; S.S.I. 2015/200, art. 2. (2), sch. (with arts. 1. (3), 4)

F80. Word in s. 271. A(6)(c) repealed (1.9.2015) by Victims and Witnesses (Scotland) Act 2014 (asp 1), ss. 11. (4)(g)(v), 34; S.S.I. 2015/200, art. 2. (2), sch. (with arts. 1. (3), 4)

F81. Word in s. 271. A(7)(a) substituted (1.9.2015) by Victims and Witnesses (Scotland) Act 2014 (asp 1), ss. 11. (4)(h)(i), 34; S.S.I. 2015/200, art. 2. (2), sch. (with arts. 1. (3), 4)

F82. Word in s. 271. A(7)(a) repealed (1.9.2015) by Victims and Witnesses (Scotland) Act 2014 (asp 1), ss. 11. (4)(h)(ii), 34; S.S.I. 2015/200, art. 2. (2), sch. (with arts. 1. (3), 4)

F83. S. 271. A(7)(b) substituted (1.4.2005, 1.4.2006, 1.4.2007 and 2.7.2007 for certain purposes and otherwise 1.4.2008) by Criminal Procedure (Amendment) (Scotland) Act 2004 (asp 5), ss. 25, 27. (1), Sch. para. 43. (e); S.S.I. 2004/405, art. 2. (2), Sch. 2 (with savings in arts. 3-5); S.S.I. 2005/168, art. 2, Sch. (with savings in art. 4); S.S.I. 2006/59, art. 2, Sch. (with art. 4. (1)); S.S.I. 2007/101, art. 2, Sch. (with art. 4); S.S.I. 2007/329, art. 2, Sch. (with art. 4); S.S.I. 2008/57, art. 2 (with art. 3)

F84. Words in s. 271. A(7)(b)(ii) substituted (28.3.2011) by Criminal Justice and Licensing (Scotland) Act 2010 (asp 13), ss. 87. (3)(d), 206. (1); S.S.I. 2011/178, art. 2, sch.

F85. Words in s. 271. A(8) substituted (1.4.2005, 1.4.2006, 1.4.2007 and 2.7.2007 for certain purposes and otherwise 1.4.2008) by Criminal Procedure (Amendment) (Scotland) Act 2004 (asp 5), ss. 25, 27. (1), Sch. para. 43. (f); S.S.I. 2004/405, art. 2. (2), Sch. 2 (with savings in arts. 3-5); S.S.I. 2005/168, art. 2, Sch. (with savings in art. 4); S.S.I. 2006/59, art. 2, Sch. (with art. 4. (1)); S.S.I. 2007/101, art. 2, Sch. (with art. 4); S.S.I. 2007/329, art. 2, Sch. (with art. 4); S.S.I. 2008/57, art. 2 (with art. 3)

F86. Words in s. 271. A(8) substituted (28.3.2011) by Criminal Justice and Licensing (Scotland) Act 2010 (asp 13), ss. 87. (3)(e), 206. (1); S.S.I. 2011/178, art. 2, sch.

F87. S. 271. A(8. A) inserted (1.4.2005, 1.4.2006, 1.4.2007 and 2.7.2007 for certain purposes and otherwise 1.4.2008) by Criminal Procedure (Amendment) (Scotland) Act 2004 (asp 5), ss. 25, 27. (1), Sch. para. 43. (g); S.S.I. 2004/405, art. 2. (2), Sch. 2 (with savings in arts. 3-5); S.S.I. 2005/168, art. 2, Sch. (with savings in art. 4); S.S.I. 2006/59, art. 2, Sch. (with art. 4. (1)); S.S.I. 2007/101, art. 2, Sch. (with art. 4); S.S.I. 2007/329, art. 2, Sch. (with art. 4); S.S.I. 2008/57, art. 2 (with art. 3)

F88. Word in s. 271. A(8. A)(a)(i) substituted (1.9.2015) by Victims and Witnesses (Scotland) Act 2014 (asp 1), ss. 11. (4)(i)(i), 34; S.S.I. 2015/200, art. 2. (2), sch. (with arts. 1. (3), 4)

F89. Word in s. 271. A(8. A)(a)(ii) repealed (1.9.2015) by Victims and Witnesses (Scotland) Act 2014 (asp 1), ss. 11. (4)(i)(ii), 34; S.S.I. 2015/200, art. 2. (2), sch. (with arts. 1. (3), 4)

F90. Words in s. 271. A(9) substituted (1.4.2005, 1.4.2006, 1.4.2007 and 2.7.2007 for certain purposes and otherwise 1.4.2008) by Criminal Procedure (Amendment) (Scotland) Act 2004 (asp 5), ss. 25, 27. (1), Sch. para. 43. (h); S.S.I. 2004/405, art. 2. (2), Sch. 2 (with savings in arts. 3-5); S.S.I. 2005/168, art. 2, Sch. (with savings in art. 4); S.S.I. 2006/59, art. 2, Sch. (with art. 4. (1)); S.S.I. 2007/101, art. 2, Sch. (with art. 4); S.S.I. 2007/329, art. 2, Sch. (with art. 4); S.S.I. 2008/57, art. 2 (with art. 3)

F91. Word in s. 271. A(9) repealed (1.9.2015) by Victims and Witnesses (Scotland) Act 2014 (asp 1), ss. 11. (4)(j), 34; S.S.I. 2015/200, art. 2. (2), sch. (with arts. 1. (3), 4)

F92. Word in s. 271. A(10) repealed (1.9.2015) by Victims and Witnesses (Scotland) Act 2014 (asp 1), ss. 11. (4)(k), 34; S.S.I. 2015/200, art. 2. (2), sch. (with arts. 1. (3), 4)

F93. Words in s. 271. A(11) substituted (1.4.2005, 1.4.2006, 1.4.2007 and 2.7.2007 for certain purposes and otherwise 1.4.2008) by Criminal Procedure (Amendment) (Scotland) Act 2004 (asp 5), ss. 25, 27. (1), Sch. para. 43. (i); S.S.I. 2004/405, art. 2. (2), Sch. 2 (with savings in arts. 3-5);

S.S.I. 2005/168, art. 2, Sch. (with savings in art. 4); S.S.I. 2006/59, art. 2, Sch. (with art. 4. (1));
S.S.I. 2007/101, art. 2, Sch. (with art. 4); S.S.I. 2007/329, art. 2, Sch. (with art. 4); S.S.I. 2008/57,
art. 2 (with art. 3)

F94. Word in s. 271. A(11)(a) repealed (1.9.2015) by Victims and Witnesses (Scotland) Act 2014
(asp 1), ss. 11. (4)(l), 34; S.S.I. 2015/200, art. 2. (2), sch. (with arts. 1. (3), 4)

F95. Words in s. 271. A(12) substituted (1.4.2005, 1.4.2006, 1.4.2007 and 2.7.2007 for certain
purposes and otherwise 1.4.2008) by Criminal Procedure (Amendment) (Scotland) Act 2004 (asp
5), ss. 25, 27. (1), Sch. para. 43. (j); S.S.I. 2004/405, art. 2. (2), Sch. 2 (with savings in arts. 3-5);
S.S.I. 2005/168, art. 2, Sch. (with savings in art. 4); S.S.I. 2006/59, art. 2, Sch. (with art. 4. (1));
S.S.I. 2007/101, art. 2, Sch. (with art. 4); S.S.I. 2007/329, art. 2, Sch. (with art. 4); S.S.I. 2008/57,
art. 2 (with art. 3)

F96. Words in s. 271. A(12) substituted (28.3.2011) by Criminal Justice and Licensing (Scotland)
Act 2010 (asp 13), ss. 87. (3)(g), 206. (1); S.S.I. 2011/178, art. 2, sch.

F97. Word in s. 271. A(13) substituted (1.9.2015) by Victims and Witnesses (Scotland) Act 2014
(asp 1), ss. 11. (4)(m), 34; S.S.I. 2015/200, art. 2. (2), sch. (with arts. 1. (3), 4)

F98. Words in s. 271. A(13) inserted (1.9.2015) by Victims and Witnesses (Scotland) Act 2014
(asp 1), ss. 13. (c), 34; S.S.I. 2015/200, art. 2. (2), sch. (with arts. 1. (3), 4)

F99. S. 271. A(13. A) inserted (1.4.2005, 1.4.2006, 1.4.2007 and 2.7.2007 for certain purposes and
otherwise 1.4.2008) by Criminal Procedure (Amendment) (Scotland) Act 2004 (asp 5), ss. 25, 27.
(1), Sch. para. 43. (k); S.S.I. 2004/405, art. 2. (2), Sch. 2 (with savings in arts. 3-5); S.S.I.
2005/168, art. 2, Sch. (with savings in art. 4); S.S.I. 2006/59, art. 2, Sch. (with art. 4. (1)); S.S.I.
2007/101, art. 2, Sch. (with art. 4); S.S.I. 2007/329, art. 2, Sch. (with art. 4); S.S.I. 2008/57, art. 2
(with art. 3)

F100. Words in s. 271. A(13. A)(c) substituted (28.3.2011) by Criminal Justice and Licensing
(Scotland) Act 2010 (asp 13), ss. 87. (3)(h), 206. (1); S.S.I. 2011/178, art. 2, sch.

F101. Words in s. 271. A(14)(a) repealed (1.9.2015) by Victims and Witnesses (Scotland) Act
2014 (asp 1), ss. 12. (a)(i), 34; S.S.I. 2015/200, art. 2. (2), sch. (with arts. 1. (3), 4)

F102. Words in s. 271. A(14)(c) repealed (1.9.2015) by Victims and Witnesses (Scotland) Act
2014 (asp 1), ss. 12. (a)(ii), 34; S.S.I. 2015/200, art. 2. (2), sch. (with arts. 1. (3), 4)

F103. S. 271. A(15) inserted (1.9.2015) by Victims and Witnesses (Scotland) Act 2014 (asp 1), ss.
12. (b), 34; S.S.I. 2015/200, art. 2. (2), sch. (with arts. 1. (3), 4)

Modifications etc. (not altering text)

C7. Ss. 271-271. M applied (with modifications) (23.12.2015) by The Justice of the Peace Courts
(Special Measures) (Scotland) Order 2015 (S.S.I. 2015/447), arts. 1. (2), 3 (with art. 1. (3))

C8. Ss. 271-271. M applied by Criminal Justice (Scotland) Act 2003 (asp 7), s. 15. A (as inserted
(1.4.2005, 30.11.2005, 1.4.2006, 1.4.2007 and 2.7.2007 for certain purposes and otherwise
1.4.2008) by Vulnerable Witnesses (Scotland) Act 2004 (asp 3), ss. 3, 25; S.S.I. 2005/168, art. 2,
Sch. (with savings in art. 4); S.S.I. 2005/590, art. 2, Sch. (with art. 4); S.S.I. 2006/59, art. 2, Sch.
(with art. 4); S.S.I. 2007/101, art. 2, Sch. (with art. 4); S.S.I. 2007/329, art. 2, Sch. (with art. 4));
S.S.I. 2008/57, art. 2 (with art. 3)

[F104271. BFurther special provision for child witnesses under the age of 12. S

(1) This section applies where a child witness—

(a) is to give evidence at, or for the purposes of, [F105a hearing in relevant criminal
proceedings] in respect of any offence specified in subsection (2) below, and

(b) is under the age of 12 on the date of commencement of the proceedings in which [F106the
hearing] is being or to be held.

(2) The offences referred to in subsection (1)(a) above are—

(a) murder,

(b) culpable homicide,

(c) any offence to which section 288. C of this Act applies,

(d) any offence which involves an assault on, or injury or a threat of injury to, any person (including any offence involving neglect or ill-treatment of, or other cruelty to, a child),

(e) abduction, and

(f) plagium.

[F107. (3)Subsection (4) applies if the child witness expresses a wish to be present in the court-room for the purpose of giving evidence.

(4) The court must make an order under section 271. A or, as the case may be, 271. D which has the effect of requiring the child witness to be present in the court-room for the purpose of giving evidence unless the court considers that it would not be appropriate for the child witness to be present there for that purpose.

(5) Subsection (6) applies if the child witness—

(a) does not express a wish to be present in the court-room for the purpose of giving evidence, or

(b) expresses a wish to give evidence in some other way.

(6) The court may not make an order under section 271. A or 271. D having the effect mentioned in subsection (4) unless the court considers that—

(a) the giving of evidence by the child witness in some way other than by being present in the court-room for that purpose would give rise to a significant risk of prejudice to the fairness of the trial or otherwise to the interests of justice, and

(b) that risk significantly outweighs any risk of prejudice to the interests of the child witness if the order were to be made.]]

Amendments (Textual)

F104. Ss. 271-271. M and preceding cross-heading substituted for s. 271 (1.4.2005, 30.11.2005, 1.4.2006. 1.4.2007 and 2.7.2007 for certain purposes and otherwise 1.4.2008) by Vulnerable Witnesses (Scotland) Act 2004 (asp 3), ss. 1, 25; S.S.I. 2005/168, art. 2, Sch. (with savings in art. 4); S.S.I. 2005/590, art. 2, Sch. (with art. 4); S.S.I. 2006/59, art. 2, Sch. (with art. 4. (1)); S.S.I. 2007/101, art. 2, Sch. (with art. 4); S.S.I. 2007/329, art. 2, Sch. (with art. 4); S.S.I. 2008/57, art. 2 (with art. 3)

F105. Words in s. 271. B(1)(a) substituted (28.3.2011) by Criminal Justice and Licensing (Scotland) Act 2010 (asp 13), ss. 87. (4)(a), 206. (1); S.S.I. 2011/178, art. 2, sch.

F106. Words in s. 271. B(1)(b) substituted (28.3.2011) by Criminal Justice and Licensing (Scotland) Act 2010 (asp 13), ss. 87. (4)(b), 206. (1); S.S.I. 2011/178, art. 2, sch.

F107. S. 271. B(3)-(6) substituted for s. 271. B(3) (1.9.2015) by Victims and Witnesses (Scotland) Act 2014 (asp 1), ss. 14. (1), 34; S.S.I. 2015/200, art. 2. (2), sch. (with arts. 1. (3), 4)

Modifications etc. (not altering text)

C7. Ss. 271-271. M applied (with modifications) (23.12.2015) by The Justice of the Peace Courts (Special Measures) (Scotland) Order 2015 (S.S.I. 2015/447), arts. 1. (2), 3 (with art. 1. (3))

C9. Ss. 271-271. M applied by Criminal Justice (Scotland) Act 2003 (asp 7), s. 15. A (as inserted (1.4.2005, 30.11.2005, 1.4.2006, 1.4.2007 and 2.7.2007 for certain purposes and otherwise 1.4.2008) by Vulnerable Witnesses (Scotland) Act 2004 (asp 3), ss. 3, 25; S.S.I. 2005/168, art. 2, Sch. (with savings in art. 4); S.S.I. 2005/590, art. 2, Sch. (with art. 4); S.S.I. 2006/59, art. 2, Sch. (with art. 4); S.S.I. 2007/101, art. 2, Sch. (with art. 4); S.S.I. 2007/329, art. 2, Sch. (with art. 4)); S.S.I. 2008/57, { art. 2} (with art. 3)

[F108271. BAAssessment of witnessesS

(1) This section applies where a party intends to cite a witness other than a child witness or a deemed vulnerable witness to give evidence at, or for the purposes of, a hearing in relevant criminal proceedings.

(2) The party intending to cite the witness must take reasonable steps to carry out an assessment under subsection (3).

(3) An assessment must determine whether the person—

(a) is likely to be a vulnerable witness, and

(b) if so, what special measure or combination of special measures ought to be used for the purpose of taking the person's evidence.

(4) In determining under subsection (3)(a) whether a person is likely to be a vulnerable witness the party must—

(a) take into account the matters mentioned in section 271. (2),

(b) have regard to the best interests of the person, and

(c) take account of any views expressed by the person.]

Amendments (Textual)

F108. S. 271. BA inserted (1.9.2015) by Victims and Witnesses (Scotland) Act 2014 (asp 1), ss. 16. (1), 34; S.S.I. 2015/200, art. 2. (2), sch. (with arts. 1. (3), 4)

Modifications etc. (not altering text)

C7. Ss. 271-271. M applied (with modifications) (23.12.2015) by The Justice of the Peace Courts (Special Measures) (Scotland) Order 2015 (S.S.I. 2015/447), arts. 1. (2), 3 (with art. 1. (3))

[F109271. C[F110. Vulnerable witness application]S

(1) This section applies where a party citing or intending to cite a person (other than a child witness [F111or a deemed vulnerable witness]) to give evidence at, or for the purposes of, [F112a hearing in relevant criminal proceedings] (such a person being referred to in this section as "the witness") [F113and, having carried out an assessment under section 271. BA,] considers—

(a) that the witness is likely to be a vulnerable witness, and

(b) that a special measure or combination of special measures ought to be used for the purpose of taking the witness's evidence.

(2) Where this section applies, the party citing or intending to cite the witness shall, [F114 by the required time], make an application (referred to as a " vulnerable witness application ") to the court for an order authorising the use of one or more of the special measures for the purpose of taking the witness's evidence.

(3) A vulnerable witness application shall—

(a) specify the special measure or measures which the party making the application considers to be the most appropriate for the purpose of taking the evidence of the witness to whom the application relates, and

(b) contain or be accompanied by—

(i) a summary of any views expressed for the purposes of section 271. E(2)(b) of this Act, and

(ii) such other information as may be prescribed by Act of Adjournal.

(4) The court may, on cause shown, allow a vulnerable witness application to be made after the [F115the required time].

[F116. (4. A)Any party to the proceedings may, not later than 7 days after a vulnerable witness application has been lodged, lodge with the court a notice (referred to in this section as "an objection notice") stating—

(a) an objection to any special measure specified in the vulnerable witness application that the party considers to be inappropriate, and

(b) the reasons for that objection.

(4. B)The court may, on cause shown, allow an objection notice to be lodged after the period referred to in subsection (4. A).

(4. C)If an objection notice is lodged in accordance with subsection (4. A) or (4. B)—

(a) subsection (5) does not apply to the vulnerable witness application, and

(b) the court must make an order under subsection (5. A).]

(5) The court shall, not [F117earlier than 7 days and not later than 14] days after a vulnerable witness application is made to it, consider the application in the absence of the parties and—

(a) make an order authorising the use of the special measure or measures specified in the application if satisfied on the basis of the application that—

(i) the witness in respect of whom the application is made is a vulnerable witness,

(ii) the special measures or measures specified in the application are the most appropriate for the purpose of taking the witness's evidence, and

(iii) it is appropriate to do so after having complied with the duty in subsection (8) below, or

(b) if not satisfied as mentioned in paragraph (a) above, [F118make an order under subsection (5. A) below.]

[F119. (5. A)That order is an order—

(a) in the case of proceedings in the High Court where the preliminary hearing is yet to be held, appointing the vulnerable witness application to be disposed of at that hearing,

(b) in the case of proceedings on indictment in the sheriff court where the first diet is yet to be held, appointing the vulnerable witness application to be disposed of at that diet, or

(c) in any other case, appointing a diet to be held before [F120the hearing at which the evidence is to be given] and requiring the parties to attend the diet.]

(6) On making an order under subsection [F121. (5. A)(c)] above, the court may postpone [F122the hearing at which the evidence is to be given].

[F123. (6. A)Subsection (7) below applies to—

(a) a preliminary hearing or first diet so far as the court is, by virtue of an order under subsection (5. A)(a) or (b) above disposing of a vulnerable witness application at the hearing or diet, and

(b) a diet appointed under subsection (5. A)(c) above.]

(7) At a [F124hearing or diet to which this subsection applies], the court may—

(a) after giving the parties an opportunity to be heard, and

(b) if satisfied that the witness in respect of whom the application is made is a vulnerable witness,

make an order authorising the use of such special measure or measures as the court considers to be the most appropriate for the purpose of taking the witness's evidence.

(8) In deciding whether to make an order under subsection (5)(a) or (7) above, the court shall—

(a) have regard to—

(i) the possible effect on the witness if required to give evidence without the benefit of any special measure, and

(ii) whether it is likely that the witness would be better able to give evidence with the benefit of a special measure, and

(b) take into account the matters specified in subsection (2)(a) to (f) of section 271 of this Act.

(9) A [F125hearing or diet to which subsection (7) above applies] may—

(a) on the application of the party citing or intending to cite the witness in respect of whom the diet is to be held, or

(b) of the court's own motion,

be held in chambers.

(10) A diet [F126appointed under subsection (5. A)(c) above in any case may be conjoined with any other diet to be held before [F127the hearing at which the evidence is to be given].]

(11) A party making a vulnerable witness application [F128or an objection notice] shall, at the same time, intimate the application [F129or, as the case may be, the notice] to the other parties to the proceedings.

[F130. (12) In subsections (2) and (4) above, "the required time" means—

(a) in the case of proceedings in the High Court, no later than 14 clear days before the preliminary hearing,

(b) in the case of proceedings on indictment in the sheriff court, no later than 7 clear days before the first diet,

(c) in any other case, no later than 14 clear days before [F131the hearing at which the evidence is to be given].]]

Amendments (Textual)

F109. Ss. 271-271. M and preceding cross-heading substituted for s. 271 (1.4.2005, 30.11.2005,

1.4.2006. 1.4.2007 and 2.7.2007 for certain purposes, otherwise 1.4.2008) by Vulnerable Witnesses (Scotland) Act 2004 (asp 3), ss. 1, 25; S.S.I. 2005/168, art. 2, Sch. (with savings in art. 4); S.S.I. 2005/590, art. 2, Sch. (with art. 4); S.S.I. 2006/59, art. 2, Sch. (with art. 4. (1)); S.S.I. 2007/101, art. 2, Sch. (with art. 4); S.S.I. 2007/329, art. 2, Sch. (with art. 4); S.S.I. 2008/57, art. 2 (with art. 3)

F110. S. 271. C title substituted (1.9.2015) by Victims and Witnesses (Scotland) Act 2014 (asp 1), ss. 11. (6), 34; S.S.I. 2015/200, art. 2. (2), sch. (with arts. 1. (3), 4)

F111. Words in s. 271. C(1) inserted (1.9.2015) by Victims and Witnesses (Scotland) Act 2014 (asp 1), ss. 16. (2)(a), 34; S.S.I. 2015/200, art. 2. (2), sch. (with arts. 1. (3), 4)

F112. Words in s. 271. C(1) substituted (28.3.2011) by Criminal Justice and Licensing (Scotland) Act 2010 (asp 13), ss. 87. (5)(a), 206. (1); S.S.I. 2011/178, art. 2, sch.

F113. Words in s. 271. C(1) inserted (1.9.2015) by Victims and Witnesses (Scotland) Act 2014 (asp 1), ss. 16. (2)(b), 34; S.S.I. 2015/200, art. 2. (2), sch. (with arts. 1. (3), 4)

F114. Words in s. 271. C(2) substituted (1.4.2005, 1.4.2006, 1.4.2007 and 2.7.2007 for certain purposes and otherwise 1.4.2008) by Criminal Procedure (Amendment) (Scotland) Act 2004 (asp 5), ss. 25, 27. (1), Sch. para. 44. (a); S.S.I. 2004/405, art. 2. (2), Sch. 2 (subject to arts. 3-5); S.S.I. 2005/168, art. 2, Sch. (with savings in art. 4); S.S.I. 2006/59, art. 2, Sch. (with art. 4. (1)); S.S.I. 2007/101, art. 2, Sch. (with art. 4); S.S.I. 2007/329, art. 2, Sch. (with art. 4); S.S.I. 2008/57, art. 2 (with art. 3)

F115. Words in s. 271. C(4) substituted (1.4.2005, 1.4.2006, 1.4.2007 and 2.7.2007 for certain purposes and otherwise 1.4.2008) by Criminal Procedure (Amendment) (Scotland) Act 2004 (asp 5), ss. 25, 27. (1), Sch. para. 44. (b); S.S.I. 2004/405, art. 2. (2), Sch. 2 (subject to arts. 3-5); S.S.I. 2005/168, art. 2, Sch. (with savings in art. 4); S.S.I. 2006/59, art. 2, Sch. (with art. 4. (1)); S.S.I. 2007/101, art. 2, Sch. (with art. 4); S.S.I. 2007/329, art. 2, Sch. (with art. 4); S.S.I. 2008/57, art. 2 (with art. 3)

F116. S. 271. C(4. A)-(4. C) inserted (1.9.2015) by Victims and Witnesses (Scotland) Act 2014 (asp 1), ss. 17. (a), 34; S.S.I. 2015/200, art. 2. (2), sch. (with arts. 1. (3), 4)

F117. Words in s. 271. C(5) substituted (1.9.2015) by Victims and Witnesses (Scotland) Act 2014 (asp 1), ss. 17. (b), 34; S.S.I. 2015/200, art. 2. (2), sch. (with arts. 1. (3), 4)

F118. Words in s. 271. C(5)(b) substituted (1.4.2005, 1.4.2006, 1.4.2007 and 2.7.2007 for certain purposes and otherwise 1.4.2008) by Criminal Procedure (Amendment) (Scotland) Act 2004 (asp 5), ss. 25, 27. (1), Sch. para. 44. (c); S.S.I. 2004/405, art. 2. (2), Sch. 2 (subject to arts. 3-5); S.S.I. 2005/168, art. 2, Sch. (with savings in art. 4); S.S.I. 2006/59, art. 2, Sch. (with art. 4. (1)); S.S.I. 2007/101, art. 2, Sch. (with art. 4); S.S.I. 2007/329, art. 2, Sch. (with art. 4); S.S.I. 2008/57, art. 2 (with art. 3)

F119. S. 271. C(5. A) inserted (1.4.2005, 1.4.2006, 1.4.2007 and 2.7.2007 for certain purposes and otherwise 1.4.2008) by Criminal Procedure (Amendment) (Scotland) Act 2004 (asp 5), ss. 25, 27. (1), Sch. para. 44. (d); S.S.I. 2004/405, art. 2. (2), Sch. 2 (subject to arts. 3-5); S.S.I. 2005/168, art. 2, Sch. (with savings in art. 4); S.S.I. 2006/59, art. 2, Sch. (with art. 4. (1)); S.S.I. 2007/101, art. 2, Sch. (with art. 4); S.S.I. 2007/329, art. 2, Sch. (with art. 4); S.S.I. 2008/57, art. 2 (with art. 3)

F120. Words in s. 271. C(5. A)(c) substituted (28.3.2011) by Criminal Justice and Licensing (Scotland) Act 2010 (asp 13), ss. 87. (5)(b), 206. (1); S.S.I. 2011/178, art. 2, sch.

F121. Words in s. 271. C(6) substituted (1.4.2005, 1.4.2006, 1.4.2007 and 2.7.2007 for certain purposes and otherwise 1.4.2008) by Criminal Procedure (Amendment) (Scotland) Act 2004 (asp 5), ss. 25, 27. (1), Sch. para. 44. (e); S.S.I. 2004/405, art. 2. (2), Sch. 2 (subject to arts. 3-5); S.S.I. 2005/168, art. 2, Sch. (with savings in art. 4); S.S.I. 2006/59, art. 2, Sch. (with art. 4. (1)); S.S.I. 2007/101, art. 2, Sch. (with art. 4); S.S.I. 2007/329, art. 2, Sch. (with art. 4); S.S.I. 2008/57, art. 2 (with art. 3)

F122. Words in s. 271. C(6) substituted (28.3.2011) by Criminal Justice and Licensing (Scotland) Act 2010 (asp 13), ss. 87. (5)(c), 206. (1); S.S.I. 2011/178, art. 2, sch.

F123. S. 271. C(6. A) inserted (1.4.2005, 1.4.2006, 1.4.2007 and 2.7.2007 for certain purposes and otherwise 1.4.2008) by Criminal Procedure (Amendment) (Scotland) Act 2004 (asp 5), ss. 25, 27. (1), Sch. para. 44. (f); S.S.I. 2004/405, art. 2. (2), Sch. 2 (subject to arts. 3-5); S.S.I. 2005/168, art.

2, Sch. (with savings in art. 4); S.S.I. 2006/59, art. 2, Sch. (with art. 4. (1)); S.S.I. 2007/101, art. 2, Sch. (with art. 4); S.S.I. 2007/329, art. 2, Sch. (with art. 4); S.S.I. 2008/57, art. 2 (with art. 3)

F124. Words in s. 271. C(7) substituted (1.4.2005, 1.4.2006, 1.4.2007 and 2.7.2007 for certain purposes and otherwise 1.4.2008) by Criminal Procedure (Amendment) (Scotland) Act 2004 (asp 5), ss. 25, 27. (1), Sch. para. 44. (g); S.S.I. 2004/405, art. 2. (2), Sch. 2 (subject to arts. 3-5); S.S.I. 2005/168, art. 2, Sch. (with savings in art. 4); S.S.I. 2006/59, art. 2, Sch. (with art. 4. (1)); S.S.I. 2007/101, art. 2, Sch. (with art. 4); S.S.I. 2007/329, art. 2, Sch. (with art. 4); S.S.I. 2008/57, art. 2 (with art. 3)

F125. Words in s. 271. C(9) substituted (1.4.2005, 1.4.2006, 1.4.2007 and 2.7.2007 for certain purposes and otherwise 1.4.2008) by Criminal Procedure (Amendment) (Scotland) Act 2004 (asp 5), ss. 25, 27. (1), Sch. para. 44. (h); S.S.I. 2004/405, art. 2. (2), Sch. 2 (subject to arts. 3-5); S.S.I. 2005/168, art. 2, Sch. (with savings in art. 4); S.S.I. 2006/59, art. 2, Sch. (with art. 4. (1)); S.S.I. 2007/101, art. 2, Sch. (with art. 4); S.S.I. 2007/329, art. 2, Sch. (with art. 4); S.S.I. 2008/57, art. 2 (with art. 3)

F126. Words in s. 271. C(10) substituted (1.4.2005, 1.4.2006, 1.4.2007 and 2.7.2007 for certain purposes and otherwise 1.4.2008) by Criminal Procedure (Amendment) (Scotland) Act 2004 (asp 5), ss. 25, 27. (1), Sch. para. 44. (i); S.S.I. 2004/405, art. 2. (2), Sch. 2 (subject to arts. 3-5); S.S.I. 2005/168, art. 2, Sch. (with savings in art. 4); S.S.I. 2006/59, art. 2, Sch. (with art. 4. (1)); S.S.I. 2007/101, art. 2, Sch. (with art. 4); S.S.I. 2007/329, art. 2, Sch. (with art. 4); S.S.I. 2008/57, art. 2 (with art. 3)

F127. Words in s. 271. C(10) substituted (28.3.2011) by Criminal Justice and Licensing (Scotland) Act 2010 (asp 13), ss. 87. (5)(d), 206. (1); S.S.I. 2011/178, art. 2, sch.

F128. Words in s. 271. C(11) inserted (1.9.2015) by Victims and Witnesses (Scotland) Act 2014 (asp 1), ss. 17. (c)(i), 34; S.S.I. 2015/200, art. 2. (2), sch. (with arts. 1. (3), 4)

F129. Words in s. 271. C(11) inserted (1.9.2015) by Victims and Witnesses (Scotland) Act 2014 (asp 1), ss. 17. (c)(ii), 34; S.S.I. 2015/200, art. 2. (2), sch. (with arts. 1. (3), 4)

F130. S. 271. C(12) inserted (1.4.2005, 1.4.2006, 1.4.2007 and 2.7.2007 for certain purposes and otherwise 1.4.2008) by Criminal Procedure (Amendment) (Scotland) Act 2004 (asp 5), ss. 25, 27. (1), Sch. para. 44. (j); S.S.I. 2004/405, art. 2. (2), Sch. 2 (subject to arts. 3-5); S.S.I. 2005/168, art. 2, Sch. (with savings in art. 4); S.S.I. 2006/59, art. 2, Sch. (with art. 4. (1)); S.S.I. 2007/101, art. 2, Sch. (with art. 4); S.S.I. 2007/329, art. 2, Sch. (with art. 4); S.S.I. 2008/57, art. 2 (with art. 3)

F131. Words in s. 271. C(12)(c) substituted (28.3.2011) by Criminal Justice and Licensing (Scotland) Act 2010 (asp 13), ss. 87. (5)(e), 206. (1); S.S.I. 2011/178, art. 2, sch.

Modifications etc. (not altering text)

C7. Ss. 271-271. M applied (with modifications) (23.12.2015) by The Justice of the Peace Courts (Special Measures) (Scotland) Order 2015 (S.S.I. 2015/447), arts. 1. (2), 3 (with art. 1. (3))

C10. Ss. 271-271. M applied by Criminal Justice (Scotland) Act 2003 (asp 7), s. 15. A (as inserted (1.4.2005, 30.11.2005, 1.4.2006, 1.4.2007 and 2.7.2007 for certain purposes and otherwise 1.4.2008) by Vulnerable Witnesses (Scotland) Act 2004 (asp 3), ss. 3, 25; S.S.I. 2005/168, art. 2, Sch. (with savings in art. 4); S.S.I. 2005/590, art. 2, Sch. (with art. 4); S.S.I. 2006/59, art. 2, Sch. (with art. 4); S.S.I. 2007/101, art. 2, Sch. (with art. 4); S.S.I. 2007/329, art. 2, Sch. (with art. 4)); S.S.I. 2008/57, art. 2 (with art. 3)

[F132271. DReview of arrangements for vulnerable witnessesS

(1) In any case in which a person who is giving or is to give evidence at or for the purposes of [F133a hearing in relevant criminal proceedings] (referred to in this section as the "witness") is or appears to the court to be a vulnerable witness, the court may at any stage in the proceedings (whether before or after the commencement of [F134the hearing] or before or after the witness has begun to give evidence)—

    (a) on the application of [F135any party to the proceedings], or

    (b) of its own motion,

review the current arrangements for taking the witness's evidence and, after giving the parties an opportunity to be heard, make an order under subsection (2) below.

(2) The order which may be made under this subsection is—

(a) where the current arrangements for taking the witness's evidence include the use of a special measure or combination of special measures authorised by an order under section 271. A or 271. C of this Act or under this subsection (referred to as the "earlier order"), an order varying or revoking the earlier order, or

(b) where the current arrangements for taking the witness's evidence do not include any special measure, an order authorising the use of such special measure or measures as the court considers most appropriate for the purpose of taking the witness's evidence.

(3) An order under subsection (2)(a) above varying an earlier order may—

(a) add to or substitute for any special measure authorised by the earlier order such other special measure as the court considers most appropriate for the purpose of taking the witness's evidence, or

(b) where the earlier order authorises the use of a combination of special measures for that purpose, delete any of the special measures so authorised.

(4) The court may make an order under subsection (2)(a) above revoking an earlier order only if satisfied—

(a) where the witness has expressed a wish to give or, as the case may be, continue to give evidence without the benefit of any special measure, that it is appropriate for the witness so to give evidence, or

(b) in any other case, that—

(i) the use, or continued use, of the special measure or measures authorised by the earlier order for the purpose of taking the witness's evidence would give rise to a significant risk of prejudice to the fairness of [F136the hearing] or otherwise to the interests of justice, and

(ii) that risk significantly outweighs any risk of prejudice to the interests of the witness if the order is made.

(5) Subsection (8) of section 271. C of this Act applies to the making of an order under subsection (2)(b) of this section as it applies to the making of an order under subsection (5)(a) or (7) of that section but as if the references to the witness were to the witness within the meaning of this section.

(6) In this section, "current arrangements" means the arrangements in place at the time the review under this section is begun.

[F137. (7)This section is subject to section 271. B.]]

Amendments (Textual)

F132. Ss. 271-271. M and preceding cross-heading substituted for s. 271 (1.4.2005, 30.11.2005, 1.4.2006. 1.4.2007 and 2.7.2007 for certain purposes, otherwise 1.4.2008) by Vulnerable Witnesses (Scotland) Act 2004 (asp 3), ss. 1, 25; S.S.I. 2005/168, art. 2, Sch. (with savings in art. 4); S.S.I. 2005/590, art. 2, Sch. (with art. 4); S.S.I. 2006/59, art. 2, Sch. (with art. 4. (1)); S.S.I. 2007/101, art. 2, Sch. (with art. 4); S.S.I. 2007/329, art. 2, Sch. (with art. 4); S.S.I. 2008/57, art. 2 (with art. 3)

F133. Words in s. 271. D(1) substituted (28.3.2011) by Criminal Justice and Licensing (Scotland) Act 2010 (asp 13), ss. 87. (6)(a)(i), 206. (1); S.S.I. 2011/178, art. 2, sch.

F134. Words in s. 271. D(1) substituted (28.3.2011) by Criminal Justice and Licensing (Scotland) Act 2010 (asp 13), ss. 87. (6)(a)(ii), 206. (1); S.S.I. 2011/178, art. 2, sch.

F135. Words in s. 271. D(1)(a) substituted (1.9.2015) by Victims and Witnesses (Scotland) Act 2014 (asp 1), ss. 18, 34; S.S.I. 2015/200, art. 2. (2), sch. (with arts. 1. (3), 4)

F136. Words in s. 271. D(4)(b)(i) substituted (28.3.2011) by Criminal Justice and Licensing (Scotland) Act 2010 (asp 13), ss. 87. (6)(b), 206. (1); S.S.I. 2011/178, art. 2, sch.

F137. S. 271. D(7) added (1.9.2015) by Victims and Witnesses (Scotland) Act 2014 (asp 1), ss. 14. (3), 34; S.S.I. 2015/200, art. 2. (2), sch. (with arts. 1. (3), 4)

Modifications etc. (not altering text)

C7. Ss. 271-271. M applied (with modifications) (23.12.2015) by The Justice of the Peace Courts

(Special Measures) (Scotland) Order 2015 (S.S.I. 2015/447), arts. 1. (2), 3 (with art. 1. (3))
C11. Ss. 271-271. M applied by Criminal Justice (Scotland) Act 2003 (asp 7), s. 15. A (as inserted (1.4.2005, 30.11.2005, 1.4.2006, 1.4.2007 and 2.7.2007 for certain purposes and otherwise 1.4.2008) by Vulnerable Witnesses (Scotland) Act 2004 (asp 3), ss. 3, 25; S.S.I. 2005/168, art. 2, Sch. (with savings in art. 4); S.S.I. 2005/590, art. 2, Sch. (with art. 4); S.S.I. 2006/59, art. 2, Sch. (with art. 4); S.S.I. 2007/101, art. 2, Sch. (with art. 4); S.S.I. 2007/329, art. 2, Sch. (with art. 4)); S.S.I. 2008/57, art. 2 (with art. 3)

[F138271. EVulnerable witnesses: supplementary provisionS

(1) Subsection (2) below applies where—

(a) a party is considering for the purposes of a [F139vulnerable] witness notice or a vulnerable witness application which of the special measures is or are the most appropriate for the purpose of taking the evidence of the person to whom the notice or application relates, or

(b) the court is making an order under section 271. A(5)(a)(ii) or (b) or (9), 271. C or 271. D of this Act.

(2) The party or, as the case may be, the court shall—

(a) have regard to the best interests of the witness, and

(b) take account of any views expressed by—

(i) the witness (having regard, where the witness is a child witness, to the witness's age and maturity), and

(ii) where the witness is a child witness, the witness's parent (except where the parent is the accused).

(3) For the purposes of subsection (2)(b) above, where the witness is a child witness—

(a) the witness shall be presumed to be of sufficient age and maturity to form a view if aged 12 or older, and

(b) in the event that any views expressed by the witness are inconsistent with any views expressed by the witness's parent, the views of the witness shall be given greater weight.

(4) In this section—

"parent", in relation to a child witness, means any person having parental responsibilities within the meaning of section 1. (3) of the Children (Scotland) Act 1995 (c. 36) in relation to the child witness,

"the witness" means—

- in the case referred to in subsection (1)(a) above, the person to whom the notice or application relates,

- in the case referred to in subsection (1)(b) above, the person to whom the order would relate.]

Amendments (Textual)
F138. Ss. 271-271. M and preceding cross-heading substituted for s. 271 (1.4.2005, 30.11.2005, 1.4.2006. 1.4.2007 and 2.7.2007 for certain purposes, otherwise 1.4.2008) by Vulnerable Witnesses (Scotland) Act 2004 (asp 3), ss. 1, 25; S.S.I. 2005/168, art. 2, Sch. (with savings in art. 4); S.S.I. 2005/590, art. 2, Sch. (with art. 4); S.S.I. 2006/59, art. 2, Sch. (with art. 4. (1)); S.S.I. 2007/101, art. 2, Sch. (with art. 4); S.S.I. 2007/329, art. 2, Sch. (with art. 4); S.S.I. 2008/57, art. 2 (with art. 3)
F139. Word in s. 271. E(1)(a) substituted (1.9.2015) by Victims and Witnesses (Scotland) Act 2014 (asp 1), ss. 11. (7), 34; S.S.I. 2015/200, art. 2. (2), sch. (with arts. 1. (3), 4)
Modifications etc. (not altering text)
C7. Ss. 271-271. M applied (with modifications) (23.12.2015) by The Justice of the Peace Courts (Special Measures) (Scotland) Order 2015 (S.S.I. 2015/447), arts. 1. (2), 3 (with art. 1. (3))
C12. Ss. 271-271. M applied by Criminal Justice (Scotland) Act 2003 (asp 7), s. 15. A (as inserted (1.4.2005, 30.11.2005, 1.4.2006, 1.4.2007 and 2.7.2007 for certain purposes and otherwise 1.4.2008) by Vulnerable Witnesses (Scotland) Act 2004 (asp 3), ss. 3, 25; S.S.I. 2005/168, art. 2, Sch. (with savings in art. 4); S.S.I. 2005/590, art. 2, Sch. (with art. 4); S.S.I. 2006/59, art. 2, Sch.

(with art. 4); S.S.I. 2007/101, art. 2, Sch. (with art. 4); S.S.I. 2007/329, art. 2, Sch. (with art. 4)); S.S.I. 2008/57, art. 2 (with art. 3)

[F140271. FThe accusedS

(1) For the purposes of the application of subsection (1) of section 271 of this Act to the accused (where the accused is giving or is to give evidence at or for the purposes of [F141a hearing in relevant criminal proceedings]), subsection (2) of that section shall have effect as if—

(a) for paragraph (c) there were substituted—

"(c)whether the accused is to be legally represented at [F142the hearing] and, if not, the accused's entitlement to be so legally represented,", and

(b) for paragraph (e) there were substituted—

"(e)any behaviour towards the accused on the part of—

(i) any co-accused or any person who is likely to be a co-accused in the proceedings,

(ii) any witness or any person who is likely to be a witness in the proceedings, or

(iii) members of the family or associates of any of the persons mentioned in sub-paragraphs (i) and (ii) above.".

(2) Where, if the accused were to give evidence at or for the purposes of [F143the hearing], he would be a child witness—

(a) section 271. A of this Act shall apply in relation to the accused subject to the following modifications—

(i) references to a [F144witness] shall be read as if they were references to the accused,

(ii) references to the party citing or intending to cite a F145... witness shall be read as if they were references to the accused, and

(iii) subsection (6) shall have effect as if for paragraph (a) there were substituted—

"(a)it appears to the court that the accused, if he were to give evidence at or for the purposes of [F146a hearing in relevant criminal proceedings], would be a child witness,", and

(b) section 271. B of this Act shall apply in relation to the accused as if—

(i) for subsection (1) there were substituted—

"(1)This section applies where the accused—

(a) if he were to give evidence at or for the purposes of [F147a hearing in relevant criminal proceedings] would be a child witness, and

(b) is under the age of 12 on the date of commencement of the proceedings.", and

(ii) in subsection (3), references to the child witness were references to the accused.

(3) Subsection (4) below applies where the accused—

(a) considers that, if he were to give evidence at or for the purposes of [F148a hearing in relevant criminal proceedings], he would be a vulnerable witness other than a child witness, and

(b) has not decided to give evidence without the benefit of any special measures.

(4) Where this subsection applies, subsections (2) to (11) of section 271. C of this Act shall apply in relation to the accused subject to the following modifications—

(a) references to the witness shall be read as if they were references to the accused,

(b) references to the party citing or intending the cite the witness shall be read as if they were references to the accused, and

(c) in subsection (8)(b), the reference to subsection (2)(a) to (f) of section 271 of this Act shall be read as if it were a reference to that subsection as modified by subsection (1) above.

(5) Section 271. D of this Act shall apply in any case where it appears to the court that the accused, if he were to give evidence at or for the purposes of [F149the hearing], would be a vulnerable witness as it applies in the case referred to in subsection (1) of that section but subject to the following modifications—

(a) references to the witness shall be read as if they were references to the accused,

(b) references to the party citing or intending to cite the witness shall be read as if they were references to the accused.

(6) Where the witness within the meaning of section 271. E of this Act is the accused, that section shall have effect in relation to the witness as if—

(a) in subsection (1), paragraph (a) were omitted, and

(b) in subsection (2), the words "The party or, as the case may be," were omitted.

(7) Section 271. M of this Act shall have effect, where the vulnerable witness is the accused, as if the reference in subsection (2) to the party citing the vulnerable witness were a reference to the accused.

(8) The following provisions of this Act shall not apply in relation to a vulnerable witness who is the accused—

(a) section 271. H(1)(c) [F150and (ea)],

(b) section 271. I(3).]

Amendments (Textual)

F140. Ss. 271-271. M and preceding cross-heading substituted for s. 271 (1.4.2005, 30.11.2005, 1.4.2006. 1.4.2007 and 2.7.2007 for certain purposes, otherwise 1.4.2008) by Vulnerable Witnesses (Scotland) Act 2004 (asp 3), ss. 1, 25; S.S.I. 2005/168, art. 2, Sch. (with savings in art. 4); S.S.I. 2005/590, art. 2, Sch. (with art. 4); S.S.I. 2006/59, art. 2, Sch. (with art. 4. (1)); S.S.I. 2007/101, art. 2, Sch. (with art. 4); S.S.I. 2007/329, art. 2, Sch. (with art. 4); S.S.I. 2008/57, art. 2 (with art. 3)

F141. Words in s. 271. F(1) substituted (28.3.2011) by Criminal Justice and Licensing (Scotland) Act 2010 (asp 13), ss. 87. (7)(a)(i), 206. (1); S.S.I. 2011/178, art. 2, sch.

F142. Words in s. 271. F(1)(a) substituted (28.3.2011) by Criminal Justice and Licensing (Scotland) Act 2010 (asp 13), ss. 87. (7)(a)(ii), 206. (1); S.S.I. 2011/178, art. 2, sch.

F143. Words in s. 271. F(2) substituted (28.3.2011) by Criminal Justice and Licensing (Scotland) Act 2010 (asp 13), ss. 87. (7)(b)(i), 206. (1); S.S.I. 2011/178, art. 2, sch.

F144. Word in s. 271. F(2)(a)(i) substituted (1.9.2015) by Victims and Witnesses (Scotland) Act 2014 (asp 1), ss. 11. (8)(a), 34; S.S.I. 2015/200, art. 2. (2), sch. (with arts. 1. (3), 4)

F145. Word in s. 271. F(2)(a)(ii) repealed (1.9.2015) by Victims and Witnesses (Scotland) Act 2014 (asp 1), ss. 11. (8)(b), 34; S.S.I. 2015/200, art. 2. (2), sch. (with arts. 1. (3), 4)

F146. Words in s. 271. F(2) substituted (28.3.2011) by Criminal Justice and Licensing (Scotland) Act 2010 (asp 13), ss. 87. (7)(b)(ii), 206. (1); S.S.I. 2011/178, art. 2, sch.

F147. Words in s. 271. F(2) substituted (28.3.2011) by Criminal Justice and Licensing (Scotland) Act 2010 (asp 13), ss. 87. (7)(b)(iii), 206. (1); S.S.I. 2011/178, art. 2, sch.

F148. Words in s. 271. F(3) substituted (28.3.2011) by Criminal Justice and Licensing (Scotland) Act 2010 (asp 13), ss. 87. (7)(c), 206. (1); S.S.I. 2011/178, art. 2, sch.

F149. Words in s. 271. F(5) substituted (28.3.2011) by Criminal Justice and Licensing (Scotland) Act 2010 (asp 13), ss. 87. (7)(d), 206. (1); S.S.I. 2011/178, art. 2, sch.

F150. Words in s. 271. F(8)(a) inserted (1.9.2015) by Victims and Witnesses (Scotland) Act 2014 (asp 1), ss. 20. (3), 34; S.S.I. 2015/200, art. 2. (2), sch. (with arts. 1. (3), 4)

Modifications etc. (not altering text)

C7. Ss. 271-271. M applied (with modifications) (23.12.2015) by The Justice of the Peace Courts (Special Measures) (Scotland) Order 2015 (S.S.I. 2015/447), arts. 1. (2), 3 (with art. 1. (3))

C13. Ss. 271-271. M applied by Criminal Justice (Scotland) Act 2003 (asp 7), s. 15. A (as inserted (1.4.2005, 30.11.2005, 1.4.2006, 1.4.2007 and 2.7.2007 for certain purposes and otherwise 1.4.2008) by Vulnerable Witnesses (Scotland) Act 2004 (asp 3), ss. 3, 25; S.S.I. 2005/168, art. 2, Sch. (with savings in art. 4); S.S.I. 2005/590, art. 2, Sch. (with art. 4); S.S.I. 2006/59, art. 2, Sch. (with art. 4); S.S.I. 2007/101, art. 2, Sch. (with art. 4); S.S.I. 2007/329, art. 2, Sch. (with art. 4)); S.S.I. 2008/57, art. 2 (with art. 3)

[F151271. GSaving provisionS

Nothing in sections 271. A to 271. F of this Act affects any power or duty which a court has otherwise than by virtue of those sections to make or authorise any special arrangements for taking the evidence of any person.]

Amendments (Textual)

F151. Ss. 271-271. M and preceding cross-heading substituted for s. 271 (1.4.2005, 30.11.2005, 1.4.2006. 1.4.2007 and 2.7.2007 for certain purposes, otherwise 1.4.2008) by Vulnerable Witnesses (Scotland) Act 2004 (asp 3), ss. 1, 25; S.S.I. 2005/168, art. 2, Sch. (with savings in art. 4); S.S.I. 2005/590, art. 2, Sch. (with art. 4); S.S.I. 2006/59, art. 2, Sch. (with art. 4. (1)); S.S.I. 2007/101, art. 2, Sch. (with art. 4); S.S.I. 2007/329, art. 2, Sch. (with art. 4); S.S.I. 2008/57, art. 2 (with art. 3)

Modifications etc. (not altering text)

C7. Ss. 271-271. M applied (with modifications) (23.12.2015) by The Justice of the Peace Courts (Special Measures) (Scotland) Order 2015 (S.S.I. 2015/447), arts. 1. (2), 3 (with art. 1. (3))

C14. Ss. 271-271. M applied by Criminal Justice (Scotland) Act 2003 (asp 7), s. 15. A (as inserted (1.4.2005, 30.11.2005, 1.4.2006, 1.4.2007 and 2.7.2007 for certain purposes and otherwise 1.4.2008) by Vulnerable Witnesses (Scotland) Act 2004 (asp 3), ss. 3, 25; S.S.I. 2005/168, art. 2, Sch. (with savings in art. 4); S.S.I. 2005/590, art. 2, Sch. (with art. 4); S.S.I. 2006/59, art. 2, Sch. (with art. 4); S.S.I. 2007/101, art. 2, Sch. (with art. 4); S.S.I. 2007/329, art. 2, Sch. (with art. 4)); S.S.I. 2008/57, art. 2 (with art. 3)

[F152271. HThe special measuresS

(1) The special measures which may be authorised to be used under section 271. A, 271. C or 271. D of this Act for the purpose of taking the evidence of a vulnerable witness are—

(a) taking of evidence by a commissioner in accordance with section 271. I of this Act,

(b) use of a live television link in accordance with section 271. J of this Act,

(c) use of a screen in accordance with section 271. K of this Act,

(d) use of a supporter in accordance with section 271. L of this Act,

(e) giving evidence in chief in the form of a prior statement in accordance with section 271. M of this Act, and

[F153. (ea)excluding the public during the taking of the evidence in accordance with section 271. HB of this Act,]

F154. (f)...............................

[F155. (1. A)The Scottish Ministers may, by order subject to the affirmative procedure—

(a) modify subsection (1),

(b) in consequence of any modification made under paragraph (a)—

(i) prescribe the procedure to be followed when special measures are used, and

(ii) so far as is necessary, modify sections 271. A to 271. M of this Act.]

F156. (2)...............................

(3) Provision may be made by Act of Adjournal regulating, so far as not regulated by sections 271. I to 271. M of this Act, the use in any proceedings of any special measure authorised to be used by virtue of section 271. A, 271. C or 271. D of this Act.]

Amendments (Textual)

F152. Ss. 271-271. M and preceding cross-heading substituted for s. 271 (1.4.2005, 30.11.2005, 1.4.2006. 1.4.2007 and 2.7.2007 for certain purposes, otherwise 1.4.2008) by Vulnerable Witnesses (Scotland) Act 2004 (asp 3), ss. 1, 25; S.S.I. 2005/168, art. 2, Sch. (with savings in art. 4); S.S.I. 2005/590, art. 2, Sch. (with art. 4); S.S.I. 2006/59, art. 2, Sch. (with art. 4. (1)); S.S.I. 2007/101, art. 2, Sch. (with art. 4); S.S.I. 2007/329, art. 2, Sch. (with art. 4); S.S.I. 2008/57, art. 2 (with art. 3)

F153. S. 271. H(1)(ea) inserted (1.9.2015) by Victims and Witnesses (Scotland) Act 2014 (asp 1), ss. 20. (1), 34; S.S.I. 2015/200, art. 2. (2), sch. (with arts. 1. (3), 4)

F154. S. 271. H(1)(f) repealed (1.9.2015) by Victims and Witnesses (Scotland) Act 2014 (asp 1), ss. 21. (a), 34; S.S.I. 2015/200, art. 2. (2), sch.

F155. S. 271. H(1. A) inserted (1.9.2015) by Victims and Witnesses (Scotland) Act 2014 (asp 1), ss. 21. (b), 34; S.S.I. 2015/200, art. 2. (2), sch.

F156. S. 271. H(2) repealed (1.9.2015) by Victims and Witnesses (Scotland) Act 2014 (asp 1), ss. 21. (c), 34; S.S.I. 2015/200, art. 2. (2), sch.

Modifications etc. (not altering text)

C7. Ss. 271-271. M applied (with modifications) (23.12.2015) by The Justice of the Peace Courts (Special Measures) (Scotland) Order 2015 (S.S.I. 2015/447), arts. 1. (2), 3 (with art. 1. (3))

C15. Ss. 271-271. M applied by Criminal Justice (Scotland) Act 2003 (asp 7), s. 15. A (as inserted (1.4.2005, 30.11.2005, 1.4.2006, 1.4.2007 and 2.7.2007 for certain purposes and otherwise 1.4.2008) by Vulnerable Witnesses (Scotland) Act 2004 (asp 3), ss. 3, 25; S.S.I. 2005/168, art. 2, Sch. (with savings in art. 4); S.S.I. 2005/590, art. 2, Sch. (with art. 4); S.S.I. 2006/59, art. 2, Sch. (with art. 4); S.S.I. 2007/101, art. 2, Sch. (with art. 4); S.S.I. 2007/329, art. 2, Sch. (with art. 4)); S.S.I. 2008/57, art. 2 (with art. 3)

[F157271. HATemporary additional special measuresS

(1) The Scottish Ministers may, by order subject to the affirmative procedure, specify additional measures which for the time being are to be treated as special measures listed in section 271. H(1).

(2) An order under subsection (1)

(3) An order under subsection (1) must specify—

   (a) the area in which the additional measures may be used,

   (b) the period during which the additional measures may be used, and

   (c) the procedure to be followed when the additional measures are used.]

Amendments (Textual)

F157. S. 271. HA inserted (1.9.2015) by Victims and Witnesses (Scotland) Act 2014 (asp 1), ss. 19, 34; S.S.I. 2015/200, art. 2. (2), sch.

Modifications etc. (not altering text)

C7. Ss. 271-271. M applied (with modifications) (23.12.2015) by The Justice of the Peace Courts (Special Measures) (Scotland) Order 2015 (S.S.I. 2015/447), arts. 1. (2), 3 (with art. 1. (3))

[F158271. HBExcluding the public while taking evidenceS

(1) This section applies where the special measure to be used in respect of a vulnerable witness is excluding the public during the taking of the evidence of the vulnerable witness.

(2) The court may direct that all or any persons other than those mentioned in subsection (3) are excluded from the court during the taking of the evidence.

(3) The persons are—

   (a) members or officers of the court,

   (b) parties to the case before the court, their counsel or solicitors or persons otherwise directly concerned in the case,

   (c) bona fide representatives of news gathering or reporting organisations present for the purpose of the preparation of contemporaneous reports of the proceedings,

   (d) such other persons as the court may specially authorise to be present.]

Amendments (Textual)

F158. S. 271. HB inserted (1.9.2015) by Victims and Witnesses (Scotland) Act 2014 (asp 1), ss. 20. (2), 34; S.S.I. 2015/200, art. 2. (2), sch. (with arts. 1. (3), 4)

Modifications etc. (not altering text)

C7. Ss. 271-271. M applied (with modifications) (23.12.2015) by The Justice of the Peace Courts (Special Measures) (Scotland) Order 2015 (S.S.I. 2015/447), arts. 1. (2), 3 (with art. 1. (3))

[F159271. ITaking of evidence by a commissionerS

(1) Where the special measure to be used is taking of evidence by a commissioner, the court shall appoint a commissioner to take the evidence of the vulnerable witness in respect of whom the special measure is to be used.

[F160. (1. A)Proceedings before a commissioner appointed under subsection (1) above shall, if the court so directed when authorising such proceedings, take place by means of a live television link between the place where the commissioner is taking, and the place from which the witness is giving, evidence.]

(2) Proceedings before a commissioner appointed under subsection (1) above shall be recorded by video recorder.

(3) An accused—

(a) shall not, except by leave of the court on special cause shown, be [F161 present—

(i) in the room where such proceedings are taking place; or

(ii) if such proceedings are taking place by means of a live television link, in the same room as the witness], but

(b) is entitled by such means as seem suitable to the court to watch and hear the proceedings.

(4) The recording of the proceedings made in pursuance of subsection (2) above shall be received in evidence without being sworn to by witnesses.

[F162. (5)Sections—

(a) 274;

(b) 275;

(c) 275. B except subsection (2)(b);

(d) 275. C;

(e) 288. C;

(f) 288. E; and

(g) 288. F,

of this Act apply in relation to proceedings before a commissioner appointed under subsection (1) above as they apply in relation to a trial.

(6) In the application of those sections in relation to such proceedings—

(a) the commissioner acting in the proceedings is to perform the functions of the court as provided for in those sections;

(b) references—

(i) in those sections, except section 275. (3)(c) and (7)(c), to a trial or a trial diet;

(ii) in those sections, except sections 275. (3)(e) and 288. F(2), (3) and (4), to the court, shall be read accordingly;

(c) the reference in section 275. B(1) to 14 days shall be read as a reference to 7 days.

(7) In a case where it falls to the court to appoint a commissioner under subsection (1) above, the commissioner shall be a person described in subsection (8) below.

(8) The persons are—

(a) where the proceedings before the commissioner are for the purposes of a trial in the High Court, a judge of the High Court; or

(b) in any other case, a sheriff.]]

Amendments (Textual)

F159. Ss. 271-271. M and preceding cross-heading substituted for s. 271 (1.4.2005, 30.11.2005, 1.4.2006. 1.4.2007 and 2.7.2007 for certain purposes, otherwise 1.4.2008) by Vulnerable Witnesses (Scotland) Act 2004 (asp 3), ss. 1, 25; S.S.I. 2005/168, art. 2, Sch. (with savings in art. 4); S.S.I. 2005/590, art. 2, Sch. (with art. 4); S.S.I. 2006/59, art. 2, Sch. (with art. 4. (1)); S.S.I. 2007/101, art. 2, Sch. (with art. 4); S.S.I. 2007/329, art. 2, Sch. (with art. 4); S.S.I. 2008/57, art. 2 (with art. 3)

F160. S. 271. I(1. A) inserted (23.4.2007) by Criminal Proceedings etc. (Reform) (Scotland) Act 2007 (asp 6), ss. 35. (3)(a), 84; S.S.I. 2007/250, art. 3. (a)

F161. Words in s. 271. I(3)(a) substituted (23.4.2007) by Criminal Proceedings etc. (Reform) (Scotland) Act 2007 (asp 6), ss. 35. (3)(b), 84; S.S.I. 2007/250, art. 3. (a)

F162. S. 271. I(5)-(8) added (23.4.2007) by Criminal Proceedings etc. (Reform) (Scotland) Act

2007 (asp 6), ss. 35. (3)(c), 84; S.S.I. 2007/250, art. 3. (a)

Modifications etc. (not altering text)

C7. Ss. 271-271. M applied (with modifications) (23.12.2015) by The Justice of the Peace Courts (Special Measures) (Scotland) Order 2015 (S.S.I. 2015/447), arts. 1. (2), 3 (with art. 1. (3))

C16. Ss. 271-271. M applied by Criminal Justice (Scotland) Act 2003 (asp 7), s. 15. A (as inserted (1.4.2005, 30.11.2005, 1.4.2006, 1.4.2007 and 2.7.2007 for certain purposes and otherwise 1.4.2008) by Vulnerable Witnesses (Scotland) Act 2004 (asp 3), ss. 3, 25; S.S.I. 2005/168, art. 2, Sch. (with savings in art. 4); S.S.I. 2005/590, art. 2, Sch. (with art. 4); S.S.I. 2006/59, art. 2, Sch. (with art. 4); S.S.I. 2007/101, art. 2, Sch. (with art. 4); S.S.I. 2007/329, art. 2, Sch. (with art. 4)); S.S.I. 2008/57, art. 2 (with art. 3)

[F163271. JLive television linkS

(1) Where the special measure to be used is a live television link, the court shall make such arrangements as seem to it appropriate for the vulnerable witness in respect of whom the special measure is to be used to give evidence from a place outside the court-room where [F164the hearing] is to take place by means of a live television link between that place and the court-room.

(2) The place from which the vulnerable witness gives evidence by means of the link—

(a) may be another part of the court building in which the court-room is located or any other suitable place outwith that building, and

(b) shall be treated, for the purposes of the proceedings at [F165the hearing], as part of the court-room whilst the witness is giving evidence.

(3) Any proceedings conducted by means of a live television link by virtue of this section shall be treated as taking place in the presence of the accused.

(4) Where—

(a) the live television link is to be used in proceedings in a sheriff court, but

(b) that court lacks accommodation or equipment necessary for the purpose of receiving such a link,

the sheriff may by order transfer the proceedings to any other sheriff court in the same sheriffdom which has such accommodation or equipment available.

(5) An order may be made under subsection (4) above—

(a) at any stage in the proceedings (whether before or after the commencement of [F166the hearing]), or

(b) in relation to any part of the proceedings.]

Amendments (Textual)

F163. Ss. 271-271. M and preceding cross-heading substituted for s. 271 (1.4.2005, 30.11.2005, 1.4.2006. 1.4.2007 and 2.7.2007 for certain purposes, otherwise 1.4.2008) by Vulnerable Witnesses (Scotland) Act 2004 (asp 3), ss. 1, 25; S.S.I. 2005/168, art. 2, Sch. (with savings in art. 4); S.S.I. 2005/590, art. 2, Sch. (with art. 4); S.S.I. 2006/59, art. 2, Sch. (with art. 4. (1)); S.S.I. 2007/101, art. 2, Sch. (with art. 4); S.S.I. 2007/329, art. 2, Sch. (with art. 4); S.S.I. 2008/57, art. 2 (with art. 3)

F164. Words in s. 271. J(1) substituted (28.3.2011) by Criminal Justice and Licensing (Scotland) Act 2010 (asp 13), ss. 87. (8)(a), 206. (1); S.S.I. 2011/178, art. 2, sch.

F165. Words in s. 271. J(2)(b) substituted (28.3.2011) by Criminal Justice and Licensing (Scotland) Act 2010 (asp 13), ss. 87. (8)(b), 206. (1); S.S.I. 2011/178, art. 2, sch.

F166. Words in s. 271. J(5)(a) substituted (28.3.2011) by Criminal Justice and Licensing (Scotland) Act 2010 (asp 13), ss. 87. (8)(c), 206. (1); S.S.I. 2011/178, art. 2, sch.

Modifications etc. (not altering text)

C7. Ss. 271-271. M applied (with modifications) (23.12.2015) by The Justice of the Peace Courts (Special Measures) (Scotland) Order 2015 (S.S.I. 2015/447), arts. 1. (2), 3 (with art. 1. (3))

C17. Ss. 271-271. M applied by Criminal Justice (Scotland) Act 2003 (asp 7), s. 15. A (as inserted (1.4.2005, 30.11.2005, 1.4.2006, 1.4.2007 and 2.7.2007 for certain purposes and otherwise

1.4.2008) by Vulnerable Witnesses (Scotland) Act 2004 (asp 3), ss. 3, 25; S.S.I. 2005/168, art. 2, Sch. (with savings in art. 4); S.S.I. 2005/590, art. 2, Sch. (with art. 4); S.S.I. 2006/59, art. 2, Sch. (with art. 4); S.S.I. 2007/101, art. 2, Sch. (with art. 4); S.S.I. 2007/329, art. 2, Sch. (with art. 4)); S.S.I. 2008/57, art. 2 (with art. 3)

[F167271. KScreensS

(1) Where the special measure to be used is a screen, the screen shall be used to conceal the accused from the sight of the vulnerable witness in respect of whom the special measure is to be used.

(2) However, the court shall make arrangements to ensure that the accused is able to watch and hear the vulnerable witness giving evidence.

(3) Subsections (4) and (5) of section 271. J of this Act apply for the purpose of the use of a screen under this section as they apply for the purpose of the use of a live television link under that section but as if—

(a) references to the live television link were references to the screen, and

(b) the reference to receiving such a link were a reference to the use of a screen.]

Amendments (Textual)

F167. Ss. 271-271. M and preceding cross-heading substituted for s. 271 (1.4.2005, 30.11.2005, 1.4.2006. 1.4.2007 and 2.7.2007 for certain purposes, otherwise 1.4.2008) by Vulnerable Witnesses (Scotland) Act 2004 (asp 3), ss. 1, 25; S.S.I. 2005/168, art. 2, Sch. (with savings in art. 4); S.S.I. 2005/590, art. 2, Sch. (with art. 4); S.S.I. 2006/59, art. 2, Sch. (with art. 4. (1)); S.S.I. 2007/101, art. 2, Sch. (with art. 4); S.S.I. 2007/329, art. 2, Sch. (with art. 4); S.S.I. 2008/57, art. 2 (with art. 3)

Modifications etc. (not altering text)

C7. Ss. 271-271. M applied (with modifications) (23.12.2015) by The Justice of the Peace Courts (Special Measures) (Scotland) Order 2015 (S.S.I. 2015/447), arts. 1. (2), 3 (with art. 1. (3))

C18. Ss. 271-271. M applied by Criminal Justice (Scotland) Act 2003 (asp 7), s. 15. A (as inserted (1.4.2005, 30.11.2005, 1.4.2006, 1.4.2007 and 2.7.2007 for certain purposes and otherwise 1.4.2008) by Vulnerable Witnesses (Scotland) Act 2004 (asp 3), ss. 3, 25; S.S.I. 2005/168, art. 2, Sch. (with savings in art. 4); S.S.I. 2005/590, art. 2, Sch. (with art. 4); S.S.I. 2006/59, art. 2, Sch. (with art. 4); S.S.I. 2007/101, art. 2, Sch. (with art. 4); S.S.I. 2007/329, art. 2, Sch. (with art. 4)); S.S.I. 2008/57, art. 2 (with art. 3)

[F168271. LSupportersS

(1) Where the special measure to be used is a supporter, another person ("the supporter") nominated by or on behalf of the vulnerable witness in respect of whom the special measure is to be used may be present alongside the witness to support the witness while the witness is giving evidence.

(2) Where the person nominated as the supporter is to give evidence at [F169that or any other hearing in the proceedings], that person may not act as the supporter at any time before giving evidence.

(3) The supporter shall not prompt or otherwise seek to influence the witness in the course of giving evidence.]

Amendments (Textual)

F168. Ss. 271-271. M and preceding cross-heading substituted for s. 271 (1.4.2005, 30.11.2005, 1.4.2006. 1.4.2007 and 2.7.2007 for certain purposes, otherwise 1.4.2008) by Vulnerable Witnesses (Scotland) Act 2004 (asp 3), ss. 1, 25; S.S.I. 2005/168, art. 2, Sch. (with savings in art. 4); S.S.I. 2005/590, art. 2, Sch. (with art. 4); S.S.I. 2006/59, art. 2, Sch. (with art. 4. (1)); S.S.I. 2007/101, art. 2, Sch. (with art. 4); S.S.I. 2007/329, art. 2, Sch. (with art. 4); S.S.I. 2008/57, art. 2 (with art. 3)

F169. Words in s. 271. L(2) substituted (28.3.2011) by Criminal Justice and Licensing (Scotland) Act 2010 (asp 13), ss. 87. (9), 206. (1); S.S.I. 2011/178, art. 2, sch.
Modifications etc. (not altering text)
C7. Ss. 271-271. M applied (with modifications) (23.12.2015) by The Justice of the Peace Courts (Special Measures) (Scotland) Order 2015 (S.S.I. 2015/447), arts. 1. (2), 3 (with art. 1. (3))
C19. Ss. 271-271. M applied by Criminal Justice (Scotland) Act 2003 (asp 7), s. 15. A (as inserted (1.4.2005, 30.11.2005, 1.4.2006, 1.4.2007 and 2.7.2007 for certain purposes and otherwise 1.4.2008) by Vulnerable Witnesses (Scotland) Act 2004 (asp 3), ss. 3, 25; S.S.I. 2005/168, art. 2, Sch. (with savings in art. 4); S.S.I. 2005/590, art. 2, Sch. (with art. 4); S.S.I. 2006/59, art. 2, Sch. (with art. 4); S.S.I. 2007/101, art. 2, Sch. (with art. 4); S.S.I. 2007/329, art. 2, Sch. (with art. 4); S.S.I. 2008/57, art. 2 (with art. 3)

[F170271. MGiving evidence in chief in the form of a prior statementS

(1) This section applies where the special measure to be used in respect of a vulnerable witness is giving evidence in chief in the form of a prior statement.

(2) A statement made by the vulnerable witness which is lodged in evidence for the purposes of this section by or on behalf of the party citing the vulnerable witness shall, subject to subsection (3) below, be admissible as the witness's evidence in chief, or as part of the witness's evidence in chief, without the witness being required to adopt or otherwise speak to the statement in giving evidence in court.

(3) Section 260 of this Act shall apply to a statement lodged for the purposes of this section as it applies to a prior statement referred to in that section but as if—

(a) references to a prior statement were references to the statement lodged for the purposes of this section,

(b) in subsection (1), the words "where a witness gives evidence in criminal proceedings" were omitted, and

(c) in subsection (2), paragraph (b) were omitted.

(4) This section does not affect the admissibility of any statement made by any person which is admissible otherwise than by virtue of this section.

(5) In this section, "statement" has the meaning given in section 262. (1) of this Act.]

Amendments (Textual)
F170. Ss. 271-271. M and preceding cross-heading substituted for s. 271 (1.4.2005, 30.11.2005, 1.4.2006. 1.4.2007 and 2.7.2007 for certain purposes, otherwise 1.4.2008) by Vulnerable Witnesses (Scotland) Act 2004 (asp 3), ss. 1, 25; S.S.I. 2005/168, art. 2, Sch. (with savings in art. 4); S.S.I. 2005/590, art. 2, Sch. (with art. 4); S.S.I. 2006/59, art. 2, Sch. (with art. 4. (1)); S.S.I. 2007/101, art. 2, Sch. (with art. 4); S.S.I. 2007/329, art. 2, Sch. (with art. 4); S.S.I. 2008/57, art. 2 (with art. 3)
Modifications etc. (not altering text)
C7. Ss. 271-271. M applied (with modifications) (23.12.2015) by The Justice of the Peace Courts (Special Measures) (Scotland) Order 2015 (S.S.I. 2015/447), arts. 1. (2), 3 (with art. 1. (3))
C20. Ss. 271-271. M applied by Criminal Justice (Scotland) Act 2003 (asp 7), s. 15. A (as inserted (1.4.2005, 30.11.2005, 1.4.2006, 1.4.2007 and 2.7.2007 for certain purposes and otherwise 1.4.2008) by Vulnerable Witnesses (Scotland) Act 2004 (asp 3), ss. 3, 25; S.S.I. 2005/168, art. 2, Sch. (with savings in art. 4); S.S.I. 2005/590, art. 2, Sch. (with art. 4); S.S.I. 2006/59, art. 2, Sch. (with art. 4); S.S.I. 2007/101, art. 2, Sch. (with art. 4); S.S.I. 2007/329, art. 2, Sch. (with art. 4)); S.S.I. 2008/57, art. 2 (with art. 3)

[F171 Witness anonymity orders S

Amendments (Textual)

F171. Ss. 271. N-271. Z inserted (28.3.2011) by Criminal Justice and Licensing (Scotland) Act 2010 (asp 13), ss. 90. (1), 206. (1); S.S.I. 2011/178, art. 2, sch.

Modifications etc. (not altering text)

C21. Ss. 271. N-271. Z applied (28.3.2011) by Criminal Justice and Licensing (Scotland) Act 2010 (asp 13), ss. 90. (3)(4), 206. (1); S.S.I. 2011/178, art. 2, sch.

271. NWitness anonymity ordersS

(1) A court may make an order requiring such specified measures to be taken in relation to a witness in criminal proceedings as the court considers appropriate to ensure that the identity of the witness is not disclosed in or in connection with the proceedings.

(2) The court may make such an order only on an application made in accordance with sections 271. P and 271. Q, if satisfied of the conditions set out in section 271. R having considered the matters set out in section 271. S.

(3) The kinds of measures that may be required to be taken in relation to a witness include in particular measures for securing one or more of the matters mentioned in subsection (4).

(4) Those matters are—

(a) that the witness's name and other identifying details may be—

(i) withheld,

(ii) removed from materials disclosed to any party to the proceedings,

(b) that the witness may use a pseudonym,

(c) that the witness is not asked questions of any specified description that might lead to the identification of the witness,

(d) that the witness is screened to any specified extent,

(e) that the witness's voice is subjected to modulation to any specified extent.

(5) Nothing in this section authorises the court to require—

(a) the witness to be screened to such an extent that the witness cannot be seen by the judge or the jury,

(b) the witness's voice to be modulated to such an extent that the witness's natural voice cannot be heard by the judge or the jury.

(6) An order made under this section is referred to in this Act as a "witness anonymity order".

(7) In this section "specified" means specified in the order concerned.

271. PApplicationsS

(1) An application for a witness anonymity order to be made in relation to a witness in criminal proceedings may be made to the court by the prosecutor or the accused.

(2) Where an application is made by the prosecutor, the prosecutor—

(a) must (unless the court directs otherwise) inform the court of the identity of the witness, but

(b) is not required to disclose in connection with the application—

(i) the identity of the witness, or

(ii) any information that might enable the witness to be identified,

to any other party to the proceedings (or to the legal representatives of any other party to the proceedings).

(3) Where an application is made by the accused, the accused—

(a) must inform the court and the prosecutor of the identity of the witness, but

(b) if there is more than one accused, is not required to disclose in connection with the application—

(i) the identity of the witness, or

(ii) any information that might enable the witness to be identified,

to any other accused (or to the legal representatives of any other accused).

(4) Subsections (5) and (6) apply where the prosecutor or the accused proposes to make an application under this section in respect of a witness.

(5) Any relevant information which is disclosed by or on behalf of that party before the determination of the application must be disclosed in such a way as to prevent—

    (a) the identity of the witness, or

    (b) any information that might enable the witness to be identified,

from being disclosed except as required by subsection (2)(a) or (3)(a).

(6) Despite any provision in this Act to the contrary, any relevant list, application or notice lodged, made or given by that party before the determination of the application must not—

    (a) disclose the identity of the witness, or

    (b) contain any other information that might enable the witness to be identified,

but the list, application or notice must, instead, refer to the witness by a pseudonym.

(7) "Relevant information" means any document or other material which falls to be disclosed, or is sought to be relied on, by or on behalf of the party concerned in connection with the proceedings or proceedings preliminary to them.

(8) "Relevant list, application or notice" means—

    (a) a list of witnesses,

    (b) a list of productions,

    (c) a notice under section 67. (5) or 78. (4) relating to the witness,

    (d) a motion or application under section 268, 269 or 270 relating to the witness,

    (e) any other motion, application or notice relating to the witness.

(9) The court must give every party to the proceedings the opportunity to be heard on an application under this section.

(10) Subsection (9) does not prevent the court from hearing one or more of the parties to the proceedings in the absence of an accused and the accused's legal representatives, if it appears to the court to be appropriate to do so in the circumstances of the case.

(11) Nothing in this section is to be taken as restricting any power to make rules of court.

271. QMaking and determination of applicationsS

(1) In proceedings on indictment, an application under section 271. P is a preliminary issue (and sections 79 and 87. A and other provisions relating to preliminary issues apply accordingly).

(2) No application under section 271. P may be made in summary proceedings by any party unless notice of the party's intention to do so has been given—

    (a) if an intermediate diet has been fixed, before that diet,

    (b) if no intermediate diet has been fixed, before the commencement of the trial.

(3) Subsection (2) is subject to subsections (4) and (8).

(4) In summary proceedings in which an intermediate diet has been fixed, the court may, on cause shown, grant leave for an application under section 271. P to be made without notice having been given in accordance with subsection (2)(a).

(5) Subsection (6) applies where—

    (a) the court grants leave for a party to make an application under section 271. P without notice having been given in accordance with subsection (2)(a), or

    (b) notice of a party's intention to make such an application is given in accordance with subsection (2)(b).

(6) The application must be disposed of before the commencement of the trial.

(7) Subsection (8) applies where a motion or application is made under section 268, 269 or 270 to lead the evidence of a witness.

(8) Despite section 79. (1) and subsection (2) above, an application under section 271. P may be made in respect of the witness at the same time as the motion or application under section 268, 269 or 270 is made.

(9) The application must be determined by the court before continuing with the trial.

(10) Where an application is made under section 271. P, the court may postpone or adjourn (or further adjourn) the trial diet.

(11) In this section, " commencement of the trial " means the time when the first witness for the prosecution is sworn.

271. RConditions for making ordersS

(1) This section applies where an application is made for a witness anonymity order to be made in relation to a witness in criminal proceedings.

(2) The court may make the order only if it is satisfied that Conditions A to D below are met.

(3) Condition A is that the proposed order is necessary—

(a) in order to protect the safety of the witness or another person or to prevent any serious damage to property, or

(b) in order to prevent real harm to the public interest (whether affecting the carrying on of any activities in the public interest or the safety of a person involved in carrying on such activities or otherwise).

(4) Condition B is that, having regard to all the circumstances, the effect of the proposed order would be consistent with the accused's receiving a fair trial.

(5) Condition C is that the importance of the witness's testimony is such that in the interests of justice the witness ought to testify.

(6) Condition D is that—

(a) the witness would not testify if the proposed order were not made, or

(b) there would be real harm to the public interest if the witness were to testify without the proposed order being made.

(7) In determining whether the measures to be specified in the order are necessary for the purpose mentioned in subsection (3)(a), the court must have regard in particular to any reasonable fear on the part of the witness—

(a) that the witness or another person would suffer death or injury, or

(b) that there would be serious damage to property,

if the witness were to be identified.

271. SRelevant considerationsS

(1) When deciding whether Conditions A to D in section 271. R are met in the case of an application for a witness anonymity order, the court must have regard to—

(a) the considerations mentioned in subsection (2), and

(b) such other matters as the court considers relevant.

(2) The considerations are—

(a) the general right of an accused in criminal proceedings to know the identity of a witness in the proceedings,

(b) the extent to which the credibility of the witness concerned would be a relevant factor when the witness's evidence comes to be assessed,

(c) whether evidence given by the witness might be material in implicating the accused,

(d) whether the witness's evidence could be properly tested (whether on grounds of credibility or otherwise) without the witness's identity being disclosed,

(e) whether there is any reason to believe that the witness—

(i) has a tendency to be dishonest, or

(ii) has any motive to be dishonest in the circumstances of the case,

having regard in particular to any previous convictions of the witness and to any relationship between the witness and the accused or any associates of the accused,

(f) whether it would be reasonably practicable to protect the witness's identity by any means other than by making a witness anonymity order specifying the measures that are under consideration by the court.

271. TDirection to juryS

(1) Subsection (2) applies where, in a trial on indictment, any evidence has been given by a witness at a time when a witness anonymity order applied to the witness.

(2) The judge must give the jury such direction as the judge considers appropriate to ensure that the fact that the order was made in relation to the witness does not prejudice the accused.

271. UDischarge and variation of orderS

(1) This section applies where a court has made a witness anonymity order in relation to any criminal proceedings.

(2) The court may discharge or vary (or further vary) the order if it appears to the court to be appropriate to do so in view of the provisions of sections 271. R and 271. S that applied to the making of the order.

(3) The court may do so—

    (a) on an application made by a party to the proceedings if there has been a material change of circumstances since the relevant time, or

    (b) on its own initiative.

(4) The court must give every party to the proceedings the opportunity to be heard—

    (a) before determining an application made to it under subsection (3)(a), and

    (b) before discharging or varying the order on its own initiative.

(5) Subsection (4) does not prevent the court from hearing one or more of the parties to the proceedings in the absence of an accused and the accused's legal representatives, if it appears to the court to be appropriate to do so in the circumstances of the case.

(6) In subsection (3)(a) "the relevant time" means—

    (a) the time when the order was made, or

    (b) if a previous application has been made under that subsection, the time when the application (or the last application) was made.

271. VAppealsS

(1) The prosecutor or the accused may appeal to the [F172appropriate Appeal Court] against—

    (a) the making of a witness anonymity order under section 271. N,

    (b) the kinds of measures that are required to be taken in relation to a witness under a witness anonymity order made under that section,

    (c) the refusal to make a witness anonymity order under that section,

    (d) the discharge of a witness anonymity order under section 271. U,

    (e) the variation of a witness anonymity order under that section, or

    (f) the refusal to discharge or vary a witness anonymity order under that section.

(2) The appeal may be brought only with the leave of the court of first instance, granted—

    (a) on the motion of the party making the appeal, or

    (b) on its own initiative.

(3) The procedure in relation to the appeal is to be prescribed by Act of Adjournal.

(4) If an appeal is brought under this section—

    (a) the period between the lodging of the appeal and its determination does not count towards any time limit applying in respect of the case,

    (b) the court of first instance or the [F173appropriate Appeal Court] may do either or both of the following—

(i) postpone or adjourn (or further adjourn) the trial diet,

(ii) extend any time limit applying in respect of the case.

(5) An appeal under this section does not affect any right of appeal in relation to any other decision of any court in the criminal proceedings.

[F174. (6)In this section, "appropriate Appeal Court" means—

(a) in the case of an appeal under this section against a decision made in proceedings on indictment, the High Court;

(b) in the case of an appeal under this section against a decision made in summary proceedings, the Sheriff Appeal Court.]

Amendments (Textual)

F172. Words in s. 271. V(1) substituted (22.9.2015) by The Courts Reform (Scotland) Act 2014 (Consequential Provisions No. 2) Order 2015 (S.S.I. 2015/338), art. 1, sch. 2 para. 5. (10)(a) (with art. 4)

F173. Words in s. 271. V(4)(b) substituted (22.9.2015) by The Courts Reform (Scotland) Act 2014 (Consequential Provisions No. 2) Order 2015 (S.S.I. 2015/338), art. 1, sch. 2 para. 5. (10)(a) (with art. 4)

F174. S. 271. V(6) inserted (22.9.2015) by The Courts Reform (Scotland) Act 2014 (Consequential Provisions No. 2) Order 2015 (S.S.I. 2015/338), art. 1, sch. 2 para. 5. (10)(b) (with art. 4)

271. WAppeal against the making of a witness anonymity orderS

(1) This section applies where—

(a) an appeal is brought under section 271. V(1)(a) against the making of a witness anonymity order, and

(b) the [F175court hearing the appeal] determines that the decision of the judge at first instance was wrong in law.

(2) The [F176court hearing the appeal] must discharge the order and the trial is to proceed as if the order had not been made.

Amendments (Textual)

F175. Words in s. 271. W(1)(b) substituted (22.9.2015) by The Courts Reform (Scotland) Act 2014 (Consequential Provisions No. 2) Order 2015 (S.S.I. 2015/338), art. 1, sch. 2 para. 5. (11) (with art. 4)

F176. Words in s. 271. W(2) substituted (22.9.2015) by The Courts Reform (Scotland) Act 2014 (Consequential Provisions No. 2) Order 2015 (S.S.I. 2015/338), art. 1, sch. 2 para. 5. (11) (with art. 4)

271. XAppeal against the refusal to make a witness anonymity orderS

(1) This section applies where—

(a) an appeal is brought under section 271. V(1)(c) against the refusal to make a witness anonymity order in relation to a witness in criminal proceedings, and

(b) the [F177court hearing the appeal] determines that the decision of the judge at first instance was wrong in law.

(2) The [F178court hearing the appeal] must make an order requiring such specified measures to be taken in relation to the witness in the proceedings as the court considers appropriate to ensure that the identity of the witness is not disclosed in or in connection with the proceedings.

Amendments (Textual)

F177. Words in s. 271. X(1)(b) substituted (22.9.2015) by The Courts Reform (Scotland) Act 2014 (Consequential Provisions No. 2) Order 2015 (S.S.I. 2015/338), art. 1, sch. 2 para. 5. (12) (with art. 4)

271. YAppeal against a variation of a witness anonymity orderS

(1) This section applies where—

(a) an appeal is brought under section 271. V(1)(e) against a variation of a witness anonymity order, and

(b) the [F179court hearing the appeal] determines that the decision of the judge at first instance was wrong in law.

(2) The [F180court hearing the appeal] must discharge the variation.

(3) If the [F181court hearing the appeal] determines that it is appropriate to make an additional variation in view of the provisions of sections 271. R and 271. S, the court may do so.

Amendments (Textual)

271. ZAppeal against a refusal to vary or discharge a witness anonymity orderS

(1) This section applies where—

(a) an appeal is brought under section 271. V(1)(f) against a refusal to discharge or vary a witness anonymity order, and

(b) the [F182court hearing the appeal] determines that the decision of the judge at first instance was wrong in law.

(2) The [F183court hearing the appeal] must discharge the order, or make the variation, as the case requires.

(3) If, in the case of a variation, the [F184court hearing the appeal] determines that it is appropriate to make an additional variation in view of the provisions of sections 271. R and 271. S, the court may do so.]

Amendments (Textual)

Evidence on commission and from abroadS

272 Evidence by letter of request or on commission.S

(1) In any criminal proceedings in the High Court or the sheriff court the prosecutor or the defence may, at an appropriate time, apply to a judge of the court in which the trial is to take place (or, if that is not yet known, to a judge of the High Court) for—

(a) the issue of a letter of request to a court, or tribunal, exercising jurisdiction in a country or territory outside the United Kingdom, Channel Islands and Isle of Man for the examination of a witness resident in that country or territory; or

(b) the appointment of a commissioner to examine, at any place in the United Kingdom, Channel Islands, or Isle of Man, a witness who—

(i) by reason of being ill or infirm is unable to attend the trial diet; or

(ii) is not ordinarily resident in, and is, at the time of the trial diet, unlikely to be present in, the United Kingdom, Channel Islands or the Isle of Man.

(2) A hearing, as regards any application under subsection (1) above by a party, shall be conducted in chambers but may be dispensed with if the application is not opposed.

(3) An application under subsection (1) above may be granted only if the judge is satisfied that—

(a) the evidence which it is averred the witness is able to give is necessary for the proper adjudication of the trial; and

(b) there would be no unfairness to the other party were such evidence to be received in the form of the record of an examination conducted by virtue of that subsection.

(4) Any such record as is mentioned in paragraph (b) of subsection (3) above shall, without being sworn to by witnesses, be received in evidence in so far as it either accords with the averment mentioned in paragraph (a) of that subsection or can be so received without unfairness to either party.

(5) Where any such record as is mentioned in paragraph (b) of subsection (3) above, or any part of such record, is not a document in writing, that record or part shall not be received in evidence under subsection (4) above unless it is accompanied by a transcript of its contents.

(6) The procedure as regards the foregoing provisions of this section shall be prescribed by Act of Adjournal; and without prejudice to the generality of the power to make it, such an Act of Adjournal may provide for the appointment of a person before whom evidence may be taken for the purposes of this section.

(7) In subsection (1) above, "appropriate time" means as regards—

(a) solemn proceedings, any time before the oath is administered to the jury;

(b) summary proceedings, any time before the first witness is sworn,

or (but only in relation to an application under paragraph (b) of that subsection) any time during the course of the trial if the circumstances on which the application is based had not arisen, or would not have merited such application, within the period mentioned in paragraph (a) or, as the case may be, (b) of this subsection.

(8) In subsection (3) and (4) above, "record" includes, in addition to a document in writing—

(a) any disc, tape, soundtrack or other device in which sounds or other data (not being visual images) are recorded so as to be capable (with or without the aid of some other equipment) of being reproduced therefrom; and

(b) any film (including microfilm), negative, tape, disc or other device in which one or more visual images are recorded so as to be capable (as aforesaid) of being reproduced therefrom.

(9) This section is without prejudice to any existing power at common law to adjourn a trial diet to the place where a witness is.

[F185. (10)Sections—

(a) 274;

(b) 275;

(c) 275. B except subsection (2)(b);

(d) 275. C; and

(e) 288. C,

of this Act apply in relation to proceedings in which a commissioner examines a witness under subsection (1)(b) above as they apply in relation to a trial.

(11) In the application of those sections in relation to such proceedings—

(a) the commissioner acting in the proceedings is to perform the functions of the court as provided for in those sections;

(b) references—

(i) in those sections, except section 275. (3)(c) and (7)(c), to a trial or a trial diet;

(ii) in those sections, except section 275. (3)(e), to the court,

shall be read accordingly;

(c) the reference in section 275. B(1) to 14 days shall be read as a reference to 7 days.

(12) In a case where it falls to the court to appoint a commissioner for the purposes of subsection (1)(b) above, the commissioner shall be a person described in subsection (13) below.

(13) The persons are—

(a) where the proceedings before the commissioner are for the purposes of a trial in the High Court, a judge of the High Court; or

(b) in any other case, a sheriff.]

[F186. (14)This section does not apply to a witness who or evidence that is the subject of a European investigation order made under Part 2 of the Criminal Justice (European Investigation Order) Regulations 2017.]

Amendments (Textual)

F185. S. 272. (10)-(13) added (23.4.2007) by Criminal Proceedings etc. (Reform) (Scotland) Act 2007 (asp 6), ss. 35. (4), 84; S.S.I. 2007/250, art. 3. (a)

F186. S. 272. (14) inserted (31.7.2017) by The Criminal Justice (European Investigation Order) Regulations 2017 (S.I. 2017/730), reg. 1. (1), Sch. 3 para. 3. (4) (with reg. 3)

273 Television link evidence from abroad.S

(1) In any [F187criminal] proceedings in the High Court or the sheriff court a person other than the accused may give evidence through a live television link if—

(a) the witness is outside the United Kingdom;

(b) an application under subsection (2) below for the issue of a letter of request has been granted; and

(c) the court is satisfied as to the arrangements for the giving of evidence in that manner by that witness.

(2) The prosecutor or the defence in any proceedings referred to in subsection (1) above may apply to a judge of the court in which the trial is to take place (or, if that court is not yet known, to a judge of the High Court) for the issue of a letter of request to—

(a) a court or tribunal exercising jurisdiction in a country or territory outside the United Kingdom where a witness is ordinarily resident; or

(b) any authority which the judge is satisfied is recognised by the government of that country or territory as the appropriate authority for receiving requests for assistance in facilitating the giving of evidence through a live television link,

requesting assistance in facilitating the giving of evidence by that witness through a live television link.

(3) An application under subsection (2) above shall be granted only if the judge is satisfied that—

(a) the evidence which it is averred the witness is able to give is necessary for the proper adjudication of the trial; and

(b) the granting of the application —

(i) is in the interests of justice; and

(ii) in the case of an application by the prosecutor, is not unfair to the accused.

[F188. (5)This section does not apply to a witness who or evidence that is the subject of a

European investigation order made under Part 2 of the Criminal Justice (European Investigation Order) Regulations 2017.]

Amendments (Textual)
F187. Word in s. 273. (1) substituted (28.3.2011) by Criminal Justice and Licensing (Scotland) Act 2010 (asp 13), ss. 91. (2), 206. (1); S.S.I. 2011/178, art. 2, sch.
F188. S. 273. (5) inserted (31.7.2017) "after subsection (4)" by virtue of The Criminal Justice (European Investigation Order) Regulations 2017 (S.I. 2017/730), reg. 1. (1), Sch. 3 para. 3. (5) (with reg. 3)

[F189. Evidence from other parts of the United KingdomS

Amendments (Textual)
F189. S. 273. A inserted (28.3.2011) by Criminal Justice and Licensing (Scotland) Act 2010 (asp 13), ss. 91. (3), 206. (1); S.S.I. 2011/178, art. 2, sch.

273. ATelevision link evidence from other parts of the United KingdomS

(1) In any criminal proceedings in the High Court or the sheriff court a person other than the accused may give evidence through a live television link if—
 (a) the witness is within the United Kingdom but outside Scotland,
 (b) an application under this section for the issue of a letter of request has been granted, and
 (c) the court is satisfied as to the arrangements for the giving of evidence in that manner by that witness.
(2) The prosecutor or the defence in any proceedings referred to in subsection (1) may apply for the issue of a letter of request.
(3) The application must be made to a judge of the court in which the trial is to take place or, if that court is not yet known, to a judge of the High Court.
(4) The judge may, on an application under this section, issue a letter to a court or tribunal exercising jurisdiction in the place where the witness is ordinarily resident requesting assistance in facilitating the giving of evidence by that witness through a live television link, if the judge is satisfied of the matters set out in subsection (5).
(5) Those matters are—
 (a) that the evidence which it is averred the witness is able to give is necessary for the proper adjudication of the trial,
 (b) that the granting of the application—
(i) is in the interests of justice, and
(ii) in the case of an application by the prosecutor, is not unfair to the accused.]

Evidence relating to sexual offencesS

[F190274 Restrictions on evidence relating to sexual offences.S

(1) In the trial of a person charged with an offence to which section 288. C of this Act applies, the court shall not admit, or allow questioning designed to elicit, evidence which shows or tends to show that the complainer—
 (a) is not of good character (whether in relation to sexual matters or otherwise);
 (b) has, at any time, engaged in sexual behaviour not forming part of the subject matter of the charge;
 (c) has, at any time (other than shortly before, at the same time as or shortly after the acts which

form part of the subject matter of the charge), engaged in such behaviour, not being sexual behaviour, as might found the inference that the complainer—

(i) is likely to have consented to those acts; or

(ii) is not a credible or reliable witness; or

(d) has, at any time, been subject to any such condition or predisposition as might found the inference referred to in sub-paragraph (c) above.

(2) In subsection (1) above—

"complainer" means the person against whom the offence referred to in that subsection is alleged to have been committed; and

the reference to engaging in sexual behaviour includes a reference to undergoing or being made subject to any experience of a sexual nature.]

Amendments (Textual)

F190. S. 274 substituted (1.11.2002) by Sexual Offences (Procedure and Evidence) (Scotland) Act 2002 (asp 9), s. 7; S.S.I. 2002/443, art. 3 (with art. 4. (5))

[F191275 Exceptions to restrictions under section 274.S

(1) The court may, on application made to it, admit such evidence or allow such questioning as is referred to in subsection (1) of section 274 of this Act if satisfied that—

(a) the evidence or questioning will relate only to a specific occurrence or occurrences of sexual or other behaviour or to specific facts demonstrating—

(i) the complainer's character; or

(ii) any condition or predisposition to which the complainer is or has been subject;

(b) that occurrence or those occurrences of behaviour or facts are relevant to establishing whether the accused is guilty of the offence with which he is charged; and

(c) the probative value of the evidence sought to be admitted or elicited is significant and is likely to outweigh any risk of prejudice to the proper administration of justice arising from its being admitted or elicited.

(2) In subsection (1) above—

(a) the reference to an occurrence or occurrences of sexual behaviour includes a reference to undergoing or being made subject to any experience of a sexual nature;

(b) "the proper administration of justice" includes—

(i) appropriate protection of a complainer's dignity and privacy; and

(ii) ensuring that the facts and circumstances of which a jury is made aware are, in cases of offences to which section 288. C of this Act applies, relevant to an issue which is to be put before the jury and commensurate to the importance of that issue to the jury's verdict,

and, in that subsection and in sub-paragraph (i) of paragraph (b) above, "complainer" has the same meaning as in section 274 of this Act.

(3) An application for the purposes of subsection (1) above shall be in writing and shall set out—

(a) the evidence sought to be admitted or elicited;

(b) the nature of any questioning proposed;

(c) the issues at the trial to which that evidence is considered to be relevant;

(d) the reasons why that evidence is considered relevant to those issues;

(e) the inferences which the applicant proposes to submit to the court that it should draw from that evidence; and

(f) such other information as is of a kind specified for the purposes of this paragraph in Act of Adjournal.

(4) The party making such an application shall, when making it, send a copy of it—

(a) when that party is the prosecutor, to the accused; and

(b) when that party is the accused, to the prosecutor and any co-accused.

(5) The court may reach a decision under subsection (1) above without considering any evidence; but, where it takes evidence for the purposes of reaching that decision, it shall do so as if

determining the admissibility of evidence.

(6) The court shall state its reasons for its decision under subsection (1) above, and may make that decision subject to conditions which may include compliance with directions issued by it.

(7) Where a court admits evidence or allows questioning under subsection (1) above, its decision to do so shall include a statement—

(a) of what items of evidence it is admitting or lines of questioning it is allowing;

(b) of the reasons for its conclusion that the evidence to be admitted or to be elicited by the questioning is admissible;

(c) of the issues at the trial to which it considers that that evidence is relevant.

(8) A condition under subsection (6) above may consist of a limitation on the extent to which evidence—

(a) to be admitted; or

(b) to be elicited by questioning to be allowed,

may be argued to support a particular inference specified in the condition.

(9) Where evidence is admitted or questioning allowed under this section, the court at any time may—

(a) as it thinks fit; and

(b) notwithstanding the terms of its decision under subsection (1) above or any condition under subsection (6) above,

limit the extent of evidence to be admitted or questioning to be allowed.]

Amendments (Textual)

F191. S. 275 substituted (1.11.2002) by Sexual Offences (Procedure and Evidence) (Scotland) Act 2002 (asp 9), s. 8. (1); S.S.I. 2002/443, art. 3 (with art. 4. (5))

[F192275. A Disclosure of accused's previous convictions where court allows questioning or evidence under section 275. S

(1) Where, under section 275 of this Act, a court [F193. (or, in proceedings before a commissioner appointed under section 271. I(1) or by virtue of section 272. (1)(b) of this Act, a commissioner)] on the application of the accused allows such questioning or admits such evidence as is referred to in section 274. (1) of this Act, the prosecutor shall forthwith place before the presiding judge any previous relevant conviction of the accused.

(2) Any conviction placed before the judge under subsection (1) above shall, unless the accused objects, be—

(a) in proceedings on indictment, laid before the jury;

(b) in summary proceedings, taken into consideration by the judge.

(3) An extract of such a conviction may not be laid before the jury or taken into consideration by the judge unless such an extract was appended to the notice, served on the accused under section 69. (2) or, as the case may be, 166. (2) of this Act, which specified that conviction.

(4) An objection under subsection (2) above may be made only on one or more of the following grounds—

(a) where the conviction bears to be a relevant conviction by virtue only of paragraph (b) of subsection (10) below, that there was not a substantial sexual element present in the commission of the offence for which the accused has been convicted;

(b) that the disclosure or, as the case may be, the taking into consideration of the conviction would be contrary to the interests of justice;

(c) in proceedings on indictment, that the conviction does not apply to the accused or is otherwise inadmissible;

(d) in summary proceedings, that the accused does not admit the conviction.

(5) Where—

(a) an objection is made on one or more of the grounds mentioned in paragraphs (b) to (d) of subsection (4) above; and

(b) an extract of the conviction in respect of which the objection is made was not appended to the notice, served on the accused under section 69. (2) or, as the case may be, 166. (2) above, which specified that conviction,

the prosecutor may, notwithstanding subsection (3) above, place such an extract conviction before the judge.

(6) In summary proceedings, the judge may, notwithstanding subsection (2)(b) above, take into consideration any extract placed before him under subsection (5) above for the purposes only of considering the objection in respect of which the extract is disclosed.

(7) In entertaining an objection on the ground mentioned in paragraph (b) of subsection (4) above, the court shall, unless the contrary is shown, presume that the disclosure, or, as the case may be, the taking into consideration, of a conviction is in the interests of justice.

(8) An objection on the ground mentioned in paragraph (c) of subsection (4) above shall not be entertained unless the accused has, under subsection (2) of section 69 of this Act, given intimation of the objection in accordance with subsection (3) of that section.

(9) In entertaining an objection on the ground mentioned in paragraph (d) of subsection (4) above, the court shall require the prosecutor to withdraw the conviction or adduce evidence in proof thereof.

(10) For the purposes of this section a "relevant conviction" is, subject to subsection (11) below—

(a) a conviction for an offence to which section 288. C of this Act applies by virtue of subsection (2) thereof; F194. . .

[F195. (aa)a conviction by a court in England and Wales, Northern Ireland or a member State of the European Union other than the United Kingdom of an offence that is equivalent to one to which section 288. C of this Act applies by virtue of subsection (2) thereof; or]

(b) where a substantial sexual element was present in the commission of any other offence in respect of which the accused has previously been convicted, a conviction for that offence, which is specified in a notice served on the accused under section 69. (2) or, as the case may be, 166. (2) of this Act.

[F196. (10. A)Any issue of equivalence arising in pursuance of subsection (10)(aa) is for the court to determine.]

(11) A conviction for an offence other than an offence to which section 288. C of this Act applies by virtue of subsection (2) thereof is not a relevant conviction for the purposes of this section unless an extract of that conviction containing information which indicates that a sexual element was present in the commission of the offence was appended to the notice, served on the accused under section 69. (2) or, as the case may be, 166. (2) of this Act, which specified that conviction.

Amendments (Textual)

F192. Ss. 275. A, 275. B inserted (1.11.2002) by Sexual Offences (Procedure and Evidence) (Scotland) Act 2002 (asp 9), s. 10. (4); S.S.I. 2002/443, art. 3 (with art. 4. (5))

F193. Words in s. 275. A(1) inserted (23.4.2007) by Criminal Proceedings etc. (Reform) (Scotland) Act 2007 (asp 6), ss. 35. (5), 84; S.S.I. 2007/250, art. 3. (a)

F194. Word in s. 275. A(10) repealed (13.12.2010 for all purposes in respect of offences committed on or after this date) by Criminal Justice and Licensing (Scotland) Act 2010 (asp 13), ss. 71. (1), 206. (1), Sch. 4 para. 7. (a)(i); S.S.I. 2010/413, art. 2, Sch.

F195. S. 275. A(10)(aa) inserted (13.12.2010 for all purposes in respect of offences committed on or after this date) by Criminal Justice and Licensing (Scotland) Act 2010 (asp 13), ss. 71. (1), 206. (1), Sch. 4 para. 7. (a)(ii); S.S.I. 2010/413, art. 2, Sch.

F196. S. 275. A(10. A) inserted (13.12.2010 for all purposes in respect of offences committed on or after this date) by Criminal Justice and Licensing (Scotland) Act 2010 (asp 13), ss. 71. (1), 206. (1), Sch. 4 para. 7. (b); S.S.I. 2010/413, art. 2, Sch.

275. B Provisions supplementary to sections 275 and 275. AS

(1) An application for the purposes of subsection (1) of section 275 of this Act shall not, unless on

special cause shown, be considered by the court unless made

[F197. (a)in the case of proceedings in the High Court, not less than 7 clear days before the preliminary hearing; or

(b) in any other case,]

not less than 14 clear days before the trial diet.

(2) Where—

(a) such an application is considered; or

(b) any objection under subsection (2) of section 275. A of this Act is entertained,

during the course of the trial, the court shall consider that application or, as the case may be, entertain that objection in the absence of the jury, the complainer, any person cited as a witness and the public.]

Amendments (Textual)

F192. Ss. 275. A, 275. B inserted (1.11.2002) by Sexual Offences (Procedure and Evidence) (Scotland) Act 2002 (asp 9), s. 10. (4); S.S.I. 2002/443, art. 3 (with art. 4. (5))

F197. Words in s. 275. B inserted (1.2.2005) by Criminal Procedure (Amendment) (Scotland) Act 2004 (asp 5), ss. 25, 27. (1), Sch. para. 45; S.S.I. 2004/405, art. 2, Sch. 1 (with savings in arts. 3-5)

[F198. Expert evidence as to subsequent behaviour of complainerS

Amendments (Textual)

F198. S. 275. C and preceding cross-heading inserted (1.4.2005) by Vulnerable Witnesses (Scotland) Act 2004 (asp 3), ss. 5, 25; S.S.I. 2005/168, art. 2, Sch. (with savings in art. 4)

275. CExpert evidence as to subsequent behaviour of complainer in certain casesS

(1) This section applies in the case of proceedings in respect of any offence to which section 288. C of this Act applies.

(2) Expert psychological or psychiatric evidence relating to any subsequent behaviour or statement of the complainer is admissible for the purpose of rebutting any inference adverse to the complainer's credibility or reliability as a witness which might otherwise be drawn from the behaviour or statement.

(3) In subsection (2) above—

"complainer" means the person against whom the offence to which the proceedings relate is alleged to have been committed,

"subsequent behaviour or statement" means any behaviour or statement subsequent to, and not forming part of the acts constituting, the offence to which the proceedings relate and which is not otherwise relevant to any fact in issue at the trial.

(4) This section does not affect the admissibility of any evidence which is admissible otherwise than by virtue of this section.]

Biological materialS

276 Evidence of biological material.S

(1) Evidence as to the characteristics and composition of any biological material deriving from human beings or animals shall, in any criminal proceedings, be admissible notwithstanding that neither the material nor a sample of it is lodged as a production.

(2) A party wishing to lead such evidence as is referred to in subsection (1) above shall, where neither the material nor a sample of it is lodged as a production, make the material or a sample of it available for inspection by the other party unless the material constitutes a hazard to health or has been destroyed in the process of analysis.

Transcripts and recordsS

277 Transcript of police interview sufficient evidence.S

(1) Subject to subsection (2) below, for the purposes of any criminal proceedings, a document certified by the person who made it as an accurate transcript made for the prosecutor of the contents of a tape (identified by means of a label) purporting to be a recording of an interview between—

(a) a police officer and an accused person; F199...

(b) a person commissioned, appointed or authorised under section 6. (3) of the M1. Customs and Excise Management Act 1979 and an accused person[F200; or

(c) a person authorised by the Scottish Environment Protection Agency under section 108 of the Environment Protection Act 1995 and an accused person.]

shall be received in evidence and be sufficient evidence of the making of the transcript and of its accuracy.

(2) Subsection (1) above shall not apply to a transcript—

(a) unless a copy of it has been served on the accused not less than 14 days before

[F201. (i)in the case of proceedings in the High Court, the preliminary hearing;

(ii) in any other case,]

his trial; or

(b) if the accused, not less than

[F202. (i)in the case of proceedings in the High Court, seven days before the preliminary hearing;

(ii) in any other case, six days before his trial;

or (in either case)] by such later time before his trial as the court may in special circumstances allow, has served notice on the prosecutor that the accused challenges the making of the transcript or its accuracy.

(3) A copy of the transcript or a notice under subsection (2) above shall be served in such manner as may be prescribed by Act of Adjournal; and a written execution purporting to be signed by the person who served the transcript or notice, together with, where appropriate, the relevant post office receipt shall be sufficient evidence of such service.

(4) Where subsection (1) above does not apply to a transcript, if the person who made the transcript is called as a witness his evidence shall be sufficient evidence of the making of the transcript and of its accuracy.

[F203. (5)Subsection (1) is without prejudice to section 108. (12) of the Environment Act 1995.]

Amendments (Textual)

F199. Word in s. 277. (1) repealed (30.6.2014) by Regulatory Reform (Scotland) Act 2014 (asp 3), s. 61. (2), sch. 3 para. 31. (2)(a)(i); S.S.I. 2014/160, art. 2. (1)(2), sch.

F200. S. 277. (1)(c) and word inserted (30.6.2014) by Regulatory Reform (Scotland) Act 2014 (asp 3), s. 61. (2), sch. 3 para. 31. (2)(a)(ii); S.S.I. 2014/160, art. 2. (1)(2), sch.

F201. Words in s. 277. (2)(a) inserted (1.2.2005) by Criminal Procedure (Amendment) (Scotland) Act 2004 (asp 5), ss. 25, 27. (1), Sch. para. 46. (a); S.S.I. 2004/405, art. 2, Sch. 1 (with savings in arts. 3-5)

F202. Words in s. 277. (2)(b) substituted (1.2.2005) by Criminal Procedure (Amendment) (Scotland) Act 2004 (asp 5), ss. 25, 27. (1), Sch. para. 46. (b); S.S.I. 2004/405, art. 2, Sch. 1 (with savings in arts. 3-5)

F203. S. 277. (5) added (30.6.2014) by Regulatory Reform (Scotland) Act 2014 (asp 3), s. 61. (2),

sch. 3 para. 31. (2)(b); S.S.I. 2014/160, art. 2. (1)(2), sch.
Marginal Citations
M11979 c.2.

F204278 Record of proceedings at examination as evidence.S

. . . .

Amendments (Textual)
F204. S. 278 repealed (17.1.2017) by Criminal Justice (Scotland) Act 2016 (asp 1), ss. 78. (2)(e), 117. (2); S.S.I. 2016/426, art. 2, sch. (with art. 3)

Documentary evidenceS

279 Evidence from documents.S

Schedule 8 to this Act, which makes provision regarding the admissibility in criminal proceedings of copy documents and of evidence contained in business documents, shall have effect.

[F205 Evidence from certain official documentsS

Amendments (Textual)
F205. S. 279. A and preceding cross-heading inserted (1.8.1997) by 1997 c. 48, s. 28. (2); S.I. 1997/1712, art. 3, Sch. (subject to arts. 4, 5)

F206279. A Evidence from certain official documents.S

(1) Any letter, minute or other official document issuing from the office of or in the custody of any of the departments of state or government in the United Kingdom [F207or any part of the Scottish Administration] which—

(a) is required to be produced in evidence in any prosecution; and

(b) according to the rules and regulations applicable to such departments may competently be so produced,

shall when so produced be prima facie evidence of the matters contained in it without being produced or sworn to by any witness.

(2) A copy of any such document as is mentioned in subsection (1) above bearing to be certified by any person having authority to certify it shall be treated as equivalent to the original of that document and no proof of the signature of the person certifying the copy or of his authority to certify it shall be necessary.

(3) Any order by any of the departments of state or government [F208or the Scottish Parliament] or any local authority or public body made under powers conferred by any statute or a print or a copy of such an order, shall when produced in a prosecution be received as evidence of the due making, confirmation, and existence of the order without being sworn to by any witness and without any further or other proof.

(4) Subsection (3) above is without prejudice to any right competent to the accused to challenge any order such as is mentioned in that subsection as being ultra vires of the authority making it or on any other competent ground.

(5) Where an order such as is mentioned in subsection (3) above is referred to in the indictment or, as the case may be, the complaint, it shall not be necessary to enter it in the record of the proceedings as a documentary production.

(6) The provisions of this section are in addition to, and not in derogation of, any powers of

proving documents conferred by statute or existing at common law.]

Amendments (Textual)

F206. S. 279. A and preceding cross-heading inserted (1.8.1997) by 1997 c. 48, s. 28. (2); S.I. 1997/1712, art. 3, Sch. (subject to arts. 4, 5)

F207. Words in s. 279. A(1) inserted (1.7.1999) by S.I. 1999/1820, arts. 1. (2), 4, Sch. 2 Pt. I para. 122. (4)(a); S.I. 1998/3178, art. 3

F208. Words in s. 279. A(3) inserted (1.7.1999) by S.I. 1999/1820, arts. 1. (2), 4, Sch. 2 Pt. I para. 122. (4)(b); S.I. 1998/3178, arts. 3

Routine evidenceS

280 Routine evidence.S

(1) For the purposes of any proceedings for an offence under any of the enactments specified in column 1 of Schedule 9 to this Act, a certificate purporting to be signed by a person or persons specified in column 2 thereof, and certifying the matter specified in column 3 thereof shall, subject to subsection (6) below, be sufficient evidence of that matter and of the qualification or authority of that person or those persons.

(2) The Secretary of State may by order—

    (a) amend or repeal the entry in Schedule 9 to this Act in respect of any enactment; or

    (b) insert in that Schedule an entry in respect of a further enactment.

(3) An order under subsection (2) above may make such transitional, incidental or supplementary provision as the Secretary of State considers necessary or expedient in connection with the coming into force of the order.

[F209. (3. A)For the purposes of any criminal proceedings, a report purporting to be signed by a person authorised by the Scottish Environment Protection Agency for the purpose of this subsection is sufficient evidence of any fact or conclusion as to fact contained in the report and of the authority of the signatory.]

(4) For the purposes of any criminal proceedings, a report purporting to be signed by two authorised forensic scientists shall, subject to subsection (5) below, be sufficient evidence of any fact or conclusion as to fact contained in the report and of the authority of the signatories.

(5) A forensic scientist is authorised for the purposes of subsection (4) above if—

    (a) he is authorised for those purposes by the Secretary of State; or

    (b) he—

F210. (i). . . . .

(ii) possesses such qualifications and experience as the Secretary of State may for the purposes of that subsection by order prescribe; and

F210. (iii). . . . .

(6) Subsections (1) [F211, (3. A)] and (4) above shall not apply to a certificate or, as the case may be, report tendered on behalf of the prosecutor or the accused—

    (a) unless a copy has been served on the other party not less than fourteen days before

[F212. (i)in the case of proceedings in the High Court, the preliminary hearing;

(ii) in any other case,]

 the trial; or

    (b) where the other party, not more than seven days after the date of service of the copy on him under paragraph (a) above or by such later time as the court may in special circumstances allow, has served notice on the first party that [F213he] challenges the matter, qualification or authority mentioned in subsection (1) above or as the case may be the fact, conclusion or authority mentioned in subsection [F214. (3. A) or] (4) above.

(7) A copy of a certificate or, as the case may be, report required by subsection (6) above, to be served on the accused or the prosecutor or of a notice required by that subsection or by subsection

(1) or (2) of section 281 of this Act to be served on the prosecutor shall be served in such manner as may be prescribed by Act of Adjournal; and a written execution purporting to be signed by the person who served such certificate or notice, together with, where appropriate, the relevant post office receipt shall be sufficient evidence of service of such a copy.

(8) Where, following service of a notice under subsection (6)(b) above, evidence is given in relation to a report referred to in subsection (4) above by both of the forensic scientists purporting to have signed the report, the evidence of those forensic scientists shall be sufficient evidence of any fact (or conclusion as to fact) contained in the report.

(9) At any trial of an offence it shall be presumed that the person who appears in answer to the complaint is the person charged by the police with the offence unless the contrary is alleged.

(10) An order made under subsection (2) or (5)(b)(ii) above shall be made by statutory instrument.

(11) No order shall be made under subsection (2) above unless a draft of the order has been laid before, and approved by a resolution of, each House of Parliament.

(12) A statutory instrument containing an order under subsection (5)(b)(ii) above shall be subject to annulment pursuant to a resolution of either House of Parliament.

Amendments (Textual)

F209. S. 280. (3. A) inserted (30.6.2014) by Regulatory Reform (Scotland) Act 2014 (asp 3), s. 61. (2), sch. 3 para. 31. (3)(a); S.S.I. 2014/160, art. 2. (1)(2), sch.

F210. S. 280. (5)(b)(i)(iii) repealed (1.4.2013) by Police and Fire Reform (Scotland) Act 2012 (asp 8), s. 129. (2), sch. 8 Pt. 1; S.S.I. 2013/51, art. 2 (with transitional provisions and savings in S.S.I. 2013/121)

F211. Word in s. 280. (6) inserted (30.6.2014) by Regulatory Reform (Scotland) Act 2014 (asp 3), s. 61. (2), sch. 3 para. 31. (3)(b)(i); S.S.I. 2014/160, art. 2. (1)(2), sch.

F212. Words in s. 280. (6)(a) inserted (1.2.2005) by Criminal Procedure (Amendment) (Scotland) Act 2004 (asp 5), ss. 25, 27. (1), Sch. para. 48; S.S.I. 2004/405, art. 2, Sch. 1 (with savings in arts. 3-5)

F213. Word in s. 280. (6)(b) substituted (1.8.1997) by 1997 c. 48, s. 62. (1), Sch. 1 para. 21. (32); S.I. 1997/1712, art. 3, Sch. (subject to arts. 4, 5)

F214. Words in s. 280. (6)(b) inserted (30.6.2014) by Regulatory Reform (Scotland) Act 2014 (asp 3), s. 61. (2), sch. 3 para. 31. (3)(b)(ii); S.S.I. 2014/160, art. 2. (1)(2), sch.

281 Routine evidence: autopsy and forensic science reports.S

(1) Where in a trial an autopsy report is lodged as a production by the prosecutor it shall be presumed that the body of the person identified in that report is the body of the deceased identified in the indictment or complaint, unless the accused not less than

[F215. (i)in the case of proceedings in the High Court, seven days before the preliminary hearing; (ii) in any other case, six days before the trial; or (in either case)] by such later time before the trial as the court may in special circumstances allow, gives notice that the contrary is alleged.

(2) At the time of lodging an autopsy or forensic science report as a production the prosecutor may intimate to the accused that it is intended that only one of the pathologists or forensic scientists F216. . . purporting to have signed the report shall be called to give evidence in respect thereof; and [F217, where such intimation is given,] the evidence of [F218one of those pathologists or forensic scientists] shall be sufficient evidence of any fact or conclusion as to fact contained in the report and of the qualifications of the signatories, unless the accused, not less than

[F219. (i)in the case of proceedings in the High Court, seven days before the preliminary hearing; (ii) in any other case, six days before the trial; or (in either case)] by such later time before the trial as the court may in special circumstances allow, serves notice on the prosecutor that he requires the attendance at the trial of the other pathologist or forensic scientist also.

(3) Where, following service of a notice by the accused under subsection (2) above, evidence is

given in relation to an autopsy or forensic science report by both of the pathologists or forensic scientists purporting to have signed the report, the evidence of those pathologists or forensic scientists shall be sufficient evidence of any fact (or conclusion as to fact) contained in the report.

Amendments (Textual)

F215. Words in s. 281. (1) substituted (1.2.2005) by Criminal Procedure (Amendment) (Scotland) Act 2004 (asp 5), ss. 25, 27. (1), Sch. para. 49. (a); S.S.I. 2004/405, art. 2. (1), Sch. 1 (with savings in arts. 3-5)

F216. Words in s. 281. (2) repealed (1.2.2005) by Criminal Procedure (Amendment) (Scotland) Act 2004 (asp 5), ss. 25, 27. (1), Sch. para. 49. (b)(i); S.S.I. 2004/405, art. 2. (1), Sch. 1 (with savings in arts. 3-5)

F217. Words in s. 281. (2) inserted (1.2.2005) by Criminal Procedure (Amendment) (Scotland) Act 2004 (asp 5), ss. 25, 27. (1), Sch. para. 49. (b)(ii); S.S.I. 2004/405, art. 2. (1), Sch. 1 (with savings in arts. 3-5)

F218. Words in s. 281. (2) substituted (1.2.2005) by Criminal Procedure (Amendment) (Scotland) Act 2004 (asp 5), ss. 25, 27. (1), Sch. para. 49. (b)(iii); S.S.I. 2004/405, art. 2. (1), Sch. 1 (with savings in arts. 3-5)

F219. Words in s. 281. (2) substituted (1.2.2005) by Criminal Procedure (Amendment) (Scotland) Act 2004 (asp 5), ss. 25, 27. (1), Sch. para. 49. (b)(iv); S.S.I. 2004/405, art. 2. (1), Sch. 1 (with savings in arts. 3-5)

[F220281. ARoutine evidence: reports of identification prior to trialS

(1) Where in a trial the prosecutor lodges as a production a report naming—

(a) a person identified in an identification parade or other identification procedure by a witness, and

(b) that witness,

it shall be presumed, subject to subsection (2) below, that the person named in the report as having been identified by the witness is the person of the same name who appears in answer to the indictment or complaint.

(2) That presumption shall not apply—

(a) unless the prosecutor has, [F221by the required time], served on the accused a copy of the report and a notice that he intends to rely on the presumption, or

(b) if the accused—

(i) not more than 7 days after the date of service of the copy of the report, or

(ii) by such later time as the court may in special circumstances allow,

has served notice on the prosecutor that he intends to challenge the facts stated in the report.

[F222. (3)In subsection (2)(a) above, "the required time" means—

(a) in the case of proceedings in the High Court—

(i) not less than 14 clear days before the preliminary hearing; or

(ii) such later time, being not less than 14 clear days before the trial, as the court may, in special circumstances, allow;

(b) in any other case, not less than 14 clear days before the trial.]]

Amendments (Textual)

F220. S. 281. A inserted (1.4.2005) by Vulnerable Witnesses (Scotland) Act 2004 (asp 3), ss. 4, 25; S.S.I. 2005/168, art. 2, Sch. (with savings in art. 4)

F221. Words in s. 281. A(2)(a) substituted (1.4.2005) by Criminal Procedure (Amendment) (Scotland) Act 2004 (asp 5), ss. 25, 27. (1), Sch. para. 50. (a); S.S.I. 2004/405, art. 2. (2), Sch. 2 (with savings in arts. 3-5)

F222. S. 281. A(3) inserted (1.4.2005) by Criminal Procedure (Amendment) (Scotland) Act 2004 (asp 5), ss. 25, 27. (1), Sch. para. 50. (b); S.S.I. 2004/405, art. 2. (2), Sch. 2 (with savings in arts. 3-5) (as amended (31.1.2005) by S.S.I. 2005/40, art. 3. (5))

Sufficient evidenceS

282 Evidence as to controlled drugs and medicinal products.S

(1) For the purposes of any criminal proceedings, evidence given by an authorised forensic scientist, either orally or in a report purporting to be signed by him, that a substance which satisfies either of the conditions specified in subsection (2) below is—

(a) a particular controlled drug or medicinal product; or

(b) a particular product which is listed in the British Pharmacopoeia as containing a particular controlled drug or medicinal product,

shall, subject to subsection (3) below, be sufficient evidence of that fact notwithstanding that no analysis of the substance has been carried out.

(2) Those conditions are—

(a) that the substance is in a sealed container bearing a label identifying the contents of the container; or

(b) that the substance has a characteristic appearance having regard to its size, shape, colour and manufacturer's mark.

(3) A party proposing to rely on subsection (1) above ("the first party") shall, not less than 14 days before the [F223relevant] diet, serve on the other party ("the second party")—

(a) a notice to that effect; and

(b) where the evidence is contained in a report, a copy of the report,

and if the second party serves on the first party, not more than seven days after the date of service of the notice on him, a notice that he does not accept the evidence as to the identity of the substance, subsection (1) above shall not apply in relation to that evidence.

[F224. (3. A)In subsection (3) above, "the relevant diet" means—

(a) in the case of proceedings in the High Court, the preliminary hearing;

(b) in any other case, the trial diet.]

(4) A notice or copy report served in accordance with subsection (3) above shall be served in such manner as may be prescribed by Act of Adjournal; and a written execution purporting to be signed by the person who served the notice or copy together with, where appropriate, the relevant post office receipt shall be sufficient evidence of such service.

(5) In this section—

"controlled drug" has the same meaning as in the M2. Misuse of Drugs Act 1971; and

"medicinal product" has the same meaning as in the M3. Medicines Act 1968.

Amendments (Textual)

F223. Word in s. 282. (3) substituted (1.2.2005) by Criminal Procedure (Amendment) (Scotland) Act 2004 (asp 5), ss. 25, 27. (1), Sch. para. 51. (a); S.S.I. 2004/405, art. 2. (1), Sch. 1 (with savings in arts. 3-5)

F224. S. 282. (3. A) inserted (1.2.2005) by Criminal Procedure (Amendment) (Scotland) Act 2004 (asp 5), ss. 25, 27. (1), Sch. para. 51. (b); S.S.I. 2004/405, art. 2. (1), Sch. 1 (with savings in arts. 3-5)

Marginal Citations

M21971 c.38.

M31968 c.67.

283 Evidence as to time and place of video surveillance recordings.S

(1) For the purposes of any criminal proceedings, a certificate purporting to be signed by a person

responsible for the operation of a video surveillance system and certifying—

    (a) the location of the camera;

    (b) the nature and extent of the person's responsibility for the system; and

    (c) that visual images [F225. (and any sounds) recorded on a particular device are images (and sounds), recorded by the system, of (or relating to)] events which occurred at a place specified in the certificate at a time and date so specified,

shall, subject to subsection (2) below, be sufficient evidence of the matters contained in the certificate.

(2) A party proposing to rely on subsection (1) above ("the first party") shall, not less than 14 days before the [F226relevant] diet, serve on the other party ("the second party") a copy of the certificate and, if the second party serves on the first party, not more than seven days after the date of service of the copy certificate on him, a notice that he does not accept the evidence contained in the certificate, subsection (1) above shall not apply in relation to that evidence.

[F227. (2. A)In subsection (2) above, "the relevant diet" means—

    (a) in the case of proceedings in the High Court, the preliminary hearing;

    (b) in any other case, the trial diet.]

(3) A copy certificate or notice served in accordance with subsection (2) above shall be served in such manner as may be prescribed by Act of Adjournal; and a written execution purporting to be signed by the person who served the copy or notice together with, where appropriate, the relevant post office receipt shall be sufficient evidence of such service.

(4) In this section, "video surveillance system" means apparatus consisting of a camera mounted in a fixed position and associated equipment for transmitting and recording visual images of events occurring in any place [F228. (and includes associated equipment for transmitting and recording sounds relating to such events)].

Amendments (Textual)

F225. Words in s. 283. (1)(c) substituted (10.12.2007) by Criminal Proceedings etc. (Reform) (Scotland) Act 2007 (asp 6), ss. 80, 84, Sch. para. 23. (a); S.S.I. 2007/479, art. 3. (1), Sch. (as amended by 2007/527)

F226. Word in s. 283. (2) substituted (1.2.2005) by Criminal Procedure (Amendment) (Scotland) Act 2004 (asp 5), ss. 25, 27. (1), Sch. para. 52. (a); S.S.I. 2004/405, art. 2. (1), Sch. 1 (with savings in arts. 3-5)

F227. S. 283. (2. A) inserted (1.2.2005) by Criminal Procedure (Amendment) (Scotland) Act 2004 (asp 5), ss. 25, 27. (1), Sch. para. 52. (b); S.S.I. 2004/405, art. 2. (1), Sch. 1 (with savings in arts. 3-5)

F228. Words in s. 283. (4) inserted (10.12.2007) by Criminal Proceedings etc. (Reform) (Scotland) Act 2007 (asp 6), ss. 80, 84, Sch. para. 23. (b); S.S.I. 2007/479, art. 3. (1), Sch. (as amended by 2007/527)

284 Evidence in relation to fingerprints.S

(1) For the purpose of any criminal proceedings, a certificate purporting to be signed by [F229a person authorised in that behalf by a chief constable] and certifying that [F229relevant physical data (within the meaning of section 18. (7. A) of this Act) was taken from or provided by] a person designated in the certificate at a time , date and place specified therein shall, subject to subsetion (2) below, be sufficient evidence of the facts contained in the certificate.

[F230. (2)A party proposing to rely on subsection (1) above ("the first party") shall, not less than 14 days before the [F231relevant] diet, serve on any other party to the proceedings a copy of the certificate, and [F232, if that other party serves on the first party, not more than seven days after the date of service of the copy on him, a notice that he does not accept the evidence contained in the certificate, subsection (1) above shall not apply in relation to that evidence.]

(2. A)Where the first party does not serve a copy of the certificate on any other party as mentioned in subsection (2) above, he shall not be entitled to rely on subsection (1) above as respects that

party.]

[F233. (2. B)In subsection (2) above, "the relevant diet" means—

(a) in the case of proceedings in the High Court, the preliminary hearing;

(b) in any other case, the trial diet.]

(3) A copy certificate or notice served in accordance with subsection (2) above shall be served in such manner as may be prescribed by Act of Adjournal; and a written execution purporting to be signed by the person who served the copy or notice together with, where appropriate, the relevant post office receipt shall be sufficient evidence of such service.

Amendments (Textual)

F229. Words in s. 284. (1) substituted (1.8.1997) by 1997 c. 48, s. 47. (4)(a)(i)(ii); S.I. 1997/1712, art. 3, Sch. (subject to arts. 4, 5)

F230. S. 284. (2)(2. A) substituted (1.8.1997) for s. 284. (2) by 1997 c. 48, s. 47. (4)(b); S.I. 1997/1712, art. 3, Sch. (subject to arts. 4, 5)

F231. Word in s. 284. (2) substituted (1.2.2005) by Criminal Procedure (Amendment) (Scotland) Act 2004 (asp 5), ss. 25, 27. (1), Sch. para. 53. (a); S.S.I. 2004/405, art. 2. (1), Sch. 1 (with savings in arts. 3-5)

F232. Words in s. 284. (2) substituted (27.6.2003) by Criminal Justice (Scotland) Act 2003 (asp 7), ss. 54, 89 (with savings in S.S.I. 2003/287, art. 3); S.S.I. 2003/288, art. 2, Sch.

F233. S. 284. (2. B) inserted (1.2.2005) by Criminal Procedure (Amendment) (Scotland) Act 2004 (asp 5), ss. 25, 27. (1), Sch. para. 53. (b); S.S.I. 2004/405, art. 2. (1), Sch. 1 (with savings in arts. 3-5)

Proof of previous convictionsS

285 Previous convictions: proof, general.S

(1) A previous conviction may be proved against any person in any criminal proceedings by the production of such evidence of the conviction as is mentioned in this subsection and subsections (2) to (6) below and by showing that his fingerprints and those of the person convicted are the fingerprints of the same person.

(2) A certificate purporting to be signed by [F234or on behalf of] the [F235chief constable of the Police Service of Scotland] or the Commissioner of Police of the Metropolis, containing particulars relating to a conviction extracted from the criminal records kept [F236by the person by whom, or on whose behalf, the certificate is signed], and certifying that the copies of the fingerprints contained in the certificate are copies of the fingerprints appearing from the said records to have been taken in pursuance of rules for the time being in force under sections 12 and 39 of the M4. Prisons (Scotland) Act 1989, or regulations for the time being in force under section 16 of the M5. Prison Act 1952, from the person convicted on the occasion of the conviction or on the occasion of his last conviction, shall be sufficient evidence of the conviction or, as the case may be, of his last conviction and of all preceding convictions and that the copies of the fingerprints produced on the certificate are copies of the fingerprints of the person convicted.

(3) Where a person has been apprehended and detained in the custody of the police in connection with any criminal proceedings, a certificate purporting to be signed by the chief constable concerned or a person authorised on his behalf, certifying that the fingerprints produced thereon were taken from him while he was so detained, shall be sufficient evidence in those proceedings that the fingerprints produced on the certificate are the fingerprints of that person.

(4) A certificate purporting to be signed by or on behalf of the governor of a prison or of a remand centre in which any person has been detained in connection with any criminal proceedings, certifying that the fingerprints produced thereon were taken from him while he was so detained, shall be sufficient evidence in those proceedings that the fingerprints produced on the certificate are the fingerprints of that person.

(5) A certificate purporting to be signed by [F237or on behalf of] the [F238chief constable of the Police Service of Scotland], and certifying that the fingerprints, copies of which are certified as mentioned in subsection (2) above by F239[F240... or on behalf of] [F241the chief constable of the Police Service of Scotland] or the Commissioner of Police of the Metropolis to be copies of the fingerprints of a person previously convicted and the fingerprints certified by or on behalf of a chief constable or a governor as mentioned in subsection (3) or (4) above, or otherwise shown, to be the fingerprints of the person against whom the previous conviction is sought to be proved, are the fingerprints of the same person, shall be sufficient evidence of the matter so certified.

(6) An extract conviction of any crime committed in any part of the United Kingdom bearing to have been issued by an officer whose duties include the issue of extract convictions shall be received in evidence without being sworn to by witnesses.

(7) It shall be competent to prove a previous conviction or any fact relevant to the admissibility of the conviction by witnesses, although the name of any such witness is not included in the list served on the accused; and the accused shall be entitled to examine witnesses with regard to such conviction or fact.

(8) An official of any prison in which the accused has been detained on such conviction shall be a competent and sufficient witness to prove its application to the accused, although he may not have been present in court at the trial to which such conviction relates.

(9) The method of proving a previous conviction authorised by this section shall be in addition to any other method of proving the conviction.

[F242. (10)In this section "fingerprint" includes any record of the skin of a person's finger created by a device approved by the Secretary of State under section 18. (7. B) of this Act.]

Amendments (Textual)

F234. Words in s. 285. (2) inserted (1.4.2013) by The Police and Fire Reform (Scotland) Act 2012 (Consequential Modifications and Savings) Order 2013 (S.S.I. 2013/119), art. 1, sch. 1 para. 16. (a)(i)

F235. Words in s. 285. (2) substituted (1.4.2013) by The Police and Fire Reform (Scotland) Act 2012 (Consequential Modifications and Savings) Order 2013 (S.S.I. 2013/119), art. 1, sch. 1 para. 16. (a)(ii)

F236. Words in s. 285. (2) substituted (1.4.2013) by The Police and Fire Reform (Scotland) Act 2012 (Consequential Modifications and Savings) Order 2013 (S.S.I. 2013/119), art. 1, sch. 1 para. 16. (a)(iii)

F237. Words in s. 285. (5) inserted (1.4.2013) by The Police and Fire Reform (Scotland) Act 2012 (Consequential Modifications and Savings) Order 2013 (S.S.I. 2013/119), art. 1, sch. 1 para. 16. (b)(i)

F238. Words in s. 285. (5) inserted (1.4.2013) by The Police and Fire Reform (Scotland) Act 2012 (Consequential Modifications and Savings) Order 2013 (S.S.I. 2013/119), art. 1, sch. 1 para. 16. (b)(ii)

F239. Words in s. 285. (5) omitted (1.4.2013) by virtue of The Police and Fire Reform (Scotland) Act 2012 (Consequential Modifications and Savings) Order 2013 (S.S.I. 2013/119), art. 1, sch. 1 para. 16. (b)(iii)

F240. Words in s. 285. (5) substituted (1.8.1997) by 1997 c. 48, s. 59. (3)(a)(b); S.I. 1997/1712, art. 3, Sch. (subject to arts. 4, 5)

F241. Words in s. 285. (5) inserted (1.4.2013) by The Police and Fire Reform (Scotland) Act 2012 (Consequential Modifications and Savings) Order 2013 (S.S.I. 2013/119), art. 1, sch. 1 para. 16. (b)(iv)

F242. S. 285. (10) inserted (1.8.1997) by 1997 c. 48, s. 47. (5); S.I. 1997/1712, art. 3, Sch. (subject to arts. 4, 5)

Marginal Citations

M41989 c.45.

M51952 c.52.

286 Previous convictions: proof in support of substantive charge.S

(1) Without prejudice to section 285. (6) to (9) or, as the case may be, section 166 of this Act, where proof of a previous conviction is competent in support of a substantive charge, any such conviction or an extract of it shall, if—

(a) it purports to relate to the accused and to be signed by the clerk of court having custody of the record containing the conviction; and

(b) a copy of it has been served on the accused not less than 14 days before the [F243relevant] diet,

be sufficient evidence of the application of the conviction to the accused unless, within seven days of the date of service of the copy on him, he serves notice on the prosecutor that he denies that it applies to him.

[F244. (1. A)In subsection (1)(b) above, "the relevant diet" means—

(a) in the case of proceedings in the High Court, the preliminary hearing;

(b) in any other case, the trial diet.]

(2) A copy of a conviction or extract conviction served under subsection (1) above shall be served on the accused in such manner as may be prescribed by Act of Adjournal, and a written execution purporting to be signed by the person who served the copy together with, where appropriate, the relevant post office receipt shall be sufficient evidence of service of the copy.

[F245. (3)The reference in subsection (1)(a) above to "the clerk of court having custody of the record containing the conviction" includes, in relation to a previous conviction by a court in another member State of the European Union, a reference to any officer of that court or of that State having such custody.]

Amendments (Textual)

F243. Word in s. 286. (1)(b) substituted (1.2.2005) by Criminal Procedure (Amendment) (Scotland) Act 2004 (asp 5), ss. 25, 27. (1), Sch. para. 54. (a); S.S.I. 2004/405, art. 2. (1), Sch. 1 (with savings in arts. 3-5)

F244. S. 286. (1. A) inserted (1.2.2005) by Criminal Procedure (Amendment) (Scotland) Act 2004 (asp 5), ss. 25, 27. (1), Sch. para. 54. (b); S.S.I. 2004/405, art. 2. (1), Sch. 1 (with savings in arts. 3-5)

F245. S. 286. (3) added (27.6.2003) by Criminal Justice (Scotland) Act 2003 (asp 7), ss. 57. (3), 89; S.S.I. 2003/288, art. 2, Sch.

[F246286. AProof of previous conviction by court in other member StateS

(1) A previous conviction by a court in another member State of the European Union may be proved against any person in any criminal proceedings by the production of evidence of the conviction and by showing that his fingerprints and those of the person convicted are the fingerprints of the same person.

(2) A certificate—

(a) bearing—

(i) to have been sealed with the official seal of a Minister of the State in question; and

(ii) to contain particulars relating to a conviction extracted from the criminal records of that State; and

(b) including copies of fingerprints and certifying that those copies—

(i) are of fingerprints appearing from those records to have been taken from the person convicted on the occasion of the conviction, or on the occasion of his last conviction; and

(ii) would be admissible in evidence in criminal proceedings in that State as a record of the skin of that person's fingers,

shall be sufficient evidence of the conviction or, as the case may be, of the person's last conviction and of all preceding convictions and that the copies of the fingerprints included in the certificate are copies of the fingerprints of the person convicted.

(3) A conviction bearing to have been—

(a) extracted from the criminal records of the State in question; and

(b) issued by an officer of that State whose duties include the issuing of such extracts,

shall be received in evidence without being sworn to by witnesses.

(4) Subsection (9) of section 285 of this Act applies in relation to this section as it does in relation to that section.]

Amendments (Textual)

F246. S. 286. A inserted (27.6.2003) by Criminal Justice (Scotland) Act 2003 (asp 7), ss. 57. (4), 89; S.S.I. 2003/288, art. 2, Sch.

PART XIII Miscellaneous

PART XIII Miscellaneous

287[F1. Demission from office of Lord Advocate and Solicitor General for Scotland].S

(1) All indictments which have been raised [F2at the instance of Her Majesty's Advocate] shall remain effective notwithstanding [F3the holder of the office of Lord Advocate] subsequently having died or demitted office and may be taken up and proceeded with by his successor [F4or the Solicitor General].

(2) During any period when the office of Lord Advocate is vacant it shall be lawful to indict accused persons [F5at the instance of Her Majesty's Advocate or] the Solicitor General F6. . . .

[F7. (2. A)Any such indictments in proceedings at the instance of the Solicitor General may be signed by the Solicitor General.

(2. B)All indictments which have been raised at the instance of the Solicitor General shall remain effective notwithstanding the holder of the office of Solicitor General subsequently having died or demitted office and may be taken up and proceeded with by his successor or the Lord Advocate.

(2. C)Subsection (2. D) applies during any period when the offices of Lord Advocate and Solicitor General are both vacant.

(2. D)It is lawful to indict accused persons at the instance of Her Majesty's Advocate.]

(3) The advocates depute shall not demit office when a Lord Advocate dies or demits office but shall continue in office until their successors receive commissions.

(4) The advocates depute and procurators fiscal shall have power, notwithstanding any vacancy in the office of Lord Advocate [F8or Solicitor General], to take up and proceed with any indictment which—

(a) by virtue of subsection (1) [F9or (2. B)] above, remains effective; or

(b) by virtue of subsection (2) above, is [F10raised at the instance] of the Solicitor General.

[F11. (c)by virtue of subsection (2. D) above, is raised at the instance of Her Majesty's Advocate]

(5) For the purposes of this Act, where, but for this subsection, demission of office by one Law Officer would result in the offices of both being vacant, he or, where both demit office on the same day, the person demitting the office of Lord Advocate shall be deemed to continue in office until the warrant of appointment of the person succeeding to the office of Lord Advocate is granted.

(6) The Lord Advocate shall enter upon the duties of his office immediately upon the grant of his warrant of appointment; F12. . ..

Amendments (Textual)
F1. S. 287 title substituted (13.12.2010) by Criminal Justice and Licensing (Scotland) Act 2010 (asp 13), ss. 60. (3), 206. (1); S.S.I. 2010/413, art. 2, Sch. (with art. 5)
F2. Words in s. 287. (1) substituted (13.12.2010) by Criminal Justice and Licensing (Scotland) Act 2010 (asp 13), ss. 60. (4)(a)(i), 206. (1); S.S.I. 2010/413, art. 2, Sch. (with art. 5)
F3. Words in s. 287. (1) substituted (13.12.2010) by Criminal Justice and Licensing (Scotland) Act 2010 (asp 13), ss. 60. (4)(a)(ii), 206. (1); S.S.I. 2010/413, art. 2, Sch. (with art. 5)
F4. Words in s. 287. (1) inserted (13.12.2010) by Criminal Justice and Licensing (Scotland) Act 2010 (asp 13), ss. 60. (4)(a)(iii), 206. (1); S.S.I. 2010/413, art. 2, Sch. (with art. 5)
F5. Words in s. 287. (2) substituted (13.12.2010) by Criminal Justice and Licensing (Scotland) Act 2010 (asp 13), ss. 60. (4)(b)(i), 206. (1); S.S.I. 2010/413, art. 2, Sch. (with art. 5)
F6. Words in s. 287. (2) repealed (13.12.2010) by Criminal Justice and Licensing (Scotland) Act 2010 (asp 13), ss. 60. (4)(b)(ii), 206. (1); S.S.I. 2010/413, art. 2, Sch. (with art. 5)
F7. S. 287. (2. A)-(2. D) inserted (13.12.2010) by Criminal Justice and Licensing (Scotland) Act 2010 (asp 13), ss. 60. (4)(c), 206. (1); S.S.I. 2010/413, art. 2, Sch. (with art. 5)
F8. Words in s. 287. (4) inserted (13.12.2010) by Criminal Justice and Licensing (Scotland) Act 2010 (asp 13), ss. 60. (4)(d)(i), 206. (1); S.S.I. 2010/413, art. 2, Sch. (with art. 5)
F9. Words in s. 287. (4)(a) inserted (13.12.2010) by Criminal Justice and Licensing (Scotland) Act 2010 (asp 13), ss. 60. (4)(d)(ii), 206. (1); S.S.I. 2010/413, art. 2, Sch. (with art. 5)
F10. Words in s. 287. (4)(b) substituted (13.12.2010) by Criminal Justice and Licensing (Scotland) Act 2010 (asp 13), ss. 60. (4)(d)(iii), 206. (1); S.S.I. 2010/413, art. 2, Sch. (with art. 5)
F11. S. 287. (4)(c) inserted (13.12.2010) by Criminal Justice and Licensing (Scotland) Act 2010 (asp 13), ss. 60. (4)(d)(iv), 206. (1); S.S.I. 2010/413, art. 2, Sch. (with art. 5)
F12. Words in s. 287. (6) repealed (20.5.1999) by S.I. 1999/1042, arts. 1. (2)(b), 4, Sch. 2 Pt. I para. 11, Pt. III; S.I. 1998/3178, art. 2. (2), Sch. 4

288 Intimation of proceedings in High Court to Lord Advocate.S

(1) In any proceeding in the High Court (other than a proceeding to which the Lord Advocate or a procurator fiscal is a party) it shall be competent for the court to order intimation of such proceeding to the Lord Advocate.

(2) On intimation being made to the Lord Advocate under subsection (1) above, the Lord Advocate shall be entitled to appear and be heard in such proceeding.

[F13[F14. Convention rights and EU law compatibility issues, and devolution issues] S

Amendments (Textual)
F13. Ss. 288. A, 288. B and cross-heading inserted (20.5.1999) by 1998 c. 46, s. 125, Sch. 8 para. 32. (2) (with s. 126. (3)-(11)); S.I. 1998/3178, art. 2. (2), Sch. 4
F14. Cross-heading substituted (22.4.2013) by Scotland Act 2012 (c. 11), ss. 34. (2), 44. (5); S.I. 2013/6, art. 2. (a)

[F15288. ZARight of Advocate General to take part in proceedingsS

(1) The Advocate General for Scotland may take part as a party in criminal proceedings so far as they relate to a compatibility issue.

(2) In this section "compatibility issue" means a question, arising in criminal proceedings, as to—
    (a) whether a public authority has acted (or proposes to act)—
(i) in a way which is made unlawful by section 6. (1) of the Human Rights Act 1998, or

(ii) in a way which is incompatible with EU law, or

(b) whether an Act of the Scottish Parliament or any provision of an Act of the Scottish Parliament is incompatible with any of the Convention rights or with EU law.

(3) In subsection (2)—

(a) "public authority" has the same meaning as in section 6 of the Human Rights Act 1998;

(b) references to acting include failing to act;

(c) "EU law" has the meaning given by section 126. (9) of the Scotland Act 1998.]

Amendments (Textual)

F15. S. 288. ZA inserted (22.4.2013) by Scotland Act 2012 (c. 11), ss. 34. (3), 44. (5); S.I. 2013/6, art. 2. (a)

Modifications etc. (not altering text)

C1. S. 288. ZA(1) modified (22.4.2013) by The Scotland Act 2012 (Transitional and Consequential Provisions) Order 2013 (S.I. 2013/7), arts. 1. (1), 8

[F16288. ZBReferences of compatibility issues to the High Court or Supreme CourtS

(1) Where a compatibility issue has arisen in criminal proceedings before a court, other than a court consisting of two or more judges of the High Court, the court may, instead of determining it, refer the issue to the High Court.

(2) The Lord Advocate or the Advocate General for Scotland, if a party to criminal proceedings before a court, other than a court consisting of two or more judges of the High Court, may require the court to refer to the High Court any compatibility issue which has arisen in the proceedings.

(3) The High Court may, instead of determining a compatibility issue referred to it under subsection (2), refer it to the Supreme Court.

(4) Where a compatibility issue has arisen in criminal proceedings before a court consisting of two or more judges of the High Court, otherwise than on a reference, the court may, instead of determining it, refer it to the Supreme Court.

(5) The Lord Advocate or the Advocate General for Scotland, if a party to criminal proceedings before a court consisting of two or more judges of the High Court, may require the court to refer to the Supreme Court any compatibility issue which has arisen in the proceedings otherwise than on a reference.

(6) On a reference to the Supreme Court under this section—

(a) the powers of the Supreme Court are exercisable only for the purpose of determining the compatibility issue;

(b) for that purpose the Court may make any change in the formulation of that issue that it thinks necessary in the interests of justice.

(7) When it has determined a compatibility issue on a reference under this section, the Supreme Court must remit the proceedings to the High Court.

(8) An issue referred to the High Court or the Supreme Court under this section is referred to it for determination.

(9) In this section "compatibility issue" has the meaning given by section 288. ZA.]

Amendments (Textual)

F16. S. 288. ZB inserted (22.4.2013) by Scotland Act 2012 (c. 11), ss. 35, 44. (5); S.I. 2013/6, art. 2. (b)

Modifications etc. (not altering text)

C2. S. 288. ZB(1)(4)(5)(7) modified (22.4.2013) by The Scotland Act 2012 (Transitional and Consequential Provisions) Order 2013 (S.I. 2013/7), arts. 1. (1), 6

288. AF17 Rights of appeal for Advocate General: [F18compatibility issues and] devolution issues.S

(1) This section applies where—

   (a) a person is acquitted or convicted of a charge (whether on indictment or in summary proceedings), and

   (b) the Advocate General for Scotland was a party to the proceedings F19....

[F20. (2)Where the Advocate General for Scotland was a party in pursuance of paragraph 6 of Schedule 6 to the Scotland Act 1998 (devolution issues), the Advocate General may refer to the High Court for their opinion any devolution issue which has arisen in the proceedings.

(2. A)Where the Advocate General for Scotland was a party in pursuance of section 288. ZA, the Advocate General may refer to the High Court for their opinion any compatibility issue (within the meaning of that section) which has arisen in the proceedings.

(2. B)If a reference is made under subsection (2) or (2. A) the Clerk of Justiciary shall send to the person acquitted or convicted and to any solicitor who acted for that person at the trial a copy of the reference and intimation of the date fixed by the Court for a hearing.]

(3) The person may, not later than seven days before the date so fixed, intimate in writing to the Clerk of Justiciary and to the Advocate General for Scotland either—

   (a) that he elects to appear personally at the hearing, or

   (b) that he elects to be represented by counsel at the hearing,

but, except by leave of the Court on cause shown, and without prejudice to his right to attend, he shall not appear or be represented at the hearing other than by and in conformity with an election under this subsection.

(4) Where there is no intimation under subsection (3)(b), the High Court shall appoint counsel to act at the hearing as amicus curiae.

(5) The costs of representation elected under subsection (3)(b) or of an appointment under subsection (4) shall, after being taxed by the Auditor of the Court of Session, be paid by the Advocate General for Scotland out of money provided by Parliament.

(6) The opinion on the point referred under subsection (2) [F21or (2. A)] shall not affect the acquittal or (as the case may be) conviction in the trial.

Amendments (Textual)

F17. Ss. 288. A-288. B and preceding cross-heading inserted (20.5.1999) by 1998 c. 46, s. 125, Sch. 8 para. 32. (2) (with s. 126. (3)-(11)); S.I. 1998/3178, art. 2. (2), Sch. 4

F18. Words in s. 288. A heading inserted (22.4.2013) by Scotland Act 2012 (c. 11), ss. 34. (5), 44. (5); S.I. 2013/6, art. 2. (a)

F19. Words in s. 288. A(1) omitted (22.4.2013) by virtue of Scotland Act 2012 (c. 11), ss. 34. (6), 44. (5); S.I. 2013/6, art. 2. (a)

F20. S. 288. A(2)-(2. B) substituted for s. 288. A(2) (22.4.2013) by Scotland Act 2012 (c. 11), ss. 34. (7), 44. (5); S.I. 2013/6, art. 2. (a)

F21. Words in s. 288. A(6) inserted (22.4.2013) by Scotland Act 2012 (c. 11), ss. 34. (8), 44. (5); S.I. 2013/6, art. 2. (a)

[F22288. AAAppeals to the Supreme Court: compatibility issuesS

(1) For the purpose of determining any compatibility issue an appeal lies to the Supreme Court against a determination in criminal proceedings by a court of two or more judges of the High Court.

(2) On an appeal under this section—

   (a) the powers of the Supreme Court are exercisable only for the purpose of determining the compatibility issue;

   (b) for that purpose the Court may make any change in the formulation of that issue that it thinks necessary in the interests of justice.

(3) When it has determined the compatibility issue the Supreme Court must remit the proceedings to the High Court.

(4) In this section "compatibility issue" has the same meaning as in section 288. ZA.

(5) An appeal under this section against a determination lies only with the permission of the High Court or, failing that permission, with the permission of the Supreme Court.

(6) Subsection (5) does not apply if it is an appeal by the Lord Advocate or the Advocate General for Scotland against a determination by the High Court of a compatibility issue referred to it under section 288. ZB(2).

(7) An application to the High Court for permission under subsection (5) must be made—

(a) within 28 days of the date of the determination against which the appeal lies, or

(b) within such longer period as the High Court considers equitable having regard to all the circumstances.

(8) An application to the Supreme Court for permission under subsection (5) must be made—

(a) within 28 days of the date on which the High Court refused permission under that subsection, or

(b) within such longer period as the Supreme Court considers equitable having regard to all the circumstances.]

Amendments (Textual)

F22. S. 288. AA inserted (22.4.2013) by Scotland Act 2012 (c. 11), ss. 36. (6), 44. (5); S.I. 2013/6, art. 2. (c)

Modifications etc. (not altering text)

C3. S. 288. AA(1)(5) modified (22.4.2013) by The Scotland Act 2012 (Transitional and Consequential Provisions) Order 2013 (S.I. 2013/7), arts. 1. (1), 7

C4. S. 288. AA(7) modified (22.4.2013) by The Scotland Act 2012 (Transitional and Consequential Provisions) Order 2013 (S.I. 2013/7), arts. 1. (1), 9

C5. S. 288. AA applied (22.4.2013) by The Scotland Act 2012 (Transitional and Consequential Provisions) Order 2013 (S.I. 2013/7), arts. 1. (1), 14

F24288. B [F23. Appeals to the Supreme Court: general].S

(1) This section applies where the [F25. Supreme Court] determines an appeal under [F26section 288. AA of this Act or] paragraph 13. (a) of Schedule 6 to the Scotland Act 1998 against a determination F27... by the High Court in the ordinary course of proceedings.

(2) The determination of the appeal shall not affect any earlier acquittal or earlier quashing of any conviction in the proceedings.

(3) Subject to subsection (2) above, the High Court shall have the same powers in relation to the proceedings when remitted to it by the [F28. Supreme Court] as it would have if it were considering the proceedings otherwise than as a trial court.]

Amendments (Textual)

F23 S. 288. B heading substituted (22.4.2013) by Scotland Act 2012 (c. 11), ss. 36. (8), 44. (5); S.I. 2013/6, art. 2. (c)

F24. Ss. 288. A-288. B and preceding cross-heading inserted (20.5.1999) by 1998 c. 46, s. 125, Sch. 8 para. 32. (2) (with s. 126. (3)-(11)); S.I. 1998/3178, art. 2. (2), Sch. 4

F25. Words in s. 288. B(1) and in sidenote substituted (1.10.2009) by Constitutional Reform Act 2005 (c. 4), ss. 40, 148, Sch. 9 para. 86. (a); S.I. 2009/1604, art. 2. (d)

F26. Words in s. 288. B(1) inserted (22.4.2013) by Scotland Act 2012 (c. 11), ss. 36. (9)(a), 44. (5); S.I. 2013/6, art. 2. (c)

F27. Words in s. 288. B(1) omitted (22.4.2013) by virtue of Scotland Act 2012 (c. 11), ss. 36. (9)(b), 44. (5); S.I. 2013/6, art. 2. (c)

F28. Words in s. 288. B(3) substituted (1.10.2009) by Constitutional Reform Act 2005 (c. 4), ss. 40, 148, Sch. 9 para. 86. (b); S.I. 2009/1604, art. 2. (d)

[F29. Dockets and charges in sex casesS

Amendments (Textual)
F29. Ss. 288. BA-288. BC inserted (1.12.2010) by Criminal Justice and Licensing (Scotland) Act 2010 (asp 13), ss. 63, 206. (1); S.S.I. 2010/357, art. 2. (b)

288. BADockets for charges of sexual offencesS

(1) An indictment or a complaint may include a docket which specifies any act or omission that is connected with a sexual offence charged in the indictment or complaint.

(2) Here, an act or omission is connected with such an offence charged if it—

(a) is specifiable by way of reference to a sexual offence, and

(b) relates to—

(i) the same event as the offence charged, or

(ii) a series of events of which that offence is also part.

(3) The docket is to be in the form of a note apart from the offence charged.

(4) It does not matter whether the act or omission, if it were instead charged as an offence, could not competently be dealt with by the court (including as particularly constituted) in which the indictment or complaint is proceeding.

(5) Where under subsection (1) a docket is included in an indictment or a complaint, it is to be presumed that—

(a) the accused person has been given fair notice of the prosecutor's intention to lead evidence of the act or omission specified in the docket, and

(b) evidence of the act or omission is admissible as relevant.

(6) The references in this section to a sexual offence are to—

(a) an offence under the Sexual Offences (Scotland) Act 2009,

(b) any other offence involving a significant sexual element.

288. BBMixed charges for sexual offencesS

(1) An indictment or a complaint may include a charge that is framed as mentioned in subsection (2) or (3) (or both).

(2) That is, framed so as to comprise (in a combined form) the specification of more than one sexual offence.

(3) That is, framed so as to—

(a) specify, in addition to a sexual offence, any other act or omission, and

(b) do so in any manner except by way of reference to a statutory offence.

(4) Where a charge in an indictment or a complaint is framed as mentioned in subsection (2) or (3) (or both), the charge is to be regarded as being a single yet cumulative charge.

(5) The references in this section to a sexual offence are to an offence under the Sexual Offences (Scotland) Act 2009.

288. BCAggravation by intent to rapeS

(1) Subsection (2) applies as respects a qualifying offence charged in an indictment or a complaint.

(2) Any specification in the charge that the offence is with intent to rape (however construed) may be given by referring to the statutory offence of rape.

(3) In this section—

(a) the reference to a qualifying offence is to an offence of assault or abduction (and includes attempt, conspiracy or incitement to commit such an offence),

(b) the reference to the statutory offence of rape is (as the case may be) to—

(i) the offence of rape under section 1 of the Sexual Offences (Scotland) Act 2009, or

(ii) the offence of rape of a young child under section 18 of that Act.]

[F30. Trials for sexual offencesS

Amendments (Textual)

F30. S. 288. C and cross-heading inserted (1.11.2002) by Sexual Offences (Procedure and Evidence) (Scotland) Act 2002 (asp 9), s. 1; S.S.I. 2002/443, art. 3 (with art. 4. (1)(2))

288. C Prohibition of personal conduct of defence in cases of certain sexual offencesS

[F31. (1)An accused charged with a sexual offence to which this section applies is prohibited from conducting his case in person at, or for the purposes of, any relevant hearing in the course of proceedings (other than proceedings in a JP court) in respect of the offence.

(1. A) In subsection (1), "relevant hearing" means a hearing at, or for the purposes of, which a witness is to give evidence.]

(2) This section applies to the following sexual offences—

(a) rape [F32. (whether at common law or under section 1. (1) of the Sexual Offences (Scotland) Act 2009 (asp 9))];

(b) sodomy;

(c) clandestine injury to women;

(d) abduction of a woman or girl with intent to rape;

[F33. (da)abduction with intent to commit the statutory offence of rape;]

(e) assault with intent to rape;

[F34. (ea)assault with intent to commit the statutory offence of rape;]

(f) indecent assault;

(g) indecent behaviour (including any lewd, indecent or libidinous practice or behaviour);

(h) an offence under section [F35311 (non-consensual sexual acts) or 313 (persons providing care services: sexual offences) of the Mental Health (Care and Treatment)(Scotland) Act 2003];

(i) an offence under any of the following provisions of the Criminal Law (Consolidation)(Scotland) Act 1995 (c.39)—

(i) sections 1 to 3 (incest and related offences);

(ii) section 5 (unlawful sexual intercourse with girl under 13 or 16);

(iii) section 6 (indecent behaviour toward girl between 12 and 16);

(iv) section 7. (2) and (3)(procuring by threats etc.);

(v) section 8 (abduction and unlawful detention);

(vi) section 10 (seduction, prostitution, etc. of girl under 16);

(vii) section 13. (5)(b) or (c)(homosexual offences);

[F36. (j)an offence under any of the following provisions of the Sexual Offences (Scotland) Act 2009 (asp 9)—

(i) section 2 (sexual assault by penetration),

(ii) section 3 (sexual assault),

(iii) section 4 (sexual coercion),

(iv) section 5 (coercing a person into being present during a sexual activity),

(v) section 6 (coercing a person into looking at a sexual image),

(vi) section 7. (1) (communicating indecently),

(vii) section 7. (2) (causing a person to see or hear an indecent communication),

(viii)section 8 (sexual exposure),

(ix) section 9 (voyeurism),

(x) section 18 (rape of a young child),

(xi) section 19 (sexual assault on a young child by penetration),

(xii) section 20 (sexual assault on a young child),

(xiii)section 21 (causing a young child to participate in a sexual activity),

(xiv) section 22 (causing a young child to be present during a sexual activity),

(xv) section 23 (causing a young child to look at a sexual image),

(xvi) section 24. (1) (communicating indecently with a young child),

(xvii)section 24. (2) (causing a young child to see or hear an indecent communication),

(xviii)section 25 (sexual exposure to a young child),

(xix) section 26 (voyeurism towards a young child),

(xx) section 28 (having intercourse with an older child),

(xxi) section 29 (engaging in penetrative sexual activity with or towards an older child),

(xxii)section 30 (engaging in sexual activity with or towards an older child),

(xxiii)section 31 (causing an older child to participate in a sexual activity),

(xxiv)section 32 (causing an older child to be present during a sexual activity),

(xxv) section 33 (causing an older child to look at a sexual image),

(xxvi)section 34. (1) (communicating indecently with an older child),

(xxvii)section 34. (2) (causing an older child to see or hear an indecent communication),

(xxviii)section 35 (sexual exposure to an older child),

(xxix)section 36 (voyeurism towards an older child),

(xxx) section 37. (1) (engaging while an older child in sexual conduct with or towards another older child),

(xxxi)section 37. (4) (engaging while an older child in consensual sexual conduct with another older child),

(xxxii)section 42 (sexual abuse of trust) but only if the condition set out in section 43. (6) of that Act is fulfilled,

(xxxiii)section 46 (sexual abuse of trust of a mentally disordered person);]

[F37. (k)attempting to commit any of the offences set out in paragraphs (a) to (j).]

(3) This section applies also to an offence in respect of which a court having jurisdiction to try that offence has made an order under subsection (4) below.

(4) Where, in the case of any offence, other than one set out in subsection (2) above, that court is satisfied that there appears to be such a substantial sexual element in the alleged commission of the offence that it ought to be treated, for the purposes of this section, in the same way as an offence set out in that subsection, the court shall, either on the application of the prosecutor or ex proprio motu, make an order under this subsection.

(5) The making of such an order does not affect the validity of anything which—

(a) was done in relation to the alleged offence to which the order relates; and

(b) was done before the order was made.

(6) The Scottish Ministers may by order made by statutory instrument vary the sexual offences to which this section applies by virtue of subsection (2) above by modifying that subsection.

(7) No such statutory instrument shall be made, however, unless a draft of it has been laid before and approved by resolution of the Scottish Parliament.

[F38. (8)F39. . . . .]

[F40. (9)In subsection (2)—

(a) the references to "rape" in paragraphs (d) and (e) are to the offence of rape at common law; and

(b) the references to "the statutory offence of rape" in paragraphs (da) and (ea) are (as the case may be) to?

(i) the offence of rape under section 1 of the Sexual Offences (Scotland) Act 2009, or

(ii) the offence of rape of a young child under section 18 of that Act.]]

Amendments (Textual)

F31. S. 288. C(1)(1. A) substituted for s. 288. C(1) (28.3.2011) by Criminal Justice and Licensing (Scotland) Act 2010 (asp 13), ss. 69. (2)(a), 206. (1); S.S.I. 2011/178, art. 2, sch.

F32. Words in s. 288. C(2)(a) inserted (1.12.2010) by Sexual Offences (Scotland) Act 2009 (asp 9), ss. 61, 62. (2), Sch. 5 para. 2. (7)(a); S.S.I. 2010/357, art. 2. (a)

F33. S. 288. C(2)(da) inserted (1.12.2010) by The Sexual Offences (Scotland) Act 2009

(Supplemental and Consequential Provisions) Order 2010 (S.S.I. 2010/421), art. 2, Sch. para. 1. (4)(a)(i)

F34. S. 288. C(2)(ea) inserted (1.12.2010) by The Sexual Offences (Scotland) Act 2009 (Supplemental and Consequential Provisions) Order 2010 (S.S.I. 2010/421), art. 2, Sch. para. 1. (4)(a)(ii)

F35. Words in s. 288. C(2)(h) substituted (27.9.2005) by The Mental Health (Care and Treatment) (Scotland) Act 2003 (Modification of Enactments) Order 2005 (S.S.I. 2005/465), art. 2, Sch. 1 para. 27. (5)

F36. S. 288. C(2)(j) substituted (1.12.2010) by Sexual Offences (Scotland) Act 2009 (asp 9), ss. 61, 62. (2), Sch. 5 para. 2. (7)(b); S.S.I. 2010/357, art. 2. (a)

F37. S. 288. C(2)(k) inserted (1.12.2010) by Sexual Offences (Scotland) Act 2009 (asp 9), ss. 61, 62. (2), Sch. 5 para. 2. (7)(c); S.S.I. 2010/357, art. 2. (a)

F38. S. 288. C(8) inserted (1.2.2005) by Criminal Procedure (Amendment) (Scotland) Act 2004 (asp 5), ss. 25, 27. (1), Sch. para. 55. (b); S.S.I. 2004/405, art. 2. (1), Sch. 1 (with savings in arts. 3-5)

F39. S. 288. C(8) repealed (28.3.2011) by Criminal Justice and Licensing (Scotland) Act 2010 (asp 13), ss. 69. (2)(b), 206. (1); S.S.I. 2011/178, art. 2, sch.

F40. S. 288. C(9) inserted (1.12.2010) by The Sexual Offences (Scotland) Act 2009 (Supplemental and Consequential Provisions) Order 2010 (S.S.I. 2010/421), art. 2, Sch. para. 1. (4)(b)

[F41288. D Appointment of solicitor by court in such casesS

(1) This section applies in the case of proceedings [F42. (other than proceedings in a JP court)] in respect of a sexual offence to which section 288. C above applies.

(2) Where the court ascertains that—

(a) the accused has not engaged a solicitor for the purposes of

[F43. (i)the conduct of his case at, or for the purposes of, any relevant hearing (within the meaning of section 288. C(1. A)) in the proceedings; or]

[F44. (iii)the conduct of his case at any commissioner proceedings; or]

(b) having engaged a solicitor for those purposes, the accused has dismissed him; or

(c) the accused's solicitor has withdrawn,

then, where the court is not satisfied that the accused intends to engage a solicitor or, as the case may be, another solicitor for those purposes, it shall, at its own hand, appoint a solicitor for those purposes.

(3)

A solicitor so appointed is not susceptible to dismissal by the accused or obliged to comply with any instruction by the accused to dismiss counsel.

(4) Subject to subsection (3) above, it is the duty of a solicitor so appointed—

(a) to ascertain and act upon the instructions of the accused; and

(b) where the accused gives no instructions or inadequate or perverse instructions, to act in the best interests of the accused.

(5) In all other respects, a solicitor so appointed has, and may be made subject to, the same obligations and has, and may be given, the same authority as if engaged by the accused; and any employment of and instructions given to counsel by the solicitor shall proceed and be treated accordingly.

(6) Where the court is satisfied that a solicitor so appointed is no longer able to act upon the instructions, or in the best interests, of the accused, the court may relieve that solicitor of his appointment and appoint another solicitor for the purposes [F45referred to in subsection (2)(a) above.]

[F46. (6. A)Where, in relation to commissioner proceedings, the commissioner is satisfied that a solicitor so appointed is no longer able to act upon the instructions, or in the best interests, of the accused, the commissioner is (for the purpose of the application of subsection (6) above) to refer the case to the court.]

(7) The references in subsections (3) to ([F47. (6. A)]) above to "a solicitor so appointed" include references to a solicitor appointed under subsection (6) above.

(8) In this section "counsel" includes a solicitor who has right of audience in the High Court of Justiciary under section 25. A (rights of audience in various courts including the High Court of Justiciary) of the Solicitors (Scotland) Act 1980 (c.46).

[F48. (9) In this section, "commissioner proceedings" means proceedings before a commissioner appointed under section 271. I(1) or by virtue of section 272. (1)(b) of this Act.]]

Amendments (Textual)

F41. S. 288. D inserted (S.) (1.11.2002) by Sexual Offences (Procedure and Evidence) (Scotland) Act 2002 (asp 9), s. 2. (1); S.S.I. 2002/443, art. 3 (with art. 4. (1)(2))

F42. Words in s. 288. D(1) inserted (28.3.2011) by Criminal Justice and Licensing (Scotland) Act 2010 (asp 13), ss. 69. (3)(a), 206. (1); S.S.I. 2011/178, art. 2, sch.

F43. S. 288. D(2)(a)(i) substituted for s. 288. D(2)(a)(i)(ii) (28.3.2011) by Criminal Justice and Licensing (Scotland) Act 2010 (asp 13), ss. 69. (3)(b), 206. (1); S.S.I. 2011/178, art. 2, sch.

F44. S. 288. D(2)(a)(iii) inserted (23.4.2007) by Criminal Proceedings etc. (Reform) (Scotland) Act 2007 (asp 6), ss. 35. (6)(a), 84; S.S.I. 2007/250, art. 3. (a)

F45. Words in s. 288. D(6) substituted (28.3.2011) by Criminal Justice and Licensing (Scotland) Act 2010 (asp 13), ss. 69. (3)(c), 206. (1); S.S.I. 2011/178, art. 2, sch.

F46. S. 288. D(6. A) inserted (23.4.2007) by Criminal Proceedings etc. (Reform) (Scotland) Act 2007 (asp 6), ss. 35. (6)(c), 84; S.S.I. 2007/250, art. 3. (a)

F47. Word in s. 288. D(7) substituted (23.4.2007) by Criminal Proceedings etc. (Reform) (Scotland) Act 2007 (asp 6), ss. 35. (6)(d), 84; S.S.I. 2007/250, art. 3. (a)

F48. S. 288. D(9) added (23.4.2007) by Criminal Proceedings etc. (Reform) (Scotland) Act 2007 (asp 6), ss. 35. (6)(e), 84; S.S.I. 2007/250, art. 3. (a)

[F49. Jury directions relating to sexual offencesS

Amendments (Textual)

F49. Ss. 288. DA, 288. DB and cross-heading inserted (24.4.2017) by Abusive Behaviour and Sexual Harm (Scotland) Act 2016 (asp 22), ss. 6, 45. (2)(3) (with s. 44); S.S.I. 2017/93, reg. 2 (with reg. 5)

288. DAJury direction relating to lack of communication about offenceS

(1) Subsection (2) applies where, in a trial on indictment for a sexual offence—

(a) evidence is given which suggests that the person against whom the offence is alleged to have been committed—

(i) did not tell, or delayed in telling, anyone, or a particular person, about the offence, or

(ii) did not report, or delayed in reporting, the offence to any investigating agency, or a particular investigating agency, or

(b) a question is asked, or a statement is made, with a view to eliciting, or drawing attention to, evidence of that nature.

(2) In charging the jury, the judge must advise that—

(a) there can be good reasons why a person against whom a sexual offence is committed may not tell others about it or report it to an investigating agency, or may delay in doing either of those things, and

(b) this does not, therefore, necessarily indicate that an allegation is false.

(3) Subsection (2) does not apply if the judge considers that, in the circumstances of the case, no

reasonable jury could consider the evidence, question or statement by reason of which subsection (2) would otherwise apply to be material to the question of whether the alleged offence is proved.

(4) For the purposes of this section—

"investigating agency" means—

- a police force maintained for the area where the offence is alleged to have been committed,

- any other person who has functions (to any extent) of investigating crime in the area where the offence is alleged to have been committed,

"sexual offence" has the same meaning as in section 210. A, except that it does not include—

- an offence under section 170 of the Customs and Excise Management Act 1979, or

- an offence under section 52. A of the Civic Government (Scotland) Act 1982.

288. DBJury direction relating to absence of physical resistance or physical forceS

(1) Subsection (2) applies where, in a trial on indictment for a sexual offence—

(a) evidence is given which suggests that the sexual activity took place without physical resistance on the part of the person against whom the offence is alleged to have been committed, or

(b) a question is asked, or a statement is made, with a view to eliciting, or drawing attention to, evidence of that nature.

(2) In charging the jury, the judge must advise that—

(a) there can be good reasons why a person against whom a sexual offence is committed might not physically resist the sexual activity, and

(b) an absence of physical resistance does not, therefore, necessarily indicate that an allegation is false.

(3) Subsection (2) does not apply if the judge considers that, in the circumstances of the case, no reasonable jury could consider the evidence, question or statement by reason of which subsection (2) would otherwise apply to be material to the question of whether the alleged offence is proved.

(4) Subsection (5) applies where, in a trial on indictment for a sexual offence—

(a) evidence is given which suggests that the sexual activity took place without the accused using physical force to overcome the will of the person against whom the offence is alleged to have been committed, or

(b) a question is asked, or a statement is made, with a view to eliciting, or drawing attention to, evidence of that nature.

(5) In charging the jury, the judge must advise that—

(a) there can be good reasons why a person may, in committing a sexual offence, not need to use physical force to overcome the will of the person against whom the offence is committed, and

(b) an absence of physical force does not, therefore, necessarily indicate that an allegation is false.

(6) Subsection (5) does not apply if the judge considers that, in the circumstances of the case, no reasonable jury could consider the evidence, question or statement by reason of which subsection (5) would otherwise apply to be material to the question of whether the alleged offence is proved.

(7) For the purposes of this section—

"sexual activity" means the sexual activity which is the subject of the alleged sexual offence,

"sexual offence" means—

- rape (whether at common law or under section 1. (1) of the Sexual Offences (Scotland) Act 2009),

- indecent assault,

- sodomy,

- clandestine injury to women,

- an offence under section 2 of the Sexual Offences (Scotland) Act 2009 (sexual assault by penetration),

- an offence under section 3 of that Act (sexual assault),
- an offence under section 4 of that Act (sexual coercion).]

[F50. Trials involving vulnerable witnessesS

Amendments (Textual)
F50 Ss. 288. E, 288. F and preceding cross-heading inserted (1.4.2005, 1.4.2006 and 1.4.2007 for certain purposes and otherwise 1.4.2008) by Vulnerable Witnesses (Scotland) Act 2004 (asp 3), ss. 6, 25; S.S.I. 2005/168, art. 2, Sch. (with savings in art. 4); S.S.I. 2006/59, art. 2, Sch. (with art. 4); S.S.I. 2007/101, art. 2, Sch. (with art. 4); S.S.I. 2008/57, art. 2 (with art. 3)

288. EProhibition of personal conduct of defence in certain cases involving child witnesses under the age of 12. S

F51. (1). . . . .
(2) This section applies to any proceedings (other than proceedings in the [F52. JP court])—
   (a) in respect of any offence specified in subsection (3) below, and
   (b) in which a child witness who is under the age of 12 on the date of commencement of the proceedings is to give evidence at or for the purposes of [F53any hearing in the course of the proceedings].
[F54. (2. A)The accused is prohibited from conducting his case in person at, or for the purposes of, any hearing at, or for the purposes of, which the child witness is to give evidence.]
(3) The offences referred to in subsection (2)(a) above are—
   (a) murder,
   (b) culpable homicide,
   (c) any offence which—
(i) involves an assault on, or injury or threat of injury to, any person (including any offence involving neglect or ill-treatment of, or other cruelty to, a child), but
(ii) is not an offence to which section 288. C of this Act applies,
   (d) abduction, and
   (e) plagium.
(4) Section 288. D of this Act applies in the case of proceedings to which this section applies as it applies in the case of proceedings in respect of a sexual offence to which section 288. C of this Act applies [F55and as if references to a relevant hearing were references to a hearing referred to in subsection (2. A) above].
(5) In proceedings to which this section applies, the prosecutor shall, at the same time as intimating to the accused under section 271. A(13) of this Act a [F56vulnerable] witness notice in respect of [F57the trial], serve on the accused a notice under subsection (6).
(6) A notice under this subsection shall contain intimation to the accused—
   [F58. (a)that his case at, or for the purposes of, any hearing in the course of the proceedings at, or for the purposes of, which the child witness is to give evidence may be conducted only by a lawyer,]
   (b) that it is therefore in his interests, if he has not already done so, to get the professional assistance of a solicitor, and
   (c) that if he does not engage a solicitor for the purposes of [F59the conduct of his case at or for the purposes of the] [F60hearing], the court will do so.
(7) A failure to comply with subsection (5) or (6) above does not affect the validity or lawfulness of any [F61vulnerable] witness notice or any other element of the proceedings against the accused.
F62. (8). . . . .
(9) For the purposes of subsection (2)(b) above, proceedings shall be taken to have commenced when the indictment or, as the case may be, the complaint is served on the accused.

Amendments (Textual)

F51 S. 288. E(1) repealed (28.3.2011) by Criminal Justice and Licensing (Scotland) Act 2010 (asp 13), ss. 69. (4)(a), 206. (1); S.S.I. 2011/178, art. 2, sch.

F52 Words in s. 288. E substituted (10.3.2008, 2.6.2008, 8.12.2008, 23.2.2009 and 14.12.2009 for certain purposes, otherwise 22.2.2010) by Criminal Proceedings etc. (Reform) (Scotland) Act 2007 (asp 6), ss. 80, 84, Sch. para. 26. (q); S.S.I. 2008/42, art. 3, Sch.; S.S.I. 2008/192, art. 3, Sch.; S.S.I. 2008/329, art. 3, Sch.; S.S.I. 2008/362, art. 3, Sch.; S.S.I. 2009/432, art. 3, Schs. 1, 2

F53 Words in s. 288. E(2)(b) substituted (28.3.2011) by Criminal Justice and Licensing (Scotland) Act 2010 (asp 13), ss. 69. (4)(b), 206. (1); S.S.I. 2011/178, art. 2, sch.

F54 S. 288. E(2. A) inserted (28.3.2011) by Criminal Justice and Licensing (Scotland) Act 2010 (asp 13), ss. 69. (4)(c), 206. (1); S.S.I. 2011/178, art. 2, sch.

F55 Words in s. 288. E(4) inserted (28.3.2011) by Criminal Justice and Licensing (Scotland) Act 2010 (asp 13), ss. 69. (4)(d), 206. (1); S.S.I. 2011/178, art. 2, sch.

F56. Word in s. 288. E(5) substituted (1.9.2015) by Victims and Witnesses (Scotland) Act 2014 (asp 1), ss. 11. (9), 34; S.S.I. 2015/200, art. 2. (2), sch. (with arts. 1. (3), 4)

F57 Words in s. 288. E(5) substituted (28.3.2011) by Criminal Justice and Licensing (Scotland) Act 2010 (asp 13), ss. 87. (10), 206. (1); S.S.I. 2011/178, art. 2, sch.

F58 S. 288. E(6)(a) substituted for s. 288. E(6)(za)(a) (28.3.2011) by Criminal Justice and Licensing (Scotland) Act 2010 (asp 13), ss. 69. (4)(e)(i), 206. (1); S.S.I. 2011/178, art. 2, sch.

F59 Words in s. 288. E(6)(c) inserted (1.4.2005, 1.4.2006 and 1.4.2007 for certain purposes, otherwise 1.4.2008) by Criminal Procedure (Amendment) (Scotland) Act 2004 (asp 5), ss. 4. (3)(b)(ii), 27. (1); S.S.I. 2004/405, art. 2. (2), Sch. 2 (with savings in arts. 3-5); S.S.I. 2005/168, art. 2, Sch. (with savings in art. 4); S.S.I. 2006/59, art. 2, Sch. (with art. 4. (1)); S.S.I. 2007/101, art. 2, Sch. (with art. 4); S.S.I. 2008/57, art. 2 (with art. 3)

F60 Word in s. 288. E(6)(c) substituted (28.3.2011) by Criminal Justice and Licensing (Scotland) Act 2010 (asp 13), ss. 69. (4)(e)(ii), 206. (1); S.S.I. 2011/178, art. 2, sch.

F61. Word in s. 288. E(7) substituted (1.9.2015) by Victims and Witnesses (Scotland) Act 2014 (asp 1), ss. 11. (9), 34; S.S.I. 2015/200, art. 2. (2), sch. (with arts. 1. (3), 4)

F62 S. 288. E(8) repealed (28.3.2011) by Criminal Justice and Licensing (Scotland) Act 2010 (asp 13), ss. 69. (4)(f), 206. (1); S.S.I. 2011/178, art. 2, sch.

Modifications etc. (not altering text)

C6. S. 288. E applied (with modifications) (23.12.2015) by The Justice of the Peace Courts (Special Measures) (Scotland) Order 2015 (S.S.I. 2015/447), arts. 1. (2), 4 (with art. 1. (3))

288. FPower to prohibit personal conduct of defence in other cases involving vulnerable witnessesS

(1) This section applies in the case of proceedings in respect of any offence, other than proceedings—

    (a) in the [F63. JP court],

    (b) in respect of a sexual offence to which section 288. C of this Act applies, or

    (c) to which section 288. E of this Act applies,

where a vulnerable witness is to give evidence at, or for the purposes of, [F64any hearing in the course of the proceedings].

(2) If satisfied that it is in the interests of the vulnerable witness to do so, the court may—

    (a) on the application of the prosecutor, or

    (b) of its own motion,

make an order prohibiting the accused from conducting his [F65case in person at any hearing at, or for the purposes of, which the vulnerable witness is to give evidence.]

(3) However, the court shall not make an order under subsection (2) above if it considers that—

    (a) the order would give rise to a significant risk of prejudice to the fairness of the [F66hearing] or otherwise to the interests of justice, and

(b) that risk significantly outweighs any risk of prejudice to the interests of the vulnerable witness if the order is not made.

(4) The court may make an order under subsection (2) above [F67in relation to a hearing after, as well as before, the hearing has commenced.]

F68. (4. A). . . . .

(5) Section 288. D of this Act applies in the case of proceedings in respect of which an order is made under this section as it applies in the case of proceedings in respect of a sexual offence to which section 288. C of this Act applies [F69 and as if references to a relevant hearing were references to any hearing in respect of which an order is made under this section].

F70. (6). . . . .]

Amendments (Textual)

F63. Words in s. 288. F(1)(a) substituted (10.3.2008, 2.6.2008, 8.12.2008, 23.2.2009 and 14.12.2009 for certain purposes, otherwise 22.2.2010) by Criminal Proceedings etc. (Reform) (Scotland) Act 2007 (asp 6), ss. 80, 84, Sch. para. 26. (r); S.S.I. 2008/42, art. 3, Sch.; S.S.I. 2008/192, art. 3, Sch.; S.S.I. 2008/329, art. 3, Sch.; S.S.I. 2008/362, art. 3, Sch.; S.S.I. 2009/432, art. 3, Schs. 1, 2

F64. Words in s. 288. F(1) substituted (28.3.2011) by Criminal Justice and Licensing (Scotland) Act 2010 (asp 13), ss. 69. (5)(a), 206. (1); S.S.I. 2011/178, art. 2, sch.

F65. Words in s. 288. F(2) substituted (28.3.2011) by Criminal Justice and Licensing (Scotland) Act 2010 (asp 13), ss. 69. (5)(b), 206. (1); S.S.I. 2011/178, art. 2, sch.

F66. Word in s. 288. F(3)(a) substituted (28.3.2011) by Criminal Justice and Licensing (Scotland) Act 2010 (asp 13), ss. 69. (5)(c), 206. (1); S.S.I. 2011/178, art. 2, sch.

F67. Words in s. 288. F(4) substituted (28.3.2011) by Criminal Justice and Licensing (Scotland) Act 2010 (asp 13), ss. 69. (5)(d), 206. (1); S.S.I. 2011/178, art. 2, sch.

F68. S. 288. F(4. A) repealed (28.3.2011) by Criminal Justice and Licensing (Scotland) Act 2010 (asp 13), ss. 69. (5)(e), 206. (1); S.S.I. 2011/178, art. 2, sch.

F69. Words in s. 288. F(5) inserted (28.3.2011) by Criminal Justice and Licensing (Scotland) Act 2010 (asp 13), ss. 69. (5)(f), 206. (1); S.S.I. 2011/178, art. 2, sch.

F70. S. 288. F(6) repealed (28.3.2011) by Criminal Justice and Licensing (Scotland) Act 2010 (asp 13), ss. 69. (5)(g), 206. (1); S.S.I. 2011/178, art. 2, sch.

Modifications etc. (not altering text)

C7. S. 288. F applied (with modifications) (23.12.2015) by The Justice of the Peace Courts (Special Measures) (Scotland) Order 2015 (S.S.I. 2015/447), arts. 1. (2), 5 (with art. 1. (3))

[F71. Application of vulnerable witnesses provisions to proceedings in the district courtS

Amendments (Textual)

F71. S. 288. G and crossheading inserted (1.7.2015) by Vulnerable Witnesses (Scotland) Act 2004 (asp 3), ss. 10, 25. (1); S.S.I. 2015/244, art. 2

288. GApplication of vulnerable witnesses provisions to proceedings in the district courtS

(1) The Scottish Ministers may by order made by statutory instrument provide for any of sections—

(a) 271 to 271. M,

(b) 288. E, and

(c) 288. F,

of this Act to apply, subject to such modifications (if any) as may be specified in the order, to proceedings in the district court.

(2) An order under subsection (1) may—

(a) make such incidental, supplemental, consequential, transitional, transitory or saving provision as the Scottish Ministers think necessary or expedient,

(b) make different provision for different district courts or descriptions of district court or different proceedings or types of proceedings,

(c) modify any enactment.

(3) An order under this section shall not be made unless a draft of the statutory instrument containing the order has been laid before, and approved by resolution of, the Scottish Parliament.]

[F72. Use of live television linkS

Amendments (Textual)
F72. Ss. 288. H-288. L and cross-heading inserted (25.1.2018) by Criminal Justice (Scotland) Act 2016 (asp 1), ss. 110. (1), 117. (2); S.S.I. 2017/345, art. 3, sch.

288. HParticipation through live television linkS

(1) Where the court so determines at any time before or at a specified hearing, a detained person is to participate in the hearing by means of a live television link.

(2) The court—

(a) must give the parties in the case an opportunity to make representations before making a determination under subsection (1),

(b) may make such a determination only if it considers that to do so is not contrary to the interests of justice.

(3) The court may require a detained person to participate by means of a live television link in any proceedings at a specified hearing or otherwise in the case for the sole purpose of considering whether to make a determination under subsection (1) with respect to a specified hearing.

(4) Where a detained person participates in any specified hearing or other proceedings by means of a live television link—

(a) a place of detention is, for the purposes of the hearing or other proceedings, deemed to be part of the court-room, and

(b) accordingly, the hearing is or other proceedings are deemed to take place in the presence of the detained person.

(5) In this section—

"court-room" includes chambers,

"live television link" means live television link between a place of detention and the court-room in which any specified hearing is or other proceedings are to be held or (as the case may be) any specified hearing is or other proceedings are being held.

288. IEvidence and personal appearanceS

(1) No evidence as to a charge on any complaint or indictment may be led or presented at a specified hearing in respect of which there is a determination under section 288. H(1).

(2) The court—

(a) may, at any time before or at a specified hearing, revoke a determination under section 288. H(1),

(b) must do so in relation to a detained person if it considers that it is in the interests of justice for the detained person to appear in person.

(3) The court may postpone a specified hearing to a later day if, on the day on which a specified hearing takes place or is due to take place—

(a) the court decides not to make a determination under section 288. H(1) with respect to the hearing, or

(b) the court revokes such a determination under subsection (2).

288. JEffect of postponementS

(1) Except where a postponement under section 288. I(3) is while section 21. (2) of the Criminal Justice (Scotland) Act 2016 applies to a detained person, the following do not count towards any time limit arising in the person's case if the postponement in the case is to the next day on which the court is sitting—

(a) that next day,

(b) any intervening Saturday, Sunday or court holiday.

(2) Even while section 21. (2) of the Criminal Justice (Scotland) Act 2016 applies to a detained person, that section does not prevent a postponement under section 288. I(3) in the person's case.

(3) In section 288. I and this section, "postpone" includes adjourn.

288. KSpecified hearingsS

(1) The Lord Justice General may by directions specify types of hearing at the High Court, [F73. Sheriff Appeal Court,] sheriff court and JP court in which a detained person may participate in accordance with section 288. H(1).

(2) Directions under subsection (1) may specify types of hearing by reference to—

(a) the venues at which they take place,

(b) particular places of detention,

(c) categories of cases or proceedings to which they relate.

(3) Directions under subsection (1) may—

(a) vary or revoke earlier such directions,

(b) make different provision for different purposes.

(4) The validity of any proceedings is not affected by the participation of a detained person by means of a live television link in a hearing that is not a specified hearing.

(5) In this section, "hearing" includes any diet or hearing in criminal proceedings which may be held in the presence of an accused, a convicted person or an appellant in the proceedings.

Amendments (Textual)

F73. Words in s. 288. K(1) inserted (25.1.2018) by The Criminal Justice (Scotland) Act 2016 (Consequential and Supplementary Modifications) Regulations 2017 (S.S.I. 2017/452), reg. 1, sch. para. 12. (3)

288. LDefined termsS

For the purpose of sections 288. H to 288. K—

"detained person" means person who is—

- an accused, a convicted person or an appellant in the case to which a specified hearing relates, and

- imprisoned or otherwise lawfully detained (whether or not in connection with an offence) at any place in Scotland,

"place of detention" means place in which a detained person is imprisoned or detained,

"specified hearing" means hearing of a type specified in directions having effect for the time being under section 288. K.]

Treason trialsS

289 Procedure and evidence in trials for treason.S

The procedure and rules of evidence in proceedings for treason and misprision of treason shall be the same as in proceedings according to the law of Scotland for murder.

Certain rights of accusedS

290 Accused's right to request identification parade.S

(1) Subject to subsection (2) below, the sheriff may, on an application by an accused at any time after the accused has been charged with an offence, order that, in relation to the alleged offence, the prosecutor shall hold an identification parade in which the accused shall be one of those constituting the parade.

(2) The sheriff shall make an order in accordance with subsection (1) above only after giving the prosecutor an opportunity to be heard and only if—

(a) an identification parade, such as is mentioned in subsection (1) above, has not been held at the instance of the prosecutor;

(b) after a request by the accused, the prosecutor has refused to hold, or has unreasonably delayed holding, such an identification parade; and

(c) the sheriff considers the application under subsection (1) above to be reasonable.

291 Precognition on oath of defence witnesses.S

(1) The sheriff may, on the application of an accused, grant warrant to cite any person (other than a co-accused), who is alleged to be a witness in relation to any offence of which the accused has been charged, to appear before the sheriff in chambers at such time or place as shall be specified in the citation, for precognition on oath by the accused or his solicitor in relation to that offence, if the court is satisfied that it is reasonable to require such precognition on oath in the circumstances.

(2) Any person who, having been duly cited to attend for precognition under subsection (1) above and having been given at least 48 hours notice, fails without reasonable excuse to attend shall be guilty of an offence and shall be liable on summary conviction to a fine not exceeding level 3 on the standard scale or to imprisonment for a period not exceeding 21 days; and the court may issue a warrant for the apprehension of the person concerned, ordering him to be brought before a sheriff for precognition on oath.

(3) Any person who, having been duly cited to attend for precognition under subsection (1) above, attends but—

(a) refuses to give information within his knowledge or to produce evidence in his possession; or

(b) prevaricates in his evidence,

shall be guilty of an offence and shall be liable to be summarily subjected forthwith to a fine not exceeding level 3 on the standard scale or to imprisonment for a period not exceeding 21 days.

[F74. (4)This section does not, however, extend to the citation of the complainer for precognition by the accused in person.

(5) In subsection (4) above, "complainer" has the same meaning as in section 274 of this Act.]

[F75. (6)A warrant is not to be granted under this section for the citation for precognition by the accused in person of any child under the age of 12 on the relevant date where the offence in relation to which the child is alleged to be a witness is one specified in section 288. E(3) of this Act.

(7) In subsection (6) above, "the relevant date" means—

(a) where an indictment or complaint in respect of the offence has been served on the accused at the time of the application, the date on which the indictment or complaint was so served, or

(b) where an indictment or complaint in respect of the offence has not been so served, the date on which the application under subsection (1) above is made.]

Amendments (Textual)

F74. S. 291. (4)(5) inserted (1.11.2002) by Sexual Offences (Procedure and Evidence) (Scotland) Act 2002 (asp 9), s. 4; S.S.I. 2002/443, art. 3

F75. S. 291. (6)(7) inserted (1.4.2005 for certain purposes and 1.4.2007 for further purposes and otherwise prosp.) by Vulnerable Witnesses (Scotland) Act 2004 (asp 3), ss. 8, 25; S.S.I. 2005/168, art. 2, Sch. (with savings in art. 4); S.S.I. 2007/101, art. 2, Sch. (with art. 4)

Mode of trialS

292 Mode of trial of certain offences.S

(1) Subject to subsection (6) below, the offences mentioned (and broadly described) in Schedule 10 to this Act shall be triable only summarily.

(2) An offence created by statute shall be triable only summarily if—

(a) the enactment creating the offence or any other enactment expressly so provides (in whatever words); or

(b) subject to subsections (4) and (5)(a) below, the offence was created by an Act passed on or before 29 July 1977 (the date of passing of the M1. Criminal Law Act 1977) and the penalty or maximum penalty in force immediately before that date, on any conviction of that offence, did not include any of the following—

(i) a fine exceeding £400;

(ii) F76. . . imprisonment for a period exceeding 3 months;

(iii) a fine exceeding £50 in respect of a specified quantity or number of things, or in respect of a specified period during which a continuing offence is committed.

(3) F77. . . . .

(4) An offence created by statute which is triable only on indictment shall continue only to be so triable.

(5) An offence created by statute shall be triable either on indictment or summarily if—

(a) the enactment creating the offence or any other enactment expressly so provides (in whatever words); or

(b) it is an offence to which neither subsection (2) nor subsection (4) above applies.

(6) An offence which may under any enactment (including an enactment in this Act or passed after this Act) be tried only summarily, being an offence which, if it had been triable on indictment, could competently have been libelled as an additional or alternative charge in the indictment, may (the provisions of this or any other enactment notwithstanding) be so libelled, and tried accordingly.

(7) Where an offence is libelled and tried on indictment by virtue of subsection (6) above, the penalty which may be imposed for that offence in that case shall not exceed that which is competent on summary conviction.

Amendments (Textual)

F76. Words in s. 292. (2)(b)(ii) repealed (10.12.2007) by Criminal Proceedings etc. (Reform) (Scotland) Act 2007 (asp 6), ss. 80, 84; Sch. para. 26. (a); S.S.I. 2007/479, art. 3. (1), Sch. (as amended by S.S.I. 2007/527)

F77. S. 292. (3) repealed (10.12.2007) by Criminal Proceedings etc. (Reform) (Scotland) Act 2007 (asp 6), ss. 80, 84; Sch. para. 26. (b); S.S.I. 2007/479, art. 3. (1), Sch. (as amended by S.S.I. 2007/527)

Marginal Citations

M11977 c.45.

Art and part and attemptS

293 Statutory offences: art and part and aiding and abetting.S

(1) A person may be convicted of, and punished for, a contravention of any enactment, notwithstanding that he was guilty of such contravention as art and part only.

(2) Without prejudice to subsection (1) above or to any express provision in any enactment having the like effect to this subsection, any person who aids, abets, counsels, procures or incites any other person to commit an offence against the provisions of any enactment shall be guilty of an offence and shall be liable on conviction, unless the enactment otherwise requires, to the same punishment as might be imposed on conviction of the first-mentioned offence.

Modifications etc. (not altering text)

C8. S. 293. (2) excluded (1.4.1996) by 1995 c. 40, ss. 3, 7. (2), Sch. 3 Pt. II para. 11

294 Attempt at crime.S

(1) Attempt to commit any indictable crime is itself an indictable crime.

(2) Attempt to commit any offence punishable on complaint shall itself be an offence punishable on complaint.

Legal custodyS

295 Legal custody.S

[F78. Without prejudice to section 13 of the Prisons (Scotland) Act 1989 (c. 45)(legal custody of prisoners),] any person required or authorised by or under this Act or any other enactment to be taken to any place, or to be detained or kept in custody [F79is], while being so taken or detained or kept, F80. . . in legal custody.

Amendments (Textual)

F78. Words in s. 295 inserted (27.6.2003) by Criminal Justice (Scotland) Act 2003 (asp 7), ss. 24. (2)(a), 89; S.S.I. 2003/288, art. 2, Sch.

F79. Word in s. 295 substituted (27.6.2003) by Criminal Justice (Scotland) Act 2003 (asp 7), ss. 24. (2)(b), 89; S.S.I. 2003/288, art. 2, Sch.

F80. Words in s. 295 repealed (27.6.2003) by Criminal Justice (Scotland) Act 2003 (asp 7), ss. 24. (2)(c), 89; S.S.I. 2003/288, art. 2, Sch.

WarrantsS

296 Warrants for search and apprehension to be signed by judge.S

Any warrant for search or apprehension granted under this Act shall be signed by the judge granting it, and execution upon any such warrant may proceed either upon the warrant itself or upon an extract of the warrant issued and signed by the clerk of court.

297 Execution of warrants and service of complaints, etc.S

(1) Any warrant granted by a justice may, without being backed or endorsed by any other justice, be executed throughout Scotland in the same way as it may be executed within the jurisdiction of the justice who granted it.

(2) Any complaint, warrant, or other proceeding for the purposes of any summary proceedings under this Act may without endorsation be served or executed at any place within Scotland by any officer of law, and such service or execution may be proved either by the oath in court of the officer or by production of his written execution.

(3) A warrant issued in the Isle of Man for the arrest of a person charged with an offence may, after it has been endorsed by a justice in Scotland, be executed there by the person bringing that warrant, by any person to whom the warrant was originally directed or by any officer of law of the sheriff court district where the warrant has been endorsed in like manner as any such warrant issued in Scotland.

(4) In subsection (3) above, "endorsed" means endorsed in the like manner as a process to which section 4 of the M2. Summary Jurisdiction (Process) Act 1881 applies.

(5) The M3. Indictable Offences Act Amendment Act 1868 shall apply in relation to the execution in Scotland of warrants issued in the Channel Islands.

Extent Information

E1. S. 297 extends to Scotland only except s. 297. (3)and(4) which also extend to the Isle of Man

Marginal Citations

M21881 c.24.

M31868 c.107.

[F81297. ARe-execution of apprehension warrantsS

(1) This section applies where a person has been apprehended under a warrant (the "original warrant") granted under this Act in relation to any proceedings.

(2) If the person absconds, the person may be re-apprehended under the original warrant (and as if that warrant had not been executed to any extent).

(3) If, for any reason, it is not practicable to bring the person before the court as required under a provision of this Act applying in the case, the person is to be brought before the court as soon as practicable after the relevant reason ceases to prevail.

(4) Despite subsection (3) above, if—

    (a) the original warrant was granted in solemn proceedings; and

    (b) the impracticability arises because the person needs medical treatment or care,

the person may be released.

(5) A person released under subsection (4) above may be re-apprehended under the original warrant (and as if that warrant had not been executed to any extent).

(6) Subsection (3) above does not affect the operation of section 22. (1. B) of this Act (which relates to liberation on an undertaking of persons apprehended under warrant granted in summary proceedings).

(7) Nothing in this section prevents a court from granting a fresh warrant for the apprehension of the person.

(8) Subject to this section are—

    (a) any rule of law as to bringing a person before a court in pursuance of a warrant granted on petition (as referred to in section 34 of this Act);

    (b) section 102. A(10) of this Act;

    (c) section 135. (3) (including as applying in relation to sections 22. (1. B) and 156) of this Act;

    (d) section 90. A(9) of this Act.]

Amendments (Textual)

F81. S. 297. A inserted (10.12.2007) by Criminal Proceedings etc. (Reform) (Scotland) Act 2007

Trial judge's reportS

298 Trial judge's report.S

(1) Without prejudice to [F82section 113] of this Act, the High Court may, in relation to—
    (a) an appeal under section 106. (1), 108 [F83or 108. A] of this Act;
    (b) an appeal by way of bill of suspension or advocation; or
    (c) a petition to the nobile officium,
at any time before the appeal is finally determined or, as the case may be, petition finally disposed of, order the judge who presided at the trial, passed sentence or otherwise disposed of the case to provide to the Clerk of Justiciary a report in writing giving the judge's opinion on the case generally or in relation to any particular matter specified in the order.
(2) The Clerk of Justiciary shall send a copy of a report provided under subsection (1) above to the convicted person or his solicitor, the Crown Agent and, in relation to cases referred under [F84. Part XA of this Act, the Commission].
[F85. (2. A)Without prejudice to section 186. (3)(b) of this Act, the Sheriff Appeal Court may, in relation to—
    (a) an appeal under section 175. (2) to (4) of this Act; or
    (b) an appeal by way of bill of suspension or advocation,
at any time before the appeal is finally determined order the judge who presided at the trial, passed sentence or otherwise disposed of the case to provide to the Clerk of the Sheriff Appeal Court a report in writing giving the judge's opinion in the case generally or in relation to any particular matter specified in the order.
(2. B)The Clerk of the Sheriff Appeal Court must send a copy of the report provided under subsection (2. A) above to the convicted person or their solicitor, the prosecutor and, in relation to cases referred under Part XA of this Act, the Commission.]
(3) Subject to [F86subsections (2) and (2. B)] above, the report of the judge shall be available only to the High Court [F87or the Sheriff Appeal Court (as the case may be)], the parties and, on such conditions as may be prescribed by Act of Adjournal, such other persons or classes of persons as may be so prescribed.
Amendments (Textual)
F82. Words in s. 298. (1) substituted (22.9.2015) by The Courts Reform (Scotland) Act 2014 (Consequential Provisions No. 2) Order 2015 (S.S.I. 2015/338), art. 1, sch. 2 para. 5. (15)(a) (with art. 4)
F83. Words in s. 298. (1)(a) substituted (22.9.2015) by The Courts Reform (Scotland) Act 2014 (Consequential Provisions No. 2) Order 2015 (S.S.I. 2015/338), art. 1, sch. 2 para. 5. (15)(b) (with art. 4)
F84. Words in s. 298. (2) substituted (1.4.1999) by 1998 c. 48, s. 62. (1), Sch. 1 para. 21. (33)(b); S.I. 1999/652, art. 2, Sch.(subject to savings and transitional provisions in art. 3)
F85. S. 298. (2. A)(2. B) inserted (22.9.2015) by The Courts Reform (Scotland) Act 2014 (Consequential Provisions No. 2) Order 2015 (S.S.I. 2015/338), art. 1, sch. 2 para. 5. (15)(c) (with art. 4)
F86. Words in s. 298. (3) substituted (22.9.2015) by The Courts Reform (Scotland) Act 2014 (Consequential Provisions No. 2) Order 2015 (S.S.I. 2015/338), art. 1, sch. 2 para. 5. (15)(d)(i) (with art. 4)
F87. Words in s. 298. (3) inserted (22.9.2015) by The Courts Reform (Scotland) Act 2014 (Consequential Provisions No. 2) Order 2015 (S.S.I. 2015/338), art. 1, sch. 2 para. 5. (15)(d)(ii) (with art. 4)
Modifications etc. (not altering text)

C9. S. 298. (2. B) excluded by 2006 asp 10, s 96. A(5) (as inserted (22.9.2015) by The Courts Reform (Scotland) Act 2014 (Consequential Provisions No. 2) Order 2015 (S.S.I. 2015/338), art. 1, sch. 2 para. 9. (6) (with art. 4))

[F88. Intimation of certain applications to the High CourtS

Amendments (Textual)
F88. S. 298. A and cross-heading inserted (10.12.2007) by Criminal Proceedings etc. (Reform) (Scotland) Act 2007 (asp 6), ss. 38, 84; S.S.I. 2007/479, art. 3. (1), Sch. (as amended by S.S.I. 2007/527)

298. AIntimation of bills and of petitions to the nobile officiumS

(1) This subsection applies where the prosecutor requires to intimate to the respondent—
    (a) a bill of advocation;
    (b) a petition to the nobile officium; F89...
    (c) an order of the High Court [F90or the Sheriff Appeal Court] relating to such a bill or (as the case may be) petition.
(2) Where subsection (1) above applies, the requirement may be met by serving on the respondent or the respondent's solicitor a copy of the bill, petition or (as the case may be) order.
(3) Service under subsection (2) above may (in relation to any proceedings) be effected—
    (a) on the respondent, in the same manner as citation under section 141 of this Act;
    (b) on the respondent's solicitor, by post.
(4) This subsection applies where a person requires to intimate to the prosecutor—
    (a) a bill of suspension or advocation;
    (b) a petition to the nobile officium; F91...
    (c) an order of the High Court [F92or the Sheriff Appeal Court] relating to such a bill or (as the case may be) petition.
(5) Where subsection (4) above applies, the requirement may be met by serving on the prosecutor a copy of the bill, petition or (as the case may be) order.
(6) Service under subsection (5) above may (in relation to any proceedings) be effected by post.
(7) It is sufficient evidence that service has been effected under subsection (3) or (6) above if there is produced a written execution—
    (a) in the form prescribed by Act of Adjournal or as nearly as may be in such form; and
    (b) signed by the person who effected service.
(8) In relation to service effected by means of registered post or the recorded delivery service, the relevant post office receipt requires to be produced along with the execution mentioned in subsection (7) above.
(9) A party who has service effected under subsection (3) or (6) above must, as soon as practicable thereafter, lodge with the Clerk of Justiciary [F93or the Clerk of the Sheriff Appeal Court (as the case may be)] a copy of the execution mentioned in subsection (7) above.
(10) For the purpose of subsection (3)(a) above, section 141 of this Act is to be read with such modifications as are necessary for its application in the circumstances.
(11) This section is without prejudice to any rule of law or practice by virtue of which things of the kinds mentioned in subsections (1) and (4) above (including copies) may be intimated or served.]

Amendments (Textual)
F89. Word in s. 298. A(1)(b) repealed (22.9.2015) by The Courts Reform (Scotland) Act 2014 (Consequential Provisions No. 2) Order 2015 (S.S.I. 2015/338), art. 1, sch. 2 para. 5. (16)(a)(i) (with art. 4)
F90. Words in s. 298. A(1)(c) inserted (22.9.2015) by The Courts Reform (Scotland) Act 2014 (Consequential Provisions No. 2) Order 2015 (S.S.I. 2015/338), art. 1, sch. 2 para. 5. (16)(a)(ii)

(with art. 4)

F91. Word in s. 298. A(4)(b) repealed (22.9.2015) by The Courts Reform (Scotland) Act 2014 (Consequential Provisions No. 2) Order 2015 (S.S.I. 2015/338), art. 1, sch. 2 para. 5. (16)(b)(i) (with art. 4)

F92. Words in s. 298. A(4)(c) inserted (22.9.2015) by The Courts Reform (Scotland) Act 2014 (Consequential Provisions No. 2) Order 2015 (S.S.I. 2015/338), art. 1, sch. 2 para. 5. (16)(b)(ii) (with art. 4)

F93. Words in s. 298. A(9) inserted (22.9.2015) by The Courts Reform (Scotland) Act 2014 (Consequential Provisions No. 2) Order 2015 (S.S.I. 2015/338), art. 1, sch. 2 para. 5. (16)(c) (with art. 4)

Correction of entriesS

299 Correction of entries.S

(1) Subject to the provisions of this section, it shall be competent to correct any entry in—
    (a) the record of proceedings in a prosecution; or
    (b) the extract of a sentence passed or an order of court made in such proceedings,
in so far as that entry constitutes an error of recording or is incomplete.

(2) An entry mentioned in subsection (1) above may be corrected—
    (a) by the clerk of the court, at any time before either the sentence or order of the court is executed or, on appeal, the proceedings are transmitted to the Clerk of Justiciary [F94or the Clerk of the Sheriff Appeal Court (as the case may be)];
    (b) by the clerk of the court, under the authority of the court which passed the sentence or made the order, at any time after the execution of the sentence or order of the court but before such transmission as is mentioned in paragraph (a) above; or
    (c) by the clerk of the court under the authority of the High Court [F95or the Sheriff Appeal Court (as the case may be)] in the case of a remit under subsection (4)(b) below.

(3) A correction in accordance with paragraph (b) or (c) of subsection (2) above shall be intimated to the prosecutor and to the former accused or his solicitor.

(4) Where during the course of an appeal, the [F96court hearing the appeal] becomes aware of an erroneous or incomplete entry, such as is mentioned in subsection (1) above, the court—
    (a) may consider and determine the appeal as if such entry were corrected; and
    (b) either before or after the determination of the appeal, may remit the proceedings to the court of first instance for correction in accordance with subsection (2)(c) above.

(5) Any correction under subsections (1) and (2) above by the clerk of the court shall be authenticated by his signature and, if such correction is authorised by a court, shall record the name of the judge or judges authorising such correction and the date of such authorisation.

Amendments (Textual)

F94. Words in s. 299. (2)(a) inserted (22.9.2015) by The Courts Reform (Scotland) Act 2014 (Consequential Provisions No. 2) Order 2015 (S.S.I. 2015/338), art. 1, sch. 2 para. 5. (17)(a)(i) (with art. 4)

F95. Words in s. 299. (2)(c) inserted (22.9.2015) by The Courts Reform (Scotland) Act 2014 (Consequential Provisions No. 2) Order 2015 (S.S.I. 2015/338), art. 1, sch. 2 para. 5. (17)(a)(ii) (with art. 4)

F96. Words in s. 299. (4) substituted (22.9.2015) by The Courts Reform (Scotland) Act 2014 (Consequential Provisions No. 2) Order 2015 (S.S.I. 2015/338), art. 1, sch. 2 para. 5. (17)(b) (with art. 4)

300 Amendment of records of conviction and sentence in

summary proceedings.S

(1) Without prejudice to section 299 of this Act, where, on an application in accordance with subsection (2) below, the [F97. Sheriff Appeal Court] is satisfied that a record of conviction or sentence in summary proceedings inaccurately records the identity of any person, it may authorise the clerk of the court which convicted or, as the case may be, sentenced the person to correct the record.

(2) An application under subsection (1) above shall be made after the determination of the summary prosecution and may be made by any party to the summary proceedings or any other person having an interest in the correction of the alleged inaccuracy.

(3) The [F98. Sheriff Appeal Court] shall order intimation of an application under subsection (1) above to such persons as it considers appropriate and shall not determine the application without affording to the parties to the summary proceedings and to any other person having an interest in the correction of the alleged inaccuracy an opportunity to be heard.

(4) The power of the High Court under this section may be exercised by a single judge of the High Court in the same manner as it may be exercised by the High Court, and subject to the same provisions.

Amendments (Textual)

F97. Words in s. 300. (1) substituted (22.9.2015) by The Courts Reform (Scotland) Act 2014 (Consequential Provisions No. 2) Order 2015 (S.S.I. 2015/338), art. 1, sch. 2 para. 5. (18) (with art. 4)

F98. Words in s. 300. (3) substituted (22.9.2015) by virtue of The Courts Reform (Scotland) Act 2014 (Consequential Provisions No. 2) Order 2015 (S.S.I. 2015/338), art. 1, sch. 2 para. 5. (18) (with art. 4)

[F99. Excusal of irregularities

Amendments (Textual)

F99. S. 300. A and cross-heading inserted (10.12.2007) by Criminal Proceedings etc. (Reform) (Scotland) Act 2007 (asp 6), ss. 40, 84; S.S.I. 2007/479, art. 3. (1), Sch. (subject to art. 11) (as amended by S.S.I. 2007/527)

300. APower of court to excuse procedural irregularitiesS

(1) Any court may excuse a procedural irregularity—
    (a) of a kind described in subsection (5) below; and
    (b) which has occurred in relation to proceedings before that court,
if the conditions mentioned in subsection (4) below are met.

(2) In appeal proceedings, the [F100court hearing the appeal] may excuse a procedural irregularity—
    (a) of that kind; and
    (b) which has occurred in relation to earlier proceedings in the case that is the subject of the appeal,
if those conditions are met.

(3) A court may proceed under subsection (1) or (2) above on the application of the prosecutor or an accused person (having given the other an opportunity to be heard).

(4) The conditions are that—
    (a) it appears to the court that the irregularity arose because of—
(i) mistake or oversight; or
(ii) other excusable reason; and
    (b) the court is satisfied in the circumstances of the case that it would be in the interests of

justice to excuse the irregularity.

(5) A procedural irregularity is an irregularity arising at any stage of proceedings—

    (a) from—

(i) failure to call or discharge a diet properly;

(ii) improper adjournment or continuation of a case;

(iii) a diet being fixed for a non-sitting day;

    (b) from failure of—

(i) the court; or

(ii) the prosecutor or the accused,

to do something within a particular period or otherwise comply with a time limit;

    (c) from failure of the prosecutor to serve properly a notice or other thing;

    (d) from failure of the accused to—

(i) intimate properly a preliminary objection;

(ii) intimate properly a plea or defence;

(iii) serve properly a notice or other thing;

    (e) from failure of—

(i) the court; or

(ii) the prosecutor or the accused,

to fulfil any other procedural requirement.

(6) Subsection (1) above does not authorise a court to excuse an irregularity arising by reason of the detention in custody of an accused person for a period exceeding that fixed by this Act.

(7) Subsection (1) above does not apply in relation to any requirement as to proof including, in particular, any matter relating to—

    (a) admissibility of evidence;

    (b) sufficiency of evidence; or

    (c) any other evidential factor.

[F101. (7. A)Subsection (1) does not authorise a court to excuse a failure to do any of the following things timeously—

    (a) lodge written intimation of intention to appeal in accordance with section 109. (1),

    (b) lodge a note of appeal in accordance with section 110. (1)(a),

    (c) make an application for a stated case under section 176. (1),

    (d) lodge a note of appeal in accordance with section 186. (2)(a).]

(8) Where a court excuses an irregularity under subsection (1) above, it may make such order as is necessary or expedient for the purpose of—

    (a) restoring the proceedings as if the irregularity had never occurred;

    (b) facilitating the continuation of the proceedings as if it had never occurred, for example—

(i) altering a diet;

(ii) extending any time limit;

(iii) appointing a diet for further procedure or granting an adjournment or continuation of a diet;

    (c) protecting the rights of the parties.

(9) For the purposes of this section—

    (a) a reference to an accused person, except the reference in subsection (6) above, includes reference to a person who has been convicted of an offence;

    (b) something is done properly if it is done in accordance with a requirement of an enactment or any rule of law.

(10) In subsection (5)(a)(iii) above, a "non-sitting day" is a day on which the court is under this Act not required to sit.

(11) This section is without prejudice to any provision of this Act under which a court may—

    (a) alter a diet; or

    (b) extend—

(i) a period within which something requires to be done; or

(ii) any other time limit.

(12) This section is without prejudice to any rule of law by virtue of which it may be determined

by a court that breach, in relation to criminal proceedings—

(a) of a requirement of an enactment; or

(b) of a rule of law,

does not render the proceedings, or anything done (or purported to have been done) for the purposes of or in connection with proceedings, invalid.]

Amendments (Textual)

F100. Words in s. 300. A(2) substituted (22.9.2015) by The Courts Reform (Scotland) Act 2014 (Consequential Provisions No. 2) Order 2015 (S.S.I. 2015/338), art. 1, sch. 2 para. 5. (19) (with art. 4)

F101. S. 300. A(7. A) inserted (17.1.2017) by Criminal Justice (Scotland) Act 2016 (asp 1), ss. 91, 117. (2); S.S.I. 2016/426, art. 2, sch.

Rights of audienceS

301 Rights of audience.S

(1) Without prejudice to section 103. (8) of this Act, any solicitor who has, by virtue of section 25. A (rights of audience) of the M4. Solicitors (Scotland) Act 1980, a right of audience in relation to the High Court of Justiciary shall have the same right of audience in that court as is enjoyed by an advocate.

(2) Any person who has complied with the terms of a scheme approved under section 26 of the M5. Law Reform (Miscellaneous Provisions) (Scotland) Act 1990 (consideration of applications made under section 25) shall have such rights of audience before the High Court of Justiciary as may be specified in an Act of Adjournal made under subsection (7)(b) of that section.

Marginal Citations

M41980 c.46.

M51990 c.40.

[F102. Recovery of documentsS

Amendments (Textual)

F102. S. 301. A and cross-heading inserted (10.12.2007) by Criminal Proceedings etc. (Reform) (Scotland) Act 2007 (asp 6), ss. 37, 84; S.S.I. 2007/479, art. 3. (1), Sch. (subject to art. 10) (as amended by S.S.I. 2007/527)

301. ARecovery of documentsS

(1) It is competent for the sheriff court to make, in connection with any criminal proceedings mentioned in subsection (2) below, the orders mentioned in subsection (3) below.

(2) The proceedings are—

(a) solemn proceedings in that sheriff court;

(b) summary proceedings—

(i) in that sheriff court;

(ii) in any JP court in that sheriff court's district.

(3) The orders are—

(a) an order granting commission and diligence for the recovery of documents;

(b) an order for the production of documents.

(4) An application for the purpose may not be made—

(a) in connection with solemn proceedings, until the indictment has been served on the accused or the accused has been cited under section 66. (4)(b) of this Act;

(b) in connection with summary proceedings, until the accused has answered the complaint.

(5) A decision of the sheriff on an application for an order under subsection (1) above may be appealed to the [F103appropriate Appeal Court].

(6) In an appeal under subsection (5) above, the [F104appropriate Appeal Court] may uphold, vary or quash the decision of the sheriff.

(7) The prosecutor is entitled to be heard in any—

(a) application for an order under subsection (1) above;

(b) appeal under subsection (5) above,

even if the prosecutor is not a party to the application or (as the case may be) appeal.

(8) The competence of the High Court to make, in connection with criminal proceedings, the orders mentioned in subsection (3) above is restricted to making them in connection with proceedings in that court.

[F105. (9)In this section, "appropriate Appeal Court" means—

(a) in the case of an appeal under subsection (5) against a decision made in solemn proceedings, the High Court;

(b) in the case of an appeal under subsection (5) against a decision made in summary proceedings, the Sheriff Appeal Court.]]

Amendments (Textual)

F103. Words in s. 301. A(5) substituted (22.9.2015) by The Courts Reform (Scotland) Act 2014 (Consequential Provisions No. 2) Order 2015 (S.S.I. 2015/338), art. 1, sch. 2 para. 5. (20)(a) (with art. 4)

F104. Words in s. 301. A(6) substituted (22.9.2015) by The Courts Reform (Scotland) Act 2014 (Consequential Provisions No. 2) Order 2015 (S.S.I. 2015/338), art. 1, sch. 2 para. 5. (20)(a) (with art. 4)

F105. S. 301. A(9) inserted (22.9.2015) by The Courts Reform (Scotland) Act 2014 (Consequential Provisions No. 2) Order 2015 (S.S.I. 2015/338), art. 1, sch. 2 para. 5. (20)(b) (with art. 4)

Modifications etc. (not altering text)

C10. S. 301. A(2)(b)(ii) applied (10.12.2007) by The District Courts and Justices of the Peace (Scotland) Order 2007 (S.S.I. 2007/480), art. 4. (1)(d)

Fixed penalties

302 Fixed penalty: conditional offer by procurator fiscal.S

(1) Where a procurator fiscal receives a report that a relevant offence has been committed he may send to the alleged offender a notice under this section (referred to in this section as a conditional offer); and where he issues a conditional offer the procurator fiscal shall notify the clerk of court specified in it of the issue of the conditional offer and of its terms.

(2) A conditional offer—

(a) shall give such particulars of the circumstances alleged to constitute the offence to which it relates as are necessary for giving reasonable information about the alleged offence;

(b) shall state—

(i) the amount of the appropriate fixed penalty for that offence;

[F106. (ii)if the penalty is to be payable by instalments, the amount of the instalments and the intervals at which they should be paid;] F107. . .

(iii) F107 . . .

(c) shall indicate that if, within 28 days of the date on which the conditional offer was issued, or such longer period as may be specified in the conditional offer, the alleged offender accepts the offer by making payment [F108in respect of the fixed penalty] to the clerk of court specified in the conditional offer at the address therein mentioned, any liability to conviction of the offence shall be discharged;

[F109. (ca)shall indicate—

(i) that the alleged offender may refuse the conditional offer by giving notice to the clerk of court in the manner specified in the conditional offer before the expiry of 28 days, or such longer period as may be specified in the conditional offer, beginning on the day on which the conditional offer is made;

(ii) that unless the alleged offender gives such notice, the alleged offender will be deemed to have accepted the conditional offer (even where no payment is made in respect of the offer);

(iii) that where the alleged offender is deemed as described in sub-paragraph (ii) above to have accepted the conditional offer any liability to conviction of the offence shall be discharged except where the offer is recalled under section 302. C of this Act;]

(d) shall state that proceedings against the alleged offender shall not be commenced in respect of that offence until the end of a period of 28 days from the date on which the conditional offer was issued, or such longer period as may be specified in the conditional offer; F110. . .

[F111. (e)shall state—

(i) that the acceptance of the offer in the manner described in paragraph (c) above, or deemed acceptance of the offer as described in paragraph (ca)(ii) above, shall not be a conviction nor be recorded as such;

(ii) that the fact that the offer has been accepted, or deemed to have been accepted, may be disclosed to the court in any proceedings for an offence committed by the alleged offender within the period of two years beginning on the day of acceptance of the offer;

[F112. (iia)that that fact may be disclosed to the court also in any proceedings for an offence to which the alleged offender is, or is liable to become, subject at such time as the offer is accepted;]

(iii) that if the offer is not accepted, that fact may be disclosed to the court in any proceedings for the offence to which the conditional offer relates;

(f) shall state that refusal of a conditional offer under paragraph (ca)(i) above will be treated as a request by the alleged offender to be tried for the offence; and

(g) shall explain the right to request a recall of the fixed penalty under section 302. C of this Act.]

(3) A conditional offer may be made in respect of more than one relevant offence and shall, in such a case, state the amount of the appropriate fixed penalty for all the offences in respect of which it is made.

[F113. (4)The clerk of court shall—

(a) without delay, notify the procurator fiscal who issued the conditional offer when a notice as described in subsection (2)(ca)(i) above has been received in respect of the offer; or

(b) following the expiry of the period of 28 days referred to in subsection (2)(c) above or such longer period as may be specified in the offer, notify the procurator fiscal if no such notice has been received.]

[F114. (4. A)A conditional offer is accepted by the alleged offender making any payment in respect of the appropriate fixed penalty.

(4. B)Where an alleged offender to whom a conditional offer of a fixed penalty is made does not give notice as described in subsection (2)(ca)(i) above, the alleged offender is deemed to have accepted the conditional offer.

(4. C)Where—

(a) an alleged offender accepts a conditional offer as described in subsection (4. A) above; or

(b) an alleged offender is deemed to have accepted a conditional offer under subsection (4. B) above and the fixed penalty is not recalled,

no proceedings shall be brought against the alleged offender for the offence.]

(5) F115. . . . .

(6) F115. . . . .

(7) The Secretary of State shall, by order, prescribe a scale of fixed penalties for the purpose of this section F116. . . .

[F117. (7. A)The amount of the maximum penalty on the scale prescribed under subsection (7) above may not exceed £300 or such higher sum as the Scottish Ministers may by order specify.]

(8) An order under subsection (7) [F118or (7. A)] above—

(a) may contain provision as to the payment of fixed penalties by instalments; and

(b) shall be made by statutory instrument, which shall [F119not be made unless a draft of the instrument has been laid before, and approved by resolution of, the Scottish Parliament].

[F120. (8. A)The alleged offender shall be presumed to have received a conditional offer under subsection (1) above if the offer is sent to—

(a) the address given by the alleged offender in a request for recall under section 302. C(1) of this Act of an earlier offer in the same matter; or

(b) any address given by the alleged offender to the clerk of court specified in the offer, or to the procurator fiscal, in connection with the offer.

(8. B)For the purposes of section 141. (4) of this Act, the accused shall be presumed to have received any citation effected at—

(a) the address to which a conditional offer under subsection (1) above was sent provided it is proved that the accused received the offer; or

(b) any address given by the accused to the clerk of court specified in the offer, or to the procurator fiscal, in connection with the offer.]

(9) In this section—

(a) "a relevant offence" means any offence in respect of which an alleged offender could [F121be tried summarily], but shall not include a fixed penalty offence within the meaning of section 51 of the M6. Road Traffic Offenders Act 1988 nor any other offence in respect of which a conditional offer within the meaning of sections 75 to 77 of that Act may be sent ; and

(b) "the appropriate fixed penalty" means such fixed penalty on the scale prescribed under subsection (7) above as the procurator fiscal thinks fit having regard to the circumstances of the case.

Amendments (Textual)

F106. S. 302. (2)(b)(ii) substituted (10.3.2008) by Criminal Proceedings etc. (Reform) (Scotland) Act 2007 (asp 6), ss. 50. (1)(a)(i), 84; S.S.I. 2008/42, art. 3, Sch. (subject to arts. 4 - 6)

F107. S. 302. (2)(b)(iii) and preceding word repealed (10.3.2008) by Criminal Proceedings etc. (Reform) (Scotland) Act 2007 (asp 6), ss. 50. (1)(a)(ii), 84; S.S.I. 2008/42, art. 3, Sch. (subject to arts. 4 - 6)

F108. Words in s. 302. (2)(c) substituted (10.3.2008) by Criminal Proceedings etc. (Reform) (Scotland) Act 2007 (asp 6), ss. 50. (1)(a)(iii), 84; S.S.I. 2008/42, art. 3, Sch. (subject to arts. 4 - 6)

F109. S. 302. (2)(ca) inserted (10.3.2008) by Criminal Proceedings etc. (Reform) (Scotland) Act 2007 (asp 6), ss. 50. (1)(a)(iv), 84; S.S.I. 2008/42, art. 3, Sch. (subject to arts. 4 - 6)

F110. Word immediately following s. 302. (2)(d) repealed (10.3.2008) by Criminal Proceedings etc. (Reform) (Scotland) Act 2007 (asp 6), ss. 50. (1)(a)(v), 84; S.S.I. 2008/42, art. 3, Sch. (subject to arts. 4 - 6)

F111. S. 302. (2)(e)-(g) substituted (10.3.2008) for s. 302. (2)(e) by Criminal Proceedings etc. (Reform) (Scotland) Act 2007 (asp 6), ss. 50. (1)(a)(vi), 84; S.S.I. 2008/42, art. 3, Sch. (subject to arts. 4 - 6)

F112. S. 302. (2)(e)(iia) inserted (28.3.2011) by Criminal Justice and Licensing (Scotland) Act 2010 (asp 13), ss. 70. (3), 206. (1); S.S.I. 2011/178, art. 2, sch.

F113. S. 302. (4) substituted (10.3.2008) by Criminal Proceedings etc. (Reform) (Scotland) Act 2007 (asp 6), ss. 50. (1)(b), 84; S.S.I. 2008/42, art. 3, Sch. (subject to arts. 4 - 6)

F114. S. 302. (4. A)-(4. C) inserted (10.3.2008) by Criminal Proceedings etc. (Reform) (Scotland) Act 2007 (asp 6), ss. 50. (1)(c), 84; S.S.I. 2008/42, art. 3, Sch. (subject to arts. 4 - 6)

F115. S. 302. (5)(6) repealed (10.3.2008) by Criminal Proceedings etc. (Reform) (Scotland) Act 2007 (asp 6), ss. 50. (1)(d), 84; S.S.I. 2008/42, art. 3, Sch. (subject to arts. 4 - 6)

F116. Words in s. 302. (7) repealed (10.3.2008) by Criminal Proceedings etc. (Reform) (Scotland) Act 2007 (asp 6), ss. 50. (1)(e), 84; S.S.I. 2008/42, art. 3, Sch. (subject to arts. 4 - 6)

F117. S. 302. (7. A) inserted (10.3.2008) by Criminal Proceedings etc. (Reform) (Scotland) Act 2007 (asp 6), ss. 50. (1)(f), 84; S.S.I. 2008/42, art. 3, Sch. (subject to arts. 4 - 6)

F118. Words in s. 302. (8) inserted (10.3.2008) by Criminal Proceedings etc. (Reform) (Scotland) Act 2007 (asp 6), ss. 50. (1)(g)(i), 84; S.S.I. 2008/42, art. 3, Sch. (subject to arts. 4 - 6)
F119. Words in s. 302. (8)(b) substituted (10.3.2008) by Criminal Proceedings etc. (Reform) (Scotland) Act 2007 (asp 6), ss. 50. (1)(g)(ii), 84; S.S.I. 2008/42, art. 3, Sch. (subject to arts. 4 - 6)
F120. S. 302. (8. A)(8. B) inserted (10.3.2008) by Criminal Proceedings etc. (Reform) (Scotland) Act 2007 (asp 6), ss. 50. (1)(h), 84; S.S.I. 2008/42, art. 3, Sch. (subject to arts. 4 - 6)
F121. Words in s. 302. (9) substituted (10.3.2008) by Criminal Proceedings etc. (Reform) (Scotland) Act 2007 (asp 6), ss. 50. (1)(i), 84; S.S.I. 2008/42, art. 3, Sch. (subject to arts. 4 - 6)
Marginal Citations
M61988 c.53.

[F122302. ACompensation offer by procurator fiscalS

(1) Where a procurator fiscal receives a report that a relevant offence has been committed he may send to the alleged offender a notice under this section (referred to in this section as a compensation offer); and where he issues a compensation offer the procurator fiscal shall notify the clerk of court specified in it of the issue of the offer and of its terms.
(2) A compensation offer—
(a) shall give such particulars of the circumstances alleged to constitute the offence to which it relates as are necessary for giving reasonable information about the alleged offence;
(b) shall state—
(i) the amount of compensation payable;
(ii) if the compensation is to be payable by instalments, the amount of the instalments and the intervals at which they should be paid;
(c) shall indicate that if, within 28 days of the date on which the offer was issued, or such longer period as may be specified in the offer, the alleged offender accepts the offer by making payment in respect of the offer to the clerk of court specified in the offer at the address therein mentioned, any liability to conviction of the offence shall be discharged;
(d) shall indicate—
(i) that the alleged offender may refuse the offer by giving notice to the clerk of court in the manner specified in the offer before the expiry of 28 days, or such longer period as may be specified in the offer, beginning on the day on which the offer is made;
(ii) that unless the alleged offender gives such notice, the alleged offender will be deemed to have accepted the offer (even where no payment is made in respect of the offer);
(iii) that where the alleged offender is deemed as described in sub-paragraph (ii) above to have accepted the offer any liability to conviction of the offence shall be discharged except where the offer is recalled under section 302. C of this Act;
(e) shall state that proceedings against the alleged offender shall not be commenced in respect of that offence until the end of a period of 28 days from the date on which the offer was made, or such longer period as may be specified in the offer;
(f) shall state—
(i) that the acceptance of the offer in the manner described in paragraph (c) above, or deemed acceptance of the offer as described in paragraph (d)(ii) above, shall not be a conviction nor be recorded as such;
(ii) that the fact that the offer has been accepted, or deemed to have been accepted, may be disclosed to the court in any proceedings for an offence committed by the alleged offender within the period of two years beginning on the day of acceptance of the offer;
[F123. (iia)that that fact may be disclosed to the court also in any proceedings for an offence to which the alleged offender is, or is liable to become, subject at such time as the offer is accepted;]
(iii) that if the offer is not accepted, that fact may be disclosed to the court in any proceedings for the offence to which the offer relates;
(g) shall state that refusal of an offer under paragraph (d)(i) above will be treated as a request by

the alleged offender to be tried for the offence; and

(h) shall explain the right to request a recall of the offer under section 302. C of this Act.

(3) A compensation offer may be made in respect of more than one relevant offence and shall, in such a case, state the amount payable in respect of the offer for all the offences in relation to which it is issued.

(4) The clerk of court shall—

(a) without delay, notify the procurator fiscal who issued the compensation offer when a notice as described in subsection (2)(d)(i) above has been received in respect of the offer; or

(b) following the expiry of the period of 28 days referred to in subsection (2)(c) above or such longer period as may be specified in the offer, notify the procurator fiscal if no such notice has been received.

(5) A compensation offer is accepted by the alleged offender making any payment in respect of the offer.

(6) Where an alleged offender to whom a compensation offer is made does not give notice as described in subsection (2)(d)(i) above, the alleged offender is deemed to have accepted the offer.

(7) Where—

(a) an alleged offender accepts a compensation offer as described in subsection (5) above; or

(b) an alleged offender is deemed to have accepted a compensation offer under subsection (6) above and the offer is not recalled,

no proceedings shall be brought against the alleged offender for the offence.

(8) The Scottish Ministers shall by order prescribe the maximum amount of a compensation offer; but that amount shall not exceed level 5 on the standard scale.

(9) An order under subsection (8) above shall be made by statutory instrument; and any such instrument shall be subject to annulment in pursuance of a resolution of the Scottish Parliament.

(10) The alleged offender shall be presumed to have received a compensation offer under subsection (1) above if the offer is sent to—

(a) the address given by the alleged offender in a request for recall under section 302. C(1) of this Act of an earlier offer in the same matter; or

(b) any address given by the alleged offender to the clerk of court specified in the offer, or to the procurator fiscal, in connection with the offer.

(11) For the purposes of section 141. (4) of this Act, the accused shall be presumed to have received any citation effected at—

(a) the address to which a compensation offer under subsection (1) above was sent provided it is proved that the accused received the offer; or

(b) any address given by the accused to the clerk of court specified in the offer, or to the procurator fiscal, in connection with the offer.

(12) The clerk of court shall account for the amount paid under a compensation offer to the person entitled thereto.

(13) In this section, a "relevant offence" means any offence—

(a) in respect of which an alleged offender could be tried summarily; and

(b) on conviction of which it would be competent for the court to make a compensation order under section 249 of this Act.

Amendments (Textual)

F122. Ss. 302. A-302. C inserted (10.3.2008) by Criminal Proceedings etc. (Reform) (Scotland) Act 2007 (asp 6), ss. 50. (2), 84; S.S.I. 2008/42, art. 3, Sch.

F123. S. 302. A(2)(f)(iia) inserted (28.3.2011) by Criminal Justice and Licensing (Scotland) Act 2010 (asp 13), ss. 70. (4), 206. (1); S.S.I. 2011/178, art. 2, sch.

302. BCombined fixed penalty and compensation offerS

(1) The procurator fiscal may send to an alleged offender a notice under sections 302. (1) and 302. A(1) of this Act in respect of the same relevant offence (referred to in this section as a "combined

offer").

(2) A combined offer shall be contained in the one notice.

(3) In addition to the information required to be provided under sections 302. (2) and 302. A(2) of this Act, the combined offer shall state—

(a) that the combined offer consists of both a fixed penalty offer and a compensation offer;

(b) the whole amount of the combined offer; and

(c) that liability to conviction of the offence shall not be discharged unless the whole of the combined offer is accepted.

(4) Any acceptance or deemed acceptance of part of a combined offer shall be treated as applying to the whole of the offer.

Amendments (Textual)

F122. Ss. 302. A-302. C inserted (10.3.2008) by Criminal Proceedings etc. (Reform) (Scotland) Act 2007 (asp 6), ss. 50. (2), 84; S.S.I. 2008/42, art. 3, Sch.

302. CRecall of fixed penalty or compensation offerS

(1) Where an alleged offender is deemed to have accepted—

(a) a fixed penalty offer by virtue of section 302. (2)(ca)(ii) of this Act; or

(b) a compensation offer by virtue of section 302. A(2)(d)(ii) of this Act,

the alleged offender may request that it be recalled.

(2) A request for recall under subsection (1) above is valid only if—

(a) the alleged offender claims that he—

(i) did not receive the offer concerned; and

(ii) would (if he had received it) have refused the offer; or

(b) the alleged offender claims that—

(i) although he received the offer concerned, it was not practicable by reason of exceptional circumstances for him to give notice of refusal of the offer; and

(ii) he would (but for those circumstances) have refused the offer.

(3) A request for recall of a fixed penalty offer or a compensation offer requires to be made—

(a) to the clerk of court referred to in the offer; and

(b) no later than 7 days after the expiry of the period specified in the offer for payment of the fixed penalty or compensation offer or, where a notice is sent in pursuance of section 303. (1. A)(a) of this Act, no later than 7 days after it is sent.

(4) The clerk of court may, on cause shown by reference to subsection (2) above, consider a request for recall of such an offer despite its being made outwith the time limit applying by virtue of subsection (3)(b) above.

(5) The clerk of court may, following receipt of such a request—

(a) uphold the fixed penalty offer or compensation offer; or

(b) recall it.

(6) The alleged offender may, within 7 days of a decision under subsection (5)(a) above, apply to the court specified in the offer for a review of the decision (including as it involves a question which arose by reference to subsections (2) to (4) above).

(7) In a review under subsection (6) above, the court may—

(a) confirm or quash the decision of the clerk;

(b) in either case, give such direction to the clerk as the court considers appropriate.

(8) The decision of the court in a review under subsection (6) above shall be final.

(9) The clerk of court shall, without delay, notify the procurator fiscal of—

(a) a request for recall under subsection (1) above;

(b) an application for review under subsection (6) above;

(c) any decision under subsection (5) or (7) above.

(10) For the purposes of this section, a certificate given by the procurator fiscal as to the date on which a fixed penalty offer or compensation order was sent shall be sufficient evidence of that

fact.]

Amendments (Textual)
F122. Ss. 302. A-302. C inserted (10.3.2008) by Criminal Proceedings etc. (Reform) (Scotland) Act 2007 (asp 6), ss. 50. (2), 84; S.S.I. 2008/42, art. 3, Sch.

303 Fixed penalty: enforcement.

[F124. (1)Subject to subsections (1. A) and (2) below, where an alleged offender accepts a fixed penalty offer under section 302 of this Act or a compensation offer under section 302. A of this Act, any amount of it which is outstanding at any time shall be treated as if the penalty or offer were a fine imposed by the court (the clerk of which is specified in the notice).]

[F125. (1. A)No action shall be taken to enforce a fixed penalty or compensation offer which an alleged offender is deemed to have accepted by virtue of section 302. (2)(ca)(ii) or section 302. A(2)(d)(ii) of this Act unless—

(a) the alleged offender is sent a notice—

(i) of the intention to take enforcement action; and

(ii) which explains the right to request a recall of the penalty or offer under section 302. C of this Act;

(b) any request for recall made under that section has been finally disposed of.]

(2) In the enforcement of a [F126fixed penalty or compensation offer] which is to be treated as a fine in pursuance of subsection (1) above—

(a) any reference, howsoever expressed, in any enactment whether passed or made before or after the coming into force of this section to—

(i) the imposition of imprisonment or detention in default of payment of a fine shall be construed as a reference to enforcement by means of civil diligence;

(ii) the finding or order of the court imposing the fine shall be construed as a reference to a certificate given in pursuance of subsection (3) below;

(iii) the offender shall be construed as a reference to the alleged offender;

(iv) the conviction of the offender shall be construed as a reference to the acceptance of the conditional offer by the alleged offender;

(b) the following sections of this Act shall not apply—

section 211. (7)

section 213. (2);

section 214. (1) to (6);

section 216. (7);

section 219, except subsection (1)(b);

section 220;

section 221. (2) to (4);

section 222. (8); and

section 224.

(3) For the purposes of any proceedings in connection with, or steps taken for, the enforcement of any amount of a fixed penalty [F127or compensation offer] which is outstanding, a document purporting to be a certificate signed by the clerk of court for the time being responsible for the collection or enforcement of the penalty as to any mater relating to the penalty shall be conclusive of the matter so certified.

(4) The Secretary of State may, by order made by statutory instrument subject to annulment in pursuance of a resolution of either House of Parliament, make such provision as he considers necessary for the enforcement in England and Wales F128. . . of any penalty, treated in pursuance of subsection (1) above as a fine, which is transferred as a fine to a court in England and Wales F128. . . .

[F129. (5)The Department of Justice in Northern Ireland may by order make such provision as it considers necessary for the enforcement in Northern Ireland of any penalty, treated in pursuance of subsection (1) above as a fine, which is transferred as a fine to a court in Northern Ireland.

(6) The power of the Department of Justice to make an order under subsection (5) is exercisable by statutory rule for the purposes of the Statutory Rules (Northern Ireland) Order 1979.

(7) An order made by the Department of Justice under subsection (5) is subject to negative resolution (within the meaning of section 41. (6) of the Interpretation Act (Northern Ireland) 1954).]

Extent Information

E2. S. 303. (4) extends to UK.

Amendments (Textual)

F124. S. 303. (1) substituted (10.3.2008 for S.) by Criminal Proceedings etc. (Reform) (Scotland) Act 2007 (asp 6), ss. 50. (3)(a), 84; S.S.I. 2008/42, art. 3, Sch. (subject to arts. 4 - 6)

F125. S. 303. (1. A) inserted (10.3.2008) by Criminal Proceedings etc. (Reform) (Scotland) Act 2007 (asp 6), ss. 50. (3)(b), 84; S.S.I. 2008/42, art. 3, Sch.

F126. Words in s. 303. (2) substituted (10.3.2008) by Criminal Proceedings etc. (Reform) (Scotland) Act 2007 (asp 6), ss. 50. (3)(c), 84; S.S.I. 2008/42, art. 3, Sch.

F127. Words in s. 303. (3) inserted (10.3.2008) by Criminal Proceedings etc. (Reform) (Scotland) Act 2007 (asp 6), ss. 50. (3)(d), 84; S.S.I. 2008/42, art. 3, Sch.

F128. Words in s. 303. (4) omitted (12.4.2010) by virtue of The Northern Ireland Act 1998 (Devolution of Policing and Justice Functions) Order 2010 (S.I. 2010/976), arts. 1. (2), 12, Sch. 14 para. 32. (2)(a) (with arts. 28-31); S.I. 2010/977, art. 1. (2)

F129. S. 303. (5)-(7) inserted (12.4.2010) by The Northern Ireland Act 1998 (Devolution of Policing and Justice Functions) Order 2010 (S.I. 2010/976), arts. 1. (2), 12, Sch. 14 para. 32. (2)(b) (with arts. 28-31); S.I. 2010/977, art. 1. (2)

[F130303. ZAWork ordersS

(1) Where a procurator fiscal receives a report that a relevant offence has been committed he may send the alleged offender a notice under this section (referred to in this section as a work offer) which offers the alleged offender the opportunity of performing unpaid work.

(2) The total number of hours of unpaid work shall be not less than 10 nor more than 50.

(3) A work offer—

(a) shall give such particulars of the circumstances alleged to constitute the offence to which it relates as are necessary for giving reasonable information about the alleged offence;

(b) shall state—

(i) the number of hours of unpaid work which the alleged offender is required to perform;

(ii) the date by which that work requires to be completed;

(c) shall indicate that if the alleged offender—

(i) accepts the work offer; and

(ii) completes the work to the satisfaction of the supervising officer,

any liability to conviction of the offence shall be discharged;

(d) shall state that proceedings against the alleged offender shall not be commenced in respect of that offence until the end of a period of 28 days from the date on which the offer was issued, or such longer period as may be specified in the offer;

(e) shall state—

(i) that acceptance of a work offer in the manner described in subsection (5) below shall not be a conviction nor be recorded as such;

[F131. (ia)that if a work offer is not accepted, that fact may be disclosed to the court in any proceedings for the offence to which the offer relates;]

(ii) that the fact that [F132a resultant work order has been completed] may be disclosed to the court in any proceedings for an offence committed by the alleged offender within the period of two years beginning on the day of acceptance of the offer;

[F133. (iia)that that fact may be disclosed to the court also in any proceedings for an offence to

515

which the alleged offender is, or is liable to become, subject at such time as the offer is accepted;]

(iii) that if a [F134resultant work order] is not completed, that fact may be disclosed to the court in any proceedings for the offence to which the order relates.

(4) A work offer may be made in respect of more than one relevant offence and shall, in such a case, state the total amount of work requiring to be performed in respect of the offences in relation to which it is made.

(5) An alleged offender accepts a work offer by giving notice to the procurator fiscal specified in the order before the expiry of 28 days, or such longer period as may be specified in the offer, beginning on the day on which the offer is made.

(6) If (and only if) the alleged offender accepts a work offer, the procurator fiscal may make an order (referred to in this section as a work order) against the alleged offender.

(7) Notice of a work order—

(a) shall be sent to the alleged offender as soon as reasonably practicable after acceptance of the work offer; and

(b) shall contain—

(i) the information mentioned in subsection (3)(b) above; and

(ii) the name and contact details of the person who is to act as supervisor ("the supervising officer") in relation to the alleged offender.

(8) The procurator fiscal shall notify the local authority which will be responsible for supervision of an alleged offender of the terms of any work order sent to the alleged offender.

(9) Where a work order is made, the supervising officer shall—

(a) determine the nature of the work which the alleged offender requires to perform;

(b) determine the times and places at which the alleged offender is to perform that work;

(c) give directions to the alleged offender in relation to that work;

(d) provide the procurator fiscal with such information as the procurator fiscal may require in relation to the alleged offender's conduct in connection with the requirements of the order.

(10) In giving directions under subsection (9)(c) above, a supervising officer shall, so far as practicable, avoid—

(a) any conflict with the alleged offender's religious beliefs;

(b) any interference with the times at which the alleged offender normally—

(i) works (or carries out voluntary work); or

(ii) attends an educational establishment.

(11) The supervising officer shall, on or as soon as practicable after the date referred to in subsection (3)(b)(ii) above, notify the procurator fiscal whether or not the work has been performed to the supervising officer's satisfaction.

(12) Where an alleged offender completes the work specified in the work order to the satisfaction of the supervising officer, no proceedings shall be brought against the alleged offender for the offence.

(13) The Scottish Ministers may, by regulations, make provision for the purposes of subsection (9) above (including, in particular, the kinds of activity of which the work requiring to be performed may (or may not) consist).

(14) Regulations under subsection (13) above shall be made by statutory instrument which shall be subject to annulment in pursuance of a resolution of the Scottish Parliament.

(15) For the purposes of section 141. (4) of this Act, the accused shall be presumed to have received any citation effected at—

(a) the address to which a work offer was sent provided it is proved that the accused received the offer; or

(b) any address given, in connection with the offer, by the accused to the procurator fiscal specified in the offer.

(16) In this section, a "relevant offence" means any offence in respect of which an alleged offender could be tried summarily.]

Amendments (Textual)

F130. S. 303. ZA inserted (2.6.2008 for specified purposes, 1.4.2011 for specified purposes) by

Criminal Proceedings etc. (Reform) (Scotland) Act 2007 (asp 6), ss. 51, 84. (1); S.S.I. 2008/192, art. 3, sch.; S.S.I. 2011/188, art. 2

F131. S. 303. ZA(3)(e)(ia) inserted (28.3.2011) by Criminal Justice and Licensing (Scotland) Act 2010 (asp 13), ss. 70. (5)(a), 206. (1); S.S.I. 2011/178, art. 2, sch.

F132. Words in s. 303. ZA(3)(e)(ii) substituted (28.3.2011) by Criminal Justice and Licensing (Scotland) Act 2010 (asp 13), ss. 70. (5)(b), 206. (1); S.S.I. 2011/178, art. 2, sch.

F133. S. 303. ZA(3)(e)(iia) inserted (28.3.2011) by Criminal Justice and Licensing (Scotland) Act 2010 (asp 13), ss. 70. (5)(c), 206. (1); S.S.I. 2011/178, art. 2, sch.

F134. Words in s. 303. ZA(3)(e)(iii) substituted (28.3.2011) by Criminal Justice and Licensing (Scotland) Act 2010 (asp 13), ss. 70. (5)(d), 206. (1); S.S.I. 2011/178, art. 2, sch.

[F135303. ZBSetting aside of offers and ordersS

(1) Where this subsection applies, the procurator fiscal may set aside—
    (a) a fixed penalty offer made under section 302. (1) of this Act;
    (b) a compensation offer made under section 302. A(1) of this Act;
    (c) a work offer made under section 303. ZA(1) of this Act;
    (d) a work order made under section 303. ZA(6) of this Act.

(2) Subsection (1) above applies where, on the basis of information which comes to the procurator fiscal's attention after the offer or (as the case may be) order has been made, the procurator fiscal considers that the offer or (as the case may be) order should not have been made in respect of the alleged offender.

(3) The procurator fiscal may act under subsection (1)(a) to (c) above even where the offer has been accepted (including, in the case of an offer mentioned in subsection (1)(a) or (b) above, deemed to have been accepted).

(4) Where the procurator fiscal acts under subsection (1) above, the procurator fiscal shall give the alleged offender notice—
    (a) of the setting aside of the offer or (as the case may be) order; and
    (b) indicating that any liability of the alleged offender to conviction of the alleged offence is discharged.]

Amendments (Textual)
F135. S. 303. ZB inserted (10.3.2008) by Criminal Proceedings etc. (Reform) (Scotland) Act 2007 (asp 6), ss. 52, 84; S.S.I. 2008/42, art. 3, Sch. (subject to arts. 4 - 6)

[F136 Transfer of rights of appeal of deceased person]

Amendments (Textual)
F136. S. 303. A and preceding cross-heading inserted (1.8.1997 for specified purposes and otherwise 1.4.1999) by 1997 c. 48, s. 20; S.I. 1997/1712, art. 3, Sch. (subject to arts. 4, 5); S.I. 1999/652, art. 2, Sch.(subject to savings and transitional provisions in art. 3)

303. A[F137 Transfer of rights of appeal of deceased person.]

(1) Where a person convicted of an offence has died, any person may, subject to the provisions of this section, apply to the [F138appropriate Appeal Court] for an order authorising him to institute or continue any appeal which could have been or has been instituted by the deceased.

(2) An application for an order under this section may be lodged with the [F139clerk of the appropriate Appeal Court] within three months of the deceased's death or at such later time as the [F140appropriate Appeal Court] may, on cause shown, allow.

(3) Where the Commission makes a reference to the High Court under section 194. B of this Act in respect of a person who is deceased, any application under this section must be made within one

month of the reference.

(4) Where an application is made for an order under this section and the applicant—

(a) is an executor of the deceased; or

(b) otherwise appears to the [F141appropriate Appeal Court] to have a legitimate interest, the [F141appropriate Appeal Court] shall make an order authorising the applicant to institute or continue any appeal which could have been instituted or continued by the deceased; and, subject to the provisions of this section, any such order may include such ancillary or supplementary provision as the [F141appropriate Appeal Court] thinks fit.

(5) The person in whose favour an order under this section is made shall from the date of the order be afforded the same rights to carry on the appeal as the deceased enjoyed at the time of his death and, in particular, where any time limit had begun to run against the deceased the person in whose favour an order has been made shall have the benefit of only that portion of the time limit which remained unexpired at the time of the death.

(6) In this section "appeal" includes any sort of application, whether at common law or under statute, for the review of any conviction, penalty or other order made in respect of the deceased in any criminal proceedings whatsoever.

[F142. (7)In this section—

"appropriate Appeal Court" means—

- in the case of an appeal proposed to be instituted or continued before the High Court, the High Court;

- in the case of an appeal proposed to be instituted or continued before the Sheriff Appeal Court, the Sheriff Appeal Court; and

"the clerk of the appropriate Appeal Court" means—

- in a case where the High Court is the appropriate Appeal Court, the Clerk of Justiciary;

- in a case where the Sheriff Appeal Court is the appropriate Appeal Court, the Clerk of that Court.]

Amendments (Textual)

F137. S. 303. A and preceding cross-heading inserted (1.8.1997 for specified purposes and otherwise 1.4.1999) by 1997 c. 48, s. 20; S.I. 1997/1712, art. 3, Sch. (subject to arts. 4, 5); S.I. 1999/652, art. 2, Sch.(subject to savings and transitional provisions in art. 3)

F138. Words in s. 303. A(1) substituted (22.9.2015) by The Courts Reform (Scotland) Act 2014 (Consequential Provisions No. 2) Order 2015 (S.S.I. 2015/338), art. 1, sch. 2 para. 5. (21)(a) (with art. 4)

F139. Words in s. 303. A(2) substituted (22.9.2015) by The Courts Reform (Scotland) Act 2014 (Consequential Provisions No. 2) Order 2015 (S.S.I. 2015/338), art. 1, sch. 2 para. 5. (21)(b) (with art. 4)

F140. Words in s. 303. A(2) substituted (22.9.2015) by The Courts Reform (Scotland) Act 2014 (Consequential Provisions No. 2) Order 2015 (S.S.I. 2015/338), art. 1, sch. 2 para. 5. (21)(c) (with art. 4)

F141. Words in s. 303. A(4) substituted (22.9.2015) by The Courts Reform (Scotland) Act 2014 (Consequential Provisions No. 2) Order 2015 (S.S.I. 2015/338), art. 1, sch. 2 para. 5. (21)(c) (with art. 4)

F142. S. 303. A(7) inserted (22.9.2015) by The Courts Reform (Scotland) Act 2014 (Consequential Provisions No. 2) Order 2015 (S.S.I. 2015/338), art. 1, sch. 2 para. 5. (21)(d) (with art. 4)

[F143. Electronic proceedingsS

Amendments (Textual)

F143. S. 303. B and cross-heading inserted (10.12.2007 for certain purposes and 1.11.2012 in so far as not already in force) by Criminal Proceedings etc. (Reform) (Scotland) Act 2007 (asp 6), ss. 41. (1), 84; S.S.I. 2007/479, art. 3. (1), Sch. (as amended by S.S.I. 2007/527); S.S.I 2012/274, art.

303. BElectronic summary proceedingsS

(1) For the purposes of section 138. (1) of this Act—
   (a) institution of proceedings may be effected by electronic complaint;
   (b) the requirement for signing is satisfied in relation to an electronic complaint by an electronic signature;
   (c) the requirement for signing may be satisfied in relation to any other complaint by an electronic signature.
(2) The references in the other provisions of this Act to a complaint include an electronic complaint unless the context otherwise requires.
(3) Where proceedings are instituted by electronic complaint, in the event of any conflict between—
   (a) the principal electronic complaint kept by the clerk of court for the purposes of the proceedings; and
   (b) any other document (whether in electronic or other form) purporting to be the complaint, the principal electronic complaint prevails.
(4) The requirement in section 85. (4) of this Act for signing may be satisfied by electronic signature.
(5) The requirement in section 136. B(2) of this Act for signing may be satisfied by electronic signature.
(6) The requirement in section 141. (3)(a) of this Act for signing may be satisfied by electronic signature.
(7) The requirement in section 159. (3) of this Act for authentication by initials is satisfied in relation to an electronic complaint by authentication by electronic signature.
(8) The requirements in section 172. (2) of this Act for signing by the clerk of court may be satisfied by electronic signature.
(9) The requirements in section 258. (2) and (9) of this Act for signing may be satisfied in relation to summary proceedings by electronic signature.
(10) The requirement in section 299. (5) of this Act for authentication by signature is satisfied in relation to—
   (a) proceedings which are recorded in electronic form;
   (b) any extract of sentence, or order made, which is recorded in electronic form,
by authentication by electronic signature.]

PART XIV General

PART XIV General

304 Criminal Courts Rules Council.S

(1) There shall be established a body, to be known as the Criminal Courts Rules Council (in this section referred to as "the Council") which shall have the functions conferred on it by subsection (9) below.
(2) The Council shall consist of—
   (a) the Lord Justice General, the Lord Justice Clerk and the Clerk of Justiciary;
   (b) a further Lord Commissioner of Justiciary appointed by the Lord Justice General;
   (c) the following persons appointed by the Lord Justice General after such consultation as he

considers appropriate—

[F1. (zi)one Appeal Sheriff;]

(i) two sheriffs;

(ii) two members of the Faculty of Advocates;

(iii) two solicitors;

(iv) one sheriff clerk; and

(v) one person appearing to him to have a knowledge of the procedures and practices of the [F2. JP court];

(d) two persons appointed by the Lord Justice General after consultation with the Lord Advocate, at least one of whom must be a procurator fiscal;

(e) two persons appointed by the Lord Justice General after consultation with the Secretary of State, at least one of whom must be a person appearing to the Lord Justice General to have—

(i) a knowledge of the procedures and practices of the courts exercising criminal jurisdiction in Scotland; and

(ii) an awareness of the interests of victims of crime and of witnesses in criminal proceedings; and

(f) any persons appointed under subsection (3) below.

(3) The Lord Justice General may appoint not more than two further persons, and the Secretary of State may appoint one person, to membership of the Council.

(4) The chairman of the Council shall be the Lord Justice General or such other member of the Council, being a Lord Commissioner of Justiciary, as the Lord Justice General may nominate.

(5) The members of the Council appointed under paragraphs (b) to (f) of subsection (2) above shall, so long as they retain the respective qualifications mentioned in those paragraphs, hold office for three years and be eligible for reappointment.

(6) Any vacancy in the membership of the Council by reason of the death or demission of office, prior to the expiry of the period for which he was appointed, of a member appointed under any of paragraphs (b) to (f) of subsection (2) above shall be filled by the appointment by the Lord Justice General or, as the case may be, the Secretary of State, after such consultation as is required by the paragraph in question, of another person having the qualifications required by that paragraph, and a person so appointed shall hold office only until the expiry of that period.

(7) The Council shall meet—

(a) at intervals of not more than 12 months; and

(b) at any time when summoned by the chairman or by three members of the Council,

but shall, subject to the foregoing, have power to regulate the summoning of its meetings and the procedure at such meetings.

(8) At any meeting of the Council six members shall be a quorum.

(9) The functions of the Council shall be—

(a) to keep under general review the procedures and practices of the courts exercising criminal jurisdiction in Scotland (including any matters incidental or relating to those procedures or practices); and

(b) to consider and comment on any draft Act of Adjournal submitted to it by the High Court, which shall, in making the Act of Adjournal, take account to such extent as it considers appropriate of any comments made by the Council under this paragraph.

(10) In the discharge of its functions under subsection (9) above the Council may invite representations on any aspect of the procedures and practices of the courts exercising criminal jurisdiction in Scotland (including any matters incidental or relating to those procedures or practices) and shall consider any such representations received by it, whether or not submitted in response to such an invitation.

Amendments (Textual)

F1. S. 304. (2)(c)(zi) inserted (22.9.2015) by Courts Reform (Scotland) Act 2014 (asp 18), s. 138. (2), sch. 5 para. 15; S.S.I. 2015/247, art. 2, sch.

F2. Words in s. 304. (2)(c)(v) substituted (10.3.2008 and 2.6.2008 for certain purposes, otherwise 8.12.2008) by Criminal Proceedings etc. (Reform) (Scotland) Act 2007 (asp 6), ss. 80, 84, Sch. para. 26. (t); S.S.I. 2008/42, art. 3, Sch.; S.S.I. 2008/192, art. 3, Sch.; S.S.I. 2008/329, art. 3, Sch.

305 Acts of Adjournal.S

(1) The High Court may by Act of Adjournal—

(a) regulate the practice and procedure in relation to criminal procedure;

(b) make such rules and regulations as may be necessary or expedient to carry out the purposes and accomplish the objects of any enactment (including an enactment in this Act) in so far as it relates to criminal procedure;

(c) subject to subsection (5) below, to fix and regulate the fees payable in connection with summary criminal proceedings; and

(d) to make provision for the application of sums paid under section 220 of this Act and for any matter incidental thereto.

[F3. (1. A)Subsection (1) above extends to making provision by Act of Adjournal for something to be done in electronic form or by electronic means.]

(2) The High Court may by Act of Adjournal modify, amend or repeal any enactment (including an enactment in this Act) in so far as that enactment relates to matters with respect to which an Act of Adjournal may be made under subsection (1) above.

(3) No rule, regulation or provision which affects the governor or any other officer of a prison shall be made by Act of Adjournal except with the consent of the Secretary of State.

(4) The Clerk of Justiciary may, with the sanction of the Lord Justice General and the Lord Justice Clerk, vary the forms set out in an Act of Adjournal made under subsection (1) above or any other Act whether passed before or after this Act from time to time as may be found necessary for giving effect to the provisions of this Act relating to solemn procedure.

(5) Nothing in paragraph (c) of subsection (1) above shall empower the High Court to make any [F4provision that the Scottish Ministers are empowered to make under section 107. (1) of the Courts Reform (Scotland) Act 2014].

Amendments (Textual)

F3. S. 305. (1. A) inserted (17.1.2017) by Criminal Justice (Scotland) Act 2016 (asp 1), ss. 111. (1), 117. (2); S.S.I. 2016/426, art. 2, sch.

F4. Words in s. 305. (5) substituted (22.9.2015) by The Courts Reform (Scotland) Act 2014 (Consequential Provisions No. 2) Order 2015 (S.S.I. 2015/338), arts. 1, 2

Modifications etc. (not altering text)

C1. S. 305 modified (27.7.2001) by 2001 asp 7, s. 4, Sch. paras. 68, 77 (with Sch. para. 65); S.S.I. 2001/274, art. 3. (1)(b)(c)(d)

C2. S. 305 modified (27.7.2001) by 1993 c. 9, s. 10. (2. U) (as substituted by 2001 asp 7, s. 3. (1)(b); S.S.I. 2001/274, art. 3. (1)(a))

C3. S. 305 modified (27.7.2001) by 2001 asp 7, s. 4, Sch. para. 21 (with Sch. para. 18); S.S.I. 2001/274, art. 3. (1)(b)(c)

306 Information for financial and other purposes.S

(1) The Secretary of State shall in each year publish such information as he considers expedient for the purpose of—

(a) enabling persons engaged in the administration of criminal justice to become aware of the financial implications of their decisions; or

(b) facilitating the performance by such persons of their duty to avoid discriminating against any persons on the ground of race or sex or any other improper ground.

(2) Publication under subsection (1) above shall be effected in such manner as the Secretary of State considers appropriate for the purpose of bringing the information to the attention of the persons concerned.

307. Interpretation.S

(1) In this Act, unless the context otherwise requires—

[F5 "alcohol treatment requirement" has the meaning given in section 227. V(1);]

F6. . . . .

[F7 "assessment order" has the meaning given by section 52. D of this Act;]

"bail" means release of an accused or an appellant on conditions, or conditions imposed on bail, as the context requires;

F8. . . . .

"child", except in section 46. (3) of and Schedule 1 to this Act, has the meaning assigned to that expression for the purposes of [F9section 199 of the Children's Hearings (Scotland) Act 2011 (asp 1)]

[F10 "child witness" shall be construed in accordance with section 271. (1)(a) of this Act;]

"children's hearing" [F11is to be construed in accordance with section 5 of the Children's Hearings (Scotland) Act 2011 (asp 1)]

"Clerk of Justiciary" shall include assistant clerk of justiciary and shall extend and apply to any person duly authorised to execute the duties of Clerk of Justiciary or assistant clerk of justiciary;

[F12"Clerk of the Sheriff Appeal Court" includes Deputy Clerk of the Sheriff Appeal Court and any person authorised to carry out the functions of Clerk of the Sheriff Appeal Court;]

[F13 "the Commission" has the meaning given by section 194. A(1) of this Act;]

"commit for trial" means commit until liberation in due course of law;

[F14 "community payback order" means a community payback order (within the meaning of section 227. A(2)) imposed under section 227. A(1) or (4) or 227. M(2);]

F6. . . . .

[F15 "compensation requirement" has the meaning given in section 227. H(1);]

"complaint" includes a copy of the complaint laid before the court;

[F16 "compulsion order" means an order under section 57. (2)(a) or 57. A(2) of this Act;]

[F17"compulsory supervision order" has the meaning given by section 83 of the Children's Hearings (Scotland) Act 2011 (asp 1),]

[F18 "conduct requirement" has the meaning given in section 227. W(1);]

"constable" has the same meaning as in the [F19. Police and Fire Reform (Scotland) Act 2012];

[F20 "conviction", in relation to a previous conviction by a court outside Scotland, means a final decision of a criminal court establishing guilt of a criminal offence;]

"court of summary jurisdiction" means a court of summary criminal jurisdiction;

"court of summary criminal jurisdiction" includes the sheriff court and [F21. JP court];

"crime" means any crime or offence at common law or under any Act of Parliament whether passed before or after this Act, and includes an attempt to commit any crime or offence;

[F22 "devolution issue" has the same meaning as in Schedule 6 to the Scotland Act 1998;]

"diet" includes any continuation of a diet;

[F23 "drug treatment and testing order" has the meaning assigned to it in section 234. B(2) of this Act;]

[F24 "drug treatment requirement" has the meaning given in section 227. U(1);]

"enactment" includes an enactment contained in a local Act and any order, regulation or other instrument having effect by virtue of an Act;

"examination of facts" means an examination of facts held under section 55 of this Act;

"existing" means existing immediately before the commencement of this Act;

"extract conviction" and "extract of previous conviction" include certified copy conviction, certificate of conviction, and any other document lawfully issued from any court of justice of the United Kingdom as evidence of a conviction [F25and also include a conviction extracted and issued as mentioned in section 286. A(3)(a) and (b) of this Act];

"fine" includes—

 - any pecuniary penalty, (but not a pecuniary forfeiture or pecuniary compensation); and

- an instalment of a fine;

"governor" means, in relation to a contracted out prison within the meaning of section 106. (4) of the M1. Criminal Justice and Public Order Act 1994, the director of the prison;

"guardian", in relation to a child, includes any person who, in the opinion of the court having cognizance of any case in relation to the child or in which the child is concerned, has for the time being the charge of or control over the child;

"guardianship order" has the meaning assigned to it by section 58 of this Act;

"High Court" and "Court of Justiciary" shall mean "High Court of Justiciary" and shall include any court held by the Lords Commissioners of Justiciary, or any of them;

"hospital" means—

- any hospital vested in the Secretary of State under the M2. National Health Service (Scotland) Act 1978;

- [F26any hospital managed by a National Health Service Trust established under section 12. A of that Act;]

- any private hospital [F27as defined in section 12. (2)] of the M3. Mental Health (Scotland) Act 1984; and

- any State hospital;

[F28 "hospital direction" has the meaning assigned to it by section 59. A(1) of this Act;]

F29. . . . .

"impose detention" or "impose imprisonment" means pass a sentence of detention or imprisonment, as the case may be, or make an order for committal in default of payment of any sum of money or for contempt of court;

"indictment" includes any indictment whether in the sheriff court or the High Court framed in the form set out an Act of Adjournal or as nearly as may be in such form;

[F30 "interim compulsion order" has the meaning given by section 53 of this Act;]

[F31"interim compulsory supervision order" has the meaning given by section 86 of the Children's Hearings (Scotland) Act 2011 (asp 1),]

[F32 "JP court" means a justice of the peace court;]

"judge", in relation to solemn procedure, means a judge of a court of solemn criminal jurisdiction and, in relation to summary procedure, means any sheriff or any judge of a [F21. JP court];

"justice" includes the sheriff and any F33... justice of the peace;

[F34 "justice of the peace" means a justice of the peace appointed under section 67 of the Criminal Proceedings etc. (Reform) (Scotland) Act 2007 (asp 6);]

"legalised police cells" has the like meaning as in the M4. Prisons (Scotland) Act 1989;

"local authority" has the meaning assigned to it by section 1. (2) of the M5. Social Work (Scotland) Act 1968;

[F35 "local probation board" means a local probation board established under section 4 of the Criminal Justice and Court Services Act 2000]

"Lord Commissioner of Justiciary" includes Lord Justice General and Lord Justice Clerk;

[F36 "mental disorder" has the meaning given by section 328. (1) of the Mental Health (Care and Treatment)(Scotland) Act 2003 (asp 13);

[F37 "mental health treatment requirement" has the meaning given in section 227. R(1);]

"Mental Welfare Commission" means the Mental Welfare Commission for Scotland;]

"offence" means any act, attempt or omission punishable by law;

[F38 "offender supervision requirement" has the meaning given in section 227. G(1);]

"officer of law" includes, in relation to the service and execution of any warrant, citation, petition, indictment, complaint, list of witnesses, order, notice, or other proceeding or document—

- any macer, messenger-at-arms, sheriff officer or other person having authority to execute a warrant of the court;

- any constable;

- F39[F40... an officer of Revenue and Customs acting with the authority (which may be general or specific) of the Commissioners for Her Majesty's Revenue and Customs;]

- [F41subject to subsection (1. AA) below, an immigration officer acting with the authority (which may be general or specific) of the Secretary of State;]

- [F42any person who is appointed under section 26 of the Police and Fire Reform (Scotland) Act 2012 who is either authorised by the chief constable of the Police Service of Scotland in relation to such service and execution or is a police custody and security officer;]

- where the person upon whom service or execution is effected is in prison at the time of service on him, any prison officer; and

- any person or [F43class of persons] authorised in that regard for the time being by the Lord Advocate or by the Secretary of State;

"order" means any order, byelaw, rule or regulation having statutory authority;

[F44 "order for lifelong restriction" means an order under section 210. F(1) of this Act;]

[F45"organisation" means—

- a body corporate;
- an unincorporated association;
- a partnership;
- a body of trustees;
- a government department;
- a part of the Scottish Administration;
- any other entity which is not an individual;]

"patient" means a person suffering or appearing to be suffering from mental disorder;

"place of safety", in relation to a person not being a child, means any police station, prison or remand centre, or any hospital the board of management of which are willing temporarily to receive him, and in relation to a child [F46has the meaning given by section 202. (1) of the Children's Hearings (Scotland) Act 2011 (asp 1),]

[F47"postal operator" has the meaning assigned to it by [F48section 27 of the Postal Services Act 2011].]

[F49 "preliminary hearing" shall be construed in accordance with section 66. (6)(b) of this Act and, where in any case a further preliminary hearing is held or to be held under this Act, includes the diet consisting of that further preliminary hearing;]

[F50 "preliminary issue" shall be construed in accordance with section 79. (2)(b) of this Act;]

[F51 "preliminary plea" shall be construed in accordance with section 79. (2)(a) of this Act;]

"the prescribed sum" has the meaning given by section 225. (8) of this Act;

"prison" does not include a naval, military or air force prison;

"prison officer" and "officer of a prison" means, in relation to a contracted out prison within the meaning of section 106. (4) of the M6. Criminal Justice and Public Order Act 1994, a prisoner custody officer within the meaning of section 114. (1) of that Act;

F6. . . . .

F6. . . . .

F6. . . . .

"procurator fiscal" means the procurator fiscal for a sheriff court district, and includes assistant procurator fiscal and procurator fiscal depute and any person duly authorised to execute the duties of the procurator fiscal;

[F52 "programme requirement" has the meaning given in section 227. P(1);]

"prosecutor"—

- for the purposes of proceedings other than summary proceedings, includes Crown Counsel, procurator fiscal, any other person prosecuting in the public interest and any private prosecutor; and

- for the purposes of summary proceedings, includes procurator fiscal, and any other person prosecuting in the public interest and complainer and any person duly authorised to represent or act for any public prosecutor;

"remand" means an order adjourning the proceedings or continuing the case and giving direction as to detention in custody or liberation during the period of adjournment or continuation and references to remanding a person or remanding in custody or on bail shall be construed accordingly;

"remand centre" has the like meaning as in the M7. Prisons (Scotland) Act 1989;

[F53 "registered psychologist" means a person registered in the part of the register maintained under [F54the Health and Social Work Professions Order 2001] which relates to practitioner psychologists;]

F55. . . . .

F56. . . . .

[F57 "residence requirement" has the meaning given in section 227. Q(1);]

[F58 "responsible officer", in relation to a community payback order, is to be construed in accordance with section 227. C;]

[F59 "restricted movement requirement" has the meaning given in section 227. ZF(1);]

"restriction order" has the meaning assigned to it by section 59 of this Act;

[F60 "risk assessment order" means an order under section 210. B(2) of this Act;]

[F61 "risk assessment report" has the meaning given by section 210. B(3)(a) of this Act;]

"sentence", whether of detention or of imprisonment, means a sentence passed in respect of a crime or offence and does not include an order for committal in default of payment of any sum of money or for contempt of court;

"sheriff clerk" includes sheriff clerk depute, and extends and applies to any person duly authorised to execute the duties of sheriff clerk;

"sheriff court district" extends to the limits within which the sheriff has jurisdiction in criminal matters whether by statute or at common law;

"State hospital" has the meaning assigned to it in Part VIII of the Mental Health (Scotland) Act 1984;

"statute" means any Act of Parliament, public general, local, or private, and any Provisional Order confirmed by Act of Parliament;

F62...

F63...

"training school order" has the same meaning as in the Social Work (Scotland) Act 1968;

[F64 "treatment order" has the meaning given by section 52. M of this Act;]

[F65"unfit for trial" has the meaning given by section 53. F of this Act;]

[F66"the unified citation provisions"means section 216. (5) and (6)(a) and (b) of this Act;]

[F67 "unpaid work or other activity requirement" has the meaning given in section 227. I(1), and "level 1 unpaid work or other activity requirement" and "level 2 unpaid work or other activity requirement" are to be construed in accordance with section 227. I(5) and (6) respectively;]

[F68 "vulnerable witness" shall be construed in accordance with section 271. (1) of this Act;]

"witness" includes haver;

"young offenders institution" has the like meaning as in the M8. Prisons (Scotland) Act 1989.

F69[F70. (1. A). . . . .

[F71. (1. AA)The inclusion of immigration officers as "officers of law" shall have effect only in relation to immigration offences and nationality offences F72....]

[F73. (1. AB)In subsection (1. AA)—

"immigration offence" means—

- an offence involving conduct which relates to the entitlement of one or more persons who are not nationals of the United Kingdom to enter, transit across, or be in, the United Kingdom (including conduct which relates to conditions or other controls on any such entitlement); or

- (insofar as it is not an offence within paragraph (a)) an offence under the Immigration Acts or in relation to which a power of arrest is conferred on an immigration officer by the Immigration Acts;

"nationality offence" means an offence involving conduct which is undertaken for the purposes of, or otherwise in relation to, an enactment in—

- the British Nationality Act 1981;
- the Hong Kong Act 1985;
- the Hong Kong (War Wives and Widows) Act 1996;
- the British Nationality (Hong Kong) Act 1997;

- the British Overseas Territories Act 2002;

- an instrument made under any of those Acts.

(1. AC)In subsection (1. AB), "the Immigration Acts" has the meaning given by section 61 of the UK Borders Act 2007.]

(1. B)In any proceedings (whether civil or criminal) under or arising from [F74this Act—

(a) a certificate of the Commissioners for Her Majesty's Revenue and Customs that an officer of Revenue of Customs, or

(b) a certificate of the Secretary of State that an immigration officer,

had the authority] to exercise a power or function conferred by a provision of this Act shall be conclusive evidence of that fact.]

(2) References in this Act to a court do not include references to a [F75service court]; and nothing in this Act shall be construed as affecting the punishment which may be awarded by a [F75service court][F76for an offence under section 42 of the Armed Forces Act 2006.]

[F77. (2. A) In subsection (2), "service court" means—

(a) the Court Martial;

(b) the Summary Appeal Court;

(c) the Court Martial Appeal Court; or

(d) the Supreme Court on an appeal brought from the Court Martial Appeal Court.]

(3) F78. . . . .

(4) Any reference in this Act to a previous sentence of imprisonment shall be construed as including a reference to a previous sentence of penal servitude; any such reference to a previous sentence of Borstal training shall be construed as including a reference to a previous sentence of detention in a Borstal institution.

[F79. (5)Except where the context requires otherwise—

(a) any reference in this Act to a previous conviction is to be construed as a reference to a previous conviction by a court in any part of the United Kingdom or in any other member State of the European Union;

(b) any reference in this Act to a previous sentence is to be construed as a reference to a previous sentence passed by any such court;

(c) any reference to a previous conviction of a particular offence is to be construed, in relation to a previous conviction by a court outside Scotland, as a reference to a previous conviction of an equivalent offence; and

(d) any reference to a previous sentence of a particular kind is to be construed, in relation to a previous sentence passed by a court outside Scotland, as a reference to a previous sentence of an equivalent kind.]

(6) References in this Act to an offence punishable with imprisonment shall be construed, in relation to any offender, without regard to any prohibition or restriction imposed by or under any enactment, including this Act, upon the imprisonment of offenders of his age.

(7) Without prejudice to section 46 of this Act, where the age of any person at any time is material for the purposes of any provision of this Act regulating the powers of a court, his age at the material time shall be deemed to be or to have been that which appears to the court, after considering any available evidence, to be or to have been his age at that time.

(8) References in this Act to findings of guilty and findings that an offence has been committed shall be construed as including references to pleas of guilty and admissions that an offence has been committed.

Amendments (Textual)

F5. Words in s. 307. (1) inserted (1.2.2011) by Criminal Justice and Licensing (Scotland) Act 2010 (asp 13), ss. 14. (2), 206. (1), Sch. 2 para. 28. (a)(i); S.S.I. 2010/413, art. 2, Sch. (with art. 3)

F6. Definitions in s. 307. (1) repealed (1.2.2011) by Criminal Justice and Licensing (Scotland) Act 2010 (asp 13), ss. 14. (2), 206. (1), Sch. 2 para. 28. (a)(ii); S.S.I. 2010/413, art. 2, Sch. (with art. 3)

F7. S. 307. (1): definition of "assessment order" inserted (5.10.2005) by Mental Health (Care and Treatment) (Scotland) Act 2003 (asp 13), ss. 333. (1), 333. (2)-(4), Sch. 4 para. 8. (16)(a); S.S.I. 2005/161, art. 3

F8. S. 307: definition of "chartered psychologist" omitted (1.7.2009) by virtue of The Health Care and Associated Professions (Miscellaneous Amendments and Practitioner Psychologists) Order 2009 (S.I. 2009/1182), art. 4. (2), Sch. 5 para. 3. (b) (with arts. 9, 10); S.I. 2009/1357, art. 2. (d)

F9. Words in s. 307. (1) substituted (24.6.2013) by The Childrens Hearings (Scotland) Act 2011 (Modification of Primary Legislation) Order 2013 (S.S.I. 2013/211), art. 1, sch. 1 para. 10. (8)(a)

F10. Definition of "child witness" in s. 307. (1) inserted (2.7.2007 for certain purposes and otherwise 1.4.2008) by Vulnerable Witnesses (Scotland) Act 2004 (asp 3), ss. 1. (2), 25; S.S.I. 2007/329, art. 2, Sch. (with art. 4); S.S.I. 2008/57, art. 2 (with art. 3)

F11. Words in s. 307. (1) substituted (24.6.2013) by The Childrens Hearings (Scotland) Act 2011 (Modification of Primary Legislation) Order 2013 (S.S.I. 2013/211), art. 1, sch. 1 para. 10. (8)(b)

F12. Definition in s. 307 inserted (22.9.2015) by Courts Reform (Scotland) Act 2014 (asp 18), s. 138. (2), sch. 3 para. 26; S.S.I. 2015/247, art. 2, sch. (with art. 6)

F13. Definition in s. 307. (1) inserted (1.4.1999) by 1997 c. 48, s. 62. (1), Sch. 1 para. 21. (34)(a); S.I. 1999/652, art. 2, Sch. (subject to savings and transitional provisions in art. 3)

F14. Words in s. 307. (1) inserted (1.2.2011) by Criminal Justice and Licensing (Scotland) Act 2010 (asp 13), ss. 14. (2), 206. (1), Sch. 2 para. 28. (a)(i); S.S.I. 2010/413, art. 2, Sch. (with art. 3)

F15. Words in s. 307. (1) inserted (1.2.2011) by Criminal Justice and Licensing (Scotland) Act 2010 (asp 13), ss. 14. (2), 206. (1), Sch. 2 para. 28. (a)(i); S.S.I. 2010/413, art. 2, Sch. (with art. 3)

F16. Definition in s. 307. (1) substituted (30.6.2017) by Mental Health (Scotland) Act 2015 (asp 9), ss. 53. (2), 61. (2); S.S.I. 2017/197, art. 2, sch.

F17. Definition in s. 307. (1) inserted (24.6.2013) by The Childrens Hearings (Scotland) Act 2011 (Modification of Primary Legislation) Order 2013 (S.S.I. 2013/211), art. 1, sch. 1 para. 10. (8)(c)

F18. Words in s. 307. (1) inserted (1.2.2011) by Criminal Justice and Licensing (Scotland) Act 2010 (asp 13), ss. 14. (2), 206. (1), Sch. 2 para. 28. (a)(i); S.S.I. 2010/413, art. 2, Sch. (with art. 3)

F19. Words in s. 307. (1) substituted (1.4.2013) by Police and Fire Reform (Scotland) Act 2012 (asp 8), s. 129. (2), sch. 7 para. 12. (10)(a); S.S.I. 2013/51, art. 2 (with transitional provisions and savings in S.S.I. 2013/121)

F20. Words in s. 307. (1) inserted (13.12.2010 for all purposes in respect of offences committed on or after this date) by Criminal Justice and Licensing (Scotland) Act 2010 (asp 13), ss. 71. (1), 206. (1), Sch. 4 para. 8. (a); S.S.I. 2010/413, art. 2, Sch.

F21. S. 307. (1): words in the definition of "court of summary criminal jurisdiction" and "judge" substituted (10.3.2008, 2.6.2008, 8.12.2008, 23.2.2009 and 14.12.2009 for certain purposes, otherwise 22.2.2010) by Criminal Proceedings etc. (Reform) (Scotland) Act 2007 (asp 6), ss. 80, 84, Sch. para. 25. (a); S.S.I. 2008/42, art. 3, Sch.; S.S.I. 2008/192, art. 3, Sch.; S.S.I. 2008/329, art. 3, Sch.; S.S.I. 2008/362, art. 3, Sch.; S.S.I. 2009/432, art. 3, Schs. 1, 2

F22. Definition in s. 307. (1) inserted (20.5.1999) by 1998 c. 46, s. 125, Sch. 8 para. 32. (3) (with s. 126-(3)-(11)); S.I. 1998/3178, art. 2. (2), Sch. 4

F23. Definition in s. 307. (1) inserted (30.9.1998) by 1998 c. 37, s. 95. (2); S.I. 1998/2327, art. 2. (1)(s) (subject to arts. 5-8)

F24. Words in s. 307. (1) inserted (1.2.2011) by Criminal Justice and Licensing (Scotland) Act 2010 (asp 13), ss. 14. (2), 206. (1), Sch. 2 para. 28. (a)(i); S.S.I. 2010/413, art. 2, Sch. (with art. 3)

F25. S. 307. (1): words in the definition of "extract conviction" and "extract of previous conviction" added (27.6.2003) by Criminal Justice (Scotland) Act 2003 (asp 7), ss. 57. (5)(a), 89; S.S.I. 2003/288, art. 2, Sch.

F26. S. 307. (1): para. (aa) in definition of "hospital" inserted (1.8.1997) by 1997 c. 48, s. 62. (1), Sch. 1 para. 21. (34)(b); S.I. 1997/1712, art. 3, Sch. (subject to arts. 4, 5)

F27. Words in s. 307. (1) substituted (1.10.2001) by 2001 asp 8, s. 79, Sch. 3 para. 20; S.S.I. 2001/304, art. 2. (1)(b)(d)

F28. Definition in s. 307. (1) inserted (1.1.1998) by 1997 c. 48, s. 6. (5); S.I. 1997/2323, art. 4, Sch. 2 (subject to art. 7)

F29. S. 307. (1): definition of "hospital order" repealed (5.10.2005) by Mental Health (Care and Treatment) (Scotland) Act 2003 (asp 13), ss. 331. (2)(3), 333. (2)-(4), Sch. 5 Pt. 1; S.S.I. 2005/161, art. 3

F30. S. 307. (1): definition of "interim compulsion order" inserted (5.10.2005) by Mental Health (Care and Treatment) (Scotland) Act 2003 (asp 13), ss. 333. (1), 333. (2)-(4), Sch. 4 para. 8. (16)(c); S.S.I. 2005/161, art. 3

F31. Definition in s. 307. (1) inserted (24.6.2013) by The Childrens Hearings (Scotland) Act 2011 (Modification of Primary Legislation) Order 2013 (S.S.I. 2013/211), art. 1, sch. 1 para. 10. (8)(d)

F32. S. 307. (1): definition of "JP court" inserted (10.3.2008) by Criminal Proceedings etc. (Reform) (Scotland) Act 2007 (asp 6), ss. 80, 84, Sch. para. 25. (c); S.S.I. 2008/42, art. 3, Sch.

F33. Words in s. 307. (1) repealed (1.4.2016) by Courts Reform (Scotland) Act 2014 (asp 18), s. 138. (2), sch. 5 para. 39. (7)(a); S.S.I. 2016/13, art. 2, sch. (with art. 3)

F34. S. 307. (1): definition of "justice of the peace" substituted (10.12.2007) by Criminal Proceedings etc. (Reform) (Scotland) Act 2007 (asp 6), ss. 80, 84, Sch. para. 25. (b); S.S.I. 2007/479, art. 3. (1), Sch. (as amended by S.S.I. 2007/527)

F35. S. 307. (1): definition of "local probation board" inserted (1.4.2001) by 2000 c. 43, s. 74, Sch. 7 para. 126; S.I. 2001/919, art. 2. (f)(ii)

F36. S. 307. (1): definitions of "mental disorder" and "Mental Welfare Commission" inserted (5.10.2005) by Mental Health (Care and Treatment) (Scotland) Act 2003 (asp 13), ss. 333. (1), 333. (2)-(4), Sch. 4 para. 8. (16)(d); S.S.I. 2005/161, art. 3

F37. Words in s. 307. (1) inserted (1.2.2011) by Criminal Justice and Licensing (Scotland) Act 2010 (asp 13), ss. 14. (2), 206. (1), Sch. 2 para. 28. (a)(i); S.S.I. 2010/413, art. 2, Sch. (with art. 3)

F38. Words in s. 307. (1) inserted (1.2.2011) by Criminal Justice and Licensing (Scotland) Act 2010 (asp 13), ss. 14. (2), 206. (1), Sch. 2 para. 28. (a)(i); S.S.I. 2010/413, art. 2, Sch. (with art. 3)

F39. Words in s. 307. (1) omitted (27.4.2017 for specified purposes, 27.6.2017 in so far as not already in force) by virtue of Criminal Finances Act 2017 (c. 22), ss. 18. (3)(a), 58. (4)(6)

F40. S. 307. (1): paragraph (ba) in the definition of "officer of law" substituted (1.12.2007) by Finance Act 2007 (c. 11), s. 85, Sch. 23 paras. 9,14; S.I. 2007/3166, art. 3. (b)

F41. Words in s. 307. (1) inserted (25.6.2013) by Crime and Courts Act 2013 (c. 22), ss. 55. (13)(a), 61. (2) (with Sch. 21 para. 40); S.I. 2013/1042, art. 4. (g)

F42. Words in s. 307. (1) substituted (1.4.2013) by Police and Fire Reform (Scotland) Act 2012 (asp 8), s. 129. (2), sch. 7 para. 12. (10)(b); S.S.I. 2013/51, art. 2 (with transitional provisions and savings in S.S.I. 2013/121)

F43. S. 307. (1): words in para. (e) of the definition of "officer of law" substituted (30.9.1998) by 1998 c. 37, s. 119, Sch. 8 para. 124. (b); S.I. 1998/2327, arts. 2. (1)(y)(2)(kk) (subject to arts. 5-8)

F44. S. 307. (1): definition of "order for lifelong restriction" inserted (19.6.2006 for certain purposes and otherwise prosp.) by Criminal Justice (Scotland) Act 2003 (asp 7), ss. 1. (2), 89, Sch. 1 para. 2. (7); S.S.I. 2006/332, art. 2. (1) (subject to art. 2. (2))

F45. Words in s. 307. (1) inserted (28.3.2011) by Criminal Justice and Licensing (Scotland) Act 2010 (asp 13), ss. 65, 206. (1); S.S.I. 2011/178, art. 2, sch.

F46. Words in s. 307. (1) substituted (24.6.2013) by The Childrens Hearings (Scotland) Act 2011 (Modification of Primary Legislation) Order 2013 (S.S.I. 2013/211), art. 1, sch. 1 para. 10. (8)(e)

F47. Words in s. 307. (1) inserted (26.3.2001) by S.I. 2001/1149, s. 3. (1), Sch. para. 104. (7) (subject to art. 1. (3))

F48. Words in s. 307. (1) substituted (1.10.2011) by Postal Services Act 2011 (c. 5), s. 93. (2)(3), Sch. 12 para. 146; S.I. 2011/2329, art. 3

F49. S. 307. (1): definition of "preliminary hearing" inserted (1.2.2005) by Criminal Procedure (Amendment) (Scotland) Act 2004 (asp 5), ss. 25, 27. (1), Sch. para. 57; S.S.I. 2004/405, art. 2. (1), Sch. 1

F50. S. 307. (1): definition of "preliminary issue" inserted (1.2.2005) by Criminal Procedure (Amendment) (Scotland) Act 2004 (asp 5), ss. 25, 27. (1), Sch. para. 57; S.S.I. 2004/405, art. 2. (1), Sch. 1

F51. S. 307. (1): definition of "preliminary plea" inserted (1.2.2005) by Criminal Procedure (Amendment) (Scotland) Act 2004 (asp 5), ss. 25, 27. (1), Sch. para. 57; S.S.I 2004/405, {art. 2. (1)}, Sch. 1

F52. Words in s. 307. (1) inserted (1.2.2011) by Criminal Justice and Licensing (Scotland) Act

2010 (asp 13), ss. 14. (2), 206. (1), Sch. 2 para. 28. (a)(i); S.S.I. 2010/413, art. 2, Sch. (with art. 3)

F53. S. 307: definition of "registered psychologist" inserted (1.7.2009) by The Health Care and Associated Professions (Miscellaneous Amendments and Practitioner Psychologists) Order 2009 (S.I. 2009/1182), art. 4. (2), Sch. 5 para. 3. (b) (with arts. 9, 10); S.I. 2009/1357, art. 2. (d)

F54. Words in s. 307. (1) substituted (1.8.2012) by Health and Social Care Act 2012 (c. 7), ss. 213. (8)(a), 306. (4) (with s. 230. (6)); S.I. 2012/1319, art. 2. (4)

F55. S. 307. (1): definition of "residential establishment" repealed (5.10.2005) by Mental Health (Care and Treatment) (Scotland) Act 2003 (asp 13), ss. 331. (2)(3), 333. (2)-(4), Sch. 5 Pt. 1; S.S.I. 2005/161, art. 3

F56. S. 307. (1): definition of "responsible medical officer" repealed (5.10.2005) by Mental Health (Care and Treatment) (Scotland) Act 2003 (asp 13), ss. 331. (2)(3), 333. (2)-(4), Sch. 5 Pt. 1; S.S.I. 2005/161, art. 3

F57. Words in s. 307. (1) inserted (1.2.2011) by Criminal Justice and Licensing (Scotland) Act 2010 (asp 13), ss. 14. (2), 206. (1), Sch. 2 para. 28. (a)(i); S.S.I. 2010/413, art. 2, Sch. (with art. 3)

F58. Words in s. 307. (1) inserted (1.2.2011) by Criminal Justice and Licensing (Scotland) Act 2010 (asp 13), ss. 14. (2), 206. (1), Sch. 2 para. 28. (a)(i); S.S.I. 2010/413, art. 2, Sch. (with art. 3)

F59. Words in s. 307. (1) inserted (1.2.2011) by Criminal Justice and Licensing (Scotland) Act 2010 (asp 13), ss. 14. (2), 206. (1), Sch. 2 para. 28. (a)(i); S.S.I. 2010/413, art. 2, Sch. (with art. 3)

F60. S. 307. (1): definition of "risk assessment order" inserted (19.6.2006 for certain purposes and otherwise prosp.) by Criminal Justice (Scotland) Act 2003 (asp 7), ss. 1. (2), 89, Sch. 1 para. 2. (7); S.S.I. 2006/332, art. 2. (1) (subject to art. 2. (2))

F61. S. 307. (1): definition of "risk assessment report" inserted (19.6.2006 for certain purposes and otherwise prosp.) by Criminal Justice (Scotland) Act 2003 (asp 7), ss. 1. (2), 89, Sch. 1 para. 2. (7); S.S.I. 2006/332, art. 2. (1) (subject to art. 2. (2))

F62. Definition in s. 307. (1) repealed (1.4.2016) by Courts Reform (Scotland) Act 2014 (asp 18), s. 138. (2), sch. 5 para. 39. (7)(b); S.S.I. 2016/13, art. 2, sch. (with art. 3)

F63. Definition in s. 307. (1) repealed (24.6.2013) by The Childrens Hearings (Scotland) Act 2011 (Modification of Primary Legislation) Order 2013 (S.S.I. 2013/211), art. 1, sch. 2

F64. S. 307. (1): definition of "treatment order" inserted (5.10.2005) by Mental Health (Care and Treatment) (Scotland) Act 2003 (asp 13), ss. 333. (1), 333. (2)-(4), Sch. 4 para. 8. (16)(e); S.S.I. 2005/161, art. 3

F65. Words in s. 307. (1) inserted (with application in accordance with art. 3 of the commencing S.S.I.) by Criminal Justice and Licensing (Scotland) Act 2010 (asp 13), s. 206. (1), sch. 7 para. 62; S.S.I. 2012/160, art. 3, sch.

F66. S. 307. (1): definition of "the unified citation provisions" inserted (27.10.2003) by Criminal Justice (Scotland) Act 2003 (asp 7), ss. 60. (2), 89; S.S.I. 2003/475, art. 2, Sch.

F67. Words in s. 307. (1) inserted (1.2.2011) by Criminal Justice and Licensing (Scotland) Act 2010 (asp 13), ss. 14. (2), 206. (1), Sch. 2 para. 28. (a)(i); S.S.I. 2010/413, art. 2, Sch. (with art. 3)

F68. Definition of "vulnerable witness" in s. 307. (1) inserted (2.7.2007 for certain purposes and 1.4.2008) by Vulnerable Witnesses (Scotland) Act 2004 (asp 3), ss. 1. (2), 25; S.S.I. 2007/329, art. 2. (1), Sch. (with art. 4); S.S.I. 2008/57, art. 2 (with art. 3)

F69. S. 307. (1. A) omitted (27.4.2017 for specified purposes, 27.6.2017 in so far as not already in force) by virtue of Criminal Finances Act 2017 (c. 22), ss. 18. (3)(b), 58. (4)(6)

F70. S. 307. (1. A)(1. B) inserted (1.12.2007) by Finance Act 2007 (c. 11), s. 85, Sch. 23 paras. 10, 14; S.I. 2007/3166, art. 3. (b)

F71. S. 307. (1. AA) inserted (25.6.2013) by Crime and Courts Act 2013 (c. 22), ss. 55. (13)(b), 61. (2) (with Sch. 21 para. 40); S.I. 2013/1042, art. 4. (g)

F72. Words in s. 307. (1. AA) repealed (25.1.2018) by The Criminal Justice (Scotland) Act 2016 (Consequential Provisions) Order 2018 (S.I. 2018/46), arts. 2. (2)(c), 15. (3) (with art. 15. (2))

F73. S. 307. (1. AB)(1. AC) inserted (25.1.2018) by The Criminal Justice (Scotland) Act 2016 (Consequential Provisions) Order 2018 (S.I. 2018/46), arts. 2. (2)(c), 15. (4) (with art. 15. (2))

F74. Words in s. 307. (1. B) substituted (25.6.2013) by Crime and Courts Act 2013 (c. 22), ss. 55. (13)(c), 61. (2) (with Sch. 21 para. 40); S.I. 2013/1042, art. 4. (g)

F75. Words in s. 307. (2) substituted (28.3.2009 for certain purposes and otherwise 31.10.2009) by Armed Forces Act 2006 (c. 52), ss. 378, 383, Sch. 16 para. 133. (a)(i); S.I. 2009/812, art. 3; S.I. 2009/1167, art. 4 (with transitional provisions in S.I. 2009/1059)

F76. Words in s. 307. (2) substituted (28.3.2009 for certain purposes and otherwise 31.10.2009) by Armed Forces Act 2006 (c. 52), ss. 378, 383, Sch. 16 para. 133. (a)(ii); S.I. 2009/812, art. 3; S.I. 2009/1167, art. 4 (with transitional provisions in S.I. 2009/1059)

F77. S. 307. (2. A) inserted (28.3.2009 for certain purposes and otherwise 31.10.2009) by Armed Forces Act 2006 (c. 52), ss. 378, 383, Sch. 16 para. 133. (b); S.I. 2009/812, art. 3; S.I. 2009/1167, art. 4 (with transitional provisions in S.I. 2009/1059)

F78. S. 307. (3) repealed (1.2.2011) by Criminal Justice and Licensing (Scotland) Act 2010 (asp 13), ss. 14. (2), 206. (1), Sch. 2 para. 28. (b); S.S.I. 2010/413, art. 2, Sch. (with art. 3)

F79. S. 307. (5) substituted (13.12.2010 for all purposes in respect of offences committed on or after this date) by Criminal Justice and Licensing (Scotland) Act 2010 (asp 13), ss. 71. (1), 206. (1), Sch. 4 para. 8. (b); S.S.I. 2010/413, art. 2, Sch.

Modifications etc. (not altering text)

C4. S. 307. (2) modified (24.4.2009 for certain purposes and otherwise 31.10.2009) by The Armed Forces Act 2006 (Transitional Provisions etc) Order 2009 (S.I. 2009/1059), art. 205, Sch. 1 para. 35

Marginal Citations

M11994 c.33.

M21978 c.29.

M31984 c.36.

M41989 c.45.

M51968 c.49.

M61994 c.33.

M71989 c.45.

M81989 c.45.

308 Construction of enactments referring to detention etc.S

In any enactment—

(a) any reference to a sentence of imprisonment as including a reference to a sentence of any other form of detention shall be construed as including a reference to a sentence of detention under section 207 of this Act; and

(b) any reference to imprisonment as including any other form of detention shall be construed as including a reference to detention under that section.

[F80308. AExpressions relating to electronic proceedingsS

(1) In this Act, an "electronic complaint" is a complaint in electronic form which is capable of being—

(a) transmitted by means of electronic communication;

(b) kept in legible form.

(2) In this Act, unless the context otherwise requires—

"electronic communication" is to be construed in accordance with section 15. (1) of the Electronic Communications Act 2000 (c. 7);

"electronic signature" is to be construed in accordance with section 7. (2) of the Electronic Communications Act 2000, but includes a version of an electronic signature which is reproduced on a paper document.

(3) The Scottish Ministers may by order modify the meaning of "electronic signature" provided for in subsection (2) above for the purpose of such provisions of this Act as are specified in the order.

(4) An order under subsection (3) above shall be made by statutory instrument subject to annulment in pursuance of a resolution of the Scottish Parliament.]

Amendments (Textual)

F80. S. 308. A inserted (10.12.2007 for specified purposes, 1.11.2012 in so far as not already in force) by Criminal Proceedings etc. (Reform) (Scotland) Act 2007 (asp 6), ss. 41. (2), 84. (1); S.S.I. 2007/479, art. 3, sch.; S.S.I. 2012/274, art. 2, sch.

309 Short title, commencement and extent.

(1) This Act may be cited as the Criminal Procedure (Scotland) Act 1995.

(2) This Act shall come into force on 1 April 1996.

(3) Subject to subsections (4) and (5) below, this Act extends to Scotland only.

(4) The following provisions of this Act and this section extend to England and Wales—
- section 44;
- section 47;
- section 209. (3) and (7);
- section 234. (4) to (11);
- section 244;
- section 252 for the purposes of the construction mentioned in subsection (1) of that subsection;
- section [F81303. (4) to (7)].
- [F82. Part 1 of Schedule 13 (and section 227. ZO)]

(5) The following provisions of this Act and this section extend to Northern Ireland—
- section 44;
- section 47;
- section 244;
- section 252 for the purposes of the construction mentioned in subsection (1) of that subsection;
- section [F83303. (4) to (7)].
- [F84. Part 2 of Schedule 13 (and section 227. ZO)]

(6) Section 297. (3) and (4) of this Act and this section also extend to the Isle of Man.

Amendments (Textual)

F81. Words in s. 309. (4) substituted (12.4.2010) by The Northern Ireland Act 1998 (Devolution of Policing and Justice Functions) Order 2010 (S.I. 2010/976), arts. 1. (2), 12, Sch. 14 para. 32. (3) (with arts. 28-31); S.I. 2010/977, art. 1. (2)

F82. Words in s. 309. (4) inserted (16.9.2011) by The Criminal Justice and Licensing (Scotland) Act 2010 (Consequential Provisions and Modifications) Order 2011 (S.I. 2011/2298), art. 1, Sch. para. 8 (with art. 4. (4))

F83. Words in s. 309. (5) substituted (12.4.2010) by The Northern Ireland Act 1998 (Devolution of Policing and Justice Functions) Order 2010 (S.I. 2010/976), arts. 1. (2), 12, Sch. 14 para. 32. (4) (with arts. 28-31); S.I. 2010/977, art. 1. (2)

F84. Words in s. 309. (5) inserted (16.9.2011) by The Criminal Justice and Licensing (Scotland) Act 2010 (Consequential Provisions and Modifications) Order 2011 (S.I. 2011/2298), art. 1, Sch. para. 9 (with art. 4. (4))

Schedules

Schedule 1. Offences Against Children Under the Age of 17 Years to which Special Provisions Apply

1. Any offence under Part I of the M1. Criminal Law (Consolidation) (Scotland) Act 1995.S

Marginal Citations

M11995 c.39.

Prospective

[F11. AAny offence under section 18 (rape of a young child) or 28 (having intercourse with an older child) of the Sexual Offences (Scotland) Act 2009 (asp 9).S

Amendments (Textual)

F1. Sch. 1 paras. 1. A -1. D inserted (1.12.2010) by Sexual Offences (Scotland) Act 2009 (asp 9), ss. 61, 62. (2), Sch. 5 para. 2. (8)(a); S.S.I. 2010/357, art. 2. (a)

Prospective

1. BAny offence under section 19 (sexual assault on a young child by penetration) or 29 (engaging in penetrative sexual activity with or towards an older child) of that Act.S

Amendments (Textual)

F1. Sch. 1 paras. 1. A -1. D inserted (1.12.2010) by Sexual Offences (Scotland) Act 2009 (asp 9), ss. 61, 62. (2), Sch. 5 para. 2. (8)(a); S.S.I. 2010/357, art. 2. (a)

Prospective

1. CAny offence under section 20 (sexual assault on a young child) or 30 (engaging in sexual activity with or towards an older child) of that Act.S

Amendments (Textual)

F1. Sch. 1 paras. 1. A -1. D inserted (1.12.2010) by Sexual Offences (Scotland) Act 2009 (asp 9), ss. 61, 62. (2), Sch. 5 para. 2. (8)(a); S.S.I. 2010/357, art. 2. (a)

Prospective

1. DAny offence under section 42 of that Act (sexual abuse of trust) towards a child under the age of 17 years but only if the condition set out in section 43. (6) of that Act is fulfilled.]S

Amendments (Textual)

F1. Sch. 1 paras. 1. A -1. D inserted (1.12.2010) by Sexual Offences (Scotland) Act 2009 (asp 9), ss. 61, 62. (2), Sch. 5 para. 2. (8)(a); S.S.I. 2010/357, art. 2. (a)

2. Any offence under section 12, 15, 22 or 33 of the M2. Children and Young Persons (Scotland) Act 1937.S

Marginal Citations

M21987 c. 41.

[F22. AAny offence under the Prohibition of Female Genital Mutilation (Scotland) Act 2005 where the person mutilated or, as the case may be, proposed to be mutilated, is a child under the age of 17 years.]S

Amendments (Textual)

F2. Sch. 1 para. 2. A inserted (1.9.2005) by Prohibition of Female Genital Mutilation (Scotland) Act 2005 (asp 8), ss. 7. (1), 8. (2)

[F32. BAny offence under section 52 or 52. A of the Civic Government (Scotland) Act 1982 in relation to an indecent photograph [F4or pseudo-photograph] of a child under the age of 17 years.S

Amendments (Textual)

F3. Sch. 1 para. 2. B, 2. C inserted (7.10.2005) by Protection of Children and Prevention of Sexual Offences (Scotland) Act 2005 (asp 9), ss. 18, 20. (2), Sch. para. 2; S.S.I. 2005/480, art. 2 (with savings in art. 3)

F4. Words in Sch. 1 para. 2. B inserted (13.12.2010) by Criminal Justice and Licensing (Scotland) Act 2010 (asp 13), ss. 41. (2), 206. (1); S.S.I. 2010/413, art. 2, Sch.

2. CAny offence under section 1, 9, 10, 11 or 12 of the Protection of Children and Prevention of Sexual Offences (Scotland) Act 2005 in respect of a child under the age of 17 years.]S

Amendments (Textual)

F3. Sch. 1 para. 2. B, 2. C inserted (7.10.2005) by Protection of Children and Prevention of Sexual Offences (Scotland) Act 2005 (asp 9), ss. 18, 20. (2), Sch. para. 2; S.S.I. 2005/480, art. 2 (with savings in art. 3)

3. Any other offence involving bodily injury to a child under the age of 17 years.S

4. Any offence involving the use of lewd, indecent or libidinous practice or behaviour towards a child under the age of 17 years.S

Prospective

[F54. AAny offence under section 5 (coercing a person into being present during a sexual activity), 6 (coercing a person into looking at a sexual image), 7 (communicating indecently etc.), 8 (sexual exposure) or 9 (voyeurism) of the Sexual Offences (Scotland) Act 2009 (asp 9) towards a child under the age of 17 years.S

Amendments (Textual)

F5. Sch. 1 paras. 4. A, 4. B inserted (1.12.2010) by Sexual Offences (Scotland) Act 2009 (asp 9), ss. 61, 62. (2), Sch. 5 para. 2. (8)(b); S.S.I. 2010/357, art. 2. (a)

Prospective

4. BAny offence under any of sections 21 to 26 or 31 to 37 of that Act (certain sexual offences relating to children).]S

Amendments (Textual)

F5. Sch. 1 paras. 4. A, 4. B inserted (1.12.2010) by Sexual Offences (Scotland) Act 2009 (asp 9), ss. 61, 62. (2), Sch. 5 para. 2. (8)(b); S.S.I. 2010/357, art. 2. (a)

Schedule 2. Examples of Indictments

Sections 34 & 64. (2)

"A.B.(name and address, that given in the declaration being sufficient), you are indicted at the instance of F1. . . Her Majesty's Advocate, and the charge against you is that on 20th 199 , in a shop in George Street, Edinburgh, occupied by John Cruikshank, draper, you did steal a shawl and a boa."

".................... You did rob Charles Doyle, a cattle dealer, of Biggar, Lanarkshire, of a watch and chain and £36 of money...................."

".................... You did break into the house occupied by Andrew Howe, banker's clerk, and did there steal twelve spoons, a ladle, and a candlestick...................."

".................... You did force open (or attempt to force open) a lockfast cupboard and did thus attempt to steal therefrom...................."

".................... You did place your hand in one of the packets of Thomas Kerr, commercial traveller, 115 Main Street, Perth, and did thus attempt to steal...................."

".................... You did assault Lewis Mann, station-master of Earlston, and compress his throat and attempt to take from him a watch and chain...................."

".................... You did, while in the employment of James Pentland, accountant in Frederick Street, Edinburgh, embezzle £4,075 of money...................."

".................... You did, while acting as commercial traveller to Brown and Company, merchants in Leith, at the times and places specified in the inventory hereto subjoined, receive from the persons therein set forth the respective sums of money therein specified for the said Brown and Company, and did embezzle the same (or did embezzle £470 of money, being part thereof)...................."

".................... You did pretend to Norah Omond, residing there, that you were a collector of subscriptions for a charitable society, and did thus induce her to deliver to you £15 of money as a subscription thereto, which you appropriated to your own use...................."

".................... You did reset a watch and chain, pocket book and £15.55 of money, the same having been dishonestly appropriated by theft or robbery...................."

".................... You did utter as genuine a bill, on which the name of John Jones bore to be signed as acceptor, such signature being forged by (here describe in general terms how the bill was uttered, and add where the bill is produced), and said bill of exchange is No. of the productions lodged herewith...................."

"................... You did utter as genuine a letter bearing to be a certificate of character of you, as a domestic servant, by Mary Watson, of 15 Bon Accord Street, Aberdeen, what was written above the signature of Mary Watson having been written there by some other person without her authority by handing it to Ellen Chisholm of Panmore Street, Forfar, to whom you were applying for a situation (here add when the letter is produced), and said letter is No. of the productions lodged herewith...................."

"................... You did utter a cheque signed by Henry Smith for £8 sterling, which had been altered without his authority by adding the letter Y to eight and the figure 0 to figure 8, so as to make it read as a cheque for £80 sterling, by presenting such altered cheque for payment to Allen Brown, Cashier of the Bank of Scotland at Callander (here add when the cheque is produced), and said cheque is No. of the productions lodged herewith...................."

"................... You did, when examined under section 45 of the M1. Bankruptcy (Scotland) Act 1985 before Hubert Hamilton Esquire, sheriff of the Lothians and Borders, depone (here state the general nature of the false statement), in order to defraud your creditors...................."

"................... You did, sequestration having been awarded on your estate on the 20th March 1991, conceal property consisting of (here state generally the property concealed), falling under your sequestration, in order to defraud your creditor, by burying it in the garden of your house in Troon Street, Kilmarnock (or by removing it to the house of James Kidd, your son, No. 17 Greek Street, Port-Glasgow)...................."

"................... You did set fire to a warehouse occupied by Peter Cranston in Holly Lane, Greenock, and the fire took effect on said warehouse, and this you did wilfully (or culpably and recklessly)...................."

"................... You did set fire to the shop in Brown Street, Blairgowrie, occupied by you, with intent to defraud the Liverpool, London, and Globe Insurance Company, and the fire took effect on said shop...................."

"................... You did assault Theresa Unwin, your wife, and did beat her and did murder her...................."

"................... You did stab Thomas Underwood, baker, of Shiels Place, Oban, and did murder him...................."

"................... You did administer poison to Vincent Wontner, your son, and did murder him...................."

"................... You did strangle Mary Shaw, mill-worker, daughter of John Shaw, residing at Juniper Green, in the county of Midlothian, and did murder her...................."

"................... You were delivered of a child now dead or amissing, and you did conceal your pregnancy and did not call for or use assistance at the birth, contrary to the Concealment of Birth (Scotland) Act 1809...................."

"................... You did assault Hector Morrison, carter, of 20 Buccleuch Street, Dalkeith, and did beat him with your fists and with a stick, and did break his arm...................."

"................... You did ravish Harriet Cowan, mill-worker, of 27 Tweed Row, Peebles...................."

"................... You did attempt to ravish Jane Peters, servant, at Glen House, near Dunbar...................."

"................... You did, when acting as railway signalman, cancel a danger signal and allow a train to enter on a part of the line protected by the signals under your charge, and did cause a collision, and did kill William Peters, commercial traveller, of Brook Street, Carlisle, a passenger in said train...................."

"................... You formed part of a riotous mob, which, acting of common purpose, obstructed A. B., C. D., and E. F., constables of the Northern constabulary on duty, and assaulted them, and forcibly took two persons whom they had arrested from their custody...................."

"................... You did, being the lawful husband of Helen Hargreaves, of 20 Teviot Row, Edinburgh, and she being still alive, bigamously marry Dorothy Rose, a widow, of 7 Blacks Row, Brechin, and did cohabit with her as her husband...................."

"................... You being sworn as a witness in a civil cause, then proceeding in the sheriff court, deponed (here set forth the statements said to be false) the truth as you knew being that (here state the true facts)..................."

"................... You did suborn James Carruthers, scavenger, 12 Hercles Street, Edinburgh, to depone as a witness in the sheriff court of Edinburgh, that (here set forth the statements said to be false), and he did (time and place) depone to that effect, the truth as you knew being (here state the true facts)..................."

"................... You did deforce John Macdonald, a sheriff officer of Renfrewshire, and prevent him serving a summons issued by the sheriff of Renfrewshire upon Peter M'Innes, market gardener in Renfrew..................."

Amendments (Textual)

F1. Words in Sch. 2 repealed (13.12.2010) by Criminal Justice and Licensing (Scotland) Act 2010 (asp 13), ss. 60. (5), 206. (1); S.S.I. 2010/413, art. 2, Sch. (with art. 5)

Marginal Citations

M11985 c. 66.

Schedule 3. Indictments and Complaints

Sections 64. (6) and 138. (4)

1. An accused may be named and designed—S

(a) according to the existing practice; or

(b) by the name given by him and designed as of the place given by him as his residence when he is examined or further examined; or

(c) by the name under which he is committed until liberated in due course of law.

2. It shall not be necessary to specify by any nomen juris the offence which is charged, but it shall be sufficient that the indictment or complaint sets forth facts relevant and sufficient to constitute an indictable offence or, as the case may be, an offence punishable on complaint.S

3. It shall not be necessary to allege that any act or commission or omission charged was done or omitted to be done "wilfully" or "maliciously", or "wickedly and feloniously", or "falsely and fraudulently" or "knowingly", or "culpably and recklessly", or "negligently", or in "breach of duty", or to use such words as "knowing the same to be forged", or "having good reason to know", or "well knowing the same to have been stolen", or to use any similar words or expressions qualifying any act charged, but such qualifying allegation shall be implied in every case.S

4. (1)The latitude formerly used in stating time shall be implied in all statements of time where an exact time is not of the essence of the charge.S

(2) The latitude formerly used in stating any place by adding to the word "at", or to the word "in", the words "or near", or the words "or in the near neighbourhood thereof" or similar words, shall be implied in all statements of place where the actual place is not of the essence of the charge.

(3) Subject to sub-paragraph (4) below, where the circumstances of the offence charged make it necessary to take an exceptional latitude in regard to time or place it shall not be necessary to set forth the circumstances in the indictment, or to set forth that the particular time or the particular place is to the prosecutor unknown.

(4) Where exceptional latitude is taken as mentioned in sub-paragraph (3) above, the court shall, if satisfied that such exceptional latitude was not reasonable in the circumstances of the case, give such remedy to the accused by adjournment of the trial or otherwise as shall seem just.

(5) Notwithstanding sub-paragraph (4) above, nothing in any rule of law shall prohibit the amendment of an indictment or, as the case may be, a complaint to include a time outwith the exceptional latitude if it appears to the court that the amendment would not prejudice the accused.

(6) The latitude formerly used in describing quantities by the words "or thereby", or the words "or part thereof", or the words "or some other quantity to the prosecutor unknown" or similar words, shall be implied in all statements of quantities.

(7) The latitude formerly used in stating details connected with the perpetration of any act regarding persons, things or modes by inserting general alternative statements followed by the words "to the prosecutor unknown" or similar words, shall be implied in every case.

(8) In this paragraph references to latitude formerly used are references to such use before the commencement of—

(a) in the case of proceedings on indictment, the M1. Criminal Procedure (Scotland) Act 1887; and

(b) in the case of summary proceedings, M2the Summary Jurisdiction (Scotland) Act 1908.

Marginal Citations

M150 & 51 Vict. c. 35.

M21954 c. 48.

5. The word "money" shall include cheques, banknotes, postal orders, money orders and foreign currency.S

6. Any document referred to shall be referred to by a general description and, where it is to be produced in proceedings on indictment, by the number given to it in the list of productions for the prosecution.S

7. In an indictment which charges a crime importing personal injury inflicted by the accused, resulting in death or serious injury to the person, the accused may be lawfully convicted of the aggravation that the assault or other injurious act was committed with intent to commit such crime.S

8. (1)In an indictment or a complaint charging the resetting of property dishonestly appropriated— S

(a) having been taken by theft or robbery; or

(b) by breach of trust, embezzlement or falsehood, fraud and wilful imposition,

it shall be sufficient to specify that the accused received the property, it having been dishonestly appropriated by theft or robbery, or by breach of trust and embezzlement, or by falsehood, fraud and wilful imposition, as the case may be.

(2) Under an indictment or a complaint for robbery, theft, breach of trust and embezzlement or falsehood, fraud and wilful imposition, an accused may be convicted of reset.

(3) Under an indictment or a complaint for robbery, breach of trust and embezzlement, or falsehood, fraud and wilful imposition, an accused may be convicted of theft.

[F1. (3. A)Under an indictment or a complaint for breach of trust and embezzlement, an accused may be convicted of falsehood, fraud and wilful imposition.

(3. B)Under an indictment or a complaint for falsehood, fraud and wilful imposition, an accused may be convicted of breach of trust and embezzlement.]

(4) Under an indictment or a complaint for theft, an accused may be convicted of breach of trust and embezzlement, or of falsehood, fraud and wilful imposition, or may be convicted of theft, although the circumstances proved may in law amount to robbery.

(5) The power conferred by sub-paragraphs (2) to (4) above to convict a person of an offence other than that with which he is charged shall be exercisable by the sheriff court before which he is tried notwithstanding that the other offence was committed outside the jurisdiction of that sheriff court.

Amendments (Textual)

F1. Sch. 3 para. 8. (3. A)(3. B) inserted (28.3.2011) by Criminal Justice and Licensing (Scotland) Act 2010 (asp 13), ss. 48, 206. (1); S.S.I. 2011/178, art. 2, sch.

9. (1)Where two or more crimes or acts of crime are charged cumulatively, it shall be lawful to convict of any one or more of them.S

(2) Any part of the charge in an indictment or complaint which itself constitutes an indictable offence or, as the case may be an offence punishable on complaint, shall be separable and it shall be lawful to convict the accused of that offence.

(3) Where any crime is charged as having been committed with a particular intent or with particular circumstances of aggravation, it shall be lawful to convict of the crime without such intent or aggravation.

10. (1)Under an indictment or, as the case may be, a complaint which charges a completed offence, the accused may be lawfully convicted of an attempt to commit the offence.S

(2) Under an indictment or complaint charging an attempt, the accused may be convicted of such attempt although the evidence is sufficient to prove the completion of the offence said to have been attempted.

(3) Under an indictment or complaint which charges an offence involving personal injury inflicted by the accused, resulting in death or serious injury to the person, the accused may be lawfully convicted of the assault or other injurious act, and may also be lawfully convicted of the aggravation that the assault or other injurious act was committed with intent to commit such offence.

11. In an indictment or complaint charging a contravention of an enactment the description of the offence in the words of the enactment contravened, or in similar words, shall be sufficient.S

12. In a complaint charging a contravention of an enactment—S

(a) the statement that an act was done contrary to a enactment shall imply a statement—

(i) that the enactment applied to the circumstances existing at the time and place of the offence;

(ii) that the accused was a person bound to observe the enactment;

(iii) that any necessary preliminary procedure had been duly gone through; and

(iv) that all the circumstances necessary to a contravention existed,

and, in the case of the contravention of a subordinate instrument, such statement shall imply a statement that the instrument was duly made, confirmed, published and generally made effectual according to the law applicable, and was in force at the time and place in question; and

(b) where the offence is created by more than one section of one or more statutes or subordinate instruments, it shall be necessary to specify only the leading section or one of the leading sections.

13. In the case of an offence punishable under any enactment, it shall be sufficient to allege that the offence was committed contrary to the enactment and to refer to the enactment founded on without setting out the words of the enactment at length.S

14. Where—S

(a) any act alleged in an indictment or complaint as contrary to any enactment is also criminal at common law; or

(b) where the facts proved under the indictment or complaint do not amount to a contravention of the enactment, but do amount to an offence at common law,

it shall be lawful to convict of the common law offence.

15. Where the evidence in a trial is sufficient to prove the identity of any person, corporation or company, or of any place, or of anything, it shall not be a valid objection to the sufficiency of the evidence that any particulars specified in the indictment or complaint relating to such identity have not been proved.S

16. Where, in relation to an offence created by or under an enactment any exception, exemption, proviso, excuse, or qualification, is expressed to have effect whether by the same or any other enactment, the exception, exemption, proviso, excuse or qualification need not be specified or negatived in the indictment or complaint, and the prosecution is not required to prove it, but the accused may do so.S

17. It shall be competent to include in one indictment or complaint both common law and statutory charges.S

18. In any proceedings under the Merchant Shipping Acts it shall not be necessary to produce the official register of the ship referred to in the proceedings in order to prove the nationality of the ship, but the nationality of the ship as stated in the indictment or, as the case may be, complaint shall, in the absence of evidence to the contrary, be presumed.S

19. In offences inferring dishonest appropriation of property brought before a court whose power to deal with such offences is limited to cases in which the value of such property does not exceed level 4 on the standard scale it shall be assumed, and it shall not be necessary to state in the charge, that the value of the property does not exceed that sum.S

Schedule 4. Supervision and Treatment Orders

Section 57. (5).

Part IS Preliminary

1. (1)In this Schedule "supervision and treatment order" means an order requiring the person in respect of whom it is made ("the supervised person")—S
(a) to be under the supervision of a social worker who is an officer of the local authority for the area where the supervised person resides or is to reside (in this Schedule referred to as "the supervising officer") for such period, not being more than three years, as is specified in the order;
(b) to comply during that period with instructions given to him by the supervising officer regarding his supervision; and
(c) to submit during that period to treatment by or under the direction of a medical practitioner with a view to the improvement of his mental condition.
(2) The Secretary of State may by order amend sub-paragraph (1) above by substituting, for the period for the time being specified in that sub-paragraph, such period as may be specified in the order.
(3) An order under sub-paragraph (2) above may make any amendment to paragraph 8. (2) below which the Secretary of State considers necessary in consequence of the order.
(4) The power of the Secretary of State to make orders under sub-paragraph (2) above shall be exercisable by statutory instrument subject to annulment in pursuance of a resolution of either House of Parliament.

Part IIS Making and Effect of Orders

Circumstances in which orders may be madeS

2. (1)The court shall not make a supervision and treatment order unless it is satisfied—S
(a) that, having regard to all the circumstances of the case, the making of such an order is the most suitable means of dealing with the person; and
(b) on the written or oral evidence of two or more [F1approved medical practitioners] , that the mental condition of the person—
(i) is such as requires and may be susceptible to treatment; but
(ii) is not such as to warrant the making of an order under paragraph (a) of subsection (2) of section 57 of this Act (whether with or without an order under paragraph (b) of that subsection) or an order under paragraph (c) of that subsection.
(2) The court shall not make a supervision and treatment order unless it is also satisfied—
(a) that the supervising officer intended to be specified in the order is willing to undertake the supervision; and
(b) that arrangements have been made for the treatment intended to be specified in the order.
(3) Subsections (3) to (5) of section 61 of this Act shall have effect with respect to proof of a person's mental condition for the purposes of sub-paragraph (1) above as they have effect with respect to proof of an offender's mental condition for the purposes of section 58. (1)(a) of this Act.
[F2. (4)In this Schedule "approved medical practitioner" has the meaning given by section 22. (4) of the Mental Health (Care and Treatment)(Scotland) Act 2003 (asp 13).]
Amendments (Textual)
F1. Words in Sch. 4 para. 2. (1)(b) substituted (27.9.2005) by The Mental Health (Care and Treatment) (Scotland) Act 2003 (Modification of Enactments) Order 2005 (S.S.I. 2005/465), art. 2, Sch. 1 para. 27. (6)(a)

F2. Sch. 4 para. 2. (4) inserted (27.9.2005) by The Mental Health (Care and Treatment) (Scotland) Act 2003 (Modification of Enactments) Order 2005 (S.S.I. 2005/465), art. 2, Sch. 1 para. 27. (6)(b)

Making of orders and general requirementsS

3. (1)A supervision and treatment order shall specify the local authority area in which the supervised person resides or will reside.S

(2) Before making such an order, the court shall explain to the supervised person in ordinary language—

(a) the effect of the order (including any requirements proposed to be included in the order in accordance with paragraph 5 below); and

(b) that the sheriff court for the area in which the supervised person resides or will reside (in this Schedule referred to as "the relevant sheriff court") has power under paragraphs 6 to 8 below to review the order on the application either of the supervised person or of the supervising officer.

(3) After making such an order, the court shall forthwith give a copy of the order to—

(a) the supervised person;

(b) the supervising officer;

[F3. (bb)the medical practitioner by whom or under whose supervision the supervised person is to be treated under the order;] and

(c) the person in charge of any institution in which the supervised person is required by the order to reside.

(4) After making such an order, the court shall also send to the relevant sheriff court—

(a) a copy of the order; and

(b) such documents and information relating to the case as it considers likely to be of assistance to that court in the exercise of its functions in relation to the order.

(5) Where such an order is made, the supervised person shall comply with such instructions as he may from time to time be given by the supervising officer regarding his supervision and shall keep in touch with that officer and notify him of any change of address.

Amendments (Textual)

F3. Sch. 4 para. 3. (3)(bb) inserted (1.1.1998) by 1997 c. 48, s. 62. (1), Sch. 1 para. 21. (35)(a); S.I. 1997/2323, art. 4, Sch. 2 (subject to art. 7)

Obligatory requirements as to medical treatmentS

4. (1)A supervision and treatment order shall include a requirement that the supervised person shall submit, during the period specified in the order, to treatment by or under the direction of a medical practitioner with a view to the improvement of his mental condition.S

(2) The treatment required by the order shall be such one of the following kinds of treatment as may be specified in the order, that is to say—

(a) treatment as a non-resident patient at such institution or place as may be specified in the order; and

(b) treatment by or under the direction of such medical practitioner as may be so specified;

but the nature of the treatment shall not be specified in the order except as mentioned in paragraph (a) or (b) above.

(3) Where the medical practitioner by whom or under whose direction the supervised person is being treated for his mental condition in pursuance of a supervision and treatment order is of the opinion that part of the treatment can be better or more conveniently given at an institution or place which—

(a) is not specified in the order; and

(b) is one at which the treatment of the supervised person will be given by or under the direction of a medical practitioner, he may, with the consent of the supervised person, make arrangements for him to be treated accordingly.

(4) Where any such arrangements as are mentioned in sub-paragraph (3) above are made for the treatment of a supervised person—

(a) the medical practitioner by whom the arrangements are made shall give notice in writing to the supervising officer, specifying the institution or place at which the treatment is to be carried out; and

(b) the treatment provided for by the arrangements shall be deemed to be treatment to which he is required to submit in pursuance of the supervision and treatment order.

Optional requirements as to residenceS

5. (1)Subject to sub-paragraphs (2) to (4) below, a supervision and treatment order may include requirements as to the residence of the supervised person.S

(2) Such an order may not require the supervised person to reside as a resident patient in a hospital.

(3) Before making such an order containing any such requirement, the court shall consider the home surroundings of the supervised person.

(4) Where such an order requires the supervised person to reside in any institution, the period for which he is so required to reside shall be specified in the order.

Part IIIS Revocation and Amendment of Orders

Revocation of order in interests of health or welfareS

6. Where a supervision and treatment order is in force in respect of any person and, on the application of the supervised person or the supervising officer, it appears to the relevant sheriff court that, having regard to circumstances which have arisen since the order was made, it would be in the interests of the health or welfare of the supervised person that the order should be revoked, the court may revoke the order.S

Amendment of order by reason of change of residenceS

7. (1)This paragraph applies where, at any time while a supervision and treatment order is in force in respect of any person, the relevant sheriff court is satisfied that—S

(a) the supervised person proposes to change, or has changed, his residence from the area specified in the order to the area of another local authority;

(b) a social worker who is an officer of the other local authority ("the new supervising officer") is willing to undertake the supervision; and

(c) the requirements of the order as respects treatment will continue to be complied with.

(2) Subject to sub-paragraph (3) below the court may, and on the application of the supervising officer shall, amend the supervision and treatment order by substituting the other area for the area specified in the order and the new supervising officer for the supervising officer specified in the order.

(3) Where a supervision and treatment order contains requirements which, in the opinion of the court, can be complied with only if the supervised person continues to reside in the area specified in the order, the court shall not amend the order under this paragraph unless it also, in accordance with paragraph 8 below, either—

(a) cancels those requirements; or

(b) substitutes for those requirements other requirements which can be complied with if the supervised person ceases to reside in that area.

Amendment of requirements of orderS

8. (1)Without prejudice to paragraph 7 above, but subject to sub-paragraph (2) below, the relevant sheriff court may, on the application of the supervised person or the supervising officer, by order amend a supervision and treatment order—S
(a) by cancelling any of the requirements of the order; or
(b) by inserting in the order (either in addition to or in substitution for any such requirement) any requirement which the court could include if it were the court by which the order was made and were then making it.
(2) The power of the court under sub-paragraph (1) above shall not include power to amend an order by extending the period specified in it beyond the end of three years from the date of the original order.

Amendment of requirements in pursuance of medical reportS

9. (1)Where the medical practitioner by whom or under whose direction the supervised person is being treated for his mental condition in pursuance of any requirement of a supervision and treatment order—S
(a) is of the opinion mentioned in sub-paragraph (2) below; or
(b) is for any reason unwilling to continue to treat or direct the treatment of the supervised person, he shall make a report in writing to that effect to the supervising officer and that officer shall apply under paragraph 8 above to the relevant sheriff court for the variation or cancellation of the requirement.
(2) The opinion referred to in sub-paragraph (1) above is—
(a) that the treatment of the supervised person should be continued beyond the period specified in the supervision and treatment order;
(b) that the supervised person needs different treatment, being treatment of a kind to which he could be required to submit in pursuance of such an order;
(c) that the supervised person is not susceptible to treatment; or
(d) that the supervised person does not require further treatment.

SupplementalS

10. (1)On the making under paragraph 6 above of an order revoking a supervision and treatment order, the sheriff clerk shall forthwith give a copy of the revoking order to the supervising officer [F4and to the medical practitioner by whom or under whose supervision the supervised person was treated under the supervision and treatment order].S
(2) On receipt of a copy of the revoking order the supervising officer shall give a copy to the supervised person and to the person in charge of any institution in which the supervised person was required by the order to reside.
Amendments (Textual)
F4. Words in Sch. 4 para. 10. (1) inserted (1.1.1998) by 1997 c. 48, s. 62. (1), Sch. 1 para. 21. (35)(b); S.I. 1997/2323, art. 4, Sch. 2 (subject to art. 7)
11. (1)On the making under paragraph 7 or 8 above of an order amending a supervision and treatment order, the sheriff clerk shall forthwith—S
(a) if the order amends the supervision and treatment order otherwise than by substituting a new area or a new place for the one specified in that order, give a copy of the amending order to the supervising officer [F5and to the medical practitioner by whom or under whose supervision the supervised person has been treated under the supervision and treatment order];

(b) if the order amends the supervision and treatment order in the manner excepted by paragraph (a) above, send to the new relevant sheriff court—

(i) a copy of the amending order; and

(ii) such documents and information relating to the case as he considers likely to be of assistance to that court in exercising its functions in relation to the order;

and in a case falling within paragraph (b) above, the sheriff clerk shall give a copy of the amending order to the supervising officer.

(2) On receipt of a copy of an amending order the supervising officer shall give a copy to the supervised person and to the person in charge of any institution in which the supervised person is or was required by the order to reside.

Amendments (Textual)

F5. Words in Sch. 4 para. 11. (1)(a) inserted (1.1.1998) by 1997 c. 48, s. 62. (1), Sch. 1 para. 21. (35)(c); S.I. 1997/2323, art. 4, Sch. 2 (subject to art. 7)

12. On the making, revocation or amendment of a supervision and treatment order the supervising officer shall give a copy of the order or, as the case may be, of the order revoking or amending it, to the Mental Welfare Commission for Scotland.S

Schedule 5. Forms of Complaint and Charges

Section 138. (2).

The following Forms are additional to those contained in Schedule 2 to this Act, all of which, in so far as applicable to charges which may be tried summarily, are deemed to be incorporated in this Schedule:—

You did assault A.L. and strike him with your fists.

You did conduct yourself in a disorderly manner and commit a breach of the peace.

You did threaten violence to the lieges and commit a breach of the peace.

You did fight and commit a breach of the peace.

You did publicly expose your person in a shameless and indecent manner in presence of the lieges.

You did obtain from A.N. board and lodging to the value of £16 without paying and intending not to pay therefor.

You did maliciously knock down 20 metres of the coping of a wall forming the fence between two fields on the said farm.

You did maliciously place a block of wood on the railway line and attempt to obstruct a train.

You did drive a horse and cart recklessly to the danger of the lieges.

You did break into a poultry house and steal three fowls.

You did steal a coat which you obtained from R.O. on the false representation that you had been sent for it by her husband.

having received from D.G. £6 to hand to E.R., you did on(date) at(place) steal the said sum.

having received from G.R. a watch in loan, you did on at , sell it to E.G., and steal it.

having found a watch, you did, without trying to discover its owner, sell it on at , to O.R., and steal it.

You did acquire from K.O., a private in the Third Battalion a military jacket and waist belt, contrary to section 195 of the Army Act 1955.

You, being a person whose estate has been sequestrated, did obtain credit from W.A. to the extent of £260 without informing him that your estate had been sequestrated and that you had not received your discharge, contrary to section 67. (9) of the Bankruptcy (Scotland) Act 1985.

You, being the occupier of the said house, did use the same for the purpose of betting with persons resorting thereto, contrary to section 1 of the Betting, Gaming and Lotteries Act 1963.

You did frequent and loiter in the said street for the purpose of betting and receiving bets, contrary to section 8 of the Betting, Gaming and Lotteries Act 1963.

You did assault L.S., a constable of the Police, while engaged in the execution of his duty, and with a stick strike him on the face to the great effusion of blood contrary to section 41 of the Police (Scotland) Act 1967.

F1.............................

Amendments (Textual)

F1. Sch. 5: entry repealed (3.11.2006) by The Animal Health and Welfare (Scotland) Act 2006 (Consequential Provisions) Order 2006 (S.S.I. 2006/536), art. 2. (3), Sch. 3

You did wilfully neglect your children K.I., aged seven years; J.I., aged five years; and H.I., aged three years, by failing to provide them with adequate food and clothing, and by keeping them in a filthy and verminous condition, contrary to section 12 of the Children and Young Persons (Scotland) Act 1937.

You are the owner of a dog which is dangerous and not kept under proper control, and which on in did chase a flock of sheep, contrary to section 2 of the Dogs Act 1871, section 2, as amended by section 1 of the Dogs Act 1906, whereby you are liable to be ordered to keep the said dog under proper control or to destroy it.

You, being a parent of D.U., a child of school age, aged , who has attended school, and the said child having failed, between and , without reasonable excuse, to attend regularly at the said school, you are thereby guilty of an offence against section 35 of the Education (Scotland) Act 1980.

F2.............................

Amendments (Textual)

F2. Sch. 5: entry repealed (26.4.2005) by The Manufacture and Storage of Explosives Regulations 2005 (S.I. 2005/1082), art. 28. (1)(2)(3), Sch. 5 para. 21. (a), Sch. 6 Pt. 1

F3.............................

Amendments (Textual)

F3. Sch. 5: entry repealed (26.4.2005) by The Manufacture and Storage of Explosives Regulations 2005 (S.I. 2005/1082), art. 28. (1)(2)(3), Sch. 5 para. 21. (b), Sch. 6 Pt. 1

You did sell and deliver to N.C. to his prejudice an article of food namely; gallons of sweet milk which was not of the nature, substance and quality of the article demanded by him and was not genuine sweet milk in respect that it was deficient in milk fat to the extent of per cent, or thereby in that it contained only per cent, of milk fat, conform to certificate of analysis granted on (date) by A.N. analytical chemist (address), public analyst for (a copy of which certificate of analysis is annexed hereto) of a sample of the said milk taken (specify time and place) by L.O., duly appointed sampling officer for , acting under the direction of the local authority for the said burgh, while the said milk was in course of delivery to the said N.C. contrary to the Food Act 1984, and the Sale of Milk Regulations 1901.

You did take part in gaming in the street contrary to sections 5 and 8 of the Gaming Act 1968.

F4...

Amendments (Textual)

F4. Words in Sch. 5 repealed (2.7.2012) by The Wildlife and Natural Environment (Scotland) Act 2011 (Consequential Modifications) Order 2012 (S.S.I. 2012/215), reg. 1, sch. pt. 3

F4...

F4...

F4...

You did present or cause to be presented to W.E., Assessors for a return in which you falsely stated that the yearly rent of your House. No. Street, , was £20, instead of £30, contrary to section 7 of the Lands Valuation (Scotland) Act 1854.

F5.............................

Amendments (Textual)

F5. Sch. 5: entries relating to "sections 74. (2) and 76 of the Licensing (Scotland) Act 1976" repealed (1.9.2009 at 5.00 a.m.) by The Licensing (Scotland) Act 2005 (Consequential Provisions) Order 2009 (S.S.I. 2009/248), arts. 1. (2), 2. (2), Sch. 2

F5.............................

You did drive a motor car recklessly contrary to section 2 of the Road Traffic Act 1988.

You did act as a pedlar without having obtained a certificate, contrary to section 4 of the Pedlars'

Act 1871.

F6. . . . .

Amendments (Textual)

F6. Words in Sch. 5 repealed (26.3.2001) by S.I. 2001/1149, art. 3. (2), Sch. 2

You did travel in a railway carriage without having previously paid your fare, and with intent to avoid payment thereof, contrary to section 5. (3)(a) of the Regulation of Railways Act 1889.

having on within the house No. Street, given birth to a female child, you did fail, within twenty-one days thereafter, to attend personally and give information to C.W., registrar of births, deaths, and marriages for (Registration District), of the particulars required to be registered concerning the birth, contrary to sections 14 and 53 of the Registration of Births, Deaths, and Marriages (Scotland) Act 1965.

You did take two salmon during the annual close time by means of cobles and sweep nets, contrary to section 15 of the Salmon Fisheries (Scotland) Act 1868.

You had in your possession for use for trade a counter balance which was false, and two weights, which were unjust, contrary to the Weights and Measures Act 1985, section 17.

Schedule 6. Documentary Evidence in Criminal Proceedings

Section 279.

Production of copy documentsS

1. (1)For the purposes of any criminal proceedings a copy of, or of a material part of, a document, purporting to be authenticated in such manner and by such person as may be prescribed, shall unless the court otherwise directs, be—S

(a) deemed a true copy; and

(b) treated for evidential purposes as if it were the document, or the material part, itself, whether or not the document is still in existence.

(2) For the purposes of this paragraph it is immaterial how many removes there are between a copy and the original.

(3) In this paragraph "copy" includes a transcript or reproduction.

Statements in business documentsS

2. (1)Except where it is a statement such as is mentioned in paragraph 3. (b) and (c) below, a statement in a document shall be admissible in criminal proceedings as evidence of any fact or opinion of which direct oral evidence would be admissible, if the following conditions are satisfied—S

(a) the document was created or received in the course of, or for the purposes of, a business or undertaking or in pursuance of the functions of the holder of a paid or unpaid office;

(b) the document is, or at any time was, kept by a business or undertaking or by or on behalf of the holder of such an office; and

(c) the statement was made on the basis of information supplied by a person (whether or not the maker of the statement) who had, or may reasonably be supposed to have had, personal knowledge of the matters dealt with in it.

(2) Sub-paragraph (1) above applies whether the information contained in the statement was supplied directly or indirectly unless, in the case of information supplied indirectly, it appears to the court that any person through whom it was so supplied did not both receive and supply it in the

course of a business or undertaking or as or on behalf of the holder of a paid or unpaid office.

(3) Where in any proceedings a statement is admitted as evidence by virtue of this paragraph—

(a) any evidence which, if—

(i) the maker of the statement; or

(ii) where the statement was made on the basis of information supplied by another person, such supplier,

had been called as a witness, would have been admissible as relevant to the witness's credibility shall be so admissible in those proceedings;

(b) evidence may be given of any matter which, if the maker or as the case may be the supplier had been called as a witness, could have been put to him in cross-examination as relevant to his credibility but of which evidence could not have been adduced by the cross-examining party; and

(c) evidence tending to prove that the maker or as the case may be the supplier, whether before or after making the statement or supplying the information on the basis of which the statement was made, made (in whatever manner) some other representation which is inconsistent with the statement shall be admissible for the purpose of showing that he has contradicted himself.

(4) In sub-paragraph (3)(c) above, "representation" does not include a representation in a precognition.

3. A statement in a document shall be admissible in criminal proceedings as evidence of the fact that the statement was made if—S

(a) the document satisfies the conditions mentioned in sub-paragraph (1)(a) and (b) of paragraph 2 above;

(b) the statement is made, whether directly or indirectly, by a person who in those proceedings is an accused; and

(c) the statement, being exculpatory only, exculpates the accused.

Documents kept by businesses etc.S

4. Unless the court otherwise directs, a document may in any criminal proceedings be taken to be a document kept by a business or undertaking or by or on behalf of the holder of a paid or unpaid office if it is certified as such by a docquet in the prescribed form and purporting to be authenticated, in such manner as may be prescribed—S

(a) by a person authorised to authenticate such a docquet on behalf of the business or undertaking by which; or

(b) by, or by a person authorised to authenticate such a docquet on behalf of, the office-holder by whom,

the document was kept.

Statements not contained in business documentsS

5. (1)In any criminal proceedings, the evidence of an authorised person that—S

(a) a document which satisfies the conditions mentioned in paragraph 2. (1)(a) and (b) above does not contain a relevant statement as to a particular matter; or

(b) no document, within a category of documents satisfying those conditions, contains such a statement,

shall be admissible evidence whether or not the whole or any part of that document or of the documents within that category and satisfying those conditions has been produced in the proceedings.

(2) For the purposes of sub-paragraph (1) above, a relevant statement is a statement which is of the kind mentioned in paragraph 2. (1)(c) above and which, in the ordinary course of events—

(a) the document; or

(b) a document within the category and satisfying the conditions mentioned in that sub-paragraph, might reasonably have been expected to contain.

(3) The evidence referred to in sub-paragraph (1) above may, unless the court otherwise directs, be given by means of a certificate by the authorised person in the prescribed form and purporting to be authenticated in such manner as may be prescribed.

(4) In this paragraph, "authorised person" means a person authorised to give evidence—

(a) on behalf of the business or undertaking by which; or

(b) as or on behalf of the office-holder by or on behalf of whom,

the document is or was kept.

Additional evidence where evidence from business documents challengedS

6. (1)This sub-paragraph applies where—S

(a) evidence has been admitted by virtue of paragraph 2. (3) above; or

(b) the court has made a direction under paragraph 1. (1), 4 or 5. (3) above.

(2) Where sub-paragraph (1) above applies the judge may, without prejudice to sections 268 and 269 of this Act—

(a) in solemn proceedings, on a motion of the prosecutor or defence at any time before the commencement of the speeches to the jury;

(b) in summary proceedings, on such a motion at any time before the prosecutor proceeds to address the judge on the evidence,

permit him to lead additional evidence of such description as the judge may specify.

(3) Subsections (3) and (4) of section 268 of this Act shall apply in relation to sub-paragraph (2) above as they apply in relation to subsection (1) of that section.

GeneralS

7. (1)Nothing in this Schedule—S

(a) shall prejudice the admissibility of a statement made by a person other than in the course of giving oral evidence in court which is admissible otherwise than by virtue of this Schedule;

(b) shall affect the operation of the M1. Bankers' Books Evidence Act 1879;

(c) shall apply to—

(i) proceedings commenced; or

(ii) where the proceedings consist of an application to the sheriff by virtue of section 42. (2)(c) of the M2. Social Work (Scotland) Act 1968, an application made,

before this Schedule comes into force.

(2) For the purposes of sub-paragraph (1)(c)(i) above, solemn proceedings are commenced when the indictment is served.

Marginal Citations

M11879 c. 11.

M21968 c. 45.

8. In this Schedule—S

"business" includes trade, profession or other occupation;

"criminal proceedings" includes any hearing by the sheriff [F1of an application made by virtue of section 93. (2)(a) or 94. (2)(a) of the Children's Hearings (Scotland) Act 2011 (asp 1) to determine whether a ground is established, in so far as the application relates to the commission of an offence by the child, or for a review of such a determination,]

"document" includes, in addition to a document in writing—

- any map, plan, graph or drawing;

- any photograph;

- any disc, tape, sound track or other device in which sounds or other data (not being visual images) are recorded so as to be capable, with or without the aid of some other equipment, of being reproduced therefrom; and

- any film, negative, tape, disc or other device in which one or more visual images are recorded so as to be capable (as aforesaid) of being produced therefrom;

"film"includes a microfilm;

"made" includes allegedly made;

"prescribed" means prescribed by Act of Adjournal;

"statement" includes any representation (however made or expressed) of fact or opinion, including an instruction, order or request, but, except in paragraph 7. (1)(a) above, does not include a statement which falls within one or more of the following descriptions—

- a statement in a precognition;

- a statement made for the purposes of or in connection with—

pending or contemplated criminal proceedings; or

a criminal investigation; or

- a statement made by an accused person in so far as it incriminates a co-accused; and

"undertaking" includes any public or statutory undertaking, any local authority and any government department.

Amendments (Textual)

F1. Words in Sch. 8 para. 8 substituted (24.6.2013) by The Childrens Hearings (Scotland) Act 2011 (Modification of Primary Legislation) Order 2013 (S.S.I. 2013/211), art. 1, sch. 1 para. 10. (9)

Schedule 7. Certificates as to Proof of Certain Routine Matters

Modifications etc. (not altering text)

C1. Sch. 9: power to amend or repeal conferred (1.4.1996) by 1995 c. 46, ss. 280. (2), 309. (2)

Enactment | Persons who may purport to sign certificates | Matters which may be certified |

That, on a date specified in the certificate—

(a) copies of regulations made under those Acts, prohibiting such activity as may be so specified, were displayed at a location so specified;

(b) in so far as those regulations prohibited persons from carrying out a specified activity in the park without written permission, such permission had not been given to a person so specified.

F1. . . . . | F1. . . . . | F1. . . . . . .
. . . . |

F2. . . . . | F2. . . . . | F2. . . . . . .
. . . . |

F2. . . . . | F2. . . . . | F2. . . . . . .
. . . . |

In relation to a person identified in the certificate, that on a date specified therein—

(a) he held, or as the case may be did not hold, a firearm certificate or shotgun certificate (within the meaning of that Act);

(b) he possessed, or as the case may be did not possess, an authority (which as regards a possessed authority, shall be described in the certificate) given under section 5 of that Act by the Secretary of State [F5or, by virtue of provision made under section 63 of the Scotland Act 1998, the Scottish Ministers].

The Misuse of Drugs Act 1971 (c.38) Sections 4, 5, 6, 8, 9, 12, 13, 19 and 20 (various offences concerning controlled drugs).

The Immigration Act 1971 (c.77) Section 24. (1)(a) in so far as it relates to entry in breach of a deportation order, section 24. (1)(b) and section 26. (1)(f) in so far as it relates to a requirement of regulations (various offences concerning persons entering, or remaining in, the United Kingdom).

In relation to a person identified in the certificate—

(a) the date, place or means of his arrival in, or any removal of him from, the United Kingdom;

(b) any limitation on, or condition attached to, any leave for him to enter or remain in the United Kingdom;

(c) the date and method of service of any notice of, or of variations of conditions attached to, such leave.

F6. . . . . | F6. . . . . | F6. . . . . . .
. . . . |

F7. . . . . | F7. . . . . | F7. . . . . . .
. . . . |

Customs and Excise Management Act 1979 The following provisions in so far as they have effect in relation to the prohibitions contained in sections 20 and 21 of the Forgery and Counterfeiting Act 1981 namely:—

Sections 50. (2) and (3)

Section 68; and

Section 170

(various offences committed in connection with contraventions of prohibitions on the import and export of counterfeits or currency notes or protected coins).

The Forgery and Counterfeiting Act 1981 Sections 14 to 16 (certain offences relating to counterfeiting). | Two officials authorised to do so by the Secretary of State, being officials of the authority or body which may lawfully issue the currency notes or protected coins referred to in column 3 hereof. | That the coin or note identified in the certificate by reference to a label or otherwise is a counterfeit of a currency note or protected coin; where "currency note" has the meaning assigned to it by section 27(1)(a) of the Forgery and Counterfeiting Act 1981, and "protected coin" means any coin which is customarily used as money in the United Kingdom, any of the Channel Islands, the Isle of Man or the Republic of Ireland. |

The Wildlife and Countryside Act 1981 (c. 69) [F8. Sections 1, 5, 6. (1) to (3), 7, 8, 9. (1), (2), (4) and (5), 10. A(1), 11. (1) and (2), 11. G(1), 11. I(1), 13. (1) and (2), 14, 14. ZC and 14. A] (certain offences relating to protection of wild animals or wild plants).

In relation to a person specified in the certificate that, on a date so specified, he held, or as the case may be did not hold, a licence under section 16 of that Act and, where he held such a licence—

(a) the purpose for which the licence was granted; and

(b) the terms and conditions of the licence.

The Civic Government (Scotland) Act 1982 (c.45) | A person authorised to do so by the Secretary of State. | In relation to a person identified in the certificate, that on a date specified therein he held, or as the case may be, did not hold, a licence under a provision so specified of that Act. | The accuracy of any particular—

(a) speedometer fitted to a police vehicle;

(b) odometer fitted to a police vehicle;

(c) radar meter; or

(d) apparatus for measuring speed, time or distance, identified in the certificate by reference to its number or otherwise.

The Video Recordings Act 1984 (c. 39) Sections 9 to 14 (offences relating to the supply and possession of video recordings in contravention of that Act).

[F9. A person authorised to do so by the Secretary of State, being a person who has examined the record maintained in pursuance of arrangements made by the designated authority and in the case of a certificate in terms of—

(a) sub-paragraph (a) in column 3, the video work mentioned in that sub-paragraph;

(b) sub-paragraph (b) in that column, both video works mentioned in that sub-paragraph.]

[That the record shows any of the following-

(a) in respect of a video work (or part of a video work) contained in a video recording identified by the certificate, that by a date specified no classification certificate had been issued;

(b) in respect of a video work which is the subject of a certificate under sub-paragraph (a) above, that the video work differs in a specified way from another video work contained in a video recording identified in the certificate under this sub-paragraph and that, on a date specified, a classification certificate was issued in respect of that other video work;

(c) that, by a date specified, no classification certificate had been issued in respect of a video work having a particular title

(d) that on the date specified, a classification certificate was issued in respect of a video work having a particular title and that a document which is identified in the certificate under this sub-paragraph is a copy of the classification certificate so issued;

 expressions used in column 2, or in this column, of this entry being construed in accordance with that Act; and in each of sub-paragraphs (a) to (d) above "specified" means specified in the certificate under that sub-paragraph.]

The Road Traffic Act 1988 (c. 52) Section 165. (3) (offence of failure to give name and address and to produce vehicle documents when required by constable).

The Control of Pollution (Amendment) Act 1989 (c.14) Section 1 (offence of transporting controlled waste without registering).

The Environmental Protection Act 1990 (c.43) Section 33(1)(a) and (b) (prohibition on harmful depositing, treatment or disposal of waste). | An officer of a waste regulation authority within the meaning of that Act authorised to do so by the authority. | In relation to a person specified in the certificate that, on a date so specified, he held, or as the case may be he did not hold, a waste management licence. |

Section 34(1)(c) (duty of care as respects transfer of waste). | An officer of a waste regulation authority within the meaning of that Act authorised to do so by the authority. | In relation to a person specified in the certificate, that on a date so specified he was not an authorised person within the meaning of section 34(3)(b) or (d) of that Act. |

The Social Security Administration Act 1992 (c.5) [F10. Section 112. (1)] (false statements etc. to obtain payments).

Any officer authorised to do so by the Secretary of State.

In relation to a person identified in the certificate—

(a) the assessment , award, or nature of any benefit applied for by him;

(b) the transmission or handing over of any payment to him.

The Criminal Justice and Public Order Act 1994 (c. 33) Paragraph 5 of Schedule 6 (offence of making false statements to obtain certification as prisoner custody officer).

That—

(a) on a date specified in the certificate, an application for a certificate under section 114 of that Act was received from a person so specified;

(b) the application contained a statement so specified;

(c) a person so specified made, on a date so specified, a statement in writing in terms so specified.

This Act. Sections 24. (3) to (8), [F1125, 27 to 29 and 90. C(1)]

In relation to a person specified in the certificate, that—

(a) an order granting bail under that Act was made on a date so specified by a court so specified;

(b) the order or a condition of it so specified was in force on a date so specified;

(c) notice of the time and place appointed for a diet so specified was given to him in a manner so specified;

(d) as respects a diet so specified, he failed to appear.

Section 150(8) (offence of failure of accused to appear at diet after due notice). | The clerk of court. | That, on a date specified in the certificate, he gave a person so specified, in a manner so specified, notice of the time and place appointed for a diet so specified. |

[F12. The Communications Act 2003

Section 363. (1) and (2)(offence of unauthorised installation or use of a television receiver)

[F13The Antisocial Behaviour etc. (Scotland) Act 2004 (asp 8), section 45(1). | An officer of a local authority within the meaning of that Act authorised to do so by the authority. | That a level of noise specified in the certificate was measured at a time and in a place specified in the certificate using an approved device within the meaning of that Act.] |

[F14The Building (Scotland) Act 2003 (asp 8) | | | |

In relation to a building specified in the certificate, that on a date so specified, the local authority had not—

    - granted a warrant under section 9 for the work or, as the case may be, conversion, or

    - received a copy of such a warrant granted by a verifier other than the authority

That, on a date specified in the certificate, the local authority had not—

    - accepted under section 18. (1) a completion certificate in respect of construction or conversion in relation to a building so specified,

    - received a copy of such a certificate accepted under section 18. (1) by a verifier other than the authority, or

    - received a copy of a permission for temporary occupation or use of the building so specified granted under section 21. (3)

Section 43(1) (offence of occupying building, following evacuation, without notice from local authority) | An officer of a local authority authorised to do so by the authority | That, on a date specified in the certificate, the local authority had not given a person notice under section 42(7)] |

F15. . . | F15. . . | F15. . . |

In relation to a person identified in the certificate, that on a date specified in that certificate that person held, or as the case may be did not hold, a licence issued under that Act.

| | In relation to a premises licence or occasional licence issued under that Act and held by a person identified in the certificate, the conditions to which that licence is subject.] |

[F17The Water Environment (Controlled Activities) (Scotland) Regulations 2011 (S.S.I. 2011/209) | | | |

Regulation 44 | A person authorised to do so by the Scottish Environment Protection Agency | That the person has analysed a sample identified in the certificate (by label or otherwise) and that the sample is of a nature and composition specified in the certificate. |

Regulations made by virtue of section 18 of the Regulatory Reform (Scotland) Act 2014 (asp 3) | A person authorised to do so by a regulator (within the meaning of paragraph 3(1) of schedule 2 to that Act) | That the person has analysed a sample identified in the certificate (by label or otherwise) and that the sample is of a nature and composition specified in the certificate. |

| | In relation to a person specified in the certificate that, on a date and in relation to an activity so specified, the person held or, as the case may be, did not hold a permit (within the meaning of paragraph 34 of schedule 2 to that Act) granted by such a regulator and, where the person held such a permit, any condition to which the permit is subject. |

In relation to a person specified in the certificate that, on a date and in relation to an activity so specified, the person held or, as the case may be, did not hold registration (within the meaning of paragraph 34 of schedule 2 to that Act) granted by such a regulator and, where the person held such registration—

    - any condition to which the registration is subject;

    - whether the registration subsisted on the date specified in the certificate.

| | In relation to a person specified in the certificate that, on a date and in relation to an activity so specified, the person had given notification (within the meaning of paragraph 34 of schedule 2 to that Act) to such a regulator and, where the person gave such notification, whether the notification subsisted on the date specified in the certificate. |

| | In relation to a permit or registration (in each case within the meaning of paragraph 34 of schedule 2 to that Act) a description of any variation, transfer, surrender, suspension or revocation of the permit or registration. |

| | In relation to a person specified in the certificate that, on a date so specified, such regulator served on the person a notice mentioned in paragraph 18 of schedule 2 to that Act. |

| | That such a regulator has, in pursuance of paragraph 4(3)(d) of schedule 2 to that Act, made general binding rules as mentioned in that paragraph, or has, in pursuance of paragraph 11 of that schedule, made standard rules as mentioned in that paragraph; and the content of those general binding rules or standard rules.] |

[F18The Air Weapons and Licensing (Scotland) Act 2015 | A constable or a person employed by the Scottish Police Authority, if the constable or person is authorised to do so by the chief constable of the Police Service of Scotland. | in relation to a person identified in the certificate, that on the date specified in the certificate the person held, or as the case may be, did not hold, an air weapon certificate (within the meaning of Part 1 of that Act).] |

Amendments (Textual)

F1. Sch. 9 Table: entry repealed (1.4.2004) by Communications Act 2003 (c. 21), ss. 406, 411. (2)(3), Sch. 19. (1); S.I. 2003/3142, art. 4. (2), Sch. 2 (with savings in art. 11)

F2. Sch. 9 Table: entry repealed (1.5.2005) by Building (Scotland) Act 2003 (asp 8), ss. 58, 59, Sch. 6 para. 22. (a); S.S.I. 2004/404, art. 2. (1)

F3. Words in Sch. 9 substituted (1.4.2013) by Police and Fire Reform (Scotland) Act 2012 (asp 8), s. 129. (2), sch. 7 para. 12. (11); S.S.I. 2013/51, art. 2 (with transitional provisions and savings in S.S.I. 2013/121)

F4. Words in Sch. 9 inserted (1.7.1999) by S.I. 1999/1820, arts. 1. (2), 4, Sch. 2 Pt. I para. 122. (5)(a); S.I. 1998/3178, art. 3

F5. Words in Sch. 9 inserted (1.7.1999) by S.I. 1999/1820, arts. 1. (2), 4, Sch. 2 Pt. I para. 122. (5)(b); S.I. 1998/3178, art. 3

F6. Sch. 9 Table: entry repealed (1.4.2006) by The Water Environment (Consequential and Savings Provisions) (Scotland) Order 2006 (S.S.I. 2006/181), art. 2, Sch. Pt. IV para. 9. (2)(a)

F7. Sch. 9: entry relating to "the Licensing (Scotland) Act 1976" repealed (1.9.2009 at 5.00 a.m.) by The Licensing (Scotland) Act 2005 (Consequential Provisions) Order 2009 (S.S.I. 2009/248), arts. 1. (1), 2. (2), Sch. 2

F8. Words in Sch. 9 substituted (2.7.2012) by The Wildlife and Natural Environment (Scotland) Act 2011 (Consequential Modifications) Order 2012 (S.S.I. 2012/215), reg. 1, sch. para. 1

F9. Words in Sch. 9 substituted (1.8.1997) by 1997 c. 48, s. 30. (2)(3); S.I. 1997/1712, art. 3, Sch. (subject to arts. 4, 5)

F10. Words in Sch. 9 substituted (4.7.1996) by 1996 c. 25, s. 73. (4)

F11. Sch. 9 Table: words substituted (1.2.2005) by Criminal Procedure (Amendment) (Scotland) Act 2004 (asp 5), ss. 25, 27. (1), Sch. para. 58; S.S.I. 2004/405, art. 2. (1), Sch. 1 (subject to transitional provisions and savings in arts. 3-5)

F12. Sch. 9 Table: words inserted (1.4.2004) by Communications Act 2003 (c. 21), ss. 406, 411. (2)(3), Sch. 17 para. 133. (3); S.I. 2003/3142, {art. 4. (2)}, Sch. 2 (with savings in art. 11)

F13. Sch. 9 Table: entry inserted (1.12.2004) by Antisocial Behaviour etc. (Scotland) Act 2004 (asp 8), ss. 144. (1), 145. (2), Sch. 4 para. 5. (12); S.S.I. 2004/420, art. 3, Sch. 3

F14. Sch. 9 Table: entries inserted (1.5.2005) by Building (Scotland) Act 2003 (asp 8), ss. 58, 59, Sch. 6 para. 22. (b); S.S.I. 2004/404, art. 2. (1)

F15. Words in Sch. 9 omitted (30.6.2014) by virtue of Regulatory Reform (Scotland) Act 2014 (asp 3), s. 61. (2), sch. 3 para. 31. (4)(a); S.S.I. 2014/160, art. 2. (1)(2), sch.

F16. Sch. 9 Table: entries inserted (1.9.2009 at 5.00 a.m.) by The Licensing (Scotland) Act 2005 (Consequential Provisions) Order 2009 (S.S.I. 2009/248), arts. 1. (1), 2. (1), Sch. 1 para. 6

F17. Words in Sch. 9 inserted (30.6.2014) by Regulatory Reform (Scotland) Act 2014 (asp 3), s. 61. (2), sch. 3 para. 31. (4)(b); S.S.I. 2014/160, art. 2. (1)(2), sch.

F18. Words in Sch. 9 inserted (31.12.2016) by Air Weapons and Licensing (Scotland) Act 2015 (asp 10), s. 88. (2), sch. 2 para. 2; S.S.I. 2016/130, art. 3. (c)

Schedule 8. The Commission: Further Provisions

Amendments (Textual)

F1. Sch. 9. A inserted (1.1.1998) by 1997 c. 48, s. 25. (2); S.I. 1997/3004, art. 2, Sch. (subject to arts. 4, 5)

MembershipS

1. Her Majesty shall, on the recommendation of the Secretary of State, appoint one of the members of the Commission to be the chairman of the Commission.S

2. (1)Subject to the following provisions of this paragraph, a person shall hold and vacate office as a member of the Commission, or as chairman of the Commission, in accordance with the terms of his appointment.S

(2) An appointment as a member of the Commission may be full-time or part-time.

(3) The appointment of a person as a member of the Commission, or as chairman of the Commission, shall be for a fixed period of not longer than five years.

(4) Subject to sub-paragraph (5) below, a person whose term of appointment as a member of the Commission, or as chairman of the Commission, expires shall be eligible for re-appointment.

(5) No person may hold office as a member of the Commission for a continuous period which is longer than ten years.

(6) A person may at any time resign his office as a member of the Commission, or as chairman of the Commission, by notice in writing addressed to Her Majesty.

(7) Her Majesty may at any time remove a person from office as a member of the Commission if satisfied—

(a) that he has without reasonable excuse failed to discharge his functions as a member for a continuous period of three months beginning not earlier than six months before that time;

(b) that he has been convicted of a criminal offence;

(c) that a bankruptcy order has been made against him, or his estate has been sequestrated, or he has made a composition or arrangement with, or granted a trust deed for, his creditors; or

(d) that he is unable or unfit to discharge his functions as a member.

(8) If the chairman of the Commission ceases to be a member of the Commission he shall also cease to be chairman.

Members and employeesS

3. (1)The Commission shall—S

(a) pay to members of the Commission such remuneration;

(b) pay to or in respect of members of the Commission any such allowances, fees, expenses and gratuities; and

(c) pay towards the provisions of pensions to or in respect of members of the Commission any such sums,

as the Commission are required to pay by or in accordance with directions given by the Secretary of State.

(2) Where a member of the Commission was, immediately before becoming a member, a participant in a scheme under section 1 of the M1. Superannuation Act 1972, the Minister for the Civil Service may determine that his term of office as a member shall be treated for the purposes of the scheme as if it were service in the employment or office by reference to which he was a participant in the scheme; and his rights under the scheme shall not be affected by sub-paragraph (1)(c) above.

(3) Where—

(a) a person ceases to hold office as a member of the Commission otherwise than on the expiry of his term of appointment; and

(b) it appears to the Secretary of State that there are special circumstances which make it right for him to receive compensation,

the Secretary of State may direct the Commission to make to him a payment of such amount as the Secretary of State may determine.

Marginal Citations

M11972 c. 11.

4. (1)The Commission may appoint a chief executive and such other employees as the Commission think fit, subject to the consent of the Secretary of State as to their number and terms and conditions of service.S

(2) The Commission shall—

(a) pay to employees of the Commission such remuneration; and

(b) pay to or in respect of employees of the Commission any such allowances, fees, expenses and gratuities,

as the Commission may, with the consent of the Secretary of State, determine.

(3) Employment by the Commission shall be included among the kinds of employment to which a scheme under section 1 of the Superannuation Act 1972 may apply.

5. The Commission shall pay to the Minister for the Civil Service, at such times as he may direct, such sums as he may determine in respect of any increase attributable to paragraph 3. (2) or 4. (3) above in the sums payable out of money provided by Parliament under the M2. Superannuation Act 1972.S

Marginal Citations

M21972 c. 11.

ProcedureS

6. (1)The arrangements for the procedure of the Commission (including the quorum for meetings) shall be such as the Commission may determine.S

(2) The arrangements may provide for the discharge, under the general direction of the Commission, of any function of the Commission—

(a) in the case of the function specified in sub-paragraph (3) below, by a committee consisting of not fewer than three members of the Commission; and

(b) in any other case, by any committee of, or by one or more of the members or employees of, the Commission.

(3) The function referred to in sub-paragraph (2)(a) above is making a reference to the High Court under section 194. B of this Act.

(4) The validity of any proceedings of the Commission (or of any committee of the Commission) shall not be affected by—

(a) any vacancy among the members of the Commission or in the office of chairman of the Commission; or

(b) any defect in the appointment of any person as a member of the Commission or as chairman of the Commission.

(5) Where—

(a) a document or other material has been produced to the Commission under section 194. I of this Act, or they have been given access to a document or other material under that section, and the Commission have taken away the document or other material (or a copy of it); and

(b) the person who produced the document or other material to the Commission, or gave them access to it, has notified the Commission that he considers that its disclosure to others may be contrary to the interests of national security,

the Commission shall, after consulting that person, deal with the document or material (or copy) in a manner appropriate for safeguarding the interests of national security.

EvidenceS

7. A document purporting to be—S

(a) duly executed under the seal of the Commission; or

(b) signed on behalf of the Commission,

shall be received in evidence and, unless the contrary is proved, taken to be so executed or signed.

Annual reports and accountsS

8. (1)As soon as possible after the end of each financial year of the Commission, the Commission shall send to the Secretary of State a report on the discharge of their functions during that year.S
(2) Such a report may include an account of the working of the provisions of Part XA of this Act and recommendations relating to any of those provisions.
(3) The Secretary of State shall lay before each House of Parliament, and cause to be published, a copy of every report sent to him under sub-paragraph (1).
9. (1)The Commission shall—S
(a) keep proper accounts and proper records in relation to the accounts; and
(b) prepare a statement of accounts in respect of each financial year of the Commission.
(2) The statement of accounts shall contain such information and shall be in such form as the Secretary of State may F2. . . direct.
(3) The Commission shall send F3. . . the statement of accounts to the Secretary of State F3. . . within such period after the end of the financial year to which the statement relates as the Secretary of State may direct.
[F4. (3. A)The Scottish Ministers shall send the statement of accounts to the Auditor General for Scotland for auditing.]
F5. (4). . . . .
Amendments (Textual)
F2. Words in Sch. 9. A para. 9. (2) repealed (1.7.1999) by S.I. 1999/1820, arts. 1. (2), 4, Sch. 2 Pt. I para. 122. (3), Pt. IV; S.I. 1998/3178, art. 3
F3. Words in Sch. 9. A para. 9. (3) repealed (1.4.2000) by 2000 asp 1, s. 26, Sch. 4 para. 14. (a); S.S.I. 2000/10, art. 2. (3)
F4. Sch. 9. A para. 9. (3. A) inserted (1.4.2000) by 2000 asp 1, s. 26, Sch. 4 para. 14. (b); S.S.I. 2000/10, art. 2. (3)
F5. Sch. 9. A para. 9. (4) repealed (1.4.2000) by 2000 asp 1, s. 26, Sch. 4 para. 14. (c); S.S.I. 2000/10, art. 2. (3)
10. For the purposes of this Schedule the Commission's financial year shall be the period of twelve months ending with 31st March; but the first financial year of the Commission shall be the period beginning with the date of establishment of the Commission and ending with the first 31st March which falls at least six months after that date.S

ExpensesS

11. The Secretary of State shall defray the expenses of the Commission up to such amount as may be approved by him.]S

Schedule 9. Certain Offences Triable only Summarily

Section 292. (1).

Night Poaching Act 1828 (c. 69)S

F11. . . . . .S
Amendments (Textual)
F1. Words in Sch. 10 repealed (2.7.2012) by The Wildlife and Natural Environment (Scotland) Act 2011 (Consequential Modifications) Order 2012 (S.S.I. 2012/215), reg. 1, sch. Pt. 3

Public Meeting Act 1908 (c.66)S

2. Offences under section 1. (1) of the Public Meeting Act 1908 (endeavour to break up a public meeting).S

Post Office Act 1953 (c. 36)S

F23. . . . . .S
Amendments (Textual)
F2. Sch. 10 para. 3 repealed (26.3.2001) by S.I. 2001/1149, art. 3. (2), Sch. 2

Betting, Gaming and Lotteries Act 1963 (c. 2)S

4. Offences under the following provisions of the Betting, Gaming and Lotteries Act 1963—S
(a) section 7 (restriction of betting on dog racecourses);
(b) section 10. (5) (advertising licensed betting offices);
(c) section 11. (6) (person holding bookmaker's or betting agency permit employing a person disqualified from holding such a permit);
(d) section 18. (2) (making unauthorised charges to bookmakers on licensed track);
(e) section 19 (occupiers of licensed tracks not to have any interest in bookmaker thereon);
(f) section 21 (betting with young persons); and
(g) section 22 (betting circulars not to be sent to young persons).

Theatres Act 1968 (c.54)S

5. Offences under section 6 of the Theatres Act 1968 (provocation of breach of the peace by means of public performance of play).S

Criminal Law (Consolidation) (Scotland) Act 1995 (c. 39)S

6. Offences under section 12. (1) of the Criminal Law (Consolidation) (Scotland) Act 1995 (allowing child under 16 to be in brothel).S

Schedule 10. FINANCIAL PENALTIES SUITABLE FOR ENFORCEMENT IN SCOTLAND

Section 223. F(7)
Amendments (Textual)
F1. Sch. 11 inserted (12.10.2009) by The Mutual Recognition of Criminal Financial Penalties in the European Union (Scotland) Order 2009 (S.S.I. 2009/342), art. 8 (with art. 2)

Person residing in ScotlandS

1. The financial penalty is suitable for enforcement in Scotland if the certificate states that the person required to pay the penalty is normally resident in Scotland.S

Person having property etc. in ScotlandS

2. The financial penalty is suitable for enforcement in Scotland if—S
(a) the certificate states that the person required to pay the penalty has property or a source of income in Scotland, and
(b) the certificate does not state—
(i) that the person has property or a source of income in England and Wales, or Northern Ireland, or
(ii) that the person is normally resident in the United Kingdom.

Person having property etc. in Scotland and England and WalesS

3. (1)This paragraph applies if—S
(a) the certificate states that the person required to pay the financial penalty has property or a source of income in Scotland,
(b) the certificate also states that the person has property or a source of income in England and Wales, and
(c) the certificate does not state—
(i) that the person has property or a source of income in Northern Ireland, or
(ii) that the person is normally resident in the United Kingdom.
(2) The financial penalty is suitable for enforcement in Scotland unless sub-paragraph (3) applies.
(3) This sub-paragraph applies if—
(a) the central authority was given the certificate by the competent authority or central authority of another member State (and not by the authority designated as the central authority for England and Wales, or the central authority for Northern Ireland), and
(b) the central authority thinks that it is more appropriate for the financial penalty to be enforced in England and Wales than in Scotland.

Person having property etc. in Scotland and Northern IrelandS

4. (1)This paragraph applies if—S
(a) the certificate states that the person required to pay the financial penalty has property or a source of income in Scotland,
(b) the certificate also states that the person has property or a source of income in Northern Ireland, and
(c) the certificate does not state—
(i) that the person has property or a source of income in England and Wales, or
(ii) that the person is normally resident in the United Kingdom.
(2) The financial penalty is suitable for enforcement in Scotland unless sub-paragraph (3) applies.
(3) This sub-paragraph applies if—
(a) the central authority was given the certificate by the competent authority or central authority of another member State (and not by the authority designated as the central authority for England and Wales, or the central authority for Northern Ireland), and
(b) the central authority thinks that it is more appropriate for the financial penalty to be enforced in Northern Ireland than in Scotland.

Person having property etc. in Scotland and England and Wales and Northern IrelandS

5. (1)This paragraph applies if—S

(a) the certificate states that the person required to pay the financial penalty has property or a source of income in Scotland,

(b) the certificate also states that the person has property or a source of income in England and Wales, and Northern Ireland, and

(c) the certificate does not state that the person is normally resident in the United Kingdom.

(2) The financial penalty is suitable for enforcement in Scotland unless the penalty is suitable for enforcement in England and Wales, or in Northern Ireland by virtue of sub?paragraph (3).

(3) The financial penalty is suitable for enforcement in England and Wales, or in Northern Ireland for the purposes of sub-paragraph (2) if—

(a) the central authority was given the certificate by the central authority or, as the case may be, the competent authority of another member State (and not by the authority designated as the central authority for England and Wales, or the central authority for Northern Ireland), and

(b) the central authority thinks that it is more appropriate for the financial penalty to be enforced in England and Wales, or in Northern Ireland, than in Scotland.

InterpretationS

6. Where the person required to pay the financial penalty is a body corporate or a partnership (including a Scottish partnership), this Schedule applies as if—S

(a) the reference in paragraph 1 to the person being normally resident in Scotland were a reference to the person having its registered office or, as the case may be, its principal office of the partnership in Scotland, and

(b) any reference to the person being normally resident in the United Kingdom were a reference to the person having its registered office or, as the case may be, its principal office of the partnership in the United Kingdom.

7. In this Schedule, unless the context otherwise requires, references to the central authority are to the central authority for Scotland.]S

Schedule 11. GROUNDS FOR REFUSAL TO ENFORCE FINANCIAL PENALTIES

Section 223. H(5)

Amendments (Textual)

F1. Sch. 12 inserted (12.10.2009) by The Mutual Recognition of Criminal Financial Penalties in the European Union (Scotland) Order 2009 (S.S.I. 2009/342), art. 8 (with art. 2)

PART 1. STHE GROUNDS FOR REFUSAL

1. A penalty (of any kind) has been imposed on the liable person in respect of the conduct to which the certificate relates under the law of any part of the United Kingdom (whether or not the penalty has been enforced).S

2. A penalty (of any kind) has been imposed on the liable person in respect of that conduct under the law of any member State, other than the United Kingdom and the issuing State, and that penalty has been enforced.S

3. The decision was made in respect of conduct—S

(a) that is not specified in Part 2 of this Schedule, and

(b) would not constitute an offence under the law of Scotland if it occurred there.

4. The decision F2... was made in respect of conduct—S

(a) that occurred outside the territory of the issuing State, and

(b) would not constitute an offence under the law of Scotland if it occurred outwith Scotland.

Amendments (Textual)

F2. Words in Sch. 12 paras. 4, 5 omitted (1.12.2014) by virtue of The Mutual Recognition of Criminal Financial Penalties in the European Union (Scotland) (No. 1) Order 2014 (S.S.I. 2014/322), arts. 1, 8. (a)

5. The decision F2... was made in respect of conduct by a person who, at the time the conduct took place, was under the age of criminal responsibility under the law of Scotland.S

[F35. A.The certificate—S

(a) is incomplete (including by reason of not being signed, or its contents not being certified as accurate); or

(b) manifestly does not correspond to the decision.]

Amendments (Textual)

F3. Sch. 12 para. 5. A inserted (1.12.2014) by The Mutual Recognition of Criminal Financial Penalties in the European Union (Scotland) (No. 1) Order 2014 (S.S.I. 2014/322), arts. 1, 8. (b)

[F46.Where the proceedings in which the decision was made were conducted in writing, the certificate does not confirm that the liable person was informed of the right to contest the proceedings and of the time limits that applied to the exercise of that right.S

Amendments (Textual)

F4. Sch. 12 paras. 6, 6. A substituted for Sch. 12 para. 6 (1.12.2014) by The Mutual Recognition of Criminal Financial Penalties in the European Union (Scotland) (No. 2) Order 2014 (S.S.I. 2014/336), arts. 1, 5

6. A.(1)The certificate—S

(a) indicates that the decision is neither the result of—

(i) proceedings conducted in writing; nor

(ii) a trial at which the liable person appeared in person; and

(b) does not state that something which is described in paragraph (i) or (j) of Article 7. (2) of the Framework Decision happened.

(2) In sub-paragraph (1), "the Framework Decision" means Council Framework Decision 2005/214/JHA on the application of the principle of mutual recognition to financial penalties as amended by Council Framework Decision 2009/299/JHA.]

7. (1)The financial penalty is for an amount of less than 70 euros.S

(2) For the purposes of sub-paragraph (1), if the amount of a financial penalty is specified in a currency other than the euro, that amount must be converted to euros by reference to the London closing exchange rate on the date on which the decision was made.

PART 2. SEUROPEAN FRAMEWORK LIST (FINANCIAL PENALTIES)

8. Participation in a criminal organisation.S

9. Terrorism.S

10. Trafficking in human beings.S

11. Sexual exploitation of children and child pornography.S

12. Illicit trafficking in narcotic drugs and psychotropic substances.S

13. Illicit trafficking in weapons, munitions and explosives.S

14. Corruption.S

15. Fraud, including that affecting the financial interests of the European Communities within the meaning of the Convention of 26th July 1995 on the protection of the European Communities' financial interests.S

16. Laundering of the proceeds of crime.S

17. Counterfeiting currency, including of the euro.S

18. Computer-related crime.S

19. Environmental crime, including illicit trafficking in endangered animal species and in

endangered plant species and varieties.S

20. Facilitation of unauthorised entry and residence.S
21. Murder, grievous bodily injury.S
22. Illicit trade in human organs and tissue.S
23. Kidnapping, illegal restraint and hostage-taking.S
24. Racism and xenophobia.S
25. Organised or armed robbery.S
26. Illicit trafficking in cultural goods, including antiques and works of art.S
27. Swindling.S
28. Racketeering and extortion.S
29. Counterfeiting and piracy of products.S
30. Forgery of administrative documents and trafficking therein.S
31. Forgery of means of payment.S
32. Illicit trafficking in hormonal substances and other growth promoters.S
33. Illicit trafficking in nuclear or radioactive materials.S
34. Trafficking in stolen vehicles.S
35. Rape.S
36. Arson.S
37. Crimes within the jurisdiction of the International Criminal Court.S
38. Unlawful seizure of aircraft or ships.S
39. Sabotage.S
40. Conduct which infringes road traffic regulations, including breaches of regulations pertaining to driving hours and rest periods and regulations on hazardous goods.S
41. Smuggling of goods.S
42. Infringements of intellectual property rights.S
43. Threats and acts of violence against persons, including violence during sporting events.S
44. Criminal damage.S
45. Theft.S
46. Offences created by the issuing State and serving the purpose of implementing obligations arising from instruments adopted under [F5the EC Treaty or Title VI of the EU Treaty (as they had effect before 1 December 2009) or under the Treaty on the Functioning of the European Union] .S

Amendments (Textual)

F5. Words in Sch. 12 para. 46 substituted (1.8.2012) by The Treaty of Lisbon (Changes in Terminology or Numbering) Order 2012 (S.I. 2012/1809), art. 2. (1), Sch. Pt. 1 (with art. 2. (2))

PART 3. SINTERPRETATION

47. (1)In this Schedule—S
[F6. (za)"certificate" means the certificate referred to in section 223. F(1)(a)(i);]
(a) "conduct" includes any act or omission;
[F7. (aa)"decision" means the decision to which the certificate relates;]
(b) "liable person" means the person required to pay the financial penalty to which the certificate relates.
(2) If the decision was made in respect of conduct by a person other than the liable person, the references in paragraphs 6 to the liable person are to be read as references to that other person.]

Amendments (Textual)

F6. Sch. 12 para. 47. (1)(za) inserted (1.12.2014) by The Mutual Recognition of Criminal Financial Penalties in the European Union (Scotland) (No. 1) Order 2014 (S.S.I. 2014/322), arts. 1, 8. (c)(i)

F7. Sch. 12 para. 47. (1)(aa) inserted (1.12.2014) by The Mutual Recognition of Criminal Financial Penalties in the European Union (Scotland) (No. 1) Order 2014 (S.S.I. 2014/322), arts.

Schedule 12. TRANSFER OF COMMUNITY PAYBACK ORDERS TO ENGLAND AND WALES OR NORTHERN IRELAND

Section 227. ZO
Amendments (Textual)
F1. Sch. 13 inserted (16.9.2011) by The Criminal Justice and Licensing (Scotland) Act 2010 (Consequential Provisions and Modifications) Order 2011 (S.I. 2011/2298), art. 1, Sch. para. 6 (with art. 4. (4))

PART 1. SENGLAND AND WALES

1.(1)This paragraph applies where the court is considering imposing a community payback order under section 227. A of this Act on an offender who—S
(a) resides in England and Wales, or
(b) when the order takes effect, will reside in England and Wales.
(2) The court must not impose the order unless—
(a) the offender has attained the age of 16 years, and
(b) the court is satisfied that arrangements have been, or can be, made in the relevant area—
(i) for the offender to comply with the requirements imposed by the order in accordance with arrangements that exist in the relevant area for offenders to comply with the same or broadly similar requirements imposed by the corresponding order, and
(ii) for the appointment of a responsible officer.
2.(1)This paragraph applies where—S
(a) an offender on whom a community payback order has been imposed under section 227. A of this Act proposes to change, or has changed, residence to a locality in England and Wales ("the new locality"), and
(b) the court is considering varying the order so as to specify the relevant area in which the offender resides or will reside.
(2) The court must not vary the order unless—
(a) the offender has attained the age of 16 years, and
(b) the court is satisfied as mentioned in paragraph 1. (2)(b).
(3) If the court considers that a requirement ("the requirement concerned") imposed by the order cannot be complied with if the offender resides in the new locality, the court must not vary the order so as to specify the relevant area unless it also varies the order so as to—
(a) revoke or discharge the requirement concerned, or
(b) substitute for the requirement concerned another requirement that can be so complied with.
(4) The court must not make a variation under sub-paragraph (3) unless it is satisfied as mentioned in paragraph 1. (2)(b) (reading the reference there to the order as a reference to the order as proposed to be varied).
3.(1)This paragraph applies where the court is considering—S
(a) imposing a community payback order by virtue of paragraph 1, or
(b) varying a community payback order by virtue of paragraph 2.
(2) Before imposing or, as the case may be, varying the order, the court must explain to the offender in ordinary language—
(a) the requirements of the legislation relating to the corresponding order,
(b) the powers of the home court under that legislation and this Schedule, and

(c) the court's powers under this Act.

(3) The court must not impose or, as the case may be, vary the order unless the offender has, after the court has explained those matters, confirmed that the offender—

(a) understands those matters, and

(b) is willing to comply with the requirements referred to in sub-paragraph (2)(a).

(4) Sub-paragraphs (2) and (3) do not affect sections 227. B(8) and (9) and 227. ZA(6) and (7) of this Act.

(5) Sections 227. B(4), 227. ZA(2), 227. ZG(2) and 227. ZH(2) of this Act have effect as if the references in them to a report by an officer of a local authority or a report by the responsible officer included references to a report by an officer of a relevant service.

(6) Sections 227. R and 227. S of this Act have effect as if the references in them to an approved medical practitioner (within the meaning of the Mental Health (Care and Treatment) (Scotland) Act 2003) included references to a registered medical practitioner approved for the purposes of section 12 of the Mental Health Act 1983.

4.(1)The court may not, in a community payback order imposed by virtue of paragraph 1, impose a compensation requirement.S

(2) Where the court would, but for sub-paragraph (1), have imposed a compensation requirement, the court must instead make a compensation order under section 249. (1) of this Act.

(3) Sub-paragraph (4) applies where—

(a) the court varies a community payback order by virtue of paragraph 2, and

(b) the order imposes a compensation requirement.

(4) The court must—

(a) also vary the order so as to revoke the compensation requirement, and

(b) make a compensation order under section 249. (1) of this Act in respect of the amount remaining to be paid under the compensation requirement.

(5) Sub-paragraphs (2) and (4)(b) are subject to sub-paragraph (8).

(6) Paragraph (ab) of section 249. (2) of this Act does not apply to the making of a compensation order by virtue of this paragraph.

(7) Before making a compensation order by virtue of this paragraph, the court must explain to the offender in ordinary language—

(a) the purpose and effect of the compensation order, and

(b) the consequences which may follow if the offender fails to comply with the order in England and Wales.

(8) The court must not make the compensation order unless the offender has, after the court has explained those matters, confirmed that the offender—

(a) understands those matters, and

(b) is willing to comply with the order.

5.(1)This paragraph applies where the court—S

(a) imposes a community payback order by virtue of paragraph 1, or

(b) varies a community payback order by virtue of paragraph 2.

(2) The court must, in the order—

(a) specify the relevant area in which the offender resides or will reside,

(b) specify, in relation to each requirement imposed by the order, the requirement of the corresponding order which the court considers to be the same as or broadly similar to those imposed by the community payback order,

(c) where—

(i) the order imposes a restricted movement requirement, and

(ii) a corresponding order imposing the same or broadly similar requirement would also impose an electronic monitoring requirement,

specify in accordance with sub-paragraph (3) the person responsible for monitoring compliance with the restricted movement requirement.

(3) The person specified under sub-paragraph (2)(c) must be of a description specified in an order made by the Secretary of State by virtue of section 215. (3) of the 2003 Act.

(4) The clerk of the court must ensure that a copy of the order, and such other documents and information relating to the case as may be useful, are given to—

(a) the clerk of the home court,

(b) the relevant service in the area in which the offender resides or will reside, and

(c) if a person is specified under sub-paragraph (2)(c), that person.

(5) Sections 227. C and 227. D(4)(a)(ii) and (b) of this Act do not apply in relation to a community payback order imposed by virtue of paragraph 1.

6.(1)This paragraph applies where the court has—S

(a) imposed a community payback order by virtue of paragraph 1, or

(b) varied a community payback order by virtue of paragraph 2.

(2) The order has effect in England and Wales as if it were a corresponding order made by a court in that jurisdiction.

(3) The home court may exercise in relation to the order any power under the legislation relating to the corresponding order that the home court could exercise, other than—

(a) a power to discharge or revoke the order (other than in circumstances where the offender is convicted of a further offence and the court imposes a custodial sentence),

(b) a power to deal with the offender in respect of the offence in relation to which the order was imposed as the offender could have been dealt with had the order not been imposed,

(c) where the order imposes an unpaid work or other activity requirement, a power to vary the order by substituting for the number of hours of work specified in it a greater number than the court which imposed the order could have specified,

(d) where the order imposed a restricted movement requirement, a power to vary the order by substituting for the period specified in it a longer period than the court which imposed it could have specified.

(4) Sub-paragraph (5) applies where it appears to the home court—

(a) on information from the responsible officer, that the offender has failed to comply with any of the requirements of the order, or

(b) on the application of the offender or the responsible officer, that it would be in the interests of justice to—

(i) discharge the order, or

(ii) revoke the order and deal with the offender as mentioned in sub-paragraph (3)(b).

(5) The home court may—

(a) refer the matter to the appropriate Scottish court, and

(b) require the offender to appear before that court.

(6) Where the matter is referred under sub-paragraph (5) to the appropriate Scottish court, that court may—

(a) if the offender fails to appear as required under sub-paragraph (5)(b), issue a warrant for the offender's arrest, and

(b) deal with the matter—

(i) where it is referred by virtue of sub-paragraph (4)(a), in accordance with section 227. ZC of this Act, or

(ii) where it is referred by virtue of sub-paragraph (4)(b), as if it were an application under section 227. Y of this Act to vary, revoke or discharge the order.

(7) Where the matter is referred by virtue of sub-paragraph (4)(a), the home court must also send to the appropriate Scottish court—

(a) a certificate signed by the clerk of the home court certifying that the offender has failed to comply with such requirements of the order as are specified in the certificate, and

(b) such other documents and information relating to the case as may be useful.

(8) The certificate mentioned in sub-paragraph (7)(a) is, for the purposes of any proceedings before the appropriate Scottish court, sufficient evidence of the failure mentioned in the certificate.

(9) Where, in dealing with the matter by virtue of sub-paragraph (6)(b), the appropriate Scottish court is considering varying the order (or has varied the order) the provisions of this Part apply in relation to the proposed variation (or the order as varied) as they apply where the court is

considering imposing a community payback order (or has imposed a community payback order) by virtue of paragraph 1.

(10) Section 227. G(3) of this Act does not apply where the appropriate Scottish court is considering imposing a restricted movement requirement by virtue of sub-paragraph (6)(b)(i).

7.(1)In this Part—S

"the 2003 Act" means the Criminal Justice Act 2003;

"the 2008 Act" means the Criminal Justice and Immigration Act 2008;

"the appropriate Scottish court" means, in relation to an order to which paragraph 6 applies—

- the court in Scotland which imposed the order by virtue of paragraph 1, or

- where the order has been varied by virtue of paragraph 2 or 6. (6)(b), the court in Scotland which made the last such variation;

"corresponding order" means—

- in relation to an offender who is under the age of 18, a youth rehabilitation order within the meaning of Part 1 of the 2008 Act,

- in relation to any other offender, a community order within the meaning of Part 12 of the 2003 Act;

"the home court" means the magistrates' court acting for the local justice area in which the offender resides or will reside;

"relevant area" means—

- in relation to an offender who is under the age of 18, the area of the local authority (within the meaning given by section 7. (1) of the 2008 Act) where the offender resides or will reside,

- in relation to any other offender, the local justice area where the offender resides or will reside;

"relevant service" means—

- in relation to an offender who is under the age of 18, a youth offending team within the meaning given by section 7. (1) of the 2008 Act,

- in relation to any other offender, a provider of a probation service within the meaning of Part 1 of the Offender Management Act 2007;

"responsible officer"—

- in relation to an offender who is under the age of 18, has the meaning given in section 4 of the 2008 Act,

- in relation to any other offender, has the meaning given in section 197 of the 2003 Act.

(2) Subject to sub-paragraph (1), any word or expression used in this Part which is also used in any of sections 227. A to 227. ZK of this Act has the same meaning as it has for the purposes of those sections.

PART 2. SNORTHERN IRELAND

8.(1)This paragraph applies where the court is considering imposing a community payback order under section 227. A of this Act on an offender who—S

(a) resides in Northern Ireland, or

(b) when the order takes effect, will reside in Northern Ireland.

(2) The court must not impose the order unless—

(a) the offender has attained the age of 16 years, and

(b) the court is satisfied that arrangements have been, or can be, made in the relevant area—

(i) for the offender to comply with the requirements imposed by the order in accordance with arrangements that exist in the relevant area for offenders to comply with the same or broadly similar requirements imposed by the corresponding order, and

(ii) for the supervision of the offender by the relevant service.

9.(1)This paragraph applies where—S

(a) an offender on whom a community payback order has been imposed under section 227. A of this Act proposes to change, or has changed, residence to a locality in Northern Ireland ("the new locality"), and

(b) the court is considering varying the order so as to specify the relevant area in which the offender resides or will reside.

(2) The court must not vary the order unless—

(a) the offender has attained the age of 16 years, and

(b) the court is satisfied as mentioned in paragraph 8. (2)(b).

(3) If the court considers that a requirement ("the requirement concerned") imposed by the order cannot be complied with if the offender resides in the new locality, the court must not vary the order so as to specify the relevant area unless it also varies the order so as to—

(a) revoke or discharge the requirement concerned, or

(b) substitute for the requirement concerned another requirement that can be so complied with.

(4) The court must not make a variation under sub-paragraph (3) unless it is satisfied as mentioned in paragraph 8. (2)(b) (reading the reference there to the order as a reference to the order as proposed to be varied).

10.(1)This paragraph applies where the court is considering—S

(a) imposing a community payback order by virtue of paragraph 8, or

(b) varying a community payback order by virtue of paragraph 9.

(2) Before imposing or, as the case may be, varying the order, the court must explain to the offender in ordinary language—

(a) the requirements of the legislation relating to the corresponding order,

(b) the powers of the home court under that legislation and this Schedule, and

(c) the court's powers under this Act.

(3) The court must not impose or, as the case may be, vary the order unless the offender has, after the court has explained those matters, confirmed that the offender—

(a) understands those matters, and

(b) is willing to comply with the requirements referred to in sub-paragraph (2)(a).

(4) Sub-paragraphs (2) and (3) do not affect sections 227. B(8) and (9) and 227. ZA(6) and (7) of this Act.

(5) Sections 227. B(4), 227. ZA(2), 227. ZG(2) and 227. ZH(2) of this Act have effect as if the references in them to a report by an officer of a local authority or a report by the responsible officer included references to a report by a relevant service or an officer of a relevant service.

(6) Sections 227. R and 227. S of this Act have effect as if the references in them to an approved medical practitioner (within the meaning of the Mental Health (Care and Treatment) (Scotland) Act 2003) included references to a registered medical practitioner approved by the Health and Social Care Regulation and Quality Improvement Authority for the purposes of Part 2 of the Mental Health (Northern Ireland) Order 1986.

11.(1)The court may not, in a community payback order imposed by virtue of paragraph 8, impose a compensation requirement.S

(2) Where the court would, but for sub-paragraph (1), have imposed a compensation requirement, the court must instead make a compensation order under section 249. (1) of this Act.

(3) Sub-paragraph (4) applies where—

(a) the court varies a community payback order by virtue of paragraph 9, and

(b) the order imposes a compensation requirement.

(4) The court must—

(a) also vary the order so as to revoke the compensation requirement, and

(b) make a compensation order under section 249. (1) of this Act in respect of the amount remaining to be paid under the compensation requirement.

(5) Sub-paragraphs (2) and (4)(b) are subject to sub-paragraph (8).

(6) Paragraph (ab) of section 249. (2) of this Act does not apply to the making of a compensation order by virtue of this paragraph.

(7) Before making a compensation order by virtue of this paragraph, the court must explain to the offender in ordinary language—

(a) the purpose and effect of the compensation order, and

(b) the consequences which may follow if the offender fails to comply with the order in Northern Ireland.

(8) The court must not make the compensation order unless the offender has, after the court has explained those matters, confirmed that the offender—

(a) understands those matters, and

(b) is willing to comply with the order.

12.(1)This paragraph applies where the court—S

(a) imposes a community payback order by virtue of paragraph 8, or

(b) varies a community payback order by virtue of paragraph 9.

(2) The court must, in the order—

(a) specify the relevant area in which the offender resides or will reside,

(b) specify, in relation to each requirement imposed by the order, the requirement of the corresponding order which the court considers to be the same as or broadly similar to those imposed by the community payback order,

(c) where—

(i) the order imposes a restricted movement requirement, and

(ii) a corresponding order imposing the same or broadly similar requirement would also impose an electronic monitoring requirement,

specify in accordance with sub-paragraph (3) the person responsible for monitoring compliance with the restricted movement requirement.

(3) The person specified under sub-paragraph (2)(c) must be of a description specified in an order made by virtue of article 40. (3) of the Criminal Justice (Northern Ireland) Order 2008.

(4) The clerk of the court must ensure that a copy of the order, and such other documents and information relating to the case as may be useful, are given to—

(a) the clerk of the home court,

(b) the relevant service in the area in which the offender resides or will reside, and

(c) if a person is specified under sub-paragraph (2)(c), that person.

(5) Sections 227. C and 227. D(4)(a)(ii) and (b) of this Act do not apply in relation to a community payback order imposed by virtue of paragraph 8.

13.(1)This paragraph applies where the court has—S

(a) imposed a community payback order by virtue of paragraph 8, or

(b) varied a community payback order by virtue of paragraph 9.

(2) The order has effect in Northern Ireland as if it were a corresponding order made by a court in that jurisdiction.

(3) The home court may exercise in relation to the order any power under the legislation relating to the corresponding order that the home court could exercise, other than—

(a) a power to discharge or revoke the order (other than in circumstances where the offender is convicted of a further offence and the court imposes a custodial sentence),

(b) a power to deal with the offender in respect of the offence in relation to which the order was imposed as the offender could have been dealt with had the order not been imposed,

(c) where the order imposes an unpaid work or other activity requirement, a power to vary the order by substituting for the number of hours of work specified in it a greater number than the court which imposed the order could have specified,

(d) where the order imposed a restricted movement requirement, a power to vary the order by substituting for the period specified in it a longer period than the court which imposed it could have specified.

(4) Sub-paragraph (5) applies where it appears to the home court—

(a) on information from the responsible officer, that the offender has failed to comply with any of the requirements of the order, or

(b) on the application of the offender or the responsible officer, that it would be in the interests of justice to—

(i) discharge the order, or

(ii) revoke the order and deal with the offender as mentioned in sub-paragraph (3)(b).

(5) The home court may—

(a) refer the matter to the appropriate Scottish court, and

(b) require the offender to appear before that court.

(6) Where the matter is referred under sub-paragraph (5) to the appropriate Scottish court, that court may—

(a) if the offender fails to appear as required under sub-paragraph (5)(b), issue a warrant for the offender's arrest, and

(b) deal with the matter—

(i) where it is referred by virtue of sub-paragraph (4)(a), in accordance with section 227. ZC of this Act, or

(ii) where it is referred by virtue of sub-paragraph (4)(b), as if it were an application under section 227. Y of this Act to vary, revoke or discharge the order.

(7) Where the matter is referred by virtue of sub-paragraph (4)(a), the home court must also send to the appropriate Scottish court—

(a) a certificate signed by the clerk of the home court certifying that the offender has failed to comply with such requirements of the order as are specified in the certificate, and

(b) such other documents and information relating to the case as may be useful.

(8) The certificate mentioned in sub-paragraph (7)(a) is, for the purposes of any proceedings before the appropriate Scottish court, sufficient evidence of the failure mentioned in the certificate.

(9) Where, in dealing with the matter by virtue of sub-paragraph (6)(b), the appropriate Scottish court is considering varying the order (or has varied the order) the provisions of this Part apply in relation to the proposed variation (or the order as varied) as they apply where the court is considering imposing a community payback order (or has imposed a community payback order) by virtue of paragraph 1.

(10) Section 227. G(3) of this Act does not apply where the appropriate Scottish court is considering imposing a restricted movement requirement by virtue of sub-paragraph (6)(b)(i).

14.(1)In this Part—S

"the 1996 Order" means the Criminal Justice (Northern Ireland) Order 1996;

"the appropriate Scottish court" means, in relation to an order to which paragraph 13 applies—

- the court in Scotland which imposed the order by virtue of paragraph 8, or

- where the order has been varied by virtue of paragraph 9 or 13. (6)(b), the court in Scotland which made the last such variation;

"corresponding order" means a community order, within the meaning of article 2 of the 1996 Order";

"the home court" means a court of summary jurisdiction acting for the petty sessions district in which an offender resides or proposes to reside;

"relevant area" means the petty sessions district in Northern Ireland where the offender resides or will reside;

"relevant service" means the Probation Board for Northern Ireland;

"responsible officer" has the meaning given in article 17. (3) of the 1996 Order;

(2) Subject to sub-paragraph (1), any word or expression used in this Part which is also used in any of sections 227. A to 227. ZK of this Act has the same meaning as it has for the purposes of those sections.]

Schedule 13. TABLE OF DERIVATIONS

Notes:S

1. This Table shows the derivation of the provisions of the Bill.

2. The following abbreviations are used in the Table:—S

Acts of Parliament

1975 | = Criminal Procedure (Scotland) Act 1975 (c.21) |
1977 | = Criminal Law Act 1977 (c.45) |
1978 | = Community Service by Offenders (Scotland) Act 1978 (c.49) |
1980B | = Bail (Scotland) Act 1980 (c.4) |
1980LR | = Law Reform (Miscellaneous Provisions) (Scotland) Act 1980 (c.55) |
1980CJ | = Criminal Justice (Scotland) Act 1980 (c.62) |
1982 | = Criminal Justice Act 1982 (c.48) |
1983 | = Mental Health (Amendment) (Scotland) Act 1983 (c.39) |
1984 | = Mental Health (Scotland) Act 1984 (c.36) |
1985 | = Law Reform (Miscellaneous Provisions) (Scotland) Act 1985 (c.73) |
1987 | = Criminal Justice (Scotland) Act 1987 (c.41) |
1988 | = Criminal Justice Act 1988 (c.33) |
1990 | = Law Reform (Miscellaneous Provisions) (Scotland) Act 1990 (c.40) |
1991 | = Criminal Justice Act 1991 (c.53) |
1993P | = Prisoners and Criminal Proceedings (Scotland) Act 1993 (c.9) |
1993CJ | = Criminal Justice Act 1993 (c.36) |
1994 | = Criminal Justice and Public Order Act 1994 (c.33) |
1995 | = Criminal Justice (Scotland) Act 1995 (c. 20) |
1995C | = Children (Scotland) Act 1995 (c. 36) |
Provision | Derivation |
1(1) | Court of Session (Scotland) Act 1830 (11 Geo 4 & 1 Will 4 c.69) s. 18. |
(2) | 1975 s. 113(1). |
(3) | 1975 s. 113(2). |
(4), (5) | 1975 s. 113(4). |
2 | 1975 s.114; 1987 s.57(2). |
3(1) | 1975 s.2(1). |
(2) | 1975 s.112; 1987 s.57(1). |
(3) to (5) | 1975 s.2(2) to (4); 1987 s.58(1). |
(6) | 1975 s.8; Drafting. |
4(1) | 1975 ss.3(1), 288(1). |
(2) | 1975 ss. 3(4), 288(5); 1990 s.60; drafting. |
(3) | 1975 ss.3(2), 288(2). |
(4) | 1975 s.288(4); drafting. |
5(1) | Drafting. |
(2) | 1975 s.289; 1977 Sch.11 §.4. |
(3) | 1975 s. 290. |
(4) | 1975 s.291(2), (3); 1980 s.38. |
6(1) | District Courts (Scotland) Act 1975 (1975 c.20) s.2(1), (1A). |
(2) | District Courts (Scotland) Act 1975 (1975 c.20) s.2(2). |
(3) | District Courts (Scotland) Act 1975 (1975 c.20) s.6(1) (part). |
(4) | District Courts (Scotland) Act 1975 (1975 c.20) s.6(2) (part), (3) (part). |
(5) | District Courts (Scotland) Act 1975 (1975 c.20) s.6(9). |
(6) | Drafting. |
7(1) | District Courts (Scotland) Act 1975 (1975 c.20) s.3(1). |
(2) | District Courts (Scotland) Act 1975 (1975 c.20) s.3(4). |
(3) | 1980CJ s.7(1); 1995 s.60. |
(4) | 1980CJ s.7(3); 1982 Sch.7 §14. |
(5) | District Courts (Scotland) Act 1975 (1975 c.20) s.3(2). |

(6) | 1975 s.284; 1977 Sch.11 §.3; 1982 Sch.7 §§.4, 5. |
(7) | 1980CJ s. 7(1A); 1995 s.60. |
(8) | 1975 s.285; 1980CJ s.7(3); 1982 Sch.7 §.6. |
(9), (10) | 1975 s.286. |
8 | 1980B s.10; 1985 s.21. |
9(1) | 1975 ss.4(1), 3(3), 287(1). |
(2) | 1975 ss.4(2), 287(2). |
(3) | 1975 ss.4(3), 287(3). |
(4), (5) | 1975 ss.4(4), (5), 287(4), (5). |
10 | 1975 s.5; 1987 Sch.1 §.4. |
11(1), (2) | 1975 s.6(1), (2). |
(3) | 1975 s.6(3); 1995 Sch.6 §.7. |
(4) | 1975 ss.7(1), (2), 292(1), (2). |
12 | 1975 ss.9, 293. |
13 | 1980CJ s.1. |
14(1) | 1980CJ s.2(1); 1994 s.129(1). |
(2) | 1980CJ s.2(2); 1987 Sch.1 §.16(a), (b), 1993P Sch.7. |
(3) | 1980CJ s.2(3). |
(4) | 1980CJ s.2(3A); 1987 Sch.1 §.16(c); 1994 Sch.10 §.47; 1995 s.59. |
(5) | 1980CJ s.2(3B); 1994 Sch.10 §.47. |
(6) | 1980CJ s.2(4); 1994 s.129(2). |
(7) to (9) | 1980CJ s.2(5) to (7). |
15(1), (2) | 1980CJ s.3(1); 1994 s.129(3). |
(3) to (5) | 1980CJ s.3(2) to (4). |
(6) | 1980CJ s.3(5); 1985 Sch.2 §.23. |
16 | 1980CJ s.5. |
17(1) | 1975 ss.19(1), 305; 1980CJ Sch.7 §. 25; 1995 Sch.6 §§.11, 106. |
(2) | 1975 ss.19(2), 305; 1995 Sch.6 §§.11, 106. |
18(1), (2) | 1993P s.28(1), (2). |
(3) | 1993P s.28(3); 1995 s.58(2), Sch.6 §.179(5). |
(4) | 1993P s.28(3A), (3C); 1995 s.58(3). |
(5) | 1993P s.28(3B); 1995 s.58(3). |
(6) | 1993P s.28(4); 1995 s.58(4). |
(7), (8) | 1993P s.28(5), (6). |
19 | 1993P s.28A; 1995 s.58(5). |
20 | 1993P s.28B; 1995 s.58(5). |
21(1) | 1975 ss.18(1), 294(1). |
(2) to (5) | 1975 ss.18(2) to (5), 294(2) to (5); 1980B s.7(1), (2). |
22(1) to (3) | 1975 s.295(1), (2); 1980B s.8. |
(4), (5) | 1975 ss.294(4), (5), 295(3); 1980B ss.7(2), 8. |
23(1) | 1975 s.26(2); 1995 Sch.6. §.15(a). |
(2) | 1975 s.26(3); 1995 Sch.6 §.15(b). |
(3) | 1975 s.26(4). |
(4) | 1975 s.27. |
(5) | 1975 s.28(1). |
(6) | 1975 s.298(1) (part). |
(7) | 1975 ss.28(2), 298(2). |
(8) | 1975 ss.28(3), 298(3); 1980CJ Sch.7 §§.26, 51. |
24(1) | 1975 ss.26(1), 298(1) (part). |
(2) | 1975 s.35. |
(3) | 1980B s.1(1); drafting. |
(4) to (8) | 1980B s.1(2) to (5); 1995 s.1. |
25 | 1980B s.2. |

26 | 1975 s.28A; 1995 s.3. |

27(1), (2) | 1980B s.3(1), (2); 1995 s.2(2), (3). |

(3) to (6) | 1980B s.3(2A) to (2D); 1995 s.2(4). |

(7) to (10) | 1980B s.3(3) to (6). |

(11) | 1980B s.3(12). |

28 | 1980B s.3(7) to (11). |

29 | 1980B s.4. |

30(1) | 1975 ss.30(1), 299(1); 1980B s.1(4). |

(2) | 1975 ss.30(2), 299(2); 1980B Sch.1 §§.4, 6. |

(3) | 1975 ss.30(3), 299(3). |

(4) | 1975 ss.30(4), 299(4); 1980B s.1(4). |

31 | 1975 ss.30A, 299A; 1995 s.4. |

32(1) | 1975 ss.31(1), 300(1) (part). |

(2) | 1975 ss.31(2), 300(1) (part); 1987 s.62(4)(a). |

(3), (4) | 1975 ss.31(3), (4), 300(2), (3). |

(5) | 1975 ss.31(4A), 300(3A); 1995 Sch.6 §§.16, 105(a). |

(6) | 1975 ss.31(5), 300(6)(part) |

(7), (8) | 1975 ss.33(1), 300(4); 1995 Sch.6 §§.17(a), 105(b). |

(9) | 1975 s.300(4A); 1987 s.62(4)(b). |

(10) | 1975 s.33(2); 1995 Sch.6 §.17(b). |

33 | 1975 s.32, 300(6)(part) |

34(1) | 1975 s.12. |

(2) | 1975 s.74(7). |

35(1), (2) | 1975 s.19(2) (part), (3), s.305(3). |

(3) | 1975 s.20(1); 1980CJ s.6(1). |

(4) | 1975 s.20(3); 1980CJ s.6(1). |

(5) to (7) | 1975 s.20(3A) to (3C); 1980CJ s.6(1). |

(8) | 1975 s.20(4). |

36(1) to (4) | 1975 s.20A(1); 1980CJ s.6(2); 1995 s.10(2). |

(5) | 1975 s.20A(2); 1980CJ s.6(2). |

(6) | 1975 s.20A(3), (3A); 1980CJ s.6(2); 1995 s.10(3). |

(7) | 1975 s.20A(4); 1980CJ s.6(2). |

(8) | 1975 s.20A(5); 1980CJ s.6(2). |

(9) | 1975 s.20A(6); 1980CJ s.6(2). |

(10), (11) | 1975 s.20A(7), (8); 1995 s.10(4). |

37(1) | 1975 s.20B(1); 1980CJ s.6(2); 1993P Sch.5 §.1(2). |

(2) to (4) | 1975 s.20B(1A) to (1C); 1993P Sch.5 §.1(2). |

(5) | 1975 s.20B(2); 1993P Sch.5 §.1(2). |

(6) | 1975 s.20B(3); 1980CJ s.6(2). |

(7), (8) | 1975 s.20B(5); 1980CJ s.6(2). |

(9) | 1975 s.20B(6); 1980CJ s.6(2). |

(10) | 1975 s.20B(9); 1980CJ s.6(2); 1995 Sch.6 §13. |

38 | 1975 s.20B(4), (7) and (8); 1980CJ s.6(2). |

39 | 1975 s.21. |

40 | 1975 s.22. |

41 | 1975 ss.170, 369. |

42(1) | Social Work (Scotland) Act 1968 (1968 c.49) s.31(1); Health and Social Services and Social Security Adjudications Act 1983 (1983 c.41) Sch.2 §.7. |

(2) to (4) | 1975 ss.39(1) to (3), 307(1) to (3). |

(5), (6) | 1975 ss.39(4), (5), 307(4), (5); 1995C Sch.4 §.24(5), (11). |

(7), (8) | 1975 ss.40(1), (2), 308(1), (2). |

(9), (10) | 1975 ss.38, 306. |

43(1) to (3) | 1975 s.296(1); 1980B s.9(a); 1995 Sch.6 §.104. |

(4) | 1975 s.296(2); 1995 Sch.6 §.104. |

(5), (6) | 1975 s.296(3), (4); 1995C Sch.4 §.24(9). |

(7), (8) | 1975 s.296(5), (6); 1980B s.9(b). |

44(1) | 1975 s.413(1); 1987 s.59(1); 1993P Sch. 5 §.1(32); 1995 Sch.6 §.141; 1995C Sch.4 §.24(17). |

(2) | 1975 s.413(2); 1987 s.59(1). |

(3), (4) | 1975 s.413(3A), (4); 1987 s.59(1); 1995C Sch.4 §.24(17). |

(5) | 1975 s.413(5); 1993P s.8. |

(6) to (8) | 1975 s.413(6A) to (6C); 1993P s.8; 1995C Sch.4 §.24(17). |

(9) | 1975 s.413(7); 1987 s.59(1); 1993P Sch.5 §.1(32). |

(10) | 1975 s.413(3); 1987 s.59(1). |

45(1) to (4) | 1975 ss.37(1) to (3), 304(1) to (3). |

(5) | 1975 ss.37(4), 304(4); 1995C Sch.4 §.24(4), (10). |

46(1), (2) | 1975 ss.171(1), (2), 368(1), (2); 1995C Sch.4 §.24(7), (15); drafting. |

(3) | 1975 ss.171(3), 368(3); Sexual Offences (Scotland) Act 1976 (c.67) Sch.1; Incest and Related Offences (Scotland) Act 1986 (c.36) Sch.1 §§.1, 3; 1988 Sch.15 §.48. |

(4) | 1975 ss.171(4), 368(4). |

(5), (6) | 1975 ss.171(1), (2), 368(1), (2); 1995C Sch.4 §24(7), (15). |

(7) | 1975 ss.171(6), 368(6). |

47(1) to (3) | 1975 ss.169(1), 374(1); 1980CJ s.22. |

(4) | 1975 ss.169(2), 374(2); 1980CJ s.22; Cable and Broadcasting Act 1986 (c.46) Sch.5 §.30; Broadcasting Act 1990 (c.42) Sch.20 §.21. |

(5), (6) | 1975 ss.169(3), (4), 374(3), (4); 1980CJ s.22. |

48 | 1975 ss.168, 364; 1980CJ Sch.7 §§.34, 57; 1995C Sch.4 §.24(6), (14). |

49(1) | 1975 ss.173(1), 372(1); Local Government etc. (Scotland) Act 1994 (c.39) Sch.13 §.97(2). |

(2) | 1975 ss.173(2), 372(2). |

(3) | 1975 ss.173(3), 372(3); 1980CJ Sch.7 §.35; Local Government etc. (Scotland) Act 1994 (c.39) Sch.13 §.97(2). |

(4), (5) | 1975 ss.173(4), (5), 372(4), (5). |

(6), (7) | 1975 s.373; Local Government etc. (Scotland) Act 1994 (c.39) Sch.13 §97(2). |

50(1), (2) | 1975 ss.165, 361. |

(3), (4) | 1975 ss.166(1), (2), 362(1), (2); 1995 Sch.6 §.64. |

(5) | 1975 ss.167, 363. |

(6) | 1975 ss.172, 371. |

51(1) | 1975 ss.23(1), s.329(1); 1987 s.62(2); 1995 Sch.6 §.14; 1995C Sch.4 §.24(13). |

(2) to (4) | 1975 ss.23(2) to (4), 329(2) to (4); 1995 Sch.6 §.14; 1995C Sch.4 §.24(13). |

52(1) | 1975 ss.175(2), 376(5). |

(2) | 1975 ss.25(1), 330(1). |

(3) | 1975 ss.25(2), 330(2); 1984 Sch.3 §§.24, 31. |

(4), (5) | 1975 ss.25(3), (4), 330(3), (4). |

(6), (7) | 1975 ss.25(5), (6), 330(5), (6); 1995 s.53. |

53(1) | 1974 ss.174A(1) (part), 375A(1) (part); 1983 s.34(a); 1984 Sch.3 §§. 25, 32. |

(2) to (10) | 1975 ss.174A(2) to (10), 375A(3) to (11); 1983 s.34(a). |

(11), (12) | 1975 ss.174A(1) (part), 375A(1) (part), (2); 1983 s.34(a). |

54(1) to (4) | 1975 ss.174(1) to (1C), 375(2) to (2C); 1995 s.47(1). |

(5) | 1975 ss.174(5), 375(4). |

(6) | 1975 ss.174(2), 375(3A); 1995 s.48, Sch.6 §.65. |

(7) | 1975 s.375(3); 1995 Sch.6 §.132. |

(8) | Drafting. |

55 | 1975 ss.174ZA, 375ZA; 1995 s.49(1), (2). |

56 | 1975 ss.174ZB, 375ZB; 1995 s.49(1), (2). |

57(1) to (4) | 1975 ss.174ZC, 375ZC; 1995 s.50(1), (2). |

(5) | Drafting. |

58(1), (2) | 1975 ss.175(1), 376(1); 1983 Sch.2 §§.31, 34(a); 1984 Sch.3 §§.26, 33. |

(3) | 1975 s.376(3); 1995 Sch.6 §.133(b). |

(4) | 1975 ss.175(3), 376(6). |

(5) | 1975 ss.175(4), 376(7). |

(6) | 1975 ss.175(5), 376(8); 1983 Sch.2 §§. 31, 34. |

(7) | 1975 ss.175(6), 376(9); 1983 Sch.2 §§. 31, 34. |

(8) | 1975 ss.175(7), 376(10); 1983 Sch.2 §§. 31, 34. |

(9) | 1975 ss.177, 378; 1995C Sch.4 §.24(8), (16). |

(10) | 1975 s.376(4). |

59(1) | 1975 ss.178(1), 379(1); 1983 s.22(2); 1984 Sch.3 §§.28, 35; 1995 s.54. |

(2) | 1975 ss.178(2), 379(2); 1983 Sch.2 §§.33, 36; 1984 Sch.3 §§.28, 35; |

(3) | 1975 ss.178(3), 379(3); 1983 Sch.2 §§.33, 36; 1984 Sch.3 §§.28, 35; 1995 Sch.6 §§.67, 135. |

60 | 1975 ss.280, 443; 1980CJ Sch.2 §.32, Sch.3 §.2; 1983 s.34(b), (d). |

61(1) | 1975 ss.176(1), 377(1); 1983 Sch.2 §§.32, 35; 1984 Sch.3 §§.27, 34; 1995 Sch.6 §§.66(a), 134(a). |

(2) | 1975 ss.176(1A), 377(1A); 1983 s.35(a), (b). |

(3) | 1975 ss.176(2), 377(2); 1995 Sch.6 §§.66(b), 134(b). |

(4) | 1975 ss.176(3), 377(3). |

(5) | 1975 ss.176(4), 377(4); 1995 Sch.6 §§.66(c), 134(c). |

62 | 1975 ss.174ZD, 375ZD; 1995 s.51. |

63(1) to (5) | 1975 ss.174ZE, 375ZE; 1995 s.52. |

(6) | Drafting. |

64(1) to (4) | 1975 s.41. |

(5) | 1975 s.57. |

(6) | Drafting. |

65(1) to (3) | 1975 s.101(1); 1980CJ s.14(1). |

(4) to (9) | 1975 s.101(2) to (6); 1980CJ s.14(1). |

(10) | 1975 s.101(1A); 1995 s.15. |

66(1), (2) | 1975 s.69(1); 1980CJ Sch.4 §.2; 1995 Sch.6 §.26(a). |

(3) | 1975 s.69(2); 1995 Sch.6 §.26(b). |

(4) | 1975 s.70. |

(5) | 1975 s.78(1); 1980CJ Sch.4 §.8; 1995 Sch.6 §.30. |

(6) | 1975 s.75; 1980CJ Sch.4 §.4; 1995 s.13(1). |

(7) | 1975 s.71; 1980CJ Sch.7 §.27. |

(8) | 1975 s.73(1); 1995 Sch.6 §.28. |

(9) | 1975 s.72(1); 1995 Sch.6 §.27(a), (b). |

(10) | 1975 s.72(2); 1995 Sch.6 §.27(c). |

(11) | 1975 s.73(2) |

(12) to (14) | 1975 s.58; 1995 Sch.6 §.22. |

67(1) | 1975 s.79(1) (part); 1995 Sch.6 §.31. |

(2) | 1975 s.79(2). |

(3) | 1975 s.80(1); 1980CJ Sch.4 §.9; 1995 Sch.6 §.32. |

(4) | 1975 s.80(2); 1980CJ Sch 4 §.9; |

(5) | 1975 s.81; 1980CJ Sch.7 §.28; 1995 Sch.6 §.33. |

(6) | 1975 s.82A; 1980CJ s.27. |

68(1) | 1975 s.78(2); 1980CJ Sch.4 §.8. |

(2) | 1975 s.83; 1980CJ Sch.4 §.11. |

(3), (4) | 1975 s.84; 1980CJ Sch.4 §.12; 1995 s.23. |

69(1) | 1975 s.68(1). |

(2) | 1975 s.68(2); 1995 Sch.6 §.25. |

(3) | 1975 s.68(3) (part); 1980CJ Sch.4 §.1. |

(4) | 1975 s.68(4) (part); 1995 Sch.6 §.25. |

(5) | 1975 s.68(3) (part) and (4) (part); 1980CJ Sch 4 §.1; 1995 Sch.6 §.25. |

70(1) | Drafting. |
(2), (3) | 1975 s.74(1). |
(4) | 1975 s.74(2). |
(5) | 1975 s.74(4); 1980CJ Sch.4 §.3(b). |
(6) | 1975 s.74(5) |
(7) | 1975 ss.74(6), 103(4). |
(8) | 1975 s.74(8) |
71 | 1975 s.75A; 1995 s.13(2). |
72(1) | 1975 s.76(1) (part) and (2), s.108(1) (part); 1980CJ Sch.4 §.5, §.19; 1985 Sch.2 §.18; 1993P s.39(2), Sch.5 §.1(3); 1995 s.13(3)(a), Sch.6 §.39. |
(2) | 1975 s.76(1) (part); 1980CJ Sch.4 §.5. |
(3) to (6) | 1975 s.76(3) to (5), (7). |
73(1), (2) | 1975 s.76(6) (part). |
(3) to (6) | 1975 s.76(6A) to (6D); 1995 s.13(3)(b). |
(7) | 1975 s.109(part). |
(8) | 1975 s.76(6) (part); drafting. |
74 | 1975 s.76A; 1980CJ Sch.4 §.5; 1995 s.13(4). |
75 | 1975 s.111A; 1980CJ Sch.7 §.31. |
76 | 1975 s.102; 1980CJ s.16. |
77(1) | 1975 s.103(1) and (4), s.124 (part); 1980CJ Sch.4 §.14; 1995 Sch.6 §.38. |
(2), (3) | 1975 s.103(2), (3); 1980CJ Sch.4 §.14. |
78(1) | 1975 s.82(1) (part); Act of Adjournal (Consolidation) 1988 (S.I. 1988/110) s.68 (part); 1980CJ s.13; 1995 Sch.6 §.34(a). |
(2) | 1975 s.82(1A); 1995 s.11. |
(3) | 1975 s.82(1) (part); Act of Adjournal (Consolidation) 1988 (S.I. 1988/110) s.68 (part); 1980CJ s.13; 1995 Sch.6 §.34(a). |
(4) | 1975 s.82(2); 1980CJ Sch.4 §.10; 1995 Sch.6 §.34(b). |
(5) | 1975 s.82(3); 1980CJ Sch.4 §.10. |
79(1) | 1975 s.108(1) (part) and (2); 1980CJ Sch.4 §.19; 1985 Sch.2 §.18; 1995 Sch.6 §.39. |
(2) | 1975 s.108(1) (part); 1980CJ Sch.4 §.19; 1985 Sch.2 §.18; 1995 Sch.6 §.39. |
80(1) | 1975 s.77; 1980CJ Sch.4 §.6; 1995 Sch.6 §.29. |
(2) to (4) | 1975 s.77A(1) to (3); 1980CJ Sch.4 §.7. |
(5), (6) | 1975 s.77A(4), drafting; 1980CJ Sch.4 §.7. |
81(1) | 1975 s.127(1); 1980CJ Sch.4 §.27; 1995 Sch.6 §44(a). |
(2) | 1975 s.127(1ZA); 1995 Sch.6 §.44(b). |
(3) | 1975 s.127(1A); 1980CJ s.18(1). |
(4) to (6) | 1975 s.127(2) to (4); 1995 Sch.6 §44(c). |
(7) | 1975 s.127(5); 1995 Sch.6 §.44(d). |
82 | 1975 s.111. |
83 | 1975 s.114A; 1995 Sch.6 §.41. |
84(1) | 1975 s.85; 1995 Sch.6 §.35. |
(2) | 1975 s.86(1); 1987 Sch.1 §.5. |
(3) | 1975 s.86(2); 1987 Sch.1 §.5. |
(4) | 1975 s.89; 1985 Sch.2 §.16. |
(5) | 1975 s.90; 1985 Sch.2 §.16. |
(6) | 1975 s.91; 1980LR Sch.2 §.6; 1985 Sch.2 §.16 . |
(7) | 1975 s.92. |
(8) | 1975 s.93; 1995 Sch.6 §.36. |
(9) | 1975 s.94 |
(10) | 1975 s.95. |
85(1) | 1975 s.96(1); 1980CJ Sch.4 §.13. |
(2) | 1975 s.96(2). |
(3) | 1975 s.97. |

(4), (5) | 1975 s.98; 1980CJ Sch.7 §.29; 1985 Sch.2 §.17. |
(6), (7) | 1975 s.99; 1980LR s.2(3). |
(8) | 1975 s.100(1); 1995 Sch.6 §.37. |
86(1) | 1975 s.130(3A); 1995 s.8. |
(2) | 1975 s.130(4). |
(3) | 1975 s.130(5); 1980LR Sch.2 §.7. |
(4) | 1975 s.130(6). |
87 | 1975 s.128; 1995 s.30(2), (3). |
88(1) | 1975 s.125; 1995 Sch.6 §.43. |
(2) | 1975 s.129 (part); 1987 Sch.1 §.7; 1995 Sch.6 §.45. |
(3) | 1975 s.131, drafting. |
(4) | 1975 s.132(1). |
(5), (6) | 1975 s.135(1); 1995 Sch.6 §.48(a), (b); drafting. |
(7) | 1975 s.133. |
(8) | 1975 s.137. |
89 | 1975 s.135(2) to (4); 1995 Sch.6 §.48(c). |
90 | 1975 s.134; 1995 Sch.6 §.47. |
91 | 1975 s.136. |
92(1), (2) | 1975 s.145(1); 1980CJ s.21. |
(3) | 1975 s.145(3). |
93 | 1975 s.274; 1980CJ Sch.8; 1995 Sch.6 §.98. |
94 | 1975 s.275; 1993P Sch.5 §.1(27). |
95 | 1975 s.137A; 1993P Sch.1 §.1(5). |
96 | 1975 s.123. |
97(1) | 1975 s.140A(1); 1980CJ s.19(1); 1995 Sch.6 §.49. |
(2), (3) | 1975 s.140A(3), (4); 1980CJ s.19(1). |
(4) | 1975 s.140A(2); 1980CJ s.19(1). |
98 | 1975 s.152. |
99(1) | 1975 s.153(2); 1980CJ s.24(1). |
(2), (3) | 1975 s.153(3); 1980CJ s.24(1); 1995 Sch.6 §.57(b). |
(4) | 1975 s.153(3A); 1980CJ s.24(1). |
(5) | 1975 s.153(4). |
(6) | 1975 s.155A; 1993P s.40(1). |
100(1), (2) | 1975 s.154; 1980CJ s.24(2). |
(3) | 1975 s.155(part); drafting. |
101(1) | 1975 s.160(1). |
(2) | 1975 ss.160(2), 161(5); 1995 s.24(3). |
(3) | 1975 s.161(1). |
(4), (5) | 1975 s.161(2). |
(6) | 1975 s.161(4). |
(7) | 1975 s.159(2). |
(8) | 1975 s.161(3). |
102(1) | 1975 s.156(1) and (2); 1995 Sch.6 §.58. |
(2) | 1975 s.157(1); 1995 Sch.6 §.59. |
(3) | 1975 ss.156(3) and 157(3). |
(4) | 1975 s.156(6). |
(5) | 1975 s.158. |
103(1) | 1975 s.245(2); 1987 Sch.1 §.13(2); drafting. |
(2) | 1975 s.245(1); 1987 Sch.1 §.13(1); 1995 s.43(1). |
(3) | 1975 s.245(1A); 1995 s.43(1). |
(4) | 1975 s.245(3); 1980CJ Sch.8. |
(5) | 1975 ss.247(part), 248; 1980CJ Sch.2 §.15, Sch.8. |
(6) | 1975 s.247(part); 1980CJ Sch.2 §.15, Sch.8. |

(7) | 1975 s.249. |
(8) | 1975 s.250. |
104(1) | 1975 s.252; 1980CJ Sch.2 §.16; 1993P Sch.5 §.1(18). |
(2), (3) | 1975 s.253; 1980CJ Sch.8. |
105(1) to (4) | 1975 s.251(1) to (4) |
(5) | 1975 s.251(5); 1980CJ Sch.7 §.44. |
(6) | 1975 s.251(6). |
106(1), (2) | 1975 s.228(1); 1980CJ Sch.2 §.1; 1993CJ s.68(1); 1995 s.42(1). |
(3) | 1975 s.228(2); 1980CJ Sch.2 §.1. |
(4) | 1975 s.270(1). |
(5) to (9) | 1975 s.270(2) to (4); 1980CJ Sch.2 §.26; 1995 Sch.6 §.96. |
107 | 1975 s.230A; 1995 s.42(2). |
108 | 1975 s.228A; 1993P s.42(1); 1993CJ s.68(2). |
109(1) | 1975 s.231(1) (part) and (2); 1980CJ Sch.2 §.3; 1987 s.45(6)(a). |
(2) | 1975 s.231(1) (part); 1980CJ Sch.2 §.3; 1987 s.45(6)(a). |
(3) | 1975 s.231(3); 1980CJ Sch.2 §.3. |
(4), (5) | 1975 s.231(4); 1987 s.45(6)(b). |
(6) | 1975 s.231(5); 1987 s.45(6)(c). |
110(1), (2) | 1975 s.233(1); 1980CJ Sch.2 §.5; 1993P Sch.5 §.1(9); 1993CJ Sch.5 §.2(4). |
(3), (4) | 1975 s.233(2), (3); 1980CJ Sch.2 §.5. |
(5) | 1975 s.233(3A); 1995 s.42(3). |
(6) | 1975 s.233(4); 1980CJ Sch.2 §.5; 1993CJ Sch.5 §.2(4). |
111 | 1975 s.236B; 1980CJ Sch.2 §.8; 1993P Sch.5 §1(11). |
112(1) | 1975 s.238(1); 1993CJ Sch.5 §.2(5); 1995 s.5(2). |
(2) | 1975 s.238(1A); 1995 s.5(3). |
(3), (4) | 1975 s.238(2); 1980CJ Sch.2 §.10(a); 1995 Sch.6 §.81. |
(5) | 1975 s.238(3); 1980CJ Sch.2 §.10(b). |
113 | 1975 s.236A; 1980CJ Sch.2 §.8; 1995 Sch.6 §.78. |
114 | 1975 s.235; 1995 Sch.6 §.77. |
115(1), (2) | 1975 s.234(1); 1980CJ Sch.8. |
(3), (4) | 1975 s.234(2), (3); 1980CJ Sch.8. |
116(1) | 1975 s.244(1); 1980CJ Sch.2 §.13. |
(2) | 1975 s.244(2); 1980CJ Sch.2 §.13; 1993CJ Sch.5 §.2(6). |
117(1), (2) | 1975 s.241; 1980CJ Sch.7 §.41. |
(3) | 1975 s.240; 1993P Sch.5 §.1(15); 1995 Sch.6 §.83. |
(4), (5), (6) | 1975 s.242; 1980CJ Sch.7 §.42. |
(7) | 1975 s.242A; 1993P Sch.5 §.1(16). |
(8) | 1975 s.243; 1980CJ Sch.7; 1993P Sch.5 §.1(17). |
(9) | 1975 s.239(1); 1980CJ Sch.2 §.11; 1993 Sch.5 §.1(14); 1995 Sch.6 §.82. |
118(1), (2) | 1975 s.254(1); 1980CJ Sch.2 §.18; 1993CJ Sch.5 §.2(7). |
(3) | 1975 s.254(2); 1993CJ Sch.5 §.2(7). |
(4) | 1975 s.254(3), (4A); 1993CJ Sch.5 §.2(7). |
(5) | 1975 s.254(4); 1993CJ Sch.5 §.2(7); 1995 Sch.6 §.85. |
(6) | 1975 s.254(5); 1995 Sch.6 §.85. |
(7) | 1975 s.254A(1); 1995 s.34(1). |
(8) | 1975 s.254B; 1995 Sch.6 §.86. |
119(1), | 1975 s.255(1) (part);1980CJ Sch.2 §.19; 1995 s.46(1). |
(2) | 1975 s.255(1A); 1995 s.46(1). |
(3) | 1975 s.255(1) (part); 1980CJ Sch.2 §.19; 1995 s.46(1). |
(4) | 1975 s.255(2); 1980CJ Sch.2 §.19. |
(5) | 1975 s.255(3) (part); 1980 Sch.2 §.19. |
(6) | 1975 s.255(1B); 1995 s.46(1). |
(7) | 1975 s.255(1C); 1995 s.46(1). |

(8) | 1975 s.255(3) (part); 1980CJ Sch.2 §.19. |
(9) | 1975 s.255(4); 1980CJ Sch.2 §.19. |
(10), (11) | 1975 s.255(5), (6); 1995 s.46(1)(c) |
120(1) | 1975 s.257; 1980CJ Sch.8; 1995 Sch.6 §.88. |
(2) | 1975 s.258; 1993P Sch.5 §.1(19). |
(3) | 1975 s.260. |
(4) | 1975 s.261; 1980CJ Sch.7 §.45; 1993P Sch.5 §.1(20) |
121(1), (2) | 1975 s.264(1), (2); 1980CJ Sch.2 §.23; 1995 Sch.6 §.92(a). |
(3) | 1975 s.264(3); 1987 s.68(3). |
(4) | 1975 s.264(4); 1995 Sch.6 §.92(b). |
122(1), (2) | 1975 s.265(1), (2); 1995 Sch.6 §.93. |
(3) | 1975 s.265(4). |
(4) | 1975 s.265(4A); 1993P Sch.5 §.1(22). |
123 | 1975 s.263A; 1980CJ s.37; 1995 Sch.6 §.91. |
124(1) | 1975 s.263(1) (part); 1980CJ Sch.2 §.22. |
(2) | 1975 ss.262, 281. |
(3) | 1975 s.263(1) (part); 1980CJ Sch.2 §.22. |
(4) | 1975 s.263(2); 1987 Sch.2. |
(5) | 1975 s.263(3); 1995 Sch.6 §.90. |
125(1) | 1975 s.268(1); 1987 Sch.1 §.14(1); 1993P Sch.5 §.1(23); 1993CJ Sch.5 §.2(8). |
(2) | 1975 s.268(2); 1987 Sch.1 §.14(2); 1993P Sch.5 §.1(23); 1993CJ Sch.5 §.2(8). |
(3) | 1975 s.268(3); 1987 Sch.1 §.14(3); 1993P Sch.5 §.1(23). |
(4) | 1975 s.268(4); 1980CJ Sch.7 §.46; 1995 Sch.6 §.94. |
126 | 1975 s.269; 1980CJ Sch.2 §.25; 1993P Sch.5 §.1(24); 1995 Sch.6 §.95. |
127 | 1975 s.271; 1980CJ Sch.2 §.27; 1985 Sch.2 §.19. |
128 | 1975 ss.266, 267. |
129(1), (2) | 1975 s.277(1); 1980CJ Sch.8. |
(3) | 1975 s.277(2); 1980 CJ Sch.2 §.31, Sch.8; 1995 Sch.6 §.100. |
(4) | 1975 s.277(1) (part). |
130 | 1975 s.230. |
131 | 1975 s.280A; 1980CJ s.35. |
132 | 1975 s.279. |
133(1) | 1975 s.283(1); 1995 Sch.6 §.102. |
(2) | 1975 s.283(1A); 1995 Sch.6 §.102. |
(3) | 1975 s.283(2) (part). |
(4) | 1975 s.283(3); drafting. |
(5) | 1975 s.310A; 1995 s.63. |
134 | 1975 s.310; 1995 Sch.6 §.108; drafting. |
135(1) | 1975 s.321(1); 1995 Sch.6 §.117(a). |
(2) | 1975 s.321(2). |
(3), (4) | 1975 s.321(3); 1980B Sch.1 §.7; 1995 Sch.6 §.117(b). |
(5) | 1975 s.321(4). |
136 | 1975 s.331; Incest and Related Offences (Scotland) Act 1986 (1986 c.36) Sch.1 §.2; 1995 s.62. |
137(1) | 1975 s.314(3); 1980CJ Sch.8. |
(2) | 1975 s.314(4); 1980CJ s.11. |
(3) | 1975 s.314(4A); 1995 Sch.6 §.111(b). |
(4), (5) | 1975 s.314(5), (6); 1980CJ s.11. |
138(1) | 1975 s.311(1) (part) & (2); 1995 Sch.6 §.109; drafting. |
(2) | 1975 s.312 (part); drafting. |
(3) | 1975 s.311(3). |
(4) | 1975 s.312(a) — (z), drafting. |
139(1) | 1975 s.314(1); 1995 Sch.6 §.111(a). |

(2) | 1975 s.314(2); 1980CJ s.11. |

140 | 1975 s.315; 1995 Sch.6 §.112. |

141(1) | 1975 s.316(1) & (2) (part). |

(2) | 1975 s.316(2) (part). |

(3), (4) | 1975 s.316(3); 1995 Sch.6 §.113. |

(5) | 1975 s.316(4). |

(6), (7) | 1975 s.319; 1995 Sch.6 §.115; drafting. |

142(1) | 1975 s.366(1); 1995 Sch.6 §131. |

(2) to (4) | 1975 s.367. |

(5) | 1975 s.370; 1980CJ Sch.7 §.58. |

143 | 1975 s.333. |

144(1) | 1975 s.334(1) (part); 1980CJ Sch.7 §.54(a); 1993P Sch.5 §.1(30). |

(2), (3) | 1975 s.334(3). |

(4), (5) | 1975 s.334(1) (part) & (2) (part); 1980CJ Sch.7 §.54(b). |

(6) to (8) | 1974 S.334(4) to (6). |

(9) | 1975 s.334(1) (part); 1980CJ Sch.7 §.54(a); drafting. |

145 | 1975 s.333A; 1993P s.38(1). |

146(1) | 1975 s.337(part). |

(2) | 1975 s.337(a); 1980B Sch.2. |

(3) | 1975 s.337(b). |

(4), (5) | 1975 s.337(c). |

(6) | 1975 s.337(d); 1980B Sch.1 §.8; 1987 s.62(3). |

(7) to (9) | 1975 s.337(f) to (h). |

147 | 1975 s.331A; 1980CJ s.14(2). |

148 | 1975 s.337A; 1980CJ s.15; 1995 s.14; drafting. |

149 | 1975 s.339; 1995 Sch.6 §.121. |

150(1) | 1975 s.338(1) (part); 1995 Sch.6 §.120. |

(2) | 1975 s.338(1)(a) (part). |

(3) | 1975 s.338(1)(c). |

(4) | 1975 s.338(1)(a) (part). |

(5), (6), (7) | 1975 s.338(1)(b). |

(8), (9), (10) | 1975 s.338(2) to (4); 1980CJ s.17. |

151 | 1975 s.331B; 1995 s.30(4). |

152 | 1975 s.338A; 1980CJ s.18(2). |

153 | 1975 s.337B; 1995 s.31. |

154 | 1975 s.353. |

155(1) | 1975 s.344(1); 1980CJ s.46(1)(c); 1982 Sch.7 §.7; 1995 Sch.6 §.122. |

(2), (3) | 1975 s.344(2), (3). |

(4) | 1975 s.344(4); 1980CJ Sch.7 §.55. |

156(1), (2) | 1975 s.320; 1995 Sch.6 §.116. |

(3), (4) | 1975 s.321(5), (6); 1995 Sch.6 §.117. |

157 | 1975 s.359; 1995 Sch.6 §.128. |

158 | 1975 s.360A(1); 1993P s.40(2); 1995 Sch.6 §.130. |

159 | 1975 s.335; 1995 Sch.6 §.118. |

160 | 1975 345A; 1980CJ s.19(2). |

161 | 1975 s.351. |

162 | 1975 s.355. |

163(1) | 1975 s.440; 1995 Sch.6 §.145. |

(2) | 1975 s.441; 1995 Sch.6 §.146. |

164 | 1975 s.427. |

165 | 1975 s.429. |

166(1) to (6) | 1975 s.357(1); 1980CJ s.40; 1995 Sch.6 §.127(a). |

(7) | 1975 s.356(2). |

(8) | 1975 s.357(5); 1995 s.24(6). |

167(1) | 1975 s.433. |

(2), (3), (4) | 1975 s.430(1); 1995 Sch.6 §.142(a). |

(5), (6) | 1975 s.430(2), (3). |

(7) | 1975 s.430(4); 1995 Sch.6 §.142(b). |

(8) | 1975 s.434. |

168 | 1975 s.303(1). |

169 | 1975 s.424; 1980CJ Sch.7 §.68. |

170 | 1975 s.456. |

171 | 1975 s.332. |

172(1) | 1975 s.309(1); 1995 Sch.6 §.107. |

(2), (3) | 1975 s.309(2) (part), (3). |

173 | 1975 s.451A; 1995 s.43(2). |

174 | 1975 s.334(2A) to (2D); 1980CJ s.36. |

175(1) to (4) | 1975 s.442(1); 1980 Sch.3 §.1; 1993CJ s.68(3); 1995 s.42(4). |

(5), (6) | 1974 s.442(2), (3); 1980 Sch.3 §.1. |

(7), (8) | 1975 s.442A(1), (2); 1980CJ Sch.3 §.1. |

(9) | 1975 s.442B; 1980CJ Sch.3 §.1; 1993CJ Sch.5 §.2(1). |

(10) | 1975 s.283(2) (part). |

176(1) | 1975 s.444(1); 1980CJ Sch.3 §.3; 1993CJ Sch.5 §.2(12); 1995 Sch.6 §.148. |

(2) | 1975 s.444(1A); 1980CJ Sch.3 §.3. |

(3) | 1975 s.444(1B); 1980CJ Sch.3 §.3. |

(4) | 1975 s.444(2). |

(5) | 1975 s.450; 1980CJ Sch.3 §.9; drafting. |

177(1) | 1975 s.446(1); 1980CJ Sch.3 §.5. |

(2), (3) | 1975 s.446(2). |

(4) | 1975 s.446(3). |

(5) to (7) | 1975 s.446(4) to (6); 1995 Sch.6 §.149. |

178(1) | 1975 s.447(1); 1980CJ Sch.3 §.6; 1985 Sch.2 §.20. |

(2) | 1975 s.447(2); 1980CJ Sch.8. |

179 | 1975 s.448(1) — (5); 1980CJ Sch.3 §.7; 1985 Sch.4. |

180 | 1975 s.442ZA; 1995 s.42(5). |

181(1), (2) | 1975 ss.444(3), (4), 448(6), (7); 1980CJ Sch.3 §.7. |

(3) | 1975 ss.444(5), 448(8); 1980B Sch.1 §.10, §.12; 1980CJ Sch.3 §.3, §.7. |

182 | 1975 s.452; 1980CJ Sch.3 §.11; 1995 s.42(6). |

183(1), (2) | 1975 s.452A(1); 1980CJ Sch.3 §.11; 1993P Sch.5 §.1(35). |

(3) | 1975 s.452A(2) (part); 1980CJ Sch.3 §.11; 1993P Sch.5 §.1(35)(b); 1993CJ Sch.5 §.2(13). |

(4) | 1975 s.452A(3); 1980CJ Sch.3 §.11. |

(5) | 1975 s.452A(2) (part); 1980CJ Sch.3 §.11; 1993P Sch.5 §.1(35)(b); 1993CJ Sch.5 §.2(13). |

(6), (7) | 1975 s.452A(7); 1980CJ Sch.3 §.11. |

(8) | 1975 s.452A(4A); 1993CJ Sch.5 §.2(13). |

(9) | 1975 s.452A(5); 1980CJ Sch.3 §.11. |

(10) | 1975 s.452A(6); 1980CJ Sch.3 §.11. |

184 | 1975 s.449; 1980CJ Sch.3 §.8. |

185(1) | 1975 s.452B(1) (part); 1980CJ Sch.3 §.11; 1995 s.46(2). |

(2) | 1975 s.452B(1A); 1995 s.46(2). |

(3) | 1975 s.452B(1) (part);1980CJ Sch.3 §.11. |

(4) | 1975 s.452B(2); 1980CJ Sch.3 §.11. |

(5) | 1975 s.452B(3) (part); 1980CJ Sch.3 §.11. |

(6), (7) | 1975 s.452B(1B), (1C); 1995 s.46((2). |

(8) | 1975 s.452B(3) (part); 1980CJ Sch.3 §.11. |

(9) | 1975 s.452B(4); 1980CJ Sch.3 §.11. |

(10) | 1975 s.452B(5); 1995 s.46(2)(c) |

186(1), (2) | 1975 s.453B(1), (2); 1980CJ Sch.3 §.13; 1993P Sch.5 §.1(36); 1993CJ Sch.5 §.2(14). |

(3) | 1975 s.453B(3); 1980CJ Sch.3 §.13; 1993CJ Sch.5 §.2(14). |
(4), (5) | 1975 s.453B(4); 1980CJ Sch.3 §.13; 1993CJ Sch.5 §.2(14); 1995 s.45(2). |
(6) | 1975 s.453B(4A); 1995 Sch.6 §.152. |
(7) | 1975 s.453B(5); 1980CJ Sch.3 §.13; 1993P Sch.5 §.1(36). |
(8), (9) | 1975 s.453B(6), (7); 1980CJ Sch.3 §.13; 1993P Sch.5 §.1(36); 1993CJ Sch.5 §.2(14). |
(10) | 1975 s.453B(8); 1980CJ Sch.3 §.13. |
187 | 1975 s.453AA; 1995 s.42(7). |
188(1) | 1975 s.453(1); 1993P s.43; 1995 Sch.6 §.151(2). |
(2), (3) | 1975 s.453(2), (3); 1993P s.43. |
(4) | 1975 s.453(4); 1993P s.43; 1995 Sch.6 §.151(3). |
(5), (6), (7) | 1975 s.453(5), (6), (7); 1993P s.43. |
189(1), (2) | 1975 s.453C(1); 1980CJ Sch.3 §.13. |
(3) | 1975 s.453C(2); 1980 Sch.3 §.13. |
(4) | 1975 s.453C(3); 1980CJ Sch.3 §.13; 1993P Sch.5 §.1(37); 1993CJ Sch.5 §.2(15). |
(5), (6) | 1975 s.453C(4), (5); 1993CJ Sch.5 §.2(15). |
(7) | 1975 s.455A(1); 1995 s.34(2). |
190 | 1975 s.453D; 1980CJ Sch.3 §.13; 1995 Sch.6 §.153. |
191(1), (2) | 1975 s.453A(1); 1980CJ Sch.3 §.13. |
(3), (4) | 1975 s.453A(2), (3); 1980CJ Sch.3 §.13. |
192(1), (2) | 1975 s.453E; 1980CJ Sch.3 §.13. |
(3) | 1975 s.454(1); 1995 Sch.6 §.154. |
(4), (5) | 1975 s.455(1), (2). |
193(1), (2) | 1975 s.443A(1), (2); 1987 s.68(1); 1993CJ Sch.5 §.2(11). |
(3) | 1975 s.443A(3); 1995 Sch.6 §.147. |
194(1) | 1975 s.451(1); 1980CJ Sch.3 §.10. |
(2) | 1975 s.451(2); 1980CJ Sch.3 §.10; 1995 s.45(1). |
(3) | 1975 s.451(3); 1980CJ Sch.3 §.10; 1995 Sch.6 §.150. |
195(1) | 1975 104(1); 1980CJ Sch.4 §.15. |
(2) | 1975 s.104(1A); 1987 s.58(2). |
(3), (4) | 1975 s.104(2), (3); 1980CJ Sch.4 §.15. |
196 | 1975 ss.217A, 430A; 1995 s.33. |
197 | 1975 ss.254A(2), 455A(2); 1995 s.34. |
198(1) | 1975 s.217(1) (part); drafting. |
(2), (3) | 1975 s.217(2), (3); drafting. |
199 | 1975 ss.193, 394; 1977 Sch.13 §.7; 1980CJ s.46(2), Sch.8; 1982 Sch.7 §.10; drafting. |
200(1), (2) | 1975 ss.180(1) (part), 381(1) (part); 1995 s.55(2). |
(3), (4), (5) | 1975 ss.180(1A) to (1C), 381(1A) to (1C); 1995 s.55(3). |
(6) | 1975 ss.180(2), 381(2); 1980B Sch.1 §.5, Sch.2. |
(7) | 1975 ss.180(4), 381(4); 1995 s.55(4). |
(8) | 1975 ss.180(4A), 381(4A); 1995 s.55(5). |
(9) | 1975 ss.180(5), 381(5); 1980B s.6(b); 1995 s.55(6). |
(10), (11) | 1975 ss.180(6), (7), 381(6), (7); 1995 s.55(7). |
201(1) to (3) | 1975 ss.179(1), 380(1); 1980B s.5(a); 1980CJ Sch.7 §.36(a), §.59(a); 1995 Sch.6 §.68. |
(4) | 1975 s.179(2), s.380(2); 1980B s.5(b); 1980CJ Sch.7 §.36(b), §.59(b). |
202 | 1975 ss.219, 432; 1980CJ s.54; 1995 Sch.6 §.143. |
203(1) | 1975 ss.179A, 380A(1); 1995 s.37. |
(2) | 1975 s.380A(2); 1995 s.37(2). |
(3) | 1975 ss.192(part), 393(part); 1995 Sch.6 §.74. |
204(1) | 1980CJ s.41(1). |
(2) | 1980 s.42(1). |

(3) | 1980CJ s.42(2). |

(4) | 1980CJ ss.41(2), 42(3) (part); 1987 Sch.1 §.17; 1988 Sch.9 §.5. |

(5) | 1980CJ ss.41(3), 42(3) (part). |

(6) | 1980CJ s.41(4). |

205(1) to (3) | 1975 s.205(1) to (3); 1980CJ s.43. |

(4) to (6) | 1975 s.205A(1) to (3); 1980CJ s.43. |

206 | 1975 s.425. |

207(1) to (4) | 1975 ss.207(1) to (4), 415(1) to (4); 1980CJ s.45(1). |

(5) | 1975 ss.207(5), 415(5); 1980CJ ss.45(1); 1985 s.43(a); 1988 s.124. |

208 | 1975 s.206; 1980CJ s.44; Prisons (Scotland) Act 1989 (1989 c.45) Sch.2 §.12. |

209(1) | 1975 s.212A(1); 1993P s.14(1). |

(2) | 1975 s.212A(1A); 1995 s.36. |

(3), (4) | 1975 s.212A(2), (3); 1993P s.14(1); 1994 s.132. |

(5) to 97) | 1975 s.212A(4) to (6). |

(8) | 1975 s.212A(7); 1993CJ s.69. |

210(1) | 1975 ss.218(1), 431(1); 1980 Sch.7 §.70, Sch.8; 1993P s.41. |

(2), (3) | 1975 ss.218(2), (3), 431(2), (3); 1993P s.41. |

211(1) | 1975 s.193A(1); 1977 Sch.11 §.1; 1980CJ Sch.7 §.37; 1982 Sch.15 §.17. |

(2) | 1975 s.193A(2); 1982 Sch.15 §.17. |

(3) | 1975 ss.196(1), 402; 1995 Sch.6 §.75. |

(4) | 1975 s.196(2); 1980CJ s.48. |

(5) | 1975 s.203. |

(6) | 1975 s.412. |

(7) | 1975 ss.194, 395(1). |

212(1), (2) | 1975 s.395(2) (part); 1980CJ Sch.7 §.60. |

(3) to (7) | 1975 s.395(3) to (7). |

(8), (9) | 1975 s.395(2) (part); 1980CJ Sch.7 §.60. |

213 | 1975 ss.194, 395A(1) to (3); 1980CJ ss.47, 49. |

214(1) to (6) | 1975 ss.194, 396(1) to (6); 1980CJ s.47; drafting. |

(7) | 1975 ss.194, 396(7); 1980CJ s.47; 1995 Sch.6 §.137. |

(8) | 1975 ss.194, 399(1); 1980CJ s.47. |

(9) | 1975 ss.194, 399(2) & (3); 1980CJ s.47, Sch.7 §.62(b). |

215(1), (2) | 1975 ss.194, 397; 1977 Sch.11 §.8; Magistrates' Courts Act 1980 (1980 c.43) Sch.7 §.136; 1980CJ s.47. |

(3), (4) | 1975 ss.194, 397(2), (3); 1980CJ s.47. |

216(1), (2) | 1975 ss.194, 398(1); 1980CJ s.47, Sch.7 §.61; 1995 Sch.6 §.138. |

(3) | 1975 ss.194, 398(2); 1980CJ s.47. |

(4) | 1975 ss.194, 398(3); 1980CJ s.47. |

(5) | 1975 ss.194, 318(1); 1980CJ s.47.. |

(6) | 1975 ss.194, 318(2) & (3), 398(4) & (5); 1980CJ s.47; 1995 Sch.6 §.114. |

(7) | 1975 ss.194, 406; 1980CJ s.47; 1995 Sch.6 §.139. |

217 | 1975 ss.194, 400; 1980CJ s.47. |

218(1), (2) | 1975 ss.194, 401(1), (2); 1980CJ s.47. |

(3) | 1975 ss.194, 401(3); 1980CJ s.47, Sch.7 §.63. |

219(1) | 1975 ss.194, 407(1); 1980CJ ss.47, 50; 1990 Sch.8 §.27(3). |

(2) | 1975 ss.194, 407(1A); 1980CJ ss.47, 50; 1985; 1987 s.67(1); 1991 s.23(2). |

(3) to (5) | 1975 ss.194, 407(1B) to (1D); 1980CJ s.47, 50. |

(6) | 1975 ss.194, 407(2); 1980CJ s.47. |

(7) | 1975 ss.194, 407(4); 1980CJ s.47. |

(8) | 1975 ss.194, 407(5); 1980CJ s47; 1987 s.67(2). |

220(1), (2) | 1975 ss.194, 409(1); 1980CJ s.47, Sch.7 §.65. |

(3) | 1975 s.194, Sch.7; 1980CJ s.47. |

(4) | 1975 ss.194, 409(2); 1980CJ s.47. |

221(1) | 1975 ss.194, 411(1); 1980CJ s.47; Debtors (Scotland) Act 1987 (1987 c.18) Sch.6 §.18. |
(2), (3) | 1975 ss.194, 411(3); 1980CJ s.47. |
(4) | 1980CJ s.52(part). |
222(1) | 1975 ss.194, 403(1); 1977 Sch.7 §.2; 1980CJ s.47. |
(2) | 1975 ss.194, 403(2); 1980CJ s.47. |
(3) | 1975 ss.194, 403(3); 1980CJ s.47; 1995 s.67(2). |
(4) | 1975 ss.194, 403(3A); 1980CJ s.47; 1995 s.67(3). |
(5) | 1975 ss.194, 403(3B); 1980CJ s.47; 1995 s.67(3). |
(6) | 1975 ss.194, 403(4); 1977 Sch.7 §.2; 1980CJ s.47. |
(7) | 1975 ss.194, 403(4A); 1980CJ s.47; 1994 s.47(4). |
(8) | 1975 ss.194, 403(6); 1977 Sch.7 §.2; 1980CJ s.47. |
223 | 1975 s.404. |
224 | 1975 ss.194, 408; 1980CJ s.47; 1995 Sch.6 §.140. |
225(1) | 1975 s.289G(1); 1982 s.54. |
(2) | 1975 s.289G(2); 1982 s.54; S.I. 1984/526; 1991 s.17(1). |
(3) | 1975 s.289G(3); 1982 s.54. |
(4) | 1975 s.289D(1); 1977 Sch.11 §.5; 1982 s.53(a). |
(5) | 1975 s.289D(1A); 1982 s.53(a); 1994 s.157(7). |
(6) | 1975 s.289D(1B); 1982 s.53(a); drafting. |
(7) | 1975 s.289D(4); 1977 Sch.11 §.5; 1987 Sch.2. |
(8) | 1975 s.289B(6) (part); drafting. |
226 | 1975 s.289GB; 1987 s.66(2). |
227 | 1975 s.182A; 1995 Sch.6 §.69. |
228(1) | 1975 ss.183(1), 384(1); 1980CJ s.53(1); 1987 Sch.1 §.10; 1990 s.61(1); 1995 s.38(3)(a). |
(2) | 1975 ss.183(1A), 384(1A); 1990 s.61; 1991 Sch.3 §.7(2). |
(3), (4) | 1975 ss.183(2), 384(2). |
(5) | 1975 ss.183(6), 384(6); 1987 s.65(4); 1995 s.38(3)(c). |
(6) | 1975 ss.183(7), 384(7); 1995 Sch.6 §.70. |
229(1) | 1975 ss.183(4), 384(4); 1978 s.7; 1987 s.65(3); 1990 s.61(1). |
(2), (3) | 1975 ss.183(5), 384(5). |
(4), (5) | 1975 ss.183(5A), 384(5A); 1978 s.7; 1982 Sch.13 §.3; 1995 s.38(1), (3)(b); drafting. |
(6), (7) | 1975 ss.183(5B), (5C), 384(5B), (5C); 1987 s.65. |
230(1) | 1975 ss.184(1), 385(1); 1984 Sch.3 §§.29, 36; 1995 s.39(1). |
(2) | 1975 ss.184(2), 385(2); 1984 Sch.3 §§.29, 36; 1995 s.39(1). |
(3) | 1975 ss.184(3), 385(3). |
(4) | 1975 ss.184(5), 385(5); 1983 s.36(2); 1995 s.39(1). |
(5) | 1975 ss.184(5A), 385(5A); 1983 s.36(2). |
(6) | 1975 ss.184(5B), 385(5B); 1983 s.36(2); 1995 s.39(1). |
(7) | 1975 ss.184(6), 385(6); 1983 s.36(3). |
(8), (9) | 1975 ss.184(7), (8), 385(7), (8). |
231 | 1975 ss.185, 386. |
232(1) | 1975 ss.186(1), 387(1); 1978 s.8; 1990 s.61(2); Local Government etc. (Scotland) Act 1994 (c.39) Sch.13 §.97(3); 1995 Sch.6 §.71. |
(2) | 1975 ss.186(2), 387(2); 1978 s.8; 1980CJ s.46(1); 1982 Sch.7 §§.3, 9; 1987 s.65(5); 1995 s.38(2); . |
(3) | 1975 ss.186(2A), 387(2A); 1993P Sch.5 §.1(7). |
(4) to (6) | 1975 ss.186(3) to (5), 387(3) to (5). |
(7) | 1975 s.317. |
233(1), (2) | 1975 ss.187(1), (2), 388(1), (2). |
(3) to (5) | 1975 ss.187(3) to (5), 388(3) to (5); 1995 s.40(1), (2). |
234(1), (2) | 1975 ss.188(1), 389(1); 1978 Sch.2 §§.2, 3; 1991 Sch.3 §.7(3). |
(3) to (10) | 1975 ss.188(2) to (8), 389(2) to (8); 1991 Sch.3 §.7(3). |
(11) | Drafting. |

235 | 1990 s.62; 1995 s.35(2) to (7). |
236 | 1975 s.412A; 1995 s.35(11). |
237 | 1975 s.412B; 1995 s.35(11). |
238(1) | 1978 s.1(1); 1990 s.61(3). |
(2) to (7) | 1978 s.1(2) to (7). |
(8), (9) | 1978 s.2(1), (2). |
(10), (11) | 1978 s.2(3), (4); 1995 Sch.6. §.161. |
239(1) to (3) | 1978 s.3(1) to (3). |
(4) | 1978 s.4(1); 1995 Sch.6 §.162. |
(5) | 1978 s.4(2); 1982 Sch.7 §.12. |
(6) | 1978 s.4(3); 1990 Sch.8 §.28. |
240 | 1978 s.5. |
241 | 1978 s.5A; 1995 s.40(3). |
242 | 1978 s.6; 1982 Sch.13 §.4. |
243(1) | 1978 s.6A(1); 1982 Sch.13 §.5. |
(2) | 1978 s.6A(2); 1982 Sch.13 §.5; S.I. 1989/1345. |
(3) | 1978 s.6A(3); 1982 Sch.13 §.5. |
244 | 1978 s.6B; 1982 Sch.13 §.5. |
245(1) to (3) | 1978 s.10(1) to (3). |
(4) | 1978 s.11. |
(5) | 1978 s.12(1). |
246(1) | 1975 ss.181, 382; 1993CJ Sch.5 §.2(2). |
(2) | 1975 s.182. |
(3) | 1975 s.383. |
247(1) | 1975 ss.191(1) (part), 392(1) (part). |
(2) | 1975 ss.191(2), 392(2). |
(3) | 1975 ss.191(3) (part), 392(3) (part); 1993CJ Sch.5 §.2(3), (9). |
(4) | 1975 ss.191(4), 392(5); 1995 Sch.6 §§.73, 136. |
(5) | 1975 s.392(4); 1995 Sch.6 §.136. |
(6) | 1975 ss.191(1) (part), 392(1) (part). |
248(1) to (4) | 1975 ss.223A, 436A; Road Traffic Act 1991 (c.40) s.39. |
249(1), (2) | 1980CJ s.58(1). |
(3), (4) | 1980CJ s.58(2), (3). |
(5), (6) | 1980CJ s.59(1). |
(7), (8) | 1980CJ s.59(2), (3). |
(9), (10) | 1980CJ s.60(1), (2). |
250(1) | 1980CJ s.61. |
(2) | 1980CJ s.62. |
(3), (4) | 1980CJ s.63(1), (2). |
251 | 1980CJ s.64. |
252 | 1980CJ s.66. |
253 | 1980CJ s.67; Armed Forces Act 1991 (c.62) Sch.2 §.9(2). |
254 | 1975 ss.224, 437. |
255 | 1975 ss.67, 312(x); drafting. |
256(1) | 1975 ss.150(1), 354(1); 1995 Sch.6 §§.55(a), 126; drafting. |
(2) | 1975 ss.150(2), 354(2) (part); 1995 Sch.6 §.55(b). |
(3) | 1975 ss.150(3), 354(2) (part); drafting. |
257 | 1975 ss.84A, 333B; 1995 s.12. |
258 | 1995 s.16. |
259 | 1995 s.17. |
260 | 1995 s.18. |
261 | 1995 s.19. |
262 | 1995 s.20. |

263(1) to (3) | 1975 ss.148(1) to (3), 340(1) to (3); 1995 Sch.6 §.54. |
(4) | 1975 ss.147, 349. |
(5) | 1975 ss.148A, 349A; 1982 s.73(1), (2). |
264(1) to (3) | 1975 ss.143(1) to (3), 348(1) to (3); 1980CJ s.29. |
(4) | Criminal Justice Administration Act 1914 (c.58) s.28(3). |
265(1) | 1975 ss.138(1), (2), 341(1), (2). |
(2) | 1975 ss.138(4), 341(4). |
(3), (4) | 1975 ss.139, 342. |
266(1) | 1975 ss.141(1) (part), 346(1) (part); Criminal Evidence Act 1979 (1979 c.16) s.1(1); 1980CJ s.28, Sch.7 §.56; 1995 s.24. |
(2) | 1975 ss.141(1)(a), 346(1)(a). |
(3) | 1975 ss.141(1)(e), 346(1)(e). |
(4) | 1975 ss.141(1)(f), 346(1)(f); Criminal Evidence Act 1979 (c.16) s.1(1); 1995 s.24(1)(a), (4)(a). |
(5) | 1975 ss.141(1A), 346(1A): 1995 s.24(1)(b), (4)(b). |
(6) | 1975 s.141(1B); 1995 s.24(1)(b). |
(7) | 1975 ss.141(1C), 346(1B); 1995 s.24(1)(c), (4)(b). |
(8) | 1975 ss.141(1)(g), 346(1)(g). |
(9) | 1975 ss.141(2), 346(2); 1980CJ s.28. |
(10) | 1975 ss.141(3), 346(3); 1980CJ s.28. |
(11) | 1975 ss.142, 347; 1995 Sch.6 §§.50, 124. |
267(1) | 1975 ss.139A, 342A; 1987 s.63. |
(2) | 1975 ss.140, 343. |
268(1), (2) | 1975 ss.149(1), 350(1); 1980CJ s.30; 1985 s.37; 1987 Sch.1 §.9; 1993P Sch.5 §.1(31). |
(3), (4) | 1975 ss.149(2), (3), 350(2), (3); 1980CJ s.30. |
(5) | Drafting. |
269(1) | 1975 ss.149A(1), 350A(1); 1980CJ s.30; 1985 s.37. |
(2), (3) | 1975 ss.149A(2), (3), 350A(2), (3); 1980CJ s.30. |
(4) | Drafting. |
270(1), (2) | 1975 ss.141ZA(1), (2), 346ZA(1), (2); 1995 s.24(2), (5). |
(3) | 1975 s.141ZA(3); 1995 s.24(2). |
(4) | 1975 ss.141ZA(4), 346ZA(3); 1995 s.24(2), (5). |
271(1) to (3) | 1993P s.33(1) to (3). |
(4) | 1993P s.33(4); 1995 Sch.6 §.179(6). |
(5) | 1990 s.56(1); 1995 Sch.6 §.175(a). |
(6) | 1993P s.34; 1995 Sch.6 §.179(7). |
(7) | 1990 s.56(2); 1995 Sch.6 §.175(b). |
(8) | 1990 s.56(3). |
(9) | 1990 s.57(1). |
(10) | 1990 s.57(2). |
(11) | 1990 s.58; 1995 Sch.6 §.176. |
(12) | 1990 s.59. |
272(1) | 1980CJ s.32(1); 1987 s.61. |
(2), (3) | 1980CJ s.32(2). |
(4) | 1980CJ s.32(3). |
(5) | 1980CJ s.32(3A); 1993P s.30. |
(6) | 1980CJ s.32(4); 1987 s.61. |
(7) | 1980CJ s.32(5). |
(8) | 1980CJ s.32(5A); 1993P s.30. |
(9) | 1980CJ s.32(6). |
273 | 1980CJ s.32A; 1993P s.32. |
274(1) | 1975 ss.141A(1), 346A(1); 1985 s.36. |

(2) | 1975 ss.141A(2), 346A(2); 1985 s.36; 1995 s.28. |

(3), (4) | 1975 ss.141A(3), (4), 346A(3), (4); 1985 s.36. |

275 | 1975 ss.141B, 346B; 1985 s.36. |

276 | 1995 s.21. |

277(1) | 1987 s.60(1); 1993P s.31. |

(2) | 1987 s.60(2). |

(3) | 1987 s.60(3); 1995 Sch.6 §.170. |

(4) | 1987 s.60(4). |

278(1) | 1975 ss.151(1), 352(1); 1980CJ s.6. |

(2), (3) | 1975 ss.151(2), 352(2); 1995 Sch.6 §§.56, 125. |

(4) | 1975 s.352(4). |

(5) | 1975 ss.151(3), 352(3). |

279 | 1993P s.29. |

280(1) | 1980CJ s.26(1). |

(2), (3) | 1980 s.26(1A), (1B); 1995 s.22(2). |

(4) | 1980CJ s.26(2); 1995 s.22(3). |

(5) | 1980CJ s.26(2A); 1995 s.22(4). |

(6) | 1980CJ s.26(3); 1995 s.22(5). |

(7) | 1980CJ s.26(4); 1995 s. 22(6), Sch.6 §.163. |

(8) | 1980CJ s.26(4A); 1995 s.22(7). |

(9) | 1980CJ s.26(5); 1995 s.22(8). |

(10) to (12) | 1980 s.26(7B) to (7D); 1995 s.22(9). |

281(1), (2) | 1980CJ s.26(6), (7). |

(3) | 1980CJ s.26(7A); 1995 s.22(9). |

282 | 1995 s.25. |

283 | 1995 s.26. |

284 | 1995 s.27. |

285(1) to (5) | 1975 ss.164(1) to (5), 358(1) to (5). |

(6) | 1975 ss.162(1), 357(2) (part). |

(7) | 1975 s.162(2). |

(8) | 1975 ss.162(3), 357(2) (part); 1995 Sch.6 §§.62, 127(b). |

(9) | 1975 ss.164(6), 357(2) (part), 358(6). |

286 | 1975 ss.162(4), (5), 357(6), (7); 1995 s.29. |

287 | 1975 s.42; 1995 Sch.6 §.18. |

288(1) | 1975 s.10. |

(2) | 1975 s.11. |

289 | 1980CJ s.39. |

290 | 1980CJ s.10(1), (2). |

291(1) | 1980CJ s.9(1). |

(2) | 1980CJ s.9(2); 1982 Sch.6 §.64. |

(3) | 1980CJ s.9(3); 1982 Sch.7 |

292(1) | 1975 ss.283A(1), (2); 1977 Sch.11 §.2; 1980CJ Sch.7 §.49. |

(2) to (7) | 1975 s.457A(1) to (4); 1982 s.55(1). |

293 | 1975 ss.216, 428; 1987 s.64(1). |

294(1) | 1975 s.63(1) (part). |

(2) | 1975 s.312(o) (part). |

295 | 1975 ss.215, 426; 1980CJ Sch.7 §§.39, 69; 1987 Sch.1 §.12; |

296 | 1975 ss.15A, 309(2) (part); 1995 Sch.6 §.9. |

297(1) | 1975 ss.15, 327; 1995 s.9. |

(2) | 1975 s.326(1) (part) |

(3), (4) | 1975 ss.16(1), (2), 324(1), (2). |

(5) | 1975 s.326(1) (part). |

298 | 1995 s.44 |

299 | 1975 ss.227A, 439; 1980CJ s.20. |
300 | 1975 s.439A; 1995 s.41. |
301(1) | 1975 s.282A; 1990 Sch.8 §.27. |
(2) | 1975 s.282B; 1990 Sch.8 §.27. |
302(1) | 1987 s.56(1). |
(2) | 1987 s.56(3); 1995 s.61(3). |
(3) | 1987 s.56(3A); 1995 s.61(4). |
(4) to (6) | 1987 s.56(4) to (6); 1995 s.61(5). |
(7), (8) | 1987 s.56(7), (7A); 1995 s.61(6). |
(9) | 1987 s.56(2), (2A); Road Traffic (Consequential Provisions) Act 1988 (1988 c.54) Sch.3 §.34; 1995 s.61(2). |
303(1) to (4) | 1987 s.56(8) to (11); 1995 s.61(8). |
304 | 1995 s.56(1) to (10). |
305(1) | 1975 ss.409(3), 457ZA(1) (part); Summary Jurisdiction (Scotland) Act 1954 (c.48) s.76(1)(d); 1995 Sch.6 §.156. |
(2) | 1975 s.457ZA(2); 1995 Sch.6 §.156. |
(3) | 1975 s457ZA(1) (part); 1995 Sch.6 §.156. |
(4) | 1975 s.278. |
(5) | Summary Jurisdiction (Scotland) Act 1954 (1954 c.48) s.76(3). |
306 | 1995 s.57. |
307(1) | 1975 s.462(1); 1977 Sch.11 §.10; National Health Service (Scotland) Act 1978 (1978 c.29) Sch.16 §.41; 1980B Sch.1 §.14; 1980CJ s.25, Sch.7 §.76; 1982 Sch.15 §.19; 1983 Sch.2 §.37; 1984 Sch.3 §.37; National Health Service and Community Care Act 1990 (c.19) Sch.9 §.14; 1995 s.39(2), Sch.6 §.157; 1995C Sch.4 §.24(18). |
(2) | 1975 s.462(2). |
(3) to (8) | 1975 s.462(4) to (9). |
308 | 1975 ss.458, 459; 1980CJ Sch.7 §§.73, 74. |
309 | Drafting. |
Sch. 1 | 1975 Sch.1; Sexual Offences (Scotland) Act 1976 (1976 c.67) Schs.1, 2; 1988 Sch.15 §§.50, 51. |
Sch. 2 | Criminal Procedure (Scotland) Act 1887 (c.35) Sch.A |
Sch. 3 | |
§.1 | 1975 ss.43 (part), 312(a). |
§.2 | 1975 ss.44, 312(b). |
§.3 | 1975 ss.48, 312(e). |
§.4(1) | 1975 ss.50(1), 312(f) (part). |
(2) | 1975 ss.50(2), 312(f) (part). |
(3) | 1975 ss.50(3) (part), 312(f) (part). |
(4) | 1975 ss.50(3) (part), 312(f) (part). |
(5) | 1975 ss.50(4), 312(f) (part); 1995 Sch.6 §§.20, 110(a). |
(6) | 1975 ss.51 (part), 312(g) (part). |
(7) | 1975 ss.51 (part), 312(g) (part). |
(8) | Drafting. |
§.5 | 1975 ss.54, 312(j); 1995 Sch.6 §§.21, 110(b). |
§.6 | 1975 ss.55, 312(k). |
§.7 | 1975 s.63(2). |
§.8(1) | 1975 ss.59 (part), 312(l) (part). |
(2) | 1975 ss.60(1), 312(m) (part). |
(3) | 1975 ss.60(2), 312(m) (part). |
(4) | 1975 ss.60(3), 312(m) (part). |
(5) | 1975 ss.60(4), 312(m) (part). |
§.9(1) | 1975 ss.61(1), 312(n) (part). |
(2) | 1975 ss.61(2), 312(n) (part). |

(3) | 1975 ss.61(3), 312(n) (part). |
§.10(1) | 1975 ss.63(1) (part), 312(o) (part). |
(2) | 1975 ss.63(1) (part), 312(o) (part). |
(3) | 1975 ss.63(2), 312(o) (part). |
§.11 | 1975 ss.48B, 312(p); 1995 Sch.6 §.19. |
§.12 | 1975 s.312(q), (r). |
§.13 | 1975 ss.49, 312(s). |
§.14 | 1975 ss.64, 312(t). |
§.15 | 1975 ss.65, 312(u). |
§.16 | 1975 ss.66, 312(v). |
§.17 | 1975 ss.48A, 312(w); 1995 Sch.6 §.19. |
§.18 | 1975 ss.60A, 312(y); 1995 Sch.6 §.23. |
§.19 | 1975 s.312(z); 1977 Sch.11 §.6; 1980CJ s.46(b); 1982 Sch.7 §.7. |
Sch. 4 | 1975 Sch.5A; 1995 Sch.2. |
Sch. 5 | Summary Jurisdiction (Scotland) Act 1954 (c.48) Sch.2 Part II |
Sch. 6 |
§.1 | 1975 Sch.5. §.1. |
§.2 | 1975 Sch.5 §.2. |
§.3 | 1975 Sch.5 §.3 |
§.4 | 1975 Sch.5 §.4; 1983 s.36(4); 1995 Sch.6 §.158. |
§.5 | 1975 Sch.5 §.5. |
§.6 | 1975 Sch.5 §.6. |
Sch. 7 |
§.1 | 1990 Sch.6 §.1; 1995 s.35(8)(a). |
§.2 | 1990 Sch.6 §.2; 1995 Sch.6 §.177(a). |
§.3 | 1990 Sch.6 §.3. |
§.4 | 1990 Sch.6 §.4; 1995 s.35(8)(b), Sch.6 §.177(b). |
§.5 | 1990 Sch.6 §.5; 1995 s.35(8)(c). |
§.6 | 1990 Sch.6 §.6. |
§.7 | 1990 Sch.6 §.7. |
§.8 | 1990 Sch.6 §.9. |
Sch. 8 | 1993P Sch.3; 1995 Sch.6 §.179(8) |
Sch. 9 | 1980CJ Sch.1; Forgery and Counterfeiting Act 1981 (1981 c.45) s.26; Road Traffic Regulation Act 1984 (1984 c.27) Sch.13 §.37; Video Recording Act 1984 (1984 c.39) s.20; 1987 Sch.1 §.18(2); 1993P Sch.4; 1995 Sch.1. |
Sch. 10 | 1975 Sch.7A; 1977 Sch.11 §.11. |

Open Government Licence v3.0

Printed in Great Britain
by Amazon